Collins
RUSSIAN
DICTIONARY
ESSENTIAL EDITION

W9-AAC-724

Published by Collins
An imprint of HarperCollins Publishers
Westerhill Road
Bishopbriggs
Glasgow G64 2QT

HarperCollins*Publishers*
1st Floor, Watermarque
Building, Ringsend Road
Dublin 4, Ireland

1st Edition 2018

10 9 8 7 6 5

ISBN 978-0-00-827070-4

collinsdictionary.com

Typeset by Davidson Publishing Solutions,
Glasgow

Printed and bound in the UK using
100% renewable electricity at CPI
Group (UK) Ltd

If you would like to comment on any
aspect of this book, please contact
us at the given address or online.
E-mail: dictionaries@harpercollins.co.uk
 facebook.com/collinsdictionary
 @collinsdict

Acknowledgements
We would like to thank those authors and
publishers who kindly gave permission for
copyright material to be used in the Collins
Corpus. We would also like to thank Times
Newspapers Ltd for providing valuable data.

СОДЕРЖАНИЕ

CONTENTS

ТОВАРНЫЕ ЗНАКИ

Слова, которые, по нашему мнению, являются товарными знаками, получили соответствующее обозначение. Начилие или отсутствие обозначения не влияет на юридический статус того или иного товарного знака.

TRADEMARKS

Words which we have reason to believe constitute trademarks have been designated as such. However, neither the presence nor the absence of such designation should be regarded as affecting the legal status of any trademark.

ВВЕДЕНИЕ

Мы рады, что вы выбрали словарь, подготовленный издательством Collins. Мы надеемся, что он окажется вам полезен, где бы вы им ни пользовались – дома, на отдыхе или на работе.

В настоящем введении излагаются некоторые советы по эффективному использованию данного издания: его обширного словника и сведений, содержащихся в каждой словарной статье. Данная информация поможет вам не только читать и понимать современный английский, но также овладеть устной речью.

О ПОЛЬЗОВАНИИ СЛОВАРЁМ

Заглавные слова

Заглавными называются слова, начинающие словарную статью. Они напечатаны жирным шрифтом и расположены в алфавитном порядке. При многих из них приводятся словосочетания и сращения. Они напечатаны жирным шрифтом меньшего размера.

Перевод

Перевод заглавных слов напечатан обычным шрифтом. Варианты перевода, разделённые запятой, синонимичны. Различные значения многозначного слова разделены точкой с запятой.

Переводы для значений производных слов часто разделены только точкой с запятой, и перед ними даётся одна помета типа (*см прил*). Это означает, что последовательное разделение значений рассматриваемого слова и его переводов даётся при слове, от которого это слово образовано. Например, **careful/carefully**.

В случаях, когда точный перевод невозможен, даётся приблизительный эквивалент. Он обозначается знаком ≈. Если же таковой отсутствует, то приводится толкование.

Пометы

Пометы служат для разделения значений многозначного слова. Их цель – помочь читателю выбрать перевод, наиболее подходящий в том или ином контексте. Пометы напечатаны курсивом и заключены в круглые скобки.

При заглавных словах даны необходимые стилистические пометы. Нецензурные слова помечены восклицательным знаком (!).

Произношение

В англо-русской части словаря все заглавные слова снабжены транскрипцией. Транскрипция не даётся для производных слов, о произношении которых можно судить, исходя из произношения исходного слова, например, **enjoy/enjoyment**. Список фонетических знаков приводится на страницах xiii.

В русско-английской части все русские слова снабжены знаком ударения. Омографы (слова, имеющие одинаковое написание, но различное ударение и значение) приводятся как отдельные заглавные слова в том порядке, в котором в них проставлено ударение, например, первым даётся слово **за́мок**, затем – **замо́к**. Более подробную информацию о принципах русского произношения читатель может найти в разделе на страницах xii.

Служебные слова

В словаре уделяется особое внимание русским и английским словам, которые обладают сложной грамматической структурой. Таковыми являются в первую очередь служебные слова, вспомогательные глаголы, местоимения, частицы итп. Они обозначены пометой **KEYWORD** или **КЛЮЧЕВОЕ СЛОВО**.

Английские фразовые глаголы

Фразовыми глаголами называются устойчивые сочетания глагола с элементами **in, up** итп, типа **blow up**, **cut down** итп. Они приводятся при базовых глаголах, таких как **blow**, **cut**, и расположены в алфавитном порядке.

Употребление *or/или*, косой черты и скобок

Между взаимозаменяемыми вариантами перевода фраз в англо-русской части употребляется союз "*or*", в русско-английской – "*или*". Косая черта (/) означает, что приведённые варианты перевода не являются взаимозаменяемыми. В круглые скобки заключаются возможные, но необязательные в данном выражении слова.

INTRODUCTION

We are delighted that you have decided to use the Collins Russian Dictionary and hope that you will enjoy and benefit from using it at home, on holiday or at work.

This introduction gives you a few tips on how to get the most out of your dictionary – not simply from its wide-ranging wordlist but also from the information provided in each entry. This will help you to read and understand modern Russian, as well as communicate and express yourself in the language.

USING THE DICTIONARY

Headwords

The **headword** is the word you look up in a dictionary. They are listed in alphabetical order, and printed in bold type. Each headword may contain phrases, which are in smaller bold type. The two headwords appearing at the top of each page indicate the first (if it appears on a left-hand page) and last word (if it appears on a right-hand page) of the page in question. Where appropriate, words related to headwords are grouped together (eg. **enjoy**, **enjoyment**) in smaller bold type than the headword.

Translations

The translations of the headword are printed in ordinary roman type. Translations separated by a comma are interchangeable, while those separated by a semi-colon are not interchangeable. Where it is not possible to give an exact translation equivalent, an approximate (cultural) equivalent is given, preceded by ≈. If this isn't possible either, then a gloss is given to explain the source item.

Indicators

Indicators are pieces of information given in italic type and in brackets. They offer contexts in which the headword might appear, or provide synonyms, guiding you to the most appropriate translation.

Informal language in the dictionary is labelled. Rude or offensive translations are also marked with (!).

Pronunciation

On the English-Russian side of the dictionary you will find the phonetic spelling of the word in square brackets after the headword, unless the word is grouped under another headword and the pronunciation can be easily derived eg. **enjoy/enjoyment**. A list of the symbols used is given on page xiii.

For Russian-English, stress is given on all Russian words as a guide to pronunciation. Words which are spelt in the same way, but have different stress positions are treated as separate entries, the order following the order of the stress eg. **за́мок** comes before **замо́к**. The section on page xii explains Russian phonetics in more detail.

Keywords

In the dictionary, special status is given to "key" Russian and English words. These words can be grammatically complex and are labelled **KEYWORD** in English and **КЛЮЧЕВОЕ СЛОВО** in Russian.

"You" in phrases

The Russian formal form is used to translate "you/your" and imperative phrases, unless the informal form would be more natural.

Use of *or*/*или*, oblique and brackets

"*or*" on the English-Russian side, and "*или*" on the Russian-English side are used between interchangeable parts of a translation or phrase, whereas the oblique (/) is used between non-interchangeable alternatives. Round brackets are used to show the optional parts of the translation or phrase.

American variants

American spelling variants are generally shown at the British headword eg. **colour/color**. Variant forms are generally shown as separate headwords eg. **trousers/pants**, unless the British and American forms are alphabetically adjacent, when the American form is only shown separately if phonetics are required eg. **cut-price/cut-rate**.

Russian reflexive verbs

Russian reflexive verbs eg. **мы́ться**, **кра́ситься** are listed under the basic verb eg. **мыть**, **кра́сить**.

STYLE AND LAYOUT OF THE DICTIONARY

RUSSIAN–ENGLISH

Inflectional and grammatical information

Inflectional information is shown in the dictionary in brackets straight after the headword and before the part of speech eg. **стол (-á)** *м.*

Grammatical information is shown after the part of speech and refers to the whole entry eg. **завид|овать (-ую**; *pf* **позави́довать)** *несов* +*dat.* Note that transitive verbs are labelled *перех* and intransitive verbs have no label other than aspect. Where grammatical information eg. *no pf* is given in the middle of the entry, it then governs all of the following senses.

Use of the hairline (|)

The hairline is used in headwords to show where the inflection adds on eg. **кни́г|а (-и)**.

Stress

Stress changes are shown where they occur, the last form given being indicative of the rest of the pattern eg. **игр|á (-ы́**; *nom pl* **-ы)**. In this example the stress is on the last syllable in the singular moving to the first syllable throughout the plural.

Nouns, numerals and pronouns

In order to help you determine the declension and stress pattern of nouns, numerals and pronouns, we have shown the genitive in each case. This is given as the first piece of information after the headword and is not labelled eg. **стол (-á)**.

Where the headword has further irregularities in declension these are shown at the headword and labelled eg. **я́блок|о (-а**; *nom pl* **-и)**.

Verbs

The majority of verbs are dealt with in aspectual pairs, and the translation is shown at the base form of the pair. The other aspect is generally shown separately and cross-referred to the base form. To help you see how a verb conjugates, inflections are shown immediately after the headword.

In phrases both aspects are shown if both work in the context.

The past tense is shown at the headword if it is irregularly formed.

Inflections given as separate entries

Some irregular inflected forms are also shown at their alphabetical position and cross-referred to the base headword.

Spelling rules

The following spelling rules apply to Russian:
– after **ж, ч, ш, щ, г, к** and **х, ы** is replaced by **и, я** by **а** and **ю** by **у**.
– after **ж, ч, ш, щ** and **ц, е** replaces an unstressed **о**.

Latin letters in Russian

With the increase in popularity of the internet, some words in Russian are now normally spelt with Latin rather than Cyrillic characters eg. **SMS, MP3-плеер**. These words are listed in alphabetical order of their Cyrillic transliterations, so for example **MP3** and **MP3-плеер** are listed between **моя́** and **мрак**.

ENGLISH–RUSSIAN

Gender

The gender of Russian noun translations is only shown for:

– nouns ending in **-ь**
– neuter nouns ending in **-я**
– masculine nouns ending in **-a**
– nouns with a common gender
– indeclinable nouns
– substantivized adjectives
– plural noun translations if a singular form exists.

Feminine forms

The feminine forms of masculine nouns are shown as follows:

– the feminine ending adds on to the masculine form eg. учи́тель(ница)
– the feminine ending substitutes part of the masculine form, the last common letter of both forms being shown before the feminine ending (unless it is a substantivized adjective) eg. актёр(три́са)
– the feminine form is given in full eg. чех (че́шка).

Adjectives

Russian translations of adjectives are always given in the masculine, unless the adjective relates only to a feminine noun eg. бере́менная.

Verbs

Imperfective and perfective aspects are shown in translation where they both apply eg. **to do** де́лать (сде́лать *pf*). If only one aspect is shown, it means that only one aspect works for this sense. The same applies to translations of infinitive phrases eg. **to buy sth** покупа́ть (купи́ть *pf*) что-н.

Where the English phrases contains the construction "to do" standing for any verb, it has been translated by +*infin*/+*impf infin*/+*pf infin*, depending on which aspects of the Russian verb work in the context.

Where the English phrase contains the past tense of a verb in the 1st person singular, the Russian translation gives only the masculine form eg. **I was glad** я был рад.

Prepositions

Unless bracketed, prepositions and cases which follow verbs, adjectives etc are obligatory as part of the translation eg. **to inundate with** зава́ливать (завали́ть *pf*) +*instr*.

Where they are separated by *or* they are interchangeable.

An oblique (/) is used to separate prepositions when the preposition depends on the following noun not the preceding verb eg. идти́ в/на.

RUSSIAN ABBREVIATIONS

aviation	*Авиа*	авиация
automobiles	*Авт*	автомобильное дело
administration	*Админ*	администрация
anatomy	*Анат*	анатомия
architecture	*Архит*	архитектура
impersonal	*безл*	безличный
biology	*Био*	биология
botany	*Бот*	ботаника
parenthesis	*вводн сл*	вводное слово
military	*Воен*	военный термин
reflexive	*возв*	возвратный глагол
geography	*Гео*	география
geometry	*Геом*	геометрия
verb	*глаг*	глагол
offensive	*груб!*	грубо
singular	*ед*	единственное число
feminine	*ж*	женский род
zoology	*Зоол*	зоология
history	*Ист*	история
et cetera	*итп*	и тому подобное
predicate	*как сказ*	как сказуемое
commercial	*Комм*	коммерция
computing	*Комп*	компьютер
somebody	*кто-н*	кто-нибудь
culinary	*Кулин*	кулинария
linguistics	*Линг*	лингвистика
masculine	*м*	мужской род
mathematics	*Мат*	математика
medicine	*Мед*	медицина
exclamation	*межд*	междометие
pronoun	*мест*	местоимение
plural	*мн*	множественное число
nautical	*Мор*	морской термин
music	*Муз*	музыка
adverb	*нареч*	наречие
invariable	*неизм*	неизменяемое
intransitive	*неперех*	непереходный глагол
indeclinable	*нескл*	несклоняемое
imperfective	*несов*	несовершенный вид
figurative	*перен*	в переносном значении
transitive	*перех*	переходный
subject	*подлеж*	подлежащее
politics	*Полит*	политика
superlative	*превос*	превосходная степень
preposition	*предл*	предлог
pejorative	*пренебр*	пренебрежительное
adjective	*прил*	прилагательное

possessive	*притяж*	притяжательный
school	*Просвещ*	просвещение
psychology	*Психол*	психология
informal	*разг*	разговорное
religion	*Рел*	религия
agriculture	*С.-Х.*	сельское хозяйство
see	*см*	смотри
collective	*собир*	собирательное
perfective	*сов*	совершенный вид
abbreviation	*сокр*	сокращение
neuter	*ср*	средний род
comparative	*сравн*	сравнительная степень
construction	*Строит*	строительство
noun	*сущ*	имя существительное
television	*Тел*	телевидение
technology	*Тех*	техника
printing	*Типог*	типографский термин
diminutive	*уменьш*	уменьшительное
physics	*Физ*	физика
photography	*Фото*	фотография
chemistry	*Хим*	химия
particle	*част*	частица
somebody's	*чей-н*	чей-нибудь
numeral	*чис*	числительное
something	*что-н*	что-нибудь
economics	*Экон*	экономика
electricity	*Элек*	электроника
law	*Юр*	юридический термин
registered trademark	®	зарегистрированный торговый знак
introduces a cultural equivalent	≈	вводит культурный эквивалент

АНГЛИЙСКИЕ СОКРАЩЕНИЯ

сокращение	*abbr*	abbreviation
винительный падеж	*acc*	accusative
прилагательное	*adj*	adjective
администрация	*Admin*	administration
наречие	*adv*	adverb
сельское хозяйство	*Agr*	agriculture
анатомия	*Anat*	anatomy
архитектура	*Archit*	architecture
автомобильное дело	*Aut*	automobiles
вспомогательный глагол	*aux vb*	auxiliary verb
авиация	*Aviat*	aviation
биология	*Bio*	biology
ботаника	*Bot*	botany
британский английский	*Brit*	British English
химия	*Chem*	chemistry
коммерция	*Comm*	commerce
компьютер	*Comput*	computing
союз	*conj*	conjunction
строительство	*Constr*	construction
сращение	*cpd*	compound
кулинария	*Culin*	culinary
дательный падеж	*dat*	dative
склоняется	*decl*	declines
определённый артикль	*def art*	definite article
уменьшительное	*dimin*	diminutive
экономика	*Econ*	economics
электроника	*Elec*	electricity
особенно	*esp*	especially
и тому подобное	*etc*	et cetera
междометие	*excl*	exclamation
женский род	*f*	feminine
в переносном значении	*fig*	figurative
родительный падеж	*gen*	genitive
география	*Geo*	geography
геометрия	*Geom*	geometry
безличный	*impers*	impersonal
несовершенный вид	*impf*	imperfective
несклоняемое	*ind*	indeclinable
неопределённый артикль	*indef art*	indefinite article
разговорное	*inf*	informal
грубо	*inf!*	offensive
инфинитив	*infin*	infinitive
творительный падеж	*instr*	instrumental
неизменяемое	*inv*	invariable
неправильный	*irreg*	irregular
лингвистика	*Ling*	linguistics
местный падеж	*loc*	locative
мужской род	*m*	masculine

субстантивированное прилагательное	*m/f/nt adj*	adjectival noun
математика	*Math*	mathematics
медицина	*Med*	medicine
военный термин	*Mil*	military
музыка	*Mus*	music
имя существительное	*n*	noun
морской термин	*Naut*	nautical
существительное во множественном числе	*npl*	plural noun
средний род	*nt*	neuter
числительное	*num*	numeral
себя	*o.s.*	oneself
пренебрежительное	*pej*	pejorative
совершенный вид	*pf*	perfective
фотография	*Phot*	photography
физика	*Phys*	physics
физиология	*Physiol*	physiology
множественное число	*pl*	plural
политика	*Pol*	politics
страдательное причастие	*pp*	past participle
предлог	*prep*	preposition
местоимение	*pron*	pronoun
предложный падеж	*prp*	prepositional
психология	*Psych*	psychiatry
прошедшее время	*pt*	past tense
религия	*Rel*	religion
кто-нибудь	*sb*	somebody
просвещение	*Scol*	school
единственное число	*sg*	singular
что-нибудь	*sth*	something
подлежащее	*subj*	subject
превосходная степень	*superl*	superlative
техника	*Tech*	technology
телесвязь	*Tel*	telecommunications
театр	*Theat*	theatre
телевидение	*TV*	television
типографский термин	*Typ*	printing
американский английский	*US*	American English
обычно	*usu*	usually
глагол	*vb*	verb
непереходный глагол	*vi*	intransitive verb
звательный падеж	*voc*	vocative
фразовый глагол	*vt fus*	phrasal verb
переходный глагол	*vt*	transitive verb
зоология	*Zool*	zoology
зарегистрированный торговый знак	®	registered trademark
вводит культурный эквивалент	≈	introduces a cultural equivalent

RUSSIAN PRONUNCIATION

Vowels and diphthongs

Letter	Symbol	Russian example	English example/explanation
А,а	[a]	да́ть	after
Е,е	[ɛ]	се́л	get
Ё,ё	[jo]	ёлка, моё	yawn
И,и	[i]	их, ни́ва	sheet
Й,й	[j]	йод, мой	yield
О́,о́	[o]	кот	dot
О,о	[ʌ]	нога́	cup
У,у	[u]	ум	shoot
Ы,ы	[+]	сын	*pronounced like "ee", but with the tongue arched further back in the mouth*
Э,э	[æ]	э́то	cat
Ю,ю	[ju]	юг	you, youth
Я,я	[ja]	я́сно	yak

Consonants

Б,б	[b]	банк	but
В,в	[v]	вот	vat
Г,г	[g]	гол	got
Д,д	[d]	дом	dog
Ж,ж	[ʒ]	жена́	measure
З,з	[z]	за́втра	doze
К,к	[k]	кот	cat
Л,л	[l]	ло́дка	lot
М,м	[m]	мать	mat
Н,н	[n]	нас	no
П,п	[p]	пасть	put
Р,р	[r]	рот	*pronounced like rolled Scots "r"*
С,с	[s]	сад	sat
Т,т	[t]	ток	top
Ф,ф	[f]	фо́рма	fat
Х,х	[x]	ход	*pronounced like Scots "ch" in "loch"*
Ц,ц	[ts]	цель	bits
Ч,ч	[tʃ]	ча́сто	chip
Ш,ш	[ʃ]	шу́тка	shoot
Щ,щ	[ʃʃ]	щит	fresh sheets

Russian vowels are inherently short. Russian stressed vowels tend to be slightly longer than unstressed vowels. In unstressed positions all vowels are "reduced". Unstressed "o" sounds like "a" eg. города́ [gərʌˈda], except in some loanwords and acronyms eg. ра́дио [ˈraḓio], госба́нк [gosˈbank]. Unstressed "e" is pronounced like "bit" eg. село́ [şiˈlo]. The same is true of "я" before stressed syllables eg. пяти́ [piˈţi], and of "a" when it follows "ч" or "щ" eg. щади́ть [ʃʃiˈḓiţ].

The letter "ё" is used only in grammar books, dictionaries etc to avoid ambiguity eg. не́бо and нёбо.

Latin characters in Russian are pronounced as if they were their Cyrillic equivalents, so for example MP3 is pronounced [ɛmpɛtri]

АНГЛИЙСКОЕ ПРОИЗНОШЕНИЕ

Гласные и дифтонги

Знак	Английский пример	Русское соответствие/описание
[ɑː]	father	ма́ма
[ʌ]	but, come	алья́нс
[æ]	man, cat	э́тот
[ə]	father, ago	ра́на
[əː]	bird, heard	Фёдор
[ɛ]	get, bed	жест
[ɪ]	it, big	кит
[iː]	tea, sea	и́ва
[ɔ]	hot, wash	ход
[ɔː]	saw, all	о́чень
[u]	put, book	бук
[uː]	too, you	у́лица
[aɪ]	fly, high	ла́й
[au]	how, house	а́ут
[ɛə]	there, bear	*произно́сится как сочета́ние "э" и кра́ткого "а"*
[eɪ]	day, obey	эй
[ɪə]	here, hear	*произно́сится как сочета́ние "и" и кра́ткого "а"*
[əu]	go, note	о́у
[ɔɪ]	boy, oil	бой
[uə]	poor, sure	*произно́сится как сочета́ние "у" и кра́ткого "а"*
[juə]	pure	*произно́сится как сочета́ние "ю" и кра́ткого "а"*

Согласные

[b]	but	бал
[d]	dot	дом
[g]	go, get, big	гол, миг
[dʒ]	gin, judge	джи́нсы, и́мидж
[ŋ]	sing	*произно́сится как ру́сское "н", но не ко́нчиком языка́, а за́дней ча́стью его́ спи́нки*
[h]	house, he	ха́ос, хи́мия
[j]	young, yes	йод, Йе́мен
[k]	come, mock	ка́мень, рок
[r]	red, tread	рот, трава́
[s]	sand, yes	сад, рис
[z]	rose, zebra	ро́за, зе́бра
[ʃ]	she, machine	ши́на, маши́на
[tʃ]	chin, rich	чин, кули́ч
[v]	valley	вальс
[w]	water, which	уо́тергейт, уик-э́нд
[ʒ]	vision	ва́жный
[θ]	think, myth	*произно́сится как ру́сское "с", но ко́нчик языка́ нахо́дится ме́жду зуба́ми*
[ð]	this, the	*произно́сится как ру́сское "з", но ко́нчик языка́ нахо́дится ме́жду зуба́ми*
[f]	face	фа́кт
[l]	lake, lick	лай, лом
[m]	must	мат
[n]	nut	нет
[p]	pat, pond	пар, пот
[t]	take, hat	э́тот, нет
[x]	loch	ход

АНГЛИЙСКИЕ НЕПРАВИЛЬНЫЕ ГЛАГОЛЫ

present	pt	pp	present	pt	pp
arise	arose	arisen	dwell	dwelt	dwelt
awake	awoke	awaked	eat	ate	eaten
be (am, is, are; being)	was, were	been	fall	fell	fallen
			feed	fed	fed
bear	bore	born(e)	feel	felt	felt
beat	beat	beaten	fight	fought	fought
become	became	become	find	found	found
begin	began	begun	flee	fled	fled
behold	beheld	beheld	fling	flung	flung
bend	bent	bent	fly (flies)	flew	flown
beseech	besought	besought	forbid	forbade	forbidden
beset	beset	beset	forecast	forecast	forecast
bet	bet, betted	bet, betted	forget	forgot	forgotten
bid	bid, bade	bid, bidden	forgive	forgave	forgiven
bind	bound	bound	forsake	forsook	forsaken
bite	bit	bitten	freeze	froze	frozen
bleed	bled	bled	get	got	got, (US) gotten
blow	blew	blown			
break	broke	broken	give	gave	given
breed	bred	bred	go (goes)	went	gone
bring	brought	brought	grind	ground	ground
build	built	built	grow	grew	grown
burn	burnt, burned	burnt, burned	hang	hung, hanged	hung, hanged
burst	burst	burst	have (has; having)	had	had
buy	bought	bought	hear	heard	heard
can	could	(been able)	hide	hid	hidden
cast	cast	cast	hit	hit	hit
catch	caught	caught	hold	held	held
choose	chose	chosen	hurt	hurt	hurt
cling	clung	clung	keep	kept	kept
come	came	come	kneel	knelt, kneeled	knelt, kneeled
cost	cost	cost			
creep	crept	crept	know	knew	known
cut	cut	cut	lay	laid	laid
deal	dealt	dealt	lead	led	led
dig	dug	dug	lean	leant, leaned	leant, leaned
do (3rd person: he/she/it/does)	did	done	leap	leapt, leaped	leapt, leaped
			learn	learnt, learned	learnt, learned
draw	drew	drawn	leave	left	left
dream	dreamed, dreamt	dreamed, dreamt	lend	lent	lent
			let	let	let
drink	drank	drunk	lie (lying)	lay	lain
drive	drove	driven	light	lit, lighted	lit, lighted

present	pt	pp	present	pt	pp
lose	lost	lost	speak	spoke	spoken
make	made	made	speed	sped, speeded	sped, speeded
may	might	—			
mean	meant	meant	spell	spelt, spelled	spelt, spelled
meet	met	met	spend	spent	spent
mistake	mistook	mistaken	spill	spilt, spilled	spilt, spilled
mow	mowed	mown, mowed	spin	spun	spun
			spit	spat	spat
must	(had to)	(had to)	split	split	split
pay	paid	paid	spoil	spoiled, spoilt	spoiled, spoilt
put	put	put	spread	spread	spread
quit	quit, quitted	quit, quitted	spring	sprang	sprung
read	read	read	stand	stood	stood
rid	rid	rid	steal	stole	stolen
ride	rode	ridden	stick	stuck	stuck
ring	rang	rung	sting	stung	stung
rise	rose	risen	stink	stank	stunk
run	ran	run	stride	strode	stridden
saw	sawed	sawn	strike	struck	struck, stricken
say	said	said			
see	saw	seen	strive	strove	striven
seek	sought	sought	swear	swore	sworn
sell	sold	sold	sweep	swept	swept
send	sent	sent	swell	swelled	swollen, swelled
set	set	set			
shake	shook	shaken	swim	swam	swum
shall	should	—	swing	swung	swung
shear	sheared	shorn, sheared	take	took	taken
			teach	taught	taught
shed	shed	shed	tear	tore	torn
shine	shone	shone	tell	told	told
shoot	shot	shot	think	thought	thought
show	showed	shown	throw	threw	thrown
shrink	shrank	shrunk	thrust	thrust	thrust
shut	shut	shut	tread	trod	trodden
sing	sang	sung	wake	woke, waked	woken, waked
sink	sank	sunk			
sit	sat	sat	wear	wore	worn
slay	slew	slain	weave	wove, weaved	woven, weaved
sleep	slept	slept			
slide	slid	slid	wed	wedded, wed	wedded, wed
sling	slung	slung	weep	wept	wept
slit	slit	slit	win	won	won
smell	smelt, smelled	smelt, smelled	wind	wound	wound
			wring	wrung	wrung
sow	sowed	sown, sowed	write	wrote	written

ЧИСЛИТЕЛЬНЫЕ/NUMBERS

Количественные числительные   Cardinal numbers

оди́н (одна́, одно́, одни́)	**1**	one
два (две)	**2**	two
три	**3**	three
четы́ре	**4**	four
пять	**5**	five
шесть	**6**	six
семь	**7**	seven
во́семь	**8**	eight
де́вять	**9**	nine
де́сять	**10**	ten
оди́ннадцать	**11**	eleven
двена́дцать	**12**	twelve
трина́дцать	**13**	thirteen
четы́рнадцать	**14**	fourteen
пятна́дцать	**15**	fifteen
шестна́дцать	**16**	sixteen
семна́дцать	**17**	seventeen
восемна́дцать	**18**	eighteen
девятна́дцать	**19**	nineteen
два́дцать	**20**	twenty
два́дцать оди́н (одна́, одно́, одни́)	**21**	twenty-one
два́дцать два́ (две́)	**22**	twenty-two
три́дцать	**30**	thirty
со́рок	**40**	forty
пятьдеся́т	**50**	fifty
шестьдеся́т	**60**	sixty
се́мьдесят	**70**	seventy
во́семьдесят	**80**	eighty
девяно́сто	**90**	ninety
сто	**100**	a hundred
сто оди́н (одна́, одно́, одни́)	**101**	a hundred and one
две́сти	**200**	two hundred
две́сти оди́н (одна́, одно́, одни́)	**201**	two hundred and one
три́ста	**300**	three hundred
четы́реста	**400**	four hundred
пятьсо́т	**500**	five hundred
ты́сяча	**1 000**	a thousand
миллио́н	**1 000 000**	a million

Собирательные числительные/Collective numerals

дво́е
тро́е
че́тверо
пя́теро
ше́стеро
се́меро

Порядковые числительные

пе́рвый	1-й
второ́й	2-й
тре́тий	3-й
четвёртый	4-й
пя́тый	5-й
шесто́й	6-й
седьмо́й	7-й
восьмо́й	8-й
девя́тый	9-й
деся́тый	10-й
оди́ннадцатый	
двена́дцатый	
трина́дцатый	
четы́рнадцатый	
пятна́дцатый	
шестна́дцатый	
семна́дцатый	
восемна́дцатый	
девятна́дцатый	
двадца́тый	
два́дцать пе́рвый	
два́дцать второ́й	
тридца́тый	
сороково́й	
пятидеся́тый	
восьмидеся́тый	
девяно́стый	
со́тый	
сто пе́рвый	
ты́сячный	
миллио́нный	

Ordinal numbers

first	1st
second	2nd
third	3rd
fourth	4th
fifth	5th
sixth	6th
seventh	7th
eighth	8th
ninth	9th
tenth	10th
eleventh	
twelfth	
thirteenth	
fourteenth	
fifteenth	
sixteenth	
seventeenth	
eighteenth	
nineteenth	
twentieth	
twenty-first	
twenty-second	
thirtieth	
fortieth	
fiftieth	
eightieth	
ninetieth	
hundredth	
hundred-and-first	
thousandth	
millionth	

Дроби

полови́на	½
треть (f)	⅓
че́тверть (f)	¼
одна́ пя́тая	⅕
три че́тверти	¾
две тре́ти	⅔
полтора́ (полторы́)	1½
ноль це́лых (и) пять деся́тых	0,5
три це́лых (и) четы́ре деся́тых	3,4
шесть це́лых (и) во́семьдесят де́вять со́тых	6,89
де́сять проце́нтов	10%
сто проце́нтов	100%

Fractions

a half	½
a third	⅓
a quarter	¼
a fifth	⅕
three quarters	¾
two thirds	⅔
one and a half	1½
(nought) point five	0.5
three point four	3.4
six point eight nine	6.89
ten per cent	10%
a hundred per cent	100%

ВРЕМЯ И ДАТЫ/TIME AND DATE

Время	**Time**
кото́рый час?	what time is it?
сейча́с 5 часо́в	it is *or* it's 5 o'clock
в како́е вре́мя?	at what time?
в +*acc*...	at ...
в час дня	at one p.m.
по́лночь (*f*)	00.00 midnight
де́сять мину́т пе́рвого	00.10, ten past midnight, ten past twelve a.m.
де́сять мину́т второ́го, час де́сять	01.10, ten past one, one ten
че́тверть второ́го, час пятна́дцать	01.15, a quarter past one, one fifteen
полвторо́го, полови́на второ́го, час три́дцать	01.30, half past one, one thirty
без че́тверти два, час со́рок пять	01.45, a quarter to two, one forty-five
без десяти́ два, час пятьдеся́т	01.50, ten to two, one fifty
по́лдень (*m*)	12.00, midday
полпе́рвого, полови́на первого, двена́дцать три́дцать	12.30, half past twelve, twelve thirty p.m.
час дня	13.00, one (o'clock) (in the afternoon), one p.m.
семь часо́в ве́чера	19.00, seven (o'clock) (in the evening), seven p.m.
де́вять три́дцать ве́чера	21.30, nine thirty (p.m. *or* at night)
без че́тверти двена́дцать, оди́ннадцать со́рок пять	23.45, a quarter to twelve, eleven forty-five p.m.
че́рез два́дцать мину́т	in twenty minutes
два́дцать минут наза́д	twenty minutes ago
в ближа́йшие два́дцать мину́т	in the next twenty minutes
за два́дцать мину́т	within twenty minutes
спустя́ два́дцать мину́т	after twenty minutes
сейча́с два́дцать мину́т четвёртого	it's twenty past *or* after (*US*) three
полчаса́	half an hour
че́тверть ча́са	quarter of an hour
полтора́ часа́	an hour and a half
час с че́твертью	an hour and a quarter
че́рез час	in an hour's time
ка́ждый час	every hour, on the hour
че́рез час, ка́ждый час	hourly
че́рез час	in an hour from now
разбуди́те меня́ в семь часо́в	wake me up at seven
уже́ нача́ло пя́того	it's just gone four
с девяти́ до пяти́	from nine to five
с двух до трёх (часо́в)	between two and three (o'clock)
сего́дня с девяти́ утра́	since nine o'clock this morning
до десяти́ часо́в ве́чера	till ten o'clock tonight
о́коло трёх часо́в дня	at about three o'clock in the afternoon
три часа́ по Гри́нвичу	three o'clock GMT

Даты / Date

сего́дня	today
за́втра	tomorrow
вчера́	yesterday
сего́дня у́тром	this morning
за́втра днём/ве́чером	tomorrow afternoon/night
позавчера́ ве́чером/позапро́шлой но́чью	the night before last
позавчера́	the day before yesterday
вчера́ ве́чером, про́шлой но́чью	last night
послеза́втра	the day after tomorrow
два дня/шесть лет наза́д	two days/six years ago
ка́ждый день/вто́рник	every day/Tuesday
в сре́ду	on Wednesday
он хо́дит туда́ по сре́дам	he goes there on Wednesdays
"закры́то по пя́тницам"	"closed on Fridays"
с понеде́льника до пя́тницы	from Monday to Friday
к четвергу́	by Thursday
как-то в ма́рте, в суббо́ту	one Saturday in March
че́рез неде́лю	in a week's time
во вто́рник на сле́дующей неде́ле	a week on or next Tuesday
в воскресе́нье на про́шлой неде́ле	a week last Sunday
че́рез понеде́льник	Monday week
на э́той/сле́дующей/про́шлой неде́ле	this/next/last week
че́рез две неде́ли	in two weeks or a fortnight
в понеде́льник че́рез две неде́ли	two weeks on Monday
в э́тот день шесть лет наза́д	six years to the day
пе́рвая/после́дняя пя́тница ме́сяца	the first/last Friday of the month
в сле́дующем ме́сяце	next month
в про́шлом году́	last year
в конце́ ме́сяца	at the end of the month
два ра́за в неде́лю/ме́сяц/год	twice a week/month/year
како́е сего́дня число́?	what's the date?, what date is it today?
сего́дня 28-е	today's date is the 28th, today is the 28th
пе́рвое января́	the first of January, January the first
ты́сяча девятьсо́т девяно́сто девя́тый год	1999, nineteen (hundred and) ninety nine
две ты́сячи трина́дцатый год	2013, two thousand and thirteen or twenty thirteen
роди́лся в 1980-м году́	I was born in 1980
у него́ день рожде́ния 5 ию́ня	his birthday is on June 5th (BRIT) or 5th June
18 а́вгуста 2018	on 18th August (BRIT) or August 18th 2018 (US)
с 19-го по 3-е	from the 19th to the 3rd
в 99-м году́	in '99
весна́ 97-го го́да	the Spring of '97
в 1930-х года́х	in (or during) the 1930s
в 1940-х года́х	in 1940 something
в 2019-м году́	in the year 2019
в XIII ве́ке	in the 13th century
4 год до н. э.	4 BC
70 год н. э.	70 AD

а

автозапра́вочная ста́нция) filling
station; **автомагистра́л|ь (-и)** ж
motorway (*Brit*), expressway (*US*);
автомаши́н|а (-ы) ж (motor)car,
automobile (*US*); **автомеха́ник (-а)** м
car mechanic; **автомоби́л|ь (-я)** м
(motor)car, automobile (*US*); **легково́й
автомоби́ль** (passenger) car
автоно́мный *прил* autonomous
автоотве́тчик (-а) м answering machine,
answer phone, voice mail
а́втор (-а) м author
авторите́т (-а) м authority
авторуч|ка (-ки; *gen pl* **-ек)** ж fountain
pen
автостра́д|а (-ы) ж motorway (*Brit*),
expressway (*US*)
аге́нт (-а) м agent; **аге́нтств|о (-а)** *ср*
agency
агити́р|овать (-ую) *несов*: **агити́ровать
(за** +*acc*) to campaign (for)
аго́ни|я (-и) ж death throes мн
агрега́т (-а) м machine
агре́сси|я (-и) ж aggression
ад (-а) м hell
адапти́р|оваться (-уюсь) (*не)сов возв*
to adapt
адвока́т (-а) м counsel; (*в суде*)
≈ barrister (*Brit*), ≈ attorney (*US*)
адеква́тный *прил* adequate
администра́ци|я (-и) ж administration;
(*гостиницы*) management
а́дрес (-а; *nom pl* **-а́)** м address;
а́дресный *прил*: **а́дресный стол**
residents' registration office; **адрес|ова́ть
(-у́ю)** (*не)сов перех*: **адресова́ть что-н
кому́-н** to address sth to sb
ажу́рный *прил* lace
аза́рт (-а) м ardour (*Brit*), ardor (*US*)
а́збук|а (-и) ж alphabet; (*букварь*) first
reading book
Азербайджа́н (-а) м Azerbaijan
А́зи|я (-и) ж Asia
азо́т (-а) м nitrogen
ай *межд* (*выражает боль*) ow, ouch
а́йсберг (-а) м iceberg
акаде́ми|я (-и) ж academy
акваре́л|ь (-и) ж watercolours мн (*Brit*),
watercolors мн (*US*); (*картина*)
watercolo(u)r
аква́риум (-а) м aquarium, fish tank
аккомпани́р|овать (-ую) *несов* +*dat* to
accompany
акко́рд (-а) м chord
аккура́тный *прил* (*посещение*) regular;
(*работник*) meticulous; (*работа*) accurate;
(*костюм*) neat
акселера́тор (-а) м accelerator
акт (-а) м act; (*документ*) formal document
актёр (-а) м actor
акти́в (-а) м assets мн
акти́вный *прил* active
актри́с|а (-ы) ж actress
актуа́льный *прил* topical; (*задача*) urgent

а *союз* **1** but; **он согласи́лся, а я
отказа́лась** he agreed, but I refused
2 (*выражает присоединение*) and
3 (*во фразах*): **а (не) то** or (else); **а вот** but
▷ *част* (*обозначает отклик*): **иди́ сюда́! —
а, что тако́е!** come here! — yes, what is it?;
а как же (*разг*) of course, certainly
▷ *межд* ah; (*выражает ужас, боль*) oh; **а
ну** (*разг*) go on; **а ну́ его!** (*разг*) stuff him!

абажу́р (-а) м lampshade
абза́ц (-а) м paragraph
абитурие́нт (-а) м entrant to university,
college etc
абонеме́нт (-а) м season ticket
або́рт (-а) м abortion
абрико́с (-а) м (*плод*) apricot
абсолю́тный *прил* absolute
абстра́ктный *прил* abstract
абсу́рдный *прил* absurd
авантю́р|а (-ы) ж adventure
авари́йный *прил* emergency; (*дом*)
unsafe; **авари́йный сигна́л** alarm signal
ава́ри|я (-и) ж accident; (*повреждение*)
breakdown
а́вгуст (-а) м August
а́виа *нескл* (*авиапочта*) air mail
авиакомпа́ни|я (-и) ж airline
авиано́с|ец (-ца) м aircraft carrier
Австра́ли|я (-и) ж Australia
А́встри|я (-и) ж Austria
автоба́з|а (-ы) ж depot
автобиогра́фи|я (-и) ж autobiography
авто́бус (-а) м bus
автовокза́л (-а) м bus station
авто́граф (-а) м autograph
авто-: **автозаво́д (-а)** м car (*Brit*) или
automobile (*US*) plant;
автозапра́вочн|ая (-ой) ж (*также*

аку́л|а (-ы) ж shark
акуше́р|ка (-ки; gen pl -ок) ж midwife
акце́нт (-а) м accent
акци́з (-а) м excise (tax)
акционе́р (-а) м shareholder
а́кци|я (-и) ж (Комм) share; (действие) action
а́либи ср нескл alibi
алиме́нт|ы (-ов) мн alimony ед, maintenance ед
алкого́лик (-а) м alcoholic
алкого́л|ь (-я) м alcohol
аллерги́|я (-и) ж allergy
алле́|я (-и) ж alley
алло́ межд hello
алма́з (-а) м diamond
алфави́т (-а) м alphabet
альбо́м (-а) м album
альт (-а́) м (инструмент) viola
альтернати́в|а (-ы) ж alternative
алья́нс (-а) м alliance
алюми́ни|й (-я) м aluminium (Brit), aluminum (US)
амбулато́ри|я (-и) ж doctor's surgery (Brit) или office (US)
Аме́рик|а (-и) ж America
америка́нск|ий прил American
амнисти́р|овать (-ую) (не)сов перех to grant (an) amnesty to
амни́сти|я (-и) ж amnesty
амора́льный прил immoral
амортиза́тор (-а) м (Tex) shock absorber
а́мпул|а (-ы) ж ampoule (Brit), ampule (US)
АН ж сокр (= Акаде́мия нау́к) Academy of Sciences
ана́лиз (-а) м analysis
анализи́р|овать (-ую; perf проанализи́ровать) несов перех to analyse (Brit), analyze (US)
анали́тик (-а) м analyst
аналоги́чный прил analogous
анало́ги|я (-и) ж analogy; по анало́гии (с +instr) in a similar way (to)
анана́с (-а) м pineapple
ана́рхи|я (-и) ж anarchy
анато́ми|я (-и) ж anatomy
а́нгел (-а) м (также разг) angel
анги́н|а (-ы) ж tonsillitis
англи́йский прил English; англи́йский язы́к English
англича́н|ин (-ина; nom pl -е, gen pl -) м Englishman (мн Englishmen)
А́нгли|я (-и) ж England
анекдо́т (-а) м joke
анеми́|я (-и) ж anaemia (Brit), anemia (US)
анестезио́лог (-а) м anaesthetist (Brit), anesthiologist (US)
анестези́|я (-и) ж anaesthesia (Brit), anesthesia (US)
анке́т|а (-ы) ж (опросный лист) questionnaire; (бланк для сведений) form; (сбор сведений) survey

анони́мный прил anonymous
Антаркти́д|а (-ы) ж Antarctica
Анта́рктик|а (-и) ж the Antarctic
анте́нн|а (-ы) ж aerial (Brit), antenna (US); анте́нна косми́ческой свя́зи satellite dish
антибио́тик (-а) м antibiotic
антиви́русный прил antivirus; антиви́русное програ́ммное обеспече́ние antivirus software
антиква́рный прил antique
анти́чный прил classical; анти́чный мир the Ancient World
антра́кт (-а) м interval
аню́тины прил: аню́тины гла́зки pansy ед
А/О ср сокр (= акционе́рное о́бщество) joint-stock company
апа́ти|я (-и) ж apathy
апелли́р|овать (-ую) (не)сов (Юр) to appeal
апелля́ци|я (-и) ж (также Юр) appeal
апельси́н (-а) м orange
аплоди́р|овать (-ую) несов +dat to applaud
аплодисме́нт|ы (-ов) мн applause ед
аппара́т (-а) м apparatus; (Физиология) system; (штат) staff
аппарату́р|а (-ы) ж собир equipment
аппендици́т (-а) м appendicitis
аппети́т (-а) м appetite; прия́тного аппети́та! bon appétit!
апре́л|ь (-я) м April
апте́к|а (-и) ж pharmacy; апте́кар|ь (-я) м pharmacist
ара́б (-а) м Arab; ара́бский прил (страны) Arab; ара́бский язы́к Arabic
ара́хис (-а) м peanut
арби́тр (-а) м (в спорах) arbitrator; (в футболе) referee
арбитра́ж (-а) м arbitration
арбу́з (-а) м watermelon
аргуме́нт (-а) м argument; аргументи́р|овать (-ую) (не)сов перех to argue
аре́н|а (-ы) ж arena; (цирка) ring
аре́нд|а (-ы) ж (наём) lease; аре́ндн|ый прил lease; аре́ндная пла́та rent; аренд|ова́ть (-у́ю) (не)сов перех to lease
аре́ст (-а) м (преступника) arrest; аресто́ванн|ый (-ого) м person held in custody; арест|ова́ть (-у́ю); impf аресто́вывать) сов перех (преступника) to arrest
арифме́тик|а (-и) ж arithmetic
а́р|ка (-ки; gen pl -ок) ж arch
А́рктик|а (-и) ж the Arctic
армату́р|а (-ы) ж steel framework
арме́йский прил army
Арме́ни|я (-и) ж Armenia
а́рми|я (-и) ж army
армяни́н (-а; nom pl армя́не, gen pl армя́н) м Armenian
арома́т (-а) м (цветов) fragrance; (кофе итп) aroma

арте́ри|я (-и) ж (также перен) artery
арти́кл|ь (-я) м (Линг) article
арти́ст (-а) м actor
арти́ст|ка (-ки; gen pl -ок) ж actress
артри́т (-а) м arthritis
а́рф|а (-ы) ж harp
архео́лог (-а) м archaeologist (Brit), archeologist (US)
архи́в (-а) м archive
архиепи́скоп (-а) м archbishop
архите́ктор (-а) м architect; **архитекту́р|а** (-ы) ж architecture
аспе́кт (-а) м aspect
аспира́нт (-а) м postgraduate (doing PhD); **аспиранту́р|а** (-ы) ж postgraduate studies мн (leading to PhD)
аспири́н (-а) м aspirin
ассамбле́|я (-и) ж assembly
ассигн|ова́ть (-у́ю) (не)сов перех to allocate
ассимили́р|оваться (-уюсь) (не)сов возв to become assimilated
ассисте́нт (-а) м assistant; (в вузе) assistant lecturer
ассортиме́нт (-а) м range
ассоциа́ци|я (-и) ж association
ассоции́р|овать (-ую) (не)сов перех to associate
а́стм|а (-ы) ж asthma
астроло́ги|я (-и) ж astrology
астрономи́ческий прил (также перен) astronomic(al)
ата́к|а (-и) ж attack; **атак|ова́ть** (-у́ю) (не)сов перех to attack
атама́н (-а) м ataman (Cossack leader)
атеи́ст (-а) м atheist
ателье́ ср нескл studio; (мод) tailor's shop; **телевизио́нное ателье́** television repair shop; **ателье́ прока́та** rental shop
атланти́ческий прил: **Атланти́ческий океа́н** the Atlantic (Ocean)
а́тлас (-а) м atlas
атле́тик|а (-и) ж: **лёгкая атле́тика** track and field events; **тяжёлая атле́тика** weight lifting
атмосфе́р|а (-ы) ж atmosphere
а́том (-а) м atom
АТС ж сокр (= автомати́ческая телефо́нная ста́нция) automatic telephone exchange
аттеста́т (-а) м certificate; **аттеста́т зре́лости** ≈ GCSE

■ **Аттеста́т зре́лости**
●
● Certificate of Secondary Education. This
■ was formerly obtained by school-leavers
● after sitting their final exams. This
■ system has now been replaced by the
■ ЕГЭ.

аттест|ова́ть (-у́ю) (не)сов перех to assess
аттракцио́н (-а) м (в цирке) attraction; (в парке) amusement

ауди́т (-а) м audit
аудито́ри|я (-и) ж lecture hall ▷ собир (слушатели) audience
аукцио́н (-а) м auction
а́ут (-а) м (в теннисе) out; (в футболе): **мяч в ау́те** the ball is out of play
афи́ш|а (-и) ж poster
А́фрик|а (-и) ж Africa
ах межд: **ах!** oh!, ah!; **ах да!** (разг) ah yes!
АЦАЛ ж сокр (= асимметри́чная цифрова́я абоне́нтская ли́ния) ADSL (= Asymmetric Digital Subscriber Line)
аэро́бик|а (-и) ж aerobics
аэровокза́л (-а) м air terminal (esp Brit)
аэрозо́л|ь (-я) м aerosol, spray
аэропо́рт (-а; loc sg -у́) м airport
АЭС ж сокр (= а́томная электроста́нция) atomic power station

б част см **бы**

ба́б|а (**-ы**) ж (разг) woman; **ба́б|а-яг|а́** (**-ы**, **-й**) ж Baba Yaga (old witch in Russian folk-tales); **ба́б|ка** (**-ки**; gen pl **-ок**) ж grandmother

ба́боч|ка (**-ки**; gen pl **-ек**) ж butterfly; (галстук) bow tie

ба́буш|ка (**-ки**; gen pl **-ек**) ж grandmother, grandma

бага́ж (**-а́**) м luggage (Brit), baggage (US); **бага́жник** (**-а**) м (в автомобиле) boot (Brit), trunk (US); (на велосипеде) carrier

багро́вый прил crimson

бадминто́н (**-а**) м badminton

ба́з|а (**-ы**) ж basis; (Воен, Архит) base; (для туристов) centre (Brit), center (US); (товаров) warehouse

база́р (**-а**) м market; (книжный) fair; (перен: разг) racket

бази́р|овать (**-ую**) несов перех: **бази́ровать что-н на** +prp to base sth on; **бази́роваться** несов возв: **бази́роваться** (**на** +prp) to be based (on)

байда́р|ка (**-ки**; gen pl **-ок**) ж canoe

Байка́л (**-а**) м Lake Baikal

бак (**-а**) м tank

бакале́|я (**-и**) ж grocery section; (товары) groceries мн

ба́кен (**-а**) м buoy

бакенба́рд|ы (**-**) мн sideburns

баклажа́н (**-а**; gen pl **—** или **-ов**) м aubergine (Brit), eggplant (US)

бакс (**-а**) м (разг) dollar

бал (**-а**; loc sg **-у́**, nom pl **-ы́**) м ball

балала́|йка (**-йки**; gen pl **-ек**) ж balalaika

бала́нс (**-а**) м balance; **баланси́р|овать** (**-ую**) несов: **баланси́ровать** (**на** +prp) to balance (on)

балери́н|а (**-ы**) ж ballerina

бале́т (**-а**) м ballet

ба́л|ка (**-ки**; gen pl **-ок**) ж beam

Балка́н|ы (**-**) мн the Balkans

балко́н (**-а**) м (Архит) balcony; (Театр) circle (Brit), balcony (US)

балл (**-а**) м mark; (Спорт) point

балло́н (**-а**) м (газовый) cylinder; (для жидкости) jar

баллоти́р|овать (**-ую**) несов перех to vote for; **баллоти́роваться** несов возв: **баллоти́роваться в** +асс или **на пост** +gen to stand (Brit) или run (US) for

бал|ова́ть (**-у́ю**; perf **избалова́ть**) несов перех to spoil; **балова́ться** несов возв (ребёнок) to be naughty

балти́йск|ий прил: **Балти́йское мо́ре** the Baltic (Sea)

ба́льн|ый прил: **ба́льное пла́тье** ball gown

ба́мпер (**-а**) м bumper

бана́н (**-а**) м banana

ба́нд|а (**-ы**) ж gang

бандеро́л|ь (**-и**) ж package

банк (**-а**) м bank

ба́н|ка (**-ки**; gen pl **-ок**) ж jar; (жестяная) tin (Brit), can (US)

банке́т (**-а**) м banquet

банки́р (**-а**) м banker

банкно́т (**-а**; gen pl **-**) м banknote

ба́нковский прил bank

банкома́т (**-а**) м cash machine

банкро́т (**-а**) м bankrupt

банкро́тств|о (**-а**) ср bankruptcy

бант (**-а**) м bow

ба́н|я (**-и**; gen pl **-ь**) ж bathhouse

бар (**-а**) м bar

бараба́н (**-а**) м drum; **бараба́н|ить** (**-ю**, **-ишь**) несов to drum

бара́к (**-а**) м barracks мн

бара́н (**-а**) м sheep; **бара́нин|а** (**-ы**) ж mutton; (молодая) lamb

барахло́ (**-а́**) ср собир junk

барахо́л|ка (**-ки**; gen pl **-ок**) ж flea market

барда́к (**-а́**) м (груб!: беспорядок) hell broke loose (!)

ба́рж|а (**-и**) ж barge

ба́рмен (**-а**) м barman (мн barmen), bartender (US)

баро́метр (**-а**) м barometer

баррика́д|а (**-ы**) ж barricade

барсу́к (**-а́**) м badger

ба́рхат (**-а**) м velvet

барье́р (**-а**) м (в беге) hurdle; (на скачках) fence; (перен) barrier

бас (**-а**; nom pl **-ы́**) м bass

баскетбо́л (**-а**) м basketball

бассе́йн (**-а**) м (swimming) pool; (реки, озера итп) basin

баст|ова́ть (**-у́ю**) несов to be on strike

батаре́|йка (**-йки**; gen pl **-ек**) ж (Элек) battery

батаре́|я (**-и**) ж (отопительная) radiator; (Воен, Элек) battery

бато́н (**-а**) м (white) loaf (long or oval)

ба́тюш|ка (**-ки**; gen pl **-ек**) м father

бахром|а́ (-ы́) ж fringe (*Brit*), bangs мн (*US*)

ба́ш|ня (-ни; *gen pl* -ен) ж tower

баюка|ть (-ю) *несов перех* to lull to sleep

баян (-а) м bayan (*kind of concertina*)

бди́тельный *прил* vigilant

бег (-а) м run, running; **на бегу́** hurriedly; см также **бега́**

бег|а́ (-о́в) мн the races мн

бе́га|ть (-ю) *несов* to run

бегемо́т (-а) м hippopotamus, hippo (*inf*)

беги́(те) *несов см* бежа́ть

бегов·о́й *прил* (*лошадь*) race; **беговая доро́жка** running track

бего́м *нареч* quickly; (*перен: разг*) in a rush

бе́гств|о (-а) *ср* flight; (*из плена*) escape

бегу́ *итп несов см* бежа́ть

бегу́н (-а́) м runner

бегу́н|ья (-ьи; *gen pl* -ий) ж runner

бед|а́ (-ы́; *nom pl* -ы) ж tragedy; (*несчастье*) misfortune, trouble; **про́сто беда́!** it's just awful!; **не беда́!** (*разг*) (it's) nothing!, not to worry!

бедне́|ть (-ю; *perf* обедне́ть) *несов* to become poor

бе́дность (-и) ж poverty; **бе́дный** *прил* poor

бедня́г|а (-и) м/ж (*разг*) poor thing

бедня́к (-а́) м poor man

бедр|о́ (-а́; *nom pl* бёдра, *gen pl* бёдер) *ср* thigh; (*таз*) hip

бе́дственный *прил* disastrous; **бе́дстви|е** (-я) *ср* disaster; **бе́дств|овать** (-ую) *несов* to live in poverty

бе|жа́ть (см *Table 20*) *несов* to run; (*время*) to fly

бе́жевый *прил* beige

бе́жен|ец (-ца) м refugee

без *предл* +*gen* without; **без пяти́/десяти́ минут шесть** five to/ten to six

безала́берный *прил* (*разг*) sloppy

безалкого́льный *прил* nonalcoholic, alcohol-free; **безалкого́льный напи́ток** soft drink

безбиле́тник (-а) м fare dodger

безбо́жный *прил* (*разг*) shameless

безве́тренный *прил* calm

безвку́сный *прил* tasteless

безвла́сти|е (-я) *ср* anarchy

безвы́ходный *прил* hopeless

безгра́мотный *прил* illiterate; (*работник*) incompetent

безде́йств|овать (-ую) *несов* to stand idle; (*человек*) to take no action

безде́льнича|ть (-ю) *несов* (*разг*) to loaf или lounge about

бездо́мный *прил* (*человек*) homeless; (*собака*) stray

безду́мный *прил* thoughtless

безду́шный *прил* heartless

безе́ *ср нескл* meringue

безжа́лостный *прил* ruthless

беззабо́тный *прил* carefree

беззасте́нчивый *прил* shameless

беззащи́тный *прил* defenceless (*Brit*), defenseless (*US*)

безли́чный *прил* impersonal

безмо́лвный *прил* silent

безмяте́жный *прил* tranquil

безнадёжный *прил* hopeless

безнра́вственный *прил* immoral

безо *предл* = **без**

безоби́дный *прил* harmless

безобра́зный *прил* ugly; (*поступок*) outrageous, disgraceful

безогово́рочный *прил* unconditional

безопа́сность (-и) ж safety; (*международная*) security

безопа́сный *прил* safe

безору́жный *прил* unarmed

безотве́тственный *прил* irresponsible

безотка́зный *прил* reliable

безотлага́тельный *прил* urgent

безотноси́тельно *нареч*: **безотноси́тельно к** +*dat* irrespective of

безоши́бочный *прил* correct

безрабо́тиц|а (-ы) ж unemployment

безрабо́т|ный *прил* unemployed ▷ (-ого) м unemployed person

безразли́чный *прил* indifferent

безразме́р|ный *прил*: **безразме́рные носки́** one-size socks

безрука́в|ка (-ки; *gen pl* -ок) ж (*кофта*) sleeveless top; (*куртка*) sleeveless jacket

безу́мный *прил* mad; (*о чувстве*) wild

безуспе́шный *прил* unsuccessful

безуча́стный *прил* indifferent

безымя́нный *прил* (*герой, автор*) anonymous; **безымя́нный па́лец** ring finger

бей(ся) *несов см* би́ть(ся)

Белару́сь (-и) ж Belarus

белору́с (-а) м Belorussian

беле́|ть (-ю; *perf* побеле́ть) *несов* (*лицо*) to go или turn white; (*no perf*: *цветы*) to show white

бели́л|а (-) *мн* emulsion ед

бел|и́ть (-ю́, -ишь; *perf* побели́ть) *несов перех* to whitewash

бе́л|ка (-ки; *gen pl* -ок) ж squirrel

бел|о́к (-ка́) м protein; (*яйца*) (egg) white; (*Анат*) white (of the eye)

белокро́ви|е (-я) *ср* (*Мед*) leukaemia (*Brit*), leukemia (*US*)

белоку́рый *прил* (*человек*) fair(-haired); (*волосы*) fair

бе́лый *прил* white; **бе́лый медве́дь** polar bear

Бе́льги|я (-и) ж Belgium

бель|ё (-я́) *ср собир* linen; **ни́жнее бельё** underwear

бельэта́ж (-а) м (*Театр*) dress circle

бемо́л|ь (-я) м (*Муз*) flat

бензи́н (-а) м petrol (*Brit*), gas (*US*)

бензоба́к (-а) м petrol (*Brit*) или gas (*US*) tank

бензоколо́н|ка (-ки; gen pl -ок) ж petrol (Brit) или gas (US) pump

бенуа́р (-а) м (Театр) boxes мн

бе́рег (-а; loc sg -ý, nom pl -á) м (моря, озера) shore; (реки) bank

бе́режный прил caring

берёз|а (-ы) ж birch (tree)

берём несов см брать

бере́мене|ть (-ю; perf забере́менеть) несов to get pregnant

бере́менн|ая прил pregnant ▷ (-ой) ж pregnant woman

бере́менность (-и) ж pregnancy

берёт см несов см брать

бер|е́чь (-егу́, -ежёшь etc, -егу́т; pt -ёг, -егла́) несов перех (здоровье, детей) to look after, take care of; (деньги) to be careful with; (время) to make good use of; **бере́чься** (perf побере́чься) несов возв: **бере́чься** +gen to watch out for; **береги́тесь!** watch out!

Берли́н (-а) м Berlin

беру́(сь) etc несов см брать(ся)

бесе́д|а (-ы) ж conversation; (популярный доклад) talk

бесе́д|ка (-ки; gen pl -ок) ж pavilion

бесе́дов|ать (-ую) несов: бесе́довать (c +instr) to talk (to)

бесконта́ктный прил contactless

бесперспекти́вный прил (работа) without prospects

беспе́чный прил carefree

беспла́тный прил free

беспод́обный прил (разг) fantastic

беспоко́|ить (-ю, -ишь) несов перех (perf побеспоко́ить) (мешать) to disturb, trouble ▷ (perf обеспоко́ить) (тревожить) to worry; **беспоко́иться** несов возв (утруждать себя) to trouble o.s.; (тревожиться): беспоко́иться о +prp или за +acc to worry about

беспоко́йный прил anxious; (ребёнок) restless; (время) troubled

беспоко́йств|о (-а) ср anxiety; (хлопоты) trouble; **прости́те за беспоко́йство!** sorry to trouble you!

бесполе́зный прил useless

беспо́мощный прил helpless

беспоря́дк|и (-ов) мн disturbances

беспоря́д|ок (-ка) м disorder; **в беспоря́дке** (комната, дела) in a mess; см также беспоря́дки

беспо́шлинный прил duty-free

беспоща́дный прил merciless

бесправный прил without (civil) rights

беспрецеде́нтный прил unprecedented

беспризо́рный прил homeless

беспристра́стный прил unbias(s)ed

беспроводно́й прил wireless; беспроводна́я связь Wi-Fi (connection)

бессерде́чный прил heartless

бесси́льный прил feeble, weak; (гнев) impotent; (президент) powerless

бессме́ртный прил immortal

бессодержа́тельный прил (речь) empty

бессозна́тельн|ый прил (действия) instinctive; **быть** (impf) **в бессозна́тельном состоя́нии** to be unconscious

бессо́нниц|а (-ы) ж insomnia

бесстра́шный прил fearless

бессты́дный прил shameless

беста́ктный прил tactless

бестолко́вый прил stupid

бестсе́ллер (-а) м best seller

бесхозя́йственный прил (руководитель) inefficient

бесцве́тный прил colourless (Brit), colorless (US)

бесце́нный прил priceless

бесце́нок м: за бесце́нок dirt cheap, for next to nothing

бесчи́сленный прил countless

бето́н (-а) м concrete

бетони́р|овать (-ую; perf забетони́ровать) несов перех to concrete

бефстро́ганов м нескл boeuf или beef stroganoff

бе́шенств|о (-а) ср (Мед) rabies; (раздражение) rage

бе́шеный прил (взгляд) furious; (характер, ураган) violent; (разг: цены) crazy

Би-би-си́ ж сокр (= Брита́нская радиовеща́тельная корпора́ция) BBC (= British Broadcasting Corporation)

библиоте́к|а (-и) ж library

библиоте́кар|ь (-я) м librarian

библиоте́чный прил library

Би́бли|я (-и) ж the Bible

бигуди́ ср/мн нескл curlers мн

бижуте́ри|я (-и) ж costume jewellery

би́знес (-а) м business; бизнесме́н (-а) м businessman ▷ (-а) м businessmen

бики́ни ср нескл bikini

биле́т (-а) м ticket; (членский) (membership) card; **обра́тный биле́т** return (Brit) или roundtrip (US) ticket; **входно́й биле́т** entrance ticket (for standing room)

биллио́н (-а) м billion (one thousand million)

бино́кл|ь (-я) м binoculars мн

бинт (-а́) м bandage; **бинт|ова́ть** (-у́ю; perf забинтова́ть) несов перех to bandage

биогра́фи|я (-и) ж biography

биоло́ги|я (-и) ж biology

би́рж|а (-и) ж (Комм) exchange; фо́ндовая би́ржа stock exchange или market; **биржеви́к** (-а́) м stockbroker

би́р|ка (-ки; gen pl -ок) ж tag

бирюз|а́ (-ы́) ж turquoise

бис межд: Бис! encore!

би́сер (-а) м собир glass beads мн

бискви́т (-а) м sponge (cake)

бит (-а) *м* (*Комп*) byte

би́тв|а (-ы) *ж* battle

бить (бью, бьёшь; *imper* бей(те), *perf* **поби́ть**) *несов перех* to beat; (*стёкла*) to break ▷ (*perf* **проби́ть**) *неперех* (*часы*) to strike; **бить** (*impf*) **в** +*acc* (*в дверь*) to bang at; (*дождь, ветер*) to beat against; (*орудие*) to hit; **его́ бьёт озно́б** he's got a fit of the shivers; **би́ться** *несов возв* (*сердце*) to beat; (*стекло*) to be breakable; (*сражаться*) to fight; **би́ться** (*impf*) **о** +*acc* to bang against; **би́ться** (*impf*) **над** +*instr* (*над задачей*) to struggle with

бифште́кс (-а) *м* steak

бла́г|а (-) *мн* rewards *мн*; **всех благ!** all the best!

бла́г|о (-а) *ср* benefit; *см также* **бла́га**

благови́дный *прил* plausible

благодар|и́ть (-ю́, -и́шь; *perf* **поблагодари́ть**) *несов перех* to thank

благода́рность|ь (-и) *ж* gratitude, thanks *мн*

благода́р|ный *прил* grateful; (*тема*) rewarding; **я Вам о́чень благода́рен** I am very grateful to you

благодаря́ *предл* +*dat* thanks to ▷ *союз*: **благодаря́ тому́, что** owing to the fact that

благ|о́й *прил*: **благи́е наме́рения** good intentions *мн*

благополу́чи|е (-я) *ср* (*в семье*) welfare; (*материальное*) prosperity

благополу́чный *прил* successful; **благополу́чная семья́** good family

благоприя́тный *прил* favourable (*Brit*), favorable (*US*)

благоразу́мный *прил* prudent

благоро́дный *прил* noble

благослов|и́ть (-лю́, -и́шь; *impf* **благословля́ть**) *сов перех* to bless

благотвори́тельность|ь (-и) *ж* charity; **благотвори́тельн|ый** *прил* charitable; **благотвори́тельная организа́ция** charity (organization); **благотвори́тельный конце́рт** charity concert

благоустро́енный *прил* (*дом*) with all modern conveniences

блаже́нств|о (-а) *ср* bliss

бланк (-а) *м* form; (*организации*) headed notepaper

блат (-а) *м* (*разг*) connections *мн*; **по бла́ту** (*разг*) through (one's) connections

бледне́|ть (-ю; *perf* **побледне́ть**) *несов* to (grow) pale

бле́дный *прил* pale; (*перен*) dull

блесн|у́ть (-у́, -ёшь) *сов* to flash; (*на экзамене*) to do brilliantly

бле|сте́ть (-щу́, -сти́шь *или*, -щешь) *несов* (*звёзды, металл*) to shine; (*глаза*) to sparkle

ближа́йший *прил* (*город, дом*) the nearest; (*год*) the next; (*планы*) immediate; (*друг, участие*) closest; **ближа́йший ро́дственник** next of kin

бли́же *сравн прил от* **бли́зкий** ▷ *сравн нареч от* **бли́зко**

бли́жний *прил* (*город*) neighbouring; **бли́жнее зарубе́жье** former Soviet republics; **Бли́жний Восто́к** Middle East

бли́зк|ие (-их) *мн* relatives *мн*

бли́зкий *прил* close; (*конец*) imminent; **бли́зкий кому́-н** (*интересы, тема*) close to sb's heart; **бли́зкий по** +*dat* (*по содержанию, по цели*) similar *или* close in; **бли́зко** *нареч* near *или* close by ▷ *как сказ* not far off; **бли́зко от** +*gen* near, close to

близне́ц (-а́) *м* (*обычно мн*) twin; **бра́тья/ сёстры-близнецы́** twin brothers/sisters

Близнец|ы́ (-о́в) *мн* Gemini *ед*

близору́кий *прил* short-sighted (*Brit*), nearsighted (*US*)

блин (-а́) *м* pancake

блог (-а) *ж* blog; **бло́гер** (-а) *м* blogger

блок (-а) *м* bloc; (*Тех*) unit

блока́д|а (-ы) *ж* (*Воен*) siege; (*экономическая*) blockade

блоки́р|овать (-ую) *(не)сов перех* to block; (*город*) to blockade

блонди́н (-а) *м*: **он — блонди́н** he is blond; **блонди́н|ка** (-ки; *gen pl* -ок) *ж* blonde

блох|а́ (-и́; *nom pl* -и) *ж* flea

блужда́|ть (-ю) *несов* to wander *или* roam (around)

блю́д|о (-а) *ср* dish

блю|сти́ (-ду́, -дёшь; *pt* -л, -ла́, -ло́, *perf* **соблюсти́**) *несов перех* (*интересы*) to guard; (*чистоту*) to maintain

боб (-а́) *м* (*обычно мн*) bean

бобр (-а́) *м* beaver

Бог (-а; *voc* Бо́же) *м* God; **не дай Бог!** God forbid!; **ра́ди Бо́га!** for God's sake!; **сла́ва Бо́гу** (*к счастью*) thank God

богате́|ть (-ю; *perf* **разбогате́ть**) *несов* to become rich

бога́тств|а (-) *мн* (*природные*) resources

бога́тств|о (-а) *ср* wealth, riches *мн*; *см также* **бога́тства**

бога́тый *прил* rich; **бога́тый урожа́й** bumper harvest

богаты́р|ь (-я́) *м* *warrior hero of Russian folk epics*; (*перен*) Hercules

бога́ч (-а́) *м* rich man (*мн* men)

боги́н|я (-и) *ж* goddess

Богоро́диц|а (-ы) *ж* the Virgin Mary

богосло́ви|е (-я) *ср* theology

богослуже́ни|е (-я) *ср* service

боготвор|и́ть (-ю́, -и́шь) *несов перех* to worship

бо́дрый *прил* energetic; (*настроение, музыка*) cheerful

боеви́к (-а́) *м* militant; (*фильм*) action movie

боево́й *прил* military; (*настроение, дух*) fighting

боеприпа́с|ы (-ов) *мн* ammunition *ед*

бо|е́ц (-йца́) *м* (*солдат*) soldier

Бо́же *сущ см* **Бог** ▷ *межд*: **Бо́же (ты мой)!** good Lord *или* God!; **Бо́же! кака́я**

красота́! God, it's beautiful!; **Бо́же упаси́** (*разг*) God forbid; **боже́ственный** *прил* divine; **Бо́ж|ий** *прил* God's; **ка́ждый бо́жий день** (*разг*) every single day; **бо́жья коро́вка** ladybird

бо|й (**-я**; *loc sg* **-ю́**, *nom pl* **-и́**, *gen pl* **-ёв**) *м* battle; (*боксёров*) fight; (*барабанов*) beating; (*часов*) striking

бо́йкий *прил* (*речь, ответ*) quick; (*продавец*) smart; (*место*) busy

бойко́т (**-а**) *м* boycott

бойкоти́р|овать (**-ую**) (*не*)*сов перех* to boycott

бок (**-а**; *loc sg* **-у́**, *nom pl* **-а́**) *м* side

бо́ком *нареч* sideways

бокс (**-а**) *м* (*Спорт*) boxing; (*Мед*) isolation ward

боксёр (**-а**) *м* boxer

Болга́ри|я (**-и**) *ж* Bulgaria

бо́лее *нареч* more; **бо́лее или ме́нее** more or less; **бо́лее того́** what's more; **тем бо́лее** all the more so

боле́зненный *прил* sickly; (*укол*) painful; (*перен: подозрительность*) unhealthy; (*самолюбие*) unnatural

боле́зн|ь (**-и**) *ж* illness; (*заразная*) disease

боле́льщик (**-а**) *м* fan

бол|е́ть (**-е́ю**) *несов*: **боле́ть** (+*instr*) to be ill (with); (*Спорт*): **боле́ть за** +*acc* to be a fan of ▷ (*3sg* **-и́т**) (*руки итп*) to ache

болеутоля́ющ|ий *прил*: **болеутоля́ющее сре́дство** painkiller

боло́нь|я (**-и**) *ж* (*ткань*) lightweight waterproof material

боло́т|о (**-а**) *ср* marsh, bog

болт (**-а́**) *м* bolt

болта́|ть (**-ю**) *несов перех* (*разг: вздор*) to talk ▷ *неперех* (*разговаривать*) to chat; (: *много*) to chatter; **болта́ть** (*impf*) **нога́ми** to dangle one's legs

бол|ь (**-и**) *ж* pain; **зубна́я боль** toothache; **головна́я боль** headache

больни́ц|а (**-ы**) *ж* hospital

больни́чный *прил* hospital; **больни́чный лист** medical certificate

бо́льно *нареч* (*удариться, упасть*) badly, painfully; (*обидеть*) deeply; **бо́льно!** that hurts!; **мне бо́льно** I am in pain

больн|о́й *прил* (*рука итп*) sore; (*воображение*) morbid; (*нездоров*) ill, sick ▷ (**-о́го**) *м* (*болеющий*) sick person; (*пациент*) patient; **больно́й вопро́с** a sore point

бо́льше *сравн прил от* **большо́й** ▷ *сравн нареч от* **мно́го** ▷ *нареч* (+*gen*: *часа, килограмма итп*) more than; (*не хотеть, не жить*) anymore; **бо́льше не бу́ду** (*разг*) I won't do it again; **бо́льше так не де́лай** don't do that again

большинств|о́ (**-а́**) *ср* majority

больш|о́й *прил* big, large; (*радость*) great; (*дети*) grown-up; **бо́льшей ча́стью**, **по бо́льшей ча́сти** for the most part; **больша́я бу́ква** capital letter

боля́ч|ка (**-ки**; *gen pl* **-ек**) *ж* sore

бо́мб|а (**-ы**) *ж* bomb

бомбардиро́вщик (**-а**) *м* bomber

бомб|и́ть (**-лю́, -и́шь**) *несов перех* to bomb

бомбоубе́жищ|е (**-а**) *ср* bomb shelter

бомж (**-а́**) *м* homeless person

бордо́вый *прил* dark red, wine colour

бордю́р (**-а**) *м* (*тротуара*) kerb (*Brit*), curb (*US*); (*салфетки*) border

борм|ота́ть (**-очу́, -о́чешь**) *несов перех* to mutter

бор|ода́ (*acc sg* **-оду**, *gen sg* **-оды́**, *nom pl* **-оды**, *gen pl* **-о́д**, *dat pl* **-ода́м**) *ж* beard

борода́в|ка (**-ки**; *gen pl* **-ок**) *ж* wart

бор|о́ться (**-ю́сь, -ешься**) *несов возв* (*Спорт*) to wrestle; **боро́ться** (*impf*) (**с** +*instr*) to fight (with *или* against)

борт (**-а**; *acc sg* **за́ борт** *или* **за бо́рт**, *instr sg* **за бо́ртом** *или* **за бортом**, *loc sg* **-у́**, *nom pl* **-а́**) *м* side; **на борту́** *или* **борт** on board, aboard; **челове́к за бо́ртом!** man overboard!

бортпроводни́к (**-а́**) *м* steward (*on plane*); **бортпроводни́ц|а** (**-ы**) *ж* air hostess, stewardess (*on plane*)

борщ (**-а́**) *м* borsch (*beetroot-based soup*)

борьб|а́ (**-ы́**) *ж* (*за мир*) fight, struggle; (*Спорт*) wrestling

босико́м *нареч* barefoot

босо́й *прил* barefoot

боти́н|ок (**-ка**) *м* (*обычно мн*) ankle boot

бо́ч|ка (**-ки**; *gen pl* **-ек**) *ж* barrel

бо|я́ться (**-ю́сь, -и́шься**) *несов возв*: **боя́ться** (+*gen*) to be afraid (of) +*infin* to be afraid of doing *или* to do

бразд|ы́ *мн*: **бразды́ правле́ния** the reins of power

брак (**-а**) *м* (*супружество*) marriage; (*продукция*) rejects *мн*; (*дефект*) flaw

брако́ванный *прил* reject

брак|ова́ть (**-у́ю**; *perf* **забракова́ть**) *несов перех* to reject

бракосочета́ни|е (**-я**) *ср* marriage ceremony

бран|и́ть (**-ю́, -и́шь**) *несов* to scold

брат (**-а**; *nom pl* **-ья**, *gen pl* **-ьев**) *м* brother; **двою́родный брат** cousin

бра|ть (**беру́, берёшь**; *pt* **-л, -ла́, -ло**, *perf* **взять**) *несов перех* to take; (*билет*) to get; (*работника*) to take on; (*барьер*) to clear; (*разг: арестовать*) to nick; **бра́ться** (*perf* **взя́ться**) *несов возв*: **бра́ться за** +*acc* (*хватать рукой*) to take hold of; (*за работу*) to get down to; (*за книгу*) to begin; (*за решение проблемы*) to take on; **бра́ться** (*perf* **взя́ться**) **за ум** to see sense

бра́тья *etc сущ см* **брат**

бревн|о́ (**-а́**; *nom pl* **брёвна**, *gen pl* **брёвен**) *ср* log; (*Спорт*) the beam

бре́|дить (**-жу, -дишь**) *несов* to be delirious; **бре́дить** (*impf*) **кем-н/чем-н** to be mad about sb/sth

бре́зг|овать (-ую; *perf* **побре́зговать**) *несов* +*instr* to be fastidious about

бре́м|я (-ени; *как* **вре́мя**; *см* Table 4) *ср* burden

бригади́р (-а) *м* team leader

бриллиа́нт (-а) *м* (cut) diamond

брита́н|ец (-ца) *м* Briton; **брита́нцы** the British

Брита́ни|я (-и) *ж* Britain

брита́нский *прил* British

бри́тв|а (-ы) *ж* razor; **безопа́сная бри́тва** safety razor

бр|ить (-е́ю, -е́ешь; *perf* **побри́ть**) *несов перех* (*человека*) to shave; (*бо́роду*) to shave off; **бри́ться** (*perf* **побри́ться**) *несов возв* to shave

бри́финг (-а) *м* briefing

бров|ь (-и; *gen pl* -е́й) *ж* eyebrow

бро|ди́ть (-жу́, -дишь) *несов* to wander

бродя́г|а (-и) *м/ж* tramp

бро́кер (-а) *м* broker

бронежиле́т (-а) *м* bullet-proof jacket

бронетранспортёр (-а) *м* armoured (*Brit*) *или* armored (*US*) personnel carrier

бро́нз|а (-ы) *ж* bronze

брони́р|овать (-ую; *perf* **заброни́ровать**) (*не*)*сов перех* to reserve

бронх (-а) *м* bronchial tube

бронхи́т (-а) *м* bronchitis

бро́н|я (-и) *ж* reservation

брон|я́ (-и́) *ж* armour (*Brit*) *или* armor (*US*) plating

броса́|ть (-ю) *несов от* **бро́сить**; **броса́ться** *несов от* **бро́ситься** ▷ *возв*: **броса́ться снежка́ми/камня́ми** to throw snowballs/stones at each other

бро́|сить (-шу, -сишь; *impf* **броса́ть**) *сов перех* (*камень, мяч итп*) to throw; (*якорь, сети*) to cast; (*семью, друга*) to abandon; (*во́йска*) to dispatch; (*спорт*) to give up; **меня́ бро́сило в жар** I broke out in a sweat; **броса́ть** (*perf* **бро́сить**) +*infin* to give up doing; **бро́ситься** (*impf* **броса́ться**) *сов возв*: **броса́ться на** +*acc* (*на врага́*) to throw o.s. at; **броса́ться** (*perf* **бро́ситься**) **в ата́ку** to rush to the attack

бро́ш|ка (-ки; *gen pl* -ек) *ж* brooch; **брош|ь** (-и) *ж* = **бро́шка**

брошю́р|а (-ы) *ж* (*книжка*) booklet

брус (-а; *nom pl* -ья, *gen pl* -ьев) *м* beam; *см также* **бру́сья**

бру́сь|я (-ев) *мн* parallel bars *мн*

бру́тто *прил неизм* gross

бры́з|гать (-жу, -жешь) *несов* to splash ▷ (-гаю) (*опрыскивать*): **бры́згать на** +*acc* to spray

бры́зг|и (-) *мн* splashes; (*мелкие*) spray *ед*

бры́нз|а (-ы) *ж* feta cheese

брю́кв|а (-ы) *ж* swede

брю́к|и (-) *мн* trousers, pants (*US*)

брюне́т (-а) *м*: **он брюне́т** he has dark hair; **брюне́т|ка** (-ки; *gen pl* -ок) *ж* brunette

Брюссе́л|ь (-я) *м* Brussels

БТР *сокр* = **бронетранспортёр**

бу́блик (-а) *м* ≈ bagel

бу́б|ны (-ён; *dat pl* -нам) *мн* (*Карты*) diamonds

буго́р (-ра́) *м* mound; (*на коже*) lump

Будапе́шт (-а) *м* Budapest

бу́дем *несов см* **быть**

бу́дет *несов см* **быть** ▷ *част* that's enough; **бу́дет тебе́**! that's enough from you!

бу́дешь *etc несов см* **быть**

буди́льник (-а) *м* alarm clock

бу|ди́ть (-жу́, -дишь; *perf* **разбуди́ть**) *несов перех* to wake (up), awaken

бу́д|ка (-ки; *gen pl* -ок) *ж* (*сторожа*) hut; (*для собаки*) kennel; **телефо́нная бу́дка** telephone box

бу́дн|и (-ей) *мн* working *или* week days; (*перен: повседневность*) routine *ед*

бу́дто *союз* (*якобы*) supposedly; (*словно*): (**как**) **бу́дто** (**бы**) as if; **он уверя́ет, бу́дто сам её ви́дел** he claims to have seen her himself

бу́ду *etc несов см* **быть**

бу́дущ|ее (-его) *ср* the future; **в бу́дущем** in the future

бу́дущ|ий *прил* (*следующий*) next; (*предстоящий*) future; **бу́дущее вре́мя** future tense

бу́дь(те) *несов см* **быть** ▷ *союз*: **будь то** be it

бужени́н|а (-ы) *ж* cold cooked and seasoned pork

бу|й (-я; *nom pl* -и́) *м* buoy

бу́йвол (-а) *м* buffalo

бук (-а) *м* beech

бу́кв|а (-ы) *ж* letter

буква́льный *прил* literal

буква́р|ь (-я́) *м* first reading book

буке́т (-а) *м* bouquet

букинисти́ческий *прил*: **букинисти́ческий магази́н** second-hand bookshop

букле́т (-а) *м* booklet

була́в|ка (-ки; *gen pl* -ок) *ж* pin

бу́л|ка (-ки; *gen pl* -ок) *ж* roll; (*белый хлеб*) loaf; **бу́лоч|ка** (-ки; *gen pl* -ек) *ж* small roll

бу́лочн|ая (-ой) *ж* baker, baker's (shop)

булы́жный *прил*: **булы́жная мостова́я** cobbled street

бульдо́зер (-а) *м* bulldozer

бульо́н (-а; *part gen* -у) *м* stock

бум (-а) *м* boom

бума́г|а (-и) *ж* paper; **це́нные бума́ги** securities

бума́ж|ка (-ки; *gen pl* -ек) *ж* piece of paper

бума́жник (-а) *м* wallet, pocketbook (*US*)

бума́жный *прил* paper

бу́нкер (-а) *м* bunker

бунт (-а) *м* (*мятеж*) riot; (: *на корабле*) mutiny

бунт|ова́ть (-у́ю) *несов* (*см сущ*) to riot; to mutiny

бура́в|ить (-лю, -ишь; *perf* **пробура́вить**) *несов перех* to drill

бур|и́ть (-ю́, -и́шь; *perf* **пробури́ть**) *несов перех* to bore, drill

бу́рный *прил* (*погода, океан*) stormy; (*чувство*) wild; (*рост*) rapid

бу́рый *прил* brown

бу́р|я (-и) *ж* storm

бу́с|ы (-) *мн* beads

бутафо́ри|я (-и) *ж* (*Театр*) props *мн* (= *properties*); (*перен*) sham

бутербро́д (-а) *м* sandwich

буто́н (-а) *м* bud

бу́тс|а (-ы) *ж* football boot

буты́л|ка (-ки; *gen pl* -ок) *ж* bottle

бу́фер (-а; *nom pl* -а́) *м* buffer

буфе́т (-а) *м* snack bar; (*шкаф*) sideboard

буфе́тчик (-а) *м* barman, barmen *мн*

буха́н|ка (-ки; *gen pl* -ок) *ж* loaf

Бухаре́ст (-а) *м* Bucharest

бу́хт|а (-ы) *ж* bay

буш|ева́ть (-у́ю) *несов* (*пожар, ураган*) to rage

⬤ **КЛЮЧЕВО́Е СЛО́ВО**

бы *част* **1** (*выражает возможность*) **купи́л бы, е́сли бы бы́ли де́ньги** I would buy it if I had the money; **я бы давно́ уже́ купи́л э́ту кни́гу, е́сли бы у меня́ бы́ли де́ньги** I would have bought this book long ago if I had had the money

2 (*выражает пожелание*) **я бы хоте́л поговори́ть с тобо́й** I would like to speak to you

3 (*выражает сове́т*) **ты бы написа́л ей** you should write to her

4 (*выражает опасе́ние*) **не захвати́л бы нас дождь** I hope we don't get caught in the rain; **отдохну́ть/погуля́ть бы** it would be nice to have a rest/go for a walk

быва́ло *част* expresses repeated action in the past; **быва́ло сиди́м и разгова́риваем** we used to *или* would sit and talk

быва́|ть (-ю) *несов* (*посещать*) to be; (*случаться*) to happen, take place; **он быва́ет у нас ча́сто** he often comes to see us; **как ни в чём не быва́ло** (*разг*) as if nothing had happened

бы́вший *прил* former

бык (-а́) *м* bull; (*рабочий*) ox

был etc *несов см* **быть**

были́н|а (-ы) *ж* heroic poem

быль (-и) *ж* true story

бы́стро *нареч* quickly

бы́стрый *прил* (*машина итп*) fast; (*руки, взгляд, речь*) quick

быт (-а; *loc sg* -у́) *м* life; (*повседневность*) everyday life; **слу́жба бы́та** consumer services

бытов|о́й *прил* everyday; **бытово́е**

обслу́живание населе́ния consumer services; **бытова́я те́хника** household electrical appliances

⬤ **КЛЮЧЕВО́Е СЛО́ВО**

быть (*см Table 21*) *несов* **1** (*omitted in present tense*) to be; **кни́га на столе́** the book is on the table; **за́втра я бу́ду в шко́ле** I will be at school tomorrow; **дом был на краю́ го́рода** the house was *или* stood on the edge of the town; **на ней краси́вое пла́тье** she is wearing a beautiful dress; **вчера́ был дождь** it rained yesterday

2 (*часть составно́го сказ*) to be; **я хочу́ быть учи́телем** I want to be a teacher; **я был рад ви́деть тебя́** I was happy to see you; **так и быть!** so be it!; **как быть?** what is to be done?; **э́того не мо́жет быть** that's impossible; **кто/како́й бы то ни был** whoever/whatever it might be; **бу́дьте добры́!** excuse me!; **бу́дьте добры́, позови́те его́!** would you be so good *или* kind as to call him?; **бу́дьте здоро́вы!** take care!

3 (*образует будущее время*) +*impf vb*; **ве́чером я бу́ду писа́ть пи́сьма** I'll be writing letters this evening; **я бу́ду люби́ть тебя́ всегда́** I'll love you forever

бью(сь) etc *несов см* **бить(ся)**

бюдже́т (-а) *м* budget; **дохо́дный бюдже́т** revenue; **расхо́дный бюдже́т** expenditure

бюдже́тник (-а) *м* person working in a state-funded institution

бюллете́н|ь (-я) *м* bulletin; (*на выборах*) ballot paper; (*справка*) medical certificate

бюро́ *ср нескл* office; **бюро́ нахо́док** lost property office

бюрокра́т (-а) *м* bureaucrat

бюрокра́ти|я (-и) *ж* bureaucracy

бюст (-а) *м* bust

бюстга́льтер (-а) *м* bra (= *brassiere*)

покрывающем): **ру́ки в кра́ске/са́же** hands covered in paint/soot; **това́р в упако́вке** packaged goods

11 (*об одежде*) in; **мужчи́на в очка́х/в ша́пке** a man in *или* wearing glasses/a hat

12 (*о состоянии*): **быть в у́жасе/негодова́нии** to be terrified/indignant

в. *сокр* (= **век**) с (= *century*); (= **восто́к**) E (= *East*)

ваго́н (-**а**) м (*пассажирский*) carriage (*Brit*), coach (*Brit*), car (*US*); (*товарный*) wagon (*Brit*), truck (*US*); **спа́льный ваго́н** couchette car; **мя́гкий ваго́н** ≈ sleeping car; **ваго́н-рестора́н** dining (*Brit*) *или* club (*US*) car

ва́жный *прил* important

ва́з|а (-**ы**) ж vase

вазели́н (-**а**) м Vaseline

вака́нси|я (-**и**) ж vacancy

вака́нт|ный *прил* vacant; **вака́нтная до́лжность** vacancy

ва́куум (-**а**) м vacuum

вакци́н|а (-**ы**) ж vaccine

вакцини́р|овать (-**ую**) (*не*)*сов перех* to vaccinate

ва́лен|ок (-**ка**) м felt boot

валериа́нк|а (-**и**) ж valerian drops *мн*

вале́т (-**а**) м (*Карты*) jack

вал|и́ть (-**ю́**, -**ишь**; *perf* **свали́ть** *или* **повали́ть**) *несов перех* (*заставить падать*) to knock over; (*рубить*) to fell ▷ (*perf* **свали́ть**) (*разг: бросать*) to dump ▷ *неперех* (*дым, пар*) to pour out; **вали́ть** (*perf* **свали́ть**) **вину́ на** +*acc* (*разг*) to point the finger at; **вали́ться** (*perf* **свали́ться** *или* **повали́ться**) *несов возв* (*падать*) to fall; **вали́ться** (*impf*) **с ног** (*разг*) to be dead on one's feet

валово́й *прил* (*доход*) gross

валу́н (-**а́**) м boulder

вальс (-**а**) м waltz

валю́т|а (-**ы**) ж currency ▷ *собир* foreign currency

валю́тный *прил* currency; **валю́тный курс** rate of exchange

валя́|ть (-**ю**) *несов перех* (*катать*) to roll ▷ (*perf* **свала́ть**) (*скатывать*) to shape; **валя́ться** *несов возв* (*кататься*) to roll about; (*разг: человек, бумаги итп*) to lie about

вам *etc мест см* **вы**

вампи́р (-**а**) м vampire

вани́л|ь (-**и**) ж vanilla

ва́нн|а (-**ы**) ж bath; **ва́нн|ая** (-**ой**) ж bathroom

варёный *прил* boiled

варе́нь|е (-**я**) *ср* jam

вариа́нт (-**а**) м variant

вар|и́ть (-**ю́**, -**ишь**; *perf* **свари́ть**) *несов перех* (*обед*) to cook; (*суп, кофе*) to make; (*картофель*) to boil; (*Тех*) to weld; **вари́ться** (*perf* **свари́ться**) *несов возв* (*обед*) to be cooking

○ **КЛЮЧЕВОЕ СЛОВО**

в *предл* +*acc* **1** (*о месте направления*) in(to); **я положи́л кни́гу в портфе́ль** I put the book in(to) my briefcase; **я сел в маши́ну** I got in(to) the car

2 (*уехать, пойти*) to; **он уе́хал в Москву́** he went to Moscow

3 (*об изменении состояния*): **погружа́ться в рабо́ту** to be absorbed in one's work

4 (*об объекте физического действия*): **он постуча́л в дверь** he knocked on the door; **он посмотре́л мне в глаза́** he looked me in the eyes; **мать поцелова́ла меня́ в щёку** mother kissed me on the cheek

5 (*о времени совершения чего-н*): **он пришёл в понеде́льник** he came on Monday; **я ви́дел его́ в про́шлом году́** I saw him last year; **я встре́тил его́ в два часа́** I met him at two o'clock; **э́то случи́лось в ма́рте/в двадца́том ве́ке** it happened in March/in the twentieth century

6 (*о размере, количестве*): **ве́сом в 3 то́нны** 3 tons *или* tonnes in weight: +*prp*; **дра́ма в трёх частя́х** a drama in three acts; **в пяти́ ме́трах от доро́ги** five metres (*Brit*) *или* meters (*US*) from the road

7 (*о соотношении величин*): **в два ра́за бо́льше/длинне́е** twice as big/long; **во мно́го раз лу́чше/умне́е** much better/cleverer

8 (*обозначает форму, вид*): **брю́ки в кле́тку** checked trousers; **лека́рство в табле́тках** medicine in tablet form

9 (+*prp: о месте*) in; **ко́шка сиди́т в корзи́не** the cat is sitting in the basket; **я живу́ в дере́вне** I live in the country; **сын у́чится в шко́ле** my son is at school

10 (*о чём-н облегчающем,*

Варша́в|а (-ы) ж Warsaw
варьете́ ср нескл variety show
варьи́р|овать (-ую) несов (не)перех to vary
вас мест см вы
ва́т|а (-ы) ж cotton wool (Brit), (absorbent) cotton (US)
ва́тман (-а) м heavy paper for drawing etc
ва́тный прил cotton-wool (Brit), absorbent cotton (US)
ватру́ш|ка (-ки; gen pl -ек) ж curd tart
ватт (-а) м watt
ва́учер (-а) м voucher
ва́хт|а (-ы) ж watch; **сто́ять** (impf) на **ва́хте** to keep watch
вахтёр (-а) м caretaker, janitor (esp US, Scottish)
ваш (-его; f-а, nt-е, pl-и; как наш; см Table 9) притяж мест your; **э́то ва́ше** this is yours
вбе|жа́ть (как бежа́ть; см Table 20; impf **вбега́ть**) сов: **вбежа́ть (в +acc)** to run in(to)
вбить (вобью́, вобьёшь; impf **вбива́ть**) сов перех: **вбить (в +acc)** to drive или hammer in(to)
вблизи́ нареч nearby ▷ предл: **вблизи́ +gen или от +gen** near (to)
вбок нареч sideways
вбро́|сить (-шу, -сишь; impf **вбра́сывать**) сов перех to throw in
ввали́ться (-ю́сь, -ишься; impf **вва́ливаться**) сов возв (щёки, глаза) to become sunken
введе́ни|е (-я) ср introduction
ввез|ти́ (-у́, -ёшь; pt ввёз, -ла́, -ло́, impf **ввози́ть**) сов перех (в дом итп) to take in; (в страну) to import
вверх нареч up ▷ предл: **вверх по +dat** up; **вверх по тече́нию** upstream; **в до́ме всё вверх дном** (разг) everything in the house is topsy-turvy; **вверх нога́ми** (разг) upside down
вверху́ нареч up ▷ предл +gen at the top of
вв|ести́ (-еду́, -едёшь; pt -ёл, -ела́, impf **вводи́ть**) сов перех to take in; (лекарство) to inject; (в компьютер) to enter; (закон) to introduce; (сделать действующим): **ввести́ что-н в +acc** to put sth into
ввиду́ предл +gen in view of ▷ союз: **ввиду́ того́, что** in view of the fact that
ввод (-а) м bringing in; (данных) input, feeding in
вво|ди́ть (-жу́, -дишь) несов от ввести́
вво|зи́ть (-жу́, -зишь) несов от ввезти́
вглубь нареч (down) into the depths ▷ предл (+gen: вниз) into the depths of; (внутрь) into the heart of
вда|ва́ться (-ю́сь) несов от вда́ться
вдав|и́ть (-лю́, -ишь; impf **вда́вливать**) сов перех: **вдави́ть (в +acc)** to press in(to)
вдалеке́ нареч in the distance; **вдалеке́**

от +gen a long way from
вдали́ нареч = вдалеке́
вдаль нареч into the distance
вда́ться (как дать; см Table 16; impf **вдава́ться**) сов возв: **вда́ться в +acc** to jut out into; (перен: в рассуждения) to get caught up in; **вдава́ться (perf вда́ться) в подро́бности** to go into details
вдво́е нареч (сложить) in two; **вдво́е сильне́е** twice as strong
вдвоём нареч: **они́ живу́т вдвоём** the two of them live together
вдвойне́ нареч double (the amount)
вде|ть (-ну, -нешь; impf **вдева́ть**) сов перех to put in
вдоба́вок нареч (разг) in addition ▷ предл: **вдоба́вок к +dat** in addition to
вдов|а́ (-ы́; nom pl -ы) ж widow
вдов|е́ц (-ца́) м widower
вдо́воль нареч to one's heart's content
вдоль нареч (сломаться) lengthways ▷ предл +gen along
вдохнове́ни|е (-я) ср inspiration
вдохнов|и́ть (-лю́, -и́шь; impf **вдохновля́ть**) сов перех to inspire
вдохн|у́ть (-у́; impf **вдыха́ть**) сов перех (воздух) to breathe in; (дым, лекарство) to inhale
вдре́безги нареч to smithereens
вдруг нареч suddenly; (а если) what if
вду́ма|ться (-юсь; impf **вду́мываться**) сов возв: **вду́маться в +acc** to think over
вдыха́|ть (-ю) несов от вдохну́ть
веб-а́дрес (-а; nom pl -а́) м web address
веб-ка́мер|а (-ы) ж webcam
вегетариа́н|ец (-ца) м vegetarian
вегетариа́нский прил vegetarian
ве́да|ть (-ю) несов (+instr: управля́ть) to be in charge of
ве́дени|е (-я) ср authority
ведёт(ся) etc несов см вести́(сь)
ве́дом|о ср: **с/без ве́дома кого́-н** (согласие) with/without sb's consent; (уведомление) with/without sb's knowledge
ве́домств|о (-а) ср department
ведр|о́ (-а́; nom pl вёдра, gen pl вёдер) ср bucket, pail
веду́щ|ий прил leading ▷ (-его) м presenter
ведь нареч (в вопросе): **ведь ты хо́чешь пое́хать?** you do want to go, don't you?; (в утверждении): **ведь она́ не спра́вится одна́!** she can't surely manage alone! ▷ союз (о причине) seeing as; **пое́шь, ведь ты го́лоден** you should eat, seeing as you're hungry
ве́дьм|а (-ы) ж witch
ве́ер (-а; nom pl -а́) м fan
ве́жливый прил polite
везде́ нареч everywhere; **везде́ и всю́ду** everywhere you go
вездехо́д (-а) м ≈ Landrover
везе́ни|е (-я) ср luck

вез|ти́ (-у́, -ёшь) *несов перех* to transport, take; (*сани*) to pull; (*тачку*) to push ▷ *perf* **повезти́** *безл* (+*dat: разг*) to be lucky

век (-а; *nom pl* -á) *м* century; (*период*) age; **на века́, во ве́ки веко́в** forever

ве́к|о (-а) *ср* eyelid

веково́й *прил* ancient

ве́ксел|ь (-я; *nom pl* -я́) *м* promissory note

вел|е́ть (-ю́, -и́шь) (*не*)*сов* +*dat* to order

велика́н (-а) *м* giant

вели́к|ий *прил* great ▷ *как сказ*: **сапоги́ мне велики́** the boots are too big for me; **вели́кие держа́вы** the Great Powers

Великобрита́ни|я (-и) *ж* Great Britain

великоду́шный *прил* magnanimous, big-hearted

великору́сский *прил* Great Russian

великоле́пный *прил* magnificent

величин|а́ (-ы́) *ж* size; (*Мат*) quantity

велого́н|ка (-ки; *gen pl* -ок) *ж* cycle race

велосипе́д (-а) *м* bicycle

вельве́т (-а) *м* corduroy

Ве́н|а (-ы) *ж* Vienna

ве́н|а (-ы) *ж* vein

Ве́нгри|я (-и) *ж* Hungary

вен|о́к (-ка́) *м* wreath

вентиля́тор (-а) *м* (ventilator) fan

венча́|ть (-ю; *perf* **обвенча́ть** *или* **повенча́ть**) *несов перех* to marry (*in church*); **венча́ть** (*impf*) **на ца́рство кого́-н** to crown sb; **венча́ться** (*perf* **обвенча́ться**) *несов возв* to be married (*in church*)

ве́р|а (-ы) *ж* faith; (*в Бога*) belief

ве́рб|а (-ы) *ж* pussy willow

верблю́д (-а) *м* camel

ве́рбный *прил*: **Ве́рбное воскресе́нье** ≈ Palm Sunday

верб|ова́ть (-у́ю; *perf* **завербова́ть**) *несов перех* to recruit

верёв|ка (-ки; *gen pl* -ок) *ж* (*толстая*) rope; (*тонкая*) string

ве́р|ить (-ю, -ишь; *perf* **пове́рить**) *несов* +*dat* to believe; (*доверять*) to trust; **ве́рить** (*perf* **пове́рить**) **в кого́-н/что-н** to believe in sb/sth; **ве́рить** (*perf* **пове́рить**) **на́ слово кому́-н** to take sb at his *итп* word; **ве́риться** *несов безл*: **не ве́рится, что э́то пра́вда** it's hard to believe it's true

верне́е *вводн сл* or rather; **верне́е всего́** most likely

ве́рно *нареч* (*преданно*) faithfully; (*правильно*) correctly ▷ *как сказ* that's right

верн|у́ть (-у́, -ёшь) *сов перех* to return, give back; (*долг*) to pay back; (*здоровье, надежду*) to restore; **верну́ться** *сов возв*: **верну́ться** (**к** +*dat*) to return (to)

ве́рный *прил* (*друг*) faithful; (*надёжный*) sure; (*правильный*) correct; **ве́рный сло́ву** true to one's word

верова́ни|е (-я) *ср* (*обычн мн*) faith

вероиспове́дани|е (-я) *ср* faith

вероя́тно *как сказ* it is probable ▷ *вводн сл* probably

вероя́тн|ый *прил* probable; **вероя́тнее всего́** most likely *или* probably

ве́рси|я (-и) *ж* version

верста́к (-а́) *м* (*Тех*) (work)bench

вертика́льный *прил* vertical

вертолёт (-а) *м* helicopter

верф|ь (-и) *ж* shipyard

верх (-а; *loc sg* -у́, *nom pl* -и́) *м* (*дома, стола*) top; (*обуви*) upper; **верх соверше́нства/глу́пости** the height of perfection/stupidity; *см также* **верхи́**

верхи́ (-о́в) *мн*: **в верха́х** at the top; **встре́ча/перегово́ры в верха́х** summit meeting/talks

ве́рхн|ий *прил* top; **ве́рхняя оде́жда** outer clothing *или* garments; **Ве́рхняя пала́та** Upper Chamber

верхо́вный *прил* supreme; **Верхо́вный Суд** High Court (*Brit*), Supreme Court (*US*)

верхово́й *прил*: **верхова́я езда́** horse (*Brit*) *или* horseback (*US*) riding

верши́н|а (-ы) *ж* top; (*горы*) summit

вес (-а; *nom pl* -á) *м* weight; (*перен: влияние*) authority

весел|е́ть (-ю; *perf* **повеселе́ть**) *несов* to cheer up

весел|и́ть (-ю́, -и́шь; *perf* **развесели́ть**) *несов перех* to amuse; **весели́ться** *несов возв* to have fun

ве́село *нареч* (*сказать*) cheerfully ▷ *как сказ*: **здесь ве́село** it's fun here; **мне ве́село** I'm having fun

весёлый *прил* cheerful

весе́нний *прил* spring

ве́|сить (-шу, -сишь) *несов* to weigh

ве́ский *прил* (*аргумент*) potent

весл|о́ (-а́; *nom pl* **вёсла**, *gen pl* **вёсел**) *ср* oar

весн|а́ (-ы́; *nom pl* **вёсны**, *gen pl* **вёсен**) *ж* spring

весно́й *нареч* in (the) spring

весну́ш|ка (-ки; *gen pl* -ек) *ж* freckle

весо́мый *прил* (*вклад*) substantial

ве|сти́ (-ду́, -дёшь; *pt* **вёл, -ла́, -ло́**) *несов перех* to take; (*машину*) to drive; (*корабль*) to navigate; (*отряд*) to lead; (*заседание*) to chair; (*работу*) to conduct; (*хозяйство*) to run; (*записи*) to keep ▷ (*perf* **привести́**) *неперех*: **вести́ к** +*dat* to lead to; **вести́** (*impf*) **себя́** to behave; **вести́сь** *несов возв* (*расследование*) to be carried out; (*переговоры*) to go on

вестибю́л|ь (-я) *м* lobby

вест|ь (-и) *ж* news; **пропада́ть** (*perf* **пропа́сть**) **без ве́сти** (*Воен*) to go missing; **бе́з вести пропа́вший** (*Воен*) missing feared dead; **Бог весть кто/что** (*разг*) God knows who/what

вес|ы́ (-о́в) *мн* scales; (*созвездие*): **Весы́** Libra

весь (всего́; *f* **вся**, *nt* **всё**, *pl* **все**; *см Table 13*) *мест* all; **всего́ хоро́шего** *или* до́брого! all the best!

ветв|**ь** (-и; gen pl -е́й) ж branch; **ветвь дискуссии** (Комп) thread

ве́т|**ер** (-ра) м wind

ветера́н (-а) м veteran

ветерина́р (-а) м vet (Brit), veterinarian (US)

ве́т|**ка** (-ки; gen pl -ок) ж branch; **ве́тка дискуссии** (Комп) thread

ве́то ср нескл veto

ве́треный прил windy

ветров|**о́й** прил: **ветрово́е стекло́** windscreen (Brit), windshield (US)

ветря́н|**ка** (-ки) ж (Мед) chickenpox

ветрян|**о́й** прил wind-powered; **ветряна́я электроста́нция** wind farm; **ветряна́я о́спа** chickenpox

ве́тхий прил (дом) dilapidated; (одежда) shabby; **Ве́тхий Заве́т** the Old Testament

ветч|**ина́** (-и́ны; nom pl -и́ны) ж ham

ве́х|**а** (-и) ж landmark

ве́чер (-а; nom pl -а́) м evening; (праздник) party; **вече́рний** прил evening

○ **ВЕЧЕ́РНЕЕ ОТДЕЛЕ́НИЕ**

○ A degree can be obtained by taking
○ courses in the evening. People who do
○ not want to give up their job may opt for
○ this method. This course runs over 4
○ days a week with over 20 contact hours a
○ week and is very much like the day-time
○ course. The entire degree takes 6 years to
○ complete. See also notes at **зао́чный** and
○ **о́чный**.

ве́чером нареч in the evening

ве́чно нареч eternally

ве́чность (-и) ж eternity

ве́чный прил eternal, everlasting

ве́шал|**ка** (-ки; gen pl -ок) ж (планка) rack; (стойка) hatstand; (плечики) coat hanger; (гардероб) cloakroom; (петля) loop

ве́ша|**ть** (-ю; perf **пове́сить**) несов перех to hang ▷ (perf **све́шать**) (товар) to weigh; **ве́шаться** (perf **пове́ситься**) несов возв to hang o.s.

веща́|**ть** (3sg -ет) несов to broadcast

веще́ственный прил material

вещество́ (-а́) ср substance

вещ|**ь** (-и; gen pl -е́й) ж thing; (книга, фильм) piece

ве́|**ять** (-ю, -ешь) несов (ветер) to blow lightly

взаи́мный прил mutual

взаимоде́йстви|**е** (-я) ср (связь) interaction

взаимоотноше́ни|**е** (-я) ср (inter) relationship

взаимопо́мощь (-и) ж mutual assistance или aid

взаимопонима́ни|**е** (-я) ср mutual understanding

взаймы́ нареч: дава́ть/брать де́ньги взаймы́ to lend/borrow money

взаме́н нареч in exchange ▷ предл (+gen: вместо) instead of; (в обмен) in exchange for

взаперти́ нареч under lock and key

взбить (взобью́, взобьёшь; imper взбе́й(те), impf **взбива́ть**) сов перех (яйца) to beat; (сливки) to whip; (волосы) to fluff up; (подушки) to plump up

взвал|**и́ть** (-ю́, -ишь; impf **взва́ливать**) сов перех: взвали́ть что-н на +acc to haul sth up onto

взве́|**сить** (-шу, -сишь; impf **взве́шивать**) сов перех (товар) to weigh; (факты) to weigh up

взве|**сти́** (-ду́, -дёшь; pt взвёл, -ла́, impf **взводи́ть**) сов перех: взвести́ куро́к to cock a gun

взве́шива|**ть** (-ю) несов от **взве́сить**

взвин|**ти́ть** (-чу́, -ти́шь; impf **взви́нчивать**) сов перех (разг: цены) to jack up

взво|**ди́ть** (-жу́, -дишь) несов от **взвести́**

взволн|**ова́ть(ся)** (-у́ю(сь)) сов от **волнова́ть(ся)**

взв|**ыть** (-о́ю, -о́ешь) сов to howl; (сирена) to wail

взгляд (-а) м glance; (выражение) look; (перен: мнение) view; **на мой/твой взгляд** in my/your view

взгля́н|**уть** (-у́, -ешь) сов: взгляну́ть на +acc to look at

вздор (-а) м (разг) rubbish; **вздо́рный** прил (нелепый) absurd

вздох (-а) м sigh; (ужаса) gasp

вздохн|**у́ть** (-у́, -ёшь) сов to sigh

вздро́гн|**уть** (-у; impf **вздра́гивать**) сов to shudder

взду́ма|**ть** (-ю) сов (разг): не взду́майте лга́ть! don't even think of lying!

вздыха́|**ть** (-ю) несов to sigh

взима́|**ть** (-ю) несов перех (налоги) to collect

взлёт (-а) м (самолёта) takeoff

взле|**те́ть** (-чу́, -ти́шь; impf **взлета́ть**) сов (птица) to soar; (самолёт) to take off; **взлета́ть** (perf **взлете́ть**) **на во́здух** to explode

взлётн|**ый** прил: **взлётная полоса́** runway; airstrip

взлома́|**ть** (-ю; impf **взла́мывать**) сов перех to break open, force; (Комп) to hack into

взло́мщик (-а) м burglar

взмахн|**у́ть** (-у́, -ёшь; impf **взма́хивать**) сов (+instr рукой) to wave; (крылом) to flap

взнос (-а) м payment; (в фонд) contribution; (членский) fee

взойти́ (как идти́; см Table 18; impf **всходи́ть** или **восходи́ть**) сов to rise; (семена) to come up; (на трон) to ascend

взорв|а́ть (-у́, -ёшь; *impf* **взрыва́ть**) *сов перех* (*бомбу*) to detonate; (*дом, мост*) to blow up; **взорва́ться** (*impf* **взрыва́ться**) *сов возв* (*бомба*) to explode; (*мост, дом*) to be blown up

взрев|е́ть (-у́, -ёшь) *сов* to roar

взросле́|ть (-ю; *perf* **повзросле́ть**) *несов* to grow up; (*духовно*) to mature

взро́сл|ый *прил* (*человек*) grown-up; (*фильм*) adult ▷ (**-ого**) *м* adult

взрыв (-а) *м* explosion; (*дома*) blowing up; (+*gen*: *возмущения*) outburst of

взрыва́|ть(ся) (-ю(сь)) *несов от* **взорва́ть(ся)**

взрывоопа́сный *прил* explosive

взрывча́т|ка (-ки; *gen pl* -ок) *ж* explosive (substance)

взы|ска́ть (-щу́, -щешь; *impf* **взы́скивать**) *сов перех* (*долг*) to recover; (*штраф*) to exact ▷ *неперех*: **взыска́ть с кого́-н** to call sb to account

взя́т|ка (-ки; *gen pl* -ок) *ж* bribe

взя|ть (**возьму́, возьмёшь**) *сов от* **брать** ▷ *перех*: **возьму́ (да) и откажу́сь** (*разг*) I could refuse just like that; **с чего́** *или* **отку́да ты взял?** (*разг*) whatever gave you that idea?; **взя́ться** *сов от* **бра́ться**

вид (-а; *part gen* -у, *loc sg* -ý) *м* (*внешность*) appearance; (*предмета, искусства*) form; (*панорама*) view; (*растений, животных*) species; (*спорта*) type; (*Линг*) aspect; **в ви́де** +*gen* in the form of; **на виду́ у** +*gen* in full view of; **под ви́дом** +*gen* in the guise of; **вид на о́зеро/го́ры** a view of the lake/hills; **име́ть** (*impf*) **в виду́** to mean; (*учитывать*) to bear in mind; **де́лать** (*perf* **сде́лать**) **вид** to pretend; **упуска́ть** (**упусти́ть** *perf*) **из ви́ду что-н** (*факт*) to lose sight of sth; **теря́ть** (**потеря́ть** *perf*) **кого́-н из ви́ду** to lose sight of sb; **вид на жи́тельство** residence permit

вида́|ть (*pt* -л, -ла, -ло, *perf* **повида́ть**) *несов перех* (*разг*) to see; (*испытать*) to know; **вида́ться** (*perf* **повида́ться**) *несов возв* (*разг*) to see each other

ви́део *ср нескл* video

видеобло́г (-а) *м* vlog; **видеобло́гер** (-а) *м* vlogger

видеоза́пис|ь (-и) *ж* video recording

видеоигр|а́ (-ы́; *nom pl* -ы) *ж* video game

видеока́мер|а (-ы) *ж* camcorder, videocamera

видеокассе́т|а (-ы) *ж* video cassette

видеомагнитофо́н (-а) *м* video (recorder)

ви́|деть (-жу, -дишь) *несов* to see ▷ (*perf* **уви́деть**) *перех* to see; (*испытать*) to know; **ви́дите ли** you see; **ви́деться** (*perf* **уви́деться**) *несов возв* to see each other

ви́димо *вводн сл* apparently

ви́димо-неви́димо *нареч* (*разг*): **наро́ду в го́роде ви́димо-неви́димо** there are masses of people in the city

ви́димост|ь (-и) *ж* visibility; (*подобие*) appearance; **по всей ви́димости** apparently

видне́|ться (*3sg* -ется) *несов возв* to be visible

ви́дно *как сказ* one can see; (*понятно*) clearly ▷ *вводн сл* probably; **тебе́ видне́е** you know best; **там ви́дно бу́дет** we'll see

ви́дный *прил* (*заметный*) visible; (*известный*) prominent

ви́жу(сь) *несов см* **ви́деть(ся)**

ви́з|а (-ы) *ж* visa

визажи́ст (-а) *м* make-up artist

визи́т (-а) *м* visit

визи́т|ка (-ки; *gen pl* -ок) *ж* business card

визи́тн|ый *прил*: **визи́тная ка́рточка** (business) card

виктори́н|а (-ы) *ж* quiz game

ви́л|ка (-ки; *gen pl* -ок) *ж* fork; (*штепсельная*) **ви́лка** plug

ви́лл|а (-ы) *ж* villa

ви́л|ы (-) *мн* pitchfork *ед*

вин|а́ (-ы́) *ж* blame; (*чувство*) guilt

винегре́т (-а) *м* beetroot salad

вини́тельный *прил*: **вини́тельный паде́ж** accusative (case)

вин|и́ть (-ю́, -и́шь) *несов перех*: **вини́ть кого́-н в** +*prp* to blame sb for; (*упрекать*: *за лень*): **вини́ть кого́-н за** +*acc* to accuse sb of

вин|о́ (-а́; *nom pl* -а) *ср* wine

винова́тый *прил* (*взгляд итп*) guilty; **винова́тый в** +*prp* (*в неудаче*) responsible *или* to blame (for); **винова́т!** sorry!, excuse me!

вино́вност|ь (-и) *ж* guilt

вино́вн|ый *прил* guilty ▷ (**-ого**) *м* guilty party

виногра́д (-а) *м* (*растение*) (grape)vine; (*ягоды*) grapes *мн*; **виногра́дник** (-а) *м* vineyard

винт (-а́) *м* screw

винто́в|ка (-ки; *gen pl* -ок) *ж* rifle

виолонче́л|ь (-и) *ж* cello

вира́ж (-а́) *м* (*поворот*) turn

виртуа́льный *прил* virtual

ви́рус (-а) *м* virus

ви|се́ть (-шу́, -си́шь) *несов* to hang; (*Комп*) to freeze

ви́ски *ср нескл* whisky (*Brit*), whiskey (*US, Ireland*)

вис|о́к (-ка́) *м* (*Анат*) temple

високо́сный *прил*: **високо́сный год** leap year

витами́н (-а) *м* vitamin

вита́|ть (-ю) *несов* to hang in the air

вит|о́к (-ка́) *м* (*спирали*) twist

витра́ж (-а́) *м* stained-glass window

витри́н|а (-ы) *ж* (*в магазине*) shop window; (*в музее*) display case

ви|ть (**вью, вьёшь**; *imper* **вей(те)**, *perf* **свить**) *несов перех* (*венок*) to weave; (*гнездо*) to build; **ви́ться** *несов возв* (*растения*) to trail; (*волосы*) to curl

ви́це-президе́нт (-а) м vice president
ВИЧ м сокр (= ви́рус иммунодефици́та челове́ка) HIV (= human immunodeficiency virus); ВИЧ-инфици́рованный HIV-positive
ви́шн|я (-ни; gen pl -ён) ж cherry
вка́лыва|ть (-ю) несов от **вколо́ть**
вка|ти́ть (-чу́, -тишь; impf **вка́тывать**) сов перех (что-н на колёсах) to wheel in; (что-н кру́глое) to roll in
вклад (-а) м (в нау́ку) contribution; (в ба́нке) deposit; **вкла́дчик** (-а) м investor
вкла́дыва|ть (-ю) несов от **вложи́ть**
включа́|ть (-ю) несов от **включи́ть**
▷ перех: **включа́ть** (в себя́) to include; **включа́ться** несов от **включи́ться**
включа́я предл +acc including
включи́тельно нареч inclusive
включ|и́ть (-у́, -и́шь; impf **включа́ть**) сов перех to turn или switch on; **включа́ть** (perf включи́ть) кого́-н/что-н во что-н to include sb/sth in sth; **включи́ться** (impf **включа́ться**) сов возв to come on; (в спор): **включи́ться в** +acc to join in
вкол|о́ть (-ю́, -ешь; impf **вка́лывать**) сов перех to stick in
вкра́тце нареч briefly
вкривь нареч: вкривь и вкось (разг) all over the place
вкру|ти́ть (-чу́, -тишь; impf **вкру́чивать**) сов перех to screw in
вкруту́ю нареч: яйцо́ вкруту́ю hard-boiled egg
вкус (-а) м taste; она́ оде́та со вку́сом she is tastefully dressed
вку́сно нареч tastily ▷ как сказ: о́чень вку́сно it's delicious; она́ вку́сно гото́вит she is a good cook
вку́сный прил tasty; (обед) delicious
вла́г|а (-и) ж moisture
владе́л|ец (-ьца) м owner
владе́ни|е (-я) ср ownership; (поме́щика) estate
владе́|ть (-ю) несов (+instr: облада́ть) to own, possess; (языко́м) to be proficient in; (ору́жием) to handle proficiently; **владе́ть** (impf) **собо́й** to control o.s.; **владе́ть** (impf) **рука́ми/нога́ми** to have the use of one's arms/legs
вла́жност|ь (-и) ж humidity
вла́жный прил damp; (глаза́, ко́жа) moist
вла́ств|овать (-ую) несов: **вла́ствовать над** +instr to rule; (перен) to hold sway over
вла́ст|и (-е́й) мн authorities
власт|ь (-и; gen pl -е́й) ж power; (роди́тельская) authority; см также **вла́сти**
вле́во нареч (to the) left
влез|ть (-у, -ешь; pt -, -ла, impf **влеза́ть**) сов: влезть на +acc to climb (up); (на кры́шу) to climb onto; (в дом) to break in
влете́|ть (-чу́, -ти́шь; impf **влета́ть**) сов:

влете́ть в +acc to fly into
влече́ни|е (-я) ср: влече́ние (к +dat) attraction (to)
вле|чь (-ку́, -чёшь etc, -ку́т; pt влёк, -кла́, perf **повле́чь**) несов перех: влечь за собо́й to lead to; его́ влечёт нау́ка he is drawn to science
влива́ни|е (-я) ср (де́нег) injection
вли|ть (волью́, вольёшь; pt -л, -ла́, -ло, imper влей(те), impf **влива́ть**) сов перех to pour in; (де́ньги) to inject
влия́ни|е (-я) ср influence
влия́тельный прил influential
влия́|ть (-ю) несов: влия́ть на +acc to influence; (на органи́зм) to affect
влож|и́ть (-у́, -ишь; impf **вкла́дывать**) сов перех to insert; (сре́дства) to invest
влюб|и́ться (-лю́сь, -ишься; impf **влюбля́ться**) сов возв: влюби́ться в +acc to fall in love with; **влюблённ|ый** прил in love; (взгляд) loving ▷ (-ого) м: влюблённые lovers
вме́сте нареч together; вме́сте с тем at the same time
вмести́тельный прил spacious
вме|сти́ть (-щу́, -сти́шь; impf **вмеща́ть**) сов перех (о за́ле) to hold; (о гости́нице) to accommodate; **вмести́ться** (impf **вмеща́ться**) несов возв to fit in
вме́сто предл (+gen: взаме́н) instead of ▷ союз: вме́сто того́ что́бы instead of, rather than
вмеша́|ть (-ю; impf **вме́шивать**) сов перех (доба́вить) to mix in; (перен): вмеша́ть кого́-н в +acc to get sb mixed up in; **вмеша́ться** (impf **вме́шиваться**) сов возв to interfere; (в перегово́ры итп) to intervene
вмеща́|ть(ся) (-ю(сь)) несов от **вмести́ть(ся)**
вмиг нареч instantly
вмя́тин|а (-ы) ж dent
внаём нареч: отдава́ть внаём to let, rent out
внача́ле нареч at first
вне предл +gen outside; вне о́череди out of turn; он был вне себя́ he was beside himself
внедоро́жник (-а) м four-wheel drive
внедре́ни|е (-я) ср introduction
внеза́пный прил sudden
внес|ти́ (-у́, -ёшь; pt внёс, -ла́, impf **вноси́ть**) сов перех (ве́щи) to carry или bring in; (су́мму) to pay; (законопрое́кт) to bring in; (попра́вку) to insert
вне́шн|ий прил (стена́) exterior; (споко́йствие) outward; (свя́зи) external; **вне́шний мир** outside world; **вне́шний вид** appearance; **вне́шняя поли́тика/торго́вля** foreign policy/trade; **вне́шност|ь** (-и) ж appearance
внешта́тный прил freelance
вниз нареч: вниз (по +dat) down; вниз по тече́нию downstream

внизу́ *нареч* below; (*в здании*) downstairs ▷ *предл*: **внизу́ страни́цы** at the foot *или* bottom of the page

вни́к|нуть (**-ну**; *pt* **-**, **-ла**, *impf* **вника́ть**) *сов*: **вни́кнуть во что-н** to understand sth well; (*изучать*) to scrutinize sth

внима́ни|е (**-я**) *ср* attention; **внима́тельный** *прил* attentive; (*работа*) careful; (*сын*) caring

вничью́ *нареч* (*Спорт*): **сыгра́ть вничью́** to draw

вновь *нареч* again

вно|си́ть (**-шу́**, **-сишь**) *несов от* **внести́**

вну|к (**-ка**; *nom pl* **-ки** *или* **-ча́та**) *м* grandson; *см также* **вну́ки**

вну́к|и (**-ов**) *мн* grandchildren

вну́тренн|ий *прил* interior; (*побуждение, голос*) inner; (*политика, рынок*) domestic; (*рана*) internal; **Министе́рство вну́тренних дел** ≈ the Home Office (*Brit*), ≈ the Department of the Interior (*US*)

внутри́ *нареч* inside ▷ *предл* (+*gen*): **до́ма** inside; (*организации*) within

внутрь *нареч* inside ▷ *предл* +*gen* inside

вну́ч|ка (**-ки**; *gen pl* **-ек**) *ж* granddaughter

внуша́|ть (**-ю**) *несов от* **внуши́ть**

внуши́тельный *прил* imposing; (*сумма, успех*) impressive

внуш|и́ть (**-у́**, **-и́шь**; *impf* **внуша́ть**) *сов перех*: **внуши́ть что-н кому́-н** (*чувство*) to inspire sb with sth; (*идею*) to instil (*Brit*) *или* instill (*US*) sth in sb

вня́тный *прил* articulate, audible

во *предл* = **в**

вовл|е́чь (**-еку́**, **-ечёшь** *etc* **-еку́т**; *pt* **-ёк**, **-екла́**, *impf* **вовлека́ть**) *сов перех*: **вовле́чь кого́-н в** +*acc* to draw sb into

во́время *нареч* on time

во́все *нареч* (*разг*) completely; **во́все нет** not at all

во-вторы́х *вводн сл* secondly, in the second place

вод|а́ (*acc sg* **-у**, *gen sg* **-ы́**, *nom pl* **-ы**) *ж* water; *см также* **во́ды**

води́тел|ь (**-я**) *м* driver

води́тельск|ий *прил*: **води́тельские права́** driving licence (*Brit*), driver's license (*US*)

во|ди́ть (**-жу́**, **-дишь**) *несов перех* (*ребёнка*) to take; (*машину, поезд*) to drive; (*самолёт*) to fly; (*корабль*) to sail; **води́ться** *несов возв* (*рыба итп*) to be (found)

во́дк|а (**-и**) *ж* vodka

во́дный *прил* water

водоём (**-а**) *м* reservoir

водола́з (**-а**) *м* diver

Водоле́й (**-я**) *м* Aquarius

водонепроница́емый *прил* waterproof

водопа́д (**-а**) *м* waterfall

водопрово́д (**-а**) *м* water supply system; **у них в до́ме есть водопрово́д** their house has running water; **водопрово́дный** *прил* (*труба, кран*) water; (*система*) plumbing; **водопрово́дчик** (**-а**) *м* plumber

водоро́д (**-а**) *м* hydrogen

водохрани́лищ|е (**-а**) *ср* reservoir

во́д|ы (**-**) *мн* (*государственные*) waters; (*минеральные*) spa *ед*

водяно́й *прил* water

во|ева́ть (**-ю́ю**) *несов* (*страна*) to be at war; (*человек*) to fight

военача́льник (**-а**) *м* (military) commander

военкома́т (**-а**) *м сокр* (= **вое́нный комиссариа́т**) office for military registration and enlistment

вое́нно-возду́шный *прил*: **вое́нно-возду́шные си́лы** (the) air force

вое́нно-морско́й *прил*: **вое́нно-морско́й флот** (the) navy

военнообя́занн|ый (**-ого**) *м person* eligible for compulsory military service

военнопле́нн|ый (**-ого**) *м* prisoner of war

вое́нно-промы́шленный *прил*: **вое́нно-промы́шленный ко́мплекс** military-industrial complex

военнослу́жащ|ий (**-его**) *м* serviceman (*мн* servicemen)

вое́нн|ый *прил* military; (*врач*) army ▷ (**-ого**) *м* serviceman (*мн* servicemen); **вое́нное положе́ние** martial law

вожде́ни|е (**-я**) *ср* (*машины*) driving; (*судна*) steering

вожд|ь (**-я́**) *м* (*племени*) chief, chieftain; (*партии*) leader

вожж|а́ (**-и́**; *nom pl* **-и**, *gen pl* **-е́й**) *ж* rein

возб|уди́ть (**-ужу́**, **-у́дишь**; *impf* **возбужда́ть**) *сов перех* (*вызвать*) to arouse; (*взволновать*) to excite; **возбужда́ть** (*perf* **возбуди́ть**) **де́ло** *или* **проце́сс про́тив** +*gen* to bring a case *или* institute proceedings against; **возбуди́ться** *сов возв* (*человек*) to become excited

возве|сти́ (**-ду́**, **-дёшь**; *pt* **возвёл**, **-ла́**, *impf* **возводи́ть**) *сов перех* to erect

возвра́т (**-а**) *м* return; (*долга*) repayment; **без возвра́та** irrevocably

возвра|ти́ть (**-щу́**, **-ти́шь**; *impf* **возвраща́ть**) *сов перех* to return; (*долг*) to repay; (*здоровье, счастье*) to restore; **возврати́ться** (*impf* **возвраща́ться**) *сов возв*: **возврати́ться** (**к** +*dat*) to return *или* come back (to)

возвраще́ни|е (**-я**) *ср* return

возгла́в|ить (**-лю**, **-ишь**; *impf* **возглавля́ть**) *сов перех* to head

возда́ть (*как* **дать**; *см Table 16*; *impf* **воздава́ть**) *сов перех*: **возда́ть кому́-н по заслу́гам** (*в награду*) to reward sb for their services; (*в наказание*) to give sb what they deserve; **воздава́ть** (*perf* **возда́ть**) **до́лжное кому́-н** to give sb their due

воздви́г|нуть (-ну; pt -, -ла, impf **воздвига́ть**) сов перех to erect
возде́йстви|е (-я) ср effect; (идеологи́ческое) influence
возде́йств|овать (-ую) (не)сов: **возде́йствовать на** +acc to have an effect on
возде́ла|ть (-ю; impf **возде́лывать**) сов перех (по́ле) to cultivate
возде́рж|а́ться (-ержу́сь, -е́ржишься; impf **возде́рживаться**) сов возв: **воздержа́ться от** +gen to refrain from; (от голосова́ния) to abstain from
во́здух (-а) м air; **на** (откры́том) **во́здухе** outside, outdoors; **возду́шный** прил air; (деса́нт) airborne; **возду́шный флот** civil aviation; (Воен) air force
воззва́ни|е (-я) ср appeal
во|зи́ть (-жу́, -зишь) несов перех to take; **вози́ться** несов возв to potter about; **вози́ться** (impf) с +instr (разг: с рабо́той итп) to dawdle over; (с детьми́ итп) to spend a lot of time with
во́зле нареч nearby ▷ предл +gen near
возлю́бленн|ый (-ого) м beloved
возме|сти́ть (-щу́, -сти́шь; impf **возмеща́ть**) сов перех (убы́тки) to compensate for; (затра́ты) to refund, reimburse
возмо́жно как сказ it is possible ▷ вводн сл (мо́жет быть) possibly; **возмо́жност|и** (-ей) мн (тво́рческие) potential ▷ (фина́нсовые возмо́жности) financial resources; **возмо́жност|ь** (-и) ж opportunity; (вероя́тность) possibility; **по** (ме́ре) **возмо́жности** as far as possible; см также **возмо́жности**; **возмо́жный** прил possible
возмужа́|ть (-ю) сов от **мужа́ть**
возмути́тельный прил appalling; **возму|ти́ть** (-щу́, -ти́шь; impf **возмуща́ть**) сов перех to appal (Brit), appall (US); **возмути́ться** (impf **возмуща́ться**) сов возв to be appalled
вознагра|ди́ть (-жу́, -ди́шь; impf **вознагражда́ть**) сов перех to reward
возни́к|нуть (-ну; pt -, -ла, impf **возника́ть**) сов to arise
возобнов|и́ть (-лю́, -и́шь; impf **возобновля́ть**) сов перех (рабо́ту) to resume; (контра́кт) to renew; **возобнови́ться** (impf **возобновля́ться**) сов возв to resume
возобновля́емый прил renewable
возраже́ни|е (-я) ср objection; **возра|зи́ть** (-жу́, -зи́шь; impf **возража́ть**) сов: **возрази́ть** (+dat) to object (to)
во́зраст (-а) м age; **он был уже́ в во́зрасте** he was getting on in years
возр|асти́ (3sg -астёт, pt -ós, -осла́, impf **возраста́ть**) сов to grow
возро|ди́ть (-жу́, -ди́шь; impf **возрожда́ть**) сов перех to revive;

возроди́ться (impf **возрожда́ться**) сов возв to revive
возрожде́ни|е (-я) ср revival; (на́ции, ве́ры) rebirth; **Возрожде́ние** Renaissance
возьму́(сь) etc сов см **взя́ть(ся)**
во́инск|ий прил military; **во́инская обя́занность** conscription
во|й (-я) м howl
во́йлок (-а) м felt
войн|а́ (-ы́; nom pl -ы) ж war
во́йск|о (-а; nom pl -á) ср (the) forces мн
войти́ (как идти́; см Table 18; impf **входи́ть**) сов: **войти́ (в** +acc) to enter, go in(to); (в комите́т) to become a member (of); (умести́ться) to fit in(to); (Комп) to log in; **па́пка "Входя́щие"** inbox
вока́льный прил vocal; (ко́нкурс) singing
вокза́л (-а) м station
вокру́г нареч around, round ▷ предл (+gen: круго́м) around, round; (по по́воду) about, over; **ходи́ть** (impf) **вокру́г да о́коло** (разг) to beat about the bush
вол (-á) м ох (мн о́ксен), bullock
волейбо́л (-а) м volleyball
волк (-а; gen pl -о́в) м wolf (мн wolves)
волн|а́ (-ы́; nom pl во́лны) ж wave
волне́ни|е (-я) ср (ра́достное) excitement; (не́рвное) agitation; (обы́чно мн: в масса́х) unrest
волни́стый прил (во́лосы) wavy
волн|ова́ть (-у́ю; perf **взволнова́ть**) несов перех to be concerned about; (подлеж:му́зыка) to excite; **волнова́ться** (perf **взволнова́ться**) несов возв (мо́ре) to be rough; (челове́к) to worry
вол|окно́ (-окна́; nom pl -о́кна, gen pl -о́кон) ср fibre (Brit), fiber (US)
во́лос (-а; gen pl воло́с, dat pl -áм) м hair то́лько ед
волос|о́к (-ка́) м hair; **быть** (impf) или **находи́ться** (impf) **на волоске́** или **на волоске́ от** +gen to be within a hair's-breadth of
волочи́|ть (-у́, -и́шь) несов перех to drag
во́лчий прил wolf
волше́бниц|а (-ы) ж (good или white) witch
волше́бный прил magic; (му́зыка) magical
во́льно нареч freely; **во́льно!** (Воен) at ease!; **во́ль|ный** прил (свобо́дный) free ▷ как сказ: **во́лен** +infin he is free to do
во́л|я (-и) ж will; (стремле́ние): **во́ля к побе́де** the will to win
вон нареч (разг: прочь) out; (: там) (over) there; **вон отсю́да!** get out of here!; **вон (оно́) что** so that's it!
вообра|зи́ть (-жу́, -зи́шь; impf **вообража́ть**) сов перех to imagine
вообще́ нареч (в о́бщем) on the whole; (совсе́м) absolutely; (+noun: без ча́стностей) in general; **вообще́ говоря́** generally speaking

воодушев|и́ть (**-лю́**, **-и́шь**; *impf* **воодушевля́ть**) *сов перех* to inspire; **воодушеви́ться** *сов возв*: **воодушеви́ться** +*instr* to be inspired by; **воодушевле́ни|е** (**-я**) *ср* inspiration

вооружа́|ть(ся) (**-ю(сь)**) *несов см* **вооружи́ть(ся)**

вооруже́ни|е (**-я**) *ср* (*процесс*) arming; (*оружие*) arms *мн*; **вооружённ|ый** *прил* armed; **вооружённые си́лы** (the) armed forces; **вооруж|и́ть** (**-у́**, **-и́шь**; *impf* **вооружа́ть**) *сов перех* to arm; (*перен*) to equip; **вооружи́ться** (*impf* **вооружа́ться**) *сов возв* to arm o.s.

во-пе́рвых *нареч* firstly, first of all

воплоти́ть (**-щу́**, **-ти́шь**; *impf* **воплоща́ть**) *сов перех* to embody; **воплоща́ть** (*perf* **воплоти́ть**) **в жизнь** to realize; **воплоти́ться** (*impf* **воплоти́ться**) *сов возв*: **воплоти́ться в** +*prp* to be embodied in; **воплоща́ться** (*perf* **воплоти́ться**) **в жизнь** to be realized

вопл|ь (**-я**) *м* scream

вопреки́ *предл* +*dat* contrary to

вопро́с (**-а**) *м* question; (*проблема*) issue; **задава́ть** (*perf* **зада́ть**) **вопро́с** to ask a question; **вопроси́тельный** *прил* (*взгляд*) questioning; (*Линг*) interrogative; **вопроси́тельный знак** question mark

вор (**-а**; *gen pl* **-о́в**) *м* thief

ворв|а́ться (**-у́сь**, **-ёшься**; *impf* **врыва́ться**) *сов возв* to burst in

вороб|е́й (**-ья́**) *м* sparrow

вор|ова́ть (**-у́ю**) *несов перех* to steal; **воровств|о́** (**-а́**) *ср* theft

во́рон (**-а**) *м* raven

воро́н|а (**-ы**) *ж* crow

во́рот (**-а**) *м* neck (of *clothes*)

воро́т|а (**-**) *мн* gates; (*Спорт*) goal *ед*

воротни́к (**-а́**) *м* collar

воро́ча|ть (**-ю**) *несов перех* to shift
▷ *неперех* (+*instr*: *разг*: **де́ньгами**) to have control of; **воро́чаться** *несов возв* to toss and turn

ворс (**-а**) *м* (*на ткани*) nap

ворч|а́ть (**-у́**, **-и́шь**) *несов* (*зверь*) to growl; (*человек*) to grumble

восемна́дцатый *чис* eighteenth

восемна́дцат|ь (**-и**; *как* **пять**; *см Table 26*) *чис* eighteen

во́с|емь (**-ьми́**; *как* **пять**; *см Table 26*) *чис* eight; **во́с|емьдесят** (**-ьми́десяти**; *как* **пятьдеся́т**; *см Table 26*) *чис* eighty; **вос|емьсо́т** (**-ьмисо́т**; *как* **пятьсо́т**; *см Table 28*) *чис* eight hundred

воск (**-а**) *м* wax

восклица́тельный *прил* exclamatory; **восклица́тельный знак** exclamation mark (*Brit*) *или* point (*US*)

восково́й *прил* wax

воскреса́|ть (**-ю**) *несов от* **воскре́снуть**

воскресе́ни|е (**-я**) *ср* resurrection

воскресе́нь|е (**-я**) *ср* Sunday

воскре́с|нуть (**-ну**; *pt* **-**, **-ла**, *impf*

воскреса́ть) *сов* to be resurrected; (*перен*) to be revived

воскре́сный *прил* Sunday

воспале́ни|е (**-я**) *ср* inflammation; **воспале́ние лёгких** pneumonia

воспал|и́ться (*3sg* **-и́тся**, *impf* **воспаля́ться**) *сов возв* to become inflamed

воспита́ни|е (**-я**) *ср* upbringing; (*граждан*) education; (*честности*) fostering; **воспита́тел|ь** (**-я**) *м* teacher; (*в лагере*) instructor; **воспита́|ть** (**-ю**; *impf* **воспи́тывать**) *сов перех* (*ребёнка*) to bring up; (*трудолюбие*) to foster

воспо́льз|оваться (**-уюсь**) *сов от* **по́льзоваться**

воспомина́ни|е (**-я**) *ср* recollection; *см также* **воспомина́ния**

воспомина́ни|я (**-й**) *мн* memoirs *мн*, reminiscences *мн*

воспрепя́тств|овать (**-ую**) *сов от* **препя́тствовать**

воспреща́|ться (*3sg* **-ется**) *несов возв* to be forbidden

восприня́ть (**-иму́**, **-и́мешь**; *impf* **воспринима́ть**) *сов перех* (*смысл*) to comprehend

воспроизв|ести́ (**-еду́**, **-едёшь**; *pt* **-ёл**, **-ела́**, **-ело́**, *impf* **воспроизводи́ть**) *сов перех* to reproduce

воспроти́в|иться (**-люсь**, **-ишься**) *сов от* **проти́виться**

восста|ва́ть (**-ю́**, **-ёшь**) *несов от* **восста́ть**

восста́ни|е (**-я**) *ср* uprising

восстан|ови́ть (**-овлю́**, **-о́вишь**; *impf* **восстана́вливать**) *сов перех* to restore

восста́|ть (**-ну**, **-нешь**; *impf* **восстава́ть**) *сов*: **восста́ть** (**про́тив** +*gen*) to rise up (against)

восто́к (**-а**) *м* east; **Восто́к** the East, the Orient

восторжеств|ова́ть (**-у́ю**) *сов от* **торжествова́ть**

восто́чный *прил* eastern; **восто́чный ве́тер** east wind

востре́бовани|е (**-я**) *ср* (*багажа*) claim; **письмо́ до востре́бования** a letter sent poste restante (*Brit*) *или* general delivery (*US*)

восхити́тельный *прил* delightful

восхи|ти́ть (**-щу́**, **-ти́шь**; *impf* **восхища́ть**) *сов перех*: **меня́ восхища́ет он/его́ хра́брость** I admire him/his courage; **восхити́ться** (*impf* **восхища́ться**) *сов возв*: **восхити́ться** +*instr* to admire

восхище́ни|е (**-я**) *ср* admiration

восхо́д (**-а**) *м*: **восхо́д со́лнца** sunrise

восх|оди́ть (**-ожу́**, **-о́дишь**) *несов от* **взойти́**

восьмёр|ка (**-ки**; *gen pl* **-ок**) *ж* (*разг*: *цифра*) eight

восьмидеся́тый *чис* eightieth

восьмо́й чис eighth

○ **КЛЮЧЕВО́Е СЛО́ВО**

вот част **1** (*о бли́зком предме́те*): **вот моя́ ма́ма** here is my mother; **вот мои́ де́ти** here are my children
2 (*выража́ет указа́ние*) this; **вот в чём де́ло** this is what it's about; **вот где ну́жно иска́ть** this is where we need to look
3 (*при эмфа́тике*): **вот ты и сде́лай э́то** YOU do this; **вот негодя́й!** what a rascal!
4 (*во фра́зах*): **вот-вот** (*разг*: **вот и́менно**) that's it; **он вот-во́т ля́жет спать** he is just about to go to bed; **вот ещё!** (*разг*) not likely!; **вот (оно́) как** или **что!** is that so или right?; **вот тебе́ и на** или **те раз!** (*разг*) well I never!

воткн|у́ть (**-у́, -ёшь**; *impf* **втыка́ть**) *сов перех* to stick in
во́тум (**-а**) *м*: **во́тум дове́рия/недове́рия** vote of confidence/no confidence
вошёл *etc сов см* **войти́**
вошь (**вши**; *instr sg* **во́шью**, *nom pl* **вши**) *ж* louse (*мн* lice)
впада́|ть (**-ю**) *несов от* **впасть**
▷ *непере́х*: **впада́ть в** +*acc* to flow into
впа|сть (**-ду́, -дёшь**; *impf* **впада́ть**) (*щёки, глаза́*) to become sunken; **впада́ть** (*perf* **впасть**) **в** +*acc* (*в исте́рику*) to go into
впервы́е *нареч* for the first time
вперёд *нареч* (*идти́*) ahead, forward; (*заплати́ть*) in advance
впереди́ *нареч* in front; (*в бу́дущем*) ahead ▷ *предл* +*gen* in front of
впечатле́ни|е (**-я**) *ср* impression
впечатля́|ть (**-ю**) *несов* to be impressive
впи|са́ть (**-шу́, -шешь**; *impf* **впи́сывать**) *сов перех* to insert
впи́та|ть (**-ю**; *impf* **впи́тывать**) *сов перех* to absorb; **впита́ться** *сов возв* to be absorbed
вплавь *нареч* by swimming
вплотну́ю *как сказ*: (*бли́зко*) close (by) ▷ *предл*: **вплотну́ю к** +*dat* (*к го́роду*) right up close to; (*к стене́*) right up against
вплоть *предл*: **вплоть до** +*gen* (*зимы́*) right up till; (*включа́я*) right up to
вполго́лоса *нареч* softly
впо́ру *как сказ*: **пла́тье/шля́па мне впо́ру** the dress/hat fits me nicely
впосле́дствии *нареч* subsequently
впра́ве *как сказ* +*infin*: **знать, тре́бовать** to have a right to do
впра́во *нареч* to the right
впредь *нареч* in future ▷ *предл*: **впредь до** +*gen* pending
впро́голодь *нареч*: **жить впро́голодь** to live from hand to mouth
впро́чем *союз* however, though ▷ *вводн сл* but then again
впу|сти́ть (**-щу́, -стишь**; *impf* **впуска́ть**) *сов перех* to let in

враг (**-а́**) *м* enemy
вражда́ (**-ы́**) *ж* enmity, hostility; **вражде́бный** *прил* hostile
вражд|ова́ть (**-у́ю**) *несов*: **вражд ова́ть** (**с** +*instr*) to be on hostile terms (with)
вразре́з *нареч*: **вразре́з с** +*instr* in contravention of
вран|ьё (**-я́**) *ср* (*разг*) lies *мн*
врата́р|ь (**-я́**) *м* goalkeeper
врач (**-а́**) *м* doctor; **враче́бный** *прил* medical
враща́|ть (**-ю**) *несов перех* (*колесо́*) to turn; **враща́ться** *несов возв* to revolve, rotate
вред (**-а́**) *м* damage; (*челове́ку*) harm ▷ *предл*: **во вред** +*dat* to the detriment of; **вреди́тел|ь** (**-я**) *м* (*насеко́мое*) pest; **вре|ди́ть** (**-жу́, -ди́шь**; *perf* **навреди́ть**) *несов* +*dat* to harm; (*здоро́вью*) to damage; (*врагу́*) to inflict damage on; **вре́дно** *нареч*: **вре́дно влия́ть на** +*acc* to have a harmful effect on ▷ *как сказ*: **кури́ть вре́дно** smoking is bad for you; **вре́дный** *прил* harmful; (*разг*: челове́к) nasty
вре́|заться (**-жусь, -жешься**; *impf* **вреза́ться**) *сов возв*: **вре́заться в** +*acc* (*верёвка*) to cut into; (*маши́на*) to plough (*Brit*) или plow (*US*) into; (*в па́мять*) to engrave itself on
времена́ми *нареч* at times
вре́менный *прил* temporary
вре́м|я (**-ени**; *см* Table 4) *ср* time; (*Линг*) tense ▷ *предл*: **во вре́мя** +*gen* during ▷ *союз*: **в то вре́мя как** или **когда́** while; (**а**) **в то же вре́мя** (but) at the same time; **вре́мя от вре́мени** from time to time; **в после́днее вре́мя** recently; **в своё вре́мя** (*когда́ необходи́мо*) in due course; **в своё вре́мя она́ была́ краса́вицей** she was a real beauty in her day; **на вре́мя** for a while; **со вре́менем** with или in time; **тем вре́менем** meanwhile; **ско́лько вре́мени?** what time is it?; **хорошо́ проводи́ть** (*perf* **провести́**) **вре́мя** to have a good time; **вре́мя го́да** season
вро́вень *нареч*: **вро́вень с** +*instr* level with
вро́де *предл* +*gen* like ▷ *част* sort of
врозь *нареч* (*жить*) apart
вруч|и́ть (**-у́, -и́шь**; *impf* **вруча́ть**) *сов перех*: **вручи́ть что-н кому́-н** to hand sth (over) to sb
вручну́ю *нареч* (*разг*) by hand
врыва́|ться (**-юсь**) *несов от* **ворва́ться**
вряд *част*: **вряд ли** hardly; **вряд ли она́ придёт** she's unlikely to come
все *мест см* **весь**

○ **КЛЮЧЕВО́Е СЛО́ВО**

всё (**всего́**) *мест см* **весь**
▷ *ср* (*как сущ*: *без исключе́ния*) everything; **вот и всё**, **э́то всё** that's all;

ча́ще всего́ most often; лу́чше всего́
написа́ть ей письмо́ it would be best to
write to her; меня́ э́то волну́ет ме́ньше
всего́ that is the least of my worries; мне
всё равно́ it's all the same to me; Вы
хоти́те чай и́ли ко́фе? — всё равно́ do you
want tea or coffee? — I don't mind; я всё
равно́ пойду́ туда́ I'll go there all the same
▷ *нареч* **1** (*разг: всё время*) all the time
2 (*только*) all; э́то всё он винова́т it's all
his fault
3 (*о нарастании признака*): шум всё
уси́ливается the noise is getting louder
and louder
4 (*о постоянстве признака*): всё так же
still the same; всё там же still there; всё же
all the same; всё ещё still

всевозмо́жный *прил* all sorts of
всегда́ *нареч* always
всего́ *мест см* весь; всё ▷ *нареч* in all
▷ *част* only; всего́ лишь (*разг*) only; всего́-
на́всего (*разг*) only, mere
вселе́нн|ая (-ой) *ж* the whole world;
Вселе́нная universe
всел|и́ть (-ю́, -и́шь; *impf* вселя́ть) *сов*
перех (*жильцов*) to install; всели́ться
(*impf* вселя́ться) *сов возв* (*жильцы*) to
move in
всем *мест см* весь; всё; все
всеме́рный *прил* all possible
всеми́р|ный *прил* worldwide; (*конгресс*)
world; всеми́рная паути́на (*Комп*)
World-Wide Web
всенаро́дный *прил* national
всео́бщ|ий *прил* universal; всео́бщая
забасто́вка general strike
всеобъе́млющий *прил* comprehensive
всеросси́йский *прил* all-Russia
всерьёз *нареч* in earnest; ты э́то
говори́шь всерьёз? are you serious?
всесторо́нний *прил* comprehensive
всё-таки *част* still, all the same ▷ *союз*:
а всё-таки all the same, nevertheless
всеуслы́шание *ср*: во всеуслы́шание
publicly
всех *мест см* все
вска́кива|ть (-ю) *несов от* вскочи́ть
вскачь *нареч* at a gallop
вски́н|уть (-у; *impf* вски́дывать) *сов*
перех (*мешок, ружьё*) to shoulder;
(*голову*) to jerk up
вскип|е́ть (-лю́, -и́шь) *сов* кипе́ть *сов*
to boil; (*перен*) to flare up
вскользь *нареч* in passing
вско́ре *нареч* soon ▷ *предл*: вско́ре
по́сле +*gen* soon или shortly after
вскоч|и́ть (-у́, -ишь; *impf* вска́кивать)
сов: вскочи́ть в/на +*acc* to leap up onto
вскри́кн|уть (-у; *impf* вскри́кивать)
сов to cry out
вслед *нареч* (*бежать*) behind ▷ *предл*:
вслед (за +*instr*) after; (+*dat*: другу,
поезду) after

всле́дствие *предл* +*gen* as a result of,
because of ▷ *союз*: всле́дствие того́ что
because; всле́дствие чего́ as a result of
which
вслух *нареч* aloud
всмя́тку *нареч*: яйцо́ всмя́тку soft-boiled
egg
всплеск (-а) *м* (*волны*) splash
всплесн|у́ть (-у́, -ёшь; *impf*
всплёскивать) *сов* (*рыба*) to splash;
всплесну́ть (*perf*) рука́ми to throw up
one's hands
всплы́|ть (-ву́, -вёшь; *impf* всплыва́ть)
сов to surface
вспо́мн|ить (-ю, -ишь; *impf*
вспомина́ть) *сов перех* to remember
▷ *неперех*: вспо́мнить о +*prp* to
remember about
вспомога́тельный *прил*
supplementary; (*судно, отряд*) auxiliary;
вспомога́тельный глаго́л auxiliary verb
вспорхн|у́ть (-у́, -ёшь) *сов* to fly off
вспоте́|ть (-ю) *сов от* поте́ть
вспугн|у́ть (-у́, ёшь; *impf* вспу́гивать)
сов перех to scare away или off
вспу́хн|уть (-у) *сов от* пу́хнуть
вспы́хн|уть (-у; *impf* вспы́хивать) *сов*
(*зажечься*) to burst into flames; (*конфликт*)
to flare up; (*покраснеть*) to blush
вспы́шк|а (-ки; *gen pl* -ек) *ж* flash;
(*гнева*) outburst; (*болезни*) outbreak
встава́|ть (-ю́; *imper* -ва́й(те)) *несов от*
встать
вста́в|ить (-лю, -ишь; *impf* вставля́ть)
сов перех to insert, put in
вста́|ть (-ну, -нешь; *impf* встава́ть) *сов*
(*на ноги*) to stand up; (*с постели*) to get up;
(*солнце*) to rise; (*вопрос*) to arise
встрево́ж|ить(ся) (-у(сь), -ишь(ся))
несов от трево́жить(ся)
встре́|тить (-чу, -тишь; *impf* встреча́ть)
сов перех to meet; (*факт*) to come across;
(*оппозицию*) to encounter; (*праздник итп*)
to celebrate; встре́титься (*impf*
встреча́ться) *сов возв*: встре́титься с
+*instr* to meet; мне встре́тились
интере́сные фа́кты I came across some
interesting facts
встре́ч|а (-и) *ж* meeting
встреча́|ть(ся) (-ю(сь)) *несов от*
встре́тить(ся)
встре́чный *прил* (*машина*) oncoming;
(*мера*) counter; встре́чный ве́тер head
wind
встряхн|у́ть (-у́, -ёшь; *impf*
встря́хивать) *сов перех* to shake (out)
вступи́тельный *прил* (*речь, статья*)
introductory; вступи́тельный экза́мен
entrance exam
вступ|и́ть (-лю́, -ишь; *impf* вступа́ть)
сов: вступи́ть в +*acc* to enter; (*в партию*)
to join; (*в переговоры*) to enter into;
вступи́ться (*impf* вступа́ться) *сов возв*:
вступи́ться за +*acc* to stand up for

вступле́ни|е (-я) *ср* entry; (*в партию*) joining; (*в книге*) introduction
всхли́пыва|ть (-ю) *несов* to sob
всхо|ди́ть (-жу́, -дишь) *несов от* взойти́
всхо́д|ы (-ов) *мн* shoots
всю́ду *нареч* everywhere
вс|я (-ей) *мест см* весь
вся́к|ий *мест* (*каждый*) every; (*разнообразный*) all kinds of; (*любой*) any
▷ (-ого) *м* (*любой*) anyone; (*каждый*) everyone
вся́ческий *мест* all possible; (*товары*) all kinds of
вся́чин|а (-ы) *ж* (*разг*): вся́кая вся́чина all sorts of things
втащи́ть (-у́, -ишь); *impf* вта́скивать) *сов перех*: втащи́ть (в +*acc*) to drag in(to)
втере́ть (вотру́, вотрёшь, *pt* втёр, втёрла, *impf* втира́ть) *сов перех*: втере́ть (в +*acc*) to rub in(to)
втисн|уть (-у; *impf* вти́скивать) *сов перех*: вти́снуть (в +*acc*) to cram in(to)
вто́ргн|уться (-усь; *impf* вторга́ться) *сов возв*: вто́ргнуться в +*acc* to invade
втори́чный *прил* (*повторный*) second; (*фактор*) secondary
вто́рник (-а) *м* Tuesday
втор|о́е (-о́го) *ср* main course
втор|о́й *прил* second; сейча́с второ́й час it's after one; сейча́с полови́на второ́го it's half past one
второпя́х *нареч* in a hurry
второстепе́нный *прил* secondary
в-тре́тьих *вводн сл* thirdly, in the third place
втро́ем *нареч* in a group of three
втройне́ *нареч* three times as much
втыка́|ть (-ю) *несов от* воткну́ть
втян|у́ть (-у́; *impf* втя́гивать) *сов перех* (*втащить*) to pull in; втя́гивать (*perf* втяну́ть) кого́-н в +*acc* (*в дело*) to involve sb in
вуа́л|ь (-и) *ж* veil
вуз (-а) *м сокр* (= *вы́сшее уче́бное заведе́ние*) higher education establishment
вулка́н (-а) *м* volcano
вульга́рный *прил* vulgar
вход (-а) *м* (*движение*) entry; (*место*) entrance; (*Tex*) inlet; (*Комп*) input
вхо|ди́ть (-жу́, -дишь) *несов от* войти́
входн|о́й *прил* (*дверь*) entrance; (*Комп*) input
вцеп|и́ться (-лю́сь, -ишься) *сов возв*: вцепи́ться в +*acc* to seize
вчера́ *нареч, м нескл* yesterday
вчера́шний *прил* yesterday's
вче́тверо *нареч* four times
вчетверо́м *нареч* in a group of four
вши *etc сущ см* вошь
вширь *нареч* in breadth
въезд (-а) *м* (*движение*) entry; (*место*) entrance; **въездно́й** *прил* entry
въ́|ехать (*как* е́хать; *см Table 19*; *impf* въезжа́ть) *сов* to enter; (*в новый дом*) to move in; (*наверх: на машине*) to drive up; (: *на коне, велосипеде*) to ride up

Вы (**Вас**; *см Table 6b*) *мест* you (*formal*)
вы (**вас**; *см Table 6b*) *мест* you (*plural*)
вы́бе|жать (*как* бежа́ть; *см Table 20*; *impf* выбега́ть) *сов* to run out
выбива́|ть(ся) (-ю(сь)) *несов от* вы́бить(ся)
выбира́|ть (-ю) *несов от* вы́брать
вы́б|ить (-ью, -ьешь; *impf* выбива́ть) *сов перех* to knock out; (*противника*) to oust; (*ковёр*) to beat; (*надпись*) to carve; выбива́ть (*perf* вы́бить) чек (*кассир*) to ring up the total; **вы́биться** (*impf* выбива́ться) *сов возв*: вы́биться из +*gen* (*освободиться*) to get out of
вы́бор (-а) *м* choice; *см также* вы́боры; **вы́борный** *прил* (*кампания*) election; (*пост, орган*) elective; **вы́борочн|ый** *прил* selective; выборочная прове́рка spot check; **вы́бор|ы** (-ов) *мн* election *ед*; *см также* вы́бор
выбра́сыва|ть(ся) (-ю(сь)) *несов от* вы́бросить(ся)
вы́б|рать (-еру, -ерешь; *impf* выбира́ть) *сов перех* to choose; (*голосованием*) to elect
вы́брос (-а) *м* (*газа*) emission; (*отходов*) discharge; (*нефти*) spillage
вы́бро|сить (-шу, -сишь; *impf* выбра́сывать) *сов перех* to throw out; (*отходы*) to discharge; (*газы*) to emit; **вы́броситься** (*impf* выбра́сываться) *сов возв* to throw oneself out; выбра́сываться (*perf* вы́броситься) с парашю́том to bale out
вы́б|ыть (*как* быть; *см Table 21*; *impf* выбыва́ть) *сов*: вы́быть из +*gen* to leave
вы́ве|зти (*как* везти́; *см Table 20*; *impf* вывози́ть) *сов перех* to take; (*товар: из страны*) to take out
вы́ве|сить (-шу, -сишь; *impf* выве́шивать) *сов перех* (*флаг*) to put up; (*бельё*) to hang out
вы́вес|ка (-ки; *gen pl* -ок) *ж* sign
вы́ве|сти (-ду, -дешь; *impf* выводи́ть) *сов перех* to take out; (*войска: из города*) to pull out, withdraw; (*формулу*) to deduce; (*птенцов*) to hatch; (*породу*) to breed; (*уничтожить*) to exterminate; (*исключить*): вы́вести кого́-н из +*gen* (*из партии*) to expel sb from; выводи́ть (*perf* вы́вести) кого́-н из терпе́ния to exasperate sb; выводи́ть (*perf* вы́вести) кого́-н из себя́ to drive sb mad; **вы́вестись** (*impf* выводи́ться) *сов возв* (*цыплята*) to hatch (out); (*исчезнуть*) to be eradicated
выве́шива|ть (-ю) *несов от* вы́весить
вы́вод (-а) *м* (*войск*) withdrawal; (*умозаключение*) conclusion
вы|води́ть(ся) (-вожу́(сь), -во́дишь(ся)) *несов от* вы́вести(сь)
вы́воз (-а) *м* removal; (*товаров*) export
вы|вози́ть (-вожу́, -во́зишь) *несов от* вы́везти

вывора́чива|ть(ся) (-ю(сь)) несов от **вы́вернуть(ся)**

выгиба́|ть (-ю) несов от **вы́гнуть**

ВЫГЛЯ|ДЕТЬ (-жу, -дишь) несов to look

вы́гля|нуть (-у; impf **выгля́дывать**) сов to look out

вы́г|нать (-оню, -онишь; impf **выгоня́ть**) сов перех to throw out; (стадо) to drive out

вы́гн|уть (-у; impf **выгиба́ть**) сов перех to bend; (спину) to arch

вы́говор (-а) м (произношение) accent; (наказание) reprimand; **вы́говор|ить** (-ю, -ишь; impf **выгова́ривать**) сов перех (произнести) to pronounce

вы́год|а (-ы) ж advantage, benefit; (прибыль) profit

вы́годно нареч (продать) at a profit ▷ как сказ it is profitable; **мне э́то вы́годно** this is to my advantage; (прибыльно) this is profitable for me

выгоня́|ть (-ю) несов от **вы́гнать**

вы́гор|еть (3sg -ит, impf **выгора́ть**) сов (сгореть) to burn down; (выцвести) to fade

вы́гре|сти (-бу, -бешь; pt -б, -бла, -бло, impf **выгреба́ть**) сов перех to rake out

вы́гру|зить (-жу, -зишь; impf **выгружа́ть**) сов перех to unload; **вы́грузиться** (impf **выгружа́ться**) сов возв to unload

выда|ва́ть(ся) (-ю́(сь)) несов от **вы́дать(ся)**

вы́дав|ить (-лю, -ишь; impf **выда́вливать**) сов перех (лимон) to squeeze

вы́да|ть (как дать; см Table 16; impf **выдава́ть**) сов перех to give out; (патент) to issue; (продукцию) to produce; (тайну) to give away; **выдава́ть** (perf **вы́дать**) кого-н/что-н за +acc to pass sb/sth off as; **выдава́ть** (perf **вы́дать**) де́вушку за́муж to marry a girl off; **вы́даться** (impf **выдава́ться**) сов возв (берег) to jut out

вы́дач|а (-и) ж (справки) issue; (продукции) output; (заложников) release

выдаю́щийся прил outstanding

выдвига́|ть(ся) (-ю(сь)) несов от **вы́двинуть(ся)**

выдвиже́ни|е (-я) ср (кандидата) nomination

вы́дви|нуть (-у; impf **выдвига́ть**) сов перех to put forward; (ящик) to pull out; (обвинение) to level; **вы́двинуться** (impf **выдвига́ться**) сов возв to slide out; (работник) to advance

вы́дел|ить (-ю, -ишь; impf **выделя́ть**) сов перех to assign, allocate; (отличить) to pick out; (газы) to emit; **вы́делиться** (impf **выделя́ться**) сов возв (пот) to be secreted; (газ) to be emitted; **выделя́ться** (perf **вы́делиться**) чем-н to stand out by virtue of sth

выдёргива|ть (-ю) несов от **вы́дернуть**

вы́держ|ать (-у, -ишь; impf **выде́рживать**) сов перех (давление) to withstand; (боль) to bear; (экзамен) to get through ▷ неперех (человек) to hold out; (мост) to hold; **не вы́держать** (perf) (человек) to give in

вы́держ|ка (-ки; gen pl -ек) ж (самообладание) self-control; (отрывок) excerpt; (Фото) exposure

вы́дерн|уть (-у; impf **выдёргивать**) сов перех to pull out

вы́дума|ть (-ю; impf **выду́мывать**) сов перех (историю) to make up, invent; (игру) to invent

вы́дум|ка (-ки; gen pl -ок) ж invention

выдыха́|ть (-ю) несов от **вы́дохнуть**

вы́езд (-а) м (отъезд) departure; (место) way out; **игра́ на вы́езде** (Спорт) away game

выездно́й прил (документ) exit; **выездно́й спекта́кль** guest performance; **выездно́й матч** away match

вы́е|хать (как е́хать; см Table 19; impf **выезжа́ть**) сов (уехать) to leave; (машина) to drive out

вы́ж|ать (-му, -мешь; impf **выжима́ть**) сов перех (лимон) to squeeze; (бельё) to wring out

вы́ж|ечь (-гу, -жешь итп -гут; pt -ег, -гла, impf **выжига́ть**) сов перех to burn; (подлеж: солнце) to scorch

выжива́ни|е (-я) ср survival

выжива́|ть (-ю) несов от **вы́жить**

выжига́|ть (-ю) несов от **вы́жечь**

выжима́|ть (-ю) несов от **вы́жать**

вы́жи|ть (-ву, -вешь; impf **выжива́ть**) сов to survive ▷ перех (разг) to drive out

вы́з|вать (-ову, -овешь; impf **вызыва́ть**) сов перех to call; (гнев, критику) to provoke; (восторг) to arouse; (пожар) to cause; **вызыва́ть** (perf **вы́звать**) кого-н на что-н to challenge sb to sth; **вы́зваться** (impf **вызыва́ться**) сов возв: **вы́зваться** +infin to volunteer to do

вы́здорове|ть (-ю, -ешь; impf **выздора́вливать**) сов to recover

вы́зов (-а) м call; (в суд) summons; (+dat: обществу, родителям итп) challenge to; **броса́ть** (perf **бро́сить**) **вы́зов кому́-н/чему́-н** to challenge sb/sth

вы́зубр|ить (-ю, -ишь) сов от **зубри́ть**

вызыва́|ть(ся) (-ю(сь)) несов от **вы́звать(ся)**

вызыва́ющий прил challenging

вы́игра|ть (-ю; impf **выи́грывать**) сов перех to win

вы́|йти (как идти; см Table 18; impf **выходи́ть**) сов to leave; (из игры) to drop out; (из автобуса) to get off; (книга) to come out; (случиться) to ensue; (оказаться) +instr to come out; **выходи́ть** (perf **вы́йти**) за́муж (за) +acc to marry (of woman); **выходи́ть** (perf **вы́йти**) **из больни́цы** to leave hospital

выка́лыва|ть (-ю) несов от **вы́колоть**

выка́пыва|ть (-ю) *несов от* **вы́копать**

выка́рмлива|ть (-ю) *несов от* **вы́кормить**

вы́кача|ть (-ю; *impf* **выка́чивать**) *сов перех* to pump out

вы́кидыш (-а) *м* miscarriage

вы́кин|уть (-у; *impf* **выки́дывать**) *сов перех* to throw out; (*слово*) to omit

вы́кип|еть (*3sg* -ит, *impf* **выкипа́ть**) *сов* to boil away

выкла́дыва|ть (-ю) *несов от* **вы́ложить**

выключа́тель (-я) *м* switch

вы́ключ|ить (-у, -ишь; *impf* **выключа́ть**) *сов перех* to turn off; **вы́ключиться** (*impf* **выключа́ться**) *возв* (*мотор*) to go off; (*свет*) to go out

вы́к|овать (-ую; *impf* **выко́вывать**) *сов перех* (*металл*) to forge

вы́кол|оть (-ю, -ешь; *impf* **выка́лывать**) *сов перех* to poke out

вы́копа|ть (-ю) *сов от* **копа́ть** ⊳ (*impf* **выка́пывать**) *перех* (*яму*) to dig; (*овощи*) to dig up

вы́корм|ить (-лю, -ишь; *impf* **выка́рмливать**) *сов перех* to rear

вы́крик (-а) *м* shout

вы́крикн|уть (-у; *impf* **выкри́кивать**) *сов перех* to shout *или* cry out

вы́кро|йка (-йки; *gen pl* -ек) *ж* pattern

вы́купа|ть(ся) (-ю(сь)) *сов от* **купа́ть(ся)**

вы́куп|ить (-лю, -ишь; *impf* **выкупа́ть**) *сов перех* (*заложника*) to ransom; (*вещи*) to redeem

выла́влива|ть (-ю) *несов от* **вы́ловить**

выла́мыва|ть (-ю) *несов от* **вы́ломать**

вы́лез|ти (-у, -ешь; *pt* -, -ла, *impf* **вылеза́ть**) *сов* (*волосы*) to fall out; **вылеза́ть** (*perf* **вы́лезти**) **из** +*gen* to climb out of

вы́леп|ить (-лю, -ишь) *сов от* **лепи́ть**

вы́лет (-а) *м* departure

вы́ле|теть (-чу, -тишь; *impf* **вылета́ть**) *сов* to fly out; **его́ и́мя вы́летело у меня́ из головы́** his name has slipped my mind

вы́леч|ить (-у, -ишь; *impf* **выле́чивать**) *сов перех* to cure; **вы́лечиться** *несов возв* to be cured

вы́л|ить (-ью, -ьешь; *impf* **вылива́ть**) *сов перех* to pour out ⊳ (*impf* **лить**) (*деталь, статую*) to cast; **вы́литься** (*impf* **вылива́ться**) *сов возв* to pour out; **вылива́ться** (*perf* **вы́литься**) **в** +*acc* to turn into

вы́лов|ить (-лю, -ишь; *impf* **выла́вливать**) *сов перех* to catch

вы́лож|ить (-у, -ишь; *impf* **выкла́дывать**) *сов перех* to lay out; **вы́ложить** **что-н чем-н** (*плиткой*) to face sth with sth

вы́лома|ть (-ю; *impf* **выла́мывать**) *сов перех* to break open

вы́луп|иться (*3sg* -ится, *impf* **вылу́пливаться**) *сов возв* (*птенцы*) to hatch (out)

выма́чива|ть (-ю) *несов от* **вы́мочить**

вы́м|ереть (-ру, -решь; *impf* **вымира́ть**) *сов* (*динозавры*) to become extinct; (*город*) to be dead

вы́ме|сти (-ту, -тешь; *pt* -л, -ла, *impf* **вымета́ть**) *сов перех* to sweep out

вы́ме|стить (-щу, -стишь; *impf* **вымеща́ть**) *сов перех*: **вы́местить что-н на ком-н** to take sth out on sb

вымета́|ть (-ю) *несов от* **вы́мести**

вымира́|ть (*3sg* -ет) *несов от* **вы́мереть**

вы́мок|нуть (-ну, -нешь; *pt* -, -ла) *сов* to get soaked through

вы́моч|ить (-у, -ишь; *impf* **выма́чивать**) *сов перех* to soak

вы́м|ыть (-ою, -оешь) *сов от* **мыть**

вына́шива|ть (-ю) *несов перех* to nurture

вы́нес|ти (-у, -ешь; *pt* -, -ла, *impf* **выноси́ть**) *сов перех* to carry *или* take out; (*приговор*) to pass, pronounce; (*впечатления, знания*) to gain; (*боль, оскорбление*) to bear

вынима́|ть (-ю) *несов от* **вы́нуть**

вын|оси́ть (-ошу́, -о́сишь) *несов от* **вы́нести** ⊳ *перех*: **я его́ не выношу́** I can't bear *или* stand him

вы́ну|дить (-жу, -дишь; *impf* **вынужда́ть**) *сов перех*: **вы́нудить кого́-н/что-н к чему́-н** to force sb/sth into sth

вы́нужденн|ый *прил* forced; **вы́нужденная поса́дка** emergency landing

вы́н|уть (-у; *impf* **вынима́ть**) *сов перех* to take out

вы́нырн|уть (-у) *сов* (*из воды́*) to surface; (*разг*: *из-за угла́*) to pop up

выпада́|ть (-ю) *несов от* **вы́пасть**

выпада́ни|е (-я) *ср* (*осадков*) fall; (*зубов, волос*) falling out

вы́па|сть (-ду, -дешь; *impf* **выпада́ть**) *сов* to fall out; (*осадки итп*) to fall; **мне вы́пал слу́чай/вы́пало сча́стье встре́тить его́** I chanced to/had the luck to meet him

вы́пивк|а (-и) *ж* booze

вы́пи|сать (-шу, -шешь; *impf* **выпи́сывать**) *сов перех* to copy *или* write out; (*пропуск, счёт, реце́пт*) to make out; (*газету*) to subscribe to; (*пациента*) to discharge; **вы́писаться** (*impf* **выпи́сываться**) *несов возв* (*из больни́цы*) to be discharged; (*с а́дреса*) to change one's residence permit

вы́пи|ска (-ки; *gen pl* -ок) *ж* (*цита́та*) extract

вы́п|ить (-ью, -ьешь; *imper* -ей(те)) *сов от* **пить**

вы́плав|ить (-лю, -ишь; *impf* **выплавля́ть**) *сов перех* to smelt

вы́плат|а (-ы) *ж* payment

вы́пла|тить (-чу, -тишь; *impf* **выпла́чивать**) *сов перех* to pay; (*долг*) to pay off

вы́плесн|уть (-у; *impf* **выплёскивать**) *сов перех* to pour out

вы́плы|ть (-ву, -вешь; *impf* **выплыва́ть**) *сов* to swim out

вы́полз|ти (-у; *pt* -, -ла, -ло, *impf* **выполза́ть**) *сов* to crawl out

выполни́мый *прил* feasible

вы́полни|ть (-ю, -ишь; *impf* **выполня́ть**) *сов перех* (*задание, заказ*) to carry out; (*план, условие*) to fulfil (*Brit*), fulfill (*US*)

вы́потрош|ить (-у, -ишь) *сов от* **потроши́ть**

выпра́шива|ть (-ю) *несов перех* to beg for

вы́про|сить (-шу, -сишь) *сов перех*: он вы́просил у отца́ маши́ну his father to give him the car

вы́прыгн|уть (-у; *impf* **выпры́гивать**) *сов* to jump out

вы́прям|ить (-лю, -ишь; *impf* **выпрямля́ть**) *сов перех* to straighten (out); (**вы́прямиться** (*impf* **выпрямля́ться**) *несов возв* to straighten (up)

вы́пуск (-а) *м* (*продукции*) output; (*газа*) emission, release; (*книги*) publication; (*денег, акций*) issue; (*учащиеся*) school-leavers *мн*, graduates *мн* (*US*)

выпуска́|ть (-ю) *несов от* **вы́пустить**

выпускни́к (-á) *м* (*вуза*) graduate; выпускни́к шко́лы school-leaver

выпускно́й *прил* (*класс*) final-year; (*Тех*): выпускно́й кла́пан exhaust valve; выпускно́й ве́чер graduation; выпускно́й экза́мен final exam, finals *мн*

вы́пу|стить (-щу, -стишь; *impf* **выпуска́ть**) *сов* to let out; (*дым*) to exhale; (*заключённого*) to release; (*специалистов*) to turn out; (*продукцию*) to produce; (*книгу*) to publish; (*заём, марки*) to issue; (*акции*) to put into circulation; (*исключить: параграф*) to omit

вы́пью *etc сов см* **вы́пить**

вы́работа|ть (-ю; *impf* **выраба́тывать**) *сов перех* to produce; (*план*) to work out; (*привычку*) to develop

выра́внива|ть (-ю) *несов от* **вы́ровнять**

выража́|ть(ся) (-ю(сь)) *несов от* **вы́разить(ся)**

выраже́ни|е (-я) *ср* expression

вы́ра|зить (-жу, -зишь; *impf* **выража́ть**) *сов перех* to express; **вы́разиться** (*impf* **выража́ться**) *сов возв* (*чувство*) to manifest *или* express itself; (*человек*) to express o.s.

вы́р|асти (-асту, -астешь; *pt* -ос, -осла, -осли) *сов от* **расти́** ▷ (*impf* **вырасти́ть**) *неперех* (*появиться*) to rise up; **выраста́ть** (*perf* **вы́расти**) в +*acc* (*grow*) to become

вы́ра|стить (-щу, -стишь) *сов от* **расти́ть**

выра́щива|ть (-ю; *perf* **вы́растить**) *несов перех* = **расти́ть**

вы́рв|ать (-у, -ешь; *impf* **вырыва́ть**) *сов перех* to pull out; (*отнять*): **вы́рвать что́-н** у кого́-н to snatch sth from sb ▷ (*impf* **рвать**) *безл* (*разг*): её вы́рвало she threw up; (*перен*) ему́ вы́рвали зуб he had his tooth taken out; **вы́рваться** (*impf* **вырыва́ться**) *сов возв* (*из тюрьмы́*) to escape; (*перен: в теа́тр*) to manage to get away; (*пламя*) to shoot out

вы́рез (-а) *м*: пла́тье с больши́м вы́резом a low-cut dress

вы́ре|зать (-жу, -жешь; *impf* **выреза́ть**) *сов перех* to cut out; (*опухоль, гнойник*) to remove; (*из дерева, из кости итп*) to carve; (*на камне, на металле итп*) to engrave; (*убить*) to slaughter

вы́рез|ка (-ки; *gen pl* -ок) *ж* (*газетная*) cutting, clipping; (*мясная*) fillet

вы́ровня|ть (-ю) *сов от* **ровня́ть** ▷ (*impf* **выра́внивать**) *перех* to level

вы́род|иться (3sg -ится, *impf* **вырожда́ться**) *сов возв* to degenerate

вы́рон|ить (-ю, -ишь) *сов перех* to drop

вы́рос *etc сов см* **вы́расти**

вы́руб|ить (-лю, -ишь; *impf* **выруба́ть**) *сов перех* (*деревья*) to cut down; (*свет*) to cut off

вы́руга|ть(ся) (-ю(сь)) *сов от* **руга́ть(ся)**

вы́руч|ить (-у, -ишь; *impf* **выруча́ть**) *сов перех* to help out; (*деньги*) to make

вы́руч|ка (-и) *ж* rescue; (*деньги*) takings *мн*

вырыва́|ть(ся) (-ю(сь)) *несов от* **вы́рвать(ся)**

вы́р|ыть (-ою, -оешь) *сов от* **рыть** ▷ (*impf* **вырыва́ть**) *перех* to dig up; (*яму*) to dig

вы́са|дить (-жу, -дишь; *impf* **выса́живать**) *сов перех* (*растение*) to plant out; (*пассажира: дать выйти*) to drop off; (: *силой*) to throw out; (*войска*) to land; **вы́садиться** (*impf* **выса́живаться**) *сов возв*: **вы́садиться** (из +*gen*) to get off; (*войска*) to land

выса́сыва|ть (-ю) *несов от* **вы́сосать**

вы́свобо|дить (-жу, -дишь; *impf* **высвобожда́ть**) *сов перех* (*ногу, руку*) to free; (*время*) to set aside

вы́си|деть (-жу, -дишь; *impf* **выси́живать**) *сов перех* to hatch; (*перен: лекцию*) to sit out

вы́с|иться (3sg -ится) *несов возв* to tower

вы́ска|зать (-жу, -жешь; *impf* **выска́зывать**) *сов перех* to express; **вы́сказаться** (*impf* **выска́зываться**) *сов возв* to speak one's mind; **выска́зываться** (*perf* **вы́сказаться**) про́тив +*gen*/за +*acc* to speak out against/in favour of

выска́зывани|е (-я) *ср* statement

выска́кива|ть (-ю) *несов от* **вы́скочить**

вы́скользн|уть (-у; *impf* **выска́льзывать**) *сов* to slip out

вы́скоч|ить (-у, -ишь; *impf* **выска́кивать**) *сов* to jump out; **его́ и́мя вы́скочило у меня́ из головы́** (*разг*) his name has slipped my mind

вы́|слать (-шлю, -шлешь; *impf* **высыла́ть**) *сов перех* to send off; (*изгнать*) to deport

высле|дить (-жу, -дишь; *impf* **высле́живать**) *сов перех* to track down

вы́слуг|а (-и) *ж*: **за вы́слугу лет** for long service

вы́слуша|ть (-ю; *impf* **выслу́шивать**) *сов перех* to hear out

высме́|ять (-ю; *impf* **высме́ивать**) *сов перех* to ridicule

вы́сморка|ть(ся) (-ю(сь)) *сов от* **сморка́ть(ся)**

высо́выва|ть(ся) (-ю(сь)) *несов от* **вы́сунуть(ся)**

высо́кий *прил* high; (*человек*) tall; (*честь*) great; (*гость*) distinguished

высоко́ *нареч* high (up) ▷ *как сказ* it's high (up)

высо́с|ать (-у, -ешь; *impf* **выса́сывать**) *сов перех* to suck out; (*насосом*) to pump out

выс|ота́ (-оты́; *nom pl* -о́ты) *ж* height; (*Гео*) altitude; (*звука*) pitch

высо́тный *прил* (*здание*) high-rise

вы́сох|нуть (-ну; *pt* -, -ла, -ло) *сов от* **со́хнуть**

высо́честв|о (-а) *ср*: **Ва́ше** *итп* **Высо́чество** Your *etc* Highness

вы́сп|аться (-люсь, -ишься; *impf* **высыпа́ться**) *сов возв* to sleep well

вы́став|ить (-лю, -ишь; *impf* **выставля́ть**) *сов перех* (*поставить наружу*) to put out; (*грудь*) to stick out; (*кандидату́ру*) to put forward; (*товар*) to display; (*охрану*) to post; (*разг: выгнать*) to chuck out

вы́став|ка (-ки; *gen pl* -ок) *ж* exhibition

выставля́|ть (-ю) *несов от* **вы́ставить**

вы́стира|ть (-ю) *сов от* **стира́ть**

вы́стрел (-а) *м* shot

вы́стрел|ить (-ю, -ишь) *сов* to fire

вы́стро|ить(ся) (-ю(сь), -ишь(ся)) *сов от* **стро́ить(ся)**

вы́ступ (-а) *м* ledge

выступ|ить (-лю, -ишь; *impf* **выступа́ть**) *сов* (*против, в защиту*) to come out; (*из толпы*) to step out; (*актёр*) to perform; (*пот, сыпь*) to break out; (*в поход, на поиски*) to set off *или* out

выступле́ни|е (-я) *ср* (*актёра*) performance; (*в печати*) article; (*речь*) speech

вы́сун|уть (-у; *impf* **высо́вывать**) *сов перех* to stick out; **вы́сунуться** (*impf* **высо́вываться**) *сов возв* (*из окна*) to lean out; (*рука, нога*) to stick out

вы́суш|ить(ся) (-у(сь), -ишь(ся)) *сов от* **суши́ть(ся)**

высчита|ть (-ю; *impf* **высчи́тывать**) *сов*

перех to calculate

вы́сш|ий *прил* (*орган власти*) highest, supreme; **в вы́сшей сте́пени** extremely; **вы́сшая ме́ра наказа́ния** capital punishment; **вы́сшее образова́ние** higher education; **вы́сшее уче́бное заведе́ние** = вуз

высыла́|ть (-ю) *несов от* **вы́слать**

высып|ать (-лю, -лешь; *impf* **высыпа́ть**) *сов перех* to pour out; **вы́сыпаться** (*impf* **высыпа́ться**) *сов возв* to pour out

выта́лкива|ть (-ю) *несов от* **вы́толкнуть**

вы́тащ|ить (-у, -ишь) *сов от* **тащи́ть** ▷ (*impf* **выта́скивать**) *перех* (*мебель*) to drag out

вытека́|ть (*3sg* -ет) *несов от* **вы́течь** ▷ *неперех* (*вывод*) to follow; (*река*) to flow out

вы́т|ереть (-ру, -решь; *impf* **вытира́ть**) *сов перех* to wipe up; (*посуду*) to dry (up); (*руки, глаза*) to wipe; **вы́тереться** (*impf* **вытира́ться**) *сов возв* (*человек*) to dry o.s.

вы́те|чь (*3sg* -чет, *3pl* -кут, *pt* -к, -кла, *impf* **вытека́ть**) *сов* to flow out

вытира́|ть(ся) (-ю(сь)) *несов от* **вы́тереть(ся)**

вы́толкн|уть (-у; *impf* **выта́лкивать**) *сов перех* to push out

вытрезви́тель (-я) *м* overnight police cell for drunks

вы́тряхн|уть (-у; *impf* **вытря́хивать**) *сов перех* to shake out

выть (во́ю, во́ешь) *несов* (*зверь, ветер*) to howl; (*сирена*) to wail

вы́тян|уть (-у; *impf* **вытя́гивать**) *сов перех* to pull out; (*дым*) to extract; (*руки*) to stretch; **вы́тянуться** (*impf* **вытя́гиваться**) *сов возв* (*на дива́не, вдоль берега*) to stretch out; (*встать смирно*) to stand at attention

выу|дить (-жу, -дишь; *impf* **выу́живать**) *сов перех* (*рыбу*) to catch; (*разг: сведения*) to wheedle out

вы́уч|ить(ся) (-у(сь), -ишь(ся)) *сов от* **учи́ть(ся)**

выха́жива|ть (-ю) *несов от* **вы́ходить**

вы́хва|тить (-чу, -тишь; *impf* **выхва́тывать**) *сов перех* to snatch

выхлопн|о́й *прил* exhaust; **выхлопны́е га́зы** exhaust fumes

вы́ход (-а) *м* (*войск*) withdrawal; (*из кризиса*) way out; (*на сцену*) appearance; (*в море*) sailing; (*книги*) publication; (*на экран*) showing; (*место*) exit

вых|оди́ть (-ожу́, -о́дишь) *несов от* **вы́йти** ▷ *неперех*: **выходи́ть на** +*acc* (*юг, север*) to face; **окно́ выхо́дит в парк** the window looks out onto the park

выходн|о́й *прил* exit; (*платье*) best
▷ (**-о́го**) *м* (*также* **выходно́й день**) day
off (work); **сего́дня выходно́й** (*разг*) today
is a holiday; **выходны́е** weekend *ед*

вы́цве|сти (*3sg* **-тет**, *impf* **выцвета́ть**)
сов to fade

вы́черкн|уть (**-у**; *impf* **вычёркивать**)
сов перех to cross *или* score out

вы́чет (**-а**) *м* deduction ▷ *предл*: **за
вы́четом** +*gen* minus

вычисле́ни|е (**-я**) *ср* calculation;
вычисли́тельн|ый *прил* (*операция*)
computing; **вычисли́тельная маши́на**
computer; **вычисли́тельная те́хника**
computers *мн*; **вычисли́тельный центр**
computer centre (*Brit*) *или* center (*US*);
вы́числ|ить (**-ю**, **-ишь**; *impf*
вычисля́ть) *сов перех* to calculate

вычита́|ть (**-ю**) *несов от* **вы́честь**

вы́ше *сравн прил от* **высо́кий** ▷ *сравн
нареч от* **высоко́** ▷ *нареч* higher; (*в
тексте*) above ▷ *предл* +*gen* above

вы́шел *сов см* **вы́йти**

вышива́|ть (**-ю**) *несов от* **вы́шить**

вы́шив|ка (**-ки**; *gen pl* **-ок**) *ж* embroidery

вы́ш|ка (**-ки**; *gen pl* **-ек**) *ж* (*строение*)
tower; (*Спорт*) diving board

вы́шла *etc сов см* **вы́йти**

вы́яв|ить (**-лю**, **-ишь**; *impf* **выявля́ть**)
сов перех to discover;
(*недостатки*) to expose; **вы́явиться** (*impf*
выявля́ться) *сов возв* to come to light,
be revealed

вы́ясн|ить (**-ю**, **-ишь**; *impf* **выясня́ть**)
сов перех to find out; **вы́ясниться** (*impf*
выясня́ться) *сов возв* to become clear

Вьетна́м (**-а**) *м* Vietnam

вью́г|а (**-и**) *ж* snowstorm, blizzard

вяз (**-а**) *м* elm

вяза́ни|е (**-я**) *ср* knitting

вя|за́ть (**-жу́**, **-жешь**; *perf* **связа́ть**)
несов перех to tie up; (*свитер*) to knit

вя́з|нуть (**-ну**; *pt* **-**, **-ла**, **-ло**, *perf*
завя́знуть *или* **увя́знуть**) *несов*:
вя́знуть (**в** +*prp*) to get stuck (in)

вя́|нуть (**-у**; *perf* **завя́нуть** *или* **увя́нуть**)
несов (*цветы*) to wilt, wither; (*красота*) to
fade

г *сокр* (= **грамм**) g (= *gram(me)*)

г. *сокр* = **год**; **го́род**

Гаа́г|а (**-и**) *ж* The Hague

габари́т (**-а**) *м* (*Тех*) dimension

га́ван|ь (**-и**) *ж* harbour (*Brit*), harbor (*US*)

гада́|ть (**-ю**) *несов* (*предполагать*) to
guess; **гада́ть** (*perf* **погада́ть**) **кому́-н** to
tell sb's fortune

га́дост|ь (**-и**) *ж* filth

га́ечный *прил*: **га́ечный ключ** spanner

газ (**-а**) *м* gas; *см также* **га́зы**

газе́т|а (**-ы**) *ж* newspaper

газиро́ванн|ый *прил*: **газиро́ванная
вода́** carbonated water

га́зов|ый *прил* gas; **га́зовая плита́** gas
cooker

газо́н (**-а**) *м* lawn

газопрово́д (**-а**) *м* gas pipeline

га́з|ы (**-ов**) *мн* (*Мед*) wind *ед*

ГАИ *ж сокр* (= **Госуда́рственная
автомоби́льная инспе́кция**) state motor
vehicle inspectorate

га́йка (**-йки**; *gen pl* **-ек**) *ж* nut

галантере́|я (**-и**) *ж* haberdashery (*Brit*),
notions store (*US*)

галере́|я (**-и**) *ж* gallery

галло́н (**-а**) *м* gallon

галлюцина́ци|я (**-и**) *ж* hallucination

га́лоч|ка (**-ки**; *gen pl* **-ек**) *ж* (*в тексте*)
tick, check (*US*)

га́лстук (**-а**) *м* tie, necktie (*US*)

га́льк|а (**-и**) *ж собир* pebbles *мн*

га́мбургер (**-а**) *м* hamburger

га́мм|а (**-ы**) *ж* (*Муз*) scale

га́нгстер (**-а**) *м* gangster

гара́ж (**-а́**) *м* garage

гаранти́йный *прил* guarantee

гаранти́р|овать (**-ую**) (*не*)*сов перех*
to guarantee

гара́нти|я (**-и**) *ж* guarantee

гардеро́б (**-а**) *м* wardrobe; (*в
общественном здании*) cloakroom

гармони́р|овать (-ую) *несов*: **гармони́ровать с** +*instr* (*со средой*) to be in harmony with; (*одежда*) to go with

гармони́ст (-а) *м* concertina player

гармо́ни|я (-и) *ж* harmony

гармо́ш|ка (-ки; *gen pl* -ек) *ж* (*разг*) ≈ squeeze-box

гарнизо́н (-а) *м* garrison

гарни́р (-а) *м* side dish

гарниту́р (-а) *м* (*мебель*) suite

гар|ь (-и) *ж* (*угля*) cinders *мн*

га|си́ть (-шу́, -сишь; *perf* **погаси́ть**) *несов перех* (*свет*) to turn off; (*пожар*) to extinguish, put out

га́с|нуть (-ну; *pt* — *или* -нул, -ла, *perf* **пога́снуть** *или* **уга́снуть**) *несов* (*огни*) to go out

гастро́л|и (-ей) *мн* performances of touring company; **е́здить/е́хать** (*perf* **пое́хать**) **на гастро́ли** to go on tour; **гастроли́р|овать** (-ую) *несов* to be on tour

гастроно́м (-а) *м* food store; **гастроно́ми|я** (-и) *ж* delicatessen

гаши́ш (-а) *м* cannabis

гва́рди|я (-и) *ж* (*Воен*) Guards *мн*

гвозди́к|а (-и) *ж* (*цветок*) carnation; (*пряность*) cloves *мн*

гвозд|ь (-я́) *м* nail

гг *сокр* = **го́ды; господа́**

где *нареч* where; (*разг*: где-нибудь) somewhere, anywhere ▷ *союз* where; **где Вы живёте?** where do you live?

где́-либо *нареч* = **где́-нибудь**

где́-нибудь *нареч* somewhere; (*в вопросе*) anywhere

где́-то *нареч* somewhere

геморро́|й (-я) *м* piles *мн*

гель (-я) *м*: **гель для ду́ша** shower gel

ген (-а) *м* gene

генера́л (-а) *м* (*Воен*) general

генера́тор (-а) *м* generator

гене́тик|а (-и) *ж* genetics

генна́льный *прил* great

ге́ни|й (-я) *м* genius

ге́нный *прил* (*терапия*) gene

геогра́фи|я (-и) *ж* geography

геоме́три|я (-и) *ж* geometry

гера́н|ь (-и) *ж* geranium

герб (-а́) *м* coat of arms; **госуда́рственный герб** national emblem

ге́рбов|ый *прил*: **ге́рбовая бума́га** stamped paper

геркуле́с (-а) *м* (*Кулин*) porridge oats *мн*

Герма́ни|я (-и) *ж* Germany; **герма́нский** *прил* German

герои́н|я (-и) *ж* heroine; **геро́йческий** *прил* heroic; **геро́|й** (-я) *м* hero

г-жа *м сокр* = **госпожа́**

ги́бел|ь (-и) *ж* (*человека*) death; (*армии*) destruction; (*самолёта, надежды*) loss; (*карьеры*) ruin

ги́бкий *прил* flexible

ги́б|нуть (-ну; *pt* -, -ла, *perf* **поги́бнуть**)

несов to perish; (*перен*) to come to nothing

гига́нт (-а) *м* giant; **гига́нтский** *прил* gigantic

гигие́н|а (-ы) *ж* hygiene; **гигиени́чный** *прил* hygienic

гид (-а) *м* guide

гидрометце́нтр (-а) *м сокр* (= *Гидрометеорологи́ческий центр*) meteorological office

гидроэлектроста́нци|я (-и) *ж* hydroelectric power station

гимн (-а) *м*: **госуда́рственный гимн** national anthem

гимна́зи|я (-и) *ж* ≈ grammar school

- **Гимна́зия**
-
- This institution of secondary education
- strives for higher academic standards
- than comprehensive schools. Pupils can
- study subjects which are not offered by
- mainstream education, e.g. classics and
- two modern languages.

гимна́стик|а (-и) *ж* exercises *мн*; (*спорти́вная*) **гимна́стика** gymnastics; **худо́жественная гимна́стика** modern rhythmic gymnastics

гинеко́лог (-а) *м* gynaecologist (*Brit*), gynecologist (*US*)

гиперссы́л|ка (-ки; *gen pl* -ок) *ж* hyperlink

гипертони́|я (-и) *ж* high blood pressure

гипо́тез|а (-ы) *ж* hypothesis

гипотони́|я (-и) *ж* low blood pressure

гиппопота́м (-а) *м* hippopotamus, hippo (*inf*)

гипс (-а) *м* (*Искусство*) plaster of Paris; (*Мед*) plaster

гита́р|а (-ы) *ж* guitar

глав|а́ (-ы́; *nom pl* -ы) *ж* (*книги*) chapter; (*здания*) head ▷ *м* (*делегации*) head; **во главе́ с** +*instr* headed by; **во главе́** +*gen* at the head of

глава́р|ь (-я́) *м* (*банды*) leader

главнокома́ндующ|ий (-его) *м* commander in chief

гла́вный *прил* main; (*старший по положению*) senior, head; **гла́вным о́бразом** chiefly, mainly

глаго́л (-а) *м* verb

глади́льн|ый *прил*: **глади́льная доска́** ironing board

гла́|дить (-жу, -дишь; *perf* **погла́дить**) *несов перех* to iron; (*волосы*) to stroke; **гла́дкий** *прил* (*ровный*) smooth

глаз (-а; *loc sg* -ý, *nom pl* -á, *gen pl* -) *м* eye; **с гла́зу на́ глаз** tête `a tête; **на глаз** roughly

глазно́й *прил* eye

глазу́нь|я (-и) *ж* fried egg

гла́нд|а (-ы) *ж* (*обычно мн*) tonsil

гла́сн|ый (-ого) *м* vowel; (*открытый*) open, public

гли́н|а (-ы) *ж* clay; **гли́няный** *прил* clay

глоба́льный *прил* universal

гло́бус (-а) *м* globe

глота́|ть (-ю) *perf* **проглоти́ть** *несов перех* to swallow

глот|о́к (-ка́) *м* gulp, swallow; *(воды, чая)* drop

гло́х|нуть (-ну) *pt* -, -ла, *perf* **огло́хнуть** *несов* to grow deaf; *(мотор)* to stall

глу́бже *сравн прил от* **глубо́кий** ▷ *сравн нареч от* **глубоко́**

глубин|а́ (-ы́) *nom pl* -**и́ны** *ж* depth; *(леса)* heart; *(перен)*: **в глубине́ души́** in one's heart of hearts

глубо́кий *прил* deep; *(провинция)* remote; *(мысль)* profound; **глубоко́** *нареч* deeply ▷ *как сказ*: **здесь глубоко́** it's deep here

глубокоуважа́емый *прил* dear

глупе́|ть (-ю) *perf* **поглупе́ть** *несов* to grow stupid

глу́по *как сказ* it's stupid *или* silly; **глу́пост|ь** (-и) *ж* stupidity, silliness; *(поступок)* stupid *или* silly thing; *(слова)* nonsense; **глу́пый** *прил* stupid, silly

глух|о́й *прил* deaf; *(звук)* muffled

глуш|ь (-и́; *instr sg* -**ью**, *loc sg* -**и́**) *ж* wilderness

глы́б|а (-ы) *ж (ледяная)* block

глюко́з|а (-ы) *ж* glucose

гля|де́ть (-жу́, -ди́шь; *perf* **погляде́ть**) *несов* to look

гля́нцевый *прил* glossy

гна|ть (гоню́, го́нишь; *pt* -л, -ла́) *несов перех (стадо)* to drive; *(человека)* to throw out; *(машину)* to drive fast; **гна́ться** *несов возв*: **гна́ться за** +*instr* to pursue

гнезд|о́ (-а́; *nom pl* **гнёзда**, *gen pl* **гнёзд**) *ср (птиц)* nest

гнету́щий *прил* depressing

гнил|о́й *прил* rotten

гни́л|ь (-и) *ж* rotten stuff

гни|ть (-ю, -ёшь; *perf* **сгни́ть**) *несов* to rot

гно|й (-я) *м* pus

ГНС *сокр* (= *Госуда́рственная нало́говая слу́жба*) ≈ Inland Revenue

гн|уть (-у, -ёшь; *perf* **согну́ть**) *несов перех* to bend; **гну́ться** *несов возв (ветка)* to bend

говор|и́ть (-ю́, -и́шь; *perf* **сказа́ть**) *несов перех* to say; *(правду)* to tell ▷ *неперех по perf* to speak, talk; *(обсуждать)*: **говори́ть о** +*prp* to talk about; *(общаться)*: **говори́ть с** +*instr* to talk to *или* with

говя́дин|а (-ы) *ж* beef

год (-а; *loc sg* -**у́**, *nom pl* -**ы**, *gen pl* -**о́в**/**лет**) *м* year; **прошло́ 3 го́да/5 лет** 3/5 years passed; **из го́да в год** year in year out; **кру́глый год** all year round

го|ди́ться (-жу́сь, -ди́шься) *несов возв* +*dat* to suit; **годи́ться** (*impf*) **для** +*gen* to be suitable for; **го́д|ный** *прил*: **го́дный к**

+*dat или* **для** +*gen* fit *или* suitable for; **биле́т го́ден до ...** the ticket is valid until ...

годовщи́н|а (-ы) *ж* anniversary

гол (-а; *nom pl* -**ы**) *м* goal

Голла́нди|я (-и) *ж* Holland

голла́ндский *прил* Dutch; **голла́ндский язы́к** Dutch

гол|ова́ (-овы́; *acc sg* -**ову**, *dat sg* -**ове́**, *nom pl* -**о́вы**, *gen pl* -**о́в**, *dat pl* -**ова́м**) *ж* head

головно́й *прил (офис)* main; *(боль)* head

го́лод (-а) *м* hunger; *(недоедание)* starvation; *(бедствие)* famine; **голода́|ть** (-ю) *несов* to starve; *(воздерживаться от пищи)* to fast; **голо́дный** *прил* hungry

голодо́в|ка (-ки; *gen pl* -**ок**) *ж* hunger strike

гололёд (-а) *м* black ice

го́лос (-а; *part gen* -**у**, *nom pl* -**а́**) *м* voice; *(Полит)* vote; **во весь го́лос** at the top of one's voice

голосова́ни|е (-я) *ср* ballot

голос|ова́ть (-ю́, *perf* **проголосова́ть**) *несов* to vote; *(разг: на доро́ге)* to hitch (a lift)

голуб|о́й *прил* light blue ▷ (-**о́го**) *м (разг)* gay

го́луб|ь (-я; *gen pl* -**е́й**) *м* pigeon; dove

го́лый *прил (человек)* naked

гольф (-а) *м* golf; *(обычно мн: чулки)* knee sock

гомеопа́т (-а) *м* homoeopath (*Brit*), homeopath (*US*)

го́мик (-а) *м (разг)* homo(sexual)

гомосексуали́ст (-а) *м* homosexual

гоне́ни|е (-я) *ср* persecution

го́н|ка (-ки; *gen pl* -**ок**) *ж (разг: спешка)* rush; *(соревнования)* race; **го́нка вооруже́ний** arms race

гонора́р (-а) *м* fee; **а́вторский гонора́р** royalty

го́ночный *прил* racing

го́нщик (-а) *м* racing (*Brit*) *или* race car (*US*) driver; *(велосипедист)* racing cyclist

гоня́|ть (-ю, -ешь) *несов перех (ученика)* to grill ▷ *неперех* to race; **гоня́ться** *несов возв*: **гоня́ться за** +*instr (преследовать)* to chase (after); *(перен)* to pursue

гор. *сокр* = **го́род**

гор|а́ (*acc sg* -**у**, *gen sg* -**ы́**, *nom pl* -**ы**, *dat pl* -**а́м**) *ж* mountain; *(небольшая)* hill

гора́здо *нареч* much

горб (-а́; *loc sg* -**у́**) *м* hump

го́рб|ить (-лю, -ишь; *perf* **сго́рбить**) *несов перех*: **го́рбить спи́ну** to stoop; **го́рбиться** (*perf* **сго́рбиться**) *несов возв* to stoop

горбу́ш|ка (-ки; *gen pl* -**ек**) *ж* crust

гор|ди́ться (-жу́сь, -ди́шься) *несов* +*instr* to be proud of

го́рдост|ь (-и) *ж* pride; **го́рдый** *прил* proud

го́р|е (-я) *ср (скорбь)* grief; *(несчастье)*

misfortune; **гор|ева́ть (-ю́ю)** *несов* to grieve

гор|е́ть (-ю́, -и́шь) *perf* **сгоре́ть** *несов* to burn; (*no perf*: *дом*) to be on fire; (*больной*) to be burning hot; (*глаза*) to shine

горизо́нт (-а) *м* horizon; **горизонта́л|ь (-и)** *ж* horizontal; **горизонта́льный** *прил* horizontal

гори́лл|а (-ы) *ж* gorilla

гори́стый *прил* mountainous

го́р|ка (-ки; *gen pl* **-ок)** *ж* hill; (*кучка*) small pile

го́рл|о (-а) *ср* throat; **го́рлыш|ко (-ка**; *nom pl* **-ки**, *gen pl* **-ек)** *ср* (*бутылки*) neck

гормо́н (-а) *м* hormone

го́рный *прил* mountain; (*лыжи*) downhill; (*промышленность*) mining

го́род (-а; *nom pl* **-а́)** *м* (*большой*) city; (*небольшой*) town; **горожа́н|ин (-ина**; *nom pl* **-е**, *gen pl* **-)** *м* city dweller

гороско́п (-а) *м* horoscope

горо́х (-а) *м собир* peas *мн*; **горо́ш|ек (-ка)** *м собир* peas *мн*; (*на платье итп*) polka dots *мн*; **ткань в горо́шек** spotted material; **горо́шин|а (-ы)** *ж* pea

горст|ь (-и; *gen pl* **-е́й)** *ж* handful

горч|и́ть (3sg -и́т) *несов* to taste bitter

горчи́ц|а (-ы) *ж* mustard

горшо́|к (-ка́) *м* pot

го́рький *прил* bitter

го́рько *нареч* (*плакать*) bitterly ▷ *как сказ*: **во рту го́рько** I have a bitter taste in my mouth

горю́че|е (-его) *ср* fuel

горя́ч|ий *прил* hot; (*перен*: *любовь*) passionate; (: *спор*) heated; (: *желание*) burning; (: *человек*) hot-tempered; **горя́чая ли́ния** hot line

горячо́ *нареч* (*спорить, любить*) passionately ▷ *как сказ* it's hot

гос. *сокр* = **госуда́рственный**

Госба́нк (-а) *м сокр* (= *госуда́рственный банк*) state bank

госбезопа́сност|ь (-и) *ж сокр* (= *госуда́рственная безопа́сность*) national security

госбюдже́т (-а) *м сокр* (= *госуда́рственный бюдже́т*) state budget

го́спитал|ь (-я) *м* army hospital

господа́ *итп сущ см* **господи́н** ▷ *мн* (*при фамилии, при звании*) Messrs

го́споди *межд*: **Го́споди!** good Lord!

госпо|ди́н (-ди́на; *nom pl* **-да́**, *gen pl* **-д)** *м* gentleman; (*мн* gentlemen); (*хозяин*) master; (*при обращении*) sir; (*при фамилии*) Mr (= *Mister*)

госпо́дств|овать (-ую) *несов* to rule; (*мнение*) to prevail

Госпо́д|ь (-а; *voc* **Го́споди)** *м* (*также* **Госпо́дь Бог**) the Lord; **не дай Го́споди!** God forbid!; **сла́ва тебе́ Го́споди!** Glory be to God!; (*разг*) thank God!

госпож|а́ (-и́) *ж* lady; (*хозяйка*) mistress; (*при обращении, при звании*) Madam; (*при фамилии*: *замужняя*) Mrs; (: *незамужняя*) Miss; (: *замужняя или незамужняя*) Ms

госстра́х (-а) *м сокр* (= *госуда́рственное страхова́ние*) ≈ national insurance

гости́н|ая (-ой) *ж* living *или* sitting room, lounge (*Brit*)

гости́ниц|а (-ы) *ж* hotel

го|сти́ть (-щу́, -сти́шь) *несов* to stay

гост|ь (-я; *gen pl* **-е́й)** *м* guest; **идти́** (*perf* **пойти́**) **в го́сти к кому́-н** to go to see sb; **быть** (*impf*) **в гостя́х у кого́-н** to be at sb's house

госуда́рственный *прил* state; **госуда́рств|о (-а)** *ср* state

гото́в|ить (-лю, -ишь) *perf* **пригото́вить** *несов перех* to get ready; (*уроки*) to prepare; (*обед*) to prepare, make ▷ (*perf* **подгото́вить**) (*специалиста*) to train ▷ *неперех* to cook; **гото́виться** (*perf* **пригото́виться**) *несов возв*: **гото́виться к** +*dat* (*к отъезду*) to get ready for; **гото́виться** (*perf* **подгото́виться**) **к** +*dat* (*к экзамену*) to prepare for

гото́вност|ь (-и) *ж* +*infin* readiness *или* willingness to do

гото́во *как сказ* that's it; **гото́вый** *прил* (*изделие*) ready-made; **я/обе́д гото́в** I am/ dinner is ready; **гото́вый к** +*dat*/ +*infin* prepared for/to do

гр. *сокр* (= *граждани́н*) Mr (= *Mister*); (= *гражда́нка*) Mrs

грабёж (-ежа́) *м* robbery; (*дома*) burglary; **граби́тел|ь (-я)** *м* robber

гра́б|ить (-лю, -ишь) *perf* **огра́бить** *несов перех* (*человека*) to rob; (*дом*) to burgle; (*город*) to pillage

гра́бл|и (-ель *или* **-лей)** *мн* rake *ед*

гра́ви|й (-я) *м* gravel

град (-а) *м* (*также перен*) hail

гра́дус (-а) *м* degree; **гра́дусник (-а)** *м* thermometer

граждан|и́н (-а; *nom pl* **гра́ждане**, *gen pl* **гра́ждан)** *м* citizen

гражда́н|ка (-ки; *gen pl* **-ок)** *ж* citizen; **гражда́нский** *прил* civil; (*долг*) civic; (*платье*) civilian

гражда́нств|о (-а) *ср* citizenship

грамм (-а) *м* gram(me)

грамма́тик|а (-и) *ж* grammar; **граммати́ческий** *прил* grammatical; (*упражнение*) grammar

гра́мот|а (-ы) *ж* (*документ*) certificate; **гра́мотный** *прил* (*человек*) literate; (*текст*) correctly written; (*специалист, план*) competent

грампласти́нк|а (-и) *ж* record

грандио́зный *прил* grand

грани́ц|а (-ы) *ж* (*государства*) border; (*участка*) boundary; (*обычно мн*: *перен*) limit; **е́хать** (*perf* **пое́хать**) **за грани́цу** to go abroad; **жить** (*impf*) **за грани́цей** to live abroad; **из-за грани́цы** from abroad;

грани́ч|ить (-у, -ишь) несов: грани́чить с +instr to border on; (перен) to verge on

грант (-а) м grant

граф|а́ (-ы́) ж column

гра́фик (-а) м (Мат) graph; (план) schedule, timetable

графи́ческий прил graphic

гра́ци|я (-и) ж grace

гребён|ка (-ки; gen pl -ок) ж comb

гребеш|о́к (-ка́) м comb

гребл|я (-и) ж rowing

гре́йпфрут (-а) м grapefruit

грек (-а) м Greek (man) (мн men)

гре́л|ка (-ки; gen pl -ок) ж hot-water bottle

грем|е́ть (-лю́, -и́шь; perf прогреме́ть) несов (поезд) to thunder by; (гром) to rumble; греме́ть (perf прогреме́ть) +instr (ведром) to clatter

гре́н|ка (-ки; gen pl -ок) ж toast

гре|сти́ (-бу́, -бёшь; pt грёб, -бла́) несов to row; (веслом, руками) to paddle ▷ перех (листья) to rake

гре|ть (-ю) несов перех (подлеж: солнце) to heat, warm; (: шуба) to keep warm; (воду) to heat (up); (руки) to warm; гре́ться несов возв (человек) to warm o.s.; (вода) to warm или heat up

грех (-а́) м sin

Гре́ци|я (-и) ж Greece

гре́цкий прил: гре́цкий оре́х walnut

гре́ческий прил Greek; гре́ческий язы́к Greek

гре́чк|а (-и) ж buckwheat; гре́чневый прил buckwheat

греш|и́ть (-у́, -и́шь; perf согреши́ть) несов to sin

гриб (-а́) м (съедобный) (edible) mushroom; несъедо́бный гриб toadstool; грибно́й прил (суп) mushroom

гриб|о́к (-ка́) м (на коже) fungal infection; (на дереве) fungus

гримир|ова́ть (-у́ю; perf загримирова́ть) несов перех: гримирова́ть кого́-н to make sb up

грипп (-а) м flu

гри́фел|ь (-я) м (pencil) lead

гроб (-а; loc sg -у́, nom pl -ы́) м coffin

гр|оза́ (-озы; nom pl -о́зы) ж thunderstorm

грозд|ь (-и; gen pl -е́й) ж (винограда) bunch; (сирени) cluster

гро|зи́ть (-жу́, -зи́шь) несов: грози́ть (perf пригрози́ть) кому́-н чем-н to threaten sb with sth; (+instr: катастрофой) to threaten to become

грозов|о́й прил: грозова́я ту́ча storm cloud

гром (-а; gen pl -о́в) м thunder

грома́дный прил enormous, huge

гром|и́ть (-лю́, -и́шь) несов перех to destroy

гро́мкий прил (голос) loud; (скандал) big; гро́мко нареч loudly

гро́мче сравн прил от гро́мкий ▷ сравн нареч от гро́мко

гро́хот (-а) м racket; грох|ота́ть (-очу́, -о́чешь; perf прогрохота́ть) несов to rumble

грубе́|ть (-ю; perf огрубе́ть) несов (человек) to become rude ▷ (perf загрубе́ть) (кожа) to become rough

груб|и́ть (-лю́, -и́шь; perf нагруби́ть) несов +dat to be rude to; груби́я́н (-а) м rude person; гру́бо нареч (отвечать) rudely; (подсчитать) roughly; гру́бо говоря́ roughly speaking; гру́бость|ь (-и) ж rudeness; гру́бый прил (человек) rude; (ткань, пища) coarse; (кожа, подсчёт) rough; (ошибка, шутка) crude; (нарушение правил) gross

груд|а (-ы) ж pile, heap

грудно́й прил (молоко) breast; (кашель) chest; грудно́й ребёнок baby; гр|удь (-уди́; instr sg -у́дью, nom pl -у́ди) ж (Анат) chest; (: женщины) breasts мн; корми́ть (impf) гру́дью to breast-feed

гружёный прил loaded

груз (-а) м (тяжесть) weight; (товар) cargo

грузи́н (-а) м Georgian

гр|узи́ть (-ужу́, -у́зишь; perf загрузи́ть или нагрузи́ть) несов перех (корабль итп) to load (up); грузи́ть (perf погрузи́ть) (в/на +acc) (товар) to load (onto)

Гру́зи|я (-и) ж Georgia

грузови́к (-а́) м lorry (Brit), truck (US)

грузов|о́й прил (судно, самолёт) cargo; грузова́я маши́на goods vehicle; грузово́е такси́ removal (Brit) или moving (US) van

грузоподъёмност|ь (и) ж freight или cargo capacity

гру́зчик (-а) м porter; (в магазине) stockroom worker

гру́пп|а (-ы) ж group; гру́ппа кро́ви blood group

гру|сти́ть (-щу́, -сти́шь) несов to feel melancholy или very sad; грусти́ть (impf) по +dat или о +prp to pine for, miss; гру́стно нареч sadly ▷ как сказ: мне гру́стно I feel sad; гру́стный прил sad; грусть|ь (-и) ж sadness

гру́ш|а (-и) ж pear

грыз|ть (-у́, -ёшь; pt -, -ла) несов перех (яблоки) to nibble (at) ▷ (perf разгры́зть) (кость) to gnaw (on)

гря́д|ка (-ки; gen pl -ок) ж row

гря́зно как сказ безл: до́ма/на у́лице гря́зно the street/house is filthy

гря́зный прил dirty; гряз|ь (-и; loc sg -и́) ж dirt; (на дороге) mud; (перен) filth

губ|а́ (-ы́; nom pl -ы, dat pl -а́м) ж lip

губе́рни|я (-и) ж gubernia (administrative region)

губерна́тор (-а) м governor

губ|и́ть (-лю́, -ишь; perf погуби́ть) несов перех to kill; (здоровье) to ruin

гу́б|ка (-ки; gen pl -ок) ж sponge

губн|о́й _прил_: **губна́я пома́да** lipstick; **губна́я гармо́шка** harmonica

гу|де́ть (-жу́, -ди́шь) _несов_ (_шмель, провода́_) to hum; (_ветер_) to moan

гуля́|ть (-ю; _perf_ **погуля́ть**) _несов_ to stroll; (_быть на у́лице_) to be out; (_на сва́дьбе_) to have a good time, enjoy o.s.; **идти́** (_perf_ **пойти́**) **гуля́ть** to go for a walk

гуманита́рный _прил_ (_помощь_) humanitarian; (_образова́ние_) arts

гума́нный _прил_ humane

гуси́н|ый _прил_ (_яйцо́_) goose; **гуси́ная ко́жа** goose flesh, goose pimples (_Brit_) или bumps (_US_)

густе́|ть (_3sg_ -ет, _perf_ **погусте́ть**) _несов_ (_тума́н_) to become denser ▷ (_perf_ **загусте́ть**) (_ка́ша_) to thicken; **густо́й** _прил_ (_лес_) dense; (_бро́ви_) bushy; (_облака́, суп, во́лосы_) thick; (_цвет, бас_) rich

густонаселённый _прил_ densely populated

гус|ь (-я; _gen pl_ -е́й) _м_ goose

гуся́тниц|а (-ы) _ж_ casserole (dish)

ГЭС _ж сокр_ = **гидроэлектроста́нция**

КЛЮЧЕВОЕ СЛОВО

да _част_ **1** (_выража́ет согла́сие_) yes

2 (_не так ли_): **ты придёшь, да?** you're coming, aren't you?; **ты меня́ лю́бишь, да?** you love me, don't you?

3 (_пусть: в лозунгах, в призывах_): **да здра́вствует демокра́тия!** long live democracy!

4 (_во фра́зах_): **вот э́то да!** (_разг_) cool!; **ну да!** (_разг_) sure!; (_выража́ет недове́рие_) I'll bet!; **да ну!** (_разг_) no way!
▷ _союз_ (_и_) and; **у неё то́лько одно́ пла́тье, да и то ста́рое** she only has one dress and even that's old

дава́й(те) _несов см_ **дава́ть** ▷ _част_ let's; **дава́й(те) пить чай** let's have some tea; **дава́й-дава́й!** (_разг_) come on!, get on with it!

да|ва́ть (-ю́; _imper_ **дава́й(те)**) _несов от_ **дать**

дав|и́ть (-лю́, -ишь) _несов перех_ (_подлеж: о́бувь_) to pinch ▷ (_perf_ **задави́ть**) (_кале́чить_) to crush, trample; (_подлеж: маши́на_) to run over ▷ (_perf_ **раздави́ть**) (_насеко́мых_) to squash; **дави́ть** (_impf_) **на** +_acc_ (_налега́ть_) to press или weigh down on; **дави́ться** _несов возв_: **дави́ться** (_perf_ **подави́ться**) +_instr_ (_ко́стью_) to choke on

да́в|ка (-ки; _gen pl_ -ок) _ж_ crush

давле́ни|е (-я) _ср_ pressure

да́вн|ий _прил_: **с да́вних пор** for a long time; **давно́** _нареч_ (_случи́ться_) a long time ago; (_до́лго_) for a long time; **давно́ бы так!** about time too!; **давны́м-давно́** _нареч_ (_разг_) ages ago

дади́м _etc сов см_ **дать**

да́же _част_ even

да́й(те) _сов см_ **дать**

дал etc сов см **дать**

да́лее нареч further; **и так да́лее** and so on

далёкий прил distant, far-off

далеко́ нареч (о расстоянии) far away ▷ как сказ it's a long way away; **далеко́ за** +acc long after; **далеко́ не** by no means

дало́ etc сов см **дать**

дальне́йш|ий прил further; **в дальне́йшем** in the future

да́льн|ий прил distant; (поезд) long-distance; **Да́льний Восто́к** the Far East

дальнозо́ркий прил long-sighted (Brit), far-sighted (US)

да́льше сравн прил от **далёкий** ▷ сравн нареч от **далеко́**

дам сов см **дать**

да́м|а (-ы) ж lady; (Карты) queen

да́мский прил (одежда) ladies'

Да́ни|я (-и) ж Denmark

да́нн|ые (-ых) мн (сведения) data ед; (способности) talent ед

да́нный прил this, the given

дан|ь (-и) ж tribute

дар (-а; nom pl -ы́) м gift

дар|и́ть (-ю́, -ишь; perf **подари́ть**) несов перех to give

да́ром нареч (бесплатно) free, for nothing; (бесполезно) in vain

даст сов см **дать**

да́т|а (-ы) ж date

да́тельный прил: **да́тельный паде́ж** the dative (case)

дати́р|овать (-ую) (не)сов перех to date

дать (см Table 16; impf **дава́ть**) сов to give; (позволить): **дать кому́-н** +infin to allow sb to do, let sb do; **я тебе́ дам!** (угроза) I'll show you!

да́ч|а (-и) ж (дом) dacha (holiday cottage in the country); (показаний) provision

дашь сов см **дать**

дв|а (-ух; см Table 23; f **две**, nt **два**) м чис two ▷ м нескл (Просвещ) ≈ poor (school mark)

двадца́тый чис twentieth

два́дцат|ь (-и; как **пять**; см Table 26) чис twenty

два́жды нареч twice; **два́жды три — шесть** two times three is six

две ж чис см **два**

двена́дцатый чис twelfth

двена́дцат|ь (-и; как **пять**; см Table 26) чис twelve

двер|ь (-и; loc sg -и́, gen pl -е́й) ж door

дв|е́сти (-ухсо́т; см Table 28) чис two hundred

дви́гател|ь (-я) м engine, motor

дви́га|ть (-ю; perf **дви́нуть**) несов перех to move; (no perf: механизм) to drive; **дви́гаться** (perf **дви́нуться**) несов возв to move; (отправляться): **дви́гаться в/на** +acc to set off или start out for

движе́ни|е (-я) ср movement; (дорожное) traffic; (души) impulse; **пра́вила доро́жного** или **у́личного движе́ния** ≈ the Highway Code

дви́н|уть(ся) (-у(сь)) сов от **дви́гать(ся)**

дво́|е (-и́х; см Table 30a) м чис two

двоето́чи|е (-я) ср (Линг) colon

дво́|йка (-йки; gen pl -ек) ж (цифра, карта) two; (Просвещ) ≈ fail, ≈ E (school mark)

двойно́й прил double

дво́йн|я (-йни; gen pl -ен) ж twins мн

дво́йственный прил (позиция) ambiguous

двор (-а́) м yard; (короле́вский) court

двор|е́ц (-ца́) м palace

дво́рник (-а) м (работник) road sweeper; (Авт) windscreen (Brit) или windshield (US) wiper

дворня́ж|ка (-ки; gen pl -ек) ж mongrel

дворя́нств|о (-а) ср nobility

двою́родн|ый прил: **двою́родный брат** (first) cousin (male); **двою́родная сестра́** (first) cousin (female)

двум etc чис см **два**

двумста́м etc чис см **две́сти**

двусмы́сленный прил ambiguous

двуспа́льн|ый прил: **двуспа́льная крова́ть** double bed

двух чис см **два**

двухсо́т чис см **две́сти**

двухсо́тый чис two hundredth

двухста́х чис см **две́сти**

двуязы́чный прил bilingual

дебати́р|овать (-ую) несов перех to debate

деба́т|ы (-ов) мн debate ед

де́бет (-а) м debit

деби́л (-а) м mentally challenged person; (разг: глупый) idiot

деби́льный прил mentally challenged

де́в|а (-ы) ж: **ста́рая де́ва** spinster; (созвездие): **Де́ва** Virgo

дева́|ть(ся) (-ю(сь)) несов от **деть(ся)**

деви́з (-а) м motto

де́вич|ий прил: **де́вичья фами́лия** maiden name

де́воч|ка (-ки; gen pl -ек) ж (ребёнок) little girl

де́вуш|ка (-ки; gen pl -ек) ж girl

девяно́ст|о (-а; как **сто**; см Table 27) чис ninety

девяно́стый чис ninetieth

девя́т|ка (-ки; gen pl -ок) ж nine

девятна́дцатый чис nineteenth

девятна́дцат|ь (-и; как **пять**; см Table 26) чис nineteen

девя́тый чис ninth

де́вят|ь (-и; как **пять**; см Table 26) чис nine

девятьсо́т (-исо́т; как **пятьсо́т**; см Table 28) чис nine hundred

дёг|оть (-тя) м tar

дегради́р|овать (-ую) (не)сов to degenerate

дед (-а) м grandfather; **Дед Моро́з**
≈ Father Christmas, ≈ Santa (Claus)

дедовщи́н|а (-ы) ж *mental and physical
harassment in the army by older conscripts*

де́душ|ка (-ки; *gen pl* -ек) м grandad

дежу́р|ить (-ю, -ишь) *несов* to be on
duty

дежу́рн|ый *прил*: **дежу́рный врач** doctor
on duty ▷ (**-ого**) м person on duty

дезодора́нт (-а) м antiperspirant,
deodorant

де́йственный *прил* effective

де́йстви|е (-я) *ср* (*механизма*)
functioning; (*романа итп*) action; (*часть
пьесы*) act; (*лекарства*) effect; *см также*
де́йствия

действи́тельно *нареч, вводн сл* really;
действи́тельност|ь (-и) ж reality

действи́тельный *прил* real, actual;
(*документ*) valid

де́йстви|я (-й) *мн* (*поступки*) actions мн

де́йств|овать (-ую) *несов* (*человек*) to
act; (*механизмы, закон*) to operate ▷ (*perf*
поде́йствовать) (*влиять*): **де́йствовать
на** +*acc* to have an effect on

де́йствующий *прил*: **де́йствующие
ли́ца** (*персонажи*) characters мн;
де́йствующая а́рмия standing army;
де́йствующий вулка́н active volcano

декабр|ь (-я́) м December

дека́н (-а) м dean; **декана́т** (-а) м
faculty office

деклара́ци|я (-и) ж declaration;
тамо́женная деклара́ция customs
declaration

декора́ци|я (-и) ж (*Театр*) set

декре́т (-а) м (*приказ*) decree; (*разг:
отпуск*) maternity leave; **декре́тный**
прил: **декре́тный о́тпуск** maternity leave

де́ла|ть (-ю; *perf* **сде́лать**) *сов перех* to
make; (*упражнения, опыты итп*) to do;
де́лать не́чего there is nothing to be done;
де́латься (*perf* **сде́латься**) *несов возв*:
де́латься +*instr* to become

делега́т (-а) м delegate

деле́ни|е (-я) *ср* division; (*на линейке, в
термометре*) point

деликате́с (-а) м delicacy

дел|и́ть (-ю́, -ишь; *perf* **подели́ть** *или*
раздели́ть) *несов перех* (*также Мат*) to
divide; **дели́ть** (*perf* **раздели́ть**) **что-н на**
+*acc* to divide sth by; **дели́ть** (*perf*
раздели́ть) **что-н с** +*instr* to share sth with;
дели́ться (*perf* **раздели́ться**) *несов
возв*: **дели́ться** (**на** +*acc*) (*отряд*) to divide
или split up (into); **дели́ться** (*perf*
подели́ться) **чем-н с кем-н** to share sth
with sb

де́л|о (-а; *nom pl* -á) *ср* matter;
(*надобность: также Комм*) business;
(*положение*) situation; (*поступок*) act;
(*Юр*) case; (*Админ*) file; **э́то моё де́ло**
that's my business; **э́то не твоё де́ло** it's
none of your business; **как дела́?** how are

things?; **в чём де́ло?** what's wrong?; **де́ло
в том, что ...** the thing is that ...; **на
(са́мом) де́ле** in (actual) fact; **на де́ле** in
practise; **то и де́ло** every now and then

делово́й *прил* business; (*дельный*)
efficient; (*вид, тон*) businesslike

де́льный *прил* (*человек*) efficient;
(*предложение*) sensible

дельфи́н (-а) м dolphin

демисезо́нн|ый *прил*: **демисезо́нное
пальто́** coat for spring and autumn wear

демобилиз|ова́ться (-у́юсь) (*не*)*сов
возв* to be demobilized

демокра́т (-а) м democrat;
демократи́ческий *прил* democratic;
демокра́ти|я (-и) ж democracy

де́мон (-а) м demon

демонстра́ци|я (-и) ж demonstration;
(*фильма*) showing

демонстри́р|овать (-ую) (*не*)*сов*
(*Полит*) to demonstrate ▷ *несов перех* to
show

демонти́р|овать (-ую) (*не*)*сов* to
dismantle

де́нежный *прил* monetary; (*рынок*)
money; **де́нежный знак** banknote

день (**дня**) м day; (*на днях: скоро*) in the
next few days; (*недавно*) the other day;
день рожде́ния birthday

де́н|ьги (-ег; *dat pl* -ьга́м) *мн* money ед

депо́ *ср нескл* depot

депорти́р|овать (-ую) (*не*)*сов перех* to
deport

депре́сси|я (-и) ж depression

депута́т (-а) м deputy (*Pol*)

дёрга|ть (-ю) *несов перех* to tug *или* pull
(at) ▷ *неперех* (+*instr* плечом, головой)
to jerk; **дёргаться** *несов возв* (*машина,
лошадь*) to jerk; (*лицо, губы*) to twitch

дереве́нский *прил* country, village;
(*пейзаж*) rural

дере́в|ня (-ни; *gen pl* -е́нь, *dat* -ня́м)
ж (*селение*) village; (*местность*) the
country

дер|ево (-ева; *nom pl* -е́вья, *gen pl*
-е́вьев) *ср* tree; (*древесина*) wood

деревя́нный *прил* wooden

держа́в|а (-ы) ж power

держа́тел|ь (-я) м holder

держ|а́ть (-у́, -ишь) *сов перех* to keep; (*в
руках, во рту, в зубах*) to hold; **держа́ть**
(*impf*) **себя́ в рука́х** to keep one's head;
держа́ться *несов возв* to stay; (*на
колоннах, на сваях*) to be supported;
(*иметь осанку*) to stand; (*вести себя*) to
behave; **держа́ться** (*impf*) +*gen* (*берега,
стены итп*) to keep to

дёрн (-а) м turf

дёрн|уть (-у) *несов перех* to tug (at)
▷ *неперех* (+*instr* плечом, головой) to
jerk; **дёрнуться** *несов возв* (*машина*) to
start with a jerk; (*губы*) to twitch

деса́нт (-а) м landing troops мн

десе́рт (-а) м dessert

десн|а́ (-ы́; *nom pl* **дёсны**, *gen pl* **дёсен**) ж (*Анат*) gum

десятиле́ти|е (-я) *ср* (*срок*) decade

деся́тк|и (-ов) *мн*: **деся́тки люде́й/книг** scores of people/books

деся́т|ок (-ка) *м* ten

деся́тый *прил* tenth

деся́т|ь (-и́; *как* **пять**; *см Table 26*) *чис* ten

дета́л|ь (-и) ж detail; (*механизма*) component, part; **дета́льный** *прил* detailed

детдо́м (-а; *nom pl* -á) *м сокр* = **де́тский дом**

детекти́в (-а) *м* (*фильм*) detective film; (*книга*) detective novel

детёныш (-а) *м* cub

де́т|и (-е́й; *dat pl* -ям, *instr pl* -ьми́, *prp pl* -ях, *nom sg* **ребёнок**) *мн* children мн

де́тск|ий *прил* (*годы, болезнь*) childhood; (*книга, игра*) children's; (*рассуждение*) childish; **де́тская площа́дка** playground; **де́тский дом** children's home; **де́тский сад** kindergarten

● **ДЕ́ТСКИЙ САД**

● Children go to kindergarten from around
● the age of three and stay there until they
● are six or seven. The kindergartens
● provide full-time childcare and
● pre-primary education five days a week.

де́тств|о (-а) *ср* childhood

де|ть (-ну, -нешь; *impf* **дева́ть**) *сов перех* (*разг*) to put; (*время, деньги*) to do with; **де́ться** (*impf* **дева́ться**) *сов возв* (*разг*) to get to

дефе́кт (-а) *м* defect

дефици́т (-а) *м* (*Экон*) deficit; (*нехватка*): **дефици́т** +*gen* или в +*prp* shortage of; **дефици́тный** *прил* in short supply

дециме́тр (-а) *м* decimetre (*Brit*), decimeter (*US*)

дешеве́|ть (*3sg* -ет, *perf* **подешеве́ть**) *несов* to go down in price

дешёвый *прил* cheap

де́ятел|ь (-я) *м*: **госуда́рственный де́ятель** statesman; **полити́ческий де́ятель** politician; **де́ятельност|ь** (-и) ж work; (*сердца, мозга*) activity; **де́ятельный** *прил* active

джаз (-а) *м* jazz

джем (-а) *м* jam

джи́нс|ы (-ов) *мн* jeans

джу́нгл|и (-ей) *мн* jungle *ед*

дзюдо́ *ср нескл* judo

диа́гноз (-а) *м* diagnosis

диагности́р|овать (-ую) (*не*)*сов перех* to diagnose

диагона́л|ь (-и) ж diagonal

диагра́мм|а (-ы) ж diagram

диале́кт (-а) *м* dialect

диало́г (-а) *м* dialogue

диа́метр (-а) *м* diameter

диапозити́в (-а) *м* (*Фото*) slide

дива́н (-а) *м* sofa

дива́н-крова́т|ь (-и) ж sofa bed

диве́рси|я (-и) ж sabotage

дивизи|я (-и) ж division

ди́в|о (-а) *ср* wonder; **на ди́во** wonderfully

дие́з (-а) *м* (*Муз*) sharp

дие́т|а (-ы) ж diet

диза́йн (-а) *м* design; **диза́йнер** (-а) *м* designer

дика́р|ь (-я́) *м* savage

ди́кий *прил* wild; (*поступок*) absurd; (*нравы*) barbarous

дикта́тор (-а) *м* dictator

дикт|ова́ть (-у́ю; *perf* **продиктова́ть**) *несов перех* to dictate

ди́лер (-а) *м*: **ди́лер (по** +*prp*) dealer (in)

дина́мик (-а) *м* (loud)speaker

дина́мик|а (-и) ж dynamics мн

динами́чный *прил* dynamic

диноза́вр (-а) *м* dinosaur

дипло́м (-а) *м* (*университета*) degree certificate; (*училища*) diploma; (*работа*) dissertation (*for undergraduate degree*)

диплома́т (-а) *м* diplomat; (*разг: портфель*) briefcase

дире́ктор (-а; *nom pl* -á) *м* director; **дире́ктор шко́лы** headmaster; **дире́кци|я** (-и) ж (*завода*) management; (*школы*) senior management

дирижёр (-а) *м* (*Муз*) conductor; **дирижи́р|овать** (-ую) *несов* +*instr* to conduct

диск (-а) *м* (*также Комп*) disc, disk (*esp US*); (*Спорт*) discus; (*Муз*) record; **ги́бкий/жёсткий диск** floppy/hard disk

диске́т (-а) *м* diskette

дисково́д (-а) *м* (*Комп*) disc drive

дискримина́ци|я (-и) ж discrimination

диску́сси|я (-и) ж discussion

диспансе́р (-а) *м* specialized health centre

диссерта́ци|я (-и) ж ≈ PhD thesis

дистанцио́нн|ый *прил*: **дистанцио́нное управле́ние** remote control

диста́нци|я (-и) ж distance

дисципли́н|а (-ы) ж discipline

дич|ь (-и) ж *собир* game

длин|а́ (-ы́) ж length; **в длину́** lengthways

дли́нный *прил* long; (*разг: человек*) tall

дли́тельный *прил* lengthy

дли́ться (*3sg* -и́тся, *perf* **продли́ться**) *несов возв* (*урок, беседа*) to last

для *предл* +*gen* for; (*в отношении*): **для меня́ э́то о́чень ва́жно** this is very important to me; **для того́ что́бы** in order to; **крем для лица́** face cream; **альбо́м для рисова́ния** sketch pad

дневни́к (-á) *м* diary; (*Просвещ*) register

дневн|о́й *прил* daily; **дневно́е вре́мя** daytime

днём *сущ см* **день** ▷ *нареч* in the daytime; (*после обеда*) in the afternoon

дни etc сущ см **день**

дн|о (-**а**) ср (ямы) bottom; (моря, реки) bottom, bed

○ **КЛЮЧЕВОЕ СЛОВО**

до предл +gen **1** (о пределе движения) as far as, to; **мы дое́хали до реки́** we went as far as или to the river; **я проводи́л его́ до ста́нции** I saw him off at the station

2 (о расстоянии) to; **до го́рода 3 киломе́тра** it is 3 kilometres (Brit) или kilometers (US) to the town

3 (о временно́м преде́ле) till, until; **я отложи́л заседа́ние до утра́** I postponed the meeting till или until morning; **до свида́ния!** goodbye!

4 (перед) before; **мы зако́нчили до переры́ва** we finished before the break

5 (о по́лном состоянии) мне бы́ло **оби́дно до слёз** I was so hurt I cried

6 (полностью): **я о́тдал ей всё до копе́йки** I gave her everything down to my last kopeck; **он вы́пил буты́лку до дна́** he drank the bottle dry

7 (направление действия): **ребёнок дотро́нулся до игру́шки** the child touched the toy

доба́в|ить (-лю, -ишь; impf **добавля́ть**) сов перех to add

добавле́ни|е (-я) ср addition

добежа́ть (как **бежа́ть**; см Table 20; impf **добега́ть**) сов: **добежа́ть до** +gen to run to или as far as

доб|и́ться (-ью́сь, -ьёшься; impf **добива́ться**) сов возв +gen to achieve

доб|ра́ться (-еру́сь, -ерёшься; impf **добира́ться**) сов возв: **добра́ться до** +gen to get to, reach

добре́|ть (-ю; perf **подобре́ть**) несов to become kinder

добр|о́ (-а́) ср good; (разг: имущество) belongings мн, property; **добро́ пожа́ловать (в Москву́)!** welcome (to Moscow)!; **э́то не к добру́** this is a bad omen

доброво́л|ец (-ьца) м volunteer

доброво́льный прил voluntary

доброду́шный прил good-natured

доброка́чественный прил quality; (о́пухоль) benign

добросо́вестный прил conscientious

доброта́ (-ы́) ж kindness

до́бр|ый прил kind; (совет, имя) good; **бу́дьте добры́!** excuse me!; **бу́дьте добры́, позвони́те нам за́втра?** would you be so good as to phone us tomorrow?; **всего́ до́брого!** all the best!; **до́брого здоро́вья!** take care!; **до́брый день/ве́чер!** good afternoon/evening!; **до́брое у́тро!** good morning!

добы́ть (как **быть**; см Table 21; impf **добыва́ть**) сов перех to get; (нефть) to extract; (руду) to mine

довез|ти́ (-у́; pt **довёз, -ла́,** impf **довози́ть**) сов перех: **довезти́ кого́-н до** +gen to take sb to или as far as

дове́ренность (-и) ж power of attorney

дове́ренн|ый (-ого) м (также **дове́ренное лицо́**) proxy

дове́ри|е (-я) ср confidence, trust; **телефо́н** or **Слу́жба дове́рия** help line

дове́р|ить (-ю, -ишь; impf **доверя́ть**) сов перех: **дове́рить что-н кому́-н** to entrust sb with sth

дове|сти́ (-ду́, -дёшь; pt **довёл, -ла́,** impf **доводи́ть**) сов перех: **довести́ кого́-н/что-н до** +gen to take sb/sth to или as far as; **доводи́ть** (perf **довести́**) **что-н до конца́** to see sth through to the end; **доводи́ть** (perf **довести́**) **что-н до све́дения кого́-н** to inform sb of sth

дов|оди́ться (-ожу́сь, -о́дишься) несов +dat to be related to

дов|ози́ть (-ожу́, -о́зишь) несов от **довезти́**

дово́льно нареч (сильный) quite ▷ как сказ (that is) enough

догада́|ться (-юсь; impf **дога́дываться**) сов возв to guess

дога́д|ка (-ки; gen pl -ок) ж guess

дог|на́ть (-оню́, -о́нишь; impf **догоня́ть**) сов перех to catch up with

догово́р (-а) м (Полит) treaty; (Комм) agreement

договорённост|ь (-и) ж agreement

договор|и́ть (-ю́, -и́шь; impf **догова́ривать**) сов (не)перех to finish

договор|и́ться (-ю́сь, -и́шься; impf **догова́риваться**) сов возв: **договори́ться с кем-н о чём-н** (о встрече) to arrange sth with sb; (о цене) to agree sth with sb

догола́ нареч: **разде́ться догола́** to strip bare или naked

догоня́|ть (-ю) несов от **догна́ть**

догор|е́ть (-ю́, -и́шь; impf **догора́ть**) сов to burn out

доде́ла|ть (-ю; impf **доде́лывать**) сов перех to finish

доду́ма|ться (-юсь; impf **доду́мываться**) сов возв: **доду́маться до** +gen to hit on; **как ты мог до тако́го доду́маться?** what on earth gave you that idea?

доеда́|ть (-ю) несов от **дое́сть**

дое́ду etc сов см **дое́хать**

доезжа́|ть (-ю) несов от **дое́хать**

дое́м сов см **дое́сть**

дое́сть (как **есть**; см Table 15; impf **доеда́ть**) сов перех to eat up

дое́хать (как **е́хать**; см Table 19; impf **доезжа́ть**) сов: **дое́хать до** +gen to reach

дожда́|ться (-у́сь, -ёшься; imper -и́(те) сь) сов возв: **дожда́ться кого́-н/чего́-н** to wait until sb/sth comes

дождли́вый *прил* rainy

дождь (-я́) *м* rain; **дождь идёт** it's raining; **дождь пошёл** it has started to rain

дожида́ться (-юсь) *несов возв* +*gen* to wait for

дожи́ть (-ву́, -вёшь; *impf* **дожива́ть**) *сов неперех*: **дожи́ть до** +*gen* to live to

до́за (-ы) *ж* dose

дозвони́ться (-ю́сь, -и́шься; *impf* **дозва́ниваться**) *сов возв* to get through

доигра́ть (-ю; *impf* **дои́грывать**) *сов перех* to finish playing

доистори́ческий *прил* prehistoric

дои́ть (-ю́, -ишь; *perf* **подои́ть**) *несов перех* to milk

дойти́ (*как* **идти́**; *см* Table 18; *impf* **доходи́ть**) *сов*: **дойти́ до** +*gen* to reach

док (-а) *м* dock

доказа́тельство (-а) *ср* proof, evidence

доказа́ть (-ажу́, -а́жешь; *impf* **дока́зывать**) *сов перех* (*правду, виновность*) to prove

докла́д (-а) *м* (*на съезде итп*) paper; (*начальнику*) report; **докла́дчик** (-а) *м* speaker

докла́дывать (-ю) *несов от* **доложи́ть**

до́ктор (-а; *nom pl* -á) *м* doctor; **до́ктор наук** Doctor of Sciences (*postdoctoral research degree in Russia*)

до́кторский *прил* (*Мед*) doctor's; (*Просвещ*) postdoctoral

докуме́нт (-а) *м* document; **документа́льный** *прил* documentary; **документа́льный фильм** documentary; **документа́ция** (-и) *ж собир* documentation

долг (-а; *loc sg* -ý, *nom pl* -и́) *м* debt; **дава́ть** (*perf* **дать**)/**брать** (**взять** *perf*) **что-н в долг** to lend/borrow sth; **быть** (*impf*) **в долгу́ пе́ред кем-н** *или* **у кого́-н** to be indebted to sb

до́лгий *прил* long

до́лго *нареч* for a long time; **как до́лго ...?** how long ...?

долгоигра́ющий *прил*: **долгоигра́ющая пласти́нка** LP (= long-playing record)

долгосро́чный *прил* long-term

долгота́ (-ы́) *ж* length; (*Гео*) longitude

○ **КЛЮЧЕВО́Е СЛО́ВО**

до́лж|ен (-на́, -но́, -ны́) *часть сказуемого* +*infin* **1** (*обязан*): **я до́лжен уйти́** I must go; **я до́лжен бу́ду уйти́** I will have to go; **она́ должна́ была́ уйти́** she had to go

2 (*выража́ет предположе́ние*): **он до́лжен ско́ро прийти́** he should arrive soon

3 (*о до́лге*): **ты до́лжен мне 5 рубле́й** you owe me 5 roubles

4: **должно́ быть** (*вероя́тно*) probably; **должно́ быть, она́ о́чень уста́ла** she must have been very tired

должностн|о́й *прил* official; **должностно́е лицо́** official

до́лжность (-и; *gen pl* -е́й) *ж* post

доли́н|а (-ы) *ж* valley

до́ллар (-а) *м* dollar

доло|жи́ть (-ожу́, -о́жишь; *impf* **докла́дывать**) *сов перех* to report

доло́т|о (-отá; *nom pl* -óта) *ср* chisel

до́льше *сравн прил от* **до́лгий** ▷ *сравн нареч от* **до́лго**

до́льк|а (-ьки; *gen pl* -ек) *ж* segment

до́л|я (-и; *gen pl* -е́й) *ж* share; (*пирога́*) portion; (*судьба́*) fate; **до́ля секу́нды** a fraction of a second

дом (-а; *nom pl* -á) *м* house; (*своё жильё*) home; (*семья́*) household; **дом моде́лей** fashion house; (*для о́тдыха* ≈ holiday centre (*Brit*) *или* center (*US*); **до́ма** *нареч* at home; **дома́шн|ий** *прил* (*а́дрес*) home; (*еда́*) home-made; (*живо́тное*) domestic; **дома́шняя хозя́йка** housewife; **дома́шнее зада́ние** homework

домини́р|овать (-ую) *несов* to dominate

домкра́т (-а) *м* (*Тех*) jack

домовладе́л|ец (-ьца) *м* home owner; **домовладе́ни|е** (-я) *ср* (*дом*) house with grounds attached

домово́дств|о (-а) *ср* home economics

домо́й *нареч* home

домоуправле́ни|е (-я) *ср* ≈ housing department

домохозя́|йка (-йки; *gen pl* -ек) *ж* = **дома́шняя хозя́йка**

домрабо́тни|ца (-ы) *ж* (= дома́шняя рабо́тница) domestic help (*Brit*), maid (*US*)

донесе́ни|е (-я) *ср* report

донес|ти́ (-у́, -ёшь; *pt* **донёс, -ла́**, *impf* **доноси́ть**) *сов перех* to carry ▷ *неперех*: **донести́ на** +*acc* to inform on; **донести́** (*perf*) **о** +*prp* to report on; **донести́сь** (*impf* **доноси́ться**) *сов возв*: **донести́сь до** +*gen* to reach

до́низу *нареч* to the bottom; **све́рху до́низу** from top to bottom

до́нор (-а) *м* (*Мед*) donor

доно́с (-а) *м*: **доно́с (на** +*acc*) denunciation (of)

доно|си́ть (-ошу́, -о́сишь) *несов от* **донести́**

допива́|ть (-ю) *несов от* **допи́ть**

до́пинг (-а) *м* drugs *мн*

допи|са́ть (-шу́, -шешь; *impf* **допи́сывать**) *сов перех* to finish (writing)

допи́ть (**допью́, допьёшь**; *imper* **допе́й(те)**, *impf* **допива́ть**) *сов перех* to drink up

допла́т|а (-ы) *ж* surcharge; **допла́та за бага́ж** excess baggage (charge)

доплы́ть (-ву́, -вёшь; *impf* **доплыва́ть**) *сов*: **доплы́ть до** +*gen* (*на корабле́*) to sail to; (*вплавь*) to swim to

дополне́ни|е (-я) *ср* supplement; (*Линг*) object; **в дополне́ние (к** +*dat*) in addition (to)

дополни́тельный *прил* additional

допо́лн|ить (-ю, -ишь; *impf* **дополня́ть**) *сов перех* to supplement

допра́шива|ть (-ю) *несов от* **допроси́ть**

допро́с (-а) *м* interrogation

допуска́|ть (-ю; *perf* **допусти́ть**) *несов перех* to admit, allow in; (*предположить*) to assume

допу́стим *вводн сл* let us assume

допуще́ни|е (-я) *ср* assumption

дораст|и́ (-у́, -ёшь; *pt* **доро́с**, **доросла́**, **доросло́**, *impf* **дораста́ть**) *сов*: **дорасти́ до** +*gen* to grow to

доро́г|а (-и) *ж* road, way; **по доро́ге** on the way

до́рого *нареч* (*купить, продать*) at a high price ▷ *как сказ* it's expensive

дорог|о́й *прил* expensive; (*цена*) high; (*друг, мать*) dear; (*воспоминания, подарок*) cherished ▷ (**-о́го**) *м* dear, darling

дорожа́|ть (*3sg* **-ет**, *perf* **подорожа́ть**) *несов* to go up in price *или* rise in price

доро́же *сравн прил от* **дорого́й** ▷ *сравн нареч от* **до́рого**

дорож|и́ть (-у́, -и́шь) *несов* +*instr* to value

доро́жный *прил* road; (*костюм, расходы*) travelling (*Brit*), traveling (*US*); (*сумка*) travel

доск|а́ (-и́; *nom pl* **-и**, *gen pl* **-о́к**) *ж* board; (*деревянная*) plank; (*мраморная*) slab; (*чугунная*) plate; **доска́ объявле́ний** notice (*Brit*) *или* bulletin (*US*) board

доскона́льный *прил* thorough

досло́вно *нареч* word for word

дослу́ша|ть (-ю; *impf* **дослу́шивать**) *сов перех* to listen to

досмо́тр (-а) *м*: **тамо́женный досмо́тр** customs examination

досм|отре́ть (-отрю́, -о́тришь; *impf* **досма́тривать**) *сов перех* to watch the end of; (*багаж*) to check

досро́чно *нареч* ahead of time

досро́чный *прил* early

доста|ва́ть(ся) (-ю́(сь)) *несов от* **доста́ть(ся)**

доста́в|ить (-лю, -ишь; *impf* **доставля́ть**) *сов перех* (*груз*) to deliver; (*пассажиров*) to carry, transport; (*удовольствие, возможность*) to give

доста́в|ка (-ки; *gen pl* **-ок**) *ж* delivery

доста́т|ок (-ка) *м* prosperity

доста́точно *нареч*: **доста́точно хорошо́/ подро́бно** good/detailed enough ▷ *как сказ* that's enough

доста́|ть (-ну, -нешь; *imper* **доста́нь(те)**, *impf* **достава́ть**) *сов перех* to take; (*раздобыть*) to get ▷ *неперех*: **доста́ть до** +*gen* to reach; **доста́ться** (*impf* **достава́ться**) *сов возв* (*при разделе*): **мне доста́лся дом** I got the house

достига́|ть (-ю) *несов от* **дости́чь**

достиже́ни|е (-я) *ср* achievement; (*предела, возраста*) reaching

дости́|чь (-гну, -гнешь; *pt* **-г**, **-гла**, *impf* **достига́ть**) *сов* +*gen* to reach; (*результата, цели*) to achieve; (*положения*) to attain

достове́рный *прил* reliable

досто́инств|о (-а) *ср* (*книги, плана*) merit; (*уважение к себе*) dignity; (*Комм*) value

досто́йный *прил* (*награда, кара*) fitting; (*человек*) worthy

достопримеча́тельност|ь (-и) *ж* sight; (*музея*) showpiece; **осма́тривать** (*perf* **осмотре́ть**) **достопримеча́тельности** to go sightseeing

достоя́ни|е (-я) *ср* property; **станови́ться** (*perf* **стать**) **достоя́нием обще́ственности** to become public knowledge

до́ступ (-а) *м* access

досу́г (-а) *м* leisure (time); **на досу́ге** in one's spare *или* free time

дота́ци|я (-и) *ж* subsidy

дотла́ *нареч*: **сгоре́ть дотла́** to burn down (to the ground)

дотро́н|уться (-усь; *impf* **дотра́гиваться**) *сов возв*: **дотро́нуться до** +*gen* to touch

дот|яну́ть (-яну́, -я́нешь; *impf* **дотя́гивать**) *сов перех*: **дотяну́ть что-н до** +*gen* to extend sth as far as; **дотяну́ться** (*impf* **дотя́гиваться**) *сов возв* **дотяну́ться до** +*gen* to reach

до́хлый *прил* dead

до́х|нуть (-ну; *pt* **-**, **-ла**, *perf* **подо́хнуть**) *несов* (*животное*) to die

дохо́д (-а) *м* income, revenue; (*человека*) income

доходи́ть *несов от* **дойти́**

дохо́дчивый *прил* clear, easy to understand

доце́нт (-а) *м* ≈ reader (*Brit*), ≈ associate professor (*US*)

до́ч|ка (-ки; *gen pl* **-ек**) *ж* daughter

доч|ь (**-ери**; *см Table 2*) *ж* daughter

дошёл *сов см* **дойти́**

дошко́льник (-а) *м* preschool child

дошла́ *итп сов см* **дойти́**

ДПР *ж сокр* (= **Демократи́ческая Па́ртия Росси́и**) *см* **ЛДПР**

драгоце́нност|ь (-и) *ж* jewel

драгоце́нный *прил* precious

дразн|и́ть (-ю́, -ишь) *несов перех* to tease

дра́к|а (-и) *ж* fight

драко́н (-а) *м* dragon

дра́м|а (-ы) *ж* drama; **драмати́ческий** *прил* dramatic; (*актёр*) stage; **драмату́рг** (-а) *м* playwright

драматурги́|я (-и) *ж* drama ▷ *собир* plays *мн*

драпир|ова́ть (-у́ю; *perf* **задрапирова́ть**) *несов перех*: **драпирова́ть что-н (чем-н)** to drape sth (with sth)

драть (**деру́, дерёшь**; *perf* **разодра́ть**) *несов перех* (*бумагу, одежду*) to tear *или* rip up ▷ (*perf* **задра́ть**) (*подлеж: волк*) to tear to pieces ▷ (*perf* **содра́ть**) (*кору, обои*) to strip; **дра́ться** (*perf* **подра́ться**) *несов возв*: **подра́ться** (**с** +*instr*) to fight (with)

дре́безг *м*: **в дре́безги** to smithereens

древеси́н|а (**-ы**) *ж собир* timber

древе́сный *прил* wood; **древе́сный у́голь** charcoal

дре́вний *прил* ancient

дрейф|ова́ть (**-у́ю**) *несов* to drift

дрель (**-и**) *ж* drill

дрессир|ова́ть (**-у́ю**; *perf* **вы́дрессировать**) *несов перех* to train

дроб|и́ть (**-лю́, -и́шь**; *perf* **раздроби́ть**) *несов перех* to crush; (*силы*) to split

дробь (**-и**; *gen pl* **-е́й**) *ж* fraction; (*барабана*) beat

дров|а́ (**-**; *dat pl* **-а́м**) *мн* firewood *ед*

дро́гн|уть (**-у**) *сов* (*стёкла, руки*) to shake; (*голос, лицо*) to quiver

дрож|а́ть (**-у́, -и́шь**) *несов* to shake, tremble; (*лицо*) to quiver; **дрожа́ть** (*impf*) **за** +*acc* **или над** +*instr* (*разг*) to fuss over

дро́жж|и (**-е́й**) *мн* yeast *ед*

дрозд (**-а́**) *м* thrush; **чёрный дрозд** blackbird

дру|г (**-га**; *nom pl* **-зья́**, *gen pl* **-зе́й**) *м* friend; **друг дру́га** each other, one another; **друг дру́гу** (*говори́ть*) to each other *или* one another; **друг за дру́гом** one after another; **друг о дру́ге** (*говори́ть*) about each other *или* one another

друг|о́й *прил* (*иной*) another; (*второй*) the other; (*не тако́й, как э́тот*) different ▷ (**-о́го**) *м* (*кто́-то ино́й*) another (person); (*второй*) the other (one); **в друго́й раз** another time; **и тот и друго́й** both

дру́жб|а (**-ы**) *ж* friendship

дружелю́бный *прил* friendly, amicable

дру́жеский *прил* friendly

дру́жественный *прил* friendly

друж|и́ть (**-у́, -ишь**) *несов*: **дружи́ть с** +*instr* to be friends with

друж|о́к (**-ка́**) *м* (*друг*) friend, pal (*inf*)

друзья́ *etc сущ см* **друг**

дрянь (**-и**) *ж* (*разг*) rubbish (*Brit*), trash (*US*)

дуб (**-а**; *nom pl* **-ы́**) *м* (*Бот*) oak (tree); (*древеси́на*) oak

дублён|ка (**-ки**; *gen pl* **-ок**) *ж* sheepskin coat

дублика́т (**-а**) *м* duplicate

дубли́р|овать (**-ую**) *несов перех* to duplicate; (*Кино*) to dub; (*Комп*) to back up

дуг|а́ (**-и́**; *nom pl* **-и**) *ж* (*Геом*) arc

ду́л|о (**-а**) *ср* muzzle; (*ствол*) barrel

ду́м|а (**-ы**) *ж* (*размышление*) thought; **Ду́ма** (*Полит*) the Duma (*lower house of Russian parliament*)

ду́ма|ть (**-ю**) *несов*: **ду́мать** (**о чём-н**) to think (about sth); **ду́мать** (*impf*) **над чем-н**

to think sth over; **я ду́маю, что да/нет** I think/don't think so

дум|е́ц (**-ца́**) *м* (*разг*) member of the Duma

думск|о́й *прил*: **думско́е заседа́ние** meeting of the Duma

ду́н|уть (**-у**) *сов* to blow

дупл|о́ (**-а́**; *nom pl* **-а**, *gen pl* **-ел**) *ср* (*дерева*) hollow

ду́р|а (**-ы**) *ж* (*разг*) fool

дура́к (**-а́**) *м* (*разг*) fool

дура́цкий *прил* (*разг*) foolish; (*шляпа*) silly

дура́ч|ить (**-у, -ишь**; *perf* **одура́чить**) *несов перех* (*разг*) to con; **дура́читься** *несов возв* (*разг*) to play the fool

дур|и́ть (**-ю́, -ишь**; *perf* **обдури́ть**) *несов перех* to fool

ду́рно *нареч* badly

ду́роч|ка (**-ки**; *gen pl* **-ек**) *ж* (*разг*) silly girl

дуршла́г (**-а**) *м* colander

ду|ть (**-ю, -ешь**) *несов* to blow ▷ (*perf* **вы́дуть**) *перех* (*Тех*) to blow; **здесь ду́ет** it's draughty (*Brit*) *или* drafty (*US*) in here

дух (**-а**; *part gen* **-у**) *м* spirit; **быть** (*impf*) **в ду́хе/не в ду́хе** to be in high/low spirits

дух|и́ (**-о́в**) *мн* perfume *ед*, scent *ед*

духо́вк|а (**-и**) *ж* oven

духо́вный *прил* spiritual; (*религио́зный*) sacred, church

духов|о́й *прил* (*Муз*) wind; **духовы́е инструме́нты** brass section (*in orchestra*); **духово́й орке́стр** brass band

душ (**-а**) *м* shower

душ|а́ (*acc sg* **-у**, *gen sg* **-и́**, *nom pl* **-и**) *ж* soul; **на ду́шу (населе́ния)** per head (of the population); **он в ней души́ не ча́ет** she's the apple of his eye; **говори́ть** (*impf*)/**бесе́довать** (*impf*) **по душа́м** to have a heart-to-heart talk/chat; **в глубине́ души́** in one's heart of hearts

душевнобольн|о́й (**-о́го**) *м* mentally ill person

душе́вн|ый *прил* (*силы, подъём*) inner; (*разговор*) sincere; (*человек*) kindly; **душе́вное потрясе́ние** shock

душ|и́ть (**-у́, -ишь**; *perf* **задуши́ть** *или* **удуши́ть**) *несов перех* to strangle; (*свобо́ду, прогре́сс*) to stifle ▷ (*perf* **надуши́ть**) (*плато́к*) to perfume, scent

ду́шно *как сказ* it's stuffy *или* close

ды́бом *нареч*: **встава́ть ды́бом** (*волосы, шерсть*) to stand on end

дыбы́ *мн*: **станови́ться на дыбы́** (*лошадь*) to rear up

дым (**-а**; *loc sg* **-у́**) *м* smoke; **дым|и́ть** (**-лю́, -и́шь**; *perf* **надыми́ть**) *несов* (*печь, дрова*) to smoulder (*Brit*), smolder (*US*); **дыми́ться** *несов возв* (*труба*) to be smoking

дымк|а (**-и**) *ж* haze

ды́мчатый *прил* (*стёкла*) tinted

ды́н|я (**-и**) *ж* melon

дыр|а́ (-ы́; *nom pl* -ы) ж hole
ды́р|ка (-ки; *gen pl* -ок) ж hole
дыроко́л (-а) м punch
дыш|а́ть (-у́, -ишь) *несов* to breathe;
  (+*instr*: *ненавистью*) to exude; (*любовью*)
  to radiate
дья́вол (-а) м devil
дю́жин|а (-ы) ж dozen
дя́д|я (-и) м uncle; (*разг*) bloke

Ева́нгели|е (-я) *ср* the Gospels мн; (*одна
  из книг*) gospel
евре́|й (-я) м Jew
евре́йский *прил* (*народ, обычаи*)
  Jewish; **евре́йский язы́к** Hebrew
е́вро м *нескл* euro
Евро́п|а (-ы) ж Europe; **европе́|ец**
  (-йца) м European; **европе́йск|ий** *прил*
  European; **Европе́йский сове́т** Council
  of Europe; **Европе́йское соо́бщество**
  European Community
его́ *мест см* **он**; **оно́** ⊳ *притяж мест*
  (*о мужчине*) his; (*о предмете*) its
ед|а́ (-ы́) ж (*пища*) food; (*процесс*): за
  едо́й, во вре́мя еды́ at mealtimes
едва́ *нареч* (*с трудом: нашёл, достал,
  доехал итп*) only just; (*только, немного*)
  barely, hardly; (*только что*) just ⊳ *союз*
  (*как только*) as soon as; **едва́ ли** hardly
е́дем *etc сов см* **е́хать**
еди́м *несов см* **есть**
едини́ц|а (-ы) ж (*цифра*) one;
  (*измерения, часть целого*) unit; **де́нежная
  едини́ца** monetary unit
единобо́рств|о (-а) *ср* single combat
единовре́менн|ый *прил*:
  единовре́менная су́мма lump sum
единогла́сный *прил* unanimous
единоду́шный *прил* unanimous
еди́нственн|ый *прил* (the) only;
  еди́нственное число́ (*Линг*) singular
еди́н|ый *прил* (*цельный*) united; (*общий*)
  common; **все до еди́ного** to a man;
  еди́ный госуда́рственный экза́мен
  university entrance exam; **еди́ный
  (проездно́й) биле́т** travel card (*for use
  on all forms of transport*)

● **Еди́ный госуда́рственный экза́мен**
●
● This exam is sat by school-leavers
● after completing 10 years of education.

- The mark obtained determines whether
- the student can be admitted to a higher
- education institue. See note at
- **проходной балл**.

○ **Единый проездной билет**

- This is a cheap and convenient way
- of city travel. It covers many types
- of transport including the trams,
- trolleybuses and buses.

едите *несов см* **есть**

еду *etc несов см* **ехать**

едят *несов см* **есть**

её *мест см* **она** ▷ *притяж мест* (*о женщине итп*) her; (*о предмете итп*) its

ёж (-**а**) *м* hedgehog

ежегодный *прил* annual

ежедневник (-**а**) *м* diary

ежедневный *прил* daily

ежемесячный *прил* monthly

еженедельный *прил* weekly

езд|а (-**ы**) *ж* journey

ез|дить (-**жу**, -**дишь**) *несов* to go; **ездить** *impf* **на** (+*prp*) (*на лошади, на велосипеде*) to ride; (*на поезде, на автобусе итп*) to travel *или* go by

ей *мест см* **она**

ел *etc несов см* **есть**

еле *нареч* (*с трудом*) only just; (*едва*) barely, hardly; **еле-еле** with great difficulty

ёл|ка (-**ки**; *gen pl* -**ок**) *ж* fir (tree); (*праздник*) New Year party for children; (**рождественская** *или* **новогодняя**) **ёлка** ≈ Christmas tree

еловый *прил* fir

ёлочн|ый *прил*: **ёлочные игрушки** Christmas-tree decorations *мн*

ел|ь (-**и**) *ж* fir (tree)

ем *несов см* **есть**

ёмкост|ь (-**и**) *ж* (*объём*) capacity; (*вместилище сосуд*) container

ему *мест см* **он**; **оно**

ерунд|а (-**ы**) *ж* rubbish, nonsense

ЕС *сокр* EU

○ **КЛЮЧЕВОЕ СЛОВО**

если *союз* **1** (*в том случае когда*) if; **если она придёт, дай ей это письмо** if she comes, give her this letter; **если ..., то ...** (*если*) if ..., then ...; **если он опоздает, то иди один** if he is late, (then) go alone
2 (*об условном действии*): **если бы(, то** *или* **тогда)** if; **если бы я мог, (то) помог бы тебе** if I could, I would help you
3 (*выражает сильное желание*): (**ах** *или* **о**) **если бы** if only; **ах если бы он пришёл!** oh, if only he would come!; **если уж на то пошло** if it comes to it; **что если...?** (*а вдруг*) what if...?

ест *несов см* **есть**

естественно *нареч* naturally ▷ *вводн сл* (*конечно*) of course; **естественный** *прил* natural

есть[1] *несов* (*один предмет*) there is; (*много предметов*) there are; **у меня есть друг** I have a friend

есть[2] (*см Table 15; perf* **поесть** *или* **съесть**) *несов перех* (*питаться*) to eat; **мне хочется есть** I'm hungry

ехать (*см Table 19*) *несов* to go; (*поезд, автомобиль: приближаться*) to come; (: *двигаться*) to go; (*разг: скользить*) to slide; **ехать** *impf* **на** (+*prp*) (*на лошади, на велосипеде*) to ride; **ехать** (*impf*) +*instr или* **на** +*prp* (*на поезде, на автобусе*) to travel *или* go by

ехидный *прил* spiteful

ешь *несов см* **есть**

ещё *нареч* (*дополнительно*) more; **хочу ещё кофе** I want more coffee

ею *мест см* **она**

Ж

ж союз, част см **же**

жа́б|а (-ы) ж (Зоол) toad

жа́воронок (-ка) м (Зоол) lark

жа́дность (-и) ж: **жа́дность** (к +dat) (к вещам, к деньгам) greed (for)

жа́дный прил greedy

жа́жд|а (-ы) ж thirst

жаке́т (-а) м (woman's) jacket

жале́|ть (-ю; perf **пожале́ть**) несов перех to feel sorry for; (скупиться) to grudge ▷ неперех: **жале́ть** о +prp to regret; **не жаля́ сил** sparing no effort

жа́л|ить (-ю, -ишь; perf **ужа́лить**) несов перех (подлеж: оса) to sting; (: змея) to bite

жа́лкий прил (вид) pitiful, pathetic

жа́лко как сказ = **жаль**

жа́л|о (-а) ср (пчелы) sting; (змеи) bite

жа́лоб|а (-ы) ж complaint

жа́лованье (-я) ср salary

жа́л|оваться (-уюсь; perf **пожа́ловаться**) несов возв: **жа́ловаться на** +acc to complain about; (ябедничать) to tell on

жа́лость (-и) ж: **жа́лость к** +dat sympathy for; **кака́я жа́лость!** what a shame!

○ **КЛЮЧЕВОЕ СЛОВО**

жаль как сказ **1** (+acc: о сострадании): **(мне) жаль дру́га** I am sorry for my friend

2 (+acc или +gen: о сожалении, о досаде): **(мне) жаль вре́мени/де́нег** I grudge the time/money

3 +infin; **жаль уезжа́ть** it's a pity или shame to leave

жар (-а) м heat; (Мед) fever

жар|а́ (-ы́) ж heat

жарго́н (-а) м slang; (профессиональный) jargon

жа́реный прил (на сковороде) fried; (в духовке) roast

жа́р|ить (-ю, -ишь; perf **зажа́рить**) несов перех (на сковороде) to fry; (в духовке) to roast; **жа́риться** (perf **зажа́риться**) несов возв to fry

жа́ркий прил hot; (спор) heated

жа́рко нареч (спорить) heatedly ▷ как сказ it's hot; **мне жа́рко** I'm hot

жа́тв|а (-ы) ж harvest

жать¹ (**жму, жмёшь**) несов перех (руку) to shake; (лимон, сок) to squeeze; **сапоги́ мне жмут** my boots are pinching (my feet)

жать² (**жну, жнёшь**; perf **сжать**) несов перех to harvest

жва́ч|ка (-ки; gen pl -ек) ж (разг: резинка) chewing gum

жд|ать (-у, -ёшь; pt -ал, -ала́, -а́ло) несов (не)перех (+acc или +gen: письмо, гостей) to expect; (поезда) to wait for

○ **КЛЮЧЕВОЕ СЛОВО**

же союз **1** (при противопоставлении) but; **я не люблю́ матема́тику, литерату́ру же обожа́ю** I don't like mathematics, but I love literature

2 (вводит дополнительные сведения) and; **успе́х зави́сит от нали́чия ресу́рсов, ресу́рсов же ма́ло** success depends on the presence of resources, and the resources are insufficient

▷ част **1** (ведь): **вы́пей ещё ча́ю, хо́чешь же!** have more tea, you want some, don't you?

2 (именно): **приду́ сейча́с же** I'll come right now

3 (выражает сходство): **тако́й же** the same; **в э́том же году́** this very year

ж|ева́ть (-ую) несов перех to chew

жела́ни|е (-я) ср (просьба) request; **жела́ние** +gen/+infin desire for/to do

жела́тельный прил desirable

жела́|ть (-ю; perf **пожела́ть**) несов +gen to desire; **жела́ть** (perf **пожела́ть**) +infin to wish или want to do; **жела́ть** (perf **пожела́ть**) **кому́-н сча́стья/всего́ хоро́шего** to wish sb happiness/all the best

жела́ющ|ий (-его) м: **жела́ющие пое́хать/порабо́тать** those interested in going/working

желе́ ср нескл jelly (Brit), jello (US)

желе́з|а́ (-езы́; nom pl -езы, gen pl -ёз, dat pl -еза́м) ж gland

железнодоро́жный прил (вокзал) railway (Brit), railroad (US); (транспорт) rail

желе́зн|ый прил iron; **желе́зная доро́га** railway (Brit), railroad (US)

желе́з|о (-а) ср iron

жёлоб (-а; nom pl -а́) м gutter

желте́|ть (-ю; perf **пожелте́ть**) несов to turn yellow

желт|**о́к** (-ка́) *м* yolk
жёлтый *прил* yellow
желу́д|**ок** (-ка) *м* (*Анат*) stomach; (*сок*) gastric
жёлудь (-я) *м* acorn
жёлчный *прил*: жёлчный пузы́рь gall bladder
же́мчуг (-а; *nom pl* -á) *м* pearls мн
жемчу́жин|**а** (-ы) *ж* pearl
жен|**á** (-ы́; *nom pl* жёны, *gen pl* жён) *ж* wife
жена́т|**ый** *прил* married (*of man*); он жена́т на +*prp* he is married to; они́ жена́ты they are married
Жене́в|**а** (-ы) *ж* Geneva
жен|**и́ть** (-ю́, -ишь) (*не*)*сов перех* (*сына*, *внука*): жени́ть кого́-н (на +*prp*) to marry sb (off) (to); **жени́ться** (*не*)*сов возв*: жени́ться на +*prp* to marry (*of man*) ▷ (*perf* **пожени́ться**) (*разг*) to get hitched
жени́х (-á) *м* (*до свадьбы*) fiancé; (*на свадьбе*) (bride)groom
же́нский *прил* women's; (*логика*, *органы*) female; же́нский пол the female sex; же́нский род feminine gender
же́нственный *прил* feminine
же́нщин|**а** (-ы) *ж* woman
жердь (-и; *gen pl* -е́й) *ж* pole
жереб|**ёнок** (-ёнка; *nom pl* -я́та, *gen pl* -я́т) *м* foal
же́ртв|**а** (-ы) *ж* victim; (*Рел*) sacrifice; челове́ческие же́ртвы casualties
же́ртв|**овать** (-ую; *perf* **поже́ртвовать**) *несов* (+*instr*: жизнью) to sacrifice ▷ *перех* (*деньги*) to donate
жест (-а) *м* gesture
жёсткий *прил* (*кровать*, *человек*) hard; (*мясо*) tough; (*волосы*) coarse; (*условия*) strict; жёсткий ваго́н railway carriage with hard seats; жёсткий диск hard disk
жесто́кий *прил* cruel; (*мороз*) severe
жесто́кость (-и) *ж* cruelty
жето́н (-а) *м* tag; (*в метро*) token
жечь (жгу, жжёшь *etc*, жгут; *pt* жёг, жгла, *perf* **сжечь**) *несов перех* to burn
жже́ни|**е** (-я) *ср* burning sensation
живо́й *прил* alive; (*организм*) living; (*животное*) live; (*человек: энергичный*) lively
живопи́сный *прил* picturesque
жи́вопись (-и) *ж* painting
живо́т (-á) *м* stomach; (*разг*) tummy
живо́тн|**ое** (-ого) *ср* animal
живо́тный *прил* animal
живу́ *etc несов см* **жить**
жи́дкий *прил* liquid
жи́дкость (-и) *ж* liquid
жи́зненный *прил* (*вопрос*, *интересы*) vital; (*необходимость*) basic; жи́зненный у́ровень standard of living; жи́зненный о́пыт experience
жизнера́достный *прил* cheerful
жизнеспосо́бный *прил* viable

жизнь (-и) *ж* life
жил *etc несов см* **жить**
жиле́т (-а) *м* waistcoat (*Brit*), vest (*US*)
жил|**е́ц** (-ьца́) *м* (*дома*) tenant
жили́щный *прил* housing
жил|**о́й** *прил* (*дом*, *здание*) residential; жила́я пло́щадь accommodation
жиль|**ё** (-я́) *ср* accommodation
жир (-а; *nom pl* -ы́) *м* fat; (*растительный*) oil
жира́ф (-а) *м* giraffe
жи́рный *прил* (*пища*) fatty; (*человек*) fat; (*волосы*) greasy
жи́тель (-я) *м* resident; **жи́тельств**|**о** (-а) *ср* residence
жи́ть (-ву́, -вёшь; *pt* -л, -ла́, -ло) *несов* to live; жил-был there once was, once upon a time there was
жму́р|**ить** (-ю, -ишь; *perf* **зажму́рить**) *несов*: жму́рить глаза́ to screw up one's eyes; **жму́риться** (*perf* **зажму́риться**) *несов возв* to squint
жоке́й (-я) *м* jockey
жонгли́р|**овать** (-ую) *несов* +*instr* to juggle (with)
жре́би|**й** (-я) *м*: броса́ть жре́бий to cast lots
ЖСК *м сокр* (= жили́щно-строи́тельный коопера́тив) ≈ housing cooperative
жужж|**а́ть** (-ý, -и́шь) *несов* to buzz
жук (-á) *м* beetle
журна́л (-а) *м* magazine; (*классный*) register
журнали́ст (-а) *м* journalist; **журнали́стик**|**а** (-и) *ж* journalism
жу́ткий *прил* terrible
ЖЭК (-а) *м сокр* (= жили́щно-эксплуатаци́онная конто́ра) ≈ housing office
жюри́ *ср нескл* panel of judges

live on the other side of the river

2 (*вне*) outside; **жить** (*impf*) **зá городом** to live outside the town; **за границей** abroad

3 (*позади*) behind; **стоя́ть** (*impf*) **за две́рью** to stand behind the door

4 (*около: стоять, сидеть*) at; **сиде́ть** (*impf*) **за столо́м** to sit at the table

5 (*о смене событий*) after; **год за го́дом** year after year

6 (*во время чего-н*) over; **за за́втраком** over breakfast

7 (*о объекте внимания*): **смотре́ть** или **уха́живать за** +*instr* to look after

8 (*с целью получить, достать что-н*) for; **я посла́л его́ за газе́той** I sent him out for a paper

9 (*по причине*) owing to

▷ *как сказ* (*согласен*) in favour; **кто за?** who is in favour?

▷ *ср нескл* pro; **взве́сить** (*perf*) **все за и про́тив** to weigh up all the pros and cons

---

з. *сокр* (= *за́пад*) W (= *West*); (= *за́падный*) W (= *West*)

⊙ КЛЮЧЕВОЕ СЛОВО

за *предл* +*acc* **1** out (of); **выходи́ть** (*perf* **вы́йти**) **за дверь** to go out (of) the door

2 (*позади*) behind; **пря́таться** (*perf* **спря́таться**) **за де́рево** to hide behind a tree

3 (*около: сесть, встать*) at; **сади́ться** (*perf* **сесть**) **за стол** to sit down at the table

4 (*свыше какого-н предела*) over; **ему́ за со́рок** he is over forty

5 (*при указании на расстояние, на время*): **за пять киломе́тров отсю́да** five kilometres (*Brit*) или kilometers (*US*) from here; **за три часа́ до нача́ла спекта́кля** three hours before the beginning of the show

6 (*при указании объекта действия*): **держа́ться за** +*acc* to hold onto; **ухвати́ться** (*perf*) **за** +*acc* to take hold of; **брать** (*perf* **взять**) **кого́-н за́ руку** to take sb by the hand; **бра́ться** (*perf* **взя́ться**) **за рабо́ту** to start work

7 (*об объекте чувств*) for; **ра́доваться** (*impf*) **за сы́на** to be happy for one's son; **беспоко́иться** (*impf*) **за му́жа** to worry about one's husband

8 (*о цели*) for; **сража́ться** (*impf*) **за побе́ду** to fight for victory

9 (*в пользу*) for, in favour (*Brit*) или favor (*US*) of; **голосова́ть** (*perf* **проголосова́ть**) **за предложе́ние** to vote for или in favour of a proposal

10 (*по причине, в обмен*) for; **благодарю́ Вас за по́мощь** thank you for your help; **плати́ть** (*impf*) **за что-н** to pay for sth

11 (*вместо кого-н*) for; **рабо́тать** (*impf*) **за дру́га** to fill in for a friend

▷ *предл* +*instr* **1** (*по другую сторону*) on the other side of; **жить** (*impf*) **за реко́й** to

забасто́в|ка (-**ки**; *gen pl* -**ок**) *ж* strike

забасто́вщик (-**а**) *м* striker

забе́г (-**а**) *м* (*Спорт*) race (*in running*); (: *отборочный*) heat

забежа́ть (*как* **бежа́ть**; *см* Table 20; *impf* **забега́ть**) *сов*: **забежа́ть** (**в** +*acc*) (*в дом, в деревню*) to run in(to); (*разг: на недолго*) to drop in(to); **забега́ть** (*perf* **забежа́ть**) **вперёд** to run ahead

забира́|ть(ся) (-**ю(сь)**)) *несов от* **забра́ть(ся)**

заб|и́ть (-**ью́**, -**ьёшь**; *impf* **забива́ть**) *перех* (*гвоздь, сваю*) to drive in; (*Спорт: гол*) to score; (*наполнить*) to overfill; (*засорить*) to clog (up); (*скот, зверя*) to slaughter; **заби́ться** (*impf* **забива́ться**) (*сердце*) to start beating ▷ (*impf* **забива́ться**) (*спрятаться*) to hide (away)

заблуди́ться (-**ужу́сь**, -**у́дишься**) *сов возв* to get lost

заблужда́|ться (-**юсь**) *несов возв* to be mistaken; **заблужде́ни|е** (-**я**) *ср* misconception

заболева́ни|е (-**я**) *ср* illness

заболе́|ть (-**ю**; *impf* **заболева́ть**) *сов* (*нога, горло*) to begin to hurt; **заболева́ть** (*perf* **заболе́ть**) +*instr* (*гриппом*) to fall ill with

забо́р (-**а**) *м* fence

забо́т|а (-**ы**) *ж* (*беспокойство*) worry; (*уход*) care; (*обычно мн: хлопоты*) trouble; **забо́|титься** (-**чусь**, -**тишься**; *perf* **позабо́титься**) *несов возв*: **забо́титься о** +*prp* to take care of; **забо́тливый** *прил* caring

забра́сыва|ть (-**ю**) *несов от* **заброса́ть**; **забро́сить**

заб|ра́ть (-**еру́**, -**ерёшь**; *impf* **забира́ть**) *сов перех* to take; **забра́ться** (*impf* **забира́ться**) *сов возв* (*влезть*): **забра́ться на** +*acc* to climb up; (*проникнуть*): **забра́ться в** +*acc* to get into

заброса́|ть (-ю; *impf* **забра́сывать**) *сов перех* (+*instr*: канаву, яму) to fill with; (цветами) to shower with

забро́|сить (-шу, -сишь) *impf* **забра́сывать**) to fling; (*десант*) to drop; (*учёбу*) to neglect

забры́зга|ть (-ю; *impf* **забры́згивать**) *сов перех* to splash

забы́ть (*как* **быть**; см Table 21; *impf* **забыва́ть**) *сов перех* to forget

зав. *сокр* = **заве́дующий**

зава́л (-а) *м* obstruction; **зав|али́ть** (-алю́, -а́лишь; *impf* **зава́ливать**) *сов перех* (вход) to block off; (*разг*: экзамен) to mess up; **зава́ливать** (*perf* **завали́ть**) +*instr* (дорогу: снегом) to cover with; (яму: землёй) to fill with; **завали́ться** (*impf* **зава́ливаться**) *сов возв* (забор) to collapse; (*разг*: на экзамене) to come a cropper

зав|ари́ть (-арю́, -а́ришь; *impf* **зава́ривать**) *сов перех* (чай, кофе) to brew; (*Tex*) to weld

заварно́й *прил*: **заварно́й крем** custard

заведе́ни|е (-я) *ср* establishment

заве́д|овать (-ую) *несов* +*instr* to be in charge of

заве́дующ|ий (-его) *м* manager; (*лабораторией, кафедрой*) head; **заве́дующий хозя́йством** (*в школе*) bursar; (*на заводе*) person in charge of supplies

заве́р|ить (-ю, -ишь; *impf* **заверя́ть**) *сов перех* (копию, подпись) to witness; **заверя́ть** (*perf* **заве́рить**) кого́-н в чём-н to assure sb of sth

заверн|у́ть (-у́, -ёшь; *impf* **завора́чивать**) *сов перех* (рукав) to roll up; (*гайку*) to tighten up; (*налево, направо, за угол*) to turn; **завора́чивать** (*perf* **заверну́ть**) (в +*acc*) (посылку, книгу, ребёнка) to wrap (in); **заверну́ться** (*impf* **завора́чиваться**) *сов возв*: **заверну́ться в** +*acc* (в полотенце, в плед) to wrap o.s. up in

заверша́|ть (-ю) *несов от* **заверши́ть**

заверша́ющий *прил* final

заверше́ни|е (-я) *ср* completion; (*разговора, лекции*) conclusion; **заверш|и́ть** (-у́, -и́шь; *impf* **заверша́ть**) *сов перех* to complete; (*разговор*) to end

заверя́|ть (-ю) *несов от* **заве́рить**

зав|ести́ (-еду́, -едёшь; *pt* -ёл, -ела́, -ело́, *impf* **заводи́ть**) *сов перех* to take; (*приобрести*) to get; (*установить*) to introduce; (*переписку, разговор*) to initiate; (*часы*) to wind up; (*машину*) to start; **завести́сь** (*impf* **заводи́ться**) *сов возв* (появиться) to appear; (*мотор, часы*) to start working

завеща́ни|е (-я) *ср* (документ) will, testament; **завеща́|ть** (-ю) (*не*)*сов перех*: **завеща́ть что-н кому́-н** (наследство) to bequeath sth to sb

завива́|ть(ся) (-ю(сь)) *несов от* **зави́ть(ся)**

зави́дно *как сказ*: ему́ зави́дно he feels envious

зави́д|овать (-ую; *perf* **позави́довать**) *несов* +*dat* to envy, be jealous of

завин|ти́ть (-чу́, -ти́шь; *impf* **зави́нчивать**) *сов перех* to tighten (up)

зави́|сеть (-шу, -сишь) *несов*: **зави́сеть от** +*gen* to depend on; **зави́симост|ь** (-и) *ж* (отношение) correlation; **зави́симость (от** +*gen*) dependence (on); **в зави́симости от** +*gen* depending on

зави́стливый *прил* envious, jealous; **за́вист|ь** (-и) *ж* envy, jealousy

завит|о́к (-ка́) *м* (локон) curl

зав|и́ть (-ью́, -ьёшь; *impf* **завива́ть**) *сов перех* (волосы) to curl; **зави́ться** (*impf* **завива́ться**) *сов возв* (волосы) to curl; (*сделать завивку*) to curl one's hair

заво́д (-а) *м* factory; (*в часах, у игрушки*) clockwork

зав|оди́ть(ся) (-ожу́(сь), -о́дишь(ся)) *несов от* **завести́(сь)**

завоева́ни|е (-я) *ср* (страны) conquest; (*успех*) achievement; **завоева́тельный** *прил* aggressive; **заво|ева́ть** (-ю́ю; *impf* **завоёвывать**) *сов перех* to conquer

завора́чива|ть(ся) (-ю(сь)) *несов от* **заверну́ть(ся)**

за́втра *нареч, ср нескл* tomorrow; **до за́втра!** see you tomorrow!

за́втрак (-а) *м* breakfast; **за́втрака|ть** (-ю; *impf* **поза́втракать**) *несов* to have breakfast

за́втрашний *прил* tomorrow's; **за́втрашний день** tomorrow

за́вуч (-а) *м сокр* ≈ deputy head

завхо́з (-а) *м сокр* = **заве́дующий хозя́йством**

зав|яза́ть (-яжу́, -я́жешь; *impf* **завя́зывать**) *сов перех* (верёвку) to tie; (*руку, посылку*) to bind; (*разговор*) to start (up); (*дружбу*) to form; **завяза́ться** (*impf* **завя́зываться**) *сов возв* (шнурки) to be tied; (*разговор*) to start (up); (*дружба*) to form

загада́|ть (-ю; *impf* **зага́дывать**) *сов перех* (загадку) to set; (*желание*) to make

зага́д|ка (-ки; *gen pl* -ок) *ж* riddle; (*перен*) puzzle; **зага́дочный** *прил* puzzling

зага́р (-а) *м* (sun)tan

загиба́|ть(ся) (-ю(сь)) *несов от* **загну́ть(ся)**

загла́ви|е (-я) *ср* title; **загла́вн|ый** *прил*: **загла́вная бу́ква** capital letter; **загла́вная роль** title role

загла́|дить (-жу, -дишь; *impf* **загла́живать**) *сов перех* (складки) to iron

загло́хн|уть (-у) *сов от* **гло́хнуть**

заглуш|и́ть (-у́, -и́шь) *сов от* **глуши́ть**

загл|яну́ть (-яну́, -я́нешь; *impf*

загля́дывать *сов (в окно, в комнату)* to peep; *(в книгу, в словарь)* to glance; *(разг: посетить)* to pop in

заг|на́ть (**-оню́, -о́нишь**; *pt* **-на́л, -нала́, -на́ло**, *impf* **загоня́ть**) *сов перех (коров, детей)* to drive

загн|и́ть (**-ию́, -иёшь**; *impf* **загнива́ть**) *сов* to rot

загн|у́ть (**-у́, -ёшь**; *impf* **загиба́ть**) *сов перех* to bend; *(край)* to fold; **загну́ться** (*impf* **загиба́ться**) *сов возв (гвоздь)* to bend; *(край)* to fold

за́говор (**-а**) *м* conspiracy

заговор|и́ть (**-ю́, -и́шь**) *сов* to begin to speak

заголо́в|ок (**-ка**) *м* headline

заго́н (**-а**) *м (для коров)* enclosure; *(для овец)* pen

загоня́|ть (**-ю**) *несов от* **загна́ть**

загора́жива|ть (**-ю**) *несов от* **загороди́ть**

загора́|ть(ся) (**-ю(сь)**) *несов от* **загоре́ть(ся)**

загоре́лый *прил* tanned

загор|е́ть (**-ю́, -и́шь**; *impf* **загора́ть**) *сов* to go brown, get a tan; **загоре́ться** (*impf* **загора́ться**) *сов возв (дрова, костёр)* to light; *(здание итп)* to catch fire; *(лампочка, глаза)* to light up

за́город (**-а**) *м (разг)* the country

загор|оди́ть (**-ожу́, -о́дишь**; *impf* **загора́живать**) *сов перех* to block off; *(свет)* to block out

за́городный *прил (экскурсия)* out-of-town; *(дом)* country

загото́в|ить (**-лю, -ишь**; *impf* **загота́вливать**) *сов перех* to lay in; *(документы итп)* to prepare

загражде́ни|е (**-я**) *ср* barrier

заграни́ц|а (**-ы**) *ж (разг)* foreign countries *мн*

заграни́чный *прил* foreign, overseas; **заграни́чный па́спорт** passport (*for travel abroad*)

загрем|е́ть (**-лю́, -и́шь**) *сов (гром)* to crash

загро́бн|ый *прил*: **загро́бный мир** the next world; **загро́бная жизнь** the afterlife

загружа́емый *прил* downloadable

загр|узи́ть (**-ужу́, -у́зишь**) *сов от* **грузи́ть** ▷ (*impf* **загружа́ть**) *перех (машину)* to load up; *(Комп)* to boot up, to download, to upload

загру́з|ка (**-ки**; *gen pl* **-ок**) *ж* download

загрязне́ни|е (**-я**) *ср* pollution; **загрязне́ние окружа́ющей среды́** (environmental) pollution

загрязн|и́ть (**-ю́, -и́шь**; *impf* **загрязня́ть**) *сов перех* to pollute; **загрязни́ться** (*impf* **загрязня́ться**) *сов возв* to become polluted

ЗАГС (**-а**) *м сокр* (= за́пись а́ктов гражда́нского состоя́ния) ≈ registry office

зад (**-а**; *nom pl* **-ы́**, *gen pl* **-о́в**) *м (человека)* behind; *(животного)* rump; *(машины)* rear

зада|ва́ть(ся) (**-ю́(сь), -ёшь(ся)**) *несов от* **зада́ть(ся)**

зад|ави́ть (**-авлю́, -а́вишь**) *сов от* **дави́ть** ▷ *перех* to crush; **его́ задави́ла маши́на** he was run over by a car

зада́ни|е (**-я**) *ср* task; *(учебное)* exercise; *(Воен)* mission; **дома́шнее зада́ние** homework

зада́т|ок (**-ка**) *м* deposit

зада́ть (*как* **дать**; *см Table 16*; *impf* **задава́ть**) *сов перех* to set; **задава́ть** (*perf* **зада́ть**) **кому́-н вопро́с** to ask sb a question; **зада́ться** (*impf* **задава́ться**) *сов возв*: **зада́ться це́лью** +*infin* to set o.s. the task of doing

зада́ч|а (**-и**) *ж* task; *(Мат)* problem

задви́га|ть (**-ю**) *сов* +*instr* to begin to move; **задви́гаться** *сов возв* to begin to move

задви́жк|а (**-и**) *ж* bolt

задви́н|уть (**-у**) *сов перех* to push; *(ящик, занаве́ски)* to close

задева́|ть (**-ю**) *несов от* **заде́ть**

заде́ла|ть (**-ю**; *impf* **заде́лывать**) *сов перех* to seal up

задёргива|ть (**-ю**) *несов от* **задёрнуть**

зад|ержа́ть (**-ержу́, -е́ржишь**; *impf* **заде́рживать**) *сов перех* to delay, hold up; *(преступника)* to detain; **я не хочу́ Вас задержа́ть** I don't want to hold you back; **задержа́ться** (*impf* **заде́рживаться**) *сов возв* to be delayed *или* held up; *(ждать)* to pause

заде́рж|ка (**-ки**; *gen pl* **-ек**) *ж* delay, hold-up

задёрн|уть (**-у**; *impf* **задёргивать**) *сов перех (што́ры)* to pull shut

заде́|ть (**-ну, -нешь**; *impf* **задева́ть**) *сов перех (перен: самолю́бие)* to wound; **задева́ть** (*perf* **заде́ть**) **за** +*асс (за стол)* to brush against; *(кость)* to graze against

задира́|ть(ся) (**-ю**) *несов от* **задра́ть(ся)**

за́дн|ий *прил* back; **помеча́ть** (*perf* **поме́тить**) **за́дним число́м** to backdate; **опла́чивать** (*perf* **оплати́ть**) **за́дним число́м** to make a back payment

задо́лго *нареч*: **задо́лго до** +*gen* long before

задо́лженност|ь (**-и**) *ж* debts *мн*

за́дом *нареч* backwards (*Brit*), backward (*US*); **за́дом наперёд** back to front

задохн|у́ться (**-у́сь, -ёшься**; *impf* **задыха́ться**) *сов возв (в дыму́)* to suffocate; *(от бега)* to be out of breath; *(от зло́сти)* to choke

зад|ра́ть (**-еру́, -ерёшь**; *impf* **задира́ть**) *сов перех (пла́тье)* to hitch *или* hike up; **задра́ться** (*impf* **задира́ться**) *сов возв (пла́тье итп)* to ruck up

задр|ема́ть (**-емлю́, -е́млешь**) *сов* to doze off

задрож|áть (-ý, -и́шь) *сов* (*человек, голос*) to begin to tremble; (*здание*) to begin to shake

задýма|ть (-ю) *impf* **задýмывать** *сов перех* (*план*) to think up; (*карту, число*) to think of; **задýмывать** (*perf* **задýмать**) +*infin* (*уехать итп*) to think of doing; **задýматься** *сов возв* (*impf* **задýмываться**) to be deep in thought

задýмыва|ть(ся) (-ю(сь)) *несов от* **задýмать(ся)**

зад|уши́ть (-ушý, -ýшишь) *сов от* **души́ть**

задыхá|ться (-юсь) *несов от* **задохнýться**

заедá|ть (-ю) *несов от* **заéсть**

заéзд (-а) *м* (*Спорт*) race (*in horse-racing, motor-racing*)

заезжá|ть (-ю) *несов от* **заéхать**

заём (**зáйма**) *м* loan

заé|сть (*как* **есть**; *см* Table 15; *impf* **заедáть**) *сов перех* (*подлеж: комары*) to eat ▷ *безл* (*разг: ружьё*) to jam; пластúнку заéло (*разг*) the record is stuck

заéхать (*как* **éхать**; *см* Table 19; *impf* **заезжáть**) *сов*: **заéхать за кем-н** to go to fetch sb; **заезжáть** (*perf* **заéхать**) в +*acc* (*в канаву, во двор*) to drive into; (*в Москвý, в магазúн итп*) to stop off at

заж|áть (-мý, -мёшь) *impf* **зажимáть** *сов перех* (*руку*) to squeeze; (*рот, уши*) to cover

заж|éчь (-гý, -жёшь *итп*, -гýт; *pt* -ёг, -глá, *impf* **зажигáть**) *сов перех* (*спичку*) to light; (*свет*) to turn on; **зажéчься** (*impf* **зажигáться**) *сов возв* (*спичка*) to light; (*свет*) to go on

заживá|ть (-ю) *несов от* **зажúть**

зажигáл|ка (-ки; *gen pl* -ок) *ж* (cigarette) lighter; **зажигáни|е** (-я) *ср* (*Авт*) ignition

зажигá|ть(ся) (-ю(сь)) *несов от* **зажéчь(ся)**

зажимá|ть (-ю) *несов от* **зажáть**

заж|úть (-ивý, -ивёшь; *impf* **заживáть**) *сов* (*рана*) to heal (up)

заземлéни|е (-я) *ср* (*Элек: устройство*) earth (*Brit*), ground (*US*); **заземл|úть** (-ю́, -úшь; *impf* **заземля́ть**) *сов перех* to earth (*Brit*), ground (*US*)

заигрá|ть (-ю) *сов (не)перех* to begin to play ▷ *неперех* (*музыка*) to begin

зайгрыва|ть (-ю) *несов*: **зайгрывать с** +*instr* (*разг: любезничать*) to flirt with; (: *заискивать*) to woo

заикá|ться (-юсь) *несов возв* to have a stutter; **заикáться** (*perf* **заикнýться**) о +*prp* (*упомянуть*) to mention

займ|ствовать (-ую) *impf* **позаимствовать** (*не)сов перех* to borrow; (*опыт*) to take on board

заинтересóванный *прил* interested; я **заинтересóван в этом дéле** I have an interest in the matter

заинтерес|овáть (-ýю) *сов перех* to

interest; **заинтересовáться** *сов возв*: **заинтересовáться** +*instr* to become interested in

зайскива|ть (-ю) *несов*: **зайскивать пéред** +*instr* to ingratiate o.s. with

зайтú (*как* **идтú**; *см* Table 18; *impf* **заходúть**) *сов* (*солнце, луна*) to go down; (*спор, разговóр*) to start up; (*посетúть*): **зайтú (в/на** +*acc*/**к** +*dat*) to call in (at); (*попáсть*): **зайтú в/на** +*acc* to stray into; **заходúть** (*perf* **зайтú**) **за кем-н** to go to fetch sb; **заходúть** (*perf* **зайтú**) **спрáва/ слéва** to come in from the right/left

закавкáзский *прил* Transcaucasian

закáз (-а) *м* (*см глаг*) ordering; commissioning; (*закáзанный предмéт*) order; **по закáзу** to order; **зак|азáть** (-ажý, -áжешь; *impf* **закáзывать**) *сов перех* to order; to book; (*портрéт*) to commission; **заказн|óй** *прил*: **заказнóе убúйство** contract killing; **заказнóе письмó** registered letter; **закáзчик** (-а) *м* customer

закáлыва|ть (-ю) *несов от* **заколóть**

закáнчива|ть(ся) (-ю) *несов от* **закóнчить(ся)**

закáпыва|ть (-ю) *несов от* **закáпать**; **закопáть**

закáт (-а) *м* (*перен: жизни*) twilight; **закáт** (**сóлнца**) sunset

закатá|ть (-ю; *impf* **закáтывать**) *сов перех* to roll up

зак|атúть (-ачý, -áтишь; *impf* **закáтывать** *сов перех* (*что-н крýглое*) to roll; (*что-н на колёсах*) to wheel; **закатúться** (*impf* **закáтываться**) *сов возв* to roll

закидá|ть (-ю; *impf* **закúдывать**) *сов* = **заброcáть**

закúн|уть (-у; *impf* **закúдывать**) *сов перех* to throw

закип|éть (*3sg* -úт, *impf* **закипáть**) *сов* to start to boil; (*перен: рабóта*) to intensify

закúс|нуть (-ну; *pt* -, -ла, *impf* **закисáть**) *сов* to turn sour

заклáдк|а (-и) *ж* (*в кнúге*) bookmark

закладн|áя (-ой) *ж* mortgage deed

закла́дыва|ть (-ю) *несов от* **заложúть**

заклé|ить (-ю, -ишь; *impf* **заклéивать**) *сов перех* to seal (up)

заклинá|ть (-ю) *несов перех* (*дýхов, змея*) to charm; (*перен: умоля́ть*) to plead with

заклúн|ить (-ю, -ишь; *impf* **заклúнивать**) *сов перех* to jam

заключá|ть (-ю) *несов от* **заключúть**; **заключáться** *несов возв*: **заключáться в** +*prp* (*состоя́ть в*) to lie in; (*содержáться в*) to be contained in; **проблéма заключáется в том, что ...** the problem is that ...

заключённ|ый (-ого) *м* prisoner

заключ|úть (-ý, -úшь; *impf* **заключáть**) *сов перех* (*договóр, сдéлку*) to conclude

зак|олóть (-олю́, -óлешь) *сов от* **колóть**

▷ (*impf* **зака́лывать**) *перех* (*волосы*) to pin up

зако́н (-а) *м* law; **объявля́ть** (*perf* **объяви́ть**) **кого́-н вне зако́на** to outlaw sb; **зако́нный** *прил* legitimate, lawful; (*право*) legal; **законода́тельный** *прил* legislative; **законода́тельств|о** (-а) *ср* legislation

закономе́рный *прил* predictable; (*понятный*) legitimate

законопрое́кт (-а) *м* (*Полит*) bill

зако́нченный *прил* complete

зако́нч|ить (-у, -ишь; *impf* **зака́нчивать**) *сов перех* to finish; **зако́нчиться** (*impf* **зака́нчиваться**) *сов возв* to finish, end

закопа́|ть (-ю; *impf* **зака́пывать**) *сов перех* to bury; (*яму*) to fill in

закоп|ти́ть (-чу́, -ти́шь) *сов от* **копти́ть**; **закопти́ться** *сов возв* to be covered in smoke

закреп|и́ть (-лю́, -и́шь) *impf* **закрепля́ть**) *сов перех* to fasten; (*победу, пози́цию*) to consolidate; (*Фото*) to fix

закрича́|ть (-у́, -и́шь) *сов* to start shouting

закругл|и́ть (-ю́, -и́шь) *impf* **закругля́ть**) *сов перех* (*край, бесе́ду*) to round off

закр|ути́ть (-учу́, -у́тишь) *impf* **закру́чивать**) *сов перех* (*волосы*) to twist; (*га́йку*) to screw in

закрыва́|ть(ся) (-ю(сь)) *несов от* **закры́ть(ся)**

закры́ти|е (-я) *ср* closing (time)

закры́т|ый *прил* closed, shut; (*терра́са, маши́на*) enclosed; (*стадио́н*) indoor; (*собра́ние*) closed, private; (*ра́на*) internal; **в закры́том помеще́нии** indoors

закр|ы́ть (-о́ю, -о́ешь; *impf* **закрыва́ть**) *сов перех* to close, shut; (*заслони́ть, накры́ть*) to cover (up); (*прохо́д, грани́цу*) to close (off); (*во́ду, газ итп*) to shut off; **закры́ться** (*impf* **закрыва́ться**) *сов возв* to close, shut; (*магази́н*) to close *или* shut down; (*запере́ться: в до́ме итп*) to shut o.s. up

зак|ури́ть (-урю́, -у́ришь; *impf* **заку́ривать**) *сов перех* to light (up)

зак|уси́ть (-ушу́, -у́сишь; *impf* **заку́сывать**) *сов* (*пое́сть*) to have a bite to eat

заку́ск|а (-и) *ж* snack; (*обычно мн: для во́дки*) zakuska (*мн* zakuski); nibbles *мн*; (*в нача́ле обе́да*) hors d'oeuvre

заку́сочн|ая (-ой) *ж* snack bar

заку́та|ть(ся) (-ю(сь)) *сов от* **ку́тать(ся)**

зал (-а) *м* hall; (*в библиоте́ке*) room; **зал ожида́ния** waiting room

заледене́лый *прил* covered in ice; (*ру́ки*) icy; **заледене́|ть** (-ю) *сов* (*доро́га*) to ice over; (*перен: ру́ки*) to freeze

зале́з|ть (-у, -ешь; *impf* **залеза́ть**) *сов*:

зале́зть на +*асс* (*на кры́шу*) to climb onto; (*на де́рево*) to climb up; (*разг*) **зале́зть в** +*асс* (*в кварти́ру*) to break into; (*в долги́*) to fall into

зале|те́ть (-чу́, -ти́шь; *impf* **залета́ть**) *сов*: **залете́ть (в** +*асс*) to fly in(to)

зал|ечи́ть (-ечу́, -е́чишь) *impf* **зале́чивать**) *сов перех* to heal

зали́в (-а) *м* bay; (*дли́нный*) gulf

зал|и́ть (-ью́, -ье́шь; *impf* **залива́ть**) *сов перех* to flood; (*костёр*) to extinguish; **залива́ть** (*perf* **зали́ть**) **бензи́н в маши́ну** to fill a car with petrol; **зали́ться** (*impf* **залива́ться**) *сов возв* (*вода́*) to seep; **залива́ться** (*perf* **зали́ться**) **слеза́ми/ сме́хом** to burst into tears/out laughing

зало́г (-а) *м* (*де́йствие: веще́й*) pawning; (*: кварти́ры*) mortgaging; (*зало́женная вещь*) security; (*Линг*) voice

зал|ожи́ть (-ожу́, -о́жишь; *impf* **закла́дывать**) *сов перех* (*покры́ть*) to clutter up; (*отме́тить*) to mark; (*кольцо́, шу́бу*) to pawn; (*дом*) to mortgage; (*запо́лнить*) to block up; **у меня́ заложи́ло нос/го́рло** (*разг*) my nose/throat is all bunged up

зало́жник (-а) *м* hostage

за́лпом *нареч* all in one go

зама́|зать (-жу, -жешь; *impf* **зама́зывать**) *сов перех* (*ще́ли*) to fill with putty; (*запа́чкать*) to smear

зама́нчивый *прил* tempting

замахн|у́ться (-у́сь, -ёшься; *impf* **зама́хиваться**) *сов возв*: **замахну́ться на** +*асс* (*на ребёнка*) to raise one's hand to; (*перен*) to set one's sights on

зама́чива|ть (-ю) *несов от* **замочи́ть**

заме́дл|ить (-ю, -ишь; *impf* **замедля́ть**) *сов перех* to slow down; **заме́длиться** (*impf* **замедля́ться**) *сов возв* to slow down

заме́н|а (-ы) *ж* replacement; (*Спорт*) substitution; **зам|ени́ть** (-еню́, -е́нишь; *impf* **заменя́ть**) *сов перех* to replace

зам|ере́ть (-ру́, -рёшь; *pt* -ер, -ерла́, *impf* **замира́ть**) *сов* (*челове́к*) to stop dead; (*перен: се́рдце*) to stand still; (*: рабо́та, страна́*) to come to a standstill; (*звук*) to die away

замёрз|нуть (-ну; *pt* -, -ла, *impf* **замерза́ть**) *сов* to freeze; (*окно́*) to ice up; **я замёрз** I'm freezing

замести́тел|ь (-я) *м* (*дире́ктора*) deputy

заме|сти́ть (-щу́, -сти́шь) *сов от* **замеща́ть**

заме́|тить (-чу, -тишь; *impf* **замеча́ть**) *сов перех* to notice; (*сказа́ть*) to remark

заме́т|ка (-ки; *gen pl* -ок) *ж* note; (*в газе́те*) short piece *или* article

заме́тно *нареч* noticeably ▷ *как сказ* (*ви́дно*) it's obvious; **заме́тный** *прил* noticeable; (*ли́чность*) prominent

замеча́ни|е (-я) *ср* comment, remark; (*вы́говор*) reprimand

замечáтельно нареч (красив, умён) extremely; (делать что-н) wonderfully, brilliantly ▷ как сказ: **замечáтельно!** that's wonderful или brilliant!; **замечáтельный** прил wonderful, brilliant

замечá|ть (-ю) несов от **замéтить**

замешáтельств|о (-а) ср confusion

замéшива|ть (-ю) несов от **замесúть**

замещá|ть (-ю) несов перех (временно) to stand in for ▷ **заместúть** (заменять: работника итп) to replace; (: игрока) to substitute; (вакансию) to fill; **замещéни|е** (-я) ср (работника) replacement; (игрока) substitution

замúн|ка (-ки; gen pl -ок) ж hitch

замирá|ть (-ю) несов от **замерéть**

замкн|ýть (-ý, -ёшь; impf **замыкáть** сов перех to close; **замкнýться** (impf **замыкáться** (перен: обособиться) to shut o.s. off

зáм|ок (-ка) м castle

зам|óк (-ká) м lock; (также **висячий замóк**) padlock

замóлк|нуть (-ну; pt -, -ла, impf **замолкáть** сов to fall silent

замолчá|ть (-ý, -úшь) сов (человек) to go quiet; **замолчú!** be quiet!, shut up!

заморó|зить (-жу, -зишь; impf **заморáживать** сов перех to freeze

зáморозк|и (-ов) мн frosts

зам|óчить (-очý, -óчишь; impf **замáчивать** сов перех to soak

зáмуж нареч: **выходúть зáмуж** (за +acc) to get married (to), marry; **зáмужем** нареч married; **замýжеств|о** (-а) ср marriage; **замýжняя** прил married

замýч|ить (-у, -ишь) сов от **мýчить** ▷ перех: **замýчить** (perf) **кого-н до смéрти** to torture sb to death; **замýчиться** сов от **мýчиться**

зáмш|а (-и) ж suede

замыкáни|е (-я) ср (также **корóткое замыкáние**) short circuit

замыкá|ть(ся) (-ю(сь)) несов от **замкнýть(ся)**

зáмыс|ел (-ла) м scheme; **замýсл|ить** (-ю, -ишь; impf **замышлять** сов перех to think up

зáнавес (-а) м (Театр) curtain; **занавé|сить** (-шу, -сишь; impf **занавéшивать** сов перех to hang a curtain over; **занавéс|ка** (-ки; gen pl -ок) ж curtain

зан|естú (-есý, -есёшь; pt -ёс, -еслá, impf **заносúть** сов перех (принести) to bring; (записать) to take down; (доставить): **дорóгу занеслó снéгом** the road is covered (over) with snow

занимá|ть (-ю) несов от **занять**; **занимáться** несов возв (на рояле итп) to practise (Brit), practice (US); **занимáться** (impf) +instr (учиться) to study; (уборкой) to do; **занимáться** (impf) **спóртом/**

мýзыкой to play sports/music; **чем ты сейчáс занимáешься?** what are you doing at the moment?

зáново нареч again

занóз|а (-ы) ж splinter

занóс (-а) м (обычно мн) drift

зан|осúть (-ошý, -óсишь) несов от **занестú**

занóсчивый прил arrogant

зáнят прил busy; **он был óчень зáнят** he was very busy; **телефóн зáнят** the phone или line is engaged

занятú|е (-я) ср occupation; (в школе) lesson, class; (времяпрепровождение) pastime

зáнятост|ь (-и) ж employment

зан|ять (займý, займёшь; impf **занимáть** сов перех to occupy; (позицию) to take up; (деньги) to borrow; (время) to take; **занять** (perf) **пéрвое/ вторóе мéсто** to take first/second place; **заняться** сов возв: **заняться** +instr (языком, спортом) to take up; (бизнесом) to go into; **заняться** (perf) **собóй/детьмú** to devote time to o.s./one's children

заоднó нареч (вместе) as one

заóчный прил part-time

- ЗАÓЧНОЕ ОТДЕЛÉНИЕ
-
- Part-time study is one of the ways of
- obtaining a degree. It is intended for
- people who do not want to give up their
- work. Most students work independently
- with regular postal communication with
- their tutors. Two exam sessions a year
- are preceded by a month of intensive
- series of lectures and tutorials which
- prepare students for the exams. See also
- notes at **óчный** and **вечéрний**.

зáпад (-а) м west; **Зáпад** (Полит) the West; **западноевропéйский** прил West European; **зáпадный** прил western; (ветер) westerly

западн|я (-ú) ж trap

запáс (-а) м store; (руды) deposit; (Воен) the reserves мн

запасá|ть(ся) (-ю(сь)) несов от **запастú(сь)**

запасн|óй прил spare ▷ (-óго) м (Спорт: также **запаснóй игрóк**) substitute; **запаснáя часть** spare part

зап|астú (-асý, -асёшь; impf **запасáть** сов перех to lay in; **запастúсь** (impf **запасáться** сов возв: **запастúсь** (+instr) to stock up (on)

зáпах (-а) м smell

запая|ть (-ю) сов перех to solder

зап|ерéть (-рý, -рёшь; impf **запирáть** сов перех (дверь) to lock; (дом, человека) to lock up; **заперéться** (impf **запирáться** сов возв (дверь) to lock; (человек) to lock o.s. up

запéть (-ою́, -оёшь) *сов (не)перех* to start singing

запечáта|ть (-ю; *impf* **запечáтывать**) *сов перех* to seal up

запирá|ть(ся) (-ю(сь)) *несов от* **заперéть(ся)**

запи|сáть (-ишу́, -и́шешь; *impf* **запи́сывать**) *сов перех* to write down; (*концерт, пластинку*) to record; (*на курсы*) to enrol; **записáться** (*impf* **запи́сываться**) *сов возв* (*на курсы*) to enrol (o.s.); (*на плёнку*) to make a recording; **записáться** (*perf*) (*на приём*) к врачу́ to make a doctor's appointment

запи́ск|а (-и) *ж* note; (*служебная*) memo

записн|óй *прил*: **записнáя кни́жка** notebook

запи́сыва|ть(ся) (-ю(сь)) *несов от* **записáть(ся)**

запи́с|ь (-и) *ж* record; (*в дневнике*) entry; (*Муз*) recording; (*на курсы*) enrolment (*Brit*), enrollment (*US*); (*на приём к врачу*) appointment

заплá|кать (-чу, -чешь) *сов* to start crying *или* to cry

заплáт|а (-ы) *ж* patch

запл|ати́ть (-ачу́, -а́тишь) *сов от* **плати́ть**

заплы́в (-а) *м* (*Спорт*) race (*in swimming*); (: *отборочный*) heat

запл|ы́ть (-ыву́, -ывёшь; *impf* **заплывáть**) *сов перех* (*человек*) to swim off; (*глаза*) to become swollen

заповéдник (-а) *м* (*природный*) nature reserve

заподóзр|ить (-ю, -ишь) *сов перех* to suspect

запóлн|ить (-ю, -ишь; *impf* **заполня́ть**) *сов перех* to fill; (*анкету, бланк*) to fill in *или* out; **заполниться** (*impf* **заполня́ться**) *сов возв* to fill up

заполя́рный *прил* polar

запóмн|ить (-ю, -ишь; *impf* **запомина́ть**) *сов перех* to remember

зáпонк|а (-и) *ж* cuff link

запóр (-а) *м* (*Мед*) constipation; (*замок*) lock

запотé|ть (-ю) *сов* to steam up

запрáв|ить (-лю, -ишь; *impf* **заправля́ть**) *сов перех* (*рубашку*) to tuck in; (*салат*) to dress; **заправля́ть** (*perf* **запрáвить**) маши́ну to fill up the car; **запрáвиться** (*impf* **заправля́ться**) *сов возв* (*разг: горючим*) to tank up

запрáв|ка (-ки; *gen pl* -ок) *ж* (*машины, самолёта итп*) filling; (*разг: станция*) filling station; (*Кулин*) dressing

запрáвочн|ый *прил*: **запрáвочная стáнция** filling station

запрéт (-а) *м*: **запрéт** (**на что-н**/+*infin*) ban (on sth/on doing); **запре|ти́ть** (-щу́, -ти́шь) *сов перех* to ban; **запрещáть** (*perf* **запрети́ть**) кому́-н +*infin* to forbid sb to do;

запрéтный *прил* forbidden

запрóс (-а) *м* inquiry; (*обычно мн*: *требования*) expectation

запр|я́чь (-ягу́, -яжёшь итп, -ягу́т; *pt* -я́г, -ягла́, *impf* **запрягáть**) *сов перех* (*лошадь*) to harness

запугá|ть (-ю; *impf* **запу́гивать**) *сов перех* to intimidate

зáпуск (-а) *м* (*станка*) starting; (*ракеты*) launch

запу|сти́ть (-щу́, -у́стишь; *impf* **запускáть**) *сов перех* (*бросить*) to hurl; (*станок*) to start (up); (*ракету*) to launch; (*хозяйство, болезнь*) to neglect ▷ *неперех*: **запусти́ть чем-н в кого́-н** to hurl sth at sb; **запускáть** (*perf* **запусти́ть**) что-н в произвóдство to launch (production of) sth

запу́танный *прил* (*нитки, волосы*) tangled; (*дело, вопрос*) confused

запу́та|ть (-ю) *сов от* **пу́тать**; **запу́таться** *сов от* **пу́таться** ▷ (*impf* **запу́тываться**) *возв* (*человек*) to get caught up; (*дело, вопрос*) to become confused

запчáст|ь (-и) *ж сокр* = **запаснáя часть**

запя́ст|ье (-ья; *gen pl* -ий) *ср* wrist

запят|áя (-óй) *ж, decl like adj* comma

зарабóта|ть (-ю; *impf* **зарабáтывать**) *сов перех* to earn ▷ *неперех* (*по impf*: *начать работать*) to start up

зáработн|ый *прил*: **зáработная плáта** pay, wages *мн*

зáработ|ок (-ка) *м* earnings *мн*

заражá|ть(ся) (-ю(сь)) *несов от* **зарази́ть(ся)**

заráз|а (-ы) *ж* infection

зарáзный *прил* infectious

зарáнее *нареч* in advance

зар|асти́ (-асту́, -астёшь; *pt* -óс, -ослá, *impf* **зарастáть**) *сов* (*зажить: рана*) to close up; **зарастáть** (*perf* **зарасти́**) +*instr* (*травой*) to be overgrown with

зарé|зать (-жу, -жешь) *сов от* **рéзать** ▷ *перех* (*человека*) to stab to death

зарекомендовá|ть (-у́ю) *сов*: **зарекомендовáть себя́** +*instr* to prove oneself to be

зароди́ться (3*sg* -и́тся, *impf* **зарождáться**) *сов возв* (*явление*) to emerge; (*перен: чувство*) to arise

зарóдыш (-а) *м* (*Био*) embryo; (*растения, также перен*) germ

зарплáт|а (-ы) *ж сокр* (= **зáработная плáта**) pay

зарубéжный *прил* foreign; **зарубéжь|е** (-я) *ср* overseas; **бли́жнее зарубéжье** former Soviet republics

зар|ы́ть (-óю, -óешь; *impf* **зарывáть**) *сов перех* to bury; **зары́ться** (*impf* **зарывáться**) *сов возв*: **зары́ться в** +*acc* to bury o.s. in

зар|я́ (-и́; *nom pl* **зóри**, *gen pl* **зорь**, *dat pl* **зóрям**) *ж* dawn; (*вечерняя*) sunset; **ни**

свет ни заря́ at the crack of dawn

заря́д (-а) м (Воен, Элек) charge; (перен: бодрости) boost

заса́д|а (-ы) ж ambush; (отряд) ambush party

заса́сыва|ть (3sg -ет) несов от засоса́ть

засверка́|ть (-ю) сов to flash

засве|ти́ть (-чу́, -́тишь) impf **засве́чивать** сов перех (Фото) to expose

засева́|ть (-ю) несов от засе́ять

заседа́ни|е (-я) ср meeting; (парламента, суда) session

заседа́тел|ь (-я) м: прися́жный заседа́тель member of the jury

заседа́|ть (-ю) несов (на совещании) to meet; (в парламенте, в суде) to sit; (парламент, суд) to be in session

засека́|ть (-ю) несов от засе́чь

засел|и́ть (-ю́, -и́шь; impf заселя́ть) сов перех (земли) to settle; (дом) to move into

засе́|чь (-еку́, -ечёшь etc, -еку́т; pt -ёк, -екла́, -екло́, impf засека́ть) сов перех (место) to locate; засека́ть (perf засе́чь) вре́мя to record the time

засе́|ять (-ю; impf засева́ть) сов перех (земли) to sow

засло́н (-а) м shield; **заслон|и́ть** (-ю́, -и́шь; impf заслоня́ть) сов перех to shield

заслу́г|а (-и) ж (обычно мн) service; награди́ть (perf) кого́-н по заслу́гам to fully reward sb; его́ наказа́ли по заслу́гам he got what he deserved

засл|ужи́ть (-ужу́, -у́жишь; impf заслу́живать) сов перех to earn

заслу́ша|ть (-ю; impf заслу́шивать) сов перех to listen to

засме|я́ться (-ю́сь, -ёшься) сов возв to start laughing

засн|у́ть (-у́, -ёшь; impf засыпа́ть) сов to go to sleep, fall asleep

засо́в (-а) м bolt

засо́выва|ть (-ю) несов от засу́нуть

засоре́ни|е (-я) ср (рек) pollution; (туалета) blockage; **засор|и́ть** (-ю́, -и́шь; impf засоря́ть) сов перех (туалет) to clog up, block; **засори́ться** (impf засоря́ться) сов возв (туалет) to become clogged up или blocked

засос|а́ть (-у́, -ёшь; impf заса́сывать) сов перех to suck in

засо́хн|уть (-у; impf засыха́ть) сов (грязь) to dry up; (растение) to wither

заста́в|а (-ы) ж (также **пограни́чная заста́ва**) frontier post

застава́|ть (-ю́, -ёшь) несов от заста́ть

заста́в|ить (-лю, -ишь; impf заставля́ть) сов перех (занять) to clutter up; заставля́ть (perf заста́вить) кого́-н +infin to force sth to do, make sb do

заста́|ть (-ну, -нешь; impf застава́ть) сов перех to catch, find

застегн|у́ть (-у́, -ёшь; impf застёгивать) сов перех to do up;

застегн|у́ться (impf застёгиваться) сов возв (на пуговицы) to button o.s. up; (на мо́лнию) to zip o.s. up

застекл|и́ть (-ю́, -и́шь; impf застекля́ть) сов перех to glaze

застел|и́ть (-ю́, -ишь) impf застила́ть сов перех (кровать) to make up

засте́нчивый прил shy

застига́|ть (-ю) несов от засти́чь

застила́|ть (-ю) несов от застели́ть

засти́|чь (-гну, -гнешь; pt -г, -гла, -гло, impf застига́ть) сов перех to catch

засто́йный прил stagnant

застра́ива|ть (-ю) несов от застро́ить

застрах|ова́ть(ся) (-у́ю(сь)) сов от страхова́ть(ся)

застрева́|ть (-ю) несов от застря́ть

застрел|и́ть (-елю́, -е́лишь) сов перех to gun down; **застрели́ться** сов возв to shoot o.s.

застро́|ить (-ю, -ишь; impf застра́ивать) сов перех to develop

застря́|ть (-ну, -нешь; impf застрева́ть) сов to get stuck

заст|упи́ться (-уплю́сь, -у́пишься; impf заступа́ться) сов возв: заступи́ться за +acc to stand up for

засты́|ть (-ну, -нешь; impf застыва́ть) сов to freeze; (цемент) to set

засу́н|уть (-у; impf засо́вывать) сов перех: засу́нуть что-н в +acc to thrust sth into

за́сух|а (-и) ж drought

зас|уши́ть (-ушу́, -у́шишь; impf засу́шивать) сов перех to dry up

засу́шливый прил dry

засчита́|ть (-ю; impf засчи́тывать) сов перех (гол) to allow (to stand)

засы́п|ать (-лю, -лешь) impf засыпа́ть сов перех (яму) to fill (up); (покры́ть) to cover; засыпа́ть (perf засы́пать) кого́-н вопро́сами to bombard sb with questions; засыпа́ть (perf засы́пать) кого́-н пода́рками to shower sb with gifts

засыпа́|ть (-ю) несов от заснуть

засыха́|ть (-ю) несов от засо́хнуть

зата|и́ть (-ю́, -и́шь; impf зата́ивать) сов перех (неприязнь) to harbour (Brit), harbor (US); затаи́ть (perf) дыха́ние to hold one's breath; **затаи́ться** сов возв to hide

зата́плива|ть (-ю) несов от затопи́ть

зата|щи́ть (-щу́, -́щишь; impf зата́скивать) сов перех to drag

затво́р (-а) м shutter

затева́|ть (-ю) несов от зате́ять

затека́|ть (-ю) несов от зате́чь

зате́м нареч (потом) then; (для того) for that reason; зате́м что́бы in order to

зат|е́чь (3sg -ечёт, pt -ёк, -екла́, -екло́, impf затека́ть) сов (опухнуть) to swell up; (онеметь) to go numb; затека́ть (perf зате́чь) за +acc/в +acc (вода) to seep behind/into

зате́я (-и) ж (замысел) idea, scheme

зате́|ять (-ю; impf **затева́ть**) сов перех (разговор, игру) to start (up)

зати́х|нуть (-ну; pt -, -ла, impf **затиха́ть**) сов to quieten (Brit) или quiet (US) down; (буря) to die down

зати́шь|е (-я) ср lull

заткн|у́ть (-у́, -ёшь; impf **затыка́ть**) сов перех to plug; **заткну́ть** (perf) что-н за +acc/в +acc to stuff sth behind/into; **затыка́ть** (perf **заткну́ть**) или **рот** кому-н (разг) to shut sb up; **заткну́ться** (impf **затыка́ться**) сов возв (разг: замолчать) to shut up; **заткни́сь!** (разг: пренебр) shut it!

затме́ни|е (-я) ср eclipse

зато́ союз (также **но зато́**) but then (again)

зат|ону́ть (-ону́, -о́нешь) сов to sink

зат|опи́ть (-оплю́, -о́пишь; impf **зата́пливать**) сов перех (печь) to light ▷ (impf **затопля́ть**) (деревню) to flood; (судно) to sink

зато́р (-а) м congestion; (на улице) traffic jam

затра́гива|ть (-ю) несов от **затро́нуть**

затра́т|а (-ы) ж expenditure

затро́н|уть (-у; impf **затра́гивать**) сов перех (перен: тему) to touch on; (: человека) to affect

затрудне́ни|е (-я) ср difficulty; **затрудни́тельный** прил difficult, awkward; **затрудн|и́ть** (-ю́, -и́шь; impf **затрудня́ть**) сов перех: **затрудни́ть** что-н to make sth difficult; **е́сли Вас не затрудни́т** if it isn't too much trouble; **затрудни́ться** (impf **затрудня́ться**) сов возв: **затрудни́ться** +infin/с чем-н to have difficulty doing/with sth

зат|упи́ть(ся) (-уплю́, -у́пишь) сов от **тупи́ть(ся)**

зат|уши́ть (-ушу́, -у́шишь) сов от **туши́ть**

затыка́|ть(ся) (-ю(сь)) несов от **заткну́ть(ся)**

заты́л|ок (-ка) м the back of the head

зат|яну́ть (-яну́, -я́нешь; impf **затя́гивать**) сов перех (шнурки, гайку) to tighten; (дело) to drag out; (вовлечь): **затяну́ть** кого-н в +acc to drag sb into; **затяну́ться** (impf **затя́гиваться**) сов возв (петля, узел) to tighten; (рана) to close up; (дело) to overrun; (при курении) to inhale

заура́дный прил mediocre

зау́трен|я (-и) ж (Рел) dawn mass

за|учи́ть (-учу́, -у́чишь; impf **зау́чивать**) сов перех to learn, memorize

захва́т (-а) м seizure, capture; (Спорт) hold; (Тех) clamp; **захв|ати́ть** (-ачу́, -а́тишь; impf **захва́тывать**) сов перех to seize, capture; (взять с собой) to take; (подлеж: музыка) to captivate; (болезнь, пожар) to catch (in time); **дух захва́тывает** it takes your breath away; **у меня́ дух захвати́ло от волне́ния** I was breathless with excitement; **захва́тнический** прил aggressive; **захва́тывающий** прил gripping; (вид) breathtaking

захлебн|у́ться (-у́сь, -ёшься; impf **захлёбываться**) сов возв to choke

захло́па|ть (-ю) сов: захло́пать (в ладо́ши) (зрители) to start clapping

захло́пн|уть (-у; impf **захло́пывать**) сов перех to slam (shut); **захло́пнуться** (impf **захло́пываться**) сов возв to slam (shut)

захо́д (-а) м (также **захо́д со́лнца**) sunset; (в порт) call; (попытка) go; **с пе́рвого/второ́го захо́да** at the first/second go

зах|оди́ть (-ожу́, -о́дишь) несов от **зайти́**

захор|они́ть (-оню́, -о́нишь) сов перех to bury

зах|оте́ть (как **хоте́ть**; см Table 14) сов перех to want; **захоте́ться** сов безл: **мне захоте́лось есть/пить** I started to feel hungry/thirsty

зац|епи́ть (-еплю́, -е́пишь; impf **зацепля́ть**) сов перех (поддеть) to hook up; (разг: задеть) to catch against; **зацепи́ться** сов возв: зацепи́ться за +acc (задеть за) to catch или get caught on; (ухвати́ться за) to grab hold of

зача́т|ок (-ка; nom pl -ки) м (идеи итп) beginning, germ

заче́м нареч why; **заче́м-то** нареч for some reason

зачеркн|у́ть (-у́, -ёшь; impf **зачёркивать**) сов перех to cross out

зачерпн|у́ть (-у́, -ёшь; impf **заче́рпывать**) сов перех to scoop up

зач|еса́ть (-ешу́, -е́шешь; impf **зачёсывать**) сов перех to comb

зачёт (-а) м (Просвещ) test; **сдава́ть** (impf)/**сдать** (perf) **зачёт по фи́зике** to sit (Brit) или take/pass a physics test; **зачётный** прил: **зачётная рабо́та** assessed essay (Brit), term paper (US); **зачётная кни́жка** student's record book

● **ЗАЧЁТНАЯ КНИ́ЖКА**

● This is a special booklet into which all
● exam marks attained by the students are
● entered. It is the students' responsibility
● to look after their own record books.

зачи́сл|ить (-ю, -ишь; impf **зачисля́ть**) сов перех (в институт) to enrol; (на рабо́ту) to take on; (на счёт) to enter

зачита́|ть (-ю; impf **зачи́тывать**) сов перех to read out

зашёл сов см **зайти́**

заш|и́ть (-ью́, -ьёшь; impf **зашива́ть**) сов перех (дырку) to mend; (шов, рану) to stitch

зашла́ etc сов см **зайти́**

зашто́па|ть (-ю) сов от **што́пать**

защёлк|а (-и) ж (на двери) latch

защёлкн|уть (-у; impf **защёлкивать**) сов перех to shut

защи́т|а (-ы) ж (также Юр, Спорт) defence (Brit), defense (US); (от комаров, от пыли) protection; (диплома) (public) viva; **защити́ть** (-щу́, -ти́шь; impf **защища́ть**) сов перех to defend; (от солнца, от комаров итп) to protect; **защити́ться** (impf **защища́ться**) сов возв to defend o.s.; (студент) to defend one's thesis; **защи́тник** (-а) м (также Спорт) defender; (Юр) defence counsel (Brit), defense attorney (US); **ле́вый/ пра́вый защи́тник** (футбол) left/right back

защи́тный прил protective; **защи́тный цвет** khaki

защища́|ть (-ю) несов от **защити́ть** ▷ перех (Юр) to defend; **защища́ться** несов от **защити́ться**

за|яви́ть (-явлю́, -я́вишь; impf **заявля́ть**) сов перех (протест) to make ▷ неперех: **заяви́ть о** +prp to announce; **заявля́ть** (perf **заяви́ть**) **на кого́-н в мили́цию** to report sb to the police; **зая́в|ка** (-ки; gen pl -ок) ж: **зая́вка (на** +acc) application (for); **заявле́ни|е** (-я) ср (правительства) statement; (просьба): **заявле́ние (о** +prp) application (for)

заявля́|ть (-ю) несов от **заяви́ть**

за́|яц (-йца) м (Зоол) hare

зва́ни|е (-я) ср (воинское) rank; (учёное, почётное) title

звать (зову́, зовёшь; perf **позва́ть**) несов перех to call; (приглашать) to ask; (no perf: называть) to call; **звать кого́-н кем-н** to call sb sth; **как Вас зову́т?** what is your name?; **меня́/его́ зову́т Алекса́ндр** my/his name is Alexander; **звать** (perf **позва́ть**) **кого́-н в го́сти/в кино́** to ask sb over/to the cinema

звезд|а́ (-ы́; nom pl **звёзды**) ж star

звен|о́ (-а́; nom pl -ья, gen pl -ьев) ср link; (конструкции) section

звери́ный прил (wild) animal

зве́рский прил (поступок) brutal; **зве́рств|овать** (-ую) несов to commit atrocities

звер|ь (-я; gen pl -е́й) м (wild) animal, beast

звон|и́ть (-ю́, -и́шь; perf **позвони́ть**) несов to ring; (Тел): **звони́ть кому́** to ring или phone или call (US) sb

звон|о́к (-ка́; nom pl -ки́) м bell; (звук) ring; (по телефону) (telephone) call

звук (-а) м sound

звуков|о́й прил sound, audio; **звукова́я доро́жка** track (on audio tape); **звукова́я аппарату́ра** hi-fi equipment

звукоза́пис|ь (-и) ж sound recording

звуч|а́ть (3sg -и́т) несов (гитара) to sound; (гнев) to be heard

зда́ни|е (-я) ср building

здесь нареч here

здоро́ва|ться (-юсь; perf **поздоро́ваться**) несов: **здоро́ваться с** +instr to say hello to

здо́рово нареч (разг: отлично) really well ▷ как сказ (разг) it's great

здоро́в|ый прил healthy; (перен: идея) sound; (разг: большой) hefty; **бу́дьте здоро́вы!** (при прощании) take care!; (при чихании) bless you!

здоро́вь|е (-я) ср health; **как Ва́ше здоро́вье?** how are you keeping?; **за Ва́ше здоро́вье!** (to) your good health!; **на здоро́вье!** enjoy it!

здравомы́слящий прил sensible

здравоохране́ни|е (-я) ср health care; **министе́рство здравоохране́ния** ≈ Department of Health

здра́вств|овать (-ую) несов to thrive; **здра́вствуйте** hello; **да здра́вствует...!** long live ...!

здра́вый прил sound

зе́бр|а (-ы) ж zebra; (переход) zebra crossing (Brit), crosswalk (US)

зева́|ть (-ю) несов to yawn ▷ (perf **прозева́ть**) перех (разг) to miss out

зевн|у́ть (-у́, -ёшь) сов to yawn

зелене́|ть (-ю; perf **позелене́ть**) несов to go или turn green; **зелён|ый** прил green; **зе́лен|ь** (-и) ж (цвет) green ▷ собир (растительность) greenery; (овощи и травы) greens мн

земе́льный прил land; **земе́льный наде́л** или **уча́сток** plot of land

землевладе́л|ец (-ьца) м landowner

земледе́ли|е (-я) ср arable farming

земледе́льческий прил (район) agricultural; (машины) farming

землетрясе́ни|е (-я) ср earthquake

зем|ля́ (-ли́; acc sg -лю, nom pl -ли, gen pl -е́ль) ж land; (поверхность) ground; (почва) earth, soil; (планета): **Земля́** Earth

земляни́к|а (-и) ж (растение) wild strawberry (plant) ▷ собир (ягоды) wild strawberries мн

земно́й прил (поверхность, кора) earth's; (перен: желания) earthly; **земно́й шар** the globe

зе́рк|ало (-ала; nom pl -ала́, gen pl -а́л, dat pl -ала́м) ср mirror

зерн|о́ (-а́; nom pl зёрна, gen pl зёрен) ср (пшеницы) grain; (кофе) bean; (мака) seed ▷ собир (семенное, на хлеб) grain

зигза́г (-а) м zigzag

зим|а́ (-ы́; acc sg -у, dat sg -е́, nom pl -ы) ж winter; **зи́мний** прил (день) winter's; (погода) wintry; (лес, одежда) winter; **зим|ова́ть** (-у́ю; perf **прозимова́ть**) несов (человек) to spend the winter; (птицы) to winter; **зимо́й** нареч in the winter

зл|ить (-ю, -ишь; perf **разозли́ть**) несов перех to annoy; **зли́ться** (perf

разозли́ться) *несов возв* to get angry

зл|о (**-а**; *gen pl* **зол**) *ср* evil; (*неприятность*) harm ▷ *нареч* (*посмотре́ть, сказа́ть*) spitefully; **со зла** out of spite; **меня́ зло берёт** (*разг*) it makes me angry; **у меня́ на неё зла не хвата́ет** (*разг*) she annoys me no end

зло́бный *прил* mean; (*улыбка*) evil; (*го́лос*) nasty

злободне́вный *прил* topical

злове́щий *прил* sinister

злоде́й (**-я**) *м* villain

злоде́йский *прил* wicked

злой *прил* evil; (*собака*) vicious; (*глаза́, лицо́*) mean; (*карикату́ра*) scathing; **я зол на тебя́** I'm angry with you

злока́чественный *прил* malignant

зло́стный *прил* malicious

злоупотреб|и́ть (**-лю́, -и́шь**; *impf* **злоупотребля́ть**) *сов* +*instr* to abuse; (*дове́рием*) to breach; **злоупотребле́ни|е** (**-я**) *ср* (*обычно мн: преступле́ние*) malpractice *ед*; **злоупотребле́ние нарко́тиками** drug abuse; **злоупотребле́ние дове́рием** breach of confidence

змей|ный *прил* (*ко́жа*) snake; **змей|ный яд** venom

зме|й (**-я**; *gen pl* **-ев**) *м* serpent; (*также* **возду́шный змей**) kite

зм|ея́ (**-ей**; *nom pl* **-е́и**, *gen pl* **-е́й**) *ж* snake

знак (**-а**) *м* sign, symbol; (*Комп*) character; **в знак** +*gen* as a token of; **под зна́ком** +*gen* in an atmosphere of; **знак ра́венства** equals sign; **зна́ки зодиа́ка** signs of the Zodiac

знако́м|ить (**-лю, -ишь**; *perf* **познако́мить**) *несов перех*: **знако́мить кого́-н с** +*instr* to introduce sb to; **знако́миться** (*perf* **познако́миться**) *несов возв*: **знако́миться с** +*instr* (*с челове́ком*) to meet ▷ (*perf* **ознако́миться**) to study; **знако́мств|о** (**-а**) *ср* acquaintance; **знако́м|ый** *прил*: **знако́мый (с** +*instr*) familiar (with) ▷ (**-ого**) *м* acquaintance

знамена́тельный *прил* momentous

знамени́тый *прил* famous

зна́м|я (**-ени**; *как* **вре́мя**; *см* *Table 4*) *ср* banner

зна́ни|е (**-я**) *ср* knowledge *то́лько ед*; **со зна́нием де́ла** expertly

зна́тный *прил* (*род, челове́к*) noble

зна|ть (**-ю**) *несов перех* to know; **как зна́ешь** as you wish; **ну, зна́ешь!** well I never!

значе́ни|е (**-я**) *ср* (*слова́, взгля́да*) meaning; (*побе́ды*) importance

зна́чит *вводн сл* (*разг*) so ▷ *союз* (*сле́довательно*) that means

значи́тельный *прил* significant; (*вид, взгляд*) meaningful

зна́ч|ить (**-у, -ишь**) *несов* (*не*)*перех*

to mean; **зна́читься** *несов возв* (*состоя́ть*) to appear

значо́к (**-ка́**) *м* badge; (*поме́тка*) mark

зна́ющий *прил* knowledgeable

зноб|и́ть (*3sg* **-и́т**) *несов безл*: **его́ зноби́т** he's shivery

зно|й (**-я**) *м* intense heat

зов (**-а**) *м* call

зову́ *итп* *несов см* **звать**

зодиа́к (**-а**) *м* zodiac

зол|а́ (**-ы́**) *ж* cinders *мн*

золо́в|ка (**-ки**; *gen pl* **-ок**) *ж* sister-in-law, husband's sister

зо́лот|о (**-а**) *ср* gold; **золото́й** *прил* gold, golden; (*перен: челове́к, вре́мя*) wonderful

зо́н|а (**-ы**) *ж* zone; (*лесна́я*) area; (*для заключённых*) prison camp

зона́льный *прил* (*грани́ца, деле́ние*) zone; (*ме́стный*) regional

зонд (**-а**) *м* probe

зонт (**-а́**) *м* (*от дождя́*) umbrella; (*от со́лнца*) parasol

зо́нтик (**-а**) *м* = **зонт**

зооло́ги|я (**-и**) *ж* zoology

зоомагази́н (**-а**) *м* pet shop

зоопа́рк (**-а**) *м* zoo

зрач|о́к (**-ка́**) *м* (*Анат*) pupil

зре́лищ|е (**-а**) *ср* sight; (*представле́ние*) show

зре́лый *прил* mature; (*плод*) ripe

зре́ни|е (**-я**) *ср* (eye)sight

зре|ть (**-ю**; *perf* **созре́ть**) *несов* to mature; (*плод*) to ripen

зри́мый *прил* visible

зри́тел|ь (**-я**) *м* (*в теа́тре, в кино́*) member of the audience; (*на стадио́не*) spectator; (*наблюда́тель*) onlooker; **зри́тельный** *прил* (*па́мять*) visual; **зри́тельный зал** auditorium

зря *нареч* (*разг: без по́льзы*) for nothing, in vain; **зря тра́тить** (*perf* **потра́тить**) **де́ньги/вре́мя** to waste money/time; **зря ты ему́ э́то сказа́л** you shouldn't have told him about it

зуб (**-а**; *nom pl* **-ы**, *gen pl* **-о́в**) *м* tooth ▷ (*мн* teeth, *nom pl* **-ья**, *gen pl* **-ьев**) (*пилы́*) tooth (*мн* teeth); (*гра́бель, ви́лки*) prong

зубн|о́й *прил* dental; **зубна́я щётка** toothbrush; **зубно́й врач** dentist

зуд (**-а**) *м* itch

зы́бкий *прил* shaky

зыб|ь (**-и**) *ж* ripple

зят|ь (**-я**) *м* (*муж до́чери*) son-in-law; (*муж сестры́*) brother-in-law

И

идио́т (-а) м idiot

идти́ (см *Table 18*) несов to go; (*пешком*) to walk; (*годы*) to go by; (*фильм*) to be on; (*часы*) to work; (*подходить: одежда*): **идти́ к** +dat to go with; **иди́ сюда́!** come here!; **иду́!** (I'm) coming!; **идёт по́езд/авто́бус** the train/bus is coming; **идёт дождь/снег** it's raining/snowing; **дела́ иду́т хорошо́/пло́хо** things are going well/badly; **Вам идёт э́та шля́па** the hat suits you; **идти́** (*perf* **пойти́**) **пешко́м** to walk, go on foot

○ **КЛЮЧЕВОЕ СЛОВО**

из предл +gen **1** (*о направлении*) out of; **он вы́шел из ко́мнаты** he went out of the room

2 (*об источнике*) from; **све́дения из кни́ги** information from a book; **я из Москвы́** I am from Moscow

3 (*при выделении части из целого*) of; **вот оди́н из приме́ров** here is one of the examples

4 (*о материале*) made of; **э́тот стол сде́лан из сосны́** this table is made of pine; **ва́за из стекла́** a glass vase; **варе́нье из я́блок** apple jam

5 (*о причине*) out of; **из осторо́жности/за́висти** out of wariness/envy; **из эконо́мии** in order to save money

6 (*во фразах*): **из го́да в год** year in, year out; **я бежа́л изо всех сил** I ran at top speed

изба́ (-ы́; *nom pl* -ы) ж hut

изба́в|ить (-лю, -ишь; *impf* **избавля́ть**) сов перех: **изба́вить кого́-н от** +gen (*от проблем*) to free sb from; (*от врагов*) to deliver sb from; **изба́виться** (*impf* **избавля́ться**) сов возв: **изба́виться от** +gen to get rid of; (*от страха*) to get over

избега́|ть (-ю) несов от **избежа́ть** ▷ *неперех*: **избега́ть чего́-н** /+infin to avoid sth/doing

избежа́ть (как **бежа́ть**; см *Table 20*; *impf* **избега́ть**) сов +gen to avoid

избива́|ть (-ю) несов от **изби́ть**

избира́тел|ь (-я) м voter; **избира́тельн|ый** прил (*система*) electoral; **избира́тельная кампа́ния** election campaign; **избира́тельный уча́сток** polling station; **избира́тельный бюллете́нь** ballot paper

избира́|ть (-ю) несов от **избра́ть**

изби́ть (-обью́, -обьёшь; *impf* **избива́ть**) сов перех to beat up

и́збранный прил (*рассказы*) selected; (*люди, круг*) select

избра́ть (-еру́, -ерёшь; *pt* -ра́л, -рала́, -ра́ло, *impf* **избира́ть**) сов перех (*профессию*) to choose; (*президента*) to elect

избы́т|ок (-ка) м (*излишек*) surplus; (*обилие*) excess; **избы́точный** прил (*вес*) excess

○ **КЛЮЧЕВОЕ СЛОВО**

и союз **1** and; **я и мой друг** my friend and I; **и вот показа́лся лес** and then a forest came into sight

2 (*тоже*): **и он пошёл в теа́тр** he went to the theatre too; **и он не пришёл** he didn't come either

3 (*даже*) even; **и сам не рад** even he himself is not pleased

4 (*именно*): **о том и речь!** that's just it!

5 (*во фразах*): **ну и нагле́ц же ты!** what a cheek you have!; **туда́ и сюда́** here and there; **и ... и ...** both ... and ...

и́в|а (-ы) ж willow

иглоука́лывани|е (-я) ср acupuncture

иго́л|ка (-ки; *gen pl* -ок) ж = **игла́**

иго́рный прил: **иго́рный дом** gaming club

игр|а́ (-ы́; *nom pl* -ы) ж game; (*на скрипке итп*) playing; (*актёра*) performance; **игра́ слов** play on words; **игра́льн|ый** прил: **игра́льные ка́рты** playing cards мн; **игра́|ть** (-ю) несов to play ▷ (*perf* **сыгра́ть**) перех to play; (*пьесу*) to perform; **игра́ть** (*perf* **сыгра́ть**) **в** +асс (*Спорт*) to play

игри́стый прил sparkling

игро́|к (-ка́) м player

игру́шечный прил toy

игру́ш|ка (-ки; *gen pl* -ек) ж toy; **ёлочные игру́шки** Christmas tree decorations

идеа́льный прил ideal

идём несов см **идти́**

идеоло́ги|я (-и) ж ideology

идёшь etc несов см **идти́**

иде́|я (-и) ж idea; **по иде́е** (*разг*) supposedly

идио́м|а (-ы) ж idiom

изверже́ни|е (-я) *ср* eruption

изве́сти|е (-я) *ср* news; *см также* **изве́стия**

изве|сти́ть (-щу́, -сти́шь; *impf* **извеща́ть**) *сов перех*: **извести́ть кого́-н о** *+prp* to inform sb of

изве́сти|я (-й) *мн* (*издание*) bulletin *ед*

изве́стно *как сказ* **изве́стно, что ... it is** well known that ...; **мне э́то изве́стно I** know about it; **наско́лько мне изве́стно as** far as I know; **как изве́стно as is well** known; **изве́стность (-и)** *ж* fame; **ста́вить** (*perf* **поста́вить**) **кого́-н в изве́стность** to inform sb; **изве́стный** *прил* famous, well-known; (*разг: лентяй*) notorious; (*условия*) certain

и́звест|ь (-и) *ж* lime

извеща́|ть (-ю) *несов от* **извести́ть**

извива́|ться (-юсь) *несов возв* (*змея*) to slither; (*человек*) to writhe

извине́ни|е (-я) *ср* apology; (*оправдание*) excuse; **извини́|ть** (-ю́, -и́шь; *impf* **извиня́ть**) (*простить*) *сов перех*: **извини́ть что-н (кому́-н)** to excuse (sb for) sth; **извини́те!** excuse me!; **извини́те, Вы не ска́жете, где вокза́л?** excuse me, could you tell me where the station is?; **извини́ться** (*impf* **извиня́ться**) *сов возв*: **извини́ться (за** +*acc*) to apologize (for)

извл|е́чь (-еку́, -ечёшь *итп*, -еку́т; *pt* -ёк, -екла́, -екло́, *impf* **извлека́ть**) *сов перех* to remove; (*осколок*) to remove; (*перен: пользу*) to derive

изги́б (-а) *м* bend

изгиба́|ть(ся) (-ю(сь)) *несов от* **изогну́ть(ся)**

изгна́ни|е (-я) *ср* (*ссылка*) exile; **изг|на́ть** (-оню́, -о́нишь; *pt* -на́л, -нала́, -на́ло, *impf* **изгоня́ть**) *сов перех* to drive out; (*сослать*) to exile

и́згород|ь (-и) *ж* fence; **жива́я и́згородь** hedge

изгото́в|ить (-лю, -ишь; *impf* **изготовля́ть**) *сов перех* to manufacture

изда|ва́ть (-ю́, -ёшь) *несов от* **изда́ть**

издалека́ *нареч* from a long way off

и́здали *нареч* = **издалека́**

изда́ни|е (-я) *ср* publication; (*изданная вещь*) edition; **изда́тел|ь** (-я) *м* publisher; **изда́тельств|о** (-а) *ср* publisher, publishing house; **изда́ть** (*как* **дать**; *см* Table 16; *impf* **издава́ть**) *сов перех* (*книгу*) to publish; (*закон*) to issue; (*стон*) to let out

издева́тельств|о (-а) *ср* mockery; (*жестокое*) abuse; **издева́|ться** (-юсь) *несов возв*: **издева́ться над** +*instr* (*над подчинёнными*) to make a mockery of; (*над чьей-л одеждой*) to mock, ridicule

изде́ли|е (-я) *ср* (*товар*) product, article

изде́рж|ки (-ек) *мн* expenses; **суде́бные изде́ржки** legal costs

из-за *предл* (+*gen: занавески*) from behind; (*угла*) from around; (*по вине*) because of; **из-за того́ что** because

излага́|ть (-ю) *несов от* **изложи́ть**

излече́ни|е (-я) *ср* (*выздоровление*) recovery

изл|ечи́ться (-ечу́сь, -е́чишься; *impf* **изле́чиваться**) *сов возв*: **излечи́ться от** +*gen* to be cured of

изли́ш|ек (-ка) *м* (*остаток*) remainder; (+*gen: веса*) excess of

изли́шний *прил* unnecessary

изложе́ни|е (-я) *ср* presentation; **изл|ожи́ть** (-ожу́, -о́жишь; *impf* **излага́ть**) *сов перех* (*события*) to recount; (*просьбу*) to state

излуче́ни|е (-я) *ср* radiation

изме́н|а (-ы) *ж* (*родине*) treason; (*другу*) betrayal; **супру́жеская изме́на** adultery; **измене́ни|е** (-я) *ср* change; (*поправка*) alteration; **изм|ени́ть** (-еню́, -е́нишь; *impf* **изменя́ть**) *сов перех* to change ⊳ *неперех* (+*dat: родине, другу*) to betray; (*супругу*) to be unfaithful to; (*память*) to fail; **измени́ться** (*impf* **изменя́ться**) *сов возв* to change; **изме́нник** (-а) *м* traitor

изме́р|ить (-ю, -ишь) *сов от* **ме́рить** ⊳ (*impf* **измеря́ть**) *перех* to measure

изму́ч|ить (-у, -ишь) *сов от* **му́чить**

изм|я́ть (-омну́, -омнёшь) *сов от* **мять**

изна́нк|а (-и) *ж* (*одежды*) inside; (*ткани*) wrong side

изнаси́лование (-я) *ср* rape

изнаси́л|овать (-ую) *сов от* **наси́ловать**

изна́шива|ть(ся) (-ю(сь)) *несов от* **износи́ть(ся)**

изнемога́|ть (-ю) *несов от* **изнемо́чь**

изнеможе́ни|е (-я) *ср* exhaustion

изнем|о́чь (-огу́, -о́жешь *итп*, -о́гут; *pt* -о́г, -огла́, -огло́, *impf* **изнемога́ть**) to be exhausted

изно́с (-а) *м* (*механизмов*) wear

изн|оси́ть (-ошу́, -о́сишь; *impf* **изна́шивать**) *сов перех* to wear out; **износи́ться** (*impf* **изна́шиваться**) *сов возв* to wear out

изнур|и́ть (-ю́, -и́шь; *impf* **изнуря́ть**) *сов перех* to exhaust

изнутри́ *нареч* from inside

изо *предл* = **из**

изобража́|ть (-ю) *несов от* **изобрази́ть**

изобрази́тельный *прил* descriptive; **изобрази́тельное иску́сство** fine art

изобра|зи́ть (-жу́, -зи́шь; *impf* **изобража́ть**) *сов перех* to depict, portray

изобр|ести́ (-ету́, -етёшь; *pt* -ёл, -ела́, *impf* **изобрета́ть**) *сов перех* to invent; **изобрета́тел|ь** (-я) *м* inventor; **изобрете́ни|е** (-я) *ср* invention

изогн|у́ть (-у́, -ёшь; *impf* **изгиба́ть**) *сов перех* to bend; **изогну́ться** (*impf* **изгиба́ться**) *сов возв* to bend

изоля́ци|я (-и) *ж* (*см глаг*) isolation; cutting off; insulation

изощрённый *прил* sophisticated

из-под *предл* +*gen* from under(neath); (*около*) from outside; **ба́нка из-под варе́нья** jam jar

Изра́ил|ь (-я) *м* Israel

израильтя́н|ин (-ина; *nom pl* -е) *м* Israeli

изра́ильский *прил* Israeli

и́зредка *нареч* now and then

изрече́ни|е (-я) *ср* saying

изуве́ч|ить (-у, -ишь; *impf* **изуве́чивать**) *сов перех* to maim

изуми́тельный *прил* marvellous (*Brit*), marvelous (*US*), wonderful

изум|и́ть (-лю́, -и́шь; *impf* **изумля́ть**) *сов перех* to amaze, astound; **изуми́ться** (*impf* **изумля́ться**) *сов возв* to be amazed *или* astounded; **изумле́ни|е** (-я) *ср* amazement

изумру́д (-а) *м* emerald

изуча́|ть (-ю) *несов от* **изучи́ть** ▷ *перех* (*о процессе*) to study

изуче́ни|е (-я) *ср* study

из|учи́ть (-учу́, -у́чишь; *impf* **изуча́ть**) *сов перех* (*язык, предмет*) to learn; (*понять*) to get to know; (*исследовать*) to study

изъяв|и́ть (-явлю́, -я́вишь; *impf* **изъявля́ть**) *сов перех* to indicate

изъя́н (-а) *м* defect

изъя́|ть (изыму́, изы́мешь; *impf* **изыма́ть**) *сов перех* to withdraw

изы́сканный *прил* refined, sophisticated

изю́м (-а) *м собир* raisins *мн*

изя́щный *прил* elegant

ика́|ть (-ю) *несов* to hiccup

ико́н|а (-ы) *ж* (*Рел*) icon

икр|а́ (-ы́) *ж* (*чёрная, красная*) caviar(e) ▷ (*nom pl* -ы) (*Анат*) calf (*мн* calves)

ИЛ (-а) *м сокр* самолёт констру́кции С.В. Илью́шина

и́ли *союз* or; **и́ли ... и́ли ...** either ... or ...

иллюстра́ци|я (-и) *ж* illustration

иллюстри́р|овать (-ую; *perf* **иллюстри́ровать** *или* **проиллюстри́ровать**) *несов перех* to illustrate

им *мест см* **он**; **оно́**; **они́**

им. *сокр* = **и́мени**

и́мени *etc сущ см* **и́мя**

име́ни|е (-я) *ср* estate

имени́нник (-а) *м person celebrating his name day or birthday*

имени́тельный *прил* (*Линг*): **имени́тельный паде́ж** the nominative (case)

и́менно *част* exactly, precisely ▷ *союз* (*перед перечислением*): **а и́менно** namely; **вот и́менно!** exactly!, precisely!

име́|ть (-ю) *несов перех* to have; **име́ть** (*impf*) **ме́сто** to take place; **име́ть** (*impf*) **де́ло с** +*instr* to deal with; **име́ть** (*impf*) **в виду́** to bear in mind; (*подразумевать*) to mean; **име́ться** *несов возв* (*сведения*) to be available

и́ми *мест см* **они́**

иммигра́нт (-а) *м* immigrant

иммиграцио́нный *прил* immigration

иммигра́ци|я (-и) *ж* immigration

иммигри́р|овать (-ую) (*не*)*сов* to immigrate

иммуните́т (-а) *м* (*Мед: перен*): **иммуните́т (к** +*dat*) immunity (to)

импера́тор (-а) *м* emperor

импе́ри|я (-и) *ж* empire

и́мпорт (-а) *м* (*ввоз*) importation; **импорти́р|овать** (-ую) (*не*)*сов перех* to import; **и́мпортный** *прил* imported

импровизи́р|овать (-ую; *perf* **импровизи́ровать** *или* **сымпровизи́ровать**) (*не*)*сов перех* to improvise

и́мпульс (-а) *м* impulse

иму́ществ|о (-а) *ср* property; (*принадлежности*) belongings *мн*

и́м|я (-ени; *как время*; *см* Table 4) *ср* (*также перен*) name; (*также* **ли́чное и́мя**) first *или* Christian name; **во и́мя** +*gen* (*ради*) in the name of; **на и́мя** +*gen* (*письмо*) addressed to; **от и́мени** +*gen* on behalf of; **и́мя по́льзователя** user name, login

ина́че *нареч* (*по-другому*) differently ▷ *союз* otherwise, or else

инвали́д (-а) *м* person with a disability; **инвали́дный** *прил*: **инвали́дная коля́ска** wheelchair; **инвали́дный дом** home for people with disabilities; **инвали́дност|ь** (-и) *ж* disability; **получа́ть** (*perf* **получи́ть**) **инвали́дность** to be registered as having a disability

инвалю́т|а (-ы) *ж сокр* (= **иностра́нная валю́та**) foreign currency

инвести́р|овать (-ую) (*не*)*сов* (*не*)*перех* (*Экон*) to invest; **инвести́ци|я** (-и) *ж* investment

инде́|ец (-йца) *м* Native American, North American Indian

инде́|йка (-йки; *gen pl* -ек) *ж* turkey

и́ндекс (-а) *м* (*цен, книг*) index (*мн* indexes); (*также* **почто́вый и́ндекс**) post (*Brit*) *или* zip (*US*) code

индивидуа́льный *прил* individual

инди́|ец (-йца) *м* Indian

инди́йский *прил* Indian; **Инди́йский океа́н** the Indian Ocean

И́нди|я (-и) *ж* India

индустриа́льный *прил* industrial

индустри́|я (-и) *ж* industry

инжене́р (-а) *м* engineer

инициа́л|ы (-ов) *мн* initials

инициати́в|а (-ы) *ж* initiative

инициати́в|ный *прил* enterprising; **инициати́вная гру́ппа** ≈ pressure group

инкасса́тор (-а) *м* security guard (*employed to collect and deliver money*)

иногда́ *нареч* sometimes

иногоро́дн|ий *прил* from another town ▷ (-его) *м person from another town*

ин|о́й *прил* different ▷ *мест (некоторый)* some (people); **ины́ми слова́ми** in other words; **не что ино́е, как ..., не кто ино́й, как ...** none other than ...

иномáр|ка (-ки; *gen pl* -ок) *ж* foreign car

инопланетя́н|ин (-ина; *nom pl* -е) *м* alien

иноро́дн|ый *прил* alien; **иноро́дное те́ло** (*Мед*) foreign body

иностра́н|ец (-ца) *м* foreigner; **иностра́нный** *прил* foreign; **Министе́рство иностра́нных дел** Ministry of Foreign Affairs, ≈ Foreign Office (*Brit*), ≈ State Department (*US*)

инспекти́р|овать (-ую; *perf* **проинспекти́ровать**) *несов перех* to inspect

инспе́ктор (-а) *м* inspector

инспе́кци|я (-и) *ж* inspection

инста́нци|я (-и) *ж* authority

инсти́нкт (-а) *м* instinct

институ́т (-а) *м* institute

инструкти́р|овать (-ую; *perf* **проинструкти́ровать**) (*не)сов перех* to instruct

инстру́кци|я (-и) *ж* instructions *мн*; (*также* **инстру́кция по эксплуата́ции**) instructions (for use)

инструме́нт (-а) *м* instrument

инсули́н (-а) *м* insulin

инсу́льт (-а) *м* (*Мед*) stroke

инсцени́р|овать (-ую) (*не)сов перех* (*роман*) to adapt

интелле́кт (-а) *м* intellect

интеллектуа́л (-а) *м* intellectual

интеллектуа́льный *прил* intellectual

интеллиге́нт (-а) *м* member of the intelligentsia; **интеллиге́нтный** *прил* cultured and educated; **интеллиге́нци|я** (-и) *ж собир* the intelligentsia

интенси́вный *прил* intensive; (*окраска*) intense

интерва́л (-а) *м* interval

интервью́ *ср нескл* interview

интервью́|ировать (-ую; *perf* **проинтервью́ировать**) (*не)сов перех* to interview

интере́с (-а) *м*: **интере́с (к** +*dat*) interest (in)

интере́сно *нареч*: **он о́чень интере́сно расска́зывает** he is very interesting to listen to ▷ *как сказ*: **интере́сно(, что ...)** it's interesting (that ...); **мне э́то о́чень интере́сно** I find it very interesting; **интере́сно, где он э́то нашёл** I wonder where he found that

интере́сный *прил* interesting; (*внешность, женщина*) attractive

интерес|ова́ть (-у́ю) *несов перех* to interest; **интересова́ться** *несов возв*: **интересова́ться** +*instr* to be interested in; (*осведомля́ться*) to inquire after; **он интересова́лся, когда́ ты приезжа́ешь** he was asking when you would be arriving

интерна́т (-а) *м* boarding school

интернациона́льный *прил* international

Интерне́т (-а) *м* internet

интерпрета́ци|я (-и) *ж* interpretation

интерье́р (-а) *м* (*здания*) interior

инти́мный *прил* intimate

интуи́ци|я (-и) *ж* intuition

Интури́ст (-а) *м сокр* (= **Гла́вное управле́ние по иностра́нному тури́зму**) Russian tourist agency dealing with foreign tourism

интури́ст (-а) *м сокр* = **иностра́нный тури́ст**

инфа́ркт (-а) *м* (*также* **инфа́ркт миока́рда**) heart attack

инфекцио́нный *прил* infectious

инфе́кци|я (-и) *ж* infection

инфинити́в (-а) *м* infinitive

информацио́нн|ый *прил* information; **информацио́нная програ́мма** news programme (*Brit*) *или* program (*US*)

информа́ци|я (-и) *ж* information

информи́р|овать (-ую; *perf* **информи́ровать** *или* **проинформи́ровать**) *несов перех* to inform

инфраструкту́р|а (-ы) *ж* infrastructure

инциде́нт (-а) *м* incident

инъе́кци|я (-и) *ж* injection

инъя́з (-а) *м сокр* (= **факульте́т иностра́нных языко́в**) modern languages department

и.о. *сокр* (= **исполня́ющий обя́занности**) acting

Иорда́ни|я (-и) *ж* Jordan

ипоте́к|а (-и) *ж* (*Комм*) mortgage

ипоте́чн|ый *прил* mortgage; **ипоте́чная ссу́да** mortgage; **ипоте́чный банк** ≈ building society

ипподро́м (-а) *м* racecourse (*Brit*), racetrack (*US*)

Ира́к (-а) *м* Iraq

Ира́н (-а) *м* Iran

и́рис (-а) *м* (*Бот*) iris

ирла́нд|ец (-ца) *м* Irishman

Ирла́нди|я (-и) *ж* Ireland

ирла́нд|ка (-ки; *gen pl* -ок) *ж* Irishwoman

иронизи́р|овать (-ую) *несов*: **иронизи́ровать (над** +*instr*) to be ironic (about)

иро́ни|я (-и) *ж* irony

иск (-а) *м* lawsuit; **предъявля́ть** (*perf* **предъяви́ть**) **кому́-н иск** to take legal action against sb

искажа́|ть(ся) (-ю(сь)) *несов от* **искази́ть(ся)**

иска́ть (ищу́, и́щешь) *несов перех* to look *или* search for

исключе́ни|е (-я) *ср* (*из списка*) exclusion; (*из институ́та*) expulsion; (*отклоне́ние*) exception; **за исключе́нием** +*gen* with the exception of; **де́лать** (*perf* сде́лать) что-н в ви́де исключе́ния to make an exception of sth

исключи́тельный *прил* exceptional

исключ|и́ть (-у́, -и́шь; *impf* **исключа́ть**) *сов перех* (*из списка*) to exclude; (*из института*) to expel; (*ошибку*) to exclude the possibility of; **э́то исключено́** that is out of the question

исконный *прил* (*население, язык*) native, original; (*право*) intrinsic

ископа́ем|ое (-ого) *ср* fossil; (*также* **поле́зное ископа́емое**) mineral

искорен|и́ть (-ю́, -и́шь; *impf* **искореня́ть**) *сов перех* to eradicate

и́скр|а (-ы) *ж* spark

и́скренне *нареч* sincerely; **и́скренне Ваш** Yours sincerely

и́скренний *прил* sincere

искрив|и́ть (-лю́, -и́шь; *impf* **искривля́ть**) *сов перех* to bend

искупа́|ть(ся) (-ю(сь)) *сов от* **купа́ть(ся)**

иск|упи́ть (-уплю́, -у́пишь; *impf* **искупа́ть**) *сов перех* to atone for

иску́сный *прил* (*работник*) skilful (*Brit*), skillful (*US*); (*работа*) fine

иску́сственный *прил* artificial; (*ткань*) synthetic; (*мех*) fake

иску́сств|о (-а) *ср* art

искуша́|ть (-ю) *несов перех* to tempt

искуше́ни|е (-я) *ср* temptation

исла́м (-а) *м* Islam; **исла́мский** *прил* Islamic

Исла́нди|я (-и) *ж* Iceland

испа́н|ец (-ца) *м* Spaniard

Испа́ни|я (-и) *ж* Spain

испа́чка|ть(ся) (-ю(сь)) *сов от* **па́чкать(ся)**

испове́д|овать (-ую) *несов перех* (*религию, идею*) to profess ▷ *(не)сов перех* (*Рел*): **испове́довать кого́-н** to hear sb's confession; **испове́доваться** *(не)сов возв*: **испове́доваться кому́-н** *или* **у кого́-н** to confess to sb

и́споведь (-и) *ж* confession

исполко́м (-а) *м сокр* (= **исполни́тельный комите́т**) executive committee

исполне́ни|е (-я) *ср* (*приказа*) execution; (*обещания*) fulfilment (*Brit*), fulfillment (*US*); (*роли*) performance

исполни́тельный *прил* (*власть*) executive; (*работник*) efficient

испо́лн|ить (-ю, -ишь; *impf* **исполня́ть**) *сов перех* (*приказ*) to carry out; (*обещание*) to fulfil (*Brit*), fulfill (*US*); (*роль*) to perform; **испо́лниться** (*impf* **исполня́ться**) *сов возв* (*желание*) to be fulfilled; **ему́ испо́лнилось 10 лет** he is 10

испо́льзовани|е (-я) *ср* use

испо́льз|овать (-ую) *(не)сов перех* to use

испра́в|ить (-лю, -ишь; *impf* **исправля́ть**) *сов перех* (*повреждение*) to repair; (*ошибку*) to correct; (*характер*) to improve; **испра́виться** (*impf*

исправля́ться) *сов возв* (*человек*) to change (for the better)

испра́вный *прил* (*механизм*) in good working order

испу́г (-а) *м* fright; **в испу́ге, с испу́гу** *или* with fright

испу́ганный *прил* frightened

испуга́|ть(ся) (-ю(сь)) *сов от* **пуга́ть(ся)**

испыта́тельный *прил*: **испыта́тельный срок** trial period, probation

испыта́|ть (-ю; *impf* **испы́тывать**) *сов перех* (*механизм*) to test; (*нужду, радость*) to experience

иссле́довани|е (-я) *ср* (*см глаг*) research; examination; (*научный труд*) study; **иссле́довательск|ий** *прил*: **иссле́довательская рабо́та** research; **иссле́довательский институ́т** research institute; **иссле́д|овать** (-ую) *(не)сов перех* to research; (*больно́го*) to examine

исся́к|нуть (*3sg* -нет, *pt* -, -ла, *impf* **иссяка́ть**) *сов* (*запасы*) to run dry; (*перен*: *терпение*) to run out

истека́|ть (-ю) *несов от* **исте́чь**

исте́рик|а (-и) *ж* hysterics *мн*

ист|е́чь (*3sg* -ечёт, *pt* -ёк, -екла́, -екло́, *impf* **истека́ть**) *сов* (*срок*) to expire; (*время*) to run out

и́стинный *прил* true

исто́к (-а) *м* (*реки*) source

исто́рик (-а) *м* historian

истори́ческий *прил* historical; (*важный*) historic; **истори́ческий факульте́т** history department

исто́ри|я (-и) *ж* (*наука*) history; (*рассказ*) story

исто́чник (-а) *м* (*водный*) spring; (*сил*) source

истоще́ни|е (-я) *ср* exhaustion

истра́|тить (-чу, -тишь) *сов от* **тра́тить**

истреби́тель (-я) *м* (*самолёт*) fighter (plane); (*лётчик*) fighter pilot

истреб|и́ть (-лю́, -и́шь; *impf* **истребля́ть**) *сов перех* to destroy; (*крыс*) to exterminate

исхо́д (-а) *м* outcome

исх|оди́ть (-ожу́, -о́дишь) *несов*: **исходи́ть из** +*gen* (*сведения*) to originate from; (*основываться*) to be based on; **исходя́ из** +*gen* *или* **от** +*gen* on the basis of

исхо́дный *прил* primary

исходя́щий *прил* outgoing; **исходя́щий но́мер** (*Админ*) reference number

исче́з|нуть (-ну, -нешь; *pt* -, -ла, *impf* **исчеза́ть**) *сов* to disappear

исче́рпа|ть (-ю; *impf* **исче́рпывать**) *сов перех* to exhaust

исчисля́|ться (*3pl* -ются) *несов возв* +*instr* to amount to

ита́к *союз* thus, hence

Ита́ли|я (-и) *ж* Italy

италья́н|ец (-ца) *м* Italian; **италья́нский** *прил* Italian; **италья́нский язы́к** Italian

и т.д. *сокр* (= *и так да́лее*) etc. (= *et cetera*)

ито́г (**-а**) *м* (*работы итп*) result; (*общая сумма*) total; **в ито́ге** (*при подсчёте*) in total; **в (коне́чном) ито́ге** in the end; **подводи́ть** (*perf* **подвести́**) **ито́ги** to sum up

итого́ *нареч* in total, altogether

ито́говый *прил* (*сумма*) total

и т.п. *сокр* (= *и тому́ подо́бное*) etc. (= *et cetera*)

иудаи́зм (**-а**) *м* Judaism

их *мест см* **они́** ▷ *притяж мест* their

и́хн|ий *притяж мест* (*разг*) their; **по и́хнему** (in) their way

ищу́ *итп несов см* **иска́ть**

ию́л|ь (**-я**) *м* July

ию́н|ь (**-я**) *м* June

Й

йо́г|а (**-и**) *ж* yoga

йо́гурт (**-а**) *м* yoghurt

йод (**-а**) *м* íodine

K

к *предл +dat* **1** (*о направлении*) towards; **я пошёл к дому** I went towards the house; **звать** (*perf* **позвать**) **кого-н к телефону** to call sb to the phone; **мы поехали к друзьям** we went to see friends; **поставь лестницу к стене** put the ladder against the wall
2 (*о добавлении, включении*) to); **эта бабочка относится к очень редкому виду** this butterfly belongs to a very rare species
3 (*об отношении*) of; **любовь к музыке** love of music; **он привык к хорошей еде** he is used to good food; **к моему удивлению** to my surprise
4 (*назначение*) with; **приправы к мясу** seasonings for meat

кабан (**-а́**) *м* (*дикий*) wild boar
кабачо́к (**-ка́**) *м* (*телефонная*) marrow (*Brit*), squash (*US*)
ка́бель (**-я**) *м* cable
каби́на (**-ы**) *ж* (*телефонная*) booth; (*грузовика*) cab; (*самолёта*) cockpit; (*лифта*) cage
кабине́т (**-а**) *м* (*в доме*) study; (*на работе*) office; (*школьный*) classroom; (*врача*) surgery (*Brit*), office (*US*); (*Полит. также* **кабине́т мини́стров**) cabinet
каблу́к (**-а́**) *м* heel
Кавка́з (**-а**) *м* Caucasus
кавка́з|ец (**-ца**) *м* Caucasian
кавы́ч|ки (**-ек**; *dat pl* **-кам**) *мн* inverted commas, quotation marks
кадр (**-а**) *м* (*Фото, Кино*) shot
ка́др|ы (**-ов**) *мн* (*работники*) personnel *ед*, staff *ед*
ка́ждый *прил* each, every
каза́|к (**-ака́**; *nom pl* **-аки́**) *м* Cossack
каза́рм|а (**-ы**) *ж* barracks *мн*

ка|за́ться (**-жу́сь, -жешься**; *perf* **показа́ться**) *несов возв +instr* to look, seem; (**мне**) **ка́жется, что ...** it seems (to me) that ...
каза́чий *прил* Cossack
казино́ *ср нескл* casino
казн|а́ (**-ы́**) *ж* treasury
казн|и́ть (**-ю́, -и́шь**) (*не*)*сов перех* to execute
казн|ь (**-и**) *ж* execution
ка|йма́ (**-ймы́**; *nom pl* **-ймы́**, *gen pl* **-ём**) *ж* hem

как *местоимённое нареч*
1 (*вопросительное*) how; **как Вы себя чу́вствуете?** how do you feel?; **как дела?** how are things?; **как тебя́ зову́т?** what's your name?
2 (*относительное*): **я сде́лал, как ты проси́л** I did as you asked; **я не зна́ю, как э́то могло́ случи́ться** I don't know how that could have happened
3 (*насколько*): **как бы́стро/давно́** how quickly/long ago
4 (*до какой степени*): **как краси́во!** how beautiful!; **как жаль!** what a pity *или* shame!
5 (*выража́ет возмуще́ние*) what
▷ *союз* **1** (*подобно*) as; **мя́гкий, как ва́та** as soft as cotton wool; **как мо́жно скоре́е/гро́мче** as soon/loud as possible; **он оде́т, как бродя́га** he is dressed like a tramp
2 (*в качестве*) as
3 (*о временны́х отноше́ниях*: *о бу́дущем, об одновре́менности*) when; (: *о прошлом*) since; **как зако́нчишь, позвони́ мне** phone (*Brit*) *или* call (*US*) me when you finish; **прошло́ два го́да, как она́ исче́зла** two years have passed since she disappeared
4: **как бу́дто, как бы** as if; **он согласи́лся как бы не́хотя** he agreed as if unwillingly; **как же** of course; **как говоря́т** *или* **говори́тся** as it were; **как ни** however; **как ника́к** after all; **как раз во́время/то, что на́до** just in time/what we need; **это пла́тье/пальто́ мне как раз** this dress/coat is just my size; **как ..., так и ...** both ... and ...; **как то́лько** as soon as

кака́о *ср нескл* cocoa
ка́к-либо *нареч* = **ка́к-нибудь**
ка́к-нибудь *нареч* (*так или иначе*) somehow; (*когда-нибудь*) sometime

как|о́й (**-а́я, -о́е, -и́е**) *мест*
1 (*вопросительное*) what; **како́й тебе́ нра́вится цвет?** what colour do you like?
2 (*относительное*) which; **скажи́, кака́я кни́га интере́снее** tell me which book is more interesting

3 (*выражает оценку*) what; **какой подлец!** what a rascal!

4 (*разг: неопределённое*) any; **нет ли каких вопросов?** are there any questions?

5 (*во фразах*): **ни в какую** not for anything; **каким образом** in what way

какой-либо *мест* = **какой-нибудь**

как|ой-нибудь *мест* (*тот или иной*) any; (*приблизительно*) some; **он ищет какой-нибудь работы** he's looking for any kind of work

как-никак *нареч* after all

как|ой-то *мест*: **Вам како́е-то письмо** there's a letter for you; (*напоминающий*): **она какая-то стра́нная сего́дня** she is acting kind of oddly today

ка́к-то *мест* (*каким-то образом*) somehow; (*в некоторой степени*) somewhat; (*разг: раз*): **ка́к-то (раз)** once

КА́КТУС (**-а**) *м* cactus (*мн* cacti)

кале́к|а (**-и**) *м/ж* person with a disability

календа́р|ь (**-я́**) *м* calendar

кале́ч|ить (**-у, -ишь**) *perf* **покале́чить** *или* **искале́чить**) *несов перех* to cripple; (*мина*) to maim

кали́бр (**-а**) *м* calibre (*Brit*), caliber (*US*)

кали́т|ка (**-ки**; *gen pl* **-ок**) *ж* gate

кало́ри|я (**-и**) *ж* calorie

калькуля́тор (**-а**) *м* calculator

ка́льци|й (**-я**) *м* calcium

камене́|ть (**-ю**) *несов от* **окамене́ть**

ка́менный *прил* stone

ка́м|ень (**-ня**; *gen pl* **-не́й**) *м* stone

ка́мер|а (**-ы**) *ж* (*тюре́мная*) cell; (*также* **телека́мера, кинока́мера**) camera; **ка́мера хране́ния** (*на вокзале*) left-luggage office (*Brit*), checkroom (*US*); (*в музее*) cloakroom

ка́мерн|ый *прил*: **ка́мерная му́зыка** chamber music

ками́н (**-а**) *м* fireplace

кампа́ни|я (**-и**) *ж* campaign

камы́ш (**-á**) *м* rushes *мн*

кана́в|а (**-ы**) *ж* ditch

Кана́д|а (**-ы**) *ж* Canada

кана́л (**-а**) *м* canal; (*Связь, Тел*) channel

канализацио́нн|ый *прил*: **канализацио́нная труба́** sewer pipe

кана́т (**-а**) *м* cable; **кана́тн|ый** *прил*: **кана́тная доро́га** cable car

кандида́т (**-а**) *м* candidate; (*Просвещ*): **кандида́т нау́к** ≈ Doctor

кани́кул|ы (**-**) *мн* holidays *мн* (*Brit*), vacation *ед* (*US*)

кани́стр|а (**-ы**) *ж* jerry can

кано́э *ср нескл* canoe

кану́н (**-а**) *м* eve; **в кану́н** +*gen* on the eve of

канцеля́ри|я (**-и**) *ж* office; **канцеля́рский** *прил* office

ка́па|ть (**-ю**) *несов* (*вода*) to drip ▷ (*perf* **нака́пать**) *перех*: **ка́пать что-н** (*микстуру*) to pour sth out drop by drop

капе́лл|а (**-ы**) *ж* (*Муз*) choir

ка́пельниц|а (**-ы**) *ж* (*Мед*) drip

капита́л (**-а**) *м* (*Комм*) capital; **капитали́зм** (**-а**) *м* capitalism; **капиталисти́ческий** *прил* capitalist

капита́льный *прил* (*Экон, Комм*) capital; (*сооружение, труд*) main; (*ремонт, покупка*) major

капита́н (**-а**) *м* captain

капка́н (**-а**) *м* trap

ка́п|ля (**-ли**; *gen pl* **-ель**) *ж* (*также перен*) drop

капо́т (**-а**) *м* (*Авт*) bonnet (*Brit*), hood (*US*)

капри́знича|ть (**-ю**) *несов* to behave capriciously

капро́н (**-а**) *м* synthetic thread

ка́псул|а (**-ы**) *ж* capsule

капу́ст|а (**-ы**) *ж* cabbage; **цветна́я капу́ста** cauliflower

капюшо́н (**-а**) *м* hood

кара́бка|ться (**-юсь**; *perf* **вскара́бкаться**) *несов возв*: **кара́бкаться на** +*acc* (*человек*) to clamber up

караме́л|ь (**-и**) *ж собир* (*леденцы*) caramels *мн*

каранда́ш (**-á**; *gen pl* **-е́й**) *м* pencil

каранти́н (**-а**) *м* quarantine

кара́|ть (**-ю**; *perf* **покара́ть**) *несов перех* to punish

карау́л (**-а**) *м* guard

карау́л|ить (**-ю, -ишь**) *несов перех* to guard

карбюра́тор (**-а**) *м* carburettor (*Brit*), carburetor (*US*)

ка́рий *прил* (*глаза*) hazel

карка́с (**-а**) *м* framework (*of building*)

ка́рлик (**-а**) *м* person of small stature

карма́н (**-а**) *м* pocket

карнава́л (**-а**) *м* carnival

карни́з (*для штор*) curtain rail

ка́рт|а (**-ы**) *ж* (*Гео*) map; (*также* **игра́льная ка́рта**) (playing) card; **магни́тная ка́рта** (swipe)card; **ка́рта па́мяти** memory card

карти́н|а (**-ы**) *ж* picture

карти́н|ка (**-ки**; *gen pl* **-ок**) *ж* (*иллюстрация*) picture (*in book etc*)

карто́н (**-а**) *м* (*бумага*) cardboard

картоте́к|а (**-и**) *ж* card index

карто́фелин|а (**-ы**) *ж* potato (*мн* potatoes); **карто́фел|ь** (**-я**) *м* (*плод*) potatoes *мн*; **карто́фельный** *прил* potato

ка́рточ|ка (**-ки**; *gen pl* **-ек**) *ж* card; (*также* **фотока́рточка**) photo

карто́ш|ка (**-ки**; *gen pl* **-ек**) *ж* (*разг*) = **карто́фелина**; **карто́фель**

ка́ртридж (**-а**) *м* (*Комп*) cartridge

карусе́л|ь (**-и**) *ж* merry-go-round (*Brit*), carousel (*US*)

карье́р|а (**-ы**) *ж* career

каса́|ться (**-юсь**; *perf* **косну́ться**) *несов возв* (+*gen*: *дотрагиваться*) to touch;

(*затрагивать*) to touch on; (*иметь отношение*) to concern; **это тебя не касается** it doesn't concern you; **что касается Вас, то ...** as far as you are concerned ...

ка́с|ка (-**ки**; *gen pl* -**ок**) *ж* helmet

каспи́йск|ий *прил*: **Каспи́йское мо́ре** Caspian Sea

ка́сс|а (-**ы**) *ж* (*Театр, Кино*) box office; (*железнодорожная*) ticket office; (*в магазине*) cash desk

кассе́т|а (-**ы**) *ж* (*магнитофонная*) cassette; (*Фото*) cartridge

касси́р (-**а**) *м* cashier

кастрю́л|я (-**и**) *ж* saucepan

катало́г (-**а**) *м* catalogue (*Brit*), catalog (*US*)

ката́р (-**а**) *м* catarrh

катастро́ф|а (-**ы**) *ж* disaster

ката́|ть (-**ю**) *несов перех* (*что-н круглое*) to roll; (*что-н на колёсах*) to wheel; **ката́ть** (*impf*) **кого́-н на маши́не** to take sb for a drive; **ката́ться** *несов возв*: **ката́ться на маши́не/велосипе́де** to go for a drive/cycle; **ката́ться** (*impf*) **на конька́х/ло́шади** to go skating/horse (*Brit*) *или* horseback (*US*) riding

катего́ри|я (-**и**) *ж* category

ка́тер (-**а**) *м* boat

ка|ти́ть (-**чу́**, -**тишь**) *несов перех* (*что-н круглое*) to roll; (*что-н на колёсах*) to wheel; **кати́ться** *несов возв* to roll; (*капли*) to run

като́лик (-**а**) *м* Catholic; **католи́ческий** *прил* Catholic

кафе́ *ср нескл* café

ка́федр|а (-**ы**) *ж* (*Просвещ*) department; (*Рел*) pulpit; **заве́дующий ка́федрой** chair

ка́фел|ь (-**я**) *м собир* tiles *мн*

кафете́ри|й (-**я**) *м* cafeteria

кача́|ть (-**ю**) *несов перех* (*колыбель*) to rock; (*нефть*) to pump; **кача́ть** (*impf*) **голово́й** to shake one's head; **кача́ться** *несов возв* to swing; (*на волнах*) to rock, roll

каче́л|и (-**ей**) *мн* swing *ед*

ка́честв|о (-**а**) *ср* quality ▷ *предл*: **в ка́честве** +*gen* as; **в ка́честве приме́ра** by way of example

ка́ш|а (-**и**) *ж* ≈ porridge

ка́ш|ель (-**ля**) *м* cough

ка́шля|ть (-**ю**) *несов* to cough

кашта́н (-**а**) *м* chestnut

каю́т|а (-**ы**) *ж* (*Мор*) cabin

ка́|яться (-**юсь**, -**ешься**; *perf* **пока́яться**) *несов возв*: **ка́яться** (**в чём-н пе́ред кем-н**) to confess (sth to sb) ▷ (*perf* **раска́яться**) (*грешник*) to repent

кв. *сокр* (= **квадра́тный**) sq. (= *square*); (= *квартира*) Apt. (= *apartment*)

квадра́т (-**а**) *м* square; **квадра́тный** *прил* square

квалифика́ци|я (-**и**) *ж* qualification; (*специальность*) profession

квалифици́рованный *прил* (*работник*) qualified; (*труд*) skilled

кварта́л (-**а**) *м* quarter

кварти́р|а (-**ы**) *ж* flat (*Brit*), apartment (*US*); (*снимаемое жильё*) lodgings *мн*; **квартира́нт** (-**а**) *м* lodger

квартпла́т|а (-**ы**) *ж сокр* (= *кварти́рная пла́та*) rent (*for a flat*)

квас (-**а**) *м* kvass (*malted drink*)

квита́нци|я (-**и**) *ж* receipt

кг *сокр* (= *килогра́мм*) kg (= *kilogram(me)*)

КГБ *м сокр* (*Ист*) (= *Комите́т госуда́рственной безопа́сности*) KGB

ке́д|ы (-**ов**) *мн* pumps *мн*

кекс (-**а**) *м* (fruit)cake

кем *мест см* **кто**

ке́мпинг (-**а**) *м* campsite

ке́п|ка (-**ки**; *gen pl* -**ок**) *ж* cap

кера́мик|а (-**и**) *ж собир* ceramics *мн*; **керами́ческий** *прил* ceramic

кефи́р (-**а**) *м* kefir (*yoghurt drink*)

кибербу́ллинг (-**а**) *м* cyberbullying

кива́|ть (-**ю**) *несов* +*dat* to nod to; **кивн|у́ть** (-**у́**, -**ёшь**) *сов*: **кивну́ть** (+*dat*) to nod (to)

кида́|ть (-**ю**) *несов от* **ки́нуть**; **кида́ться** *несов от* **ки́нуться** ▷ *возв*: **кида́ться камня́ми** to throw stones at each other

ки́ллер (-**а**) *м* (*мн hit man*) hit man

килогра́мм (-**а**) *м* kilogram(me)

киломе́тр (-**а**) *м* kilometre (*Brit*), kilometer (*US*)

кино́ *ср нескл* cinema; (*разг: фильм*) film, movie (*US*); **идти́** (*perf* **пойти́**) **в кино́** (*разг*) to go to the pictures (*Brit*) *или* movies (*US*); **киноактёр** (-**а**) *м* (film) actor; **киноактри́с|а** (-**ы**) *ж* (film) actress; **кинокарти́н|а** (-**ы**) *ж* film; **кинотеа́тр** (-**а**) *м* cinema; **кинофи́льм** (-**а**) *м* film

ки́н|уть (-**у**; *impf* **кида́ть**) *сов перех* (*камень*) to throw; (*взгляд*) to cast; (*друзей*) to desert; (*разг: обмануть*) to cheat; **ки́нуться** (*impf* **кида́ться**) *сов возв*: **ки́нуться на** +*acc* (*на врага*) to attack; (*на еду*) to fall upon

кио́ск (-**а**) *м* kiosk

ки́п|а (-**ы**) *ж* bundle

кипе́ни|е (-**я**) *ср* boiling; **кип|е́ть** (-**лю́**, -**и́шь**; *perf* **вскипе́ть**) *несов* (*вода*) to boil; (*страсти*) to run high

кипя|ти́ть (-**чу́**, -**ти́шь**; *perf* **вскипяти́ть**) *несов перех* to boil; **кипяти́ться** *несов возв* (*овощи*) to boil; **кипят|о́к** (-**ка́**) *м* boiling water; **кипячёный** *прил* boiled

кирпи́ч (-**а́**) *м* brick

кислоро́д (-**а**) *м* oxygen

кислот|а́ (-**ы́**; *nom pl* -**о́ты**) *ж* acid

ки́с|лый *прил* sour; **ки́слая капу́ста** sauerkraut

ки́с|нуть (-**ну**; *pt* -, -**ла**, *perf* **проки́снуть** *или* **ски́снуть**) *несов* to go off

кист|ь (-**и**) *ж* (*Анат*) hand; (*гроздь*:

рябины) cluster; (: винограда) bunch; (на скатерти итп) tassel; (художника, маляра) (paint)brush

кит (-а́) м whale

кита́|ец (-йца) м Chinese; **Кита́|й** (-я) м China; **кита́йский** прил Chinese; **кита́йский язы́к** Chinese

кише́чник (-а) м intestines мн

клавиату́р|а (-ы) ж keyboard

кла́виш|а (-и) ж key

клад (-а) м treasure

кла́дбищ|е (-а) ср cemetery

кладу́ etc несов см **класть**

клад|ь (-и) ж: **ручна́я кладь** hand luggage

клал etc несов см **класть**

кла́ня|ться (-юсь; perf поклони́ться) несов возв +dat to bow to

кла́пан (-а) м valve

класс (-а) м class; (комната) classroom

кла́ссик|а (-и) ж classics мн; **класси́ческий** прил (пример, работа) classic; (музыка, литература) classical

кла́ссный прил (Просвещ) class; (разг: хороший) cool

кла|сть (-ду́, -дёшь; pt -л, -ла, perf положи́ть) несов перех to put ▷ (perf сложи́ть) (фундамент) to lay

клева́|ть (-ю́ю) несов перех (подлеж: птица) to peck ▷ неперех (рыба) to bite

кле́|ить (-ю, -ишь; perf скле́ить) несов перех to glue; **кле́иться** несов возв to stick

кле|й (-я) м glue; **кле́йк|ий** прил sticky; **кле́йкая ле́нта** sticky tape

клейм|о́ (-а́; nom pl -а) ср stamp; (на скоте, на осуждённом) brand; **клеймо́ позо́ра** stigma

клён (-а) м maple (tree)

кле́т|ка (-ки; gen pl -ок) ж (для птиц, животных) cage; (на ткани) check; (на бумаге) square; (Био) cell; **ткань в кле́тку** checked material

кле́щ|и (-ей) мн tongs

клие́нт (-а) м client

кли́макс (-а) м (Био) menopause

кли́мат (-а) м (также перен) climate; **измене́ние кли́мата** climate change

клин (-а; nom pl -ья, gen pl -ьев) м wedge

кли́ник|а (-и) ж clinic

кли́пс|ы (-ов) мн clip-on earrings

кли́ч|ка (-ки; gen pl -ек) ж (кошки итп) name; (человека) nickname

клише́ ср нескл (перен) cliché

клони́р|овать (-ую) (не)сов перех to clone

клон|и́ть (-ю́, -ишь) несов: **его́ клони́ло ко сну** he was drifting off (to sleep); **к чему́ ты кло́нишь?** what are you getting или driving at?

кло́ун (-а) м clown

клоч|о́к (-ка́) м, уменьш от **клок**; (земли) plot; (бумаги) scrap

клуб (-а) м club ▷ (nom pl -ы́) (обычно мн: дыма, пыли) cloud

клуб|и́ться (3sg -и́тся) несов возв to swirl

клубни́к|а (-и) ж собир (ягоды) strawberries мн

клуб|о́к (-ка́) м (шерсти) ball

клюв (-а) м beak

клю́кв|а (-ы) ж собир (ягоды) cranberries мн

клю́н|уть (-у) сов перех to peck

ключ (-а́) (также перен) key; (родник) spring; (Муз): **басо́вый/скрипи́чный ключ** bass/treble clef; **га́ечный ключ** spanner; **ключево́й** прил (главный) key

клю́ш|ка (-ки; gen pl -ек) ж (Хоккей) hockey stick; (Гольф) club

кля|сться (-ну́сь, -нёшься; pt -лся, -ла́сь, perf покля́сться) несов возв to swear; **кля́сться (perf покля́сться) в чём-н** to swear sth

кля́тв|а (-ы) ж oath

км. сокр (= киломе́тр) km

кни́г|а (-и) ж book

кни́ж|ка (-ки; gen pl -ек) ж, уменьш от **кни́га**; (разг) book; **трудова́я кни́жка** employment record book; **че́ковая кни́жка** chequebook (Brit), checkbook (US)

кни́жный прил: **кни́жный магази́н** bookshop

книзу́ нареч downwards

кно́п|ка (-ки; gen pl -ок) ж (звонка) button; (канцелярская) drawing pin (Brit), thumbtack (US); (застёжка) press stud, popper (Brit)

КНР ж сокр (= Кита́йская Наро́дная Респу́блика) PRC (= People's Republic of China)

княз|ь (-я; nom pl -ья́, gen pl -е́й) м prince (in Russia)

ко предл = **к**

кобы́л|а (-ы) ж mare

кова́рный прил devious

ков|ёр (-ра́) м carpet

ко́врик (-а) м rug; (дверной) mat; (Комп) mouse mat

ковш (-а́) м ladle

ковыря́|ть (-ю) несов перех to dig up; **ковыря́ть** (impf) **в зуба́х/носу́** to pick one's teeth/nose

когда́ нареч when; **когда́ как** it depends

когда́-либо нареч = **когда́-нибудь**

когда́-нибудь нареч (в вопросе) ever; (в утверждении) some или one day; **Вы когда́-нибудь там бы́ли?** have you ever been there?; **я когда́-нибудь туда́ пое́ду** I'll go there some или one day

когда́-то нареч once

кого́ мест от **кто**

ко́г|оть (-тя; gen pl -те́й) м claw

код (-а) м code

ко́декс (-а) м code

ко́е-где нареч here and there

ко́е-как нареч (небрежно) any old how; (с трудом) somehow

ко́е-како́й (**ко́е-како́го**) *мест* some

ко́е-кто (**ко́е-кого́**) *мест* (*некоторые*) some (people)

ко́е-что (**ко́е-чего́**) *мест* (*нечто*) something; (*немногое*) a little

ко́ж|а (**-и**) *ж* skin; (*материал*) leather; **ко́жаный** *прил* leather

ко́жн|ый *прил*: **ко́жные боле́зни** skin diseases

кожур|а́ (**-ы́**) *ж* (*апельсина итп*) peel

коз|а́ (**-ы́**; *nom pl* **-ы**) *ж* (nanny) goat

коз|ёл (**-ла́**) *м* (billy) goat

Козеро́г (**-а**) *м* (*созвездие*) Capricorn

ко́йка (**-йки**; *gen pl* **-ек**) *ж* (*в казарме*) bunk; (*в больнице*) bed

кокаи́н (**-а**) *м* cocaine

коклю́ш (**-а**) *м* whooping cough

кокте́йл|ь (**-я**) *м* cocktail

кол (**-а́**; *nom pl* **-ья**) *м* stake

колбас|а́ (**-ы́**) *ж* sausage

колго́т|ки (**-ок**) *мн* tights *мн* (*Brit*), pantihose *мн* (*US*)

колд|ова́ть (**-у́ю**) *несов* to practise (*Brit*) *или* practice (*US*) witchcraft

кол|еба́ть (**-е́блю, -е́блешь**) *несов перех* to rock, swing ▷ (*perf* **поколеба́ть**) (*авторитет*) to shake; **колеба́ться** *несов возв* (*Физ*) to oscillate; (*пламя итп*) to flicker; (*цены*) to fluctuate; (*сомневаться*) to waver

коле́н|о (**-а**; *nom pl* **-и**, *gen pl* **-ей**) *ср* knee

кол|есо́ (**-еса́**; *nom pl* **-ёса**) *ср* wheel

ко́личеств|о (**-а**) *ср* quantity

ко́лкост|ь (**-и**) *ж* (*насмешка*) biting remark

колле́г|а (**-и**) *м/ж* colleague

колле́ги|я (**-и**) *ж*: **адвока́тская колле́гия** ≈ the Bar; **редакцио́нная колле́гия** editorial board

колле́дж (**-а**) *м* college

коллекти́в (**-а**) *м* collective

коллекти́вный *прил* collective

коллекциони́р|овать (**-ую**) *несов перех* to collect

колле́кци|я (**-и**) *ж* collection

коло́д|а (**-ы**) *ж* (*бревно*) block; (*карт*) pack, deck

коло́д|ец (**-ца**) *м* well; (*в шахте*) shaft

ко́локол (**-а**; *nom pl* **-а́**) *м* bell

колоко́льчик (**-а**) *м* bell; (*Бот*) bluebell

коло́ни|я (**-и**) *ж* colony; **исправи́тельно-трудова́я коло́ния** penal colony

коло́н|ка (**-ки**; *gen pl* **-ок**) *ж* column; (*газовая*) water heater; (*для воды, для бензина*) pump

коло́нн|а (**-ы**) *ж* (*Архит*) column

колори́т (**-а**) *м* (*перен: эпохи*) colour (*Brit*), color (*US*); **колори́тный** *прил* colourful (*Brit*), colorful (*US*)

ко́л|ос (**-оса**; *nom pl* **-о́сья**, *gen pl* **-о́сьев**) *м* ear (of corn, wheat)

кол|оти́ть (**-очу́, -о́тишь**) *несов*: **колоти́ть по столу́/в дверь** to thump the table/on the door; **колоти́ться** *несов возв* (*сердце*) to thump

кол|о́ть (**-ю́, -ешь**; *perf* **расколо́ть**) *несов перех* (*дрова*) to chop (up); (*орехи*) to crack ▷ (*perf* **заколо́ть**) (*штыком итп*) to spear ▷ (*perf* **уколо́ть**) (*иголкой*) to prick; (*разг: делать укол*): **коло́ть кого́-н** to give sb an injection; **коло́ть** (*impf*) **кому́-н что-н** (*разг*) to inject sb with sth; **у меня́ ко́лет в боку́** I've got a stitch; **коло́ться** *несов возв* (*ёж, шипо́вник*) to be prickly; (*наркоман*) to be on drugs

колыбе́льн|ая (**-ой**) *ж* (*также* **колыбе́льная пе́сня**) lullaby

кольцев|о́й *прил* round, circular; **кольцева́я доро́га** ring road; **кольцева́я ли́ния** (*в метро*) circle line

кол|ьцо́ (**-ьца́**; *nom pl* **-ьца**, *gen pl* **-е́ц**) *ср* ring; (*в маршруте*) circle

колю́ч|ий *прил* (*куст*) prickly; **колю́чая про́волока** barbed wire; **колю́ч|ка** (**-ки**; *gen pl* **-ек**) *ж* thorn

коля́с|ка (**-ки**; *gen pl* **-ок**) *ж*: (*де́тская*) **коля́ска** pram (*Brit*), baby carriage (*US*); **инвали́дная коля́ска** wheelchair

ком *мест см* **кто** ▷ (**-а**; *nom pl* **-ья**, *gen pl* **-ьев**) *м* lump

кома́нд|а (**-ы**) *ж* command; (*судна*) crew; (*Спорт*) team

командиро́в|ка (**-ки**; *gen pl* **-ок**) *ж* (*короткая*) business trip; (*длительная*) secondment (*Brit*), posting

кома́ндовани|е (**-я**) *ср*: **кома́ндование** (+*instr*) (*судном, войском*) command (of) ▷ *собир* command

кома́нд|овать (**-ую**; *perf* **скома́ндовать**) *несов* to give orders; (+*instr*: *армией*) to command; (*мужем*) to order around

кома́р (**-а́**) *м* mosquito (*мн* mosquitoes)

комба́йн (**-а**) *м* (*С.-х.*) combine (harvester); **ку́хонный комба́йн** food processor

комбина́т (**-а**) *м* plant

комбина́ци|я (**-и**) *ж* combination; (*женское бельё*) slip

комбинезо́н (**-а**) *м* overalls *мн*; (*детский*) dungarees *мн*

комбини́р|овать (**-ую**; *perf* **скомбини́ровать**) *несов перех* to combine

коме́дийный *прил* comic; (*актёр*) comedy

коме́ди|я (**-и**) *ж* comedy

коме́т|а (**-ы**) *ж* comet

ко́мик (**-а**) *м* comedian, comic

комиссио́нный *прил*: **комиссио́нный магази́н** second-hand shop which sells goods on a commission basis

коми́сси|я (**-и**) *ж* commission

комите́т (**-а**) *м* committee

коммента́ри|й (**-я**) *м* commentary; **коммента́тор** (**-а**) *м* commentator; **комменти́р|овать** (**-ую**) (*не*)*сов перех* (*текст*) to comment on; (*матч*) to commentate on

коммерса́нт (-а) *м* businessman (*мн* businessmen)

комме́рческий *прил* commercial; **комме́рческое** **at** at symbol, @; **комме́рческий магази́н** privately-run shop

коммуна́льн|ый *прил* communal; **коммуна́льные платежи́** bills; **коммуна́льные услу́ги** utilities

● **Коммуна́льные услу́ги**

●
● The communal services include water
● supply, hot water and heating, public
● radio, rubbish collection and street
● sweeping, and building maintenance.
● All these are paid for on a standing
● charge basis. Electricity and telephone
● are the two services which are metered
● and hence paid for separately.

коммуни́зм (-а) *м* communism

коммуника́ци|я (-и) *ж* communication

коммуни́ст (-а) *м* communist

ко́мнат|а (-ы) *ж* room; **ко́мнатн|ый** *прил* indoor; **ко́мнатная температу́ра** room temperature; **ко́мнатное расте́ние** house plant

компа́кт-ди́ск (-а) *м* compact disc

компа́ктный *прил* compact

компа́ни|я (-и) *ж* (*Комм*) company; (*друзья*) group of friends

компаньо́н (-а) *м* (*Комм*) partner

компа́рти|я (-и) *ж сокр* (= **коммунисти́ческая па́ртия**) Communist Party

ко́мпас (-а) *м* compass

компенса́ци|я (-и) *ж* compensation; **компенси́р|овать** (-ую) (*не*)*сов перех*: **компенси́ровать** (**кому́-н**) to compensate (sb) for

компете́нтный *прил* (*человек*) competent; (*органы*) appropriate

ко́мплекс (-а) *м* complex; (*мер*) range

компле́кт (-а) *м* set; **комплект|ова́ть** (-у́ю; *perf* **укомплектова́ть**) *несов перех* to build up

комплиме́нт (-а) *м* compliment

компози́тор (-а) *м* composer

компоне́нт (-а) *м* component

компости́р|овать (-ую; *perf* **закомпости́ровать**) *сов перех* to punch *или* clip (*ticket*)

компромети́р|овать (-ую; *perf* **скомпромети́ровать**) *несов перех* to compromise

компроми́сс (-а) *м* compromise

компью́тер (-а) *м* computer

компью́терщик (-а) *м* (*разг*) computer specialist

кому́ *мест см* **кто**

комфо́рт (-а) *м* comfort;

комфорта́бельный *прил* comfortable

конве́йер (-а) *м* conveyor (belt)

конве́рси|я (-и) *ж* conversion

конве́рт (-а) *м* envelope

конверти́р|овать (-ую) (*не*)*сов перех* (*деньги*) to convert

конво́|й (-я) *м* escort

конгре́сс (-а) *м* (*съезд*) congress

конди́терский *прил* confectionery; **конди́терский магази́н** confectioner's

кондиционе́р (-а) *м* air conditioner

кон|ёк (-ька́) *м* (*обычно мн*: *Спорт*) skate; **ката́ться** (*impf*) **на конька́х** to skate; *см также* **коньки́**

кон|е́ц (-ца́) *м* end; **без конца́** endlessly; **в конце́ концо́в** in the end; **биле́т в оди́н коне́ц** single (*Brit*) *или* one-way ticket; **под коне́ц** towards the end

коне́чно *вводн сл* of course, certainly

коне́чност|ь (-и) *ж* (*Анат*) limb

коне́чный *прил* (*цель*, *итог*) final; (*станция*) last

конкре́тно *нареч* (*говорить*) specifically; (*именно*) actually

конкре́тный *прил* (*реальный*) concrete; (*факт*) actual

конкуре́нт (-а) *м* competitor; **конкурентоспосо́бный** *прил* competitive; **конкуре́нци|я** (-и) *ж* competition; **конкури́р|овать** (-ую) *несов*: **конкури́ровать с** +*instr* to compete with

ко́нкурс (-а) *м* competition

консе́нсус (-а) *м* consensus

консервати́вный *прил* conservative

консерва́тор (-а) *м* conservative

консервато́ри|я (-и) *ж* (*Муз*) conservatoire (*Brit*), conservatory (*US*)

консерви́р|овать (-ую) (*не*)*сов перех* to preserve; (*в жестяных банках*) to can

консе́рвн|ый *прил*: **консе́рвная ба́нка** can

консе́рв|ы (-ов) *мн* canned food *ед*

конспе́кт (-а) *м* notes *мн*; **конспекти́р|овать** (-ую; *perf* **законспекти́ровать**) *несов перех* to take notes on

конспира́ци|я (-и) *ж* conspiracy

конститу́ци|я (-и) *ж* constitution

констру́и́р|овать (-ую; *perf* **сконструи́ровать**) *несов перех* to construct

констру́ктор (-а) *м* designer; (*детская игра*) construction set; **констру́кторск|ий** *прил*: **констру́кторское бюро́** design studio; **констру́кци|я** (-и) *ж* construction

ко́нсул (-а) *м* consul; **ко́нсульств|о** (-а) *ср* consulate

консульта́нт (-а) *м* consultant; **консульта́ци|я** (-и) *ж* (*у врача*, *у юриста*) consultation; (*учреждение*) consultancy; **консульти́р|овать** (-ую; *perf* **проконсульти́ровать**) *несов перех*

to give professional advice to;
консульти́роваться (*impf*
проконсульти́роваться) *несов возв*:
консульти́роваться с кем-н to consult sb

конта́кт (-а) *м* contact; **конта́ктный**
прил (*линзы*) contact; **конта́ктный
телефо́н** contact number

конте́йнер (-а) *м* container

конте́кст (-а) *м* context

контине́нт (-а) *м* continent

конто́р|**а** (-ы) *ж* office; **конто́рский**
прил office

контраба́с (-а) *м* double bass

контра́кт (-а) *м* contract

контра́ктный *прил* contractual

контра́ст (-а) *м* contrast

контрацепти́в (-а) *м* contraceptive

контролёр (-а) *м* (*в поезде*) (ticket)
inspector; (*театральный*) ≈ usher;
(*сберкассы*) cashier; **контроли́р**|**овать**
(-ую) *несов перех* to control

контро́л|**ь** (-я) *м* (*наблюдение*)
monitoring; (*проверка*) testing, checking;
(*в транспорте*) ticket inspection; (*в
магазине*) checkout

контро́льн|**ая** (-ой) *ж* (*также*
контро́льная рабо́та) class test

контро́льн|**ый** *прил*: **контро́льная
коми́ссия** inspection team; **контро́льные
ци́фры** control figures

контрразве́дк|**а** (-и) *ж*
counterespionage

конур|**а́** (-ы́) *ж* (*собачья*) kennel

ко́нус (-а) *м* cone

конфере́нц-за́л (-а) *м* conference room

конфере́нци|**я** (-и) *ж* conference

конфе́т|**а** (-ы) *ж* sweet

конфиденциа́льный *прил* confidential

конфли́кт (-а) *м* (*военный*) conflict; (*в
семье, на работе*) tension;
конфликт|**ова́ть** (-у́ю) *несов*:
конфликтова́ть с +*instr* (*разг*) to be at
loggerheads with

конфо́р|**ка** (-ки; *gen pl* -**ок**) *ж* ring (on
cooker)

конфронта́ци|**я** (-и) *ж* confrontation

концентра́ци|**я** (-и) *ж* concentration

концентри́р|**овать** (-ую) *perf*
сконцентри́ровать) *несов перех* to
concentrate; **концентри́роваться** (*perf
сконцентри́роваться) *несов возв*
(*капитал*) to be concentrated; (*ученик*) to
concentrate

конце́пци|**я** (-и) *ж* concept

конце́рн (-а) *м* (*Экон*) concern

конце́рт (-а) *м* concert

концла́гер|**ь** (-я; *nom pl* -**я́**) *м*
(= **концентрацио́нный ла́герь**)
concentration camp

конча́|**ть(ся)** (-ю(сь)) *несов от*
ко́нчить(ся)

ко́нчик (-а) *м* tip (*of finger etc*)

ко́нч|**ить** (-у, -ишь; *impf* **конча́ть**) *сов
перех* to end; (*университет, книгу, работу*)

to finish; **ко́нчиться** (*impf* **конча́ться**)
сов возв (*разговор, книга*) to end, finish;
(*запасы*) to run out; (*лес итп*) to end

кон|**ь** (-я́; *nom pl* -**и**, *gen pl* -**е́й**) *м*
(*лошадь*) horse; (*Шахматы*) knight

конько́й (-о́в) *мн* skates *мн*

коньяк (-а́) *м* brandy, cognac

конъюнкту́р|**а** (-ы) *ж* (*Комм*) situation;
конъюнкту́ра ры́нка market conditions

коопера́тор (-а) *м member of private
enterprise*

коопера́ци|**я** (-и) *ж* cooperative
enterprise

координа́т|**а** (-ы) *ж* (*Геом*: *обычно мн*)
coordinate; (*разг*: *адрес*) number (and
address)

координи́р|**овать** (-ую) (*не*)*сов перех*
to coordinate

копа́|**ть** (-ю) *несов перех* (*землю*) to dig
▷ (*perf* **вы́копать**) (*колодец*) to sink;
(*овощи*) to dig up; **копа́ться** *несов возв*
(*в чужих вещах*) to snoop about; (*разг*:
возиться) to dawdle

копе́|**йка** (-йки; *gen pl* -**ек**) *ж* kopeck

копирова́льн|**ый** *прил*: **копирова́льная
маши́на** photocopying machine,
photocopier; **копирова́льная бума́га**
carbon paper

копи́р|**овать** (-ую; *perf* **скопи́ровать**)
несов перех to copy

коп|**и́ть** (-лю́, -ишь; *perf* **накопи́ть** *или*
скопи́ть) *перех* to save;
копи́ться (*perf* **накопи́ться** *или*
скопи́ться) *несов возв* to accumulate

ко́пи|**я** (-и) *ж* copy; (*перен*: *о человеке*)
spitting image

ко́поть (-и) *ж* layer of soot

коп|**ти́ть** (-чу́, -ти́шь) *несов* (*лампа*) to
give off soot ▷ (*perf* **закопти́ть**) *перех*
(*мясо, рыбу*) to smoke

копчёный *прил* smoked

копы́т|**о** (-а) *ср* hoof (*мн* hooves)

копь|**ё** (-я́; *nom pl* -**я**, *gen pl* -**ий**) *ср*
spear; (*Спорт*) javelin

кор|**а́** (-ы́) *ж* (*дерева*) bark; **земна́я кора́**
the earth's crust

кораблекруше́ни|**е** (-я) *ср* shipwreck

кора́бл|**ь** (-я́) *м* ship

кора́лл (-а) *м* coral

кордебале́т (-а) *м* corps de ballet

коренн|**о́й** *прил* (*население*) indigenous;
(*вопрос, реформы*) fundamental;
коренны́м о́бразом fundamentally;
коренно́й зуб molar

кореш|**о́к** (-ка́) *м* (*переплёта*) spine

Коре́|**я** (-и) *ж* Korea

корзи́н|**а** (-ы) *ж* basket

коридо́р (-а) *м* corridor

кори́ц|**а** (-ы) *ж* cinnamon

кори́чневый *прил* brown

ко́р|**ка** (-ки; *gen pl* -**ок**) *ж* (*апельсинная*)
peel

корм (-а; *nom pl* -**а́**) *м* (*для скота*) fodder,
feed; (*диких животных*) food

корма́ (-ы́) ж stern

корм|и́ть (-лю́, -ишь; perf **накорми́ть**) несов перех: корми́ть кого́-н чем-н to feed sb sth ▷ (perf **прокорми́ть**) (содержать) to feed, keep; **корми́ть** (impf) **гру́дью** to breast-feed; **корми́ться** (perf **прокорми́ться**) несов возв (животное) to feed; (человек): **корми́ться** +instr to survive

коро́б|ка (-ки; gen pl -ок) ж box; **коро́бка скоросте́й** gearbox

коро́в|а (-ы) ж cow

короле́в|а (-ы) ж queen

короле́вский прил royal

короле́вств|о (-а) ср kingdom

коро́л|ь (-я́) м king

коро́н|а (-ы) ж crown

коро́н|ка (-ки; gen pl -ок) ж (на зубе) crown

корон|ова́ть (-у́ю) (не)сов перех to crown

коро́тк|ий прил short; **коро́ткие во́лны** short wave; **коро́ткое замыка́ние** short circuit; **коро́тко** нареч briefly; (стричься) short ▷ как сказ: э́то пла́тье мне ко́ротко this dress is too short for me

коро́че сравн нареч: **коро́че говоря́** to put it briefly, in short

корпора́ци|я (-и) ж corporation

корректи́в (-а) м amendment

корректи́р|овать (-ую; perf **откорректи́ровать**) несов перех (ошибку) to correct

корреспонде́нт (-а) м correspondent; **корреспонде́нци|я** (-и) ж correspondence

коррумпи́рованный прил corrupt

корру́пци|я (-и) ж corruption

корт (-а) м (tennis) court

ко́рточ|ки (-ек) мн: присе́сть на ко́рточки to squat down; сиде́ть (impf) на ко́рточках to squat

ко́рч|иться (-усь, -ишься; perf **ско́рчиться**) несов возв (от боли) to double up

кор|ь (-и) ж measles мн

коси́л|ка (-ки; gen pl -ок) ж mower (machine)

ко|си́ть (-шу́, -сишь; perf **скоси́ть**) несов перех (газон, сено) to mow; (глаза) to slant

косме́тик|а (-и) ж make-up ▷ собир cosmetics мн

космети́ческий прил cosmetic; **космети́ческий кабине́т** beauty salon

космети́ч|ка (-ки; gen pl -ек) ж (специалистка) beautician; (сумочка) make-up bag

косми́ческ|ий прил space; **косми́ческое простра́нство** (outer) space

космона́вт (-а) м cosmonaut; (в США итп) astronaut

ко́смос (-а) м the cosmos, space

косн|у́ться (-у́сь, -ёшься) сов от **каса́ться**

ко́стный прил (Анат): **ко́стный мозг** (bone) marrow

ко́сточ|ка (-ки; gen pl -ек) ж (абрикосовая, вишнёвая) stone; (винограда) seed; (лимона) pip

косты́л|ь (-я́) м (инвалида) crutch (мн crutches)

кост|ь (-и; gen pl -е́й) ж bone

костю́м (-а) м outfit; (на сцене) costume; (пиджак и брюки/юбка) suit

костя́ш|ка (-ки; gen pl -ек) ж (пальцев) knuckle

косы́н|ка (-ки; gen pl -ок) ж (triangular) scarf

кот (-а́) м cat

кот|ёл (-ла́) м (паровой) boiler

котел|о́к (-ка́) м (кастрюля) billy(can); (шляпа) bowler (hat) (Brit), derby (US)

коте́льн|ая (-ой) ж boiler house

кот|ёнок (-ёнка; nom pl -я́та, gen pl -я́т) м kitten

ко́тик (-а) м (тюлень) fur seal

коти́р|оваться (-уюсь) несов возв (Комм): коти́роваться (в +acc) to be quoted (at); (также перен) to be highly valued

котле́т|а (-ы) ж rissole; (также **отбивна́я котле́та**) chop

⊙ **КЛЮЧЕВОЕ СЛОВО**

кото́р|ый (-ая, -ое, -ые) мест
1 (вопросительное) which; **кото́рый час?** what time is it?
2 (относительное: о предмете) which; (: о человеке) who; **же́нщина, кото́рую я люблю́** the woman I love
3 (не первый): **кото́рый день/год мы не ви́делись** we haven't seen each other for many days/years

ко́фе м нескл coffee; **ко́фе в зёрнах** coffee beans

кофе́йник (-а) м coffeepot

кофе́йный прил coffee

кофемо́л|ка (-ки; gen pl -ок) ж coffee grinder

ко́фт|а (-ы) ж blouse; (шерстяная) cardigan

коча́н (-а́) м: **коча́н капу́сты** cabbage

кочене́|ть (-ю; perf **окочене́ть**) несов (руки) to go stiff; (человек) to get stiff

коша́чий прил (мех, лапа) cat's

кошел|ёк (-ька́) м purse

ко́ш|ка (-ки; gen pl -ек) ж cat

кошма́р (-а) м nightmare

кошма́рный прил nightmarish

краб (-а) м crab

краево́й прил regional

кра́ж|а (-и) ж theft; **кра́жа со взло́мом** burglary

кра|й (-я; *loc sg* -ю́, *nom pl* -я́, *gen pl* -ёв) м edge; (*чашки, коробки*) rim; (*местность*) land; (*Полит*) край (*regional administrative unit*)

кра́йне *нареч* extremely

кра́йн|ий *прил* extreme; (*дом*) end; (*пункт маршрута*) last, final; **в кра́йнем слу́чае** as a last resort; **по кра́йней ме́ре** at least; **Кра́йний Се́вер** the Arctic; **кра́йний срок** (final) deadline

кран (-а) м tap, faucet (*US*); (*Строит*) crane

крапи́в|а (-ы) ж nettle

краси́вый *прил* beautiful; (*мужчина*) handsome; (*решение, фраза*) fine

краси́тел|ь (-я) м dye; **кра́|сить** (-шу, -сишь; *perf* **покра́сить**) *несов перех* to paint; (*волосы*) to dye ▷ (*perf* **накра́сить**) (*губы итп*) to make up; **кра́ситься** (*perf* **накра́ситься**) *несов возв* to wear make-up

кра́с|ка (-ки; *gen pl* -ок) ж paint; (*обычно мн: нежные, весенние итп*) colour (*Brit*), color (*US*)

красне́|ть (-ю; *perf* **покрасне́ть**) *несов* to turn red; (*от стыда*) to blush, flush; (*от гнева*) to go red

кра́сный *прил* red; **кра́сная ры́ба** salmon; **кра́сная строка́** new paragraph

крас|ота́ (-оты́; *nom pl* -о́ты) ж beauty

кра́сочный *прил* colourful (*Brit*), colorful (*US*)

кра|сть (-ду́, -дёшь; *perf* **укра́сть**) *несов перех* to steal; **кра́сться** *несов возв* (*человек*) to creep, steal

кра́тк|ий *прил* short; (*беседа*) brief; **кра́ткое прилага́тельное** short-form adjective

кратковре́менный *прил* short; **кратковре́менный дождь** shower

краткосро́чный *прил* short; (*заём, ссуда*) short-term

краудфа́ндинг (-а) м crowdfunding

крах (-а) м collapse

крахма́л (-а) м starch; **крахма́л|ить** (-ю, -ишь; *perf* **накрахма́лить**) *несов перех* to starch

креве́т|ка (-ки; *gen pl* -ок) ж shrimp

креди́т (-а) м credit; **креди́тный** *прил* credit; **креди́тная ка́рточка** credit card; **креди́тный счёт** credit account; **кредитоспосо́бный** *прил* solvent

крем (-а) м cream; **сапо́жный крем** shoe polish

кремл|ь (-я́) м citadel; **Кремль** the Kremlin

кре́мовый *прил* cream

креп|и́ть (-лю́, -и́шь) *несов перех* to fix

кре́п|кий *прил* strong; **кре́пко** *нареч* strongly; (*спать, любить*) deeply; (*завязать*) tightly

кре́п|нуть (-ну; *pt* -, -ла, *perf* **окре́пнуть**) *несов* to get stronger; (*уверенность*) to grow

кре́пост|ь (-и) ж (*Воен*) fortress

кре́сл|о (-ла; *gen pl* -ел) *ср* armchair; (*в театре*) seat

крест (-а́) м cross

кре|сти́ть (-щу́, -стишь; *perf* **окрести́ть**) *несов перех* to christen, baptize; **крести́ться** (не)сов возв to be christened *или* baptized; **крёстн|ый** *прил*: **крёстная мать** godmother; **крёстный оте́ц** godfather

крестья́н|ин (-ина; *nom pl* -е, *gen pl* -) м peasant; **крестья́нский** *прил* peasant

креще́ни|е (-я) *ср* christening, baptism; (*праздник*): **Креще́ние** ≈ the Epiphany

крив|о́й (-о́го, -о́й; *perf* **скриви́ть** *или* **покриви́ть**) *несов перех* to curve; (*лицо, губы*) to twist

кри́зис (-а) м crisis

крик (-а; *part gen* -у) м cry

кри́к|нуть (-у) *сов* to shout

кримина́л (-а) м crime; **кримина́лист** (-а) м specialist in crime detection; **криминальный** *прил* (*случай*) criminal; (*история, хроника*) crime

криста́лл (-а) м crystal

крите́ри|й (-я) м criterion (*мн* criteria)

кри́тик (-а) м critic; **кри́тик|а** (-и) ж criticism; **критик|ова́ть** (-у́ю) *несов перех* to criticize; **крити́ческий** *прил* critical

крич|а́ть (-у́, -и́шь) *несов* (*человек: от боли, от гнева*) to cry (out); (: *говорить громко*) to shout; **крича́ть** (*impf*) **на** +acc (*бранить*) to shout at

крова́т|ь (-и) ж bed

кро́в|ля (-ли; *gen pl* -ель) ж roof

кро́вный *прил* (*родство*) blood; **кро́вные интере́сы** vested interest *ед*; **кро́вный враг** deadly enemy

кровообраще́ни|е (-я) *ср* (*Мед*) circulation

кровопроли́тный *прил* bloody

кровоточ|и́ть (*3sg* -и́т) *несов* to bleed

кро́в|ь (-и; *loc sg* -и́) ж blood

кро|и́ть (-ю́, -и́шь) *несов перех* to cut out

крокоди́л (-а) м crocodile

кро́лик (-а) м rabbit; (*мех*) rabbit fur; **кро́личий** *прил* rabbit

кро́ме *предл* (+gen: *за исключением*) except; (*сверх чего-н*) as well as; **кро́ме того́** besides

кро́н|а (-ы) ж (*дерева*) crown

кроншт́е́йн (-а) м (*балкона*) support; (*полки*) bracket

кропотли́вый *прил* painstaking

кроссво́рд (-а) м crossword

кроссо́в|ка (-ки; *gen pl* -ок) ж (*обычно мн*) trainer

кро́хотный *прил* tiny

крош|и́ть (-у́, -ишь) *несов перех* (*хлеб*) to crumble; **кроши́ться** *несов возв* (*хлеб, мел*) to crumble

кро́ш|ка (-ки; *gen pl* -ек) ж (*кусочек*) crumb; (*ребёнок*) little one

круг (-а; *nom pl* -и́) м circle; (*Спорт*) lap ▷ (*loc sg* -у́) (*перен: знакомых*) circle; (: *обязанностей, интересов*) range

круглосу́точный *прил* (*работа*) round-the-clock; (*магазин*) twenty-four-hour

кру́гл|ый *прил* round; (*дурак*) total; **кру́глый год** all year (round); **кру́глые су́тки** twenty-four hours

круговоро́т (-а) м cycle

кругозо́р (-а) м: **он челове́к широ́кого кругозо́ра** he is knowledgeable

круго́м *нареч* around

кругосве́тный *прил* round-the-world

кружевно́й *прил* lace; **кру́жев|о** (-а; *nom pl* -а́) *ср* lace

круж|и́ть (-у́, -ишь) *несов перех* to spin ▷ *неперех* (*птица*) to circle; **кружи́ться** *несов возв* (*в танце*) to spin (around); **у меня́ голова́ кру́жится** my head's spinning

кру́ж|ка (-ки; *gen pl* -ек) ж mug

круж|о́к (-ка́) м circle; (*организация*) club

круи́з (-а) м cruise

круп|а́ (-ы́; *nom pl* -ы) ж grain

кру́пный *прил* (*размеры, фирма*) large; (*песок, соль*) coarse; (*учёный, дело*) prominent; (*событие, успех*) major; **кру́пный план** close-up

кру|ти́ть (-чу́, -тишь) *несов перех* (*руль*) to turn ▷ (*perf* **скрути́ть**) (*руки*) to twist; **крути́ться** *несов возв* (*вертеться*) to turn around; (: *колесо*) to spin; (: *дети*) to fidget

круто́й *прил* steep; (*перемены*) sharp; (*разг: хороший*) cool

крыжо́вник (-а) м *собир* (*ягоды*) gooseberries мн

крыл|о́ (-а́; *nom pl* -ья, *gen pl* -ьев) *ср* wing

крыльц|о́ (-а́) *ср* porch

Крым (-а; *loc sg* -у́) м Crimea

кры́с|а (-ы) ж rat

кры|ть (-о́ю, -о́ешь; *perf* **покры́ть**) *несов перех* to cover

кры́ш|а (-и) ж roof; (*разг: перен*) protection; **кры́ш|ка** (-ки; *gen pl* -ек) ж (*ящика, чайника*) lid

крю|к (-ка́; *nom pl* -чья, *gen pl* -чьев) м hook

крюч|о́к (-ка́) м hook; **крючо́к для вяза́ния** crochet hook

кряхт|е́ть (-чу́, -ти́шь) *несов* to groan

ксероко́пи|я (-и) ж photocopy, Xerox; **ксе́рокс** (-а) м photocopier; (*копия*) photocopy, Xerox

кста́ти *вводн сл* (*между прочим*) incidentally, by the way; (*случайно*) by any chance ▷ *нареч* (*сказать, прийти*) at the right time

КЛЮЧЕВОЕ СЛОВО

кто (кого́; см *Table 7*) *мест*
1 (*вопросительное, относительное*) who; **кто там?** who is there?

2 (*разг: кто-нибудь*) anyone; **е́сли кто позвони́т, позови́ меня́** if anyone phones, please call me

3: ма́ло ли кто many (people); **ма́ло кто** few (people); **ма́ло кто пошёл в кино́** only a few of us went to the cinema; **кто из вас ...** which of you ...; **кто (его́) зна́ет!** who knows!

кто́-либо (кого́-либо; *как кто*; см *Table 7*) *мест* = **кто́-нибудь**

кто́-нибудь (кого́-нибудь; *как кто*; см *Table 7*) *мест* (*в вопросе*) anybody, anyone; (*в утверждении*) somebody, someone

кто́-то (кого́-то; *как кто*; см *Table 7*) *мест* somebody, someone

куб (-а) м (*Геом, Мат*) cube

ку́бик (-а) м (*игрушка*) building brick *или* block

ку́б|ок (-ка) м (*Спорт*) cup

кубоме́тр (-а) м cubic metre (*Brit*) *или* meter (*US*)

кувши́н (-а) м jug (*Brit*), pitcher (*US*)

кувырка́|ться (-юсь) *несов возв* to somersault

куда́ *нареч* (*вопросительное, относительное*) where; **куда́ ты положи́л мою́ ру́чку?** where did you put my pen?; **скажи́, куда́ ты идёшь** tell me where you are going

куда́-либо *нареч* = **куда́-нибудь**

куда́-нибудь *нареч* (*в вопросе*) anywhere; (*в утверждении*) somewhere

куда́-то *нареч* somewhere

ку́др|и (-е́й) *мн* curls; **кудря́вый** *прил* (*волосы*) curly; (*человек*) curly-haired

кузне́чик (-а) м grasshopper

ку́зов (-а; *nom pl* -а́) м (*Авт*) back (*of van, lorry etc*)

кукаре́ка|ть (-ю) *несов* to crow

ку́к|ла (-лы; *gen pl* -ол) ж (*также перен*) doll; (*в театре*) puppet

ку́кольный *прил*: **ку́кольный теа́тр** puppet theatre (*Brit*) *или* theater (*US*)

кукуру́з|а (-ы) ж (*Бот*) maize; (*Кулин*) (sweet)corn

куку́ш|ка (-ки; *gen pl* -ек) ж cuckoo

кула́к (-а́) м fist

кул|ёк (-ька́) м paper bag

кулина́р (-а) м master chef

кулинари́|я (-и) ж cookery; (*магазин*) ≈ delicatessen

кули́с|а (-ы) ж (*Театр*) wing

кулуа́р|ы (-ов) *мн* (*Полит*) lobby *ед*

кульмина́ци|я (-и) ж (*перен*) high point, climax

культ (-а) м cult

культу́р|а (-ы) ж culture

культу́рный *прил* cultural; (*растение*) cultivated

куми́р (-а) м (*также перен*) idol

купа́льник (-а) м swimming *или* bathing costume (*Brit*), bathing suit (*US*);

купа́льный *прил*: купа́льный костю́м swimming *или* bathing costume (*Brit*), bathing suit (*US*)

купа́|ть (-ю; *perf* вы́купать *или* искупа́ть) *несов перех* to bath; купа́ться (*perf* вы́купаться *или* искупа́ться) *несов возв* to bathe; (*плавать*) to swim; (*в ванне*) to have a bath

купе́ *ср нескл* compartment (*in railway carriage*); купе́йный *прил*: купе́йный ваго́н Pullman (car)

купи́рованный *прил* = купе́йный

купи́|ть (-лю́, -ишь; *impf* покупа́ть) *сов перех* to buy

куплю́ *сов см* купи́ть

купо́н (-а) *м* (*ценных бумаг*) ticket; пода́рочный купо́н gift voucher

купю́р|а (-ы) *ж* (*Экон*) denomination; (*сокращение*) cut

куре́ни|е (-я) *ср* smoking; кури́льщик (-а) *м* smoker

кури́ный *прил* (*бульон*) chicken

кур|и́ть (-ю́, -ишь) *несов* (не)*перех* to smoke

ку́р|ица (-ицы; *nom pl* ку́ры) *ж* hen, chicken; (*мясо*) chicken

кур|о́к (-ка́) *м* hammer (*on gun*)

куро́рт (-а) *м* (holiday) resort

курс (-а) *м* course; (*Полит*) policy; (*Комм*) exchange rate; (*Просвещ*) year (*of university studies*); быть (*impf*) в ку́рсе (де́ла) to be well-informed; входи́ть (*perf* войти́) в курс чего́-н to bring o.s. up to date on sth; вводи́ть (*perf* ввести́) кого́-н в курс (чего́-н) to put sb in the picture (about sth)

курси́в (-а) *м* italics *мн*

курси́р|овать (-ую) *несов*: курси́ровать ме́жду +*instr* ... и +*instr* ... (*самолёт, автобус*) to shuttle between ... and ...; (*судно*) to sail between ... and ...

курсов|о́й *прил*: курсова́я рабо́та project; курсова́я ра́зница (*Комм*) difference in exchange rates

курсо́р (-а) *м* cursor

ку́рт|ка (-ки; *gen pl* -ок) *ж* jacket

ку́р|ы (-) *мн от* ку́рица

курье́р (-а) *м* messenger

куря́тин|а (-ы) *ж* chicken

куса́|ть (-ю) *несов перех* to bite; куса́ться *несов возв* (*животное*) to bite

кус|о́к (-ка́) *м* piece; кусо́к са́хара sugar lump; кусо́к мы́ла bar of soap

куст (-а́) *м* (*Бот*) bush

ку́та|ть (-ю; *perf* заку́тать) *несов перех* (*плечи*) to cover up; (*ребёнка*) to bundle up; ку́таться (*perf* заку́таться) *несов возв*: ку́таться в +*acc* to wrap o.s. up in

ку́х|ня (-ни; *gen pl* -онь) *ж* (*помещение*) kitchen; ру́сская ку́хня Russian cuisine; ку́хонный *прил* kitchen

ку́ч|а (-и) *ж* (*песка, листьев*) pile, heap; (+*gen*: *разг*: *денег, проблем*) heaps *или* loads of

ку́ша|ть (-ю; *perf* поку́шать *или* ску́шать) *несов перех* to eat

куше́т|ка (-ки; *gen pl* -ок) *ж* couch

кюве́т (-а) *м* ditch

Л

лаборант (-а) м lab(oratory) technician
лаборатори|я (-и) ж laboratory
ла́в|ка (-ки; gen pl -ок) ж (скамья) bench; (магазин) shop
лавро́вый прил: лавро́вый лист bay leaf
ла́гер|ь (-я) м camp
ла́дно част (разг) O.K., all right
ладо́н|ь (-и) ж palm
ла́зер (-а) м laser
ла́|зить (-жу, -зишь) несов to climb; (под стол) to crawl
ла́йнер (-а) м liner
лак (-а) м (для ногтей, для пола) varnish; лак для воло́с hairspray
ла́мп|а (-ы) ж lamp; (Тех) tube; ла́мпа дневно́го све́та fluorescent light
ла́мпо|чка (-ки; gen pl -ек) ж lamp; (для освещения) light bulb
ла́ндыш (-а) м lily of the valley
ла́п|а (-ы) ж (зверя) paw; (птицы) foot
лапто́п (-а) м laptop
лар|ёк (-ька́) м stall
ла́сковый прил affectionate
ла́сти|к (-а) м (разг) rubber (Brit), eraser
ла́сточ|ка (-ки; gen pl -ек) ж swallow
Ла́тви|я (-и) ж Latvia
лату́н|ь (-и) ж brass
латы́н|ь (-и) ж Latin
лауреа́т (-а) м winner (of award)
ла́цкан (-а) м lapel
ла́|ять (-ю; perf пролая́ть) несов to bark
лгать (лгу, лжёшь итп, лгут; perf солга́ть) несов to lie; **лгун** (-а́) м liar
ЛДПР ж сокр (= Либера́льно-демократи́ческая Па́ртия Росси́и) Liberal Democratic Party of Russia
ле́бед|ь (-я; gen pl -е́й) м swan
лев (льва) м lion; (созвездие): **Лев** Leo
левосторо́нний прил on the left
левш|а́ (-и́; gen pl -е́й) м/ж left-handed person
ле́вый прил left; (Полит) left-wing

лёг итп сов см **лечь**
леге́нд|а (-ы) ж legend
лёгк|ий прил (груз) light; (задача) easy; (боль, насморк) slight; (характер, человек) easy-going; **лёгкая атле́тика** athletics (Brit), track (US); **легко́** нареч easily ▷ как сказ: э́то легко́ it's easy
легкоатле́т (-а) м athlete (in track and field events)
легков|о́й прил: легкова́я маши́на, легково́й автомоби́ль car, automobile (US)
лёгк|ое (-ого) ср (обычно мн) lung
легкомы́сленный прил frivolous, flippant; (поступок) thoughtless; **легкомы́сли|е** (-я) ср frivolity
лёгкост|ь (-и) ж (задания) simplicity, easiness
ле́гче сравн прил от **лёгкий** ▷ сравн нареч от **легко́** ▷ как сказ: **больно́му сего́дня ле́гче** the patient is feeling better today
лёд (льда; loc sg льду́) м ice
леден|е́ц (-ца́) м fruit drop
ледяно́й прил (покров) ice; (вода, взгляд) icy
леж|а́ть (-у́, -и́шь) несов (человек, животное) to lie; (предмет, вещи) to be; **лежа́ть** (impf) **в больни́це** to be in hospital
лез etc несов см **лезть**
ле́зви|е (-я) ср blade
лез|ть (-у, -ешь; pt -, -ла) несов (выпадать: волосы) to fall out; (проникать): **лезть в** +acc to climb in; **лезть** (impf) **на** +acc to climb (up)
ле́й|ка (-йки; gen pl -ек) ж watering can
лейкопла́стыр|ь (-я) м sticking plaster (Brit), adhesive tape (US)
лейтена́нт (-а) м lieutenant
лека́рств|о (-а) ср medicine; лека́рство **от** +gen medicine for; **лека́рство от ка́шля** cough medicine
ле́ктор (-а) м lecturer
ле́кци|я (-и) ж lecture
лени́вый прил lazy
лен|и́ться (-ю́сь, -ишься; perf полени́ться) несов возв to be lazy
ле́нт|а (-ы) ж ribbon; (Тех) tape; (Комп) feed
лепест|о́к (-ка́) м petal
леп|и́ть (-лю́, -ишь; perf вы́лепить) несов перех to model ▷ (perf слепи́ть) (соты, гнездо́) to build
лес (-а; loc sg -у́, nom pl -а́) м (большой) forest; (небольшой) wood ▷ собир (материал) timber (Brit), lumber (US)
лесбия́н|ка (-ки; gen pl -ок) ж lesbian
ле́ск|а (-и) ж fishing line
лесно́й прил forest
ле́стниц|а (-ы) ж staircase; (ступени) stairs мн; (переносная) ladder; (стремянка) stepladder
лет|а́ (-) мн см **год**; (возраст): **ско́лько Вам лет?** how old are you?; **ему́ 16 лет** he is 16 (years old)
лета́|ть (-ю) несов to fly

ле|те́ть (-чу́, -ти́шь) несов to fly
ле́тний прил summer
ле́т|о (-а) ср summer; ле́том нареч in summer
лету́ч|ий прил: летучая мышь bat
лётчик (-а) м pilot
ле́чащий прил: ле́чащий врач ≈ consultant-in-charge (Brit), ≈ attending physician (US)
лече́бниц|а (-ы) ж clinic
лече́бный прил (учреждение) medical; (трава) medicinal
лече́ни|е (-я) ср (больных) treatment; (от простуды) cure; лечи́ть (-у́, -ишь) несов перех to treat; (больного): лечи́ть кого́-н от +gen to treat sb for; лечи́ться несов возв to undergo treatment
лечу́ несов см лете́ть
ле|чь (ля́гу, ля́жешь итп, ля́гут; pt лёг, -гла́, imper ля́г(те), impf ложи́ться) сов to lie down; (перен): лечь на +acc (задача) to fall on; ложи́ться (perf лечь) в больни́цу to go into hospital
лжец (-а́) м liar
лжи сущ см ложь
ли част (в вопросе): зна́ешь ли ты, что ... do you know that ...; (в косвенном вопросе): спроси́, смо́жет ли он нам помо́чь ask if he can help us; (в разделительном вопросе): она́ краси́вая, не так ли? she's beautiful, isn't she?
либера́льный прил liberal
ли́бо союз (или) or
ли́г|а (-и) ж (Полит, Спорт) league
ли́дер (-а) м leader; лиди́р|овать (-ую) несов to lead, be in the lead
ли|за́ть (-жу́, -жешь) несов перех (тарелку, мороженое) to lick
лизн|у́ть (-у́, -ёшь) сов перех to lick
ликёр (-а) м liqueur
ли́ли|я (-и) ж lily
лило́вый прил purple
лими́т (-а) м (на бензин) quota; (цен) limit; лимити́р|овать (-ую) (не)сов перех to limit; (цены) to cap
лимо́н (-а) м lemon; лимона́д (-а) м lemonade; лимо́нный прил lemon; лимо́нная кислота́ citric acid
лине́йк|а (-йки; gen pl -ек) ж (линия) line; (инструмент) ruler; тетра́дь в лине́йку lined notebook
ли́нз|а (-ы) ж lens
ли́ни|я (-и) ж line; по ли́нии +gen in the line of; железнодоро́жная ли́ния railway (Brit) или railroad (US) track
линя́|ть (3sg -ет, perf полиня́ть) несов to run (colour) ▷ (perf облиня́ть) (животные) to moult (Brit), molt (US)
ли́пкий прил sticky
ли́п|нуть (-ну; pt -, -ла, perf прили́пнуть) несов (грязь, тесто) to stick
липу́ч|ка (-ки; gen pl -ек) ж (разг: застёжка) Velcro fastening
ли́рик|а (-и) ж lyric poetry

лис|а́ (-ы́; nom pl -ы) ж fox
лист (-а́; nom pl -ья) м (растения) leaf ▷ (nom pl -ы́) (бумаги, железа) sheet
листа́|ть (-ю) несов перех (страницы) to turn
листв|а́ (-ы́) ж собир foliage, leaves мн
листо́в|ка (-ки; gen pl -ок) ж leaflet
листо́к (-ка́) м (бумаги) sheet
ли́стья итп сущ см лист
Литв|а́ (-ы́) ж Lithuania
литерату́р|а (-ы) ж literature; (также худо́жественная литерату́ра) fiction; литерату́рный прил literary
литр (-а) м litre (Brit), liter (US); литро́вый прил (бутылка итп) (one-)litre (Brit), (one-)liter (US)
ли|ть (лью, льёшь; pt -л, -ла́) несов перех (воду) to pour; (слёзы) to shed; (Тех: детали, изделия) to cast, mould (Brit), mold (US) ▷ неперех (вода, дождь) to pour; ли́ться несов возв (вода) to pour out
лифт (-а) м lift
ли́фчик (-а) м bra
лихора́дк|а (-и) ж fever; (на губах) cold sore
лицев|о́й прил: лицева́я сторона́ мате́рии the right side of the material
лице́|й (-я) м lycée, ≈ grammar school
лицеме́рный прил hypocritical
лице́нзи|я (-и) ж licence (Brit), license (US)
ли|цо́ (-ца́; nom pl -ца) ср face; (перен: индивидуальность) image; (ткани итп) right side; (Линг) person; от лица́ +gen in the name of, on behalf of
ли́чно нареч (знать) personally; (встретить) in person
ли́чность (-и) ж individual
ли́чный прил personal; (частный) private
лиша́|ть(ся) несов от лиши́ть(ся)
лиш|и́ть (-у́, -и́шь; impf лиша́ть) сов перех: лиши́ть кого́-н/что-н +gen (отнять: прав, привилегий) to deprive sb/sth of; (покоя, счастья) to rob sb/sth of
ли́шний прил (вес) extra; (деньги, билет) spare; ли́шний раз once again или more
лишь част (только) only ▷ союз (как только) as soon as; лишь бы она́ согласи́лась! if only she would agree!
лоб (лба; loc sg лбу) м forehead
ло́бби ср нескл lobby
лобов|о́й прил frontal; лобово́е стекло́ windscreen (Brit), windshield (US)
лов|и́ть (-лю́, -ишь; perf пойма́ть) несов перех to catch; (момент) to seize; лови́ть (impf) ры́бу to fish
лову́ш|ка (-ки; gen pl -ек) ж trap
ло́гик|а (-и) ж logic; логи́чный прил logical
логоти́п (-а) м logo
ло́д|ка (-ки; gen pl -ок) ж boat
лоды́ж|ка (-ки; gen pl -ек) ж ankle
ло́ж|а (-и) ж (в театре, в зале) box
ложи́ться (-у́сь, -и́шься) несов от лечь
ло́ж|ка (-ки; gen pl -ек) ж spoon
ло́жный прил false; (вывод) wrong

ложь (**лжи**; *instr sg* **ло́жью**) *ж* lie
лоз|а́ (**-ы́**; *nom pl* **-ы**) *ж* vine
ло́зунг (**-а**) *м* (*призыв*) slogan; (*плакат*) banner
ло́к|оть (**-тя**; *gen pl* **-те́й**, *dat pl* **-тя́м**) *м* elbow
лома́ть (**-ю**; *perf* **слома́ть**) *несов перех* to break; (*традиции*) to challenge; (*планы*) to frustrate ▷ (*perf* **слома́ть** *или* **полома́ть**) (*механизм*) to break; **лома́ть** (*impf*) **го́лову над чем-то** to rack one's brains over sth; **лома́ться** (*perf* **слома́ться**) *несов возв* to break
ло́мтик (**-а**) *м* slice
Ло́ндон (**-а**) *м* London
ло́пасть (**-и**; *gen pl* **-е́й**) *ж* blade
лопа́т|а (**-ы**) *ж* spade; **лопа́т|ка** (**-ки**; *gen pl* **-ок**) *ж*, *уменьш от* **лопа́та**; (*Анат*) shoulder blade
ло́пн|уть (**-у**; *perf* **ло́паться**) *сов* (*шар*) to burst; (*стекло*) to shatter; (*разг: банк*) to go bust
лоску́т (**-а́**) *м* (*материи*) scrap
лосо́с|ь (**-я**) *м* salmon
лосьо́н (**-а**) *м* lotion
лотере́|я (**-и**) *ж* lottery
лото́ *ср нескл* lotto
лот|о́к (**-ка́**) *м* (*прилавок*) stall
лохмо́ть|я (**-ев**) *мн* rags *мн*
ло́шад|ь (**-и**; *gen pl* **-е́й**) *ж* horse
луг (**-а**; *loc sg* **-у́**, *nom pl* **-а́**) *м* meadow
лу́ж|а (**-и**) *ж* (*на дороге*) puddle; (*на полу, на столе*) pool
лук (**-а**) *м собир* (*плоды*) onions *мн* ▷ *м* (*оружие*) bow; **зелёный лук** spring onion (*Brit*), scallion
лу́ковиц|а (**-ы**) *ж* bulb
лун|а́ (**-ы́**) *ж* moon
лу́н|ка (**-ки**; *gen pl* **-ок**) *ж* hole
лу́нный *прил*: **лу́нный свет** moonlight
лу́п|а (**-ы**) *ж* magnifying glass
луч (**-а́**) *м* ray; (*фонаря*) beam; **лучев|о́й** *прил*: **лучева́я боле́знь** radiation sickness
лу́чше *сравн прил от* **хоро́ший** ▷ *сравн нареч от* **хорошо́** ▷ *как сказ*: **так лу́чше** that's better ▷ *част*: **лу́чше не опра́вдывайся** don't try and justify yourself ▷ *вводн сл*: **лу́чше (всего́), позвони́ ве́чером** it would be better if you phone in the evening; **больно́му лу́чше** the patient is feeling better; **нам лу́чше, чем им** we're better off than them; **как нельзя́ лу́чше** couldn't be better
лу́чш|ий *прил* (*самый хороший*) best; **в лу́чшем слу́чае мы зако́нчим за́втра** the best-case scenario is that we'll finish tomorrow; **э́то (всё) к лу́чшему** it's (all) for the best
лы́ж|а (**-и**) *ж* (*обычно мн*) ski; *см также* **лы́жи**; **лы́ж|и** (**-**) *мн* (*спорт*) skiing *ед*; **во́дные лы́жи** water-skis; (*спорт*) water-skiing; **го́рные лы́жи** downhill skis; (*спорт*) downhill skiing; **лы́жник** (**-а**) *м* skier; **лы́жный** *прил* (*крепления, мазь*

итп) ski; (*соревнования*) skiing; **лыжн|я́** (**-и́**) *ж* ski track
лысе́ть (**-ю**; *perf* **облысе́ть** *или* **полысе́ть**) *несов* to go bald; **лы́син|а** (**-ы**) *ж* bald patch; **лы́сый** *прил* bald
ль *част = ли*
льго́т|а (**-ы**) *ж* benefit; (*предприятиям итп*) special term; **нало́говые льго́ты** tax relief; **льго́тный** *прил* (*тариф*) concessionary; (*условия*) privileged; (*заём*) special-rate; **льго́тный биле́т** concessionary ticket
льди́н|а (**-ы**) *ж* ice floe
льняно́й *прил* (*полотенце*) linen
любе́зност|ь (**-и**) *ж* (*одолжение*) favour (*Brit*), favor (*US*)
любе́зный *прил* polite; **бу́дьте любе́зны!** excuse me, please!; **бу́дьте любе́зны, принеси́те нам ко́фе!** could you be so kind as to bring us some coffee?
люби́м|ец (**-ца**) *м* favourite (*Brit*), favorite (*US*)
люби́мый *прил* (*женщина, брат*) beloved; (*писатель, занятие итп*) favourite (*Brit*), favorite (*US*)
люби́тел|ь (**-я**) *м* (*непрофессионал*) amateur; **люби́тель му́зыки/спо́рта** music-/sports-lover; **люби́тельский** *прил* amateur
люби́ть (**-лю́, -ишь**) *несов перех* to love; (*музыку, спорт итп*) to like
любова́ться (**-у́юсь**; *perf* **полюбова́ться**) *несов возв +instr* to admire
любо́вник (**-а**) *м* lover; **любо́вный** *прил* (*дела*) lover's; (*песня, письмо*) love; (*отношение, подход*) loving
любо́в|ь (**-ви́**; *instr sg* **-о́вью**) *ж* love; (*привязанность*): **любо́вь к +dat** (*к ро́дине, к ма́тери итп*) love for; (*к чте́нию, к иску́сству итп*) love of
любо́й *мест* (*всякий*) any ▷ (**-ого**) *м* (*любой человек*) anyone
любопы́тный *прил* (*случай*) interesting; (*человек*) curious
любопы́тств|о (**-а**) *ср* curiosity
лю́бящий *прил* loving
лю́д|и (**-е́й**; *dat pl* **-ям**, *instr pl* **-ьми́**, *prp pl* **-ях**) *мн* people *мн*; (*кадры*) staff *ед*; **молоды́е лю́ди** young men; (*молодёжь*) young people; *см также* **челове́к**; **лю́дный** *прил* (*улица итп*) busy
людско́й *прил* human
люкс (**-а**) *м* (*о вагоне*) first-class carriage; (*о каюте*) first-class cabin ▷ *прил неизм* first-class
лю́стр|а (**-ы**) *ж* chandelier
ляга́ть (**-ю**) *несов перех* (*подлеж: лошадь, корова*) to kick; **ляга́ться** *несов возв* (*лошадь, корова*) to kick
ля́гу *итп сов см* **лечь**
лягу́ш|ка (**-ки**; *gen pl* **-ек**) *ж* frog
ля́жешь *итп сов см* **лечь**
ля́ж|ка (**-ки**; *gen pl* **-ек**) *ж* thigh
ля́м|ка (**-ки**; *gen pl* **-ок**) *ж* strap

M

М *сокр* = **метро́**

м *сокр* (= **метр**) m

мавзоле́й (-я) *м* mausoleum

магази́н (-а) *м* shop

маги́стр (-а) *м* master's degree

магистра́л|ь (-и) *ж* main line

маги́ческий *прил* magic

магни́т (-а) *м* magnet

магнитофо́н (-а) *м* tape recorder

ма́|зать (-жу, -жешь; *perf* **нама́зать**
или **пома́зать**) *несов перех* to spread
▷ (*perf* **изма́зать**) (*разг: пачкать*) to get
dirty; **ма́заться** *несов возв* (*perf*
изма́заться) (*разг: пачкаться*) to get dirty;
ма́заться (*perf* **нама́заться**) **кре́мом** to
apply cream

мазо́к (-ка́) *м* (*Мед*) smear

маз|ь (-и) *ж* (*Мед*) ointment; (*Тех*) grease

ма|й (-я) *м* May

● **1 Ма́я: Пра́здник весны́ и труда́**
●
● Spring and Labour Day, formerly known
● as International Day of Workers'
● Solidarity, has been greatly depoliticized
● since the collapse of the Soviet Union.
● For most people it is simply an
● opportunity to celebrate the spring and to
● enjoy a short holiday.

ма́йка (-йки; *gen pl* -ек) *ж* vest (*Brit*),
sleeveless undershirt (*US*)

майоне́з (-а) *м* mayonnaise

майо́р (-а) *м* (*Воен*) major

мак (-а) *м* poppy

макаро́н|ы (-) *мн* pasta *ед*

мака́|ть (-ю) *несов перех* to dip

маке́т (-а) *м* model

ма́клер (-а) *м* (*Комм*) broker

макн|у́ть (-у́, -ёшь) *сов перех* to dip

максима́льный *прил* maximum

ма́ксимум (-а) *м* maximum

макулату́р|а (-ы) *ж собир* wastepaper
(*for recycling*)

мале́йший *прил* (*ошибка*) the slightest

ма́ленький *прил* small, little

мали́н|а (-ы) *ж* (*кустарник*) raspberry
cane *или* bush; (*ягоды*) raspberries *мн*

○ **КЛЮЧЕВОЕ СЛОВО**

ма́ло *чис* (+*gen: друзей, книг*) only a few;
(*работы, денег*) not much, little; **нам да́ли
ма́ло книг** they only gave us a few books;
у меня́ ма́ло де́нег I don't have much
money; **ма́ло ра́дости** little joy
▷ *нареч* not much; **она́ ма́ло измени́лась**
she hasn't changed much
▷ *как сказ*: **мне э́того ма́ло** this is not
enough for me; **ма́ло ли что** so what?;
ма́ло ли кто/где/когда́ it doesn't matter
who/where/when; **ма́ло того́** (and) what's
more; **ма́ло того́ что** not only

маловероя́тный *прил* improbable

малоду́шный *прил* cowardly

малокро́ви|е (-я) *ср* (sickle-cell) anaemia
(*Brit*) *или* anemia (*US*)

малоле́тний *прил* young

малочи́сленный *прил* small

ма́л|ый *прил* small, little; (*доход,
скорость*) low ▷ *как сказ*: **пла́тье/пальто́
мне ма́ло** the dress/coat is too small for
me; **са́мое ма́лое** at the very least

малы́ш (-а́) *м* little boy

малы́шка (-ки; *gen pl* -ек) *ж* little girl

ма́льчик (-а) *м* boy

малю́т|ка (-ки; *gen pl* -ок) *м/ж* baby

маля́р (-а́) *м* painter (and decorator)

маляри́|я (-и) *ж* malaria

ма́м|а (-ы) *ж* mummy (*Brit*), mommy (*US*)

мама́ш|а (-и) *ж* mummy (*Brit*), mommy
(*US*)

мандари́н (-а) *м* tangerine

манда́т (-а) *м* mandate

манёвр (-а) *м* manoevre (*Brit*), maneuver
(*US*)

манеке́н (-а) *м* (*портного*) dummy; (*в
витрине*) dummy, mannequin

манеке́нщиц|а (-ы) *ж* model

мане́р|а (-ы) *ж* manner; (*художника*) style

манже́т|а (-ы) *ж* cuff

маникю́р (-а) *м* manicure

манипули́р|овать (-ую) *несов* +*instr* to
manipulate

манифе́ст (-а) *м* manifesto

манифеста́ци|я (-и) *ж* rally

ма́ни|я (-и) *ж* mania

ма́нный *прил*: **ма́нная ка́ша, ма́нная
крупа́** semolina

манья́к (-а) *м* maniac

мара́зм (-а) *м* (*Мед*) dementia; (*перен:
разг*) idiocy; **ста́рческий мара́зм** senile
dementia

марафо́н (-а) *м* marathon; **марафо́н|ец**
(-ца) *м* marathon runner

маргари́н (-а) м margarine

маргари́т|ка (-ки; gen pl -ок) ж daisy

марин|ова́ть (-у́ю; perf замаринова́ть) несов перех (овощи) to pickle; (мясо, рыбу)) to marinate, marinade

марионе́т|ка (-ки; gen pl -ок) ж puppet

ма́р|ка (-ки; gen pl -ок) ж (почтовая) stamp; (сорт) brand; (качество) grade; (модель) make; (деньги) mark; **торго́вая ма́рка** trademark

ма́ркетинг (-а) м marketing

маркси́зм (-а) м Marxism

мармела́д (-а) м fruit jellies мн

Марс (-а) м Mars

март (-а) м March

8 МА́РТА: МЕЖДУНАРО́ДНЫЙ ЖЕ́НСКИЙ ДЕНЬ

International Women's Day. This is a celebration of women of all ages. Women receive gifts from men and mothers receive gifts and greetings from their children. Special variety shows are put on in major concert halls and broadcast on television.

марш (-а) м march

ма́ршал (-а) м marshal

марширова́ть (-у́ю; perf промарширова́ть) несов to march

маршру́т (-а) м route; **маршру́тный** прил: **маршру́тное такси́** fixed-route taxi

ма́с|ка (-ки; gen pl -ок) ж mask; (косметическая) face pack

маскара́д (-а) м masked ball

маскир|ова́ть (-у́ю; perf замаскирова́ть) несов перех to camouflage; **маскирова́ться** (perf замаскирова́ться) несов возв to camouflage o.s.

ма́слениц|а (-ы) ж ≈ Shrove Tuesday, Pancake Day

масли́н|а (-ы) ж (дерево) olive (tree); (плод) olive

ма́с|ло (-ла; nom pl -ла́, gen pl -ел) ср oil; (сливочное) butter

ма́сляный прил oil; (пятно) oily

масо́н (-а) м (Free)mason

ма́сс|а (-ы) ж (также Физ) mass; (древесная) pulp; (много) loads мн

масса́ж (-а) м massage; **массажи́ст** (-а) м masseur

масси́в (-а) м (водный) expanse; (земельный) tract; **го́рный масси́в** massif; **жило́й** или **жили́щный масси́в** housing estate (Brit) или project (US); **масси́вный** прил massive

ма́ссовый прил mass; **това́ры ма́ссового спро́са** consumer goods

ма́стер (-а; nom pl -а́) м master; (в цеху) foreman (мн foremen)

мастерск|а́я (-о́й) ж workshop; (художника) studio

мастерств|о́ (-а́) ср skill

масти́к|а (-и) ж floor polish

маст|ь (-и; gen pl -е́й) ж (лошади) colour (Brit), color (US); (Карты) suit

масшта́б (-а) м scale; **масшта́бный** прил scale; (большой) large-scale

мат (-а) м (Шахматы) checkmate; (половик: также Спорт) mat; (ругательства) bad language

матема́тик (-а) м mathematician; **матема́тик|а** (-и) ж mathematics

ма́тери etc сущ см **мать**

материа́л (-а) м material; (обычно мн: следствия) document

материа́льный прил material; (финансовый) financial

матери́к (-а́) м continent; (суша) mainland

матери́нский прил maternal

матери́нств|о (-а) ср motherhood

мате́ри|я (-и) ж matter; (разг: ткань) cloth

ма́тер|ь (-и) ж: **Ма́терь Бо́жья** Mother of God

ма́терью etc сущ см **мать**

ма́тов|ый прил (без блеска) mat(t); **ма́товое стекло́** frosted glass

матра́с (-а) м mattress

матрёш|ка (-ки; gen pl -ек) ж Russian doll (containing range of smaller dolls)

ма́тричный прил: **ма́тричный при́нтер** (Комп) dot-matrix printer

матро́с (-а) м sailor

ма́туш|ка (-ки; gen pl -ек) ж (мать) mother

матч (-а) м match

мат|ь (-ери; см Table 1) ж mother; **мать-одино́чка** single mother

мафио́зный прил mafia

ма́фи|я (-и) ж the Mafia

мах (-а) м (крыла) flap; (рукой) swing; **одни́м ма́хом** in a stroke; **с ма́ху** straight away

ма|ха́ть (-шу́, -шешь) несов +instr to wave; (крыльями) to flap; **маха́ть** (impf) **кому́-н руко́й** to wave to sb

махн|у́ть (-у́, -ёшь) сов to wave

махо́рк|а (-и) ж coarse tobacco

ма́чех|а (-и) ж stepmother

ма́чт|а (-ы) ж mast

маши́н|а (-ы) ж machine; (автомобиль) car

машина́льный прил mechanical

машини́ст (-а) м driver, operator; **машини́ст|ка** (-ки; gen pl -ок) ж typist

маши́н|ка (-ки; gen pl -ок) ж machine; **пи́шущая маши́нка** typewriter

маши́нный прил machine; **маши́нное отделе́ние** engine room

машиностро́ени|е (-я) ср mechanical engineering

мая́к (-а́) м lighthouse

МВД ср сокр (= Министе́рство вну́тренних дел) ≈ the Home Office (Brit), ≈ the Department of the Interior (US)

мгл|а́ (-ы́) ж haze; (вече́рняя) gloom

мгнове́ни|е (-я) ср moment

мгнове́нный прил instant; (злость) momentary

МГУ м сокр (= Моско́вский госуда́рственный университе́т) Moscow State University

ме́бел|ь (-и) ж собир furniture

мёд (-а) м honey

меда́л|ь (-и) ж medal

медве́д|ь (-я) м bear; **медвеж|о́нок** (-о́нка; nom pl -я́та, gen pl -я́т) м bear cub

медикаме́нт (-а) м medicine

медици́н|а (-ы) ж medicine

ме́дленный прил slow

медли́тельный прил slow

ме́дл|ить (-ю, -ишь) несов to delay; **ме́длить** (impf) **с реше́нием** to be slow in deciding

ме́дный прил copper; (Муз) brass

медо́вый прил honey; **медо́вый ме́сяц** honeymoon

медпу́нкт (-а) м сокр (= медици́нский пункт) ≈ first-aid centre (Brit) или center (US)

медсестр|а́ (-ы́) ж сокр (= медици́нская сестра́) nurse

меду́з|а (-ы) ж jellyfish

ме́д|ь (-и) ж copper

ме́жду предл +instr between; (+gen: в окруже́нии) amongst; **ме́жду про́чим** (попутно) in passing; (кстати) by the way; **ме́жду тем** meanwhile; **ме́жду тем как** while; **они́ договори́лись ме́жду собо́й** they agreed between them

междугоро́дный прил intercity

междунаро́дный прил international

мел (-а) м chalk

меле́|ть (3sg -ет, perf **обмеле́ть**) несов to become shallower

ме́лкий прил small; (песок, дождь) fine; (интересы) petty

мело́ди|я (-и) ж tune, melody; **мело́дия для моби́льного телефо́на** ringtone

ме́лочный прил petty

ме́лочь (-и; gen pl -е́й) ж (пустяк) triviality; (подробность) detail ▷ ж собир little things мн; (деньги) small change

мел|ь (-и; loc sg -и́) ж shallows мн; **сади́ться (perf сесть) на мель** (Мор) to run aground

мелька́|ть (-ю) несов to flash past; **мелькн|у́ть** (-у́, -ёшь) сов to flash

ме́льком нареч in passing

ме́льниц|а (-ы) ж mill

мельхио́р (-а) м nickel silver

ме́льче сравн прил от **ме́лкий**

мельч|и́ть (-у́, -и́шь; perf **измельчи́ть** или **размельчи́ть**) несов перех (ножом) to cut up into small pieces; (в ступке) to crush

мем (-а) м meme

мемориа́л (-а) м memorial

мемуа́р|ы (-ов) мн memoirs

ме́неджер (-а) м manager

ме́неджмент (-а) м management

ме́нее сравн нареч от **ма́ло** ▷ нареч (опасный) less; (года) less than; **тем не ме́нее** nevertheless

менинги́т (-а) м meningitis

менструа́ци|я (-и) ж menstruation

ме́ньше сравн прил от **ма́лый**; **ма́ленький** ▷ сравн нареч от **ма́ло** ▷ нареч less than; **ме́ньше всего́** least of all

ме́ньш|ий сравн прил от **ма́лый**; **ма́ленький** ▷ прил: **по ме́ньшей ме́ре** at least; **са́мое ме́ньшее** no less than

меньшинств|о́ (-а́) ср собир minority

меню́ ср нескл menu

мен|я́ мест см **я**

мен|я́ть (-ю; perf **поменя́ть**) несов перех to change; **меня́ть (perf поменя́ть) что-н на +acc** to exchange sth for; **меня́ться (perf поменя́ться)** несов возв to change

ме́р|а (-ы) ж measure; (предел) limit; **в по́лной ме́ре** fully; **по ме́ре** +gen with; **по ме́ре того́ как** as

ме́рзкий прил disgusting; (погода, настроение) foul

мёрзлый прил (земля) frozen

мёрз|нуть (-ну; pt -, -ла, perf **замёрзнуть**) несов to freeze

ме́р|ить (-ю, -ишь; perf **сме́рить** или **изме́рить**) несов перех to measure ▷ (perf **поме́рить**) (примерять) to try on

ме́рк|а (-ки; gen pl -ок) ж measurements мн; (перен: критерий) standard

ме́рк|нуть (3sg -нет, perf **поме́ркнуть**) несов to fade

мероприя́ти|е (-я) ср measure; (событие) event

мертве́|ть (-ю; perf **омертве́ть**) несов (от холода) to go numb ▷ (perf **помертве́ть**) (от страха, от горя) to be numb

мертве́ц (-а́) м dead person

мёртвый прил dead

мерца́|ть (3sg -ет) несов to glimmer, flicker; (звёзды) to twinkle

ме|сти́ (-ту́, -тёшь; pt мёл, -ла́, perf **подмести́**) несов перех (пол) to sweep; (мусор) to sweep up

ме́стность (-и) ж area

ме́стный прил local

ме́ст|о (-а; nom pl -а́) ср place; (действия) scene; (в театре, в поезде итп) seat; (багажа) item

местожи́тельств|о (-а) ср place of residence

местоиме́ни|е (-я) ср pronoun

местонахожде́ни|е (-я) ср location

месторожде́ни|е (-я) ср (угля, нефти) field

мест|ь (-и) ж revenge, vengeance

ме́сяц (-а; nom pl -ы) м month; (часть луны) crescent moon; (диск луны) moon

ме́сячный прил monthly

мета́лл (-а) м metal

металлоло́м (-а) м scrap metal

ме|та́ть (-чу́, -чешь) несов перех (гранату, диск итп) to throw ▷ (perf **намета́ть**) (шов) to tack (Brit), baste; **мета́ться** несов возв (в посте́ли) to toss and turn; (по комнате) to rush about

мете́л|ь (-и) ж snowstorm, blizzard

метеоро́лог (-а) м meteorologist

метеосво́д|ка (-ки; gen pl -ок) ж сокр (= метеорологи́ческая сво́дка) weather forecast или report

метеоста́нци|я (-и) ж сокр (= метеорологи́ческая ста́нция) weather station

ме́|тить (-чу, -тишь; perf **поме́тить**) несов перех to mark ▷ неперех: **ме́тить в** +acc (в цель) to aim at; **ме́титься** (perf **наме́титься**) несов возв: **ме́титься в** +acc to aim at

ме́т|ка (-ки; gen pl -ок) ж mark

ме́ткий прил (то́чный) accurate; (замеча́ние) apt

метн|у́ть (-у́, -ёшь) сов перех to throw; **метну́ться** сов возв to rush

ме́тод (-а) м method

метр (-а) м metre (Brit), meter (US); (линейка) measure

метрдоте́л|ь (-я) м head waiter

ме́трик|а (-и) ж birth certificate

метри́ческий прил metric

метро́ ср нескл metro, tube (Brit), subway (US)

мех (-а; nom pl -а́) м fur

мех|а́ (-о́в) мн (кузнечный) bellows мн

механи́зм (-а) м mechanism

меха́ник (-а) м mechanic

механи́ческий прил mechanical; (цех) machine

мехово́й прил fur

мецена́т (-а) м patron

меч (-а́) м sword

мече́т|ь (-и) ж mosque

мечт|а́ (-ы; gen pl -а́ний) ж dream

мечта́|ть (-ю) несов: **мечта́ть (о** +prp) to dream (of)

меша́|ть (-ю; perf **помеша́ть**) несов перех (суп, чай) to stir ▷ (perf **смеша́ть**) (напи́тки, краски) to mix ▷ (perf **помеша́ть**) неперех (+dat: быть помехой) to disturb, bother; (реформам) to hinder; **меша́ть** (perf **помеша́ть**) кому́-н +infin (препя́тствовать) to make it difficult for sb to do; **меша́ться** (perf **смеша́ться**) несов возв (путаться) to get mixed up

меш|о́к (-ка́) м sack

мещ|ани́н (-ани́на; nom pl -а́не, gen pl -а́н) м petty bourgeois

миг (-а) м moment

мига́|ть (-ю) несов to wink; (огни) to twinkle

мигн|у́ть (-у́, -ёшь) сов to wink

ми́гом нареч (разг) in a jiffy

мигра́ци|я (-и) ж migration

МИД (-а) м сокр (= Министе́рство иностра́нных дел) ≈ the Foreign Office (Brit), ≈ the State Department (US)

ми́довский прил (разг) Foreign Office

ми́зерный прил meagre (Brit), meager (US)

мизи́н|ец (-ца) м (на руке) little finger; (на ноге) little toe

микроавто́бус (-а) м minibus

микрорайо́н (-а) м ≈ catchment area

- ● **Микрорайо́н**
- ●
- ● These are modern housing estates with
- ● densely built blocks of flats and are a
- ● feature of all big Russian cities. They
- ● have their own infrastructure of schools,
- ● health centres, cinemas, and shops.

микроско́п (-а) м microscope

микрофо́н (-а) м microphone

ми́ксер (-а) м mixer

миксту́р|а (-ы) ж mixture

милиционе́р (-а) м policeman (in Russia) (мн policemen)

мили́ци|я (-и) ж, собир police (in Russia)

миллиа́рд (-а) м billion

миллигра́мм (-а) м milligram(me)

миллиме́тр (-а) м millimetre (Brit), millimeter (US)

миллио́н (-а) м million; **миллионе́р** (-а) м millionaire

ми́л|овать (-ую; perf **поми́ловать**) несов перех to have mercy on; (преступника) to pardon

милосе́рди|е (-я) ср compassion

ми́лостын|я (-и) ж alms мн

ми́лост|ь (-и) ж (доброта́) kind-heartedness; **ми́лости про́сим!** welcome!

ми́лый прил (симпати́чный) pleasant, nice; (дорогой) dear

ми́л|я (-и) ж mile

ми́мик|а (-и) ж expression

ми́мо нареч past ▷ предл +gen past

мимолётный прил fleeting

мимохо́дом нареч on the way; (упомяну́ть) in passing

ми́н|а (-ы) ж (Воен) mine

минда́лин|а (-ы) ж (Мед) tonsil

минда́л|ь (-я́) м almond

минера́л (-а) м mineral

минздра́в (-а) м сокр (= министе́рство здравоохране́ния) Ministry of Health

миниатю́р|а (-ы) ж miniature; (Театр) short play; **миниатю́рный** прил miniature

минима́льный прил minimum

ми́нимум (-а) м minimum ▷ нареч at least, minimum; **прожи́точный ми́нимум** minimum living wage

мини́р|овать (-ую; perf **замини́ровать**) (не)сов перех (Воен) to mine

министе́рств|о (-а) *ср* ministry; **мини́стр** (-а) *м* (*Полит*) minister

ми́нн|ый *прил* mine; **ми́нное по́ле** minefield

мин|ова́ть (-у́ю) (*не)сов перех* to pass

мину́вший *прил* past

ми́нус (-а) *м* minus

мину́т|а (-ы) *ж* minute; **мину́тный** *прил* (*стрелка*) minute; (*дело*) brief

ми́н|уть (*3sg* -ет) *сов* (*исполниться*): ей/ему́ ми́нуло 16 лет she/he has turned 16

минфи́н (-а) *м сокр* (*разг*) (= Министе́рство фина́нсов) Ministry of Finance

мир (-а; *nom pl* -ы́) *м* world; (*Вселенная*) universe ▷ (*loc sg* -у́) (*Рел*) (secular) world; (*состояние без войны*) peace

мир|и́ть (-ю́, -ишь; *perf* помири́ть *или* примири́ть) *несов перех* to reconcile; **мири́ться** (*perf* помири́ться) *несов возв*: мири́ться *с +instr* to make up *или* be reconciled with ▷ (*perf* примири́ться) (с недоста́тками) to reconcile o.s. to, come to terms with

ми́рн|ый *прил* peaceful; **ми́рное вре́мя** peacetime; **ми́рное населе́ние** civilian population; **ми́рные перегово́ры** peace talks *или* negotiations

мировоззре́ни|е (-я) *ср* philosophy of life

мирово́й *прил* world

миротво́р|ец (-ца) *м* peacemaker, peacekeeper

миротво́рческ|ий *прил* peacemaking; **миротво́рческие войска́** peacekeeping force

мирско́й *прил* secular, lay

ми́сси|я (-и) *ж* mission

ми́стер (-а) *м* Mr

ми́тинг (-а) *м* rally

митрополи́т (-а) *м* metropolitan

миф (-а) *м* myth

мише́н|ь (-и) *ж* target

младе́н|ец (-ца) *м* infant, baby

мла́дше *сравн прил от* молодо́й

мла́дший *прил* younger; (*сотрудник, класс*) junior

млекопита́ющ|ее (-его) *ср* mammal

мле́чный *прил*: Мле́чный Путь the Milky Way

мм *сокр* (= миллиме́тр) mm

мне *мест см* я

мне́ни|е (-я) *ср* opinion

мни́мый *прил* imaginary; (*ложный*) fake

мни́тельный *прил* suspicious

мно́г|ие *прил* many ▷ (-их) *мн* (*много людей*) many (people)

мно́го *чис* (+*gen*: книг, друзей) many, a lot of; (*работы*) much, a lot of ▷ *нареч* (*разговаривать, пить итп*) a lot; (+*comparative*: гораздо) much; **мно́го книг тебе́ да́ли?** did they give you many *или* a lot of books?; **мно́го рабо́ты тебе́ да́ли?** did they give you much *или* a lot of work?

многоде́тный *прил* with a lot of children

мно́г|ое (-ого) *ср* a great deal

многозначи́тельный *прил* significant

многоле́тний *прил* (*планы*) long-term; (*труд*) of many years; (*растения*) perennial

многолю́дный *прил* crowded

многонациона́льный *прил* multinational

многообеща́ющий *прил* promising

многообра́зи|е (-я) *ср* variety

многообра́зный *прил* varied

многосторо́нний *прил* (*переговоры*) multilateral; (*личность*) many-sided; (*интересы*) diverse

многоуважа́емый *прил* (*в обращении*) Dear

многочи́сленный *прил* numerous

многоэта́жный *прил* multistorey (*Brit*), multistory (*US*)

мно́жественн|ый *прил*: **мно́жественное число́** (*Линг*) the plural (number)

мно́жеств|о (-а) *ср* +*gen* a great number of

мно́жительн|ый *прил*: **мно́жительная те́хника** photocopying equipment

мно́ж|ить (-у, -ишь; *perf* умно́жить) *несов перех* to multiply

мной *мест см* я

мобилиз|ова́ть (-у́ю) (*не)сов перех* to mobilize

моби́льник (-а) *м* (*разг*) mobile

моби́льный *прил* mobile; **моби́льный телефо́н** mobile phone

мог *итп несов см* мочь

моги́л|а (-ы) *ж* grave

могу́ *etc несов см* мочь

могу́чий *прил* mighty

могу́ществ|о (-а) *ср* power, might

мо́д|а (-ы) *ж* fashion; *см также* мо́ды

модели́р|овать (-ую) (*не)сов перех* (*одежду*) to design ▷ (*perf* смодели́ровать) (*процесс, поведение*) to simulate

моде́л|ь (-и) *ж* model; **моделье́р** (-а) *м* fashion designer

моде́м (-а) *м* (*Комп*) modem

мо́дный *прил* fashionable

мо́д|ы (-) *мн* fashions; **журна́л мод** fashion magazine

мо́жет *несов см* мочь ▷ *вводн сл* (*также* мо́жет быть) maybe

мо́жно *как сказ* (*возможно*) +*infin* it is possible to do; **мо́жно (войти́)?** may I (come in)?; **как мо́жно лу́чше** as well as possible

мозг (-а; *loc sg* -у́, *nom sg* -и́) *м* brain; **спинно́й мозг** spinal cord

мой (моего́; *см* Table 8; *f* моя́, *nt* моё, *pl* мои́) *притяж мест* my; **по-мо́ему** my way; (*по моему мнению*) in my opinion

мо́к|нуть (-ну; *pt* -, -ла) *несов* to get wet; (*лежать в воде*) to be soaking

мо́крый *прил* wet

молв|а́ (-ы́) ж rumour (Brit), rumor (US)

моле́б|ен (-на) м (Рел) service

моле́кул|а (-ы) ж molecule

моли́тв|а (-ы) ж prayer; **моли́твенник** (-а) м prayer book

мол|и́ться (-ю́сь, -и́шься; perf **помоли́ться**) несов возв +dat to pray to

мо́лни|я (-и) ж lightning; (застёжка) zip (fastener) (Brit), zipper (US)

молодёжный прил youth; (мода, газета) for young people

молодёж|ь (-и) ж собир young people мн

молоде́|ть (-ю; perf **помолоде́ть**) несов to become younger

молоде́ц (-ца́) м strong fellow; **молоде́ц!** (разг) well done!; **она́/он молоде́ц!** (разг) she/he has done well!

молодо́й прил young; (картофель, листва) new; **мо́лодост|ь** (-и) ж youth

моло́же сравн прил от **молодо́й**

молок|о́ (-а́) ср milk

мо́лот (-а) м hammer

молот|о́к (-ка́) м hammer

мо́лотый прил (кофе, перец) ground

моло́ть (мелю́, ме́лешь; perf **смоло́ть** или **помоло́ть**) несов перех to grind

моло́чник (-а) м (посуда) milk jug

моло́чный прил (продукты, скот) dairy; (коктейль) milk

мо́лча нареч silently

молча́ни|е (-я) ср silence; **молч|а́ть** (-у́, -и́шь) несов о +prp to keep silent или quiet about

мол|ь (-и) ж moth

моме́нт (-а) м moment; (доклада) point; **теку́щий моме́нт** the current situation; **момента́льный** прил instant

монасты́р|ь (-я́) м (мужской) monastery; (женский) convent

мона́х (-а) м monk; **мона́хин|я** (-и; gen pl -ь) ж nun

моне́т|а (-ы) ж coin; **моне́тный** прил: **моне́тный двор** mint

монито́р (-а) м monitor

моното́нный прил monotonous

монта́ж (-а́) ж (сооружения) building; (механизма) assembly; (кадров) editing

монти́р|овать (-ую; perf **смонти́ровать**) несов перех (оборудование) to assemble; (фильм) to edit

монуме́нт (-а) м monument

мора́л|ь (-и) ж morals мн, ethics мн; (басни, сказки) moral

мора́льный прил moral

морг (-а) м morgue

морга́|ть (-ю) несов to blink; (подмигивать): **морга́ть** (+dat) to wink (at)

моргн|у́ть (-у́, -ёшь) сов to blink; (подмигнуть): **моргну́ть** (+dat) to wink (at)

мо́рд|а (-ы) ж (животного) muzzle; (разг: человека) mug

мо́р|е (-я; nom pl -я́, gen pl -е́й) ср sea

мореходный прил naval

морж (-а́) м walrus

морко́в|ь (-и) ж carrots мн

моро́жен|ое (-ого) ср ice cream

моро́женый прил frozen

моро́з (-а) м frost

морози́льник (-а) м freezer

моро́|зить (-жу, -зишь) несов перех to freeze

моро́зный прил frosty

мороси́ть (3sg -и́т) несов to drizzle

моро́ч|ить (-у, -ишь; perf **заморо́чить**) несов перех: **моро́чить го́лову кому́-н** (разг) to pull sb's leg

морск|о́й прил sea; (Био) marine; (курорт) seaside; **морско́е пра́во** maritime law; **морска́я боле́знь** seasickness; **морска́я сви́нка** guinea pig

морщи́н|а (-ы) ж (на лице) wrinkle

мо́рщ|ить (-у, -ишь; perf **намо́рщить**) несов перех (брови) to knit ▷ (perf **смо́рщить**) (нос, лоб) to wrinkle; (лицо) to screw up; **мо́рщиться** (perf **смо́рщиться**) несов возв: **мо́рщиться от** +gen (от старости) to become wrinkled from; (от боли) to wince in

моря́к (-а́) м sailor

Москв|а́ (-ы́) ж Moscow

москви́ч (-а́) м Muscovite

мост (-а; loc sg -у́) м bridge

мо́стик (-а) м bridge; **капита́нский мо́стик** bridge (Naut)

мо|сти́ть (-щу́, -сти́шь; perf **вы́мостить**) несов перех to pave

мостов|а́я (-о́й) ж road

мота́|ть (-ю; perf **намота́ть**) несов перех (нитки) to wind ▷ (perf **помота́ть**) неперех (+instr: головой) to shake; **мота́ться** несов возв to swing

моте́л|ь (-я) м motel

моти́в (-а) м (преступления) motive; (мелодия) motif

мотиви́р|овать (-ую) (не)сов перех to justify

мото́р (-а) м motor; (автомобиля, лодки) engine

моторо́ллер (-а) м (motor) scooter

мотоци́кл (-а) м motorcycle

мотыл|ёк (-ька́) м moth

мох (мха; loc sg мху, nom pl мхи) м moss

мохе́р (-а) м mohair

моч|а́ (-и́) ж urine

моча́л|ка (-ки; gen pl -ок) ж sponge

мочево́й прил: **мочево́й пузы́рь** bladder

моч|и́ть (-у́, -ишь; perf **намочи́ть**) несов перех to wet ▷ (perf **замочи́ть**) (бельё) to soak

мо́|чь (-гу́, -жешь etc, -гут; pt -г, -гла́, -гло́, perf **смочь**) несов +infin to be able to do; **я могу́ игра́ть на гита́ре/ говори́ть по-англи́йски** I can play the guitar/speak English; **он мо́жет прийти́** he can или is able to come; **я сде́лаю всё, что**

могу́ I will do all I can; **за́втра мо́жешь не приходи́ть** you don't have to come tomorrow; **он мо́жет оби́деться** he may well be offended; **не могу́ поня́ть э́того** I can't understand this; **мо́жет быть** maybe; **не мо́жет быть!** it's impossible!

мо́ш|ка (-ки; gen pl -ек) ж midge

мо́щность (-и) ж power

мо́щный прил powerful

мощь (-и) ж might, power

мо|я́ (-е́й) притяж мест см **мой**

МРЗ-плее́р (-а) м MP3 player

мрак (-а) м darkness

мра́мор (-а) м marble

мра́чный прил gloomy

мстить (мщу, мстишь; perf **отомсти́ть**) несов: **мстить кому́-н** to take revenge on sb

МТС ж сокр (= междугоро́дная телефо́нная ста́нция) ≈ intercity telephone exchange

му́дрость (-и) ж wisdom

му́дрый прил wise

муж (-а; nom pl -ья́, gen pl -е́й) м husband

мужа́|ть (-ю; perf **возмужа́ть**) несов to mature; **мужа́ться** несов возв to take heart, have courage

му́жественный прил (посту́пок) courageous

му́жеств|о (-а) ср courage

мужско́й прил men's; (хара́ктер) masculine; (о́рганы, кле́тка) male; **мужско́й род** masculine gender

мужчи́н|а (-ы) м man (мн men)

музе́|й (-я) м museum

му́зык|а (-и) ж music

музыка́льн|ый прил musical; **музыка́льная шко́ла** music school

музыка́нт (-а) м musician

му́к|а (-и) ж torment

мук|а́ (-и́) ж flour

му́льтик (-а) м (разг) cartoon

мультимеди́йный прил (Комп) multimedia

мультипликацио́нный прил: **мультипликацио́нный фильм** cartoon, animated film

мунди́р (-а) м uniform; **карто́фель в мунди́ре** jacket potatoes

муниципалите́т (-а) м municipality, city council

мурав|е́й (-ья́) м ant

мура́шки (-ек) мн: **у меня́ мура́шки по спине́ бе́гают** shivers are running down my spine

мурлы́|кать (-чу, -чешь) несов to purr

муска́т (-а) м (оре́х) nutmeg

му́скул (-а) м muscle

мускули́стый прил muscular

му́сор (-а) м rubbish (Brit), garbage (US); **му́сорн|ый** прил rubbish (Brit), garbage (US); **му́сорное ведро́** dustbin (Brit), trash can (US); **мусоропрово́д** (-а) м

refuse или garbage (US) chute

мусульма́нин (-а) м Muslim

му|ти́ть (-чу́, -ти́шь; perf **взмути́ть** или **замути́ть**) несов перех (жи́дкость) to cloud; **мути́ться** (perf **замути́ться**) несов возв (вода́, раство́р) to become cloudy

мутне́|ть (3sg -ет, perf **помутне́ть**) несов (жи́дкость) to become cloudy; (взор) to grow dull

му́тный прил (жи́дкость) cloudy; (стекло́) dull

му́х|а (-и) ж fly

мухомо́р (-а) м (Бот) fly agaric

муче́ни|е (-я) ср torment, torture

му́ченик (-а) м martyr

му́ч|ить (-у, -ишь; perf **заму́чить** или **изму́чить**) несов перех to torment; **му́читься** (perf **заму́читься**) несов возв: **му́читься** +instr (сомне́ниями) to be tormented by; **му́читься** (impf) **над** +instr to agonize over

мч|ать (-у, -ишь) несов (маши́ну) to speed along; (ло́шадь) to race along; **мча́ться** несов возв (по́езд) to speed along; (ло́шадь) to race along

мще́ни|е (-я) ср vengeance, revenge

мы (нас; см Table 6b) мест we; **мы с тобо́й/жено́й** you/my wife and I

мы́л|ить (-ю, -ишь; perf **намы́лить**) несов перех to soap; **мы́литься** (perf **намы́литься**) несов возв to soap o.s.

мы́л|о (-а) ср soap

мы́льниц|а (-ы) ж soap dish

мы́льн|ый прил (пе́на) soap; **мы́льная о́пера** soap (opera)

мыс (-а; loc sg -у́, nom pl -ы) м point

мы́сленный прил mental

мы́сл|ить (-ю, -ишь) несов to think ▷ перех to imagine

мысл|ь (-и) ж thought; (иде́я) idea; **за́дняя мысль** ulterior motive; **о́браз мы́слей** way of thinking

мыть (мо́ю, мо́ешь; perf **вы́мыть** или **помы́ть**) несов перех to wash; **мы́ться** (perf **вы́мыться** или **помы́ться**) несов возв to wash o.s.

мы́шечный прил muscular

мы́ш|ка (-ки; gen pl -ек) ж mouse; **под мы́шкой** under one's arm

мышле́ни|е (-я) ср (спосо́бность) reason; (проце́сс) thinking

мы́шц|а (-ы) ж muscle

мышь (-и) ж (Зоол, Комп) mouse

мэр (-а) м mayor

мэ́ри|я (-и) ж city hall

мя́гкий прил soft; (движе́ния) smooth; (хара́ктер, кли́мат) mild; (наказа́ние) lenient; **мя́гкий ваго́н** railway carriage with soft seats; **мя́гкий знак** soft sign (Russian letter)

мя́гко нареч gently; (отруга́ть) mildly; **мя́гко говоря́** to put it mildly

мя́коть (-и) ж flesh; (мя́со) fillet

ма́мл|ить (-ю, -ишь; *perf* **прома́млить**)
несов перех to mumble

мясни́к (-á) *м* butcher

мясно́й *прил* (*котлета*) meat; **мясно́й магази́н** the butcher's

мя́с|о (-а) *ср* meat

мя́т|а (-ы) *ж* mint

мяте́ж (-á) *м* revolt

мя́тный *прил* mint

мять (мну, мнёшь; *perf* **измя́ть** *или* **смять**) *несов перех* (*одежду*) to crease; (*бумагу*) to crumple

мяч (-á) *м* ball; **футбо́льный мяч** football

⃝ КЛЮЧЕВОЕ СЛОВО

на *предл +асс* **1** (*направление на поверхность*) on; **положи́ таре́лку на стол** put the plate on the table

2 (*направление в какое-нибудь место*) to; **сесть** (*perf*) **на по́езд** to get on(to) the train

3 (*об объекте воздействия*): **обрати́ внима́ние на э́того челове́ка** pay attention to this man; **нажми́ на педа́ль/кно́пку** press the pedal/button; **я люблю́ смотре́ть на дете́й/на звёзды** I love watching the children/the stars

4 (*о времени, сроке*) for; **он уе́хал на ме́сяц** he has gone away for a month

5 (*о цели, о назначении*) for; **де́ньги на кни́ги** money for books

6 (*о мере*) into; **дели́ть** (*impf*) **что-н на ча́сти** to divide sth into parts

7 (*при сравнении*): **я получа́ю на сто рубле́й ме́ньше** I get one hundred roubles less

8 (*об изменении состояния*) into; **на́до перевести́ текст на англи́йский** the text must be translated into English

▷ *предл +prp* **1** (*нахождение на поверхности*) on; **кни́га на по́лке** the book is on the shelf; **на де́вочке ша́пка/шу́ба** the girl has a hat/fur coat on

2 (*о пребывании где-нибудь*) in; **на Кавка́зе** in the Caucasus; **на у́лице** in the street; **быть** (*impf*) **на рабо́те/заседа́нии** to be at work/at a meeting

3 (*о времени осуществления чего-н*): **встре́тимся на сле́дующей неде́ле** let's meet next week

4 (*об объекте воздействия*) on; **сосредото́читься** (*perf*)/**останови́ться** (*perf*) **на чём-н** to concentrate/dwell on sth

5 (*о средстве осуществления чего-н*):

éздить на по́езде/велосипе́де to travel by train/bicycle; **игра́ть** (*impf*) **на роя́ле/скри́пке** to play the piano/violin; **ката́ться** (*impf*) **на лы́жах/конька́х** to go skiing/skating; **говори́ть** (*impf*) **на ру́сском/англи́йском языке́** to speak (in) English/Russian
6 (*о составной части предмета*): **ка́ша на воде́** porridge made with water

на (**на́те**) *част* (*разг*) here (you are)
набежа́ть (*как* **бежа́ть**; *см Table 20; impf* **набега́ть**) *сов* (*разг: тучи*) to gather; (*наскочить*): **набежа́ть на** +*acc* to run into; (*волны: на берег*) to lap against
на́бело *нареч*: **переписа́ть что-н на́бело** to write sth out neatly
на́бережн|ая (**-ой**) *ж* embankment
набива́|ть(ся) (**-ю(сь)**) *несов от* **наби́ть(ся)**
наби́вк|а (**-и**) *ж* stuffing
набира́|ть (**-ю**) *несов от* **набра́ть**
наби́|ть (**-ью, -ьёшь**; *impf* **набива́ть**) *сов перех*: **наби́ть** (+*instr*) to stuff (with); **набива́ть** (*perf* **наби́ть**) **це́ну** (*разг*) to talk up the price; **наби́ться** (*impf* **набива́ться**) *сов возв* (*разг*): **наби́ться в** +*acc* to be crammed into
наблюда́тел|ь (**-я**) *м* observer; **наблюда́тельный** *прил* (*человек*) observant; **наблюда́тельный пункт** observation point
наблюда́|ть (**-ю**) *несов перех* to observe ▷ *неперех*: **наблюда́ть за** +*instr* to monitor
на́бок *нареч* to one side
набра́сыва|ть (**-ю**) *несов от* **наброса́ть**; **набро́сить**; **набра́сываться** *несов от* **набро́ситься**
наб|ра́ть (**-еру́, -ерёшь**; *pt* **-ра́л, -рала́, -ра́ло**, *impf* **набира́ть**) *сов перех* (+*gen*: *цветы*) to pick; (*воду*) to fetch; (*студентов*) to take on; (*скорость, высоту, баллы*) to gain; (*код*) to dial; (*текст*) to typeset
наброса́|ть (**-ю**; *impf* **набра́сывать**) *сов перех* (*план, текст*) to sketch out ▷ (*не*) *перех* (+*acc или* +*gen*: *вещей, окурков*) to throw about
набро́|сить (**-шу, -сишь**; *impf* **набра́сывать**) *сов перех* (*пальто, платок*) to throw on; **набро́ситься** (*impf* **набра́сываться**) *сов возв*: **набро́ситься на** +*acc* (*на жертву*) to fall upon
набро́с|ок (**-ка**) *м* (*рисунок*) sketch; (*статьи*) draft
набу́х|нуть (*3sg* **-нет**, *pt* **-, -ла**, *impf* **набуха́ть**) *сов* to swell up
нав|али́ть (**-алю́, -а́лишь**; *impf* **нава́ливать**) *сов* (*не)перех* (+*acc или* +*gen*: *мусору*) to pile up; **навали́ться** (*impf* **нава́ливаться**) *сов возв*: **навали́ться на** +*acc* (*на дверь итп*) to lean into
нава́лом *как сказ* (+*gen*: *разг*) loads of; **у**

него́ де́нег нава́лом he has loads of money
наведе́ни|е (**-я**) *ср* (*порядка*) establishment; (*справок*) making
наве́к(и) *нареч* (*навсегда*) forever
наве́рно(е) *вводн сл* probably
наверняка́ *вводн сл* (*конечно*) certainly ▷ *нареч* (*несомненно*) definitely, for sure
наве́рх *нареч* up; (*на верхний этаж*) upstairs; (*на поверхность*) to the top
наверху́ *нареч* at the top; (*на верхнем этаже*) upstairs
нав|ести́ (**-еду́, -едёшь**; *pt* **-ёл, -ела́, -ело́**, *impf* **наводи́ть**) *сов перех* (*ужас, грусть итп*) to cause; (*бинокль*) to focus; (*орудие*) to aim; (*порядок*) to establish; **наводи́ть** (*perf* **навести́**) **кого́-н на** +*acc* (*на место, на след*) to lead sb to; **наводи́ть** (*perf* **навести́**) **спра́вки** to make inquiries
наве|сти́ть (**-щу́, -сти́шь**; *impf* **навеща́ть**) *сов перех* to visit
на́взничь *нареч* on one's back
навига́ци|я (**-и**) *ж* navigation
нави́с|нуть (**-ну**; *pt* **-, -ла**, *impf* **нависа́ть**) *сов*: **нави́снуть на** +*acc* (*волосы: на лоб*) to hang down over
нав|оди́ть (**-ожу́, -о́дишь**) *несов от* **навести́**
наводне́ни|е (**-я**) *ср* flood
наво́з (**-а**) *м* manure
на́волоч|ка (**-ки**; *gen pl* **-ек**) *ж* pillowcase
навре|ди́ть (**-жу́, -ди́шь**) *сов от* **вреди́ть**
навсегда́ *нареч* forever; **раз и навсегда́** once and for all
навстре́чу *предл* +*dat* towards ▷ *нареч*: **идти́ навстре́чу кому́-н** (*перен*) to give sb a hand
на́вык (**-а**) *м* skill
навы́нос *нареч* to take away (*Brit*), to go (*US*)
навы́пуск *нареч* outside, over
нав|яза́ть (**-яжу́, -я́жешь**; *impf* **навя́зывать**) *сов перех*: **навяза́ть что-н кому́-н** to impose sth on sb; **навяза́ться** (*impf* **навя́зываться**) *сов возв* to impose o.s.
навя́зчивый *прил* persistent
нагиба́|ть(ся) (**-ю(сь)**) *несов от* **нагну́ть(ся)**
нагле́|ть (**-ю**; *perf* **обнагле́ть**) *несов* to get cheeky; **нагле́ц** (**-а́**) *м* impudent upstart
нагля́дный *прил* (*пример, случай*) clear; (*метод обучения*) visual
наг|на́ть (**-оню́, -о́нишь**; *impf* **нагоня́ть**) *сов перех* (*беглеца*) to catch up with; (*упущенное*) to make up for; **нагоня́ть** (*perf* **нагна́ть**) **страх на кого́-н** to strike fear into sb
нагнета́|ть (**-ю**) *несов перех* (*воздух*) to pump; (*перен: напряжение*) to heighten
нагн|у́ть (**-у́, -ёшь**; *impf* **нагиба́ть**) *сов*

перех (*ветку*) to pull down; (*голову*) to bend; **нагну́ться** (*impf* **нагиба́ться**) *сов возв* to bend down

наго́й *прил* (*человек*) naked, nude

на́голо *нареч*: **остри́чься на́голо** to shave one's head

нагоня́|ть (-**ю**) *несов от* **нагна́ть**

наготове *нареч* at the ready

награ́д|а (-**ы**) *ж* reward, prize; (*Воен*) decoration; **награ|ди́ть** (-**жу́**, -**ди́шь**; *impf* **награжда́ть**) *сов перех*: **награди́ть кого́-н чем-н** (*орденом*) to award sb sth, award sth to sb; (*перен: талантом*) to endow sb with sth

нагрева́тельный *прил*: **нагрева́тельный прибо́р** heating appliance

нагре́|ть (-**ю**; *impf* **нагрева́ть**) *сов перех* to heat, warm; **нагре́ться** (*impf* **нагрева́ться**) *сов возв* to warm up

нагроможде́ни|е (-**я**) *ср* pile

нагруб|и́ть (-**лю́**, -**и́шь**) *сов от* **груби́ть**

нагру́дник (-**а**) *м* bib; **нагру́дный** *прил*: **нагру́дный карма́н** breast pocket

нагру|зи́ть (-**ужу́**, -**у́зишь**) *сов от* **грузи́ть** ▷ (*impf* **нагружа́ть**) *перех* to load up; (*impf* **нагружа́ть**) *перех* to load

над *предл* +*instr* above; **рабо́тать** (*impf*) **над** +*instr* to work on; **ду́мать** (*impf*) **над** +*instr* to think about; **смея́ться** (*impf*) **над** +*instr* to laugh at; **сиде́ть** (*impf*) **над кни́гой** to sit over a book

над|ави́ть (-**авлю́**, -**а́вишь**; *impf* **нада́вливать**) *сов*: **надави́ть на** +*асс* (*на дверь итп*) to lean against; (*на кно́пку*) to press

надви́н|уть (-**у**; *impf* **надвига́ть**) *сов перех*: **надви́нуть что-н** (*на* +*асс*) to pull sth down (over); **надви́нуться** (*impf* **надвига́ться**) *сов возв* (*опасность, старость*) to approach

на́двое *нареч* in half

надгро́би|е (-**я**) *ср* gravestone

надева́|ть (-**ю**) *несов от* **наде́ть**

наде́жд|а (-**ы**) *ж* hope

наде́жный *прил* reliable; (*механизм*) secure

наде́ла|ть (-**ю**) *сов (не)перех* (+*асс или* +*gen*: *ошибок*) to make lots of; **что ты наде́лал?** what have you done?

надел|и́ть (-**ю́**, -**и́шь**; *impf* **наделя́ть**) *сов перех*: **надели́ть кого́-н чем-н** (*землёй*) to grant sb sth

наде́|ть (-**ну**, -**нешь**; *impf* **надева́ть**) *сов перех* to put on

наде́|яться (-**юсь**) *несов возв* +*infin* to hope to do; **наде́яться** (*perf* **понаде́яться**) **на** +*асс* (*на друга*) to rely on; (*на улучшение*) to hope for

надзира́тел|ь (-**я**) *м* guard

надзо́р (-**а**) *м* control; (*орган*) monitoring body

надл|оми́ть (-**омлю́**, -**о́мишь**; *impf* **надла́мывать**) *сов перех* to break; (*здоровье, психику*) to damage

⬤ **КЛЮЧЕВОЕ СЛОВО**

на́до[1] *как сказ* **1** (*следует*): **на́до ему́ помо́чь** it is necessary to help him; **на́до, что́бы он пришёл во́время** he must come on time; **на́до всегда́ говори́ть пра́вду** one must always speak the truth; **мне/ему́ на́до зако́нчить рабо́ту** I/he must finish the job; **помо́чь тебе́? — не на́до!** can I help you? — there's no need!; **не на́до!** (*не де́лай э́того*) don't!

2 (*о потребности*): **на́до мно́го лет** it takes many years; **им на́до 5 рубле́й** they need 5 roubles; **что тебе́ на́до?** what do you want?; **так ему́/ей и на́до** (*разг*) it serves him/her right; **на́до же!** (*разг*) of all things!

на́до[2] *предл* = **над**

надое́|сть (*как* **есть**; *см Table 15*; *impf* **надоеда́ть**) *сов*: **надое́сть кому́-н** (+*instr*) (*разгово́рами, упрёками*) to bore sb (with); **мне надое́ло ждать** I'm tired of waiting; **он мне надое́л** I've had enough of him

надо́лго *нареч* for a long time

надорв|а́ть (-**у́**, -**ёшь**; *impf* **надрыва́ть**) *сов перех* (*перен: силы*) to tax; (: *здоровье*) to put a strain on; **надорва́ться** (*impf* **надрыва́ться**) *сов возв* to do o.s. an injury; (*перен*) to overexhaust o.s.

надсмо́трщик (-**а**) *м* (*тюре́мный*) warden

наду́|ть (-**ю**, -**ешь**; *impf* **надува́ть**) *сов перех* (*мяч, колесо́*) to inflate, blow up; **наду́ться** (*impf* **надува́ться**) *сов возв* (*матра́с, мяч*) to inflate; (*вены*) to swell; (*перен: от важности*) to swell up; (: *разг: обидеться*) to sulk

наеда́|ться (-**юсь**) *несов от* **нае́сться**

наедине́ *нареч*: **наедине́** (*с* +*instr*) alone (with); **они́ оста́лись наедине́** they were left on their own

нае́здник (-**а**) *м* rider

наезжа́|ть (-**ю**) *несов от* **нае́хать**

наёмник (-**а**) *м* mercenary; (*рабо́тник*) casual worker

наёмный *прил* (*труд, рабо́тник*) hired; **наёмный уби́йца** hitman

нае́|сться (*как* **есть**; *см Table 15*; *impf* **наеда́ться**) *сов возв* (+*gen*: *сла́дкого*) to eat a lot of; **я нае́лся** I'm full

нае́|хать (*как* **е́хать**; *см Table 19*; *impf* **наезжа́ть**) *сов* (*разг: го́сти*) to arrive in droves; **наезжа́ть** (*perf* **нае́хать**) **на** +*асс* to drive into

наж|а́ть (-**му́**, -**мёшь**; *impf* **нажима́ть**) *сов* (*перен*): **нажа́ть на** +*асс* (*на кно́пку*) to press

нажда́чн|ый *прил*: **нажда́чная бума́га** emery paper

нажи́м (-**а**) *м* pressure

нажима́|ть (-**ю**) *несов от* **нажа́ть**

нажи́ть (-ву́, -вёшь; *impf* **нажив́ать**) *сов перех* (*состояние*) to acquire;
нажи́ться (*impf* **нажив́аться**) *сов возв*: **нажи́ться (на** +*prp*) to profiteer (from)

наза́д *нареч* back; (*нагнуться, катиться итп*) backwards; (*тому*) **наза́д** ago; **де́сять лет/неде́лю (тому) наза́д** ten years/one week ago

назва́ни|е (-я) *ср* name; **торго́вое назва́ние** trade name

наз|ва́ть (-ову́, -овёшь; *impf* **называ́ть**) *сов перех* (*дать имя*) to call; (*назначить*) to name

назе́мн|ый *прил* surface; **назе́мные войска́** ground troops

на́земь *нареч* to the ground

назло́ *нареч* out of spite; **назло́ кому́-н** to spite sb; **как назло́** to make things worse

назначе́ни|е (-я) *ср* (*цены итп*) setting; (*на работу*) appointment; (*функция*) function; **пункт** *или* **ме́сто назначе́ния** destination; **назна́ч|ить** (-у, -ишь; *impf* **назнача́ть**) *сов перех* (*на работу*) to appoint; (*цену*) to set; (*встречу*) to arrange; (*лекарство*) to prescribe

назо́йливый *прил* persistent

назре́|ть (*3sg* -ет, *impf* **назрева́ть**) *сов* (*вопрос*) to become unavoidable

называ́емый *прил*: **так называ́емый** so-called

называ́|ть (-ю) *несов от* **назва́ть**; **называ́ться** *несов возв* (*носить название*) to be called

наибо́лее *нареч*: **наибо́лее интере́сный/ краси́вый** the most interesting/beautiful

наибо́льший *прил* the greatest

наи́вный *прил* naive

наизна́нку *нареч* inside out

наизу́сть *нареч*: **знать/вы́учить наизу́сть** to know/learn by heart

наиме́нее *нареч*: **наиме́нее уда́чный/ спосо́бный** the least successful/capable

наименова́ни|е (-я) *ср* name; (*книги*) title, name

наиме́ньший *прил* (*длина, вес*) the smallest; (*усилие*) the least

на|йти́ (-йду́, -йдёшь; *pt* -шёл, -шла, -шло́, *impf* **находи́ть**) *сов перех* to find; **на меня́ нашёл смех** I couldn't help laughing; **найти́сь** (*impf* **находи́ться**) *сов возв* (*потерянное*) to turn up; (*добровольцы*) to come forward; (*не растеряться*) to regain control

наказа́ни|е (-я) *ср* punishment; **нак|аза́ть** (-ажу́, -а́жешь; *impf* **нака́зывать**) *сов перех* to punish

нака́л (-а) *м* (*борьбы*) heat

накал|и́ть (-ю́, -и́шь; *impf* **накаля́ть**) *сов перех* to heat up; (*перен: обстановку*) to hot up; **накали́ться** (*impf* **накаля́ться**) *сов возв* to heat; (*перен: обстановка*) to hot up

накану́не *нареч* the day before, the previous day ▷ *предл* +*gen* on the eve of

нака́плива|ть(ся) (-ю(сь)) *несов от* **накопи́ть(ся)**

нак|ати́ть (-ачу́, -а́тишь; *impf* **нака́тывать**) *сов*: **накати́ть (на** +*acc*) (*волна*) to roll up (onto)

накача́|ть (-ю; *impf* **нака́чивать**) *сов перех* (*камеру*) to pump up

наки́д|ка (-ки; *gen pl* -ок) *ж* (*одежда*) wrap; (*покрывало*) bedspread, throw

наки́н|уть (-у; *impf* **наки́дывать**) *сов перех* (*платок*) to throw on; **наки́нуться** (*impf* **наки́дываться**) *сов возв*: **наки́нуться на** +*acc* (*на человека*) to hurl o.s. at; (*разг: на еду, на книгу*) to get stuck into

на́кип|ь (-и) *ж* (*на бульоне*) scum; (*в чайнике*) fur (*Brit*), scale (*US*)

накладн|а́я (-о́й) *ж* (*Комм*) bill of lading (*Brit*), waybill (*US*); **грузова́я накладна́я** consignment note

накла́дыва|ть (-ю) *несов от* **наложи́ть**

накле́|ить (-ю, -ишь; *impf* **накле́ивать**) *сов перех* to stick on

накле́|йка (-йка; *gen pl* -ек) *ж* label

накло́н (-а) *м* incline, slope

накл|они́ть (-оню́, -о́нишь; *impf* **наклоня́ть**) *сов перех* to tilt; **наклони́ться** (*impf* **наклоня́ться**) *сов возв* to bend down

накло́нност|ь (-и) *ж*: **накло́нность к** +*dat* (*к музыке итп*) aptitude for; **дурны́е/ хоро́шие накло́нности** bad/good habits

нак|оло́ть (-олю́, -о́лешь; *impf* **нака́лывать**) *сов перех* (*руку*) to prick; (*прикрепить*): **наколо́ть (на** +*acc*) (*на шляпу, на дверь*) to pin on(to)

наконе́ц *нареч* at last, finally ▷ *вводн сл* after all; **наконе́ц-то!** at long last!

наконе́чник (-а) *м* tip, end

накоп|и́ть (-лю́, -ишь; *сов от* **копи́ть** ▷ (*impf* **нака́пливать**) *перех* (*силы, информацию*) to store up; (*средства*) to accumulate; **накопи́ться** *сов от* **копи́ться** ▷ (*impf* **нака́пливаться**) *возв* (*силы*) to build up; (*средства*) to accumulate

нак|орми́ть (-ормлю́, -о́рмишь) *сов от* **корми́ть**

накрича́ть (-у́, -и́шь) *сов*: **накрича́ть на** +*acc* to shout at

накру|ти́ть (-чу́, -у́тишь; *impf* **накру́чивать**) *сов перех*: **накрути́ть (на** +*acc*) (*гайку*) to screw on(to); (*канат*) to wind (round)

накр|ы́ть (-о́ю, -о́ешь; *impf* **накрыва́ть**) *сов перех* to cover; **накрыва́ть** (*perf* **накры́ть**) (**на**) **стол** to lay the table; **накры́ться** (*impf* **накрыва́ться**) *сов возв*: **накры́ться** (+*instr*) (*одеялом*) to cover o.s. up (with)

налага́|ть (-ю) *несов от* **наложи́ть**

нала́|дить (-жу, -дишь; *impf* **нала́живать**) *сов перех* (*механизм*) to repair, fix; (*сотрудничество*) to initiate;

(*хозяйство*) to sort out; **нала́диться**
(*impf* **нала́живаться**) *сов возв* (*работа*)
to go well; (*отношения, здоровье*) to
improve

нале́во *нареч* (to the) left; (*разг: продать*)
on the side

налегке́ *нареч* (*ехать*) without luggage

налёт (-а) *м* raid; (*пыли, плесени*) thin
coating *или* layer; **нале|те́ть** (-чу́,
-ти́шь; *impf* **налета́ть**) *сов* (*буря*) to
spring up; **налета́ть** (*perf* **налете́ть**) **на**
+*acc* (*натолкнуться*) to fly against;
(*напасть*) to swoop down on

нал|и́ть (-ью́, -ьёшь; *impf* **налива́ть**) *сов
перех* to pour (out)

налицо́ *как сказ*: **фа́кты налицо́** the facts
are obvious; **доказа́тельство налицо́** there
is proof

нали́чи|е (-я) *ср* presence

нали́чност|ь (-и) *ж* cash

нали́чн|ые (-ых) *мн* cash *ед*

нали́чный *прил*: **нали́чные де́ньги** cash;
нали́чный расчёт cash payment;
нали́чный счёт cash account

нало́г (-а) *м* tax; **нало́г на ввоз** +*gen*
import duty on; **нало́гов|ый** *прил* tax;
нало́говая деклара́ция tax return;
налогоплате́льщик (-а) *м* taxpayer

нал|ожи́ть (-ожу́, -о́жишь; *impf*
накла́дывать) *сов перех* to put *или*
place on; (*компресс, бинт, лак*) to apply
▷ (*impf* **налага́ть**) (*штраф*) to impose

нам *мест см* **мы**

нама́|зать (-жу, -жешь) *сов от* **ма́зать**

нама́тыва|ть (-ю) *несов от* **намота́ть**

намёк (-а) *м* hint

намека́|ть (-ю; *perf* **намекну́ть**) *несов*:
намека́ть на +*acc* to hint at

намерева́|ться (-юсь) *несов возв* +*infin*
to intend to do

наме́рен *как сказ*: **он наме́рен уе́хать** he
intends to leave

наме́рени|е (-я) *ср* intention;
наме́ренный *прил* deliberate

намета́|ть (-ю) *сов от* **мета́ть**

наме́|тить (-чу, -тишь; *impf* **намеча́ть**)
сов перех to plan; (*план*) to project;
наме́титься *сов от* **ме́титься** ▷ (*impf*
намеча́ться) *возв* to begin to show;
(*событие*) to be coming up

на́ми *мест см* **мы**

намно́го *нареч* much, far; **намно́го ху́же/
интере́снее** much worse/more interesting

намо́кн|уть (-у; *impf* **намока́ть**) *сов возв* to
get wet

намо́рдник (-а) *м* muzzle

намо́рщ|ить (-у, -ишь) *сов от* **мо́рщить**

намота́|ть (-ю) *сов от* **мота́ть**

нам|очи́ть (-очу́, -о́чишь) *сов от*
мочи́ть

нан|ести́ (-есу́, -есёшь; *pt* -ёс, -есла́,
-есло́, *impf* **наноси́ть**) *сов перех* (*мазь,
краску*) to apply; (*рисунок*) to draw; (*на
карту*) to plot; (*удар*) to deliver; (*урон*) to

inflict; **нанести́** (*perf*) **кому́-н визи́т** to pay
sb a visit

нани́зыва|ть (-ю) *несов перех* to string

на|ня́ть (-йму́, -ймёшь; *impf* **нанима́ть**)
сов перех (*работника*) to hire; (*лодку,
машину*) to hire, rent; **наня́ться** (*impf*
нанима́ться) *сов возв* to get a job

наоборо́т *нареч* (*делать*) the wrong way
(round) ▷ *вводн сл, част* on the contrary

наобу́м *нареч* without thinking

напада́|ть (-ю) *несов от* **напа́сть**

напада́ющ|ий (-его) *м* (*Спорт*) forward

нападе́ни|е (-я) *ср* attack; (*Спорт*)
forwards *мн*

напа́дки (-ок) *мн* attacks

напа́сть (-аду́, -адёшь; *impf* **напада́ть**)
сов: **напа́сть на** +*acc* to attack;
(*обнаружить*) to strike; (*тоска, страх*) to
grip, seize

напе́в (-а) *м* tune, melody

напева́|ть (-ю) *несов от* **напе́ть** ▷ *перех*
(*песенку*) to hum

наперебо́й *нареч* vying with each other

наперегонки́ *нареч* (*разг*) racing each
other

наперёд *нареч* (*знать, угада́ть*)
beforehand; **за́дом наперёд** back to front

напереко́р *предл* +*dat* in defiance of

нап|е́ть (-ою́, -оёшь; *impf* **напева́ть**)
сов перех (*мотив, песню*) to sing

напива́|ться (-юсь) *несов от* **напи́ться**

напи́льник (-а) *м* file

напира́|ть (-ю) *несов*: **напира́ть на** +*acc*
(*теснить*) to push against

написа́ни|е (-я) *ср* writing; (*слова*)
spelling

нап|иса́ть (-ишу́, -и́шешь) *сов от*
писа́ть

напи́т|ок (-ка) *м* drink

напи́ться (-ью́сь, -ьёшься; *impf*
напива́ться) *сов возв*: **напи́ться** (+*gen*)
to have a good drink (of); (*разг: опьянеть*)
to get drunk

напл|ева́ть (-юю́) *сов от* **плева́ть**

наплы́в (-а) *м* (*туристов*) influx;
(*: заявлений, чувств*) flood

наплы́|ть (-ву́, -вёшь; *impf* **наплыва́ть**)
сов (*перен: воспоминания*) to come
flooding back; **наплыва́ть** (*perf* **наплы́ть**)
на +*acc* (*на мель, на камень*) to run
against

напова́л *нареч* (*убить*) outright

нап|ои́ть (-ою́, -о́ишь) *сов от* **пои́ть**

напока́з *нареч* for show

напо́лн|ить (-ю, -ишь; *impf* **наполня́ть**)
сов перех +*instr* to fill with; **напо́лниться**
(*impf* **наполня́ться**) *сов возв*:
напо́лниться +*instr* to fill with

наполови́ну *нареч* by half; (*наполнить*)
half

напомина́|ть (-ю) *несов от* **напо́мнить**
▷ *перех* (*иметь сходство*) to resemble

напо́мн|ить (-ю, -ишь; *impf*
напомина́ть) *сов (не)перех*: **напо́мнить**

кому́-н +acc или о +prp to remind sb of

напóр (-а) м pressure

напослéдок нареч finally

напрáв|**ить** (-лю, -ишь; impf **направля́ть**) сов перех to direct; (к врачу́) to refer; (послáние) to send; **напрáвиться** (impf **направля́ться**) сов возв: **напрáвиться в** +acc/к +dat итп to make for

направлéни|**е** (-я) ср direction; (дéятельности: также Воен) line; (политики) orientation; (докумéнт: в больни́цу) referral; (: на рабóту, на учёбу) directive; **по направлéнию к** +dat towards

напрáво нареч (идти́) to (the) right

напрáсно нареч in vain

напрáшива|**ться** (-юсь) несов от **напроси́ться**

напримéр вводн сл for example или instance

напрокáт нареч: **взять напрокáт** to hire; **отдавáть** (perf **отдáть**) **напрокáт** to hire out

напролёт нареч without a break

напролóм нареч stopping at nothing

напр|**оси́ться** (-ошу́сь, -óсишься; impf **напрáшиваться**) сов возв (разг: в гóсти) to force o.s.; **напрáшиваться** (perf **напроси́ться**) **на** +acc (на комплимéнт) to invite

напрóтив нареч opposite ▷ вводн сл on the contrary ▷ предл +gen opposite

напряга́|**ть(ся)** (-ю(сь)) несов от **напря́чь(ся)**

напряжéни|**е** (-я) ср tension; (Физ: механи́ческое) strain, stress; (: электри́ческое) voltage

напряжённый прил tense; (отношéния, встрéча) strained

напрями́к нареч (идти́) straight

напр|**я́чь** (-ягу́, -яжёшь итп, -ягу́т; pt -я́г, -ягла́, -ягло́ impf **напряга́ть**) сов перех to strain; **напря́чься** (impf **напряга́ться**) сов возв (му́скулы) to become tense; (человéк) to strain o.s.

напыл|**и́ть** (-ю́, -и́шь) сов от **пыли́ть**

напы́щенный прил pompous

наравнé нареч: **наравнé с** +instr (по однóй ли́нии) on a level with; (на рáвных прáвах) on an equal footing with

нарас|**ти́** (3sg -тёт, impf **нараста́ть**) сов (процéнты) to accumulate; (волнéние, сопротивлéние) to grow

нарасхвáт нареч like hot cakes

нарáщива|**ть** (-ю) несов перех (тéмпы, объём итп) to increase

нарв|**áть** (-ý, -ёшь) сов (не)перех (+acc или +gen: цветóв, ягод) to pick; **нарвáться** (impf **нарывáться**) сов возв (разг): **нарвáться на** +acc (на хулигáна) to run up against; (на неприя́тность) to run into

наре́|**зать** (-жу, -жешь; impf **нареза́ть**) сов перех to cut

наре́чи|**е** (-я) ср (Линг: часть рéчи) adverb; (: говóры) dialect

нарис|**овáть** (-ýю) сов от **рисовáть**

наркоби́знес (-а) м drug trafficking

наркодéл|**ец** (-ьцá) м drug dealer

наркóз (-а) м (Мед) anaesthesia (Brit), anesthesia (US)

наркологи́ческий прил: **наркологи́ческий диспансéр** drug-abuse clinic

наркомáн (-а) м drug addict или abuser; **наркомáни**|**я** (-и) ж (Мед) drug addiction или abuse

наркóтик (-а) м drug

наркоти́ческий прил (срéдства) drug

нарóд (-а; part gen -у) м people мн; **нарóдность** (-и) ж nation

нарóдный прил national; (фронт) popular; (искýсство) folk

нарочи́тый прил deliberate; **нарóчно** нареч purposely, on purpose; **как нарóчно** (разг) to make things worse

нарýжность (-и) ж appearance; **нарýжный** прил (двéрь, стенá) exterior; (спокóйствие) outward; **нарýжу** нареч out

нарýчник (-а) м (обычн мн) handcuff

нарýчн|**ый** прил: **нарýчные часы́** (wrist) watch ед

наруша́|**ть(ся)** (-ю(сь)) несов от **нарýшить(ся)**

нарýшител|**ь** (-я) м (закóна) transgressor; (Юр: порядка) offender; **нарýшитель грани́цы** person who illegally crosses a border; **нарýшитель дисципли́ны** troublemaker

нарýш|**ить** (-у, -ишь; impf **наруша́ть**) сов перех (покóй) to disturb; (связь) to break; (прáвила, договóр) to violate; (дисципли́ну) to breach; **нарýшить** (perf **нарýшить**) **грани́цу** to illegally cross a border; **нарýшиться** (impf **наруша́ться**) сов возв to be broken или disturbed

нары́в (-а) м (Мед) abscess, boil

наря́д (-а) м (одéжда) attire; (краси́вый) outfit; (распоряжéние) directive; (Комм) order; **наря**|**ди́ть** (-жý, -́дишь; impf **наряжáть**) сов перех (одéть) to dress; **наряжáть** (perf **наряди́ть**) **ёлку** ≈ to decorate (Brit) или trim (US) the Christmas tree; **наряди́ться** (impf **наряжáться**) сов возв: **наряди́ться** (в +acc) to dress o.s. (in); **наря́дный** прил (человéк) well-dressed; (кóмната, ýлица) nicely decorated; (шля́па, плáтье) fancy

наря́ду нареч: **наря́ду с** +instr along with; (наравнé) on an equal footing with

наряжá|**ть(ся)** (-ю(сь)) несов от **наряди́ть(ся)**

нас мест см **мы**

насекóм|**ое** (-ого) ср insect

населе́ни|е (-я) *ср* population

населённый *прил* (*район*) populated; **населённый пункт** locality

насел|и́ть (-ю́, -и́шь; *impf* **населя́ть**) *сов перех* (*регион*) to settle

населя́|ть (-ю) *несов от* **насели́ть** ▷ *перех* (*проживать*) to inhabit

насе́ч|ка (-ки; *gen pl* -ек) *ж* notch

наси́ли|е (-я) *ср* violence; **наси́л|овать** (-ую; *perf* **изнаси́ловать**) *несов перех* (*женщину*) to rape

наси́льственный *прил* violent

наска́кива|ть (-ю) *несов от* **наскочи́ть**

насквозь *нареч* through

наско́лько *нареч* so much

наско́лько *нареч* so much

наск|очи́ть (-очу́, -о́чишь; *impf* **наска́кивать**) *сов*: **наскочи́ть на** +*acc* to run into

наску́ч|ить (-у, -ишь) *сов*: **наску́чить кому́-н** to bore sb

насла|ди́ться (-жу́сь, -ди́шься; *impf* **наслажда́ться**) *сов возв* +*instr* to relish

наслажде́ни|е (-я) *ср* enjoyment, relish

насле́ди|е (-я) *ср* (*культурное*) heritage; (*идеологическое*) legacy

насле́д|овать (-ую) (*не*)*сов перех* to inherit; (*престол*) to succeed to

насле́дств|о (-а) *ср* (*имущество*) inheritance; (*культурное*) heritage; (*идеологическое*) legacy

наслы́шан *как сказ*: **я наслы́шан об э́том** I have heard a lot about it

насма́рку *нареч* (*разг*): **идти́ насма́рку** to be wasted

на́смерть *нареч* (*сражаться*) to the death; (*ранить*) fatally

насмеха́|ться (-юсь) *несов возв*: **насмеха́ться над** +*instr* to taunt

насме́ш|ить (-у́, -и́шь) *сов от* **смеши́ть**

насме́я|ться (-юсь) *сов возв*: **насмея́ться над** +*instr* to offend

на́сморк (-а) *м* runny nose

насовсе́м *нареч* (*разг*) for good

насор|и́ть (-ю́, -и́шь) *сов от* **сори́ть**

насо́с (-а) *м* pump

наста|ва́ть (*3sg* -ёт) *несов от* **наста́ть**

наста́ива|ть (-ю) *несов от* **настоя́ть**

наста́|ть (*3sg* -нет, *impf* **настава́ть**) *сов* to come; (*ночь*) to fall

на́стежь *нареч* (*открыть*) wide

насти́|чь (-гну, -гнешь; *pt* -г, -гла, *impf* **настига́ть**) *сов перех* to catch up with

насто́йчивый *прил* persistent; (*просьба*) insistent

насто́лько *нареч* so

насто́льный *прил* (*лампа, часы*) table; (*календарь*) desk

насторож|е́ *как сказ*: **он всегда́ насторо́же** he is always on the alert

насторож|и́ть (-у́, -и́шь; *impf* **настора́живать**) *сов перех* to alert; **насторожи́ться** (*impf* **настора́живаться**) *сов возв* to become more alert

настоя́ни|е (-я) *ср*: **по настоя́нию кого́-н** on sb's insistence

настоя́тельный *прил* (*просьба*) persistent; (*задача*) urgent

настоя́щ|ий *прил* real; (*момент*) present; **по-настоя́щему** (*как надо*) properly; (*преданный*) really; **настоя́щее вре́мя** (*Линг*) the present tense

настра́ива|ть(ся) (-ю(сь)) *несов от* **настро́ить(ся)**

настрое́ни|е (-я) *ср* mood; (*антивоенное*) feeling; **не в настрое́нии** in a bad mood

настро́|ить (-ю, -ишь; *impf* **настра́ивать**) *сов перех* (*пианино итп*) to tune; (*механизм*) to adjust; **настра́ивать** (*perf* **настро́ить**) **кого́-н на** +*acc* to put sb in the right frame of mind for; **настра́ивать** (*perf* **настро́ить**) **кого́-н про́тив** +*gen* to incite sb against; **настро́иться** (*impf* **настра́иваться**) *сов возв*: **настро́иться** (*perf*) +*infin* to be disposed to do

настро́|й (-я) *м* mood

настро́йщик (-а) *м*: **настро́йщик роя́ля** piano tuner

наступа́|ть (-ю) *несов от* **наступи́ть** ▷ *неперех* (*Воен*) to go on the offensive

наст|упи́ть (-уплю́, -у́пишь; *impf* **наступа́ть**) *сов* to come; (*ночь*) to fall; **наступа́ть** (*perf* **наступи́ть**) **на** +*acc* (*на ка́мень итп*) to step on

наступле́ни|е (-я) *ср* (*Воен*) offensive; (*весны, старости*) beginning; (*темноты*) fall

на́сухо *нареч*: **вы́тереть что́-н на́сухо** to dry sth thoroughly

насу́щный *прил* vital

насчёт *предл* +*gen* regarding

насчита́|ть (-ю; *impf* **насчи́тывать**) *сов перех* to count

насчи́тыва|ть (-ю) *несов от* **насчита́ть** ▷ *неперех* to have

насы́п|ать (-лю, -лешь; *impf* **насыпа́ть**) *сов перех* to pour

на́сып|ь (-и) *ж* embankment

ната́лкива|ть(ся) (-ю(сь)) *несов от* **натолкну́ть(ся)**

натвор|и́ть (-ю́, -и́шь) *сов* (*не*)*перех* (+*acc или* +*gen*: *разг*) to get up to

нат|ере́ть (-ру́, -рёшь; *pt* -ёр, -ёрла, *impf* **натира́ть**) *сов перех* (*ботинки, полы*) to polish; (*морковь, сыр итп*) to grate; (*ногу*) to chafe

на́тиск (-а) *м* pressure

наткн|у́ться (-у́сь, -ёшься; *impf* **натыка́ться**) *сов возв*: **наткну́ться на** +*acc* to bump into

НА́ТО *ср сокр* NATO (= North Atlantic Treaty Organization)

натолкн|у́ть (-у́, -ёшь; *impf* **ната́лкивать**) *сов перех*: **натолкну́ть кого́-н на** +*acc* (*на иде́ю*) to lead sb to; **натолкну́ться** (*impf* **ната́лкиваться**) *сов возв*: **натолкну́ться на** +*acc* to bump into

натоща́к *нареч* on an empty stomach

на́три|й (**-я**) *м* sodium

нату́р|а (**-ы**) *ж* (*характер*) nature; (*натурщик*) model (*Art*); **нату́рой, в нату́ре** (*Экон*) in kind; **натура́льный** *прил* natural; (*мех, кожа*) real; **нату́рщик** (**-а**) *м* model (*Art*)

натыка́|ться (**-юсь**) *несов от* **наткну́ться**

натюрмо́рт (**-а**) *м* still life

натя́гива|ть(ся) (**-ю**) *несов от* **натяну́ть(ся)**

натя́нутый *прил* strained

нат|яну́ть (**-яну́, -я́нешь**; *impf* **натя́гивать**) *сов перех* to pull tight; (*перчатки*) to pull on; **натяну́ться** (*impf* **натя́гиваться**) *сов возв* to tighten

науга́д *нареч* at random

нау́к|а (**-и**) *ж* science; **есте́ственные нау́ки** science; **гуманита́рные нау́ки** arts

нау́тро *нареч* next morning

на|учи́ть(ся) (**-учу́(сь), -у́чишь(ся)**) *сов от* **учи́ть(ся)**

нау́чно-популя́рный *прил* science

нау́чно-техни́ческий *прил* scientific

нау́чный *прил* scientific

нау́шник (**-а**) *м* (*обычно мн: также* **магнитофо́нные нау́шники**) headphones

наха́л (**-а**) *м* (*разг*) cheeky beggar; **наха́льный** *прил* cheeky

нахлы́н|уть (*3sg* **-ет**) *сов* to surge

нахму́р|ить(ся) (**-ю(сь), -ишь(ся)**) *несов от* **хму́рить(ся)**

нах|оди́ть (**-ожу́, -о́дишь**) *несов от* **найти́**; **находи́ться** *несов от* **найти́сь** ▷ *возв* (*дом, город*) to be situated; (*человек*) to be

нахо́д|ка (**-ки**; *gen pl* **-ок**) *ж* (*потерянного*) discovery; **он — нахо́дка для нас** he is a real find for us; **Бюро́ нахо́док** lost property office (*Brit*), lost and found (*US*)

нахо́дчивый *прил* resourceful

наце́л|ить (**-ю, -ишь**; *impf* **наце́ливать**) *сов перех*: **наце́лить кого́-н на** +*acc* to push sb towards; **наце́литься** *сов от* **це́литься**

наце́н|ка (**-ки**; *gen pl* **-ок**) *ж* (*на товар*) surcharge

национали́ст (**-а**) *м* nationalist

национа́льност|ь (**-и**) *ж* nationality; (*нация*) nation

национа́льный *прил* national

наци́ст (**-а**) *м* Nazi

на́ци|я (**-и**) *ж* nation; **Организа́ция Объединённых На́ций** United Nations Organization

нача|ди́ть (**-жу́, -ди́шь**) *сов от* **чади́ть**

нача́л|о (**-а**) *ср* beginning, start; **быть** (*impf*) **под нача́лом кого́-н** *или* **у кого́-н** to be under sb

нача́льник (**-а**) *м* (*руководитель*) boss; (*цеха*) floor manager; (*управления*) head

нача́льн|ый *прил* (*период*) initial; (*глава книги*) first; **нача́льная шко́ла** (*Просвещ*) primary (*Brit*) *или* elementary (*US*) school; **нача́льные кла́ссы** (*Просвещ*) the first three classes of primary school

● **НАЧА́ЛЬНЫЕ КЛА́ССЫ**
●
● Children start school at the age of six or
● seven. There are no separate primary
● schools in Russia. The first three classes
● of the 10-year education system are
● referred to as **нача́льные кла́ссы**. The
● main emphasis is on reading, writing and
● arithmetic. Other subjects taught include
● drawing, PE and singing.

нача́льств|о (**-а**) *ср* (*власть*) authority ▷ *собир* (*руководители*) management

нач|а́ть (**-ну́, -нёшь**; *impf* **начина́ть**) *сов перех* to begin, start

начеку́ *нареч*: **быть начеку́** to be on one's guard

на́черно *нареч* roughly

нач|ерти́ть (**-ерчу́, -е́ртишь**) *сов от* **черти́ть**

начина́ни|е (**-я**) *ср* initiative

начина́|ть (**-ю**) *несов от* **нача́ть**

начина́ющий *прил* (*писатель*) novice ▷ (**-его**) *м* beginner

начина́я *предл* (+*instr*: включая) including; **начина́я с** +*gen* from; (*при отсчёте*) starting from; **начина́я от** +*gen* (*включая*) including

начин|и́ть (**-ю́, -и́шь**; *impf* **начина́ть**) *сов перех* (*пирог*) to fill

начи́н|ка (**-ки**; *gen pl* **-ок**) *ж* filling

начну́ *итп см* **нача́ть**

наш (**-его**; *см Table 9*; *f* **-а**, *nt* **-е**, *pl* **-и**) *притяж мест* our; **чей э́то дом? — наш** whose is this house? — ours; **чьи э́то кни́ги? — на́ши** whose are these books? — ours; **по-на́шему** our way; (*по нашему мнению*) in our opinion

наше́стви|е (**-я**) *ср* invasion

нащу́па|ть (**-ю**; *impf* **нащу́пывать**) *сов перех* to find

НДС *м сокр* (= **нало́г на доба́вленную сто́имость**) VAT (= value-added tax)

не *част* not; **не я написа́л э́то письмо́** I didn't write this letter; **я не рабо́таю** I don't work; **не пла́чьте/опозда́йте** don't cry/be late; **не могу́ не согласи́ться/не возрази́ть** I can't help agreeing/objecting; **не мне на́до помо́чь, а ему́** I am not the one who needs help, he is; **не до** +*gen* no time for; **мне не до тебя́** I have no time for you; **не без того́** (*разг*) that's about it; **не то** (*разг*: *в противном случае*) or else

небе́сный *прил* (*тела*) celestial; (*перен*) heavenly; **небе́сный цвет** sky blue

неблагода́рный *прил* ungrateful; (*работа*) thankless

не́б|о (-а; *nom pl* **небеса́**, *gen pl* **небе́с**) *ср* sky; (*Рел*) heaven

небольшо́й *прил* small

небоскло́н (-а) *м* sky above the horizon

небоскрё́б (-а) *м* skyscraper

небре́жный *прил* careless

небыва́лый *прил* unprecedented

нева́жно *нареч* (*делать что-н*) not very well ▷ *как сказ* it's not important

нева́жный *прил* unimportant; (*не очень хороший*) poor

неве́дени|е (-я) *ср* ignorance; **он пребыва́ет в по́лном неве́дении** he doesn't know anything (about it)

неве́жественный *прил* ignorant; **неве́жеств|о** (-а) *ср* ignorance

невезе́ни|е (-я) *ср* bad luck

неве́рный *прил* (*ошибочный*) incorrect; (*муж*) unfaithful

невероя́тный *прил* improbable; (*чрезвычайный*) incredible

неве́ст|а (-ы) *ж* (*после помолвки*) fiancée; (*на свадьбе*) bride

неве́ст|ка (-ки; *gen pl* -ок) *ж* (*жена сына*) daughter-in-law; (*жена брата*) sister-in-law

невзго́д|а (-ы) *ж* adversity *ед*

невзира́|я *предл*: **невзира́я на** +*acc* in spite of

невзлюб́|и́ть (-юблю́, -ю́бишь) *сов перех* to take a dislike to

невзнача́й *нареч* (*разг*) by accident

неви́данный *прил* unprecedented

неви́димый *прил* invisible

неви́нный *прил* innocent

невино́вный *прил* innocent

невня́тный *прил* muffled

не́вод (-а) *м* fishing net

невозмо́жно *нареч* (*большой, трудный*) impossibly ▷ *как сказ* (+*infin*: сделать, найти итп) it is impossible to do; (*э́то*) **невозмо́жно** that's impossible; **невозмо́жный** *прил* impossible

нево́л|я (-и) *ж* captivity

невооружё́нный *прил* unarmed; **невооружё́нным гла́зом** (*без приборов*) with the naked eye; **э́то ви́дно невооружё́нным гла́зом** (*перен*) it's plain for all to see

невпопа́д *нареч* (*разг*) out of turn

неврасте́ник (-а) *м* neurotic

неврастени́|я (-и) *ж* (*Мед*) nervous tension

невыноси́мый *прил* unbearable, intolerable

негати́в (-а) *м* (*Фото*) negative

негати́вный *прил* negative

не́где *как сказ*: **не́где отдохну́ть** итп there is nowhere to rest итп; **мне не́где жить** I have nowhere to live

негла́сный *прил* secret

него́ *мест от* **он**; **оно́**

него́дность| (-и) *ж*: **приходи́ть** (*perf* **прийти́**) **в него́дность** (*оборудование*) to become defunct

негод|ова́ть (-у́ю) *несов* to be indignant

негра́мотный *прил* illiterate; (*работа*) incompetent

негритя́нский *прил* African-American

неда́вн|ий *прил* recent; **до неда́внего вре́мени** until recently; **неда́вно** *нареч* recently

недалёк|ий *прил* (*перен: человек, ум*) limited; **в недалёком бу́дущем** in the near future; **недалеко́** *нареч* (*жить, быть*) nearby; (*идти, ехать*) not far ▷ *как сказ*: **недалеко́** (*до* +*gen*) it isn't far (to); **недалеко́ от** +*gen* not far from

неда́ром *нареч* (*не напрасно*) not in vain; (*не без цели*) for a reason

недви́жимост|ь (-и) *ж* property; **недви́жимое иму́щество** = **недви́жимость**

неде́л|я (-и) *ж* week; **че́рез неде́лю** in a week's time; **на про́шлой/э́той/ сле́дующей неде́ле** last/this/next week

недове́ри|е (-я) *ср* mistrust, distrust

недово́льств|о (-а) *ср*: **недово́льство** (+*instr*) dissatisfaction (with)

недогово́р|и́ть (-ю́, -и́шь; *impf* **недогова́ривать**) *сов перех* to leave unsaid; **он что́-то недогова́ривает** there is something that he's not saying

недоеда́|ть (-ю) *несов* to eat badly

недолю́блива|ть (-ю) *несов перех* to dislike

недомога́ни|е (-я) *ср*: **чу́вствовать** (*impf*) **недомога́ние** to feel unwell

недомога́|ть (-ю) *несов* to feel unwell

недоно́шенный *прил*: **недоно́шенный ребёнок** premature baby

недооцен|и́ть (-еню́, -е́нишь; *impf* **недооце́нивать**) *сов перех* to underestimate

недоразуме́ни|е (-я) *ср* misunderstanding

недосмо́тр (-а) *м* oversight

недоста|ва́ть (*3sg* -ё́т) *несов безл*: **мне недостаё́т сме́лости** I lack courage; **мне недостаё́т де́нег** I need money

недоста́точно *нареч* insufficiently ▷ *как сказ*: **у нас недоста́точно еды́/де́нег** we don't have enough food/money; **я недоста́точно зна́ю об э́том** I don't know enough about it

недоста́точный *прил* insufficient

недоста́ч|а (-и) *ж* (*мало*) lack; (*при проверке*) shortfall

недостаю́щий *прил* missing

недосто́йный *прил*: **недосто́йный** (+*gen*) unworthy (of)

недоумева́|ть (-ю) *несов* to be perplexed *или* bewildered

недочё́т (-а) *м* (*в подсчётах*) shortfall; (*в работе*) deficiency

не́др|а (-) *мн* depths *мн*; **в не́драх земли́** in the bowels of the earth

неё́ *мест см* **она́**

нежда́нный *прил* unexpected

не́ж|иться (**-усь, -ишься**) *несов возв* to laze about

не́жный *прил* tender, gentle; (*кожа, пух*) soft; (*запах*) subtle

незабыва́емый *прил* unforgettable

незави́симо *нареч* independently; **незави́симо от** +*gen* regardless of; **незави́симост|ь** (**-и**) *ж* independence

незави́симый *прил* independent

незадо́лго *нареч*: **незадо́лго до** +*gen* или **пе́ред** +*instr* shortly before

незаме́тно *нареч* (*изменяться*) imperceptibly ⊳ *как сказ* it isn't noticeable; **он незаме́тно подошёл** he approached unnoticed; **незаме́тный** *прил* barely noticeable; (*перен: человек*) unremarkable

незауря́дный *прил* exceptional

не́зачем *как сказ* (*разг*): **не́зачем ходи́ть/э́то де́лать** there's no reason to go/do it

нездоро́в|иться (*3sg* **-ится**) *несов безл*: **мне нездоро́вится** I feel unwell, I don't feel well

незнако́м|ец (**-ца**) *м* stranger

незначи́тельный *прил* (*сумма*) insignificant; (*факт*) trivial

неизбе́жный *прил* inevitable

неизве́стн|ый *прил* unknown ⊳ (**-ого**) *м* stranger

неиме́ни|е (**-я**) *ср*: **за неиме́нием** +*gen* for want of

неимове́рный *прил* extreme

неиму́щий *прил* deprived

не́йстовый *прил* intense

ней *мест см* **она́**

нейло́н (**-а**) *м* nylon

нейтра́льный *прил* neutral

не́кем *мест см* **не́кого**

не́к|ий (**-ого**; *f* **-ая**, *nt* **-ое**, *pl* **-ие**) *мест* a certain

не́когда *как сказ* (*читать*) there is no time; **ей не́когда** she is busy; **ей не́когда** +*infin* … she has no time to …

не́к|ого (*как* **кто**; *см Table 7*) *мест*: **не́кого спроси́ть/позва́ть** there is nobody to ask/call

не́кому *мест см* **не́кого**

не́котор|ый (**-ого**; *f* **-ая**, *nt* **-ое**, *pl* **-ые**) *мест* some

некроло́г (**-а**) *м* obituary

некста́ти *нареч* at the wrong time ⊳ *как сказ*: **э́то некста́ти** this is untimely

не́кто *мест* a certain person

не́куда *как сказ* (*идти*) there is nowhere; **да́льше** или **ху́же/лу́чше не́куда** (*разг*) it can't get any worse/better

нелеги́тимный *прил* illegitimate

неле́пый *прил* stupid

нелётный *прил*: **нелётная пого́да** poor weather for flying

нельзя́ *как сказ* (*невозможно*) it is impossible; (*не разрешается*) it is forbidden; **нельзя́ ли?** would it be

possible?; **как нельзя́ лу́чше** as well as could be expected

нём *мест см* **он; оно́**

неме́дленно *нареч* immediately; **неме́дленный** *прил* immediate

неме́|ть (**-ю**; *perf* **онеме́ть**) *несов* (*от ужаса, от восторга*) to be struck dumb; (*нога, рука*) to go numb

не́м|ец (**-ца**) *м* German; **неме́цкий** *прил* German; **неме́цкий язы́к** German

неминуемый *прил* unavoidable

не́м|ка (**-ки**; *gen pl* **-ок**) *ж от* **не́мец**

немно́г|ие (**-их**) *мн* few

немно́го *нареч* (*отдохну́ть, ста́рше*) a little, a bit +*gen* a few; (*денег*) a bit

немно́жко *нареч* (*разг*) = **немно́го**

нем|о́й *прил* (*человек*) with a speech impairment; (*перен: вопрос*) implied; **немо́й фильм** silent film

нему́ *мест от* **он; оно́**

ненави́|деть (**-жу, -дишь**) *несов перех* to hate; **не́навист|ь** (**-и**) *ж* hatred

нена́стный *прил* wet and dismal

нена́сть|е (**-я**) *ср* awful weather

ненорма́льный *прил* abnormal; (*разг: сумасше́дший*) mad ⊳ (**-ого**) *м* (*разг*) crackpot

необита́емый *прил* (*место*) uninhabited; **необита́емый о́стров** desert island

необъя́тный *прил* vast

необходи́мо *как сказ* it is necessary; **мне необходи́мо с Ва́ми поговори́ть** I really need to talk to you; **необходи́мост|ь** (**-и**) *ж* necessity; **необходи́мый** *прил* necessary

необъя́тный *прил* vast

необыкнове́нный *прил* exceptional

необыча́йный *прил* = **необыкнове́нный**

необы́чный *прил* unusual

неожи́данност|ь (**-и**) *ж* surprise

неожи́данный *прил* unexpected

неотврати́мый *прил* inevitable

неотдели́мый *прил*: **неотдели́мый** (*от* +*gen*) inseparable (from)

не́откуда *как сказ*: **мне не́откуда де́нег взять** I can't get money from anywhere

неотло́жн|ый *прил* urgent; **неотло́жная медици́нская по́мощь** emergency medical service

неотрази́мый *прил* irresistible; (*впечатле́ние*) powerful

неохо́т|а (**-ы**) *ж* (*разг: нежела́ние*) reluctance ⊳ *как сказ*: **мне неохо́та спо́рить** I don't feel like arguing

неоцени́мый *прил* invaluable

непереходный *прил*: **непереходный глаго́л** (*Линг*) intransitive verb

неповтори́мый *прил* unique

непого́д|а (**-ы**) *ж* bad weather

неподви́жный *прил* motionless; (*взгляд*) fixed

неподде́льный *прил* genuine

непола́д|ки (**-ок**) *мн* fault *ед*

неполноце́нный прил inadequate, insufficient

непоня́тно нареч incomprehensibly ▷ как сказ it is incomprehensible; мне э́то непоня́тно I cannot understand this

непосре́дственный прил (нача́льник) immediate; (результат, участник) direct

непоча́тый прил: непоча́тый край no end, a great deal

непра́вд|а (-ы) ж lie ▷ как сказ it's not true; э́то непра́вда! this is a lie!

непра́вильно нареч (реши́ть) incorrectly, wrongly ▷ как сказ: э́то непра́вильно it's wrong; непра́вильный прил (форма, глагол) irregular

непредсказу́емый прил unpredictable

непрекло́нный прил firm

непреме́нный прил necessary

непреры́вный прил continuous

непривы́чно как сказ: мне непривы́чно +infin I'm not used to doing

неприли́чный прил indecent

непристо́йный прил obscene

неприя́зн|ь (-и) ж hostility

неприя́тно как сказ +infin it's unpleasant to; мне неприя́тно говори́ть об э́том I don't enjoy talking about it; неприя́тность (-и) ж (обычно мн: на работе, в семье) trouble; неприя́тный прил unpleasant

непромока́емый прил waterproof

нера́венств|о (-а) ср inequality

неравнопра́ви|е (-я) ср inequality (of rights)

нера́вный прил unequal

неразбери́х|а (-и) ж (разг) muddle

неразу́мный прил unreasonable

нерв (-а) м (Анат) nerve; не́рвы (вся система) nervous system

не́рвнича|ть (-ю) несов to fret

не́рвный прил nervous

нерво́зный прил (человек) nervous, highly (Brit) или high (US) strung

неря́шливый прил (человек, одежда) scruffy; (работа) careless

нёс несов см нести́

несваре́ни|е (-я) ср: несваре́ние желу́дка indigestion

несгиба́емый прил staunch

не́скольк|о (-их) чис +gen a few ▷ нареч (обидеться) somewhat

нескро́мный прил (человек) immodest; (вопрос) indelicate; (жест, предложение) indecent

неслы́ханный прил unheard of

неслы́шно нареч (сде́лать) quietly ▷ как сказ: мне неслы́шно I can't hear

несмотря́ предл: несмотря́ на +acc in spite of, despite; несмотря́ на то что ... in spite of или despite the fact that ...; несмотря́ ни на что no matter what

несовершенноле́тн|ий (-его) м minor ▷ прил: несовершенноле́тний ребёнок minor

несоверше́нный прил flawed; несоверше́нный вид (Линг) imperfective (aspect)

несовмести́мый прил incompatible

несомне́нно нареч (правильный, хороший итп) indisputably ▷ вводн сл without a doubt ▷ как сказ: э́то несомне́нно this is indisputable; несомне́нно, что он придёт there is no doubt that he will come

несправедли́вост|ь (-и) ж injustice

несправедли́вый прил (человек, суд, упрёк) unfair, unjust

непросто́ нареч (разг) for a reason

нес|ти́ (-у́, -ёшь; pt нёс, -ла́) несов от носи́ть ▷ перех to carry; (влечь: неприя́тности) to bring ▷ (perf понести́) (службу) to carry out ▷ (perf снести́) (яйцо́) to lay; нести́сь несов возв (человек, машина) to race ▷ (perf снести́сь) (курица) to lay eggs

несча́стный прил unhappy; (разг: жалкий) wretched; несча́стный слу́чай accident

несча́сть|е (-я) ср misfortune; к несча́стью unfortunately

🔵 **КЛЮЧЕВОЕ СЛОВО**

нет част 1 (при отрицании, несогла́сии) no; ты согла́сен? — нет do you agree? — no; тебе́ не нра́вится мой суп? — нет, нра́вится don't you like my soup? — yes, I do

2 (для привлечения внимания): нет, ты то́лько посмотри́ на него́! would you just look at him!

3 (выражает недоверие): нет, ты действи́тельно не се́рдишься? so you are really not angry?

▷ как сказ (+gen: не имеется: об одном предмете) there is no; (: о нескольких предметах) there are no; нет вре́мени there is no time; нет биле́тов или биле́тов нет there are no tickets; у меня́ нет де́нег I have no money; его́ нет в го́роде he is not in town

▷ союз (во фразах): нет — так нет it can't be helped; чего́ то́лько нет! what don't they have!; нет чтобы извини́ться (разг) instead of saying sorry

нетерпе́ни|е (-я) ср impatience; с нетерпе́нием ждать (impf)/слу́шать (impf) to wait/listen impatiently; с нетерпе́нием жду Ва́шего отве́та I look forward to hearing from you

нетре́звый прил drunk; в нетре́звом состоя́нии drunk

нетрудово́й прил: нетрудово́й дохо́д unearned income

нетрудоспосо́бност|ь (-и) ж disability; посо́бие по нетрудоспосо́бности disability living allowance

нетрудоспосо́бный *прил* unable to work through disability

не́тто *прил неизм* (*о весе*) net

неуда́ч|а (**-и**) *ж* bad luck; (*в делах*) failure

неуда́чный *прил* (*попытка*) unsuccessful; (*фильм, стихи*) bad

неудо́бно *нареч* (*расположенный, сидеть*) uncomfortably ▷ *как сказ* it's uncomfortable; (*неприлично*) it's awkward; **мне неудо́бно** I am uncomfortable; **неудо́бно задава́ть лю́дям таки́е вопро́сы** it's awkward to ask people such questions; **(мне) неудо́бно сказа́ть ему́ об э́том** I feel uncomfortable telling him that

неудо́бный *прил* uncomfortable

неудовлетвори́тельный *прил* unsatisfactory

неудово́льстви|е (**-я**) *ср* dissatisfaction

неуже́ли *част* really

неузнава́емость (**-и**) *ж*: **до неузнава́емости** beyond (all) recognition

неукло́нный *прил* steady

неуклю́жий *прил* clumsy

неуме́стный *прил* inappropriate

неурожа́йный *прил*: **неурожа́йный год** year with a poor harvest

неуря́диц|а (**-ы**) *ж* (*разг: обычно мн: ссоры*) squabble

неформа́льный *прил* (*организация*) informal

нефтедобыва́ющий *прил* (*промышленность*) oil

нефтедобы́ч|а (**-и**) *ж* drilling for oil

нефтеперерабо́тк|а (**-и**) *ж* oil processing

нефтепрово́д (**-а**) *м* oil pipeline

нефт|ь (**-и**) *ж* oil, petroleum

нефтя́ник (**-а**) *м* worker in the oil industry

нефтяно́й *прил* oil

нехва́тк|а (**-и**) *ж* +*gen* shortage of

нехорошо́ *нареч* badly ▷ *как сказ* it's bad; **мне нехорошо́** I'm not well

неча́янный *прил* unintentional; (*неожиданный*) chance

не́чего *как сказ*: **не́чего рассказа́ть** there is nothing to tell; (*разг: не следует*) there's no need to do; **не́ за что!** (*в ответ на благодарность*) not at all!, you're welcome! (*US*); **де́лать не́чего** there's nothing else to be done

нечётный *прил* (*число*) odd

не́что *мест* something

нея́сно *нареч*: **он нея́сно объясни́л положе́ние** he didn't explain the situation clearly ▷ *как сказ* it's not clear; **мне нея́сно, почему́ он отказа́лся** I'm not clear или it's not clear to me why he refused

нея́сный *прил* (*очертания, звук*) indistinct; (*мысль, вопрос*) vague

---

⭕ **КЛЮЧЕВО́Е СЛО́ВО**

ни *част* **1** (*усиливает отрицание*) not a; **ни оди́н** not one, not a single; **она́ не**

произнесла́ ни сло́ва she didn't say a word; **она́ ни ра́зу не пришла́** she didn't come once; **у меня́ не оста́лось ни рубля́** I don't have a single rouble left

2: **кто/что/как ни** who-/what-/however; **ско́лько ни** however much; **что ни говори́** whatever you say; **как ни стара́йся** however hard you try

▷ *союз* (*при перечислении*): **ни ..., ни ...** neither ... nor ...; **ни за что** no way

нигде́ *нареч* nowhere; **его́ нигде́ не́ было** he was nowhere to be found; **нигде́ нет мое́й кни́ги** I can't find my book anywhere, my book is nowhere to be found; **я нигде́ не мог пое́сть** I couldn't find anywhere to get something to eat

ни́же *сравн прил от* **ни́зкий** ▷ *сравн нареч от* **ни́зко** ▷ *нареч* (*далее*) later on ▷ *предл* +*gen* below

ни́жн|ий *прил* (*ступенька, ящик*) bottom; **ни́жний эта́ж** ground (*Brit*) или first (*US*) floor; **ни́жнее бельё** underwear; **ни́жняя ю́бка** underskirt

низ (**-а**) *м* (*стола, ящика итп*) bottom

ни́зкий *прил* low

ни́зко *нареч* low

ни́зший *сравн прил от* **ни́зкий**; (*звание*) junior

НИИ *м сокр* (= нау́чно-иссле́довательский институ́т) scientific research institute

ника́к *нареч* (*никаким образом*) no way; **ника́к не могу́ запо́мнить э́то сло́во** I can't remember this word at all; **дверь ника́к не открыва́лась** the door just wouldn't open

никак|о́й *мест*: **нет никако́го сомне́ния** there is no doubt at all; **никаки́е де́ньги не помогли́** no amount of money would have helped

ни́кел|ь (**-я**) *м* (*Хим*) nickel

никогда́ *нареч* never; **как никогда́** as never before

никого́ *мест см* **никто́**

ник|о́й *мест*: **нико́им о́бразом** not at all; **ни в ко́ем слу́чае** under no circumstances

ни|кто́ (**-кого́**; *как кто*; см Table 7) *мест* nobody

никуда́ *нареч*: **я никуда́ не пое́ду** I'm not going anywhere; **никуда́ я не пое́ду** I'm going nowhere; **э́то никуда́ не годи́тся** that just won't do

ниотку́да *нареч* from nowhere; **ниотку́да нет по́мощи** I get no help from anywhere

ниско́лько *нареч* not at all; (*не лучше*) no; (*не рад*) at all

ни́т|ка (**-ки**; *gen pl* **-ок**) *ж* (*обычно мн: для шитья*) thread; (*: для вязания*) yarn

ни́т|ь (**-и**) *ж* = **ни́тка**

них *мест см* **они́**

ничего́ *мест см* **ничто́** ▷ *нареч* fairly well; **(э́то) ничего́, что ...** it's all right that ...; **извини́те, я Вас побеспоко́ю — ничего́!** sorry to disturb you — it's all right!; **как живёшь? — ничегó** how are you? — all right; **ничегó себé** (*снóсно*) fairly well; **ничегó себé!** (*удивление*) well, I never!

нич|éй (**-ьегó**; *f* **-ья́**, *nt* **-ьё**, *pl* **-ьи́**; *как* чей; *см Table 5*) *мест* nobody's

ничéйн|ый *прил*: **ничéйный результáт/ ничéйная пáрти**я draw

ничкóм *нареч* face down

нич|тó (**-егó**; *как* что; *см Table 7*) *мест*, *ср* nothing; **ничегó подóбного не ви́дел** I've never seen anything like it; **ничегó подóбного!** (*разг: совсéм не так*) nothing like it!; **ни за что!** (*ни в коем слýчае*) no way!; **ни за что не соглашáйся** whatever you do, don't agree; **я здесь ни при чём** it has nothing to do with me; **ничегó не подéлаешь** there's nothing to be done

ничýть *нареч* (*нискóлько*) not at all; (*не лýчше, не бóльше*) no; (*не испугáлся, не огорчи́лся*) at all

ничь|**я́** (**-éй**) *ж* (*Спорт*) draw; **сыгрáть** (*perf*) **в ничью́** to draw (*Brit*), tie (*US*)

ни́щенск|ий *прил* (*зарплáта*) meagre (*Brit*), meager (*US*); **ни́щенская жизнь** life of begging

нищет|á (**-ы́**) *ж* poverty

но *союз* but ▷ *межд*: **но!** gee up!

нóвенький *прил* (*разг*) new

новизн|á (**-ы́**) *ж* novelty

нови́н|ка (**-ки**; *gen pl* **-ок**) *ж* new product

новичóк (**-ка́**) *м* newcomer; (*в клáссе*) new pupil

новобрáн|ец (**-ца**) *м* new recruit

новогóдн|ий *прил* New Year; **новогóдняя ёлка** ≈ Christmas tree

новорождённ|ый *прил* newborn ▷ (**-ого**) *м* newborn boy

новосёл (**-а**) *м* (*разг*) new owner

новосéль|е (**-я**; *gen pl* **-ий**) *ср* house-warming (party)

нóвост|ь (**-и**; *gen pl* **-éй**) *ж* news

нóвшеств|о (**-а**) *ср* (*явление*) novelty; (*мéтод*) innovation

нóв|ый *прил* new; **нóвая истóрия** modern history; **Нóвый Завéт** the New Testament; **Нóвая Зелáндия** New Zealand

ног|á (**-и́**; *acc sg* **-у**, *nom pl* **-и**, *gen pl* **-**, *dat pl* **-áм**) *ж* (*ступня́*) foot; (*выше ступни́*) leg; **вверх ногáми** upside down

нóг|оть (**-тя**; *gen pl* **-тéй**) *м* nail

нож (**-á**) *м* knife

нóж|ка (**-ки**; *gen pl* **-ек**, *уменьш от* ногá; (*стýла, столá итп*) leg; (*ци́ркуля*) arm

нóжниц|ы (**-**) *мн* scissors

ножнóй *прил* foot

ноздр|я́ (**-и́**; *nom pl* **-и**, *gen pl* **-éй**) *ж* (*обычно мн*) nostril

нол|ь (**-я́**) *м* (*Мат*) zero, nought; (*о температýре*) zero; (*перен: человéк*) nothing; **ноль цéлых пять деся́тых**, 0.5 zero *или* nought point five, 0.5; **в дéсять ноль-ноль** at exactly ten o'clock

номенклатýр|а (**-ы**) *ж* (*товáров*) list ▷ *собир* (*рабóтники*) nomenklatura

нóмер (**-а**; *nom pl* **-á**) *м* number; (*журнáла*) issue; (*в гости́нице*) room; **нóмер маши́ны** registration (number)

номернóй *прил*; **номернóй знак** (*автомоби́ля*) (car) number (*Brit*) *или* license (*US*) plate

номер|óк (**-ка́**) *ж* (*для пальтó*) ≈ ticket

Норвéги|я (**-и**) *ж* Norway

нóрм|а (**-ы**) *ж* standard; (*вырабóтки*) rate

нормáльно *нареч* normally ▷ *как сказ*: **э́то вполнé нормáльно** this is quite normal; **как делá? — не плóхо** how are things? — not bad; **у нас всё нормáльно** everything's fine with us

нормáльный *прил* normal

нос (**-а**; *loc sg* **-ý**, *nom pl* **-ы́**) *м* nose; (*корабля́*) bow; (*пти́цы*) beak, bill; (*боти́нка*) toe

носи́л|ки (**-ок**) *мн* stretcher *ед*

носи́льщик (**-а**) *м* porter

носи́тель (**-я**) *м* (*инфéкции*) carrier; **носи́тель языка́** native speaker

но|си́ть (**-шý**, **-сишь**) *несов перех* to carry; (*плáтье, очки́*) to wear; (*усы́, причёску*) to sport; (*фами́лию мýжа*) to use; **носи́ться** *несов возв* (*человéк*) to rush; (*слýхи*) to spread; (*одéжда*) to wear; (*разг: увлекáться*): **носи́ться с** +*instr* (*с идéей*) to be preoccupied with; (*с человéком*) to make a fuss of

носов|óй *прил* (*звук*) nasal; **носовáя часть** bow; **носовóй платóк** handkerchief

нос|óк (**-ка́**; *gen pl* **-óк**) *м* (*обычно мн: чулóк*) sock ▷ (*gen pl* **-кóв**) (*боти́нка, чулкá, ноги́*) toe

носорóг (**-а**) *м* rhinoceros, rhino

ностальги́|я (**-и**) *ж* nostalgia

нóт|а (**-ы**) *ж* note; *см также* **нóты**

нотáриус (**-а**) *м* notary (public)

нóт|ы (**-**) *мн* (*Муз*) sheet music

нóутбук (**-а**) *м* (*Комп*) laptop (computer)

ноч|евáть (**-ýю**; *perf* **переночевáть**) *несов* to spend the night

ночёв|ка (**-ки**; *gen pl* **-ок**) *ж*: **останови́ться на ночёвку** to spend the night

ночлéг (**-а**) *м* (*мéсто*) somewhere to spend the night; **останáвливаться** (*perf* **останови́ться**) **на ночлéг** to spend the night

ночн|óй *прил* (*час, хóлод*) night; **ночнáя рубáшка** nightshirt

ноч|ь (**-и**; *loc sg* **-и́**, *nom pl* **-и**, *gen pl* **-éй**) *ж* night; **на́ ночь** before bed; **споко́йной нóчи!** good night!

нóчью *нареч* at night

нóшеный *прил* second-hand

ношý(сь) *несов см* **носи́ть(ся)**

ноя́бр|ь (**-я́**) *м* November

нрав (**-а**) *м* (*человéка*) temperament; *см также* **нрáвы**

нра́в|иться (-люсь, -ишься; perf
понра́виться) несов возв: мне/им
нра́вится э́тот фильм I/they like this film;
мне нра́вится чита́ть/гуля́ть I like to read
или reading/to go for a walk
нра́вственный прил moral
нра́в|ы (-ов) мн morals
н.с. сокр (= но́вого сти́ля) NS, New Style
НТР ж сокр = нау́чно-техни́ческая
револю́ция

О **КЛЮЧЕВО́Е СЛО́ВО**

ну межд **1** (выража́ет побужде́ние) come
on; ну, начина́й! come on, get started!
2 (выража́ет восхище́ние) what; ну и
си́ла! what strength!
3 (выража́ет иро́нию) well (well)
▷ част **1** (неуже́ли): (да) ну?! not really?!
2 (уси́ливает вырази́тельность) ну
коне́чно! why of course!; ну, я тебе́
покажу́! why, I'll show you!
3 (допу́стим): ты говори́шь по-
англи́йски? - ну, говорю́ do you speak
English — what if I do
4 (во фра́зах): ну и ну! (разг) well well!;
ну-ка! (разг) come on!; ну тебя́/его́! (разг)
forget it!

ну́дный прил tedious
нужд|а́ (-ы́; nom pl -ы) ж (no pl:
бедность) poverty; (потребность): нужда́
(в +prp) need (for)
нужда́|ться (-юсь) несов возв
(бедствовать) to be needy; нужда́ться
(impf) в +prp to need, be in need of
ну́жно как сказ (необходимо): ну́жно,
что́бы им помогли́, ну́жно им помо́чь it is
necessary to help them; мне ну́жно идти́ I
have to go, I must go; мне ну́жно 10
рубле́й I need 10 roubles; о́чень ну́жно!
(разг) my foot!
ну́жный прил necessary
нулев|о́й прил: нулева́я температу́ра
temperature of zero; нулева́я отме́тка
(mark of) zero
нул|ь (-я́) м (Мат) zero, nought; (о
температуре) zero; (перен: человек)
nothing; начина́ть (perf нача́ть) с нуля́ to
start from scratch
нумер|ова́ть (-у́ю; perf
пронумерова́ть) несов перех to number
ны́не нареч today
ны́нешний прил the present
нырн|у́ть (-у́, -ёшь) сов to dive
ныря́|ть (-ю) несов to dive
ныть (но́ю, но́ешь) несов (рана) to ache;
(жаловаться) to moan
Нью-Йо́рк (-а) м New York
н.э. сокр (= на́шей э́ры) AD (= anno
Domini)
нюх (-а) м (собаки) nose
ню́ха|ть (-ю; perf поню́хать) несов
перех (цветы, воздух) to smell

ня́неч|ка (-ки; gen pl -ек) ж (разг)
= **ня́ня**
ня́нч|ить (-у, -ишь) несов перех to mind;
ня́нчиться несов возв: ня́нчиться с +instr
(с младенцем) to mind
ня́нь|ка (-ьки; gen pl -ек) ж (разг:
ребёнка) nanny
ня́н|я (-и; gen pl -ь) ж nanny;
(работающая на дому) child minder; (в
больнице) auxiliary nurse; (в детском
саду) cleaner; приходя́щая ня́ня babysitter

O

o межд oh ▷ предл +prp about; (+acc: опереться, удариться) against; (споткнуться) over

об предл = **o**

о́б|а (-**о́их**; см *Table 25*; *f* **о́бе**, *nt* **о́ба**) *м чис* both

обанкро́|титься (-**чусь, -тишься**) *сов возв* to go bankrupt

обая́ни|е (-**я**) *ср* charm; **обая́тельный** *прил* charming

обва́л (-**а**) *м* (*снежный*) avalanche; (*здания, экономики*) collapse

обвал|и́ться (*3sg* -**ится**, *impf* **обва́ливаться**) *сов возв* to collapse

обв|ести́ (-**еду́, -еде́шь**; *pt* -**ёл, -ела́**, *impf* **обводи́ть**) *сов перех* (*букву, чертёж*) to go over; **обводи́ть** (*perf* **обвести́**) **вокру́г** +*gen* to lead *или* take round

обвине́ни|е (-**я**) *ср*: **обвине́ние** (**в** +*prp*) accusation (of); (*Юр*) charge (of) ▷ *собир* (*обвиняющая сторона*) the prosecution

обвин|и́ть (-**ю́, -и́шь**; *impf* **обвиня́ть**) *сов перех*: **обвини́ть кого́-н** (**в** +*prp*) to accuse sb (of); (*Юр*) to charge sb (with)

обвиня́ем|ый (-**ого**) *м* the accused, the defendant

обвиня́|ть (-**ю**) *несов от* **обвини́ть** ▷ *перех* (*Юр*) to prosecute

обв|и́ть (-**овью́, -овье́шь**; *impf* **обвива́ть**) *сов перех* (*подлеж: плющ*) to twine around; **обвива́ть** (*perf* **обви́ть**) **кого́-н/что-н чем-н** to wind sth round sb/sth

обв|оди́ть (-**ожу́, -о́дишь**) *несов от* **обвести́**

обв|яза́ть (-**яжу́, -я́жешь**; *impf* **обвя́зывать**) *сов перех*: **обвяза́ть кого́-н/что-н чем-н** to tie sth round sb/sth; **обвяза́ться** (*impf* **обвя́зываться**) *сов возв*: **обвяза́ться чем-н** to tie sth round o.s.

обгоня́|ть (-**ю**) *несов от* **обогна́ть**

обгор|е́ть (-**ю́, -и́шь**; *impf* **обгора́ть**) *сов* (*дом*) to be burnt; (*на солнце*) to get sunburnt

обдира́|ть (-**ю**) *несов от* **ободра́ть**

обду́ма|ть (-**ю**; *impf* **обду́мывать**) *сов перех* to consider, think over

о́б|е (-**е́их**) *ж чис см* **о́ба**

обега́|ть (-**ю**) *несов от* **обежа́ть**

обе́д (-**а**) *м* lunch, dinner; (*время*) lunch *или* dinner time; **по́сле обе́да** after lunch *или* dinner; (*после 12 часов дня*) in the afternoon

обе́да|ть (-**ю**; *perf* **пообе́дать**) *несов* to have lunch *или* dinner

обе́денный *прил* (*стол, сервиз*) dinner; (*время*) lunch, dinner

обедне́|ть (-**ю**) *сов от* **бедне́ть**

обежа́ть (*как* **бежа́ть**; см *Table 20*; *impf* **обега́ть**) *сов*: **обежа́ть вокру́г** +*gen* to run round

обезбо́ливающ|ее (-**его**) *ср* painkiller

обезбо́л|ить (-**ю, -ишь**; *impf* **обезбо́ливать**) *сов перех* to anaesthetize (*Brit*), anesthetize (*US*)

обезвре́|дить (-**жу, -дишь**; *impf* **обезвре́живать**) *сов перех* (*бомбу*) to defuse; (*преступника*) to disarm

обездо́ленный *прил* deprived

обезору́ж|ить (-**у, -ишь**; *impf* **обезору́живать**) *сов перех* to disarm

обезу́ме|ть (-**ю**) *сов*: **обезуметь от** +*gen* to go out of one's mind with

обе́их *чис см* **о́бе**

оберега́|ть (-**ю**) *несов перех* (*человека*) to protect

оберн|у́ть (-**у́, -ёшь**; *impf* **обёртывать** *или* **обора́чивать**) *сов перех* to wrap (up); **оберну́ться** (*impf* **обора́чиваться**) *сов возв* (*повернуться назад*) to turn (round); **обора́чиваться** (*perf* **оберну́ться**) +*instr* (*неприятностями*) to turn out to be

обёрт|ка (-**ки**; *gen pl* -**ок**) *ж* (*конфетная*) wrapper

обёрточн|ый *прил*: **обёрточная бума́га** wrapping paper

обёртыва|ть (-**ю**) *несов от* **оберну́ть**

обеспе́чени|е (-**я**) *ср* (*мира, договора*) guarantee; (+*instr*: сырьём) provision of; **материа́льное обеспе́чение** financial security

обеспе́ченность (-**и**) *ж* (*material*) comfort; **фина́нсовая обеспе́ченность** financial security

обеспе́ч|ить (-**у, -ишь**; *impf* **обеспе́чивать**) *сов перех* (*семью*) to provide for; (*мир, успех*) to guarantee; **обеспе́чивать** (*perf* **обеспе́чить**) **кого́-н/что-н чем-н** to provide *или* supply sb/sth with sth

обесси́ле|ть (-**ю**; *impf* **обесси́левать**) *сов* to become *или* grow weak

обесцве́|тить (-**чу, -тишь**; *impf* **обесцве́чивать**) *несов перех* to bleach

обеща́ни|е (-я) ср promise

обеща́|ть (-ю; perf обеща́ть или пообеща́ть) несов (не)перех to promise

обжа́лование (-я) ср appeal; обжа́л|овать (-ую) сов перех to appeal against

об|же́чь (-ожгу́, -ожжёшь etc, -о́жгут; pt -жёг, -ожгла́, -ожгло́, impf обжига́ть) сов перех to burn; (кирпич итп) to fire; (подлеж: крапива) to sting; обже́чься (impf обжига́ться) сов возв to burn o.s.

обзо́р (-а) м view; (новостей) review; обзо́рный прил general

обива́|ть (-ю) несов от оби́ть

оби́вк|а (-и) ж upholstery

оби́д|а (-ы) ж insult; (горечь) grievance; кака́я оби́да! what a pity!; быть (impf) в оби́де на кого́-н to be in a huff with sb

оби́|деть (-жу, -дишь; impf обижа́ть) сов перех to hurt, offend; оби́деться (impf обижа́ться) сов возв: оби́деться (на +acc) to be hurt или offended (by)

оби́дно как сказ (см прил) it's offensive; it's upsetting; мне оби́дно слы́шать э́то it hurts me to hear this

обижа́|ть(ся) (-ю(сь)) несов от оби́деть(ся)

оби́льный прил abundant

обита́|ть (-ю) несов to live

об|и́ть (-обью́, -обьёшь; imper обе́й(те), impf обива́ть) сов перех: оби́ть (+instr) to cover (with)

обихо́д (-а) м: быть в обихо́де to be in use

обкле́|ить (-ю, -ишь; impf обкле́ивать) сов перех (плакатами) to cover; (обоями) to (wall)paper

обкра́дыва|ть (-ю) несов от обокра́сть

обл. сокр = о́бласть

обла́в|а (-ы) ж (на преступников) roundup

облага́|ть (-ю) несов от обложи́ть

облада́|ть (-ю) несов +instr to possess

о́блак|о (-а; nom pl -á, gen pl -о́в) ср cloud

областно́й прил ≈ regional; о́бласт|ь (-и; gen pl -е́й) ж region; (Админ) ≈ region, oblast; (науки, искусства) field

о́блачный прил cloudy

облега́|ть (-ю) несов от обле́чь ▷ перех to fit

облегче́ни|е (-я) ср (жизни) improvement; (успокоение) relief

облегч|и́ть (-у́, -и́шь; impf облегча́ть) сов перех (вес) to lighten; (жизнь) to make easier; (боль) to ease

обле́з|ть (-у, -ешь; impf облеза́ть) сов (разг) to grow mangy; (краска, обои) to peel (off)

облека́|ть (-ю) несов от обле́чь

обле|те́ть (-чу́, -ти́шь; impf облета́ть) сов перех to fly round ▷ неперех (листья) to fall off

облива́|ть (-ю) несов от обли́ть; облива́ться несов от обли́ться ▷ возв: облива́ться слеза́ми to be in floods of tears

обл|иза́ть (-ижу́, -и́жешь; impf обли́зывать) сов перех to lick

о́блик (-а) м appearance

обли́ть (-олью́, -ольёшь; impf облива́ть) сов перех: обли́ть кого́-н/ что-н чем-н (намеренно) to pour sth over sb/sth; (случайно) to spill sth over sb/sth; обли́ться (impf облива́ться) сов возв: обли́ться чем-н (водой) to sluice o.s. with sth

обл|ожи́ть (-ожу́, -о́жишь; impf облага́ть) сов перех: обложи́ть нало́гом to tax

обло́ж|ка (-ки; gen pl -ек) ж (книги, тетради) cover

облок|оти́ться (-очу́сь, -о́тишься) сов возв: облокоти́ться на +acc to lean one's elbows on

обло́м|ок (-ка) м fragment

облысе́|ть (-ю) сов от лысе́ть

обмакн|у́ть (-у́, -ёшь; impf обма́кивать) сов перех: обмакну́ть что-н в +acc to dip sth into

обма́н (-а) м deception

обм|ану́ть (-ану́, -а́нешь; impf обма́нывать) сов перех to deceive; (поступить нечестно) to cheat

обма́нчивый прил deceptive

обма́нива|ть (-ю) несов от обману́ть

обма́тыва|ть (-ю) несов от обмота́ть

обме́н (-а) м exchange; (документов) renewal; (также обме́н веще́ств: Био) metabolism; (также обме́н жилпло́щадью) exchange (of flats etc)

обме́нный прил exchange

обменя́|ть (-ю; impf обме́нивать) сов перех (вещи, билеты) to change; обменя́ться (impf обме́ниваться) сов возв: обменя́ться +instr to exchange

обморо́|зить (-жу, -зишь; impf обмора́живать) сов перех: обморо́зить но́гу to get frostbite in one's foot

о́бморок (-а) м faint; па́дать (perf упа́сть) в о́бморок to faint

обмота́|ть (-ю; impf обма́тывать) сов перех: обмота́ть кого́-н/что-н чем-н to wrap sth round sb/sth

обм|ы́ть (-о́ю, -о́ешь; impf обмыва́ть) сов перех (рану) to bathe; (разг: событие) to celebrate (by drinking)

обнагле́|ть (-ю) сов от нагле́ть

обнадёж|ить (-у, -ишь; impf обнадёживать) сов перех to reassure

обнажённый прил bare

обнаж|и́ть (-у́, -и́шь; impf обнажа́ть) сов перех to expose; (руки, ноги) to bare; (ветки) to strip bare; обнажи́ться (impf обнажа́ться) сов возв to be exposed; (человек) to strip

обнару́ж|ить (-у, -ишь; impf

обнару́живать) *сов перех* (*найти*) to find; (*проявить*) to show; **обнару́житься** (*impf* **обнару́живаться**) *сов возв* (*найтись*) to be found; (*стать явным*) to become evident

обн|ести́ (-есу́, -есёшь; *pt* -ёс, -есла́, -есло́, *impf* **обноси́ть**) *сов перех*: **обнести́ что-н/кого-н вокру́г** +*gen* to carry sth/sb round; (*огородить*): **обнести́ что-н чем-н** to surround sth with sth

обнима́|ть(ся) (-ю(сь)) *несов от* **обня́ть(ся)**

обни́мк|а *ж*: **в обни́мку** (*разг*) with their arms around each other

обнов|и́ть (-лю́, -и́шь; *impf* **обновля́ть**) *сов перех* (*оборудование, гардероб*) to replenish; (*репертуар*) to refresh; (*старую мебель*) to upcycle; **обнови́ться** (*impf* **обновля́ться**) *сов возв* (*репертуар*) to be refreshed; (*организм*) to be regenerated

обн|я́ть (-иму́, -и́мешь; *pt* -ял, -яла́, -яло, *impf* **обнима́ть**) *сов перех* to embrace; **обня́ться** (*impf* **обнима́ться**) *сов возв* to embrace (each other)

обо *предл* = **о**

обобщ|и́ть (-у́, -и́шь; *impf* **обобща́ть**) *сов перех* (*факты*) to generalize from; (*статью*) to summarize

обога|ти́ть (-щу́, -ти́шь; *impf* **обогаща́ть**) *сов перех* to enrich; **обогати́ться** (*impf* **обогаща́ться**) *сов возв* (*человек, страна*) to be enriched

обогре́|ть (-ю; *impf* **обогрева́ть**) *сов перех* (*помещение*) to heat; (*человека*) to warm

о́б|од (-ода; *nom pl* -о́дья, *gen pl* -о́дьев) *м* rim; (*ракеты*) frame

об|одра́ть (-деру́, -дерёшь; *impf* **обдира́ть**) *сов перех* (*кору, шкуру*) to strip; (*руки*) to scratch

ободр|и́ть (-ю́, -и́шь; *impf* **ободря́ть**) *сов перех* to encourage

обо́з (-а) *м* convoy

обознача́|ть (-ю) *несов от* **обозна́чить** ▷ *перех* to signify

обозна́ч|ить (-у, -ишь; *impf* **обознача́ть**) *сов перех* (*границу*) to mark; (*слово*) to mean

обозрева́тел|ь (-я) *м* (*событий*) observer; (*на радио итп*) editor

обозре́ни|е (-я) *ср* review

обо́|и (-ев) *мн* wallpaper *ед*

обо́их *чис см* **о́ба**

обойти́ (*как* **идти́**; *см Table 18*, *impf* **обходи́ть**) *сов перех* to go round; (*закон*) to get round; (*обогнать*) to pass; **обойти́сь** (*impf* **обходи́ться**) *сов возв* (*уладиться*) to turn out well; (*стоить*): **обойти́сь в** +*acc* to cost; **обходи́ться** (*perf* **обойти́сь**) **с кем-н/чем-н** to treat sb/sth; **обходи́ться** (*perf* **обойти́сь**) **без** +*gen* (*разг*) to get by without

об|окра́сть (-краду́, -крадёшь; *impf* **обкра́дывать**) *сов перех* to rob

обоня́ни|е (-я) *ср* sense of smell

обора́чива|ть(ся) (-ю(сь)) *несов от* **оберну́ть(ся)**

оборва́ть (-у́, -ёшь; *pt* -а́л, -ала́, -а́ло, *impf* **обрыва́ть**) *сов перех* (*верёвку*) to break; (*ягоды, цветы*) to pick; (*перен: разговор, дружбу*) to break off; (: *разг: говорящего*) to cut short; **оборва́ться** (*impf* **обрыва́ться**) *сов возв* (*верёвка*) to break; (*перен: жизнь, разговор*) to be cut short

оборо́н|а (-ы) *ж* defence (*Brit*), defense (*US*); **оборо́нный** *прил* defence (*Brit*), defense (*US*); **обороня́|ть** (-ю) *несов перех* to defend; **обороня́ться** *несов возв* (*защищаться*) to defend o.s.

оборо́т (-а) *м* (*полный круг*) revolution; (*Комм*) turnover; (*обратная сторона*) back; (*перен: поворот событий*) turn; (*Линг*) turn of phrase; (*употребление*) circulation

оборудова́ни|е (-я) *ср* equipment

обору́д|овать (-ую) (*не*)*сов перех* to equip

обосо́бленный *прил* (*дом*) detached; (*жизнь*) solitary

обостр|и́ть (-ю́, -и́шь; *impf* **обостря́ть**) *сов перех* (*желания, конфликт*) to intensify; (*желания, конфликт*) to sharpen; **обостри́ться** (*impf* **обостря́ться**) *сов возв* (*см перех*) to sharpen; to intensify

обошёл(ся) *etc сов см* **обойти́(сь)**

обою́дный *прил* mutual

обрабо́та|ть (-ю; *impf* **обраба́тывать**) *сов перех* (*камень*) to cut; (*кожу*) to cure; (*деталь*) to turn; (*текст*) to polish up; (*землю*) to till; (*перен: разг: человека*) to work on

обра́д|овать(ся) (-ую(сь)) *сов от* **ра́довать(ся)**

о́браз (-а) *м* image; (*Литература*) figure; (*жизни*) way; (*икона*) icon; **каки́м о́бразом?** in what way?; **таки́м о́бразом** (*следовательно*) consequently; **гла́вным о́бразом** mainly; **не́которым о́бразом** to some extent; **о́браз|е́ц** (-ца́) *м* sample; (*скромности, мужества*) model

образова́ни|е (-я) *ср* formation; (*получение знаний*) education; **образо́ванный** *прил* educated; **образ|ова́ть** (-у́ю; *impf* **образова́ть**) (*не*)*сов перех* to form; **образова́ться** (*impf* **образова́ться**) (*не*)*сов возв* to form; (*группа, комиссия*) to be formed

обра|ти́ть (-щу́, -ти́шь; *impf* **обраща́ть**) *сов перех* (*взгляд, мысли*) to turn; **обраща́ть** (*perf* **обрати́ть**) **кого́-н/что-н в** +*acc* to turn sb/sth into; **обраща́ть** (*perf* **обрати́ть**) **внима́ние на** +*acc* to pay attention to; **обрати́ться** (*impf* **обраща́ться**) *сов возв* (*взгляд*) to turn; (*превратиться*): **обрати́ться в** +*acc* to turn into; **обраща́ться** (*perf* **обрати́ться**) **к** +*dat* (*к врачу итп*) to consult; (*к проблеме*) to address; **обраща́ться** (*perf* **обрати́ться**) **в**

суд to go to court

обра́тно *нареч* back; **туда́ и обра́тно** there and back; **биле́т туда́ и обра́тно** return (*Brit*) *или* round-trip (*US*) ticket

обра́тн|ый *прил* reverse; (*дорога, путь*) return; **на обра́тном пути́** on the way back; **в обра́тную сто́рону** in the opposite direction; **обра́тная сторона́** reverse (side); **обра́тный а́дрес** return address

обраща́|ть (**-ю**) *несов от* **обрати́ть**; **обраща́ться** *несов от* **обрати́ться** ▷ *возв* (*деньги, товар*) to circulate; **обраща́ться** (*impf*) **с** +*instr* (*с машиной*) to handle; (*с человеком*) to treat

обраще́ни|е (**-я**) *ср* address; (*Экон*) circulation; **обраще́ние к** +*dat* (*к народу итп*) address to; **обраще́ние с** +*instr* (*с прибором*) handling of

обремени́|ть (**-ю́, -и́шь**; *impf* **обременя́ть**) *несов от* **обремени́ть кого́-н чем-н** to load sb down with sth

о́бруч (**-а**) *м* hoop

обруча́льн|ый *прил*: **обруча́льное кольцо́** wedding ring

обру́ш|ить (**-у, -ишь**; *impf* **обру́шивать**) *сов перех* (*стену, крышу*) to bring down; **обру́шиться** (*impf* **обру́шиваться** *сов возв* (*крыша, здание*) to collapse; **обру́шиться** (*perf* **обру́шиться**) **на** +*асс* (*на голову*) to crash down onto; (*на врага*) to fall upon

обрыва́|ть(ся) (**-ю(сь)**) *несов от* **оборва́ть(ся)**

обры́в|ок (**-ка**) *м* (*бумаги*) scrap; (*воспоминаний*) fragment

обры́зга|ть (**-ю**; *impf* **обры́згивать**) *сов перех*: **обры́згать кого́-н/что-н** +*instr* (*водой*) to splash sb/sth with; (*грязью*) to splatter sb/sth with; **обры́згаться** (*impf* **обры́згиваться** *сов возв*: **обры́згаться** +*instr* (*см перех*) to get splashed with; to get splattered with

обря́д (**-а**) *м* ritual

обслед|овать (**-ую**) (*не*)*сов перех* to inspect; (*больного*) to examine

обслу́живани|е (**-я**) *ср* service

обслуж|и́ть (**-ужу́, -у́жишь**; *impf* **обслу́живать**) *сов перех* (*клиентов*) to serve; (*подлеж*: *поликлиника*) to see to

обста́в|ить (**-лю, -ишь**; *impf* **обставля́ть**) *сов перех* (*квартиру*) to furnish

обстано́в|ка (**-ки**; *gen pl* **-ок**) *ж* situation; (*квартиры*) furnishings *мн*

обстоя́тельств|о (**-а**) *ср* circumstance; **смотря́ по обстоя́тельствам** depending on the circumstances; (*как ответ на вопрос*) it depends

обс|уди́ть (**-ужу́, -у́дишь**; *impf* **обсужда́ть**) *сов перех* to discuss

обсужде́ни|е (**-я**) *ср* discussion

обува́|ть(ся) (**-ю(сь)**) *несов от* **обу́ть(ся)**

обувно́й *прил* shoe; **о́бувь** (**-и**) *ж* footwear

обусло́в|ить (**-лю, -ишь**; *impf* **обусла́вливать**) *сов перех* (*явиться причиной*) to lead to

обу́|ть (**-ю**; *impf* **обува́ть**) *сов перех* (*ребёнка*) to put shoes on; **обу́ться** (*impf* **обува́ться** *сов возв* to put on one's shoes or boots

обуче́ни|е (**-я**) *ср* (+*dat*: *преподавание*) teaching of

обхва́т|ить (**-ачу́, -а́тишь**; *impf* **обхва́тывать**) *сов перех*: **обхвати́ть что-н** (*рука́ми*) to put one's arms round sth

обхо́д (**-а**) *м* (*путь*) way round; (*в больнице*) round; **в обхо́д** +*gen* (*озера, закона*) bypassing

обх|оди́ть(ся) (**-ожу́(сь), -о́дишь(ся)**) *несов от* **обойти́(сь)**

обходно́й *прил* (*путь*) detour

обши́рный *прил* extensive

обща́|ться (**-юсь**) *несов возв*: **обща́ться с** +*instr* to mix with; (*с одним человеком*) to see; (*вести разговор*) to communicate with

общегосуда́рственный *прил* state

общедосту́пный *прил* (*способ*) available to everyone; (*цены*) affordable; (*лекция*) accessible

о́бщ|ее (**-его**) *ср* similarity; **в о́бщем** (*разг*) on the whole; **у них мно́го о́бщего** they have a lot in common

общежи́ти|е (**-я**) *ср* (*рабочее*) hostel; (*студенческое*) hall of residence (*Brit*), dormitory *или* hall (*US*)

общеизве́стный *прил* well-known

обще́ни|е (**-я**) *ср* communication

общеобразова́тельный *прил* comprehensive

общепри́знанный *прил* universally recognized

общепри́нятый *прил* generally accepted

обще́ственност|ь (**-и**) *ж собир* community; **обще́ственн|ый** *прил* social; (*не частный*) public; (*организация*) civic; **обще́ственное мне́ние** public opinion; **о́бществ|о** (**-а**) *ср* society

о́бщ|ий *прил* general; (*труд*) communal; (*дом*) shared; (*друзья*) mutual; (*интересы*) common; (*количество*) total; (*картина, описание*) general; **в о́бщей сло́жности** altogether

общи́тельный *прил* sociable

о́бщност|ь (**-и**) *ж* (*идей*) similarity; (*социальная*) community

объединённый *прил* joint

объедин|и́ть (**-ю́, -и́шь**; *impf* **объединя́ть**) *сов перех* to join, unite; (*ресурсы*) to pool; (*компании*) to amalgamate; **объедини́ться** (*impf* **объедини́ться** *сов возв* to unite

объе́зд (**-а**) *м* detour; (*с целью осмотра*) tour

объезжа́|ть (**-ю**) *несов от* **объе́хать**

объе́кт (**-а**) *м* subject; (*Строит, Воен*) site

объекти́в (-а) *м* lens

объекти́вный *прил* objective

объём (-а) *м* volume

объе́хать (*как* **е́хать**; *см* Table 19; *impf* **объезжа́ть**) *сов перех* (*яму*) to go *или* drive round; (*друзей, страны*) to visit

объ|яви́ть (-явлю́, -я́вишь; *impf* **объявля́ть**) *сов перех* to announce; (*войну*) to declare ▷ *неперех*: **объяви́ть о** +*prp* to announce; **объявле́ни|е** (-я) *ср* announcement; (*войны*) declaration; (*реклама*) advertisement; (*извещение*) notice

объясне́ни|е (-я) *ср* explanation; **объясн|и́ть** (-ю́, -и́шь; *impf* **объясня́ть**) *сов перех* to explain; **объясни́ться** (*impf* **объясня́ться**) *сов возв*: **объясни́ться (с** +*instr*) to clear things up (with)

объясня́|ться (-юсь) *несов от* **объясни́ться** ▷ *возв* (*на английском языке*) to communicate; (+*instr*: *трудностями*) to be explained by

обыкнове́нный *прил* ordinary

о́быск (-а) *м* search; **обы|ска́ть** (-щу́, -щешь; *impf* **обы́скивать**) *сов перех* to search

обы́ча|й (-я) *м* custom

обы́чно *нареч* usually; **обы́чный** *прил* usual; (*заурядный*) ordinary

обя́занност|и (-ей) *мн* duties, responsibilities; **исполня́ть** (*impf*) **обя́занности** +*gen* to act as; **обя́занност|ь** (-и) *ж* duty; *см также* **обя́занности**; **обя́занный** *прил* (+*infin*: *сделать итп*) obliged to do

обяза́тельно *нареч* definitely; **не обяза́тельно** not necessarily; **обяза́тельный** *прил* (*правило*) binding; (*исполнение, обучение*) compulsory, obligatory; (*работник*) reliable

обяза́тельств|о (-а) *ср* commitment; (*обычно мн: Комм*) liability

ова́л (-а) *м* oval

овдове́|ть (-ю) *сов* (*женщина*) to become a widow, be widowed; (*мужчина*) to become a widower, be widowed

Ов|е́н (-на́) *м* (*созвездие*) Aries

ов|ёс (-са́) *м* собир oats *мн*

ОВИ́Р (-а) *м сокр* = **отде́л виз и регистра́ций**

овладе́|ть (-ю, -ешь; *impf* **овладева́ть**) *сов* (+*instr*: *городом, вниманием*) to capture; (*языком, профессией*) to master

о́вощ (-а) *м* vegetable

овощно́й *прил* (*суп, блюдо*) vegetable; **овощно́й магази́н** greengrocer's (*Brit*), fruit and vegetable shop

овра́г (-а) *м* ditch

овся́нк|а (-и) *ж собир* (*каша*) porridge (*Brit*), oatmeal (*US*); **овся́ный** *прил* oat

овча́р|ка (-ки; *gen pl* -ок) *ж* sheepdog

оглавле́ни|е (-я) *ср* (table of) contents

огло́хнуть (-у) *сов от* **гло́хнуть**

огл|уши́ть (-ушу́, -уши́шь; *impf* **оглуша́ть**) *сов перех*: **оглуши́ть кого́-н чем-н** to deafen sb with sth

огля|де́ть (-жу́, -ди́шь; *impf* **огля́дывать**) *сов перех* to look round; **огляде́ться** (*impf* **огля́дываться**) *сов возв* to look around

огл|яну́ться (-яну́сь, -я́нешься; *impf* **огля́дываться**) *сов возв* to look back; (**я**) **не успе́л огляну́ться, как** ... before I knew it ...

огнеопа́сный *прил* (in)flammable

огнестре́льн|ый *прил*: **огнестре́льное ору́жие** firearms *мн*; **огнестре́льная ра́на** bullet wound

огнетуши́тел|ь (-я) *м* fire-extinguisher

ог|о́нь (-ня́) *м* fire; (*фонарей, в окне*) light

огоро́д (-а) *м* vegetable *или* kitchen garden

огорче́ни|е (-я) *ср* distress; **к моему́ огорче́нию** to my dismay

огорч|и́ть (-у́, -и́шь; *impf* **огорча́ть**) *сов перех* to distress; **огорчи́ться** (*impf* **огорча́ться**) *сов возв* to be distressed *или* upset

огра́б|ить (-лю, -ишь) *сов от* **гра́бить**

ограбле́ни|е (-я) *ср* robbery

огра́д|а (-ы) *ж* (*забор*) fence; (*решётка*) railings *мн*

огра|ди́ть (-жу́, -ди́шь; *impf* **огражда́ть**) *сов перех* (*сберечь*) to shelter, protect

огражде́ни|е (-я) *ср* = **огра́да**

ограниче́ни|е (-я) *ср* limitation; (*правило*) restriction

ограни́ч|ить (-у, -ишь; *impf* **ограни́чивать**) *сов перех* to limit, restrict; **ограни́читься** (*impf* **ограни́чиваться**) *сов возв*: **ограни́читься** +*instr* (*удовлетвориться*) to content o.s. with; (*свестись*) to become limited to

огро́мный *прил* enormous

огры́з|ок (-ка) *м* (*яблока*) half-eaten bit; (*карандаша*) stub

огур|е́ц (-ца́) *м* cucumber

ода́лжива|ть (-ю) *несов от* **одолжи́ть**

одарённый *прил* gifted

одева́|ть(ся) (-ю(сь)) *несов от* **оде́ть(ся)**

оде́жд|а (-ы) *ж* clothes *мн*

одеколо́н (-а) *м* eau de Cologne

оде́ну(сь) *etc сов см* **оде́ть(ся)**

од|ержа́ть (-ержу́, -е́ржишь; *impf* **оде́рживать**) *сов перех*: **одержа́ть побе́ду** to be victorious

оде́|ть (-ну, -нешь; *impf* **одева́ть**) *сов перех* to dress; **оде́ться** (*impf* **одева́ться**) *сов возв* to get dressed; (*тепло, красиво*) to dress

одея́л|о (-а) *ср* (*шерстяное*) blanket; (*стёганое*) quilt

○ **КЛЮЧЕВОЕ СЛОВО**

од|и́н (-ного́; см Table 22; f **одна́**, nt **одно́**, pl **одни́**) м чис one; **одна́ кни́га** one book; **одни́ брю́ки** one pair of trousers
▷ прил alone; (единственный, единый) one; (одинаковый, тот же самый) the same; **он идёт в кино́ оди́н** he goes to the cinema alone; **есть то́лько оди́н вы́ход** there is only one way out; **у них одни́ взгля́ды** they hold similar views
▷ мест **1** (какой-то): **оди́н мой знако́мый** a friend of mine; **одни́ неприя́тности** nothing but problems
2 (во фразах): **оди́н из** +gen pl one of; **оди́н и то́т же** the same; **одно́ и то́ же** the same thing; **оди́н раз** once; **оди́н на оди́н** one to one; **все до одного́** all to a man; **ни оди́н** not one; **оди́н за други́м** one after the other; **по одному́** one by one; **оди́н-еди́нственный** only one

одина́ковый прил similar
оди́ннадцатый чис eleventh
оди́ннадцат|ь (-и; как **пять**; см Table 26) чис eleven
одино́кий прил (жизнь, человек) lonely; (не семейный) single; **одино́честв|о** (-а) ср loneliness
одино́чный прил single
одн|а́ (-ой) ж чис см **оди́н**
одна́жды нареч once
одна́ко союз, вводн сл however; **одна́ко!** well, I never!
одни́ (-х) мн чис см **оди́н**
одн|о́ (-ого́) ср чис см **оди́н**
одновреме́нно нареч: одновреме́нно (с +instr) at the same time (as)
одного́ etc чис см **оди́н**, **одно́**
одно-: **однообра́зный** прил monotonous; **однора́зовый** прил disposable; **одноро́дный** прил (явления) similar; (масса) homogeneous; **односторо́нний** прил unilateral; (движение) one-way; **одноцве́тный** прил plain; **одноэта́жный** прил single-storey (Brit), single-story (US), one-storey (Brit), one-story (US)
одобре́ни|е (-я) ср approval; **одобри́тельный** прил (отзыв) favourable (Brit), favorable (US); (восклицание) approving; **одобр|и́ть** (-ю, -ишь; impf **одобря́ть**) сов перех to approve
одолже́ни|е (-я) ср favour (Brit), favor (US); **одолж|и́ть** (-у́, -и́шь; impf **ода́лживать**) сов перех: одолжи́ть что-н кому́-н to lend sth to sb; **ода́лживать** (perf **одолжи́ть**) что-н у кого́-н (разг) to borrow sth from sb
одува́нчик (-а) м dandelion
ожере́л|ье (-ья; gen pl -ий) ср necklace
ожесточе́ни|е (-я) ср resentment
ожива́|ть (-ю) несов от **ожи́ть**

ожив|и́ть (-лю́, -и́шь; impf **оживля́ть**) сов перех to revive; (глаза, лицо) to light up; **ожи
ви́ться** (impf **оживля́ться**) сов возв to liven up; (лицо) to brighten; **оживлённый** прил lively; (беседа, спор) animated
ожида́ни|е (-я) ср anticipation; (обычно мн: надежды) expectation; **ожида́|ть** (-ю) несов перех (ждать) to expect; (+gen: надеяться) to expect; **э́того мо́жно бы́ло ожида́ть** that was to be expected; **ожида́ться** несов возв to be expected
ож|и́ть (-иву́, -ивёшь; impf **ожива́ть**) сов to come to life
ожо́г (-а) м burn
озабо́ченный прил worried
о́з|еро (-ера; nom pl -ёра) ср lake
озира́|ться (-юсь) несов возв: озира́ться (по сторона́м) to glance about или around
означа́|ть (-ю) несов перех to mean, signify
озо́н (-а) м ozone; **озо́новый** прил: озо́новый слой ozone layer; **озо́новая дыра́** hole in the ozone layer
ой межд: ой! (выражает испуг) argh!; (выражает боль) ouch!, ow!
ок|аза́ть (-ажу́, -а́жешь; impf **ока́зывать**) сов перех: оказа́ть по́мощь кому́-н to provide help for sb; **ока́зывать** (perf **оказа́ть**) влия́ние/давле́ние на +acc to exert influence/pressure on sb; **ока́зывать** (perf **оказа́ть**) внима́ние кому́-н to pay attention to sb; **ока́зывать** (perf **оказа́ть**) сопротивле́ние (кому́-н) to offer resistance (to sb); **ока́зывать** (perf **оказа́ть**) услу́гу кому́-н to do sb a service; **оказа́ться** (impf **ока́зываться**) сов возв (найтись: на столе итп) to appear; (очутиться: на острове итп) to end up; **ока́зываться** (perf **оказа́ться**) +instr (вором, шпионом) to turn out to be; **ока́зывается, она́ была́ права́** it turns out that she was right
окамене́|ть (impf **камене́ть**) сов (перен: лицо) to freeze; (: сердце) to turn to stone
ока́нчива|ть (-ю) несов от **око́нчить**; **ока́нчиваться** несов от **око́нчиться** ▷ возв: ока́нчиваться на гла́сную/согла́сную to end in a vowel/consonant
океа́н (-а) м ocean
оки́н|уть (-у; impf **оки́дывать**) сов перех: оки́нуть кого́-н/что-н взгля́дом to glance over at sb/sth
оккупи́р|овать (-ую) (не)сов перех to occupy
окла́д (-а) м (зарплата) salary
окле́|ить (-ю, -ишь; impf **окле́ивать**) сов перех: окле́ить что-н чем-н to cover sth with sth
ок|но́ (-на́; nom pl -на, gen pl -он) ср window
о́коло нареч nearby ▷ предл (+gen: рядом с) near; (приблизительно) about, around

околозе́мный *прил* around the earth

оконча́ни|е (**-я**) *ср* end; (*Линг*) ending; **оконча́тельно** *нареч* (*ответить*) definitely; (*победить*) completely; (*отредактировать*) finally; **оконча́тельный** *прил* final; (*победа, свержение*) complete

око́нч|ить (**-у, -ишь**) *impf* **ока́нчивать** *сов перех* to finish; (*вуз*) to graduate from; **око́нчиться** (*impf* **ока́нчиваться**) *сов возв* to finish; **око́нчиться** (*perf*) +*instr* (*скандалом*) to result in

око́п (**-а**) *м* trench

о́корок (**-а**; *nom pl* **-а́**) *м* gammon

окочене́|ть (**-ю**) *сов от* **коченеть**

окра́ин|а (**-ы**) *ж* (*города*) outskirts *мн*; (*страны*) remote parts *мн*

окра́с|ка (**-ки**; *gen pl* **-ок**) *ж* (*стены*) painting; (*животного*) colouring (*Brit*), coloring (*US*)

окре́пн|уть (**-у**) *сов от* **кре́пнуть**

окре́стность (**-и**) *ж* (*обычн мн*) environs *мн*; **окре́стный** *прил* (*деревни*) neighbouring (*Brit*), neighboring (*US*)

о́крик (**-а**) *м* shout; **окри́кн|уть** (**-у**; *impf* **окри́кивать**) *сов перех*: **окри́кнуть кого́-н** to shout to sb

о́круг (**-а**) *м* (*административный*) district; (*избирательный*) ward; (*национальный*) territory; (*города*) borough

округл|и́ть (**-ю́, -и́шь**; *impf* **округля́ть**) *сов перех* (*форму*) to round off; (*цифру*) to round up *или* down

окружа́|ть (**-ю**) *несов от* **окружи́ть** ▷ *перех* to surround

окружа́ющее (**-его**) *ср* environment; **окружа́ющи|е** (**-их**) *мн* (*также* **окружа́ющие лю́ди**) *the people around one*; **окружа́ющий** *прил* surrounding

окруже́ни|е (**-я**) *ср* (*среда*) environment; (*компания*) circles *мн*; (*Воен*) encirclement; **в окруже́нии** +*gen* (*среди*) surrounded by; **окружи́|ть** (**-у́, -и́шь**; *impf* **окружа́ть**) *сов перех* to surround

окружн|о́й *прил* regional; **окружна́я доро́га** bypass

окру́жность (**-и**) *ж* circle

октя́бр|ь (**-я́**) *м* October

окун|у́ть (**-у́, -ёшь**; *impf* **окуна́ть**) *сов перех* to dip

ок|упи́ть (**-уплю́, -у́пишь**; *impf* **окупа́ть**) *сов перех* (*расходы*) to cover; (*поездку, проект*) to cover the cost of

окур|ок (**-ка**; *nom pl* **-ки**) *м* stub, butt

ола́д|ья (**-ьи**; *gen pl* **-ий**) *ж* ≈ drop scone, ≈ (Scotch) pancake

оле́н|ь (**-я**) *м* deer (*мн* deer)

оли́вк|а (**-и**) *ж* olive

олимпиа́д|а (**-ы**) *ж* (*Спорт*) the Olympics *мн*; (*по физике итп*) Olympiad; **олимпи́йск|ий** *прил* Olympic; **олимпи́йские и́гры** the Olympic Games

о́лов|о (**-а**) *ср* (*Хим*) tin

омерзи́тельный *прил* disgusting

омле́т (**-а**) *м* omelet(te)

ОМО́Н *м сокр* (= *отря́д мили́ции осо́бого назначе́ния*) special police force

омо́ним (**-а**) *м* homonym

омо́нов|ец (**-ца**) *м* member of the special police force

он (**его́**; *см* Table 6a) *мест* (*человек*) he; (*животное, предмет*) it

она́ (**её**; *см* Table 6a) *мест* (*человек*) she; (*животное, предмет*) it

они́ (**их**; *см* Table 6a) *мест* they

онла́йновый *прил* (*Комп*) on-line

оно́ (**его́**; *см* Table 6a) *мест* it; **оно́ и ви́дно** (*разг*) sure! (used ironically); **вот оно́ что** *или* **как!** (*разг*) so that's what it is!

ОО́Н *ж сокр* (= *Организа́ция Объединённых На́ций*) UN(O) (= *United Nations (Organization)*)

опа́здыва|ть (**-ю**) *несов от* **опозда́ть**

опаса́|ться (**-юсь**) *несов возв* +*gen* to be afraid of; **опаса́ться** (*impf*) **за** +*acc* to be worried about

опа́сность (**-и**) *ж* danger

опа́сный *прил* dangerous

опека́|ть (**-ю**) *несов перех* to take care of; (*сироту*) to be guardian to

о́пер|а (**-ы**) *ж* opera

операти́вн|ый *прил* (*меры*) efficient; (*хирургический*) surgical; **операти́вная гру́ппа** ≈ task force; **операти́вное запомина́ющее устро́йство** RAM

опера́тор (**-а**) *м* operator

опера́ци|я (**-и**) *ж* operation

опере́ться (**обопру́сь, обопрёшься**; *pt* **опёрся, -ла́сь**, *impf* **опира́ться**) *сов*: **опере́ться на** +*acc* to lean on

опери́р|овать (**-ую**; *perf* **опери́ровать** *или* **проопери́ровать**) *несов перех* (*больного*) to operate on ▷ *неперех* (*no perf*: *Воен*) to operate; (+*instr*: *акциями*) to deal in; (*перен*: *цифрами, фактами*) to use

о́перный *прил* operatic; (*певец*) opera

опеча́та|ть (**-ю**; *impf* **опеча́тывать**) *сов перех* to seal

опеча́т|ка (**-ки**; *gen pl* **-ок**) *ж* misprint

опи́л|ки (**-ок**) *мн* (*древесные*) sawdust *ед*; (*металлические*) filings *мн*

опира́ться (**-юсь**) *несов от* **опере́ться**

описа́ни|е (**-я**) *ср* description

оп|иса́ть (**-ишу́, -и́шешь**; *impf* **опи́сывать**) *сов перех* to describe

опла́т|а (**-ы**) *ж* payment; **опл|ати́ть** (**-ачу́, -а́тишь**; *impf* **опла́чивать**) *сов перех* (*работу, труд*) to pay for; (*счёт*) to pay

опове|сти́ть (**-щу́, -сти́шь**; *impf* **оповеща́ть**) *сов перех* to notify

опозда́ни|е (**-я**) *ср* lateness; (*поезда, самолёта*) late arrival; **опозда́|ть** (**-ю**; *impf* **опа́здывать**) *сов*: **опозда́ть** (**в/на** +*acc*) (*в школу, на работу итп*) to be late (for)

опозна́|ть (**-ю**; *impf* **опознава́ть**) *сов перех* to identify

опозóр|ить(ся) (-ю(сь)) *сов от* позóрить(ся)

опóмн|иться (-юсь, -ишься) *сов возв* (*прийти в сознание*) to come round; (*одуматься*) to come to one's senses

опóр|а (-ы) *ж* support

опóрный *прил* supporting; опóрный прыжóк *м* vault; опóрный пункт base

оппозициóнный *прил* opposition

оппозиция (-и) *ж* opposition

оппонéнт (-а) *м* (*в споре*) opponent; (*диссертации*) external examiner

опрáв|а (-ы) *ж* frame

оправдáни|е (-я) *ср* justification; (*Юр*) acquittal; (*извинение*) excuse

оправдá|ть (-ю; *impf* опрáвдывать) *сов перех* to justify; (*надежды*) to live up to; (*Юр*) to acquit; оправдáться (*impf* опрáвдываться) *сов возв* to justify o.s.; (*расходы*) to be justified

опрáв|ить (-лю, -ишь; *impf* оправлять) *сов перех* (*платье, постель*) to straighten; (*линзы*) to frame; опрáвиться (*impf* опрáвиться) *сов возв*: опрáвиться от +*gen* to recover from

опрáшива|ть (-ю) *несов от* опросить

определéни|е (-я) *ср* determination; (*Линг*) attribute

определённый *прил* (*установленный*) definite; (*некоторый*) certain

определ|ить (-ю, -ишь; *impf* определять) *сов перех* to determine; (*понятие*) to define

оприхóд|овать (-ую) *сов от* прихóдовать

опровéргн|уть (-у; *impf* опровергáть) *сов перех* to refute

опрокин|уть (-у; *impf* опрокидывать) *сов перех* (*стакан*) to knock over; опрокинуться (*impf* опрокидываться) *сов возв* (*стакан, стул, человек*) to fall over; (*лодка*) to capsize

опрóс (-а) *м* (*свидетелей*) questioning; (*населения*) survey; опрóс общéственного мнéния opinion poll

опр|осить (-ошу, -óсишь; *impf* опрáшивать) *сов перех* (*свидетелей*) to question; (*население*) to survey

опрóсный *прил*: опрóсный лист questionnaire

опротест|овáть (-ýю) *сов перех* (*Юр*) to appeal against

опрятный *прил* neat, tidy

оптимáльный *прил* optimum

оптимизм (-а) *м* optimism

оптимистичный *прил* optimistic

оптóв|ый *прил* wholesale; оптóвые закýпки (*Комм*) bulk buying; óптом *нареч*: купить/продáть óптом to buy/sell wholesale

опускá|ть(ся) (-ю(сь)) *несов от* опустить(ся)

опустé|ть (3sg -ет) *сов от* пустéть

оп|устить (-ущу, -ýстишь; *impf* опускáть) *сов перех* to lower; (*пропустить*) to miss out; опускáть (*perf* опустить) в +*acc* (*в ящик*) to drop *или* put in(to); опуститься (*impf* опускáться) *сов возв* (*человек: на диван, на землю*) to sit (down); (*солнце*) to sink; (*мост, шлагбаум*) to be lowered; (*перен: человек*) to let o.s. go

опýхн|уть (-у) *сов от* пýхнуть ▷ (*impf* опухáть) *неперех* to swell (up); óпухол|ь (-и) *ж* (*рана*) swelling; (*внутренняя*) tumour (*Brit*), tumor (*US*); опýхший *прил* swollen

óпыт (-а) *м* experience; (*эксперимент*) experiment

óпытный *прил* (*рабочий*) experienced; (*лаборатория*) experimental

опьянé|ть (-ю) *сов от* пьянéть

опять *нареч* again; опять же (*разг*) at that

орáнжевый *прил* orange

орбит|а (-ы) *ж* orbit

óрган (-а) *м* (*также Анат*) organ; (*власти*) body; (*орудие*: +*gen*: пропагáнды) vehicle for; мéстные óрганы влáсти local authorities (*Brit*) *или* government (*US*); половы́е óрганы genitals

оргáн (-а) *м* (*Муз*) organ

организáтор (-а) *м* organizer

организáци|я (-и) *ж* organization; (*устройство*) system

организм (-а) *м* organism

организ|овáть (-ýю) (*не*)*сов перех* (*создать*) to organize

органический *прил* organic

оргкомитéт (-а) *м сокр* (= организациóнный комитéт) organizational committee

оргтéхник|а (-и) *ж* office automation equipment

óрден (-а; *nom pl* -á) *м* order

орёл (орлá; *nom pl* орлы́) *м* eagle

орéх (-а) *м* nut

оригинáл (-а) *м* original; оригинáльный *прил* original

ориентир (-а) *м* landmark

оркéстр (-а) *м* orchestra

орнáмент (-а) *м* (*decorative*) pattern

оробé|ть (-ю) *сов от* робéть

оросительный *прил* irrigation; орошéни|е (-я) *ср* irrigation

ортодоксáльный *прил* orthodox

ортопéд (-а) *м* orthopaedic (*Brit*) *или* orthopedic (*US*) surgeon; ортопедический *прил* orthopaedic (*Brit*), orthopedic (*US*)

орýди|е (-я) *ср* tool; (*Воен*) gun (*used of artillery*)

орýжи|е (-я) *ж* weapon

орфогрáфи|я (-и) *ж* spelling

ОС *ж нескл сокр* (*Комп*) (= операциóнная систéма) operating system

ос|á (-ы́; *nom pl* óсы) *ж* wasp

осáд|а (-ы) *ж* siege

осáд|ки (-ков) *мн* precipitation *ед*

осва́ива|ть(ся) (-ю(сь)) *несов от* **осво́ить(ся)**

осве́дом|ить (-лю, -ишь; *impf* **осведомля́ть**) *сов перех* to inform; **осве́домиться** (*impf* **осведомля́ться**) *сов возв*: **осве́домиться о** +*prp* to inquire about

освеж|и́ть (-у́, -и́шь; *impf* **освежа́ть**) *сов перех* (*знания*) to refresh; **освежи́ться** (*impf* **освежа́ться**) *сов возв* (*воздух*) to freshen; (*человек*) to freshen up

освети́тельный *прил*: **освети́тельный прибо́р** light

осве|ти́ть (-щу́, -ти́шь; *impf* **освеща́ть**) *сов перех* to light up; (*проблему*) to cover; **освети́ться** (*impf* **освеща́ться**) *сов возв* to be lit up

освеще́ни|е (-я) *ср* lighting; (*проблемы, дела*) coverage

освобо|ди́ть (-жу́, -ди́шь; *impf* **освобожда́ть**) *сов перех* (*из тюрьмы́*) to release; (*город*) to liberate; (*дом*) to vacate; (*время*) to free up; **освободи́ть** (*perf*) **кого́-н от до́лжности** to dismiss sb; **освободи́ться** (*impf* **освобожда́ться**) *сов возв* (*из тюрьмы́*) to be released; (*дом*) to be vacated; **освобожде́ни|е** (-я) *ср* release; (*города*) liberation; **освобожде́ние от до́лжности** dismissal

осво|ить (-ю, -ишь; *impf* **осва́ивать**) *сов перех* (*технику, язык*) to master; (*земли*) to cultivate; **осво́иться** (*impf* **осва́иваться**) *сов возв* (*на новой рабо́те*) to find one's feet

освя|ти́ть (-щу́, -ти́шь; *impf* **освяща́ть**) *сов перех* (*Рел*) to bless

оседа́|ть (-ю) *несов от* **осе́сть**

осёл (-ла́) *м* donkey

осе́нний *прил* autumn, fall (*US*)

о́сен|ь (-и) *ж* autumn, fall (*US*)

о́сенью *нареч* in autumn *или* the fall (*US*)

ос|е́сть (-я́ду, -я́дешь; *impf* **оседа́ть**) *сов* (*пыль, осадок*) to settle

осётр (-етра́) *м* sturgeon (*Zool*); **осетри́н|а** (-ы) *ж* sturgeon (*Culin*)

оси́н|ый *прил*: **оси́ное гнездо́** (*перен*) hornet's nest

оско́л|ок (-ка) *м* (*стекла́*) piece; (*снаряда*) shrapnel *ед*

оскорби́тельный *прил* offensive

оскорб|и́ть (-лю, -и́шь; *impf* **оскорбля́ть**) *сов перех* to insult; **оскорби́ться** (*impf* **оскорбля́ться**) *сов возв* to be offended, take offence *или* offense (*US*); **оскорбле́ни|е** (-я) *ср* insult

осла́б|ить (-лю, -ишь; *impf* **ослабля́ть**) *сов перех* to weaken; (*дисципли́ну*) to relax

ослеп|и́ть (-лю́, -и́шь; *impf* **ослепля́ть**) *сов перех* to blind; (*подлеж: красота́*) to dazzle

ослеп|нуть (-ну; *pt* -, -ла) *сов от* **сле́пнуть**

осложне́ни|е (-я) *ср* complication

осложн|и́ть (-ю́, -и́шь; *impf* **осложня́ть**) *сов перех* to complicate; **осложни́ться** (*impf* **осложня́ться**) *сов возв* to become complicated

осма́трива|ть(ся) (-ю(сь)) *несов от* **осмотре́ть(ся)**

осмеле́|ть (-ю) *несов от* **смеле́ть**

осме́л|иться (-юсь, -ишься; *impf* **осме́ливаться**) *сов возв* to dare

осмо́тр (-а) *м* inspection; (*больно́го*) examination; (*музея*) visit; **осм|отре́ть** (-отрю́, -о́тришь; *impf* **осма́тривать**) *сов перех* (*см сущ*) to inspect; to examine; to visit; **осмотре́ться** (*impf* **осма́триваться**) *сов возв* (*по сторона́м*) to look around; (*перен: на новом ме́сте*) to settle in

осмотри́тельный *прил* cautious

осна|сти́ть (-щу́, -сти́шь; *impf* **оснаща́ть**) *сов перех* to equip; **оснаще́ни|е** (-я) *ср* equipment

осно́в|а (-ы) *ж* basis; (*сооруже́ния*) foundations *мн*; **на осно́ве** +*gen* on the basis of; *см также* **осно́вы**

основа́ни|е (-я) *ср* base; (*теории*) basis; (*поступка*) grounds *мн*; **без вся́ких основа́ний** without any reason; **до основа́ния** completely; **на основа́нии** +*gen* on the grounds of; **на како́м основа́нии?** on what grounds?

основа́тел|ь (-я) *м* founder

основа́тельный *прил* (*ана́лиз*) thorough

основа́|ть (*pt* -л, -ла, -ло, *impf* **осно́вывать**) *сов перех* to found; **осно́вывать** (*perf* **основа́ть**) **что-н на** +*prp* to base sth on *или* upon; **основа́ться** (*impf* **осно́вываться**) *сов возв* (*компа́ния*) to be founded

осно́выва|ть(ся) (-ю(сь)) *несов от* **основа́ть(ся)**

осно́в|ы (-) *мн* (*фи́зики*) basics

осо́бенно *нареч* particularly; (*хорошо́*) especially, particularly

осо́бенный *прил* special, particular

особня́к (-а́) *м* mansion

осо́бый *прил* (*вид, случай*) special, particular; (*помеще́ние*) special

осозна́|ть (-ю; *impf* **осознава́ть**) *сов перех* to realize

оспа́рива|ть (-ю) *несов от* **оспо́рить** ▷ *перех* (*пе́рвенство*) to contend *или* compete for

оспо́р|ить (-ю, -ишь; *impf* **оспа́ривать**) *сов перех* to question

остава́|ться (-ю́сь, -ёшься) *несов от* **оста́ться**

оста́в|ить (-лю, -ишь; *impf* **оставля́ть**)

сов перех to leave; (*сохранить*) to keep; (*прекратить*) to stop; (*перен: надежды*) to give up; **оста́вь!** stop it!

остальн|о́е (**-о́го**) *ср* the rest *мн*; в **остально́м** in other respects; **остально́й** *прил* (*часть*) the remaining; **остальн|ы́е** (**-ых**) *мн* the others

остан|ови́ть (**-овлю́, -о́вишь**); *impf* **остана́вливать** *сов перех* to stop; **останови́ться** (*impf* **остана́вливаться**) *сов возв* to stop; (*в гостинице, у друзей*) to stay; **останови́ться** (*perf*) **на** +*prp* (*на вопросе*) to dwell on; (*на решении*) to come to; (*взгляд*) to rest on

остано́вк|а (**-и**) *ж* stop; (*мотора*) stopping; (*в работе*) pause

оста́т|ок (**-ка**) *м* (*пищи, дня*) the remainder, the rest; **оста́тки** (*дома*) remains; (*еды*) leftovers

оста́|ться (**-нусь**; *impf* **остава́ться**) *сов возв* (*не уйти*) to stay; (*сохраниться*) to remain; (*оказаться*) to be left

остекл|и́ть (**-ю́, -и́шь**) *сов от* **стекли́ть**

осторо́жно *нареч* (*взять*) carefully; (*ходить, говорить*) cautiously; **осторо́жно!** look out!; **осторо́жность** (**-и**) *ж* care; (*поступка, поведения*) caution; **осторо́жный** *прил* careful

остри|ё (**-я́**) *ср* point; (*ножа*) edge

остр|и́ть (**-ю́, -и́шь**; *perf* **сострить**) *несов* to make witty remarks

о́стров (**-а**; *nom pl* **-а́**) *м* island

остросюже́тный *прил* (*пьеса*) gripping; **остросюже́тный фильм, остросюже́тный рома́н** thriller

остроу́мный *прил* witty

о́стрый *прил* (*нож, память, вкус*) sharp; (*борода, нос*) pointed; (*зрение, слух*) keen; (*шутка, слово*) witty; (*еда*) spicy; (*желание*) burning; (*боль, болезнь*) acute; (*ситуация*) critical

ост|уди́ть (**-ужу́, -у́дишь**; *impf* **остужа́ть**) *сов перех* to cool

осты́|ть (**-ну, -нешь**) *сов от* **стыть** ▷ (*impf* **остыва́ть**) *неперех* to cool down

ос|уди́ть (**-ужу́, -у́дишь**; *impf* **осужда́ть**) *сов перех* to condemn; (*приговорить*) to convict

осуждённ|ый (**-ого**) *м* convict

ос|уши́ть (**-ушу́, -у́шишь**; *impf* **осуша́ть**) *сов перех* to drain

осуществ|и́ть (**-лю́, -и́шь**; *impf* **осуществля́ть**) *сов перех* (*мечту, идею*) to realize; (*план*) to implement; **осуществи́ться** (*impf* **осуществля́ться**) *сов возв* (*мечты, идея*) to be realized

осчастли́в|ить (**-лю, -ишь**) *сов перех* to make happy

осып|а́ть (**-лю, -лешь**; *impf* **осыпа́ть**) *сов перех*: **осыпа́ть** (*perf* **осы́пать**) **кого́-н/что-н чем-н** to scatter sth over sb/ sth; (*перен: подарками*) to shower sb/sth

with sth; **осы́паться** (*impf* **осыпа́ться**) *сов возв* (*насыпь*) to subside; (*штукатурка*) to crumble; (*листья*) to fall

осьмино́г (**-а**) *м* octopus (*мн* octopuses)

⊙ **КЛЮЧЕВО́Е СЛО́ВО**

от *предл* +*gen* **1** from; **он отошёл от стола́** he moved away from the table; **он узна́л об э́том от дру́га** he found out about it from a friend

2 (*указывает на причину*) **бума́га размо́кла от дождя́** the paper got wet with rain; **от зло́сти** with anger; **от ра́дости** for joy; **от удивле́ния** in surprise; **от разочарова́ния/стра́ха** out of disappointment/fear

3 (*указывает на что-н, против чего направлено действие*) for; **лека́рство от ка́шля** medicine for a cough, cough medicine

4 (*о части целого*): **ру́чка/ключ от две́ри** door handle/key; **я потеря́л пу́говицу от пальто́** I lost the button off my coat

5 (*в датах*): **письмо́ от пе́рвого февраля́** a letter *или* dated the first of February

6 (*о временной последовательности*): **год от го́да** from year to year; **вре́мя от вре́мени** from time to time

ота́плива|ть (**-ю**) *несов перех* to heat; **ота́пливаться** *несов возв* to be heated

отбежа́ть (*как* **бежа́ть**; *см Table 20*; *impf* **отбега́ть**) *сов* to run off

отбел|и́ть (**-елю́, -е́лишь**; *impf* **отбе́ливать**) *сов перех* to bleach

отбивн|а́я (**-о́й**) *ж* tenderized steak; (*также* **отбивна́я котле́та**) chop

отбира́|ть (**-ю**) *несов от* **отобра́ть**

от|би́ть (**-обью́, -обьёшь**; *impf* **отбива́ть**) *сов перех* (*отколоть*) to break off; (*мяч, удар*) to fend off; (*атаку*) to repulse; **отби́ться** (*impf* **отбива́ться**) *сов возв*: **отби́ться** (*perf*) (**от** +*gen*) (*от нападающих*) to defend o.s. (against); (*отстать*) to fall behind

отблагодар|и́ть (**-ю́, -и́шь**) *сов перех* to show one's gratitude to

отбо́р (**-а**) *м* selection

отбро́|сить (**-шу, -сишь**; *impf* **отбра́сывать**) *сов перех* to throw aside; (*сомнения*) to cast aside; (*тень*) to cast

отбро́с|ы (**-ов**) *мн* (*производства*) waste *ед*; (*пищевые*) scraps *мн*

отбы́ть (*как* **быть**; *см Table 21*; *impf* **отбыва́ть**) *сов*: **отбы́ть** (**из** +*gen*/**в** +*acc*) to depart (from/for) ▷ (*pt* **-ыл, -ыла́, -ыло**) *перех*: **отбы́ть наказа́ние** to serve a sentence

отва́жный *прил* brave

отва́р (**-а**) *м* (*мясной*) broth

отв|ари́ть (**-арю́, -а́ришь**; *impf* **отва́ривать**) *сов перех* to boil

отв|езти́ (-езу́, -езёшь; pt -ёз, -езла́, impf **отвози́ть**) сов перех (увезти) to take away; **отвози́ть** (perf **отвезти́**) кого́-н/ что́-н в го́род/на да́чу to take sb/sth off to town/the dacha

отве́ргн|уть (-у; impf **отверга́ть**) сов перех to reject

отверн|у́ть (-у́, -ёшь; impf **отвёртывать**) сов перех (гайку) to unscrew ▷ (impf **отвора́чивать**) (лицо, голову) to turn away; **отверну́ться** (impf **отвора́чиваться**) сов возв (человек) to turn away

отве́рсти|е (-я) ср opening

отвёрт|ка (-ки; gen pl -ок) ж screwdriver

отв|ести́ (-еду́, -едёшь; pt -ёл, -ела́, impf **отводи́ть**) сов перех (человека: домой, к врачу) to take (off); (: от окна) to lead away; (глаза) to avert; (кандидатуру) to reject; (участок) to allot; (средства) to allocate

отве́т (-а) м (на вопрос) answer; (реакция) response; (на письмо, на приглашение) reply; **в отве́т** (на +acc) in response (to); **быть** (impf) **в отве́те за** +acc to be answerable for

ответвле́ни|е (-я) ср branch

отве́|тить (-чу, -тишь; impf **отвеча́ть**) сов: **отве́тить** (на +acc) to answer, reply (to); **отве́тить** (perf) **за** +acc (за преступление) to answer for

отве́тственност|ь (-и) ж (за поступки) responsibility; (задания) importance; **нести́** (perf **понести́**) **отве́тственность за** +acc to be responsible for; **привлека́ть** (perf **привле́чь**) **кого́-н к отве́тственности** to call sb to account

отве́тственный прил: **отве́тственный (за** +acc) responsible (for); (важный) important; **отве́тственный рабо́тник** executive

отвеча́|ть (-ю) несов от **отве́тить** ▷ неперех (+dat: требованиям) to meet; (описанию) to answer; **отвеча́ть** (impf) **за кого́-н/что́-н** to be responsible for sb/sth

отвл|е́чь (-еку́, -ечёшь итп, -еку́т; pt -ёк, -екла́, impf **отвлека́ть**) сов перех: **отвле́чь (от** +gen) (от дел) to distract (from); (противника) to divert (from); **отвле́чься** (impf **отвлека́ться**) сов возв: **отвле́чься (от** +gen) to be distracted (from); (от темы) to digress (from)

отв|оди́ть (-ожу́, -о́дишь) несов от **отвести́**

отво|ева́ть (-юю; impf **отвоёвывать**) сов перех to win back

отв|ози́ть (-ожу́, -о́зишь) несов от **отвезти́**

отвора́чива|ть(ся) (-ю(сь)) несов от **отверну́ть(ся)**

отврати́тельный прил disgusting

отвраще́ни|е (-я) ср disgust

отвы́к|нуть (-ну; pt -, -ла, impf **отвыка́ть**) сов: **отвы́кнуть от** +gen (от людей, от работы) to become unaccustomed to; (от наркотиков) to give up

отв|яза́ть (-яжу́, -я́жешь; impf **отвя́зывать**) сов перех (верёвку) to untie; **отвяза́ться** (impf **отвя́зываться**) сов возв (разг): **отвяза́ться от** +gen (отделаться) to get rid of

отгада́|ть (-ю; impf **отга́дывать**) сов перех to guess

отговор|и́ть (-ю́, -и́шь; impf **отгова́ривать**) сов перех: **отговори́ть кого́-н от чего́-н**/+infin to dissuade sb from sth/from doing; **отгово́р|ка** (-ки; gen pl -ок) ж excuse

отгоня́|ть (-ю) несов от **отогна́ть**

отгу́л (-а) м day off

отда|ва́ть (-ю́, -ёшь) несов от **отда́ть**

отдалённый прил distant; (место, сходство) remote

отда́ть (как **дать**; см Table 16; impf **отдава́ть**) сов перех (возвратить) to return; (дать) to give; (ребёнка: в школу) to send; **отдава́ть** (perf **отда́ть**) **кого́-н под суд** to prosecute sb; **отдава́ть** (perf **отда́ть**) **кому́-н честь** to salute sb; **отдава́ть** (perf **отда́ть**) **себе́ отчёт в** +prep to realize

отде́л (-а) м (учреждения) department; (газеты) section; (истории, науки) branch; **отде́л ка́дров** personnel department

отде́ла|ть (-ю; impf **отде́лывать**) сов перех (квартиру) to do up; **отде́лывать** (perf **отде́лать**) **что́-н под** +acc: **мехом**: to trim sth with sth; **отде́латься** (impf **отде́лываться**) сов возв: **отде́латься от** +gen (разг) to get rid of; **отде́латься** (perf) +instr (разг: испугом) to get away with

отделе́ни|е (-я) ср section; (учреждения) department; (филиал) branch; (концерта) part; **отделе́ние свя́зи** post office; **отделе́ние мили́ции** police station

отд|ели́ть (-елю́, -е́лишь; impf **отделя́ть**) сов перех to separate; **отдели́ться** (impf **отделя́ться**) сов возв: **отдели́ться (от** +gen) to separate (from)

отде́л|ка (-ки; gen pl -ок) ж decoration; (на платье) trimmings мн

отде́лыва|ть(ся) (-ю(сь)) несов от **отде́лать(ся)**

отде́льный прил separate

отдохн|у́ть (-у́, -ёшь; impf **отдыха́ть**) сов to (have a) rest; (на море) to have a holiday, take a vacation (US)

о́тдых (-а) м rest; (отпуск) holiday, vacation (US); **на о́тдыхе** (в отпуске) on holiday; **дом о́тдыха** holiday centre (Brit) или center (US)

отдыха́|ть (-ю) несов от **отдохну́ть**

отдыха́ющ|ий (-его) м holidaymaker (Brit), vacationer (US)

отёк (-а) м swelling; **отека́|ть** (-ю) несов от **отечь**

отéл|ь (-я) м hotel

отéц (-цá) м father

отéчественн|ый прил (промышленность) domestic; **Отéчественная Войнá** patriotic war (fought in defence of one's country)

отéчеств|о (-а) ср fatherland

отéчь (-екý, -ечёшь итп, -екýт; pt отёк, -еклá, -екло́, impf **отекáть**) сов to swell up

óтзвук (-а) м echo

óтзыв (-а) м (рецензия) review

отзывá|ть(ся) (-ю(сь)) несов от **отозвáть(ся)**

отзы́вчивый прил ready to help

откáз (-а) м refusal; (от решения) rejection; (механизма) failure; (perf **закрути́ть**) что-н до откáза to turn sth full on; **набивáть** (perf **набить**) до откáза to cram

отк|азáть (-ажý, -áжешь; impf **откáзывать**) сов (мотор, нервы) to fail; **откáзывать** (perf **отказáть**) кому-н в чём-н to refuse sb sth; (в помощи) to deny sb sth; **отказáться** (impf **откáзываться**) сов возв: **отказáться** (от +gen) to refuse; (от отдыха, от мысли) to give up; **откáзываться** (perf **отказáться**) от свои́х слов to retract one's words

откáлыва|ть(ся) (-ю(сь)) несов от **отколóть(ся)**

откачá|ть (-ю; impf **откáчивать**) сов перех to pump (out)

откѝн|уть (-у; impf **отки́дывать**) сов перех to throw; (верх, сидение) to open; (волосы, голову) to toss back; **отки́нуться** (impf **отки́дываться**) сов возв: **отки́нуться на** +acc to lean back against

откладыва|ть (-ю) несов от **отложи́ть**

отключ|и́ть (-ý, -и́шь; impf **отключáть**) сов перех to switch off; (телефон) to cut off; **отключи́ться** (impf **отключáться**) сов возв to switch off

откорректи́р|овать (-ую) сов от **корректи́ровать**

откровéнно нареч frankly

откровéнный прил frank; (обман) blatant

откро́ю(сь) etc сов см **откры́ть(ся)**

открывáл|ка (-ки; gen pl -ок) ж (разг: для консервов) tin-opener; (для бутылок) bottle-opener

открывá|ть(ся) (-ю(сь)) несов от **откры́ть(ся)**

откры́ти|е (-я) ср discovery; (сезона, выставки) opening

откры́т|ка (-ки; gen pl -ок) ж postcard

откры́тый прил open; (голова, шея) bare; (взгляд, человек) frank

откр|ы́ть (-о́ю, -о́ешь; impf **открывáть**) сов перех to open; (намерения, правду итп) to reveal; (воду, кран) to turn on; (возможность, путь) to open up; (закон) to discover; **откры́ться** (impf **открывáться**) сов возв to open; (возможность, путь) to open up

откýда нареч where from ▷ союз from where; **Вы откýда?** where are you from?; **откýда Вы приéхали?** where have you come from?; **откýда ты э́то знáешь?** how do you know about that?; **откýда-нибудь** нареч from somewhere (or other); **откýда-то** нареч from somewhere

отк|уси́ть (-ушý, -ýсишь; impf **откýсывать**) сов перех to bite off

отлá|дить (-жу, дишь) сов перех от **отлáживать**

отлáжива|ть (-ю; perf **отлáдить**) +gen несоб перех (Комп) to debug

отлагáтельств|о (-а) ср delay

отлáмыва|ть(ся) (-ю(сь)) несов от **отломи́ть(ся)**

отле|тéть (-чý, -ти́шь; impf **отлетáть**) сов to fly off; (мяч) to fly back

отличá|ть (-ю) несов от **отличи́ть**; **отличáться** возв (быть другим): **отличáться (от** +gen) to be different (from)

отли́чи|е (-я) ср distinction; **в отли́чие от** +gen unlike

отлич|и́ть (-ý, -и́шь; impf **отличáть**) сов перех (наградить) to honour (Brit), honor (US); **отличáть** (perf **отличи́ть**) кого-н/ что-н от +gen to tell sb/sth from

отли́чник (-а) м 'A'grade pupil

отли́чно нареч extremely well ▷ как сказ it's excellent или great ▷ ср нескл (Просвещ) excellent или outstanding (school mark); **он отли́чно знáет, что он винова́т** he knows perfectly well that he's wrong; **учи́ться** (impf) **на отли́чно** to get top marks

отли́чный прил excellent; (иной): **отли́чный от** +gen distinct from

отл|ожи́ть (-ожý, -о́жишь; impf **откла́дывать**) сов перех (деньги) to put aside; (собрание) to postpone

отл|оми́ть (-омлю́, -о́мишь; impf **отлáмывать**) сов перех to break off; **отломи́ться** (impf **отлáмываться**) сов возв to break off

отмахн|ýться (-ýсь, -ёшься; impf **отмáхиваться**) сов возв: **отмахнýться от** +gen (от мухи) to brush away; (от предложения) to brush или wave aside

отмéн|а (-ы) ж (см глаг) repeal; reversal; abolition; cancellation; **отм|ени́ть** (-еню́, -éнишь; impf **отменя́ть**) сов перех (решение, приговор) to reverse; (налог) to abolish; (лекцию) to cancel; (закон) to repeal

отмé|тить (-чу, -тишь; impf **отмечáть**) сов перех (на карте, в книге) to mark; (указать) to note; (юбилей) to celebrate; **отмéтиться** (impf **отмечáться**) сов возв to register

отмéт|ка (-ки; gen pl -ок) ж mark; (в документе) note

● **ОТМЕ́ТКА**

● The Russian scale of marking is from 1 to 5, with 5 being the highest mark.

отмеча́|ть(ся) (-ю(сь)) *несов от* **отме́тить(ся)**

отморо́|зить (-жу, -зишь; *impf* **отмора́живать**) *сов перех*: **отморо́зить ру́ки/но́ги** to get frostbite in one's hands/feet

отм|ы́ть (-о́ю, -о́ешь; *impf* **отмыва́ть**) *сов перех*: **отмы́ть что-н** to get sth clean; (*грязь*) to wash sth out; (*деньги*) to launder sth

отн|ести́ (-есу́, -есёшь; *pt* -ёс, -есла́, *impf* **относи́ть**) *сов перех* to take (off); (*подлеж*: *течение*) to carry off; (*причислить к*): **отнести́ что-н к** +*dat* (*к периоду, к году*) to date sth back to; (*к число группе*) to categorize sth as; (*к категории*) to put sth into; **относи́ть** (*perf* **отнести́**) **что-н за** *или* **на счёт** +*gen* to put sth down to; **отнести́сь** (*impf* **относи́ться**) *сов возв*: **отнести́сь к** +*dat* (*к человеку*) to treat; (*к предложению, к событию*) to take

отнима́|ть (-ю) *несов от* **отня́ть**

относи́тельно *нареч* relatively ▷ *предл* (+*gen*: *в отношении*) regarding, with regard to

относи́тельный *прил* relative

отн|оси́ть (-ошу́, -о́сишь) *несов от* **отнести́**; **относи́ться** *несов от* **отнести́сь** ▷ *возв*: **относи́ться к** +*dat* to relate to; (*к классу*) to belong to; (*к году*) to date from; **он к ней хорошо́ отно́сится** he likes her; **как ты отно́сишься к нему́?** what do you think about him?; **э́то к нам не отно́сится** it has nothing to do with us

отноше́ни|е (-я) *ср* (*Мат*) ratio; **отноше́ние к** +*dat* attitude (to); (*связь*) relation (to); **в отноше́нии** +*gen* with regard to; **по отноше́нию к** +*dat* towards; **в э́том отноше́нии** in this respect *или* regard; **в не́котором отноше́нии** in certain respects; **име́ть** (*impf*) **отноше́ние к** +*dat* to be connected with; **не име́ть** (*impf*) **отноше́ния к** +*dat* to have nothing to do with

отню́дь *нареч*: **отню́дь не** by no means, far from; **отню́дь нет** absolutely not

отн|я́ть (-иму́, -и́мешь; *impf* **отнима́ть**) *сов перех* to take away; (*силы, время*) to take up

ото *предл* = **от**

от|обра́ть (-беру́, -берёшь; *pt* -обра́л, -обрала́, *impf* **отбира́ть**) *сов перех* (*отнять*) to take away; (*выбрать*) to select

отовсю́ду *нареч* from all around

от|огна́ть (-гоню́, -го́нишь; *impf* **отгоня́ть**) *сов перех* to chase away

отодви́н|уть (-у; *impf* **отодвига́ть**) *сов перех* (*шкаф*) to move; (*засов*) to slide back; (*срок, экзамен*) to put back;

отодви́нуться (*impf* **отодвига́ться**) *сов возв* (*человек*) to move

от|озва́ть (-зову́, -зовёшь; *impf* **отзыва́ть**) *сов перех* to call back; (*посла, документы*) to recall; **отзыва́ть** (*perf* **отозва́ть**) **кого́-н в сто́рону** to take sb aside; **отозва́ться** (*impf* **отзыва́ться**) *сов возв*: **отозва́ться** (**на** +*acc*) to respond (to); **хорошо́/пло́хо отозва́ться** (*perf*) **о** +*prp* to speak well/badly of

отойти́ (*как* **идти́**; *см Table 18*; *impf* **отходи́ть**) *сов* (*поезд, автобус*) to leave; (*пятно*) to come out; (*отлучиться*) to go off; **отходи́ть** (*perf* **отойти́**) **от** +*gen* to move away from; (*перен: от друзей, от взглядов*) to distance o.s. from; (*от темы*) to depart from

отом|сти́ть (-щу́, -сти́шь) *сов от* **мстить**

отопи́тельный *прил* (*прибор*) heating; **отопи́тельный сезо́н** the cold season

● **ОТОПИ́ТЕЛЬНЫЙ СЕЗО́Н**

● The heating comes on around the middle of October and goes off around the middle of May. The central heating is controlled centrally and individual home owners do not have any say over it.

отопле́ни|е (-я) *ср* heating

оторв|а́ть (-у́, -ёшь; *impf* **отрыва́ть**) *сов перех* to tear off; **отрыва́ть** (*perf* **оторва́ть**) (**от** +*gen*) to tear away (from); **оторва́ться** (*impf* **отрыва́ться**) *сов возв* (*пуговица*) to come off; **отрыва́ться** (*perf* **оторва́ться**) (**от** +*gen*) (*от работы*) to tear o.s. away (from); (*убежать*) to break away (from); (*от семьи*) to lose touch (with); **отрыва́ться** (*perf* **оторва́ться**) **от земли́** (*самолёт*) to take off

отпева́ни|е (-я) *ср* funeral service; **отпева́|ть** (-ю) *несов от* **отпе́ть**

отп|е́ть (-ою́, -оёшь; *impf* **отпева́ть**) *сов перех* (*Рел*) to conduct a funeral service for

отпеча́та|ть (-ю; *impf* **отпеча́тывать**) *сов перех* to print; **отпеча́таться** (*impf* **отпеча́тываться**) *сов возв* (*на земле*) to leave a print; (*перен: в памяти*) to imprint itself

отпеча́т|ок (-ка) *м* imprint; **отпеча́тки па́льцев** fingerprints

отпира́|ть (-ю) *несов от* **отпере́ть**

отпл|ати́ть (-ачу́, -а́тишь; *impf* **отпла́чивать**) *сов* (+*dat: наградить*) to repay; (*отомстить*) to pay back

отплы́|ть (-ву́, -вёшь; *impf* **отплыва́ть**) *сов* (*человек*) to swim off; (*корабль*) to set sail

отполз|ти́ (-у́, -ёшь; *impf* **отполза́ть**) *сов* to crawl away

отправи́тел|ь (-я) *м* sender

отпра́в|ить (-лю, -ишь; *impf* **отправля́ть**) *сов перех* to send;

отпра́виться (*impf* **отправля́ться**) *сов возв* (*человек*) to set off

отпра́в|ка (**-ки**; *gen pl* **-ок**) *ж* (*письма*) posting; (*груза*) dispatch

отправле́ни|е (**-я**) *ср* (*письма*) dispatch; (*почтовое*) item

отправн|о́й *прил*: **отправно́й пункт** point of departure; **отправна́я то́чка** (*перен*) starting point

отпр|оси́ться (**-ошу́сь**, **-о́сишься**; *impf* **отпра́шиваться**) *сов перех* to ask permission to leave

о́тпуск (**-а**) *м* holiday (*Brit*), vacation (*US*); **быть** (*impf*) **в о́тпуске** to be on holiday

отп|усти́ть (**-ущу́**, **-у́стишь**; *impf* **отпуска́ть**) *сов перех* to let out; (*из рук*) to let go of; (*товар*) to sell; (*деньги*) to release; (*бороду*) to grow

отрабо́та|ть (**-ю**; *impf* **отраба́тывать**) *сов перех* (*какое-то время*) to work; (*освоить*) to perfect, polish ⊳ *неперех* (*кончить работать*) to finish work

отр|ави́ть (**-авлю́**, **-а́вишь**; *impf* **отравля́ть**) *сов перех* to poison; (*перен*: *праздник*) to spoil; **отрави́ться** (*impf* **отравля́ться**) *сов возв* to poison o.s.; (*едой*) to get food-poisoning

отраже́ни|е (**-я**) *ср* (*см глаг*) reflection; deflection

отра|зи́ть (**-жу́**, **-зи́шь**; *impf* **отража́ть**) *сов перех* to reflect; (*удар*) to deflect; **отрази́ться** (*impf* **отража́ться**) *сов возв*: **отрази́ться в** +*prp* to be reflected; **отража́ться** (*perf* **отрази́ться**) (*в зеркале*) to be reflected in; **отража́ться** (*perf* **отрази́ться**) **на** +*prp* (*на здоровье*) to have an effect on

о́трасл|ь (**-и**) *ж* branch (*of industry*)

отр|асти́ (*3sg* **-астёт**, *pt* **-óс**, **-осла́**) *сов* to grow

отра|сти́ть (**-щу́**, **-сти́шь**; *impf* **отра́щивать**) *сов перех* to grow

отре́з (**-а**) *м* piece of fabric

отре́|зать (**-жу**, **-жешь**; *impf* **отреза́ть**) *сов перех* to cut off

отре́з|ок (**-ка**) *м* (*ткани*) piece; (*пути*) section; (*времени*) period

отрица́ни|е (**-я**) *ср* denial; (*Линг*) negation; **отрица́тельный** *прил* negative

отрица́|ть (**-ю**) *несов перех* to deny; (*моду итп*) to reject

отро́ст|ок (**-ка**) *м* (*побег*) shoot

отр|уби́ть (**-ублю́**, **-у́бишь**; *impf* **отруба́ть**) *сов перех* to chop off

отруга́|ть (**-ю**) *сов от* **руга́ть**

отры́в (**-а**) *м*: **отры́в от** +*gen* (*от семьи*) separation from; **ли́ния отры́ва** perforated line; **быть** (*impf*) **в отры́ве от** +*gen* to be cut off from

отрыва́|ть(ся) (**-ю(сь)**) *несов от* **оторва́ть(ся)**

отря́д (**-а**) *м* party, group; (*Воен*) detachment

отряхн|у́ть (**-у́**, **-ёшь**; *impf* **отря́хивать**) *сов перех* (*снег, пыль*) to shake off; (*пальто*) to shake down

отсе́к (**-а**) *м* compartment

отс|е́чь (**-еку́**, **-ечёшь** *etc*, **-еку́т**; *pt* **-ёк**, **-екла́**, *impf* **отсека́ть**) *сов перех* to cut off

отск|очи́ть (**-очу́**, **-о́чишь**; *impf* **отска́кивать**) *сов* (*в сторону, назад*) to jump; (*разг*: *пуговица, кнопка*) to come off; **отска́кивать** (*perf* **отскочи́ть**) **от** +*gen* (*мяч*) to bounce off; (*человек*) to jump off

отсро́ч|ить (**-у**, **-ишь**; *impf* **отсро́чивать**) *сов перех* to defer

отста|ва́ть (**-ю́**, **-ёшь**) *несов от* **отста́ть**

отста́в|ка (**-ки**; *gen pl* **-ок**) *ж* retirement; (*кабинета*) resignation; **подава́ть** (*perf* **пода́ть**) **в отста́вку** to offer one's resignation

отста́ива|ть(ся) (**-ю**) *несов от* **отстоя́ть(ся)**

отста́лый *прил* backward

отста́|ть (**-ну**, **-нешь**; *impf* **отстава́ть**) *сов* (*перен*: *в учёбе, в работе*) to fall behind; (*часы*) to be slow; **отстава́ть** (*perf* **отста́ть**) (**от** +*gen*) (*от группы*) to fall behind; (*от поезда, от автобуса*) to be left behind; **отста́нь от меня́!** stop pestering me!

отсто|я́ть (**-ю́**, **-и́шь**; *impf* **отста́ивать**) *сов перех* (*город, своё мнение*) to defend; (*раствор*) to allow to stand; (*два часа итп*) to wait; **отстоя́ться** (*impf* **отста́иваться**) *сов возв* to settle

отстран|и́ть (**-ю́**, **-и́шь**; *impf* **отстраня́ть**) *сов перех* (*отодвинуть*) to push away; (*уволить*): **отстрани́ть от** +*gen* to remove, dismiss; **отстрани́ться** (*impf* **отстраня́ться**) *сов возв*: **отстрани́ться от** +*gen* (*от должности*) to relinquish; (*отодвинуться*) to draw back

отст|упи́ть (**-уплю́**, **-у́пишь**; *impf* **отступа́ть**) *сов* to step back; (*Воен*) to retreat; (*перен*: *перед трудностями*) to give up

отступле́ни|е (**-я**) *ср* retreat; (*от темы*) digression

отсу́тстви|е (**-я**) *ср* (*человека*) absence; (*денег, вкуса*) lack

отсу́тств|овать (**-ую**) *несов* (*в классе итп*) to be absent; (*желание*) to be lacking

отсу́тствующ|ий *прил* (*взгляд, вид*) absent ⊳ (**-его**) *м* absentee

отсчёт (**-а**) *м* (*минут*) calculation; **то́чка отсчёта** point of reference

отсчита́|ть (**-ю**; *impf* **отсчи́тывать**) *сов перех* to count out

отсю́да *нареч* from here

отта́ива|ть (**-ю**) *несов от* **отта́ять**

отта́лкива|ть(ся) (**-ю(сь)**) *несов от* **оттолкну́ть(ся)**

отт|ащи́ть (**-ащу́**, **-а́щишь**; *impf* **отта́скивать**) *сов перех* to drag

отта́|ять (**-ю**; *impf* **отта́ивать**) *сов*

(земля) to thaw; (мясо) to thaw out

оттéн|ок (-ка) м shade

óттепел|ь (-и) ж thaw

óттиск (-а) м (ступни) impression; (рисунка) print

оттогó нареч for this reason; **оттогó что** because

оттолкн|ýть (-ý, -ёшь; impf **отта́лкивать**) сов перех to push away; **оттолкну́ться** (impf **отта́лкиваться**) сов возв: **оттолкну́ться от чего́-н** (от берега) to push o.s. away или back from sth; (перен: от данных) to take sth as one's starting point

оттýда нареч from there

отт|яну́ть (-яну́, -я́нешь; impf **отта́гивать**) сов перех to pull back; (карман) to stretch; (разг: выполнение) to delay; **отта́гивать** (**оттяну́ть** impf) вре́мя to play for time

от|учи́ть (-учу́, -у́чишь; impf **отуча́ть**) сов перех: **отучи́ть кого́-н от** +gen (от курения) to wean sb off; **отуча́ть** (**отучи́ть** perf) **кого́-н** +infin (врать) to teach sb not to do; **отучи́ться** (impf **отуча́ться**) сов возв: **отучи́ться** +infin to get out of the habit of doing

отхлы́н|уть (3sg -ет) сов (волны) to roll back

отхо́д (-а) м departure; (Воен) withdrawal; см также **отхо́ды**

отх|оди́ть (-ожу́, -о́дишь) несов от **отойти́**

отхо́д|ы (-ов) мн waste ед

отца́ etc сущ см **отéц**

отцо́вский прил father's; (чувства, права) paternal

отча́ива|ться (-юсь) несов от **отча́яться**

отча́л|ить (-ю, -ишь; impf **отча́ливать**) сов to set sail

отча́яни|е (-я) ср despair; **отча́янный** прил desperate; (смелый) daring; **отча́яться** (-юсь; impf **отча́иваться**) сов возв: **отча́яться** (+infin) to despair (of doing)

отчего́ нареч (почему) why ▷ союз (вследствие чего) which is why; **отчего́-нибудь** нареч for any reason; **отчего́-то** нареч for some reason

óтчеств|о (-а) ср patronymic

○ **Óтчество**
○
○ The full name of a Russian person must
○ include his or her patronymic. Besides
○ being the formal way of addressing
○ people, the use of the patronymic also
○ shows your respect for that person.
○ Patronymics are not as officious as they
○ sound to some foreign ears. In fact, quite
○ often the patronymic replaces the first
○ name and is used as an affectionate way
○ of addressing people you know well.

отчёт (-а) м account; **фина́нсовый отчёт** financial report; (выписка) statement; **отдава́ть** (perf **отда́ть**) **себе́ отчёт в чём-н** to realize sth

отчётливый прил distinct; (объяснение) clear

отчи́зн|а (-ы) ж mother country

óтчим (-а) м stepfather

отчисле́ни|е (-я) ср (работника) dismissal; (студента) expulsion; (обычно мн: на строительство) allocation; (: денежные: удержание) deduction; (: выделение) assignment

отчита́|ть (-ю; impf **отчи́тывать**) сов перех (ребёнка) to tell off; **отчита́ться** (impf **отчи́тываться**) сов возв to report

отъе́зд (-а) м departure; **быть** (impf) **в отъе́зде** to be away

отъ|е́хать (как **е́хать**; см Table 19; impf **отъезжа́ть**) сов to travel; **отъезжа́ть** (perf **отъе́хать**) **от** +gen to move away from

отъя́вленный прил utter

отыгра́|ть (-ю; impf **оты́грывать**) сов перех to win back; **отыгра́ться** (impf **оты́грываться**) сов возв (в ка́рты, в ша́хматы) to win again; (перен) to get one's own back

от|ыска́ть (-ыщу́, -ы́щешь; impf **оты́скивать**) сов перех to hunt out; (Комп) to retrieve

óфис (-а) м office

офице́р (-а) м (Воен) officer; (разг: Шахматы) bishop

официа́льн|ый прил official; **официа́льное лицо́** official

официа́нт (-а) м waiter

офла́йный прил off-line

оформи́тел|ь (-я) м: **оформи́тель спекта́кля** set designer; **оформи́тель витри́н** window dresser

офо́рм|ить (-лю, -ишь; impf **оформля́ть**) сов перех (докуме́нты, догово́р) to draw up; (кни́гу) to design the layout of; (витри́ну) to dress; (спекта́кль) to design the sets for; **оформля́ть** (perf **офо́рмить**) **кого́-н на рабо́ту** (+instr) to take sb on as; **офо́рмиться** (impf **оформля́ться**) сов возв (взгля́ды) to form; **оформля́ться** (perf **офо́рмиться**) **на рабо́ту** (+instr) to be taken on as

оформле́ни|е (-я) ср design; (докуме́нтов, догово́ра) drawing up; **музыка́льное оформле́ние** music

оформля́|ть(ся) (-ю(сь)) несов от **офо́рмить**

оффшо́рный прил (Комп) offshore

охладе́|ть (-ю; impf **охладева́ть**) сов (отноше́ния) to cool; **охладева́ть** (perf **охладе́ть**) **к** +dat (к му́жу) to grow cool towards

охла|ди́ть (-жу́, -ди́шь; impf **охлажда́ть**) сов перех (во́ду, чу́вства) to cool; **охлади́ться** (impf **охлажда́ться**) сов возв (печка, вода) to cool down

охо́т|а (-ы) ж hunt; (разг: желание) desire; **охо́титься** (-чусь, -тишься) несов возв: **охо́титься на** +acc to hunt (to kill); **охо́титься** (impf) **за** +instr to hunt (to catch); (перен: разг) to hunt for; **охо́тник** (-а) м hunter; **охо́тничий** прил hunting

охо́тно нареч willingly

охра́н|а (-ы) ж (защита) security; (группа людей) bodyguard; (растений, животных) protection; (здоровья) care; **охра́на труда́** health and safety regulations

охра́нник (-а) м guard

охраня́|ть (-ю) несов перех to guard; (природу) to protect

оц|ени́ть (-еню́, -е́нишь; impf **оце́нивать**) сов перех (вещь) to value; (знания) to assess; (признать достоинства) to appreciate; **оце́н|ка** (-ки; gen pl -ок) ж (вещи) valuation; (работника, поступка) assessment; (отметка) mark

оц|епи́ть (-еплю́, -е́пишь; impf **оцепля́ть**) сов перех to cordon off

оча́г (-а́) м hearth; (перен: заболевания) source

очарова́ни|е (-я) ср charm

очарова́тельный прил charming

очар|ова́ть (-у́ю; impf **очаро́вывать**) сов перех to charm

очеви́дно нареч, част obviously ▷ как сказ: очеви́дно, что он винова́т it's obvious that he is guilty ▷ вводн сл: очеви́дно, он не придёт apparently he's not coming; **очеви́дный** прил (факт) plain; (желание) obvious

о́чень нареч +adv, +adj very +vb very much

очередно́й прил next; (ближайший: задача) immediate; (: номер газеты) latest; (повторяющийся) another

о́черед|ь (-и) ж (порядок) order; (место в порядке) turn; (группа людей) queue (Brit), line (US); (в строительстве) section; **в пе́рвую о́чередь** in the first instance; **в поря́дке о́череди** when one's turn comes; **в свою́ о́чередь** in turn; **по о́череди** in turn

о́черк (-а) м (литературный) essay; (газетный) sketch

очерта́ни|е (-я) ср outline

оче́чник (-а) м spectacle case

очи́|стить (-щу, -стишь; impf **очища́ть**) сов перех to clean; (газ, воду) to purify; (город, квартиру) to clear; **очи́ститься** (impf **очища́ться**) сов возв (газ, вода) to be purified

очистн|о́й прил: **очистны́е сооруже́ния** purification plant ед

очища́|ть(ся) (-ю) несов от **очи́стить(ся)**

очк|и́ (-о́в) мн (для чтения) glasses, spectacles; (для плавания) goggles; **защи́тные очки́** safety specs

очк|о́ (-а́) ср (Спорт) point; (Карты) pip

очн|у́ться (-у́сь, -ёшься) сов возв (после сна) to wake up; (после обморока) to come round

о́чн|ый прил (обучение, институт итп) with direct contact between students and teachers; **о́чная ста́вка** (Юр) confrontation

---

● **О́чное отделе́ние**
●
● This is one of the ways of obtaining a
● degree. Most students choose this
● method. It is full time course with over
● 30 contact hours a week and two exam
● sessions. See also notes at **зао́чный** and
● **вече́рний**.

оч|ути́ться (2sg -у́тишься) сов возв to end up

оше́йник (-а) м collar

ош|иби́ться (-ибу́сь, -ибёшься; pt -и́бся, -и́блась, impf **ошиба́ться**) сов возв to make a mistake; **ошиба́ться** (perf **ошиби́ться**) **в ком-н** to misjudge sb; **оши́б|ка** (-ки; gen pl -ок) ж mistake, error; **по оши́бке** by mistake; **оши́бочный** прил (мнение) mistaken, erroneous; (суждение, вывод) wrong

ощу́па|ть (-ю; impf **ощу́пывать**) сов перех to feel; **о́щуп|ь** (-и) ж: **на о́щупь** by touch; **пробира́ться** (impf) **на о́щупь** to grope one's way through

ощу|ти́ть (-щу́, -ти́шь; impf **ощуща́ть**) сов перех (желание, боль) to feel

ощуще́ни|е (-я) ср sense; (радости, боли) feeling

П

павильо́н (-а) м pavilion

павли́н (-а) м peacock

па́да|ть (-ю; *perf* упа́сть *или* пасть)
несов to fall; (*настроение*) to sink;
(*дисциплина, нравы*) to decline

паде́ж (-á) м (*Линг*) case

паде́ни|е (-я) *ср* fall; (*нравов,
дисциплины*) decline

па́йщик (-а) м shareholder

паке́т (-а) м package; (*мешок*) (paper *или*
plastic) bag

пак|ова́ть (-у́ю; *perf* запакова́ть *или*
упакова́ть) *несов перех* to pack

пала́т|а (-ы) ж (*в больнице*) ward; (*Полит*)
chamber, house

пала́т|ка (-ки; *gen pl* -ок) ж tent

па́л|ец (-ьца) м (*руки*) finger; (*ноги*) toe;
большо́й па́лец (*руки*) thumb; (*ноги*)
big toe

па́л|ка (-ки; *gen pl* -ок) ж stick

пало́мничеств|о (-а) *ср* pilgrimage

па́лоч|ка (-ки; *gen pl* -ек) ж (*Муз*):
дирижёрская па́лочка (conductor's) baton;
волше́бная па́лочка magic wand

па́луб|а (-ы) ж (*Мор*) deck

па́льм|а (-ы) ж palm (tree)

пальто́ *ср нескл* overcoat

па́мятник (-а) м monument; (*на могиле*)
tombstone

па́мят|ь (-и) ж memory; (*воспоминание*)
memories *мн*

пана́м|а (-ы) ж Panama (hat)

пане́л|ь (-и) ж (*Строит*) panel

па́ник|а (-и) ж panic; паник|ова́ть
(-у́ю) *несов* (*разг*) to panic

панихи́д|а (-ы) ж (*Рел*) funeral service;
гражда́нская панихи́да civil funeral

панора́м|а (-ы) ж panorama

пансиона́т (-а) м boarding house

па́п|а (-ы) м dad; (*также* Ри́мский па́па)
the Pope

папиро́с|а (-ы) ж type of cigarette

папиро́сн|ый *прил*: папиро́сная
бума́га (*тонкая бумага*) tissue
paper

па́п|ка (-ки; *gen pl* -ок) ж folder
(*Brit*), file (*US*)

пар (-а; *nom pl* -ы́) м steam; см также
пары́

па́р|а (-ы) ж (*туфель итп*) pair;
(*супружеская*) couple

пара́граф (-а) м paragraph

пара́д (-а) м parade

пара́дн|ое (-ого) *ср* entrance

пара́дный *прил* (*вход, лестница*) front,
main

парадо́кс (-а) м paradox

парази́т (-а) м parasite

парали́ч (-á) м paralysis

паралле́л|ь (-и) ж parallel

парашю́т (-а) м parachute

па́рен|ь (-я) м (*разг*) guy

пари́ *ср нескл* bet

Пари́ж (-а) м Paris

пари́к (-á) м wig

парикма́хер (-а) м hairdresser;
парикма́херск|ая (-ой) ж hairdresser's
(*Brit*), beauty salon (*US*)

па́р|иться (-юсь, -ишься) *несов возв*
(*в бане*) to have a sauna

па́р|ить (-ю, -ишь) *несов* to glide

парк (-а) м park

парк|ова́ть (-у́ю) *несов перех* to
park

парла́мент (-а) м parliament

парла́ментский *прил* parliamentary

парни́к (-á) м greenhouse

парнико́вый *прил*: парнико́вый
эффе́кт greenhouse effect

парово́з (-а) м steam engine

паров|о́й *прил* steam; парово́е
отопле́ние central heating

паро́ди|я (-и) ж: паро́дия (на +*асс*)
parody (of)

паро́л|ь (-я) м password

паро́м (-а) м ferry

па́рт|а (-ы) ж desk (*in schools*)

парте́р (-а) м the stalls *мн*

парти́йный *прил* party

па́рти|я (-и) ж (*Полит*) party; (*Муз*) part;
(*груза*) consignment; (*изделий: в
производстве*) batch; (*Спорт*): па́ртия в
ша́хматы/волейбо́л a game of chess/
volleyball

партнёр (-а) м partner; партнёрств|о
(-а) *ср* partnership

па́рус (-а; *nom pl* -á) м sail

парфюме́ри|я (-и) ж *собир* perfume and
cosmetic goods

пар|ы́ (-о́в) *мн* vapour *ед* (*Brit*), vapor *ед*
(*US*)

пас (-а) м (*Спорт*) pass

па́смурный *прил* overcast, dull

па́спорт (-а; *nom pl* -á) м passport;
(*автомобиля, станка*) registration
document

ПА́СПОРТ

Russian citizens are required by law to have a passport at the age of 14. This is then renewed at the ages of 20 and 45. The passport serves as an essential identification document and has to be produced on various occasions ranging from applying for a job to collecting a parcel from the post office. Those who travel abroad have to get a separate passport for foreign travel.

пассажи́р (-а) *м* passenger
пасси́вный *прил* passive
па́ст|**а** (-ы) *ж* paste; (*тома́тная*) purée; **зубна́я па́ста** toothpaste
пас|**ти́** (-у́, -ёшь; *pt* -, -ла́) *несов перех* (*скот*) to graze; **пасти́сь** *несов возв* to graze
паст|**ила́** (-илы́; *nom pl* -и́лы) *ж* ≈ marshmallow
па́сть (-ду́, -дёшь; *pt* -л, -ла, -ло) *сов от* **па́дать** ▷ (-сти) *ж* (*зверя́*) mouth
Па́сх|**а** (-и) *ж* (*в иудаи́зме*) Passover; (*в христиа́нстве*) ≈ Easter
пате́нт (-а) *м* patent; **пате́нт**|**ова́ть** (-у́ю; *perf* **запатентова́ть**) *несов перех* to patent
патриа́рх (-а) *м* patriarch
патро́н (-а) *м* (*Воен*) cartridge; (*ла́мпы*) socket
патрули́р|**овать** (-ую) *несов (не)перех* to patrol
патру́л|**ь** (-я́) *м* patrol
па́уз|**а** (-ы) *ж* (*также Муз*) pause
пау́к (-а́) *м* spider
паути́н|**а** (-ы) *ж* spider's web, spiderweb (*US*); (*в помеще́нии*) cobweb; (*перен*) web
пах (-а; *loc sg* -у́) *м* groin
па|**ха́ть** (-шу́, -шешь; *perf* вспаха́ть) *несов перех* to plough (*Brit*), plow (*US*)
па́х|**нуть** (-ну; *pt* -, -ла) *несов*: **па́хнуть** (+*instr*) to smell (of)
пацие́нт (-а) *м* patient
па́чк|**а** (-ки; *gen pl* -ек) *ж* (*бума́г*) bundle; (*ча́я, сигаре́т итп*) packet
па́чка|**ть** (-ю; *perf* **запа́чкать** или **испа́чкать**) *несов перех*: **па́чкать что-н** to get sth dirty; **па́чкаться** (*perf* **запа́чкаться** или **испа́чкаться**) *несов возв* to get dirty
паште́т (-а) *м* pâté
пая́|**ть** (-ю) *несов перех* to solder
пев|**е́ц** (-ца́) *м* singer; **певи́ц**|**а** (-ы) *ж от* **певе́ц**
педаго́г (-а) *м* teacher; **педагоги́ческий** *прил* (*коллекти́в*) teaching; **педагоги́ческий институ́т** teacher-training (*Brit*) или teachers' (*US*) college; **педагоги́ческий сове́т** staff meeting
педа́л|**ь** (-и) *ж* pedal
педиа́тр (-а) *м* paediatrician (*Brit*), pediatrician (*US*)

пей *несов см* **пить**
пе́йджер (-а) *м* pager
пейза́ж (-а) *м* landscape
пе́йте *несов см* **пить**
пека́р|**ня** (-ни; *gen pl* -ен) *ж* bakery
пелён|**ка** (-ки; *gen pl* -ок) *ж* swaddling clothes *мн*
пельме́н|**ь** (-я; *nom pl* -и) *м* (*обы́чно мн*) ≈ ravioli *ед*
пе́н|**а** (-ы) *ж* (*мы́льная*) suds *мн*; (*морска́я*) foam; (*бульо́нная*) froth
пена́л (-а) *м* pencil case
пе́ни|**е** (-я) *ср* singing
пе́н|**иться** (3sg -ится, *perf* **вспе́ниться**) *несов возв* to foam, froth
пеницилли́н (-а) *м* penicillin
пе́нк|**а** (-и) *ж* (*на молоке́*) skin
пенсионе́р (-а) *м* pensioner
пенсио́нный *прил* (*фонд*) pension
пе́нси|**я** (-и) *ж* pension; **выходи́ть** (*perf* **вы́йти**) **на пе́нсию** to retire
пень (пня) *м* (tree) stump
пе́п|**ел** (-ла) *м* ash; **пе́пельниц**|**а** (-ы) *ж* ashtray
пе́рвенств|**о** (-а) *ср* championship; (*ме́сто*) first place
пе́рв|**ое** (-ого) *ср* first course
первокла́ссник (-а) *м* pupil in first year at school
первонача́льный *прил* (*исхо́дный*) original, initial
пе́рв|**ый** *чис* first; (*по вре́мени*) first, earliest; **пе́рвый эта́ж** ground (*Brit*) или first (*US*) floor; **пе́рвое вре́мя** at first; **в пе́рвую о́чередь** in the first place или instance; **пе́рвый час дня/но́чи** after midday/midnight; **това́р пе́рвого со́рта** top grade product (*on a scale of 1-3*); **пе́рвая по́мощь** first aid
перебежа́ть (*как* **бежа́ть**; *см Table 20*; *impf* **перебега́ть**) *сов*: **перебежа́ть** (**че́рез** +*acc*) to run across
перебива́|**ть** (-ю) *несов от* **переби́ть**
перебира́|**ть(ся)** (-ю(сь)) *несов от* **перебра́ть(ся)**
переби́ть (-ью, -ьёшь; *impf* **перебива́ть**) *сов перех* to interrupt; (*разби́ть*) to break
переболе́|**ть** (-ю) *сов* +*instr* to recover from
переб|**оро́ть** (-орю́, -о́решь) *сов перех* to overcome
переб|**ра́сыва**|**ть** (-ю) *несов от* **перебро́сить**
переб|**ра́ть** (-еру́, -ерёшь; *impf* **перебира́ть**) *сов перех* (*бума́ги*) to sort out; (*крупу́, я́годы*) to go over или through (in one's mind); **перебра́ться** (*impf* **перебира́ться**) *сов возв* (*че́рез ре́ку*) to manage to get across
перебро́|**сить** (-шу, -сишь; *impf* **перебра́сывать**) *сов перех* (*мяч*) to throw; (*войска́*) to transfer
перева́л (-а) *м* (*в гора́х*) pass

перева́лочный прил: **перева́лочный пункт/ла́герь** transit area/camp

перев|ари́ть (-арю́, -а́ришь; impf **перева́ривать**) сов перех to overcook (by boiling); (пищу, информацию) to digest; **перевари́ться** (impf **перева́риваться**) сов возв to be overcooked или overdone; (пища) to be digested

перев|езти́ (-езу́, -езёшь; pt -ёз, -езла́, impf **перевози́ть**) сов перех to take или transport across

перевер|ну́ть (-у́, -ёшь; impf **перевора́чивать**) сов перех to turn over; (изменить) to change (completely); (no impf: комнату) to turn upside down; **переверну́ться** (impf **перевора́чиваться**) сов возв (человек) to turn over; (лодка, машина) to overturn

переве́с (-а) м (преимущество) advantage

перев|ести́ (-еду́, -едёшь; pt -ёл, -ела́, impf **переводи́ть**) сов перех (помочь перейти) to take across; (текст) to translate; (: устно) to interpret; (часы) to reset; (учреждение, сотрудника) to transfer, move; (переслать: деньги) to transfer; (доллары, метры итп) to convert; **перевести́сь** (impf **переводи́ться**) сов возв to move

перево́д (-а) м transfer; (стрелки часов) resetting; (текст) translation; (деньги) remittance

перево́д|чик (-а) м translator; (устный) interpreter

перев|ози́ть (-ожу́, -о́зишь) несов от **перевезти́**

перевора́чива|ть(ся) (-ю(сь)) несов от **переверну́ть(ся)**

переворо́т (-а) м (Полит) coup (d'état); (в судьбе) turning point

перев|яза́ть (-яжу́, -я́жешь; impf **перевя́зывать**) сов перех (руку, раненого) to bandage; (рану) to dress, bandage; (коробку) to tie up

перег|на́ть (-оню́, -о́нишь; pt -на́л, -нала́, -на́ло, impf **перегоня́ть**) сов перех (обогнать) to overtake; (нефть) to refine; (спирт) to distil (Brit), distill (US)

перегова́рива|ться (-юсь) несов возв: **перегова́риваться (с** +instr) to exchange remarks (with)

перегово́рный прил: **перегово́рный пункт** telephone office (for long-distance calls)

перегово́р|ы (-ов) мн negotiations, talks; (по телефону) call ед

перегоня́|ть (-ю) несов от **перегна́ть**

перегор|е́ть (3sg -и́т, impf **перегора́ть**) сов (лампочка) to fuse; (двигатель) to burn out

перегоро|ди́ть (-жу́, -ди́шь; impf **перегора́живать**) сов перех (комнату) to partition (off); (дорогу) to block

перегру|зи́ть (-ужу́, -у́зишь; impf **перегружа́ть**) сов перех to overload

перегру́з|ка (-ки; gen pl -ок) ж overload; (обычно мн: нервные) strain

⭘ **КЛЮЧЕВО́Е СЛО́ВО**

пе́ред предл +instr 1 (о положении, в присутствии) in front of
2 (раньше чего-л) before
3 (об объекте воздействия): **пе́ред тру́дностями** in the face of difficulties; **извини́ться** (perf **извини́ться**) **пе́ред** кем-н to apologize to sb; **отчи́тываться** (perf **отчита́ться**) **пе́ред** +instr to report to
4 (по сравнению) compared to
5 (как союз): **пе́ред тем как** before; **пе́ред тем как зако́нчить** before finishing

переда|ва́ть (-ю́; imper **передава́й(те)**) несов от **переда́ть**

переда́м etc сов см **переда́ть**

переда́тчик (-а) м transmitter

переда́|ть (как **дать**; см Table 16; impf **передава́ть**) сов перех: **переда́ть что-н (кому́-н)** (письмо, подарок) to pass или hand sth (over) (to sb); (известие, интерес) to pass sth on (to sb); **переда́йте ему́ (мой) приве́т** give him my regards; **переда́йте ей, что я не приду́** tell her I am not coming; **передава́ть** (perf **переда́ть) что-н по телеви́дению/ра́дио** to televise/broadcast sth

переда́ч|а (-и) ж (денег, письма) handing over; (матча) transmission; (Тел, Радио) programme (Brit), program (US); **програ́мма переда́ч** television and radio guide

переда́шь сов см **переда́ть**

передвига́|ть(ся) (-ю(сь)) несов от **передви́нуть(ся)**

передвиже́ни|е (-я) ср movement; **сре́дства передвиже́ния** means of transport

передви́н|уть (-у; impf **передвига́ть**) сов перех to move; **передви́нуться** (impf **передвига́ться**) сов возв to move

переде́ла|ть (-ю; impf **переде́лывать**) сов перех (работу) to redo; (характер) to change

пере́дний прил front

пере́дн|яя (-ей) ж (entrance) hall

пе́редо предл = **пе́ред**

передов|а́я (-о́й) ж (также **передова́я статья́**) editorial; (также **передова́я пози́ция**: Воен) vanguard

передово́й прил (технология) advanced; (писатель, взгляды) progressive

передр|азни́ть (-азню́, -а́знишь; impf **передра́знивать**) сов перех to mimic

перее́зд (-а) м (в новый дом) move

перее́хать (как **е́хать**; см Table 19; impf

переезжа́ть) *сов* (*переселиться*) to move; **переезжа́ть** (*perf* **перее́хать**) (**че́рез** +*acc*) to cross

пережива́ни|е (-*я*) *ср* feeling

пережива́|ть (-*ю*) *несов от* **пережи́ть** ▷ *неперех*: **пережива́ть** (**за** +*acc*) to worry (about)

пережи́|ть (-*ву́*, -*вёшь*; *impf* **пережива́ть**) *сов перех* (*вытерпеть*) to suffer

перезвон|и́ть (-*ю́*, -*и́шь*; *impf* **перезва́нивать**) *сов* to phone (*Brit*) *или* call (*US*) back

пере|йти́ (*как* **идти́**; *см* Table 18; *impf* **переходи́ть**) *сов* (*не*)*перех*: **перейти́** (**че́рез** +*acc*) to cross ▷ *неперех*: **перейти́ в/на** +*acc* to go (over) to; (*на другую работу*) to move to; **переходи́ть** (*perf* **перейти́**) **к** +*dat* (*к сыну итп*) to pass to; (*к делу, к обсуждению*) to turn to; **переходи́ть** (*perf* **перейти́**) **на** +*acc* to switch to

перекин|у́ть (-*у*; *impf* **переки́дывать**) *сов перех* to throw

перекла́дыва|ть (-*ю*) *несов от* **переложи́ть**

переключа́тел|ь (-*я*) *m* switch

переключ|и́ть (-*у́*, -*и́шь*; *impf* **переключа́ть**) *сов перех* to switch; **переключи́ться** (*impf* **переключа́ться**) *сов возв*: **переключи́ться** (**на** +*acc*) (*внимание*) to shift (to)

перекопа́|ть (-*ю*) *сов перех* (*огород*) to dig up; (*разг*: *шкаф*) to rummage through

перекр|ести́ть (-*ещу́*, -*е́стишь*) *сов от* **крести́ть**; **перекрести́ться** *сов от* **крести́ться** ▷ (*impf* **перекре́щиваться**) *возв* (*дороги, интересы*) to cross

перекрёст|ок (-*ка*) *m* crossroads

перекр|ы́ть (-*о́ю*, -*о́ешь*; *impf* **перекрыва́ть**) *сов перех* (*реку*) to dam; (*воду, газ*) to cut off

перек|упи́ть (-*уплю́*, -*у́пишь*; *impf* **перекупа́ть**) *сов перех* to buy

перек|уси́ть (-*ушу́*, -*у́сишь*) *сов* (*разг*) to have a snack

переле́з|ть (-*у*, -*ешь*; *pt* -, -*ла*, *impf* **перелеза́ть**) *сов* (*не*)*перех*: **переле́зть** (**че́рез** +*acc*) (*забор, канаву*) to climb (over)

перелёт (-*а*) *m* flight; (*птиц*) migration; **переле|те́ть** (-*чу́*, -*ти́шь*; *impf* **перелета́ть**) *сов* (*не*)*перех*: **перелете́ть** (**че́рез** +*acc*) to fly over

перелива́ни|е (-*я*) *ср*: **перелива́ние кро́ви** blood transfusion

перелива́|ть (-*ю*) *несов от* **перели́ть**

перелиста́|ть (-*ю*; *impf* **перели́стывать**) *сов перех* (*просмотреть*) to leaf through

перел|и́ть (-*ью́*, -*ьёшь*; *impf* **перелива́ть**) *сов перех* to pour (*from one container to another*); **перелива́ть** (*perf* **перели́ть**) **кровь кому́-н** to give sb a blood transfusion

перел|ожи́ть (-*ожу́*, -*о́жишь*; *impf* **перекла́дывать**) *сов перех* to move; **перекла́дывать** (*perf* **переложи́ть**) **что-н на кого́-н** (*задачу*) to pass sth onto sb

перело́м (-*а*) *m* (*Мед*) fracture; (*перен*) turning point

перело́мный *прил* critical

перема́тыва|ть (-*ю*) *несов от* **перемота́ть**

переме́н|а (-*ы*) *ж* change; (*в школе*) break (*Brit*), recess (*US*); **переме́нный** *прил* (*успех, ветер*) variable; **переме́нный ток** alternating current

переме|сти́ть (-*щу́*, -*сти́шь*; *impf* **перемеща́ть**) *сов перех* (*предмет*) to move; (*людей*) to transfer; **перемести́ться** (*impf* **перемеща́ться**) *сов возв* to move

перемеша́|ть (-*ю*; *impf* **переме́шивать**) *сов перех* (*кашу*) to stir; (*угли, дрова*) to poke; (*вещи, бумаги*) to mix up

перемеща́|ть(ся) (-*ю(сь)*) *несов от* **перемести́ть(ся)**

перемеще́ни|е (-*я*) *ср* transfer

переми́ри|е (-*я*) *ср* truce

перемота́|ть (-*ю*; *impf* **перема́тывать**) *сов перех* (*нитку*) to wind; (*плёнку*) to rewind

перенапряга́|ть (-*ю*) *несов от* **перенапря́чь**

перенаселённый *прил* overpopulated

перен|ести́ (-*есу́*, -*есёшь*; *pt* -*ёс*, -*есла́*, -*есло́*, *impf* **переноси́ть**) *сов перех*: **перенести́ что-н че́рез** +*acc* to carry sth over *или* across; (*поменять место*) to move; (*встречу, заседание*) to reschedule; (*болезнь*) to suffer from; (*голод, холод итп*) to endure

перенима́|ть (-*ю*) *несов от* **переня́ть**

перено|си́ть (-*шу́*, -*сишь*) *несов от* **перенести́** ▷ *перех*: **не переноси́ть антибио́тиков/самолёта** to react badly to antibiotics/flying

переноси́ц|а (-*ы*) *ж* bridge of the nose

переносно́й *прил* portable

перено́сный *прил* (*значение*) figurative

перено́счик (-*а*) *m* (*Мед*) carrier

переноч|ева́ть (-*у́ю*) *сов от* **ночева́ть**

переоде́|ть (-*ну*, -*нешь*; *impf* **переодева́ть**) *сов перех* (*одежду*) to change (out of); **переодева́ть** (*perf* **переоде́ть**) **кого́-н** to change sb *или* sb's clothes; **переоде́ться** (*impf* **переодева́ться**) *сов возв* to change, get changed

перепа́д (-*а*) *m* +*gen* fluctuation in

переп|иса́ть (-*ишу́*, -*и́шешь*; *impf* **перепи́сывать**) *сов перех* (*написать заново*) to rewrite; (*скопировать*) to copy

перепи́сыва|ть (-*ю*) *несов от* **переписа́ть**; **перепи́сываться** *несов возв*: **перепи́сываться** (**с** +*instr*) to correspond (with)

пе́репис|ь (-*и*) *ж* (*населения*) census; (*имущества*) inventory

перепл|ести́ (-ету́, -етёшь; *pt* -ёл, -ела́, *impf* **переплета́ть**) *сов перех* (*книгу*) to bind

переплы́|ть (-ву́, -вёшь; *pt* -л, -ла́, *impf* **переплыва́ть**) *сов* (*не*)*перех*: **переплы́ть** (**че́рез** +*acc*) (**вплавь**) to swim (across); (*на ло́дке, на корабле́*) to sail (across)

переполз|ти́ (-у́, -ёшь; *pt* -, -ла́, -ло́, *impf* **переполза́ть**) *сов* (*не*)*перех*: **переползти́** (**че́рез** +*acc*) to crawl across

переправ|а (-ы) *ж* crossing

переправ|ить (-лю, -ишь; *impf* **переправля́ть**) *сов перех*: **переправить кого́-н/что-н че́рез** +*acc* to take across; **переправиться** (*impf* **переправля́ться**) *сов возв*: **переправиться че́рез** +*acc* to cross

перепры́гн|уть (-у; *impf* **перепры́гивать**) *сов* (*не*)*перех*: **перепры́гнуть** (**че́рез** +*acc*) to jump (over)

перепуга́|ть (-ю) *сов перех*: **перепуга́ть кого́-н** to scare the life out of sb

перепу́та|ть (-ю) *сов от* **пу́тать**

переpé|зать (-жу, -жешь; *impf* **перереза́ть**) *сов перех* (*провод*) to cut in two; (*путь*) to cut off

переры́в (-а) *м* break; **де́лать** (*perf* **сде́лать**) **переры́в** to take a break

перес|ади́ть (-ажу́, -а́дишь; *impf* **переса́живать**) *сов перех* to move; (*де́рево, цвето́к, се́рдце*) to transplant

переса́д|ка (-ки; *gen pl* -ок) *ж* (*на по́езд итп*) change; (*Мед: се́рдца*) transplant; (*: ко́жи*) graft

переса́жива|ть (-ю) *несов от* **пересади́ть**; **переса́живаться** *несов от* **пересе́сть**

пересека́|ть(ся) (-ю(сь)) *несов от* **пересе́чь(ся)**

пересел|и́ть (-ю́, -и́шь; *impf* **переселя́ть**) *сов перех* (*на но́вые зе́мли*) to settle; (*в но́вую кварти́ру*) to move; **пересели́ться** (*impf* **переселя́ться** *сов возв* (*в но́вый дом*) to move

перес|е́сть (-я́ду, -я́дешь; *impf* **переса́живаться**) *сов* (*на друго́е ме́сто*) to move; **переса́живаться** (*perf* **пересе́сть**) **на другой по́езд/самолёт** to change trains/planes

пересече́ни|е (-я) *ср* (*де́йствие*) crossing; (*ме́сто*) intersection

переск|аза́ть (-ажу́, -а́жешь; *impf* **переска́зывать**) *сов перех* to tell

пересла́|ть (-шлю́, -шлёшь; *impf* **пересыла́ть**) *сов перех* (*отосла́ть*) to send; (*по друго́му а́дресу*) to forward

пересм|отре́ть (-отрю́, -о́тришь; *impf* **пересма́тривать**) *сов перех* (*реше́ние, вопро́с*) to reconsider

пересн|я́ть (-иму́, -и́мешь; *pt* -я́л, -яла́, *impf* **пересни́мать**) *сов перех* (*докуме́нт*) to make a copy of

пересол|и́ть (-олю́, -о́лишь; *impf* **переса́ливать**) *сов перех*: **пересоли́ть**

что-н to put too much salt in sth

пересо́х|нуть (*3sg* -нет, *pt* -, -ла, *impf* **пересыха́ть**) *сов* (*по́чва, бельё*) to dry out; (*река́*) to dry up

переспр|оси́ть (-ошу́, -о́сишь; *impf* **переспра́шивать**) *сов перех* to ask again

переста|ва́ть (-ю́) *несов от* **переста́ть**

переста́в|ить (-лю, -ишь; *impf* **переставля́ть**) *сов перех* to move; (*измени́ть поря́док*) to rearrange

переста́ра|ться (-юсь) *сов возв* to overdo it

переста́|ть (-ну, -нешь; *impf* **перестава́ть**) *сов* to stop; **перестава́ть** (*perf* **переста́ть**) +*infin* to stop doing

перестра́ива|ть (-ю) *несов от* **перестро́ить**

перестре́л|ка (-ки; *gen pl* -ок) *ж* exchange of fire

перестро́|йка (-йки; *gen pl* -ек) *ж* (*до́ма*) rebuilding; (*эконо́мики*) reorganization; (*Ист*) perestroika

пересчита́|ть (-ю; *impf* **пересчи́тывать**) *сов перех* to count; (*повто́рно*) to re-count, count again; (*в други́х едини́цах*) to convert

пересыла́|ть (-ю) *несов от* **пересла́ть**

пересы́п|ать (-лю, -лешь; *impf* **пересыпа́ть**) *сов перех* (*насыпа́ть*) to pour

пересыха́|ть (*3sg* -ет) *несов от* **пересо́хнуть**

перет|ащи́ть (-ащу́, -а́щишь; *impf* **перета́скивать**) *сов перех* (*предме́т*) to drag over

перетр|уди́ться (-ужу́сь, -у́дишься; *impf* **перетружда́ться**) *сов возв* (*разг*) to be overworked

перет|яну́ть (-яну́, -я́нешь; *impf* **перетя́гивать**) *сов перех* (*передви́нуть*) to pull, tow; (*быть тяже́лее*) to outweigh

переубе|ди́ть (-жу́, -ди́шь; *impf* **переубежда́ть**) *сов перех*: **переубеди́ть кого́-н** to make sb change his *итп* mind

переу́л|ок (-ка) *м* lane, alley

переутом|и́ться (-лю́сь, -и́шься; *impf* **переутомля́ться**) *сов возв* to tire o.s. out; **переутомле́ни|е** (-я) *ср* exhaustion

перехитр|и́ть (-ю́, -и́шь) *сов перех* to outwit

перехо́д (-а) *м* crossing; (*к друго́й систе́ме*) transition; (*подзе́мный, в зда́нии*) passage

переход|и́ть (-ожу́, -о́дишь) *несов от* **перейти́**

перехо́дный *прил* (*промежу́точный*) transitional; **перехо́дный глаго́л** transitive verb

пе́р|ец (-ца) *м* pepper

пе́реч|ень (-ня) *м* list

перечеркн|у́ть (-у́, -ёшь; *impf* **перечёркивать**) *сов перех* to cross out

перечи́сл|ить (-ю, -ишь; *impf*

перечисля́ть сов перех (упомянуть) to
list; (Комм) to transfer
перечита́ть (-ю; impf **перечи́тывать**)
сов перех (книгу) to reread, read again
перешагн|у́ть (-у́, -ёшь; impf
переша́гивать) сов (не)перех:
перешагну́ть (**че́рез** +acc) to step over
перешёл итп сов см **перейти́**
переш|и́ть (-ью́, -ьёшь; impf
перешива́ть) сов перех (платье) to alter;
(пуговицу) to move (by sewing on
somewhere else)
пери́л|а (-) мн railing ед; (лестницы)
ban(n)isters мн
пери́метр (-а) м perimeter
пери́од (-а) м period; **пе́рвый/второ́й
пери́од игры́** (Спорт) first/second half (of
the game); **периоди́ческий** прил
periodical
перифери́|я (-и) ж the provinces мн
перло́вый прил barley
пер|о́ (-а́; nom pl -ья, gen pl -ьев) ср
(птицы) feather; (для письма) nib
перочи́нный прил: **перочи́нный нож**
penknife (мн penknives)
перро́н (-а) м platform (Rail)
пе́рсик (-а) м peach
персона́ж (-а) м character
персона́л (-а) м (Админ) personnel, staff;
персона́льный прил personal;
персона́льный компью́тер PC
(= personal computer)
перспекти́в|а (-ы) ж (Геом) perspective;
(вид) view; (обычн мн. планы) prospects; **в
перспекти́ве** (в будущем) in store
перспекти́вный прил (изображение) in
perspective; (планирование) long-term;
(ученик) promising
пе́рст|ень (-ня) м ring
перча́т|ка (-ки; gen pl -ок) ж glove
пе́рч|ить (-у, -ишь; perf **напе́рчить**) сов
перех to pepper
перш|и́ть (3sg -и́т) несов безл (разг): **у
меня́ перши́т в го́рле** I've got a frog in my
throat
пе́рья etc сущ см **перо́**
пёс (**пса**) м dog
пес|е́ц (-ца́) м arctic fox
пе́с|ня (-ни; gen pl -ен) ж song
пес|о́к (-ка́; part gen -ку́) м sand;
песо́чный прил sandy; (печенье) short
пессимисти́чный прил pessimistic
пёстрый прил (ткань) multi-coloured
(Brit), multi-colored (US)
песча́ный прил sandy
петру́шк|а (-и) ж parsley
пету́х (-а́) м cock, rooster (US)
петь (**пою́, поёшь**; imper **пой(те)**, perf
спеть) несов перех to sing
пехо́т|а (-ы) ж infantry
печа́л|ь (-и) ж (грусть) sadness, sorrow
печа́льный прил sad; (ошибка, судьба)
unhappy
печа́та|ть (-ю; perf **напеча́тать**) несов

перех (также Фото) to print;
(публиковать) to publish; (на компьютере)
to type
печён|ка (-ки; gen pl -ок) ж liver
печёный прил baked
пе́чен|ь (-и) ж (Анат) liver
пече́нь|е (-я) ср biscuit (Brit), cookie (US)
пе́ч|ка (-ки; gen pl -ек) ж stove
печь (-чи; loc sg -чи́, gen pl -е́й) ж stove;
(Тех) furnace ▷ **-ку́, -чёшь** etc, **-ку́т**; pt
пёк, -кла́, perf **испе́чь**) несов перех to
bake; **микроволно́вая печь** microwave
oven; **пе́чься** (perf **испе́чься**) несов
возв to bake
пешехо́д (-а) м pedestrian;
пешехо́дный прил pedestrian
пе́ш|ка (-ки; gen pl -ек) ж pawn
пешко́м нареч on foot
пеще́р|а (-ы) ж cave
пиани́но ср нескл (upright) piano;
пиани́ст (-а) м pianist
пивн|а́я (-о́й) ж ≈ bar, ≈ pub (Brit)
пивно́й прил (бар, бочка) beer
пи́в|о (-а) ср beer
пиджа́к (-а́) м jacket
пижа́м|а (-ы) ж pyjamas мн
пик (-а) м peak ▷ прил неизм (часы,
период, время) peak; **часы́ пик** rush hour
пи́к|и (-) мн (в картах) spades; **пи́ковый**
прил (в картах) of spades
пил|а́ (-ы́; nom pl -ы) ж saw
пил|и́ть (-ю́, -ишь) несов перех to saw;
(перен: разг) to nag
пи́л|ка (-ки; gen pl -ок) ж nail file
пило́т (-а) м pilot
пило́тный прил (пробный) pilot, trial
пина́|ть (-ю) несов перех to kick
пингви́н (-а) м penguin
пин|о́к (-ка́) м kick
пинце́т (-а) м (Мед) tweezers мн
пионе́р (-а) м pioneer; (в СССР) member
of Communist Youth organization
пир (-а; nom pl -ы́) м feast
пирами́д|а (-ы) ж pyramid
пира́т (-а) м pirate
пиро́г (-а́) м pie
пиро́жн|ое (-ого) ср cake
пирож|о́к (-ка́) м (с мясом) pie; (с
вареньем) tart
писа́ни|е (-я) ср: **Свяще́нное Писа́ние**
Holy Scripture
писа́тел|ь (-я) м writer
пи|са́ть (-шу́, -шешь; perf **написа́ть**)
несов перех to write; (картину) to paint
▷ неперех (по perf: ребёнок) to be able to
write; (ручка) to write; **писа́ться** несов
возв (слово) to be spelt или spelled
пистоле́т (-а) м pistol
пи́сьменно нареч in writing;
пи́сьменный прил (просьба, экзамен)
written; (стол, прибор) writing; **в
пи́сьменной фо́рме** in writing
письм|о́ (-ьма́; nom pl -ьма, gen pl -ем)
ср letter; (по pl: алфавитное) script

пита́ни|**е** (**-я**) *ср* (*ребёнка*) feeding; (*Тех*) supply; (*вегетарианское*) diet; **обще́ственное пита́ние** public catering

пита́|**ть** (**-ю**) *несов перех* (*перен: любовь*) to feel; **пита́ться** *несов возв*: **пита́ться** +*instr* (*человек, растение*) to live on; (*животное*) to feed on

пито́мник (**-а**) *м* (*Бот*) nursery

пи|**ть** (**пью, пьёшь**; *pt* **-л, -ла́**, *imper* **пе́й(те)**, *perf* **вы́пить**) *несов перех* to drink ▷ *неперех*: **пить за кого́-н/что́-н** to drink to sb/sth

питьев|**о́й** *прил*: **питьева́я вода́** drinking water

пи́цц|**а** (**-ы**) *ж* pizza

пи́чка|**ть** (**-ю**; *perf* **напи́чкать**) *несов перех* to stuff

пишу́ *etc несов см* **писа́ть(ся)**

пи́щ|**а** (**-и**) *ж* food

пищеваре́ни|**е** (**-я**) *ср* digestion

пищев|**о́й** *прил* food; (*соль*) edible; **пищева́я со́да** baking soda

ПК *м сокр* = **персона́льный компью́тер**

пл. *сокр* (= *пло́щадь*) Sq. (= *Square*)

пла́вани|**е** (**-я**) *ср* swimming; (*на судне*) sailing; (*рейс*) voyage

пла́вательный *прил*: **пла́вательный бассе́йн** swimming pool

пла́ва|**ть** (**-ю**) *несов* to swim; (*корабль*) to sail; (*в воздухе*) to float

пла́в|**ить** (**-лю, -ишь**; *perf* **распла́вить**) *несов перех* to smelt; **пла́виться** (*perf* **распла́виться**) *несов возв* to melt

пла́в|**ки** (**-ок**) *мн* swimming trunks

пла́вленый *прил*: **пла́вленый сыр** processed cheese

плавни́к (**-а́**) *м* (*у рыб*) fin

пла́вный *прил* smooth

плака́т (**-а**) *м* poster

пла́|**кать** (**-чу, -чешь**) *несов* to cry, weep; **пла́кать** (*impf*) **от** +*gen* (*от боли итп*) to cry from; (*от радости*) to cry

пла́м|**я** (**-ени**; *как* **вре́мя**; *см* Table 4) *ср* flame

план (**-а**) *м* plan; (*чертёж*) plan, map; **пере́дний план** foreground; **за́дний план** background

плане́р (**-а**) *м* glider

плака́т (**-а**) *м* poster *[sic?]* **планёр** *m*

плане́т|**а** (**-ы**) *ж* planet

плани́р|**овать** (**-ую**) *несов перех* to plan ▷ (*perf* **заплани́ровать**) (*намереваться*) to plan

планиро́вк|**а** (**-и**) *ж* layout

планоме́рный *прил* systematic

планше́т (**-а**) *м* (*Комп*) tablet

пла́стик (**-а**) *м* = **пластма́сса**

пласти́н|**а** (**-ы**) *ж* plate; **пласти́н**|**ка** (**-ки**; *gen pl* **-ок**) *ж, уменьш от* **пласти́на**; (*Муз*) record

пласти́ческий *прил* plastic

пласти́чный *прил* (*жесты, движения*) graceful; (*материалы, вещества*) plastic

пластма́сс|**а** (**-ы**) *ж сокр* (= *пласти́ческая ма́сса*) plastic

пла́стыр|**ь** (**-я**) *м* (*Мед*) plaster

пла́т|**а** (**-ы**) *ж* (*за труд, за услуги*) pay; (*за кварти́ру*) payment; (*за проезд*) fee; (*перен: награда*) reward

платёж (**-ежа́**) *м* payment; **платёжеспосо́бный** *прил* (*Комм*) solvent

пла|**ти́ть** (**-чу́, -тишь**; *perf* **заплати́ть** *или* **уплати́ть**) *несов перех* to pay

пла́тный *прил* (*вход, стоянка*) chargeable; (*школа*) fee-paying; (*больница*) private

плат|**о́к** (**-ка́**) *м* (*головной*) headscarf (*мн* headscarves); (*наплечный*) shawl; (*также* **носово́й плато́к**) handkerchief

платфо́рм|**а** (**-ы**) *ж* platform; (*станция*) halt; (*основание*) foundation

пла́ть|**е** (**-я**; *gen pl* **-ев**) *ср* dress ▷ *собир* (*одежда*) clothing, clothes *мн*

плафо́н (**-а**) *м* (*абажур*) shade (*for ceiling light*)

плацка́ртный *прил*: **плацка́ртный ваго́н** railway car with open berths instead of compartments

пла́чу *etc несов см* **пла́кать**

плачу́ *несов см* **плати́ть**

плащ (**-а́**) *м* raincoat

плева́|**ть** (**-юю**) *несов* to spit ▷ (*perf* **наплева́ть**) (*перен*): **плева́ть на** +*acc* (*разг: на правила, на мнение других*) to not give a damn about; **плева́ться** *несов возв* to spit

плед (**-а**) *м* (*tartan*) rug

пле́йер (**-а**) *м* Walkman

пле́м|**я** (**-ени**; *как* **вре́мя**; *см* Table 4) *ср* (*также перен*) tribe

племя́нник (**-а**) *м* nephew; **племя́нниц**|**а** (**-ы**) *ж* niece

плен (**-а**; *loc sg* **-у́**) *м* captivity; **бра́ть** (*perf* **взя́ть**) **кого́-н в плен** to take sb prisoner; **попада́ть** (*perf* **попа́сть**) **в плен** to be taken prisoner

плён|**ка** (**-ки**; *gen pl* **-ок**) *ж* film; (*кожица*) membrane; (*магнитофонная*) tape

пле́нный (**-ого**) *м* prisoner

пле́сен|**ь** (**-и**) *ж* mould (*Brit*), mold (*US*)

плеск (**-а**) *м* splash

пле́|**скаться** (**-щусь, -ещешься**) *несов возв* to splash

пле́сневе|**ть** (*3sg* **-ет**, *perf* **запле́сневеть**) *несов* to go mouldy (*Brit*) *или* moldy (*US*)

плёт|**ка** (**-ки**; *gen pl* **-ок**) *ж* whip

пле́чики (**-ов**) *мн* (*вешалка*) coat hangers; (*подкладки*) shoulder pads

плеч|**о́** (**-а́**; *nom pl* **-и**) *ср* shoulder

пли́нтус (**-а**) *м* skirting board (*Brit*), baseboard (*US*)

плиссе́ *прил неизм*: **ю́бка/пла́тье плиссе́** pleated skirt/dress

плит|**а́** (**-ы́**; *nom pl* **-ы**) *ж* (*каменная*) slab; (*металлическая*) plate; (*печь*) cooker, stove

пли́т|**ка** (**-ки**; *gen pl* **-ок**) *ж* (*керамическая*) tile; (*шоколада*) bar;

(электри́ческая) hot plate; (газовая) camping stove
плов|е́ц (-ца́) *м* swimmer
плод (-а́) *м* (Бот) fruit; (Био) foetus (*Brit*), fetus (*US*); (+gen: перен: усилий) fruits of
плод|и́ться (3sg -и́тся, perf **расплоди́ться**) несов возв to multiply
плодоро́дный (-а) прил fertile
пло́мб|а (-ы) ж (в зубе) filling; (на дверях, на сейфе) seal
пломби́р (-а) *м* rich creamy ice-cream
пломбир|ова́ть (-у́ю; perf **запломбирова́ть**) несов перех (зуб) to fill ▷ (perf **опломбирова́ть**) (дверь, сейф) to seal
пло́ский прил flat
плоскогу́бц|ы (-ев) мн pliers
пло́скост|ь (-и; gen pl -е́й) ж plane
плот (-а́; loc sg -у́) *м* raft
плоти́н|а (-ы) ж dam
пло́тник (-а) *м* carpenter
пло́тный прил (туман) dense, thick; (толпа́) dense; (бума́га, кожа) thick; (обе́д) substantial
пло́хо нареч (учи́ться, рабо́тать) badly ▷ как сказ it's bad; **мне пло́хо** I feel bad; **у меня́ пло́хо с деньга́ми** I am short of money
плохо́й прил bad
площа́д|ка (-ки; gen pl -ок) ж (детская) playground; (спортивная) ground; (строительная) site; (часть вагона) corridor; **ле́стничная площа́дка** landing; **поса́дочная площа́дка** landing pad
пло́щад|ь (-и; gen pl -е́й) ж (место) square; (пространство: также Мат) area; (также **жила́я пло́щадь**) living space
плуг (-а; nom pl -и́) *м* plough (*Brit*), plow (*US*)
плы|ть (-ву́, -вёшь; pt -л, -ла́) несов to swim; (судно) to sail; (облако) to float
плю́н|уть (-у) сов to spit; **плюнь!** (разг) forget it!
плюс *м* нескл, союз plus
пляж (-а) *м* beach
пневмони́|я (-и) ж pneumonia
ПО ср нескл сокр (= програ́ммное обеспе́чение) software; (Комм) (= произво́дственное объедине́ние) ≈ large industrial company

○ **КЛЮЧЕВО́Е СЛО́ВО**

по предл +dat **1** (о месте действия, вдоль) along; **ло́дка плывёт по реке́** the boat is sailing on the river; **спуска́ться** (perf **спусти́ться**) **по ле́стнице** to go down the stairs
2 (при глаголах движения) round; **ходи́ть** (impf) **по ко́мнате/са́ду** to walk round the room/garden; **плыть** (impf) **по тече́нию** to go downstream
3 (об объекте воздействия) on; **уда́рить** (impf) **по врагу́** to deal a blow to the enemy

4 (в соответствии с): **де́йствовать по зако́ну/пра́вилам** to act in accordance with the law/the rules; **по расписа́нию/пла́ну** according to schedule/plan
5 (об основании) to judge by appearances; **жени́ться** (impf/perf) **по любви́** to marry for love
6 (вследствие) due to; **по необходи́мости** out of necessity
7 (посредством): **говори́ть по телефо́ну** to speak on the phone; **отправля́ть** (perf **отпра́вить**) **что-н по по́чте** to send sth by post; **передава́ть** (perf **переда́ть**) **что-н по ра́дио/по телеви́дению** to broadcast/televise sth
8 (с целью, для): **о́рганы по борьбе́ с престу́пностью** organizations in the fight against crime; **я позва́л тебя́ по де́лу** I called on you on business
9 (о какой-н характеристике объекта) in; **по профе́ссии** by profession; **дед по ма́тери** maternal grandfather; **това́рищ по шко́ле** school friend
10 (о сфере деятельности) in
11 (о мере времени): **по вечера́м/утра́м** in the evenings/mornings; **по воскресе́ньям/пя́тницам** on Sundays/Fridays; **я рабо́таю по це́лым дням** I work all day long; **рабо́та рассчи́тана по мину́там** the work is planned by the minute
12 (о единичности предметов): **ма́ма дала́ всем по я́блоку** Mum gave them each an apple; **мы купи́ли по одно́й кни́ге** we bought a book each
▷ предл +асс **1** (вплоть до) up to; **с пе́рвой по пя́тую главу́** from the first to (*Brit*) или through (*US*) the fifth chapter; **я за́нят по го́рло** (разг: перен) I am up to my eyes in work; **он по́ уши в неё влюблён** he is head over heels in love with her
2 (при обозначении цены): **по два/три рубля́ за шту́ку** two/three roubles each
3 (при обозначении количества): **по два/три челове́ка** in twos/threes
▷ предл (+prp: после) on; **по прие́зде** on arrival

п/о сокр (= почто́вое отделе́ние) post office
по-англи́йски нареч in English
побегу́ etc сов см **побежа́ть**
побе́д|а (-ы) ж victory; **победи́тель** (-я) *м* (в войне) victor; (в состязании) winner; **побед|и́ть** (2sg -и́шь, 3sg -и́т, impf **побежда́ть**) сов перех to defeat ▷ неперех to win
победоно́сный прил victorious
побежа́ть (как **бежа́ть**; см Table 20) (человек, животное) to start running; (дни, годы) to start to fly by; (ручьи́, слёзы) to begin to flow
побежда́|ть (-ю) несов от **победи́ть**
побеле́|ть (-ю) сов от **беле́ть**
побел|и́ть (-ю́, -ишь) сов от **бели́ть**

побере́ж|ье (-ья; *gen pl* -ий) *ср* coast

побеспоко́ить (-ю, -ишь) *сов от* **беспоко́ить**

поби́ть (-ью, -ьёшь) *сов от* **бить** ▷ *перех* (*повредить*) to destroy; (*разбить*) to break

побли́зости *нареч* nearby ▷ *предл*: **побли́зости от** +*gen* near (to), close to

побо́рник (-а) *м* champion (*of cause*)

побор|о́ть (-орю́, -о́решь) *сов перех* (*также перен*) to overcome

побо́чный *прил* (*продукт, реакция*) secondary; **побо́чный эффе́кт** side effect

побу|ди́ть (-жу́, -ди́шь) *сов перех*: **побуди́ть кого́-н к чему́-н**/+*infin* to prompt sb into sth/to do

побужде́ни|е (-я) *ср* (*к действию*) motive

побыва́|ть (-ю) *сов*: **побыва́ть в Áфрике/у роди́телей** to visit Africa/one's parents

побы́|ть (*как* **быть**; *см* Table 21) *сов* to stay

пов|али́ть(ся) (-алю́(сь), -а́лишь(ся)) *сов от* **вали́ть(ся)**

по́вар (-а; *nom pl* -а́) *м* cook; **пова́ренный** *прил*: **пова́ренная кни́га** cookery (*Brit*) *или* cook (*US*) book; **пова́ренная соль** table salt

поведе́ни|е (-я) *ср* behaviour (*Brit*), behavior (*US*)

повез|ти́ (-у́, -ёшь; *pt* -ёз, -езла́) *сов от* **везти́** ▷ *перех* to take

пове́ренн|ый (-ого) *м*: **пове́ренный в дела́х** chargé d'affaires

пове́р|ить (-ю, -ишь) *сов от* **ве́рить**

поверн|у́ть (-у́, -ёшь; *impf* **повора́чивать**) *сов (не)перех* to turn; **поверну́ться** (*impf* **повора́чиваться**) *сов возв* to turn

пове́рх *предл* +*gen* over

пове́рхностный *прил* surface; (*перен*) superficial; **пове́рхность** (-и) *ж* surface

пове́р|ье (-ья; *gen pl* -ий) *ср* (*popular*) belief

пове́|сить(ся) (-шу(сь), -сишь(ся)) *сов от* **ве́шать(ся)**

повествова́ни|е (-я) *ср* narrative

пов|ести́ (-еду́, -едёшь; *pt* -ёл, -ла́) *сов перех* (*начать вести: ребёнка*) to take; (: *войска*) to lead; (*машину, поезд*) to drive; (*войну, следствие итп*) to begin ▷ (*impf* **поводи́ть**) *неперех* (+*instr*: *бровью*) to raise; (*плечом*) to shrug; **повести́** (*perf*) **себя́** to start behaving

по́вест|ь (-и) *ж* story

по-ви́димому *вводн сл* apparently

пови́дл|о (-а) *ср* jam (*Brit*), jelly (*US*)

повин|ова́ться (-у́юсь) *сов возв* +*dat* to obey

повинове́ни|е (-я) *ср* obedience

пови́с|нуть (-ну; *pt* -, -ла, *impf* **повиса́ть**) *сов* to hang; (*тучи*) to hang motionless

повл|е́чь (-еку́, -ечёшь *итп*, -еку́т; *pt* -ёк, -екла́, -екло́) *сов от* **влечь**

по́в|од (-ода, *loc sg* -оду́, *nom pl* -о́дья, *gen pl* -ьев) *м* (*лошади*) rein ▷ (*nom pl* -оды) (*причина*) reason ▷ *предл*: **по по́воду** +*gen* regarding, concerning

пово|ди́ть (-ожу́, -о́дишь) *несов от* **повести́**

пово|до́к (-ка́) *м* lead, leash

пово́з|ка (-ки; *gen pl* -ок) *ж* cart

повора́чива|ть(ся) (-ю(сь)) *несов от* **поверну́ть(ся)**

поворо́т (-а) *м* (*действие*) turning; (*место*) bend; (*перен*) turning point

повре|ди́ть (-жу́, -ди́шь; *impf* **поврежда́ть**) *сов перех* (*поранить*) to injure; (*поломать*) to damage

поврежде́ни|е (-я) *ср* (*см глаг*) injury; damage

повседне́вный *прил* everyday, routine; (*занятия, встречи*) daily

повсеме́стный *прил* widespread

повсю́ду *нареч* everywhere

по-вся́кому *нареч* in different ways

повторе́ни|е (-я) *ср* repetition; (*урока*) revision

повтор|и́ть (-ю́, -и́шь; *impf* **повторя́ть**) *сов перех* to repeat; **повтори́ться** (*impf* **повторя́ться**) *сов возв* (*ситуация*) to repeat itself; (*болезнь*) to recur

повы́|сить (-шу, -сишь; *impf* **повыша́ть**) *сов перех* to increase; (*интерес, культуру*) to heighten; (*качество, культуру*) to improve; (*работника*) to promote; **повыша́ть** (*perf* **повы́сить**) **го́лос** to raise one's voice; **повы́ситься** (*impf* **повыша́ться**) *сов возв* to increase; (*интерес*) to heighten; (*качество, культура*) to improve

пов|яза́ть (-яжу́, -я́жешь; *impf* **повя́зывать**) *сов перех* to tie; **повя́з|ка** (-ки; *gen pl* -ок) *ж* bandage

пога́н|ка (-ки; *gen pl* -ок) *ж* toadstool

пога|си́ть (-шу́, -а́сишь) *сов от* **гаси́ть** ▷ (*impf* **погаша́ть**) *перех* (*заплатить*) to pay (off)

погас|нуть (-ну; *pt* -, -ла) *сов от* **га́снуть**

погаша́|ть (-ю) *несов от* **погаси́ть**

поги́б|нуть (-ну; *pt* -, -ла) *сов от* **ги́бнуть**

поги́бш|ий (-его) *м* casualty (*dead*)

погл|оти́ть (-ощу́, -о́тишь; *impf* **поглоща́ть**) *сов перех* to absorb; (*время*) to take up; (*фирму*) to take over

пог|на́ться (-оню́сь, -о́нишься) *сов возв*: **погна́ться за кем-н/чем-н** to set off in pursuit of sb/sth

погово́р|ка (-ки; *gen pl* -ок) *ж* saying

пого́д|а (-ы) *ж* weather; **пого́дный** *прил* weather

поголо́в|ье (-я) *ср* (*скота*) total number

пого́н (-а) *м* (*обычно мн*) (shoulder) stripe

пого́н|я (-и) *ж*: **пого́ня за** +*instr* pursuit of

пограни́чник (-а) *м* frontier *или* border

guard; **пограни́чный** *прил* border

по́греб (-а; *nom pl* -á) *м* cellar

погреба́льный *прил* funeral

погрему́шка (-ки; *gen pl* -ек) *ж* rattle

погре́ть (-ю) *сов перех* to warm up;
погре́ться *сов возв* to warm up

погру|зи́ть (-ужу́, -у́зишь) *сов перех от*
грузи́ть ▷ (-ужу́, -у́зишь) *impf*
погружа́ть *перех*: **погрузи́ть что-н в**
+*acc* to immerse sth in; **погрузи́ться**
(*impf* **погружа́ться**) *сов возв*:
погрузи́ться в +*acc* (*человек*) to immerse
o.s. in; (*предмет*) to sink into

погря́з|нуть (-у; *impf* **погряза́ть**) *сов*:
погря́знуть в +*prp* (в долгах, во лжи) to
sink into

○ **КЛЮЧЕВО́Е СЛО́ВО**

под *предл* +*acc* **1** (*ниже*) under; **идти́**
(*impf*) **под гору** to go downhill
2 (*поддерживая снизу*) by
3 (*указывает на положение, состояние*)
under; **отдава́ть** (*perf* **отда́ть**) **кого́-н под**
суд to prosecute sb; **попада́ть** (*perf*
попа́сть) **под дождь** to be caught in the
rain
4 (*близко к*): **под у́тро/ве́чер** towards
morning/evening; **под ста́рость**
approaching old age
5 (*указывает на функцию*) as; **мы**
приспосо́били помеще́ние под магази́н
we fitted out the premises as a shop
6 (*в виде чего-н*): **сте́ны под мра́мор**
marble-effect walls
7 (*в обмен на*) on; **брать** (*perf* **взять**)
что-н под зало́г/че́стное сло́во to take sth
on security/trust
8 (*в сопровождении*): **под роя́ль/скри́пку**
to the piano/violin; **мне э́то не под си́лу**
that is beyond my powers
▷ *предл* +*instr* **1** (*ниже чего-н*) under
2 (*около*) near; **под но́сом у кого́-н** under
sb's nose; **под руко́й** to hand, at hand
3 (*об условиях существования объекта*)
under; **быть** (*impf*) **под наблюде́нием/**
аре́стом to be under observation/arrest;
под назва́нием, под и́менем under the
name of
4 (*вследствие*) under; **под влия́нием/**
тя́жестью чего́-н under the influence/
weight of sth; **понима́ть** (*impf*)/
подразумева́ть (*impf*) **под чем-н** to
understand/imply by sth

пода|ва́ть (-ю́) *несов от* **пода́ть**

под|ави́ть (-авлю́, -а́вишь; *impf*
подавля́ть) *сов перех* to suppress;
подави́ться *сов от* **дави́ться**

пода́вленный *прил* (*настроение,*
человек) depressed

подавля́|ть (-ю) *несов от* **подави́ть**

подавля́ющий *прил* (*большинство*)
overwhelming

под|ари́ть (-арю́, -а́ришь) *сов от* **дари́ть**

пода́р|ок (-ка) *м* present, gift;
пода́рочный *прил* gift

пода́ть (*как* **дать**; *см Table 16*; *impf*
подава́ть) *сов перех* to give; (*еду*) to
serve up; (*поезд, такси итп*) to bring;
(*заявление, жалобу итп*) to submit;
(*Спорт: в теннисе*) to serve; (: *в футболе*)
to pass; **подава́ть** (*perf* **пода́ть**) **го́лос за**
+*acc* to cast a vote for; **подава́ть** (*perf*
пода́ть) **в отста́вку** to hand in *или* submit
one's resignation; **подава́ть** (*perf* **пода́ть**)
на кого́-н в суд to take sb to court;
подава́ть (*perf* **пода́ть**) **кому́-н ру́ку** (*при*
встрече) to give sb one's hand

пода́ч|а (-и) *ж* (*действие: заявления*)
submission; (*Спорт: в теннисе*) serve; (: *в*
футболе) pass

подбежа́ть (*как* **бежа́ть**; *см Table 20*;
impf **подбега́ть**) *сов* to run up

подбива́|ть (-ю) *несов от* **подби́ть**

подбира́|ть (-ю) *несов от* **подобра́ть**

под|би́ть (-обью́, -обьёшь; *impf*
подбива́ть) *сов перех* (*птицу, самолёт*)
to shoot down; (*глаз, крыло*) to injure

подбо́р (-а) *м* selection

подборо́д|ок (-ка) *м* chin

подбро́|сить (-шу, -сишь; *impf*
подбра́сывать) *сов перех* (*мяч, камень*)
to toss; (*наркотик*) to plant; (*разг*:
подвезти) to give a lift

подва́л (-а) *м* cellar; (*для жилья*)
basement; **подва́льный** *прил*
(*помещение*) basement

подве|зти́ (-зу́, -зёшь; *pt* -ёз, -езла́,
impf **подвози́ть**) *сов перех* (*машину,*
товар) to take up; (*человека*) to give a lift

подве́рг|нуть (-ну; *pt* -, -ла, *impf*
подверга́ть) *сов перех*: **подве́ргнуть**
кого́-н/что-н чему́-н to subject sb/sth to
sth; **подверга́ть** (*perf* **подве́ргнуть**) **кого́-н**
ри́ску/опа́сности to put sb at risk/in
danger; **подве́ргнуться** (*impf*
подверга́ться) *сов возв*: **подве́ргнуться**
+*dat* to be subjected to

подве́рженный *прил* (+*dat*: дурному
влиянию) subject to; (*простуде*)
susceptible to

подверн|у́ть (-у́, -ёшь; *impf*
подвора́чивать) *сов перех* (*сделать*
короче) to turn up; **подвора́чивать** (*perf*
подверну́ть) **но́гу** to turn *или* twist one's
ankle; **подверну́ться** (*impf*
подвора́чиваться) *сов возв* (*разг*:
попасться) to turn up

подве́|сить (-шу, -сишь; *impf*
подве́шивать) *сов перех* to hang up

подве|сти́ (-ду́, -дёшь; *pt* -ёл, -ела́,
impf **подводи́ть**) *сов перех*
(*разочаровать*) to let down; **подводи́ть**
(*perf* **подвести́**) **к** +*dat* (*человека*) to bring
up to; (*машину*) to drive up to; (*поезд*) to
bring into; (*корабль*) to sail up to;
(*электричество*) to bring to; **подводи́ть**

(*perf* **подвести́**) **глаза́/гу́бы** to put eyeliner/lipstick on; **подводи́ть** (*perf* **подвести́**) **ито́ги** to sum up

подве́шива|ть (**-ю**) *несов от* **подве́сить**

по́двиг (**-а**) *м* exploit

подвига́|ть(ся) (**-ю(сь)**) *несов от* **подви́нуть(ся)**

подви́н|уть (**-у**; *impf* **подвига́ть**) *сов перех* (*передвинуть*) to move; **подви́нуться** (*impf* **подвига́ться**) *сов возв* (*человек итп*) to move

подвла́стный *прил* (+*dat*: *закону*) subject to; (*президенту*) under the control of

подв|оди́ть (**-ожу́, -о́дишь**) *несов от* **подвести́**

подво́дн|ый *прил* (*растение, работы*) underwater; **подво́дная ло́дка** submarine

подв|ози́ть (**-ожу́, -о́зишь**) *несов от* **подвезти́**

подвора́чива|ть (**-ю**) *несов от* **подверну́ть**

подгиба́|ть(ся) (**-ю(сь)**) *несов от* **подогну́ть(ся)**

подгля|де́ть (**-жу́, -ди́шь**; *impf* **подгля́дывать**) *сов перех* to peep through

подгор|е́ть (*3sg* **-и́т**, *impf* **подгора́ть**) *сов* to burn slightly

подгото́в|ить (**-лю, -ишь**; *impf* **подгота́вливать**) *сов перех* to prepare; **подгото́виться** (*impf* **подгота́вливаться**) *сов возв* to prepare (o.s.)

подгото́вк|а (**-и**) *ж* preparation; (*запас знаний*) training

подгу́зник (**-а**) *м* nappy (*Brit*), diaper (*US*)

подда|ва́ться (**-ю́сь**) *несов от* **подда́ться** ▷ *возв*: **не поддава́ться сравне́нию/описа́нию** to be beyond comparison/words

по́дданн|ый (**-ого**) *м* subject

по́дданств|о (**-а**) *ср* nationality

подда́|ться (*как* **дать**; *см Table 16*; *impf* **поддава́ться**) *сов возв* (*дверь итп*) to give way; **поддава́ться** (*perf* **подда́ться**) +*dat* (*влиянию, соблазну*) to give in to

подде́ла|ть (**-ю**; *impf* **подде́лывать**) *сов перех* to forge; **подде́л|ка** (**-ки**; *gen pl* **-ок**) *ж* forgery

подд|ержа́ть (**-ержу́, -е́ржишь**; *impf* **подде́рживать**) *сов перех* to support; (*падающего*) to hold on to; (*предложение итп*) to second; (*беседу*) to keep up

подде́ржива|ть (**-ю**) *несов от* **подде́ржать** ▷ *перех* (*переписку*) to keep up; (*порядок, отношения*) to maintain

подде́ржк|а (**-и**) *ж* support

поде́ла|ть (**-ю**) *сов перех* (*разг*) to do; **что поде́лаешь** (*разг*) it can't be helped

под|ели́ть(ся) (**-елю́(сь), -е́лишь(ся)**) *сов от* **дели́ть(ся)**

поде́ржанный *прил* (*одежда, мебель итп*) second-hand

под|же́чь (**-ожгу́, -ожжёшь** *etc*, **-ожгу́т**; *impf* **поджига́ть**) *сов перех* to set fire to

подзаты́льник (**-а**) *м* (*разг*) clip round the ear

подзе́мный *прил* underground

подзо́рн|ый *прил*: **подзо́рная труба́** telescope

подка́ст (**-а**) *м* podcast

подк|ати́ть (**-ачу́, -а́тишь**; *impf* **подка́тывать**) *сов перех* (*что-н круглое*) to roll; (*что-н на колёсах*) to wheel

подка́шива|ть(ся) (**-ю(сь)**) *несов от* **подкоси́ть(ся)**

подки́н|уть (**-у**; *impf* **подки́дывать**) *сов* = **подбро́сить**

подкла́д|ка (**-ки**; *gen pl* **-ок**) *ж* lining

подкла́дыва|ть (**-ю**) *несов от* **подложи́ть**

подключ|и́ть (**-у́, -и́шь**; *impf* **подключа́ть**) *сов перех* (*телефон*) to connect; (*лампу*) to plug in; (*специалистов*) to involve

подко́в|а (**-ы**) *ж* (*лошади итп*) shoe

подк|ова́ть (**-ую́**; *impf* **подко́вывать**) *сов перех* to shoe

подкра́сться (**-аду́сь, -адёшься**; *impf* **подкра́дываться**) *сов возв* to sneak *или* steal up

подкреп|и́ть (**-лю́, -и́шь**; *impf* **подкрепля́ть**) *сов перех* to support, back up

по́дкуп (**-а**) *м* bribery; **подк|упи́ть** (**-уплю́, -у́пишь**; *impf* **подкупа́ть**) *сов перех* to bribe

подлеж|а́ть (*3sg* **-и́т**) *несов* (+*dat*: *проверке, обложению налогом*) to be subject to; **э́то не подлежи́т сомне́нию** there can be no doubt about that

подлежа́щ|ее (**-его**) *ср* (*Линг*) subject

подли́в|ка (**-ки**; *gen pl* **-ок**) *ж* (*Кулин*) sauce

по́длинник (**-а**) *м* original; **по́длинный** *прил* original; (*документ*) authentic; (*чувство*) genuine; (*друг*) true

подло́г (**-а**) *м* forgery

подл|ожи́ть (**-ожу́, -о́жишь**; *impf* **подкла́дывать**) *сов перех* (*бомбу*) to plant; (*добавить*) to put; (*дров, сахара*) to add

подлоко́тник (**-а**) *м* arm(rest)

по́длый *прил* base

подмен|и́ть (**-ю́, -и́шь**; *impf* **подме́нивать**) *сов перех* to substitute; (*коллегу*) to stand in for

подм|ести́ (**-ету́, -етёшь**; *pt* **-ёл, -ела́**) *сов от* **мести́** ▷ (*impf* **подмета́ть**) *перех* (*пол*) to sweep; to sweep up

подмётк|а (**-и**) *ж* (*подошва*) sole

подмигн|у́ть (**-у́, -ёшь**; *impf* **подми́гивать**) *сов*: **подмигну́ть кому́-н** to wink at sb

поднес|ти́ (-у́, -ёшь; *impf* **подноси́ть**) *сов перех*: **поднести́** что-н к чему́-н to bring sth up to sth

поднима́|ть(ся) (-ю(сь)) *несов от* **подня́ть(ся)**

подно́жи|е (-я) *ср* (*горы*) foot

подно́ж|ка (-ки; *gen pl* -ек) *ж* (*автобуса итп*) step; **поста́вить** (*perf*) **подно́жку кому́-н** to trip sb up

подно́с (-а) *м* tray

подн|оси́ть (-ошу́, -о́сишь) *несов от* **поднести́**

подня́ть (-иму́, -и́мешь; *impf* **поднима́ть**) *сов перех* to raise; (*что-н лёгкое*) to pick up; (*что-н тяжёлое*) to lift (up); (*флаг*) to hoist; (*спящего*) to rouse; (*панику, восстание*) to start; (*экономику, дисциплину*) to improve; (*архивы, документацию итп*) to unearth; **поднима́ть** (*perf* **подня́ть**) **крик** или **шум** to make a fuss; **подня́ться** (*impf* **поднима́ться**) *сов возв* to rise; (*на этаж, на сцену*) to go up; (*с постели, со стула*) to get up; (*паника, метель, драка*) to break out; **поднима́ться** (*perf* **подня́ться**) **на́ гору** to climb a hill; **подня́лся крик** there was an uproar

подо *предл* = **под**

подоба́ющий *прил* appropriate

подо́бно *предл* +*dat* like, similar to

подо́бн|ый *прил* (+*dat*: *сходный с*) like, similar to; **и тому́ подо́бное** et cetera, and so on; **ничего́ подо́бного** (*разг*) nothing of the sort

под|обра́ть (-беру́, -берёшь; *impf* **подбира́ть**) *сов перех* to pick up; (*приподнять*) to gather (up); (*выбрать*) to pick, select

подобре́|ть (-ю) *сов от* **добре́ть**

подогн|у́ть (-у́, -ёшь; *impf* **подгиба́ть**) *сов перех* (*рукава*) to turn up; **подогну́ться** (*impf* **подгиба́ться**) *сов возв* to curl under

подогре́|ть (-ю; *impf* **подогрева́ть**) *сов перех* to warm up

пододви́н|уть (-у; *impf* **пододвига́ть**) *сов перех* to move closer

пододе́яльник (-а) *м* ≈ duvet cover

подожда́|ть (-у́, -ёшь; *pt* -а́л, -ала́) *сов перех* to wait for; **подожда́ть** (*perf*) **с чем-н** to put sth off

подозрева́|ть (-ю) *несов перех* to suspect; **подозрева́ть** (*impf*) **кого́-н в чём-н** to suspect sb of sth; **подозрева́ть** (*impf*) (**о чём-н**) to have an idea (about sth)

подозре́ни|е (-я) *ср* suspicion

подозри́тельный *прил* suspicious

подо́|ить (-ю́, -ишь) *сов от* **дои́ть**

подойти́ (*как* **идти́**; *см* Table 18; *impf* **подходи́ть**) *сов*: **подойти́ к** +*dat* to approach; (*соответствовать*): **подойти́ к** +*dat* (*юбка*) to go (well) with; **э́то мне подхо́дит** this suits me

подоко́нник (-а) *м* windowsill

подо́лгу *нареч* for a long time

подо́пытный *прил*: **подо́пытный кро́лик** (*перен*) guinea pig

подорв|а́ть (-у́, -ёшь; *pt* -а́л, -ала́, *impf* **подрыва́ть**) *сов перех* to blow up; (*перен: авторитет*) to undermine; (: *здоровье*) to destroy

подохо́дный *прил*: **подохо́дный нало́г** income tax

подо́шв|а (-ы) *ж* (*обуви*) sole

подошёл *etc сов см* **подойти́**

под|пере́ть (-опру́, -опрёшь; *pt* -пёр, -пёрла, *impf* **подпира́ть**) *сов перех*: **подпере́ть** что-н чем-н to prop sth up with sth

подп|иса́ть (-ишу́, -и́шешь; *impf* **подпи́сывать**) *сов перех* to sign; **подписа́ться** (*impf* **подпи́сываться**) *сов возв*: **подписа́ться под** +*instr* to sign; **подпи́сываться** (*perf* **подписа́ться**) **на** +*acc* (*на газету*) to subscribe to; (*аккаунт в социа́льной сети*) to follow

подпи́с|ка (-ки; *gen pl* -ок) *ж* subscription; (*о невыезде*) signed statement

по́дпис|ь (-и) *ж* signature

подплы́|ть (-ву́, -вёшь; *pt* -л, -ла́, *impf* **подплыва́ть**) *сов* (*лодка*) to sail (up); (*пловец, рыба*) to swim (up)

подполко́вник (-а) *м* lieutenant colonel

подпо́льный *прил* underground

подпо́р|ка (-ки; *gen pl* -ок) *ж* prop, support

подпры́гн|уть (-у; *impf* **подпры́гивать**) *сов* to jump

подп|усти́ть (-ущу́, -у́стишь) *сов перех* to allow to approach

подрабо́та|ть (-ю) *сов* (*не)перех* +*acc* или +*gen* to earn extra

подра́внива|ть (-ю) *несов от* **подровня́ть**

подража́ни|е (-я) *ср* imitation; **подража́|ть** (-ю) *несов* +*dat* to imitate

подраздел|я́ться (3sg -е́тся) *несов возв* to be subdivided

подразумева́|ть (-ю) *несов перех* to imply; **подразумева́ться** *несов возв* to be implied

подр|асти́ (-асту́, -асте́шь; *pt* -о́с, -осла́, *impf* **подраста́ть**) *сов* to grow

под|ра́ться (-еру́сь, -ерёшься) *сов от* **дра́ться**

подре́|зать (-жу, -жешь; *impf* **подреза́ть**) *сов перех* (*волосы*) to cut

подро́бность (-и) *ж* detail; **подро́бный** *прил* detailed

подровня́|ть (-ю; *impf* **подра́внивать**) *сов перех* to trim

подро́ст|ок (-ка) *м* teenager, adolescent

подру́г|а (-и) *ж* (girl)friend

по-друго́му *нареч* (*иначе*) differently

подр|ужи́ться (-ужу́сь, -у́жишься) *сов возв*: **подружи́ться с** +*instr* to make friends with

подру́чный *прил*: **подру́чный материа́л** the material to hand

подрыва́|ть (-ю) *несов от* **подорва́ть**

подря́д *нареч* in succession ▷ (-а) *м* (*рабо́чий догово́р*) contract; **все/всё подря́д** everyone/everything without exception; **подря́дный** *прил* contract; **подря́дчик** (-а) *м* contractor

подса́жива|ться (-юсь) *несов от* **подсе́сть**

подсве́чник (-а) *м* candlestick

подсе́|сть (-я́ду, -я́дешь; *impf* **подса́живаться**) *сов*: **подсе́сть к** +*dat* to sit down beside

подск|аза́ть (-ажу́, -а́жешь; *impf* **подска́зывать**) *сов перех* (*перен: иде́ю*) to suggest; (*разг: а́дрес*) to give out; **подска́зывать** (*perf* **подсказа́ть**) **что-н кому́-н** to prompt sb with sth

подска́з|ка (-ки; *gen pl* -ок) *ж* prompt

подслу́ша|ть (-ю; *impf* **подслу́шивать**) *сов перех* to eavesdrop on

подсм|отре́ть (-отрю́, -о́тришь; *impf* **подсма́тривать**) *сов перех* (*уви́деть*) to spy on

подсо́бный *прил* subsidiary

подсо́выва|ть (-ю) *несов от* **подсу́нуть**

подсозна́ни|е (-я) *ср* the subconscious

подсозна́тельный *прил* subconscious

подсо́лнечн|ый *прил*: **подсо́лнечное ма́сло** sunflower oil

подсо́лнух (-а) *м* (*разг*) sunflower

подста́в|ить (-лю, -ишь; *impf* **подставля́ть**) *сов перех*: **подста́вить под** +*acc* to put under

подста́в|ка (-ки; *gen pl* -ок) *ж* stand

подставля́|ть (-ю) *несов от* **подста́вить**

подстере́|чь (-гу́, -жёшь *итп*, -гу́т; *impf* **подстерега́ть**) *сов перех* to lie in wait for

подстра́ива|ть (-ю) *несов от* **подстро́ить**

подстре|ли́ть (-елю́, -е́лишь; *impf* **подстре́ливать**) *сов перех* to wound

подстри́|чь (-гу́, -жёшь *итп*, -гу́т; *pt* -г, -ла, *impf* **подстрига́ть**) *сов перех* to trim; (*для укора́чивания*) to cut; **подстри́чься** (*impf* **подстрига́ться**) *сов возв* to have one's hair cut

подстро́|ить (-ю, -ишь; *impf* **подстра́ивать**) *сов перех* to fix

по́дступ (-а) *м* (*обы́чно мн*) approach

подст|упи́ть (-уплю́, -у́пишь; *impf* **подступа́ть**) *сов* (*слёзы*) to well up; (*рыда́ния*) to rise; **подступа́ть** (*perf* **подступи́ть**) **к** +*dat* (*к го́роду, к те́ме*) to approach

подсуди́м|ый (-ого) *м* (*Юр*) the accused, the defendant

подсу́дный *прил* (*Юр*) sub judice

подсу́н|уть (-у; *impf* **подсо́вывать**) *сов перех* to shove

подсчита́|ть (-ю; *impf* **подсчи́тывать**) *сов перех* to count (up)

подта́лкива|ть (-ю) *несов от* **подтолкну́ть**

подтвер|ди́ть (-жу́, -ди́шь; *impf* **подтвержда́ть**) *сов перех* to confirm; (*фа́ктами*) to back up; **подтверди́ться** (*impf* **подтвержда́ться**) *сов* to be confirmed

подтвержде́ни|е (-я) *ср* confirmation

подтолкн|у́ть (-у́, -ёшь; *impf* **подта́лкивать**) *сов перех* to nudge; (*побуди́ть*) to urge on

подтя́гива|ть(ся) (-ю(сь)) *несов от* **подтяну́ть(ся)**

подтя́ж|ки (-ек) *мн* (*для брюк*) braces (*Brit*), suspenders (*US*)

подтя́нутый *прил* smart

подтян|у́ть (-яну́, -я́нешь; *impf* **подтя́гивать**) *сов перех* (*тяжёлый предме́т*) to haul up; (*га́йку*) to tighten; (*войска́*) to bring up; **подтяну́ться** (*impf* **подтя́гиваться**) *сов возв* (*на бру́сьях*) to pull o.s. up; (*войска́*) to move up

поду́ма|ть (-ю) *сов*: **поду́мать (о** +*prp*) to think (about); **поду́мать** (*perf*) **над** +*instr или о* +*prp* to think about; **поду́мать** (*perf*), **что...** to think that ...; **кто бы мог поду́мать!** who would have thought it!

поду́|ть (-ю) *сов* to blow; (*ве́тер*) to begin to blow

под|уши́ть (-ушу́, -у́шишь) *сов перех* to spray lightly with perfume

поду́ш|ка (-ки; *gen pl* -ек) *ж* (*для сиде́ния*) cushion; (*под го́лову*) pillow

подхв|ати́ть (-ачу́, -а́тишь; *impf* **подхва́тывать**) *сов перех* (*па́дающее*) to catch; (*подлеж: тече́ние, толпа́*) to carry away; (*иде́ю, боле́знь*) to pick up

подхо́д (-а) *м* approach

подх|оди́ть (-ожу́, -о́дишь) *несов от* **подойти́**

подходя́щий *прил* (*дом*) suitable; (*моме́нт, сло́ва*) appropriate

подчеркн|у́ть (-у́, -ёшь; *impf* **подчёркивать**) *сов перех* (*в те́ксте*) to underline; (*в ре́чи*) to emphasize

подчине́ни|е (-я) *ср* obedience; **подчинённый** *прил* subordinate ▷ (-ого) *м* subordinate

подше́фный *прил*: **подше́фный де́тский дом** children's home under patronage

подшива́|ть (-ю) *несов от* **подши́ть**

подши́в|ка (-ки; *gen pl* -ок) *ж* (*газе́т, докуме́нтов*) file

подши́пник (-а) *м* (*Тех*) bearing

под|ши́ть (-ошью́, -ошьёшь; *imper* -ше́й(те), *impf* **подшива́ть**) *сов перех* (*рука́в*) to hem; (*подо́л*) to take up

подш|ути́ть (-учу́, -у́тишь; *impf* **подшу́чивать**) *сов*: **подшути́ть над** +*instr* to make fun of

подъе́ду *etc* *сов см* **подъе́хать**

подъе́зд (-а) *м* (*к го́роду, к до́му*) approach; (*в зда́нии*) entrance

подъезжа́|ть (-ю) *несов от* **подъе́хать**

подъём (-a) м (груза) lifting; (флага) raising; (на гору) ascent; (промышленный) revival; **подъёмник** (-a) м lift (Brit), elevator (US)

подъе́хать (как е́хать; см Table 19; impf **подъезжа́ть**) сов (на автомобиле) to drive up; (на коне) to ride up

поды́ша́ть (-шу́, -шешь) сов to breathe

пое́дешь etc сов см **пое́хать**

поеди́м итп сов см **пое́сть**

поеди́те сов см **пое́сть**

пое́ду etc сов см **пое́хать**

поедя́т сов см **пое́сть**

по́езд (-a; nom pl -á) м train

пое́зд|ка (-ки; gen pl -ок) ж trip

поезжа́й(те) сов см **пое́хать**

пое́сть (как есть; см Table 15) сов от **есть** ▷ перех: **пое́сть чего́-н** to eat a little bit of sth

пое́хать (как е́хать; см Table 19) сов to set off

пое́шь сов см **пое́сть**

пожале́|ть (-ю) сов от **жале́ть**

пожа́л|овать (-ую) сов: **добро́ пожа́ловать** welcome; **пожа́ловаться** сов от **жа́ловаться**

пожа́луйста част please; (в ответ на благодарность) don't mention it (Brit), you're welcome (US); **пожа́луйста, помоги́те мне** please help me; **скажи́те, пожа́луйста, где вокза́л?** could you tell me where the station is; **мо́жно здесь сесть? — пожа́луйста!** may I sit here? — please do!

пожа́р (-a) м fire; **пожа́рник** (-a) м (разг) fireman (мн firemen); **пожа́рный** (-ого) м fireman (мн firemen) прил: **пожа́рная кома́нда** fire brigade (Brit) или department (US); **пожа́рная маши́на** fire engine

пож|а́ть (-му́, -мёшь; impf **пожима́ть**) сов перех to squeeze; **он пожа́л мне ру́ку** he shook my hand; **пожима́ть** (perf **пожа́ть**) **плеча́ми** to shrug one's shoulders

пожела́ни|е (-я) ср wish; **прими́те мой наилу́чшие пожела́ния** please accept my best wishes

пожела́|ть (-ю) сов от **жела́ть**

пож|ени́ться (-ению́сь, -е́нишься) сов возв to marry, get married

поже́ртвовани|е (-я) ср donation

пожива́|ть (-ю) несов (разг): **как ты пожива́ешь?** how are you?

пожило́й прил elderly

пожима́|ть (-ю) несов от **пожа́ть**

пож|и́ть (-иву́, -ивёшь; pt -и́л, -ила́) сов (пробыть) to live for a while

по́з|а (-ы) ж posture; (перен: поведение) pose

позавчера́ нареч the day before yesterday

позади́ нареч (сзади) behind; (в прошлом) in the past ▷ предл +gen behind

позаи́мств|овать (-ую) сов от **заи́мствовать**

позапро́шлый прил before last

поз|ва́ть (-ову́, -овёшь) сов от **звать**

позво́л|ить (-ю, -ишь; impf **позволя́ть**) сов to permit ▷ перех: **позво́лить что́-н кому́-н** to allow sb sth; **позволя́ть** (perf **позво́лить**) **себе́ что́-н** (покупку) to be able to afford sth

позвон|и́ть (-ю́, -и́шь) сов от **звони́ть**

позвоно́чник (-a) м spine, spinal column

поздне́е сравн нареч от **по́здно** ▷ нареч later ▷ предл +gen after; **(не) поздне́е** +gen (no) later than

по́здн|ий прил late; **са́мое по́зднее** (разг) at the latest

по́здно нареч late ▷ как сказ it's late

поздоро́ва|ться (-юсь) сов от **здоро́ваться**

поздра́в|ить (-лю, -ишь; impf **поздравля́ть**) сов перех: **поздра́вить кого́-н с** +instr to congratulate sb on; **поздравля́ть** (perf **поздра́вить**) **кого́-н с днём рожде́ния** to wish sb a happy birthday; **поздравле́ни|е** (-я) ср congratulations мн; (с днём рождения) greetings мн

по́зже нареч = **поздне́е**

позити́вный прил positive

пози́ци|я (-и) ж position

познако́м|ить(ся) (-лю(сь), -ишь(ся)) сов от **знако́мить(ся)**

позна́ни|я (-й) мн knowledge ед

позову́ итп сов см **позва́ть**

позо́р (-a) м disgrace; **позо́р|ить** (-ю, -ишь; perf **опозо́рить**) несов перех to disgrace; **позо́риться** (perf **опозо́риться**) несов возв to disgrace o.s.

позо́рный прил disgraceful

пойм|ка (-ки; gen pl -ок) ж capture

поинтересова́|ться (-у́юсь) сов возв +instr to take an interest in

по́иск (-a) м search; (научный) quest; см также **по́иски**

по|иска́ть (-ищу́, -и́щешь) сов перех to have a look for

по́иск|и (-ов) мн: **по́иски** (+gen) search ед (for); **в по́исках** +gen in search of

по|и́ть (-ю́, -ишь; imper **пои́(те)**, perf **напои́ть**) несов перех: **пои́ть кого́-н чем-н** to give sb sth to drink

пойду́ etc сов см **пойти́**

пойма́|ть (-ю) сов от **лови́ть** ▷ перех to catch

пойму́ etc сов см **поня́ть**

пойти́ (как идти́; см Table 18) сов to set off; (по пути реформ) to start off; (о механизмах, к цели) to start working; (дождь, снег) to begin to fall; (дым, пар) to begin to rise; (кровь) to start flowing; (фильм итп) to start showing; (подойти): **пойти́** +dat или к +dat (шляпа, поведение) to suit

◯ **КЛЮЧЕВОЕ СЛОВО**

пока́ *нареч* **1** (*некоторое время*) for a while

2 (*тем временем*) in the meantime

▷ *союз* **1** (*в то время как*) while

2 (*до того времени как*): **пока́ не** until; **пока́!** so long!; **пока́ что** for the moment

покажу́(сь) *etc сов см* **показа́ть(ся)**

пока́з (-а) *м* (*фильма*) showing; demonstration; **показа́ни|е** (-я) *ср* (*Юр: обычно мн*) evidence; (*на счётчике итп*) reading; **показа́тел|ь** (-я) *м* indicator; (*Мат, Экон*) index (*мн* indices); **показа́тельный** *прил* (*пример*) revealing

пока|за́ть (-жу́, -жешь; *impf* **пока́зывать**) *сов перех* to show ▷ *неперех* (*на суде*) to testify; **пока́зывать** (*perf* **показа́ть**) приме́р to set an example; **показа́ться** *сов от* **каза́ться** ▷ (*impf* **пока́зываться**) *возв* to appear; **пока́зываться** (*perf* **показа́ться**) врачу́ to see a doctor

поката́|ть (-ю) *сов перех*: **поката́ть кого́-н на маши́не** to take sb for a drive; **поката́ться** *сов возв* to go for a ride

пок|ати́ть (-ачу́, -а́тишь) *сов перех* (*что-н круглое*) to roll; (*что-н на колёсах*) to wheel; **покати́ться** *сов возв* to start rolling *или* to roll

покача́|ть (-ю) *сов перех* to rock ▷ *неперех*: **покача́ть голово́й** to shake one's head; **покача́ться** *сов возв* (*на каче́лях*) to swing

пока́чива|ться (-юсь) *несов возв* to rock

поки́н|уть (-у; *impf* **покида́ть**) *сов перех* to abandon

покло́н (-а) *м* (*жест*) bow; (*приветствие*) greeting

покл|они́ться (-оню́сь, -о́нишься) *сов от* **кла́няться**

покло́нник (-а) *м* admirer

поклоня́|ться (-юсь) *несов возв* +*dat* to worship

поко́|иться (3sg -ится) *несов возв*: **поко́иться на** +*prp* to rest on

поко́|й (-я) *м* peace; **оставля́ть** (*perf* **оста́вить**) **кого́-н в поко́е** to leave sb in peace

поко́йный *прил* the late ▷ (-**ого**) *м* the deceased

поколе́ни|е (-я) *ср* generation

поко́нч|ить (-у, -ишь) *сов*: **поко́нчить с** +*instr* (*с делами*) to be finished with; (*с бедностью, с проблемой*) to put an end to; **поко́нчить** (*perf*) **с собо́й** to kill o.s., commit suicide

покор|и́ть (-ю́, -и́шь; *impf* **покоря́ть**) *сов перех* (*страну, народ*) to conquer; **покоря́ть** (*perf* **покори́ть**) **кого́-н** (*заставить любить*) to win sb's heart;

покор|и́ться (*impf* **покоря́ться**) *сов возв*: **покори́ться** (+*dat*) to submit (to)

покрови́тельств|о (-а) *ср* protection

покро́|й (-я) *ср* cut (*of clothing*)

покрыва́л|о (-а) *ср* bedspread

покр|ы́ть (-о́ю, -о́ешь) *сов от* **крыть** ▷ (*impf* **покрыва́ть**) *перех* (*звуки*) to cover up; (*расходы, расстояние*) to cover; **покры́ться** (*impf* **покрыва́ться**) *сов возв*: **покры́ться** +*instr* (*одеялом*) to cover o.s. with; (*снегом итп*) to be covered in

покры́ш|ка (-ки; *gen pl* -ек) *ж* (*Авт*) tyre (*Brit*), tire (*US*)

покупа́тел|ь (-я) *м* buyer; (*в магазине*) customer; **покупа́тельский** *прил* (*спрос, интересы*) consumer

покупа́|ть (-ю) *несов от* **купи́ть**

поку́п|ка (-ки; *gen pl* -ок) *ж* purchase; **де́лать** (*perf* **сде́лать**) **поку́пки** to go shopping

покуша́|ться (-юсь) *несов возв*: **покуша́ться на** +*acc* to attempt to take; **покуше́ни|е** (-я) *ср*: **покуше́ние** (**на** +*acc*) (*на свободу, на права*) infringement (of); (*на жизнь*) attempt (on)

пол (-а; *loc sg* -у́, *nom pl* -ы́) *м* floor ▷ (*nom pl* -ы́, *gen pl* -о́в, *dat pl* -а́м) sex

полага́|ть (-ю) *несов* (*думать*) to suppose; **на́до полага́ть** supposedly

полго́да (-уго́да) *ср/мн* half a year

по́лдень (полу́дня *или* по́лдня) *м* midday, noon; **2 часа́ по́сле полу́дня** 2 p.m

по́л|е (-я; *nom pl* -я́, *gen pl* -е́й) *ср* field; **по́ле де́ятельности** sphere of activity; **по́ле зре́ния** field of vision

поле́зный *прил* useful; (*пища*) healthy; **поле́зные ископа́емые** minerals

поле́з|ть (-у, -ешь) *сов*: **поле́зть на** +*acc* (*на гору*) to start climbing *или* to climb; **поле́зть** (*perf*) **в** +*acc* (*в драку, в спор*) to get involved in; **поле́зть** (*perf*) **в карма́н** to put one's hand in(to) one's pocket

поле́н|о (-а; *nom pl* -ья, *gen pl* -ьев) *ср* log

полёт (-а) *м* flight

поле|те́ть (-чу́, -ти́шь) *сов* (*птица, самолёт*) to fly off; (*время*) to start to fly by

по́лза|ть (-ю) *несов* to crawl

полз|ти́ (-у́, -ёшь; *pt* -, -ла́) *несов* to crawl

ползунк|и́ (-о́в) *мн* rompers

полива́|ть (-ю) *несов от* **поли́ть**

поливитами́н|ы (-ов) *мн* multivitamins

полиго́н (-а) *м* (*для учений*) shooting range; (*для испытания оружия*) test(ing) site

поликли́ник|а (-и) *ж* health centre (*Brit*) *или* center (*US*)

● **Поликли́ника**

● These centres are staffed by a range of
● specialist doctors: surgeons, eye doctors,
● dermatologists etc. Patients can make an
● appointment with a number of doctors
● at any time.

полир|ова́ть (-у́ю; *perf* **отполирова́ть**) *несов перех* to polish

по́лис (-а) *м*: **страхово́й по́лис** insurance policy

поли́тик (-а) *м* politician; **поли́тик|а** (-и) *ж* (*курс*) policy; (*события, наука*) politics; **полити́ческий** *прил* political

пол|и́ть (-ью́, -ьёшь; *pt* -и́л, -ила́, *impf* **полива́ть**) *сов* (*дождь*) to start pouring *или* to pour down ▷ *перех*: **поли́ть что-н чем-н** (*соусом*) to pour sth over sth; **полива́ть** (*perf* **поли́ть**) **цветы́** to water the flowers

полице́йск|ий *прил* police ▷ (-ого) *м* policeman (*мн* policemen); **полице́йский уча́сток** police station

поли́ци|я (-и) *ж* the police

поли́чн|ое (-ого) *ср*: **пойма́ть кого́-н с поли́чным** to catch sb at the scene of a crime; (*перен*) to catch sb red-handed *или* in the act

полиэтиле́н (-а) *м* polythene

полк (-а́; *loc sg* -ý) *м* regiment

по́лк|а (-и; *gen pl* -ок) *ж* shelf; (*в поезде: для багажа́*) luggage rack; (: *для лежания*) berth; **кни́жная по́лка** bookshelf

полко́вник (-а) *м* colonel

полне́|ть (-ю; *perf* **пополне́ть**) *несов* to put on weight

полномо́чи|е (-я) *ср* authority; (*обычно мн: право*) power; **полномо́чный** *прил* fully authorized

полнопра́вный *прил* (*гражданин*) fully fledged; (*наследник*) rightful

по́лностью *нареч* fully, completely

полноце́нный *прил* proper

по́л|ночь (-ýночи) *ж* midnight

по́лный *прил* full; (*победа, счастье итп*) complete, total; (*толстый*) stout; **по́лный +gen** *или* **+instr** full of; (*тревоги, любви итп*) filled with

полови́к (-а́) *м* mat

полови́н|а (-ы) *ж* half; **на полови́не доро́ги** halfway; **сейча́с полови́на пе́рвого/второ́го** it's (now) half past twelve/one

поло́вник (-а) *м* ladle

полово́дь|е (-я) *ср* high water

полово́й *прил* (*тряпка, мастика*) floor; (*Био*) sexual

положе́ни|е (-я) *ср* situation; (*географическое*) location, position; (*тела, головы итп*) position; (*социальное, семейное итп*) status; (*правила*) regulations *мн*; (*обычно мн: тезис*) point; **она́ в положе́нии** (*разг*) she's expecting; **положе́ние дел** the state of affairs

поло́женный *прил* due

положи́тельный *прил* positive

пол|ожи́ть (-ожу́, -о́жишь) *сов от* **класть**

поло́м|ка (-ки; *gen pl* -ок) *ж* breakdown

полос|а́ (-ы́; *nom pl* **по́лосы**, *gen pl* **поло́с**, *dat pl* **поло́сам**) *ж* (*ткани*, *металла*) strip; (*на ткани, на рисунке итп*) stripe; **полоса́тый** *прил* striped, stripy; **поло́с|ка** (-ки; *gen pl* -ок) *ж* (*ткани, бумаги*) (thin) strip; (*на ткани*) (thin) stripe; **в поло́ску** striped

пол|оска́ть (-ощу́, -о́щешь; *perf* **прополоска́ть**) *несов перех* (*бельё, посуду*) to rinse; (*рот*) to rinse out

по́лост|ь (-и; *gen pl* -е́й) *ж* (*Анат*) cavity

полоте́н|це (-ца; *gen pl* -ец) *ср* towel

полотн|о́ (-отна́; *nom pl* -о́тна, *gen pl* -о́тен) *ср* (*ткань*) sheet; (*картина*) canvas

пол|о́ть (-ю́, -ешь; *perf* **прополо́ть**) *несов перех* to weed

полпути́ *м нескл* half (*of journey*); **на полпути́** halfway

пол|тора́ (-у́тора; *f* **полторы́**) *м/ср чис* one and a half

полуботи́н|ок (-ка) *м* ankle boot

полуго́ди|е (-я) *ср* (*Просвещ*) semester; (*Экон*) half (*of the year*)

полукру́г (-а) *м* semicircle

полупальто́ *ср нескл* jacket, short coat

полуфабрика́т (-а) *м* (*Кулин*) partially prepared food

полуфина́л (-а) *м* semifinal

получа́тел|ь (-я) *м* recipient

получа́|ть(ся) (-ю(сь)) *несов от* **получи́ть(ся)**

пол|учи́ть (-учу́, -у́чишь; *impf* **получа́ть**) *сов перех* to receive, get; (*урожай, насморк, удовольствие*) to get; (*известность*) to gain ▷ *неперех* (*разг: быть наказанным*) to get it in the neck; **получи́ться** (*impf* **получа́ться**) *сов возв* to turn out; (*удаться*) to work; (*фотография*) to come out; **из него́ полу́чится хоро́ший учи́тель** he'll make a good teacher; **у меня́ э́то не получа́ется** I can't do it

полу́ч|ка (-ки; *gen pl* -ек) *ж* (*разг*) pay

полчаса́ (-уча́са) *м* half an hour

по́лый *прил* hollow

по́льз|а (-ы) *ж* benefit; **в по́льзу +gen** in favour (*Brit*) *или* favor (*US*) of

по́льзовани|е (-я) *ср*: **по́льзование (+instr)** use (of); **по́льз|оваться** (-уюсь; *perf* **воспо́льзоваться**) *несов возв* **+instr** to use; (*no perf: авторитетом, успехом итп*) to enjoy

по́льский *прил* Polish; **по́льский язы́к** Polish

По́льш|а (-и) *ж* Poland

пол|юби́ть (-юблю́, -ю́бишь) *сов перех* (*человека*) to come to love; **полюби́ть** (*perf*) **что-н/+infin** to develop a love for sth/doing

по́люс (-а; *nom pl* -а́) *м* pole

пол|я́ (-е́й) *мн* (*шляпы*) brim *ед*; (*на странице*) margin *ед*

поля́рный *прил* (*Гео*) polar; (*разные*) diametrically opposed

пома́д|а (-ы) *ж* (*также* **губна́я пома́да**) lipstick

пом|аха́ть (-ашу́, -а́шешь) *сов* +*instr* to wave

поме́дл|ить (-ю, -ишь) *сов*: **поме́длить с** +*instr*/+*infin* to linger over sth/doing

поменя́|ть(ся) (-ю(сь)) *сов от* **меня́ть(ся)**

поме́р|ить (-ю, -ишь) *сов от* **ме́рить**

поме|сти́ть (-щу́, -сти́шь; *impf* **помеща́ть**) *сов перех* to put; **помести́ться** (*impf* **помеща́ться**) *сов возв* (*уместиться*) to fit

помёт (-а) *м* dung; (*птиц*) droppings *мн*; (*детёныши*) litter

поме́т|а (-ы) *ж* note

поме́|тить (-чу, -тишь) *сов от* **ме́тить** ▷ (*impf* **помеча́ть**) *перех* to note

поме́т|ка (-ки; *gen pl* -ок) *ж* note

поме́х|а (-и) *ж* hindrance; (*Связь: обычно мн*) interference

помеча́|ть (-ю) *несов от* **поме́тить**

помеша́|ть (-ю) *сов от* **меша́ть**

помеща́|ть(ся) (-ю(сь)) *несов от* **помести́ть(ся)**

помеще́ни|е (-я) *ср* room; (*под офис*) premises *мн*; **жило́е помеще́ние** living space

помидо́р (-а) *м* tomato (*мн* tomatoes)

поми́л|овать (-ую) *сов от* **ми́ловать**

поми́мо *предл* +*gen* besides; **поми́мо того́/всего́ про́чего** apart from that/anything else

поми́н|ки (-ок) *мн* wake *ед*

помину́тный *прил* at one-minute intervals; (*очень частый*) constant

помир|и́ть(ся) (-ю́(сь), -и́шь(ся)) *сов от* **мири́ть(ся)**

по́мн|ить (-ю, -ишь) *несов* (*не*)*перех*: **по́мнить (о** +*prp* **или про** +*acc*) to remember

помо́г *итп сов см* **помо́чь**

помога́|ть (-ю) *несов от* **помо́чь**

по-мо́ему *нареч* my way ▷ *вводн сл* in my opinion

помо́|и (-ев) *мн* dishwater *ед*; (*отходы*) slops *мн*

помолч|а́ть (-у́, -и́шь) *сов* to pause

помо́рщ|иться (-усь, -ишься) *сов возв* to screw up one's face

помо́ст (-а) *м* (*для обозрения*) platform; (*для выступлений*) rostrum

помо́|чь (-гу́, -ожешь итп, -гут; *pt* -г, -гла́, *impf* **помога́ть**) *сов* +*dat* to help; (*другой стране*) to aid

помо́щник (-а) *м* helper; (*должность*) assistant

по́мощ|ь (-и) *ж* help, assistance

пом|ы́ть(ся) (-о́ю(сь), -о́ешь(ся)) *сов от* **мы́ть(ся)**

пона́доб|иться (-люсь, -ишься) *сов возв* to be needed

по-настоя́щему *нареч* properly

по-на́шему *нареч* in our opinion, our way

понеде́льник (-а) *м* Monday

понемно́гу *нареч* a little; (*постепенно*) little by little

пон|ести́ (-есу́, -есёшь; *pt* -ёс, -есла́) *сов от* **нести́**; **понести́сь** *сов возв* (*человек*) to tear off; (*лошадь*) to charge off; (*машина*) to speed off

по́ни *м нескл* pony

понижа́|ть(ся) (-ю(сь)) *несов от* **пони́зить(ся)**

пони|зить (-жу, -зишь; *impf* **понижа́ть**) *сов перех* to reduce; (*в должности*) to demote; (*голос*) to lower; **пони́зиться** (*impf* **понижа́ться**) *сов возв* to be reduced

понима́|ть (-ю) *несов от* **поня́ть** ▷ *перех* to understand ▷ *неперех*: **понима́ть в** +*prp* to know about; **понима́ете** you see

поно́с (-а) *м* diarrhoea (*Brit*), diarrhea (*US*)

пон|оси́ть (-ошу́, -о́сишь) *сов перех* to carry for a while; (*одежду*) to wear

поно́шенный *прил* (*одежда*) worn

понра́в|иться (-люсь, -ишься) *сов от* **нра́виться**

по́нчик (-а) *м* doughnut (*Brit*), donut (*US*)

поня́ти|е (-я) *ср* notion; (*знание*) idea; **поня́тия не име́ю** (*разг*) I've no idea; **поня́тно** *нареч* intelligibly ▷ *как сказ*: **мне поня́тно** I understand; **поня́тно!** I see!; **поня́тно?** got it?; **поня́тный** *прил* intelligible; (*ясный*) clear; (*оправданный*) understandable

по|ня́ть (-йму́, -ймёшь; *pt* -нял, -няла́, *impf* **понима́ть**) *сов перех* to understand

поощре́ни|е (-я) *ср* encouragement

поощр|и́ть (-ю́, -и́шь; *impf* **поощря́ть**) *сов перех* to encourage

поп (-а́) *м* (*разг*) priest

попада́ни|е (-я) *ср* hit

попада́|ть(ся) (-ю(сь)) *несов от* **попа́сть(ся)**

попа́рно *нареч* in pairs

попа́|сть (-ду́, -дёшь; *impf* **попада́ть**) *сов*: **попа́сть в** +*acc* (*в цель*) to hit; (*в воро́та*) to end up in; (*в чужой город*) to find o.s. in; (*в беду*) to land in; **мы́ло попа́ло мне в глаза́** the soap got in my eyes; **попада́ть** (*perf* **попа́сть**) **в ава́рию** to have an accident; **попада́ть** (*perf* **попа́сть**) **в плен** to be taken prisoner; **попада́ть** (*perf* **попа́сть**) **под дождь** to be caught in the rain; **ему́ попа́ло** (*разг*) he got a hiding; **(Вы) не туда́ попа́ли** you've got the wrong number; **попа́сться** (*impf* **попада́ться**) *сов возв* (*преступник*) to be caught; **мне попа́лась интере́сная кни́га** I came across an interesting book; **попада́ться** (*perf* **попа́сться**) **кому́-н на глаза́** to catch sb's eye

попе́й(те) *сов см* **попи́ть**

поперёк *нареч* crossways ▷ *предл* +*gen* across

попере́чный *прил* horizontal

поперхн|у́ться (-у́сь, -ёшься) *сов возв* to choke

попе́рч|ить (-у, -ишь) сов от **пе́рчить**
попече́ни|е (-я) ср (о детях) care; (о делах, о доме) charge
поп|и́ть (-ью́, -ьёшь; pt -и́л, -ила́, imper -е́й(те)) сов перех to have a drink of
поплы|́ть (-ву́, -вёшь; pt -л, -ла́) сов to start swimming; (судно) to set sail
попола́м нареч in half; **попола́м с** +instr mixed with
попо́лн|ить (-ю, -ишь; impf **пополня́ть**) сов перех: **пополнить что-н** (запасы) to replenish sth with; (колле́кцию) to expand sth with; (коллекти́в) to reinforce sth with; **попо́лниться** (impf **пополня́ться** (запасы) to be replenished; (колле́кция) to be expanded
попра́в|ить (-лю, -ишь; impf **поправля́ть**) сов перех to correct; (галстук, платье) to straighten; (причёску) to tidy; (здоро́вье, дела́) to improve; **попра́виться** (impf **поправля́ться**) сов возв to improve; (потолсте́ть) to put on weight
попра́в|ка (-ки; gen pl -ок) ж (оши́бки) correction; (в решение, в закон) amendment
по-пре́жнему нареч as before; (всё ещё) still
попро́б|овать (-ую) сов от **про́бовать**
попро|си́ть(ся) (-ошу́(сь), -о́сишь(ся)) сов от **проси́ть(ся)**
попроща́|ться (-юсь) сов возв: **попроща́ться с** +instr to say goodbye to
попуга́|й (-я) м parrot
популя́рност|ь (-и) ж popularity
популя́рный прил popular; (поня́тный) accessible
попу́тный прил (замеча́ние) accompanying; (маши́на) passing; (ве́тер) favourable (Brit), favorable (US)
попу́тчик (-а) м travelling (Brit) или traveling (US) companion
попы́т|ка (-ки; gen pl -ок) ж attempt
попью́ итп сов см **попи́ть**
попя́|титься (-чусь, -тишься) сов возв to take a few steps backwards (Brit) или backward (US)
по́р|а (-ы) ж pore
пор|а́ (-ы́; acc sg -у, dat sg -е́, nom pl -ы) ж time ▷ как сказ it's time; **до каки́х пор?** until when?; **до сих пор** (ра́ньше) up till now; (всё ещё) still; **до тех пор** until then; **до тех пор, пока́** until; **с каки́х пор?** since when?
поравня́|ться (-юсь) сов возв: **поравня́ться с** +instr (челове́к) to draw level with; (маши́на) to come alongside
пораже́ни|е (-я) ср (це́ли) hitting; (Мед) damage; (про́игрыш) defeat; **наноси́ть** (perf **нанести́) кому́-н пораже́ние** to defeat sb; **терпе́ть** (perf **потерпе́ть) пораже́ние** to be defeated
порази́тельный прил striking; (о непри́ятном) astonishing

пора́н|ить (-ю, -ишь) сов перех to hurt
порв|а́ть(ся) (-у́, -ёшь) сов от **рва́ть(ся)**
поре́з (-а) м cut; **поре́|зать** (-жу, -жешь) сов перех to cut; **поре́заться** сов возв to cut o.s.
порногра́фи|я (-и) ж pornography
по́ровну нареч equally
поро́г (-а) м (также перен) threshold
поро́д|а (-ы) ж (живо́тных) breed; **поро́дистый** прил pedigree
поро́й нареч from time to time
пороло́н (-а) м foam rubber
порош|о́к (-ка́) м powder
порт (-а; loc sg -у́, nom pl -ы, gen pl -о́в) м port
портати́вный прил portable; **портати́вный компью́тер** laptop (computer)
портве́йн (-а) м port (wine)
по́р|тить (-чу, -тишь; perf **испо́ртить**) несов перех to damage; (настрое́ние, пра́здник, ребёнка) to spoil; **по́ртиться** (perf **испо́ртиться**) сов возв (механи́зм) to be damaged; (здоро́вье, пого́да) to deteriorate; (настрое́ние) to be spoiled; (молоко́) to go off; (мя́со, о́вощи) to go bad
портре́т (-а) м portrait
Португа́ли|я (-и) ж Portugal
португа́льский прил Portuguese; **португа́льский язы́к** Portuguese
портфе́л|ь (-я) м briefcase; (Полит, Комм) portfolio
портье́р|а (-ы) ж curtain
поруга́|ться (-юсь) сов от **руга́ться** ▷ возв (разг): **поруга́ться (с** +instr) to fall out (with)
пору́к|а (-и) ж: **брать кого́-н на пору́ки** to take sb on probation; (Юр) to stand bail for sb
по-ру́сски нареч (говори́ть, писа́ть) in Russian; **говори́ть** (impf)/**понима́ть** (impf) **по-ру́сски** to speak/understand Russian
поруча́|ть (-ю) несов от **поручи́ть**
поруче́ни|е (-я) ср (зада́ние) errand; (: ва́жное) mission
поручи́тельств|о (-а) ср guarantee
пор|учи́ть (-учу́, -у́чишь; impf **поруча́ть**) сов: **поручи́ть кому́-н что-н** to entrust sb with sth; **поруча́ть** (perf **поручи́ть) кому́-н** +infin to instruct sb to do; **поруча́ть** (perf **поручи́ть) кому́-н кого́-н/что-н** (отда́ть на попече́ние) to leave sb/sth in sb's care; **поручи́ться** сов от **руча́ться**
по́рци|я (-и) ж portion
поры́в (-а) м (ве́тра) gust
поря́д|ок (-ка) м order; (пра́вила) procedure; **в поря́дке** +gen (в ка́честве) as; **в поря́дке** in order; **всё в поря́дке** everything's O.K.; **поря́док дня** agenda
поря́дочный прил (че́стный) decent; (значи́тельный) fair
пос|ади́ть (-ажу́, -а́дишь) сов от **сажа́ть**

поса́д|ка (**-ки**; *gen pl* **-ок**) ж (*овощей*) planting; (*пассажиров*) boarding; (*самолёта итп*) landing; **поса́дочный** *прил* (*талон*) boarding; (*площадка*) landing

по-своему *нареч* his *итп* way; **он по-своему прав** he is right in his own way, he is right

посвя|ти́ть (**-щу́, -ти́шь**; *impf* **посвяща́ть**) *сов перех*: **посвяти́ть что-н +dat** to devote sth to; (*книгу*) to dedicate sth to

посе́в|ы (**-ов**) *мн* crops

поселе́ни|е (**-я**) *ср* settlement

посел|и́ть(ся) (**-елю́(сь), -е́лишь(ся)**) *сов от* **сели́ть(ся)**

посёл|ок (**-ка**) *м* village; **да́чный посёлок** village made up of dachas

посереди́не *нареч* in the middle ▷ *предл +gen* in the middle of

посети́тел|ь (**-я**) *м* visitor

посе|ти́ть (**-щу́, -ти́шь**; *impf* **посеща́ть**) *сов перех* to visit

посеще́ни|е (**-я**) *ср* visit

посе́|ять (**-ю, -ишь**) *сов от* **се́ять**

посиде́ть (**-жу́, -ди́шь**) *сов* to sit for a while

поскользн|у́ться (**-у́сь, -ёшься**) *сов возв* to slip

поско́льку *союз* as

посла́ни|е (**-я**) *ср* message; **посла́нник** (**-а**) *м* envoy

по|сла́ть (**-шлю, -шлёшь**; *impf* **посыла́ть**) *сов перех* to send

по́сле *нареч* (*потом*) afterwards (*Brit*), afterward (*US*) ▷ *предл +gen* after ▷ *союз*: **по́сле того́ как** after

после́дн|ий *прил* last; (*новости, мода*) latest; **за** *или* **в после́днее вре́мя** recently

после́дователь (**-я**) *м* follower

после́довательность (**-и**) *ж* sequence; (*политики*) consistency

после́довательный *прил* (*один за другим*) consecutive; (*логический*) consistent

после́д|овать (**-ую**) *сов от* **сле́довать**

после́дстви|е (**-я**) *ср* consequence

послеза́втра *нареч* the day after tomorrow

посло́виц|а (**-ы**) *ж* proverb, saying

послу́ша|ть (**-ю**) *сов от* **слу́шать** ▷ *перех*: **послу́шать что-н** to listen to sth for a while; **послу́шаться** *сов от* **слу́шаться**

послу́шный *прил* obedient

посме́|ть (**-ю**) *сов от* **сметь**

посм|отре́ть (**-отрю́, -о́тришь**) *сов от* **смотре́ть** ▷ *неперех*: **посмо́трим** (*разг*) we'll see; **посмотре́ться** *сов от* **смотре́ться**

посо́би|е (**-я**) *ср* (*помощь*) benefit; (*Просвещ: учебник*) textbook; (: *наглядное*) visual aids *мн*; **посо́бие по безрабо́тице** unemployment benefit; **посо́бие по инвали́дности** disability living allowance

посо́л (**-ла́**) *м* ambassador

посол|и́ть (**-олю́, -о́лишь**) *сов от* **соли́ть**

посо́льств|о (**-а**) *ср* embassy

поспе́|ть (*3sg* **-ет**) *сов от* **спеть**

поспеш|и́ть (**-у́, -и́шь**) *сов от* **спеши́ть**

поспо́р|ить (**-ю, -ишь**) *сов от* **спо́рить**

посреди́ *нареч* in the middle ▷ *предл +gen* in the middle of

посреди́не *нареч* in the middle ▷ *предл +gen* in the middle of

посре́дник (**-а**) *м* intermediary; (*при конфликте*) mediator; **торго́вый посре́дник** middleman (*мн* **middlemen**); **посре́днический** *прил* (*Комм*) intermediary; (*услуги*) agent's; **посре́дничеств|о** (**-а**) *ср* mediation

посре́дственно *нареч* (*учиться, писать*) so-so ▷ *ср нескл* (*Просвещ*) ≈ satisfactory (*school mark*); **посре́дственный** *прил* mediocre

посре́дством *предл +gen* by means of; (*человека*) through

поссо́р|ить(ся) (**-ю(сь), -ишь(ся)**) *сов от* **ссо́рить(ся)**

пост (**-а́**; *loc sg* **-у́**) *м* (*люди*) guard; (*место*) lookout post; (*должность*) post; (*Рел*) fast; (*Комп*) blogpost

поста́в|ить (**-лю, -ишь**) *сов от* **ста́вить** ▷ (*impf* **поставля́ть**) *перех* (*товар*) to supply; **поста́в|ка** (**-ки**; *gen pl* **-ок**) *ж* (*снабжение*) supply; **поставщи́к** (**-а́**) *м* supplier

постаме́нт (**-а**) *м* pedestal

постан|ови́ть (**-овлю́, -о́вишь**; *impf* **постановля́ть**) *сов +infin* to resolve to do

постано́в|ка (**-ки**; *gen pl* **-ок**) *ж* (*Театр*) production; **постано́вка вопро́са** the formulation of the question

постановле́ни|е (**-я**) *ср* (*решение*) resolution; (*распоряжение*) decree

постано́вщик (**-а**) *м* producer

постара́|ться (**-юсь**) *сов от* **стара́ться**

пост|ели́ть (**-елю́, -е́лишь**) *сов от* **стели́ть**

посте́л|ь (**-и**) *ж* bed

посте́льн|ый *прил*: **посте́льное бельё** bedclothes *мн*

постепе́нно *нареч* gradually

постепе́нный *прил* gradual

постира́|ть (**-ю**) *сов от* **стира́ть**

по|сти́ться (**-щу́сь, -сти́шься**) *несов возв* (*Рел*) to fast

по́стн|ый *прил* (*суп*) vegetarian; **по́стное ма́сло** vegetable oil

посто́льку *союз*: **посто́льку ... поско́льку** insofar as ...

посторо́нн|ий *прил* (*чужой*) strange; (*помощь, влияние*) outside; (*вопрос*) irrelevant ▷ (**-его**) *м* stranger, outsider; **посторо́нним вход воспрещён** authorized entry only

постоя́нн|ый *прил* (*работа, адрес*) permanent; (*шум*) constant; **постоя́нное**

запомина́ющее устро́йство ROM

посто|я́ть (-ю́, -и́шь) *сов от* стоя́ть
▷ *неперех (стоять недолго)* to stand for a
while

постри́|чь(ся) (-гу́(сь), -жёшь(ся) *итп*,
-гу́т(ся); *pt* -г(ся), -гла(сь)) *сов от*
стри́чь(ся)

постро́|ить (-ю, -ишь) *сов от* стро́ить

постро́|йка (-йки; *gen pl* -ек) *ж*
construction; *(здание)* building

пост|упи́ть (-уплю́, -у́пишь; *impf*
поступа́ть) *сов* *(человек)* to act; *(товар,
известия)* to come in; *(жалоба)* to be
received; поступа́ть *(perf* поступи́ть) в/на
+*асс (в университет, на работу)* to start

поступле́ни|е (-я) *ср (действие: в
универ ситет, на работу)* starting; *(обычно
мн: бюджетные)* revenue *ед*; *(в
библиотеке)* acquisition

посту́п|ок (-ка) *м* deed

постуч|а́ть(ся) (-у́(сь), -и́шь(ся)) *сов от*
стуча́ть(ся)

посу́д|а (-ы) *ж собир* crockery; ку́хонная
посу́да kitchenware; стекля́нная посу́да
glassware; мыть *(perf* помы́ть) посу́ду to
wash the dishes, wash up

посчита́|ть (-ю) *сов от* счита́ть

посыла́|ть (-ю) *несов от* посла́ть

посы́л|ка (-ки; *gen pl* -ок) *ж (действие:
книг, денег)* sending; *(посланное)* parcel

посы́п|ать (-лю, -лешь) *сов перех* to
sprinkle; посы́паться *сов от* сы́паться

пот (-а; *loc sg* -у́) *м* sweat

по-тво́ему *нареч* your way

потенциа́л (-а) *м* potential

потенциа́льный *прил* potential

потепле́ни|е (-я) *ср* warmer spell

пот|ере́ть (-ру́, -рёшь; *pt* -ёр, -ёрла)
сов перех (ушиб) to rub; *(морковь)* to
grate

потерпе́вш|ий (-его) *м (Юр)* victim

пот|ерпе́ть (-ерплю́, -е́рпишь) *сов от*
терпе́ть

поте́р|я (-и) *ж* loss

потеря́|ть(ся) (-ю(сь)) *сов от* теря́ть(ся)

поте́|ть (-ю; *impf* вспоте́ть) *несов* to
sweat

по́тный *прил* sweaty

пото́к (-а) *м* stream

потол|о́к (-ка́) *м* ceiling

пото́м *нареч (через некоторое время)*
later; *(после)* then ▷ *союз*: **а/и пото́м** and
then, anyhow; **на пото́м** for later

пото́мк|и (-ов) *мн* descendants

пото́мств|о (-а) *ср собир* descendants
мн; *(дети)* offspring *мн*

потому́ *нареч*: **потому́ (и)** that's why;
потому́ что because

пото́п (-а) *м* flood

потороп|и́ть(ся) (-лю́(сь), -ишь(ся))
сов от торопи́ть(ся)

пото́чн|ый *прил (производство)* mass;
пото́чная ли́ния production line

потра́|тить (-чу, -тишь) *сов от* тра́тить

потреби́тел|ь (-я) *м* consumer;
потреби́тельский *прил (спрос)*
consumer

потреб|и́ть (-лю́, -и́шь) *сов от*
потребля́ть; потребле́ни|е (-я) *ср
(действие)* consumption; **това́ры
широ́кого потребле́ния** consumer goods;
потребля́|ть (-ю; *perf* потреби́ть)
несов перех to consume; потре́бность|ь
(-и) *ж* need

потре́б|овать(ся) (-ую(сь)) *сов от*
тре́бовать(ся)

потроха́ (-о́в) *мн (птицы)* giblets *мн*

потрош|и́ть (-у́, -и́шь; *perf*
вы́потрошить) *несов перех (курицу,
рыбу)* to gut

потруди́ться (-жу́сь, -дишься) *сов
возв* to work +*infin* to take the trouble to
do

потряса́ющий *прил (музыка, стихи)*
fantastic; *(красота)* stunning

потрясе́ни|е (-я) *ср (нервное)*
breakdown; *(социальное)* upheaval;
(впечатление) shock

потряс|ти́ (-у́, -ёшь; *pt* -, -ла́) *сов перех*
to shake; *(взволновать)* to stun

поту́хн|уть (*3sg* -ет, *impf* потуха́ть) *сов
(лампа, свет)* to go out

пот|уши́ть (-ушу́, -у́шишь) *сов от*
туши́ть

пот|яну́ться (-яну́сь, -я́нешься; *impf*
потя́гиваться) *сов возв (в постели, в
кресле)* to stretch out

поу́жина|ть (-ю) *сов от* у́жинать

поумне́|ть (-ю) *сов от* умне́ть

похвал|а́ (-ы́) *ж* praise

похва́ста|ться (-юсь) *сов от* хва́статься

похити́тел|ь (-я) *м (см глаг)* thief;
abductor; kidnapper

похи́|тить (-щу, -тишь; *impf* похища́ть)
сов перех (предмет) to steal; *(человека)*
to abduct; *(: для выкупа)* to kidnap

похище́ни|е (-я) *ср (см глаг)* theft;
abduction; kidnap(ping)

похло́па|ть (-ю) *сов перех* to pat

похме́ль|е (-я) *ср* hangover

похо́д (-а) *м (военный)* campaign;
(туристический) hike *(walking and
camping expedition)*

пох|оди́ть (-ожу́, -о́дишь) *несов*:
походи́ть на кого́-н/что-н to resemble sb/
sth ▷ *сов* to walk

похо́ж|ий *прил*: **похо́жий (на** +*асс или с*
+*instr)* similar (to); **он похо́ж на бра́та, они́
с бра́том похо́жи** he looks like his brother;
они́ похо́жи they look alike; **похо́же на то,
что ...** it looks as if ...; **это на него́ (не)
похо́же** it's (not) like him

похолода́ни|е (-я) *ср* cold spell

похолода́|ть (*3sg* -ет) *сов от* холода́ть

похорон|и́ть (-оню́, -о́нишь) *сов от*
хорони́ть

похоро́нн|ый *прил* funeral;
похоро́нное бюро́ undertaker's

по́хор|о́ны (-о́н; *dat pl* -она́м) *мн* funeral *ед*

поцел|ова́ть(ся) (-у́ю(сь)) *сов от* **целова́ть(ся)**

поцелу́й (-я) *м* kiss

почасово́й *прил* (*оплата*) hourly

по́чв|а (-ы) *ж* soil; (*перен*) basis; **на по́чве** +*gen* arising from

почём *нареч* (*разг*) how much?

почему́ *нареч* why; **вот почему́** that is why

почему́-либо *нареч* for some reason or other

почему́-нибудь *нареч* = **почему́-либо**

почему́-то *нареч* for some reason

по́черк (-а) *м* handwriting

почерне́|ть (-ю) *сов от* **черне́ть**

почеса́|ть(ся) (-шу́(сь), -шешь(ся)) *сов от* **чеса́ть(ся)**

почёт (-а) *м* honour (*Brit*), honor (*US*)

почётный *прил* (*гость*) honoured (*Brit*), honored (*US*); (*член*) honorary; (*обязанность*) honourable (*Brit*), honorable (*US*); **почётный карау́л** guard of honour (*Brit*) *или* honor (*US*)

почин|и́ть (-иню́, -и́нишь) *сов от* **чини́ть**

почи́н|ка (-ки; *gen pl* -ок) *ж* repair

почи́|стить (-щу, -стишь) *сов от* **чи́стить**

почита́тел|ь (-я) *м* admirer

почита́|ть (-ю) *сов перех* (*книгу*) to read ▷ *несов перех* to admire

по́ч|ка (-ки; *gen pl* -ек) *ж* (*Бот*) bud; (*Анат*) kidney

по́чт|а (-ы) *ж* (*учреждение*) post office; (*письма*) post, mail; **почтальо́н** (-а) *м* postman (*Brit*) (*мн* postmen), mailman (*US*) (*мн* mailmen); **почта́мт** (-а) *м* main post office

почти́ *нареч* almost, nearly; **почти́ что** (*разг*) almost

почти́тельный *прил* respectful

почти́ть (*как* **чтить**; *см* Table 17) *сов перех* (*память*) to pay homage to

почто́вый *прил* postal; (*марка*) postage; **почто́вая откры́тка** postcard; **почто́вый и́ндекс** postcode (*Brit*), zip code (*US*); **почто́вый перево́д** (*деньги*) postal order; **почто́вый я́щик** postbox

почу́вств|овать (-ую) *сов от* **чу́вствовать**

пошатн|у́ть (-у́, -ёшь) *сов перех* (*веру*) to shake; (*здоровье*) to damage; **пошатну́ться** *сов возв* to sway; (*авторитет*) to be undermined

пошёл *сов см* **пойти́**

пошла́ *etc сов см* **пойти́**

по́шлин|а (-ы) *ж* duty

пошло́ *сов см* **пойти́**

пошлю́ *итп сов см* **посла́ть**

пош|ути́ть (-учу́, -у́тишь) *сов от* **шути́ть**

поща́д|а (-ы) *ж* mercy

поща|ди́ть (-жу́, -ди́шь) *сов от* **щади́ть**

пощёчин|а (-ы) *ж* slap across the face

поэ́зи|я (-и) *ж* poetry

поэ́м|а (-ы) *ж* poem

поэ́т (-а) *м* poet; **поэте́сс|а** (-ы) *ж от* **поэ́т**; **поэти́ческий** *прил* poetic

поэ́тому *нареч* therefore

пою́ *итп несов см* **петь**

поя|ви́ться (-влю́сь, -́вишься; *impf* **появля́ться**) *сов возв* to appear; **у него́ появи́лись иде́и/сомне́ния** he has had an idea/begun to have doubts

появле́ни|е (-я) *ср* appearance

появля́|ться (-юсь) *несов от* **появи́ться**

по́яс (-а; *nom pl* -а́) *м* (*ремень*) belt; (*талия*) waist; (*Гео*) zone

поясне́ни|е (-я) *ср* explanation; (*к схеме*) explanatory note

поясн|и́ть (-ю́, -и́шь; *impf* **поясня́ть**) *сов перех* to explain

поясни́ц|а (-ы) *ж* small of the back

пр. *сокр* = **прое́зд**; **проспе́кт**

прабáбуш|ка (-ки; *gen pl* -ек) *ж* great-grandmother

прав|а́ (-) *мн* (*также* **води́тельские права́**) driving licence *ед* (*Brit*), driver's license *ед* (*US*); *см также* **пра́во**

пра́вд|а (-ы) *ж* truth ▷ *нареч* really ▷ *вводн сл* true ▷ *как сказ* it's true; **пра́вду** *или* **по пра́вде говоря́** *или* **сказа́ть** to tell the truth

правди́вый *прил* truthful

правдоподо́бный *прил* plausible

пра́вил|о (-а) *ср* rule; **э́то не в мои́х пра́вилах** that's not my way; **как пра́вило** as a rule; **по всем пра́вилам** by the rules; **пра́вила доро́жного движе́ния** rules of the road, ≈ Highway Code

пра́вильно *нареч* correctly ▷ *как сказ* that's correct *или* right; **пра́вильный** *прил* correct; (*вывод, ответ*) right

прави́тел|ь (-я) *м* ruler; **прави́тельственный** *прил* government; **прави́тельств|о** (-а) *ср* government

пра́в|ить (-лю, -ишь) *несов перех* (*исправлять*) to correct ▷ *неперех* (+*instr*: *страной*) to rule, govern; (*машиной*) to drive; **правле́ни|е** (-я) *ср* government; (*орган*) board

пра́в|о (-а; *nom pl* -а́) *ср* (*свобода*) right; (*нормы, наука*) law; **име́ть** (*impf*) **пра́во на что-н**/+*infin* to be entitled *или* have the right to sth/to do; **на ра́вных права́х с** +*instr* on equal terms with; **права́ челове́ка** human rights

пра́во-: правонаруше́ни|е (-я) *ср* offence; **правонаруши́тел|ь** (-я) *м* offender; **правописа́ни|е** (-я) *ср* spelling; **правопоря́д|ок** (-ка) *м* law and order

правосла́ви|е (-я) *ср* orthodoxy; **правосла́вный** *прил* (*церковь, обряд*) orthodox ▷ (-ого) *м* member of the Orthodox Church

правосу́ди|е (-я) *ср* justice

пра́вый *прил* right; (*Полит*) right-wing; **он прав** he is right

пра́вящий *прил* ruling

Пра́г|а (**-и**) *ж* Prague

прадеду́ш|ка (**-ки**; *gen pl* **-ек**) *м* great-grandfather

пра́зднеств|о (**-а**) *ср* festival

пра́здник (**-а**) *м* public holiday; (*религиозный*) festival; (*нерабочий день*) holiday; (*радость, торжество*) celebration; **с пра́здником!** best wishes!; **пра́здничный** *прил* (*салют, обед*) celebratory; (*одежда, настроение*) festive; **пра́здничный день** holiday; **пра́здн|овать** (**-ую**) *несов перех* to celebrate

пра́ктик|а (**-и**) *ж* practice; (*часть учёбы*) practical experience *или* work; **на пра́ктике** in practice; **практика́нт** (**-а**) *м* trainee (*on placement*); **практик|ова́ть** (**-у́ю**) *несов перех* to practise (*Brit*), practice (*US*); **практикова́ться** *несов возв* (*обучаться*): **практикова́ться в чём-н** to practise sth

практи́чески *нареч* (*на деле*) in practice; (*по сути дела*) practically

практи́чный *прил* practical

прах (**-а**) *м* (*умершего*) ashes *мн*

пра́чечн|ая (**-ой**) *ж* laundry

пребыва́ни|е (**-я**) *ср* stay

пребыва́|ть (**-ю**) *несов* to be

превзойти́ (*как* **идти́**; *см Table 18; impf* **превосходи́ть**) *сов перех* (*врага, соперника*) to beat; (*результаты, ожидания*) to surpass; (*доходы, скорость*) to exceed

превосхо|ди́ть (**-жу́, -дишь**) *несов от* **превзойти́**

превосхо́дно *нареч* superbly ▷ *как сказ* it's superb; *част* **превосхо́дно!** (*хорошо*) excellent!

превосхо́дн|ый *прил* superb; **превосхо́дная сте́пень** (*Линг*) superlative degree

превра|ти́ть (**-щу́, -ти́шь**; *impf* **превраща́ть**) *сов перех*: **преврати́ть что-н/кого́-н в** +*acc* to turn *или* transform sth/sb into; **преврати́ться** (*impf* **превраща́ться**) *сов возв*: **преврати́ться (в** +*acc*) to turn (into)

превраще́ни|е (**-я**) *ср* transformation

превы́|сить (**-шу, -сишь**; *impf* **превыша́ть**) *сов перех* to exceed

прегра́д|а (**-ы**) *ж* barrier

прегра|ди́ть (**-жу́, -ди́шь**; *impf* **прегражда́ть**) *сов перех*: **прегради́ть кому́-н доро́гу/вход** to block *или* bar sb's way/entrance

преда|ва́ть (**-ю́**) *несов от* **преда́ть**

пре́данный *прил* devoted

преда́тель (**-я**) *м* traitor

преда́ть (*как* **дать**; *см Table 16; impf* **предава́ть**) *сов перех* to betray; **предава́ть** (*perf* **преда́ть**) **что-н гла́сности** to make sth public

предвари́тельный *прил* preliminary; (*продажа*) advance

предви́|деть (**-жу, -дишь**) *сов перех* to predict

предводи́тель (**-я**) *м* leader

преде́л (**-а**) *м* (*обычно мн: города, страны*) boundary; (*перен: приличия*) bound; (*: терпения*) limit; (*подлости, совершенства*) height; (*мечтаний*) pinnacle; **на преде́ле** at breaking point; **в преде́лах** +*gen* (*закона, года*) within; (*приличия*) within the bounds of; **за преде́лами** +*gen* (*страны, города*) outside

преде́льный *прил* maximum; (*восторг, важность*) utmost; **преде́льный срок** deadline

предисло́ви|е (**-я**) *ср* foreword, preface

предлага́|ть (**-ю**) *несов от* **предложи́ть**

предло́г (**-а**) *м* pretext; (*Линг*) preposition; **под предло́гом** +*gen* on the pretext of

предложе́ни|е (**-я**) *ср* suggestion, proposal; (*замужества*) proposal; (*Комм*) offer; (*Линг*) sentence; **де́лать** (*perf* **сде́лать**) **предложе́ние кому́-н** (*девушке*) to propose to sb; (*Комм*) to make sb an offer; **вноси́ть** (*perf* **внести́**) **предложе́ние** (*на собрании*) to propose a motion

предл|ожи́ть (**-ожу́, -о́жишь**; *impf* **предлага́ть**) *сов перех* to offer; (*план, кандидатуру*) to suggest, propose ▷ *неперех* to suggest, propose

предло́жный *прил* (*Линг*) prepositional

предме́т (**-а**) *м* object; (*обсуждения, изучения*) subject

пре́д|ок (**-ка**) *м* ancestor

предоста́в|ить (**-лю, -ишь**) *сов перех*: **предоста́вить что-н кому́-н** to give sb sth ▷ *неперех*: **предоста́вить кому́-н** +*infin* (*выбирать, решать*) to let sb do

предостереже́ни|е (**-я**) *ср* warning

предостер|е́чь (**-егу́, -ежёшь** *etc*, **-егу́т**; *pt* **-ёг, -егла́**, *impf* **предостерега́ть**) *сов перех*: **предостере́чь кого́-н (от** +*gen*) to warn sb (against)

предотвра|ти́ть (**-щу́, -ти́шь**; *impf* **предотвраща́ть**) *сов перех* to prevent; (*войну, кризис*) to avert

предохрани́тель (**-я**) *м* safety device; (*Элек*) fuse (*Brit*), fuze (*US*)

предохран|и́ть (**-ю́, -и́шь**; *impf* **предохраня́ть**) *сов перех* to protect

предположи́тельно *нареч* supposedly

предпол|ожи́ть (**-ожу́, -о́жишь**; *impf* **предполага́ть**) *сов перех* (*допустить возможность*) to assume, suppose; **предполо́жим** (*возможно*) let's assume *or* suppose

предпосле́дний *прил* (*номер, серия*) penultimate; (*в очереди*) last but one

предприи́мчивый *прил* enterprising

предпринима́тель (**-я**) *м* entrepreneur, businessman (*мн* businessmen); **предпринима́тельств|о** (**-а**) *ср* enterprise

предпринять (-иму́, -и́мешь; pt -и́нял, -иняла́, impf **предпринима́ть**) сов перех to undertake

предприя́ти|е (-я) ср plant; (Комм) enterprise, business

предрассу́д|ок (-ка) м prejudice

председа́тел|ь (-я) м chairman (мн chairmen)

предсказа́ни|е (-я) ср prediction; **предск|аза́ть** (-ажу́, -а́жешь; impf **предска́зывать**) сов перех to predict

предсме́ртный прил (агония) death; (воля) last

представи́тел|ь (-я) м representative; **представи́тельный** прил representative; **представи́тельств|о** (-а) ср (Полит) representation; дипломати́ческое представи́тельство diplomatic corps

предста́в|ить (-лю, -ишь; impf **представля́ть**) сов перех to present; **представля́ть** (perf **предста́вить**) кого́-н кому́-н (познако́мить) to introduce sb to sb; **представля́ть** (perf **предста́вить**) (себе́) to imagine; **предста́виться** (impf **представля́ться**) несов возв (при знако́мстве) to introduce o.s.; (возмо́жность) to present itself

представле́ни|е (-я) ср presentation; (Теа́тр) performance; (зна́ние) idea; не име́ть (impf) (никако́го) представле́ния о +prp to have no idea about

представля́|ть (-ю) несов от **предста́вить** ▷ перех (организа́цию, страну́) to represent; **представля́ть** (impf) (себе́) что-н (понима́ть) to understand sth; **представля́ться** несов от **предста́виться**

предсто|я́ть (3sg -и́т) несов to lie ahead

предубежде́ни|е (-я) ср prejudice

предупре|ди́ть (-жу́, -ди́шь; impf **предупрежда́ть**) сов перех to warn; (останови́ть) to prevent

предупрежде́ни|е (-я) ср warning; (ава́рии, заболева́ния) prevention

предусм|отре́ть (-отрю́, -о́тришь; impf **предусма́тривать**) сов перех (уче́сть) to foresee; (пригото́виться) to provide for; **предусмотри́тельный** прил prudent

предчу́встви|е (-я) ср premonition

предше́ствующий прил previous

предъ|яви́ть (-явлю́, -я́вишь; impf **предъявля́ть**) сов перех (па́спорт, биле́т итп) to show; (доказа́тельства) to produce; (тре́бования, прете́нзии) to make; (иск) to bring; **предъявля́ть** (perf **предъяви́ть**) пра́ва на что-н to lay claim to sth

предыду́щий прил previous

предысто́ри|я (-и) ж background

прее́мник (-а) м successor

пре́жде нареч (в про́шлом) formerly; (снача́ла) first ▷ предл +gen before; **пре́жде всего́** first of all; **пре́жде чем** before

преждевре́менный прил premature

пре́жний прил former

презента́ци|я (-и) ж presentation

презервати́в (-а) м condom

президе́нт (-а) м president

презира́|ть (-ю) несов перех to despise

презре́ни|е (-я) ср contempt

преиму́щество (-а) ср advantage

прейскура́нт (-а) м price list

преклоне́ни|е (-я) ср: преклоне́ние (пе́ред +instr) admiration (for)

преклоня́|ться (-юсь) несов возв: преклоня́ться пе́ред +instr to admire

прекра́сно нареч (сде́лать) brilliantly; част прекра́сно! excellent!; ты прекра́сно зна́ешь, что ты не прав you know perfectly well that you are wrong

прекра́сный прил beautiful; (врач, результа́т) excellent

прекра|ти́ть (-щу́, -ти́шь; impf **прекраща́ть**) сов перех to stop ▷ непере́х +infin to stop doing; **прекрати́ться** (impf **прекраща́ться**) сов возв (дождь, заня́тия) to stop; (отноше́ния) to end

преле́стный прил charming

пре́лест|ь (-и) ж charm

прелю́ди|я (-и) ж prelude

пре́ми|я (-и) ж (рабо́тнику) bonus; (победи́телю) prize; (Комм) premium

премье́р (-а) м premier

премье́р|а (-ы) ж première

премье́р-мини́стр (-а) м prime minister, premier

пренебрега́|ть (-ю) несов от **пренебре́чь**

пренебреже́ни|е (-я) ср (зако́нами итп) disregard; (: обя́занностями) neglect; (высокоме́рие) disdain

пренебре́|чь (-гу́, -жёшь etc, -гу́т; pt -ёг, -егла́, impf **пренебрега́ть**) сов (+instr. опа́сностью) to disregard; (бога́тством, пра́вилами) to scorn; (сове́том, про́сьбой) to ignore

пре́ни|я (-й) мн debate ед

преоблада́|ть (3sg -ет) несов: преоблада́ть (над +instr) to predominate (over)

преобразова́ни|е (-я) ср transformation; **преобраз|ова́ть** (-у́ю; impf **преобразо́вывать**) сов перех to transform

преодоле́|ть (-ю; impf **преодолева́ть**) сов перех to overcome; (барье́р) to clear

препара́т (-а) м (Мед: также медици́нский препара́т) drug

препина́ни|е (-я) ср: зна́ки препина́ния punctuation marks

преподава́тел|ь (-я) м (шко́лы, ку́рсов) teacher; (ву́за) lecturer

преподава́|ть (-ю́, -ёшь) несов перех to teach

преподн|ести́ (-есу́, -есёшь; pt -ёс, -есла́, impf **преподноси́ть**) сов перех:

преподнести́ что-н кому́-н to present sb with sth

препя́тстви|е (-я) *ср* obstacle

препя́тств|овать (ую; *perf* воспрепя́тствовать) *несов* +*dat* to impede

прерв|а́ть (-у́, -ёшь; *impf* прерыва́ть) *сов перех* (*разговор, работу итп*) to cut short; (*отношения*) to break off; (*говоря́щего*) to interrupt; прерва́ться (*impf* прерыва́ться) *сов возв* (*разговор, игра*) to be cut short; (*отношения*) to be broken off

пресе́|чь (-еку́, -ечёшь *etc*, -еку́т; *pt* -ёк, -екла́, *impf* пресека́ть) *сов перех* to suppress

пресле́довани|е (-я) *ср* pursuit; (*сексуальное*) harassment; (*инакомыслия*) persecution; пресле́д|овать (-ую) *несов перех* to pursue; (*инакомыслящих*) to persecute; (*насмешками*) to harass

пресловý́тый *прил* notorious

пресмыка́ющ|ееся (-егося) *ср* reptile

пресново́дный *прил* freshwater

пре́сный *прил* (*вода*) fresh; (*пища*) bland

пресс (-а) *м* (*Тех*) press

пре́сс|а (-ы) *ж собир* the press

пресс-конфере́нци|я (-и) *ж* press conference

пресс-рели́з (-а) *м* press release

пресс-секрета́р|ь (-я́) *м* press secretary

пресс-це́нтр (-а) *м* press office

престаре́л|ый *прил* aged; дом (для) престаре́лых old people's home

прести́ж (-а) *м* prestige; прести́жный *прил* prestigious

преступле́ни|е (-я) *ср* crime; престу́пник (-а) *м* criminal; престу́пность (-и) *ж* (*количество*) crime; престу́пный *прил* criminal

претенд|ова́ть (-у́ю) *несов*: претендова́ть на +*acc* (*стреми́ться*) to aspire to; (*заявля́ть права*) to lay claim to

прете́нзи|я (-и) *ж* (*обычно мн*: на насле́дство) claim; (: *на ум, на красоту итп*) pretension; (*жа́лоба*) complaint

преткнове́ни|е (-я) *ср*: ка́мень преткнове́ния stumbling block

преувели́ч|ить (-у, -ишь; *impf* преувели́чивать) *сов перех* to exaggerate

преуме́ньш|ить (-у, -ишь; *impf* преуменьша́ть) *сов перех* to underestimate

преуспе́|ть (-ю; *impf* преуспева́ть) *сов* (*в учёбе*) to be successful; (*в жизни*) to prosper, thrive

прецеде́нт (-а) *м* precedent

при *предл* (+*prp*: *возле*) by, near; (*о части*) at; (*в присутствии*) in front of; (*о времени*) under; (*о наличии чего-н у кого-н*) on; он всегда́ при деньга́х he always has money on him; я здесь ни при чём it has nothing to do with me

приба́в|ить (-лю, -ишь; *impf* прибавля́ть) *сов перех* to add; (*увеличить*) to increase; приба́виться (*impf* прибавля́ться) *сов возв* (*проблемы, работа итп*) to mount up ▷ *безл* (*воды в реке*) to rise

прибежа́ть (*как* бежа́ть; см Table 20) *сов* to come running

приб|и́ть (-ью, -ьёшь; *imper* -е́й(те), *impf* прибива́ть) *сов перех* (*гвоздями*) to nail

приближа́|ть(ся) (-ю(сь)) *несов от* прибли́зить(ся)

приближе́ни|е (-я) *ср* approach

приблизи́тельный *прил* approximate

прибли́|зить (-жу, -зишь; *impf* приближа́ть) *сов перех* (*придвинуть*) to move nearer; (*ускорить*) to bring nearer; прибли́зиться (*impf* приближа́ться) *сов возв* to approach

прибо́|й (-я) *м* breakers *мн*

прибо́р (-а) *м* (*измерительный*) device; (*оптический*) instrument; (*нагревательный*) appliance; (*бритвенный*) set; столо́вый прибо́р setting

прибыва́|ть (-ю) *несов от* прибы́ть

при́бы́л|ь (-и) *ж* profit; при́быльный *прил* profitable

прибы́ти|е (-я) *ср* arrival; прибы́ть (*как* быть; см Table 21; *impf* прибыва́ть) *сов* to arrive

приватизи́р|овать (-ую) (*не*)*сов перех* to privatize

прив|езти́ (-езу́, -езёшь; *pt* -ёз, -езла́, *impf* привози́ть) *сов перех* to bring

прив|ести́ (-еду́, -едёшь; *pt* -ёл, -ела́) *сов от* вести́ ▷ (*impf* приводи́ть) *перех* (*сопроводить*) to bring; (*подлеж: дорога: к дому*) to take; (*пример*) to give; привести́ (*perf*) в у́жас to horrify; приводи́ть (*perf* привести́) в восто́рг to delight; приводи́ть (*perf* привести́) в изумле́ние to astonish; приводи́ть (*perf* привести́) в исполне́ние to put into effect; приводи́ть (*perf* привести́) в поря́док to put in order

приве́т (-а) *м* regards *мн*; (*разг*: при встрече) hi; (: *при расставании*) bye; передава́ть (*perf* переда́ть) кому́-н приве́т to give sb one's regards; приве́тливый *прил* friendly; приве́тстви|е (-я) *ср* (*при встрече*) greeting; (*делегации*) welcome; приве́тств|овать (-ую; *perf* поприве́тствовать) *несов перех* to welcome

приви́в|ка (-ки; *gen pl* -ок) *ж* (*Мед*) vaccination

привиде́ни|е (-я) *ср* ghost

привиле́ги|я (-и) *ж* privilege

привин|ти́ть (-чу́, -ти́шь; *impf* приви́нчивать) *сов перех* to screw in

при́вкус (-а) *м* flavour (*Brit*), flavor (*US*)

привлека́тельный *прил* attractive

привлека́|ть (-ю) *несов от* привле́чь

привлечéни|е (-я) *ср* (*покупателей, внимания*) attraction; (*ресурсов*) use

привл|éчь (-екý, -ечёшь *etc*, -екýт; *pt* -ёк, -еклá, *impf* **привлекáть**) *сов перех* to attract; (*ресурсы*) to use; **привлекáть** (*perf* **привлéчь**) когó-н +*dat* (*к работе, к участию*) to involve sb in; (*к судý*) to take sb to; **привлекáть** (*perf* **привлéчь**) когó-н к отвéтственности to call sb to account

прив|одить (-ожý, -óдишь) *несов от* **привести**

прив|озить (-ожý, -óзишь) *несов от* **привезти**

привы́к|нуть (-ну; *pt* -, -ла, *impf* **привыкáть**) *сов* +*infin* to get into the habit of doing; **привыкáть** (*perf* **привы́кнуть**) к +*dat* (*к новому*) to get used to

привы́ч|ка (-ки; *gen pl* -ек) *ж* habit; **привы́чный** *прил* familiar

привя́занност|ь (-и) *ж* attachment

привя́з|áть (-яжý, -я́жешь; *impf* **привя́зывать**) *сов перех*: **привязáть что-н/когó-н к** +*dat* to tie sth/sb to; **привязáться** (*impf* **привя́зываться**) *сов возв*: **привязáться к** +*dat* (*к сиденью*) to fasten o.s. to; (*полюбить*) to become attached to

приглаcи́тельный *прил*: **приглаcи́тельный билéт** invitation

пригла|cить (-шý, -cишь; *impf* **приглашáть**) *сов перех* to invite

приглашéни|е (-я) *ср* invitation

приговор|и́ть (-ю́, -и́шь; *impf* **пригова́ривать**) *сов перех*: **приговори́ть когó-н к** +*dat* to sentence sb to

приго|ди́ться (-жýсь, -ди́шься) *сов возв* +*dat* to be useful to; **приго́дный** *прил* suitable

пригор|éть (*3sg* -и́т, *impf* **пригорáть**) *сов* to burn

при́город (-а) *м* suburb; **при́городный** *прил* suburban; (*поезд*) commuter

приготóв|ить (-лю, -ишь) *сов от* **готóвить** ▷ (*impf* **приготáвливать**) *перех* to prepare; (*постель*) to make; **приготóвиться** *сов от* **готóвиться** ▷ *возв*: **приготóвиться (к** +*dat*) (*к путешествию*) to get ready (for); (*к уроку*) to prepare (o.s.) for

приготовлéни|е (-я) *ср* preparation

пригро|зи́ть (-жý, -зи́шь) *сов от* **грози́ть**

прида|вáть (-ю́, -ёшь) *несов от* **придáть**

придáть (*как* **дать**; *см* Table 16; *impf* **придавáть**) *сов*: **придáть чегó-н комý-н** (*увéренности*) to instil (*Brit*) *или* instill (*US*) sth in sb ▷ *перех*: **придáть что-н чемý-н** (*вид, форму*) to give sth to sth; (*важность*) to attach sth to sth

придáч|а (-и) *ж*: **в придáчу** in addition

придви́н|уть (-у; *impf* **придвигáть**) *сов перех*: **придви́нуть (к** +*dat*) to move over *или* up (to)

придéла|ть (-ю; *impf* **придéлывать**) *сов перех*: **придéлать что-н к** +*dat* to attach sth to

прид|ержáть (-ержý, -éржишь; *impf* **придéрживать**) *сов перех* (*дверь*) to hold (steady); (*лошадь*) to restrain

придéржива|ться (-юсь) *несов возв* (+*gen*: *взглядов*) to hold

придирáться (-юсь) *несов от* **придрáться**

приди́рчивый *прил* (*человек*) fussy; (*замечáние, взгляд*) critical

прид|рáться (-ерýсь, -ерёшься; *impf* **придирáться**) *сов возв*: **придрáться к** +*dat* to find fault with

придý *etc сов см* **прийти́**

придýма|ть (-ю; *impf* **придýмывать**) *сов перех* (*отговóрку, причину*) to think of *или* up; (*новый прибор*) to devise; (*песню, стихотворéние*) to make up

приéду *etc сов см* **приéхать**

приéзд (-а) *м* arrival

приезжá|ть (-ю) *несов от* **приéхать**

приём (-а) *м* reception; (*у врача*) surgery (*Brit*), office (*US*); (*Спорт*) technique; (*наказания, воздéйствия*) means; **в два/три приёма** in two/three attempts; **запи́сываться** (*perf* **записáться**) **на приём к** +*dat* to make an appointment with

приёмн|ая (-ой) *ж* (*также* **приёмная кóмната**) reception

приёмник (-а) *м* receiver; (*радио*) radio

приёмный *прил* (*часы*) reception; (*день*) visiting; (*экзамены*) entrance; (*комиссия*) selection; (*родители, дети*) adoptive

приéхать (*как* **éхать**; *см* Table 19; *impf* **приезжáть**) *сов* to arrive *или* come (*by transport*)

приж|áть (-мý, -мёшь; *impf* **прижимáть**) *сов перех*: **прижáть что-н/когó-н к** +*dat* to press sth/sb to *или* against; **прижáться** (*impf* **прижимáться**) *сов возв*: **прижáться к** +*dat* to press o.s. against; (*к груди*) to snuggle up to

приз (-а; *nom pl* -ы́) *м* prize

призвáни|е (-я) *ср* (*к наукé итп*) vocation

приз|вáть (-овý, -овёшь; *pt* -вáл, -валá, *impf* **призывáть**) *сов перех* (*к борьбé, к защите*) to call; **призывáть** (*perf* **призвáть**) **к миру** to call for peace; **призывáть** (*perf* **призвáть**) **когó-н к порядку** to call sb to order; **призывáть** (*perf* **призвáть**) **в áрмию** to call up (to join the army)

приземл|и́ть (-ю́, -и́шь; *impf* **приземля́ть**) *сов перех* to land; **приземли́ться** (*impf* **приземля́ться**) *сов возв* to land

призна|вáть(ся) (-ю́(сь), -ёшь(ся)) *несов от* **признáть(ся)**

при́знак (-а) *м* (*кризиса, успéха*) sign; (*отравлéния*) symptom

признáни|е (-я) *ср* recognition; (*согласие*) acknowledgment; (*в любви*) declaration; (*в преступлении*) confession

призна́тельность (**-и**) *ж* gratitude; **призна́тельный** *прил* grateful

призна́ть (**-ю**; *impf* **признава́ть**) *сов перех* to recognize; (*счесть*): **призна́ть что-н/кого́-н** +*instr* to recognize sth/sb as; **призна́ться** (*impf* **признава́ться**) *сов возв*: **призна́ться кому́-н в чём-н** (*в преступлении*) to confess sth to sb; **признава́ться** (*perf* **призна́ться**) кому́-н в любви́ to make a declaration of love to sb

при́зрак (**-а**) *м* ghost

призы́в (**-а**) *м* call; (*в армию*) conscription, draft (*US*); (*лозунг*) slogan

призыва́ть (**-ю**) *несов от* **призва́ть**

призывни́к (**-а́**) *м* conscript

прийти́ (*как* **идти́**; *см* Table 18; *impf* **приходи́ть**) *сов* (*идя, достичь*) to come (*on foot*); (*телеграмма, письмо*) to arrive; (*весна, час свободы*) to come; (*достигнуть*): **прийти́ к** +*dat* (*к власти, к вы́воду*) to come to; (*к демокра́тии*) to achieve; **приходи́ть** (*perf* **прийти́**) в у́жас/недоуме́ние to be horrified/bewildered; **приходи́ть** (*perf* **прийти́**) в восто́рг to go into raptures; **приходи́ть** (*perf* **прийти́**) кому́-н в го́лову *или* на ум to occur to sb; **приходи́ть** (*perf* **прийти́**) в себя́ (*после обморока*) to come to *или* round; (*успоко́иться*) to come to one's senses; **прийти́сь** (*impf* **приходи́ться**) *сов возв*: **прийти́сь на** +*acc* to fall on; (**нам**) **придётся согласи́ться** we'll have to agree

прика́з (**-а**) *м* order; **приказа́ние** (**-я**) *ср* = **прика́з**; **приказа́ть** (**-ажу́, -а́жешь**; *impf* **прика́зывать**) *сов*: **приказа́ть кому́-н** +*infin* to order sb to do

прика́лывать (**-ю**) *несов от* **приколо́ть**

прикаса́ться (**-юсь**) *несов от* **прикосну́ться**

прикла́д (**-а**) *м* (*ружья́*) butt

прикла́дывать (**-ю**) *несов от* **приложи́ть**

прикле́ить (**-ю, -ишь**; *impf* **прикле́ивать**) *сов перех* to glue, stick; **прикле́иться** (*impf* **прикле́иваться**) *сов возв* to stick

приключе́ние (**-я**) *ср* adventure

прико|ло́ть (**-олю́, -о́лешь**; *impf* **прика́лывать**) *сов перех* to fasten

прикосну́|ться (**-у́сь, -ёшься**; *impf* **прикаса́ться**) *сов возв*: **прикосну́ться к** +*dat* to touch lightly

прикреп|и́ть (**-лю́, -и́шь**; *impf* **прикрепля́ть**) *сов перех*: **прикрепи́ть что-н/кого́-н к** +*dat* to attach sth/sb to

прикры́|ть (**-о́ю, -о́ешь**; *impf* **прикрыва́ть**) *сов перех* to cover; (*закры́ть*) to close (over)

прику|ри́ть (**-урю́, -у́ришь**; *impf* **прику́ривать**) *сов* to get a light (*from a lit cigarette*)

прила́в|ок (**-ка**) *м* (*в магазине*) counter; (*на ры́нке*) stall

прилага́тельн|ое (**-ого**) *ср* (*Линг*: *также* **и́мя прилага́тельное**) adjective

прилага́|ть (**-ю**) *несов от* **приложи́ть**

прилега́|ть (*3sg* **-ет**) *несов*: **прилега́ть к** чему́-н *несов* to fit sth tightly

приле|те́ть (**-чу́, -ти́шь**; *impf* **прилета́ть**) *сов* to arrive (*by air*), fly in

прил|е́чь (**-я́гу, -я́жешь** etc, **-я́гут**; *pt* **-ёг, -егла́**) *сов* to lie down for a while

прили́в (**-а**) *м* (*в мо́ре*) tide

прили́п|нуть (**-ну**; *pt* **-, -ла**, *impf* **прилипа́ть** *или* **ли́пнуть**) *сов*: **прили́пнуть к** +*dat* to stick to

прили́чный *прил* (*челове́к*) decent; (*су́мма, результа́т*) fair, decent

приложе́ни|е (**-я**) *ср* (*зна́ний, эне́ргии*) application; (*к журна́лу*) supplement; (*к докуме́нту*) addendum (*мн* addenda); (*Комп*) app

прил|ожи́ть (**-ожу́, -о́жишь**; *impf* **прилага́ть**) *сов перех* (*присоедини́ть*) to attach; (*си́лу, зна́ния*) to apply; **прикла́дывать** (*perf* **приложи́ть**) что-н +*dat* (*ру́ку: ко лбу*) to put sth to; **умá не приложу́** (*разг*) I don't have a clue

примене́ни|е (**-я**) *ср* (*ору́жия, маши́н*) use; (*лека́рств*) application; (*мер, ме́тода*) adoption

прим|ени́ть (**-еню́, -е́нишь**; *impf* **применя́ть**) *сов перех* (*ме́ры*) to implement; (*си́лу*) to use, apply; **применя́ть** (*perf* **примени́ть**) что-н (**к** +*dat*) (*ме́тод, тео́рию*) to apply sth (to)

применя́|ться (*3sg* **-ется**) *несов* (*испо́льзоваться*) to be used

приме́р (**-а**) *м* example

приме́р|ка (**-ки**; *gen pl* **-ок**) *ж* trying on

приме́рно *нареч* (*см прил*) in an exemplary fashion; (*о́коло*) approximately

при́месь (**-и**) *ж* dash

приме́т|а (**-ы**) *ж* (*при́знак*) sign; (*суеве́рная*) omen

примета́|ть (**-ю**; *impf* **примётывать**) *сов перех* to stitch on

примеча́ни|е (**-я**) *ср* note

примити́вный *прил* primitive

примо́рский *прил* seaside

принадлеж|а́ть (**-у́, -и́шь**) *несов* +*dat* to belong to; (*заслу́га*) to go to

принадле́жность (**-и**) *ж* characteristic; (*обычно мн: компле́кт*) tackle; (*: пи́сьменные*) accessories *мн*

прин|ести́ (**-есу́, -есёшь**; *pt* **-ёс, -есла́**, *impf* **приноси́ть**) *сов перех* to bring; (*извине́ния, благода́рность*) to express; (*прися́гу*) to take; **приноси́ть** (*perf* **принести́**) по́льзу to be of use to; **приноси́ть** (*perf* **принести́**) вред +*dat* to harm

принима́|ть(ся) (**-ю(сь)**) *несов от* **приня́ть(ся)**

прин|оси́ть (**-ошу́, -о́сишь**) *несов от* **принести́**

при́нтер (**-а**) *м* (*Комп*) printer

принуди́тельный *прил* forced

прину́ди́ть (**-жу, -дишь;** *impf* **принужда́ть**) *сов перех:* **принуди́ть кого́-н/что́-н к чему́-н/**+*infin* to force sb/sth into sth/to do

принц (**-а**) *м* prince; **принце́сс|а** (**-ы**) *ж* princess

при́нцип (**-а**) *м* principle

при|ня́ть (**-му́, -мешь;** *pt* **-нял, -няла́,** *impf* **принима́ть**) *сов перех* to take; (*подарок, условия*) to accept; (*пост*) to take up; (*гостей, телеграмму*) to receive; (*закон, резолюцию*) to pass; (*отношение, вид*) to take on; (*христианство итп*) to adopt; **принима́ть** (*perf* **приня́ть**) **в/на** +*acc* (*в университет, на работу*) to accept for; **принима́ть** (*perf* **приня́ть**) **что-н/кого́-н за** +*acc* to mistake sth/sb for; (*счесть*) to take sth/sb as; **приня́ться** (*impf* **принима́ться**) *сов возв:* **приня́ться** +*infin* (*приступить*) to get down to doing; **принима́ться** (*perf* **приня́ться**) **за** +*acc* (*приступить*) to get down to

приобр|ести́ (**-ету́, -етёшь;** *pt* **-ёл, -ела́,** *impf* **приобрета́ть**) *сов перех* to acquire, obtain; (*друзей, врагов*) to make

приорите́т (**-а**) *м* priority

приостан|ови́ть (**-овлю́, -о́вишь;** *impf* **приостана́вливать**) *сов перех* to suspend

припа́д|ок (**-ка**) *м* (*Мед*) attack

припа́с|ы (**-ов**) *мн* supplies; (*Воен*) ammunition *ед*

припе́в (**-а**) *м* (*песни*) chorus, refrain

припи|са́ть (**-шу́, -́шешь;** *impf* **припи́сывать**) *сов перех* to add; **припи́сывать** (*perf* **приписа́ть**) **что-н кому́-н** to attribute sth to sb

припо́лз|ти́ (**-у́, -ёшь;** *impf* **приполза́ть**) *сов перех* to crawl in

припо́мн|ить (**-ю, -ишь;** *impf* **припомина́ть**) *сов перех* to remember

приправ|а (**-ы**) *ж* seasoning

приравня́|ть (**-ю;** *impf* **приравнивать**) *сов перех:* **приравня́ть кого́-н/что́-н к** +*dat* to equate sb/sth with

приро́д|а (**-ы**) *ж* nature; (*места вне города*) countryside; **приро́дный** *прил* natural

прирост (**-а**) *м* (*населения*) growth; (*доходов, урожая*) increase

приручи́ть (**-у́, -́ишь;** *impf* **прируча́ть**) *сов перех* to tame

приса́жива|ться (**-юсь**) *несов от* **присе́сть**

присво́|ить (**-ю, -ишь;** *impf* **присва́ивать**) *сов перех* (*чужое*) to appropriate; (*дать*): **присво́ить что-н кому́-н** (*звание*) to confer sth on sb

приседа́ни|е (**-я**) *ср* squatting (*physical exercise*)

прис|е́сть (**-я́ду, -я́дешь;** *impf* **приседа́ть**) *сов* to squat ▷ (*impf* **приса́живаться**) (*на стул*) to sit down (*for a short while*)

приск|ака́ть (**-ачу́, -а́чешь;** *impf* **приска́кивать**) *сов* to gallop *или* come galloping up

при|сла́ть (**-шлю́, -шлёшь;** *impf* **присыла́ть**) *сов перех* to send

прислон|и́ть (**-ю́, -́ишь;** *impf* **прислоня́ть**) *сов перех:* **прислони́ть что-н к** +*dat* to lean sth against; **прислони́ться** (*impf* **прислоня́ться**) *сов возв:* **прислони́ться к** +*dat* to lean against

прислу́жива|ть (**-ю**) *несов* (+*dat:* *официант*) to wait on

прислу́ша|ться (**-юсь;** *impf* **прислу́шиваться**) *сов возв:* **прислу́шаться к** +*dat* (*к звуку*) to listen to

присмо́тр (**-а**) *м* care

присм|отре́ть (**-отрю́, -о́тришь;** *impf* **присма́тривать**) *сов:* **присмотре́ть за** +*instr* to look after; (*найти*) to spot

присни́ться (*3sg* **-́ится**) *сов от* **сни́ться**

присоедине́ни|е (**-я**) *ср* attachment; (*провода*) connection; (*территории*) annexation

присоедин|и́ть (**-ю́, -́ишь;** *impf* **присоединя́ть**) *сов перех:* **присоедини́ть что-н к** +*dat* to attach sth to; (*провод*) to connect sth to; (*территорию*) to annex sth to; **присоедини́ться** (*impf* **присоединя́ться**) *сов возв:* **присоедини́ться к** +*dat* to join; (*к мнению*) to support

приспосо́б|ить (**-лю, -ишь;** *impf* **приспоса́бливать**) *сов перех* to adapt; **приспосо́биться** (*impf* **приспоса́бливаться**) *сов возв* (*делать что-н*) to learn how; (*к условиям*) to adapt (*o.s.*)

приста|ва́ть (**-ю́, -ёшь**) *несов от* **приста́ть**

приста́в|ить (**-лю, -ишь;** *impf* **приставля́ть**) *сов перех:* **приста́вить что-н к** +*dat* to put sth against

приста́в|ка (**-ки;** *gen pl* **-ок**) *ж* (*Линг*) prefix; (*Тех*) attachment

приставля́|ть (**-ю**) *несов от* **приста́вить**

при́стальный *прил* (*взгляд, внимание*) fixed; (*интерес, наблюдение*) intent

при́стан|ь (**-и**) *ж* pier

приста́|ть (**-ну, -нешь;** *impf* **пристава́ть**) *сов:* **приста́ть к** +*dat* (*прилипнуть*) to stick to; (*присоединиться*) to join; (*разг: с вопросами*) to pester; (*причалить*) to moor

пристегн|у́ть (**-у́, -ёшь;** *impf* **пристёгивать**) *сов перех* to fasten; **пристегну́ться** (*impf* **пристёгиваться**) *сов возв* (*в самолёте итп*) to fasten one's seat belt

пристра́ива|ть (**-ю**) *несов от* **пристро́ить**

пристре́л|ить (**-елю́, -́елишь;** *impf* **пристре́ливать**) *сов перех* (*животное*) to put down

пристро́|ить (-ю, -ишь; *impf* **пристра́ивать**) *сов перех* (*комнату*) to build on; **пристро́|йка** (-йки; *gen pl* -ек) *ж* extension

при́ступ (-а) *м* (*атака, сердечный*) attack; (*смеха, гнева, кашля*) fit; **прист|упи́ть** (-уплю́, -у́пишь; *impf* **приступа́ть**) *сов*: **приступи́ть к** +*dat* (*начать*) to commence

прис|уди́ть (-ужу́, -у́дишь; *impf* **присужда́ть**) *сов перех*: **присуди́ть что-н кому́-н** to award sth to sb; (*учёную степень*) to confer sth on sb

прису́тстви|е (-я) *ср* presence; **прису́тств|овать** (-ую) *несов* to be present

прису́тствующ|ие (-их) *мн* those present *мн*

присыла́|ть (-ю) *несов от* **присла́ть**

прися́г|а (-и) *ж* oath

прит|ащи́ть (-ащу́, -а́щишь; *impf* **прита́скивать**) *сов перех* to drag

притвор|и́ться (-ю́сь, -и́шься; *impf* **притворя́ться**) *сов возв* +*instr* to pretend to be

прити́х|нуть (-ну, -нешь; *pt* -, -ла, *impf* **притиха́ть**) *сов* to grow quiet

прито́к (-а) *м* (*река*) tributary; (+*gen*: *энергии, средств*) supply of; (*населения*) influx of

прито́м *союз* and what's more

прито́н (-а) *м* den

при́торный *прил* sickly sweet

прит|упи́ться (*3sg* -у́пится, *impf* **притупля́ться**) *сов возв* (*нож*) to go blunt; (*перен: внимание итп*) to diminish; (: *чувства*) to fade; (: *слух*) to fail

притяза́ни|е (-я) *ср*: **притяза́ние на** +*acc* claim to

приуро́ч|ить (-у, -ишь) *сов перех*: **приуро́чить что-н к** +*dat* to time sth to coincide with

приу|чи́ть (-чу́, -у́чишь; *impf* **приуча́ть**) *сов перех*: **приучи́ть кого́-н к** +*dat*/+*infin* to train sb for/to do; **приучи́ться** (*impf* **приуча́ться**) *сов возв*: **приучи́ться к** +*dat*/+*infin* to train for/ to do

прихв|ати́ть (-ачу́, -а́тишь; *сов перех* (*разг*: взять) to take

прихо́д (-а) *м* arrival; (*Комм*) receipts *мн*; (*Рел*) parish; **прихо́д и расхо́д** (*Комм*) credit and debit

прих|оди́ть (-ожу́, -о́дишь) *несов от* **прийти́**; **приходи́ться** *несов от* **прийти́сь** ▷ *возв*: **приходи́ться кому́-н ро́дственником** to be sb's relative

прих|одова́ть (-ую; *perf* **оприхо́довать**) *несов перех* (*Комм*: *сумму*) to enter (*in receipt book*)

приходя́щ|ий *прил* nonresident; **приходя́щая ня́ня** babysitter

прихо́ж|ая (-ей) *ж* entrance hall

прихожу́(сь) *несов см* **приходи́ть(ся)**

при́хот|ь (-и) *ж* whim

прице́л (-а) *м* (*ружья, пушки*) sight

прице́л|иться (-юсь, -ишься; *impf* **прице́ливаться**) *сов возв* to take aim

прице́п (-а) *м* trailer; **прице́|пить** (-еплю́, -е́пишь; *impf* **прицепля́ть**) *сов перех* (*вагон*) to couple

прича́л (-а) *м* mooring; (*пассажирский*) quay; (*грузовой, ремонтный*) dock; **прича́л|ить** (-ю, -ишь; *impf* **прича́ливать**) *сов* (не)*перех* to moor

прича́сти|е (-я) *ср* (*Линг*) participle; (*Рел*) communion

прича|сти́ть (-щу́, -сти́шь; *impf* **причаща́ть**) *сов перех* (*Рел*) to give communion to; **причасти́ться** (*impf* **причаща́ться**) *сов возв* (*Рел*) to receive communion

прича́стный *прил* (*связанный*): **прича́стный к** +*dat* connected with

причаща́|ть(ся) (-ю(сь)) *несов от* **причасти́ть(ся)**

причём *союз* moreover

прич|еса́ть (-ешу́, -е́шешь; *impf* **причёсывать**) (*расчёской*) to comb; (*щёткой*) to brush; **причёсывать** (*perf* **причеса́ть**) **кого́-н** to comb/brush sb's hair; **причеса́ться** (*impf* **причёсываться**) *сов возв* (*см перех*) to comb one's hair; to brush one's hair

причёс|ка (-ки; *gen pl* -ок) *ж* hairstyle

причи́н|а (-ы) *ж* (*то, что вызывает*) cause; (*обоснование*) reason; **по причи́не** +*gen* on account of

причин|и́ть (-ю́, -и́шь; *impf* **причиня́ть**) *сов перех* to cause

причу́д|а (-ы) *ж* whim

пришёл(ся) *сов см* **прийти́(сь)**

приш|и́ть (-ью́, -ьёшь; *imper* -е́й(те), *impf* **пришива́ть**) *сов перех* to sew on

пришла́ *etc сов см* **прийти́**

прищем|и́ть (-лю́, -и́шь; *impf* **прищемля́ть**) *сов перех* to catch

прищу́р|ить (-ю, -ишь; *impf* **прищу́ривать**) *сов перех* (*глаза*) to screw up; **прищу́риться** (*impf* **прищу́риваться**) *сов возв* to screw up one's eyes

прию|ти́ть (-чу́, -ти́шь) *сов перех* to shelter; **приюти́ться** *сов возв* to take shelter

прия́тел|ь (-я) *м* friend

прия́тно *нареч* (*удивлён*) pleasantly ▷ *как сказ* it's nice *или* pleasant; **мне прия́тно э́то слы́шать** I'm glad to hear that; **о́чень прия́тно** (*при знакомстве*) pleased to meet you; **прия́тный** *прил* pleasant

про *предл* +*acc* about

про́б|а (-ы) *ж* (*испытание*) test; (*образец*) sample; (*золота*) standard (*of quality*); (*клеймо*) hallmark

пробе́г (-а) *м* (*Спорт*) race; (: *лыжный*) run; (*Авт*) mileage

пробежа́ть (*как* **бежа́ть**; *см Table 20*;

impf **пробега́ть**) *сов перех* (*текст*) to skim; (*5 километров*) to cover ⊳ *неперех* (*время*) to pass; (*миновать бегом*): **пробежа́ть ми́мо** +*gen* to run past; (*появиться и исчезнуть*): **пробежа́ть по** +*dat* (*шум, дрожь*) to run through; **пробежа́ться** *сов возв* to run

пробе́л (-а) *м* (*также перен*) gap

пробива́|**ть(ся)** (-ю(сь)) *несов от* **проби́ть(ся)**

пробира́|**ться** (-юсь) *несов от* **пробра́ться**

проб|**и́ть** (-ью́, -ьёшь) *сов от* **бить** ⊳ (*impf* **пробива́ть**) *перех* (*дыру*) to knock; (*крышу, стену*) to make a hole in; **проби́ться** (*impf* **пробива́ться**) *сов возв* (*прорваться*) to fight one's way through; (*растения*) to push through *или* up

про́б|**ка** (-ки; *gen pl* -ок) *ж* cork; (*перен: на дороге*) jam; (*Элек*) fuse (*Brit*), fuze (*US*)

пробле́м|**а** (-ы) *ж* problem

проблемати́чный *прил* problematic(al)

про́бный *прил* trial

про́б|**овать** (-ую, *perf* **попро́бовать**) *несов перех* (*пирог, вино*) to taste; (*пытаться*) +*infin* to try to do

пробо́ин|**а** (-ы) *ж* hole

пробо́р (-а) *м* parting (*of hair*)

проб|**ра́ться** (-еру́сь, -ерёшься; *impf* **пробира́ться**) *сов возв* (*с трудом пройти*) to fight one's way through; (*тихо пройти*) to steal past *или* through

пробы́ть (*как быть*; *см Table 21*) *сов* (*прожить*) to stay, remain

прова́л (-а) *м* (*в почве, в стене*) hole; (*перен: неудача*) flop; (: *памяти*) failure

прова́л|**ить** (-алю́, -а́лишь; *impf* **прова́ливать**) *сов перех* (*крышу, пол*) to cause to collapse; (*разг: перен: дело, затею*) to botch up; (: *студента*) to fail; **провали́ться** (*impf* **прова́ливаться**) *сов возв* (*человек*) to fall; (*крыша*) to collapse; (*разг: перен: студент, попытка*) to fail; **как сквозь зе́млю провали́лся** he disappeared into thin air

проведу́ *etc сов см* **провести́**

пров|**езти́** (-езу́, -езёшь; *pt* -ёз, -езла́, *impf* **провози́ть**) *сов перех* (*незаконно*) to smuggle; (*везя, доставить*): **провезти́ по** +*dat*/**ми́мо** +*gen*/**че́рез** +*acc* to take along/past/across

прове́р|**ить** (-ю, -ишь; *impf* **проверя́ть**) *сов перех* to check; (*знание, двигатель*) to test; **прове́риться** (*impf* **проверя́ться**) *сов возв* (*у врача*) to get a check up

прове́р|**ка** (-ки; *gen pl* -ок) *ж* (*см глаг*) check-up; test

пров|**ести́** (-еду́, -едёшь; *pt* -ёл, -ела́, *impf* **проводи́ть**) *сов перех* (*черту, границу*) to draw; (*дорогу*) to build; (*план, реформу*) to implement; (*урок, репетицию*) to hold; (*операцию*) to carry out; (*детство, день*) to spend; **проводи́ть**

(*perf* **провести́**) **ми́мо** +*gen*/**че́рез** +*acc* (*людей*) to take past/across

прове́тр|**ить** (-ю, -ишь; *impf* **прове́тривать**) *сов перех* to air; **прове́триться** (*impf* **прове́триваться**) *сов возв* (*комната, одежда*) to have an airing

провин|**и́ться** (-ю́сь, -и́шься) *сов возв*: **провини́ться** (**в** +*prp*) to be guilty (of)

провинциа́льный *прил* provincial

прови́нци|**я** (-и) *ж* province

про́вод (-а; *nom pl* -а́) *м* cable

пров|**оди́ть** (-ожу́, -о́дишь) *несов от* **провести́** ⊳ (*impf* **провожа́ть**) *сов перех* to see off; (*провести́*) глаза́ми/взгля́дом кого́-н to follow sb with one's eyes/gaze

прово́д|**ка** (-ки; *gen pl* -ок) *ж* (*Элек*) wiring

проводни́к (-а́) *м* (*в горах*) guide; (*в поезде*) steward (*Brit*), porter (*US*)

про́вод|**ы** (-ов) *мн* (*прощание*) send-off *ед*

провожа́|**ть** (-ю) *несов от* **проводи́ть**

провожу́ (*не*)*сов см* **проводи́ть**

прово́з (-а) *м* (*багажа*) transport; (*незаконный*) smuggling

провозгла|**си́ть** (-шу́, -си́шь; *impf* **провозглаша́ть**) *сов перех* to proclaim

пров|**ози́ть** (-ожу́, -о́зишь) *несов от* **провезти́**

провока́ционный *прил* provocative

про́волок|**а** (-и) *ж* wire

провоци́р|**овать** (-ую, *perf* **спровоци́ровать**) *несов перех* to provoke

прогиба́|**ть(ся)** (-ю(сь)) *несов от* **прогну́ть(ся)**

прогл|**оти́ть** (-очу́, -о́тишь; *impf* **прогла́тывать** *или* **глота́ть**) *сов перех* (*также перен*) to swallow

прог|**на́ть** (-оню́, -о́нишь; *pt* -на́л, -нала́, *impf* **прогоня́ть**) *сов перех* (*заставить уйти*) to turn out

прогно́з (-а) *м* forecast

прогоня́|**ть** (-ю) *несов от* **прогна́ть**

програ́мм|**а** (-ы) *ж* programme (*Brit*), program (*US*); (*Полит*) manifesto; (*также вещательная програ́мма*) channel; (*Просвещ*) curriculum; (*Комп*) program

программи́р|**овать** (-ую; *perf* **запрограмми́ровать**) *несов перех* (*Комп*) to program

программи́ст (-а) *м* (*Комп*) programmer

програ́ммный *прил* programme (*Brit*), programed (*US*); (*экзамен, зачёт*) set; **програ́ммное обеспе́чение** (*Комп*) software

прогре́сс (-а) *м* progress; **прогресси́вный** *прил* progressive

прогу́л (-а) *м* (*на работе*) absence; (*в школе*) truancy

прогу́лива|**ть** (-ю) *несов от* **прогуля́ть**

прогу́л|**ка** (-ки; *gen pl* -ок) *ж* walk; (*недалёкая поездка*) trip

прогу́льщик (-а) м (об ученике) truant
прогуля́|ть (-ю) несов перех (работу) to be absent from; (уроки) to miss; (гуля́ть) to walk
продава́|ть (-ю́) несов от прода́ть
продав|е́ц (-ца́) м seller; (в магазине) (shop-)assistant; **продавщи́ц|а** (-ы) ж от продаве́ц
прода́ж|а (-и) ж (дома, товара) sale; (торговля) trade
прода́ть (как дать; см Table 16; impf **продава́ть**) сов перех to sell; (перен: друга) to betray
продвига́ть(ся) (-ю(сь)) несов от продви́нуть(ся)
продвиже́ни|е (-я) ср (войск) advance; (по службе) promotion
продви́н|уть (-у; impf **продвига́ть**) сов перех to move; (перен: работника) to promote; **продви́нуться** (impf **продвига́ться**) сов возв to move; (войска) to advance; (перен: работник) to be promoted; (: работа) to progress
продева́|ть (-ю) несов от проде́ть
проде́ла|ть (-ю; impf **проде́лывать**) сов перех (отверстие) to make; (работу) to do
проде́|ть (-ну, -нешь; impf **продева́ть**) сов перех to thread
продлева́|ть (-ю) несов от продли́ть
продле́ни|е (-я) ср (см глаг) extension; prolongation
продл|и́ть (-ю́, -и́шь; impf **продлева́ть**) сов перех to extend; (жизнь) to prolong
продл|и́ться (3sg -и́тся) сов от дли́ться
продово́льственный прил food; **продово́льственный магази́н** grocer's (shop) (Brit), grocery (US)
продово́льстви|е (-я) ср provisions мн
продолжа́|ть (-ю; perf **продо́лжить**) несов перех to continue; **продолжа́ть** (perf **продо́лжить**) +impf infin to continue или carry on doing; **продолжа́ться** (perf **продо́лжиться**) несов возв to continue, carry on; **продолже́ни|е** (-я) ср (борьбы, лекции) continuation; (романа) sequel; **в продолже́ние** +gen for the duration of; **продолжи́тельность** (-и) ж duration; (сре́дняя) **продолжи́тельность жи́зни** (average) life expectancy
продо́лж|ить(ся) (-у(сь), -ишь(ся)) сов от продолжа́ть(ся)
проду́кт (-а) м product; см также **проду́кты**; **продукти́вность** (-и) ж productivity; **продукти́вный** прил productive; **продукто́вый** прил food; **проду́кт|ы** (-ов) мн (также **проду́кты пита́ния**) foodstuffs
проду́кци|я (-и) ж produce
проду́манный прил well thought-out
проду́ма|ть (-ю; impf **проду́мывать**) сов перех (действия) to think out
прое́зд (-а) м (в транспорте) journey; (место) passage; **проездно́й** прил

(документ) travel; **проездно́й биле́т** travel card; **прое́здом** нареч en route
проезжа́|ть (-ю) несов от прое́хать
прое́зж|ий прил (люди) passing through; **прое́зжая часть (у́лицы)** road
прое́кт (-а) м project; (дома) design; (зако́на, догово́ра) draft; **проекти́р|овать** (-ую; perf **спроекти́ровать**) несов перех (дом) to design; (доро́ги) to plan ⊳ (perf **запроекти́ровать**) (наме́тить) to plan
прое́ктор (-а) м (Оптика) projector
прое́хать (как е́хать; см Table 19) сов перех (минова́ть) to pass; (пропусти́ть) to miss ⊳ (impf **проезжа́ть**) неперех: **прое́хать ми́мо** +gen/**по** +dat/**че́рез** +acc итп to drive past/along/across итп; **прое́хаться** сов возв (на маши́не) to go for a drive
прож|е́чь (-гу́, -жёшь итп, -гу́т; pt -ёг, -гла́, impf **прожига́ть**) сов перех to burn a hole in
прожива́ни|е (-я) ср stay
прожива́|ть (-ю) несов от прожи́ть ⊳ неперех to live
прожига́|ть (-ю) несов от проже́чь
прож|и́ть (-иву́, -ивёшь) сов (пробы́ть живы́м) to live; (жить) to spend
про́з|а (-ы) ж prose
про́звищ|е (-а) ср nickname
прозева́|ть (-ю) сов от зева́ть
прозра́чный прил transparent; (ткань) see-through
проигра́|ть (-ю; impf **прои́грывать**) сов перех to lose; (игра́ть) to play
прои́грыватель (-я) м record player
про́игрыш (-а) м loss
произведе́ни|е (-я) ср work
произв|ести́ (-еду́, -едёшь; pt -ёл, -ела́, impf **производи́ть**) сов перех (операцию) to carry out; (впечатле́ние, сумато́ху) to create
производи́тель (-я) м producer; **производи́тельность** (-и) ж productivity; **производи́тельный** прил (продукти́вный) productive
произв|оди́ть (-ожу́, -о́дишь) несов от произвести́ ⊳ перех (изготовля́ть) to produce, manufacture
произво́дственный прил (проце́сс, план) production; **произво́дственное объедине́ние** large industrial company
произво́дств|о (-а) ср (това́ров) production, manufacture; (о́трасль) industry; (заво́д, фа́брика) factory; **промы́шленное произво́дство** industrial output; (о́трасль) industry
произво́льный прил (свобо́дный) free; (Спорт) freestyle; (вы́вод) arbitrary
произн|ести́ (-есу́, -есёшь; pt -ёс, -есла́, impf **произноси́ть**) сов перех (сло́во) to pronounce; (речь) to make
произн|оси́ть (-ошу́, -о́сишь) несов от произнести́

произноше́ни|е (-я) *ср* pronunciation

произойти́ (*как* **идти́**; *см* Table 18; *impf* **происходи́ть**) *сов* to occur

происх|оди́ть (-ожу́, -о́дишь) *несов от* **произойти́** ▷ *неперех*: **происходи́ть от/ из** +*gen* to come from

происхожде́ни|е (-я) *ср* origin

происше́стви|е (-я) *ср* event; **доро́жное происше́ствие** road accident

пройти́ (*как* **идти́**; *см* Table 18; *impf* **проходи́ть**) *сов* to pass; (*расстояние*) to cover; (*слух*) to spread; (*дорога, канал итп*) to stretch; (*дождь, снег*) to fall; (*операция, переговоры итп*) to go ▷ *перех* (*практику, службу итп*) to complete; (*изучить: тему итп*) to do; **пройти́** (*impf* **проходи́ть**) **в** +*acc* (*в институт итп*) to get into; **пройти́сь** (*impf* **проха́живаться**) *сов возв* (*по комнате*) to pace; (*по парку*) to stroll

прока́лыва|ть (-ю) *несов от* **проколо́ть**

прока́т (-а) *м* (*телевизора*) hire; (*также* **кинопрока́т**) film distribution; **брать** (*perf* **взять**) **что-н на прока́т** to hire sth

прок|ати́ть (-ачу́, -а́тишь) *сов перех*: **прокати́ть кого́-н** (*на машине итп*) to take sb for a ride; **прокати́ться** *сов возв* (*на машине*) to go for a ride

проки́с|нуть (3sg -нет, pt -, -ла) *сов от* **ки́снуть**

прокла́д|ка (-ки; *gen pl* -ок) *ж* (*действие: труб*) laying out; (: *провода*) laying; (: *защитная*) padding

прокла́дыва|ть (-ю) *несов от* **проложи́ть**

прокл|я́сть (-яну́, -янёшь; *pt* -ял, -яла́, -я́ло, *impf* **проклина́ть**) *сов перех* to curse

проко́л (-а) *м* (*см глаг*) puncturing; lancing; piercing; (*отверстие: в шине*) puncture

прокра́|сться (-ду́сь, -дёшься; *impf* **прокра́дываться**) *сов возв*: **прокра́сться в** +*acc*/**ми́мо** +*gen*/**че́рез** +*acc итп* to creep (*Brit*) *или* sneak (*US*) in(to)/past/through *итп*

прокрич|а́ть (-у́, -и́шь) *сов перех* (*выкрикнуть*) to shout out

прокру|ти́ть (-чу́, -ти́шь; *impf* **прокру́чивать**) *сов перех* (*провернуть*) to turn; (*мясо*) to mince; (*разг: деньги*) to invest illegally

пролага́|ть (-ю) *несов от* **проложи́ть**

прола́мыва|ть (-ю) *несов от* **проломи́ть**

прола́|ять (-ю) *сов от* **ла́ять**

пролеж|а́ть (-у́, -и́шь) *сов* to lie

проле́з|ть (-у, -ешь; *impf* **пролеза́ть**) *сов* to get through

проле|те́ть (-чу́, -ти́шь; *impf* **пролета́ть**) *сов* to fly; (*человек, поезд*) to fly past; (*лето, отпуск*) to fly by

проли́в (-а) *м* strait(s) (*мн*)

пролива́|ть(ся) (-ю(сь)) *несов от* **проли́ть(ся)**

прол|и́ть (-ью́, -ьёшь; *pt* -и́л, -ила́, *impf* **пролива́ть**) *сов перех* to spill; **проли́ться** (*impf* **пролива́ться**) *сов возв* to spill

прол|ожи́ть (-ожу́, -о́жишь; *impf* **прокла́дывать**) *сов перех* to lay

прол|оми́ть (-омлю́, -о́мишь; *impf* **прола́мывать**) *сов перех* (*лёд*) to break; (*череп*) to fracture

про́мах (-а) *м* miss; (*перен*) blunder

промахн|у́ться (-у́сь, -ёшься; *impf* **прома́хиваться**) *сов возв* to miss

прома́чива|ть (-ю) *несов от* **промочи́ть**

промедле́ни|е (-я) *ср* delay

промедл|ить (-ю, -ишь) *сов*: **промедлить с** +*instr* to delay

промежу́т|ок (-ка) *м* gap

промельк|ну́ть (-у́, -ёшь) *сов* to flash past; **промелькну́ть** (*perf*) **в** +*prp* (*в голове́*) to flash through; (*перед глаза́ми*) to flash past

промока́|ть (-ю) *несов от* **промо́кнуть**; **промокну́ть** ▷ *неперех* to let water through

промока́ш|ка (-ки; *gen pl* -ек) *ж* (*разг*) blotting paper

промо́к|нуть (-у; *impf* **промока́ть**) *сов* to get soaked

промок|ну́ть (-у́, -ёшь; *impf* **промока́ть**) *сов* to blot

промолч|а́ть (-у́, -и́шь) *сов* to say nothing

пром|очи́ть (-очу́, -о́чишь; *impf* **прома́чивать**) *сов перех* to get wet

промтова́рный *прил*: **промтова́рный магази́н** small department store

промтова́р|ы (-ов) *мн* = **промы́шленные това́ры**

промч|а́ться (-у́сь, -и́шься) *сов возв* (*год, лето, жизнь*) to fly by; **промча́ться** (*perf*) **ми́мо** +*gen*/**че́рез** +*acc* (*поезд, челове́к*) to fly past/through

пром|ы́ть (-о́ю, -о́ешь; *impf* **промыва́ть**) *сов перех* (*желудок*) to pump; (*рану, глаз*) to bathe

промы́шленност|ь (-и) *ж* industry

промы́шленн|ый *прил* industrial; **промы́шленные това́ры** manufactured goods

прон|ести́ (-есу́, -есёшь; *pt* -ёс, -есла́, *impf* **проноси́ть**) *сов перех* to carry; (*секретно*) to sneak in; **пронести́сь** (*impf* **проноси́ться**) *сов возв* (*машина, пуля, бегу́н*) to shoot by; (*время*) to fly by; (*буря*) to whirl past

прони́к|нуть (-ну; *pt* -, -ла, *impf* **проника́ть**) *сов перех*: **прони́кнуть в** +*acc* to penetrate; (*залезть*) to break into; **прони́кнуться** (*impf* **проника́ться**) *сов возв*: +*instr* to be filled with

прон|оси́ть(ся) (-ошу́(сь), -о́сишь(ся)) *несов от* **пронести́(сь)**

пропага́нд|а (-ы) *ж* propaganda; (*спорта*) promotion; **пропаганди́р|овать**

(-**ую**) несов перех (политику) to spread propaganda about; (знания, спорт) to promote

пропада́|ть (-ю) несов от **пропа́сть**

пропа́ж|а (-и) ж (денег, документов) loss

проп|а́сть (-аду́, -аде́шь; impf **пропада́ть**) сов to disappear; (деньги, письмо) to go missing; (аппетит, голос, слух) to go; (усилия, билет в театр) to be wasted; **пропада́ть** (perf **пропа́сть**) **бе́з вести** (человек) to go missing

пропе́ллер (-а) м (Авиа) propeller

проп|е́ть (-ою́, -о́ешь) сов от **петь**

проп|иса́ть (-ишу́, -и́шешь; impf **пропи́сывать**) сов перех (человека) to register; (лекарство) to prescribe; **прописа́ться** сов возв to register

пропи́с|ка (-ки) ж registration

● **ПРОПИ́СКА**
●
●
● By law every Russian citizen is required
● to register at his or her place of
● residence. A stamp confirming the
● registration is displayed in the passport.
● This registration stamp is as essential as
● having the passport itself. See also note
● at **па́спорт**.

пропис|но́й прил: **прописна́я бу́ква** capital letter

пропи́сыва|ть (-ю) несов от **прописа́ть**

пропита́ни|е (-я) ср food

пропл|ы́ть (-ыву́, -ыве́шь; impf **проплыва́ть**) сов (человек) to swim; (: миновать) to swim past; (судно) to sail; (: миновать) to sail past

пропове́дник (-а) м (Рел) preacher; (перен: теории) advocate

пропове́д|овать (-ую) несов перех (Рел) to preach; (теорию) to advocate

проползти́ (-у́, -ёшь; pt -, -ла́) сов: **проползти́ по** +dat/**в** +acc итп (насекомое, человек) to crawl along/into итп; (змея) to slither along/into итп

прополоска́|ть (-ю) сов от **полоска́ть**

проп|оло́ть (-олю́, -о́лешь) сов от **поло́ть**

пропо́рци|я (-и) ж proportion

про́пуск (-а) м (действие: в зал, через границу итп) admission; (в тексте, в изложении) gap; (неявка: на работу, в школу) absence ▷ (nom pl -а́) (документ) pass

пропуска́|ть (-ю) несов от **пропусти́ть** ▷ перех (свет итп) to let through; (воду, холод) to let in

проп|усти́ть (-ущу́, -у́стишь; impf **пропуска́ть**) сов перех to miss; (разрешить) to allow; **пропуска́ть** (perf **пропусти́ть**) **кого́-н вперёд** to let sb by

прорабо́та|ть (-ю; impf **прораба́тывать**) сов to work

прорв|а́ть (-у́, -ёшь; pt -а́л, -ала́, impf **прорыва́ть**) сов перех (плотину) to burst; (оборону, фронт) to break through; **прорва́ться** (impf **прорыва́ться**) сов возв (плотина, шарик) to burst; **прорыва́ться** (perf **прорва́ться**) **в** +acc to burst in(to)

проре́|зать (-жу, -жешь; impf **прореза́ть**) сов перех to cut through; **проре́заться** сов от **ре́заться**

проре́ктор (-а) м vice-principal

проро́ч|ить (-у, -ишь; perf **напроро́чить**) несов перех to predict

прор|уби́ть (-ублю́, -у́бишь; impf **проруба́ть**) сов перех to make a hole in

про́руб|ь (-и) ж ice-hole

прорыва́|ть(ся) (-ю(сь)) несов от **прорва́ть(ся)**

прор|ы́ть (-о́ю, -о́ешь; impf **прорыва́ть**) сов перех to dig

проса́чива|ться (3sg -ется) несов от **просочи́ться**

просверл|и́ть (-ю́, -и́шь; impf **просве́рливать** или **сверли́ть**) сов перех to bore, drill

просве́т (-а) м (в тучах) break; (перен: в кризисе) light at the end of the tunnel

просве́чива|ть (-ю) несов от **просвети́ть** ▷ неперех (солнце, луна) to shine through; (ткань) to let light through

просвеща́|ть (-ю) несов от **просвети́ть**

просвеще́ни|е (-я) ср education

просви|сте́ть (-щу́, -сти́шь) сов от **свисте́ть** ▷ неперех (пуля) to whistle past

просе́|ять (-ю; impf **просе́ивать**) сов перех (муку, песок) to sift

проси|де́ть (-жу́, -ди́шь; impf **проси́живать**) сов (сидеть) to sit; (пробыть) to stay

про|си́ть (-шу́, -сишь; perf **попроси́ть**) несов перех to ask; **прошу́ Вас!** if you please!; **проси́ть** (perf **попроси́ть**) **кого́-н о чём-м/** +infin to ask sb for sth/to do; **проси́ть** (perf **попроси́ть**) **кого́-н за кого́-н** to ask sb a favour (Brit) или favor (US) on behalf of sb; **проси́ться** (perf **попроси́ться**) несов возв (просьбе) to ask permission

проск|ака́ть (-ачу́, -а́чешь) сов: **проскака́ть че́рез/сквозь** +acc (лошадь) to gallop across/through

проскользн|у́ть (-у́, -ёшь; impf **проска́льзывать**) сов (монета) to slide in; (человек) to slip in; (перен: сомнение) to creep in

просла́вленный прил renowned

просле|ди́ть (-жу́, -ди́шь; impf **просле́живать**) сов перех (глазами) to follow; (исследовать) to trace ▷ неперех: **проследи́ть за** +instr to follow; (контролировать) to monitor

просмо́тр (-а) м (фильма) viewing; (документов) inspection

просм|отре́ть (-отрю́, -о́тришь; impf

просма́тривать) сов перех
(*ознакомиться: читая*) to look through;
(: *смотря*) to view; (*пропустить*) to
overlook

просну́ться (-у́сь, -ёшься; *impf*
просыпа́ться) сов возв to wake up;
(*перен: любовь, страх итп*) to be
awakened

просочи́ться (*3sg* -и́тся, *impf*
проса́чиваться) сов возв (*также перен*)
to filter through

проспа́ть (-лю́, -и́шь; *pt* -а́л, -ала́) сов
(*спать*) to sleep ▷ (*impf* **просыпа́ть**)
(*встать поздно*) to oversleep, sleep in

проспе́кт (-а) м (*в городе*) avenue;
(*издание*) brochure

просро́чить (-у, -ишь; *impf*
просро́чивать) сов перех (*платёж*) to be
late with; (*паспорт, билет*) to let expire

проста́ивать (-ю) *несов от* **простоя́ть**

простира́|ться (-юсь; *perf*
простере́ться) *несов возв* to extend

проститу́т|ка (-ки; *gen pl* -ок) ж
prostitute

прости́|ть (прощу́, прости́шь; *impf*
проща́ть) сов перех to forgive; (*impf*
проща́ть) (*perf* **прости́ть**) что-н кому-н to excuse
или forgive sb (for) sth; **прости́те, как
пройти́ на ста́нцию?** excuse me, how do I
get to the station?; **прости́ться** (*impf*
проща́ться) сов возв: **прости́ться с** +*instr*
to say goodbye to

про́сто *нареч* (*делать*) easily; (*объяснять*)
simply ▷ *част* just; **всё э́то про́сто
недоразуме́ние** all this is just a
misunderstanding; **про́сто (так)** for no
particular reason

прост|о́й *прил* simple; (*одежда*) plain;
(*задача*) easy, simple; (*человек, манеры*)
unaffected; (*обыкновенный*) ordinary
▷ (-о́я) м downtime; (*рабочих*) stoppage;
просто́й каранда́ш lead pencil

прост|она́ть (-ону́, -о́нешь) сов (*не*)
перех to groan

просто́рный *прил* spacious

простота́ (-ы́) ж (*см прил*) simplicity

просто|я́ть (-ю́, -и́шь; *impf*
проста́ивать) сов to stand; (*бездействуя*) to stand idle

простре́л|ить (-елю́, -е́лишь; *impf*
простре́ливать) сов перех to shoot
through

просту́д|а (-ы) ж (*Мед*) cold

прост|уди́ть (-ужу́, -у́дишь; *impf*
простужа́ть) сов перех: **простуди́ть
кого́-н** to give sb a cold; **простуди́ться**
(*impf* **простужа́ться**) сов возв to catch a
cold

просту́женный *прил*: **ребёнок
просту́жен** the child has got a cold

прост|упи́ть (*3sg* -у́пит, *impf*
проступа́ть) сов (*пот, пятна*) to come
through; (*очертания*) to appear

просту́п|ок (-ка) м misconduct

простын|я́ (-и́; *nom pl* про́стыни, *gen pl*
просты́нь, *dat pl* -я́м) ж sheet

просу́н|уть (-у, -ешь; *impf*
просо́вывать) сов перех: **просу́нуть в**
+*acc* to push in

просчёт (-а) м (*счёт*) counting; (*ошибка: в
подсчёте*) error; (: *в действиях*)
miscalculation

просчита́|ть (-ю; *impf* **просчи́тывать**)
сов перех (*считать*) to count; (*ошибиться*)
to miscount; **просчита́ться** (*impf*
просчи́тываться) сов возв (*при счёте*)
to miscount; (*в планах*) to miscalculate

просы́п|ать (-лю, -лешь; *impf*
просыпа́ть) сов перех to spill;
просы́паться (*impf* **просыпа́ться**) сов
возв to spill

просыпа́|ть (-ю) *несов от* **проспа́ть**
просы́пать; **просыпа́ться** *несов от*
просну́ться; **просы́паться**

про́сьб|а (-ы) ж request

прота́лкива|ть (-ю) *несов от*
протолкну́ть

прот|ащи́ть (-ащу́, -а́щишь; *impf*
прота́скивать) сов перех to drag

протека́|ть (*3sg* -ет) *несов от* **проте́чь**
▷ *неперех* (*вода*) to flow; (*болезнь,
явление*) to progress

прот|ере́ть (-ру́, -рёшь; *pt* -ёр, -ёрла,
impf **протира́ть**) сов перех (*износить*) to
wear a hole in; (*очистить*) to wipe;
протере́ться (*impf* **протира́ться**) сов
возв (*износиться*) to wear through

проте́ст (-а) м protest; (*Юр*) objection

протеста́нт (-а) м Protestant;
протеста́нтский *прил* Protestant

протест|ова́ть (-у́ю) *несов*:
протестова́ть (про́тив +*gen*) to protest
(against)

проте́ч|ка (-ки; *gen pl* -ек) ж leak

про́тив *предл* +*gen* against; (*прямо
перед*) opposite ▷ *как сказ*: **я про́тив
э́того** I am against this

про́тив|ень (-ня) м baking tray

проти́в|иться (-люсь, -ишься; *perf*
воспроти́виться) *несов возв* +*dat* to
oppose

проти́вник (-а) м opponent ▷ *собир*
(*Воен*) the enemy

проти́вно *нареч* offensively ▷ *как сказ
безл* it's disgusting

проти́вный *прил* (*мнение*) opposite;
(*неприятный*) disgusting

противоде́йств|овать (-ую) *несов* +*dat*
to oppose

противозако́нный *прил* unlawful

противозача́точный *прил*
contraceptive; **противозача́точное
сре́дство** contraceptive

противопоста́в|ить (-лю, -ишь; *impf*
противопоставля́ть) сов перех:
противопоста́вить кого́-н/что-н +*dat* to
contrast sb/sth with

противоре́чи|е (-я) ср contradiction;

(*классовое*) conflict

противоре́ч|ить (**-у, -ишь**) *несов* (+*dat*: *человеку*) to contradict; (*логике, закону итп*) to defy

противосто|я́ть (**-ю́, -и́шь**) *несов* (+*dat*: *ветру*) to withstand; (*уговорам*) to resist

противоя́ди|е (**-я**) *ср* antidote

протира́|ть(ся) (**-ю(сь)**) *несов от* **протере́ть(ся)**

проткн|у́ть (**-у́, -ёшь**; *impf* **протыка́ть**) *сов перех* to pierce

прото́к (**-а**) *м* (*рукав реки*) tributary; (*соединяющая река*) channel

протоко́л (**-а**) *м* (*собрания*) minutes *мн*; (*допроса*) transcript; (*соглашение*) protocol

протолкн|у́ть (**-у́, -ёшь**; *impf* **прота́лкивать**) *сов перех* to push through

прото́чный *прил* (*вода*) running

проту́хн|уть (*3sg* **-ет**, *impf* **протуха́ть** *или* **ту́хнуть**) *сов* to go bad *или* off

протыка́|ть (**-ю**) *несов от* **проткну́ть**

протя́гива|ть(ся) (**-ю(сь)**) *несов от* **протяну́ть(ся)**

протяже́ни|е (**-я**) *ср*: **на протяже́нии двух неде́ль/ме́сяцев** over a period of two weeks/months; **протяжённост|ь** (**-и**) *ж* length

протян|у́ть (**-у́, -ешь**) *сов от* **тяну́ть** ▷ (*impf* **протя́гивать**) *перех* (*верёвку*) to stretch; (*провод*) to extend; (*руки, ноги*) to stretch (out); (*предмет*) to hold out; **протяну́ться** (*impf* **протя́гиваться**) *сов возв* (*дорога*) to stretch; (*провод*) to extend; (*рука*) to stretch out

про|учи́ть (**-учу́, -у́чишь**; *impf* **проу́чивать**) *сов перех* (*разг*: *наказать*) to teach a lesson; **проучи́ться** *сов возв* to study

профессиона́л (**-а**) *м* professional; **профессиона́льный** *прил* professional; (*болезнь, привычка, обучение*) occupational; (*обучение*) vocational; **профессиона́льный сою́з** trade (*Brit*) *или* labor (*US*) union

профе́сси|я (**-и**) *ж* profession

профе́ссор (**-а**; *nom pl* **-á**) *м* professor

профила́ктик|а (**-и**) *ж* prevention

про́фил|ь (**-я**) *м* profile

профсою́з (**-а**) *м сокр* = **профессиона́льный сою́з**

профсою́зный *прил* trade union

проха́жива|ться (**-юсь**) *несов от* **пройти́сь**

прохла́д|а (**-ы**) *ж* cool

прохлади́тельный *прил*: **прохлади́тельный напи́ток** cool soft drink

прохла́дно *нареч* (*встретить*) coolly ▷ *как сказ* it's cool

прохла́дный *прил* cool

прохо́д (**-а**) *м* passage

прох|оди́ть (**-ожу́, -о́дишь**) *несов от* **пройти́**

проходн|а́я (**-о́й**) *ж* checkpoint (*at entrance to factory etc*)

проходно́й *прил*: **проходно́й балл** pass mark

● **Проходно́й балл**
●
● This is the score which the student has
● to achieve to be admitted into a higher
● education institution. It consists of a mark
● out of 100, obtained in the **ЕГЭ**. Each
● university and department sets its own
● pass mark.

прохо́ж|ий (**-его**) *м* passer-by

процвета́|ть (**-ю**) *несов* (*фирма, бизнесмен*) to prosper; (*театр, наука*) to flourish; (*хорошо жить*) to thrive

проц|еди́ть (**-ежу́, -е́дишь**) *сов от* **цеди́ть** ▷ (*impf* **проце́живать**) *перех* (*бульон, сок*) to strain

процеду́р|а (**-ы**) *ж* procedure; (*Мед*: *обычно мн*) course of treatment

проце́жива|ть (**-ю**) *несов от* **процеди́ть**

проце́нт (**-а**) *м* percentage; **в разме́ре 5 проце́нтов годовы́х** at a yearly rate of 5 percent; *см также* **проце́нты**; **проце́нтный** *прил* percentage; **проце́нтная ста́вка** interest rate

проце́нт|ы (**-ов**) *мн* (*Комм*) interest *ед*; (*плата*) commission *ед*

проце́сс (**-а**) *м* process; (*Юр*: *порядок*) proceedings *мн*; (: *также* **суде́бный проце́сс**) trial; **воспали́тельный проце́сс** inflammation; **в проце́ссе** +*gen* in the course of

проце́ссор (**-а**) *м* (*Комп*) processor

прочёл *сов см* **прочесть**

проч|е́сть (**-ту́, -тёшь**; *pt* **-ёл, -ла́**) *сов от* **чита́ть**

про́ч|ий *прил* other; **поми́мо всего́ про́чего** apart from anything else

прочита́|ть (**-ю**) *сов от* **чита́ть**

прочла́ *etc сов см* **прочесть**

про́чно *нареч* (*закрепить*) firmly

про́чный *прил* (*материал итп*) durable; (*постройка*) solid; (*знания*) sound; (*отношение, семья*) stable; (*мир, счастье*) lasting

прочту́ *etc сов см* **прочесть**

прочь *нареч* (*в сторону*) away; **ру́ки прочь!** hands off!

проше́дш|ий *прил* (*прошлый*) past; **проше́дшее вре́мя** past tense

прошёл(ся) *сов см* **пройти́(сь)**

проше́ни|е (**-я**) *ср* plea; (*ходатайство*) petition

прош|епта́ть (**-епчу́, -е́пчешь**) *сов перех* to whisper

прошла́ *etc сов см* **пройти́**

прошлого́дний *прил* last year's

про́шл|ое (**-ого**) *ср* the past

про́шл|ый *прил* last; (*прежний*) past; **в про́шлый раз** last time; **на про́шлой**

неде́ле last week; **в про́шлом ме́сяце/году́** last month/year

прошу́(сь) несов см проси́ть(ся)

проща́йте част goodbye

проща́льный прил parting; (вечер) farewell

проща́ни|е (-я) ср (действие) parting; **на проща́ние** on parting

проща́|ть(ся) (-ю(сь)) несов от прости́ть(ся)

про́ще сравн нареч от **про́сто** ▷ сравн прил от **просто́й**

проще́ни|е (-я) ср (ребёнка, друга итп) forgiveness; (преступника) pardon; **проси́ть** (perf попроси́ть) **проще́ния** to say sorry; **прошу́ проще́ния!** (I'm) sorry!

прояви́тел|ь (-я) м (Фото) developer

про|яви́ть (-явлю́, -я́вишь; impf **проявля́ть**) сов перех to display; (Фото) to develop; **прояви́ться** (impf **проявля́ться**) сов возв (талант, потенциал итп) to reveal itself; (Фото) to be developed

проявле́ни|е (-я) ср display

проявля́|ть(ся) (-ю(сь)) несов от прояви́ть(ся)

проясн|и́ть (-ю́, -и́шь; impf **проясня́ть**) сов перех (обстановку) to clarify; **проясни́ться** (impf **проясня́ться**) сов возв (погода, небо) to brighten или clear up; (обстановка) to be clarified; (мысли) to become lucid

пруд (-а́; loc sg -у́) м pond

пружи́н|а (-ы) ж (Tex) spring

прут (-а́; nom pl -ья) м twig

прыга́л|ка (-ки; gen pl -ок) ж skipping-rope (Brit), skip rope (US)

прыга́|ть (-ю) несов to jump; (мяч) to bounce

прыгн|уть (-у) сов to jump; (мяч) to bounce

прыгу́н (-а́) м (Спорт) jumper

прыж|о́к (-ка́) м jump; (в воду) dive; **прыжки́ в высоту́/длину́** high/long jump

прыщ (-а́) м spot

пряд|ь (-и) ж lock (of hair)

пря́ж|ка (-ки; gen pl -ек) ж (на ремне) buckle; (на юбке) clasp

пря́м|ая (-о́й) ж straight line

пря́мо нареч (о направлении) straight ahead; (ровно) upright; (непосредственно) straight; (откровенно) directly ▷ част (действительно) really

прям|о́й прил straight; (путь, слова, человек) direct; (ответ, политика) open; (вызов, обман) obvious; (улики) hard; (сообщение, обязанность итп) direct; (выгода, смысл) real; (значение слова) literal; **пряма́я трансля́ция** live broadcast; **прямо́е дополне́ние** direct object

прямоуго́льник (-а) м rectangle

пря́ник (-а) м ≈ gingerbread

пря́ност|ь (-и) ж spice; **пря́ный** прил spicy

пря́|тать (-чу, -чешь; perf **спря́тать**) несов перех to hide; **пря́таться** (perf **спря́таться**) несов возв to hide; (человек: от холода) to shelter

пря́т|ки (-ок) мн hide-and-seek ед (Brit), hide-and-go-seek ед (US)

псевдони́м (-а) м pseudonym

псих (-а) м (разг) nut

психиа́тр (-а) м psychiatrist

психиатри́ческий прил psychiatric

психи́ческий прил (заболевание) mental

психо́лог (-а) м psychologist; **психологи́ческий** прил psychological; **психоло́ги|я** (-и) ж psychology

птен|е́ц (-ца́) м chick

пти́ц|а (-ы) ж bird ▷ собир: (дома́шняя) пти́ца poultry

пти́чий прил (корм, клетка) bird

пу́блик|а (-и) ж собир audience; (общество) public

публика́ци|я (-и) ж publication

публик|ова́ть (-у́ю; perf **опубликова́ть**) несов перех to publish

публици́ст (-а) м social commentator; **публици́стик|а** (-и) ж собир sociopolitical journalism

публи́чный прил public; **публи́чный дом** brothel

пу́гал|о (-а) ср scarecrow; (перен: о человеке) fright

пуга́|ть (-ю; perf **испуга́ть** или **напуга́ть**) несов перех to frighten, scare; **пуга́ться** (perf **испуга́ться** или **напуга́ться**) несов возв to be frightened или scared

пу́говиц|а (-ы) ж button

пу́дел|ь (-я) м poodle

пу́динг (-а) м ≈ pudding

пу́др|а (-ы) ж powder; **са́харная пу́дра** icing sugar

пу́дрениц|а (-ы) ж powder compact

пу́др|ить (-ю, -ишь; perf **напу́дрить**) несов перех to powder; **пу́дриться** (perf **напу́дриться**) несов возв to powder one's face

пузы́р|ь (-я́) м (мыльный) bubble; (на коже) blister

пулемёт (-а) м machine gun

пуло́вер (-а) м pullover

пульс (-а) м (Мед: перен) pulse

пульт (-а) м panel

пу́л|я (-и) ж bullet

пункт (-а) м point; (документа) clause; (медицинский) centre (Brit), center (US); (наблюдательный, командный) post; **населённый пункт** small settlement

пункти́р (-а) м dotted line

пунктуа́льный прил (человек) punctual

пунктуа́ци|я (-и) ж punctuation

пуп|о́к (-ка́) м (Анат) navel

пург|а́ (-и́) ж snowstorm

пуск (-а) м (завода итп) launch

пуска́|ть(ся) (-ю(сь)) несов от **пусти́ть(ся)**

пусте́|ть (3sg -ет, perf **опусте́ть**) несов to become empty; (улицы) to become deserted

пу|сти́ть (-щу́, -стишь; impf **пуска́ть**) сов перех (руку, человека) to let go of; (лошадь, санки итп) to send off; (станок) to start; (в вагон, в зал) to let in; (пар, дым) to give off; (камень, снаряд) to throw; (корни) to put out; **пуска́ть** (perf **пусти́ть**) что-н на +acc/под +acc (использовать) to use sth as/for; **пуска́ть** (perf **пусти́ть**) кого́-н куда́-нибудь to let sb go somewhere; **пусти́ться** (impf **пуска́ться**) сов возв: **пусти́ться в** +acc (в объяснения) to go into; **пуска́ться** (perf **пусти́ться**) **в путь** to set off

пу́сто нареч empty ▷ как сказ (ничего нет) it's empty; (никого нет) there's no-one there

пусто́й прил empty

пуст|ота́ (-оты́; nom pl -о́ты) ж emptiness; (полое место) cavity

пусты́н|я (-и; gen pl -ь) ж desert

пусты́ш|ка (-ки; gen pl -ек) ж (разг: соска) dummy (Brit), pacifier (US)

○ **КЛЮЧЕВОЕ СЛОВО**

пусть част +3sg/pl **1** (выражает приказ, угрозу): **пусть он придёт у́тром** let him come in the morning; **пусть она́ то́лько попро́бует отказа́ться** let her just try to refuse

2 (выражает согласие): **пусть бу́дет так** so be it; **пусть бу́дет по-тво́ему** have it your way

3 (всё равно) O.K., all right

пустя́к (-а́) м trifle; (неценный предмет) trinket ▷ как сказ: **э́то пустя́к** it's nothing

пута́ниц|а (-ы) ж muddle

пу́та|ть (-ю; perf **запу́тать** или **спу́тать**) несов перех (нитки, волосы) to tangle; (сбить с толку) to confuse (perf **спу́тать** или **перепу́тать**) (бумаги, факты итп) to mix up ▷ (perf **впу́тать**) (разг): **пу́тать** кого́-н в +acc to get sb mixed up in; **я его́ с кем-то пу́таю** I'm confusing him with somebody else; **он всегда́ пу́тал на́ши имена́** he always got our names mixed up; **пу́таться** (perf **запу́таться** или **спу́таться**) несов возв to get tangled; (в рассказе, в объяснении) to get mixed up

путёв|ка (-ки; gen pl -ок) ж holiday voucher; (водителя) manifest (of cargo drivers)

путеводи́тел|ь (-я) м guidebook

путём предл +gen by means of

путеше́ственник (-а) м traveller (Brit), traveler (US)

путеше́стви|е (-я) ср journey, trip; (морское) voyage

путеше́ств|овать (-ую) несов to travel

пу́тник (-а) м traveller (Brit), traveler (US)

пут|ь (-и́; см Table 3) м (также перен) way; (платфо́рма) platform; (рельсы) track; (путеше́ствие) journey; **во́дные пути́** waterways; **возду́шные пути́** air lanes; **нам с Ва́ми не по пути́** we're not going the same way; **счастли́вого пути́!** have a good trip!; **пути́ сообще́ния** transport network

пух (-а; loc sg -у́) м (у живо́тных) fluff; (у птиц, у челове́ка) down; **ни пу́ха ни пера́!** good luck!

пу́х|нуть (-ну; pt -, -ла, perf **вспу́хнуть** или **опу́хнуть**) несов to swell (up)

пучо́к (-ка́) м bunch; (света) beam

пуши́стый прил (мех, ковёр итп) fluffy; (волосы) fuzzy; (кот) furry

пу́ш|ка (-ки; gen pl -ек) ж cannon; (на танке) artillery gun

пчел|а́ (-ы́; nom pl **пчёлы**) ж bee

пшени́ц|а (-ы) ж wheat; **пшени́чный** прил wheat

пшённ|ый прил: **пшённая ка́ша** millet porridge

пыла́|ть (-ю) несов (костёр) to blaze; (перен: лицо) to burn

пылесо́с (-а) м vacuum cleaner, hoover; **пылесо́с|ить** (-ишь; perf **пропылесо́сить**) сов перех to vacuum, hoover

пыли́н|ка (-ки; gen pl -ок) ж speck of dust

пыл|и́ть (-ю́, -и́шь; perf **напыли́ть**) несов to raise dust; **пыли́ться** (perf **запыли́ться**) несов возв to get dusty

пыл|ь (-и; loc sg -и́) ж dust; **вытира́ть** (perf **вы́тереть**) **пыль** to dust; **пы́льный** прил dusty

пыльц|а́ (-ы́) ж pollen

пыта́|ть (-ю) несов перех to torture; **пыта́ться** (perf **попыта́ться**) несов возв: **пыта́ться** +infin to try to do

пы́т|ка (-ки; gen pl -ок) ж torture

пьедеста́л (-а) м (основание) pedestal; (для победителей) rostrum

пье́с|а (-ы) ж (Литература) play; (Муз) piece

пью etc несов см **пить**

пью́щ|ий (-его) м heavy drinker

пьяне́|ть (-ю; perf **опьяне́ть**) несов to get drunk

пья́ниц|а (-ы) м/ж drunk(ard)

пья́нств|о (-а) ср heavy drinking; **пья́нств|овать** (-ую) несов to drink heavily

пья́н|ый прил (человек) drunk; (крики, песни итп) drunken ▷ (-ого) м drunk

пюре́ ср нескл (фруктовое) purée; **карто́фельное пюре́** mashed potato

пя́т|ая (-ой) ж: **одна́ пя́тая** one fifth

пятёр|ка (-ки; gen pl -ок) ж (цифра, карта) five; (Просвещ) ≈ A (school mark); (группа из пяти) group of five

пя́тер|о (**-ы́х**; *как* **че́тверо**; см *Table 30b*) чис five

пятидесяти *чис см* **пятьдеся́т**

пятидесятиле́ти|е (**-я**) *ср* fifty years мн; (*годовщина*) fiftieth anniversary

пятидеся́тый *чис* fiftieth

пя́|титься (**-чусь, -тишься**; *perf* **попя́титься**) *несов возв* to move backwards

пятиуго́льник (**-а**) *м* pentagon

пятиэта́жный *прил* five-storey (*Brit*), five-story (*US*)

пя́т|ка (**-ки**; *gen pl* **-ок**) *ж* heel

пятна́дцатый *чис* fifteenth

пятна́дцат|ь (**-и**; *как* **пять**; см *Table 26*) чис fifteen

пя́тниц|а (**-ы**) *ж* Friday

пят|но́ (**-на́**; *nom pl* **пя́тна**, *gen pl* **-ен**) *ср* (*также перен*) stain; (*другого цвета*) spot

пя́тый *чис* fifth

пят|ь (**-и́**; см *Table 26*) чис five; (*Просвещ*) ≈ A (*school mark*)

пят|ьдеся́т (**-и́десяти**; см *Table 26*) чис fifty

пят|ьсо́т (**-исо́т**; см *Table 28*) чис five hundred

р. *сокр* (= *река́*) R., r. (= *river*); (= *роди́лся*) b. (= *born*); (= *рубль*) R., r. (= *rouble*)

раб (**-а́**) *м* slave

рабо́т|а (**-ы**) *ж* work; (*источник заработка*) job; **сме́нная рабо́та** shiftwork

рабо́тать (**-ю**) *несов* to work; (*магазин*) to be open; **рабо́тать** (*impf*) **на кого́-н/ что-н** to work for sb/sth; **кем Вы рабо́таете?** what do you do for a living?

рабо́тник (**-а**) *м* worker; (*учреждения*) employee

работода́тел|ь (**-я**) *м* employer

работоспосо́бный *прил* (*человек*) able to work hard

рабо́ч|ий *прил* worker's; (*человек, одежда*) working ▷ (**-его**) *м* worker; **рабо́чая си́ла** workforce; **рабо́чий день** working day (*Brit*), workday (*US*)

ра́бств|о (**-а**) *ср* slavery; **рабы́н|я** (**-и**) *ж* slave

равви́н (**-а**) *м* rabbi

ра́венств|о (**-а**) *ср* equality; **знак ра́венства** (*Мат*) equals sign

равни́н|а (**-ы**) *ж* plain

равно́ *нареч* equally ▷ *союз*: **равно́ (как) и** as well as ▷ *как сказ*: **э́то всё равно́** it doesn't make any difference; **мне всё равно́** I don't mind; **я всё равно́ приду́** I'll come anyway

равноду́шный *прил*: **равноду́шный (к** +*dat*) indifferent (to)

равноме́рный *прил* even

равнопра́ви|е (**-я**) *ср* equality

равноси́льн|ый *прил* +*dat* equal to; **э́то равноси́льно отка́зу** this amounts to a refusal

равноце́нный *прил* of equal value *или* worth

ра́вн|ый *прил* equal; **ра́вным о́бразом** equally

равня́|ть (**-ю**; *perf* **сравня́ть**) *несов перех*: **равня́ть (с** +*instr*) (*делать равным*) to make equal (with); **равня́ться** *несов возв*: равня́ться по +*dat* to draw level with; (*считать себя равным*): равня́ться с +*instr* to compare o.s. with; (*быть равносильным*): равня́ться +*dat* to be equal to

рад *как сказ*: рад (+*dat*) glad (of) +*infin* glad or pleased to do; **рад познако́миться с Ва́ми** pleased to meet you

ра́ди *предл* +*gen* for the sake of; **ра́ди Бо́га!** (*разг*) for God's sake!

радиа́ци|я (-и) *ж* radiation

радика́льный *прил* radical

радикули́т (-а) *м* lower back pain

ра́дио *ср нескл* radio

радиоакти́вный *прил* radioactive

радиовеща́ни|е (-я) *ср* (radio) broadcasting

радиопереда́ч|а (-и) *ж* radio programme (*Brit*) или program (*US*)

радиоприёмник (-а) *м* radio (set)

радиослу́шатель (-я) *м* (radio) listener

радиоста́нци|я (-и) *ж* radio station

ра́д|овать (-ую; *perf* **обра́довать**) *несов перех*: **ра́довать кого́-н** to make sb happy, please sb; **ра́доваться** *несов возв* (*перен: душа*) to rejoice; **ра́доваться** (*perf* **обра́доваться**) +*dat* (*успехам*) to take pleasure in; **он всегда́ ра́дуется гостя́м** he is always happy to have visitors

ра́дост|ь (-и) *ж* joy; **с ра́достью** gladly

ра́дуг|а (-и) *ж* rainbow

ра́дужный *прил* (*перен: приятный*) bright; **ра́дужная оболо́чка** (*Анат*) iris

раду́шный *прил* warm

раз (-а; *nom pl* -ы́, *gen pl* -) *м* time ▷ *нескл* (*один*) one ▷ *нареч* (*разг: однажды*) once ▷ *союз* (*разг: если*) if; в тот/про́шлый раз that/last time; на э́тот раз this time; ещё раз (once) again; раз и навсегда́ once and for all; ни ра́зу not once; (оди́н) раз в день once a day; раз … то … (*разг*) if … then …

разба́в|ить (-лю, -ишь; *impf* **разбавля́ть**) *сов перех* to dilute

разбежа́ться (*как бежа́ть*; см *Table 20*; *impf* **разбега́ться**) *сов возв* to run off, scatter; (*перед прыжком*) to take a run-up; **у меня́ глаза́ разбега́ются** (*разг*) I'm spoilt for choice

разбива́|ть(ся) (-ю(сь)) *несов от* **разби́ть(ся)**

разбира́|ть (-ю) *несов от* **разобра́ть**; **разбира́ться** *несов от* **разобра́ться** ▷ *возв* (*разг: понимать*): **разбира́ться в** +*prp* to be an expert in

разби́ть (-обью́, -обьёшь; *imper* -бе́й(те), *impf* **разбива́ть**) *сов перех* to break; (*машину*) to smash up; (*армию*) to crush; (*алле́ю*) to lay; **разби́ться** (*impf* **разбива́ться**) *сов возв* to break, smash; (*в аварии*) to be badly hurt; (*на группы, на участки*) to break up

разбогате́|ть (-ю) *сов от* **богате́ть**

разбо́|й (-я) *м* robbery; **разбо́йник** (-а) *м* robber

разбра́сыва|ть (-ю) *несов от* **разброса́ть**; **разбра́сываться** *несов возв*: **разбра́сываться** (*impf*) +*instr* (*деньгами*) to waste; (*друзьями*) to underrate

разброса́|ть (-ю; *impf* **разбра́сывать**) *сов перех* to scatter

разбу́|дить (-ужу́, -у́дишь) *сов от* **буди́ть**

разва́л (-а) *м* chaos

разва́лин|а (-ы) *ж* ruins *мн*

разв|али́ть (-алю́, -а́лишь; *impf* **разва́ливать**) *сов перех* to ruin; **развали́ться** (*impf* **разва́ливаться**) *сов возв* to collapse

разв|ари́ться (*3sg* -а́рится, *impf* **разва́риваться**) *сов возв* to be overcooked

ра́зве *част* really; **ра́зве он согласи́лся/не знал?** did he really agree/not know?; **ра́зве то́лько** или **что** except that

развева́|ться (*3sg* -ется) *несов возв* (*флаг*) to flutter

разведённый *прил* (*в разводе*) divorced

разве́д|ка (-ки; *gen pl* -ок) *ж* (*Гео*) prospecting; (*шпионаж*) intelligence; (*Воен*) reconnaissance; **разве́дчик** (-а) *м* (*Гео*) prospector; (*шпион*) intelligence agent; (*Воен*) scout

разв|езти́ (-езу́, -езёшь; *pt* -ёз, -езла́, -езло́, *impf* **развози́ть**) *сов перех* (*товар*) to take

разверн|у́ть (-у́, -ёшь; *impf* **развёртывать** или **развора́чивать**) *сов перех* (*бумагу*) to unfold; (*торго́влю итп*) to launch; (*кора́бль, самолёт*) to turn around; (*батальо́н*) to deploy; **разверну́ться** (*impf* **развёртываться** или **развора́чиваться**) *сов возв* (*кампа́ния, работа*) to get under way; (*автомоби́ль*) to turn around; (*вид*) to open up

развесел|и́ть (-ю́, -и́шь) *сов от* **весели́ть**

разве́|сить (-шу, -сишь) *impf* **разве́шивать** *сов перех* to hang

разв|ести́ (-еду́, -едёшь; *pt* -ёл, -ела́, *impf* **разводи́ть**) *сов перех* (*доста́вить*) to take; (*порошо́к*) to dissolve; (*сок*) to dilute; (*живо́тных*) to breed; (*цветы́, сад*) to grow; (*мост*) to raise; **развести́сь** (*impf* **разводи́ться**) *сов возв*: **развести́сь** (с +*instr*) to divorce, get divorced (from)

разветвле́ни|е (-я) *ср* (*доро́ги*) fork

разве́|ять (-ю; *impf* **разве́ивать**) *сов перех* (*облака́*) to disperse; (*сомне́ния, грусть*) to dispel; **разве́яться** (*impf* **разве́иваться**) *сов возв* (*облака́*) to disperse; (*челове́к*) to relax

развива́|ть(ся) (-ю(сь)) *несов от* **разви́ть(ся)**

развива́ющ|ийся *прил*:
развива́ющаяся страна́ developing
country

развил|ка (**-ки**; *gen pl* **-ок**) *ж* fork (*in
road*)

разви́ти|е (**-я**) *ср* development

раз|ви́ть (**-овью́, -овьёшь**; *imper*
-ве́й(те), *impf* **развива́ть**) *сов перех* to
develop; **разви́ться** (*impf* **развива́ться**)
сов возв to develop

развлека́тельный *прил* entertaining

развлече́ни|е (**-я**) *ср* entertaining

развл|е́чь (**-еку́, -ечёшь** *etc*, **-еку́т**; *pt*
-ёк, -екла́, *impf* **развлека́ть**) *сов перех*
to entertain; **развле́чься** (*impf*
развлека́ться) *сов возв* to have fun

разво́д (**-а**) *м* (*супругов*) divorce

разв|оди́ть(ся) (**-ожу́(сь), -о́дишь(ся)**)
несов от **развести́(сь)**

развора́чива|ть(ся) (**-ю(сь)**) *несов от*
разверну́ть(ся)

разворо́т (**-а**) *м* (*машины*) U-turn; (*в
книге*) double page

развя́з|ка (**-ки**; *gen pl* **-ок**) *ж* (*конец*)
finale; (*Авт*) junction

разгада́|ть (**-ю**; *impf* **разга́дывать**) *сов
перех* (*загадку*) to solve; (*замыслы*,
тайну) to guess

разга́р (**-а**) *м*: **в разга́ре** +*gen* (*сезона*) at
the height of; (*боя*) in the heart of;
кани́кулы в (по́лном) разга́ре the holidays
are in full swing

разгиба́|ть(ся) (**-ю(сь)**) *несов от*
разогну́ть(ся)

разгла́|дить (**-жу, -дишь**; *impf*
разгла́живать) *сов перех* to smooth out

разгла|си́ть (**-шу́, -си́шь**; *impf*
разглаша́ть) *сов перех* to divulge,
disclose

разгова́рива|ть (**-ю**) *несов*:
разгова́ривать (с +*instr*) to talk (to)

разгово́р (**-а**) *м* conversation;
разгово́рник (**-а**) *м* phrase book;
разгово́рный *прил* colloquial

разго́н (**-а**) *м* (*демонстрации*) breaking
up; (*автомобиля*) acceleration

разгоня́|ть(ся) (**-ю(сь)**) *несов от*
разогна́ть(ся)

разгор|е́ться (*3sg* **-и́тся**, *impf*
разгора́ться) *сов возв* to flare up

разгоряч|и́ться (**-у́сь, -и́шься**) *сов возв*
(*от волнения*) to get het up; (*от бега*) to be
hot

разгром|и́ть (**-лю́, -и́шь**) *сов перех*
(*врага*) to crush; (*книгу*) to slam

разгр|узи́ть (**-ужу́, -у́зишь**; *impf*
разгружа́ть) *сов перех* to unload

разгры́з|ть (**-у, -ёшь**) *сов от* **грызть**

раздава́|ть(ся) (**-ю, -ёшь(ся)**) *несов от*
разда́ть(ся)

разд|ави́ть (**-авлю́, -а́вишь**) *сов от*
дави́ть

разда́ть (*как* **дать**; *см Table 16*; *impf*
раздава́ть) *сов перех* to give out,
distribute; **разда́ться** (*impf*
раздава́ться) *сов возв* (*звук*) to be heard

раздва́ива|ться (**-юсь**) *несов от*
раздвои́ться

раздви́н|уть (**-у**; *impf* **раздвига́ть**) *сов
перех* to move apart

раздво|и́ться (**-ю́сь, -и́шься**; *impf*
раздва́иваться) *сов возв* (*дорога, река*)
to divide into two; (*перен: мнение*) to be
divided

раздева́л|ка (**-ки**; *gen pl* **-ок**) *ж*
changing room

раздева́|ть(ся) (**-ю(сь)**) *несов от*
разде́ть(ся)

разде́л (**-а**) *м* (*имущества*) division;
(*часть*) section

разде́ла|ть (**-ю**; *impf* **разде́лывать**) *сов
перех* (*тушу*) to cut up; **разде́латься**
(*impf* **разде́лываться**) *сов возв* (*разг*):
разде́латься с +*instr* (*с делами*) to finish;
(*с долгами*) to settle

раздел|и́ть (**-елю́, -е́лишь**) *сов от*
дели́ть ▷ (*impf* **разделя́ть**) *перех*
(*мнение*) to share; **раздели́ться** *сов от*
дели́ться ▷ (*impf* **разделя́ться**) *возв*
(*мнения, общество*) to become divided

разде́|ть (**-ну, -нешь**; *impf* **раздева́ть**)
сов перех to undress; **разде́ться** (*impf*
раздева́ться) *сов возв* to get undressed

раздира́|ть (**-ю**) *несов перех* (*душу,
общество*) to tear apart

раздраже́ни|е (**-я**) *ср* irritation;
раздражи́тельный *прил* irritable;
раздраж|и́ть (**-у́, -и́шь**; *impf*
раздража́ть) *сов перех* to irritate, annoy;
(*нервы*) to agitate; **раздражи́ться** (*impf*
раздража́ться) *сов возв* (*кожа, глаза*) to
become irritated; (*человек*): **раздражи́ться**
(+*instr*) to be irritated (by)

раздува́|ть(ся) (**-ю(сь)**) *несов от*
разду́ть(ся)

разду́ма|ть (**-ю**; *impf* **разду́мывать**) *сов*
+*infin* to decide not to do

разду́мыва|ть (**-ю**) *несов от* **разду́мать**
▷ *неперех*: **разду́мывать (о** +*prp*) (*долго
думать*) to contemplate

разду́|ть (**-ю**; *impf* **раздува́ть**) *сов
перех* (*огонь*) to fan; **у неё разду́ло щёку**
her cheek has swollen up; **разду́ться**
(*impf* **раздува́ться**) *сов возв* (*щека*) to
swell up

раз|жа́ть (**-ожму́, -ожмёшь**; *impf*
разжима́ть) *сов перех* (*пальцы, губы*) to
relax; **разжа́ться** (*impf* **разжима́ться**)
сов возв to relax

разж|ева́ть (**-ую**; *impf* **разжёвывать**)
сов перех to chew

разлага́|ть(ся) (**-ю**) *несов от*
разложи́ть(ся)

разла́мыва|ть (**-ю**) *несов от* **разлома́ть**;
разломи́ть

разле|те́ться (**-чу́сь, -ти́шься**; *impf*
разлета́ться) *сов возв* to fly off (*in
different directions*)

разли́в (-а) *м* flooding
разли́|ть (-олью́, -ольёшь; *impf* **разлива́ть**) *сов перех* (*пролить*) to spill; **разли́ться** (*impf* **разлива́ться**) *сов возв* (*пролиться*); (*река*) to overflow
различа́|ть (-ю) *несов от* **различи́ть**; **различа́ться** *несов возв*: **различа́ться по** +*dat* to differ in
разли́чи|е (-я) *ср* difference
различ|и́ть (-у́, -и́шь; *impf* **различа́ть**) *сов перех* (*увидеть, услышать*) to make out; (*отличить*): **различи́ть (по** +*dat*) to distinguish (by)
разли́чный *прил* different
разл|ожи́ть (-ожу́, -о́жишь; *impf* **раскла́дывать**) *сов перех* (*карты*) to arrange; (*диван*) to open out ▷ (*impf* **разлага́ть**) (Хим, Био) to decompose; **разложи́ться** *сов возв* (*impf* **разлага́ться**) (Хим, Био) to decompose; (*общество*) to disintegrate
разл|оми́ть (-омлю́, -о́мишь; *impf* **разла́мывать**) *сов перех* (*на части*) to break up
разлу́к|а (-и) *ж* separation
разлуч|и́ть (-у́, -и́шь; *impf* **разлуча́ть**) *сов перех*: **разлучи́ть кого́-н с** +*instr* to separate sb from; **разлучи́ться** (*impf* **разлуча́ться**) *сов возв*: **разлучи́ться (с** +*instr*) to be separated (from)
разл|юби́ть (-юблю́, -ю́бишь) *сов перех* (+*infin*: *читать, гулять итп*) to lose one's enthusiasm for doing; **он меня́ разлюби́л** he doesn't love me any more
разма́|зать (-жу, -жешь; *impf* **разма́зывать**) *сов перех* to smear
разма́тыва|ть (-ю) *несов от* **размота́ть**
разма́х (-а) *м* (*рук*) span; (*перен: деятельности*) scope; (: *проекта*) scale; **разма́х кры́льев** wingspan
размахн|у́ться (-у́сь, -ёшься; *impf* **разма́хиваться**) *сов возв* to bring one's arm back; (*перен. разг: в делах итп*) to go to town
разме́н (-а) *м* (*денег, пленных*) exchange; **разме́н кварти́ры** flat swap (*of one large flat for two smaller ones*)
разме́нный *прил*: **разме́нный автома́т** change machine; **разме́нная моне́та** (small) change
разменя́|ть (-ю; *impf* **разме́нивать**) *сов перех* (*деньги*) to change; (*квартиру*) to exchange; **разменя́ться** (*impf* **разме́ниваться**) *сов возв* (*перен: разг*: обменя́ть жилпло́щадь) to do a flat swap (*of one large flat for two smaller ones*)
разме́р (-а) *м* size
разме|сти́ть (-щу́, -сти́шь; *impf* **размеща́ть**) *сов перех* (*в отеле*) to place; (*на столе*) to arrange; **размести́ться** (*impf* **размеща́ться**) *сов возв* (*по комнатам*) to settle o.s.
разме́|тить (-чу, -тишь; *impf* **размеча́ть**) *сов перех* to mark out

размеша́|ть (-ю; *impf* **разме́шивать**) *сов перех* to stir
размеща́|ть(ся) (-ю(сь)) *несов от* **размести́ть(ся)**
размина́|ть(ся) (-ю(сь)) *несов от* **размя́ть(ся)**
размини́р|овать (-ую) (*не)сов перех*: **размини́ровать по́ле** to clear a field of mines
размин|у́ться (-у́сь, -ёшься) *сов возв* (*не встретиться*) to miss each other; (*дать пройти*) to pass
размно́ж|ить (-у, -ишь; *impf* **размножа́ть**) *сов перех* to make (multiple) copies of; **размно́житься** (*perf* **размножа́ться**) *сов возв* (Био) to reproduce
размо́к|нуть (-ну; *pt* -, -ла, *impf* **размока́ть**) *сов* (*хлеб, картон*) to go soggy; (*почва*) to become sodden
размо́лв|ка (-ки) *ж* quarrel
размота́|ть (-ю; *impf* **разма́тывать**) *сов перех* to unwind
разм|ы́ть (3sg -о́ет, *impf* **размыва́ть**) *сов перех* to wash away
размышля́|ть (-ю) *несов*: **размышля́ть (о** +*prp*) to contemplate, reflect (on)
раз|мя́ть (-омну́, -омнёшь; *impf* **размина́ть**) *сов перех* to loosen up; **размя́ться** (*impf* **размина́ться**) *сов возв* to warm up
разна́шива|ть(ся) (-ю) *несов от* **разноси́ть(ся)**
разн|ести́ (-есу́, -есёшь; *pt* -ёс, -есла́, *impf* **разноси́ть**) *сов перех* (*письма*) to deliver; (*тарелки*) to put out; (*тучи*) to disperse; (*заразу, слухи*) to spread; (*раскритиковать*) to slam; **разнести́сь** (*impf* **разноси́ться**) *сов возв* (*слух, запах*) to spread; (*звук*) to resound
разнима́|ть (-ю) *несов от* **разня́ть**
ра́зниц|а (-ы) *ж* difference; **кака́я ра́зница?** what difference does it make?
разнови́дност|ь (-и) *ж* (Био) variety; (*людей*) type, kind
разногла́си|е (-я) *ср* disagreement
разнообра́зи|е (-я) *ср* variety
разнообра́зный *прил* various
разн|оси́ть (-ошу́, -о́сишь) *несов от* **разнести́** ▷ (*impf* **разна́шивать**) *сов перех* (*обувь*) to break in; **разноси́ться** *несов от* **разнести́сь** ▷ (*impf* **разна́шиваться**) *сов возв* (*обувь*) to be broken in
разносторо́нний *прил* (*деятельность*) wide-ranging; (*ум, личность*) multifaceted
ра́зность|ь (-и) *ж* difference
разноцве́тный *прил* multicoloured (*Brit*), multicolored (*US*)
ра́зный *прил* different
разоблач|и́ть (-у́, -и́шь; *impf* **разоблача́ть**) *сов перех* to expose
раз|обра́ть (-беру́, -берёшь; *impf* **разбира́ть**) *сов перех* (*бумаги*) to sort

out; (*текст*) to analyse (*Brit*), analyze (*US*); (*вкус, подпись итп*) to make out; **разбира́ть** (*perf* **разобра́ть**) **(на ча́сти)** to take apart; **разобра́ться** (*impf* **разбира́ться**) *сов возв:* **разобра́ться в** +*prp* (*в вопросе, в деле*) to sort out

ра́зовый *прил:* **ра́зовый биле́т** single (*Brit*) *или* one-way ticket

раз|огна́ть (**-гоню́, -го́нишь;** *impf* **разгоня́ть**) *сов перех* (*толпу*) to break up; (*тучи*) to disperse; (*машину*) to increase the speed of; **разгна́ться** (*impf* **разгоня́ться**) *сов возв* to build up speed, accelerate

разогн|у́ть (**-у́, -ёшь;** *impf* **разгиба́ть**) *сов перех* (*проволоку*) to straighten out; **разогну́ться** (*impf* **разгиба́ться**) *сов возв* to straighten up

разогре́|ть (**-ю;** *impf* **разогрева́ть**) *сов перех* (*чайник, суп*) to heat; **разогре́ться** (*impf* **разогрева́ться**) *сов возв* (*суп*) to heat up

разозл|и́ть(ся) (**-ю́(сь), -и́шь(ся)**) *сов от* **зли́ть(ся)**

разойти́сь (*как* **идти́;** см *Table 18; impf* **расходи́ться**) *сов возв* (*гости*) to leave; (*толпа*) to disperse; (*тираж*) to sell out; (*не встретиться*) to miss each other; (*супруги*) to split up; (*шов, крепления*) to come apart; (*перен: мнения*) to diverge; (*разг: дать волю себе*) to get going

ра́зом *нареч* (*разг: все вместе*) all at once; (*: в один приём*) all in one go

разорва́ть (**-у́, -ёшь**) *сов от* **рвать** ▷ (*impf* **разрыва́ть**) *перех* to tear *или* rip up; (*перен: связь*) to sever; (*: договор*) to break; **разорва́ться** *сов от* **рва́ться** ▷ (*impf* **разрыва́ться**) *возв* (*одежда*) to tear, rip; (*верёвка, цепь*) to break; (*связь*) to be severed; (*снаряд*) to explode

разор|и́ть (**-ю́, -и́шь;** *impf* **разоря́ть**) *сов перех* (*деревню, гнездо*) to plunder; (*население*) to impoverish; (*: компанию, страну*) to ruin; **разори́ться** (*impf* **разоря́ться**) *сов возв* (*человек*) to become impoverished; (*компания*) to go bust *или* bankrupt

разоруж|и́ть (**-у́, -и́шь;** *impf* **разоружа́ть**) *сов перех* to disarm; **разоружи́ться** (*impf* **разоружа́ться**) *сов возв* to disarm

разоря́|ть(ся) (**-ю(сь)**) *несов от* **разори́ть(ся)**

разо|сла́ть (**-шлю́, -шлёшь;** *impf* **рассыла́ть**) *сов перех* to send out

разостла́ть (**расстелю́, расстелешь**) *несов* = **расстели́ть**

разочарова́ни|е (**-я**) *ср* disappointment; (*потеря веры*): **разочарова́ние в** +*prp* (*в идее*) disenchantment with

разочаро́ванный *прил* disappointed; **разочаро́ванный в** +*prp* (*в идее*) disenchanted with

разочар|ова́ть (**-у́ю;** *impf*

разочаро́вывать) *сов перех* to disappoint; **разочарова́ться** (*impf* **разочаро́вываться**) *сов возв:* **разочарова́ться в** +*prp* to become disenchanted with

разрабо́та|ть (**-ю;** *impf* **разраба́тывать**) *сов перех* to develop

разрабо́т|ка (**-ки**) *ж* development; **га́зовые разрабо́тки** gas fields *мн;* **нефтяны́е разрабо́тки** oilfields *мн*

разра|зи́ться (**-жу́сь, -зи́шься;** *impf* **разража́ться**) *сов возв* to break out

разра|сти́сь (*3sg* **-стётся,** *pt* **-о́сся, -осла́сь,** *impf* **разраста́ться**) *сов возв* (*лес*) to spread

разре́з (**-а**) *м* (*на юбке*) slit; (*Геом*) section

разре́|зать (**-жу, -жешь**) *сов от* **ре́зать**

разреша́|ть (**-ю**) *несов от* **разреши́ть;** **разреша́ться** *несов от* **разреши́ться** ▷ *неперех* (*допускаться*) to be allowed *или* permitted

разреше́ни|е (**-я**) *ср* (*действие*) authorization; (*родителей*) permission; (*проблемы*) resolution; (*документ*) permit

разреш|и́ть (**-у́, -и́шь;** *impf* **разреша́ть**) *сов перех* (*решить*) to resolve; (*позволить*): **разреши́ть кому́-н** +*infin* to allow *или* permit sb to do; **разреши́те?** may I come in? **разреши́те пройти́** may I pass; **разреши́ться** (*impf* **разреша́ться**) *сов возв* to be resolved

разровня́|ть (**-ю**) *сов от* **ровня́ть**

разр|уби́ть (**-ублю́, -у́бишь;** *impf* **разруба́ть**) *сов перех* to chop in two

разруши́тельный *прил* (*война*) devastating; (*действие*) destructive

разру́ш|ить (**-у, -ишь;** *impf* **разруша́ть**) *сов перех* to destroy; **разру́шиться** (*impf* **разруша́ться**) *сов возв* to be destroyed

разры́в (**-а**) *м* (*во времени, в цифрах*) gap; (*отношений*) severance; (*снаряда*) explosion

разрыва́|ть(ся) (**-ю(сь)**) *несов от* **разорва́ть(ся)**

разря́д (**-а**) *м* (*тип*) category; (*квалификация*) grade

разря|ди́ть (**-жу́, -ди́шь;** *impf* **разряжа́ть**) *сов перех* (*ружьё*) to discharge; **разряжа́ть** (*perf* **разряди́ть**) **обстано́вку** to diffuse the situation

разря́д|ка (**-ки;** *gen pl* **-ок**) *ж* escape; (*в тексте*) spacing; **разря́дка (междунаро́дной напряжённости)** détente

разряжа́|ть (**-ю**) *несов от* **разряди́ть**

разубе|ди́ть (**-жу́, -ди́шь;** *impf* **разубежда́ть**) *сов перех:* **разубеди́ть кого́-н** (**в** +*prp*) to dissuade sb (from)

разува́|ть(ся) (**-ю(сь)**) *несов от* **разу́ть(ся)**

ра́зум (**-а**) *м* reason; **разуме́|ться** (*3sg* **-ется**) *сов возв:* **под э́тим разуме́ется, что ...** by this is meant that ...; (*само́ собо́й*) **разуме́ется** that goes without saying ▷ вводн сл: он, разуме́ется, не знал об э́том naturally, he knew nothing about it; **разу́мный** прил (существо) intelligent; (поступок, решение) reasonable

разу́тый прил (без обуви) barefoot

раз|у́ть (-у́ю; impf **разува́ть**) сов перех: **разу́ть кого́-н** to take sb's shoes off; **разу́ться** (impf **разува́ться**) сов возв to take one's shoes off

разуч|и́ть (-у́, -у́чишь; impf **разу́чивать**) сов перех to learn; **разучи́ться** (impf **разу́чиваться**) сов возв: **разучи́ться** +infin to forget how to do

разъеда́|ть (3sg -ет) несов от **разъе́сть**

разъезжа́|ть (-ю) несов (по делам) to travel; (ката́ться) to ride about; **разъезжа́ться** несов от **разъе́хаться**

разъе́хаться (как **е́хать**; см Table 19; impf **разъезжа́ться**) сов возв (гости) to leave

разъярённый прил furious

разъясн|и́ть (-ю́, -и́шь; impf **разъясня́ть**) сов перех to clarify

разыгра́|ть (-ю; impf **разы́грывать**) сов перех (Муз, Спорт) to play; (сце́ну) to act out; (в лотере́ю) to raffle; (разг: подшути́ть) to play a joke или trick on

раз|ыска́ть (-ыщу́, -ы́щешь; impf **разы́скивать**) сов перех to find

РАИС ср сокр (= Росси́йское аге́нтство интеллектуа́льной со́бственности) copyright protection agency

ра|й (-я; loc sg -ю́) м paradise

райо́н (-а) м (страны́) region; (го́рода) district

райо́нный прил district

ра́йский прил heavenly

рак (-а) м (Зоол: речной) crayfish (мн crayfish); (: морско́й) crab; (Мед) cancer; (созве́здие): **Рак** Cancer

раке́т|а (-ы) ж rocket; (Воен) missile; (су́дно) hydrofoil

раке́т|ка (-ки; gen pl -ок) ж (Спорт) racket

ра́ковин|а (-ы) ж (Зоол) shell; (для умыва́ния) sink

ра́ковый прил (Зоол, Кулин) crab; (Мед) cancer

ра́м|ка (-ки; gen pl -ок) ж frame; см также **ра́мки**

ра́м|ки (-ок) мн +gen: рассказа, обя́занностей) framework ед от; (зако́на, прили́чия) limits мн от; **в ра́мках** +gen (зако́на, прили́чия) within the bounds of; (перегово́ров) within the framework of; **за ра́мками** +gen beyond the bounds of

РАН м сокр (= Росси́йская акаде́мия нау́к) Russian Academy of Sciences

ра́н|а (-ы) ж wound

ра́неный прил injured; (Воен) wounded

ра́н|ить (-ю, -ишь) (не)сов перех to wound

ра́нний прил early

ра́но нареч early ▷ как сказ it's early; **ра́но и́ли по́здно** sooner or later

ра́ньше сравн нареч от **ра́но** ▷ нареч (пре́жде) before ▷ предл +gen before; **ра́ньше вре́мени** (ра́доваться итп) too soon

ра́порт (-а) м report

рапорт|ова́ть (-у́ю) (не)сов: **рапортова́ть** (кому́-н о чём-н) to report back (to sb on sth)

ра́с|а (-ы) ж race; **раси́зм** (-а) м racism; **раси́ст** (-а) м racist

раска́ива|ться (-юсь) несов от **раска́яться**

раскал|и́ть (-ю́, -и́шь; impf **раскаля́ть**) сов перех to bring to a high temperature; **раскали́ться** (impf **раскаля́ться**) сов возв to get very hot

раска́лыва|ть(ся) (-ю(сь)) несов от **расколо́ть(ся)**

раска́пыва|ть (-ю) несов от **раскопа́ть**

раска́|яться (-юсь; impf **раска́иваться**) сов возв: **раска́яться (в** +prp) to repent (of)

раскида́|ть (-ю; impf **раски́дывать**) сов перех to scatter

раски́н|уть (-у; impf **раски́дывать**) сов перех (ру́ки) to throw open; (се́ти) to spread out; (ла́герь) to set up; **раски́нуться** (impf **раски́дываться**) сов возв to stretch out

раскладно́й прил folding

расклад|у́шка (-ки; gen pl -ек) ж (разг) camp bed (Brit), cot (US)

раскла́дыва|ть (-ю) несов от **разложи́ть**

раско́ванный прил relaxed

раск|оло́ть (-олю́, -о́лешь; impf **раска́лывать**) сов перех to split; (лёд, оре́х) to crack; **расколо́ться** (impf **раска́лываться**) сов возв (поле́но, оре́х) to split open; (перен: организа́ция) to be split

раскопа́|ть (-ю; impf **раска́пывать**) сов перех to dig up

раско́п|ки (-ок) мн (рабо́ты) excavations; (ме́сто) (archaeological) dig ед

раскра́|сить (-шу, -сишь; impf **раскра́шивать**) сов перех to colour (Brit) или color (US) (in)

раскро́|ить (-ю́, -и́шь) сов перех to cut

раскру́т|ка (-ки; gen pl -ок) ж (разг) hyping up

раскры́|ть (-о́ю, -о́ешь; impf **раскрыва́ть**) сов перех to open; (перен: чью-нибудь та́йну, план) to discover; (: свою́ та́йну, план) to disclose; **раскры́ться** (impf **раскрыва́ться**) сов возв to open

раск|упи́ть (-уплю́, -у́пишь; impf **раскупа́ть**) сов перех to buy up

ра́совый прил racial

распада́|ться (3sg -ется) несов от

распа́сться ▷ *возв* (*состоять из частей*): **распада́ться на** +*acc* to be divided into

распахн|у́ть (-у́, -ёшь; *impf* **распа́хивать**) *сов перех* to throw open; **распахну́ться** (*impf* **распа́хиваться**) *сов возв* to fly open

распашо́н|ка (-ки; *gen pl* -ок) *ж* cotton baby top without buttons

распеча́та|ть (-ю; *impf* **распеча́тывать**) *сов перех* (*письмо, пакет*) to open; (*размножить*) to print off

распеча́т|ка (-ки; *gen pl* -ок) *ж* (*доклада*) print-out

распина́|ть (-ю) *несов от* **распя́ть**

расписа́ни|е (-я) *ср* timetable, schedule

расп|иса́ть (-ишу́, -и́шешь; *impf* **распи́сывать**) *сов перех* (*дела*) to arrange; (*стены, шкату́лку*) to paint; (*разг: женить*) to marry (*in registry office*); **расписа́ться** (*impf* **распи́сываться**) *сов возв* (*поставить подпись*) to sign one's name; **распи́сываться** (*perf* **расписа́ться**) **с** +*instr* to get married to (*in registry office*)

распи́с|ка (-ки; *gen pl* -ок) *ж* (*о получении денег*) receipt; (*о невыезде*) warrant

распла́т|а (-ы) *ж* payment; (*перен: за преступление*) retribution;

распл|ати́ться (-ачу́сь, -а́тишься; *impf* **распла́чиваться**) *сов возв*: **расплати́ться** (**с** +*instr*) to pay; (*перен: с предателем*) to revenge o.s. on

распл|еска́ть (-ещу́, -е́щешь; *impf* **расплёскивать**) *сов перех* to spill; **расплеска́ться** (*impf* **расплёскиваться**) *сов возв* to spill

расплы́вчатый *прил* (*рисунок, очертания*) blurred; (*перен: ответ, намёк*) vague

расплы́|ться (-ву́сь, -вёшься; *impf* **расплыва́ться**) *сов возв* (*краски*) to run; (*перен: фигуры*) to be blurred

распого́д|иться (3sg -ится) *сов возв* (*о погоде*) to clear up

распозна́|ть (-ю; *impf* **распознава́ть**) *сов перех* to identify

распола́га|ть (-ю) *несов от* **расположи́ть** ▷ *неперех* (+*instr*: **временем**) to have available; **распола́га́ться** *несов от* **расположи́ться** ▷ *возв* (*находиться*) to be situated *или* located

расположе́ни|е (-я) *ср* (*место: лагеря*) location; (*комнат*) layout; (*симпатия*) disposition

распо́ложенный *прил*: **распо́ложенный к** +*dat* (*к человеку*) well-disposed towards; (*к болезни*) susceptible to

распол|ожи́ть (-ожу́, -о́жишь; *impf* **распола́гать**) *сов перех* (*мебель, вещи итп*) to arrange; (*отряд*) to station; **распола́гать** (*perf* **расположи́ть**) **кого́-н к**

себе́ to win sb over; **расположи́ться** (*impf* **располага́ться**) *сов возв* (*человек*) to settle down; (*отряд*) to position itself

распоряди́тел|ь (-я) *м* (*Комм*) manager; **распоряди́тельный** *прил*: **распоряди́тельный дире́ктор** managing director

распоря|ди́ться (-жу́сь, -ди́шься; *impf* **распоряжа́ться**) *сов возв* to give out instructions

распоря́д|ок (-ка) *м* routine

распоряжа́|ться (-юсь) *несов от* **распоряди́ться** ▷ *возв*: **распоряжа́ться** (+*instr*) to be in charge of

распоряже́ни|е (-я) *ср* (*управление*) management; **ба́нковское распоряже́ние** banker's order; **в распоряже́ние кого́-н/ чего́-н** at sb's/sth's disposal

распра́в|ить (-лю, -ишь; *impf* **расправля́ть**) *сов перех* to straighten out; (*крылья*) to spread; **распра́виться** (*impf* **расправля́ться**) *сов возв* (*см перех*) to be straightened out; to spread

распределе́ни|е (-я) *ср* distribution; (*после института*) work placement

распредел|и́ть (-ю́, -и́шь; *impf* **распределя́ть**) *сов перех* to distribute; **распредели́ться** (*impf* **распределя́ться**) *сов возв*: **распредели́ться** (**по** +*dat*) (*по группам, по бригадам*) to divide up (into)

распрода́ж|а (-и) *ж* sale

распрода́ть (*как* **дать**; *см Table 16*; *impf* **распродава́ть**) *сов перех* to sell off; (*билеты*) to sell out of

распростране́ни|е (-я) *ср* spreading; (*оружия*) proliferation; (*приказа*) application

распространённый *прил* widespread

распростран|и́ть (-ю́, -и́шь; *impf* **распространя́ть**) *сов перех* to spread; (*правило, приказ*) to apply; (*газеты*) to distribute; (*запах*) to emit; **распространи́ться** (*impf* **распространя́ться**) *сов возв* to spread; **распространи́ться** (*perf*) **на** +*acc* to extend to; (*приказ*) to apply to

распрям|и́ть (-лю́, -и́шь; *impf* **распрямля́ть**) *сов перех* (*проволоку*) to straighten (out); (*плечи*) to straighten

расп|усти́ть (-ущу́, -у́стишь; *impf* **распуска́ть**) *сов перех* (*армию*) to disband; (*волосы*) to let down; (*парламент*) to dissolve; (*слухи*) to spread; (*перен: ребёнка итп*) to spoil; **распусти́ться** (*impf* **распуска́ться**) *сов возв* (*цветы, почки*) to open out; (*дети, люди*) to get out of hand

распу́хн|уть (-у; *impf* **распуха́ть**) *сов* to swell up

распыл|и́ть (-ю́, -и́шь; *impf* **распыля́ть**) *сов перех* to spray

расса́д|а (-ы) *ж собир* (*Бот*) seedlings *мн*

расс|ади́ть (-ажу́, -а́дишь; *impf*

расса́живать) *сов перех* (гостей, публику) to seat; (цветы) to thin out

рассве|сти́ (3sg -тёт, pt -ло́, impf **рассвета́ть)** *сов безл*: **рассвело́** dawn was breaking

рассве́т (-а) *м* daybreak

рассе́ива|ть(ся) (-ю(сь)) *несов от* **рассе́ять(ся)**

рассека́|ть (-ю) *несов от* **рассе́чь**

рассе|ли́ть (-елю́, -е́лишь; impf **расселя́ть)** *сов перех* (по комнатам) to accommodate

расс|ерди́ть(ся) (-ержу́(сь), -е́рдишь(ся)) *сов от* **серди́ть(ся)**

рассе́|сться (-я́дусь, -я́дешься; pt -е́лся, -е́лась) *сов возв* (по стола́м, в за́ле) to take one's seat

рассе́|чь (-еку́, -ечёшь etc, -еку́т; pt -ёк, -екла́, impf **рассека́ть)** *сов перех* to cut in two; (губу, лоб) to cut

рассе́|ять (-ю; impf **рассе́ивать)** *сов перех* (семена, людей) to scatter; (перен: сомнения) to dispel; **рассе́яться** (impf **рассе́иваться)** *сов возв* (люди) to be scattered; (тучи, дым) to disperse

расска́з (-а) *м* story; (свидетеля) account; **расск|аза́ть** (-ажу́, -а́жешь; impf **расска́зывать)** *сов перех* to tell; **расска́зчик** (-а) *м* storyteller; (автор) narrator

рассла́б|ить (-лю, -ишь; impf **расслабля́ть)** *сов перех* to relax; **рассла́биться** (impf **расслабля́ться)** *сов возв* to relax

рассле́д|овать (-ую) (не)сов перех to investigate

рассма́трива|ть (-ю) *несов от* **рассмотре́ть** ▷ *перех*: **рассма́тривать что-н как** to regard sth as

рассмеш|и́ть (-у́, -и́шь) *сов от* **смеши́ть**

рассме|я́ться (-ю́сь, -ёшься) *сов возв* to start laughing

рассм|отре́ть (-отрю́, -о́тришь; impf **рассма́тривать)** *сов перех* (изучить) to examine; (различить) to discern

расспр|оси́ть (-ошу́, -о́сишь; impf **расспра́шивать)** *сов перех*: **расспроси́ть (о +prp)** to question (about)

рассро́ч|ка (-ки; gen pl -ек) *ж* installment (Brit), instalment (US); **в рассро́чку** on hire purchase (Brit), on the installment plan (US)

расстава́ни|е (-я) *ср* parting

расста|ва́ться (-ю́сь, -ёшься) *сов от* **расста́ться**

расста́в|ить (-лю, -ишь; impf **расставля́ть)** *сов перех* to arrange

расстано́в|ка (-ки; gen pl -ок) *ж* (мебели, книг) arrangement

расста́|ться (-нусь, -нешься; impf **расстава́ться)** *сов возв*: **расста́ться с +instr** to part with

расстегн|у́ть (-у́, -ёшь; impf

расстёгивать) *сов перех* to undo; **расстегну́ться** (impf **расстёгиваться)** *сов возв* (человек) to unbutton o.s.; (рубашка, пуговица) to come undone

расст|ели́ть (-елю́, -е́лешь; impf **расстила́ть)** *сов перех* to spread out

расстоя́ни|е (-я) *ср* distance

расстра́ива|ть(ся) (-ю(сь)) *несов от* **расстро́ить(ся)**

расстре́л (-а) *м* +gen shooting или firing at; (казнь) execution (by firing squad)

расстреля́|ть (-ю; impf **расстре́ливать)** *сов перех* (демонстрацию) to open fire on; (казнить) to shoot

расстро́енный *прил* (здоровье, нервы) weak; (человек, вид) upset; (рояль) out of tune

расстро́|ить (-ю, -ишь; impf **расстра́ивать)** *сов перех* (планы) to disrupt; (человека, желудок) to upset; (здоровье) to damage; (Муз) to put out of tune; **расстро́иться** (impf **расстра́иваться)** *сов возв* (планы) to fall through; (человек) to get upset; (нервы) to weaken; (здоровье) to be damaged; (Муз) to go out of tune

расстро́йств|о (-а) *ср* (огорчение) upset; (речи) dysfunction; **расстро́йство желу́дка** stomach upset

расст|упи́ться (3sg -у́пится, impf **расступа́ться)** *сов возв* (толпа) to make way

рассу|ди́ть (-жу́, -у́дишь) *сов*: **она́ рассуди́ла пра́вильно** her judgement was correct

рассу́д|ок (-ка) *м* reason

рассужда́|ть (-ю) *несов* to reason; **рассужда́ть (impf) о +prp** to debate

рассужде́ни|е (-я) *ср* judg(e)ment

рассчита́|ть (-ю; impf **рассчи́тывать)** *сов перех* to calculate; **рассчита́ться** (impf **рассчи́тываться)** *сов возв*: **рассчита́ться (с +instr)** (с продавцом) to settle up (with)

рассчи́тыва|ть (-ю) *несов от* **рассчита́ть** ▷ *неперех*: **рассчи́тывать на +acc** (надеяться) to count или rely on; **рассчи́тываться** *несов от* **рассчита́ться**

рассыла́|ть (-ю) *несов от* **разосла́ть**

рассы́п|ать (-лю, -лешь; impf **рассыпа́ть)** *сов перех* to spill; **рассы́паться** (impf **рассыпа́ться)** *сов возв* (сахар, бусы) to spill; (толпа) to scatter

раста́плива|ть (-ю) *несов от* **растопи́ть**

раста́птыва|ть (-ю) *несов от* **растопта́ть**

раста́|ять (-ю) *сов от* **та́ять**

раство́р (-а) *м* (Хим) solution; (строительный) mortar

раствори́мый *прил* soluble; **раствори́мый ко́фе** instant coffee

раствори́тел|ь (-я) *м* solvent

раствор|и́ть (-ю́, -и́шь; *impf*
раствор|я́ть) *сов перех* (*порошок*) to
dissolve; (*окно, дверь*) to open;
раствори́ться (*impf* **раствор|я́ться**) *сов
возв* (*см перех*) to dissolve; to open

расте́ни|е (-я) *ср* plant

раст|ере́ть (разотру́, разотрёшь; *pt*
-ёр, -ёрла, *impf* **растира́ть**) *сов перех*
(*рану, тело*) to massage

расте́рянный *прил* confused

растер|я́ться (-ю́сь) *сов возв* (*человек*)
to be at a loss, be confused; (*письма*)
to disappear

раст|е́чься (*3sg* -ечётся, *pt* -ёкся,
-екла́сь, *impf* **растека́ться**) *сов возв*
(*вода*) to spill

раст|и́ (-у́, -ёшь; *pt* рос, росла́, росло́,
perf **вы́расти**) *несов* to grow

растира́|ть (-ю) *несов от* **растере́ть**

расти́тельный *прил* plant;
расти́тельное ма́сло vegetable oil

ра|сти́ть (-щу́, -сти́шь; *perf* **вы́растить**)
несов перех (*детей*) to raise; (*цветы*) to
grow

раст|опи́ть (-оплю́, -о́пишь; *impf*
раста́пливать) *сов перех* (*печку*) to
light; (*воск, жир, лёд*) to melt;
растопи́ться *сов от* **топи́ться**

раст|опта́ть (-опчу́, -о́пчешь; *impf*
раста́птывать) *сов перех* to trample on

растра́т|а (-ы) *ж* (*времени, денег*) waste;
(*хищение*) embezzlement

растро́га|ть (-ю) *сов перех:* **растро́гать**
кого́-н (+*instr*) to touch *или* move sb (by);
растро́гаться *сов возв* to be touched
или moved

раст|яну́ть (-яну́, -я́нешь; *impf*
растя́гивать) *сов перех* to stretch;
(*связки*) to strain; **растяну́ться** (*impf*
растя́гиваться) *сов возв* to stretch;
(*человек, обоз*) to stretch out; (*связки*) to
be strained

расхвата́|ть (-ю; *impf* **расхва́тывать**)
сов перех (*разг*) to snatch up

расхо́д (-а) *м* (*энергии*) consumption;
(*обычно мн: затраты*) expense; (: *Комм: в
бухгалте́рии*) expenditure

расх|оди́ться (-ожу́сь, -о́дишься)
несов от **разойти́сь**

расхо́д|овать (-ую; *perf*
израсхо́довать) *несов перех* (*деньги*) to
spend; (*материалы*) to use up

расхожде́ни|е (-я) *ср* discrepancy; (*во
взглядах*) divergence

расхоте́ть (*как* **хоте́ть**; *см* Table 14) *сов*
(+*infin*: *спать, гуля́ть итп*) to no longer
want to do; **расхоте́ться** *сов безл:* (*мне*)
расхоте́лось спать I don't feel sleepy any
more

расцв|ести́ (-ету́, -етёшь; *pt* -ёл, -ела́,
-ело́, *impf* **расцвета́ть**) *сов* to blossom

расцве́т (-а) *м* (*науки*) heyday; (*таланта*)
height; **он в расцве́те сил** he is in the
prime of life

расцве́т|ка (-ки; *gen pl* -ок) *ж* colour
(*Brit*) *или* color (*US*) scheme

расце́нива|ться (*3sg* -ется) *несов:*
расце́ниваться как to be regarded as

расцен|и́ть (-ю́, -е́ни́шь; *impf*
расце́нивать) *сов перех* to judge

расце́н|ка (-ки; *gen pl* -ок) *ж* (*работы*)
rate; (*цена*) tariff

расч|еса́ть (-ешу́, -е́шешь; *impf*
расчёсывать) *сов перех* (*волосы*) to
comb; **расчеса́ть** (*perf* **расчеса́ть**)
кого́-н to comb sb's hair

расчёс|ка (-ки; *gen pl* -ок) *ж* comb

расчёт (-а) *м* (*стоимости*) calculation;
(*выгода*) advantage; (*бережли́вость*)
economy; **из расчёта** +*gen* on the basis of;
брать (*perf* **взять**) *или* **принима́ть**
(**приня́ть** *perf*) **что-н в расчёт** to take sth
into account; **я с Ва́ми в расчёте** we are all
even

расчи́|стить (-щу, -стишь; *impf*
расчища́ть) *сов перех* to clear

расшата́|ть (-ю; *impf* **расша́тывать**)
сов перех (*стул*) to make wobbly;
(*здоровье*) to damage; **расшата́ться**
(*impf* **расша́тываться**) *сов возв* (*стул*) to
become wobbly; (*здоровье*) to be damaged

расшире́ни|е (-я) *ср* widening; (*связей,
дела*) expansion; (*знаний*) broadening

расши́р|ить (-ю, -ишь; *impf*
расширя́ть) *сов перех* to widen; (*дело*)
to expand; **расши́риться** (*impf*
расширя́ться) *сов возв* (*см перех*) to
widen; to expand

ратифици́р|овать (-ую) (*не*)*сов перех*
to ratify

ра́унд (-а) *м* (*Спорт, Полит*) round

рафина́д (-а) *м* sugar cubes *мн*

рацио́н (-а) *м* ration

рациона́льный *прил* rational;
рациона́льное пита́ние well-balanced diet

рва́ный *прил* torn; (*ботинки*) worn

рв|ать (-у, -ёшь; *perf* **порва́ть** *или*
разорва́ть) *несов перех* to tear, rip;
(*перен: дружбу*) to break off ▷ (*perf*
вы́рвать) (*предмет из рук*) to snatch
▷ (*perf* **сорва́ть**) (*цветы, траву*) to pick
▷ (*perf* **вы́рвать**) *безл:* **его́ рвёт** he is
vomiting *или* being sick; **рва́ться** (*perf*
порва́ться *или* **разорва́ться**) *несов*
возв to tear, rip; (*обувь*) to become worn
▷ (*perf* **разорва́ться**) (*снаряд*) to explode;
рва́ться (*impf*) **к вла́сти** to be hungry for
power

рве́ни|е (-я) *ср* enthusiasm

рво́т|а (-ы) *ж* vomiting

реаги́р|овать (-ую) *несов:* **реаги́ровать**
(**на** +*acc*) (*на свет*) to react (to) ▷ (*perf*
отреаги́ровать *или* **прореаги́ровать**)
(*на критику, на слова*) to react *или*
respond (to)

реакти́вный *прил:* **реакти́вный
дви́гатель** jet engine; **реакти́вный
самолёт** jet (plane)

реа́ктор (-а) м reactor

реа́кци|я (-и) ж reaction

реализа́ци|я (-и) ж (см глаг) implementation; disposal

реализ|ова́ть (-у́ю) (не)сов перех to implement; (товар) to sell

реа́льност|ь (-и) ж reality; (плана) feasibility

реа́льный прил real; (политика) realistic; (план) feasible

реанима́ци|я (-и) ж resuscitation; **отделе́ние реанима́ции** intensive care unit

ребён|ок (-ка; nom pl де́ти или ребя́та) м child (мн children); (грудно́й) baby

ребр|о́ (-а́; nom pl рёбра) ср (Анат) rib; (ку́бика итп) edge

ребя́т|а (-) мн от **ребёнок**; (разг: парни) guys мн

рёв (-а) м roar

рева́нш (-а) м revenge

реве́н|ь (-я́) м rhubarb

реве́ть (-у́, -ёшь) несов to roar

ревизио́нн|ый прил: **ревизио́нная коми́ссия** audit commission

реви́зи|я (-и) ж (Комм) audit; (теории) revision; **ревиз|ова́ть** (-у́ю) (не)сов перех (Комм) to audit; **ревизо́р** (-а) м (Комм) auditor

ревмати́зм (-а) м rheumatism

ревни́вый прил jealous

ревн|ова́ть (-у́ю) несов перех: **ревнова́ть (кого́-н)** to be jealous (of sb)

ре́вност|ь (-и) ж jealousy

революционе́р (-а) м revolutionary

револю́ци|я (-и) ж revolution

ре́гби ср нескл rugby; **регби́ст** (-а) м rugby player

регио́н (-а) м region; **региона́льный** прил regional

реги́стр (-а) м register; (на пишущей маши́нке): **ве́рхний/ни́жний реги́стр** upper/lower case

регистра́тор (-а) м receptionist; **регистрату́р|а** (-ы) ж reception

регистри́р|овать (-ую; perf **зарегистри́ровать**) несов перех to register; **регистри́роваться** (perf **зарегистри́роваться**) несов возв to register; (оформля́ть брак) to get married (at a registry office)

регла́мент (-а) м (поря́док) order of business; (вре́мя) speaking time

регули́р|овать (-ую) несов перех to regulate ▷ (perf **отрегули́ровать**) (мо́тор) to adjust

регулиро́вщик (-а) м: **регулиро́вщик у́личного движе́ния** traffic policeman

регуля́рный прил regular

редакти́р|овать (-ую; perf **отредакти́ровать**) несов перех to edit

реда́ктор (-а) м editor; (Комп) spellchecker; **редакцио́нн|ый** прил editorial; **редакцио́нная колле́гия** editorial board; **редакцио́нная статья́** editorial;

реда́кци|я (-и) ж (де́йствие: те́кста) editing; (формулиро́вка: статьи́ зако́на) wording; (учрежде́ние) editorial offices мн; (на ра́дио) desk; (на телеви́дении) division; **под реда́кцией** +gen edited by

реде́|ть (3sg -ет, perf **пореде́ть**) несов to thin out

реди́с (-а) м radish

ре́дкий прил rare; (во́лосы) thin; **ре́дко** нареч rarely, seldom

редколле́ги|я (-и) ж сокр = **редакцио́нная колле́гия**

режи́м (-а) ж regime; (больни́чный) routine; (Комп) mode

режиссёр (-а) м director (of film, play etc); **режиссёр-постано́вщик** (stage) director

ре́|зать (-жу, -жешь; perf **разре́зать**) несов перех (мета́лл, ко́жу) to cut; (хлеб) to slice ▷ (perf **заре́зать**) (разг: свинью́) to slaughter; (no perf: фигу́рки итп) to carve; **ре́заться** (perf **проре́заться**) несов возв (зу́бы, рога́) to come through

резе́рв (-а) м reserve

резиде́нци|я (-и) ж residence

рези́н|а (-ы) ж rubber; **рези́нк|а** (-ки; gen pl -ок) ж (ла́стик) rubber (Brit), eraser (esp US); (тесёмка) elastic; **рези́новый** прил rubber

ре́зкий прил sharp; (свет, го́лос) harsh; (за́пах) pungent; **ре́зко** нареч sharply

резн|я́ (-и́) ж slaughter

резолю́ци|я (-и) ж (съе́зда) resolution; (распоряже́ние) directive

результа́т (-а) м result

результати́вный прил productive

резьб|а́ (-ы́) ж carving; (винта́) thread

резюме́ ср нескл résumé, summary

рейс (-а) м (самолёта) flight; (авто́буса) run; (парохо́да) sailing

ре́йсовый прил regular

ре́йтинг (-а) м popularity rating

рейту́з|ы (-) мн long johns, thermal pants (US)

рек|а́ (-и́; acc sg -у, dat sg -е́, nom pl -и) ж river

рекла́м|а (-ы) ж (де́йствие: торго́вая) advertising; (сре́дство) advert (Brit), advertisement; **реклами́р|овать** (-ую) (не)сов перех to advertise; **рекла́мный** прил (отде́л, коло́нка) advertising; (статья́, фильм) publicity; **рекла́мный ро́лик** advertisement; (фи́льма) trailer; **реклама́датель** (-я) м advertiser

рекоменда́тельн|ый прил: **рекоменда́тельное письмо́** letter of recommendation

рекоменд|ова́ть (-у́ю) (не)сов перех to recommend

реконструи́р|овать (-ую) (не)сов перех to rebuild; (зда́ние) to reconstruct

реко́рд (-а) м record; **реко́рдный** прил record(-breaking); **рекордсме́н** (-а) м record holder

ре́ктор (-а) м ≈ principal; **ректора́т** (-а) м principal's office

религио́зный прил religious

рели́ги|я (-и) ж religion

рельс (-а) м (обычно мн) rail

рем|е́нь (-ня́) м belt; (сумки) strap; **привязны́е ремни́** seat belt

ремесл|о́ (-а́; nom pl **ремёсла**, gen pl **ремёсел**) ср trade

ремеш|о́к (-ка́) м strap

ремо́нт (-а) м repair; (здания: крупный) refurbishment; (: мелкий) redecoration; **теку́щий ремо́нт** maintenance; **ремонти́р|овать** (-ую; perf **отремонти́ровать**) несов перех to repair; (здание) to renovate; **ремо́нтн|ый** прил: **ремо́нтные рабо́ты** repairs мн; **ремо́нтная мастерска́я** repair workshop

рента́бельный прил profitable

рентге́н (-а) м (Мед) X-ray

репети́р|овать (-ую; perf **отрепети́ровать**) несов (не)перех to rehearse; **репети́тор** (-а) м private tutor; **репети́ци|я** (-и) ж rehearsal

ре́плик|а (-и) ж remark

репорта́ж (-а) м report; **репортёр** (-а) м reporter

репре́сси|я (-и) ж repression

репроду́ктор (-а) м loudspeaker

репроду́кци|я (-и) ж reproduction (of painting etc)

репута́ци|я (-и) ж reputation

ресни́ц|а (-ы) ж (обычно мн) eyelash

респу́блик|а (-и) ж republic

рессо́р|а (-ы) ж spring

реставра́ци|я (-и) ж restoration

реставри́р|овать (-ую; perf **реставри́ровать** или **отреставри́ровать**) несов перех to restore

рестора́н (-а) м restaurant

ресу́рс (-а) м (обычно мн) resource

рефле́кс (-а) м reflex

рефо́рм|а (-ы) ж reform

рецензи́р|овать (-ую; perf **прорецензи́ровать**) несов перех to review

реце́нзи|я (-и) ж: **реце́нзия (на** +acc) review (of)

реце́пт (-а) м (Мед) prescription; (Кулин: перен) recipe

речево́й прил speech

речно́й прил river

реч|ь (-и) ж speech; (разговорная итп) language; **речь идёт о том, как/где/кто ...** the matter in question is how/where/who ...; **об э́том не мо́жет быть и ре́чи** there can be absolutely no question of this; **о чём речь!** (разг) sure!, of course!

реша́|ть(ся) (-ю(сь)) несов от **реши́ть(ся)**

реше́ни|е (-я) ср decision; (проблемы) solution

реши́мост|ь (-и) ж resolve

реши́тельно нареч resolutely; (действовать) decisively

реш|и́ть (-у́, -и́шь; impf **реша́ть**) сов перех to decide; (проблему) to solve; **реши́ться** (impf **реша́ться**) сов возв (вопрос, судьба) to be decided; **реша́ться** (perf **реши́ться**) +infin to resolve to do; **реша́ться** (perf **реши́ться**) на +acc to decide on

ре́шк|а (-и) ж (на моне́те) tails; **орёл или ре́шка?** heads or tails?

ре́|ять (3sg -ет) сов (флаг) to fly

ржа́ве|ть (3sg -ет, perf **заржа́веть**) несов to rust

ржа́вчин|а (-ы) ж rust

ржа́вый прил rusty

ржано́й прил rye

рж|ать (-у, -ёшь) несов to neigh

ржи итп сущ см **рожь**

РИА ср сокр (= Росси́йское информацио́нное аге́нтство) Russian News Agency

Рим (-а) м Rome

ринг (-а) м (boxing) ring

ри́н|уться (-усь) сов возв to charge

рис (-а) м rice

риск (-а) м no pl risk; **риско́ванный** прил risky; **риск|ова́ть** (-у́ю; perf **рискну́ть**) несов to take risks; **рискова́ть** (perf **рискну́ть**) +instr (жи́знью, рабо́той) to risk

рисова́ни|е (-я) ср (карандашо́м) drawing; (кра́сками) painting; **рис|ова́ть** (-у́ю; perf **нарисова́ть**) несов перех (карандашо́м) to draw; (кра́сками) to paint

ри́совый прил rice

рису́н|ок (-ка) м drawing; (на тка́ни) pattern

ритм (-а) м rhythm; **ритми́ческий** прил rhythmic(al)

ритуа́л (-а) м ritual

риф (-а) м reef

ри́фм|а (-ы) ж rhyme

р-н сокр = **райо́н**

робе́|ть (-ю; perf **оробе́ть**) несов to go shy; **ро́бкий** прил shy

ро́бот (-а) м robot

р|ов (-ва; loc sg -у́) м ditch

рове́сник (-а) м: **он мой рове́сник** he is the same age as me

ро́вно нареч (писа́ть) evenly; (черти́ть) straight; (через год) exactly; **ро́вно в два часа́** at two o'clock sharp

ро́вный прил even; (линия) straight; **ровня́|ть** (-ю; perf **сровня́ть** или **вы́ровнять**) несов перех (строй) to straighten ▷ (perf **разровня́ть** или **сровня́ть**) (доро́жку) to level

род (-а; loc sg -у́, nom pl -ы́) м (о семье́) clan, family; (вид) type; (Линг) gender; **своего́ ро́да** a kind of; **в не́котором ро́де** to some extent; **что-то в э́том** или **тако́м ро́де** something like that

род. сокр (= роди́лся) b. (= born)

роддо́м (-а) м сокр = **роди́льный дом**

роди́льный прил: **роди́льный дом** maternity hospital

роди́м|ый прил: **роди́мое пятно́** birthmark

ро́дин|а (-ы) ж homeland

роди́тел|и (-ей) мн parents

роди́тельный прил: **роди́тельный паде́ж** the genitive (case)

роди́тельск|ий прил parental; **роди́тельское собра́ние** parents' meeting

ро|ди́ть (-жу́, -ди́шь; impf **рожа́ть** или **рожда́ть**) (не)сов перех to give birth to; **роди́ться** (impf **рожда́ться**) (не)сов возв to be born

родни́к (-а́) м spring (water)

родно́й прил (брат, мать итп) natural; (город, лесной) native; (в обраще́нии) dear; **родно́й язы́к** mother tongue; см также **родны́е**

родны́|е (-х) мн relatives

родово́й прил (поня́тие, при́знак) generic; (Линг) gender; (имение) family; (Мед: судороги, травма) birth

родосло́вн|ый прил: **родосло́вное де́рево** family tree

ро́дственник (-а) м relation, relative

ро́дственный прил family; (языки́, науки) related

родств|о́ (-а́) ср relationship; (душ, идей) affinity

ро́д|ы (-ов) мн labour ед (Brit), labor ед (US); **принима́ть** (perf **приня́ть**) **ро́ды** to deliver a baby

рожа́|ть (-ю) несов от **роди́ть**

рожда́емость (-и) ж birth rate

рожда́|ть(ся (-ю(сь)) несов от **роди́ть(ся)**

рожде́ни|е (-я) ср birth; **день рожде́ния** birthday

рожде́ственский прил Christmas

Рождеств|о́ (-а́) ср (Рел) Nativity; (праздник) Christmas; **С Рождество́м!** Happy или Merry Christmas!

рожь (ржи) ж rye

ро́з|а (-ы) ж (растение) rose(bush); (цветок) rose

розе́т|ка (-ки; gen pl -ок) ж power point

ро́зниц|а (-ы) ж retail goods мн; **продава́ть** (perf **прода́ть**) **в ро́зницу** to retail; **ро́зничный** прил retail

ро́зовый прил rose; (цвет) pink; (мечты) rosy

ро́зыск (-а) м search; **Уголо́вный ро́зыск** Criminal Investigation Department (Brit), Federal Bureau of Investigation (US)

ро|й (-я; nom pl -и́) м (пчёл) swarm

рок (-а) м (судьба) fate; (также **рок-му́зыка**) rock

роково́й прил fatal

рол|ь (-и; gen pl -е́й) ж role

ром (-а) м rum

рома́н (-а) м novel; (любо́вная связь) affair

романи́ст (-а) м novelist

рома́нс (-а) м (Муз) romance

рон|я́ть (-ю; perf **урони́ть**) несов перех to drop; (авторите́т) to lose

рос итп несов см **расти́**

рос|а́ (-ы́; nom pl -ы) ж dew

роско́шный прил luxurious, glamorous

ро́скош|ь (-и) ж luxury

ро́спис|ь (-и) ж (узор: на шкату́лке) design; (: на стена́х) mural; (по́дпись) signature

росси́йск|ий прил Russian; **Росси́йская Федера́ция** the Russian Federation

Росси́|я (-и) ж Russia

россия́н|ин (-ина; nom pl -е, gen pl -) м Russian

рост (-а) м growth; (увеличение) increase; (размер: челове́ка) height ▷ (nom pl -а́) (длина́: пальто́, пла́тья) length

ро́стбиф (-а) м roast beef

рост|о́к (-ка́) м (Бот) shoot

рот (рта; loc sg **рту**) м mouth

ро́т|а (-ы) ж (Воен) company

роя́л|ь (-я) м grand piano

РПЦ ж сокр (= Ру́сская правосла́вная це́рковь) Russian Orthodox Church

р/с сокр = **расчётный счёт**

рта etc сущ см **рот**

рту́т|ь (-и) ж mercury

руб. сокр = **рубль** R., r. (= rouble)

руба́ш|ка (-ки; gen pl -ек) ж (мужска́я) shirt; **ни́жняя руба́шка** (же́нская) slip; **ночна́я руба́шка** nightshirt

рубе́ж (-а́) м (госуда́рства) border; (: водный, лесной) boundary; **он живёт за рубежо́м** he lives abroad

руби́н (-а) м ruby

руб|и́ть (-лю́, -ишь; perf **сруби́ть**) сов перех (де́рево) to fell; (ве́тку) to chop off

рубл|ь (-я́) м rouble

ру́брик|а (-и) ж (раздел) column; (заголовок) heading

руга́|ть (-ю; perf **вы́ругать** или **отруга́ть**) несов перех to scold; **руга́ться** несов возв (брани́ть): **руга́ться с** +instr to scold ▷ (perf **вы́ругаться**) to swear; **руга́ться** (perf **поруга́ться**) с +instr (с му́жем, с дру́гом) to fall out with

руд|а́ (-ы́; nom pl -ы) ж ore; **рудни́к** (-а́) м mine

ружь|ё (-я́; nom pl -ья, gen pl -ей) ср rifle

рук|а́ (acc sg -у, gen sg -и́, nom pl -и, gen pl -, dat pl -а́м) ж hand; (ве́рхняя коне́чность) arm; **из пе́рвых рук** first hand; **под руко́й** to hand, handy; **отсю́да до го́рода руко́й пода́ть** it's a stone's throw from here to the town; **э́то ему́ на́ руку** that suits him

рука́в (-а́) м (одежды) sleeve

руководи́тел|ь (-я) м leader; (*кафедры, предприятия*) head; **руково|ди́ть** (-жу́, -ди́шь) несов +*instr* to lead; (*учреждением*) to be in charge of; (*страной*) to govern; (*аспирантами*) to supervise; **руково́дств|о** (-а) м leadership; (*заводом, институтом*) management; (*по эксплуата́ции, по ухо́ду*) instructions мн

ру́копис|ь (-и) ж manuscript

рукоя́т|ка (-ки; *gen pl* -ок) ж handle

рулев|о́й *прил:* **рулево́е колесо́** steering wheel

руле́т (-а) м (*с джемом*) ≈ swiss roll

рул|и́ть (-ю́, -и́шь) несов перех to steer

руло́н (-а) м roll

рул|ь (-я́) м steering wheel

румя́н|а (-) мн blusher ед; **румя́н|ец** (-ца) м glow; **румя́н|ить** (-ю, -ишь; *perf* **нарумя́нить**) несов перех (*щёки*) to apply blusher to; **румя́ниться** (*perf* **разрумя́ниться**) несов возв to flush ▷ (*perf* **нарумя́ниться**) (*женщина*) to apply blusher ▷ (*perf* **подрумя́ниться**) (*пирог*) to brown

РУО́П (-а) м сокр (= Региона́льное управле́ние по борьбе́ с организо́ванной престу́пностью) department fighting organised crime

руо́пов|ец (-ца) м member of the department fighting organized crime

ру́сл|о (-ла; *gen pl* -ел) ср bed (*of river*); (*перен: направление*) course

ру́сск|ий *прил* Russian ▷ (-ого) м Russian; **ру́сский язы́к** Russian

ру́сый *прил* (*волосы*) light brown

ру́хн|уть (-у) сов to collapse

руча́тельств|о (-а) ср guarantee

руча́|ться (-юсь; *perf* **поручи́ться**) несов возв: **руча́ться за** +*acc* to guarantee

руче́|й (-ья́) м stream

ру́ч|ка (-ки; *gen pl* -ек) ж, *уменьш от* **рука́**; (*двери, чемодана итп*) handle; (*кресла, дивана*) arm; (*для письма*) pen

ручн|о́й *прил* hand; (*животное*) tame; **ручна́я кладь, ручно́й бага́ж** hand luggage; **ручны́е часы́** (wrist)watch

РФ ж сокр = **Росси́йская Федера́ция**

ры́б|а (-ы) ж fish; **ни ры́ба ни мя́со** neither here nor there; **рыба́к** (-а́) м fisherman (*мн* fishermen); **рыба́л|ка** (-ки; *gen pl* -ок) ж fishing; **рыба́цкий** *прил* fishing; **ры́бий** *прил* fish; **ры́бий жир** cod-liver oil; **ры́бный** *прил* (*магазин*) fish; (*промышленность*) fishing; **рыболо́в** (-а) м angler, fisherman (*мн* fishermen)

Ры́б|ы (-) мн (*созвездие*) Pisces ед

рыв|о́к (-ка́) м jerk; (*в работе*) push

рыда́|ть (-ю) несов to sob

ры́жий *прил* (*волосы*) ginger; (*человек*) red-haired

ры́н|ок (-ка) м market; **ры́ночный** *прил* (*Комм*) market

рысц|а́ (-ы́) ж jog trot

ры́цар|ь (-я) м knight

рыча́г (-а́) м (*управления*) lever; (*перен: реформ*) instrument

рыч|а́ть (-у́, -и́шь) несов to growl

рэ́кет (-а) м racket

рюкза́к (-а́) м rucksack

рю́м|ка (-ки; *gen pl* -ок) ж ≈ liqueur glass

ряд (-а; *loc sg* -у́, *nom pl* -ы́) м row; (*явлений*) sequence ▷ (*prp sg* -е) (+*gen*: несколько: вопросов, причин) a number of; **из ря́да вон выходя́щий** extraordinary; *см также* **ряды́**; **рядов|о́й** *прил* (*обычный*) ordinary; (*член партии*) rank-and-file ▷ (-о́го) м (*Воен*) private

ря́дом *нареч* side by side; (*близко*) nearby; **ря́дом с** +*instr* next to; **э́то совсе́м ря́дом** it's really near

ряды́ (-о́в) мн (*армии*) ranks

ря́женк|а (-и) ж natural set yoghurt

C

c¹ *сокр* (= *се́вер*) N (= *North*); (= *секу́нда*) s
(= *second*)

○ **КЛЮЧЕВОЕ СЛОВО**

c² *предл* +*instr* **1** (*указывает на объект, от*
которого что-н отделяется) off; **лист упа́л**
с де́рева a leaf fell off the tree; **с рабо́ты/**
ле́кции from work/a lecture
2 (*следуя чему-н*) from; **перево́д с**
ру́сского a translation from Russian
3 (*об источнике*) from; **де́ньги с**
зака́зчика money from a customer
4 (*начиная с*) since; **жду тебя́ с утра́** I've
been waiting for you since morning; **с**
января́ по май from January to May
5 (*на основании чего-н*) with; **с**
одобре́ния парла́мента with the approval
of parliament
6 (*по причине*): **с го́лоду/хо́лода/го́ря** of
hunger/cold/grief; **я уста́л с доро́ги** I was
tired from the journey
▷ *предл* (+*асс: приблизительно*) about;
с киломе́тр/то́нну about a kilometre (*Brit*)
или kilometer (*US*)/ton(ne)
▷ *предл* +*instr* **1** (*совместно*) with; **я иду́**
гуля́ть с дру́гом I am going for a walk with
a friend; **он познако́мился с де́вушкой** he
has met a girl; **мы с ним** he and I
2 (*о наличии чего-н в чём-н*): **пиро́г с**
мя́сом a meat pie; **хлеб с ма́слом** bread
and butter; **челове́к с ю́мором** a man with
a sense of humour (*BRIT*) *или* humor (*US*)
3 (*при указании на образ действия*) with;
слу́шать (*impf*) **с удивле́нием** to listen with
или in surprise; **ждём с нетерпе́нием**
встре́чи с Ва́ми we look forward to
meeting you
4 (*при посредстве*): **с курье́ром** by courier
5 (*при наступлении чего-н*): **с во́зрастом**
with age; **мы вы́ехали с рассве́том** we left
at dawn

6 (*об объекте воздействия*) with;
поко́нчить (*perf*) **с несправедли́востью** to
do away with injustice; **спеши́ть** (*perf*
поспеши́ть) **с вы́водами** to draw hasty
conclusions; **что с тобо́й?** what's the
matter with you?

с. *сокр* (= *страни́ца*) р. (= *page*); = **село́**
са́бля (**-ли**; *gen pl* **-ель**) *ж* sabre (*Brit*),
saber (*US*)
сад (**-а**; *loc sg* **-у́**, *nom pl* **-ы́**) *м* garden;
(*фрукто́вый*) orchard; (*также* **де́тский**
сад) nursery (school) (*Brit*), kindergarten
сади́ться (**-жу́сь, -ди́шься**) *несов от*
сесть
садо́вник (**-а**) *м* (professional) gardener
садо́вый *прил* garden
сажа́|ть (**-ю**; *perf* **посади́ть**) *несов перех*
to seat; (*дерево*) to plant; (*самолёт*) to
land; **сажа́ть** (*perf* **посади́ть**) **кого́-н в**
тюрьму́ to put sb in prison
сайт (**-а**) *м* (*Комп*) site
саксофо́н (**-а**) *м* saxophone
сала́т (**-а**) *м* (*Кулин*) salad; **сала́тниц|а**
(**-ы**) *ж* salad bowl
са́л|о (**-а**) *ср* (*животного*) fat; (*Кулин*) lard
сало́н (**-а**) *м* salon; (*автобуса, самолёта*
итп) passenger section
салфе́т|ка (**-ки**; *gen pl* **-ок**) *ж* napkin
са́льто *ср нескл* mid-air somersault
салю́т (**-а**) *м* salute
сам (**-ого́**; *f* **сама́**, *nt* **само́**, *pl* **са́ми**) *мест*
(*я*) myself; (*ты*) yourself; (*он*) himself; (*как*
таково́й) itself; **сам по себе́** (*отдельно*) by
itself
сам|а́ (**-о́й**) *мест* (*я*) myself; (*ты*) yourself;
(*она*) herself; *см также* **сам**
сам|е́ц (**-ца́**) *м* male (*Zool*)
са́м|и (**-и́х**) *мест* (*мы*) ourselves; (*они*)
themselves; *см также* **сам**
са́м|ка (**-ки**; *gen pl* **-ок**) *ж* female (*Zool*)
са́ммит (**-а**) *м* summit
сам|о́ (**-ого́**) *мест* itself; **само́ собо́й**
(*разуме́ется*) it goes without saying; *см*
также **сам**
самова́р (**-а**) *м* samovar
самоде́льный *прил* home-made
самоде́ятельност|ь (**-и**) *ж* initiative;
(*также* **худо́жественная**
самоде́ятельность) amateur art and
performance; **самоде́ятельный** *прил*
(*театр*) amateur
самока́т (**-а**) *м* scooter
самолёт (**-а**) *м* (aero)plane (*Brit*), (air)
plane (*US*)
самостоя́тельный *прил* independent
самоуби́йств|о (**-а**) *ср* suicide;
поко́нчить (*perf*) **жизнь самоуби́йством** to
commit suicide; **самоуби́йц|а** (**-ы**) *м/ж*
suicide (victim)
самоуве́ренный *прил* self-confident,
self-assured
самоучи́тел|ь (**-я**) *м* teach-yourself book
самочу́встви|е (**-я**) *ср*: **как Ва́ше**

самочу́вствие? how are you feeling?

са́м|**ый** *мест* +n the very; (+*adj*: вку́сный, краси́вый итп) the most; **в са́мом нача́ле/конце́** right at the beginning/end; **в са́мом де́ле** really; **на са́мом де́ле** in actual fact

санато́ри|**й** (**-я**) *м* sanatorium (*Brit*), sanitarium (*US*) (*мн* sanatoriums *или* sanatoria)

санда́ли|**я** (**-и**) *ж* (*обычно мн*) sandal

са́н|**и** (**-е́й**) *мн* sledge *ед* (*Brit*), sled *ед* (*US*); (*спортивные*) toboggan *ед*

санита́р|**ка** (**-ки**; *gen pl* **-ок**) *ж* nursing auxiliary

санита́рн|**ый** *прил* sanitary; (*Воен*) medical; **санита́рная те́хника** collective term for plumbing equipment and bathroom accessories

са́н|**ки** (**-ок**) *мн* sledge *ед* (*Brit*), sled *ед* (*US*)

санкциони́р|**овать** (**-ую**) (*не*)*сов перех* to sanction

са́нкци|**я** (**-и**) *ж* sanction

санте́хник (**-а**) *м сокр* (= санита́рный те́хник) plumber; **санте́хник**|**а** (**-и**) *ж сокр* = санита́рная те́хника

сантиме́тр (**-а**) *м* centimetre (*Brit*), centimeter (*US*); (*линейка*) tape measure

сапо́г (**-а́**; *nom pl* **-и́**, *gen pl* **-**) *м* boot

сапфи́р (**-а**) *м* sapphire

сара́|**й** (**-я**) *м* shed; (*для сена*) barn

сарафа́н (**-а**) *м* (*платье*) pinafore (dress) (*Brit*), jumper (*US*)

сати́р|**а** (**-ы**) *ж* satire

сау́довск|**ий** *прил*: **Сау́довская Ара́вия** Saudi Arabia

са́ун|**а** (**-ы**) *ж* sauna

са́хар (**-а**; *part gen* **-у**) *м* sugar; **са́харниц**|**а** (**-ы**) *ж* sugar bowl; **са́харный** *прил* sugary; **са́харный диабе́т** diabetes; **са́харный песо́к** granulated sugar

сач|**о́к** (**-ка́**) *м* (*для ловли рыб*) landing net; (*для бабочек*) butterfly net

сба́в|**ить** (**-лю, -ишь**; *impf* **сбавля́ть**) *сов перех* to reduce

сбе́га|**ть** (**-ю**) *сов* (*разг*): **сбе́гать в магази́н** to run to the shop

сбежа́|**ть** (*как* **бежа́ть**; *см Table 20*; *impf* **сбега́ть**) *сов* (*убежать*) to run away; **сбега́ть** (*perf* **сбежа́ть**) *с* +*gen* (*с горы итп*) to run down; **сбежа́ться** (*impf* **сбега́ться**) *сов возв* to come running

сберба́нк (**-а**) *м сокр* (= сберега́тельный банк) savings bank

сберега́тельн|**ый** *прил*: **сберега́тельный банк** savings bank; **сберега́тельная ка́сса** savings bank; **сберега́тельная кни́жка** savings book

сберега́|**ть** (**-ю**) *несов от* **сбере́чь**

сбереже́ни|**е** (**-я**) *ср* (*действие*) saving; **сбереже́ния** savings *мн*

сбер|**е́чь** (**-егу́, -ежёшь** итп, **-егу́т**; *pt* **-ёг, -егла́**, *impf* **сберега́ть**) *сов перех* (*здоровье, любовь, отношение*) to preserve; (*деньги*) to save (up)

сберка́сс|**а** (**-ы**) *ж сокр* = сберега́тельная ка́сса

сберкни́ж|**ка** (**-ки**; *gen pl* **-ек**) *ж сокр* = сберега́тельная кни́жка

сбить (**собью́, собьёшь**; *imper* **сбе́й(те)**, *impf* **сбива́ть**) *сов перех* to knock down; (*птицу, самолёт*) to shoot down; (*сливки, яйца*) to beat; **сби́ться** (*impf* **сбива́ться**) *сов возв* (*шапка, повязка итп*) to slip; **сбива́ться** (*perf* **сби́ться**) **с пути́** (*также перен*) to lose one's way

сбли́|**зить** (**-жу, -зишь**; *impf* **сближа́ть**) *сов перех* to bring closer together; **сбли́зиться** (*impf* **сближа́ться**) *сов возв* (*люди, государства*) to become closer

сбо́ку *нареч* at the side

сбор (**-а**) *м* (*урожая, данных*) gathering; (*налогов*) collection; (*плата*: *страховой итп*) fee; (*прибыль*) takings *мн*, receipts *мн*; (*собрание*) assembly, gathering; **тамо́женный/ге́рбовый сбор** customs/stamp duty; **все в сбо́ре** everyone is present

сбо́р|**ка** (**-ки**; *gen pl* **-ок**) *ж* (*изделия*) assembly

сбо́рн|**ая** (**-ой**) *ж* (*разг*) = сбо́рная кома́нда

сбо́рник (**-а**) *м* collection (*of stories, articles*)

сбо́рн|**ый** *прил*: **сбо́рный пункт** assembly point; **сбо́рная ме́бель** kit furniture; **сбо́рная кома́нда** (*страны*) national team

сбо́рочный *прил* assembly

сбра́сыва|**ть(ся)** (**-ю(сь)**) *несов от* **сбро́сить(ся)**

сбр|**ить** (**-е́ю, -е́ешь**; *impf* **сбрива́ть**) *сов перех* to shave off

сбро́|**сить** (**-шу, -сишь**; *impf* **сбра́сывать**) *сов перех* (*предмет*) to throw down; (*свергнуть*) to overthrow; (*скорость, давление*) to reduce; **сбро́ситься** (*impf* **сбра́сываться**) *сов возв*: **сбра́сываться** (*perf* **сбро́ситься**) **с** +*gen* to throw o.s. from

сбру́|**я** (**-и**) *ж* harness

сбыт (**-а**) *м* sale

сбыть (*как* **быть**; *см Table 21*; *impf* **сбыва́ть**) *сов перех* (*товар*) to sell; **сбы́ться** (*impf* **сбыва́ться**) *сов возв* (*надежды*) to come true

св. *сокр* (= свято́й) St (= Saint)

сва́дьб|**а** (**-ьбы**; *gen pl* **-еб**) *ж* wedding

свал|**и́ть** (**-алю́, -а́лишь**) *сов* **вали́ть** ⊳ (*impf* **сва́ливать**) *перех* to throw down; **свали́ться** *сов от* **вали́ться**

сва́л|**ка** (**-ки**; *gen pl* **-ок**) *ж* (*место*) rubbish dump

сваля́|**ть** (**-ю**) *сов от* **валя́ть**

свари́|**ть(ся)** (**-арю́(сь), -а́ришь(ся)**) *сов от* **вари́ть(ся)**

сва́та|ть (-ю; *perf* **посва́тать** *или* **сосва́тать**) *несов перех:* **сва́тать кого́-н (за** +*acc***)** to try to marry sb off (to); **сва́таться** (*perf* **посва́таться**) *несов возв:* **сва́таться к** +*dat или* **за** +*acc* to court

сва́|я (-и) *ж* (*Строит*) pile

сведе́ни|е (-я) *ср* information *только ед*; **доводи́ть** (*perf* **довести́**) **что-н до све́дения кого́-н** to bring sth to sb's attention

сведе́ни|е (-я) *ср* (*пятна́*) removal; (*в таблицу, в график итп*) arrangement

све́жий *прил* fresh; (*журнал*) recent

свёкл|а (-ы) *ж* beetroot

свёк|ор (-ра) *м* father-in-law, husband's father

свекро́в|ь (-и) *ж* mother-in-law, husband's mother

све́ргн|уть (-у; *impf* **сверга́ть**) *сов перех* to overthrow; **сверже́ни|е** (-я) *ср* overthrow

све́р|ить (-ю, -ишь; *impf* **сверя́ть**) *сов перех:* **све́рить (с** +*instr***)** to check (against)

сверка́|ть (-ю) *несов* (*звезда, глаза*) to twinkle; (*огни*) to flicker; **сверка́ть** (*impf*) **умо́м/красото́й** to sparkle with intelligence/beauty

сверкн|у́ть (-у́, -ёшь) *сов* to flash

сверл|и́ть (-ю́, -и́шь; *perf* **просверли́ть**) *несов перех* to drill, bore

св|ерло́ (-ерла́; *nom pl* **свёрла**) *ср* drill

све́рстник (-а) *м* peer; **мы с ней све́рстники** she and I are the same age

свёрт|ок (-ка) *м* package

сверх *предл* (+*gen*: *нормы*) over and above

све́рху *нареч* (*о направлении*) from the top; (*в верхней части*) on the surface

сверхуро́чны|е (-ых) *мн* (*плата*) overtime pay *ед*

сверхуро́чны|й *прил:* **сверхуро́чная рабо́та** overtime

сверхъесте́ственный *прил* supernatural

сверч|о́к (-ка́) *м* (*Зоол*) cricket

сверя́|ть (-ю) *несов от* **све́рить**

св|ести́ (-еду́, -едёшь; *pt* -ёл, -ела́, *impf* **своди́ть**) *сов перех:* **свести́ с** +*gen* to lead down; (*пятно*) to shift; (*собрать*) to arrange; **своди́ть** (*perf* **свести́**) **кого́-н с ума́** to drive sb mad; **свести́сь** (*perf* **свести́сь**) *сов возв:* **свести́сь к** +*dat* to be reduced to

свет (-а) *м* light; (*Земля*) the world; **ни свет ни заря́** at the crack of dawn; **выходи́ть** (*perf* **вы́йти**) **в свет** (*книга*) to be published; **ни за что на све́те я не сде́лал бы э́того** (*разг*) I wouldn't do it for the world

света́|ть (*3sg* -ет) *несов безл* to get *или* grow light

свети́льник (-а) *м* lamp

све|ти́ть (-чу́, -́тишь) *несов* to shine; **свети́ть** (*perf* **посвети́ть**) **кому́-н** (*фонарём*

итп) to light the way for sb; **свети́ться** *несов возв* to shine

све́тлый *прил* light; (*комната, день*) bright; (*ум*) lucid

светофо́р (-а) *м* traffic light

свеч|а́ (-и́; *nom pl* -и, *gen pl* -е́й) *ж* candle; (*Мед*) suppository; (*Тех*) spark(ing) plug; (*Спорт*) lob

све́ч|ка (-ки; *gen pl* -ек) *ж* candle

све́ша|ть (-ю) *сов от* **ве́шать**

све́шива|ться (-юсь) *несов от* **све́ситься**

свива́|ть (-ю; *perf* **свить**) *несов перех* to weave

свида́ни|е (-я) *ср* rendezvous; (*деловое*) appointment; (*с заключённым, с больным*) visit; (*влюблённых*) date; **до свида́ния** goodbye; **до ско́рого свида́ния** see you soon

свиде́тел|ь (-я) *м* witness; **свиде́тельств|о** (-а) *ср* evidence; (*документ*) certificate; **свиде́тельство о бра́ке/рожде́нии** marriage/birth certificate; **свиде́тельств|овать** (-ую) *несов:* **свиде́тельствовать о** +*prp* to testify to

свин|е́ц (-ца́) *м* lead (*metal*)

свини́н|а (-ы) *ж* pork

сви́н|ка (-и) *ж* (*Мед*) mumps

свино́й *прил* (*сало, корм*) pig; (*из свинины*) pork

свин|ья́ (-ьи́; *nom pl* -ьи, *gen pl* -е́й) *ж* pig

свиса́|ть (*3sg* -ет) *несов* to hang

свист (-а) *м* whistle; **сви|сте́ть** (-щу́, -сти́шь; *perf* **просвисте́ть**) *несов* to whistle; **сви́стн|уть** (-у) *сов* to give a whistle

свист|о́к (-ка́) *м* whistle

сви́тер (-а) *м* sweater

свить (**совью́, совьёшь**) *сов от* **вить**; **свива́ть**

свобо́д|а (-ы) *ж* freedom; **лише́ние свобо́ды** imprisonment

свобо́дный *прил* free; (*незанятый*: *место*) vacant; (*движение, речь*) fluent; **вход свобо́дный** free admission; **свобо́дный уда́р** (*в футболе*) free kick

св|оди́ть(ся) (-ожу́(сь), -о́дишь(ся)) *несов от* **свести́(сь)**

сво́д|ка (-ки; *gen pl* -ок) *ж:* **сво́дка пого́ды/новосте́й** weather/news summary

сво́дный *прил* (*таблица*) summary; **сво́дный брат** stepbrother; **сво́дная сестра́** stepsister

сво|ё (-его́) *мест см* **свой**

своевре́менный *прил* timely

своеобра́зный *прил* original; (*необычный*) peculiar

○ **КЛЮЧЕВО́Е СЛО́ВО**

сво|й (-его́; *f* **своя́**, *nt* **своё**, *pl* **свои́**; *как* **мой**; *см Table 8*) *мест* **1** (*я*) my; (*ты*) your;

(он) his; (она) her; (оно) its; (мы) our; (вы)
your; (они) their; я люблю свою работу I
love my work; мы собрáли свои вéщи we
collected our things

2 (собственный) one's own; у неё свой
компьютер she has her own computer

3 (своеобразный) its; э́тот план имéет
свои недостáтки this plan has its
shortcomings

4 (близкий): свой человéк one of us

свóйственный прил +dat characteristic
of

свóйств|о (-а) ср characteristic, feature

сворáчива|ть(ся) (-ю(сь)) несов от
сверну́ть(ся)

сво|я́ (-éй) мест см **свой**

свы́ше предл (+gen) beyond; (больше)
over, more than

свя́занный прил: свя́занный (с +instr)
connected (to или with); (имеющий связи):
свя́занный с +instr (с деловыми кругами)
associated with; (несвободный) restricted

свя|зáть (-жу́, -жешь) сов от **вязáть**
▷ (impf **свя́зывать**) перех (верёвку итп)
to tie; (вещи, человека) to tie up;
(установить сообщение, зависимость):
связáть что-н с +instr to connect или link
sth to; **связáться** (impf **свя́зываться**)
сов возв: связáться с +instr to contact;
(разг: с невыгодным делом) to get (o.s.)
caught up in

свя́з|ка (-ки; gen pl -ок) ж (ключей)
bunch; (бумаг, дров) bundle; (Анат)
ligament; (Линг) copula

связь (-и) ж tie; (причинная) connection,
link; (почтовая итп) communications мн; в
связи́ с +instr (вследствие) due to; (по
поводу) in connection with; свя́зи с
общéственностью public relations

свят|óй прил holy; (дело, истина) sacred
▷ (-óго) м (Рел) saint

свящéнник (-а) м priest

свящéнный прил holy, sacred; (долг)
sacred

с.г. сокр = **сегó гóда**

сгиб (-а) м bend; **сгибá|ть** (-ю; perf
согну́ть) несов перех to bend;
сгибáться (perf **согну́ться**) несов возв
to bend down

сгни|ть (-ю́, -ёшь) сов от **гнить**

сгно|и́ть (-ю́, -и́шь) сов от **гнои́ть**

сгорá|ть (-ю) несов от **сгорéть**
▷ неперех: сгорáть от любопы́тства to be
burning with curiosity

сгор|éть (-ю́, -и́шь; impf **сгорáть** или
горéть) сов to burn ▷ (impf **сгорáть**)
(Элек) to fuse; (на солнце) to get burnt

сгр|ести́ (-ебу́, -ебёшь; pt -ёб, -еблá,
impf **сгребáть**) сов перех (собрать) to
rake up

сгр|узи́ть (-ужу́, -у́зишь; impf
сгружáть) сов перех: сгрузи́ть (с +gen)
to unload (from)

сгусти́ться (impf **сгущáться**) сов возв
to thicken

сгущённ|ый прил: сгущённое молокó
condensed milk

сда|вáть (-ю́, -ёшь; imper -вáй(те))
несов от **сдать** ▷ перех: сдавáть
экзáмен to sit an exam; **сдавáться**
несов от **сдáться** ▷ возв (помещение)
to be leased out; "сдаётся внаём"
"to let"

сд|ави́ть (-авлю́, -áвишь) сов перех to
squeeze

сдáвливать impf

сда́ть (как **дать**; см Table 16; impf
сдавáть) сов перех (пальто, багаж,
работу) to hand in; (дом, комнату итп)
to rent out, let; (город, позицию) to
surrender; (no impf: экзамен, зачёт итп)
to pass; **сдáться** (impf **сдавáться**) сов
возв to give up; (солдат, город) to
surrender

сдвиг (-а) м (в работе) progress

сдви́н|уть (-у; impf **сдвигáть**) сов перех
(переместить) to move; (сблизить) to
move together; **сдви́нуться** (impf
сдвигáться) сов возв: сдви́нуться (с
мéста) to move

сдéла|ть(ся) (-ю(сь)) сов от **дéлать(ся)**

сдéл|ка (-ки; gen pl -ок) ж deal

сдéржанный прил (человек) reserved

сдéрж|ивать (-ержу́, -éржишь) impf
сдéрживать сов перех to contain, hold
back; **сдéрживать** (perf **сдержáть**) слóво/
обещáние to keep one's word/promise;
сдержáться (impf **сдéрживаться**) сов
возв to restrain o.s.

сдёрн|уть (-у; impf **сдёргивать**) сов
перех to pull off

сдирá|ть (-ю) несов от **содрáть**

сдóбный прил (тесто) rich

сду́|ть (-ю; impf **сдувáть**) сов перех to
blow away

сеáнс (-а) м (Кино) show; (терапии)
session

себé мест см **себя́** ▷ част (разг): так себé
so-so; **ничегó себé** (сносно) not bad;
(ирония) well, I never!

себестóимост|ь (-и) ж cost price

⊙ **КЛЮЧЕВÓЕ СЛÓВО**

себя́ мест (я) myself; (ты) yourself; (он)
himself; (она) herself; (оно) itself; (мы)
ourselves; (вы) yourselves; (они)
themselves; он трéбователен к себé he
asks a lot of himself; онá вини́т себя́ she
blames herself; к себé (домой) home; (в
свою́ комнату) to one's room; "к себé" (на
двери) "pull"; "от себя́" (на двери)
"push"; по себé (по своим вкусам) to
one's taste; говори́ть (impf)/читáть про
себя́ to talk/read to o.s.; онá себé на
умé (разг) she is secretive; он у себя́ (в
своём доме) he is at home; (в своём
кабинете) he is in the office

се́вер (-а) м north; **Се́вер** (*Арктика*) the Arctic North; **се́верный** *прил* north; (*ветер, направление*) northerly; (*климат, полушарие*) northern; **Се́верный Ледови́тый океа́н** Arctic Ocean; **се́верное сия́ние** the northern lights мн

се́веро-восто́к (-а) м northeast

се́веро-за́пад (-а) м northwest

сего́ *мест см* **сей**

сего́дня *нареч, сущ нескл* today; **сего́дня у́тром/днём/ве́чером** this morning/afternoon/evening

седе́ть (-ю; *perf* **поседе́ть**) *несов* to go grey (*Brit*) *или* gray (*US*)

седина́ (-ины́; *nom pl* -и́ны) *ж* grey (*Brit*) *или* gray (*US*) hair

седло́ (-а́) *ср* saddle

седо́й *прил* (*волосы*) grey (*Brit*), gray (*US*)

седьмо́й *чис* seventh; **сейча́с седьмо́й час** it's after six

сезо́н (-а) м season

сезо́нный *прил* seasonal

сей (**сего́**; *см* Table 12) *мест* this

сейф (-а) м (*ящик*) safe

сейча́с *нареч* (*теперь*) now; (*скоро*) just now; **сейча́с же!** right now!

секре́т (-а) м secret

секрета́рша (-и) *ж* (*разг*) secretary

секрета́рь (-я́) м secretary; **секрета́рь-машини́стка** secretary

секре́тный *прил* secret

секс (-а) м sex

сексуа́льный *прил* sexual; (*жизнь, образова́ние*) sex; **сексуа́льное пресле́дование** *or* **домога́тельство** sexual harassment

се́кта (-ы) *ж* sect

секта́нт (-а) м sect member

се́ктор (-а) м sector

секу́нда (-ы) *ж* second

се́кция (-и) *ж* section

сел *итп сов см* **сесть**

селёдка (-ки; *gen pl* -ок) *ж* herring

селе́ктор (-а) м (*Тел*) intercom

селе́кция (-и) *ж* (*Био*) selective breeding

селе́ние (-я) *ср* village

сели́ть (-ю́, -ишь; *perf* **посели́ть**) *несов перех* (*в местности*) to settle; (*в доме*) to house; **сели́ться** (*perf* **посели́ться**) *несов возв* to settle

село́ (-а́; *nom pl* **сёла**) *ср* village

се́лфи *ср нескл* selfie

сельдере́й (-я) м celery

сельдь (-и; *gen pl* -е́й) *ж* herring

се́льский *прил* (*см сущ*) village; country, rural; **се́льское хозя́йство** agriculture

сельскохозя́йственный *прил* agricultural

сёмга (-и) *ж* salmon

семе́йный *прил* family

семе́йство (-а) *ср* family

семёрка (-ки; *gen pl* -ок) *ж* (*цифра, карта*) seven

се́меро (-ы́х; *как* **че́тверо**; *см* Table 30b) *чис* seven

семе́стр (-а) м term (*Brit*), semester (*US*)

се́мечко (-ка; *gen pl* -ек) *ср* seed; **се́мечки** sunflower seeds

семидеся́тый *чис* seventieth

семина́р (-а) м seminar

семна́дцатый *чис* seventeenth

семна́дцать (-и; *как* **пять**; *см* Table 26) *чис* seventeen

семь (-и́; *как* **пять**; *см* Table 26) *чис* seven

се́мьдесят (-и́десяти; *как* **пятьдеся́т**; *см* Table 26) *чис* seventy

семьсо́т (-исо́т; *как* **пятьсо́т**; *см* Table 28) *чис* seven hundred

семья́ (-и́; *nom pl* -и) *ж* family

се́мя (-ени; *как* **вре́мя**; *см* Table 4) *ср* seed; (*no pl: Био*) semen

сена́тор (-а) м senator

сенно́й *прил*: **сенна́я лихора́дка** hay fever

се́но (-а) м hay

сенса́ция (-и) *ж* sensation

сентимента́льный *прил* sentimental

сентя́брь (-я́) м September

се́ра (-ы) *ж* sulphur (*Brit*), sulfur (*US*); (*в уша́х*) (ear)wax

серва́нт (-а) м buffet unit

се́рвер (-а) м (*Комп*) server

серви́з (-а) м: **столо́вый/ча́йный серви́з** dinner/tea service

се́рвис (-а) м service (*in shop etc*)

серде́чный *прил* heart, cardiac; (*челове́к*) warm-hearted; (*приём, разгово́р*) cordial; **серде́чный при́ступ** heart attack

серди́тый *прил* angry

серди́ть (-жу́, -дишь; *perf* **рассерди́ть**) *несов перех* to anger, make angry; **серди́ться** (*perf* **рассерди́ться**) *несов возв*: **серди́ться (на кого́-н/что-н)** to be angry (with sb/about sth)

се́рдце (-ца; *nom pl* -ца́) *ср* heart; **в глубине́ се́рдца** in one's heart of hearts; **от всего́ се́рдца** from the bottom of one's heart

сердцебие́ние (-я) *ср* heartbeat

серебро́ (-а́) *ср, собир* silver; **сере́бряный** *прил* silver

середи́на (-ы) *ж* middle

серёжка (-ки; *gen pl* -ек) *ж, уменьш от* **серьга́**

сержа́нт (-а) м sergeant

сериа́л (-а) м (*Тел*) series

се́рия (-и) *ж* series; (*кинофи́льма*) part

се́рный *прил*: **се́рная кислота́** sulphuric (*Brit*) *или* sulfuric (*US*) acid

сертифика́т (-а) м certificate; (*това́ра*) guarantee (certificate)

серфи́ть (-лю, -ишь) *несов перех* (*Комп*) to surf

се́рый *прил* grey (*Brit*), gray (*US*); **се́рый хлеб** brown bread

сер|ьга (-ьги; *nom pl* -ьги, *gen pl* -ёг, *dat pl* -ьгам) ж earring

серьёзно *нареч, вводн сл* seriously

серьёзный *прил* serious

сесси|я (-и) ж (*суда, парламента*) session; (*также* **экзаменацио́нная се́ссия**) examinations мн

сестр|а́ (-ы́; *nom pl* **сёстры**, *gen pl* **сестёр**) ж sister; (*также* **медици́нская сестра́**) nurse

сесть (**ся́ду, ся́дешь**; *pt* **сел, се́ла**, *impf* **сади́ться**) *сов* to sit down; (*птица, самолёт*) to land; (*солнце, луна*) to go down; (*одежда*) to shrink; (*батаре́йка*) to run down; **сади́ться** (*perf* **сесть**) **в по́езд/ на самолёт** to get on a train/plane; **сади́ться** (*perf* **сесть**) **в тюрьму́** to go to prison

сетево́й *прил* (*Комп*) net; (*магазин*) chain

се́т|ка (-ки; *gen pl* -ок) ж net; (*сумка*) net bag

сет|ь (-и; *prp sg* -и́, *gen pl* -е́й) ж (*для ло́вли рыб итп*) net; (*дорог*) network; (*магазинов*) chain; (*Комп*) the Net; **социа́льные се́ти** social media

сече́ни|е (-я) *ср* section; **ке́сарево сече́ние** Caesarean (*Brit*) *или* Cesarean (*US*) (section)

сечь (**секу́, сечёшь** итп, **секу́т**; *pt* **сёк, секла́**) *несов перех* (*руби́ть*) to cut up

се́|ять (-ю; *perf* **посе́ять**) *несов перех* to sow

сжа́л|иться (-юсь, -ишься) *сов возв*: **сжа́литься (над** +*instr*) to take pity (on)

сжать (**сожму́, сожмёшь**; *impf* **сжима́ть**) *сов перех* to squeeze; (*воздух, газ*) to compress; **сжа́ться** (*impf* **сжима́ться**) *сов возв* (*пружина*) to contract; (*человек: от боли, от испуга*) to tense up; (*перен: сердце*) to seize up

сжечь (**сожгу́, сожжёшь** итп, **сожгу́т**; *pt* **сжёг, сожгла́**, *impf* **сжига́ть** *или* **жечь**) *сов перех* to burn

сжима́|ть(ся) (-ю(сь)) *несов от* **сжа́ть(ся)**

сза́ди *нареч* (*подойти́*) from behind; (*находиться*) behind ▷ *предл* +*gen* behind

сзыва́|ть (-ю) *несов от* **созва́ть**

сиби́рский *прил* Siberian

Сиби́р|ь (-и) ж Siberia

сибиря́к (-а́) м Siberian

сигаре́т|а (-ы) ж cigarette

сигна́л (-а) м signal; **сигнализа́ци|я** (-и) ж (*в кварти́ре*) burglar alarm

сиде́нь|е (-я) *ср* seat

си|де́ть (-жу́, -ди́шь) *несов* to sit; (*одежда*) to fit

си́дя *нареч*: **рабо́тать/есть си́дя** to work/ eat sitting down

сидя́чий *прил* (*положение*) sitting; **сидя́чие места́** seats мн

си́л|а (-ы) ж strength; (*тока, ветра, зако́на*) force; (*во́ли, сло́ва*) power; (*обычно мн: душе́вные, тво́рческие*) energy; **в си́лу**

того́ что ... owing to the fact that ...; **от си́лы** (*разг*) at (the) most; **вступа́ть** (*perf* **вступи́ть**) *или* **входи́ть** (**войти́** *perf*) **в си́лу** to come into *или* take effect; *см также* **си́лы**

си́лой *нареч* by force

силуэ́т (-а) м (*ко́нтур*) silhouette

си́л|ы (-) *мн* forces; **си́лами кого́-н** through the efforts of sb; **свои́ми си́лами** by oneself

си́льно *нареч* strongly; (*уда́рить*) hard; (*хоте́ть, понра́виться* итп) very much

си́льный *прил* strong; (*моро́з*) hard; (*впечатле́ние*) powerful; (*дождь*) heavy

СИМ-ка́рт|а (-ы) ж SIM card

си́мвол (-а) м symbol; (*Комп*) character

симметри́ческий *прил* symmetrical

симметри́|я (-и) ж symmetry

симпатизи́р|овать (-ую) *несов*: **симпатизи́ровать кому́-н** to like *или* be fond of sb

симпати́чный *прил* nice, pleasant

симпа́ти|я (-и) ж liking, fondness

симпто́м (-а) м symptom

симфо́ни|я (-и) ж (*Муз*) symphony

синаго́г|а (-и) ж synagogue

синдро́м (-а) м (*Мед*) syndrome

сине́|ть (-ю; *perf* **посине́ть**) *несов* to turn blue

си́ний *прил* blue

сини́ц|а (-ы) ж tit (*Zool*)

сино́ним (-а) м synonym

сино́птик (-а) м weather forecaster

синтети́ческий *прил* synthetic

синя́к (-а́) м bruise

сире́н|а (-ы) ж (*гудо́к*) siren

сире́невый *прил* lilac

сире́н|ь (-и) ж (*куста́рник*) lilac bush ▷ *собир* (*цветы́*) lilac

сиро́п (-а) м syrup

сир|ота́ (-оты́; *nom pl* -о́ты) м/ж orphan

систе́м|а (-ы) ж system

системати́ческий *прил* regular

си́т|ец (-ца) м cotton

си́течк|о (-ка; *gen pl* -ек) *ср* (*для ча́я*) (tea) strainer

си́т|о (-а) *ср* sieve

ситуа́ци|я (-и) ж situation

си́тцевый *прил* (*ткань*) cotton

сия́|ть (-ю) *несов* (*со́лнце, звезда́*) to shine; (*ого́нь*) to glow

ск|аза́ть (-ажу́, -а́жешь) *сов от* **говори́ть** ▷ *перех*: **ска́жем** (*разг*) let's say; **скажи́те!** (*разг*) I say!; **так сказа́ть** so to speak; **сказа́ться** (*impf* **ска́зываться**) *сов возв* (*ум, о́пыт* итп) to show; (*отрази́ться*): **сказа́ться на** +*prp* to take its toll on

ска́з|ка (-ки; *gen pl* -ок) ж fairy tale

ска́зочный *прил* fairy-tale

сказу́емо|е (-ого) *ср* (*Линг*) predicate

ск|ака́ть (-ачу́, -а́чешь) *несов* (*челове́к*) to skip; (*мяч*) to bounce; (*ло́шадь, вса́дник*) to gallop

скаков|о́й *прил:* **скакова́я ло́шадь** racehorse

скаку́н (**-а́**) *м* racehorse

скал|а́ (**-ы́**; *nom pl* **-а́лы**) *ж* cliff

скали́стый *прил* rocky

скаме́йка (**-йки**; *gen pl* **-ек**) *ж* bench

скам|ья́ (**-ьи́**; *gen pl* **-е́й**) *ж* bench; **скамья́ подсуди́мых** (*Юр*) the dock

сканда́л (**-а**) *м* scandal; (*ссора*) quarrel

сканда́л|ить (**-ю**, **-ишь**; *perf* **поскандалить**) *несов* to quarrel

ска́нер (**-а**) *м* (*Комп*) scanner

ска́плива|ться (**-юсь**) *несов от* **скопи́ться**

скарлати́н|а (**-ы**) *ж* scarlet fever

скат (**-а**) *м* slope; (*Авт: колесо́*) wheel

ската́|ть (**-ю**; *impf* **ска́тывать**) *сов перех* to roll up

ска́терт|ь (**-и**) *ж* tablecloth

ск|ати́ть (**-ачу́**, **-а́тишь**; *impf* **ска́тывать**) *сов перех* to roll down; **скати́ться** (*impf* **ска́тываться**) *сов возв* (*слеза*) to roll down; (*перен*): **скати́ться к** +*dat/*на +*acc* to slide towards/into

ска́ч|ки (**-ек**) *мн* the races

скач|о́к (**-ка́**) *м* leap

СКВ *ж сокр* (= *свобо́дно конверти́руемая валю́та*) convertible currency

сквер (**-а**) *м* small public garden

скве́рный *прил* foul

сквоз|и́ть (*3sg* **-и́т**) *несов безл*: **здесь сквози́т** it's draughty here

сквозня́к (**-а́**) *м* (*в ко́мнате*) draught (*Brit*), draft (*US*)

сквозь *предл* +*acc* through

скворе́чник (**-а**) *м* nesting box

скеле́т (**-а**) *м* skeleton

скепти́ческий *прил* sceptical

ски́д|ка (**-ки**; *gen pl* **-ок**) *ж* (*с цены́*) discount, reduction

ски́|нуть (**-у**; *impf* **ски́дывать**) *сов перех* (*сбросить*) to throw down

ски́с|нуть (**-ну**, **-нешь**; *pt* **-**, **-ла**, **-ло**, *impf* **скиса́ть**) *сов* (*молоко́*) to turn sour

склад (**-а**) *м* (*това́рный*) store; (*ору́жия итп*) cache; (*о́браз: мы́слей*) way

скла́д|ка (**-ки**; *gen pl* **-ок**) *ж* (*на оде́жде*) pleat

складно́й *прил* folding

скла́дыва|ть(ся) (**-ю(сь)**) *несов от* **сложи́ть(ся)**

скле́|ить (**-ю**, **-ишь**) *сов от* **кле́ить** ▷ (*impf* **скле́ивать**) *перех* to glue together

склон (**-а**) *м* slope

склоне́ни|е (**-я**) *ср* (*Линг*) declension

скл|они́ть (**-оню́**, **-о́нишь**; *impf* **склоня́ть**) *сов перех* (*опусти́ть*) to lower; **склоня́ть** (*perf* **склони́ть**) **кого́-н к побе́гу/ на преступле́ние** to persuade sb to escape/ commit a crime; **склони́ться** (*impf* **склоня́ться**) *сов возв* (*нагну́ться*) to bend; (*перен*): **склони́ться к** +*dat* to come round to

скло́нност|ь (**-и**) *ж*: **скло́нность к** +*dat* (*к му́зыке*) aptitude for; (*к меланхо́лии, к полноте́*) tendency to

скло́нный *прил*: **скло́нный к** +*dat* (*к просту́дам*) prone *или* susceptible to; (+*infin*: **помири́ться**) inclined to do

склоня́емый *прил* declinable

склоня́|ть (**-ю**) *несов от* **склони́ть** ▷ (*perf* **просклоня́ть**) *перех* (*Линг*) to decline; **склоня́ться** *несов от* **склони́ться** ▷ *возв* (*Линг*) to decline

ск|оба́ (**-обы́**; *nom pl* **-о́бы**) *ж* (*для опо́ры*) clamp; (*для крепле́ния*) staple

скоб|ка (**-ки**; *gen pl* **-ок**) *ж*, *уменьш от* **скоба́**; (*обы́чно мн: в те́ксте*) bracket, parentheses *мн*

ск|ова́ть (**-ую**; *impf* **ско́вывать**) *сов перех* (*челове́ка*) to paralyse

сковород|а́ (**-ы́**; *nom pl* **ско́вороды**) *ж* frying-pan (*Brit*), skillet (*US*)

сколь *нареч* (*как*) how; (*возмо́жно*) as much as; **сколь ... сто́ль (же) ...** as much ... as ...

скольз|и́ть (**-жу́**, **-зи́шь**) *несов* to glide; (*па́дая*) to slide

ско́льзкий *прил* slippery; (*ситуа́ция, вопро́с*) sensitive

скользн|у́ть (**-у́**, **-ёшь**) *сов* to glide; (*быстро пройти́*) to slip

⭕ **КЛЮЧЕВО́Е СЛО́ВО**

ско́льк|о (**-их**) *местоиме́нное нареч*
1 (+*gen*: *книг, часо́в, дней итп*) how many; (*са́хара, сил, рабо́ты итп*) how much; **ско́лько люде́й пришло́?** how many people came?; **ско́лько де́нег тебе́ на́до?** how much money do you need?; **ско́лько э́то сто́ит?** how much is it?; **ско́лько тебе́ лет?** how old are you?
2 (*относи́тельное*) as much; **бери́, ско́лько хо́чешь** take as much as you want; **ско́лько уго́дно** as much as you like ▷ *нареч* **1** (*наско́лько*) as far as; **ско́лько по́мню, он всегда́ был агресси́вный** as far as I remember, he was always aggressive
2 (*мно́го*): **ско́лько люде́й!** what a lot of people!; **не сто́лько ... ско́лько ...** not so much ... as ...

ско́мка|ть (**-ю**) *сов от* **ко́мкать**

сконча́|ться (**-юсь**) *сов возв* to pass away

скоп|и́ть (**-лю́**, **-ишь**) *сов от* **копи́ть**; **скопи́ться** *сов от* **копи́ться** ▷ (*impf* **ска́пливаться**) *возв* (*лю́ди*) to gather; (*рабо́та*) to mount up

ско́р|ая (**-ой**) *ж* (*разг: та́кже* **ско́рая по́мощь**) ambulance

скорб|ь (**-и**; *gen pl* **-е́й**) *ж* grief

скоре́е *сравн прил от* **ско́рый** ▷ *сравн нареч от* **ско́ро** ▷ *част* rather; **скоре́е... чем** *или* **нежели** (*в бо́льшей сте́пени*) more likely ... than; (*лу́чше, охо́тнее*) rather ... than; **скоре́е всего́ они́ до́ма** it's most likely they'll be (at) home; **скоре́е бы он верну́лся** I wish he would come back soon

скорл|упа́ (-упы́; *nom pl* -у́пы) ж shell

ско́ро *нареч* soon ▷ *как сказ* it's soon; **ско́ро зима́** it will soon be winter

скоропости́жн|ый *прил*: **скоропости́жная смерть** sudden death

ско́рост|ь (-и; *gen pl* -е́й) ж speed

скоросшива́тель (-я) м (loose-leaf) binder

скорпио́н (-а) м scorpion; (*созвездие*): **Скорпио́н** Scorpio

ско́р|ый *прил* (*движение*) fast; (*разлука, визит*) impending; **в ско́ром вре́мени** shortly; **ско́рая по́мощь** (*учреждение*) ambulance service; (*автомашина*) ambulance; **ско́рый по́езд** express (train)

скот (-а́) м *собир* livestock; **моло́чный/мясно́й скот** dairy/beef cattle

скреп|и́ть (-лю́, -и́шь; *impf* **скрепля́ть**) *сов перех* (*соединить*) to fasten together

скре́п|ка (-ки; *gen pl* -ок) ж paperclip

скре|сти́ть (-щу́, -сти́шь; *impf* **скре́щивать**) *сов перех* to cross; (*животных*) to cross-breed; **скрести́ться** (*impf* **скре́щиваться**) *сов возв* to cross

скри́п|ка (-ки; *gen pl* -ок) ж violin

скро́мность (-и) ж modesty

скро́мн|ый *прил* modest; (*служащий, должность*) humble

скр|ути́ть (-учу́, -у́тишь) *сов перех* от **крути́ть** ▷ (*impf* **скру́чивать**) *перех* (*провода, волосы*) to twist together; **скрути́ться** *сов возв* to twist together

скрыва́|ть (-ю) *несов* от **скрыть**; **скрыва́ться** *несов* от **скры́ться** ▷ *возв* (*от полиции*) to hide

скры́тый *прил* secretive

скры́тый *прил* (*тайный*) hidden, secret

скры́ть (-о́ю, -о́ешь; *impf* **скрыва́ть**) *сов перех* (*спрятать*) to hide; (*факты*) to conceal; **скры́ться** (*impf* **скрыва́ться**) *сов возв* (*от дождя, от погони*) to take cover; (*стать невидимым*) to disappear

ску́дный *прил* (*запасы*) meagre (*Brit*), meager (*US*)

ску́к|а (-и) ж boredom

скул|и́ть (-ю́, -и́шь) *несов* to whine

скульптор (-а) м sculptor; **скульпту́р|а** (-ы) ж sculpture

ску́мбри|я (-и) ж mackerel

ск|упи́ть (-уплю́, -у́пишь; *impf* **скупа́ть**) *сов перех* to buy up

скупо́й *прил* mean

скуча́|ть (-ю) *несов* to be bored; (*тосковать*): **скуча́ть по** +*dat или* о +*prp* to miss

ску́чно *нареч* (*жить, рассказывать итп*) boringly ▷ *как сказ*: **здесь ску́чно** it's boring here; **мне ску́чно** I'm bored

ску́чный *прил* boring, dreary

слабе́|ть (-ю; *perf* **ослабе́ть**) *несов* to grow weak; (*дисциплина*) to slacken

слаби́тельн|ое (-ого) *ср* laxative

сла́бо *нареч* (*вскрикнуть*) weakly; (*нажать*) lightly; (*знать*) badly

сла́бость (-и) ж weakness

сла́бый *прил* weak; (*ветер*) light; (*знания, доказательство итп*) poor; (*дисциплина итп*) slack

сла́в|а (-ы) ж (*героя*) glory; (*писателя, актёра итп*) fame; **сла́ва Бо́гу**! thank God!

славя́н|ин (-яни́на; *nom pl* -я́не, *gen pl* -я́н) м Slav; **славя́нский** *прил* Slavonic

слага́|ть (-ю) *несов* от **сложи́ть**

сла́дкий *прил* sweet

сла́дко *нареч* (*пахнуть*) sweet; (*спать*) deeply

сла́дк|ое (-ого) *ср* sweet things *мн*; (*разг: десерт*) afters (*Brit*), dessert (*US*)

слайд (-а) м (*Фото*) slide

сла|ть (шлю, шлёшь) *несов перех* to send

сла́ще *сравн прил* от **сла́дкий** ▷ *сравн нареч* от **сла́дко**

сле́ва *нареч* on the left

слегка́ *нареч* slightly

след (-а; *nom pl* -ы́) м trace; (*ноги*) footprint

сле|ди́ть (-жу́, -ди́шь) *несов*: **следи́ть за** +*instr* to follow; (*заботиться*) to take care of; (*за шпионом*) to watch

сле́довани|е (-я) *ср* (*моде*) following; **по́езд/авто́бус да́льнего сле́дования** long-distance train/bus

сле́дователь (-я) м detective

сле́довательно *вводн сл* consequently ▷ *союз* therefore

сле́д|овать (-ую; *perf* **после́довать**) *несов* (*вывод, неприятность*) to follow ▷ *безл*: **Вам сле́дует поду́мать об э́том** you should think about it; **как сле́дует** properly

сле́дом *предл*: **сле́дом за** +*instr* following

сле́дстви|е (-я) *ср* (*последствие*) consequence; (*Юр*) investigation

сле́дующий *прил* next ▷ *мест* following; **на сле́дующий день** the next day

слез|а́ (-ы́; *nom pl* -ёзы, *dat pl* -еза́м) ж tear

сле́за|ть (-ю) *несов* от **слезть**

слез|и́ться (*3sg* -и́тся) *несов возв* (*глаза*) to water

слезоточи́вый *прил*: **слезоточи́вый газ** tear gas

слез|ть (-у, -ешь; *pt* -, -ла, *impf* **слеза́ть**) *сов* (*кожа, краска*) to peel off; **слеза́ть** (*perf* **слезть**) (с +*gen*) (*с дерева*) to climb down

слеп|и́ть (*3sg* -и́т) *сов перех*: **слепи́ть глаза́ кому́-н** to blind sb

сл|епи́ть (-еплю́, -е́пишь) *сов* от **лепи́ть**

слеп|ну́ть (-у; *perf* **осле́пнуть**) *несов* to go blind

слеп|о́й *прил* blind ⊳ (**-о́го**) *м* blind person (*мн* people)

слеса́р|ь (**-я**; *nom pl* **-я́**, *gen pl* **-е́й**) *м* maintenance man

слете́ть (**-чу́, -ти́шь**; *impf* **слета́ть**) *сов*: **слете́ть** (**с** +*gen*) (*птица*) to fly down (from); **слете́ться** (*impf* **слета́ться**) *сов возв* (*птицы*) to flock

сли́в|а (**-ы**) *ж* (*дерево*) plum (tree); (*плод*) plum

слива́|ть(ся) (**-ю(сь)**) *несов от* **сли́ть(ся)**

сли́в|ки (**-ок**) *мн* cream *ед*

сли́вочн|ый *прил* made with cream; **сли́вочное ма́сло** butter

сли́зист|ый *прил*: **сли́зистая оболо́чка** mucous membrane

слип|ну́ться (*3sg* **-нется**, *pt* **-ся, -лась**, *impf* **слипа́ться**) *сов возв* to stick together

сли|ть (**солью́, сольёшь**; *pt* **-л, -ла́**, *imper* **сле́й(те)**, *impf* **слива́ть**) *сов перех* to pour; (*перен: соединить*) to merge; **сли́ться** (*impf* **слива́ться**) *сов возв* to merge

сли́шком *нареч* too; **э́то уже́ сли́шком** (*разг*) that's just too much

слова́рный *прил* (*работа, статья*) dictionary, lexicographic(al); **слова́рный запа́с** vocabulary

словар|ь (**-я́**) *м* (*книга*) dictionary; (*запас слов*) vocabulary

слове́сный *прил* oral; (*протест*) verbal

сло́вно *союз* (*как*) like; (*как будто*) as if

сло́в|о (**-а**; *nom pl* **-а́**) *ср* word

сло́вом *вводн сл* in a word

словосочета́ни|е (**-я**) *ср* word combination

слог (**-а**; *nom pl* **-и**, *gen pl* **-о́в**) *м* syllable

слоёный *прил*: **слоёное те́сто** puff pastry

сложе́ни|е (**-я**) *ср* (*в математике*) addition; (*фигура*) build

сл|ожи́ть (**-ожу́, -о́жишь**; *impf* **скла́дывать** *сов перех* (*вещи*) to put; (*чемодан итп*) to pack; (*придавая форму*) to fold (up) ⊳ (*impf* **скла́дывать** *или* **слага́ть**) (*числа*) to add (up); (*песню, стихи*) to make up; **сиде́ть** (*impf*) **сложа́ ру́ки** to sit back and do nothing; **сложи́ться** (*impf* **скла́дываться**) *сов возв* (*ситуация*) to arise; (*характер*) to form; (*зонт, палатка*) to fold up; (*впечатление*) to be formed

сло́жно *нареч* (*делать*) in a complicated way ⊳ *как сказ* it's difficult

сло́жность (**-и**) *ж* (*многообразие*) complexity; (*обычно мн: трудность*) difficulty; **в о́бщей сло́жности** all in all

сло́жный *прил* complex; (*узор*) intricate; (*трудный*) difficult

сло|й (**-я**; *nom pl* **-й**) *м* layer

слома́|ть(ся) (**-ю(сь)**) *сов от* **лома́ть(ся)**

слом|и́ть (**-лю́, -ишь**) *сов перех* to break; **сломя́ го́лову** (*разг*) at breakneck speed;

сломи́ться (*перен: человек*) to crack

слон (**-а́**) *м* elephant; (*Шахматы*) bishop;

слон|ёнок (**-ёнка**; *nom pl* **-я́та**, *gen pl* **-я́т**) *м* elephant calf (*мн* calves);

слони́х|а (**-и**) *ж* cow (*elephant*);

слоно́вый *прил* elephant; **слоно́вая кость** ivory

слуг|а́ (**-и́**; *nom pl* **-и**) *м* servant;

служа́н|ка (**-ки**; *gen pl* **-ок**) *ж* maid

слу́жащ|ий (**-его**) *м* white collar worker; **госуда́рственный слу́жащий** civil servant; **конто́рский слу́жащий** clerk

слу́жб|а (**-ы**) *ж* service; (*работа*) work; (*орган*) agency; **срок слу́жбы** durability; **Слу́жба бы́та** consumer services; **Слу́жба за́нятости** ≈ Employment Agency

служе́бный *прил* (*дела итп*) official

служи́тел|ь (**-я**) *м* (*в музее, на автозаправке*) attendant; (*в зоопарке*) keeper; **служи́тель це́ркви** clergyman (*мн* clergymen)

сл|ужи́ть (**-ужу́, -у́жишь**) *несов* to serve; (*в банке*) to work; **чем могу́ служи́ть?** what can I do for you?

слух (**-а**) *м* hearing; (*музыкальный*) ear; (*известие*) rumour (*Brit*), rumor (*US*)

слухово́й *прил* (*нерв, орган*) auditory; **слуховой аппара́т** hearing aid

слу́ча|й (**-я**) *м* occasion; (*случайность*) chance; **в слу́чае** +*gen* in the event of; **во вся́ком слу́чае** in any case; **на вся́кий слу́чай** just in case

случа́йно *нареч* by chance ⊳ *вводн сл* by any chance

случа́йность (**-и**) *ж* chance

случа́йный *прил* (*встреча*) chance

случ|и́ться (**-у́сь, -и́шься**; *impf* **случа́ться**) *сов возв* to happen

слу́шани|я (**-й**) *мн* hearing *ед*

слу́шател|ь (**-я**) *м* listener; (*Просвещ*) student

слу́ша|ть (**-ю**) *несов перех* (*музыку, речь*) to listen to; (*Юр*) to hear ⊳ (*perf* **послу́шать**) (*совет*) to listen to; **слу́шаться** (*perf* **послу́шаться**) *несов возв*: **слу́шаться** +*gen* to obey; (*совета*) to follow

слы́ш|ать (**-у, -ишь**) *несов* to hear ⊳ (*perf* **услы́шать**) *перех* to hear; **слы́шать** (*impf*) **о** +*prp* to hear about; **он пло́хо слы́шит** he's hard of hearing; **слы́шаться** *несов возв* to be heard

слы́шно *как сказ* it can be heard; **мне ничего́ не слы́шно** I can't hear a thing; **о ней ничего́ не слы́шно** there's no news of her

слы́шный *прил* audible

слюн|а́ (**-ы́**) *ж* saliva

слю́н|ки (**-ок**) *мн*: **у меня́ слю́нки теку́т** my mouth's watering

см *сокр* (= **санти́метр**) cm (= *centimetre* (*Brit*), centimeter (*US*))

смайл (-а) м (Комп) emoticon

смартфо́н (-а) м smart phone

сма́тыва|ть (-ю) несов от **смота́ть**

смахн|у́ть (-у́, -ёшь; impf сма́хивать) сов перех to brush off

сме́жный прил (комната) adjoining, adjacent; (предприятие) affiliated

смеле́|ть (-ю; perf осмеле́ть) несов to grow bolder

сме́лост|ь (-и) ж (храбрость) courage, bravery

сме́лый прил courageous, brave; (идея, проект) ambitious

сме́н|а (-ы) ж (руководства) change; (на производстве) shift

см|ени́ть (-еню́, -е́нишь; impf сменя́ть) сов перех to change; (коллегу) to relieve; **смени́ться** (impf сменя́ться) сов возв (руководство) to change

смерте́льный прил mortal; (скука) deadly; **смерте́льный слу́чай** fatality

сме́ртный прил mortal; (разг: скука) deadly; **сме́ртный пригово́р** death sentence; **сме́ртная казнь** the death penalty, capital punishment

смерт|ь (-и) ж death; **я уста́л до́ сме́рти** I am dead tired

смеси́тел|ь (-я) м mixer

сме|си́ть (-шу́, -сишь) сов от **меси́ть**

см|ести́ (-ету́, -ете́шь; pt -ёл, -ела́, -ело́, impf смета́ть) сов перех to sweep

сме|сти́ть (-щу́, -сти́шь; impf смеща́ть) сов перех (уволить) to remove; **смести́ться** (impf смеща́ться) сов возв to shift

смес|ь (-и) ж mixture; **моло́чная смесь** powdered baby milk

сме́т|а (-ы) ж (Экон) estimate

смета́н|а (-ы) ж sour cream

смета́|ть (-ю) несов от **смести́**

сме|ть (-ю; perf посме́ть) несов +infin to dare to do

смех (-а) м laughter

смехотво́рный прил ludicrous

смеша́|ть (-ю) сов от **меша́ть** ⊳ (impf сме́шивать) перех (спутать) to mix up; **смеша́ться** сов от **меша́ться** ⊳ (impf сме́шиваться) возв (слиться) to mingle; (краски, цвета) to blend

смеш|и́ть (-у́, -и́шь; perf насмеши́ть или рассмеши́ть) несов перех: **смеши́ть кого́-н** to make sb laugh

смешно́ нареч (смотреться) funny ⊳ как сказ it's funny; (глупо) it's ludicrous

смешно́й прил funny

смеща́|ть(ся) (-ю(сь)) несов от **смести́ть(ся)**

смеще́ни|е (-я) ср (руководства) removal; (понятий, критериев) shift

смея́|ться (-ю́сь) несов возв to laugh

СМИ сокр (= сре́дства ма́ссовой информа́ции) mass media

смир|и́ть (-ю́, -и́шь; impf смиря́ть) сов перех to suppress; **смири́ться** (impf смиря́ться) сов возв (покориться) to submit; (примириться): **смири́ться с** +instr to resign o.s. to

сми́рно нареч (сидеть, вести себя) quietly; (Воен): **сми́рно!** attention!

смог etc сов см **смочь**

смо́жешь etc сов см **смочь**

смол|а́ (-ы́; nom pl -ы) ж (дерево) resin; (дёготь) tar

смо́лк|нуть (-ну; pt -, -ла, impf смолка́ть) сов to fade away

сморка́|ть (-ю; perf вы́сморкать) несов перех: **сморка́ть нос** to blow one's nose; **сморка́ться** (perf вы́сморкаться) несов возв to blow one's nose

сморо́дин|а (-ы) ж: **кра́сная сморо́дина** (ягоды) redcurrants мн; **чёрная сморо́дина** (ягоды) blackcurrants мн

смо́рщить(ся) (-у(сь), -ишь(ся)) сов от **мо́рщить(ся)**

смота́|ть (-ю; impf сма́тывать) сов перех to wind

смотр (-а) м presentation; (музыкальный) festival

см|отре́ть (-отрю́, -о́тришь; perf посмотре́ть) несов ⊳ перех (фильм, игру) to watch; (картину) to look at; (музей, выставку) to look round; (следить): **смотре́ть за** +instr to look after; **смотре́ть** (impf) **в/на** +acc to look onto; **смотря́ по** +dat depending on; **смотре́ться** (perf посмотре́ться) несов возв: **смотре́ться в** +acc (в зеркало) to look at o.s. in

смотри́тел|ь (-я) м attendant

смо́|чь (-гу́, -жешь etc, -гут; pt -г, -гла́, -гло́) сов от **мочь**

SMS ср нескл text (message)

сму́зи м нескл smoothie

сму́т|а (-ы) ж unrest

сму|ти́ть (-щу́, -ти́шь; impf смуща́ть) сов перех to embarrass; **смути́ться** (impf смуща́ться) сов возв to get embarrassed

сму́тный прил vague; (время) troubled

смуще́ни|е (-я) ср embarrassment; **смущённый** прил embarrassed

смысл (-а) м sense; (назначение) point

см|ыть (-о́ю, -о́ешь; impf смыва́ть) сов перех to wash off; (подлеж: волна) to wash away; **смы́ться** (impf смыва́ться) сов возв to wash off

смыч|о́к (-ка́) м (Муз) bow

смягч|и́ть (-у́, -и́шь; impf смягча́ть) сов перех (кожу, удар) to soften; (боль) to ease; (наказание) to mitigate; (человека) to appease; **смягчи́ться** (impf смягча́ться) сов возв to soften

смя́ть(ся) (**сомну́(сь)**, **сомнёшь(ся)**) сов от **мя́ть(ся)**

сна etc сущ см **сон**

снаб|ди́ть (-жу́, -ди́шь; impf снабжа́ть) сов перех: **снабди́ть кого́-н/что-н чем-н** to supply sb/sth with sth

снабже́ни|е (**-я**) *ср* supply

сна́йпер (**-а**) *м* sniper

снару́жи *нареч* on the outside; (*закрыть*) from the outside

снаря́д (**-а**) *м* (*Воен*) shell; (*Спорт*) apparatus

снаря|ди́ть (**-жу́, -ди́шь**) *impf* **снаряжа́ть** *сов перех* to equip; **снаряже́ни|е** (**-я**) *ср* equipment

снача́ла *нареч* at first; (*ещё раз*) all over again

СНГ *м сокр* (= *Содру́жество Незави́симых Госуда́рств*) CIS (= *Commonwealth of Independent States*)

снег (**-а**; *loc sg* **-у́**, *nom pl* **-а́**) *м* snow; **идёт снег** it's snowing

снегови́к (**-а́**) *м* snowman (*мн* snowmen)

Снегу́роч|ка (**-ки**; *gen pl* **-ек**) *ж* Snow Maiden

● **СНЕГУ́РОЧКА**
●
● The Snow Maiden accompanies Father
● Christmas on his visits to children's New
● Year parties, where she organizes games
● and helps with the important task of
● giving out the presents.

сне́жный *прил* snow; (*зима*) snowy

снеж|о́к (**-ка́**) *м* snowball

сн|ести́ (**-есу́, -есёшь**; *pt* **-ёс, -есла́, -есло́**, *impf* **сноси́ть**) *сов перех* (*отнести*) to take; (*подлеж: буря*) to tear down; (*перен: вытерпеть*) to take; (*дом*) to demolish

снижа́|ть(ся) (**-ю(сь)**) *несов от* **сни́зить(ся)**

сниже́ни|е (**-я**) *ср* (*цен итп*) lowering; (*самолёта*) descent; (*выдачи*) reduction

сни́|зить (**-жу, -зишь**; *impf* **снижа́ть**) *сов перех* (*цены, давление итп*) to lower; (*скорость*) to reduce; **сни́зиться** (*impf* **снижа́ться**) *сов возв* to fall; (*самолёт*) to descend

сни́зу *нареч* (*внизу*) at the bottom; (*о направлении*) from the bottom

снима́|ть(ся) (**-ю(сь)**) *несов от* **снять(ся)**

сни́м|ок (**-ка**) *м* (*Фото*) snap(shot)

сн|и́ться (**-ю́сь, -и́шься**; *perf* **присни́ться**) *несов безл*: **мне сни́лся стра́шный сон** I was having a terrible dream; **мне сни́лось, что я в гора́х** I dreamt I was in the mountains; **ты ча́сто сни́шься мне** I often dream of you

сно́ва *нареч* again

снос (**-а**) *м* demolition

сно́с|ка (**-ки**; *gen pl* **-ок**) *ж* footnote

снотво́рн|ое (**-ого**) *ср* sleeping pill

снох|а́ (**-и́**) *ж* daughter-in-law (*of husband's father*)

сн|ять (**-иму́, -и́мешь**; *impf* **снима́ть**) *сов перех* to take down; (*плод*) to pick; (*одежду*) to take off; (*запрет, ответственность*) to remove;

(*фотографировать*) to photograph; (*копию*) to make; (*нанять*) to rent; (*уволить*) to dismiss; **снима́ть** (*perf* **снять**) **фотогра́фию** to take a picture; **снима́ть** (*perf* **снять**) **фильм** to shoot a film; **сня́ться** (*impf* **снима́ться**) *сов возв* (*сфотографироваться*) to have one's photograph taken; (*в фильме*) to appear

со *предл* = **с**

соба́к|а (**-и**) *ж* dog

собе́с (**-а**) *м* social security; (*орган*) social security department

собесе́дник (**-а**) *м*: **мой собесе́дник замолча́л** the person I was talking to fell silent

собесе́довани|е (**-я**) *ср* interview

собира́тел|ь (**-я**) *м* collector

собира́|ть (**-ю**) *несов от* **собра́ть**; **собира́ться** *несов от* **собра́ться** ▷ *возв*: **я собира́юсь пойти́ туда́** I'm going to go there

соблазн|и́ть (**-ю́, -и́шь**; *impf* **соблазня́ть**) *сов перех* to seduce; (*прельстить*): **соблазни́ть кого́-н чем-н** to tempt sb with sth; **соблазни́ться** (*impf* **соблазня́ться**) *сов возв*: **соблазни́ться +instr +infin** to be tempted by/to do

соблюда́|ть (**-ю**) *несов от* **соблюсти́** ▷ *перех* (*дисциплину, порядок*) to maintain

соблю|сти́ (**-ду́, -дёшь**) *сов от* **блюсти́** ▷ (*impf* **соблюда́ть**) *перех* (*закон, правила*) to observe

соболе́зновани|е (**-я**) *ср* condolences *мн*

собо́р (**-а**) *м* cathedral

СОБР (**-а**) *м сокр* (= *Сво́дный отря́д бы́строго реаги́рования*) flying squad

собра́ни|е (**-я**) *ср* meeting; (*Полит*) assembly; (*картин итп*) collection; **собра́ние сочине́ний** collected works

соб|ра́ть (**-еру́, -ерёшь**; *pt* **-ра́л, -рала́, -ра́ло**, *impf* **собира́ть**) *сов перех* to gather (together); (*ягоды, грибы*) to pick; (*механизм*) to assemble; (*налоги, подписи*) to collect; **собра́ться** (*impf* **собира́ться**) *сов возв* (*гости*) to assemble, gather; (*приготовиться*): **собра́ться +infin** to get ready to do; **собира́ться** (*perf* **собра́ться**) **с +instr** (*с силами, с мыслями*) to gather

собро́в|ец (**-ца**) *м* member of the flying squad

со́бственник (**-а**) *м* owner

со́бственно *част* actually ▷ *вводн сл*: **со́бственно** (**говоря́**) as a matter of fact

со́бственност|ь (**-и**) *ж* property; **со́бственный** *прил* (one's) own

собы́ти|е (**-я**) *ср* event

сов|а́ (**-ы́**; *nom pl* **-ы**) *ж* owl

соверша́|ть(ся) (**-ю**) *несов от* **соверши́ть(ся)**

соверше́ни|е (**-я**) *ср* (*сделки*) conclusion; (*преступления*) committing

соверше́нно *нареч* (*очень хорошо*) perfectly; (*совсем*) absolutely, completely

совершеннолétн|ий *прил*: **стать совершеннолéтним** to come of age

совершéнный *прил* (*хороший*) perfect; (*абсолютный*) absolute, complete; **совершéнный вид** (*Линг*) perfective (aspect); **совершéнств|о** (-а) *ср* perfection; **совершéнств|овать** (-ую; *perf* **усовершéнствовать**) *несов перех* to perfect; **совершéнствоваться** (*perf* **усовершéнствоваться**) *несов возв*: **совершéнствоваться в** +*prp* to perfect

соверш|и́ть (-у́, -и́шь; *impf* **совершáть**) *сов перех* to make; (*сделку*) to conclude; (*преступление*) to commit; (*обряд, подвиг*) to perform; **совершиться** (*impf* **совершáться**) *сов возв* (*событие*) to take place

со́вест|ь (-и) *ж* conscience; **на со́весть** (*сделанный*) very well

совéт (-а) *м* advice *только ед*; (*военный*) council; **совéтник** (-а) *м* (*юстиции итп*) councillor; (*президента*) adviser

совéт|овать (-ую; *perf* **посовéтовать**) *несов*: **совéтовать кому́-н** +*infin* to advise sb to do; **совéтоваться** (*perf* **посовéтоваться**) *несов возв*: **совéтоваться с кем-н** (*с другом*) to ask sb's advice; (*с юристом*) to consult sb

совéтский *прил* Soviet

совещáни|е (-я) *ср* (*собрание*) meeting; (*конгресс*) conference

совещá|ться (-юсь) *несов возв* to deliberate

совмести́мый *прил* compatible

совме|сти́ть (-щу́, -сти́шь; *impf* **совмещáть**) *сов перех* to combine

совмéстный *прил* (*общий*) joint

сов|óк (-кá) *м* (*для мусора*) dustpan; (*для муки*) scoop

совоку́пност|ь (-и) *ж* combination; **в совоку́пности** in total

совоку́пный *прил* (*усилия*) joint

совпа|сть (*3sg* -дёт, *impf* **совпадáть**) *сов* (*события*) to coincide; (*данные, цифры итп*) to tally; (*интересы, мнения*) to meet

совр|áть (-у́, -ёшь) *сов от* **врать**

совремéнник (-а) *м* contemporary

совремéнност|ь (-и) *ж* the present day; (*идей*) modernity

совремéнный *прил* contemporary; (*техника*) up-to-date; (*человек, идеи*) modern

совсéм *нареч* (*новый*) completely; (*молодой*) very; (*нисколько*: не **пригодный, не нужный**) totally: **не совсéм** not quite

соглáси|е (-я) *ср* consent; (*в семье*) harmony, accord

согла|си́ться (-шу́сь, -си́шься; *impf* **соглашáться**) *сов возв* to agree

соглáсно *предл*: **соглáсно** +*dat или* с +*instr* in accordance with

соглáсн|ый (-ого) *м* (*также* **соглáсный звук**) consonant ▷ *прил*: **соглáсный на** +*acc* (*на условия*) agreeable to; **Вы соглáсны (со мной)?** do you agree (with me)?

соглас|овáть (-у́ю; *impf* **согласóвывать**) *сов перех* (*действия*) to coordinate; (*обговорить*): **согласовáть что-н с** +*instr* (*план, цену*) to agree sth with; **согласовáться** (*не*)*сов возв*: **согласовáться с** +*instr* to correspond with

соглашá|ться (-юсь) *несов от* **соглаcи́ться**

соглашéни|е (-я) *ср* agreement

согн|у́ть (-у́, -ёшь) *сов от* **гнуть**; **сгибáть**

согрé|ть (-ю; *impf* **согревáть**) *сов перех* (*воду*) to heat up; (*ноги, руки*) to warm up; **согрéться** (*impf* **согревáться**) *сов возв* to warm up; (*вода*) to heat up

сóд|а (-ы) *ж* soda

содéйстви|е (-я) *ср* assistance

содéйств|овать (-ую) (*не*)*сов* +*dat* to assist

содержáни|е (-я) *ср* (*семьи, детей*) upkeep; (*магазина, фермы*) keeping; (*книги*) contents *мн*; (*сахара, витаминов*) content; (*оглавление*) (table of) contents *мн*

содержáтельный *прил* (*статья, доклад*) informative

сод|ержáть (-ержу́, -éржишь) *несов перех* (*детей, родителей, магазин*) to keep; (*ресторан*) to own; (*сахар, ошибки, информацию итп*) to contain; **содержáться** *несов возв* (*под арестом*) to be held

содр|áть (*сдеру́, сдерёшь*; *pt* -áл, -алá, *impf* **сдирáть**) *сов перех* (*слой, одежду*) to tear off

содрýжеств|о (-а) *ср* (*дружба*) cooperation; (*союз*) commonwealth; **Содрýжество Независи́мых Госудáрств** the Commonwealth of Independent States

сóевый *прил* soya

соедин|и́ть (-ю́, -и́шь; *impf* **соединя́ть**) *сов перех* (*силы, детали*) to join; (*людей*) to unite; (*провода, трубы, по телефону*) to connect; (*города*) to link; **соедини́ться** (*impf* **соединя́ться**) *сов возв* (*люди, отряды*) to join together

сожалéни|е (-я) *ср* (*сострадание*) pity; **сожалéние (о** +*prp*) (*о прошлом, о потере*) regret (about); **к сожалéнию** unfortunately

сожалé|ть (-ю) *несов*: **сожалéть о чём-н/, что** to regret sth/that

созвон|и́ться (-ю́сь, -и́шься; *impf* **созвáниваться**) *сов возв*: **созвони́ться с** +*instr* to phone (*Brit*) *или* call (*US*)

созда|вáть(ся) (-ю́, -ёшь) *несов от* **создáть(ся)**

создáни|е (-я) *ср* creation; (*существо*)

creature; **созда́тел|ь** (-я) *м* creator

созда|ть (*как* **дать**; *см Table 16*; *impf* **создава́ть**) *сов перех* to create; **созда́ться** (*impf* **создава́ться**) *сов возв* (*обстановка*) to emerge; (*впечатление*) to be created

созна|ва́ть (-ю́, -ёшь) *несов от* **созна́ть** ▷ *перех* to be aware of; **сознава́ться** *несов от* **созна́ться**

созна́ни|е (-я) *ср* consciousness; (*вины, долга*) awareness; **приходи́ть** (*perf* **прийти́**) **в созна́ние** to come round

созна́тельност|ь (-и) *ж* awareness; **созна́тельный** *прил* (*человек, возраст*) mature; (*жизнь*) adult; (*обман, поступок*) intentional

созна́|ть (-ю; *impf* **сознава́ть**) *сов перех* (*вину, долг*) to realize; **созна́ться** (*impf* **сознава́ться**) *сов возв*: **созна́ться** (**в** +*prp*) (*в ошибке*) to admit (to); (*в преступлении*) to confess (to)

созре́|ть (-ю) *сов от* **зреть**

созыва́|ть (-ю) *несов от* **созва́ть**

сойти́ (*как* **идти́**; *см Table 18*; *impf* **сходи́ть**) *сов* (*с горы, с лестницы*) to go down; (*с дороги*) to leave; (*разг*): **сойти́ с** +*instr* (*с поезда, с автобуса*) to get off; **сходи́ть** (*perf* **сойти́**) **с ума́** to go mad; **сойти́сь** (*impf* **сходи́ться**) *сов возв* (*собраться*) to gather; (*цифры, показания*) to tally

сок (-а) *м* juice

сокра|ти́ть (-щу́, -ти́шь; *impf* **сокраща́ть**) *сов перех* to shorten; (*расходы*) to reduce; **сократи́ться** (*impf* **сокраща́ться**) *сов возв* (*расстояние, сроки*) to be shortened; (*расходы, снабжение*) to be reduced; **сокраще́ни|е** (-я) *ср* (*см глаг*) shortening; reduction; (*сокращённое название*) abbreviation; (*также* **сокраще́ние шта́тов**) staff reduction

сокро́вищ|е (-а) *ср* treasure

соку́рсник (-а) *м*: **он мой соку́рсник** he is in my year

сол|га́ть (-гу́, -жёшь *etc*, -гу́т) *сов от* **лгать**

солда́т (-а; *gen pl* -) *м* soldier; **солда́тик** (-а) *м* (*игрушка*) toy soldier

солёный *прил* (*пища*) salty; (*овощи*) pickled in brine; (*вода*) salt

соли́дный *прил* (*постройка*) solid; (*фирма*) established

соли́ст (-а) *м* soloist

сол|и́ть (-ю́, -ишь; *perf* **посоли́ть**) *несов перех* to salt; (*засаливать*) to preserve in brine

со́лнечн|ый *прил* solar; (*день, погода*) sunny; **со́лнечный уда́р** sunstroke; **со́лнечные очки́** sunglasses

со́лнц|е (-а) *ср* sun

со́ло *ср нескл, нареч* solo

соло́м|а (-ы) *ж* straw; **соло́менный** *прил* (*шляпа*) straw

соло́н|ка (-ки; *gen pl* -ок) *ж* saltcellar

сол|ь (-и) *ж* salt

со́льный *прил* solo

сомнева́|ться (-юсь) *несов возв*: **сомнева́ться в чём-н/, что** to doubt sth/ that

сомне́ни|е (-я) *ср* doubt; **сомни́тельный** *прил* (*дело, личность*) shady; (*предложение, знакомство*) dubious

сон (**сна**) *м* sleep; (*сновидение*) dream; **со́нный** *прил* (*заспанный*) sleepy

соображ́а|ть (-ю) *несов от* **сообрази́ть**

соображе́ни|е (-я) *ср* (*мысль*) idea; (*обычно мн: мотивы*) reasoning

сообрази́тельный *прил* smart

сообра|зи́ть (-жу́, -зи́шь; *impf* **сообража́ть**) *сов* to work out

сообща́ *нареч* together

сообща́|ть (-ю) *несов от* **сообщи́ть**

сообще́ни|е (-я) *ср* (*информация*) report; (*правительственное*) announcement; (*связь*) communications *мн*

сообществ|о (-а) *ср* association; **мирово́е** *или* **междунаро́дное сообщество** international community

сообщи́ть (-у́, -и́шь; *impf* **сообща́ть**) *сов*: **сообщи́ть кому́-н о** +*prp* to inform sb of ▷ *перех* (*новости, тайну*) to tell

сообщник (-а) *м* accomplice

соотве́тственно *предл* (+*dat*: *обстановке*) according to; **соотве́тственный** *прил* (*оплата*) appropriate; (*результаты*) fitting

соотве́тстви|е (-я) *ср* (*интересов, стилей итп*) correspondence; **в соотве́тствии с** +*instr* in accordance with; **соотве́тств|овать** (-ую) *несов* +*dat* to correspond to; (*требованиям*) to meet

соотве́тствующий *прил* appropriate

соотноше́ни|е (-я) *ср* correlation

сопе́рник (-а) *м* rival; (*в спорте*) competitor

сопе́рнича|ть (-ю) *несов*: **сопе́рничать с кем-н в чём-н** to rival sb in sth

сопра́но *ср нескл* soprano

сопровожда́|ть (-ю; *perf* **сопроводи́ть**) *несов перех* to accompany; **сопровожде́ни|е** (-я) *ср*: **в сопровожде́нии** +*gen* accompanied by

сопротивле́ни|е (-я) *ср* resistance

сопротивля́|ться (-юсь) *несов возв* +*dat* to resist

сор (-а) *м* rubbish

сорв|а́ть (-у́, -ёшь; *impf* **срыва́ть**) *сов перех* (*цветок, яблоко*) to pick; (*дверь, крышу, одежду*) to tear off; (*лекцию, переговоры*) to sabotage; (*планы*) to frustrate; **сорва́ться** (*impf* **срыва́ться**) *сов возв* (*человек*) to lose one's temper; (*планы*) to be frustrated; **срыва́ться** (*perf* **сорва́ться**) **с** +*gen* (*с петель*) to come away from

соревновáни|**е** (-я) *ср* competition
соревн|**овáться** (-ýюсь) *несов возв* to compete
сор|**ить** (-ю, -ишь; *perf* **насорить**) *несов* to make a mess
сорняк (-á) *м* weed
со́рок (-á; см *Table 27*) *чис* forty
сороковóй *чис* fortieth
сорт (-а; *nom pl* -á) *м* sort; (*пшеницы*) grade; **сортир**|**овáть** (-ýю; *perf* **рассортировáть**) *несов перех* to sort; (*по качеству*) to grade
сос|**áть** (-ý, -ёшь) *несов перех* to suck
сосéд (-а; *nom pl* -и, *gen pl* -ей) *м* neighbour (*Brit*), neighbor (*US*); **сосéдний** *прил* neighbouring (*Brit*), neighboring (*US*); **сосéдств**|**о** (-а) *ср*: **жить по сосéдству** to live nearby; **в сосéдстве с** +*instr* near
сосиск|**а** (-ки, *gen pl* -ок) *ж* sausage
соск|**очи́ть** (-очу́, -о́чишь; *impf* **соскáкивать**) *сов* to jump off
соскуч|**иться** (-усь, -ишься) *сов возв* to be bored; **соскучиться** (*perf*) **по** +*dat* (*по детям*) to miss
сослагáтельн|**ый** *прил*: **сослагáтельное наклонéние** subjunctive mood
со|**слáть** (-шлю́, -шлёшь; *impf* **ссылáть**) *сов перех* to exile; **сослáться** (*impf* **ссылáться**) *сов возв*: **сослáться на** +*acc* to refer to
сослужи́в|**ец** (-ца) *м* colleague
сос|**нá** (-ны́; *nom pl* -ны, *gen pl* -ен) *ж* pine (tree); **сосно́вый** *прил* pine
сос|**óк** (-кá) *м* nipple
сосредотóч|**ить** (-у, -ишь; *impf* **сосредотáчивать**) *сов перех* to concentrate; **сосредотóчиться** (*impf* **сосредотáчиваться**) *сов возв* (*войска*) to be concentrated; (*внимание*): **сосредотóчиться на** +*acc* to focus on
состáв (-а) *м* (*классовый*) structure; (+*gen*: *комитета*) members *мн* of; (*вещества*) composition of
состáв|**ить** (-лю, -ишь; *impf* **составлять**) *сов перех* (*словарь, список*) to compile; (*план*) to draw up; (*сумму*) to constitute; (*команду*) to put together; **состáвиться** (*impf* **составляться**) *сов возв* to be formed
составн|**óй** *прил*: **составнáя часть** component
состáр|**ить** (-ю, -ишь) *сов от* **стáрить**; **состáриться** *сов возв* (*человек*) to grow old
состоя́ни|**е** (-я) *ср* state; (*больного*) condition; (*собственность*) fortune; **быть** (*impf*) **в состоя́нии** +*infin* to be able to do
состоя́тельный *прил* (*богатый*) well-off
состо|**я́ть** (-ю́, -и́шь) *несов*: **состоя́ть из** +*gen* (*книга*) to consist of; (*заключаться*): **состоя́ть в** +*prp* to be; (*в партии*) to be a member of; (+*instr*: *директором итп*) to be;

состоя́ться *несов возв* (*собрание*) to take place
сострадáни|**е** (-я) *ср* compassion
состязáни|**е** (-я) *ср* contest
состяз|**áться** (-ю́сь) *несов возв* to compete
сосýд (-а) *м* vessel
сот *чис см* **сто**
сотворéни|**е** (-я) *ср*: **сотворéние ми́ра** Creation
со́т|**ня** (-ни, *gen pl* -ен) *ж* (*сто*) a hundred
со́тов|**ый** *прил*: **со́товый телефо́н** mobile phone; **со́товая связь** network
сотрýдник (-а) *м* (*служащий*) employee; **нау́чный сотрýдник** research worker; **сотрýднича**|**ть** (-ю) *несов* to cooperate; (*работать*) to work; **сотрýдничеств**|**о** (-а) *ср* (*см глаг*) cooperation; work
сотряс|**ти́** (-ý, -ёшь; *impf* **сотрясáть**) *сов перех* to shake; **сотрясти́сь** (*impf* **сотрясáться**) *сов возв* to shake
со́т|**ы** (-ов) *мн*: (*пчели́ные*) **со́ты** honeycomb *ед*
со́тый *чис* hundredth
со́ус (-а) *м* sauce
соучáстник (-а) *м* accomplice
соф|**á** (-ы́; *nom pl* -ы) *ж* sofa
со́х|**нуть** (-ну; *pt* -, -ла, *perf* **вы́сохнуть**) *несов* to dry; (*растения*) to wither
сохран|**и́ть** (-ю́, -и́шь; *impf* **сохраня́ть**) *сов перех* to preserve; (*Комп*) to save; **сохрани́ться** (*impf* **сохраня́ться**) *сов возв* to be preserved
сохра́нност|**ь** (-и) *ж* (*вкладов, документов*) security; **в (по́лной) сохра́нности** (fully) intact
соци́ал-демокра́т (-а) *м* social democrat
социали́зм (-а) *м* socialism; **социалисти́ческий** *прил* socialist
социа́льн|**ый** *прил* social; **социа́льная защищённость** social security
социоло́ги|**я** (-и) *ж* sociology
соцсе́т|**ь** (-и) *ж* social networking site
сочета́ни|**е** (-я) *ср* combination
сочета́|**ть** (-ю) (*не*)*сов перех* to combine; **сочета́ться** (*не*)*сов возв* (*соедини́ться*) to combine; (*гармони́ровать*) to match
сочине́ни|**е** (-я) *ср* (*литерату́рное*) work; (*музыка́льное*) composition; (*Просвещ*) essay
сочин|**и́ть** (-ю́, -и́шь; *impf* **сочиня́ть**) *сов перех* (*му́зыку*) to compose; (*стихи, песню*) to write
со́чный *прил* (*плод*) juicy; (*трава*) lush; (*краски*) vibrant
сочу́встви|**е** (-я) *ср* sympathy
сочу́вств|**овать** (-ую) *несов* +*dat* to sympathize with
сошёл(ся) *etc сов см* **сойти́(сь)**
сошью́ *итп сов см* **сши́ть**
сою́з (-а) *м* union; (*вое́нный*) alliance; (*Линг*) conjunction; **сою́зник** (-а) *м* ally; **сою́зный** *прил* (*а́рмия*) allied

со́|я (-и) ж собир soya beans мн

спад (-а) м drop; экономи́ческий спад recession

спада́|ть (3sg -ет) несов от спасть

спазм (-а) м spasm

спа́льный прил (ме́сто) sleeping; спа́льный ваго́н sleeping car; спа́льный мешо́к sleeping bag

спа́л|ьня (-ьни; gen pl -ен) ж (ко́мната) bedroom; (ме́бель) bedroom suite

Спас (-а) м (Рел) the Day of the Saviour (in Orthodox Church)

спаса́тельн|ый прил (ста́нция) rescue; спаса́тельная ло́дка lifeboat; спаса́тельный жиле́т life jacket; спаса́тельный по́яс life belt

спаса́|ть(ся) (-ю(сь)) несов от спасти́(сь)

спасе́ни|е (-я) ср rescue; (Рел) Salvation

спаси́бо част: спаси́бо (Вам) thank you; большо́е спаси́бо! thank you very much!; спаси́бо за по́мощь thanks for the help

спас|ти́ (-у́, -ёшь; impf спаса́ть) сов перех to save; спасти́сь (impf спаса́ться) сов возв: спасти́сь (от +gen) to escape

спа|сть (3sg -дёт, impf спада́ть) сов (вода́) to drop

сп|ать (-лю, -ишь) несов to sleep; ложи́ться (perf лечь) спать to go to bed; спа́ться несов возв: мне не спи́тся I can't (get to) sleep

СПБ сокр (= Санкт-Петербу́рг) St Petersburg

спекта́кл|ь (-я) м performance

спектр (-а) м spectrum

спе́лый прил ripe

спе́реди нареч in front

спе́рм|а (-ы) ж sperm

сп|еть (3sg -е́ет, perf поспе́ть) несов (фру́кты, о́вощи) to ripen ▷ (-ою́, -оёшь) сов от петь

спех (-а) м: мне не к спе́ху (разг) I'm in no hurry

специализи́р|оваться (-уюсь) (не)сов возв: специализи́роваться в +prp или по +dat to specialize in

специали́ст (-а) м specialist

специа́льност|ь (-и) ж (профе́ссия) profession

специа́льный прил special

специ́фик|а (-и) ж specific nature

специфи́ческий прил specific

спе́ци|я (-и) ж spice

спецко́р (-а) м сокр (= специа́льный корреспонде́нт) special correspondent

спецку́рс (-а) м сокр (в ву́зе) (= специа́льный курс) course of lectures in a specialist field

спецна́з (-а) м special task force

спецна́зов|ец (-ца) м member of the special task force

спецоде́жд|а (-ы) ж сокр (= специа́льная оде́жда) work clothes мн

спецслу́жб|а (-ы) ж сокр (обычно мн) (= специа́льная слу́жба) special service

спеш|и́ть (-у́, -и́шь) несов (часы́) to be fast; (челове́к) to be in a rush; спеши́ть (perf поспеши́ть) +infin/c +instr to be in a hurry to do/with; спеши́ть (impf) на по́езд to rush for the train

спе́шк|а (-и) ж (разг) hurry, rush

спе́шный прил urgent

СПИД (-а) м сокр (= синдро́м приобретённого иммунодефици́та) AIDS (= acquired immune deficiency syndrome)

спидо́метр (-а) м speedometer

спи́кер (-а) м speaker

спин|а́ (-ы́; acc sg -у, dat sg -е́, nom pl -ы) ж (челове́ка, живо́тного) back

спи́нк|а (-и; gen pl -ок) ж, уменьш от спина́; (дива́на, сту́ла итп) back; (крова́ти: ве́рхняя) headboard; (: ни́жняя) foot

спинно́й прил (позвоно́к) spinal; спинно́й мозг spinal cord

спира́л|ь (-и) ж (ли́ния) spiral; (та́кже внутрима́точная спира́ль) coil (contraceptive)

спирт (-а) м (Хим) spirit

спиртн|о́е (-о́го) ср alcohol

спиртно́й прил: спиртно́й напи́ток alcoholic drink

спи́с|ать (-ишу́, -и́шешь; impf спи́сывать) сов перех to copy; (Комм) to write off

спи́с|ок (-ка) м list

спи́ц|а (-ы) ж (для вяза́ния) knitting needle; (колеса́) spoke

спи́чк|а (-и; gen pl -ек) ж match

спла́чива|ть(ся) (-ю) несов от сплоти́ть(ся)

сплетнича|ть (-ю) несов to gossip

сплет|ня (-ни; gen pl -ен) ж gossip

спло|ти́ть (-чу́, -ти́шь; impf спла́чивать) сов перех to unite; сплоти́ться (impf спла́чиваться) сов возв to unite

сплошно́й прил (степь) continuous; (пе́репись) universal; (разг: неуда́чи) utter

сплошь нареч (по всей пове́рхности) all over; (без исключе́ния) completely; сплошь и ря́дом (разг) everywhere

сплю несов см спать

споко́йный прил (у́лица, жизнь) quiet; (мо́ре, взгляд) calm

сполз|ти́ (-у́, -ёшь; pt -, -ла́, impf сполза́ть) сов to climb down

спонси́р|овать (-ую) (не)сов to sponsor

спо́нсор (-а) м sponsor

спор (-а) м debate; (Юр) dispute; на́ спор (разг) as a bet

спо́р|ить (-ю, -ишь; perf поспо́рить) несов (вести спор) to argue; (держа́ть пари́) to bet; спо́рить (impf) с кем-н о чём-н или за что-н (о насле́дстве) to dispute sth with sb

спо́рный прил (де́ло) disputed; (побе́да) doubtful; спо́рный вопро́с moot point

спорт (-а) м sport

спортза́л (-а) м сокр (= спорти́вный зал) sports hall

спортсме́н (-а) м sportsman (мн sportsmen)

спо́соб (-а) м way

спосо́бност|**ь** (-и) ж ability

спосо́бный прил capable; (тала́нтливый) able

спосо́бствовать (-ую) сов (+dat: успе́ху, разви́тию) to encourage

споткн|**у́ться** (-у́сь, -ёшься; impf **спотыка́ться**) сов возв to trip

спою́ итп несов см **спеть**

спра́ва нареч to the right; **спра́ва от** +gen to the right of

справедли́вост|**ь** (-и) ж justice

справедли́вый прил fair, just; (вы́вод) correct

спра́виться (impf **справля́ться**) сов возв: **спра́виться с** +instr (с рабо́той) to cope with, manage; (с проти́вником) to deal with; (узна́ть): **спра́виться о** +prp to enquire или ask about

спра́в|**ка** (-ки; gen pl -ок) ж (све́дения) information; (докуме́нт) certificate

спра́вочник (-а) м directory; (граммати́ческий) reference book

спра́вочный прил (литерату́ра) reference; **спра́вочное бюро́** information office или bureau

спра́шива|**ть(ся)** (-ю(сь)) несов от **спроси́ть(ся)**

спрос (-а) м: **спрос на** +acc (на това́ры) demand for; (тре́бование): **спрос с** +gen (с роди́телей) demands мн on; **без спро́са** или **спро́су** without permission

спр|**оси́ть** (-ошу́, -о́сишь; impf **спра́шивать**) сов перех (доро́гу, вре́мя) to ask; (сове́та, де́нег) to ask for; (взыска́ть): **спроси́ть что-н с** +gen to call sb to account for sth; (осве́домиться): **спроси́ть кого́-н о чём-н** to ask sb about sth; **спра́шивать** (perf **спроси́ть**) ученика́ to question или test a pupil; **спроси́ться** (impf **спра́шиваться**) сов возв: **спроси́ться** +gen или у +gen (у учи́теля итп) to ask permission of

спры́г|**нуть** (-ну; impf **спры́гивать**) сов: **спры́гнуть с** +gen to jump off

спряже́ни|**е** (-я) ср (Линг) conjugation

спря́|**тать(ся)** (-чу(сь), -чешь(ся)) сов от **пря́тать(ся)**

спуска́|**ть** (-ю) несов от **спусти́ть** ▷ перех: **я не спуска́л глаз с неё** I didn't take my eyes off her; **спуска́ться** несов от **спусти́ться**

спу|**сти́ть** (-щу́, -стишь; impf **спуска́ть**) сов перех to lower; (соба́ку) to let loose; (газ, во́ду) to drain; **спусти́ться** (impf **спуска́ться**) сов возв to go down

спустя́ нареч: **спустя́ три дня/год** three days/a year later

спу́та|**ть(ся)** (-ю(сь)) сов от **пу́тать(ся)**

спу́тник (-а) м (в пути́) travelling (Brit) или traveling (US) companion; (Астроно́мия) satellite; (Ко́смос: также **иску́сственный спу́тник**) sputnik, satellite

сравне́ни|**е** (-я) ср comparison; **в сравне́нии** или **по сравне́нию с** +instr compared with

сра́внива|**ть** (-ю) несов от **сравни́ть**; **сравня́ть**

сравни́тельный прил comparative

сравн|**и́ть** (-ю́, -и́шь; impf **сра́внивать**) сов перех: **сравни́ть что-н/кого́-н (с** +instr) to compare sth/sb (with); **сравни́ться** сов возв: **сравни́ться с** +instr to compare with

сраже́ни|**е** (-я) ср battle

сра́зу нареч (неме́дленно) straight away; (в оди́н приём) (all) at once

сраст|**и́сь** (3sg -ётся, impf **сраста́ться**) сов возв (ко́сти) to knit (together)

сред|**а́** (-ы́; nom pl -ы) ж medium; (no pl: приро́дная, социа́льная) environment ▷ (acc sg -у) (день неде́ли) Wednesday; **окружа́ющая среда́** environment; **охра́на окружа́ющей среды́** conservation

среди́ предл +gen in the middle of; (в числе́) among

средизе́мный прил: **Средизе́мное мо́ре** the Mediterranean (Sea)

среднеазиа́тский прил Central Asian

средневеко́вый прил medieval

среднегодово́й прил average annual

сре́дний прил average; (разме́р) medium; (в середи́не) middle; (шко́ла) secondary

- **СРЕ́ДНЯЯ ШКО́ЛА**
-
- Children in Russia start school at the age
- of six or seven. They stay in the same
- school throughout their education. They
- can leave school after eight years if they
- plan to continue into further education.
- Those who stay on study for a further
- two or three years before sitting their
- final exams. On completing the final
- exams they receive the Certificate of
- Secondary Education. See also note
- at ЕГЭ.

сре́дств|**о** (-а) ср means мн; (лека́рство) remedy

срез (-а) м (ме́сто) cut; (то́нкий слой) section

сре́|**зать** (-жу, -жешь; impf **среза́ть**) сов перех to cut

срок (-а) м (дли́тельность) time, period; (да́та) date; **в срок** (во́ время) in time; **после́дний** или **преде́льный срок** deadline; **срок го́дности** (това́ра) sell-by date; **срок де́йствия** period of validity

сро́чный прил urgent

срыв (-а) м disruption; (на экза́мене итп) failure

срыва́|ть(ся) (-ю(сь)) *несов от*
сорва́ть(ся)

сса́дин|а (-ы) *ж* scratch

ссо́р|а (-ы) *ж* quarrel

ссо́р|ить (-ю, -ишь; *perf* **поссо́рить**)
несов перех (*друзей*) to cause to quarrel;
ссо́риться (*perf* **поссо́риться**) *несов
возв* to quarrel

СССР *м сокр* (Ист) (= *Сою́з Сове́тских
Социалисти́ческих Респу́блик*) USSR
(= *Union of Soviet Socialist Republics*)

ссу́д|а (-ы) *ж* loan

ссу|ди́ть (-жу́, -дишь; *impf* **ссужа́ть**)
сов перех (*деньги*) to lend

ссыла́|ть (-ю) *несов от* **сосла́ть**;
ссыла́ться *несов от* **сосла́ться** ▷ *возв*:
ссыла́ясь на +*acc* with reference to

ссы́л|ка (-ки; *gen pl* **-ок**) *ж* exile;
(*цита́та*) quotation

ст. *сокр* = **ста́нция**

ста *чис см* **сто**

стабилизи́р|овать (-ую) (*не*)*сов перех*
to stabilize

стаби́льный *прил* stable

ста́в|ить (-лю, -ишь; *perf* **поста́вить**)
несов перех to put; (*назнача́ть*:
мини́стром) to appoint; (*о́перу*) to stage;
ста́вить (*perf* **поста́вить**) **часы́** to set a
clock

ста́в|ка (-ки; *gen pl* **-ок**) *ж* (*та́кже* Комм)
rate; (Воен) headquarters *мн*; (*в ка́ртах*)
stake; (*перен*): **ста́вка на** +*acc* (*расчёт*)
reliance on more

стадио́н (-а) *м* stadium (*мн* stadia)

ста́ди|я (-и) *ж* stage

ста́д|о (-а; *nom pl* **-а́**) *ср* (*коро́в*) herd;
(*ове́ц*) flock

стаж (-а) *м* (*рабо́чий*) experience

стажир|ова́ться (-у́юсь) *несов возв* to
work on probation

стажиро́в|ка (-ки; *gen pl* **-ок**) *ж*
probationary period

стака́н (-а) *м* glass; **бума́жный стака́н**
paper cup

стал *сов см* **стать**

ста́лкива|ть(ся) (-ю(сь)) *несов от*
столкну́ть(ся)

сталь (-и) *ж* steel

стам *итп чис см* **сто**

станда́рт (-а) *м* standard

стан|ови́ться (-овлю́сь, -о́вишься)
несов от **стать**

становле́ни|е (-я) *ср* formation

стан|о́к (-ка́) *м* machine (tool)

ста́ну *итп сов см* **стать**

ста́нци|я (-и) *ж* station; **телефо́нная
ста́нция** telephone exchange

стара́ни|е (-я) *ср* effort

стара́|ться (-юсь; *perf* **постара́ться**)
несов +*infin* to try to do

старе́|ть (-ю; *perf* **постаре́ть**) *несов*
(*челове́к*) to grow old(er), age ▷ (*perf*
устаре́ть) (*обору́дование*) to become
out of date

стари́к (-а́) *м* old man

стари́нный *прил* ancient

ста́р|ить (-ю, -ишь; *perf* **соста́рить**)
несов перех to age

старомо́дный *прил* old-fashioned

ста́рост|а (-ы) *м* (*ку́рса*) senior student;
(*кла́сса*: *ма́льчик*) head boy; (: *де́вочка*)
head girl; (*клу́ба*) head, president

ста́рост|ь (-и) *ж* old age

старт (-а) *м* (Спорт) start; (*раке́ты*) takeoff;
(*ме́сто*) takeoff point

старт|ова́ть (-у́ю) (*не*)*сов* (Спорт) to
start; (*раке́та*) to take off

стару́х|а (-и) *ж* old woman (*мн* women)

стару́ш|ка (-ки; *gen pl* **-ек**) *ж* = **стару́ха**

ста́рше *сравн прил от* **ста́рый** ▷ *как
сказ*: **я ста́рше сестры́ на́ год** I am a year
older than my sister

старшекла́ссник (-а) *м* senior pupil

старшеку́рсник (-а) *м* senior student

ста́рший *прил* senior; (*сестра́, брат*)
elder

ста́рый *прил* old

стати́стик|а (-и) *ж* statistics

ста́тус (-а) *м* status

ста́ту|я (-и) *ж* statue

ста|ть (-ти -ну) *сов*: **под стать кому́-н/чему́-н**
like sb/sth ▷ (**-ну, -нешь**; *impf*
станови́ться) *сов* to stand; (*по impf*:
останови́ться) to stop; (+*infin*: *нача́ть*) to
begin *или* start doing ▷ *безл*
(*наличествовать*): **нас ста́ло бо́льше/тро́е**
there are more/three of us; **с како́й ста́ти?**
(*разг*) why?; **станови́ться** (*perf* **стать**)
+*instr* (*учи́телем*) to become; **не ста́ло
де́нег/сил** I have no more money/energy
left; **ста́ло быть** (*зна́чит*) so; **во что бы то
ни ста́ло** no matter what

стать|я́ (-и́; *gen pl* **-е́й**) *ж* (*в газе́те*)
article; (*в зако́не, в догово́ре*) paragraph,
clause

ствол (-а́) *м* (*де́рева*) trunk; (*ружья́,
пу́шки*) barrel

сте́б|ель (-ля) *м* (*цветка́*) stem

стега́|ть (-ю; *perf* **простега́ть**) *несов
перех* (*одея́ло*) to quilt; (*по perf*: *хлысто́м*)
to lash

стеж|о́к (-ка́) *м* stitch

стека́|ть(ся) (3sg **-ет(ся)**) *несов от*
сте́чь(ся)

стекл|и́ть (-ю́, -и́шь; *perf* **остекли́ть**)
несов перех (*окно́*) to glaze

стекл|о́ (-а́; *nom pl* **стёкла**, *gen pl*
стёкол) *ср* glass; (*та́кже* **око́нное
стекло́**) (window) pane; (*для очко́в*)
lenses *мн* ▷ *собир* (*изде́лия*) glassware

стёклыш|ко (-ка; *gen pl* **-ек**) *ср*
(*оско́лок*) piece of glass

стекля́нный *прил* glass

стел|и́ть (-ю́, -ишь; *perf* **постели́ть**)
несов перех (*ска́терть, подсти́лку*) to
spread out ▷ (*perf* **настели́ть**) (*парке́т*)
to lay; **стели́ть** (*perf* **постели́ть**) **посте́ль**
to make up a bed

стемне́|ть (*3sg -ет*) *сов от* **темне́ть**

стен|а́ (*-ы́*; *acc sg -у*, *dat sg -е́*, *nom pl -ы*, *dat pl -а́м*) *ж* wall

сте́н|ка (*-ки*; *gen pl -ок*) *ж*, *уменьш от* **стена́**; (*разг: мебель*) wall unit

стенн|о́й *прил* wall; **стенна́я ро́спись** mural

стенографи́р|овать (*-ую*; *perf* **застенографи́ровать**) *несов перех*: **стенографи́ровать что-н** to take sth down in shorthand (*Brit*) *или* stenography (*US*)

стенографи́ст (*-а*) *м* shorthand typist (*Brit*), stenographer (*US*)

сте́пен|ь (*-и*; *gen pl -е́й*) *ж* (*также Просвещ*) degree; (*Мат*) power

степ|ь (*-и*; *gen pl -е́й*) *ж* the steppe

стереосисте́м|а (*-ы*) *ж* stereo

стереоти́п (*-а*) *м* stereotype

стере́|ть (*сотру́*, *сотрёшь*; *pt* **стёр**, **стёрла**, *impf* **стира́ть**) *сов перех* to wipe off; **стере́ться** (*impf* **стира́ться**) *сов возв* (*надпись*, *краска*) to be worn away; (*подошвы*) to wear down

стер|е́чь (*-егу́*, *-ежёшь итп*, *-егу́т*; *pt -ёг*, *-егла́*) *несов перех* to watch over

сте́рж|ень (*-ня*) *м* rod; (*шариковой ручки*) (ink) cartridge

стерилиз|ова́ть (*-у́ю*) (*не*)*сов перех* to sterilize

сте́рлинг (*-а*) *м* (*Экон*) sterling; **10 фу́нтов сте́рлингов** 10 pounds sterling

стесни́тельный *прил* shy

стесня́|ться (*-юсь*; *perf* **постесня́ться**) *несов возв*: **стесня́ться** (*+gen*) to be shy (of)

стече́ни|е (*-я*) *ср* (*народа*) gathering; (*случайностей*) combination

стил|ь (*-я*) *м* style

сти́мул (*-а*) *м* incentive, stimulus (*мн* stimuli)

стимули́р|овать (*-ую*) (*не*)*сов перех* to stimulate; (*работу*, *прогресс*) to encourage

стипе́нди|я (*-и*) *ж* grant

стира́льный *прил* washing

стира́|ть (*-ю*) *несов от* **стере́ть** ▷ (*perf* **вы́стирать** *или* **постира́ть**) *перех* to wash; **стира́ться** *несов от* **стере́ться**

сти́р|ка (*-ки*) *ж* washing

стиха́|ть (*-ю*) *несов от* **сти́хнуть**

стих|и́ (*-ов*) *мн* poetry *мн*

стихи́|я (*-и*) *ж* (*вода*, *огонь итп*) element; (*рынка*) natural force

сти́х|нуть (*-ну*; *pt -*, *-ла*, *impf* **стиха́ть**) *сов* to die down

стихотворе́ни|е (*-я*) *ср* poem

сто (*ста*; *см Table 27*) *чис* one hundred

стог (*-а*; *nom pl -а́*) *м*: **стог се́на** haystack

сто́имост|ь (*-и*) *ж* (*затраты*) cost; (*ценность*) value

сто́|ить (*-ю*, *-ишь*) *несов* (*не*)*перех* (*+acc или +gen: денег*) to cost ▷ *неперех* (*+gen: внимания*, *любви*) to be worth ▷ *безл* *+infin* to be worth doing; **мне ничего́ не**

сто́ит сде́лать э́то it's no trouble for me to do it; **спаси́бо! — не сто́ит** thank you! — don't mention it; **сто́ит (то́лько) захоте́ть** you only have to wish

сто́й|ка (*-йки*; *gen pl -ек*) *ж* (*положение тела*) stance; (*прилавок*) counter

стол (*-а́*) *м* table; (*письменный*) desk

столб (*-а́*) *м* (*пограничный*) post; (*телеграфный*) pole; (*перен: пыли*) cloud

сто́лбик (*-а*) *м*, *уменьш от* **столб**; (*цифр*) column

столе́ти|е (*-я*) *ср* (*срок*) century; (*+gen: годовщина*) centenary of

сто́лик (*-а*) *м*, *уменьш от* **стол**

столи́ц|а (*-ы*) *ж* capital (city)

столкнове́ни|е (*-я*) *ср* clash; (*машин*) collision

столкн|у́ть (*-у́*, *-ёшь*; *impf* **ста́лкивать**) *сов перех*: **столкну́ть** (*с +gen*) to push off; (*подлеж: случай*) to bring together; **столкну́ться** (*impf* **ста́лкиваться**) *сов возв* (*машины*) to collide; (*интересы*, *характеры*) to clash; (*встретиться*): **столкну́ться** *с +instr* to come into contact with; (*случайно*) to bump *или* run into; (*с трудностями*) to encounter

столо́в|ая (*-ой*) *ж* (*заведение*) canteen; (*комната*) dining room

столо́в|ый *прил* (*мебель*) dining-room; **столо́вая ло́жка** tablespoon; **столо́вая соль** table salt; **столо́вый серви́з** dinner service

столп|и́ться (*3sg -и́тся*) *сов возв* to crowd

столь *нареч* so; **столь же ... ско́лько ...** as ... as ...

сто́льк|о *нареч* (*книг*) so many; (*сахара*) so much ▷ (*-их*) *мест* (*см нареч*) this many; this much

сто́лько-то *нареч* (*книг*) X number of; (*сахара*) X amount of

столя́р (*-а́*) *м* joiner

стомато́лог (*-а*) *м* dental surgeon

стоматологи́ческий *прил* dental

стометро́вый *прил*: **стометро́вая диста́нция** one hundred metres (*Brit*) *или* meters (*US*)

стон (*-а*) *м* groan

стон|а́ть (*-у́*, *-ешь*) *несов* to groan

стоп *межд* stop

стоп|а́ (*-ы́*; *nom pl -ы*) *ж* (*Анат*) sole

сто́п|ка (*-ки*; *gen pl -ок*) *ж* (*бумаг*) pile

стоп-кра́н (*-а*) *м* emergency handle (*on train*)

сто́пор (*-а*) *м* (*Тех*) lock

стоп|та́ть (*-чу́*, *-чешь*; *impf* **ста́птывать**) *сов перех* to wear out; **стопта́ться** (*impf* **ста́птываться**) *сов возв* to wear out

сторож|и́ть (*-у́*, *-и́шь*) *несов перех* = **стере́чь**

сторон|а́ (*-оны́*; *acc sg -ону*, *dat sg -оне́*, *nom pl -оны*, *gen pl -о́н*, *dat pl -она́м*) *ж* side; (*направление*): **ле́вая/пра́вая**

сторона́ the left/right; **в стороне́** a little way off; **в сто́рону** +gen towards; **э́то о́чень любе́зно с Ва́шей стороны́** that is very kind of you; **с одно́й стороны́ ... с друго́й стороны́ ...** on the one hand ... on the other hand ...

сторо́нник (-а) м supporter

сто́я нареч standing up

стоя́н|ка (-ки; gen pl -ок) ж (остано́вка) stop; (автомоби́лей) car park (Brit), parking lot (US); (гео́логов) camp; **стоя́нка такси́** taxi rank

стоя́|ть (-ю́, -и́шь; imper сто́й(те)) несов to stand; (безде́йствовать) to stand idle ▷ (perf постоя́ть) (защища́ть): **стоя́ть за** +acc to stand up for

сто́ящий прил (де́ло) worthwhile; (челове́к) worthy

страда́ни|е (-я) ср suffering

страда́тельный прил (Линг): **страда́тельный зало́г** passive voice

страда́|ть (-ю) несов to suffer

стра́ж|а (-и) ж собир guard; **под стра́жей** in custody

стран|а́ (-ы́; nom pl -ы) ж country

страни́ц|а (-ы) ж page

стра́нно нареч strangely ▷ как сказ that is strange или odd; **мне стра́нно, что ...** I find it strange that ...

стра́нный прил strange

стра́стный прил passionate

страст|ь (-и) ж passion

страте́ги|я (-и) ж strategy

страх (-а) м fear

страхова́ни|е (-я) ср insurance; **госуда́рственное страхова́ние** national insurance (Brit); **страхова́ние жи́зни** life insurance

страхова́тел|ь (-я) м person taking out insurance

страх|ова́ть (-у́ю; perf застрахова́ть) несов перех: **страхова́ть от** +gen (иму́щество) to insure (against); (принима́ть ме́ры) to protect (against); **страхова́ться** (perf застрахова́ться) несов возв: **страхова́ться (от** +gen) to insure o.s. (against); (принима́ть ме́ры) to protect o.s. (from)

страхо́в|ка (-ки; gen pl -ок) ж insurance

страхов|о́й прил (фи́рма, аге́нт) insurance; **страхово́й взнос** или **страхова́я пре́мия** insurance premium

стра́шно нареч (крича́ть) in a frightening way; (разг: уста́лый, дово́льный) terribly ▷ как сказ it's frightening; **мне стра́шно** I'm frightened или scared

стра́шн|ый прил (фильм, сон) terrifying; (хо́лод итп) terrible, awful; **ничего́ стра́шного** it doesn't matter

стрек|оза́ (-озы́; nom pl -о́зы) ж dragonfly (мн dragonflies)

стрел|а́ (-ы́; nom pl -ы) ж (для стрельбы́) arrow; (по́езд) express (train)

стрел|е́ц (-ьца́) м (созве́здие): **Стреле́ц** Sagittarius

стре́л|ка (-ки; gen pl -ок) ж, уменьш от **стрела́**; (часо́в) hand; (ко́мпаса) needle; (знак) arrow

стреля́|ть (-ю) несов: **стреля́ть (в** +acc) to shoot (at) ▷ перех (убива́ть) to shoot; **стреля́ться** несов возв to shoot o.s.

стреми́тельный прил (движе́ние, ата́ка) swift; (измене́ния) rapid

стрем|и́ться (-лю́сь, -и́шься) несов возв: **стреми́ться в/на** +acc (в университе́т) to aspire to go to; (на ро́дину) to long to go to; (добива́ться): **стреми́ться к** +dat (к сла́ве) to strive for

стремле́ни|е (-я) ср: **стремле́ние (к** +dat) striving (for), aspiration (to)

стремя́н|ка (-ки; gen pl -ок) ж stepladder

стресс (-а) м stress

стриж (-а́) м swift

стри́ж|ка (-ки; gen pl -ек) ж (см глаг) cutting; mowing; pruning; (причёска) haircut

стри́|чь (-гу́, -жёшь итп, -гу́т; pt -г, -гла, perf постри́чь) несов перех (во́лосы, тра́ву) to cut; (газо́н) to mow; (кусты́) to prune; **стричь (perf постри́чь) кого́-н** to cut sb's hair; **стри́чься (perf постри́чься)** несов возв (в парикма́херской) to have one's hair cut

стро́гий прил strict; (причёска, наказа́ние) severe

строе́ни|е (-я) ср (зда́ние) building; (организа́ции, вещества́) structure

стро́же сравн прил от **стро́гий** ▷ сравн нареч от **стро́го**

строи́тел|ь (-я) м builder

строи́тельный прил building, construction

строи́тельств|о (-а) ср (зда́ний) building, construction

стро́|ить (-ю, -ишь; perf вы́строить или постро́ить) несов перех to build, construct ▷ (perf постро́ить) (о́бщество, семью́) to create; (план) to make; (отря́д) to draw up; **стро́иться (perf вы́строиться)** несов возв (солда́ты) to form up

стро|й (-я) м (социа́льный) system; (языка́) structure ▷ (loc sg -ю́) (Воен: шере́нга) line

стро́|йка (-йки; gen pl -ек) ж (ме́сто) building или construction site

стро́йный прил (фигу́ра) shapely; (челове́к) well-built

строк|а́ (-и́; nom pl -и, dat pl -а́м) ж (в те́ксте) line

стро́ч|ка (-ки; gen pl -ек) ж, уменьш от **строка́**; (шов) stitch

стро́чный прил: **стро́чная бу́ква** lower case или small letter

структу́р|а (-ы) ж structure

струн|а́ (-ы́; nom pl -ы) ж string

стручкÓв|ый *прил*: **стручкÓвый пéрец** chilli; **стручкÓвая фасÓль** runner beans *мн*

стру|я́ (**-и́**; *nom pl* **-и**) *ж* stream

стряхн|у́ть (**-у́, -ёшь**; *impf* **стря́хивать**) *сов перех* to shake off

студéнт (**-а**) *м* student

студéнческий *прил* student; **студéнческий билéт** student card

стýд|ень (**-ня**) *м* jellied meat

стýди|я (**-и**) *ж* studio; (*школа*) school (*for actors, dancers, artists etc*); (*мастерская*) workshop

стýж|а (**-и**) *ж* severe cold

стук (**-а**) *м* (*в дверь*) knock; (*сердца*) thump; (*падающего предмета*) thud

стýкн|уть (**-у**) *сов* (*в дверь, в окно*) to knock; (*по столу*) to bang; **стýкнуться** (*impf* **стýкаться**) *сов возв* to bang o.s.

стул (**-а**; *nom pl* **-ья**, *gen pl* **-ьев**) *м* chair

ступéн|ь (**-и**) *ж* step ▷ (*gen pl* **-éй**) (*процесса*) stage

ступéнька (**-ьки**; *gen pl* **-ек**) *ж* step

стýп|ка (**-ки**; *gen pl* **-ок**) *ж* mortar

ступн|я́ (**-и́**) *ж* (*стопа*) foot (*мн* feet)

стуч|а́ть (**-у́, -и́шь**; *perf* **постуча́ть**) *несов* (*в дверь, в окно*) to knock; (*по столу*) to bang; (*сердце*) to thump; (*зубы*) to chatter; **стуча́ться** (*perf* **постуча́ться**) *несов возв*: **стуча́ться** (*в* +*acc*) to knock (at); **стуча́ться** (*perf* **постуча́ться**) **к кому́-н** to knock at sb's door

стыд (**-á**) *м* shame

сты|ди́ть (**-жу́, -ди́шь**; *perf* **пристыди́ть**) *несов перех* to (put to) shame; **стыди́ться** (*perf* **постыди́ться**) *несов возв*: **стыди́ться** +*gen*/+*infin* to be ashamed of/to do

сты́дно *как сказ* it's a shame; **мне сты́дно** I am ashamed; **как тебé не сты́дно!** you ought to be ashamed of yourself!

сты|ть (**-ну, -нешь**; *perf* **осты́ть**) *несов* to go cold ▷ (*perf* **просты́ть**) (*мёрзнуть*) to freeze

стюардéсс|а (**-ы**) *ж* air hostess

стян|у́ть (**-у́, -ешь**; *impf* **стя́гивать**) *сов перех* (*пояс, шнуровку*) to tighten; (*войска*) to round up

суббóт|а (**-ы**) *ж* Saturday

субси́ди|я (**-и**) *ж* subsidy

субти́тр (**-а**) *м* subtitle

субъекти́вный *прил* subjective

сувени́р (**-а**) *м* souvenir

сувере́нный *прил* sovereign

сугрóб (**-а**) *м* snowdrift

суд (**-á**) *м* (*орган*) court; (*заседание*) court session; (*процесс*) trial; (*мнение*) judgement, verdict; **отдава́ть** (*perf* **отда́ть**) **кого́-н под суд** to prosecute sb; **подава́ть** (*perf* **пода́ть**) **на кого́-н в суд** to take sb to court

судéбн|ый *прил* (*заседание, органы*) court; (*издержки, практика*) legal;

судéбное решéние adjudication; **судéбное дéло** court case

су|ди́ть (**-жу́, -дишь**) *несов перех* (*преступника*) to try; (*матч*) to referee; (*укорять*) to judge; **судя́ по** +*dat* judging by; **суди́ться** *несов возв*: **суди́ться с кем-н** to be involved in a legal wrangle with sb

сýд|но (**-на**; *nom pl* **-á**, *gen pl* **-óв**) *ср* vessel

судовéрф|ь (**-и**) *ж сокр* (= **судострои́тельная верфь**) shipyard

судов|óй *прил*: **судова́я кома́нда** ship's crew; **судовóй журна́л** ship's log

судóку *ср нескл* sudoku

судопроизвóдств|о (**-а**) *ср* legal proceedings *мн*

судорог|а (**-и**) *ж* (*от боли*) spasm

судострóени|е (**-я**) *ср* ship building

судохóдств|о (**-а**) *ср* navigation

судь|ба́ (**-ьбы́**; *nom pl* **-ьбы**, *gen pl* **-еб**) *ж* fate; (*будущее*) destiny; **каки́ми судьба́ми!** what brought you here?

судь|я́ (**-и́**; *nom pl* **-и**, *gen pl* **-éй**) *м* judge; (*Спорт*) referee

суевéри|е (**-я**) *ср* superstition

суевéрный *прил* superstitious

суе|ти́ться (**-чу́сь, -ти́шься**) *несов возв* to fuss (about)

суетли́вый *прил* fussy; (*жизнь, работа*) busy

суéтный *прил* futile; (*хлопотный*) busy; (*человек*) vain

сужа́|ть (**-ю**) *несов от* **сузи́ть**

суждéни|е (**-я**) *ср* (*мнение*) opinion

суждено́ *как сказ*: (**нам**) **не суждено́ было встрéтиться** we weren't fated to meet

су|зи́ть (**-жу, -зишь**; *impf* **сужа́ть**) *сов перех* to narrow

сýк|а (**-и**) *ж* bitch (*also !*); **сýкин сын** (*разг*) son of a bitch (!)

сумасшéдш|ий *прил* mad; (*разг: успех*) amazing ▷ (**-его**) *м* madman (*мн* madmen)

сумасшéстви|е (**-я**) *ср* madness, lunacy

суматóх|а (**-и**) *ж* chaos

сýмер|ки (**-ек**) *мн* twilight *ед*, dusk *ед*

сумé|ть (**-ю**) *сов* +*infin* to manage to do

сýм|ка (**-ки**; *gen pl* **-ок**) *ж* bag

сýмм|а (**-ы**) *ж* sum

сумми́р|овать (**-ую**) (*не*)*сов перех* (*затраты итп*) to add up; (*информацию*) to summarize

сýмоч|ка (**-ки**; *gen pl* **-ек**) *ж*, *уменьш от* **сýмка**; (*дамская, вечерняя*) handbag

сýмрак (**-а**) *м* gloom

сундýк (**-á**) *м* trunk, chest

суп (**-а**; *nom pl* **-ы́**) *м* soup

супермáркет (**-а**) *м* supermarket

супероблóж|ка (**-ки**; *gen pl* **-ек**) *ж* (dust) jacket

супрýг (**-а**; *nom pl* **-и**) *м* spouse; **супрýги** husband and wife

супру́г|а (-и) ж spouse
супру́жеский прил marital
сургу́ч (-á) м sealing wax
суро́вый прил harsh
су́слик (-а) м ground squirrel (Brit), gopher (US)
суста́в (-а) м (Анат) joint
су́т|ки (-ок) мн twenty four hours; кру́глые су́тки round the clock
су́точный прил twenty-four-hour
суту́л|ить (-ю, -ишь; perf ссуту́лить) несов перех to hunch; **суту́литься** (perf ссуту́литься) несов возв to stoop
сут|ь (-и) ж essence; суть де́ла the crux of the matter; по су́ти (де́ла) as a matter of fact
су́ффикс (-а) м suffix
сухожи́ли|е (-я) ср tendon
сухо́й прил dry; (засушенный) dried; сухо́й зако́н prohibition
сухопу́тн|ый прил land; сухопу́тные войска́ ground forces мн
сухофру́кт|ы (-ов) мн dried fruit ед
су́ш|а (-и) ж (dry) land
су́ше сравн прил от сухо́й
суше́ный прил dried
суш|и́ть (-у́, -ишь; perf вы́сушить) несов перех to dry; **суши́ться** (perf вы́сушиться) несов возв to dry
суще́ственный прил essential; (изменения) substantial
существи́тельн|ое (-ого) ср (также и́мя существи́тельное) noun
существ|о́ (-á) ср (вопроса, дела итп) essence ▷ (nom pl -á) (животное) creature; по существу́ (говорить) to the point; (вводн сл) essentially
существова́ни|е (-я) ср existence; сре́дства к существова́нию livelihood
существ|ова́ть (-у́ю) несов to exist
су́щность (-и) ж essence
СФ м сокр (= Сове́т Федера́ций) upper chamber of Russian parliament
сфе́р|а (-ы) ж sphere; (производства, науки) area; в сфе́ре +gen in the field of; сфе́ра обслу́живания или услу́г service industry
схва|ти́ть (-чу́, -тишь) сов от хвата́ть ▷ (impf схва́тывать) перех (мысль, смысл) to grasp; **схвати́ться** сов от хвата́ться
схва́т|ка (-ки; gen pl -ок) ж fight; см также схва́тки
схва́т|ки (-ок) мн (Мед) contractions
схе́м|а (-ы) ж (метро, улиц) plan; (Элек: радио, цепи) circuit board
схо|ди́ть (-жу́, -дишь) сов (разг: в театр, на прогулку) to go ▷ несов от сойти́; **сходи́ться** несов от сойти́сь
схо́дный прил similar
схо́дств|о (-а) ср similarity
сце́н|а (-ы) ж (подмостки) stage; (в пьесе, на улице) scene
сцена́ри|й (-я) м (фильма) script

сча́стливо нареч (жить, рассмеяться) happily; сча́стливо отде́латься (perf) to have a lucky escape
счастли́во нареч: счастли́во! all the best!; счастли́во остава́ться! good luck!
счастли́в|ый прил happy; (удачный) lucky; счастли́вого пути́! have a good journey!
сча́сть|е (-я) ср happiness; (удача) luck; к сча́стью luckily, fortunately; на на́ше сча́стье luckily for us
счесть (сочту́, сочтёшь; pt счёл, сочла́) сов от счита́ть
счёт (-а; loc sg -у́, nom pl -á) м (действие) counting; (Комм: в банке) account; (: накладная) invoice; (ресторанный, телефонный) bill; (по pl: Спорт) score; в счёт +gen in lieu of; за счёт +gen (фирмы) at the expense of; (внедрений итп) due to; на счёт кого́-н at sb's expense; на э́тот счёт in this respect; э́то не в счёт that doesn't count
счётн|ый прил: счётная маши́на calculator
счётчик (-а) м meter
счёт|ы (-ов) мн (приспособление) abacus ед; (деловые) dealings
счи́танн|ый прил: счи́танные дни/ мину́ты only a few days/minutes; счи́танное коли́чество very few
счита́|ть (-ю) несов to count ▷ (perf посчита́ть или сосчита́ть) перех (деньги итп) to count ▷ (perf посчита́ть или счесть); счита́ть кого́-н/что-н +instr to regard sb/sth as; я счита́ю, что ... I believe или think that ...; **счита́ться** несов возв: счита́ться +instr to be considered to be; (уважать): счита́ться с +instr to respect
США мн сокр (= Соединённые Шта́ты Аме́рики) USA (= United States of America)
сшить (сошью́, сошьёшь; imper сше́й(те)) сов от шить ▷ (impf сшива́ть) перех (соединить шитьём) to sew together
съеда́|ть (-ю) несов от съесть
съедо́бный прил edible
съезд (-а) м (партийный) congress
съе́з|дить (-жу, -дишь) сов to go
съезжа́|ть(ся) (-ю(сь)) несов от съе́хать(ся)
съём сов см съесть
съём|ка (-ки; gen pl -ок) ж (обычно мн: фильма) shooting
съёмочн|ый прил: съёмочная площа́дка film set; съёмочная гру́ппа film crew
съёмщик (-а) м tenant
съесть (как есть; см Table 15; impf съеда́ть или съеда́ть) сов перех (хлеб, кашу) to eat; (подлеж: моль, тоска́) to eat away at
съе́хать (как е́хать; см Table 19; impf съезжа́ть) сов: (спуститься) to go down; съезжа́ть (perf

съе́хать) (с кварти́ры) to move out (of one's flat); **съеха́ться** (*impf* **съезжа́ться**) *сов возв* (*делега́ты*) to gather

съешь *сов см* **съесть**

сыгра́|ть (-ю) *сов от* **игра́ть**

сын (-а; *nom pl* **-овья́**, *gen pl* **-ове́й**, *dat pl* **-овья́м**) *м* son

сы́п|ать (-лю, -лешь; *imper* **сы́пь(те)**) *несов перех* to pour; **сы́паться** (*perf* **посы́паться**) *несов возв* to pour

сып|ь (-и) *ж* rash

сыр (-а; *nom pl* **-ы́**) *м* cheese

сыре́|ть (*3sg* **-ет**) *несов* to get damp

сыро́й *прил* damp; (*мя́со, о́вощи*) raw

сыр|о́к (-ка́) *м*: **творо́жный сыро́к** sweet curd cheese; **пла́вленный сыро́к** processed cheese

сырь|ё (-я́) *ср собир* raw materials *мн*

сыск (-а) *м* criminal detection

сы́тный *прил* filling

сы́тый *прил* (*не голо́дный*) full

сэконо́м|ить (-лю, -ишь) *сов от* **эконо́мить**

сы́щик (-а) *м* detective

сюда́ *нареч* here

сюже́т (-а) *м* plot

сюрпри́з (-а) *м* surprise

ся́ду *итп сов см* **сесть**

та (**той**) *мест см* **тот**

таба́к (-а́) *м* tobacco

та́бел|ь (-я) *м* (*Просвещ*) school report (*Brit*), report card (*US, Scottish*); (*гра́фик*) chart

табле́т|ка (-ки; *gen pl* **-ок**) *ж* tablet

табли́ц|а (-ы) *ж* table; (*Спорт*) (league) table; **табли́ца умноже́ния** multiplication table

табло́ *ср нескл* (*information*) board; (*на стадио́не*) scoreboard

табу́н (-а́) *м* herd

таз (-а; *nom pl* **-ы́**) *м* (*сосу́д*) basin; (*Ана́т*) pelvis

таи́нственный *прил* mysterious

таи́|ть (-ю, -и́шь) *несов перех* to conceal; **таи́ться** *несов возв* (*скрыва́ться*) to hide; (*опа́сность*) to lurk

тайг|а́ (-и́) *ж* the taiga

тайм (-а) *м* (*Спорт*) period; **пе́рвый/ второ́й тайм** (*Футбо́л*) the first/second half

та́йн|а (-ы) *ж* (*ли́чная*) secret; (*собы́тия*) mystery

тайни́к (-а́) *м* hiding place

та́йный *прил* secret

⭕ **КЛЮЧЕВОЕ СЛОВО**

так *нареч* **1** (*указа́тельное: таки́м о́бразом*) like this, this way; **пусть бу́дет так** so be it

2 (*насто́лько*) so

3 (*разг: без како́го-н наме́рения*) for no (special) reason; **почему́ ты пла́чешь? — да так** why are you crying? — for no reason

▷ *част* **1** (*разг: ничего́*) nothing; **что с тобо́й? — так** what's wrong? — nothing

2 (*разг: приблизи́тельно*) about; **дня так че́рез два** in about two days

3 (*наприме́р*) for example

4 (*да*) O.K.; **так, всё хорошо́** O.K. that's fine

▷ *союз* **1** (*в таком случае*) then; **éхать, так éхать** if we are going, (then) let's go **2** (*таким образом*) so; **так ты поéдешь?** so, you are going?
3 (*в разделительных вопросах*): **э́то поле́зная кни́га, не так ли?** it's a useful book, isn't it?; **он хоро́ший челове́к, не так ли?** he's a good person, isn't he?
4 (*во фразах*): **и так** (*и без того уже*) anyway; **éсли** *или* **раз так** in that case; **так и быть!** so be it!; **так и есть** (*разг*) sure enough; **так ему́!** serves him right!; **та́к себе** (*разг*) so-so; **так как** since; **так что** so; **так что́бы** so that

та́кже *союз, нареч* also; **С Но́вым Го́дом! — И Вас та́кже** Happy New Year! — the same to you
тако́в (**-а́, -о́, -ы́**) *как сказ* such
таково́й *мест*: **как таково́й** as such
тако́|е (**-́ого**) *ср* (*о чём-н интересном, важном итп*) something; **что тут тако́го?** what is so special about that?
тако́й *мест* such; **что тако́е?** what is it?
та́кс|а (**-ы**) *ж* (*Комм*) (fixed) rate
такси́ *ср нескл* taxi
такси́ст (**-а**) *м* taxi driver
таксопа́рк (**-а**) *м сокр* (= **таксомото́рный парк**) taxi depot
такт (**-а**) *м* (*тактичность*) tact; (*Муз*) bar (*Brit*), measure (*US*)
такти́чный *прил* tactful
тала́нт (**-а**) *м* talent; **тала́нтливый** *прил* talented
та́ли|я (**-и**) *ж* waist
тало́н (**-а**) *м* ticket; (*на продукты итп*) coupon
там *нареч* there; **там посмо́трим** (*разг*) we'll see
тамо́женник (**-а**) *м* customs officer
тамо́женн|ый *прил* (*досмотр*) customs; **тамо́женная по́шлина** customs (duty)
тамо́ж|ня (**-ни**; *gen pl* **-ен**) *ж* customs
тампо́н (**-а**) *м* tampon
та́н|ец (**-ца**) *м* dance
танк (**-а**) *м* tank
та́нкер (**-а**) *м* tanker (*ship*)
танц|ева́ть (**-у́ю**) *несов (не)перех* to dance
танцо́вщик (**-а**) *м* dancer
танцо́р (**-а**) *м* dancer
та́поч|ка (**-ки**; *gen pl* **-ек**) *ж* (*обычно мн. домашняя*) slipper; (: *спортивная*) plimsoll (*Brit*), sneaker (*US*)
та́р|а (**-ы**) *ж собир* containers *мн*
тарака́н (**-а**) *м* cockroach
таре́л|ка (**-ки**; *gen pl* **-ок**) *ж* plate; **я здесь не в свое́й таре́лке** (*разг*) I feel out of place here
тари́ф (**-а**) *м* tariff
тас|ова́ть (**-у́ю**; *perf* **стасова́ть**) *несов перех* to shuffle
ТАСС *м сокр* (= **Телегра́фное аге́нтство Сове́тского Сою́за**) Tass

татуиро́в|ка (**-ки**; *gen pl* **-ок**) *ж* tattoo
та́ч|ка (**-ки**; *gen pl* **-ек**) *ж* wheelbarrow
тащ|и́ть (**-у́, -ишь**) *несов перех* to drag; (*тянуть*) to pull; (*нести*) to haul ▷ (*perf* **вы́тащить**) (*перен*: *в театр, на прогулку*) to drag out; **тащи́ться** *несов возв* (*медленно éхать*) to trundle along
та́|ять (**-ю**; *perf* **раста́ять**) *несов* to melt
ТВ *м сокр* (= **телеви́дение**) TV (= *television*)
тверде́|ть (*3sg* **-ет**, *perf* **затверде́ть**) *несов* to harden
твёрдо *нареч* (*верить, сказать*) firmly; (*запо́мнить*) properly; **я твёрдо зна́ю, что ...** I know for sure that ...
твёрдый *прил* (*Физ*) solid; (*земля, предмет*) hard; (*решение, сторонник, тон*) firm; (*цены, ставки*) stable; (*знания*) solid; (*характер*) tough; **твёрдый знак** (*Линг*) hard sign
твёрже *сравн прил от* **твёрдый** ▷ *сравн нареч от* **твёрдо**
твит (**-а**) *м* tweet
тво|й (**-его́**; *f* **-я́**, *nt* **-ё**, *pl* **-и́**; *как* **мой**; *см* Table 8) *притяж мест* your; **как по-тво́ему?** what is your opinion?; **дава́й сде́лаем по-тво́ему** let's do it your way
творе́ни|е (**-я**) *ср* creation
твори́тельный *прил*: **твори́тельный паде́ж** (*Линг*) the instrumental (case)
твор|и́ть (**-ю́, -ишь**) *несов* to create ▷ (*perf* **сотвори́ть**) *перех* to create ▷ (*perf* **натвори́ть**) (*разг*) to get up to; **твори́ться** *несов возв*: **что тут твори́тся?** what's going on here?
творо́г (**-а́**) *м* ≈ curd cheese
тво́рческий *прил* creative
тво́рчеств|о (**-а**) *ср* creative work; (*писателя*) work
тво|я́ (**-е́й**) *притяж мест см* **твой**
те (**тех**) *мест см* **тот**
т.е. *сокр* (= **то́ есть**) i.e. (= *id est*)
теа́тр (**-а**) *м* theatre (*Brit*), theater (*US*); **театра́льный** *прил* (*афиша, сезон*) theatre (*Brit*), theater (*US*); (*деятельность*) theatrical; **театра́льный институ́т** drama school
теб|я́ *итп мест см* **ты**
текст (**-а**) *м* text; (*песни*) words *мн*, lyrics *мн*
теку́чий *прил* fluid
теку́щий *прил* (*год*) current; **теку́щий счёт** (*Комм*) current (*Brit*) *или* checking (*US*) account
тел. *сокр* (= **телефо́н**) tel. (= *telephone*)
телеви́дени|е (**-я**) *ср* television
телевизио́нный *прил* television; **телевизио́нный фильм** television drama
телеви́зор (**-а**) *м* television (set)
телегра́мм|а (**-ы**) *ж* telegram
телеграфи́р|овать (**-ую**) *(не)сов перех* to wire
теле́ж|ка (**-ки**; *gen pl* **-ек**) *ж* (*для багажа, в супермаркете*) trolley
телезри́тел|ь (**-я**) *м* viewer

телека́мер|а (-ы) ж television camera

тел|ёнок (-ёнка; *nom pl* -я́та) м calf (*мн* calves)

телепереда́ч|а (-и) ж TV programme (*Brit*) *или* program (*US*)

телеско́п (-а) м telescope

телесту́ди|я (-и) ж television studio

телета́йп (-а) м teleprinter (*Brit*), teletypewriter (*US*), Teletype

телефо́н (-а) м telephone; **телефо́нный** *прил* telephone; **телефо́нная кни́га** telephone book *или* directory

Тел|е́ц (-ьца́) м (*созвездие*) Taurus

телеце́нтр (-а) м television centre (*Brit*) *или* center (*US*)

те́л|о (-а; *nom pl* -а́) *ср* body

телогре́|йка (-йки; *gen pl* -ек) ж body warmer

телохрани́тел|ь (-я) м bodyguard

теля́тин|а (-ы) ж veal

тем *мест см* **тот; то** ▷ *союз* +*comparative*; **чем бо́льше, тем лу́чше** the more the better; **тем бо́лее!** all the more so!; **тем бо́лее что ...** especially as ...; **тем не ме́нее** nevertheless; **тем са́мым** thus

те́м|а (-ы) ж topic; (*Муз, Литература*) theme

те́ми *мест см* **тот; то**

темне́|ть (*3sg* -ет, *perf* **потемне́ть**) *несов* to darken ▷ (*perf* **стемне́ть**) *безл* to get dark

темно́ *как сказ*: **на у́лице темно́** it's dark outside

темнот|а́ (-ы́) ж darkness

тёмный *прил* dark

темп (-а) м speed; **в те́мпе** (*разг*) quickly

темпера́мент (-а) м temperament

температу́р|а (-ы) ж temperature

тенде́нци|я (-и) ж tendency; (*предвзятость*) bias

те́н|и (-ей) *мн* (*также* **те́ни для век**) eye shadow *ед*

те́ннис (-а) м tennis; **тенниси́ст** (-а) м tennis player

тен|ь (-и; *prp sg* -и́, *gen pl* -е́й) ж (*место*) shade; (*предмета, человека*) shadow; (*перен*: +*gen*: *волнения, печали*) flicker of; *см также* **те́ни**

тео́ри|я (-и) ж theory

тепе́рь *нареч* now

тепле́|ть (*3sg* -ет, *perf* **потепле́ть**) *несов* to get warmer

тепл|о́ *нареч* warmly ▷ (-а́) *ср* (*также перен*) warmth ▷ *как сказ* it's warm; **мне тепло́** I'm warm

теплово́й *прил* thermal

теплохо́д (-а) м motor ship *или* vessel

тепло(электро)центра́л|ь (-и) ж generator plant (*supplying central heating systems*)

тёплый *прил* warm

терапе́вт (-а) м ≈ general practitioner

тера́кт (-а) м *сокр* (= террористи́ческий акт) terrorist attack

терапи́|я (-и) ж (*Мед*: *наука*) (internal) medicine; (*лечение*) therapy

тере́|ть (**тру, трёшь**, *pt* **тёр, тёрла, тёрло**) *несов перех* to rub; (*овощи*) to grate

терза́|ть (-ю; *perf* **растерза́ть**) *несов перех* (*добычу*) to savage ▷ (*perf* **истерза́ть**) (*перен*: *упрёками, ревностью*) to torment; **терза́ться** *несов возв*: **терза́ться** +*instr* (*сомнениями*) to be racked by

тёр|ка (-ки; *gen pl* -ок) ж grater

те́рмин (-а) м term

термина́л (-а) м terminal

термо́метр (-а) м thermometer

те́рмос (-а) м Thermos

терпели́вый *прил* patient

терпе́ни|е (-я) *ср* patience

терпе́|ть (-лю́, -ишь) *несов перех* (*боль, холод*) to suffer, endure ▷ (*perf* **потерпе́ть**) (*неудачу*) to suffer; (*грубость*) to tolerate; **терпе́ть** (*perf* **потерпе́ть**) **круше́ние** (*корабль*) to be wrecked; (*поезд*) to crash; **терпе́ть не могу́ таки́х люде́й** (*разг*) I can't stand people like that; **терпе́ть не могу́ спо́рить** (*разг*) I hate arguing; **терпе́ться** *несов безл*: **мне не те́рпится** +*infin* I can't wait to do

терпи́мост|ь (-и) ж: **терпи́мость (к** +*dat*) tolerance (of)

терпи́мый *прил* tolerant

терра́с|а (-ы) ж terrace

террито́ри|я (-и) ж territory

терроризи́р|овать (-ую) (*не*)*сов перех* to terrorize

террори́зм (-а) м terrorism

террори́ст (-а) м terrorist

террористи́ческий *прил* terrorist

теря́|ть (-ю; *perf* **потеря́ть**) *несов перех* to lose; **теря́ться** (*perf* **потеря́ться**) *несов возв* to get lost; (*робеть*) to lose one's nerve

тесн|и́ть (-ю́, -и́шь; *perf* **потесни́ть**) *несов перех* (*в толпе*) to squeeze; (*к стене*) to press

те́сно *нареч* (*располагать(ся)*) close together; (*сотрудничать*) closely ▷ *как сказ*: **в кварти́ре о́чень те́сно** the flat is very cramped; **мы с ним те́сно знако́мы** he and I know each other very well

те́сный *прил* (*проход*) narrow; (*помещение*) cramped; (*одежда*) tight; (*дружба*) close; **мир те́сен** it's a small world

тест (-а) м test

тести́р|овать (-ую) (*не*)*сов* to test

те́ст|о (-а) *ср* (*дрожжевое*) dough; (*слоёное, песо́чное*) pastry (*Brit*), paste (*US*)

тест|ь (-я) м father-in-law, wife's father

тесьм|а́ (-ы́) ж tape

тёт|ка (-ки; *gen pl* -ок) ж auntie

тетра́д|ь (-и) ж exercise book

тёт|я (-и; *gen pl* -ь) ж aunt; (*разг*: *женщина*) lady

тéфтел|и (-ей) мн meatballs

тех мест см **те**

тéхник|а (-и) ж technology; (приёмы) technique ▷ собир (машины) machinery; (разг: Муз) hi-fi; **тéхника безопáсности** industrial health and safety

тéхникум (-а) м technical college

техни́ческ|ий прил technical; **техни́ческий осмо́тр** (Авт) ≈ MOT (Brit) (annual roadworthiness check); **техни́ческое обслу́живание** maintenance, servicing

технологи́ческий прил technical

техноло́ги|я (-и) ж technology

течéни|е (-я) ср current; (в искусстве) trend; **в течéние** +gen during

те́|чь (3sg -чёт, pt тёк, теклá) несов to flow; (крыша, лодка итп) to leak ▷ (-чи) ж leak

тёщ|а (-и) ж mother-in-law, wife's mother

тигр (-а) м tiger

ти́ка|ть (3sg -ет) несов to tick

тип (-а) м type; **ти́па** +gen (разг) sort of

типи́чный прил: **типи́чный (для** +gen) typical (of)

типогрáфи|я (-и) ж press, printing house

тир (-а) м shooting gallery

тирé ср нескл dash

тиск|и́ (-óв) мн: **в тискáх** +gen (перен) in the grip of

ти́тр (-а) м (обычно мн) credit (of film)

ти́тул (-а) м title

ти́тульный прил: **ти́тульный лист** title page

ти́хий прил quiet; **ти́хий у́жас!** (разг) what a nightmare!; **Ти́хий океáн** the Pacific (Ocean)

ти́хо нареч (говори́ть, жить) quietly ▷ как сказ: **в до́ме ти́хо** the house is quiet; **ти́хо!** (be) quiet!

ти́ше сравн прил от **ти́хий** ▷ сравн нареч от **ти́хо** ▷ как сказ: **ти́ше!** quiet!, hush!

тишин|á (-ы́) ж quiet

т.к. сокр = **так как**

ткан|ь (-и) ж fabric, material; (Анат) tissue

тк|ать (-у, -ёшь; perf соткáть) несов перех to weave

тле|ть (3sg -ет) несов (дрова, угли) to smoulder (Brit), smolder (US)

тмин (-а) м (Кулин) caraway seeds мн

т.н. сокр = **так называемый**

то¹ союз (условный): **éсли ... то ...** if ... then ...; (разделительный): **то ... то ...** sometimes ... sometimes ...; **и то** even; **то есть** that is

то² (того́) мест см **тот**

т.о. сокр = **таки́м о́бразом**

-то част (для выделения): **письмó-то ты получи́л?** did you (at least) receive the letter?

тобóй мест см **ты**

товáр (-а) м product; (Экон) commodity

товáрищ (-а) м (приятель) friend; (по партии) comrade; **товáрищеский** прил comradely; **товáрищеский матч** (Спорт) friendly (match)

товáриществ|о (-а) ср (Комм) partnership

товáрн|ый прил (производство) goods; (рынок) commodity; **товáрная би́ржа** commodity exchange; **товáрный знак** trademark

товарооборóт (-а) м turnover

тогдá нареч then; **тогдá как** (хотя) while; (при противопоставлении) whereas

того́ мест см **тот**; **то**

тóже нареч (также) too, as well, also

той мест см **та**

ток (-а) м (Элек) current

толк (-а) м (в рассуждениях) sense; (разг: польза) use; **сбивáть** (perf **сбить) когó-н с тóлку** to confuse sb

толкá|ть (-ю; perf **толкнýть**) несов перех to push; (перен): **толкáть когó-н на** +acc to force sb into; **толкáться** несов возв (в толпе) to push (one's way)

толк|овáть (-ýю) несов перех to interpret

толкóвый прил intelligent

толп|á (-ы́; nom pl -ы) ж crowd

толп|и́ться (3sg -и́тся) несов возв to crowd around

толсте́|ть (-ю; perf **потолсте́ть**) несов to get fatter

тóлстый прил thick; (человек) fat

толч|óк (-кá) м (в спину) shove; (при торможении) jolt; (при землетрясении) tremor; (перен: к работе) incentive

тóлще сравн прил от **тóлстый**

толщин|á (-ы́) ж thickness

○ **КЛЮЧЕВÓЕ СЛÓВО**

тóлько част **1** only

2 (+pron/+adv: усиливает выразительность): **попро́буй тóлько отказáться!** just try to refuse!; **подýмать тóлько!** imagine that!

▷ союз **1** (сразу после) as soon as

2 (однако, но) only; **позвони́, тóлько разговáривай недóлго** phone (Brit) или call (US), only don't talk for long

▷ нареч **1** (недавно) (only) just; **ты давнó здесь?- нет, тóлько вошлá** have you been here long? — no, I've (only) just come in

2 (во фразах): **тóлько лишь** (разг) only; **тóлько и всегó** (разг) that's all; **как** или **лишь** или **едвá тóлько** as soon as; **не тóлько ..., но и ...** not only ... but also ...; **тóлько бы** if only; **тóлько что** only just

том мест см **тот**; **то** ▷ (-а; nom pl -á) м volume

томáтный прил: **томáтный сок** tomato juice

томý мест см **тот**; **то**

тон (-а) м tone

тонзилли́т (-а) м tonsillitis

тонизи́рующ|ий прил (напиток) refreshing; **тонизи́рующее сре́дство** tonic

то́нкий прил thin; (фигура) slender; (черты лица, работа, ум) fine; (различия, намёк) subtle

тонне́л|ь (-я) м tunnel

тон|у́ть (-у́, -ешь; perf **утону́ть**) несов (человек) to drown ▷ (perf **затону́ть**) (корабль) to sink

то́ньше сравн прил от **то́нкий**

то́па|ть (-ю) несов: **то́пать нога́ми** to stamp one's feet

топ|и́ть (-лю́, -ишь) несов перех (печь) to stoke (up); (масло, воск) to melt ▷ (perf **утопи́ть**) (корабль) to sink; (человека) to drown; **топи́ться** несов возв (печь) to burn ▷ (perf **утопи́ться**) (человек) to drown o.s.

то́пливо (-а) ср fuel

то́пол|ь (-я) м poplar

топо́р (-а́) м axe (Brit), ax (US)

то́пот (-а) м clatter

топ|та́ть (-чу́, -чешь; perf **потопта́ть**) несов перех (траву) to trample; **топта́ться** несов возв to shift from one foot to the other

торг|и́ (-о́в) мн (аукцион) auction ед; (состязание) tender ед

торг|ова́ть (-у́ю) несов (магазин) to trade; **торгова́ть** (impf) +instr (мясом, мебелью) to trade in; **торгова́ться** (perf **сторгова́ться**) несов возв to haggle

торго́в|ец (-ца) м merchant; (мелкий) trader

торго́вл|я (-и) ж trade

торго́в|ый прил trade; (судно, флот) merchant; **торго́вая сеть** retail network; **торго́вая то́чка** retail outlet; **торго́вое представи́тельство** trade mission; **торго́вый центр** shopping centre (Brit), mall (US)

торгпре́д (-а) м сокр (= торго́вый представи́тель) head of the trade mission

торгпре́дств|о (-а) ср сокр = **торго́вое представи́тельство**

торже́ственный прил (день, случай) special; (собрание) celebratory; (вид, обстановка) festive; (обещание) solemn

торжеств|о́ (-а́) ср celebration; (в голосе, в словах) triumph; **торжеств|ова́ть** (-у́ю; perf **восторжествова́ть**) несов: **торжествова́ть (над** +instr) to triumph (over)

то́рмоз (-а; nom pl -а́) м brake

тормо|зи́ть (-жу́, -зи́шь; perf **затормози́ть**) несов перех (машину) to slow down ▷ неперех (машина) to brake; **тормози́ться** (perf **затормози́ться**) несов возв (работа итп) to be hindered

тор|опи́ть (-оплю́, -о́пишь; perf **поторопи́ть**) несов перех to hurry; **торопи́ться** (perf **поторопи́ться**) несов возв to hurry

торопли́вый прил (человек) hasty

торпе́д|а (-ы) ж torpedo (мн torpedoes)

торт (-а) м cake

торф (-а) м peat

торч|а́ть (-у́, -и́шь) несов (вверх) to stick up; (в стороны) to stick out; (разг: на улице) to hang around

торше́р (-а) м standard lamp

тоск|а́ (-и́) ж (на сердце) anguish; (скука) boredom; **тоска́ по ро́дине** homesickness; **тоскли́вый** прил gloomy; **тоск|ова́ть** (-у́ю) несов to pine away; **тоскова́ть** (impf) по +dat или о +prp to miss

тост (-а) м toast

O **КЛЮЧЕВО́Е СЛО́ВО**

то|т (-го́; f та, nt то, pl те; см Table 11) мест **1** that; **тот дом** that house

2 (о ранее упомянутом) that; **в тот раз/день** that time/day

3 (в главных предложениях): **э́то тот челове́к, кото́рый приходи́л вчера́** it's the man who came yesterday

4 (о последнем из названных лиц): **я посмотре́л на дру́га, тот стоя́л мо́лча** I looked at my friend, who stood silently

5 (обычно с отрицанием): **зашёл не в тот дом** I called at the wrong house

6 (об одном из перечисляемых предметов): **ни тот ни друго́й** neither one nor the other; **тем или ины́м спо́собом** by some means or other; **тот же** the same

7 (во фразах): **до того́** so; **мне не до того́** I have no time for that; **к тому́ же** moreover; **ни с того́ ни с сего́** (разг) out of the blue; **тому́ наза́д** ... ago; **и тому́ подо́бное** et cetera, and so on

---

тоталита́рный прил totalitarian

тота́льный прил total; (война) all-out

то-то част (разг: вот именно) exactly, that's just it; (вот почему) that's why; (выражает удовлетворение): **то-то же** pleased to hear it; **то-то он удиви́тся!** he WILL be surprised!

то́тчас нареч immediately

точи́л|ка (-ки; gen pl -ок) ж pencil sharpener

точ|и́ть (-у́, -ишь; perf **наточи́ть**) несов перех to sharpen; (no perf: подлеж: червь, ржавчина) to eat away at

то́ч|ка (-ки; gen pl -ек) ж point; (пятнышко) dot; (Линг) full stop (Brit), period (esp US); **то́чка зре́ния** point of view; **то́чка с запято́й** semicolon

точне́е вводн сл to be exact или precise

то́чно нареч exactly; (объясни́ть) precisely; (подсчита́ть, перевести́) accurately ▷ част (разг: действи́тельно) exactly, precisely

то́чност|ь (-и) ж accuracy

то́чный прил exact; (часы, перевод, попадание) accurate

точь-в-точь нареч (разг) just like

тошн|и́ть (3sg -и́т, perf стошни́ть) несов безл: меня́ тошни́т I feel sick

тошнот|а́ (-ы́) ж (чувство) nausea

тóщий прил (человек) skinny

т.п. сокр (= тому́ подóбное) etc. (= et cetera)

трав|а́ (-ы́; nom pl -ы) ж grass; (лекарственная) herb

трав|и́ть (-лю́, -ишь) несов перех (также перен) to poison ▷ (perf затрави́ть) (дичь) to hunt; (перен: разг: притеснять) to harass, hound; трави́ть в Интерне́те to bully online, cyberbully; трави́ться (perf отрави́ться) несов возв to poison o.s.

тра́вм|а (-ы) ж (физическая) injury; (психическая) trauma

травматóлог (-а) м doctor working in a casualty department

травматологи́ческий прил: травматологи́ческий отде́л casualty; травматологи́ческий пункт first-aid room

травми́р|овать (-ую) (не)сов перех to injure; (перен: психически) to traumatize

траге́ди|я (-и) ж tragedy

траги́ческий прил tragic

традициóнный прил traditional

тради́ци|я (-и) ж tradition

тра́ктор (-а) м tractor; трактори́ст (-а) м tractor driver

трамва́|й (-я) м tram (Brit), streetcar (US)

транзи́стор (-а) м (приёмник) transistor (radio)

транзи́т (-а) м transit

транс (-а) м transport document

трансге́нный прил (овощи) genetically modified

трансли́р|овать (-ую) (не)сов перех to broadcast; трансли́ровать в режи́ме онла́йн to stream

трансля́ци|я (-и) ж (передача) broadcast

транспара́нт (-а) м banner

транспланта́ци|я (-и) ж transplant

тра́нспорт (-а) м transport

транспортёр (-а) м (конвейер) conveyor belt; (Воен) army personnel carrier

транспорти́р|овать (-ую) (не)сов перех to transport

тра́нспортный прил transport

транше́|я (-и) ж trench

тра́сс|а (-ы) ж (лыжная) run; (трубопровода) line; автомоби́льная тра́сса motorway (Brit), expressway (US)

тра́|тить (-чу, -тишь; perf истра́тить или потра́тить) несов перех to spend

тра́ур (-а) м mourning

тре́бовани|е (-я) ср demand; (правило) requirement

тре́бовательный прил demanding

тре́б|овать (-ую; perf потре́бовать) несов перех: тре́бовать что-н/+infin to demand sth/to do; тре́боваться (perf потре́боваться) несов возв to be needed или required

трево́г|а (-и) ж (волнение) anxiety; возду́шная трево́га air-raid warning

трево́ж|ить (-у, -ишь; perf встрево́жить) несов перех to alarm ▷ (perf потрево́жить) (мешать) to disturb; трево́житься (perf встрево́житься) несов возв (за детей) to be concerned

трево́жный прил (голос, взгляд) anxious; (сведения) alarming

трезве́|ть (-ю; perf отрезве́ть) несов to sober up

тре́звый прил (человек) sober; (перен: идея) sensible

трём etc чис см три

тре́мста́м etc чис см три́ста

тренажёр (-а) м equipment used for physical training

тре́нер (-а) м coach

тре́ни|е (-я) ср friction

трениро́в|ать (-у́ю; perf натренирова́ть) несов перех to train; (спортсменов) to coach; тренирова́ться (perf натренирова́ться) несов возв (спортсмен) to train

трениро́в|ка (-ки; gen pl -ок) ж training; (отдельное занятие) training (session)

трениро́вочный прил training; трениро́вочный костю́м tracksuit

треп|а́ть (-лю́, -лешь; perf потрепа́ть) несов перех (подлеж: ветер) to blow about; (человека: по плечу) to pat ▷ (perf истрепа́ть или потрепа́ть) (разг: обувь, книги) to wear out; трепа́ться (perf истрепа́ться или потрепа́ться) несов возв (одежда) to wear out

треп|ета́ть (-ещу́, -е́щешь) несов (флаги) to quiver; (от ужаса) to quake, tremble

треск|а́ (-и́) ж cod

тре́ска|ться (3sg -ется, perf потре́скаться) несов возв to crack

тре́сн|уть (3sg -ет) сов (ветка) to snap; (стакан, кожа) to crack

трест (-а) м (Экон) trust

тре́т|ий чис third; тре́тье лицо́ (Линг) the third person

трет|ь (-и; nom pl -и, gen pl -е́й) ж third

тре́ть|е (-его) ср (Кулин) sweet (Brit), dessert

треуго́льник (-а) м triangle

треуго́льный прил triangular

треф|ы (-) мн (Карты) clubs

трёх чис см три

трёхме́рный прил 3-D, three-dimensional

трёхсо́т чис см три́ста

трёхсо́тый чис three hundredth

треща́ть (-у́, -и́шь) несов (лёд, доски) to crack; (кузнечики) to chip

тре́щин|а (-ы) ж crack

тр|и (-ёх; см Table 24) чис three ▷ нескл (Просвещ) ≈ C (school mark)

трибу́н|а (-ы) ж platform; (стадиона) stand

трибуна́л (-а) м tribunal; вое́нный трибуна́л military court

тридца́тый *чис* thirtieth

три́дцат|ь (-и; *как* пять; см *Table 26*) *чис* thirty

три́жды *нареч* three times

трико́ *ср нескл* leotard

трина́дцатый *чис* thirteenth

трина́дцат|ь (-и; *как* пять; см *Table 26*) *чис* thirteen

три́ста (трёхсо́т; *как* сто; см *Table 28*) *чис* three hundred

триу́мф (-а) *м* triumph

тро́гательный *прил* touching

тро́га|ть (-ю; *perf* тро́нуть) *несов перех* to touch; (*подлеж*: рассказ, событие) to move; **тро́гаться** (*perf* тро́нуться) *несов возв* (поезд) to move off

тр|о́е (-ои́х; см *Table 30a*) *чис* three

тро́иц|а (-ы) *ж* (также Свята́я тро́ица) the Holy Trinity; (*праздник*) ≈ Trinity Sunday

Тро́ицын *прил*: Тро́ицын день ≈ Trinity Sunday

тро́йк|а (-йки; *gen pl* -ек) *ж* (цифра, карта) three; (*Просвещ*) ≈ C (*school mark*); (*лошадей*) troika; (*костюм*) three-piece suit

тройни́к (-а́) *м* (*Элек*) (three-way) adaptor

тройно́й *прил* triple

тролле́йбус (-а) *м* trolleybus

тромбо́н (-а) *м* trombone

трон (-а) *м* throne

тро́н|уть(ся) (-у(сь)) *сов от* тро́гать(ся)

тро́пик (-а) *м*: се́верный/ю́жный тро́пик the tropic of Cancer/Capricorn

тропи́н|ка (-ки; *gen pl* -ок) *ж* footpath

тропи́ческий *прил* tropical

трос (-а) *м* cable

тростни́к (-а́) *м* reed; са́харный тростни́к sugar cane

трост|ь (-и) *ж* walking stick

тротуа́р (-а) *м* pavement (*Brit*), sidewalk (*US*)

трофе́|й (-я) *м* trophy

трою́родн|ый *прил*: трою́родный брат second cousin (*male*); трою́родная сестра́ second cousin (*female*)

тро́йкий *прил* triple

труб|а́ (-ы́; *nom pl* -ы) *ж* pipe; (*дымовая*) chimney; (*Муз*) trumpet

труби́|ть (-лю́, -и́шь; *perf* протруби́ть) *несов* (труба) to sound; (*Муз*): труби́ть в +*acc* to blow

тру́б|ка (-ки; *gen pl* -ок) *ж* tube; (*курительная*) pipe; (*телефона*) receiver

труд (-а́) *м* work; (*Экон*) labour (*Brit*), labor (*US*); без труда́ without any difficulty; с (больши́м) трудо́м with (great) difficulty; труди́ться (-жу́сь, -дишься) *несов возв* to work hard

тру́дно *как сказ* it's hard *или* difficult; у меня́ тру́дно с деньга́ми I've got money problems; мне тру́дно поня́ть э́то I find it hard to understand; (мне) тру́дно бе́гать/ стоя́ть I have trouble running/standing up; тру́дно сказа́ть it's hard to say

тру́дност|ь (-и) *ж* difficulty

тру́дный *прил* difficult

трудово́й *прил* working; трудова́я кни́жка *employment record book*

трудоёмкий *прил* labour-intensive (*Brit*), labor-intensive (*US*)

трудолюби́вый *прил* hard-working, industrious

труп (-а) *м* corpse

тру́пп|а (-ы) *ж* (*Театр*) company

трус (-а) *м* coward

тру́сик|и (-ов) *мн* (детские) knickers (*Brit*), panties (*US*)

тру́|сить (-шу, -сишь; *perf* стру́сить) *несов* to get scared

трусли́вый *прил* cowardly

трус|ы́ (-о́в) *мн* (бельё: обычно мужские) (under)pants; (*спортивные*) shorts

трущо́б|а (-ы) *ж* slum

трюм (-а) *м* hold (*of ship*)

трюмо́ *ср нескл* (*мебель*) dresser

тря́п|ка (-ки; *gen pl* -ок) *ж* (половая) cloth; (*лоскут*) rag; тря́пки (*разг*) clothes *мн*

тряс|ти́ (-у́, -ёшь) *несов перех* to shake; **трясти́сь** *несов возв*: трясти́сь пе́ред +*instr* (перед начальством) to tremble before; (*трясти́сь* (*impf*) над +*instr* (*разг*: над ребёнком) to fret over *или* about

тряхн|у́ть (-у́, -ёшь) *сов перех* to shake

ТУ *м сокр* самолёт констру́кции А.Н.Ту́полева

туале́т (-а) *м* toilet; (*одежда*) outfit; **туале́тн|ый** *прил*: туале́тная бума́га toilet paper; туале́тное мы́ло toilet soap; туале́тные принадле́жности toiletries; туале́тный сто́лик dressing table

туго́й *прил* (струна, пружина) taut; (узел, одежда) tight; он туг на́ ухо (*разг*) he's a bit hard of hearing

туда́ *нареч* there; туда́ и обра́тно there and back; биле́т туда́ и обра́тно return (*Brit*) *или* round-trip (*US*) ticket

туда́-сюда́ *нареч* all over the place; (*раскачиваться*) backwards and forwards

ту́же *сравн прил от* туго́й

туз (-а́) *м* (*Карты*) ace

тузе́м|ец (-ца) *м* native

тума́н (-а) *м* mist

тума́нный *прил* misty; (идеи) nebulous

ту́мбоч|ка (-ки; *gen pl* -ек) *ж*, уменьш от ту́мба; (*мебель*) bedside cabinet

тун|е́ц (-ца́) *м* tuna (fish)

тунея́д|ец (**-ца**) м parasite (*fig*)

тунне́л|ь (**-я**) м = **тонне́ль**

тупи́к (**-а́**) м (*улица*) dead end, cul-de-sac; (*для поездов*) siding; (*перен: в переговорах итп*) deadlock

тупи́ть (**-лю́, -ишь**; *perf* **затупи́ть**) *несов перех* to blunt; **тупи́ться** (*perf* **затупи́ться**) *несов возв* to become blunt

тупо́й *прил* (*нож, карандаш*) blunt; (*человек*) stupid; (*боль, ум*) dull; (*покорность*) blind

тур (**-а**) м (*этап*) round; (*в танце*) turn

тури́зм (**-а**) м tourism; **тури́ст** (**-а**) м tourist; (*в походе*) hiker; **туристи́ческий** *прил* tourist

турне́ *ср нескл* (*Театр, Спорт*) tour

турни́р (**-а**) м tournament

Ту́рци|я (**-и**) ж Turkey

ту́склый *прил* (*стекло*) opaque; (*краска*) mat(t); (*свет, взгляд*) dull

тус|ова́ться (**-у́юсь**; *perf* **потусова́ться**) *несов* (*разг*) to hang out

тусо́вк|а (**-и**) ж (*разг: на улице*) hanging about; (*вечеринка*) party

тут *нареч* here; **и всё тут** (*разг*) and that's that; **не тут-то бы́ло** (*разг*) it wasn't to be

ту́фл|я (**-и**; *gen pl* **-ель**) ж shoe

ту́х|нуть (*3sg* **-нет**, *pt* **-, -ла,** *perf* **поту́хнуть**) *несов* (*костёр, свет*) to go out ▷ (*perf* **протухнуть**) (*мясо*) to go off

ту́ч|а (**-и**) ж rain cloud

тушён|ка (**-ки**; *gen pl* **-ок**) ж (*разг*) tinned (*Brit*) *или* canned meat

туш|ь (**-и**) ж (*для ресниц*) mascara

т/ф м *сокр* = **телевизио́нный фильм**

ТЦ м *сокр* (= **телевизио́нный центр**) television centre (*Brit*) *или* center (*US*)

тща́тельный *прил* thorough

тщесла́ви|е (**-я**) *ср* vanity; **тщесла́вный** *прил* vain

ты (**тебя́**; см *Table 6a*) *мест* you; **быть** (*impf*) **с кем-н на ты** to be on familiar terms with sb

ты́|кать (**-чу, -чешь**; *perf* **ткнуть**) *несов перех* (*разг: ударять*): **ты́кать что-н/ кого́-н чем-н** to poke sth/sb with sth

ты́кв|а (**-ы**) ж pumpkin

тыл (**-а**; *loc sg* **-у́,** *nom pl* **-ы́**) м (*Воен: территория*) the rear; **ты́льный** *прил* back

тыс. *сокр* = **ты́сяча**

ты́сяч|а (**-и**; см *Table 29*) ж *чис* thousand

ты́сячный *чис* thousandth; (*толпа, армия*) of thousands

тьм|а (**-ы**) ж (*мрак*) darkness, gloom

ТЭЦ ж *сокр* = **тепло(электро)центра́ль**

тю́бик (**-а**) м tube

ТЮЗ (**-а**) м *сокр* (= **теа́тр ю́ного зри́теля**) children's theatre (*Brit*) *или* theater (*US*)

тюле́н|ь (**-я**) м (*Зоол*) seal

тюльпа́н (**-а**) м tulip

тюре́мн|ый *прил* prison; **тюре́мное заключе́ние** imprisonment

тюрьм|а́ (**-ы́**) ж prison

тя́г|а (**-и**) ж (*в печи*) draught (*Brit*), draft (*US*); (*насоса, пылесоса*) suction; **тя́га к** +*dat* (*перен*) attraction to

тяготе́ни|е (**-я**) *ср* (*Физ*) gravity

тя́гот|ы (**-**) мн hardships

тя́жб|а (**-ы**) ж dispute

тяжеле́|ть (**-ю**; *perf* **отяжеле́ть** *или* **потяжеле́ть**) *несов* to get heavier

тяжело́ *нареч* heavily; (*больной*) seriously ▷ *как сказ* (*нести*) it's heavy; (*понять*) it's hard; **мне тяжело́ здесь** I find it hard here; **больно́му тяжело́** the patient is suffering

тяжёл|ый *прил* heavy; (*труд, день*) hard; (*сон*) restless; (*запах*) strong; (*воздух*) stale; (*преступление, болезнь, рана*) serious; (*зрелище, мысли, настроение*) grim; (*трудный: человек, характер*) difficult; **тяжёлая атле́тика** weightlifting; **тяжёлая промы́шленность** heavy industry

тя́жкий *прил* (*труд*) arduous; (*преступление*) grave

тяну́ть (**-у́, -ешь**) *несов перех* (*канат, сеть итп*) to pull; (*шею, руку*) to stretch out; (*дело*) to drag out ▷ (*perf* **протяну́ть**) (*кабель*) to lay ▷ (*perf* **вы́тянуть**) (*жребий*) to draw ▷ *неперех*: **тяну́ть с** +*instr* (*с ответом, с письма*) to delay; **меня́ тя́нет в Петербу́рг** I want to go to Petersburg; **тяну́ться** *несов возв* to stretch; (*дело, время*) to drag on; (*дым, запах*) to waft; **тяну́ться** (*impf*) **к** +*dat* to be attracted *или* drawn to

У

перех to kill; (*о преступлении*) to murder

убо́гий *прил* wretched

убо́й (**-я**) *м* slaughter

убо́р (**-а**) *м*: **головно́й убо́р** hat

убо́рк|а (**-и**) *ж* (*помещения*) cleaning; **убо́рка урожа́я** harvest

убо́рн|ая (**-ой**) *ж* (*артиста*) dressing room; (*туалет*) lavatory

убо́рщиц|а (**-ы**) *ж* cleaner

убра́ть (**уберу́, уберёшь;** *impf* **убира́ть**) *сов перех* (*унести: вещи*) to take away; (*комнату*) to tidy; (*урожай*) to gather (in); **убира́ть** (*perf* **убра́ть**) **со стола́** to clear the table

у́был|ь (**-и**) *ж* decrease; **идти́** (*impf*) **на у́быль** to decrease

убы́т|ок (**-ка**) *м* loss

убью́ *итп сов см* **уби́ть**

уважа́ем|ый *прил* respected, esteemed; **уважа́емый господи́н** Dear Sir; **уважа́емая госпожа́** Dear Madam

уважа́|ть (**-ю**) *несов перех* to respect

уваже́ни|е (**-я**) *ср* respect

УВД *ср сокр* (= *Управле́ние вну́тренних дел*) *administration of internal affairs within a town/region*

уве́дом|ить (**-лю, -ишь;** *impf* **уведомля́ть**) *сов перех* to notify

уведомле́ни|е (**-я**) *ср* notification

увез|ти́ (**-у́, -ёшь;** *pt* **увёз, -ла́,** *impf* **увози́ть**) *сов перех* to take away

увеличи́тельн|ый *прил*: **увеличи́тельное стекло́** magnifying glass

увели́ч|ить (**-у, -ишь;** *impf* **увели́чивать**) *сов перех* to increase; (*фотографию*) to enlarge; **увели́читься** (*impf* **увели́чиваться**) *сов возв* to increase

уве́ренност|ь (**-и**) *ж* confidence

уве́ренный *прил* confident

уверя́|ть (**-ю**) *несов перех*: **уверя́ть кого́-н/что-н (в чём-н)** to assure sb/sth (of sth)

ув|ести́ (**-еду́, -едёшь;** *pt* **-ёл, -ела́,** *impf* **уводи́ть**) *сов перех* to lead off

уви́деть(ся) (**-жу(сь), -дишь(ся)**) *сов от* **ви́деть(ся)**

увлека́тельный *прил* (*рассказ*) absorbing; (*поездка*) entertaining

увлече́ни|е (**-я**) *ср* passion

увл|е́чь (**-еку́, -ечёшь** *итп*, **-еку́т;** *pt* **-ёк, -екла́,** *impf* **увлека́ть**) *сов перех* to lead away; (*перен: захватить*) to captivate; **увле́чься** (*impf* **увлека́ться**) *сов возв*: **увле́чься** +*instr* to get carried away with; (*влюбиться*) to fall for; (*шахматами итп*) to become keen on

ув|оди́ть (**-ожу́, -о́дишь**) *несов от* **увести́**

ув|ози́ть (**-ожу́, -о́зишь**) *несов от* **увезти́**

увол|ить (**-ю, -ишь;** *impf* **увольня́ть**) *сов перех* (*с работы*) to dismiss, sack; **уво́литься** (*impf* **увольня́ться**) *сов возв*: **уво́литься (с рабо́ты)** to leave one's job

 КЛЮЧЕВОЕ СЛОВО

у *предл* +*gen* **1** (*около*) by; **у окна́** by the window

2 (*обозначает обладателя чего-н*): **у меня́ есть дом/де́ти** I have a house/children

3 (*обозначает объект, с которым соотносится действие*): **я живу́ у друзе́й** I live with friends; **я учи́лся у него́** I was taught by him

4 (*указывает на источник получения чего-н*) from; **я попроси́л у дру́га де́нег** I asked for money from a friend

▷ *межд* (*выражает испуг, восторг*) oh

убега́|ть (**-ю**) *несов от* **убежа́ть**

убеди́тельный *прил* (*пример*) convincing; (*просьба*) urgent

убед|и́ть (**2sg** -**и́шь, 3sg** -**и́т,** *impf* **убежда́ть**) *сов перех*: **убеди́ть кого́-н** +*infin* to persuade sb to do; **убежда́ть** (*perf* **убеди́ть**) **кого́-н в чём-н** to convince sb of sth; **убеди́ться** (*impf* **убежда́ться**) *сов возв*: **убеди́ться в чём-н** to be convinced of sth

убежа́|ть (*как* **бежа́ть;** *см* Table 20; *impf* **убега́ть**) *сов* to run away

убежде́ни|е (**-я**) *ср* (*взгляд*) conviction

убе́жищ|е (**-а**) *ср* (*от дождя, от бомб*) shelter; **полити́ческое убе́жище** political asylum

убер|е́чь (**-егу́, -ежёшь** *итп*, **-егу́т;** *pt* **-ёг, -егла́,** *impf* **уберега́ть**) *сов перех* to protect; **убере́чься** (*impf* **убере́чься** *от опасности итп*) *сов возв* (*от опасности итп*) to protect o.s.

убива́|ть (**-ю**) *несов от* **уби́ть**

уби́йств|о (**-а**) *ср* murder

уби́йц|а (**-ы**) *м/ж* murderer

убира́|ть (**-ю**) *несов от* **убра́ть**

уби́т|ый (**-ого**) *м* dead man (*мн* men)

уб|и́ть (**-ью, -ьёшь;** *impf* **убива́ть**) *сов*

увольне́ни|е (-я) *ср* (*со службы*) dismissal; (*Воен*) leave

увя́н|уть (-у) *сов от* **вя́нуть**

угада́|ть (-ю; *impf* **уга́дывать**) *сов перех* to guess

уга́рный *прил*: **уга́рный газ** carbon monoxide

угаса́|ть (-ю; *perf* **уга́снуть**) *несов* (*огонь*) to die down

угла́ *итп сущ см* **у́гол**

углево́д (-а) *м* carbohydrate

углеки́слый *прил*: **углеки́слый газ** carbon dioxide

углеро́д (-а) *м* (*Хим*) carbon

углово́й *прил* corner; (*также* **углово́й уда́р**: *Спорт*) corner

углуб|и́ть (-лю́, -и́шь; *impf* **углубля́ть**) *сов перех* to deepen; **углуби́ться** (*impf* **углубля́ться**) *сов возв* to deepen

угля́ *итп сущ см* **у́голь**

угн|а́ть (угоню́, уго́нишь; *impf* **угоня́ть**) *сов перех* to drive off; (*самолёт*) to hijack

угнета́|ть (-ю) *несов перех* to oppress; (*тяготить*) to depress

угово́р|и́ть (-ю́, -и́шь; *impf* **угова́ривать**) *сов перех* to persuade

уго|ди́ть (-жу́, -ди́шь; *impf* **угожда́ть**) *сов* (*попасть*) to end up; **угожда́ть** (*perf* **угоди́ть**) +*dat* to please

уго́дно *част*: **что уго́дно** whatever you like ▷ *как сказ*: **что Вам уго́дно?** what can I do for you?; **кто уго́дно** anyone; **когда́/ како́й уго́дно** whenever/whichever you like; **от них мо́жно ожида́ть чего́ уго́дно** they might do anything

уго́дный *прил* +*dat* pleasing to

угожда́|ть (-ю) *несов от* **угоди́ть**

у́г|ол (-ла́; *loc sg* -лу́) *м* corner; (*Геом*) angle; **у́гол зре́ния** perspective

уголо́вник (-а) *м* criminal

уголо́вн|ый *прил* criminal; **уголо́вное преступле́ние** felony; **уголо́вный престу́пник** criminal; **уголо́вный ро́зыск** Criminal Investigation Department

у́г|оль (-ля́) *м* coal

угоня́|ть (-ю) *несов от* **угна́ть**

уго|сти́ть (-щу́, -сти́шь; *impf* **угоща́ть**) *сов перех*: **угости́ть кого́-н чем-н** (*пирогом, вином*) to offer sb sth

угоща́|ться (-юсь) *несов возв*: **угоща́йтесь!** help yourself!

угрожа́|ть (-ю) *несов*: **угрожа́ть кому́-н (чем-н)** to threaten sb (with sth)

угро́з|а (-ы) *ж* (*обычно мн*) threat

угрызе́ни|е (-я) *ср*: **угрызе́ния со́вести** pangs *мн* of conscience

уда|ва́ться (3sg -ётся) *несов от* **уда́ться**

удал|и́ть (-ю́, -и́шь; *impf* **удаля́ть**) *сов перех* (*отослать*) to send away; (*игрока*) to send off; (*пятно, занозу, орган*) to remove

уда́р (-а) *м* blow; (*ногой*) kick; (*инсульт*) stroke; (*сердца*) beat

ударе́ни|е (-я) *ср* stress

уда́р|ить (-ю, -ишь; *impf* **ударя́ть**) *сов перех* to hit; (*ногой*) to kick; (*подлеж*: *часы*) to strike; **уда́риться** (*impf* **ударя́ться**) *сов возв*: **уда́риться о** +*acc* to bang (o.s.) against

уда́рный *прил* (*инструмент*) percussion; (*слог*) stressed

уда́|ться (*как* **дать**; *см* Table 16; *impf* **удава́ться**) *сов возв* (*опыт, дело*) to be successful, work; (*пирог*) to turn out well; **нам удало́сь поговори́ть/зако́нчить рабо́ту** we managed to talk to each other/ finish the work

уда́ч|а (-и) *ж* (good) luck; **жела́ю уда́чи!** good luck!

уда́чный *прил* successful; (*слова*) apt

удво́|ить (-ю, -ишь; *impf* **удва́ивать**) *сов перех* to double

удел|и́ть (-ю́, -и́шь; *impf* **уделя́ть**) *сов перех*: **удели́ть что-н кому́-н/чему́-н** to devote sth to sb/sth

уд|ержа́ть (-ержу́, -е́ржишь; *impf* **уде́рживать**) *сов перех* to restrain; (*де́ньги*) to deduct; **уде́рживать** (*perf* **удержа́ть**) (**за собо́й**) to retain; **уде́рживать** (*perf* **удержа́ть**) **кого́-н от пое́здки** to keep sb from going on a journey; **удержа́ться** (*impf* **уде́рживаться**) *сов возв* to stop *или* restrain o.s.

удиви́тельный *прил* amazing

удив|и́ть (-лю́, -и́шь; *impf* **удивля́ть**) *сов перех* to surprise; **удиви́ться** (*impf* **удивля́ться**) *сов возв*: **удиви́ться** +*dat* to be surprised at *или* by

удивле́ни|е (-я) *ср* surprise

уди́ть (ужу́, у́дишь) *несов* to angle

удо́бно *нареч* (*сесть*) comfortably ▷ *как сказ* it's comfortable; (*прилично*) it's proper; **не удо́бно так говори́ть/де́лать** it is not proper to say so/do so; **мне не удо́бно** I feel awkward; **мне здесь удо́бно** I'm comfortable here; **мне удо́бно прийти́ ве́чером** it's convenient for me to come in the evening

удо́бный *прил* comfortable; (*время, место*) convenient

удобре́ни|е (-я) *ср* fertilizer

удо́бств|о (-а) *ср* comfort; **кварти́ра со все́ми удо́бствами** a flat with all (modern) conveniences

удовлетвори́тельный *прил* satisfactory

удовлетвор|и́ть (-ю́, -и́шь; *impf* **удовлетворя́ть**) *сов перех* to satisfy; (*потребности, про́сьбу*) to meet; (*жалобу*) to respond to; **удовлетвори́ться** (*impf* **удовлетворя́ться**) *сов возв*: **удовлетвори́ться** +*instr* to be satisfied with

удово́льстви|е (-я) *ср* pleasure

удостовере́ни|е (-я) *ср* identification (card); **удостовере́ние ли́чности** identity card

удочер|и́ть (-ю́, -и́шь; *impf* **удочеря́ть**)

сов перех to adopt (*daughter*)

у́доч|**ка** (-**ки**; *gen pl* -**ек**) ж (fishing-)rod

уе́хать (*как* **е́хать**; *см* Table 19; *impf* **уезжа́ть**) *сов* to leave, go away

уж (-**а́**) *част* (*при усилении*): **здесь не так уж пло́хо** it's not as bad as all that here

ужа́л|**ить** (-**ю**, -**ишь**) *сов от* **жа́лить**

у́жас (-**а**) *м* horror; (*страх*) terror ⊳ *как сказ* (*разг*): (**э́то**) **у́жас!** it's awful *или* terrible!; **ти́хий у́жас!** (*разг*) what a nightmare!; **до у́жаса** (*разг*) terribly

ужа́сно *нареч* (*разг: очень*) awfully, terribly ⊳ *как сказ*: **э́то ужа́сно** it's awful *или* terrible

ужа́сный *прил* terrible, horrible, awful

у́же *сравн прил от* **у́зкий**

уже́ *нареч, част* already; **ты же уже́ не ма́ленький** you're not a child any more

ужива́|ться (-**юсь**) *несов от* **ужи́ться**

у́жин (-**а**) *м* supper

у́жина|ть (-**ю**; *perf* **поу́жинать**) *несов* to have supper

ужи́|ться (-**ву́сь**, -**вёшься**; *impf* **ужива́ться**) *сов возв*: **ужи́ться с кем-н** to get on with sb

узако́н|ить (-**ю**, -**ишь**) *impf* **узако́нивать**) *сов перех* to legalize

у́з|**ел** (-**ла́**) *м* knot; (*мешок*) bundle; **телефо́нный у́зел** telephone exchange; **железнодоро́жный у́зел** railway junction; **санита́рный у́зел** bathroom and toilet

у́зкий *прил* narrow; (*тесный*) tight; (*перен: человек*) narrow-minded

узна́|ть (-**ю**; *impf* **узнава́ть**) *сов перех* to recognize; (*новости*) to learn

у́зок *прил см* **у́зкий**

узо́р (-**а**) *м* pattern

уйти́ (*как* **идти́**; *см* Table 18; *impf* **уходи́ть**) *сов* (*человек*) to go away, leave; (*автобус, поезд*) to go, leave; (*избежать*): **уйти́ от** +*gen* (*от опасности итп*) to get away from; (*потребоваться*): **уйти́ на** +*acc* (*деньги, время*) to be spent on

ука́з (-**а**) *м* (*президента*) decree

указа́ни|е (-**я**) *ср* indication; (*разъяснение*) instruction; (*приказ*) directive

указа́тел|ь (-**я**) *м* (*дорожный*) sign; (*книга*) guide; (*список в книге*) index; (*прибор*) indicator

указа́тельный *прил*; **указа́тельное местоиме́ние** demonstrative pronoun; **указа́тельный па́лец** index finger

ук|**аза́ть** (-**ажу́**, -**а́жешь**; *impf* **ука́зывать**) *сов перех* to point out; (*сообщить*) to indicate

укача́|ть (-**ю**; *impf* **ука́чивать**) *сов перех* (*усыпить*) to rock to sleep; **его́ укача́ло** (**в маши́не/на парохо́де**) he got (car-/sea-) sick

укла́дыва|ть (-**ю**) *несов от* **уложи́ть**; **укла́дываться** *несов от* **уложи́ться** ⊳ *возв*: **э́то не укла́дывается в обы́чные ра́мки** this is out of the ordinary; **э́то не**

укла́дывается в голове́ *или* **в созна́нии** it's beyond me

укло́н (-**а**) *м* slant; **под укло́н** downhill

уко́л (-**а**) *м* prick; (*Мед*) injection

ук|**оло́ть** (-**олю́**, -**о́лешь**) *сов от* **коло́ть**

укра́|сить (-**шу**, -**сишь**; *impf* **украша́ть**) *сов перех* to decorate; (*жизнь итп*) to brighten up

укра́|сть (-**ду́**, -**дёшь**) *сов от* **красть**

украша́|ть (-**ю**) *несов от* **укра́сить**

украше́ни|е (-**я**) *ср* decoration; (*коллекции*) jewel; (*также* **ювели́рное украше́ние**) jewellery (*Brit*), jewelry (*US*)

укреп|**и́ть** (-**лю́**, -**и́шь**; *impf* **укрепля́ть**) *сов перех* to strengthen; (*стену*) to reinforce; **укрепи́ться** (*impf* **укрепля́ться**) *сов возв* to become stronger

укро|**ти́ть** (-**щу́**, -**ти́шь**; *impf* **укроща́ть**) *сов перех* to tame

укры́ти|е (-**я**) *ср* shelter

укр|**ы́ть** (-**о́ю**, -**о́ешь**; *impf* **укрыва́ть**) *сов перех* (*закрыть*) to cover; (*беженца*) to shelter; **укры́ться** (*impf* **укрыва́ться**) *сов возв* to cover o.s.; (*от дождя*) to take cover

у́ксус (-**а**) *м* vinegar

уку́с (-**а**) *м* bite

ук|**уси́ть** (-**ушу́**, -**у́сишь**) *сов перех* to bite

укута́|ть (-**ю**; *impf* **уку́тывать**) *сов перех* to wrap up; **уку́таться** (*impf* **уку́тываться**) *сов возв* to wrap o.s. up

ул. *сокр* (= **у́лица**) St (= *street*)

ула́влива|ть (-**ю**) *несов от* **улови́ть**

ула́|дить (-**жу**, -**дишь**; *impf* **ула́живать**) *сов перех* to settle

у́ле|й (-**ья**) *м* (bee-)hive

уле|те́ть (-**чу́**, -**ти́шь**; *impf* **улета́ть**) *сов* (*птица*) to fly away; (*самолёт*) to leave

ули́к|а (-**и**) *ж* (piece of) evidence (*мн* evidence)

ули́т|ка (-**ки**; *gen pl* -**ок**) *ж* snail

у́лиц|а (-**ы**) *ж* street; **на у́лице** outside

у́личный *прил* street; **у́личное движе́ние** traffic

уло́в (-**а**) *м* catch (*of fish*)

улови́мый *прил*: **едва́** *или* **чуть** *или* **е́ле улови́мый** barely perceptible

ул|**ови́ть** (-**овлю́**, -**о́вишь**; *impf* **ула́вливать**) *сов перех* to detect; (*мысль, связь*) to grasp

ул|**ожи́ть** (-**ожу́**, -**о́жишь**; *impf* **укла́дывать**) *сов перех* (*ребёнка*) to put to bed; (*вещи, чемодан*) to pack; **уложи́ться** (*impf* **укла́дываться**) *сов возв* (*сложить вещи*) to pack; **укла́дываться** (*perf* **уложи́ться**) **в сро́ки** to keep to the time limit

улу́чш|**ить** (-**у**, -**ишь**; *impf* **улучша́ть**) *сов перех* to improve

улыба́|ться (-**юсь**; *perf* **улыбну́ться**) *несов возв*: **улыба́ться** (+*dat*) to smile (at)

улы́б|**ка** (-**ки**; *gen pl* -**ок**) *ж* smile

ультрафиоле́товый прил:
ультрафиоле́товые лучи́ ultraviolet rays
мн

ум (-а́) м mind; **быть** (impf) **без ума́ от
кого́-н/чего́-н** to be wild about sb/sth; **в
уме́** (считать) in one's head; **бра́ться** (perf
взя́ться) за ум to see sense; **сходи́ть** (perf
сойти́) с ума́ to go mad; **своди́ть** (perf
свести́) кого́-н с ума́ to drive sb mad;
(перен: увлечь) to drive sb wild; **ума́ не
приложу́, куда́/ско́лько/кто …** I can't think
where/how much/who …

ума́лчива|ть (-ю) несов от **умолча́ть**
уме́лый прил skilful (Brit), skillful (US)
уме́ни|е (-я) ср ability, skill
уме́ньш|ить (-у, -ишь; impf
уменьша́ть) сов перех to reduce;
уме́ньшиться (impf **уменьша́ться**) сов
возв to diminish

ум|ере́ть (-ру́, -рёшь; impf **умира́ть**)
сов to die

уме́р|ить (-ю, -ишь; impf **умеря́ть**) сов
перех to moderate

уме|сти́ть (-щу́, -сти́шь; impf **умеща́ть**)
сов перех to fit; **умести́ться** (impf
умеща́ться) сов возв to fit

уме́|ть (-ю) несов can, to be able to;
(иметь способность) to know how to; **он
уме́ет пла́вать/чита́ть** he can swim/read
умеща́|ть(ся) (-ю(сь)) несов от
умести́ть(ся)

умира́|ть (-ю) несов от **умере́ть**
▷ неперех (перен): **умира́ю, как хочу́
есть/спать** I'm dying for something to eat/
to go to sleep; **я умира́ю от ску́ки** I'm
bored to death

умне́|ть (-ю; perf **поумне́ть**) несов
(человек) to grow wiser

у́мниц|а (-ы) м/ж: **он/она́ у́мница** he's/
she's a clever one; (разг): **вот у́мница!**
good for you!, well done!

у́мно нареч (сделанный) cleverly; (вести
себя) sensibly; (говорить) intelligently
умножа́|ть (-ю) несов от **умно́жить**
умноже́ни|е (-я) ср (см глаг)
multiplication; increase

умно́ж|ить (-у, -ишь; impf **мно́жить**
или **умножа́ть**) сов перех (Мат) to
multiply

у́мный прил clever, intelligent
умозаключе́ни|е (-я) ср (вывод)
deduction

умол|и́ть (-ю́, -ишь; impf **умоля́ть**) сов
перех: **умоли́ть кого́-н** (+infin) to prevail
upon sb (to do)

умо́лкн|уть (-у; impf **умолка́ть**) сов to
fall silent

умолч|а́ть (-у́, -и́шь; impf **ума́лчивать**)
сов: **умолча́ть о чём-н** to keep quiet about
sth

умоля́|ть (-ю) несов от **умоли́ть** ▷ перех
to implore

умру́ итп сов см **умере́ть**
умо́ю(сь) сов см **умы́ть(ся)**

у́мственно нареч: **у́мственно отста́лый**
with learning difficulties

у́мственный прил (способности)
mental; **у́мственный труд** intellectual work
умудр|и́ться (-ю́сь, -и́шься; impf
умудря́ться) сов возв to manage

умч|а́ть (-у́, -и́шь) сов перех to whisk off
или away; **умча́ться** сов возв to dash off
умы́ть (умо́ю, умо́ешь; impf **умыва́ть**)
сов перех to wash; **умы́ться** (impf
умыва́ться) сов возв to wash

ун|ести́ (-есу́, -есёшь; pt -ёс, -есла́,
impf **уноси́ть**) сов перех to take away;
унести́сь (impf **уноси́ться**) сов возв to
speed off

универма́г (-а) м = **универса́льный
магази́н**

универса́льный прил universal;
(образование) all-round; (человек,
машина) versatile; **универса́льный
магази́н** department store

универса́м (-а) м supermarket
университе́т (-а) м university
унижа́|ть(ся) (-ю(сь)) несов от
уни́зить(ся)

униже́ни|е (-я) ср humiliation
уни́|зить (-жу, -зишь; impf **унижа́ть**)
сов перех to humiliate; **унижа́ть** (perf
уни́зить) себя́ to abase o.s.; **уни́зиться**
(impf **унижа́ться**) сов возв: **уни́зиться
(пе́ред** +instr) to abase o.s. (before)

уника́льный прил unique
унита́з (-а) м toilet
уничто́ж|ить (-у, -ишь; impf
уничтожа́ть) сов перех to destroy
ун|оси́ть(ся) (-ошу́(сь), -о́сишь(ся))
несов от **унести́(сь)**

уныва́|ть (-ю) несов (человек) to be
downcast или despondent

ун|я́ть (-уйму́, уймёшь; pt -л, -ла́, -ло,
impf **унима́ть**) сов перех (волнение) to
suppress

упа́д|ок (-ка) м decline
упак|ова́ть (-у́ю) сов от **пакова́ть**
упако́вк|а (-и) ж packing; (материал)
packaging

упасти́ сов перех: **упаси́ Бог** или **Бо́же**
или **Го́споди!** God forbid!

упа́|сть (-ду́, -дёшь) сов от **па́дать**
упере́ть (упру́, упрёшь; pt упёр,
упёрла, упёрло, impf **упира́ть**) сов
перех: **упере́ть что-н в** +acc (в стену итп)
to prop sth against; **упере́ться** (impf
упира́ться) сов возв: **упере́ться чем-н в**
+acc (в землю) to dig sth into;
(натолкнуться): **упере́ться в** +acc (в стену)
to come up against

упива́|ться (-юсь) несов возв (+instr:
перен: счастьем) to be intoxicated by
упира́|ть (-ю) несов от **упере́ть**;
упира́ться несов от **упере́ться** ▷ возв
(иметь причиной): **упира́ться в** +prp to be
down to

упла́т|а (-ы) ж payment

упл|ати́ть (-ачу́, -а́тишь) *сов от* **плати́ть**

уплы́|ть (-ву́, -вёшь; *impf* **уплыва́ть**) *сов* (*человек, рыба итп*) to swim away или off; (*корабль*) to sail away или off

уподо́б|ить (-лю, -ишь; *impf* **уподобля́ть**) *сов перех*: **уподо́бить что-н/кого-н** +*dat* to compare sth/sb to; **уподо́биться** (*impf* **уподобля́ться**) *сов возв*: **уподо́биться** +*dat* to become like

уполз|ти́ (-у́, -ёшь; *pt* -, -ла́) *сов* (*змея*) to slither away

уполномо́чи|е (-я) *ср*: **по уполномо́чию** +*gen* on behalf of

уполномо́ч|ить (-у, -ишь; *impf* **уполномо́чивать**) *сов перех*: **уполномо́чить кого-н** +*infin* to authorize sb to do

упомяну́|ть (-яну́, -я́нешь; *impf* **упомина́ть**) *сов (не)перех* (*назвать*): **упомяну́ть** +*acc или* (**о** +*prp*) to mention

упо́р (-а) *м* (*для ног*) rest; **в упо́р** (*стрелять*) point-blank; (*смотреть*) intently; **де́лать** (*perf* **сде́лать**) **упо́р на** +*prp* to put emphasis on

упо́рный *прил* persistent

употреби́тельный *прил* frequently used

употреб|и́ть (-лю́, -и́шь; *impf* **употребля́ть**) *сов перех* to use

употребле́ни|е (-я) *ср* (*слова*) usage; (*лекарства*) taking; (*алкоголя, пищи*) consumption

управле́ни|е (-я) *ср* (*делами*) administration; (*фирмой*) management; (*учреждение*) office; (*система приборов*) controls *мн*

управля́|ть (-ю) *несов* (+*instr*: *автомобилем*) to drive; (*судном*) to navigate; (*государством*) to govern; (*учреждением, фирмой*) to manage; (*оркестром*) to conduct

управля́ющ|ий (-его) *м* (*хозяйством*) manager; (*имением*) bailiff

упражне́ни|е (-я) *ср* exercise

упражня́|ть (-ю) *несов перех* to exercise; **упражня́ться** *несов возв* to practise

упраздн|и́ть (-ю́, -и́шь; *impf* **упраздня́ть**) *сов перех* to abolish

упра́шива|ть (-ю) *несов от* **упроси́ть**

упрека́|ть (-ю; *perf* **упрекну́ть**) *несов перех*: **упрека́ть кого-н** (**в** +*prp*) to reproach sb (for)

упр|оси́ть (-ошу́, -о́сишь; *impf* **упра́шивать**) *сов перех*: **упроси́ть кого-н** +*infin* to persuade sb to do

упро|сти́ть (-щу́, -сти́шь; *impf* **упроща́ть**) *сов перех* to simplify

упро́ч|ить (-у, -ишь; *impf* **упро́чивать**) *сов перех* to consolidate; **упро́читься** (*impf* **упро́чиваться**) *сов возв* (*положение, позиции*) to be consolidated

упроща́|ть (-ю) *несов от* **упрости́ть**

упря́ж|ка (-ки; *gen pl* -ек) *ж* team (of horses, dogs etc); (*упряжь*) harness

у́пряж|ь (-и) *ж по pl* harness

упря́мый *прил* obstinate, stubborn

упуска́|ть (-ю; *perf* **упусти́ть**) *несов перех* (*мяч*) to let go of; (*момент*) to miss; **упуска́ть** (*perf* **упусти́ть**) **из ви́ду** to overlook

упуще́ни|е (-я) *ср* error, mistake

ура́ *межд* hooray, hurrah

уравне́ни|е (-я) *ср* (*Мат*) equation

ура́внива|ть (-ю) *несов от* **уравня́ть**

уравнове́|сить (-шу, -сишь; *impf* **уравнове́шивать**) *сов перех* to balance; **уравнове́ситься** (*impf* **уравнове́шиваться**) *сов возв* (*силы*) to be counterbalanced

уравнове́шенный *прил* balanced

уравня́|ть (-ю; *impf* **ура́внивать**) *сов перех* to make equal

урага́н (-а) *м* hurricane

урага́нный *прил*: **урага́нный ве́тер** gale

ура́н (-а) *м* uranium

урегули́р|овать (-ую) *сов перех* to settle

у́рн|а (-ы) *ж* (*погребальная*) urn; (*для мусора*) bin; **избира́тельная у́рна** ballot box

у́ров|ень (-ня) *м* level; (*техники*) standard; (*зарплаты*) rate; **встре́ча на вы́сшем у́ровне** summit meeting; **у́ровень жи́зни** standard of living

уро́д (-а) *м* person with a deformity

урожа́|й (-я) *м* harvest

уро́к (-а) *м* lesson; (*задание*) task; (*обычно мн*: *домашняя работа*) homework; **де́лать** (*perf* **сде́лать**) **уро́ки** to do one's homework

ур|они́ть (-оню́, -о́нишь) *сов от* **роня́ть**

ус|ади́ть (-ажу́, -а́дишь; *impf* **уса́живать**) *сов перех* (*заставить делать*): **усади́ть кого-н за что-н/**+*infin* to sit sb down to sth/to do

уса́жива|ть (-ю) *несов от* **усади́ть**; **уса́живаться** *несов от* **усе́сться**

уса́тый *прил*: **уса́тый мужчи́на** man with a moustache (*Brit*) или mustache (*US*)

ус|е́сться (-я́дусь, -я́дешься; *pt* -е́лся, -е́лась, *impf* **уса́живаться**) *сов возв* to settle down; **уса́живаться** (*perf* **усе́сться**) **за** +*acc* (*за работу*) to sit down to work

уси́лива|ть (-ю) *несов от* **уси́лить**

уси́ли|е (-я) *ср* effort

уси́л|ить (-ю, -ишь; *impf* **уси́ливать**) *сов перех* to intensify; (*охрану*) to heighten; (*внимание*) to increase; **уси́литься** (*impf* **уси́ливаться**) *сов возв* (*ветер*) to get stronger; (*волнение*) to increase

ускользн|у́ть (-у́, -ёшь; *impf* **ускольза́ть**) *сов* to slip away

усло́ви|е (-я) *ср* condition; (*договора*) term; (*обычно мн*: *правила*) requirement; *см также* **усло́вия**

усло́в|иться (-люсь, -ишься; *impf*

усла́вливаться) *сов возв*: **усло́виться о** +*prp* (*договори́ться*) to agree on

усло́ви|я (-й) *мн* (*природные*) conditions *мн*; (*задачи*) factors *мн*; **жили́щные усло́вия** housing; **усло́вия труда́** working conditions; **в усло́виях** +*gen* in an atmosphere of; **по усло́виям догово́ра** on the terms of the agreement; **на льго́тных усло́виях** on special terms

усло́вный *прил* conditional; (*сигнал*) code

усложн|и́ть (-ю́, -и́шь; *impf* **усложня́ть**) *сов перех* to complicate; **усложни́ться** (*impf* **усложня́ться**) *возв* to get more complicated

услу́г|а (-и) *ж* (*одолжение*) favour (*Brit*), favor (*US*); (*обычно мн*: *обслуживание*) service; **к Ва́шим услу́гам!** at your service!

услы́ш|ать (-у, -ишь) *сов от* **слы́шать**

усма́трива|ть (-ю) *несов от* **усмотре́ть**

усмехн|у́ться (-у́сь, -ёшься; *impf* **усмеха́ться**) *сов возв* to smile slightly

усме́шк|а (-и) *ж* slight smile; **зла́я усме́шка** sneer

усмир|и́ть (-ю́, -и́шь; *impf* **усмиря́ть**) *сов перех* (*зверя*) to tame

усмотре́ни|е (-я) *ср* discretion

усм|отре́ть (-отрю́, -о́тришь; *impf* **усма́тривать**) *сов перех* (*счесть*): **усмотре́ть что-н в** +*prp* to see sth in

усн|у́ть (-у́, -ёшь) *сов* to fall asleep, go to sleep

усоверше́нствовани|е (-я) *ср* improvement

усомн|и́ться (-ю́сь, -и́шься) *сов возв*: **усомни́ться в** +*prp* to doubt

успева́емост|ь (-и) *ж* performance (*in studies*)

успе́|ть (-ю; *impf* **успева́ть**) *сов* (*о работе*) to manage; (*прийти вовремя*) to be *или* make it in time

успе́х (-а) *м* success; (*обычно мн*: *в спорте, в учёбе*) achievement; **как Ва́ши успе́хи?** how are you getting on?

успе́шный *прил* successful

успоко́|ить (-ю, -ишь; *impf* **успока́ивать**) *сов перех* to calm (down); **успоко́иться** (*impf* **успока́иваться**) *возв* (*человек*) to calm down

уста́в (-а) *м* (*партийный*) rules *мн*; (*воинский*) regulations *мн*; (*фирмы*) statute

уста|ва́ть (-ю́, -ёшь) *несов от* **уста́ть**

уста́в|ить (-лю, -ишь; *impf* **уставля́ть**) *сов перех* (*занять*): **уста́вить что-н чем-н** to cover sth with sth; (*разг: устремить*): **уста́вить что-н в** +*acc* to fix sth on; **уста́виться** (*impf* **уставля́ться**) *сов возв* (*разг*): **уста́виться на/в** +*acc* to stare at

уста́лост|ь (-и) *ж* tiredness, fatigue

уста́лый *прил* tired

устан|ови́ть (-овлю́, -о́вишь; *impf* **устана́вливать**) *сов перех* to establish;

(*сроки*) to set; (*прибор*) to install; **установи́ться** (*impf* **устана́вливаться**) *сов возв* to be established

устано́вк|а (-и) *ж* installation

устаре́|ть (-ю) *сов от* **старе́ть** ▷ (*impf* **устарева́ть**) *неперех* (*оборудование*) to become obsolete

уста́|ть (-ну, -нешь; *impf* **устава́ть**) *сов* to get tired

у́стн|ый *прил* (*экзамен*) oral; (*обещание, приказ*) verbal; **у́стная речь** spoken language

усто́йчив|ый *прил* stable; **усто́йчивое (сло́во)сочета́ние** set phrase

усто|я́ть (-ю́, -и́шь) *сов* (*не упасть*) to remain standing; (*в борьбе итп*) to stand one's ground; (*перед соблазном*) to resist

устра́ива|ть(ся) (-ю(сь)) *несов от* **устро́ить(ся)**

устран|и́ть (-ю́, -и́шь; *impf* **устраня́ть**) *сов перех* to remove

устрем|и́ть (-лю́, -и́шь; *impf* **устремля́ть**) *сов перех* to direct; **устреми́ться** (*impf* **устремля́ться**) *сов возв*: **устреми́ться на** +*acc* (*толпа*) to charge at

у́стриц|а (-ы) *ж* oyster

устро́|ить (-ю, -ишь; *impf* **устра́ивать**) *сов перех* to organize; (*подлеж: цена*) to suit; **э́то меня́ устро́ит** that suits me; **устро́иться** (*impf* **устра́иваться**) *сов возв* (*расположиться*) to settle down; (*прийти в порядок*) to work out; **устра́иваться** (*perf* **устро́иться**) **на рабо́ту** to get a job

устро́йств|о (-а) *ср* (*прибора*) construction; (*техническое*) device, mechanism

усту́п (-а) *м* foothold

уст|упи́ть (-уплю́, -у́пишь; *impf* **уступа́ть**) *сов перех*: **уступи́ть что-н кому́-н** to give sth up for sb; (*победу*) to concede sth to sb ▷ *неперех*: **уступи́ть кому́-н/чему́-н** (*силе, желанию*) to yield to sb/sth; **уступа́ть** (*perf* **уступи́ть**) **в** +*prp* (*в силе, в уме*) to be inferior in

усту́п|ка (-ки; *gen pl* **-ок**) *ж* conciliation; (*скидка*) discount; **пойти́** (*perf*) **на усту́пку** to compromise

у́сть|е (-я) *ср* (*реки*) mouth

ус|ы́ (-о́в) *мн* (*у человека*) moustache *ед* (*Brit*), mustache *ед* (*US*); (*у животных*) whiskers

усынов|и́ть (-лю́, -и́шь; *impf* **усыновля́ть**) *сов перех* to adopt (*son*)

усып|и́ть (-лю́, -и́шь; *impf* **усыпля́ть**) *сов перех* (*больного*) to anaesthetize (*Brit*), anesthetize (*US*); (*ребёнка*) to lull to sleep

ут|ащи́ть (-ащу́, -а́щишь; *impf* **ута́скивать**) *сов перех* (*унести*) to drag away *или* off

утверд|и́ть (-жу́, -ди́шь; *impf* **утвержда́ть**) *сов перех* (*закон*) to pass;

(*договор*) to ratify; (*план*) to approve; (*порядок*) to establish; **утверди́ться** (*impf* **утвержда́ться**) *сов возв* to be established

утвержда́|ть (-ю) *несов от* **утверди́ть** ▷ *перех* (*настаивать*) to maintain; **утвержда́ться** *несов от* **утверди́ться**

утвержде́ни|е (-я) *ср* (*см глаг*) passing; ratification; approval; establishment; (*мысль*) statement

утёс (-а) *м* cliff

уте́чк|а (-и) *ж* (*также перен*) leak; (*кадров*) turnover; **уте́чка мозго́в** brain drain

ут|е́чь (*3sg* -ечёт, *pt* -ёк, -екла́, -екло́, *impf* **утека́ть**) *сов* (*вода*) to leak out

уте́ш|ить (-у, -ишь; *impf* **утеша́ть**) *сов перех* to comfort, console

утихн|уть (-у; *impf* **утиха́ть**) *сов* (*спор*) to calm down; (*звук*) to die away; (*вьюга*) to die down

у́тк|а (-и; *gen pl* -ок) *ж* duck

уткн|у́ть (-у́, -ёшь) *сов перех* (*разг: лицо*) to bury; **уткну́ться** *сов возв* (*разг*): **уткну́ться в** +*acc* (*в книгу*) to bury one's nose in

утол|и́ть (-ю́, -и́шь; *impf* **утоля́ть**) *сов перех* to satisfy; (*жажду*) to quench

утоми́тельный *прил* tiring

утом|и́ть (-лю́, -и́шь; *impf* **утомля́ть**) *сов перех* to tire; **утоми́ться** (*impf* **утомля́ться**) *сов возв* to get tired

ут|ону́ть (-ону́, -о́нешь) *сов от* **тону́ть**

утопа́|ть (-ю) *несов* (*тонуть*) to drown

ут|опи́ть(ся) (-оплю́(сь), -о́пишь(ся)) *сов от* **топи́ть(ся)**

уточн|и́ть (-ю́, -и́шь; *impf* **уточня́ть**) *сов перех* to clarify

утра́т|а (-ы) *ж* loss

утра́|тить (-чу, -тишь; *impf* **утра́чивать**) *сов перех* (*потерять*) to lose; **утра́чивать** (*perf* **утра́тить**) **си́лу** (*документ*) to become invalid

у́тренний *прил* morning; (*событие*) this morning's

у́тренник (-а) *м* matinée; (*для детей*) children's party

у́тр|о (-а́; *nom pl* -а, *gen pl* -, *dat pl* -ам) *ср* morning; **до́брое у́тро!, с до́брым у́тром!** good morning!; **на у́тро** next morning; **под у́тро, к утру́** in the early hours of the morning

утро́б|а (-ы) *ж* (*матери*) womb

утро́|ить (-ю, -ишь) *сов перех* to treble, triple; **утро́иться** *сов возв* to treble, triple

у́тром *нареч* in the morning

утружда́|ть (-ю) *несов перех*: **утружда́ть кого́-н чем-н** to trouble sb with sth; **утружда́ться** *несов возв* to trouble o.s.

утю́г (-а́) *м* iron (*appliance*)

утю́ж|ить (-у, -ишь; *perf* **вы́утюжить** *или* **отутю́жить**) *несов перех* to iron

уф *межд*: уф! phew!

ух *межд*: ух! ooh!

ух|а́ (-и́) *ж* fish broth

уха́жива|ть (-ю) *несов*: **уха́живать за** +*instr* (*за больным*) to nurse; (*за садом*) to tend; (*за женщиной*) to court

ухв|ати́ть (-ачу́, -а́тишь; *impf* **ухва́тывать**) *сов перех* (*человека: за руку*) to get hold of; (*перен: идею, смысл*) to grasp; **ухвати́ться** (*impf* **ухва́тываться**) *сов возв*: **ухвати́ться за** +*acc* to grab hold of; (*за идею*) to jump at

у́х|о (-а; *nom pl* **у́ши**, *gen pl* **уше́й**) *ср* ear; (*у шапки*) flap

ухо́д (-а) *м* departure; (*из семьи*) desertion; (*со сцены*) exit; (*за больным, за ребёнком*) care; **ухо́д в отста́вку** resignation; **ухо́д на пе́нсию** retirement

ух|оди́ть (-ожу́, -о́дишь) *несов от* **уйти́**

уху́дш|ить (-у, -ишь; *impf* **ухудша́ть**) *сов перех* to make worse; **уху́дшиться** (*impf* **ухудша́ться**) *сов возв* to deteriorate

уцеле́|ть (-ю) *сов* to survive

уцен|и́ть (-ю́, -ишь; *impf* **уце́нивать**) *сов перех* to reduce (the price of)

уце́нк|а (-и; *gen pl* -ок) *ж* reduction

уча́ств|овать (-ую) *сов*: **уча́ствовать в** +*prp* to take part in

участко́в|ый *прил* local ▷ (-ого) *м* (*разг: также* **участко́вый инспе́ктор**) local policeman; (: *также* **участко́вый врач**) local GP *или* doctor

уча́стник (-а) *м* participant; (*экспедиции*) member

уча́ст|ок (-ка) *м* (*земли, кожи итп*) area; (*реки, фронта*) stretch; (*врачебный*) catchment area; (*земельный*) plot; (*строительный*) site; (*работы*) field; **садо́вый уча́сток** allotment

у́част|ь (-и) *ж* lot

учаща́|ть(ся) (-ю) *несов от* **участи́ть(ся)**

уча́щ|ийся (-егося) *м* (*школы*) pupil; (*училища*) student

учёб|а (-ы) *ж* studies *мн*

уче́бник (-а) *м* textbook

уче́бн|ый *прил* (*работа*) academic; (*фильм*) educational; (*бой*) mock; (*судно*) training; (*методы*) teaching; **уче́бная програ́мма** curriculum; **уче́бное заведе́ние** educational establishment; **уче́бный год** academic year

уче́ни|е (-я) *ср* (*теория*) teachings *мн*; *см также* **уче́ния**

учени́к (-а́) *м* (*школы*) pupil; (*училища*) student; (*мастера*) apprentice

учени́ческий *прил* (*тетради*) school

уче́ни|я (-й) *мн* exercises *мн*

учён|ый *прил* academic; (*труды*) scholarly; (*человек*) learned, scholarly ▷ (-ого) *м* academic, scholar; (*в области точных и естественных наук*) scientist

уч|е́сть (-ту́, -тёшь; *pt* -ёл, -ла́, *impf* **учи́тывать**) *сов перех* to take into account; **учти́те, что …** bear in mind that …

учёт (-а) *м* (*факторов*) consideration; (*военный, медицинский*) registration; (*затрат*) record; **брать** (*perf* **взять**) **на учёт** to register; **вести** (*impf*) **учёт** to keep a record

учётн|ый *прил*: **учётная ка́рточка** registration form

учи́лищ|е (-а) *ср* college

учи́тел|ь (-я; *nom pl* -я́) *м* teacher

учи́тельск|ая (-ой) *ж* staffroom

учи́тыва|ть (-ю) *несов от* **уче́сть**

уч|и́ть (-у́, -ишь; *perf* **вы́учить**) *несов перех* (*урок, роль*) to learn ▷ (*perf* **научи́ть** *или* **обучи́ть**); **учи́ть кого́-н чему́-н/**+*infin* to teach sb sth/to do; **учи́ться** *несов возв* (*в школе, в учи́лище*) to study ▷ (*perf* **вы́учиться** *или* **научи́ться**): **учи́ться чему́-н/**+*infin* to learn sth/to do

учреди́тел|ь (-я) *м* founder

учреди́тельн|ый *прил*: **учреди́тельное собра́ние** inaugural meeting

учрежда́ть (-жу́, -ди́шь; *impf* **учрежда́ть**) *сов перех* (*организацию*) to set up; (*контроль, порядок*) to introduce

учрежде́ни|е (-я) *ср* (*организация итп*) setting up; (*научное*) establishment; (*финансовое, общественное*) institution

уша́н|ка (-ки; *gen pl* -ок) *ж* cap with ear-flaps

ушёл *сов см* **уйти́**

у́ши *etc сущ см* **у́хо**

уши́б (-а) *м* bruise

ушиб|и́ть (-у́, -ёшь; *pt* -, -ла, *impf* **ушиба́ть**) *сов перех* to bang; **ушиби́ться** *сов возв* to bruise

уш|и́ть (-ью́, -ьёшь; *impf* **ушива́ть**) *сов перех* (*одежду*) to take in

у́шк|о (-а; *nom pl* -ки, *gen pl* -ек) *ср*, *уменьш от* **у́хо**; (*иголки*) eye

ушла́ *etc сов см* **уйти́**

ушн|о́й *прил* ear; **ушна́я боль** earache

уще́ль|е (-ья; *gen pl* -ий) *ср* gorge, ravine

ущем|и́ть (-лю́, -и́шь; *impf* **ущемля́ть**) *сов перех* (*палец*) to trap; (*права*) to limit

ущипн|у́ть (-у́, -ёшь) *сов перех* to nip, pinch

ую́тно *нареч* (*расположиться*) comfortably ▷ *как сказ*: **здесь ую́тно** it's cosy here; **мне здесь ую́тно** I feel comfortable here

ую́тный *прил* cosy

уязви́мый *прил* vulnerable

уязв|и́ть (-лю́, -и́шь) *сов перех* to wound, hurt

уясн|и́ть (-ю́, -и́шь; *impf* **уясня́ть**) *сов перех* (*значение*) to comprehend

фа́брик|а (-и) *ж* factory; (*ткацкая, бумажная*) mill

фабри́чный *прил* factory

фа́з|а (-ы) *ж* phase

фаза́н (-а) *м* pheasant

файл (-а) *м* (*Комп*) file

фа́кел (-а) *м* torch

факс (-а) *м* fax

факт (-а) *м* fact

факти́чески *нареч* actually, in fact

факти́ческий *прил* factual

фа́ктор (-а) *м* factor

факту́р|а (-ы) *ж* texture; (*Комм*) invoice

факультати́вный *прил* optional

факульте́т (-а) *м* faculty

фами́ли|я (-и) *ж* surname; **де́вичья фами́лия** maiden name

фан (-а) *м* fan

фана́тик (-а) *м* fanatic

фантази́р|овать (-ую) *несов* (*мечтать*) to dream; (*выдумывать*) to make up stories

фанта́ст (-а) *м* writer of fantasy; (*научный*) science-fiction writer

фанта́стик|а (-и) *ж*, *собир* (*Литература*) fantasy; **нау́чная фанта́стика** science fiction

фантасти́ческий *прил* fantastic

фа́р|а (-ы) *ж* (*Авт, Авиа*) light

фармаце́вт (-а) *м* chemist, pharmacist

фа́ртук (-а) *м* apron

фарши́р|ова́ть (-ую; *perf* **зафарширова́ть**) *несов перех* to stuff

фаса́д (-а) *м* (*передняя сторона*) facade, front; **за́дний фаса́д** back

фасо́л|ь (-и) *ж* (*растение*) bean plant ▷ *собир* (*семена*) beans *мн*

фасо́н (-а) *м* style

фат|а́ (-ы́) *ж* veil

ФБР *ср сокр* (= **Федера́льное бюро́ рассле́дований (США)**) FBI (= *Federal Bureau of Investigation*)

февра́л|ь (-я́) *м* February

● **23 ФЕВРАЛЯ́: ДЕНЬ ЗАЩИ́ТНИКА**
● **ОТЕ́ЧЕСТВА**

● This is an official celebration of the
● Russian army, though various sections of
● the armed forces have their own special
● holidays. Men of all ages and walks of life
● receive gifts and greetings, mainly from
● women.

федера́льный *прил* federal

федерати́вный *прил* federal

федера́ци|я (-и) *ж* federation

фе́льдшер (-а) *м* (*в поликли́нике*) ≈ practice nurse; **фе́льдшер ско́рой по́мощи** ≈ paramedic

фельето́н (-а) *м* satirical article

фемини́ст|ка (-ки; *gen pl* -ок) *ж* feminist

фен (-а) *м* hairdryer

ферз|ь (-я́) *м* (*Ша́хматы*) queen

фе́рм|а (-ы) *ж* farm

фе́рмер (-а) *м* farmer

фе́рмерск|ий *прил*: **фе́рмерское хозя́йство** farm

фестива́л|ь (-я) *м* festival

фетр (-а) *м* felt

фехтова́ни|е (-я) *ср* (*Спорт*) fencing

фе́|я (-и) *ж* fairy

фиа́л|ка (-ки; *gen pl* -ок) *ж* violet

фиа́ско *ср нескл* fiasco

фи́г|а (-и) *ж* (*Бот*) fig; (*разг*) fig (*gesture of refusal*); **иди́ на́ фиг!** get lost!; **ни фига́** nothing at all

фигу́р|а (-ы) *ж* figure; (*Ша́хматы*) (chess) piece

фигури́р|овать (-ую) *несов* to be present; (*и́мя, те́ма*) to feature

фигури́ст (-а) *м* figure skater

фи́зик (-а) *м* physicist

фи́зик|а (-и) *ж* physics

физиотерапи́|я (-и) *ж* physiotherapy

физи́ческ|ий *прил* physical; (*труд*) manual; **физи́ческая культу́ра** physical education

физкульту́р|а (-ы) *ж сокр* (= *физи́ческая культу́ра*) PE (= *physical education*)

фикси́р|овать (-ую); *perf* **зафикси́ровать** *несов перех* to fix; (*отмеча́ть*) to record

филармо́ни|я (-и) *ж* (*зал*) concert hall; (*организа́ция*) philharmonic society

филе́ *ср нескл* fillet

фило́лог (-а) *м* specialist in language and literature

филоло́ги|я (-и) *ж* language and literature

филологи́ческий *прил* philological; **филологи́ческий факульте́т** department of language and literature

фило́соф (-а) *м* philosopher

филосо́фи|я (-и) *ж* philosophy

фильм (-а) *м* film

фильтр (-а) *м* filter

фильтр|ова́ть (-ую; *perf* **профильтрова́ть**) *несов перех* to filter

фина́л (-а) *м* finale; (*Спорт*) final

фина́льный *прил* final

финанси́р|овать (-ую) *несов перех* to finance

фина́нсовый *прил* financial; (*год*) fiscal; (*отде́л, инспе́ктор*) finance

фина́нс|ы (-ов) *мн* finances; **Министе́рство фина́нсов** ≈ the Treasury (*Brit*), ≈ the Department of the Treasury (*US*)

фи́ник (-а) *м* (*плод*) date

фи́ниш (-а) *м* (*Спорт*) finish

финиши́р|овать (-ую) (*не*)*сов* to finish

Финля́нди|я (-и) *ж* Finland

финн (-а) *м* Finn

фи́нский *прил* Finnish; **фи́нский язы́к** Finnish; **фи́нский зали́в** Gulf of Finland

Ф.И.О. *сокр* (= *фами́лия, и́мя, о́тчество*) surname, first name, patronymic

фиоле́товый *прил* purple

фи́рм|а (-ы) *ж* firm

фи́рменный *прил* (*магази́н*) chain; (*разг: това́р*) quality; **фи́рменный знак** brand name

фи́ш|ка (-ки; *gen pl* -ек) *ж* counter, chip

флаг (-а) *м* flag

флако́н (-а) *м* bottle

фланг (-а) *м* flank

флане́л|ь (-и) *ж* flannel

фле́йт|а (-ы) *ж* flute

фле́ш|ка (-ки; *gen pl* -ек) *ж* (*разг*) USB stick; **флеш-накопи́тел|ь** (-я) *м* USB stick

фли́гел|ь (-я) *м* (*Архит*) wing

флома́стер (-а) *м* felt-tip (pen)

флот (-а) *м* (*Воен*) navy; (*Мор*) fleet; **возду́шный флот** air force

фойе́ *ср нескл* foyer

фо́кус (-а) *м* trick; (*Тех: перен*) focus

фольг|а́ (-и́) *ж* foil

фолькло́р (-а) *м* folklore

фон (-а) *м* background

фона́р|ь (-я́) *м* (*у́личный*) lamp; (*карма́нный*) torch

фо́ндов|ый *прил*: **фо́ндовая би́ржа** stock exchange

фоне́тик|а (-и) *ж* phonetics

фоноте́к|а (-и) *ж* music collection

фонта́н (-а) *м* fountain

форе́л|ь (-и) *ж* trout

фо́рм|а (-ы) *ж* form; (*оде́жда*) uniform; (*Тех*) mould (*Brit*), mold (*US*); (*Кули́н*) (cake) tin

форма́льност|ь (-и) *ж* formality

форма́т (-а) *м* format

форма́ци|я (-и) *ж* (*обще́ственная*) system

фо́рменн|ый *прил*: **фо́рменный бланк** standard form; **фо́рменная оде́жда** uniform

формирова́ни|е (-я) *ср* formation; **вое́нное формирова́ние** military unit

формир|ова́ть (-у́ю; *perf*

сформирова́ть) *несов перех* to form;
формирова́ться (*perf*
сформирова́ться) *несов возв* to form
фо́рмул|а (-ы) ж formula
формули́р|овать (-ую; *perf*
сформули́ровать) *несов перех* to
formulate
формулиро́в|ка (-ки; *gen pl* -ок) ж
(*определе́ние*) definition
фортепья́но *ср нескл* (grand) piano
фо́рточ|ка (-ки; *gen pl* -ек) ж hinged,
upper pane in window for ventilation
фо́рум (-а) м forum
фо́то-: фотоаппара́т (-а) м camera;
фото́граф (-а) м photographer;
фотографи́р|овать (-ую; *perf*
сфотографи́ровать) *несов перех* to
photograph; **фотографи́роваться** (*perf*
сфотографи́роваться) *несов возв* to
have one's photo(graph) taken;
фотогра́фи|я (-и) ж photography;
(*сни́мок*) photograph; **фотока́рточ|ка**
(-ки; *gen pl* -ек) ж photo
фра́з|а (-ы) ж phrase
фрак (-а) м tail coat, tails *мн*
фра́кци|я (-и) ж faction
Фра́нци|я (-и) ж France
францу́жен|ка (-ки) ж Frenchwoman
(*мн* Frenchwomen)
францу́з (-а) м Frenchman (*мн* Frenchmen)
францу́зский *прил* French;
францу́зский язы́к French
фрахт (-а) м freight
фрахт|ова́ть (-у́ю; *perf* **зафрахтова́ть)**
несов перех to charter
фрикаде́л|ька (-ьки; *gen pl* -ек) ж
meatball
фронт (-а; *nom pl* -ы́) м front
фронтови́к (-а́) м front line soldier;
(*ветера́н*) war veteran
фрукт (-а) м (*Бот*) fruit; **фрукто́вый**
прил fruit
ФСБ ж нескл сокр (= Федера́льная слу́жба
безопа́сности) Department of State
Security
ФСК ж нескл сокр (= Федера́льная слу́жба
контрразве́дки) counterespionage
intelligence service
фтор (-а) м fluorin(e)
фу *межд*: **фу!** ugh!
фунда́мент (-а) м (*Строит*) foundations
мн, base; (*перен: семьи, нау́ки*)
foundation, basis
фундамента́льный *прил* (*зда́ние*)
sound, solid; (*перен: зна́ния*) profound
функционе́р (-а) м official
функциони́р|овать (-ую) *несов* to
function
фу́нкци|я (-и) ж function
фунт (-а) м pound
фура́ж|ка (-ки; *gen pl* -ек) ж cap; (*Воен*)
forage cap
фурго́н (-а) м (*Авт*) van; (*пово́зка*)
(covered) wagon

фуру́нкул (-а) м boil
футбо́л (-а) м football (*Brit*), soccer;
футболи́ст (-а) м football (*Brit*) *или*
soccer player; **футбо́л|ка** (-ки; *gen pl*
-ок) ж T-shirt, tee shirt; **футбо́льный**
прил football (*Brit*), soccer; **футбо́льный
мяч** football
футля́р (-а) м case
фы́ркн|уть (-у) *сов* (*живо́тное*) to give a
snort

X

ха́кер (-а) м (*Комп*) hacker

хала́т (-а) м (*домашний*) dressing gown; (*врача*) gown

ха́мство (-а) *ср* rudeness

ха́ос (-а) м chaos

хаоти́чный *прил* chaotic

хара́ктер (-а) м character, nature; (*человека*) personality; **характеризова́ть** (-у́ю) *несов перех* to be typical of ⊳ (*perf* **охарактеризова́ть**) (*человека, ситуацию*) to characterize; **характери́стик**|**а** (-и) ж (*документ*) (character) reference; (*описание*) description; **характе́рный** *прил* (*свойственный*): **характе́рный (для** +*gen*) characteristic (of); (*случай*) typical

хвале́бный *прил* complimentary

хвал|**и́ть** (-ю́, -ишь; *perf* **похвали́ть**) *несов перех* to praise

хва́ста|ться (-юсь; *perf* **похва́statься**) *несов возв*: **хва́statься** (+*instr*) to boast (about)

хвата́|ть (-ю; *perf* **схвати́ть**) *несов перех* to grab (hold of), snatch; (*преступника*) to arrest ⊳ (*perf* **хвати́ть**) *безл* (+*gen*: *денег, времени*) to have enough; **мне хвата́ет де́нег на еду́** I've got enough to buy food; **э́того ещё не хвата́ло!** (*разг*) I'm not having this!; **не хвата́ет то́лько, что́бы он отказа́лся** (*разг*) now all we need is for him to refuse; **хвата́ться** (*perf* **схвати́ться**) *несов возв*: **хвата́ться за** +*acc* (*за ручку, за ору́жие*) to grab

хва|ти́ть (-чу́, -тишь) *сов от* **хвата́ть** ⊳ *безл* (*разг*): **хва́тит!** that's enough!; **с меня́ хва́тит!** I've had enough!

хва́т|ка (-ки; *gen pl* -ок) ж grip; **делова́я хва́тка** business acumen

хво́рост (-а) м *собир* firewood

хвост (-а́) м tail; (*поезда*) tail end; (*причёска*) ponytail

хво́стик (-а) м (*мыши, реди́ски*) tail; (*причёска*) pigtail

хек (-а) м whiting

хе́рес (-а) м sherry

хи́жин|**а** (-ы) ж hut

хи́лый *прил* sickly

хи́мик (-а) м chemist; **химика́т** (-а) м chemical; **хими́ческ**|**ий** *прил* chemical; (*факульте́т, кабине́т*) chemistry; **хими́ческая чи́стка** (*процесс*) dry-cleaning; (*пункт приёма*) dry-cleaner's

хи́ми|**я** (-и) ж chemistry

химчи́ст|**ка** (-ки; *gen pl* -ок) ж *сокр* = **хими́ческая чи́стка**

хиру́рг (-а) м surgeon; **хирурги́**|**я** (-и) ж surgery

хитр|**и́ть** (-ю́, -и́шь; *perf* **схитри́ть**) *несов* to act slyly; **хи́трост**|**ь** (-и) ж cunning; **хи́трый** *прил* cunning

хихи́ка|ть (-ю) *несов* (*разг*) to giggle

хи́щник (-а) м predator

хлам (-а) м *собир* junk

хлеб (-а) м bread; (*зерно*) grain

хле́бниц|**а** (-ы) ж bread basket; (*для хранения*) breadbin (*Brit*), breadbox (*US*)

хлеб|ну́ть (-у́, -ёшь) *сов перех* (*разг: чай итп*) to take a gulp of

хлебозаво́д (-а) м bakery

хлестн|**у́ть** (-у́, -ёшь) *сов перех* to whip; (*по щеке*) to slap

хло́па|ть (-ю) *несов перех* (*ладонью*) to slap ⊳ *неперех* (+*instr: дверью, крышкой*) to slam; (+*dat: арти́сту*) to clap

хло́пковый *прил* cotton

хло́пн|уть (-у) *сов перех* (*по спине́*) to slap ⊳ *неперех* (*в ладони*) to clap; (*дверь*) to slam shut

хло́п|ок (-ка) м cotton

хлоп|о́к (-ка́) м (*удар в ладоши*) clap

хлоп|ота́ть (-очу́, -о́чешь) *несов* (*по дому*) to busy o.s.; **хлопота́ть** (*impf*) о +*prp* (*о разреше́нии*) to request

хлопотли́вый *прил* (*человек*) busy; (*работа*) troublesome

хло́п|оты (-о́т; *dat pl* -о́там) мн (*по дому итп*) chores; (*прося чего-н*) efforts

хлопу́ш|ка (-ки; *gen pl* -ек) ж (*игру́шка*) (Christmas) cracker

хлопчатобума́жный *прил* cotton

хло́пь|я (-ев) мн (*снега, мыла*) flakes мн; **кукуру́зные хло́пья** cornflakes

хлор (-а) м chlorine; **хло́рк**|**а** (-и) ж (*разг*) bleaching powder; **хло́рн|ый** *прил*: **хло́рная и́звесть** bleaching powder

хлын|у́ть (*3sg* -ет) *сов* to flood

хмеле́|ть (-ю; *perf* **захмеле́ть**) *несов* to be drunk

хны́ка|ть (-ю) *несов* (*разг: плакать*) to whimper

хо́бби *ср нескл* hobby

хо́бот (-а) м (*слона*) trunk

ход (-а; *part gen* -у, *loc sg* -у́) м (*машины, поршня*) movement; (*событий, дела*) course; (*часов, двигателя*) run; (*Карты*) go; (*манёвр: также Шахматы*) move; (*возможность*) chance; (*вход*) entrance; **в хо́де** +*gen* in the course of; **ход мы́слей** train of thought; **идти́** (*perf* **пойти́**) **в ход** to come into use; **быть** (*impf*) **в (большо́м) ходу́** to be (very) popular; **на ходу́** (*есть, разгова́ривать*) on the move; (*пошути́ть*) in passing; **с хо́ду** straight off; **дава́ть** (*perf* **дать**) **ход де́лу** to set things in motion

хода́тайств|о (-a) *ср* petition; **ходатайств|овать** (-ую) *perf* **походатайствовать** *несов*: **ходатайствовать о чём-н/за кого-н** to petition for sth/on sb's behalf

хо|ди́ть (-жу́, -дишь) *несов* to walk; (*по магази́нам, в го́сти*) to go (*on foot*); (*по́езд, авто́бус итп*) to go; (*слу́хи*) to go round; (*часы́*) to work; (*носить*): **ходи́ть в** +*prp* (*в пальто́, в сапога́х итп*) to wear; (+*instr*: *ту́зом итп*) to play; (*конём, пешко́й итп*) to move

хожу́ *несов см* **ходи́ть**

хоздогово́р (-a) *м сокр* (= **хозя́йственный догово́р**) business deal (*between companies*)

хозрасчёт (-a) *м* (= **хозя́йственный расчёт**) system of management based on self-financing and self-governing principles

хозрасчётн|ый *прил*: **хозрасчётное предпри́ятие** self-financing, self-governing enterprise

хозя́|ин (-ина; *nom pl* -ева, *gen pl* -ев) *м* (*владе́лец*) owner; (*сдаю́щий жильё*) landlord; (*принима́ющий госте́й*) host; (*перен: распоряди́тель*) master; **хозя́|йка** (-йки; *gen pl* -ек) *ж* (*владе́лица*) owner; (*сдаю́щая жильё*) landlady; (*принима́ющая госте́й*) hostess; (*в до́ме*) housewife; **хозя́йнича|ть** (-ю) *несов* (*в до́ме, на ку́хне*) to be in charge; (*кома́ндовать*) to be bossy

хозя́йственн|ый *прил* (*де́ятельность*) economic; (*постро́йка, инвента́рь*) domestic; (*челове́к*) thrifty; **хозя́йственные това́ры** hardware; **хозя́йственный магази́н** hardware shop

хозя́йств|о (-a) *ср* (*Экон*) economy; (*фе́рмерское*) enterprise; (*предме́ты бы́та мн*; *дома́шнее*) household goods *мн*; (*дома́шнее*) housekeeping; **хозя́йств|овать** (-ую) *несов*: **хозя́йствовать на предприя́тии** to manage a business

хоккеи́ст (-a) *м* hockey player

хокке́|й (-я) *м* hockey

холл (-a) *м* (*теа́тра, гости́ницы*) lobby; (*в кварти́ре, в до́ме*) hall

холм (-á) *м* hill; **холми́стый** *прил* hilly

хо́лод (-a; *nom pl* -á) *м* cold; (*пого́да*) cold weather; **холода́|ть** (*3sg* -ет, *perf* **похолода́ть**) *несов безл* to turn cold; **холоде́|ть** (-ю; *perf* **похолоде́ть**) *несов* to get cold; (*от стра́ха*) to go cold

холоди́льник (-a) *м* (*дома́шний*) fridge; (*промы́шленный*) refrigerator

хо́лодно *нареч* coldly ▷ *как сказ* it's cold; **мне/ей хо́лодно** I'm/she's cold

холо́дный *прил* cold

холосто́й *прил* (*мужчи́на*) single, unmarried; (*вы́стрел, патро́н*) blank; **холостя́к** (-а́) *м* bachelor

холст (-а́) *м* canvas

хомя́к (-а́) *м* hamster

хор (-a) *м* choir; (*насме́шек*) chorus

Хорва́ти|я (-и) *ж* Croatia

хо́ром *нареч* in unison

хор|они́ть (-оню́, -о́нишь; *perf* **похорони́ть**) *несов перех* to bury

хоро́шенький *прил* (*лицо́*) cute

хороше́нько *нареч* (*разг*) properly

хороше́|ть (-ю; *perf* **похороше́ть**) *несов* to become more attractive

хоро́ш|ий *прил* good; **он хоро́ш (собо́ю)** he's good-looking; **всего́ хоро́шего!** all the best!

хорошо́ *нареч* well ▷ *как сказ* it's good; **мне хорошо́** I feel good ▷ *част, вводн сл* O.K., all right ▷ *ср нескл* (*Просве́щ*) ≈ good (*school mark*); **мне здесь хорошо́** I like it here; **ну, хорошо́!** right then!; **хорошо́ бы пое́сть/поспа́ть** (*разг*) I wouldn't mind a bite to eat/getting some sleep

хо|те́ть (см *Table 14*) *несов перех* +*infin* to want to do; **как хоти́те** (*как вам уго́дно*) as you wish; (*а всё-таки*) no matter what you say; **хо́чешь не хо́чешь** whether you like it or not; **хоте́ть** (*impf*) **есть/пить** to be hungry/thirsty; **хоте́ться** *несов безл*: **мне хо́чется пла́кать/есть** I feel like crying/something to eat

хот-спо́т (-a) *м* (wireless) hotspot

○ **КЛЮЧЕВОЕ СЛОВО**

хоть *союз* **1** (*несмотря́ на то, что*) (al) though; **хоть я и оби́жен, я помогу́ тебе́** although I am hurt, I will help you
2 (*до тако́й сте́пени, что*) even if; **не соглаша́ется, хоть до утра́ проси́** he won't agree, even if you ask all night; **хоть убе́й, не могу́ пойти́ на э́то** I couldn't do that to save my life; **хоть..., хоть...** either..., or...; **езжа́й хоть сего́дня, хоть че́рез ме́сяц** go either today, or in a month's time
▷ *част* **1** (*слу́жит для усиле́ния*) at least; **подвези́ его́ хоть до ста́нции** take him to the station at least; **пойми́ хоть ты** you of all people should understand
2 (*во фра́зах*): **хоть бы** at least; **хоть бы ты ему́ позвони́л** you could at least phone him!; **хоть бы зако́нчить сего́дня!** if only we could get finished today!; **хоть кто** anyone; **хоть како́й** any; **ему́ хоть бы что** it doesn't bother him; **хоть куда́!** (*разг*) excellent!; **хоть бы и так!** so what!

хотя́ *союз* although; **хотя́ и** even though; **хотя́ бы** at least

хо́хот (-а) *м* loud laughter

хохот|а́ть (-очу́, -о́чешь) *несов* to guffaw; **хохота́ть** (*impf*) (**над** +*instr*) to laugh (at)

хочу́ *etc несов см* **хоте́ть**

хра́брост|ь (-и) *ж* courage, bravery

хра́брый *прил* courageous, brave

храм (-а) *м* (*Рел*) temple

хране́ни|е (-я) *ср* (*денег*) keeping; **хране́ние ору́жия** possession of firearms; **ка́мера хране́ния** (*на вокза́ле*) left-luggage office (*Brit*) *или* checkroom (*US*)

храни́лищ|е (-а) *ср* store

хран|и́ть (-ю́, -и́шь) *несов перех* to keep; (*достоинство*) to protect; (*традиции*) to preserve; **храни́ться** *несов возв* to be kept

храп|е́ть (-лю́, -и́шь) *несов* to snore

хреб|е́т (-та́) *м* (*Анат*) spine; (*Гео*) ridge; **го́рный хребе́т** mountain range

хрен (-а) *м* horseradish

хрип|е́ть (-лю́, -и́шь) *несов* to wheeze

хри́плый *прил* (*голос*) hoarse

хри́пн|уть (-у; *perf* **охри́пнуть**) *несов* to become *или* grow hoarse

христиан|и́н (-ани́на; *nom pl* -а́не, *gen pl* -а́н) *м* Christian; **христиа́нский** *прил* Christian; **христиа́нств|о** (-а) *ср* Christianity

Христ|о́с (-а́) *м* Christ

хром (-а) *м* (*Хим*) chrome

хрома́|ть (-ю) *несов* to limp

хромо́й *прил* lame

хро́ник|а (-и) *ж* chronicle; (*в газеты*) news items

хрони́ческий *прил* chronic

хру́пкий *прил* fragile; (*печенье, кости*) brittle; (*перен: фигура*) delicate; (*: здоровье, организма*) frail

хруст (-а) *м* crunch

хруста́лик (-а) *м* (*Анат*) lens

хруста́л|ь (-я́) *м, собир* crystal

хруста́льный *прил* crystal

хру|сте́ть (-щу́, -сти́шь) *несов* to crunch; **хрустя́щий** *прил* crunchy, crisp

хрю́ка|ть (-ю) *несов* to grunt

худе́|ть (-ю) *несов* to grow thin; (*быть на диете*) to slim

худо́жественн|ый *прил* artistic; (*школа, выставка*) art; **худо́жественная литерату́ра** fiction; **худо́жественная самоде́ятельность** amateur performing arts; **худо́жественный сало́н** (*выставка*) art exhibition; (*магазин*) art gallery and craft shop; **худо́жественный фильм** feature film

худо́жник (-а) *м* artist

худо́й *прил* thin

ху́дший *превос прил* the worst

ху́же *сравн прил, нареч* worse

хулига́н (-а) *м* hooligan; **хулига́н|ить** (-ю, -ишь; *perf* **нахулига́нить**) *несов* to act like a hooligan

цара́па|ть (-ю; *perf* **оцара́пать**) *несов перех* (*руку*) to scratch; **цара́паться** (*perf* **оцара́паться**) *несов возв* to scratch

цара́пин|а (-ы) *ж* scratch

цари́ц|а (-ы) *ж* tsarina (*wife of tsar*)

ца́рский *прил* tsar's, royal; (*режим, правительство*) tsarist

ца́рств|о (-а) *ср* reign

ца́рств|овать (-ую) *несов* to reign

цар|ь (-я́) *м* tsar

цве|сти́ (-ту́, -тёшь) *несов* (*Бот*) to blossom, flower

цвет (-а; *nom pl* -а́) *м* (*окраска*) colour (*Brit*), color (*US*) ▷ (*prep sg* -ý) (*Бот*) blossom

цветно́й *прил* (*карандаш*) coloured (*Brit*), colored (*US*); (*фото, фильм*) colour (*Brit*), color (*US*)

цвет|о́к (-ка́; *nom pl* -ы́) *м* flower (*bloom*); (*комнатный*) plant

цвето́чный *прил* flower

це|ди́ть (-жу́, -дишь; *perf* **процеди́ть**) *несов перех* (*жидкость*) to strain; (*перен: слова*) to force out

це́др|а (-ы) *ж* (*dried*) peel *ед*

целе́бный *прил* medicinal; (*воздух*) healthy

целенапра́вленный *прил* single-minded; (*политика*) consistent

целико́м *нареч* (*без ограничений*) wholly, entirely; (*сварить*) whole

це́л|иться (-юсь, -ишься; *perf* **наце́литься**) *несов возв*: **це́литься в** +*acc* to (take) aim at

целлофа́н (-а) *м* cellophane

цел|ова́ть (-у́ю; *perf* **поцелова́ть**) *несов перех* to kiss; **целова́ться** (*perf* **поцелова́ться**) *несов возв* to kiss (each other)

це́л|ое (-ого) *ср* whole

це́лый *прил* whole, entire; (*неповреждённый*) intact; **в це́лом**

(*полностью*) as a whole; (*в общем*) on the whole

цел|ь (-и) ж (*при стрельбе*) target; (*перен*) aim, goal; **с це́лью** +*infin* with the object *или* aim of doing; **с це́лью** +*gen* for; **в це́лях** +*gen* for the purpose of

це́льный *прил* (*кусок*) solid; (*характер*) complete

цеме́нт (-а) м cement; **цементи́р|овать** (-ую) *perf* **зацементи́ровать**) *несов перех* to cement

цен|а́ (-ы́; *acc sg* -у, *dat sg* -е́, *nom pl* -ы) ж price; (*перен: человека*) value; **цено́ю** +*gen* at the expense of

цензу́р|а (-ы) ж censorship

цен|и́ть (-ю́, -ишь) *несов перех* (*вещь*) to value; (*помощь*) to appreciate

це́нность (-и) ж value; **це́нности** valuables; **материа́льные це́нности** commodities

це́нный *прил* valuable; (*письмо*) registered

це́нтнер (-а) м centner (*100kg*)

центр (-а) м centre (*Brit*), center (*US*); **в це́нтре внима́ния** in the limelight; **торго́вый центр** shopping centre (*Brit*) *или* mall (*US*)

центра́льный *прил* central

---

* **ЦЕНТРА́ЛЬНОЕ ОТОПЛЕ́НИЕ**
*
* The vast majority of Russians live in flats
* for which hot water and central heating
* are provided by huge communal boiler
* systems. Each city borough has a boiler
* system of its own. These systems
* distribute hot water for domestic use all
* year round and radiators are heated
* during the cold months. The heating is
* controlled centrally and individual home
* owners do not have any say over it. See
* also note at **отопи́тельный сезо́н**.

Центроба́нк м *сокр* = **Центра́льный банк (Росси́и)**

цепля́|ться (-юсь) *несов возв*: **цепля́ться за** +*acc* to cling *или* hang on to

цепно́й *прил* chain

цепо́ч|ка (-ки; *gen pl* -ек) ж (*тонкая цепь*) chain; (*машин, людей*) line

цеп|ь (-и; *loc sg* -и́) ж chain; (*Элек*) circuit; **го́рная цепь** mountain range

церемо́ни|я (-и) ж ceremony

церко́вный *прил* church

це́рк|овь (-ви; *instr sg* -овью, *nom pl* -ви, *gen pl* -ве́й) ж church

цех (-а; *loc sg* -у́, *nom pl* -а́) м (work)shop (*in factory*)

цивилиза́ци|я (-и) ж civilization; **цивилизо́ванный** *прил* civilized

цикл (-а) м cycle; (*лекций*) series

цикл|ева́ть (-ю́ю; *perf* **отциклева́ть**) *несов перех* to sand

цикло́н (-а) м cyclone

цили́ндр (-а) м cylinder; (*шляпа*) top hat

цини́чный *прил* cynical

цирк (-а) м circus

циркули́р|овать (*3sg* -ует) *несов* to circulate

ци́ркул|ь (-я) м (a pair of) compasses мн

циркуля́р (-а) м decree

цита́т|а (-ы) ж quote, quotation; **цити́р|овать** (-ую; *perf* **процити́ровать**) *несов перех* to quote

цифербла́т (-а) м dial; (*на часах*) face

ци́фр|а (-ы) ж number; (*арабские, римские*) numeral; (*обычно мн: расчёт*) figure

ЦРУ *ср сокр* (= **Центра́льное разве́дывательное управле́ние (США)**) CIA (= *Central Intelligence Agency*)

ЦСУ *ср сокр* = **Центра́льное статисти́ческое управле́ние**

ЦТ *ср сокр* = **Центра́льное телеви́дение**

цыга́н (-а; *nom pl* -е) м gypsy

цыпл|ёнок (-ёнка; *nom pl* -я́та, *gen pl* -я́т) м chick

цы́поч|ки (-ек) мн: **на цы́почках** on tiptoe

Ч

ча|ди́ть (-жу́, -ди́шь; *perf* **начади́ть**) *несов* to give off fumes

чаеви́|е (-ых) *мн* tip *ед*

ча|й (-я; *part gen* -ю, *nom pl* -и́) *м* tea; **зава́ривать** (*perf* **завари́ть**) **чай** to make tea; **дава́ть** (*perf* **дать**) **кому́-н на чай** to give sb a tip

ча́|йка (-йки; *gen pl* -ек) *ж* (sea)gull

ча́йник (-а) *м* kettle; (*для заварки*) teapot

ча́йн|ый *прил*: **ча́йная ло́жка** teaspoon

час (-а; *nom pl* -ы́) *м* hour; **академи́ческий час** (*Просвещ*) ≈ period; **кото́рый час?** what time is it?; **сейча́с 3 часа́ но́чи/дня** it's 3 o'clock in the morning/afternoon; *см также* **часы́**

часо́в|ня (-ни; *gen pl* -ен) *ж* chapel

часово́й *прил* (*лекция*) one-hour; (*механизм: ручных часов*) watch; (*: стенных часов*) clock ▷ (-о́го) *м* sentry; **часова́я стре́лка** the small hand; **часово́й по́яс** time zone

части́ц|а (-ы) *ж* (*стекла*) fragment; (*желания*) bit; (*количества*) fraction; (*Физ, Линг*) particle

части́чный *прил* partial

ча́стник (-а) *м* (*собственник*) (private) owner

ча́стност|ь (-и) *ж* (*деталь*) detail; (*подробность*) particular; **в ча́стности** for instance

ча́стн|ый *прил* private; (*случай*) isolated; **ча́стная со́бственность** private property

ча́сто *нареч* (*много раз*) often; (*тесно*) close together

част|ота́ (-оты́; *nom pl* -о́ты) *ж* (*Тех*) frequency

ча́стый *прил* frequent

част|ь (-и; *gen pl* -е́й) *ж* part; (*отдел*) department; (*симфонии*) movement; (*Воен*) unit; **часть ре́чи** part of speech; **часть све́та** continent

час|ы́ (-о́в) *мн* (*карманные*) watch *ед*; (*стенные*) clock *ед*

чат (-а) *м* (*Интернет*) chat; **ча́т-ко́мнат|а** (-ы) *ж* chat room

ча́ш|ка (-ки; *gen pl* -ек) *ж* cup

ча́ще *сравн прил от* **ча́стый** ▷ *сравн нареч от* **ча́сто**

чего́ *мест см* **что**

чей (**чьего́**; *см Table 5*; *f* **чья**, *nt* **чьё**, *pl* **чьи**) *мест* whose; **чей бы то ни́ был** no matter whose it is

че́й-либо (**чьего́-либо**; *как* **чей**; *см Table 5*; *f* **чья́-либо**, *nt* **чьё-либо**, *pl* **чьи́-либо**) *мест* = **че́й-нибудь**

че́й-нибудь (**чьего́-нибудь**; *как* **чей**; *см Table 5*; *f* **чья́-нибудь**, *nt* **чьё-нибудь**, *pl* **чьи́-нибудь**) *мест* anyone's

че́й-то (**чьего́-то**; *как* **чей**; *см Table 5*; *f* **чья́-то**, *nt* **чьё-то**, *pl* **чьи́-то**) *мест* someone's, somebody's

чек (-а) *м* (*банковский*) cheque (*Brit*), check (*US*); (*товарный, кассовый*) receipt

че́ковый *прил* cheque (*Brit*), check (*US*)

чёл|ка (-ки; *gen pl* -ок) *ж* (*человека*) fringe (*Brit*), bangs *мн* (*US*)

челн|о́к (-ка́) *м* shuttle; (*торговец*) small trader buying goods abroad and selling them on local markets

челове́к (-а; *nom pl* **лю́ди**, *gen pl* **люде́й**) *м* human (being); (*некто, личность*) person (*мн* people)

челове́ческий *прил* human; (*человечный*) humane

челове́честв|о (-а) *ср* humanity, mankind

челове́чный *прил* humane

че́люст|ь (-и) *ж* (*Анат*) jaw

чем *мест см* **что** ▷ *союз* than; (*разг*: *вместо того чтобы*) instead of; **чем бо́льше/ра́ньше, тем лу́чше** the bigger/earlier, the better

чемода́н (-а) *м* suitcase

чемпио́н (-а) *м* champion; **чемпиона́т** (-а) *м* championship

чему́ *мест см* **что**

чепух|а́ (-и́) *ж* nonsense

че́рв|и (-е́й) *мн* (*Карты*) hearts *мн*

черв|ь (-я́; *nom pl* -и, *gen pl* -е́й) *м* worm; (*личинка*) maggot

червя́к (-а́) *м* worm

черда́к (-а́) *м* attic, loft

черед|ова́ть (-у́ю) *несов перех*: **чередова́ть что-н с** +*instr* to alternate sth with

⦿ **КЛЮЧЕВОЕ СЛОВО**

че́рез *предл* +*acc* **1** (*поперёк*) across, over; **переходи́ть** (*perf* **перейти́**) **че́рез доро́гу** to cross the road

2 (*сквозь*) through; **че́рез окно́** through the window

3 (*поверх*) over; **че́рез забо́р** over the fence

4 (*спустя*) in; **чéрез час** in an hour('s time)

5 (*минуя какое-н пространство*): **чéрез три квартáла — стáнция** the station is three blocks away

6 (*при помощи*) via; **он передáл письмó чéрез знакóмого** he sent the letter via a friend

7 (*при повторении действия*) every; **принимáйте таблéтки чéрез кáждый час** take the tablets every hour

чéреп (-а) м skull

черепáх|а (-и) ж tortoise; (*морская*) turtle

черепúц|а (-ы) ж собир tiles мн

черéш|ня (-ни; *gen pl* -ен) ж cherry

черне́|ть (-ю; *perf* **почерне́ть**) несов (*становиться чёрным*) to turn black

чернúл|а (-) мн ink ед

черновúк (-á) м draft

чёрный (-ен, -нá, -нó) прил black; (*ход*) back

чéрпа|ть (-ю) несов перех (*жидкость*) to ladle

черстве́|ть (-ю; *perf* **зачерстве́ть**) несов (*хлеб*) to go stale

чёрствый прил (*хлеб*) stale; (*человек*) callous

чёрт (-а; *nom pl* **чéрти**, *gen pl* **чертéй**) м (*дьявол*) devil; **идú к чёрту!** (*разг*) go to hell!

черт|á (-ы́) ж (*линия*) line; (*признак*) trait; **в óбщих чертáх** in general terms; *см также* **черты́**

чертёж (-á) м draft

чер|тúть (-чý, -тишь; *perf* **начертúть**) несов перех (*линию*) to draw; (*график*) to draw up

черт|ы́ (-) мн (*также* **черты́ лицá**) features

че|сáть (-шý, -шешь; *perf* **почесáть**) несов перех (*спину*) to scratch; **чесáться** (*perf* **почесáться**) несов возв to scratch o.s.; (*no perf: зудеть*) to itch

чеснóк (-á) м garlic

чéстно нареч (*сказать*) honestly; (*решить*) fairly ▷ *как сказ*: **так бýдет чéстно** that'll be fair

чéстност|ь (-и) ж honesty; **чéстный** прил honest; **чéстное слóво** honestly

честолюбúвый прил ambitious

чест|ь (-и) ж honour (*Brit*), honor (*US*) ▷ (*loc sg* -ú) (*почёт*) glory; **к чéсти когó-н** to sb's credit; **отдавáть** (*perf* **отдáть**) **комý-н честь** to salute sb

четвéрг (-á) м Thursday

четвере́н|ьки (-ек) мн: **на четвере́ньках** on all fours

четвёр|ка (-ки; *gen pl* -ок) ж (*цифра, карта*) four; (*Просвещ*) ≈ B (*school mark*)

чéтвер|о (см *Table 30a*; -ы́х) чис four

четвёртый чис fourth; **сейчáс четвёртый час** it's after three

чéтверт|ь (-и) ж quarter; (*Просвещ*) term

четвертьфинáл (-а) м (*Спорт*) quarter final

чёткий прил clear; (*движения*) precise

чётный прил (*число*) even

четы́р|е (-ёх; *instr sg* **-ьмя́**; см *Table 24*) чис (*цифра, число*) four; (*Просвещ*) ≈ B (*school mark*)

четы́р|еста (-ёхсóт; см *Table 28*) чис four hundred

четы́рнадцатый чис fourteenth

четы́рнадцат|ь (-и; *как* **пять**; см *Table 26*) чис fourteen

Чéхи|я (-и) ж the Czech Republic

чех|óл (-лá) м (*для мебели*) cover; (*для гитары, для оружия*) case

чешу|я́ (-и́) ж собир scales мн

чин (-а; *nom pl* -ы́) м rank

чин|úть (-ю́, -ишь; *perf* **починúть**) несов перех to mend, repair ▷ (*perf* **очинúть**) (*карандаш*) to sharpen

чинóвник (-а) м (*служащий*) official

чúпс|ы (-ов) мн crisps

чúсленност|ь (-и) ж (*армии*) numbers мн; (*учащихся*) number; **чúсленность населéния** population

чис|лó (-лá; *nom pl* -ла, *gen pl* -ел) ср number; (*день месяца*) date; **быть** (*impf*) **в числé** +*gen* to be among(st)

чú|стить (-щу, -стишь; *perf* **вы́чистить** *или* **почúстить**) несов перех to clean; (*зубы*) to brush, clean ▷ (*perf* **почúстить**) (*яблоко, картошку*) to peel; (*рыбу*) to scale

чúсто нареч (*только*) purely; (*убранный, сделанный*) neatly ▷ *как сказ*: **в дóме чúсто** the house is clean

чистовúк (-á) м fair copy

чистосердéчный прил sincere

чистот|á (-ы́) ж purity; **у негó в дóме всегдá чистотá** his house is always clean

чúстый прил (*одежда, комната*) clean; (*совесть, небо*) clear; (*золото, спирт, случайность*) pure; (*прибыль, вес*) net; **экологúчески чúстый** organic

читáльный прил: **читáльный зал** reading room

читáтел|ь (-я) м reader

читá|ть (-ю; *perf* **прочéсть** *или* **прочитáть**) несов перех to read; (*лекцию*) to give; (*в Твиттере*) to follow

чихá|ть (-ю; *perf* **чихнýть**) несов to sneeze

член (-а) м member; (*обычно мн: конечности*) limb; **половóй член** penis; **член предложéния** part of a sentence

чó|каться (-юсь; *perf* **чóкнуться**) несов возв to clink glasses (*during toast*)

черевáтый прил +*instr* fraught with

чрезвычáйно нареч extremely

чрезвычáйный прил (*исключительный*) extraordinary; (*экстренный*) emergency; **чрезвычáйное положéние** state of emergency

чрезмéрный прил excessive

чтéни|е (-я) ср reading

⊙ КЛЮЧЕВОЕ СЛОВО

что (**чего́**; см *Table 7*) *мест*
1 (*вопросительное*) what; **что ты сказа́л?** what did you say?; **что Вы говори́те!** you don't say!
2 (*относительное*) which; **она́ не поздоро́валась, что мне бы́ло неприя́тно** she did not say hello, which was unpleasant for me; **что ни говори́ ...** whatever you say ...
3 (*столько сколько*): **она́ закрича́ла что бы́ло сил** she shouted with all her might
4 (*разг: что-нибудь*) anything; **я е́сли что случи́тся** if anything happens, should anything happen; **в слу́чае чего́** if anything happens; **чуть что — сра́зу скажи́ мне** get in touch at the slightest thing
▷ *нареч* (*почему*) why; **что ты грусти́шь?** why are you sad?
▷ *союз* **1** (*при сообщении, высказывании*): **я зна́ю, что на́до де́лать** I know what must be done; **я зна́ю, что он прие́дет** I know that he will come
2 (*во фразах*): **а что?** (*разг*) why (do you ask)?; **к чему́** (*зачем*) why; **не за что!** not at all! (*Brit*), you're welcome! (*US*); **ни за что!** (*разг*) no way!; **ни за что ни про что** (*разг*) for no (good) reason at all; **что ты!** (*при возражении*) what!; **я здесь ни при чём** it has nothing to do with me; **что к чему́** (*разг*) what's what

чтоб *союз* = **чтобы**

⊙ КЛЮЧЕВОЕ СЛОВО

что́бы *союз* (+*infin*: *выражает цель*) in order *или* so as to do
▷ *союз* +*pt* **1** (*выражает цель*) so that
2 (*выражает желательность*): **я хочу́, чтобы она́ пришла́** I want her to come
3 (*выражает возможность*): **не мо́жет быть, чтобы он так поступи́л** it can't be possible that he could have acted like that
▷ *част* **1** (*выражает пожелание*): **чтобы она́ заболе́ла!** I hope she gets ill!
2 (*выражает требование*): **чтобы я его́ здесь бо́льше не ви́дел!** I hope (that) I never see him here again!

что́-либо (**чего́-либо**; *как что*; см *Table 7*) *мест* = **что́-нибудь**
что́-нибудь (**чего́-нибудь**; *как что*; см *Table 7*) *мест* (*в утверждении*) something; (*в вопросе*) anything
что́-то (**чего́-то**; *как что*; см *Table 7*) *мест* something; (*приблизительно*) something like ▷ *нареч* (*разг: почему-то*) somehow
чувстви́тельный *прил* sensitive
чу́вств|о (**-а**) *ср* feeling; (+*gen*: *юмора, долга*) sense of
чу́вств|овать (**-ую**; *perf* **почу́вствовать**) *несов перех* to feel;

(*присутствие, опасность*) to sense; **чу́вствовать** (*impf*) **себя́ хорошо́/нело́вко** to feel good/awkward; **чу́вствоваться** *несов возв* (*жара, усталость*) to be felt
чугу́н (**-а́**) *м* cast iron
чуда́к (**-а́**) *м* eccentric
чудеса́ *итп сущ см* **чу́до**
чуде́сный *прил* (*очень хороший*) marvellous (*Brit*), marvelous (*US*), wonderful; (*необычный*) miraculous
чу́д|о (**-а**; *nom pl* **-еса́**, *gen pl* **-е́с**, *dat pl* **-еса́м**) *ср* miracle
чудо́вищ|е (**-а**) *ср* monster
чудо́м *нареч* by a miracle
чу́ждый *прил* alien
чужо́й *прил* (*вещь*) someone *или* somebody else's; (*речь, обычай*) foreign; (*человек*) strange
чул|о́к (**-ка́**; *gen pl* **-о́к**, *dat pl* **-ка́м**) *м* (*обычно мн*) stocking
чум|а́ (**-ы́**) *ж* plague
чу́точку *нареч* (*разг*) a tiny bit
чуть *нареч* (*разг: едва*) hardly; (*немного*) a little ▷ *союз* (*как только*) as soon as; **чуть (бы́ло) не** almost, nearly; **чуть что** (*разг*) at the slightest thing
чуть-чуть *нареч* (*разг*) a little
чу́чел|о (**-а**) *ср* scarecrow
чушь (**-и**) *ж* (*разг*) rubbish (*Brit*), garbage (*US*), nonsense
чу́|ять (**-ю**) *несов перех* (*собака*) to scent; (*предвидеть*) to sense
чьё (**чьего́**) *мест см* **чей**
чьи (**чьих**) *мест см* **чей**
чья (**чьей**) *мест см* **чей**

шаг (-а; *nom pl* -**и**) *м* step
шага́ть (-ю) *несов* to march
шагну́ть (-у́, -ёшь) *сов* to step, take a step
ша́й|ка (-йки; *gen pl* -ек) *ж* gang
шал|ь (-и) *ж* shawl
шампа́нск|ое (-ого) *ср* champagne
шампиньо́н (-а) *м* (*Бот*) (field) mushroom
шампу́н|ь (-я) *м* shampoo
шанс (-а) *м* chance
шанта́ж (-а́) *м* blackmail
шантажи́р|овать (-ую) *несов перех* to blackmail
ша́п|ка (-ки; *gen pl* -ок) *ж* hat
шар (-а; *nom pl* -ы́) *м* (*Геом*) sphere ▷ (*gen sg* -а́) (*бильярдный итп*) ball; **возду́шный шар** balloon
ша́рик (-а) *м* (*детский*) balloon
ша́риков|ый *прил*: **ша́риковая ру́чка** ballpoint pen
ша́рка|ть (-ю) *несов* +*instr* to shuffle
шарф (-а) *м* scarf
шата́|ть (-ю) *несов перех* (*раскачивать*) to rock; **шата́ться** *несов возв* (*зуб*) to be loose *или* wobbly; (*стол*) to be wobbly; (*от ветра*) to shake; (*от усталости*) to reel; (*по улицам*) to hang around
шах (-а) *м* (*в шахматах*) check
ша́хматный *прил* chess
ша́хмат|ы (-) *мн* (*игра*) chess *ед*; (*фигуры*) chessmen
ша́хт|а (-ы) *ж* mine; (*лифта*) shaft
шахтёр (-а) *м* miner
ша́ш|ки (-ек) *мн* (*игра*) draughts *ед* (*Brit*), checkers *ед* (*US*)
шашлы́к (-а́) *м* shashlik, kebab
шва́бр|а (-ы) *ж* mop
шварт|ова́ть (-у́ю; *perf* **пришвартова́ть**) *несов перех* to moor
швед (-а) *м* Swede
шве́дский *прил* Swedish

шве́йный *прил* sewing
швейца́р|ец (-ца) *м* Swiss
Швейца́ри|я (-и) *ж* Switzerland
швейца́рский *прил* Swiss
Шве́ци|я (-и) *ж* Sweden
шевел|и́ть (-ю́, -и́шь; *perf* **пошевели́ть**) *несов перех* (*сено*) to turn over; (*подлеж*: *ветер*) to stir ▷ *неперех* (+*instr*: *пальцами, губами*) to move; **шевели́ться** (*perf* **пошевели́ться**) *несов возв* to stir
шеде́вр (-а) *м* masterpiece
шёл *несов см* **идти́**
шёлк (-а; *nom pl* -а́) *м* silk
шёлковый *прил* silk
шелуш|и́ться (-у́сь, -и́шься) *несов возв* to peel
шепн|у́ть (-у́, -ёшь) *сов перех* to whisper
шёпот (-а) *м* whisper
шёпотом *нареч* in a whisper
шеп|та́ть (-чу́, -чешь) *несов перех* to whisper; **шепта́ться** *несов возв* to whisper to each other
шере́нг|а (-и; *солдат*) rank
шерст|ь (-и) *ж* (*животного*) hair; (*пряжа, ткань*) wool
шерстяно́й *прил* (*пряжа, ткань*) woollen (*Brit*), woolen (*US*)
шерша́вый *прил* rough
шесть́ро (-ы́х; *см* Table 30b) *чис* six
шестидеся́тый *чис* sixtieth
шестна́дцатый *чис* sixteenth
шестна́дцат|ь (-и; *как пять*; *см* Table 26) *чис* sixteen
шесто́й *чис* sixth
шест|ь (-и́; *как пять*; *см* Table 26) *чис* six
шест|ьдеся́т (-и́десяти; *как пятьдеся́т*; *см* Table 26) *чис* sixty
шест|ьсо́т (-исо́т; *как пятьсо́т*; *см* Table 28) *чис* six hundred
шеф (-а) *м* (*полиции*) chief; (*разг*: *начальник*) boss; (*благотворитель: лицо*) patron; (*организация*) sponsor
ше́фств|о (-а) *ср*: **ше́фство над** +*instr* (*лица*) patronage of; (*организация*) sponsorship of
ше́фств|овать (-ую) *несов*: **ше́фствовать над** +*instr* (*лицо*) to be patron of; (*организация*) to sponsor
ше́|я (-и) *ж* (*Анат*) neck
ши́ворот (-а) *м* (*разг*): **за ши́ворот** by the collar
шизофре́ник (-а) *м* schizophrenic
шика́рный *прил* (*разг*) glamorous, chic
шимпанзе́ *м нескл* chimpanzee
шин|а (-ы) *ж* (*Авт*) tyre (*Brit*), tire (*US*)
шине́л|ь (-и) *ж* overcoat
шинк|ова́ть (-у́ю; *perf* **нашинкова́ть**) *несов перех* (*овощи*) to shred
шип (-а́) *м* (*растения*) thorn; (*на колесе*) stud; (*на ботинке*) spike
шипу́чий *прил* fizzy
ши́ре *сравн прил от* **широ́кий** ▷ *сравн нареч от* **широко́**

ширин|а́ (**-ы́**) *ж* width; **доро́жка метр ширино́й** *или* **в ширину́** a path a metre (Brit) *или* meter (US) wide

ши́рм|а (**-ы**) *ж* screen

широ́к|ий *прил* wide; (степи, планы) extensive; (перен: общественность) general; (: смысл) broad; (: натура, жест) generous; **това́ры широ́кого потребле́ния** (Экон) consumer goods

широко́ *нареч* (раскинуться) widely; (улыбаться) broadly

широкополо́сный *прил* broadband; **широкополо́сная связь** broadband connection; **широкополо́сный до́ступ** broadband access

широкоэкра́нный *прил* (фильм) widescreen

шир|ота́ (**-оты́**) *ж* breadth ▷ (*nom pl* **-о́ты**) (Гео) latitude

ширпотре́б (**-а**) *м сокр* = **широ́кое потребле́ние** (разг: о товарах) consumer goods *мн*; (: о плохом товаре) shoddy goods *мн*

шить (**шью, шьёшь**; *perf* **сшить**) *несов перех* (платье итп) to sew

ши́фер (**-а**) *м* slate

шиш (**-а́**) *м* (разг) gesture of refusal; (**ни**) **шиша́** (разг: ничего) nothing at all

ши́шк|а (**-ки**; *gen pl* **-ек**) *ж* (Бот) cone; (на лбу) bump, lump

шкал|а́ (**-ы́**; *nom pl* **-ы**) *ж* scale

шкаф (**-а**; *loc sg* **-у́**, *nom pl* **-ы́**) *м* (для одежды) wardrobe; (для посуды) cupboard; **кни́жный шкаф** bookcase

шки́пер (**-а**) *м* (Мор) skipper

шко́л|а (**-ы**) *ж* school; (милиции) academy; **сре́дняя шко́ла** secondary (Brit) *или* high (US) school

шко́л|а-интерна́т (**-ы, -а**) *ж* boarding school

шко́льник (**-а**) *м* schoolboy; **шко́льниц|а** (**-ы**) *ж* schoolgirl

шко́льный *прил* (здание) school

шку́р|а (**-ы**) *ж* (животного) fur; (убитого животного) skin; (: обработанная) hide

шла *несов см* **идти́**

шлагба́ум (**-а**) *м* barrier

шланг (**-а**) *м* hose

шлем (**-а**) *м* helmet

шли *несов см* **идти́**

шлиф|ова́ть (**-у́ю**; *perf* **отшлифова́ть**) *несов перех* (Тех) to grind

шло *несов см* **идти́**

шлю́п|ка (**-ки**; *gen pl* **-ок**) *ж* (Мор) dinghy; **спаса́тельная шлю́пка** lifeboat

шля́п|а (**-ы**) *ж* hat

шля́п|ка (**-ки**; *gen pl* **-ок**) *ж* hat; (гвоздя) head; (гриба) cap

шмель (**-я́**) *м* bumblebee

шмы́га|ть (**-ю**) *несов*: **шмы́гать но́сом** to sniff

шнур|ова́ть (**-у́ю**; *perf* **зашнурова́ть**) *несов перех* (ботинки) to lace up

шнур|о́к (**-ка́**) *м* (ботинка) lace

шок (**-а**) *м* (Мед: перен) shock

шоки́р|овать (**-ую**) (не)сов перех to shock

шокола́д (**-а**) *м* chocolate

шокола́дный *прил* chocolate

шо́рт|ы (**-**) *мн* shorts

шоссе́ *ср нескл* highway

шотла́нд|ец (**-ца**) *м* Scotsman (*мн* Scotsmen)

Шотла́нди|я (**-и**) *ж* Scotland

шотла́ндский *прил* Scottish, Scots

шо́у *ср нескл* (также перен) show

шофёр (**-а**) *м* driver

шпа́г|а (**-и**) *ж* sword

шпага́т (**-а**) *м* (бечёвка) string

шпакл|ева́ть (**-ю́ю**; *perf* **зашпаклева́ть**) *несов перех* to fill

шпа́л|а (**-ы**) *ж* sleeper (Rail)

шпиль (**-я**) *м* spire

шпи́ль|ка (**-ьки**; *gen pl* **-ек**) *ж* (для волос) hairpin; (каблук) stiletto (heel)

шпина́т (**-а**) *м* spinach

шпингале́т (**-а**) *м* (на окне) catch

шпио́н (**-а**) *м* spy

шпиона́ж (**-а**) *м* espionage

шпио́н|ить (**-ю, -ишь**) *несов* (разг) to spy

шприц (**-а**) *м* syringe

шпро́т|ы (**-ов**) *мн* sprats

шрам (**-а**) *м* (на теле) scar

шрифт (**-а**; *nom pl* **-ы́**) *м* type

штаб (**-а**) *м* headquarters *мн*

штамп (**-а**) *м* (печать) stamp

штамп|ова́ть (**-у́ю**; *perf* **проштампова́ть**) *несов перех* (документы) to stamp ▷ (*perf* **отштампова́ть**) (детали) to punch, press

шта́нг|а (**-и**) *ж* (Спорт: в тяжёлой атлетике) weight; (: ворот) post

штан|ы́ (**-о́в**) *мн* trousers

штат (**-а**) *м* (государства) state; (работники) staff

шта́тный *прил* (сотрудник) permanent

шта́тск|ий *прил* (одежда) civilian ▷ (**-ого**) *м* civilian

што́псель|ь (**-я**) *м* (Элек) plug

што́пор (**-а**) *м* corkscrew

шторм (**-а**) *м* gale

штормов|о́й *прил* stormy; **штормово́е предупрежде́ние** storm warning

штраф (**-а**) *м* (денежный) fine; (Спорт) punishment; **штрафн|о́й** *прил* penal ▷ (**-о́го**) *м* (Спорт: также **штрафно́й уда́р**) penalty (kick)

штраф|ова́ть (**-у́ю**; *perf* **оштрафова́ть**) *несов перех* to fine; (Спорт) to penalize

штрих (**-а́**) *м* (черта) stroke

штрихово́й *прил*: **штрихово́й код** bar code

шту́к|а (**-и**) *ж* (предмет) item

штукату́р|ить (**-ю, -ишь**; *perf*

отштукату́рить или **оштукату́рить)**
несов перех to plaster
штукату́рк|а (**-и**) ж plaster
штурм (**-а**) м (Воен) storm
штурм|ова́ть (**-у́ю**) несов перех (Воен)
to storm
шу́б|а (**-ы**) ж (меховая) fur coat
шум (**-а**; part gen **-у**) м (звук) noise
шум|е́ть (**-лю́, -и́шь**) несов to make a
noise
шу́мный прил noisy; (разговор,
компания) loud; (оживлённый: улица)
bustling
шу́рин (**-а**) м brother-in-law (wife's
brother)
шуру́п (**-а**) м (Тех) screw
шу|ти́ть (**-чу́, -тишь**; perf **пошути́ть**)
несов to joke; (смеяться): **шути́ть над**
+instr to make fun of; (no perf, +instr:
пренебрегать: здоровьем) to disregard
шу́т|ка (**-ки**; gen pl **-ок**) ж joke; **без**
шу́ток joking apart, seriously
шутли́вый прил humourous (Brit),
humorous (US)
шу́точный прил (рассказ) comic, funny
шучу́ несов см **шути́ть**
шью итп несов см **шить**

щаве́л|ь (**-я́**) м sorrel
ща|ди́ть (**-жу́, -ди́шь**; perf **пощади́ть**)
несов перех to spare
ще́дрост|ь (**-и**) ж generosity
ще́дрый прил generous
щека́ (**щеки́**; nom pl **щёки**, gen pl **щёк**,
dat pl **щека́м**) ж cheek
щек|ота́ть (**-очу́, -о́чешь**; perf
пощекота́ть) несов перех to tickle
щекотли́вый прил (вопрос итп) delicate
щёлк|а (**-и**) ж small hole
щёлка|ть (**-ю**) несов (+instr: языком) to
click; (кнутом) to crack
щёлкн|уть (**-у**) сов от **щёлкать**
щёлоч|ь (**-и**) ж alkali
щелч|о́к (**-ка́**) м flick; (звук) click
щел|ь (**-и**; loc sg **-и́**, gen pl **-е́й**) ж (в полу)
crack; **смотрова́я щель** peephole
щен|о́к (**-ка́**; nom pl **-я́та**, gen pl **-я́т**) м
(собаки) pup; (лисы, волчицы) cub
щепети́льный прил scrupulous
ще́п|ка (**-ки**; gen pl **-ок**) ж splinter; (для
растопки): **ще́пки** chippings
щепо́т|ка (**-ки**; gen pl **-ок**) ж pinch
щети́н|а (**-ы**) ж (животных, щётки) bristle;
(у мужчины) stubble
щёт|ка (**-ки**; gen pl **-ок**) ж brush; **щётка**
для воло́с hairbrush
щи (**щей**; dat pl **щам**) мн cabbage soup ед
щи́колот|ка (**-ки**; gen pl **-ок**) ж ankle
щип|а́ть (**-лю́, -лешь**) несов перех (до
боли) to nip, pinch; (no perf: подлеж:
мороз) to bite ▷ (perf **ощипа́ть**) (волосы,
курицу) to pluck; **щипа́ться** несов возв
(разг) to nip, pinch
щипц|ы́ (**-о́в**) мн: хирурги́ческие щипцы́
forceps; **щипцы́ для са́хара** sugar-tongs
щи́пчик|и (**-ов**) мн (для ногтей) tweezers
щит (**-а́**) м shield; (рекламный,
баскетбольный) board; (Тех) panel
щитови́дн|ый прил: **щитови́дная**
железа́ thyroid gland

щу́к|а (-и) ж pike (мн pike)

щу́пальце (-ьца; nom pl -ьца, gen pl -ец) ср (осьминога) tentacle; (насекомых) feeler

щу́па|ть (-ю; perf пощу́пать) несов перех to feel for

щу́р|ить (-ю, -ишь; perf сощу́рить) несов перех: щу́рить глаза́ to screw up one's eyes; **щу́риться** (perf сощу́риться) несов возв (от солнца) to squint

эвакуа́ци|я (-и) ж evacuation

эвакуи́р|овать (-ую) (не)сов перех to evacuate

ЭВМ ж сокр (= электро́нная вычисли́тельная маши́на) computer

эволю́ци|я (-и) ж evolution

эгои́ст (-а) м egoist

эгоисти́чный прил egotistic(al)

эква́тор (-а) м equator

эквивале́нт (-а) м equivalent

экза́мен (-а) м: экза́мен (по +dat) (по исто́рии) exam(ination) (in); выпускны́е экза́мены Finals; сдава́ть (impf) экза́мен to sit (Brit) или take an exam(ination); сдать (perf) экза́мен to pass an exam(ination); **экзамена́тор** (-а) м examiner; **экзаменацио́нный** прил examination; (вопрос) exam

экземпля́р (-а) м copy

экзоти́ческий прил exotic

экипа́ж (-а) м crew

экологи́ческий прил ecological

эколо́ги|я (-и) ж ecology

эконо́мик|а (-и) ж economy; (наука) economics

экономи́ст (-а) м economist

эконо́м|ить (-лю, -ишь; perf сэконо́мить) несов перех (энергию, деньги) to save; (выгадывать): эконо́мить на +prp to economize или save on

экономи́ческий прил economic

эконо́ми|я (-и) ж economy

эконо́мный прил (хозяин) thrifty; (метод) economical

экра́н (-а) м screen

экскава́тор (-а) м excavator, digger

экску́рси|я (-и) ж excursion

экскурсово́д (-а) м guide

экспеди́ци|я (-и) ж (научная) field work; (группа людей) expedition

экспериме́нт (-а) м experiment

эксперименти́р|овать (-ую) несов:

экспериментировать (над или с +instr) to experiment (on или with)

эксперт (-а) м expert

эксплуатация|я (-и) ж exploitation; (машин) utilization

эксплуатир|овать (-ую) несов перех to exploit; (машины) to use

экспонат (-а) м exhibit

экспорт (-а) м export; экспортёр (-а) м exporter; экспортир|овать (-ую) несов перех to export

экстремальный прил extreme

экстренный прил urgent; (заседание) emergency

ЭКЮ сокр ECU (= European Currency Unit)

эластичный прил stretchy

элеватор (-а) м (С.-х.) grain store или elevator (US)

элегантный прил elegant

электрик (-а) м electrician

электрический прил electric

электричество (-а) ср electricity

электричк|а (-и; gen pl -ек) ж (разг) electric train

электробытов|ой прил: электробытовые приборы electrical appliances мн

электрогитар|а (-ы) ж electric guitar

электромонтёр (-а) м electrician

электрон (-а) м electron

электроник|а (-и) ж electronics

электронн|ый прил electronic; электронный микроскоп electron microscope; электронная почта (Комп) email, electronic mail; электронный адрес email address; электронная страница webpage

электропередач|а (-и) ж power transmission; линия электропередачи power line

электропоезд (-а) м electric train

электроприбор (-а) м electrical device

электропроводк|а (-и) ж (electrical) wiring

электростанци|я (-и) ж (electric) power station

электротехник (-а) м electrical engineer

электроэнерги|я (-и) ж electric power

элемент (-а) м element; элементарный прил elementary; (правила) basic

элит|а (-ы) ж собир élite

элитный прил (лучший) élite; (дом, школа) exclusive

эмалевый прил enamel

эмалированный прил enamelled

эмал|ь (-и) ж enamel

эмбарго ср нескл embargo

эмблем|а (-ы) ж emblem

эмбрион (-а) м embryo

эмигрант (-а) м emigrant

эмиграционный прил emigration

эмиграци|я (-и) ж emigration

эмигрир|овать (-ую) (не)сов to emigrate

эмоциональный прил emotional

эмоци|я (-и) ж emotion

эмульси|я (-и) ж emulsion

энергетик|а (-и) ж power industry; энергетический прил energy

энергичный прил energetic

энерги|я (-и) ж energy

энн|ый прил: энное число/количество X number/amount; в энный раз yet again

энтузиазм (-а) м enthusiasm

энциклопеди|я (-и) ж encyclopaedia (Brit), encyclopedia (US)

эпиграф (-а) м epigraph

эпидеми|я (-и) ж epidemic

эпизод (-а) м episode

эпизодический прил (явление) random

эпилепси|я (-и) ж epilepsy

эпилог (-а) м epilogue (Brit), epilog (US)

эпицентр (-а) м epicentre (Brit), epicenter (US)

эпопе|я (-и) ж epic

эпос (-а) м epic literature

эпох|а (-и) ж epoch

эр|а (-ы) ж era; первый век нашей эры/до нашей эры the first century AD/BC

эрози|я (-и) ж erosion

эротический прил erotic

эскалатор (-а) м escalator

эскалаци|я (-и) ж escalation

эскиз (-а) м (к картине) sketch; (к проекту) draft

эскимо ср нескл choc-ice, Eskimo (US)

эскорт (-а) м escort

эссенци|я (-и) ж (Кулин) essence

эстакад|а (-ы) ж (на дороге) flyover (Brit), overpass

эстафет|а (-ы) ж (Спорт) relay (race)

эстетик|а (-и) ж aesthetics (Brit), esthetics (US); эстетический прил aesthetic (Brit), esthetic (US)

эстон|ец (-ца) м Estonian

Эстони|я (-и) ж Estonia

эстрад|а (-ы) ж (для оркестра) platform; (вид искусства) variety; эстрадный прил: эстрадный концерт variety show

эт|а (-ой) мест см этот

этаж (-а) м floor, storey (Brit), story (US); первый/второй/третий этаж ground/first/second floor (Brit), first/second/third floor (US)

этажёр|ка (-ки; gen pl -ок) ж stack of shelves

эталон (-а) м (меры) standard; (перен: красоты) model

этап (-а) м (работы) stage; (гонки) lap

эт|и (-их) мест см этот

этик|а (-и) ж ethics

этикет (-а) м etiquette

этикет|ка (-ки; gen pl -ок) ж label

этим мест см этот

этими мест см эти

этимологи|я (-и) ж etymology

этичный прил ethical

э́т|о (-ого; см *Table 10*) *мест*
1 (*указательное*) this; **э́то бу́дет тру́дно** this will be difficult; **он на всё соглаша́ется — э́то о́чень стра́нно** he is agreeing to everything, this is most strange
2 (*связка в сказуемом*): **любо́вь — э́то проще́ние** love is forgiveness
3 (*как подлежащее*): **с кем ты разгова́ривал? — э́то была́ моя́ сестра́** who were you talking to? — that was my sister; **как э́то произошло́?** how did it happen?
4 (*для усиления*): **э́то он во всём винова́т** he is the one who is to blame for everything
▷ *част* **1** (*служит для усиления*): **кто э́то звони́л?** who was it who phoned (*Brit*) *или* called (*US*)?

э́т|от (-ого; *f* **э́та**, *nt* **э́то**, *pl* **э́ти**; см *Table 10*) *мест* **1** (*указательное*: *о близком предмете*) this; (: *о близких предметах*) these; **э́тот дом** this house; **э́ти кни́ги** these books
2 (*о данном времени*) this; **э́тот год осо́бенно тру́дный** this year is particularly hard; **в э́ти дни я при́нял реше́ние** in the last few days I have come to a decision; **э́тот са́мый** that very
3 (*о чём-то только что упомянутом*) this; **он ложи́лся в 10 часо́в ве́чера — э́та привы́чка меня́ всегда́ удивля́ла** he used to go to bed at 10 p.m., this habit always amazed me
▷ *ср* (*как сущ: об одном предмете*) this one; (: *о многих предметах*) these ones; **дай мне вот э́ти** give me these ones; **э́тот на всё спосо́бен** this one is capable of anything; **при э́том** at that

этю́д (-а) *м* sketch
эфи́р (-а) *м* (*Хим*) ether; (*воздушное пространство*) air; **выходи́ть** (*perf* **вы́йти**) **в эфи́р** to go on the air; **прямо́й эфи́р** live broadcast
эффе́кт (-а) *м* effect
эффекти́вный *прил* effective
эффе́ктный *прил* (*одежда*) striking; (*речь*) impressive
э́х|о (-а) *ср* echo (*мн* echoes)
эшело́н (-а) *м* echelon; (*поезд*) special train

ю. *сокр* (= *юг*) S (= *South*); (= *южный*) S (= *South*)
ю́б|ка (-ки; *gen pl* -ок) *ж* skirt
ювели́р (-а) *м* jeweller (*Brit*), jeweler (*US*); **ювели́рный** *прил* jewellery (*Brit*), jewelery (*US*)
юг (-а) *м* south
южа́нин (-а) *м* southerner
ю́жный *прил* southern
ю́мор (-а) *м* humour (*Brit*), humor (*US*)
юмори́ст (-а) *м* comedian; **юмористи́ческий** *прил* humorous
ЮНЕ́СКО *ср сокр* UNESCO (= *United Nations Educational Scientific and Cultural Organization*)
юнио́р (-а) *м* (*Спорт*) junior
ю́ность (-и) *ж* youth
ю́нош|а (-и; *nom pl* -и, *gen pl* -ей) *м* young man; **ю́ношеский** *прил* youthful; (*организация*) youth
ю́ный *прил* (*молодой*) young
юриди́ческ|ий *прил* (*сила*) juridical; (*образование*) legal; **юриди́ческий факульте́т** law faculty; **юриди́ческая консульта́ция** ≈ legal advice office
юрисди́кци|я (-и) *ж* jurisdiction
юриско́нсульт (-а) *м* ≈ solicitor, ≈ lawyer
юри́ст (-а) *м* lawyer

Я

я (меня́; см Table 6a) мест I ▷ сущ нескл (ли́чность) the self, the ego

я́бед|а (-ы) м/ж sneak; **я́бедничаjть** (-ю; perf **наябедничать**) несов: **я́бедничать на** +acc (разг) to tell tales about

я́блок|о (-а; nom pl -и) ср apple; **я́блон|я** (-и) ж apple tree; **я́блочный** прил apple

яв|и́ться (-лю́сь, -ишься; impf **явля́ться**) сов возв to appear; (домой, в гости) to arrive; **явля́ться** (perf **яви́ться**) +instr (причиной) to be

я́в|ка (-ки; gen pl -ок) ж appearance

явле́ни|е (-я) ср phenomenon (мн phenomena); (Рел) manifestation

явля́|ться (-юсь) несов от **яви́ться** ▷ возв +instr to be

я́вно нареч (очевидно) obviously

я́вный прил (вражда) overt; (ложь) obvious

яв|ь (-и) ж reality

ягн|ёнок (-ёнка; nom pl -я́та, gen pl -я́т) м lamb

я́год|а (-ы) ж berry

я́годиц|а (-ы) ж (обычно мн) buttock

яд (-а) м poison

я́дерный прил nuclear

ядови́тый прил poisonous

яд|ро́ (-ра́; nom pl -ра, gen pl -ер) ср nucleus; (Земли, древесины) core; (Спорт) shot

я́зв|а (-ы) ж (Мед) ulcer

язв|и́ть (-лю́, -и́шь; perf **съязви́ть**) несов +dat to sneer at

язы́к (-а́) м tongue; (русский, разговорный) language; **владе́ть** (impf) **языко́м** to speak a language

языково́й прил language

язычо́к (-ка́) м (ботинка) tongue

яи́чниц|а (-ы) ж fried eggs мн

яи́чн|ый прил: **яи́чный бело́к** egg white; **яи́чная скорлупа́** eggshell

яйц|о́ (яйца́; nom pl я́йца, gen pl яи́ц, dat pl я́йцам) ср egg; **яйцо́ всмя́тку/вкруту́ю** soft-boiled/hard-boiled egg

ЯК (-а) м сокр самолёт констру́кции А.С. Я́ковлева

я́кобы союз (будто бы) that ▷ част supposedly

я́кор|ь (-я; nom pl -я́) м (Мор) anchor

я́м|а (-ы) ж (в земле) pit

я́моч|ка (-ки; gen pl -ек) ж dimple

янва́р|ь (-я́) м January

янта́р|ь (-я́) м amber

Япо́ни|я (-и) ж Japan

я́ркий прил bright; (перен: человек, речь) brilliant

ярлы́к (-а́) м label

я́рмар|ка (-ки; gen pl -ок) ж fair; **междунаро́дная я́рмарка** international trade fair

я́ростный прил (взгляд, слова) furious; (атака, критика) fierce

я́рост|ь (-и) ж fury

я́рус (-а) м (в теа́тре) circle

я́сл|и (-ей) мн (также **де́тские я́сли**) crèche ед, day nursery ед (Brit)

я́сно нареч clearly ▷ как сказ (о погоде) it's fine; (понятно) it's clear

я́сност|ь (-и) ж clarity

я́сный прил clear

я́стреб (-а) м hawk

я́хт|а (-ы) ж yacht

яхтсме́н (-а) м yachtsman (мн yachtsmen)

ячме́нный прил barley

ячме́н|ь (-я́) м barley

я́щериц|а (-ы) ж lizard

я́щик (-а) м (вместилище: большой) chest; (: маленький) box; (в пи́сьменном столе итп) drawer; **мусорный я́щик** dustbin (Brit), garbage can (US); **почто́вый я́щик** (на у́лице) postbox; (до́ма) letter box

я́щур (-а) м foot-and-mouth disease

Russian Grammar

1 Spelling Rules

Note that certain vowels in Russian cannot be written after 'hushing' consonants, even where these vowels would be expected according to the normal rules of conjugation or declension. These spelling rules are:

- After **ж, ч, ш, щ, г, к** and **х**:
  ы becomes **и** e.g. **ногá** (*nom sg*) → **ноги́** (*gen sg*)
  я becomes **а** e.g. **молчáть** (*infin*) → **молчáт** (*3rd person pl*)
  ю becomes **у** e.g. **молчáть** (*infin*) → **молчý** (*1st person sg*)

- After **ж, ч, ш, щ** and **ц**:
  о becomes **е** when unstressed e.g. **хорóший** (*m nom sg*) → **хорóшего** (*m gen sg*)

2 Verbs

2.1 Conjugation of Verbs

Russian verbs can be divided into two groups according to their endings when conjugated. The two groups are referred to as first conjugation and second conjugation. The following examples show the pattern encountered in the imperfective present tense and perfective future tense.

infinitive	1st conjugation	2nd conjugation
	рабóтать	говори́ть
я	рабóтаю	говорю́
ты	рабóтаешь	говори́шь
он/онá/онó	рабóтает	говори́т
мы	рабóтаем	говори́м
вы	рабóтаете	говори́те
они́	рабóтают	говоря́т

First Conjugation Verbs

These include verbs with infinitive endings in **–ать** (e.g. **рабóтать**), in **–ять** (e.g. **стреля́ть**), in **–овать/–евать** (e.g. **интересовáть, танцевáть**), in **–уть** (e.g. **махнýть**), in **–авать** (e.g. **узнавáть**), in **–ыть** (e.g. **мыть**) and in **–зть**, **–оть**, **–сть** and **–ти**, as well as monosyllabic verbs in **–ить** (e.g. **шить**).

Many first-conjugation verbs undergo a stem change in conjugation:

- Particularly common are consonant mutations in the final consonant before the ending. As general rules, **г** becomes **ж, д** becomes **ж, з** becomes **ж, к** becomes **ч, с** becomes **ш, ск** becomes **щ, ст** becomes **щ, т** becomes **ч**. For example **писáть** conjugates as пишý, пи́шешь... пи́шут, and **искáть** conjugates as ищý, и́щешь... и́щут.

- Another common stem change occurs in verbs ending in **–овать/–евать**. In the conjugation of these verbs, the **–ева–/–ова–** particle is replaced by **–у–**. This category of verbs is important as it contains many borrowed and new verbs. For example, **фотографи́ровать** conjugates as фотографи́рую, фотографи́руешь ... фотографи́руют.

2

Second Conjugation Verbs

These include most verbs with infinitive endings in **–ить** (the main exception being monosyllabic ones), many verbs in **–еть** (e.g. **смотре́ть**), some in **–ать** (e.g. **молча́ть**) and two in **–ять(ся)** (**боя́ться** and **стоя́ть**).

Note that spelling rules (see page 2) may apply to the first person singular and third person plural of second-conjugation verbs. For example **слы́шать** conjugates **слы́шу, слы́шишь**... **слы́шат**.

As with first-conjugation verbs, many second-conjugation verbs have consonant mutations in the stem when conjugated. However, in the second conjugation, these mutations only affect the first person of the verb. For example, **плати́ть** conjugates as **плачу́, пла́тишь**... **пла́тят** and **суди́ть** conjugates as **сужу́, су́дишь**... **су́дят**.

Furthermore, a salient feature of the second conjugation is the addition of the letter **л** in the first person singular of verbs whose stem ends in **б, в, м, п** and **ф**, e.g. **люби́ть: я люблю́** and **корми́ть: я кормлю́**.

Irregular Verbs

Some common Russian verbs have irregular conjugations. Below are the conjugations of three of the most useful irregular verbs (**дать, есть** and **быть**):

дать	
я дам	мы дади́м
ты дашь	вы дади́те
он/она́/оно́ даст	они́ даду́т

есть	
я ем	мы еди́м
ты ешь	вы еди́те
он/она́/оно́ ест	они́ едя́т

Note that the invariable form **есть** is sometimes used as the present tense of **быть**.

быть	
я бу́ду	мы бу́дем
ты бу́дешь	вы бу́дете
он/она́/оно́ бу́дет	они́ бу́дут

Note that **быть** has no present tense form – the form given here is the future tense. For more about the future tense, please see page 5.

2.2 Past Tense

The past tense of most Russian verbs is formed by replacing the infinitive ending by **–л, –ла, –ло, –ли**, giving the masculine, feminine, neuter, and plural forms respectively.

For example:

	молчáть	упáсть	кóнчить
m	он молчáл	он упáл	он кóнчил
f	онá молчáла	онá упáла	онá кóнчила
nt	онó молчáло	онó упáло	онó кóнчило
pl	они́ молчáли	они́ упáли	они́ кóнчили

The singular past tense always agrees with the gender of the subject, so that even after the personal pronouns **я** and **ты** the gender is always marked, e.g. **я сказáл** (masculine subject), **я сказáла** (feminine subject).

Verbs with infinitives ending in **–ереть**, **–зть**, **–чь**, and many in **–ти** have no **–л** in the masculine past tense, e.g. **умерéть** (**ýмер, умерлá**), **лезть** (**лез, лéзла**). This is also the case with some verbs in **–нуть**, e.g. **привы́кнуть** (**привы́к, привы́кла**).

The verb **идти́** has an irregular stem in the past tense formed as follows: **он шёл, онá шла, онó шло, они́ шли**. Compounds of **идти́** such as **прийти́** and **уйти́** form the past tense similarly, e.g. **прийти́** becomes **он пришёл, онá пришлá** etc.

2.3 Imperative Mood

The imperative mood has two forms – the familiar and the formal – which are used in accordance with the mode of address (i.e. the familiar **ты** or the formal **Вы**) appropriate in any given situation:

• The formal imperative is formed by adding **–те** to the end of the familiar form.

• The familiar imperative is formed by replacing the third person plural ending of a verb by **–й** if it is directly preceded by a vowel, and **–и** if it is preceded by a consonant and has mobile or end stress in conjugation.

For example:

дéлать (*infin*) → **дéлают** (3rd person pl) → **дéлай(те)** (*imperative*)

держáть → **дéржат** → **держи́(те)**

The imperative ending **–ь(те)** is used where the third person plural ending is preceded by no more than one consonant and the verb has fixed stem stress in conjugation e.g.:

постáвить → **постáвят** → **постáвь(те)**

Some common exceptions:

• **давáть** and its compounds have **давáй(те)**

• **пить** has imperative **пéй(те)** (compare **петь** which has imperative **пóй(те)**). **бить, вить, лить** and **шить** also form the imperative like **пить**.

• The imperative of **быть** is **бýдь(те)**.

2.4 Aspect

The majority of Russian verbs have two verb aspects: the imperfective (for conveying the frequency of an action, describing repeated or habitual actions or describing a process), and the perfective (for emphasis on a single or a completed action). Each verb has two infinitives: an imperfective one and a perfective one. The conjugated form of an imperfective verb is the present tense, whereas the conjugated form of a perfective verb is a future tense. Perfective verbs have no present tense form.

Consider the following examples:

Я не чита́ю кни́гу.   *I am not reading the book.*
Я не прочита́ю кни́гу.   *I won't finish reading the book.*

There is no one simple way to differentiate aspectual pairs of infinitives. Some of the more common ways are:

- by the presence of a prefix in the perfective aspect e.g. **сде́лать** (cf. imperfective **де́лать**)

- by the presence of a suffix in the imperfective aspect e.g. **пока́зывать** (cf. perfective **показа́ть**)

- by a change in conjugation e.g. the perfective **ко́нчить** and its imperfective counterpart **конча́ть**.

In addition, some aspectual pairs have infinitives deriving from two different roots, e.g. **говори́ть** (*impf*)/**сказа́ть** (*perf*), **брать** (*impf*)/**взять** (*perf*).

A minority of verbs exist only in one aspect, e.g. **сто́ить** (*impf*), while some verbs incorporate the two aspects in one form, e.g. **иссле́довать** (*impf/perf*).

Aspect also has a bearing on the use of the imperative, where, generally speaking, the perfective aspect is used in positive commands (i.e. telling someone to do something), while the imperfective is used in negative commands (i.e. telling someone not to do something).

2.5 Future Tense

There are two forms of the future tense in Russian: the perfective form and the imperfective form. The perfective future is formed by conjugating a perfective infinitive (see above). The imperfective future is formed by combining the future tense of **быть** with an imperfective infinitive as follows:

я	бу́ду	чита́ть
ты	бу́дешь	чита́ть
он/она́/оно́	бу́дет	чита́ть
мы	бу́дем	чита́ть
вы	бу́дете	чита́ть
они́	бу́дут	чита́ть

For example:

Я не прочита́ю кни́гу.   *I won't finish reading the book.*
Я не бу́ду чита́ть кни́гу.   *I won't read the book.*
Я сде́лаю поку́пки в суббо́ту.   *I will do the shopping on Saturday.*
Я бу́ду де́лать поку́пки   *I will do the shopping every Saturday.*
   ка́ждую суббо́ту.

3 Nouns

3.1 Gender of Nouns

All Russian nouns are either masculine, feminine or neuter. In most cases the gender is determinable by the ending:

> дом *m*
> карти́на *f*
> кре́сло *nt*

Noun gender is significant since, for example, it determines the ending of a qualifying adjective:

> большо́й дом
> больша́я картина
> большо́е кресло

Masculine Noun Categories

- All nouns ending in a hard consonant, e.g. **кот**, **собо́р**, and all nouns ending in –**й** e.g. **музе́й**.
- Some nouns ending in –**а**/–**я** including natural masculine nouns e.g. **мужчи́на**, **дя́дя** and masculine first names, including familiar forms e.g. **Фома́**, **Ми́тя**.
- Numerous nouns ending in a soft sign, including: natural masculines e.g. **па́рень**, **коро́ль**; months of the year e.g. **ию́ль**.

Feminine Noun Categories

- The majority of nouns ending in –**а**/–**я** e.g. **доро́га**, **ко́мната**, **тётя**.
- The majority of nouns ending in a soft sign including: natural feminines e.g. **мать**; all nouns ending in –**жь**, –**чь**, –**шь**, –**щь**, –**знь**, –**мь**, –**пь**, –**фь**; most nouns ending in –**сть**, –**бь**, –**вь**, –**дь**, –**зь**, –**сь**, –**ть**.

Neuter Noun Categories

- Almost all nouns ending in –**о** and –**е** e.g. **ме́сто**, **со́лнце**.
- All nouns ending in –**ё** and –**мя** e.g. **копьё**, **вре́мя**, **и́мя**.
- Most indeclinable loan words e.g. **ви́ски**, **ра́дио** (a notable exception being **ко́фе**, which is masculine).

3.2 Noun Cases

Russian nouns can decline into six cases:

Nominative: this case is used for the subject of a sentence.

Accusative: this case is used for the direct object of a sentence and after **на** and **в** to indicate movement towards something or someone.

Genitive: this case is used to indicate possession and with certain verbs and prepositions.

Dative: this case is used for the indirect object of a sentence and with certain verbs and prepositions.

Instrumental: this case is used to indicate the means by which an action is done, or the passive agent and with certain verbs and prepositions.

Prepositional: this case is used after **на** and **в** to indicate location, and with other prepositions, most notably **о**.

3.3 Declension of Nouns

Regular Declensions

There are three declension patterns for nouns:

• The first declension contains most masculine and neuter nouns

• The second declension contains most feminine nouns

• The third declension is specific to feminine nouns ending in a soft sign.

For the first declension, hard-ending masculine and neuter nouns (e.g. **мост**, **óзеро**) have the genitive singular ending **–а**, whereas soft-ending masculine and neuter nouns (e.g. **гость**, **гóре**) have the genitive ending **–я**. Similarly, the second declension pattern has a split between hard-ending feminine nouns (e.g. **лáмпа**) with the genitive ending **–ы** and soft-ending feminine nouns (e.g. **бáшня**) with the genitive ending **–и**. All nouns in the third declension pattern, as they are soft-ending, have the genitive ending **–и**. The genitive singular declension generally sets the pattern for the other oblique cases.

Plural animate nouns, (nouns referring to living things such as people and animals), take genitive endings in the accusative case. In the singular, this rule applies to masculine animate nouns only.

The following tables set out the most common declension patterns:

Masculine

nom	Singular					Plural					
	acc	gen	dat	instr	prep	nom	acc	gen	dat	instr	prep
завóд	–	–а	–у	–ом	о –е	–ы	–ы	–ов	–ам	–ами	о –ах
музéй|й	–й	–я	–ю	–ем	о –е	–и	–и	–ев	–ям	–ями	о –ях
гость|ь	–я	–я	–ю	–ем	о –е	–и	–éй	–éй	–я́м	–я́ми	о –я́х
писáтел|ь	–я	–я	–ю	–ем	о –е	–и	–ей	–ей	–ям	–ями	о –ях
двúгател|ь	–ь	–я	–ю	–ем	о –е	–и	–и	–ей	–ям	–ями	о –ях

Feminine

nom	Singular					Plural					
	acc	gen	dat	instr	prep	nom	acc	gen	dat	instr	prep
лáмп|а	–у	–ы	–е	–ой	о –е	–ы	–ы	–	–ам	–ами	о –ах
бáш|ня	–ню	–ни	–не	–ней	о –не	–ни	–ни	–ен	–ням	–нями	–нях
двер|ь	–ь	–и	–и	–ью	о –и	–и́	–и́	–éй	–я́м	–я́ми	о –я́х
стáнци|я	–ю	–и	–и	–ей	о –и	–и	–и	–й	–ям	–ями	–ях

7

Neuter

Singular						Plural					
nom	acc	gen	dat	instr	prep	nom	acc	gen	dat	instr	prep
мéст|о	–о	–а	–у	–ом	о –е	–á	–á	–	–áм	–áми	о –áх
пóл|е	–е	–я	–ю	–ем	о –е	–я́	–я́	–éй	–я́м	–я́ми	о –я́х
здáни|е	–е	–я	–ю	–ем	о –и	–я	–я	–й	–ям	–ями	о –ях

Where nouns have no ending in the genitive plural, a buffer vowel (**e**, **o** or **ë**) may need to be inserted between the last two consonants. For example **окнó** has the genitive plural form **óкон**, **сестрá** → **сестёр**, **бáшня** → **бáшен**.

Feminine and neuter nouns ending in **–ия/–ие** take the ending **–и** in the singular prepositional case.

Irregular Declensions

The table below shows the declensions of two of the most common irregular nouns, **врéмя** *time* and **мать** *mother*:

Singular		
nom	врéмя	мать
acc	врéмя	мать
gen	врéмени	мáтери
dat	врéмени	мáтери
instr	врéменем	мáтерью
prep	о врéмени	о мáтери

Plural		
nom	временá	мáтери
acc	временá	матерéй
gen	времён	матерéй
dat	временáм	матеря́м
instr	временáми	матеря́ми
prep	о временáх	о матеря́х

Other nouns ending in **–мя** such as **и́мя** *name* and **плéмя** *tribe* follow the same pattern as **врéмя**. **Дочь** *daughter* follows the same pattern as **мать** with the exception of the instrumental plural which is **дочерьми́**.

4 Adjectives

4.1 Long Form Adjectives

Russian adjectives generally have a long (attributive) form e.g. **вéжливый** *polite* and a short (predicative) form e.g. **вéжлив**. Russian long adjectives are used attributively and the majority have hard endings, the first vowel of the ending being **–ы**, **–a**, or **–o**. Note that the animate accusative/genitive rule which affects nouns also applies to long adjectives.

The following table shows the declension of hard-ending adjectives:

	m	f	nt	pl
nom	стáрый	стáрая	стáрое	стáрые
acc	стáрый/ого	стáрую	стáрое/ого	стáрые/ых
gen	стáрого	стáрой	стáрого	стáрых
dat	стáрому	стáрой	стáрому	стáрым
instr	стáрым	стáрой	стáрым	стáрыми
prep	о стáром	о стáрой	о стáром	о стáрых

The alternative forms of the accusative are animate and identical with the genitive. The feminine instrumental ending **–ою** also exists.

Adjectives ending in **–ой**, such as **живóй** *alive*, decline similarly, with the only difference being the masculine nominative singular and inanimate accusative singular, where the ending **–ой** replaces **–ый**.

Note that Russian spelling rules (see page 2) may apply in some cases, so that adjectives such as **глáдкий** *smooth*, **тúхий** *quiet* and **дóлгий** *long* decline as above with **–и–** in place of **–ы–**.

Adjectives ending in **–ний** are known as soft adjectives. They decline as follows:

	m	f	nt	pl
nom	осéнний	осéнняя	осéннее	осéнние
acc	осéнний/его	осéннюю	осéннее/его	осéнние/их
gen	осéннего	осéнней	осéннего	осéнних
dat	осéннему	осéнней	осéннему	осéнним
instr	осéнним	осéнней	осéнним	осéнними
prep	о осéннем	о осéнней	о осéннем	о осéнних

The alternative forms of the accusative are animate and identical with the genitive. The feminine instrumental ending **–ею** also exists.

Due to spelling rules (see page 2), adjectives ending in **–ший**, **–щий**, **–чий** and **–жий** (e.g. **хорóший** *good*, **горячий** *hot*) also decline like soft adjectives.

4.2 Short Form Adjectives

Short adjectives can be derived from most long adjectives. These are formed by replacing the long form endings with contracted ones. For example, the adjective **вежливый** *polite* declines as follows:

	long form	short form
m	ве́жливый	ве́жлив
f	ве́жливая	ве́жлива
nt	ве́жливое	ве́жливо
pl	ве́жливые	ве́жливы

The masculine short form of many adjectives needs a buffer vowel (**e**, **o** or **ё**) to be inserted between the last two consonants or to replace a soft sign. For example **ва́жный** has the masculine short form **ва́жен**, **лёгкий → лёгок**, **у́мный → умён**. Masculine short forms of adjectives ending in **-енный** (i.e. unstressed) generally have **-ен** endings whereas those in **-énный** (i.e. stressed) are replaced by the short form **-énен**.

4.3 Usage

Long adjectives are typically used attributively – immediately before the noun to which they refer. For example:

На у́лице стои́т бе́лая маши́на.	*A white car is parked in the street.*
Он во́дит бе́лую маши́ну.	*He drives a white car.*

Long adjectives may be used predicatively when they denote characteristics inherent to the nouns they refer to:

Эта у́лица – дли́нная.	*This street is long.*
Этот груз – тяжёлый.	*This load is heavy.*

In contrast, the short form is typically used predicatively, and when talking about a temporary state. For example:

Он плох.	*He is unwell.*
Он плохо́й.	*He is bad.*

4.4 Possessive Adjectives

These follow one of two declension patterns. Possessive adjectives like **соба́чий** *the dog's* and **де́вичий** *the girl's* decline as follows:

	m	f	nt	pl
nom	соба́чий	соба́чья	соба́чье	соба́чьи
acc	соба́чий/ьего	соба́чью	соба́чье	соба́чьи/ьих
gen	соба́чьего	соба́чьей	соба́чьего	соба́чьих
dat	соба́чьему	соба́чьей	соба́чьему	соба́чьим
instr	соба́чьим	соба́чьей	соба́чьим	соба́чьими
prep	о соба́чьем	о соба́чьей	о соба́чьем	о соба́чьих

The alternative forms of the accusative are animate and identical with the genitive. The feminine instrumental ending **-ьею** also exists. The ordinal numeral **третий** *third* also declines according to the above table.

In addition, there are possessive adjectives formed by adding the suffixes **-ин**, **-нин** or **-ов** to the stems of nouns. This form is mainly used with reference to particular family members such as **мáмин** *mother's*, **мýжнин** *husband's*, and **дéдов** *grandfather's*, but can also be derived from the familiar forms of first names e.g. **Сáшин**. These decline as follows:

	m	f	nt	pl
nom	Сáшин	Сáшина	Сáшино	Сáшины
acc	Сáшин/ого	Сáшину	Сáшино	Сáшины/ых
gen	Сáшиного	Сáшиной	Сáшиного	Сáшиных
dat	Сáшину	Сáшиной	Сáшину	Сáшиным
instr	Сáшиным	Сáшиной	Сáшиным	Сáшиными
prep	о Сáшином	о Сáшиной	о Сáшином	о Сáшиных

The alternative forms of the accusative are animate and identical with the genitive. The feminine instrumental ending **-ьою** also exists.

5 Pronouns

The following pages give the declensions of various Russian pronouns. For more details on their translation and usage, see the entries in the main dictionary text.

5.1 Personal Pronouns

Singular

nom	я	ты	он	онá	онó
acc/gen	меня	тебя	егó	её	егó
dat	мне	тебé	емý	ей	емý
instr	мной *or* мнóю	тобóй *or* тобóю	им	ей *or* éю	им
prep	обо мне	о тебé	о нём	о ней	о нём

The reflexive pronoun **себя** declines like **тебя**.

Plural

nom	мы	вы	они
acc/gen	нас	вас	их
dat	нам	вам	им
instr	нáми	вáми	и́ми
prep	о нас	о вас	о них

5.2 Interrogative Pronouns

The alternatives given at the accusative are animate forms which are identical with the genitive.

кто *who*, **что** *what* (**никто** *nobody* and **ничто** *nothing* decline in the same way)

nom	кто	что
acc	кого	что
gen	кого	чего
dat	кому	чему
instr	кем	чем
prep	о ком	о чём

чей *whose*

	m	f	nt	pl
nom	чей	чья	чьё	чьи
acc	чей/чьего	чью	чьё	чьи/чьих
gen	чьего	чьей	чьего	чьих
dat	чьему	чьей	чьему	чьим
instr	чьим	чьей *or* чьёю	чьим	чьими
prep	о чьём	о чьей	о чьём	о чьих

5.3 Possessive Pronouns

мой *my* (**твой** *your* (*sg*) and the reflexive possessive pronoun **свой** decline like **мой**)

	m	f	nt	pl
nom	мой	моя	моё	мои
acc	мой/моего	мою	моё	мои/моих
gen	моего	моей	моего	моих
dat	моему	моей	моему	моим
instr	моим	моей *or* моею	моим	моими
prep	о моём	о моей	о моём	о моих

наш *our* (**ваш** *your* (*pl*) declines like **наш**)

	m	f	nt	pl
nom	наш	наша	наше	наши
acc	наш/нашего	нашу	наше	наши/наших
gen	нашего	нашей	нашего	наших
dat	нашему	нашей	нашему	нашим
instr	нашим	нашей *or* нашею	нашим	нашими
prep	о нашем	о нашей	о нашем	о наших

The possessive pronouns **его**, **её** and **их** are invariable.

5.4 Demonstrative Pronouns

этот *this*

	m	f	nt	pl
nom	э́тот	э́та	э́то	э́ти
acc	э́тот/э́того	э́ту	э́то	э́ти/э́тих
gen	э́того	э́той	э́того	э́тих
dat	э́тому	э́той	э́тому	э́тим
instr	э́тим	э́той *or* э́тою	э́тим	э́тими
prep	об э́том	об э́той	об э́том	об э́тих

тот *that*

	m	f	nt	pl
nom	тот	та	то	те
acc	тот/того́	ту	то	те/тех
gen	того́	той	того́	тех
dat	тому́	той	тому́	тем
instr	тем	той *or* то́ю	тем	те́ми
prep	о то́м	о той	о то́м	о те́х

сей *this*

	m	f	nt	pl
nom	сей	сия́	сиé	сий
acc	сей/сего́	сию́	сиé	сий/сих
gen	сего́	сей	сего́	сих
dat	сему́	сей	сему́	сим
instr	сим	сей *or* се́ю	сим	си́ми
prep	о сём	о сей	о сём	о сих

весь *all*

	m	f	nt	pl
nom	весь	вся	всё	все
acc	весь/всего́	всю	всё	все/всех
gen	всего́	всей	всего́	всех
dat	всему́	всей	всему́	всем
instr	всем	всей *or* все́ю	всем	все́ми
prep	обо всём	обо всей	обо всём	обо всех

6 Numbers

6.1 Cardinal Numbers

The alternatives given at the accusative are animate forms which are identical with the genitive.

оди́н 1 *one*

	m	f	nt	pl
nom	оди́н	одна́	одно́	одни́
acc	оди́н/одного́	одну́	одно́	одни́/одни́х
gen	одного́	одно́й	одного́	одни́х
dat	одному́	одно́й	одному́	одни́м
instr	одни́м	одно́й *or* одно́ю	одни́м	одни́ми
prep	об одно́м	об одно́й	об одно́м	об одни́х

два 2 *two*

	m	f	nt
nom	два	две	два
acc	два/двух	две/двух	два/двух
gen	двух	двух	двух
dat	двум	двум	двум
instr	двумя́	двумя́	двумя́
prep	о двух	о двух	о двух

óба *both*

	m/nt	f
nom	óба	óбе
acc	óба/обóих	óбе/обéих
gen	обóих	обéих
dat	обóим	обéим
instr	обóими	обéими
prep	об обóих	об обéих

три 3 *three*

nom	три
acc	три/трёх
gen	трёх
dat	трём
instr	тремя́
prep	о трёх

четы́ре 4 *four*

nom	четы́ре
acc	четы́ре/четырёх
gen	четырёх
dat	четырём
instr	четырьмя́
prep	о четырёх

пять 5 *five*

nom	пять
acc	пять
gen	пяти́
dat	пяти́
instr	пятью́
prep	о пяти́

The numerals **шесть** to **два́дцать** 6–20 and **три́дцать** 30 decline like **пять**.

со́рок 40 *forty*

nom	со́рок
acc	со́рок
gen	сорока́
dat	сорока́
instr	сорока́
prep	о сорока́

пятьдеся́т 50 *fifty*

nom	пятьдеся́т
acc	пятьдеся́т
gen	пяти́десяти
dat	пяти́десяти
instr	пятью́десятью
prep	о пяти́десяти

шестьдеся́т 60 and **се́мьдесят** 70 decline like **пятьдеся́т**.

сто 100 *a hundred*

nom	сто
acc	сто
gen	ста
dat	ста
instr	ста
prep	о ста

девяно́сто 90 declines like **сто**.

две́сти 200 *two hundred*

nom	две́сти
acc	две́сти
gen	двухсо́т
dat	двумста́м
instr	двумяста́ми
prep	о двухста́х

три́ста 300 *three hundred*

nom	три́ста
acc	три́ста
gen	трёхсо́т
dat	трёмста́м
instr	тремяста́ми
prep	о трёхста́х

четы́реста 400 *four hundred*

nom	четы́реста
acc	четы́реста
gen	четырёхсот
dat	четырёмста́м
instr	четырьмяста́ми
prep	о четырёхста́х

пятьсо́т 500 *five hundred*

nom	пятьсо́т
acc	пятьсо́т
gen	пятисо́т
dat	пятиста́м
instr	пятьюста́ми
prep	о пятиста́х

шестьсо́т 600, **семьсо́т** 700, **восемьсо́т** 800 and **девятьсо́т** 900 decline like **пятьсо́т**.

ты́сяча 1000 *one thousand*

	singular	plural
nom	ты́сяча	ты́сячи
acc	ты́сячу	ты́сячи
gen	ты́сячи	ты́сяч
dat	ты́сяче	ты́сячам
instr	ты́сячей *or* ты́сячью	ты́сячами
prep	о ты́сяче	о ты́сячах

6.2 Collective Numerals

The following tables show how the collective numerals 2–7 decline. Other collective numerals decline like **че́тверо**.

The alternatives given at the accusative are animate forms which are identical with the genitive.

nom	дво́е	тро́е	че́тверо
acc	дво́е/двои́х	тро́е/трои́х	че́тверо/четверы́х
gen	двои́х	трои́х	четверы́х
dat	двои́м	трои́м	четверы́м
instr	двои́ми	трои́ми	четверы́ми
prep	о двои́х	о трои́х	о четверы́х

nom	пя́теро	ше́стеро	се́меро
acc	пя́теро/пятеры́х	ше́стеро/шестеры́х	се́меро/семеры́х
gen	пятеры́х	шестеры́х	семеры́х
dat	пятеры́м	шестеры́м	семеры́м
instr	пятеры́ми	шестеры́ми	семеры́ми
prep	о пятеры́х	о шестеры́х	о семеры́х

Грамматика Английского Языка

1 Глаголы

Существует три основных вида глаголов:

- основные глаголы, например, *look*, *run*, *want*, *make*, *expect*, обозначающие действия и состояния;
- вспомогательные глаголы *be*, *have* и *do*, используемые для образования различных времён, вопросительной и отрицательной форм;
- модальные глаголы, например, *can*, *could*, *may*, *might*, *would*, используемые для придания различных дополнительных значений, таких как возможность и обязанность.

1.1 Основные глаголы

Правильные или неправильные глаголы

Основные глаголы могут быть либо правильными, либо неправильными. Правильные глаголы имеют окончание *–s* в третьем лице единственного числа простого настоящего времени (*He talks*), окончание *-ing* в причастии настоящего времени (*He is talking*) и окончание *-ed* в простом прошедшем времени и причастии прошедшего времени (*He talked*, *He has talked*). У неправильных глаголов в некоторых из перечисленных форм могут быть иные окончания.

Правильные:	*talk*, *talks*, *talking*, *talked*
Неправильные:	*go*, *goes*, *going*, *went*, *gone*

Переходные или непереходные глаголы

Основные глаголы бывают либо переходными, либо непереходными. Если глагол является переходным, за ним следует прямое дополнение. Если глагол непереходный, то у него нет прямого дополнения.

Переходный:	*We enjoyed the party.*
Непереходный:	*They waited.*

Многие глаголы могут быть как переходными, так и непереходными, например, *read*.

Переходный:	*Ann was reading a letter.*
Непереходный:	*Ann was reading.*

Некоторые глаголы также имеют косвенное дополнение, которое указывает на лицо, в отношении которого выполняется действие, или которое является получателем чего–либо. Например, если речь идет о *giving something*, как правило, необходимо сообщить, кто при этом является получателем. В следующем предложении *a box of chocolates* выступает в роли прямого дополнения, а *me* – косвенного дополнения.

Rob gave me a box of chocolates.

1.2 Вспомогательные глаголы

Вспомогательный глагол – это глагол, который употребляется вместе с основным глаголом. Важнейшие вспомогательные глаголы включают в себя *be*, *have* и *do*.

Be относится к неправильным глаголам. Ниже приведены его формы:

Базовая форма		be
Простое настоящее время	1-е лицо единственного числа	I **am**
	3-е лицо единственного числа	He/she/it **is**
	2-е лицо единственного числа, все лица множественного числа	You/we/they **are**
Простое прошедшее время	1-е и 3-е лицо единственного числа	I/he/she/it **was**
	2-е лицо единственного числа, все лица множественного числа	You/we/they **were**
Причастие настоящего времени		**being**
Причастие прошедшего времени		**been**

Be используется в формах длительного времени (см. раздел 1.4).

> I **am working**.
> We **were waiting** for a long time.

Be также используется в страдательном залоге (см. раздел 1.6).

> His car **was stolen**.

Have относится к неправильным глаголам. Ниже приведены его формы:

Базовая форма		have
Простое настоящее время	1-е и 2-е лицо единственного числа, все лица множественного числа	I/you/we/they **have**
	3-е лицо единственного числа	He/she/it **has**
Простое прошедшее время	Все формы	I/you/he/she/it/we/they **had**
Причастие настоящего времени		**having**
Причастие прошедшего времени		**had**

Have используется в совершенных формах глагола (см. раздел 1.4).

> We **have** already **eaten** lunch.
> The train **had left** before we arrived.
> I **'ve been thinking**.

Do относится к неправильным глаголам. Ниже приведены его формы:

Базовая форма		do
Простое настоящее время	1-е и 2-е лицо единственного числа, все лица множественного числа	I/you/we/they **do**
	3-е лицо единственного числа	He/she/it **does**
Простое прошедшее время	Все формы	I/you/he/she/it/we/they **did**
Причастие настоящего времени		**doing**
Причастие прошедшего времени		**done**

Do используется в отрицательных и вопросительных предложениях.

> I **don't like** eggs at all.
> **Does** she **like** eggs?

Обратите внимание, что **be**, **have** и **do** также выступают в роли основных глаголов, например:

> I **am** tall.
> Vineeta **has** three brothers.
> We **do** the shopping together.

1.3 Модальные глаголы

Модальные глаголы представляют собой особый тип вспомогательных глаголов. Модальные глаголы используются в тех случаях, когда вы хотите придать основному глаголу особое значение, например, для выражения уверенности, обращения за разрешением, указания на необходимость чего-либо. В отличие от основных глаголов модальные глаголы не изменяются по лицам и числам, не имеют неопределенной формы: I **can** swim, She **can** swim, You **can** swim, и т.д. Модальные глаголы употребляются с инфинитивом без частицы **to**.

Выражение способности

Глаголы **can** и **could** используются для обозначения умения или способности совершить какое-либо действие. Если речь идет о прошлом, то используется форма **could**. К отрицательным формам относятся **cannot** или **can't**, а также **could not** или **couldn't**.

> Morag **can** speak French quite well now.
> When I was younger I **could** play tennis.
> I **can't** come tomorrow.
> We **couldn't** open the door.

Для этого также можно использовать оборот **be able to**. Оборот **be able to** отличается от других модальных глаголов тем, что он может изменяться. Он состоит из глагола **be** + **able to**.

> **Are** you **able to** walk to the car?
> We **weren't able to** find a solution.

В отличие от **can** и **could**, оборот **be able to** можно использовать для выражения способности в будущем.

> I hope you**'ll be able to** come to the party.
> **Will** you **be able to** manage on your own?

Обращение за разрешением и выражение разрешения

Для обращения за разрешением используются глаголы **can**, **could** и **may**. При этом **could** и **may** несут более формальный и вежливый оттенок по сравнению с **can**.

> **Can** I borrow your car tomorrow, Mum?
> **Could** I come with you on the trip?
> **May** I take this book home with me?

Для разрешения используется глагол **may**. Отрицательная форма имеет вид **may not**. В случаях, когда вы хотите решительно запретить что-либо, используется **must not**.

> You **may** go now.
> You **may not** download forms from this website.
> Students **must not** plagiarise.

Выражение просьбы

Для выражения просьбы употребляются *can*, *will*, *could* или *would*. *Could* и *would* несут более вежливый и формальный оттенок.

> *Can* you lend me £5, please?
> *Will* you help me look for my purse?
> *Could* you help me for a minute?
> *Would* you mind moving your bag?

Выражение обязательств и советов

Для выражения обязательств, а также советов и указаний используются *should* и *ought to*. Отрицательные формы имеют вид *should not* или *shouldn't*, а также *ought not to* или *oughtn't to*.

> They *should* do what you suggest.
> You *shouldn't* drink that.
> We *ought to* leave now.

Для выражения сожаления о несовершенном действии используется *should have* или *ought to have* с причастием прошедшего времени основного глагола.

> He *should have* stopped at the red light.
> I *ought to have* told you earlier. I'm sorry.

Выражение долженствования и приказов

Для выражения долженствования и строгих приказов используются *must* и *have (got) to*. *Must* употребляется только в настоящем и будущем времени, а *have (got) to* можно использовать и для выражения совершения действия в прошлом. Отрицательная форма *must* имеет вид *must not* или *mustn't*. *Have (got) to* не имеет отрицательной формы.

> All passengers *must* show their tickets when asked.
> You *must* go to sleep now.
> You *must not* cross the road when the light is red.
> We *had to* leave immediately.

Выражение отсутствия необходимости

Для выражения отсутствия необходимости действия используется *don't have to* или *don't need to*. Прошедшие формы имеют вид *didn't have to* и *didn't need to*.

> You *don't have to* go yet.
> She *didn't need to* drive here – I could have picked her up.

Выражение предложений и рекомендаций

Will используется для дачи предложений или обещаний.

> I'*ll* call you tomorrow.
> Don't worry – we'*ll* help you.

Shall используется для дачи рекомендаций или предложения помощи.

> *Shall* we go to the cinema tonight?
> *Shall* I cook supper?

1.4 Времена глаголов

В этом разделе разъясняются способы употребления и формы основных времён глаголов.

В таблице форм глаголов приведены полные формы глаголов.

В разговорном английском языке эти формы зачастую сокращаются. Основные сокращения включают в себя n't (not), 'm (am), 's (is or has), 're (are), 'll (will), 've (have) и 'd (had or would):

do not, does not, did not	→	don't, doesn't, didn't
will not	→	won't
is not, are not, was not, were not	→	isn't, aren't, wasn't, weren't
have not, has not, had not	→	haven't, hasn't, hadn't
I am	→	I'm
he is, she is, it is	→	he's, she's, it's
you are, we are, they are	→	you're, we're, they're
I have, you have, they have, we have	→	I've, you've, they've, we've
he has, she has, it has	→	he's, she's, it's
I had, he had, she had, etc	→	I'd, he'd, she'd, etc
I would, he would, she would, etc	→	I'd, he'd, she'd, etc
I will, he will, she will, etc	→	I'll, he'll, she'll, etc

Простое настоящее время

	Утвердительная форма	Отрицательная форма	Вопросительная форма
1–е и 2–е лицо единственного числа, все лица множественного числа	I/you/we/they **work**.	I/you/we/they **do not work**.	**Do** I/you/we/they **work**?
3–е лицо единственного числа	He/she/it **works**.	He/she/it **does not work**.	**Does** he/she/it **work**?

Простое настоящее время употребляется в отношении:

- привычек, предпочтений и регулярно повторяющихся действий. Оно часто используется с наречиями, указывающими на частоту действия, такими как **always**, **often**, **usually**, **sometimes** or **never**, а также с выражениями, обозначающими время, такими как **on Sundays** или **in the summer**.
    I **like** coffee for breakfast but everyone else in my family **prefers** tea.
    I **never drive** to work.
    They **often go** to the cinema **on Saturdays**.

- фактов и постоянных явлений
    Do you **live** in India?
    Birds **fly** south in the winter.

- мнений и убеждений
    I **think** he's a very good teacher.
    I **don't agree**.

- определенных планов на будущее, как, например, планов путешествий и расписаний
    The train **leaves** at 10.40 a.m. and **arrives** at 3.30 p.m.

- будущего с определенными выражениями, обозначающими время. В одной части предложения употребляется простое настоящее время со словом **when**, **until**, **before** или **as soon as**, а в другой – **will** или другой модальный глагол.
    As soon as I **finish** my work, I'll phone you.
    I must do the shopping **before** they **arrive**.

22

Простое прошедшее время

	Утвердительная форма	Отрицательная форма	Вопросительная форма
Все лица и числа	I/you/he/she/it/we/they **arrived**.	I/you/he/she/it/we/they **did not arrive**.	**Did** I/you/he/she/it/we/they **arrive**?

Простое прошедшее время употребляется в отношении:

- одиночных действий в прошлом
  > He **locked** the door and **left** the house.
  > **Did** you **see** Roger last week?

- привычных действий в прошлом. Оно часто используется вместе с наречиями времени и частоты действия.
  > When I lived in Cambridge I **cycled** to work **every day**.

Настоящее длительное время

Настоящее длительное время образуется с помощью формы настоящего времени глагола **be** + the present participle основного глагола.

	Утвердительная форма	Отрицательная форма	Вопросительная форма
1-е лицо единственного числа	I **am working**.	I **am not working**.	**Am** I **working**?
3-е лицо единственного числа	He/she/it **is working**.	He/she/it **is not working**.	**Is** he/she/it **working**?
2-е лицо единственного числа, все лица множественного числа	You/we/they **are working**.	You/we/they **are not working**.	**Are** you/we/they **working**?

Настоящее длительное время употребляется в отношении:

- явлений, происходящих сейчас, в момент речи
  > What **are** you **doing**? — I'**m finishing** my essay.

- действий и ситуаций, носящих временный характер
  > I'**m studying** accountancy at college.
  > Fiona **is working** as a waitress at the moment.

- планов на будущее с указанием времени
  > I'**m flying** to New York **next week**.

- часто происходящих раздражающих явлений. В этом случае с глаголом употребляется такое наречие, как **always** или **constantly**.
  > She'**s always complaining** about work.

Прошедшее длительное время

Прошедшее длительное время образуется с помощью формы прошедшего времени глагола **be** + the present participle основного глагола.

	Утвердительная форма	Отрицательная форма	Вопросительная форма
1-е и 3-е лицо единственного числа	I/he/she/it **was working**.	I/he/she/it **was not working**.	**Was** I/he/she/it **working**?
2-е лицо единственного числа, все лица множественного числа	You/we/they **were working**.	You/we/they **were not working**.	**Were** you/we/they **working**?

Прошедшее длительное время употребляется в отношении:

- действий, которые происходили в определенный момент или период времени в прошлом

    What were you doing at eight o'clock last night? — I was standing at the bus stop.

- прерванных действий. Для описания события, из-за которого действие было прервано, следует употреблять простое прошедшее время.

    We were leaving the house when the phone rang.

Настоящее совершенное время

Настоящее совершенное время образуется с помощью формы настоящего времени глагола *have + the past participle* основного глагола.

	Утвердительная форма	Отрицательная форма	Вопросительная форма
1-е и 2-е лицо единственного числа, все лица множественного числа	I/you/we/they **have finished**.	I/you/we/they **have not finished**.	**Have** I/you/we/they **finished**?
3-е лицо единственного числа	He/she/it **has finished**.	He/she/it **has not finished**.	**Has** he/she/it **finished**?

Настоящее совершенное время употребляется в отношении:

- событий, произошедших в прошлом, но имеющих отношение к настоящему. Если событие произошло недавно, можно использовать слово *just*. Если событие не произошло, можно использовать слово *never*. Если вы спрашиваете, произошло ли событие или нет, можно использовать слово *ever*.

    Her daughter has had an accident.
    I have just handed in my essay.
    I've never met him.
    Have you ever been to Europe?

- периодов времени. В вопросительных предложениях следует использовать выражение *How long*. При указании длительности события следует использовать предлог *for*. При указании момента времени следует использовать слово *since*.

    How long have you lived in Delhi?
    I've lived in Delhi for fifteen years.
    James has worked here since 2008.

Прошедшее совершенное время

Прошедшее совершенное время образуется с помощью вспомогательного глагола *had + the past participle* основного глагола.

	Утвердительная форма	Отрицательная форма	Вопросительная форма
Все лица и числа	I/he/she/it/you/we/they **had finished**.	I/he/she/it/you/we/they **had not finished**.	**Had** I/he/she/it/you/we/they **finished**?

Прошедшее совершенное время употребляется в отношении действий, произошедших в прошлом перед тем, как случилось другое событие:

    She had just made some coffee when I arrived.

Настоящее совершенное длительное время

Настоящее совершенное длительное время образуется с помощью формы настоящего времени глагола *have + been + the present participle* основного глагола.

	Утвердительная форма	Отрицательная форма	Вопросительная форма
1-е и 2-е лицо единственного числа, все лица множественного числа	I/you/we/they **have been waiting**.	I/you/we/they **have not been waiting**.	**Have** I/you/we/they **been waiting**?
3-е лицо единственного числа	He/she/it **has been waiting**.	He/she/it **has not been waiting**.	**Has** he/she/it **been waiting**?

Настоящее совершенное длительное время употребляется в отношении:

• действий и состояний, которые начались в прошлом и продолжаются в данный момент

How long **have** you **been learning** English?

• действий и состояний, которые начались в прошлом и закончились только что

Thank goodness you're here! I'**ve been waiting** for hours!

Прошедшее совершенное длительное время

Прошедшее совершенное длительное время образуется с помощью вспомогательного глагола *had + been + the present participle* основного глагола.

	Утвердительная форма	Отрицательная форма	Вопросительная форма
Все лица и числа	I/he/she/it/you/we/they **had been waiting**.	I/he/she/it/you/we/they **had not been waiting**.	**Had** I/he/she/it/you/we/they **been waiting**?

Прошедшее совершенное длительное время употребляется в отношении действий, которые начались в прошлом и завершились до того, как случилось другое событие:

I **had been studying** for hours, so I stopped and went for a walk.

1.5 Выражение действия в будущем

В английском языке нет будущего времени. При разговоре о будущем можно использовать простое настоящее или настоящее длительное время, описанные выше. Ниже приведены другие способы выражения действия в будущем.

Will

	Утвердительная форма	Отрицательная форма	Вопросительная форма
Все лица и числа	I/he/she/it/you/we/they **will wait**.	I/he/she/it/you/we/they **will not wait**.	**Will** I/he/she/it/you/we/they **wait**?

Глагол **will** + базовая форма основного глагола употребляется:

- в отношении обстоятельств в будущем
  I'll **be** on the plane this time tomorrow.
- обещаний
  We **will call** you next week.
- с такими глаголами, как **think** и **believe**, для выражения мнения о событиях в будущем
  Do you think **he will** pass the exam?

Будущее длительное время

	Утвердительная форма	Отрицательная форма	Вопросительная форма
Все лица и числа	I/he/she/it/you/we/they **will be waiting**.	I/he/she/it/you/we/they **will not be waiting**.	**Will** I/he/she/it/you/we/they be **waiting**?

Глагол **will** + **be** + the present participle основного глагола употребляется в отношении процессов, осуществляемых в определенный момент в будущем:

  Will you **be working** here next week?

Будущее совершенное время

	Утвердительная форма	Отрицательная форма	Вопросительная форма
Все лица и числа	I/he/she/it/you/we/they **will have waited**.	I/he/she/it/you/we/they **will not have waited**.	**Will** I/he/she/it/you/we/**they have waited**?

Глагол **will** + **have** + the past participle основного глагола употребляется в отношении действий, которые завершатся к определенному моменту в будущем:

  Do you want to go out next Saturday? — Yes, I'll **have finished** my exams by then.

Будущее совершенное длительное время

	Утвердительная форма	Отрицательная форма	Вопросительная форма
Все лица и числа	I/he/she/it/you/we/they **will have been waiting**.	I/he/she/it/you/we/they **will not have been waiting**.	**Will** I/he/she/it/you/we/they **have been waiting**?

Глагол **will** + **have** + **been** + the present participle основного глагола употребляется в отношении продолжающихся действий, которые завершатся к определенному моменту в будущем:

  She'll be here at 2 o'clock. We'll **have been waiting** for three hours by then.

Be going to

Be going to состоит из глагола **be** + **going to** + инфинитив. Фраза **be going to** употребляется:

- при разговоре об определенных планах на будущее
  I'm **going to visit** Amir tonight.
- для выражения прогноза о том, что должно произойти в скором времени, основанного на происходящем в данный момент
  Sally never does any work; she's **going to fail** her exams.

Be about to

Be about to состоит из глагола *be* + *about to* + инфинитив. Фраза *be about to* употребляется в отношении событий в ближайшем будущем.

> *Come on! We're about to leave!*

1.6 Действительный и страдательный залоги

В предложении с глаголом в действительном залоге подлежащее – это лицо или предмет, выполняющий действие, описываемое глаголом. В предложении с глаголом в страдательном залоге в роли подлежащего выступает лицо или предмет, на который оказывается воздействие. Страдательный залог образуется при помощи формы глагола *be* + *the past participle* основного глагола.

> Действительный залог:
> *The postman **delivers** thousands of letters every day.*
> Страдательный залог:
> *Thousands of letters **are delivered** every day.*

Страдательный залог употребляется в тех случаях, когда вы желаете обратить внимание на самый важный элемент действия. В приведенном выше примере нам не нужно знать, кто доставляет письма. Самое важное здесь – это количество доставляемых писем. Страдательный залог также можно использовать, если вам не известно лицо или предмет, выполняющий действие, или когда эта информация не имеет значения.

Страдательный залог можно употреблять с любым из основных времен глагола.

2 Существительные

2.1 Виды существительных

Исчисляемые существительные

К исчисляемым существительным относятся те, что обозначают предметы, которые можно сосчитать: *one cat*, *two cats*, *seventeen cats* и т.д. Они могут быть в единственном или во множественном числе. В единственном числе эти существительные употребляются с определяющим словом (например, *a*, *the*, *my* или *that*).

> *Could you fetch me **a chair**?*
> *We've bought **six new chairs**.*

Неисчисляемые существительные

К неисчисляемым существительным относятся те, что обозначают предметы, которые обычно невозможно сосчитать, например, чувства или мысли. Как правило, они не имеют формы множественного числа, и за ними следует глагол в единственном числе. Обычно эти существительные не употребляются с артиклем *a* или *an*.

К наиболее часто встречающимся неисчисляемым существительным относятся следующие: *advice, beauty, behaviour, evidence, furniture, happiness, help, homework, information, knowledge, luggage, money, news, progress, research.*

> *John asked me for some **advice**.*
> *Do you have enough **money**?*

Если необходимо указать количество какого-нибудь из этих существительных, то следует использовать определяющее слово (например, *some*) или такое выражение, как *a piece of* или *a bit of*.

> *Let me give you a piece of advice.*
> *He handed me a bowl of rice.*

В зависимости от своего значения некоторые существительные могут быть как исчисляемыми, так и неисчисляемыми. К ним относятся слова *hair*, *time*, *light* и *paper*.

> *Time passed slowly.*
> *She sat the exam four times.*

Вещественные существительные

Вещественные существительные обозначают вещества, которые можно разделить, но невозможно посчитать. Например: *bread*, *cheese*, *coffee*, *sugar* и *tea*. В большинстве случаев они подобны неисчисляемым существительным, то есть, они не имеют формы множественного числа, за ними следует глагол в форме единственного числа, и с ними не употребляется артикль *a* или *an*.

> *Meat is usually more expensive than cheese.*

Однако употребление вещественных существительных во множественном числе возможно, если речь идет об отдельном виде этого вещества или о его порции:

> *Rebecca brought out a selection of French cheeses.*
> *Two coffees please, and a slice of cake.*

Существительные, которые всегда употребляются во множественном числе

Некоторые существительные всегда употребляются только во множественном числе, даже если речь идет об одном предмете. Например: *clothes*, *trousers*, *jeans*, *glasses* и *scissors*. За ними следует глагол во множественном числе.

> *These trousers are very expensive.*
> *Put the scissors in the drawer when you have finished with them.*

При упоминании предметов, состоящих из двух частей, можно использовать выражение *a pair of*.

> *I bought a new pair of jeans.*
> *Liz has two pairs of glasses.*

2.2 Обозначение принадлежности существительных

Принадлежность можно обозначить:

- путем добавления 's к существительному в единственном числе или к существительному с особой формой множественного числа, которая не оканчивается на -s

one *dog*	one *boy*	several *children*
the *dog's* bones	the *boy's* book	the *children's* toys

- путем добавления ' к существительному с обычной формой множественного числа

the *dogs'* bones	the *boys'* books

- путем добавления после существительного предложной фразы с *of*
  *the side **of the ship**   the end **of the queue***

Принадлежность, выражаемую при помощи *'s*, обычно используют с существительными, которые обозначают людей и животных, а также во фразах, обозначающих время.

  ***Maria's** coat   **today's** newspaper*

Принадлежность, выражаемую при помощи *of* обычно используют с существительными, которые обозначают предметы и абстрактные понятия.

  *the leg **of the table**   the growth **of modern industry***

Например, можно сказать **This is the girl's book**, но нельзя сказать ~~This is the book of the girl~~. Можно сказать **We waited at the end of the queue**, но нельзя сказать ~~We waited at the queue's end~~.

Принадлежность употребляется для обозначения:

- предмета, принадлежащему кому-то
  *Is this your **sister's bag**?*
- места, где кто-то живет или работает
  *I'm going to the **doctor's** after work.*

2.3 Употребление артиклей с существительными

Неопределенный артикль: a или an

Артикль *a* употребляется перед словами, начинающимися с согласного звука. Артикль *an* ставится перед словами, которые начинаются с гласного звука. Обратите внимание, что форму артикля (*a* или *an*) определяет звучание последующего слова. Например, несмотря на то, что в начале слова *university* стоит гласная буква, оно начинается со звука [j].

  a child   an engineer   a green apple
  an old man   a university   an umbrella

Артикль *a* или *an* употребляется с исчисляемыми существительными в единственном числе:

- для указания лица или предмета, упоминаемого впервые
  A man was seen driving away in a black car.
- для указания неконкретного лица или предмета
  I went into a shop to buy a newspaper.
- когда речь идет о профессиях
  Her father is a dentist and her mother is a teacher.
- для обозначения того, сколько раз было совершено действие за определенный период времени
  I brush my teeth twice a day.

Определенный артикль: the

Артикль **the** употребляется с существительными в единственном и во множественном числе. Использовать **the** можно как с исчисляемыми, так и с неисчисляемыми существительными.

Артикль **the** употребляется для указания того, что упоминалось ранее, а также что уже известно. Во втором примере ниже говорящий и слушатель знают, о какой библиотеке идет речь.

  *That's **the man** I was telling you about.*
  *Let's go to **the library**.*

Отсутствие артикля

Имеются случаи, в которых артикль не используется:

- перед существительным во множественном числе, а также перед неисчисляемым существительным, если речь идет о предмете в целом
  Tigers are becoming extinct.
  Do you like rice?

- перед видами транспорта после *by*: *bicycle*, *car*, *bus*, *train*, *boat*, *plane*
  Ruth went by bicycle but Lucy went by car.

- перед словами, обозначающими прием пищи
  She met Diane for lunch.
  I made breakfast.

- перед названиями организаций, если используется предлог *to* или *at*:
  hospital, *prison*, *school*, *university*, *college*, *work*.
  Jamal was taken to hospital with a broken ankle.
  I was at university with her.

(При этом, если речь идет о конкретном месте, необходимо использовать артикль *a* или *the*, например: *How do I get to the hospital from here?*)

3 Местоимения

3.1 Личные местоимения

	Единственное число		Множественное число	
	Субъект	Объект	Субъект	Объект
1–е лицо	I	me	we	us
2–е лицо	you			
3–е лицо (мужской род)	he	him	they	them
3–е лицо (женский род)	she	her		
3–е лицо (средний род)	it			

Обратите внимание на то, что в английском языке существует одна форма *you* для единственного и множественного числа 2–го лица личных местоимений. Для того чтобы ясно выразить обращение к более чем одному человеку, используются такие слова, как *both (of)* или *all (of)*.

I'd like both of you to come for dinner on Sunday.
You must all stop writing now.

3.2 Возвратные местоимения

	Единственное число	Множественное число
1–е лицо	myself	ourselves
2–е лицо	yourself	yourselves
3–е лицо (мужской род)	himself	
3–е лицо (женский род)	herself	themselves
3–е лицо (средний род)	itself	

I looked at myself in the mirror.
Gita made herself a sandwich.

Как правило, возвратные местоимения не употребляются для описания процессов, которые человек делает самостоятельно, как, например, принятие душа или процесс бритья.

*Jeremy **washed** and **dressed**, then went out.*

3.3 Неопределенные местоимения

Неопределенные местоимения используются, когда деятель или субъект неизвестен или мы не хотим его упоминать. К неопределенным местоимениям относятся:

- объемы и количества: *most, some, none, any, all, both, half, several, enough, many, each*.

    *Although we lost a lot of our books in the fire, **some** were saved.*
    *I've run out of sugar. Do you have **any**?*

- неопределенные люди или предметы:

someone	somebody	something
no one	nobody	nothing
anyone	anybody	anything
everyone	everybody	everything

После этих местоимений используется единственное число глагола.

Nothing has *been written on the subject yet.*

Когда используются такие слова, как *someone/somebody*, *no one/nobody*, *anyone/anybody* и *everyone/everybody*, возможно употребление местоимений или определяющих слов в форме множественного числа, таких как *they*, *them* или *their*.

*Has **everyone** finished **their** lunch?*
*If **anyone** calls, please tell **them** I've gone out.*

4 Прилагательные

4.1 Прилагательные с существительными

Большинство прилагательных в предложении ставится перед существительным или после глагола-связки *be* или *seem*:

*There was a **tall man** waiting in the office.*
*My father **is** very **tall**.*

Однако некоторые прилагательные ставятся только после глагола-связки. Их расположение перед существительным невозможно. К таким прилагательным относятся: *afraid, alike, alive, alone, ashamed, asleep, awake, glad* и *hurt*. К примеру, можно сказать *She was glad that he came*, но нельзя сказать ~~She was a glad woman~~. В большинстве подобных случаев перед существительным ставится другое прилагательное с аналогичным значением.

*They **seem afraid** of you.*
*He was acting like a **frightened child**.*
*Chris **was asleep** on the sofa.*
*We stared at the **sleeping baby**.*

4.2 Степени сравнения прилагательных

Сравнительная степень используется для сравнения двух людей, предметов или состояний. Перед второй частью сравнения используется **than**.

> *Anna is **taller than** Mary but Mary is **older**.*

Превосходная степень используется для сравнения более чем двух людей, предметов или состояний, при этом подчеркивается, что один из предметов лучше или хуже остальных. Как правило, перед прилагательными в превосходной степени ставится **the**, но его можно опускать в случаях, если прилагательное используется после глагола–связки, такого как **be** или **seem**.

> *This is **the smallest** camera I have ever seen.*
> *Which of them is (the) **tallest**?*

Сравнительная и превосходная формы прилагательных образуются следующим образом:

- В односложных прилагательных к основе добавляется **-er** (сравнительная) или **-est** (превосходная). Если односложное или двусложное прилагательное заканчивается на **-e**, к слову просто прибавляется **-r** или **-st**.

bright	*brighter*	*the brightest*
long	*longer*	*the longest*
wise	*wiser*	*the wisest*

- Если односложное прилагательное заканчивается на единичную согласную, которой предшествует единичная гласная, то согласная в конце слова удваивается. (Не применяется для двусложных прилагательных.)

big	*bigger*	*the biggest*
hot	*hotter*	*the hottest*

- Если прилагательное имеет два слога и заканчивается на **-y**, то к основе добавляется **-er** или **-est**. При этом **-y** заменяется на **-i**.

pretty	*prettier*	*the prettiest*

- В прилагательных, содержащих три и более слога, перед прилагательными используется **more** для формирования сравнительной степени и **most** для формирования превосходной степени.

relevant	*more relevant*	*the most relevant*
interesting	*more interesting*	*the most interesting*

- Следующие прилагательные имеют неправильные формы сравнительных и превосходных степеней:

good	*better*	*the best*
bad	*worse*	*the worst*
far	*further*	*the furthest*

a

A [eɪ] n (Mus) ля nt ind

a [ə] (before vowel or silent h: **an**) indef art
1: **a book** кни́га; **an apple** я́блоко; **she's a
student** она́ студе́нтка
2 (instead of the number "one"): **a week
ago** неде́лю наза́д; **a hundred pounds** сто
фу́нтов
3 (in expressing time) в +acc; **3 a day** 3 в
день; **10 km an hour** 10 км в час
4 (in expressing prices): **30p a kilo** 30
пе́нсов килогра́мм; **£5 a person** £5 с
ка́ждого

AA n abbr (Brit) (= Automobile
Association) автомоби́льная ассоциа́ция
AAA n abbr (= American Automobile
Association) америка́нская
автомоби́льная ассоциа́ция
aback [ə'bæk] adv: **I was taken aback** я
был поражён
abandon [ə'bændən] vt (person)
покида́ть (perf поки́нуть); (search)
прекраща́ть (perf прекрати́ть); (hope)
оставля́ть (perf оста́вить); (idea)
отка́зываться (perf отказа́ться) от +gen
abbey ['æbɪ] n абба́тство
abbreviation [əbriːvɪ'eɪʃən] n
сокраще́ние
abdomen ['æbdəmɛn] n брюшна́я
по́лость f, живо́т
abide [ə'baɪd] vt: **I can't abide it/him** я
э́того/его́ не выношу́; **abide by** vt fus
соблюда́ть (perf соблюсти́)
ability [ə'bɪlɪtɪ] n (capacity) спосо́бность
f; (talent, skill) спосо́бности fpl
able ['eɪbl] adj (capable) спосо́бный;
(skilled) уме́лый; **he is able to ...** он
спосо́бен +infin ...
abnormal [æb'nɔːml] adj ненорма́льный

aboard [ə'bɔːd] prep (position: Naut,
Aviat) на борту́ +gen; (: train, bus) в +prp;
(motion: Naut, Aviat) на борт +gen; (: train,
bus) в +acc ▷ adv: **to climb aboard** (train)
сади́ться (perf сесть) в по́езд
abolish [ə'bɔlɪʃ] vt отменя́ть (perf
отмени́ть)
abolition [æbə'lɪʃən] n отме́на
abortion [ə'bɔːʃən] n або́рт; **to have an
abortion** де́лать (perf сде́лать) або́рт

about [ə'baut] adv **1** (approximately:
referring to time, price etc) о́коло +gen,
приме́рно +acc; **at about two (o'clock)**
приме́рно в два (часа́), о́коло двух
(часо́в); **I've just about finished** я почти́
зако́нчил
2 (approximately: referring to height, size
etc) о́коло +gen, приме́рно +nom; **the
room is about 10 metres wide** ко́мната
приме́рно 10 ме́тров в ширину́; **she is
about your age** она́ приме́рно Ва́шего
во́зраста
3 (referring to place) повсю́ду; **to leave
things lying about** разбра́сывать (perf
разброса́ть) ве́щи повсю́ду; **to run/walk
about** бе́гать (impf)/ходи́ть (impf) вокру́г
4: **to be about to do** собира́ться (perf
собра́ться) +infin; **he was about to go to
bed** он собра́лся лечь спать
▷ prep **1** (relating to) о(б) +prp; **a book
about London** кни́га о Ло́ндоне; **what is it
about?** о чём э́то?; **what or how about
doing ...?** как насчёт того́, что́бы +infin ...?
2 (referring to place) по +dat; **to walk
about the town** ходи́ть (impf) по го́роду;
her clothes were scattered about the room
её оде́жда была́ разбро́сана по ко́мнате

above [ə'bʌv] adv (higher up) наверху́
▷ prep (higher than) над +instr; (: in rank
etc) вы́ше +gen; **from above** све́рху;
mentioned above вышеупомя́нутый;
above all пре́жде всего́
abroad [ə'brɔːd] adv (to be) за грани́цей
or рубежо́м; (to go) за грани́цу or рубе́ж;
(to come from) из-за грани́цы or рубежа́
abrupt [ə'brʌpt] adj (action, ending)
внеза́пный; (person, manner) ре́зкий
absence ['æbsəns] n отсу́тствие
absent ['æbsənt] adj отсу́тствующий
absolute ['æbsəluːt] adj абсолю́тный;
absolutely [æbsə'luːtlɪ] adv абсолю́тно,
соверше́нно; (certainly) безусло́вно
absorb [əb'zɔːb] vt (liquid, information)
впи́тывать (perf впита́ть); (light, firm)
поглоща́ть (perf поглоти́ть); **he is
absorbed in a book** он поглощён кни́гой;
absorbent cotton n (US)
гигроскопи́ческая ва́та; **absorbing** adj
увлека́тельный
abstract ['æbstrækt] adj абстра́ктный

absurd [əb'sə:d] *adj* абсу́рдный, неле́пый

abundant [ə'bʌndənt] *adj* оби́льный

abuse [*n* ə'bju:s, *vb* ə'bju:z] *n* (*insults*) брань *f*; (*ill-treatment*) жесто́кое обраще́ние; (*misuse*) злоупотребле́ние ▷ *vt* (*see n*) оскорбля́ть (*perf* оскорби́ть); жесто́ко обраща́ться (*impf*) с +*instr*; злоупотребля́ть (*perf* злоупотреби́ть) +*instr*

abusive [ə'bju:sɪv] *adj* (*person*) гру́бый, жесто́кий

academic [ækə'dɛmɪk] *adj* (*system*) академи́ческий; (*qualifications*) учёный; (*work, books*) нау́чный; (*person*) интеллектуа́льный ▷ *n* учёный(-ая) *m(f) adj*

academy [ə'kædəmɪ] *n* (*learned body*) акаде́мия; (*college*) учи́лище; (*in Scotland*) сре́дняя шко́ла; **academy of music** консервато́рия

accelerate [æk'sɛləreɪt] *vi* (*Aut*) разгоня́ться (*perf* разогна́ться)

acceleration [æksɛlə'reɪʃən] *n* (*Aut*) разго́н

accelerator [æk'sɛləreɪtə^r] *n* акселера́тор

accent [æksɛnt] *n* акце́нт; (*stress mark*) знак ударе́ния

accept [ək'sɛpt] *vt* принима́ть (*perf* приня́ть); (*fact, situation*) мири́ться (*perf* примири́ться) с +*instr*; (*responsibility, blame*) принима́ть (*perf* приня́ть) на себя́; **acceptable** *adj* прие́млемый; **acceptance** *n* приня́тие; (*of fact*) прия́тие

access [æksɛs] *n* до́ступ; **accessible** [æk'sɛsəbl] *adj* досту́пный

accessory [æk'sɛsərɪ] *n* принадле́жность *f*; **accessories** *npl* (*Dress*) аксессуа́ры *mpl*

accident [æksɪdənt] *n* (*disaster*) несча́стный слу́чай; (*in car etc*) ава́рия; **by accident** случа́йно; **accidental** [æksɪ'dɛntl] *adj* случа́йный; **accidentally** [æksɪ'dɛntəlɪ] *adv* случа́йно

acclaim [ə'kleɪm] *n* призна́ние

accommodate [ə'kɔmədeɪt] *vt* (*subj: person*) предоставля́ть (*perf* предоста́вить) жильё +*dat*; (: *car, hotel etc*) вмеща́ть (*perf* вмести́ть)

accommodation [əkɔmə'deɪʃən] *n* (*to live in*) жильё; (*to work in*) помеще́ние; **accommodations** *npl* (*US: lodgings*) жильё *ntsg*

accompaniment [ə'kʌmpənɪmənt] *n* сопровожде́ние; (*Mus*) аккомпанеме́нт

accompany [ə'kʌmpənɪ] *vt* сопровожда́ть (*perf* сопроводи́ть); (*Mus*) аккомпани́ровать (*impf*) +*dat*

accomplice [ə'kʌmplɪs] *n* соо́бщник(-ица)

accomplish [ə'kʌmplɪʃ] *vt* (*task*) заверша́ть (*perf* заверши́ть); (*goal*)

достига́ть (дости́гнуть *or* дости́чь *perf*) +*gen*

accord [ə'kɔ:d] *n*: **of his own accord** по со́бственному жела́нию; **of its own accord** сам по себе́; **accordance** *n*: **in accordance with** в согла́сии *or* соотве́тствии с +*instr*; **according** *prep*: **according to** согла́сно +*dat*; **accordingly** *adv* соотве́тствующим о́бразом; (*as a result*) соотве́тственно

account [ə'kaunt] *n* (*bill*) счёт; (*in bank*) (расчётный) счёт; (*report*) отчёт; **accounts** *npl* (*Comm*) счета́ *mpl*; (*books*) бухга́лтерские кни́ги *fpl*; **to keep an account of** вести́ (*impf*) счёт +*gen or* +*dat*; **to bring sb to account for sth** призыва́ть (*perf* призва́ть) кого́-н к отве́ту за что-н; **by all accounts** по всем сведе́ниям; **it is of no account** э́то не ва́жно; **on account** в креди́т; **on no account** ни в ко́ем слу́чае; **on account of** по причи́не +*gen*; **to take into account, take account of** принима́ть (*perf* приня́ть) в расчёт; **account for** *vt fus* (*expenses*) отчи́тываться (*perf* отчита́ться) за +*acc*; (*absence, failure*) объясня́ть (*perf* объясни́ть); **accountable** *adj* отчётный; **to be accountable to sb for sth** отвеча́ть (*impf*) за что-н пе́ред кем-н; **accountancy** *n* бухгалте́рия, бухга́лтерское де́ло; **accountant** *n* бухга́лтер

accumulate [ə'kju:mjuleɪt] *vt* нака́пливать (*perf* накопи́ть) ▷ *vi* нака́пливаться (*perf* накопи́ться)

accuracy ['ækjurəsɪ] *n* то́чность *f*

accurate ['ækjurɪt] *adj* то́чный; (*person, device*) аккура́тный; **accurately** *adv* то́чно

accusation [ækju'zeɪʃən] *n* обвине́ние

accuse [ə'kju:z] *vt*: **to accuse sb (of sth)** обвиня́ть (*perf* обвини́ть) кого́-н (в чём-н); **accused** *n* (*Law*): **the accused** обвиня́емый(-ая) *m(f) adj*

accustomed [ə'kʌstəmd] *adj*: **I'm accustomed to working late/to the heat** я привы́к рабо́тать по́здно/к жаре́

ace [eɪs] *n* (*Cards*) туз; (*Tennis*) вы́игрыш с пода́чи, эйс

ache [eɪk] *n* боль *f* ▷ *vi* боле́ть (*impf*); **my head aches** у меня́ боли́т голова́

achieve [ə'tʃi:v] *vt* (*result*) достига́ть (дости́гнуть *or* дости́чь *perf*); (*success*) добива́ться (*perf* доби́ться) +*gen*; **achievement** *n* достиже́ние

acid ['æsɪd] *adj* (*Chem*) кисло́тный; (*taste*) ки́слый ▷ *n* (*Chem*) кислота́

acknowledge [ək'nɔlɪdʒ] *vt* (*letter etc: also* **acknowledge receipt of**) подтвержда́ть (*perf* подтверди́ть) получе́ние +*gen*; (*fact*) признава́ть (*perf* призна́ть); **acknowledgement** *n* (*of letter etc*) подтвержде́ние получе́ния

acne ['æknɪ] *n* угри́ *mpl*, прыщи́ *mpl*

acorn ['eɪkɔ:n] *n* жёлудь *m*

acquaintance n знако́мый(-ая) m(f) adj
acquire [ə'kwaɪə^r] vt приобрета́ть (perf
приобрести́)
acquisition [ækwɪ'zɪʃən] n
приобрете́ние
acre ['eɪkə^r] n акр
across [ə'krɔs] prep (over) че́рез +acc; (on
the other side of) на друго́й стороне́ +gen,
по ту сто́рону +gen; (crosswise over)
че́рез +acc, поперёк +gen ▷ adv на ту or
другу́ю сто́рону; (measurement: width)
ширино́й; **to walk across the road**
переходи́ть (perf перейти́) доро́гу; **to take
sb across the road** переводи́ть (perf
перевести́) кого́-н че́рез доро́гу; **the lake
is 12 km across** ширина́ о́зера — 12 км;
across from напро́тив +gen
act [ækt] n (also Law) акт; (deed)
посту́пок; (of play) де́йствие, акт ▷ vi (do
sth) поступа́ть (perf поступи́ть),
де́йствовать (impf); (behave) вести́ (perf
повести́) себя́; (have effect) де́йствовать
(perf поде́йствовать); (Theat) игра́ть (perf
сыгра́ть); **in the act of** в проце́ссе +gen; **to
act as** де́йствовать (impf) в ка́честве +gen;
acting adj: **acting director** исполня́ющий
обя́занности дире́ктора ▷ n (profession)
актёрская профе́ссия
action ['ækʃən] n (deed) посту́пок,
де́йствие; (motion) движе́ние; (Mil)
вое́нные де́йствия ntpl; (Law) иск; **the
machine was out of action** маши́на вы́шла
из стро́я; **to take action** принима́ть (perf
приня́ть) ме́ры
active ['æktɪv] adj акти́вный; (volcano)
де́йствующий; **actively** adv (participate)
акти́вно; (discourage, dislike) си́льно
activist ['æktɪvɪst] n активи́ст(ка)
activity [æk'tɪvɪtɪ] n (being active)
акти́вность f; (action) де́ятельность f;
(pastime) заня́тие
actor ['æktə^r] n актёр
actress ['æktrɪs] n актри́са
actual ['æktjuəl] adj (real)
действи́тельный; **the actual work hasn't
begun yet** сама́ рабо́та ещё не начала́сь;
actually adv (really) действи́тельно; (in
fact) на са́мом де́ле, факти́чески; (even)
да́же
acupuncture ['ækjupʌŋktʃə^r] n
иглоука́лывание, акупункту́ра
acute [ə'kju:t] adj о́стрый; (anxiety)
си́льный; **acute accent** аку́т
AD adv abbr (= Anno Domini) н.э. (= на́шей
э́ры)
ad [æd] n abbr (inf) = **advertisement**
adamant ['ædəmənt] adj непрекло́нный
adapt [ə'dæpt] vt (alter) приспоса́бливать
(perf приспосо́бить) ▷ vi: **to adapt (to)**
приспоса́бливаться (perf приспосо́биться)
(к +dat), адапти́роваться (impf/perf) (к
+dat)
add [æd] vt (to collection etc) прибавля́ть
(perf приба́вить); (comment) добавля́ть

(perf доба́вить); (figures: also **add up**)
скла́дывать (perf сложи́ть) ▷ vi: **to add to**
(workload) увели́чивать (perf увели́чить);
(problems) усугубля́ть (perf усугуби́ть)
addict ['ædɪkt] n (also **drug addict**)
наркома́н; **addicted** [ə'dɪktɪd] adj: **to be
addicted to** (drugs etc) пристрасти́ться
(perf) к +dat; (fig): **he's addicted to football**
он за́ядлый люби́тель футбо́ла;
addiction [ə'dɪkʃən] n пристра́стие; **drug
addiction** наркома́ния; **addictive**
[ə'dɪktɪv] adj (drug) вызыва́ющий
привыка́ние
addition [ə'dɪʃən] n (sum) сложе́ние;
(thing added) добавле́ние; (to collection)
пополне́ние; **in addition** вдоба́вок,
дополни́тельно; **in addition to** в
дополне́ние к +dat; **additional** adj
дополни́тельный
address [ə'drɛs] n а́дрес; (speech) речь f
▷ vt адресова́ть (impf/perf); (person)
обраща́ться (perf обрати́ться) к +dat;
(problem) занима́ться (perf заня́ться)
+instr; **address book** n записна́я кни́жка
adequate ['ædɪkwɪt] adj (sufficient)
доста́точный; (satisfactory) адеква́тный
adhere [əd'hɪə^r] vi: **to adhere to** (fig)
приде́рживаться (impf) +gen
adhesive [əd'hi:zɪv] adj кле́йкий ▷ n
клей
adjacent [ə'dʒeɪsənt] adj: **adjacent (to)**
сме́жный (с +instr)
adjective ['ædʒɛktɪv] n прилага́тельное
nt adj
adjust [ə'dʒʌst] vt (plans, views)
приспоса́бливать (perf приспосо́бить);
(clothing) поправля́ть (perf попра́вить);
(mechanism) регули́ровать (perf
отрегули́ровать) ▷ vi: **to adjust (to)**
приспоса́бливаться (perf приспосо́биться)
(к +dat); **adjustable** adj регули́руемый;
adjustment n (to surroundings)
адапта́ция; (of prices, wages)
регули́рование; **to make adjustments to**
вноси́ть (perf внести́) измене́ния в +acc
administer [əd'mɪnɪstə^r] vt (country,
department) управля́ть (impf) +instr,
руководи́ть (impf) +instr; (justice)
отправля́ть (impf); (test) проводи́ть (perf
провести́)
administration [ədmɪnɪs'treɪʃən] n
(management) администра́ция
administrative [əd'mɪnɪstrətɪv] adj
администрати́вный
admiration [ædmə'reɪʃən] n восхище́ние
admire [əd'maɪə^r] vt восхища́ться (perf
восхити́ться) +instr; (gaze at) любова́ться
(impf) +instr; **admirer** n покло́нник(-ица)
admission [əd'mɪʃən] n (admittance)
до́пуск; (entry fee) входна́я пла́та;
"admission free", **"free admission"** "вход
свобо́дный"
admit [əd'mɪt] vt (confess, accept)
признава́ть (perf призна́ть); (permit to

enter) впуска́ть (perf впусти́ть); (to hospital) госпитализи́ровать (impf/perf); **admit to** vt fus (crime) сознава́ться (perf созна́ться) в +prp;
admittedly [əd'mɪtɪdlɪ] adv: **admittedly it is not easy** призна́ться, э́то не легко́
adolescent [ædəu'lɛsnt] adj подро́стковый ▷ n подро́сток
adopt [ə'dɔpt] vt (son) усыновля́ть (perf усынови́ть); (daughter) удочеря́ть (perf удочери́ть); (policy) принима́ть (perf приня́ть); **adopted** adj (child) приёмный; **adoption** [ə'dɔpʃən] n (see vt) усыновле́ние; удочере́ние; приня́тие
adore [ə'dɔːʳ] vt обожа́ть (impf)
Adriatic [eɪdrɪ'ætɪk] n: **the Adriatic** Адриа́тика
ADSL abbr (= Asymmetric Digital Subscriber Line) АЦАЛ f (= асимметри́чная цифрова́я абоне́нтская ли́ния)
adult ['ædʌlt] n взро́слый(-ая) m(f) adj ▷ adj (grown-up) взро́слый; **adult film** фильм для взро́слых
adultery [ə'dʌltərɪ] n супру́жеская неве́рность f
advance [əd'vɑːns] n (progress) успе́х; (Mil) наступле́ние; (money) ава́нс ▷ adj (booking) предвари́тельный ▷ vt (theory, idea) выдвига́ть (perf вы́двинуть) ▷ vi продвига́ться (perf продви́нуться) вперёд; (Mil) наступа́ть (impf); **in advance** зара́нее, предвари́тельно; **to advance sb money** плати́ть (perf заплати́ть) кому́-н ава́нсом; **advanced** adj (studies) для продви́нутого у́ровня; (course) продви́нутый; (child, country) развито́й; **advanced maths** вы́сшая матема́тика
advantage [əd'vɑːntɪdʒ] n преиму́щество; **to take advantage of** (person) испо́льзовать (perf); **to our advantage** в на́ших интере́сах
adventure [əd'vɛntʃəʳ] n приключе́ние
adventurous [əd'vɛntʃərəs] adj (person) сме́лый
adverb ['ædvəːb] n наре́чие
adversary ['ædvəsərɪ] n проти́вник(-ница)
adverse ['ædvəːs] adj неблагоприя́тный
advert ['ædvəːt] n abbr (Brit) = **advertisement**
advertise ['ædvətaɪz] vt, vi реклами́ровать (impf); **to advertise on television/in a newspaper** дава́ть (perf дать) объявле́ние по телеви́дению/в газе́ту; **to advertise a job** объявля́ть (perf объяви́ть) ко́нкурс на ме́сто; **to advertise for staff** дава́ть (perf дать) объявле́ние, что тре́буются рабо́тники; **advertisement** [əd'vəːtɪsmənt] n рекла́ма; (classified) объявле́ние
advice [əd'vaɪs] n сове́т; **a piece of advice** сове́т; **to take legal advice** обраща́ться (perf обрати́ться) (за сове́том) к юри́сту
advisable [əd'vaɪzəbl] adj целесообра́зный

advise [əd'vaɪz] vt сове́товать (perf посове́товать) +dat; (professionally) консульти́ровать (perf проконсульти́ровать) +gen; **to advise sb of sth** извеща́ть (perf извести́ть) кого́-н о чём-н; **to advise (sb) against doing** отсове́товать (perf) (кому́-н) +impf infin
adviser (US **advisor**) n сове́тник, консульта́нт; **legal adviser** юриско́нсульт
advisory [əd'vaɪzərɪ] adj консультати́вный
advocate [vb 'ædvəkeɪt, n 'ædvəkɪt] vt выступа́ть (perf вы́ступить) за +acc ▷ n (Law) защи́тник, адвока́т; (supporter): **advocate of** сторо́нник(-ица) +gen
Aegean [iː'dʒiːən] n: **the Aegean** Эге́йское мо́ре
aerial ['ɛərɪəl] n анте́нна ▷ adj возду́шный; **aerial photography** аэрофотосъёмка
aerobics [ɛə'rəubɪks] n аэро́бика
aeroplane ['ɛərəpleɪn] n (Brit) самолёт
aerosol ['ɛərəsɔl] n аэрозо́ль m
affair [ə'fɛəʳ] n (matter) де́ло; (also **love affair**) рома́н
affect [ə'fɛkt] vt (influence) де́йствовать (perf поде́йствовать) or влия́ть (perf повлия́ть) на +acc; (afflict) поража́ть (perf порази́ть); (move deeply) тро́гать (perf тро́нуть)
affection [ə'fɛkʃən] n привя́занность f; **affectionate** adj не́жный
affluent ['æfluənt] adj благополу́чный
afford [ə'fɔːd] vt позволя́ть (perf позво́лить) себе́; **I can't afford it** мне э́то не по карма́ну; **I can't afford the time** мне вре́мя не позволя́ет; **affordable** adj досту́пный
Afghanistan [æf'gænɪstæn] n Афганиста́н
afraid [ə'freɪd] adj испу́ганный; **to be afraid of sth/sb/of doing** боя́ться (impf) чего́-н/кого́-н/+infin; **to be afraid to** боя́ться (perf побоя́ться) +infin; **I am afraid that** (apology) бою́сь, что; **I am afraid so/not** бою́сь, что да/нет
Africa ['æfrɪkə] n А́фрика; **African** adj африка́нский
after ['ɑːftəʳ] prep (time) по́сле +gen, спустя́ +acc, че́рез +acc; (place, order) за +instr ▷ adv пото́м, по́сле ▷ conj по́сле того́ как; **after three years they divorced** спустя́ or че́рез три го́да они́ развели́сь; **who are you after?** кто Вам ну́жен?; **to name sb after sb** называ́ть (perf назва́ть) кого́-н в честь кого́-н; **it's twenty after eight** (US) сейча́с два́дцать мину́т девя́того; **to ask after sb** справля́ться (perf спра́виться) о ком-н; **after all** в конце́ концо́в; **after he left** по́сле того́ как он ушёл; **after having done this** сде́лав э́то; **aftermath** n после́дствия ntpl; **afternoon** n втора́я полови́на дня; **in the afternoon** днём; **after-shave (lotion)** n

одеколо́н по́сле бритья́; **afterwards** (*US* **afterward**) *adv* впосле́дствии, пото́м

again [ə'gɛn] *adv* (*once more*) ещё раз, сно́ва; (*repeatedly*) опя́ть; **I won't go there again** я бо́льше не пойду́ туда́; **again and again** сно́ва и сно́ва

against [ə'gɛnst] *prep* (*lean*) к +*dat*; (*hit, rub*) о +*acc*; (*stand*) у +*gen*; (*in opposition to*) про́тив +*gen*; (*at odds with*) вопреки́ +*dat*; (*compared to*) по сравне́нию с +*instr*

age [eɪdʒ] *n* во́зраст; (*period in history*) век; **aged** ['eɪdʒd] *adj*: **a boy aged ten** ма́льчик десяти́ лет

agency ['eɪdʒənsɪ] *n* (*Comm*) бюро́ *nt ind*, аге́нтство; (*Pol*) управле́ние

agenda [ə'dʒɛndə] *n* (*of meeting*) пове́стка (дня)

agent ['eɪdʒənt] *n* аге́нт; (*Comm*) посре́дник; (*Chem*) реакти́в

aggression [ə'grɛʃən] *n* агре́ссия

aggressive [ə'grɛsɪv] *adj* (*belligerent*) агресси́вный

AGM *n abbr* = **annual general meeting**

ago [ə'gəu] *adv*: **two days ago** два дня наза́д; **not long ago** неда́вно; **how long ago?** как давно́?

agony ['ægənɪ] *n* мучи́тельная боль *f*; **to be in agony** му́читься (*impf*) от бо́ли

agree [ə'gri:] *vt* согласо́вывать (*perf* согласова́ть) ▷ *vi*: **to agree with** (*have same opinion*) соглаша́ться (*perf* согласи́ться) с +*instr*; (*correspond*) согласо́вываться (*impf/perf*) с +*instr*; **to agree that** соглаша́ться (*perf* согласи́ться), что; **garlic doesn't agree with me** я не переношу́ чеснока́; **to agree to sth/to do** соглаша́ться (*perf* согласи́ться) на что-н/+*infin*; **agreeable** *adj* (*pleasant*) прия́тный; (*willing*): **I am agreeable** я согла́сен; **agreement** *n* (*consent*) согла́сие; (*arrangement*) соглаше́ние, догово́р; **in agreement with** в согла́сии с +*instr*; **we are in complete agreement** ме́жду на́ми по́лное согла́сие

agricultural [ægrɪ'kʌltʃərəl] *adj* сельскохозя́йственный; **agricultural land** земе́льные уго́дья

agriculture ['ægrɪkʌltʃə'] *n* се́льское хозя́йство

ahead [ə'hɛd] *adv* впереди́; (*direction*) вперёд; **ahead of** впереди́ +*gen*; (*earlier than*) ра́ньше +*gen*; **ahead of time** *or* **schedule** досро́чно; **go right** *or* **straight ahead** иди́те вперёд *or* пря́мо; **go ahead!** (*giving permission*) приступа́йте!, дава́йте!

aid [eɪd] *n* (*assistance*) по́мощь *f*; (*device*) приспособле́ние ▷ *vt* помога́ть (*perf* помо́чь) +*dat*; **in aid of** в по́мощь +*dat*; *see also* **hearing**

aide [eɪd] *n* помо́щник

AIDS [eɪdz] *n abbr* (= *acquired immune deficiency syndrome*) СПИД (= *синдро́м приобретённого иммунодефици́та*)

aim [eɪm] *n* (*objective*) цель *f* ▷ *vi* (*also* **take aim**) наце́литься (*perf* наце́литься) ▷ *vt*: **to aim (at)** (*gun, camera*) наводи́ть (*perf* навести́) (на +*acc*); (*missile, blow*) це́лить (*perf* наце́лить) (на +*acc*); (*remark*) направля́ть (*perf* напра́вить) (на +*acc*); **to aim to do** ста́вить (*perf* поста́вить) свое́й це́лью +*infin*; **he has a good aim** он ме́ткий стрело́к

ain't [eɪnt] (*inf*) = **am not**; **are not**; **is not**

air [ɛə'] *n* (*appearance*) вид ▷ *vt* (*room, bedclothes*) прове́тривать (*perf* прове́трить); (*views*) обнаро́довать (*perf*) ▷ *cpd* возду́шный; **by air** по во́здуху; **on the air** (*be*) в эфи́ре; (*go*) в эфи́р; **airborne** *adj* (*attack*) возду́шный; **air conditioning** *n* кондициони́рование; **aircraft** *n inv* самолёт; **Air Force** *n* Вое́нно-Возду́шные Си́лы *fpl*; **air hostess** *n* (*Brit*) бортпроводни́ца, стюарде́сса; **airline** *n* авиакомпа́ния; **airmail** *n*: **by airmail** авиапо́чтой; **airplane** *n* (*US*) самолёт; **airport** *n* аэропо́рт; **air raid** *n* возду́шный налёт

airy ['ɛərɪ] *adj* (*room*) просто́рный

aisle [aɪl] *n* прохо́д

alarm [ə'lɑ:m] *n* (*anxiety*) трево́га; (*device*) сигнализа́ция ▷ *vt* трево́жить (*perf* встрево́жить); **alarm clock** *n* буди́льник

Albania [æl'beɪnɪə] *n* Алба́ния

album ['ælbəm] *n* альбо́м

alcohol ['ælkəhɔl] *n* алкого́ль *m*; **alcoholic** [ælkə'hɔlɪk] *adj* алкого́льный ▷ *n* алкого́лик(-и́чка)

alcove ['ælkəuv] *n* алько́в

alert [ə'lə:t] *adj* внима́тельный; (*to danger*) бди́тельный ▷ *vt* (*police etc*) предупрежда́ть (*perf* предупреди́ть); **to be on the alert** (*also Mil*) быть (*impf*) начеку́

A LEVELS

A levels — квалификацио́нные экза́мены. Шко́льники сдаю́т их в во́зрасте 17-18 лет. Полу́ченные результа́ты определя́ют приём в университе́т. Экза́мены сдаю́тся по трём предме́там. Вы́бор предме́тов дикту́ется специа́льностью, кото́рую выпускники́ плани́руют изуча́ть в университе́те.

Algeria [æl'dʒɪərɪə] *n* Алжи́р

alias ['eɪlɪəs] *n* вы́мышленное и́мя *nt* ▷ *adv*: **alias John** он же Джон

alibi ['ælɪbaɪ] *n* а́либи *nt ind*

alien ['eɪlɪən] *n* (*extraterrestrial*) инопланетя́нин(-я́нка) ▷ *adj*: **alien (to)** чу́ждый (+*dat*); **alienate** ['eɪlɪəneɪt] *vt* отчужда́ть (*impf*), отта́лкивать (*perf* оттолкну́ть)

alight [ə'laɪt] *adj*: **to be alight** горе́ть

(*impf*); (*eyes, face*) сия́ть (*impf*)

alike [ə'laɪk] *adj* одина́ковый ▷ *adv* одина́ково; **they look alike** они́ похо́жи друг на дру́га

alive [ə'laɪv] *adj* (*place*) оживлённый; **he is alive** он жив

◯ **KEYWORD**

all [ɔːl] *adj* весь (*f* вся, *nt* всё, *pl* все); **all day** весь день; **all night** всю ночь; **all five stayed** все пя́теро оста́лись; **all the books** все кни́ги; **all the time** всё вре́мя
▷ *pron* **1** всё; **I ate it all, I ate all of it** я всё съел; **all of us stayed** мы все оста́лись; **we all sat down** мы все се́ли; **is that all?** э́то всё?
2 (*in phrases*): **above all** пре́жде всего́; **after all** в конце́ концо́в; **all in all** в це́лом *or* о́бщем; **not at all** (*in answer to question*) совсе́м *or* во́все нет; (*in answer to thanks*) не́ за что; **I'm not at all tired** я совсе́м не уста́л
▷ *adv* совсе́м; **I am all alone** я совсе́м оди́н; **I did it all by myself** я всё сде́лал сам; **it's not as hard as all that** э́то во́все не так уж тру́дно; **all the more/better** тем бо́лее/лу́чше; **I have all but finished** я почти́ (что) зако́нчил; **the score is two all** счёт 2:2

allegation [ælɪ'geɪʃən] *n* обвине́ние
allegedly [ə'ledʒɪdlɪ] *adv* я́кобы
allegiance [ə'liːdʒəns] *n* ве́рность *f*; (*to idea*) приве́рженность *f*
allergic [ə'lɜːdʒɪk] *adj*: **he is allergic to ...** у него́ аллерги́я на +*acc* ...
allergy [ˈælədʒɪ] *n* (*Med*) аллерги́я
alleviate [ə'liːvɪeɪt] *vt* облегча́ть (*perf* облегчи́ть)
alley [ˈælɪ] *n* переу́лок
alliance [ə'laɪəns] *n* сою́з; (*Pol*) алья́нс
allied [ˈælaɪd] *adj* сою́зный
alligator [ˈælɪgeɪtər] *n* аллига́тор
all-in [ˈɔːlɪn] *adj* (*Brit*): **it cost me £100 all-in** в о́бщей сло́жности мне э́то сто́ило £100
allocate [ˈæləkeɪt] *vt* выделя́ть (*perf* вы́делить); (*tasks*) поруча́ть (*perf* поручи́ть)
all-out [ˈɔːlaut] *adj* (*effort*) максима́льный; (*attack*) масси́рованный
allow [ə'lau] *vt* (*permit*) разреша́ть (*perf* разреши́ть); (: *claim, goal*) признава́ть (*perf* призна́ть) действи́тельным; (*set aside: sum*) выделя́ть (*perf* вы́делить); (*concede*): **to allow that** допуска́ть (*perf* допусти́ть), что; **to allow sb to do** разреша́ть (*perf* разреши́ть) *or* позволя́ть (*perf* позво́лить) кому́-н +*infin*; **allow for** *vt fus* учи́тывать (*perf* уче́сть), принима́ть (*perf* приня́ть) в расчёт; **allowance** *n* (*Comm*) де́ньги *pl* на расхо́ды; (*pocket money*) карма́нные де́ньги; (*welfare*

payment) посо́бие; **to make allowances for** (*perf* сде́лать) ски́дку для +*gen*
all right *adv* хорошо́, норма́льно; (*positive response*) хорошо́, ла́дно ▷ *adj* неплохо́й, норма́льный; **is everything all right?** всё норма́льно *or* в поря́дке?; **are you all right?** как ты?, ты в поря́дке? (*разг*) **do you like him? — he's all right** он Вам нра́вится? — ничего́
ally [ˈælaɪ] *n* сою́зник
almighty [ɔːl'maɪtɪ] *adj* (*tremendous*) колосса́льный
almond [ˈaːmənd] *n* минда́ль *m*
almost [ˈɔːlməust] *adv* почти́; (*all but*) чуть *or* едва́ не
alone [ə'ləun] *adj, adv* оди́н (*f* одна́); **to leave sb/sth alone** оставля́ть (*perf* оста́вить) кого́-н/что-н в поко́е; **let alone ... не говоря́ уже́ о +*prp* ...
along [ə'lɔŋ] *prep* (*motion*) по +*dat*, вдоль +*gen*; (*position*) вдоль +*gen* ▷ *adv*: **is he coming along (with us)?** он идёт с на́ми?; **he was limping along** он шёл хромая; **along with** вме́сте с +*instr*; **all along** с са́мого нача́ла; **alongside** *prep* (*position*) ря́дом с +*instr*, вдоль +*gen*; (*motion*) к +*dat* ▷ *adv* ря́дом
aloud [ə'laud] *adv* (*read, speak*) вслух
alphabet [ˈælfəbɛt] *n* алфави́т
Alps [ælps] *npl*: **the Alps** А́льпы *pl*
already [ɔːl'rɛdɪ] *adv* уже́
alright [ˈɔːlraɪt] *adv* (*Brit*) = **all right**
also [ˈɔːlsəu] *adv* (*about subject*) та́кже, то́же; (*about object*) та́кже; (*moreover*) кро́ме того́, к тому́ же; **he also likes apples** он та́кже *or* то́же лю́бит я́блоки; **he likes apples also** он лю́бит та́кже я́блоки
altar [ˈɔltər] *n* алта́рь *m*
alter [ˈɔltər] *vt* изменя́ть (*perf* измени́ть) ▷ *vi* изменя́ться (*perf* измени́ться); **alteration** [ɔltə'reɪʃən] *n* измене́ние
alternate [*adj* ɔl'tɜːnɪt, *vb* 'ɔltəneɪt] *adj* череду́ющийся; (*US: alternative*) альтернати́вный ▷ *vi*: **to alternate (with)** чередова́ться (*impf*) (с +*instr*); **on alternate days** че́рез день
alternative [ɔl'tɜːnətɪv] *adj* альтернати́вный ▷ *n* альтернати́ва; **alternatively** *adv*: **alternatively one could ...** кро́ме того́ мо́жно ...
although [ɔːl'ðəu] *conj* хотя́
altitude [ˈæltɪtjuːd] *n* (*of plane*) высота́; (*of place*) высота́ над у́ровнем мо́ря
altogether [ɔːltə'gɛðər] *adv* (*completely*) соверше́нно; (*in all*) в о́бщем, в о́бщей сло́жности
aluminium [ælju'mɪnɪəm] (*US* **aluminum** [ə'luːmɪnəm]) *n* алюми́ний
always [ˈɔːlweɪz] *adv* всегда́
am [æm] *vb see* **be**
a.m. *adv abbr* (= *ante meridiem*) до полу́дня
amateur [ˈæmətər] *n* люби́тель *m*; **amateur dramatics** люби́тельский теа́тр;

amateur photographer фотограф-
люби́тель m
amazement [ə'meɪzmənt] n изумле́ние
amazing [ə'meɪzɪŋ] adj (surprising)
порази́тельный; (fantastic) изуми́тельный,
замеча́тельный
ambassador [æm'bæsədəʳ] n посо́л
ambiguous [æm'bɪɡjuəs] adj нея́сный,
двусмы́сленный
ambition [æm'bɪʃən] n (see adj)
честолю́бие; амби́ция; (aim) цель f
ambitious [æm'bɪʃəs] adj (positive)
честолюби́вый; (negative) амбицио́зный
ambulance ['æmbjuləns] n ско́рая
по́мощь f
ambush ['æmbuʃ] n заса́да ▷ vt
устра́ивать (perf устро́ить) заса́ду +dat
amend [ə'mend] vt (law, text)
пересма́тривать (perf пересмотре́ть) ▷ n:
to make amends загла́живать (perf
загла́дить) (свою́) вину́; **amendment** n
попра́вка
amenities [ə'mi:nɪtɪz] npl удо́бства ntpl
America [ə'merɪkə] n Аме́рика;
American adj америка́нский ▷ n
америка́нец(-нка)
amicable ['æmɪkəbl] adj (relationship)
дру́жеский
amid(st) [ə'mɪd(st)] prep посреди́ +gen
ammunition [æmju'nɪʃən] n (for gun)
патро́ны mpl
amnesty ['æmnɪstɪ] n амни́стия
among(st) [ə'mʌŋ(st)] prep среди́ +gen
amount [ə'maunt] n коли́чество ▷ vi: **to
amount to** (total) составля́ть (perf
соста́вить)
amp(ère) ['æmp(εəʳ)] n ампе́р
ample ['æmpl] adj (large) соли́дный;
(abundant) оби́льный; (enough)
доста́точный; **to have ample time/room**
име́ть (impf) доста́точно вре́мени/ме́ста
amuse [ə'mju:z] vt развлека́ть (perf
развле́чь); **amusement** n (mirth)
удово́льствие; (pastime) развлече́ние;
amusement arcade n павильо́н с
игровы́ми аппара́тами
an [æn] indef art see **a**
anaemia [ə'ni:mɪə] (US anemia) n
анеми́я, малокро́вие
anaesthetic [ænɪs'θetɪk] (US anesthetic)
n нарко́з
analyse ['ænəlaɪz] (US analyze) vt
анализи́ровать (perf проанализи́ровать)
analysis [ə'næləsɪs] n (pl analyses) n
ана́лиз
analyst ['ænəlɪst] n (political) анали́тик,
коммента́тор; (financial, economic)
экспе́рт; (US: psychiatrist) психиа́тр
analyze ['ænəlaɪz] vt (US) = **analyse**
anarchy ['ænəkɪ] n ана́рхия
anatomy [ə'nætəmɪ] n анато́мия; (body)
органи́зм
ancestor ['ænsɪstəʳ] n пре́док
anchor ['æŋkəʳ] n я́корь m

anchovy ['æntʃəvɪ] n анчо́ус
ancient ['eɪnʃənt] adj (civilization, person)
дре́вний; (monument) стари́нный
and [ænd] conj и; **my father and I** я и мой
оте́ц, мы с отцо́м; **bread and butter** хлеб с
ма́слом; **and so on** и так да́лее; **try and
come** постара́йтесь прийти́; **he talked and
talked** он всё говори́л и говори́л
anemia [ə'ni:mɪə] n (US) = **anaemia**
anesthetic [ænɪs'θetɪk] n (US)
= **anaesthetic**
angel ['eɪndʒəl] n а́нгел
anger ['æŋɡəʳ] n гнев, возмуще́ние
angle ['æŋɡl] n (corner) у́гол
angler ['æŋɡləʳ] n рыболо́в
Anglican ['æŋɡlɪkən] adj англика́нский
▷ n англика́нец(-а́нка)
angling ['æŋɡlɪŋ] n ры́бная ло́вля
angrily ['æŋɡrɪlɪ] adv серди́то, гне́вно
angry ['æŋɡrɪ] adj серди́тый, гне́вный;
(wound) воспалённый; **to be angry with
sb/at sth** серди́ться (impf) на кого́-н/что-н;
to get angry серди́ться (perf
рассерди́ться)
anguish ['æŋɡwɪʃ] n му́ка
animal ['ænɪməl] n живо́тное nt adj; (wild
animal) зверь m; (pej: person) зверь,
живо́тное ▷ adj живо́тный
animated adj оживлённый, живо́й; (film)
мультипликацио́нный
animation [ænɪ'meɪʃən] n (enthusiasm)
оживле́ние
ankle ['æŋkl] n лоды́жка
anniversary [ænɪ'və:sərɪ] n годовщи́на
announce [ə'nauns] vt (engagement,
decision) объявля́ть (perf объяви́ть) (о
+prp); (birth, death) извеща́ть (perf
извести́ть) о +prp; **announcement** n
объявле́ние; (in newspaper etc)
сообще́ние
annoy [ə'nɔɪ] vt раздража́ть (perf
раздражи́ть); **annoying** adj (noise)
раздража́ющий; (mistake, event)
доса́дный
annual ['ænjuəl] adj (meeting)
ежего́дный; (income) годово́й; **annually**
adv ежего́дно
annum ['ænəm] n see **per**
anonymous [ə'nɔnɪməs] adj анони́мный
anorak ['ænəræk] n ку́ртка
anorexia [ænə'reksɪə] n анорекси́я
another [ə'nʌðəʳ] pron друго́й ▷ adj:
another book (additional) ещё одна́ кни́га;
(different) друга́я кни́га; see also **one**
answer ['ɑ:nsəʳ] n отве́т; (to problem)
реше́ние ▷ vi отвеча́ть (perf отве́тить)
▷ vt (letter, question) отвеча́ть (perf
отве́тить) на +acc; (person) отвеча́ть (perf
отве́тить) +dat; **in answer to your letter** в
отве́т на Ва́ше письмо́; **to answer the
phone** подходи́ть (perf подойти́) к
телефо́ну; **to answer the bell** or **the door**
открыва́ть (perf откры́ть) дверь;
answering machine n автоотве́тчик

ant [ænt] n муравей
Antarctic [ænt'ɑːktɪk] n: the Antarctic
Антарктика
antelope ['æntɪləup] n антилопа
anthem ['ænθəm] n: national anthem
государственный гимн
antibiotic [æntɪbaɪ'ɔtɪk] n антибиотик
antibody ['æntɪbɔdɪ] n антитело
anticipate [æn'tɪsɪpeɪt] vt (expect)
ожидать (impf) +gen; (foresee)
предугадывать (perf преугадать);
(forestall) предвосхищать (perf
предвосхитить)
anticipation [æntɪsɪ'peɪʃən] n
(expectation) ожидание; (eagerness)
предвкушение
antics ['æntɪks] npl (of child) шалости fpl
antidote ['æntɪdəut] n противоядие
antifreeze ['æntɪfriːz] n антифриз
antique [æn'tiːk] n антикварная вещь f,
предмет старины ▷ adj антикварный
antiseptic [æntɪ'septɪk] n антисептик
antivirus [æntɪ'vaɪrəs] adj (Comput)
антивирусный; **antivirus software**
антивирусное программное обеспечение
anxiety [æŋ'zaɪətɪ] n тревога
anxious ['æŋkʃəs] adj (person, look)
беспокойный, озабоченный; (time)
тревожный; **she is anxious to do** она
очень хочет +infin; **to be anxious about**
беспокоиться (impf) о +prp

🔵 **KEYWORD**

any ['ɛnɪ] adj 1 (in questions etc): **have
you any butter/children?** у Вас есть масло/
дети?; **do you have any questions?** у Вас
есть какие-нибудь вопросы?; **if there are
any tickets left** если ещё остались билеты
2 (with negative): **I haven't any bread/
books** у меня нет хлеба/книг; **I didn't buy
any newspapers** я не купил газет
3 (no matter which) любой; **any colour
will do** любой цвет подойдёт
4 (in phrases): **in any case** в любом
случае; **any day now** в любой день; **at any
moment** в любой момент; **at any rate** во
всяком случае; (anyhow) так или иначе;
any time (at any moment) в любой
момент; (whenever) в любое время; (as
response) не за что
▷ pron 1 (in questions etc): **I need some
money, have you got any?** мне нужны
деньги, у Вас есть?; **can any of you sing?**
кто-нибудь из вас умеет петь?
2 (with negative) ни один (f одна, nt
одно, pl одни); **I haven't any (of those)** у
меня таких нет
3 (no matter which one(s)) любой; **take
any you like** возьмите то, что Вам
нравится
▷ adv 1 (in questions etc): **do you want
any more soup?** хотите ещё супу?; **are you
feeling any better?** Вам лучше?

2 (with negative): **I can't hear him any
more** я больше его не слышу; **don't wait
any longer** не ждите больше; **he isn't any
better** ему не лучше

anybody ['ɛnɪbɔdɪ] pron = anyone
anyhow ['ɛnɪhau] adv (at any rate) так
или иначе; **the work is done anyhow**
(haphazardly) работа сделана кое-как;
I shall go anyhow я так или иначе пойду
anyone ['ɛnɪwʌn] pron (in questions etc)
кто-нибудь; (with negative) никто; (no
matter who) любой, всякий; **can you see
anyone?** Вы видите кого-нибудь?; **I can't
see anyone** я никого не вижу; **anyone
could do it** любой or всякий может это
сделать; **you can invite anyone** Вы можете
пригласить кого угодно
anything ['ɛnɪθɪŋ] pron (in questions etc)
что-нибудь; (with negative) ничего; (no
matter what) (всё,) что угодно; **can you
see anything?** Вы видите что-нибудь?;
I can't see anything я ничего не вижу;
anything (at all) will do всё, что угодно
подойдёт
anyway ['ɛnɪweɪ] adv всё равно; (in
brief): **anyway, I didn't want to go** в
общем, я не хотел идти; **I will be there
anyway** я всё равно там буду; **anyway,
I couldn't stay even if I wanted to** в любом
случае, я не мог остаться, даже если бы я
хотел; **why are you phoning, anyway?** а
всё-таки, почему Вы звоните?

🔵 **KEYWORD**

anywhere ['ɛnɪwɛə'] adv 1 (in questions
etc: position) где-нибудь; (: motion)
куда-нибудь; **can you see him anywhere?**
Вы его где-нибудь видите?; **did you go
anywhere yesterday?** Вы вчера
куда-нибудь ходили?
2 (with negative: position) нигде;
(: motion) никуда; **I can't see him
anywhere** я нигде его не вижу; **I'm not
going anywhere today** сегодня я никуда
не иду
3 (no matter where: position) где угодно;
(: motion) куда угодно; **anywhere in the
world** где угодно в мире; **put the books
down anywhere** положите книги куда
угодно

apart [ə'pɑːt] adv (position) в стороне;
(motion) в сторону; (separately)
раздельно, врозь; **they are ten miles apart**
они находятся на расстоянии десяти
миль друг от друга; **to take apart**
разбирать (perf разобрать) (на части);
apart from кроме +gen
apartment [ə'pɑːtmənt] n (US)
квартира; (room) комната
apathy ['æpəθɪ] n апатия
ape [eɪp] n человекообразная обезьяна

▷ *vt* копи́ровать (*perf* скопи́ровать)

aperitif [ə'pɛrɪtiːf] *n* аперити́в

apologize [ə'pɔlədʒaɪz] *vi*: **to apologize (for sth to sb)** извиня́ться (*perf* извини́ться) (за что-н пе́ред кем-н)

apology [ə'pɔlədʒɪ] *n* извине́ние

app [æp] *n* приложе́ние

appalling [ə'pɔːlɪŋ] *adj* (*awful*) ужа́сный; (*shocking*) возмути́тельный

apparatus [æpə'reɪtəs] *n* аппарату́ра; (*in gym*) (гимнасти́ческий) снаря́д; (*of organization*) аппара́т

apparent [ə'pærənt] *adj* (*seeming*) ви́димый; (*obvious*) очеви́дный; **apparently** *adv* по всей ви́димости

appeal [ə'piːl] *vi* (*Law*) апелли́ровать (*impf/perf*), подава́ть (*perf* пода́ть) апелля́цию ▷ *n* (*attraction*) привлека́тельность *f*; (*plea*) призы́в; (*Law*) апелля́ция, обжа́лование; **to appeal (to sb) for** (*help, funds*) обраща́ться (*perf* обрати́ться) (к кому́-н) за +*instr*; (*calm, order*) призыва́ть (*perf* призва́ть) (кого́-н) к +*dat*; **to appeal to** (*attract*) привлека́ть (*perf* привле́чь), нра́виться (*perf* понра́виться) +*dat*; **appealing** *adj* привлека́тельный

appear [ə'pɪə'] *vi* появля́ться (*perf* появи́ться); (*seem*) каза́ться (*perf* показа́ться); **to appear in court** представа́ть (*perf* предста́ть) пе́ред судо́м; **to appear on TV** выступа́ть (*perf* вы́ступить) по телеви́дению; **it would appear that ...** похо́же (на то), что ...; **appearance** *n* (*arrival*) появле́ние; (*look, aspect*) вне́шность *f*; (*in public, on TV*) выступле́ние

appendices [ə'pɛndɪsiːz] *npl of* **appendix**

appendicitis [əpɛndɪ'saɪtɪs] *n* аппендици́т

appendix [ə'pɛndɪks] (*pl* **appendices**) *n* приложе́ние; (*Anat*) аппе́ндикс

appetite [æpɪtaɪt] *n* аппети́т

applaud [ə'plɔːd] *vi* аплоди́ровать (*impf*), рукоплеска́ть (*impf*) ▷ *vt* аплоди́ровать (*impf*) +*dat*, рукоплеска́ть (*impf*) +*dat*; (*praise*) одобря́ть (*perf* одо́брить)

applause [ə'plɔːz] *n* аплодисме́нты *pl*

apple [æpl] *n* я́блоко

applicable [ə'plɪkəbl] *adj*: **applicable (to)** примени́мый (к +*dat*)

applicant [æplɪkənt] *n* (*for job, scholarship*) кандида́т; (*for college*) абитурие́нт

application [æplɪ'keɪʃən] *n* (*for job, grant etc*) заявле́ние; **application form** *n* заявле́ние-анке́та

apply [ə'plaɪ] *vt* (*paint, make-up*) наноси́ть (*perf* нанести́) ▷ *vi*: **to apply to** применя́ться (*impf*) к +*dat*; (*ask*) обраща́ться (*perf* обрати́ться) (с про́сьбой) к +*dat*; **to apply o.s. to** сосредота́чиваться (*perf* сосредото́читься) на +*prp*; **to apply for a**

grant/job подава́ть (*perf* пода́ть) заявле́ние на стипе́ндию/о приёме на рабо́ту

appoint [ə'pɔɪnt] *vt* назнача́ть (*perf* назна́чить); **appointment** *n* (*of person*) назначе́ние; (*post*) до́лжность *f*; (*arranged meeting*) приём; **to make an appointment (with sb)** назнача́ть (*perf* назна́чить) (кому́-н) встре́чу; **I have an appointment with the doctor** я записа́лся (на приём) к врачу́

appraisal [ə'preɪzl] *n* оце́нка

appreciate [ə'priːʃɪeɪt] *vt* (*value*) цени́ть (*impf*); (*understand*) оце́нивать (*perf* оцени́ть) ▷ *vi* (*Comm*) повыша́ться (*perf* повы́ситься) в цене́

appreciation [əpriːʃɪ'eɪʃən] *n* (*understanding*) понима́ние; (*gratitude*) призна́тельность *f*

apprehensive [æprɪ'hɛnsɪv] *adj* (*glance etc*) опа́сливый

apprentice [ə'prɛntɪs] *n* учени́к, подмасте́рье

approach [ə'prəutʃ] *vi* приближа́ться (*perf* прибли́зиться) ▷ *vt* (*ask, apply to*) обраща́ться (*perf* обрати́ться) к +*dat*; (*come to*) приближа́ться (*perf* прибли́зиться) к +*dat*; (*consider*) подходи́ть (*perf* подойти́) к +*dat* ▷ *n* подхо́д; (*advance: also fig*) приближе́ние

appropriate [ə'prəuprɪeɪt] *adj* (*behaviour*) подоба́ющий; (*remarks*) уме́стный; (*tools*) подходя́щий

approval [ə'pruːvəl] *n* одобре́ние; (*permission*) согла́сие; **on approval** (*Comm*) на про́бу

approve [ə'pruːv] *vt* (*motion, decision*) одобря́ть (*perf* одо́брить); (*product, publication*) утвержда́ть (*perf* утверди́ть); **approve of** *vt fus* одобря́ть (*perf* одо́брить)

approximate [ə'prɔksɪmɪt] *adj* приблизи́тельный; **approximately** *adv* приблизи́тельно

apricot ['eɪprɪkɔt] *n* абрико́с

April ['eɪprəl] *n* апре́ль *m*

apron ['eɪprən] *n* фа́ртук

apt [æpt] *adj* уда́чный, уме́стный; **apt to do** скло́нный +*infin*

aquarium [ə'kwɛərɪəm] *n* аква́риум

Aquarius [ə'kwɛərɪəs] *n* Водоле́й

Arab [ærəb] *adj* ара́бский ▷ *n* ара́б(ка); **Arabian** [ə'reɪbɪən] *adj* ара́бский; **Arabic** *adj* ара́бский

arbitrary ['aːbɪtrərɪ] *adj* произво́льный

arbitration [aːbɪ'treɪʃən] *n* трете́йский суд; (*Industry*) арбитра́ж; **the dispute went to arbitration** спо́р пе́редан в арбитра́ж

arc [aːk] *n* (*also Math*) дуга́

arch [aːtʃ] *n* а́рка, свод; (*of foot*) свод ▷ *vt* (*back*) выгиба́ть (*perf* вы́гнуть)

archaeology [aːkɪ'ɔlədʒɪ] (*US* **archeology**) *n* археоло́гия

archbishop [aːtʃ'bɪʃəp] *n* архиепи́скоп

archeology [ɑːkɪˈɔlədʒɪ] n (US)
= **archaeology**
architect [ˈɑːkɪtɛkt] n (of building)
архите́ктор; **architecture** n архитекту́ра
archive [ˈɑːkaɪv] n архи́в; **archives** npl
(documents) архи́в msg
Arctic [ˈɑːktɪk] adj аркти́ческий ▷ n: the
Arctic Áрктика
are [ɑːʳ] vb see **be**
area [ˈɛərɪə] n о́бласть f; (part: of place)
уча́сток; (: of room) пло́щадь f
arena [əˈriːnə] n (also fig) аре́на
aren't [ɑːnt] = **are not**
Argentina [ɑːdʒənˈtiːnə] n Аргенти́на
arguably [ˈɑːgjuəblɪ] adv возмо́жно
argue [ˈɑːgjuː] vi (quarrel) ссо́риться (perf
поссо́риться); (reason) дока́зывать (perf
доказа́ть)
argument [ˈɑːgjumənt] n (quarrel)
ссо́ра; (reasons) аргуме́нт, до́вод
Aries [ˈɛərɪz] n Ове́н
arise [əˈraɪz] (pt **arose**, pp **arisen**) vi
(occur) возника́ть (perf возни́кнуть)
arithmetic [əˈrɪθmətɪk] n (Math)
арифме́тика; (calculation) подсчёт
arm [ɑːm] n рука́; (of chair) ру́чка; (of
clothing) рука́в ▷ vt вооружа́ть (perf
вооружи́ть); **arms** npl (Mil) вооруже́ние
ntsg; (Heraldry) герб; **arm in arm** по́д руку;
armchair n кре́сло; **armed** adj
вооружённый
armour [ˈɑːməʳ] (US **armor**) n (also **suit
of armour**) доспе́хи mpl
army [ˈɑːmɪ] n (also fig) а́рмия
aroma [əˈrəumə] n арома́т;
aromatherapy [ərəuməˈθɛrəpɪ] n
ароматерапи́я
arose [əˈrəuz] pt of **arise**
around [əˈraund] adv вокру́г ▷ prep
(encircling) вокру́г +gen; (near, about)
о́коло +gen
arouse [əˈrauz] vt (interest, passions)
возбужда́ть (perf возбуди́ть)
arrange [əˈreɪndʒ] vt (organize)
устра́ивать (perf устро́ить); (put in order)
расставля́ть (perf расста́вить) ▷ vi: **we
have arranged for a car to pick you up** мы
договори́лись, чтобы за Ва́ми зае́хала
маши́на; **to arrange to do** догова́риваться
(perf договори́ться) +infin; **arrangement**
n (agreement) договорённость f; (order,
layout) расположе́ние; **arrangements**
npl (plans) приготовле́ния ntpl
array [əˈreɪ] n: **array of** ряд +gen
arrears [əˈrɪəz] npl задо́лженность fsg; **to
be in arrears with one's rent** име́ть (impf)
задо́лженность по кварти́рной
arrest [əˈrɛst] vt (Law) аресто́вывать (perf
арестова́ть) ▷ n аре́ст; **under arrest** под
аре́стом
arrival [əˈraɪvl] n (of person, vehicle)
прибы́тие; **new arrival** новичо́к; (baby)
новорождённый(-ая) m(f) adj
arrive [əˈraɪv] vi (traveller) прибыва́ть

(perf прибы́ть); (letter, news) приходи́ть
(perf прийти́); (baby) рожда́ться (perf
роди́ться)
arrogance [ˈærəgəns] n высокоме́рие
arrogant [ˈærəgənt] adj высокоме́рный
arrow [ˈærəu] n (weapon) стрела́; (sign)
стре́лка
arse [ɑːs] n (Brit: infl) жо́па (!)
arson [ˈɑːsn] n поджо́г
art [ɑːt] n иску́сство; **Arts** npl (Scol)
гуманита́рные нау́ки fpl
artery [ˈɑːtərɪ] n (also fig) арте́рия
art gallery n (national) карти́нная
галере́я; (private) (арт-)галере́я
arthritis [ɑːˈθraɪtɪs] n артри́т
artichoke [ˈɑːtɪtʃəuk] n (also **globe
artichoke**) артишо́к; (also **Jerusalem
artichoke**) земляна́я гру́ша
article [ˈɑːtɪkl] n (object) предме́т; (Ling)
арти́кль m; (in newspaper, document)
статья́
articulate [vb ɑːˈtɪkjuleɪt, adj ɑːˈtɪkjulɪt]
vt (ideas) выража́ть (perf вы́разить)
▷ adj: **she is very articulate** она́ чётко
выража́ет свои́ мы́сли
artificial [ɑːtɪˈfɪʃl] adj иску́сственный;
(affected) неесте́ственный
artist [ˈɑːtɪst] n худо́жник(-ица);
(performer) арти́ст(ка); **artistic** [ɑːˈtɪstɪk]
adj худо́жественный

◯ **KEYWORD**

as [æz, əz] conj **1** (referring to time) когда́;
he came in as I was leaving он вошёл,
когда́ я уходи́л; **as the years went by** с
года́ми; **as from tomorrow** с за́втрашнего
дня
2 (in comparisons): **as big as** тако́й же
большо́й, как; **twice as big as** в два ра́за
бо́льше, чем; **as white as snow** бе́лый, как
снег; **as much money/many books as**
сто́лько же де́нег/книг, ско́лько; **as soon
as** как то́лько; **as soon as possible** как
мо́жно скоре́е
3 (since, because) поско́льку, так как
4 (referring to manner, way) как; **do as you
wish** де́лайте, как хоти́те; **as she said** как
она́ сказа́ла
5 (concerning): **as for** or **to** что каса́ется
+gen
6: **as if** or **though** как бу́дто; **he looked as
if he had been ill** он вы́глядел так, как
бу́дто он был бо́лен
▷ prep (in the capacity of): **he works as a
waiter** он рабо́тает официа́нтом; **as
chairman of the company, he … as** глава́
компа́нии он …; see also **long**; **same**;
such; **well**

a.s.a.p. adv abbr = **as soon as possible**
ascent [əˈsɛnt] n (slope) подъём; (climb)
восхожде́ние
ash [æʃ] n (of fire) зола́, пе́пел; (of

cigarette) пе́пел; (*wood, tree*) я́сень *m*

ashamed [əˈʃeɪmd] *adj*: **to be ashamed (of)** стыди́ться (*impf*) (+*gen*); **I'm ashamed of ...** мне сты́дно за +*acc* ...

ashore [əˈʃɔːʳ] *adv* (*be*) на берегу́; (*swim, go*) на бе́рег

ashtray [ˈæʃtreɪ] *n* пе́пельница

Asia [ˈeɪʃə] *n* А́зия; **Asian** *adj* азиа́тский ▷ *n* азиа́т(ка)

aside [əˈsaɪd] *adv* в сто́рону ▷ *n* ре́плика

ask [ɑːsk] *vt* (*inquire*) спра́шивать (*perf* спроси́ть); (*invite*) звать (*perf* позва́ть); **to ask sb for sth/sb to do** проси́ть (*perf* попроси́ть) что-н у кого́-н/кого́-н +*infin*; **to ask sb about** спра́шивать (*perf* спроси́ть) кого́-н о +*prp*; **to ask (sb) a question** задава́ть (*perf* зада́ть) (кому́-н) вопро́с; **to ask sb out to dinner** приглаша́ть (*perf* пригласи́ть) кого́-н в рестора́н; **ask for** *vt fus* проси́ть (*perf* попроси́ть); (*trouble*) напра́шиваться (*perf* напроси́ться) на +*acc*

asleep [əˈsliːp] *adj*: **to be asleep** спать (*impf*); **to fall asleep** засыпа́ть (*perf* засну́ть)

asparagus [əsˈpærəgəs] *n* спа́ржа

aspect [ˈæspɛkt] *n* (*element*) аспе́кт, сторона́; (*quality, air*) вид

aspirin [ˈæsprɪn] *n* аспири́н

ass [æs] *n* (*also fig*) осёл; (*US: infl*) жо́па (*!*)

assassin [əˈsæsɪn] *n* (полити́ческий) уби́йца *m/f*

assault [əˈsɔːlt] *n* нападе́ние; (*Mil, fig*) ата́ка ▷ *vt* напада́ть (*perf* напа́сть) на +*acc*; (*sexually*) наси́ловать (*perf* изнаси́ловать)

assemble [əˈsɛmbl] *vt* собира́ть (*perf* собра́ть) ▷ *vi* собира́ться (*perf* собра́ться)

assembly [əˈsɛmblɪ] *n* (*meeting*) собра́ние; (*institution*) ассамбле́я, законода́тельное собра́ние; (*construction*) сбо́рка

assert [əˈsəːt] *vt* (*opinion, authority*) утвержда́ть (*perf* утверди́ть); (*rights, innocence*) отста́ивать (*perf* отстоя́ть); **assertion** [əˈsəːʃən] *n* (*claim*) утвержде́ние

assess [əˈsɛs] *vt* оце́нивать (*perf* оцени́ть); **assessment** *n*: **assessment (of)** оце́нка (+*gen*)

asset [ˈæsɛt] *n* (*quality*) досто́инство; **assets** *npl* (*property, funds*) акти́вы *mpl*; (*Comm*) акти́в *msg* бала́нса

assignment [əˈsaɪnmənt] *n* зада́ние

assist [əˈsɪst] *vt* помога́ть (*perf* помо́чь) +*dat*; (*financially*) соде́йствовать (*perf* посоде́йствовать) +*dat*; **assistance** *n* (*see vt*) по́мощь *f*; соде́йствие; **assistant** *n* помо́щник(-ица); (*in office etc*) ассисте́нт(ка); (*Brit: also* **shop assistant**) продаве́ц-вщи́ца)

associate [*n* əˈsəʊʃɪɪt, *vb* əˈsəʊʃɪeɪt] *n*

(*colleague*) колле́га *m/f* ▷ *adj* (*member, professor*) ассоции́рованный ▷ *vt* (*mentally*) ассоции́ровать (*impf/perf*); **to associate with sb** обща́ться (*impf*) с кем-н

association [əsəʊsɪˈeɪʃən] *n* ассоциа́ция; (*involvement*) связь *f*

assorted [əˈsɔːtɪd] *adj* разнообра́зный

assortment [əˈsɔːtmənt] *n* (*of clothes, colours*) ассортиме́нт; (*of books, people*) подбо́р

assume [əˈsjuːm] *vt* (*suppose*) предполага́ть (*perf* предположи́ть), допуска́ть (*perf* допусти́ть); (*responsibility*) принима́ть (*perf* приня́ть) (на себя́); (*air*) напуска́ть (*perf* напусти́ть) на себя́; (*power*) брать (*perf* взять)

assumption [əˈsʌmpʃən] *n* предположе́ние; (*of responsibility*) приня́тие на себя́; **assumption of power** прихо́д к вла́сти

assurance [əˈʃʊərəns] *n* (*promise*) завере́ние; (*confidence*) уве́ренность *f*; (*insurance*) страхова́ние

assure [əˈʃʊəʳ] *vt* (*reassure*) заверя́ть (*perf* заве́рить); (*guarantee*) обеспе́чивать (*perf* обеспе́чить)

asthma [ˈæsmə] *n* а́стма

astonishment [əˈstɔnɪʃmənt] *n* изумле́ние

astrology [əsˈtrɔlədʒɪ] *n* астроло́гия

astronomical [æstrəˈnɔmɪkl] *adj* (*also fig*) астрономи́ческий

astronomy [əsˈtrɔnəmɪ] *n* астроно́мия

astute [əsˈtjuːt] *adj* (*person*) проница́тельный

🔵 **KEYWORD**

at [æt] *prep* **1** (*referring to position*) в/на +*prp*; **at school** в шко́ле; **at the theatre** в теа́тре; **at a concert** на конце́рте; **at the station** на ста́нции; **at the top** наверху́; **at home** до́ма; **they are sitting at the table** они́ сидя́т за столо́м; **at my friend's (house)** у моего́ дру́га; **at the doctor's** у врача́

2 (*referring to direction*) в/на +*acc*; **to look at** смотре́ть (*perf* посмотре́ть) на +*acc*; **to throw sth at sb** (*stone*) броса́ть (*perf* бро́сить) что-н *or* чем-н в кого́-н

3 (*referring to time*) **at four o'clock** в четы́ре часа́; **at half past two** в полови́не тре́тьего; **at a quarter to two** без че́тверти два; **at a quarter past two** че́тверть тре́тьего; **at dawn** на заре́; **at night** но́чью; **at Christmas** на Рождество́; **at lunch** за обе́дом; **at times** времена́ми

4 (*referring to rates*): **at one pound a kilo** по фу́нту за килогра́мм; **two at a time** по́ дво́е; **at fifty km/h** со ско́ростью пятьдеся́т км/ч; **at full speed** на по́лной ско́рости

5 (*referring to manner*): **at a stroke** одни́м ма́хом; **at peace** в ми́ре

6 (*referring to activity*): **to be at home/
work** быть (*impf*) до́ма/на рабо́те; **to play
at cowboys** игра́ть (*impf*) в ковбо́и; **to be
good at doing** хорошо́ уме́ть (*impf*) +*infin*
7 (*referring to cause*): **he is surprised/
annoyed at sth** он удивлён/раздражён
чем-н; **I am surprised at you** Вы меня́
удивля́ете; **I stayed at his suggestion** я
оста́лся по его́ предложе́нию
8 (@ *symbol*) комме́рческое at *nt ind*

ate [eɪt] *pt of* **eat**
atheist ['eɪθɪɪst] *n* атеи́ст(ка)
Athens ['æθɪnz] *n* Афи́ны *pl*
athlete ['æθliːt] *n* спортсме́н(ка)
athletic [æθ'lɛtɪk] *adj* спорти́вный;
athletics [æθ'lɛtɪks] *n* лёгкая атле́тика
Atlantic [ət'læntɪk] *n*: **the Atlantic
(Ocean)** Атланти́ческий океа́н
atlas ['ætləs] *n* а́тлас
atmosphere ['ætməsfɪəʳ] *n* атмосфе́ра
atom ['ætəm] *n* а́том; **atomic** [ə'tɔmɪk]
adj а́томный
attach [ə'tætʃ] *vt* прикрепля́ть (*perf*
прикрепи́ть); (*document, letter*) прилага́ть
(*perf* приложи́ть); **he is attached to** (*fond
of*) он привя́зан к +*dat*; **to attach
importance to** придава́ть (*perf* прида́ть)
значе́ние +*dat*; **attachment** *n* (*device*)
приспособле́ние, наса́дка; **attachment (to
sb)** (*love*) привя́занность *f* (к кому́-н)
attack [ə'tæk] *vt* (*Mil, fig*) атакова́ть
(*impf/perf*); (*assault*) напада́ть (*perf
напа́сть*) на +*acc* ▷ *n* (*Mil, fig*) ата́ка;
(*assault*) нападе́ние; (*of illness*) при́ступ;
attacker *n*: his/her attacker
напа́вший(-ая) *m(f) adj* на него́/неё
attain [ə'teɪn] *vt* (*happiness, success*)
достига́ть (*dostи́гнуть or* дости́чь *perf*)
+*gen*, добива́ться (*perf* доби́ться) +*gen*
attempt [ə'tɛmpt] *n* попы́тка ▷ *vt*: **to
attempt to do** пыта́ться (*perf* попыта́ться)
+*infin*; **to make an attempt on sb's life**
соверша́ть (*perf* соверши́ть) покуше́ние
на кого́-н
attend [ə'tɛnd] *vt* (*school, church*)
посеща́ть (*impf*); **attend to** *vt fus* (*needs,
patient*) занима́ться (*perf* заня́ться) +*instr*;
(*customer*) обслу́живать (*perf* обслужи́ть);
attendance *n* прису́тствие; (*Scol*)
посеща́емость *f*; **attendant** *n*
сопровожда́ющий(-ая) *m(f) adj*; (*in garage*)
служи́тель(ница) *m(f)*
attention [ə'tɛnʃən] *n* внима́ние; (*care*)
ухо́д; **for the attention of ...** (*Admin*) к
све́дению +*gen* ...
attic ['ætɪk] *n* (*living space*) манса́рда;
(*storage space*) черда́к
attitude ['ætɪtjuːd] *n*: **attitude (to** or
towards) отноше́ние (к +*dat*)
attorney [ə'təːnɪ] *n* (*US: lawyer*) юри́ст;
Attorney General *n* (*Brit*) мини́стр
юсти́ции; (*US*) Генера́льный прокуро́р
attract [ə'trækt] *vt* привлека́ть (*perf*

привле́чь); **attraction** [ə'trækʃən] *n*
(*appeal*) привлека́тельность *f*; **attractive**
adj привлека́тельный
attribute [*n* 'ætrɪbjuːt, *vb* ə'trɪbjuːt] *n*
при́знак, атрибу́т ▷ *vt*: **to attribute sth to**
(*cause*) относи́ть (*perf* отнести́) что-н за
счёт +*gen*; (*painting, quality*) припи́сывать
(*perf* приписа́ть) что-н +*dat*
aubergine ['əubəʒiːn] *n* баклажа́н
auction ['ɔːkʃən] *n* (*also* **sale by auction**)
аукцио́н ▷ *vt* продава́ть (*perf* прода́ть)
на аукцио́не
audible ['ɔːdɪbl] *adj* слы́шный
audience ['ɔːdɪəns] *n* аудито́рия, пу́блика
audit ['ɔːdɪt] *vt* (*Comm*) проводи́ть (*perf*
провести́) реви́зию +*gen*
audition [ɔː'dɪʃən] *n* прослу́шивание
auditor ['ɔːdɪtəʳ] *n* реви́зия, ауди́тор
auditorium [ɔːdɪ'tɔːrɪəm] *n* зал
August ['ɔːgəst] *n* а́вгуст
aunt [ɑːnt] *n* тётя; **auntie** ['ɑːntɪ] *n
dimin of* **aunt**
au pair ['əu'pɛəʳ] *n* (*also* **au pair girl**)
молода́я ня́ня-иностра́нка, живу́щая в
семье́
aura ['ɔːrə] *n* (*fig: air*) орео́л
Australia [ɔs'treɪlɪə] *n* Австра́лия
Austria ['ɔstrɪə] *n* А́встрия
authentic [ɔː'θɛntɪk] *adj* по́длинный
author ['ɔːθəʳ] *n* (*of text, plan*) а́втор;
(*profession*) писа́тель(ница) *m(f)*
authority [ɔː'θɔrɪtɪ] *n* (*power*) власть *f*;
(*Pol*) управле́ние; (*expert*) авторите́т;
(*official permission*) полномо́чие;
authorities *npl* (*ruling body*) вла́сти *fpl*
autobiography [ɔːtəbaɪ'ɔgrəfɪ] *n*
автобиогра́фия
autograph ['ɔːtəgrɑːf] *n* авто́граф ▷ *vt*
надпи́сывать (*perf* надписа́ть)
automatic [ɔːtə'mætɪk] *adj*
автомати́ческий ▷ *n* (*US: gun*)
(самозаря́дный) пистоле́т; (*car*)
автомоби́ль *m* с автомати́ческим
переключе́нием скоросте́й;
automatically *adv* автомати́чески
automobile ['ɔːtəməbiːl] *n* (*US*)
автомоби́ль *m*
autonomous [ɔː'tɔnəməs] *adj* (*region*)
автоно́мный; (*person, organization*)
самостоя́тельный
autonomy [ɔː'tɔnəmɪ] *n* автоно́мия,
самостоя́тельность *f*
autumn ['ɔːtəm] *n* о́сень *f*; **in autumn**
о́сенью
auxiliary [ɔːg'zɪlɪərɪ] *adj*
вспомога́тельный ▷ *n* помо́щник
avail [ə'veɪl] *n*: **to no avail** напра́сно
availability [əveɪlə'bɪlɪtɪ] *n* нали́чие
available [ə'veɪləbl] *adj* досту́пный;
(*person*) свобо́дный
avalanche ['ævəlɑːnʃ] *n* лави́на
avenue ['ævənjuː] *n* (*street*) у́лица; (*drive*)
алле́я
average ['ævərɪdʒ] *n* сре́днее *nt adj* ▷ *adj*

сре́дний ▷ vt достига́ть (perf дости́чь) в сре́днем +gen; (sum) составля́ть (perf соста́вить) в сре́днем; **on average** в сре́днем

avert [ə'vəːt] vt (perf предотвраща́ть (perf предотврати́ть); (blow, eyes) отводи́ть (perf отвести́)

avid ['ævɪd] adj (keen) стра́стный

avocado [ævə'kɑːdəu] n авока́до nt ind

avoid [ə'vɔɪd] vt избега́ть (perf избежа́ть)

await [ə'weɪt] vt ожида́ть (impf) +gen

awake [ə'weɪk] (pt awoke or awoken or awaked) adj: **he is awake** он просну́лся; **he was still awake** он ещё не спал

award [ə'wɔːd] n награ́да ▷ vt награжда́ть (perf награди́ть); (Law) присужда́ть (perf присуди́ть)

aware [ə'wɛər] adj: **to be aware (of)** (realize) сознава́ть (impf) (+acc); **to become aware of sth/that** осознава́ть (perf осозна́ть) что-н/, что; **awareness** n осозна́ние

away [ə'weɪ] adv (movement) в сто́рону; (position) в стороне́; (far away) далеко́; **the holidays are two weeks away** до кани́кул (оста́лось) две неде́ли; **away from** (movement) от +gen; (position) в стороне́ от +gen; **two kilometres away from the town** в двух киломе́трах от го́рода; **two hours away by car** в двух часа́х езды́ на маши́не; **he's away for a week** он в отъе́зде на неде́лю; **to take away (from)** (remove) забира́ть (perf забра́ть) (у +gen); (subtract) отнима́ть (perf отня́ть) (от +gen); **he is working away** (continuously) он продолжа́ет рабо́тать

awe [ɔː] n благогове́ние

awful ['ɔːfəl] adj ужа́сный; **an awful lot (of)** ужа́сно мно́го (+gen); **awfully** adv ужа́сно

awkward ['ɔːkwəd] adj (clumsy) неуклю́жий; (inconvenient) неудо́бный; (embarrassing) нело́вкий

awoke [ə'wəuk] pt of **awake**; **awoken** pp of **awake**

axe [æks] (US **ax**) n топо́р ▷ vt (project) отменя́ть (perf отмени́ть); (jobs) сокраща́ть (perf сократи́ть)

B [biː] n (Mus) си nt ind

BA n abbr = **Bachelor of Arts**

baby ['beɪbɪ] n ребёнок; (newborn) младе́нец; **baby carriage** n (US) коля́ска; **baby-sit** vi смотре́ть (impf) за детьми́; **baby-sitter** n приходя́щая ня́ня

bachelor ['bætʃələr] n холостя́к; **Bachelor of Arts/Science** ≈ бакала́вр гуманита́рных/есте́ственных нау́к

○ **KEYWORD**

back [bæk] n **1** (of person, animal) спина́; **the back of the hand** ты́льная сторона́ ладо́ни

2 (of house, car etc) за́дняя часть f; (of chair) спи́нка; (of page, book) оборо́т

3 (Football) защи́тник

▷ vt **1** (candidate: also **back up**) подде́рживать (perf поддержа́ть)

2 (financially: horse) ста́вить (perf поста́вить) на +acc; (: person) финанси́ровать (impf)

3: he backed the car into the garage он дал за́дний ход и поста́вил маши́ну в гара́ж

▷ vi (car etc: also **back up**) дава́ть (perf дать) за́дний ход

▷ adv **1** (not forward) обра́тно, наза́д; **he ran back** он побежа́л обра́тно or наза́д

2 (returned): **he's back** он верну́лся

3 (restitution): **to throw the ball back** кида́ть (perf ки́нуть) мяч обра́тно

4 (again): **to call back** (visit again) заходи́ть (perf зайти́) ещё раз; (Tel) перезва́нивать (perf перезвони́ть)

▷ cpd **1** (payment) за́дним число́м

2 (Aut: seat, wheels) за́дний

back down vi отступа́ть (perf отступи́ть)

back out vi (of promise) отступа́ться (perf отступи́ться)

back up vt (person, theory etc) подде́рживать (perf поддержа́ть)

back: **backache** n прострел, боль f в
пояснице; **backbencher** n (Brit)
заднескамеечник; **backbone** n
позвоночник; he's the backbone of the
organization на нём держится вся
организация; **background** n (of picture)
задний план; (of events) предыстория;
(experience) опыт; he's from a working
class background он из рабочей семьи;
against a background of ... на фоне +gen
...; **backing** n: (support) поддержка;
backlog n: backlog of work
невыполненная работа; **backpack** n
рюкзак; **backstage** adv за кулисами;
backward adj (movement) обратный;
(person, country) отсталый; **backwards**
adv назад; (list) наоборот; (fall)
навзничь; to walk backwards пятиться
(perf попятиться); **backyard** n (of house)
задний двор

bacon ['beɪkən] n бекон

bacteria [bæk'tɪərɪə] npl бактерии fpl

bad [bæd] adj плохой; (mistake)
серьёзный; (injury, crash) тяжёлый; (food)
тухлый; his bad leg его больная нога; to
go bad (food) тухнуть (perf протухнуть),
портиться (perf испортиться)

badge [bædʒ] n значок

badger ['bædʒər] n барсук

badly ['bædlɪ] adv плохо; badly wounded
тяжело раненый; he needs it badly он
сильно в этом нуждается; to be badly off
(for money) нуждаться (impf) (в деньгах)

badminton ['bædmɪntən] n бадминтон

bag [bæg] n сумка; (paper, plastic) пакет;
(handbag) сумочка; (satchel) ранец; (case)
портфель m; bags of (inf) уйма +gen

baggage ['bægɪdʒ] n (US) багаж

baggy ['bægɪ] adj мешковатый

bail [beɪl] n (money) залог ▷ vt (also to
grant bail to) выпускать (perf выпустить)
под залог; he was released on bail он был
выпущен под залог; **bail out** vt (Law)
платить (perf заплатить) залоговую
сумму за +acc; (boat) вычерпывать (perf
вычерпать) воду из +gen

bait [beɪt] n (for fish) наживка; (for animal,
criminal) приманка ▷ vt (hook, trap)
наживлять (perf наживить)

bake [beɪk] vt печь (perf испечь) ▷ vi
(bread etc) печься (perf печься); (make
cakes etc) печь (impf); **baked beans** npl
консервированная фасоль fsg (в томате);
baker n пекарь m; (also the baker's)
булочная f adj; **bakery** n пекарня;
(shop) булочная f adj

baking ['beɪkɪŋ] n выпечка; she does her
baking once a week она печёт раз в
неделю; **baking powder** n
разрыхлитель m

balance ['bæləns] n (equilibrium)
равновесие; (Comm: in account) баланс;
(: remainder) остаток; (scales) весы pl ▷ vt
(budget, account) балансировать (perf

сбалансировать); (make equal)
уравновешивать (perf уравновесить);
balance of payments/trade платёжный/
торговый баланс; **balanced** adj (diet)
сбалансированный

balcony ['bælkənɪ] n балкон

bald [bɔːld] adj (head) лысый; (tyre)
стёртый

ball [bɔːl] n (for football, tennis) мяч; (for
golf) мячик; (of wool, string) клубок;
(dance) бал

ballerina [bælə'riːnə] n балерина

ballet ['bæleɪ] n балет

balloon [bə'luːn] n воздушный шар; (also
hot air balloon) аэростат

ballot ['bælət] n голосование,
баллотировка

ballroom ['bɔːlrum] n бальный зал

Baltic ['bɔːltɪk] n: the Baltic Балтийское
море ▷ adj: the Baltic States страны fpl
Балтии, прибалтийские государства ntpl

bamboo [bæm'buː] n бамбук

ban [bæn] vt (prohibit) запрещать (perf
запретить); (suspend, exclude) отстранять
(perf отстранить) ▷ n (prohibition) запрет

banana [bə'nɑːnə] n банан

band [bænd] n (group: of people, rock
musicians) группа; (: of jazz, military
musicians) оркестр

bandage ['bændɪdʒ] n повязка ▷ vt
бинтовать (perf забинтовать)

B & B n abbr = bed and breakfast

bang [bæŋ] n стук; (explosion) выстрел;
(blow) удар ▷ excl бах ▷ vt (door)
хлопать (perf хлопнуть) +instr; (head etc)
ударять (perf ударить) ▷ vi (door)
захлопываться (perf захлопнуться)

bangs [bæŋz] npl (US) чёлка fsg

banish ['bænɪʃ] vt высылать (perf
выслать)

bank [bæŋk] n банк; (of river, lake) берег;
(of earth) насыпь f; **bank on** vt fus
полагаться (perf положиться) на +acc;
bank account n банковский счёт; **bank
card** n банковская карточка; **bank
holiday** n (Brit) нерабочий день m
(обычно понедельник); **banknote** n
банкнот

bankrupt ['bæŋkrʌpt] adj
обанкротившийся; to go bankrupt
обанкротиться (perf); I am bankrupt я —
банкрот, я обанкротился; **bankruptcy** n
банкротство, несостоятельность f

banner ['bænər] n транспарант

bannister ['bænɪstər] n (usu pl) перила
pl

banquet ['bæŋkwɪt] n банкет

baptism ['bæptɪzəm] n крещение

bar [bɑːr] n (pub) бар; (counter) стойка;
(rod) прут; (of soap) брусок; (of chocolate)
плитка; (Mus) такт ▷ vt (door, way)
загораживать (perf загородить); (person)
не допускать (perf допустить); **bars** npl
(on window) решётка fsg; **behind bars** за

решёткой; **the Bar** адвокату́ра; **bar none** без исключе́ния

barbaric [bɑːˈbærɪk] *adj* ва́рварский

barbecue [ˈbɑːbɪkjuː] *n* барбекю́ *nt ind*

barbed wire [ˈbɑːbd-] *n* колю́чая про́волока

barber [ˈbɑːbəʳ] *n* парикма́хер

bare [bɛəʳ] *adj* (*body*) го́лый, обнажённый; (*trees*) оголённый ▷ *vt* (*one's body*) оголи́ть (*perf* оголя́ть), обнажа́ть (*perf* обнажи́ть); (*teeth*) ска́лить (*perf* оска́лить); **in** *or* **with bare feet** босико́м; **barefoot** *adj* босо́й ▷ *adv* босико́м; **barely** *adv* едва́

bargain [ˈbɑːɡɪn] *n* сде́лка; (*good buy*) вы́годная поку́пка

barge [bɑːdʒ] *n* ба́ржа

bark [bɑːk] *n* (*of tree*) кора́ ▷ *vi* (*dog*) ла́ять (*impf*)

barley [ˈbɑːlɪ] *n* ячме́нь *m*

barman [ˈbɑːmən] *irreg n* ба́рмен

barn [bɑːn] *n* амба́р

barometer [bəˈrɔmɪtəʳ] *n* баро́метр

baron [ˈbærən] *n* баро́н; (*of press, industry*) магна́т

barracks [ˈbærəks] *npl* каза́рма *fsg*

barrage [ˈbærɑːʒ] *n* (*fig*) лави́на

barrel [ˈbærəl] *n* (*of wine, beer*) бо́чка; (*of oil*) барре́ль *m*; (*of gun*) ствол

barren [ˈbærən] *adj* (*land*) беспло́дный

barricade [bærɪˈkeɪd] *n* баррика́да ▷ *vt* баррикади́ровать (*perf* забаррикади́ровать); **to barricade o.s. in** баррикади́роваться (*perf* забаррикади́роваться)

barrier [ˈbærɪəʳ] *n* (*at entrance*) барье́р; (*at frontier*) шлагба́ум; (*fig: to progress*) препя́тствие

barring [ˈbɑːrɪŋ] *prep* за исключе́нием +*gen*

barrister [ˈbærɪstəʳ] *n* (*Brit*) адвока́т

barrow [ˈbærəu] *n* (*also* **wheelbarrow**) та́чка

base [beɪs] *n* основа́ние; (*of monument etc*) ба́за, постаме́нт; (*Mil*) ба́за; (*for organization*) местонахожде́ние ▷ *adj* ни́зкий ▷ *vt*: **to base sth on** (*opinion*) осно́вывать (*impf*) что-н на +*prp*; **baseball** *n* бейсбо́л; **basement** *n* подва́л

basic [ˈbeɪsɪk] *adj* (*fundamental*) фундамента́льный; (*elementary*) нача́льный; (*primitive*) элемента́рный; **basically** *adv* по существу́; (*on the whole*) в основно́м; **basics** *npl*: **the basics** осно́вы *fpl*

basil [ˈbæzl] *n* базили́к

basin [ˈbeɪsn] *n* (*also* **washbasin**) ра́ковина; (*Geo*) бассе́йн

basis [ˈbeɪsɪs] (*pl* **bases**) *n* основа́ние; **on a part-time basis** на непо́лной ста́вке; **on a trial basis** на испыта́тельный срок

basket [ˈbɑːskɪt] *n* корзи́на; **basketball** *n* баскетбо́л

bass [beɪs] *n* бас ▷ *adj* ба́ссовый

bastard [ˈbɑːstəd] *n* внебра́чный ребёнок; (*infl*) ублю́док (*!*)

bat [bæt] *n* (*Zool*) летучая мышь *f*; (*Sport*) бита́; (*Brit: Table Tennis*) раке́тка

batch [bætʃ] *n* (*of bread*) вы́печка; (*of papers*) па́чка

bath [bɑːθ] *n* ва́нна ▷ *vt* купа́ть (*perf* вы́купать); **to have a bath** принима́ть (*perf* приня́ть) ва́нну; **bathe** [beɪð] *vi* (*swim*) купа́ться (*impf*); (*US: have a bath*) принима́ть (*perf* приня́ть) ва́нну ▷ *vt* (*wound*) промыва́ть (*perf* промы́ть); **bathroom** [ˈbɑːθrum] *n* ва́нная *f adj*; **baths** [bɑːðz] *npl* (*also* **swimming baths**) пла́вательный бассе́йн *msg*; **bath towel** *n* ба́нное полоте́нце

baton [ˈbætən] *n* (*Mus*) дирижёрская па́лочка; (*Police*) дуби́нка; (*Sport*) эстафе́тная па́лочка

batter [ˈbætəʳ] *vt* (*person*) бить (*perf* изби́ть); (*subj: wind, rain*) бить (*perf* поби́ть) ▷ *n* (*Culin*) жи́дкое те́сто

battery [ˈbætərɪ] *n* (*of torch etc*) батаре́йка; (*Aut*) аккумуля́тор

battle [ˈbætl] *n* би́тва, бой

bay [beɪ] *n* зали́в; (*smaller*) бу́хта; **loading bay** погру́зочная площа́дка; **to hold sb at bay** держа́ть (*impf*) кого́-н на расстоя́нии

bazaar [bəˈzɑːʳ] *n* база́р, ры́нок; (*fete*) благотвори́тельный база́р

BBC *n abbr* (= *British Broadcasting Corporation*) Би-Би-Си *nt ind*

BC *adv abbr* (= *before Christ*) до рождества́ Христо́ва

🅞 **KEYWORD**

be [biː] (*pt* **was, were**, *pp* **been**) *aux vb*
1 (*with present participle: forming continuous tenses*): **what are you doing?** что Вы де́лаете?; **it is raining** идёт дождь; **they're working tomorrow** они́ рабо́тают за́втра; **the house is being built** дом стро́ится; **I've been waiting for you for ages** я жду Вас уже́ це́лую ве́чность
2 (*with pp: forming passives*): **he was killed** он был уби́т; **the box had been opened** я́щик откры́ли; **the thief was nowhere to be seen** во́ра нигде́ не́ было ви́дно
3 (*in tag questions*) не так *or* пра́вда ли, да; **she's back again, is she?** она́ верну́лась, да *or* не так *or* пра́вда ли?; **she is pretty, isn't she?** она́ хоро́шенькая, не пра́вда ли *or* да?
4 (*to +infin*): **the house is to be sold** дом должны́ прода́ть; **you're to be congratulated for all your work** Вас сле́дует поздра́вить за всю Ва́шу рабо́ту; **he's not to open it** он не до́лжен открыва́ть это
▷ *vb* **1** (+ *complement: in present tense*): **he is English** он англича́нин; (*in past/future*

tense) быть (*impf*) +*instr*; **he was a doctor** он был врачо́м; **she is going to be very tall** она́ бу́дет о́чень высо́кой; **I'm tired** я уста́л; **I was hot/cold** мне бы́ло жа́рко/ хо́лодно; **two and two are four** два́жды два — четы́ре; **she's tall** она́ высо́кая; **be careful!** бу́дьте осторо́жны!; **be quiet!** ти́хо!, ти́ше!

2 (*of health*): **how are you feeling?** как Вы себя́ чу́вствуете?; **he's very ill** он о́чень бо́лен; **I'm better now** мне сейча́с лу́чше

3 (*of age*): **how old are you?** ско́лько Вам лет?; **I'm sixteen (years old)** мне шестна́дцать (лет)

4 (*cost*): **how much is the wine?** ско́лько сто́ит вино́?; **that'll be £5.75, please** с Вас £5,75, пожа́луйста

▷ *vi* **1** (*exist*) быть (*impf*); **there are people who ...** есть лю́ди, кото́рые ...; **there is one drug that ...** есть одно́ лека́рство, кото́рое ...; **is there a God?** Бог есть?

2 (*occur*) быва́ть (*impf*); **there are frequent accidents on this road** на э́той доро́ге ча́сто быва́ют ава́рии; **be that as it may** как бы то ни́ было; **so be it** так и быть, быть по сему́

3 (*referring to place*): **I won't be here tomorrow** меня́ здесь за́втра не бу́дет; **the book is on the table** кни́га на столе́; **there are pictures on the wall** на стене́ карти́ны; **Edinburgh is in Scotland** Эдинбу́рг нахо́дится в Шотла́ндии; **there is someone in the house** в до́ме кто-то есть; **we've been here for ages** мы здесь уже́ це́лую ве́чность

4 (*referring to movement*) быть (*impf*); **where have you been?** где Вы бы́ли?; **I've been to the post office** я был на по́чте

▷ *impers vb* **1** (*referring to time*): **it's five o'clock (now)** сейча́с пять часо́в; **it's the 28th of April (today)** сего́дня 28-ое апре́ля

2 (*referring to distance, weather. in present tense*): **it's 10 km to the village** до дере́вни 10 км; (*: in past/future tense*) быть (*impf*); **it's hot/cold (today)** сего́дня жа́рко/ хо́лодно; **it was very windy yesterday** вчера́ бы́ло о́чень ве́трено; **it will be sunny tomorrow** за́втра бу́дет со́лнечно

3 (*emphatic*): **it's (only) me/the postman** э́то я/почтальо́н; **it was Maria who paid the bill** и́менно Мари́я оплати́ла счёт

beach [biːtʃ] *n* пляж

beacon ['biːkən] *n* (*marker*) сигна́льный ого́нь *m*

bead [biːd] *n* бу́сина; (*of sweat*) ка́пля

beak [biːk] *n* клюв

beam [biːm] *n* (*Archit*) ба́лка, стропи́ло; (*of light*) луч

bean [biːn] *n* боб; **French bean** фасо́ль *f* *no pl*; **runner bean** фасо́ль о́гненная; **coffee bean** кофе́йное зерно́

bear [bɛəʳ] (*pt* **bore**, *pp* **borne**) *n*

медве́дь(-е́дица) *m(f)* ▷ *vt* (*cost, responsibility*) нести́ (*perf* понести́); (*weight*) нести́ (*impf*) ▷ *vi*: **to bear right/ left** (*Aut*) держа́ться (*impf*) пра́вого/ ле́вого поворо́та; **bear out** *vt* подде́рживать (*perf* поддержа́ть)

beard [bɪəd] *n* борода́

bearing ['bɛərɪŋ] *n* (*connection*) отноше́ние; **bearings** *npl* (*also* **ball bearings**) ша́рики *mpl* подши́пника; **to take a bearing** ориенти́роваться (*impf/ perf*)

beast [biːst] *n* (*also inf*) зверь *m*

beat [biːt] (*pt* **beat**, *pp* **beaten**) *n* (*of heart*) бие́ние; (*Mus: rhythm*) ритм; (*Police*) уча́сток ▷ *vt* (*wife, child*) бить (*perf* поби́ть); (*eggs etc*) взбива́ть (*perf* взби́ть); (*opponent, record*) побива́ть (*perf* поби́ть); (*drum*) бить (*impf*) в +*acc* ▷ *vi* (*heart*) би́ться (*impf*); (*rain, wind*) стуча́ть (*impf*); **beat it!** (*inf*) кати́сь!; **off the beaten track** по непротоённому пути́; **beat up** *vt* (*person*) избива́ть (*perf* изби́ть); **beating** *n* избие́ние; (*thrashing*) по́рка

beautiful ['bjuːtɪful] *adj* краси́вый; (*day, experience*) прекра́сный; **beautifully** ['bjuːtɪflɪ] *adv* (*play, sing etc*) краси́во, прекра́сно

beauty ['bjuːtɪ] *n* красота́; (*woman*) краса́вица

beaver ['biːvəʳ] *n* (*Zool*) бобр

became [bɪ'keɪm] *pt of* **become**

because [bɪ'kɔz] *conj* потому́ что; (*since*) так как; **because of** из-за +*gen*

become [bɪ'kʌm] (*irreg like* **come**) *vi* станови́ться (*perf* стать) +*instr*; **to become fat** толсте́ть (*perf* потолсте́ть); **to become thin** худе́ть (*perf* похуде́ть)

bed [bɛd] *n* крова́ть *f*; (*of river, sea*) дно; (*of flowers*) клу́мба; **to go to bed** ложи́ться (*perf* лечь) спать; **bed and breakfast** *n* ма́ленькая ча́стная гости́ница с за́втраком; (*terms*) ночле́г и за́втрак; **bedclothes** *npl* посте́льное бельё *ntsg*; **bedding** *n* посте́льные принадле́жности *fpl*; **bedroom** *n* спа́льня; **bedside** *n*: **at sb's bedside** у посте́ли кого́-н; **bedspread** *n* покрыва́ло; **bedtime** *n* вре́мя *nt* ложи́ться спать

bee [biː] *n* пчела́

beech [biːtʃ] *n* бук

beef [biːf] *n* говя́дина; **roast beef** ро́стбиф

been [biːn] *pp of* **be**

beer [bɪəʳ] *n* пи́во

beet [biːt] *n* (*vegetable*) кормова́я свёкла; (*US: also* **red beet**) свёкла

beetle ['biːtl] *n* жук

beetroot ['biːtruːt] *n* (*Brit*) свёкла

before [bɪ'fɔːʳ] *prep* пе́ред +*instr*, до +*gen* ▷ *conj* до того́ *or* пе́ред тем, как ▷ *adv* (*time*) ра́ньше, пре́жде; **the day before yesterday** позавчера́; **do this before you forget** сде́лайте э́то, пока́ Вы не забы́ли;

before going пе́ред ухо́дом; **before she goes** до того́ or пе́ред тем, как она́ уйдёт; **the week before** неде́лю наза́д, на про́шлой неде́ле; **I've never seen it before** я никогда́ э́того ра́ньше не ви́дел; **beforehand** adv зара́нее

beg [bɛg] vi попроша́йничать (impf), ни́щенствовать (impf) ▷ vt (also **beg for**: food, money) проси́ть (impf); (: mercy, forgiveness) умоля́ть (perf умоли́ть) о +prp; **to beg sb to do** умоля́ть (perf умоли́ть) кого́-н +infin

began [bɪ'gæn] pt of **begin**

beggar ['bɛgəᵊ] n попроша́йка, ни́щий(-ая) m(f) adj

begin [bɪ'gɪn] (pt **began**, pp **begun**) vt начина́ть (perf нача́ть) ▷ vi начина́ться (perf нача́ться); **to begin doing** or **to do** начина́ть (perf нача́ть) +impf infin; **beginner** n начина́ющий(-ая) m(f) adj; **beginning** n нача́ло

begun [bɪ'gʌn] pp of **begin**

behalf [bɪ'hɑːf] n: **on** or (US) **in behalf of** от и́мени +gen; (for benefit of) в по́льзу +gen, в интере́сах +gen; **on my/his behalf** от моего́/его́ и́мени

behave [bɪ'heɪv] vi вести́ (impf) себя́; (also **behave o.s.**) вести́ (impf) себя́ хорошо́

behaviour [bɪ'heɪvjəᵊ] (US **behavior**) n поведе́ние

behind [bɪ'haɪnd] prep (at the back of) за +instr, позади́ +gen; (supporting) за +instr; (lower in rank etc) ни́же +gen ▷ adv сза́ди, позади́ ▷ n (buttocks) зад; **to be behind schedule** отстава́ть (perf отста́ть) от гра́фика

beige [beɪʒ] adj бе́жевый

Beijing [beɪ'dʒɪŋ] n Пеки́н

Belarus [bɛlə'rus] n Белару́сь f

belated [bɪ'leɪtɪd] adj запозда́лый

Belgian ['bɛldʒən] n бельги́ец(-и́йка)

Belgium ['bɛldʒəm] n Бе́льгия

belief [bɪ'liːf] n (conviction) убежде́ние; (trust, faith) ве́ра; **it's beyond belief** э́то невероя́тно; **in the belief that** полага́я, что

believe [bɪ'liːv] vt ве́рить (perf пове́рить) +dat or в +acc ▷ vi ве́рить (impf); **to believe in** ве́рить (perf пове́рить) в +acc

bell [bɛl] n ко́локол; (small) колоко́льчик; (on door) звоно́к

belly ['bɛlɪ] n (of animal) брю́хо; (of person) живо́т

belong [bɪ'lɔŋ] vi: **to belong to** принадлежа́ть (impf) +dat; (club) состоя́ть (impf) в +prp; **this book belongs here** ме́сто э́той кни́ги здесь; **belongings** npl ве́щи fpl

beloved [bɪ'lʌvɪd] adj люби́мый

below [bɪ'ləu] prep (position) под +instr; (motion) под +acc; (less than) ни́же +gen ▷ adv (position) внизу́; (motion) вниз; see **below** смотри́ ни́же

belt [bɛlt] n (leather) реме́нь m; (cloth)

по́яс; (of land) по́яс, зо́на; (Tech) приводно́й реме́нь

bemused [bɪ'mjuːzd] adj озада́ченный

bench [bɛntʃ] n скамья́; (Brit: Pol) места́ ntpl па́ртий в парла́менте; (in workshop) верста́к; (in laboratory) лаборато́рный стол; **the Bench** (Law) суде́йская колле́гия

bend [bɛnd] (pt, pp **bent**) vt гнуть (perf согну́ть), сгиба́ть (impf) ▷ vi (person) гну́ться (perf согну́ться) ▷ n (Brit: in road) поворо́т; (in pipe) изги́б; (in river) излу́чина; **bend down** vi наклоня́ться (perf наклони́ться), нагиба́ться (perf нагну́ться)

beneath [bɪ'niːθ] prep (position) под +instr; (motion) под +acc; (unworthy of) ни́же +gen ▷ adv внизу́

beneficial [bɛnɪ'fɪʃəl] adj: **beneficial (to)** благотво́рный (для +gen)

benefit ['bɛnɪfɪt] n (advantage) вы́года; (money) посо́бие ▷ vt приноси́ть (perf принести́) по́льзу +dat ▷ vi: **he'll benefit from it** он полу́чит от э́того вы́году

benign [bɪ'naɪn] adj добросерде́чный; (Med) доброка́чественный

bent [bɛnt] pt, pp of **bend** ▷ adj (wire, pipe) погну́тый; **he is bent on doing** он настро́ился +infin

bereaved [bɪ'riːvd] adj поне́сший тяжёлую утра́ту ▷ n: **the bereaved** друзья́ mpl и ро́дственники mpl поко́йного

Berlin [bəː'lɪn] n Берли́н

Bermuda [bəː'mjuːdə] n Берму́дские острова́ mpl

berry ['bɛrɪ] n я́года

berth [bəːθ] n (in caravan, on ship) ко́йка; (on train) по́лка; (mooring) прича́л

beside [bɪ'saɪd] prep ря́дом с +instr, о́коло +gen, у +gen; **to be beside o.s. (with)** быть (impf) вне себя́ (от +gen); **that's beside the point** э́то к де́лу не отно́сится

besides [bɪ'saɪdz] adv кро́ме того́ ▷ prep кро́ме +gen, помимо +gen

best [bɛst] adj лу́чший ▷ adv лу́чше всего́; **the best part of** (quantity) бо́льшая часть +gen; **at best** в лу́чшем слу́чае; **to make the best of sth** испо́льзовать (impf) что-н наилу́чшим о́бразом; **to do one's best** де́лать (perf сде́лать) всё возмо́жное; **to the best of my knowledge** наско́лько мне изве́стно; **to the best of my ability** в ме́ру мои́х спосо́бностей; **best man** n ша́фер; **bestseller** n бестсе́ллер

bet [bɛt] (pt, pp **bet** or **betted**) n (wager) пари́ nt ind; (in gambling) ста́вка ▷ vi (wager) держа́ть (impf) пари́; (expect, guess) би́ться (impf) об закла́д ▷ vt: **to bet sb sth** спо́рить (perf поспо́рить) с кем-н на что-н; **to bet money on sth** ста́вить (perf поста́вить) де́ньги на что-н

betray [bɪ'treɪ] vt (friends) предава́ть (perf преда́ть); (trust) обма́нывать (perf обману́ть)

better ['bɛtə^r] adj лучший ▷ adv лучше
▷ vt (score) улучшать (perf улучшить)
▷ n: **to get the better of** брать (perf взять)
верх над +instr; **I feel better** я чувствую
себя лучше; **to get better** (Med)
поправляться (perf поправиться); **I had
better go** мне лучше уйти; **he thought
better of it** он передумал
betting ['bɛtɪŋ] n пари nt ind
between [bɪ'twi:n] prep между +instr
▷ adv: **in between** между тем
beware [bɪ'wɛə^r] vi: **to beware (of)**
остерегаться (perf остеречься) (+gen)
bewildered [bɪ'wɪldəd] adj изумлённый
beyond [bɪ'jɔnd] prep (position) за +instr;
(motion) за +acc; (understanding) выше
+gen; (expectations) сверх +gen; (doubt)
вне +gen; (age) больше +gen; (date) после
+gen ▷ adv (position) вдали; (motion)
вдаль; **it's beyond repair** это невозможно
починить
bias ['baɪəs] n (against) предубеждение;
(towards) пристрастие
bib [bɪb] n (child's) нагрудник
Bible ['baɪbl] n Библия
bicycle ['baɪsɪkl] n велосипед
bid [bɪd] (pt **bade** or **bid**, pp **bid(den)**) n
(at auction) предложение цены; (attempt)
попытка ▷ vt (offer) предлагать (perf
предложить) ▷ vi: **to bid for** (at auction)
предлагать (perf предложить) цену за
+acc; **bidder** n: **the highest bidder** лицо,
предлагающее наивысшую цену
big [bɪg] adj большой; (important)
важный; (bulky) крупный; (older: brother,
sister) старший
bike [baɪk] n (inf: bicycle) велик
bikini [bɪ'ki:nɪ] n бикини nt ind
bilateral [baɪ'lætərl] adj двусторонний
bilingual [baɪ'lɪŋgwəl] adj двуязычный
bill [bɪl] n (invoice) счёт; (Pol)
законопроект; (US: banknote)
казначейский билет, банкнот; (beak)
клюв; **billboard** n доска объявлений
billion ['bɪljən] n (Brit) биллион; (US)
миллиард
bin [bɪn] n (Brit: also **rubbish bin**)
мусорное ведро; (container) ящик
bind [baɪnd] (pt, pp **bound**) vt (tie)
привязывать (perf привязать); (hands,
feet) связывать (perf связать); (oblige)
обязывать (perf обязать); (book)
переплетать (perf переплести)
bingo ['bɪŋgəu] n лото nt ind
binoculars [bɪ'nɔkjuləz] npl бинокль
msg
biography [baɪ'ɔgrəfɪ] n биография
biological [baɪə'lɔdʒɪkl] adj (science)
биологический; (warfare)
бактериологический; (washing powder)
содержащий биопрепараты
biology [baɪ'ɔlədʒɪ] n биология
birch [bə:tʃ] n берёза
bird [bə:d] n птица

Biro ['baɪərəu] n шариковая ручка
birth [bə:θ] n рождение; **to give birth to**
рожать (perf родить); **birth certificate** n
свидетельство о рождении; **birth
control** n (policy) контроль m
рождаемости; (methods)
противозачаточные меры fpl; **birthday** n
день m рождения ▷ cpd: **birthday card**
открытка ко дню рождения; see also
happy; **birthplace** n родина
biscuit ['bɪskɪt] n (Brit) печенье; (US)
≈ кекс
bishop ['bɪʃəp] n (Rel) епископ; (Chess)
слон
bit [bɪt] pt of **bite** ▷ n (piece) кусок,
кусочек; (Comput) бит; **a bit of** немного
+gen; **a bit dangerous** слегка опасный; **bit
by bit** мало-помалу, понемногу
bitch [bɪtʃ] n (also infl) сука (also !)
bite [baɪt] (pt **bit**, pp **bitten**) vt кусать
(perf укусить) ▷ vi кусаться (impf) ▷ n
(insect bite) укус; **to bite one's nails** кусать
(impf) ногти; **let's have a bite (to eat)** (inf)
давайте перекусим; **he had a bite of cake**
он откусил кусок пирога
bitter ['bɪtə^r] adj горький; (wind)
пронизывающий; (struggle)
ожесточённый
bizarre [bɪ'zɑ:^r] adj странный,
причудливый
black [blæk] adj чёрный; (tea) без
молока; (person): **Black** чернокожий ▷ n
(colour) чёрный цвет, чёрное nt adj; **black
and blue** в синяках; **to be in the black**
иметь (impf) деньги в банке; **blackberry**
n ежевика f no pl; **blackbird** n (чёрный)
дрозд; **blackboard** n классная доска;
black coffee n чёрный кофе m ind;
blackcurrant n чёрная смородина;
blackmail n шантаж ▷ vt
шантажировать (impf); **black market** n
чёрный рынок; **blackout** n (Elec)
обесточивание; (TV, Radio) приостановление
передач; (Med) обморок; **black pepper**
n чёрный перец; **Black Sea** n: **the Black
Sea** Чёрное море
bladder ['blædə^r] n мочевой пузырь m
blade [bleɪd] n (of propeller, oar)
лопасть f; **a blade of grass** травинка
blame [bleɪm] n вина ▷ vt: **to blame sb
for sth** винить кого́-н в чём-н; **he is
to blame (for sth)** он виноват (в чём-н)
bland [blænd] adj (food) пресный
blank [blæŋk] adj (paper) чистый; (look)
пустой ▷ n (of memory) провал; (on form)
пропуск; (for gun) холостой патрон
blanket ['blæŋkɪt] n одеяло; (of snow)
покров; (of fog) пелена
blast [blɑ:st] n (explosion) взрыв ▷ vt
(blow up) взрывать (perf взорвать)
blatant ['bleɪtənt] adj (obvious) явный
blaze [bleɪz] n (fire) пламя nt; (of colour)
полыхание
blazer ['bleɪzə^r] n форменный пиджак

bleach [bli:tʃ] n (also **household bleach**) отбеливатель m ▷ vt (fabric) отбеливать (perf отбелить)

bleak [bli:k] adj (day, face) унылый; (prospect) мрачный

bleed [bli:d] (pt, pp **bled**) vi кровоточить (impf); **my nose is bleeding** у меня из носа идёт кровь

blend [blɛnd] n (of tea, whisky) букет ▷ vt (Culin) смешивать (perf смешать) ▷ vi (also **blend in**) сочетаться (impf)

bless [blɛs] (pt, pp **blessed** or **blest**) vt благословлять (perf благословить); **bless you!** будьте здоровы!; **blessing** n благословение; (godsend) Божий дар

blew [blu:] pt of **blow**

blind [blaɪnd] adj слепой ▷ n штора; (also **Venetian blind**) жалюзи pl ind ▷ vt ослеплять (perf ослепить); **to be blind (to)** (fig) не видеть (impf) (+acc)

blink [blɪŋk] vi моргать (impf); (light) мигать (impf)

bliss [blɪs] n блаженство

blizzard ['blɪzəd] n вьюга

bloated ['bləutɪd] adj (face, stomach) вздутый; **I feel bloated** я весь раздулся

blob [blɒb] n (of glue, paint) сгусток; (shape) смутное очертание

bloc [blɒk] n блок

block [blɒk] n (of buildings) квартал; (of stone etc) плита ▷ vt (barricade) блокировать (perf заблокировать), загораживать (perf загородить); (progress) препятствовать (impf); **block of flats** (Brit) многоквартирный дом; **mental block** провал памяти; **blockade** [blɔ'keɪd] n блокада; **blockage** ['blɔkɪdʒ] n блокирование

blog [blɒg] n блог f ▷ vi писать (perf написать) в блог; **blogger** n блогер; **blogpost** n пост, статья

bloke [bləuk] n (Brit: inf) парень m

blond(e) [blɒnd] adj белокурый ▷ n: **blonde** (woman) блондинка

blood [blʌd] n кровь f; **blood donor** n донор; **blood pressure** n кровяное давление; **bloodshed** n кровопролитие; **bloodstream** n кровообращение; **bloody** adj (battle) кровавый; (Brit: inf!): **this bloody weather** эта проклятая погода

blossom ['blɔsəm] n цвет, цветение

blot [blɔt] n (on text) клякса

blow [bləu] (pt **blew**, pp **blown**) n удар ▷ vi (wind, person) дуть (perf подуть); (fuse) перегорать (perf перегореть) ▷ vt (subj: wind) гнать (impf); (instrument) дуть (impf) в +acc; **to blow one's nose** сморкаться (perf высморкаться); **blow away** vt сдувать (perf сдуть); **blow up** vi (storm, crisis) разражаться (perf разразиться) ▷ vt (bridge) взрывать (perf взорвать); (tyre) надувать (perf надуть)

blue [blu:] adj (colour: light) голубой; (: dark) синий; (unhappy) грустный; **blues**

npl (Mus) блюз msg; **out of the blue** (fig) как гром среди ясного неба; **bluebell** n колокольчик

bluff [blʌf] n: **to call sb's bluff** заставлять (perf заставить) кого-н раскрыть карты

blunder ['blʌndəʳ] n грубая ошибка

blunt [blʌnt] adj тупой; (person) прямолинейный

blur [blɜ:ʳ] n (shape) смутное очертание ▷ vt (vision) затуманивать (perf затуманить); (distinction) стирать (perf стереть)

blush [blʌʃ] vi краснеть (perf покраснеть)

board [bɔ:d] n доска; (card) картон; (committee) комитет; (in firm) правление ▷ vt (ship, train) садиться (perf сесть) на +acc; **on board** (Naut, Aviat) на борту; **full board** (Brit) полный пансион; **half board** (Brit) пансион с завтраком и ужином; **board and lodging** проживание и питание; **boarding card** n (Aviat, Naut) посадочный талон; **boarding school** n школа-интернат

boast [bəust] vi: **to boast (about** or **of)** хвастаться (perf похвастаться) (+instr)

boat [bəut] n (small) лодка; (large) корабль m

bob [bɔb] vi (boat: also **bob up and down**) покачиваться (impf)

body ['bɔdɪ] n тело; (of car) корпус; (torso) туловище; (fig: group) группа; (: organization) орган; **bodyguard** n телохранитель m; **bodywork** n корпус

bog [bɔg] n (Geo) болото, трясина

bogus ['bəugəs] adj (claim) фиктивный

boil [bɔɪl] vt (water) кипятить (perf вскипятить); (eggs, potatoes) варить (perf сварить) ▷ vi кипеть (perf вскипеть) ▷ n фурункул; **to come to the** (Brit) or **a** (US) **boil** вскипеть (perf); **boiled egg** n варёное яйцо; **boiler** n (device) паровой котёл, бойлер

bold [bəuld] adj (brave) смелый; (pej: cheeky) наглый; (pattern, colours) броский

bolt [bəult] n (lock) засов; (with nut) болт ▷ adv: **bolt upright** вытянувшись в струнку

bomb [bɔm] n бомба ▷ vt бомбить (impf)

bomber ['bɔməʳ] n (Aviat) бомбардировщик

bond [bɔnd] n узы pl; (Finance) облигация

bone [bəun] n кость f ▷ vt отделять (perf отделить) от костей

bonfire ['bɔnfaɪəʳ] n костёр

bonnet ['bɔnɪt] n (hat) капор; (Brit: of car) капот

bonus ['bəunəs] n (payment) премия; (fig) дополнительное преимущество

boo [bu:] excl фу ▷ vt освистывать (perf освистать)

book [buk] n книга; (of stamps, tickets) книжечка ▷ vt (ticket, table) заказывать (*perf* заказа́ть); (*seat, room*) брони́ровать (*perf* заброни́ровать); (*subj: police officer, referee*) штрафова́ть (*perf* оштрафова́ть); **books** *npl* (*accounts*) бухга́лтерские кни́ги *fpl*; **bookcase** *n* кни́жный шкаф; **booklet** *n* брошю́ра; **bookmark** *n* закла́дка; **bookshop** *n* кни́жный магази́н

boom [buːm] *n* (*noise*) ро́кот; (*growth*) бум

boost [buːst] *n* (*to confidence*) сти́мул ▷ *vt* стимули́ровать (*impf*)

boot [buːt] *n* (*for winter*) сапо́г; (*for football*) бу́тса; (*for walking*) боти́нок; (*Brit: of car*) бага́жник

booth [buːð] *n* (*at fair*) ларёк; (*Tel, for voting*) бу́дка

booze [buːz] (*inf*) *n* вы́пивка

border ['bɔːdər] *n* (*of country*) грани́ца; (*for flowers*) бордю́р; (*on cloth etc*) кайма́ ▷ *vt* (*road, river etc*) окаймля́ть (*perf* окайми́ть); (*country: also* **border on**) грани́чить (*impf*) с +*instr*; **borderline** *n*: **on the borderline** на гра́ни

bore [bɔːr] *pt of* **bear** ▷ *vt* (*hole*) сверли́ть (*perf* просверли́ть); (*person*) наску́чить (*perf*) +*dat* ▷ *n* (*person*) зану́да *m/f*; **to be bored** скуча́ть (*impf*); **boredom** *n* (*condition*) ску́ка; (*boring quality*) зану́дство

boring ['bɔːrɪŋ] *adj* ску́чный

born [bɔːn] *adj* рождённый; **to be born** рожда́ться (*perf* роди́ться)

borne [bɔːn] *pp of* **bear**

borough ['bʌrə] *n* администрати́вный о́круг

borrow ['bɔrəu] *vt*: **to borrow sth from sb** занима́ть (*perf* заня́ть) что-н у кого́-н

Bosnia ['bɔznɪə] *n* Бо́сния; **Bosnia-Herzegovina** [-hз:tsəgəuˈviːnə] *n* Бо́сния-Герцегови́на

bosom ['buzəm] *n* (*Anat*) грудь *f*

boss [bɔs] *n* (*employer*) хозя́ин(-я́йка), босс ▷ *vt* (*also* **boss around, boss about**) распоряжа́ться (*impf*), кома́ндовать (*impf*) +*instr*; **bossy** *adj* вла́стный

both [bəuθ] *adj, pron* о́ба (*f* о́бе) *adv*: **both A and B** и A, и B; **both of us went, we both went** мы о́ба пошли́

bother ['bɔðər] *vt* (*worry*) беспоко́ить (*perf* обеспоко́ить); (*disturb*) беспоко́ить (*perf* побеспоко́ить) ▷ *vi* (*also* **bother o.s.**) беспоко́иться (*impf*) ▷ *n* (*trouble*) беспоко́йство; (*nuisance*) хло́поты *pl*; **to bother doing** брать (*perf* взять) на себя́ труд +*infin*

bottle ['bɔtl] *n* буты́лка; **bottle-opener** *n* што́пор

bottom ['bɔtəm] *n* (*of container, sea*) дно; (*Anat*) зад; (*of page, list*) низ; (*of class*) отстаю́щий(-ая) *m(f) adj* ▷ *adj* (*lowest*) ни́жний; (*last*) после́дний

bought [bɔːt] *pt, pp of* **buy**

boulder ['bəuldər] *n* валу́н

bounce [bauns] *vi* (*ball*) отска́кивать (*perf* отскочи́ть); (*cheque*) верну́ться (*perf*) (*ввиду отсу́тствия де́нег на счету́*) ▷ *vt* (*ball*) ударя́ть (*perf* уда́рить); **bouncer** *n* (*inf*) вышиба́ла *m*

bound [baund] *pt, pp of* **bind** ▷ *vi* (*leap*) пры́гать (*perf* пры́гнуть) ▷ *adj*: **he is bound by law to ...** его́ обя́зывает зако́н +*infin* ... ▷ *npl*: **bounds** (*limits*) преде́лы *mpl*

boundary ['baundrɪ] *n* грани́ца

bouquet ['bukeɪ] *n* буке́т

bout [baut] *n* (*of illness*) при́ступ; (*of activity*) всплеск

boutique [buːˈtiːk] *n* ла́вка

bow¹ [bəu] *n* (*knot*) бант; (*weapon*) лук; (*Mus*) смычо́к

bow² [bau] *n* (*of head, body*) покло́н; (*Naut: also* **bows**) нос ▷ *vi* (*with head, body*) кла́няться (*perf* поклони́ться); (*yield*): **to bow to** *or* **before** поддава́ться (*perf* подда́ться) +*dat or* на +*acc*

bowels ['bauəlz] *npl* кише́чник *msg*

bowl [bəul] *n* (*plate, food*) ми́ска, ча́ша; (*ball*) шар

bowling ['bəulɪŋ] *n* (*game*) кегельба́н

bowls [bəulz] *n* (*game*) игра́ в шары́

box [bɔks] *n* я́щик, коро́бка; (*also* **cardboard box**) карто́нная коро́бка; (*Theat*) ло́жа; (*inf: TV*) я́щик; **boxer** *n* боксёр; **boxing** *n* бокс; **Boxing Day** *n* (*Brit*) день по́сле Рождества́

● **BOXING DAY**
●
● Boxing Day — пе́рвый день по́сле
● Рождества́. Буква́льно "День коро́бок".
● Этот день явля́ется пра́здничным.
● Его́ назва́ние свя́зано с обы́чаем
● де́лать пода́рки, упако́ванные в
● рожде́ственские коро́бки, почтальо́нам,
● разно́счикам газе́т и други́м
● рабо́тникам, ока́зывающим услу́ги
● на дому́.

box office *n* театра́льная ка́сса

boy [bɔɪ] *n* ма́льчик; (*son*) сыно́к

boycott ['bɔɪkɔt] *n* бойко́т ▷ *vt* бойкоти́ровать (*impf/perf*)

boyfriend ['bɔɪfrɛnd] *n* друг

bra [brɑː] *n* ли́фчик

brace [breɪs] *n* (*on leg*) ши́на; (*on teeth*) пласти́нка ▷ *vt* (*knees, shoulders*) напряга́ть (*perf* напря́чь); **braces** *npl* (*Brit: for trousers*) подтя́жки *pl*; **to brace o.s.** (*for shock*) собира́ться (*perf* собра́ться) с ду́хом

bracelet ['breɪslɪt] *n* брасле́т

bracket ['brækɪt] *n* (*Tech*) кронште́йн; (*group, range*) катего́рия; (*also* **brace bracket**) ско́бка; (*also* **round bracket**) кру́глая ско́бка; (*also* **square bracket**) квадра́тная ско́бка ▷ *vt* (*word, phrase*) заключа́ть (perf заключи́ть) в ско́бки

brain [breɪn] n мозг; **brains** npl (also Culin) мозги́ mpl

brake [breɪk] n то́рмоз ▷ vi тормози́ть (perf затормози́ть)

bran [bræn] n о́труби pl

branch [brɑ:ntʃ] n (of tree) ве́тка, ветвь f; (of bank, firm etc) филиа́л

brand [brænd] n (also brand name) фи́рменная ма́рка ▷ vt (cattle) клейми́ть (perf заклейми́ть)

brand-new ['brænd'nju:] adj соверше́нно но́вый

brandy ['brændɪ] n бре́нди nt ind, конья́к

brash [bræʃ] adj наха́льный

brass [brɑ:s] n (metal) лату́нь f; the brass (Mus) духовы́е инструме́нты mpl

brat [bræt] n (pej) озо́рник

brave [breɪv] adj сме́лый, хра́брый ▷ vt сме́ло or хра́бро встреча́ть (perf встре́тить); **bravery** ['breɪvərɪ] n сме́лость f, хра́брость f

brawl [brɔ:l] n дра́ка

Brazil [brə'zɪl] n Брази́лия

breach [bri:tʃ] vt (defence, wall) пробива́ть (perf проби́ть) ▷ n (gap) брешь f; breach of contract/of the peace наруше́ние догово́ра/обще́ственного поря́дка

bread [brɛd] n (food) хлеб; **breadbin** n (Brit) хле́бница; **breadbox** n (US) = breadbin; **breadcrumbs** npl (Culin) паниро́вочные сухари́ mpl

breadth [brɛtθ] n ширина́; (fig: of knowledge, subject) широта́

break [breɪk] (pt broke, pp broken) vt (crockery) разбива́ть (perf разби́ть); (leg, arm) лома́ть (perf слома́ть); (law, promise) наруша́ть (perf нару́шить); (record) побива́ть (perf поби́ть) ▷ vi (crockery) разбива́ться (perf разби́ться); (storm) разража́ться (perf разрази́ться); (weather) по́ртиться (perf испо́ртиться); (dawn) бре́зжить (perf забре́зжить); (story, news) сообща́ть (perf сообщи́ть) ▷ n (gap) пробе́л; (chance) шанс; (fracture) перело́м; (playtime) переме́на; to break even (Comm) зака́нчивать (perf зако́нчить) без убы́тка; to break free or loose вырыва́ться (perf вы́рваться) на свобо́ду; **break down** vt (figures etc) разбива́ть (perf разби́ть) по статья́м ▷ vi (machine, car) лома́ться (perf слома́ться); (person) сломи́ться (perf); (talks) срыва́ться (perf сорва́ться); **break in** vi (burglar) вла́мываться (perf вломи́ться); (interrupt) вме́шиваться (perf вмеша́ться); **break into** vt fus (house) вла́мываться (perf вломи́ться) в +acc; **break off** vi (branch) отла́мываться (perf отломи́ться); (speaker) прерыва́ть (perf прерва́ть) речь ▷ vt (engagement) расторга́ть (perf расто́ргнуть); **break out** vi (begin) разража́ться (perf разрази́ться); (escape)

сбега́ть (perf сбежа́ть); **to break out in spots/a rash** покрыва́ться (perf покры́ться) прыща́ми/сы́пью; **break up** vi (ship) разбива́ться (perf разби́ться); (crowd, meeting) расходи́ться (perf разойти́сь); (marriage, partnership) распада́ться (perf распа́сться); (Scol) закрыва́ться (perf закры́ться) на кани́кулы ▷ vt разла́мывать (perf разломи́ть); (journey) прерыва́ть (perf прерва́ть); (fight) прекраща́ть (perf прекрати́ть); **breakdown** n (in communications) наруше́ние, срыв; (of marriage) распа́д; (also **nervous breakdown**) не́рвный срыв

breakfast ['brɛkfəst] n за́втрак

breakthrough ['breɪkθru:] n (in technology) перело́мное откры́тие

breast [brɛst] n грудь f; (of meat) груди́нка; (of poultry) бе́лое мя́со; **breast-feed** (irreg like feed) vt корми́ть (perf покорми́ть) гру́дью ▷ vi корми́ть (impf) (гру́дью)

breath [brɛθ] n вдох; (breathing) дыха́ние; **to be out of breath** запыха́ться (perf запыха́ться); **breathe** [bri:ð] vi дыша́ть (impf); **breathe in** vt вдыха́ть (perf вдохну́ть) ▷ vi де́лать (perf сде́лать) вдох; **breathe out** vi де́лать (perf сде́лать) вы́дох; **breathing** ['bri:ðɪŋ] n дыха́ние; **breathless** ['brɛθlɪs] adj (from exertion) запыха́вшийся; **breathtaking** ['brɛθteɪkɪŋ] adj захва́тывающий дух

bred [brɛd] pt, pp of breed

breed [bri:d] (pt, pp bred) vt (animals, plants) разводи́ть (perf развести́) ▷ vi размножа́ться (impf) ▷ n (Zool) поро́да

breeze [bri:z] n бриз

breezy ['bri:zɪ] adj (manner, tone) оживлённый; (weather) прохла́дный

brew [bru:] vt (tea) зава́ривать (perf завари́ть); (beer) вари́ть (perf свари́ть) ▷ vi (storm) надвига́ться (perf надви́нуться); (fig: trouble) назрева́ть (perf назре́ть); **brewery** n пивова́ренный заво́д

bribe [braɪb] n взя́тка, по́дкуп ▷ vt (person) подкупа́ть (perf подкупи́ть), дава́ть (perf дать) взя́тку; **bribery** ['braɪbərɪ] n по́дкуп

brick [brɪk] n (for building) кирпи́ч

bride [braɪd] n неве́ста; **bridegroom** n жени́х; **bridesmaid** n подру́жка неве́сты

bridge [brɪdʒ] n мост; (Naut) капита́нский мо́стик; (Cards) бридж; (of nose) перено́сица ▷ vt (fig: gap) преодолева́ть (perf преодоле́ть)

bridle ['braɪdl] n узде́чка, узда́

brief [bri:f] adj (period of time) коро́ткий; (description) кра́ткий; (task) зада́ние ▷ vt знако́мить (perf ознако́мить) с +instr; **briefs** npl (for men) трусы́ pl; (for women) тру́сики pl; **briefcase** n портфе́ль m;

(*attaché case*) диплома́т; **briefing** n инструкта́ж; (*Press*) бри́финг; **briefly** adv (*glance, smile*) бе́гло; (*explain*) вкра́тце

bright [braɪt] adj (*light, colour*) я́ркий; (*room, future*) све́тлый; (*clever: person, idea*) блестя́щий; (*lively: person*) живо́й, весёлый

brilliant ['brɪljənt] adj блестя́щий; (*sunshine*) я́ркий; (*inf: holiday etc*) великоле́пный

brim [brɪm] n (*of cup*) край; (*of hat*) поля́ pl

bring [brɪŋ] (*pt, pp* **brought**) vt (*thing*) приноси́ть (*perf* принести́); (*person: on foot*) приводи́ть (*perf* привести́); (: *by transport*) привози́ть (*perf* привезти́); (*satisfaction, trouble*) доставля́ть (*perf* доста́вить); **bring about** vt (*cause: unintentionally*) вызыва́ть (*perf* вы́звать); (: *intentionally*) осуществля́ть (*perf* осуществи́ть); **bring back** vt (*restore*) возрожда́ть (*perf* возроди́ть); (*return*) возвраща́ть (*perf* возврати́ть), верну́ть (*perf*); **bring down** vt (*government*) сверга́ть (*perf* све́ргнуть); (*plane*) сбива́ть (*perf* сбить); (*price*) снижа́ть (*perf* сни́зить); **bring forward** vt (*meeting*) переноси́ть (*perf* перенести́) на бо́лее ра́нний срок; **bring out** vt (*publish*) выпуска́ть (*perf* вы́пустить); **bring up** vt (*carry up*) приноси́ть (*perf* принести́) наве́рх; (*child*) воспи́тывать (*perf* воспита́ть); (*subject*) поднима́ть (*perf* подня́ть); **he brought up his food** его́ стошни́ло

brink [brɪŋk] n: **on the brink of** (*fig*) на гра́ни +gen

brisk [brɪsk] adj (*tone*) отры́вистый; (*person, trade*) оживлённый; **business is brisk** дела́ иду́т по́лным хо́дом

Britain ['brɪtən] n (*also* **Great Britain**) Брита́ния

British ['brɪtɪʃ] adj брита́нский; npl: **the British** брита́нцы mpl; **British Isles** npl: **the British Isles** Брита́нские острова́ mpl

Briton ['brɪtən] n брита́нец(-нка)

brittle ['brɪtl] adj хру́пкий, ло́мкий

broad [brɔːd] adj (*wide, general*) широ́кий; (*strong*) си́льный; **in broad daylight** средь бе́ла дня; **broadband** ['brɔːdb[ae]nd] adj широкополо́сный; **broadband connection** широкополо́сная связь; **broadband access** широкополо́сный доступ; **broadcast** (*pt, pp* **broadcast**) n (*радио*)переда́ча; (*TV*) (*теле*)переда́ча ▷ vt транслировать (*impf*) ▷ vi веща́ть (*impf*); **broaden** vt расширя́ть (*perf* расши́рить) ▷ vi расширя́ться (*perf* расши́риться); **broadly** adv вообще́

broccoli ['brɔkəlɪ] n бро́кколи nt ind

brochure ['brəʊʃjʊə'] n брошю́ра

broke [brəʊk] *pt of* **break** ▷ adj: **I am broke** (*inf*) я на мели́; **broken** *pp of* **break** ▷ adj (*window, cup etc*) разби́тый;

(*machine, leg*) сло́манный; **in broken Russian** на ло́маном ру́сском

broker ['brəʊkə'] n (*in shares*) бро́кер; (*in insurance*) страхово́й аге́нт

bronchitis [brɔŋ'kaɪtɪs] n бронхи́т

bronze [brɔnz] n (*metal*) бро́нза; (*sculpture*) бро́нзовая скульпту́ра

brooch [brəʊtʃ] n брошь f

Bros. abbr (*Comm*) (= **brothers**) бра́тья mpl

broth [brɔθ] n похлёбка

brothel ['brɔθl] n публи́чный дом, борде́ль m

brother ['brʌðə'] n брат; **brother-in-law** n (*sister's husband*) зять m; (*wife's brother*) шу́рин; (*husband's brother*) де́верь m

brought [brɔːt] *pt, pp of* **bring**

brow [brau] n (*forehead*) лоб, чело́; (*also* **eyebrow**) бровь f; (*of hill*) гре́бень m

brown [braun] adj кори́чневый; (*hair*) тёмно-ру́сый; (*eyes*) ка́рий; (*tanned*) загоре́лый ▷ n (*colour*) кори́чневый цвет ▷ vt (*Culin*) подрумя́нивать (*perf* подрумя́нить); **brown bread** n чёрный хлеб; **brown sugar** n неочи́щенный са́хар

browse [brauz] vi осма́триваться (*perf* осмотре́ться); **to browse through a book** проли́стывать (*perf* пролиста́ть) кни́гу; **browser** n (*Comput*) бра́узер

bruise [bruːz] n (*on face etc*) синя́к ▷ vt ушиба́ть (*perf* ушиби́ть)

brunette [bruː'nɛt] n брюне́тка

brush [brʌʃ] n (*for cleaning*) щётка; (*for painting*) кисть f; (*for shaving*) помазо́к ▷ vt (*sweep*) подмета́ть (*perf* подмести́); (*groom*) чи́стить (*perf* почи́стить) щёткой; (*also* **brush against**) задева́ть (*perf* заде́ть)

Brussels ['brʌslz] n Брюссе́ль m; **Brussels sprout** n брюссе́льская капу́ста

brutal ['bruːtl] adj (*person, action*) жесто́кий, зве́рский; (*honesty*) жёсткий

bubble ['bʌbl] n пузы́рь m; **bubble bath** n пе́нистая ва́нна

bucket ['bʌkɪt] n ведро́

buckle ['bʌkl] n пря́жка

bud [bʌd] n (*of tree*) по́чка; (*of flower*) буто́н

Buddhism ['budɪzəm] n будди́зм

buddy ['bʌdɪ] n (*US*) прия́тель m, дружо́к

budge [bʌdʒ] vt (*fig: person*) заставля́ть (*perf* заста́вить) уступи́ть ▷ vi сдвига́ться (*perf* сдви́нуться) (с ме́ста)

budgerigar ['bʌdʒərɪgɑː'] n волни́стый попуга́йчик

budget ['bʌdʒɪt] n бюдже́т

budgie ['bʌdʒɪ] n = **budgerigar**

buff [bʌf] adj кори́чневый ▷ n (*inf: enthusiast*) спец, знато́к

buffalo ['bʌfələu] (*pl* **buffalo** *or* **buffaloes**) n (*Brit*) бу́йвол; (*US: bison*) бизо́н

buffer ['bʌfə^r] n буфер
buffet ['bufeɪ] n (Brit: in station) буфет; (food) шведский стол
bug [bʌg] n (insect) насекомое nt adj; (Comput: glitch) ошибка; (virus) вирус; (fig: germ) вирус; (hidden microphone) подслушивающее устройство ▷ vt (room etc) прослушивать (impf); (inf: annoy): to **bug sb** действовать (impf) кому-н на нервы
buggy ['bʌgɪ] n (also **baby buggy**) складная (детская) коляска
build [bɪld] (pt, pp **built**) n (of person) (тело)сложение ▷ vt строить (perf построить); **build up** vt (forces, production) наращивать (impf); (stocks) накапливать (perf накопить); **builder** n строитель m; **building** n строение; **building society** n (Brit) ≈ "строительное общество"

● BUILDING SOCIETY
●
● **Building society** — строительные
● общества или ипотечные банки. Они
● были созданы для предоставления
● ипотечного жилищного кредитования.
● Одновременно строительные общества
● функционировали как сберегательные
● банки. В последние годы они стали
● предоставлять более широкий объём
● банковских услуг.

built [bɪlt] pt, pp of **build** ▷ adj: **built-in** встроенный
bulb [bʌlb] n (Bot) луковица; (Elec) лампа, лампочка
Bulgaria [bʌl'gɛərɪə] n Болгария
bulimia [bə'lɪmɪə] n булимия
bulk [bʌlk] n громада; **in bulk** оптом; the **bulk of** большая часть +gen; **bulky** adj громоздкий
bull [bul] n (Zool) бык
bulldozer ['buldəuzə^r] n бульдозер
bullet ['bulɪt] n пуля
bulletin ['bulɪtɪn] n (journal) бюллетень m; **news bulletin** сводка новостей; **bulletin board** n (Comput) доска объявлений
bully ['bulɪ] n задира m/f, преследователь m ▷ vt травить (perf затравить)
bum [bʌm] n (inf: backside) задница; (esp US: tramp) бродяга m/f; (: good-for-nothing) бездельник
bumblebee ['bʌmblbiː] n шмель m
bump [bʌmp] n (minor accident) столкновение; (jolt) толчок; (swelling) шишка ▷ vt (strike) ударять (perf ударить); **bump into** vt fus наталкиваться (perf натолкнуться) на +acc; **bumper** n (Aut) бампер ▷ adj: **bumper crop** or **harvest** небывалый урожай; **bumpy** adj (road) ухабистый

bun [bʌn] n (Culin) сдобная булка; (of hair) узел
bunch [bʌntʃ] n (of flowers) букет; (of keys) связка; (of bananas) гроздь f; (of people) компания; **bunches** npl (in hair) хвостики mpl
bundle ['bʌndl] n (of clothes) узел; (of sticks) вязанка; (of papers) пачка ▷ vt (also **bundle up**) связывать (perf связать) в узел; **to bundle sth/sb into** заталкивать (perf затолкнуть) что-н/кого-н в +acc
bungalow ['bʌŋgələu] n бунгало nt ind
bunk [bʌŋk] n (bed) койка; **bunk beds** npl двухъярусная кровать fsg
bunker ['bʌŋkə^r] n бункер
bunny ['bʌnɪ] n (also **bunny rabbit**) зайчик
buoy [bɔɪ] n буй, бакен
buoyant ['bɔɪənt] adj (fig: economy, market) оживлённый; (: person) жизнерадостный
burden ['bəːdn] n (responsibility) бремя nt; (load) ноша ▷ vt: **to burden sb with** обременять (perf обременить) кого-н +instr
bureau ['bjuərəu] (pl **bureaux**) n (Brit) бюро nt ind; (US) комод
bureaucracy [bjuə'rɔkrəsɪ] n (Pol, Comm) бюрократия; (system) бюрократизм
bureaucrat ['bjuərəkræt] n бюрократ
bureaux ['bjuərəuz] npl of **bureau**
burger ['bəːgə^r] n бургер
burglar ['bəːglə^r] n взломщик; **burglar alarm** n сигнализация; **burglary** n (crime) кража со взломом, квартирный разбой
burial ['bɛrɪəl] n погребение, похороны pl
burn [bəːn] (pt, pp **burned** or **burnt**) vt жечь (perf сжечь), сжигать (perf сжечь); (intentionally) поджигать (perf поджечь) ▷ vi (house, wood) гореть (perf сгореть), сгорать (perf сгореть); (cakes) подгорать (perf подгореть) ▷ n ожог; **burning** adj (building, forest) горящий; (issue, ambition) жгучий
burst [bəːst] (pt, pp **burst**) vt (bag etc) разрывать (perf разорвать) ▷ vi (tyre, balloon, pipe) лопаться (perf лопнуть) ▷ n (of gunfire) залп; (of energy) прилив; (also **burst pipe**) прорыв; **to burst into flames** вспыхивать (perf вспыхнуть); **to burst into tears** расплакаться (perf); **to burst out laughing** расхохотаться (perf); **to be bursting with** (pride, anger) раздуваться (perf раздуться) от +gen; **burst into** vt fus (room) врываться (perf ворваться)
bury ['bɛrɪ] vt (object) зарывать (perf зарыть), закапывать (perf закопать); (person) хоронить (perf похоронить); **many people were buried in the rubble** много людей было погребено под обломками

bus [bʌs] n автобус; (*double decker*) (двухэтажный) автобус

bush [buʃ] n куст; **to beat about the bush** ходить (*impf*) вокруг да около

business ['bɪznɪs] n (*matter*) дело; (*trading*) бизнес, дело; (*firm*) предприятие; (*occupation*) занятие; **to be away on business** быть (*impf*) в командировке; **it's none of my business** это не моё дело; **he means business** он настроен серьёзно; **businesslike** adj деловитый; **businessman** irreg n бизнесмен; **businesswoman** irreg n бизнесменка

bus-stop ['bʌsstɔp] n автобусная остановка

bust [bʌst] n бюст, грудь f; (*measurement*) объём груди; (*sculpture*) бюст ▷ adj: **to go bust** (*firm*) прогореть (*perf* прогореть)

bustling ['bʌslɪŋ] adj оживлённый, шумный

busy ['bɪzɪ] adj (*person*) занятой; (*street*) оживлённый, шумный; (*Tel*): **the line is busy** линия занята ▷ vt: **to busy o.s. with** заниматься (*perf* заняться) +instr

KEYWORD

but [bʌt] conj 1 (*yet*) но; (: *in contrast*) а; **he's not very bright, but he's hard-working** он не очень умён, но усёрден; **I'm tired but Paul isn't** я устал, а Павел нет
2 (*however*) но; **I'd love to come, but I'm busy** я бы с удовольствием пришёл, но я занят
3 (*showing disagreement, surprise etc*) но; **but that's fantastic!** но это же потрясающе!
▷ prep (*apart from, except*) **no-one but him can do it** никто, кроме него, не может это сделать; **nothing but trouble** сплошные or одни неприятности; **but for you/your help** если бы не Вы/Ваша помощь; **I'll do anything but that** я сделаю всё, что угодно, но только не это
▷ adv (*just, only*): **she's but a child** она всего лишь ребёнок; **had I but known** если бы я только это знал; **I can but try** конечно, я могу попробовать; **the work is all but finished** работа почти закончена

butcher ['butʃə'] n мясник; (*also* **butcher's (shop)**) мясной магазин

butt [bʌt] n (*large barrel*) бочка; (*of rifle*) приклад; (*of pistol*) рукоятка; (*of cigarette*) окурок; (*Brit: of teasing*) предмет

butter ['bʌtə'] n (*sliv.*) сливочное масло ▷ vt намазывать (*perf* намазать) (сливочным) маслом; **buttercup** n лютик

butterfly ['bʌtəflaɪ] n бабочка; (*also* **butterfly stroke**) баттерфляй

buttocks ['bʌtəks] npl ягодицы fpl

button ['bʌtn] n (*on clothes*) пуговица; (*on machine*) кнопка; (*US: badge*) значок ▷ vt (*also* **button up**) застёгивать (*perf* застегнуть)

buy [baɪ] (*pt, pp* **bought**) vt покупать (*perf* купить) ▷ n покупка; **to buy sb sth/ sth from sb** покупать (*perf* купить) кому-н что-н/что-н у кого-н; **to buy sb a drink** покупать (*perf* купить) кому-н выпить; **buyer** n покупатель(ница)

buzz [bʌz] n жужжание; **buzzer** n зуммер, звонок

KEYWORD

by [baɪ] prep 1 (*referring to cause, agent*): **he was killed by lightning** его убило молнией; **a painting by Van Gogh** картина Ван Гога; **it's by Shakespeare** это Шекспир
2 (*referring to manner, means*): **by bus/ train** автобусом/поездом; **by car** на машине; **by phone** по телефону; **to pay by cheque** платить (*perf* заплатить) чёком; **by moonlight** при свете луны; **by candlelight** при свечах; **by working constantly, he ...** благодаря тому, что он работал без остановки, он ...
3 (*via, through*) через +acc; **by the back door** через заднюю дверь; **by land/sea** по суше/морю
4 (*close to*) y +gen, около +gen; **the house is by the river** дом находится y or около реки; **a holiday by the sea** отпуск на море
5 (*past*) мимо +gen; **she rushed by me** она пронеслась мимо меня
6 (*not later than*) к +dat; **by four o'clock** к четырём часам; **by the time I got here ...** к тому времени, когда я добрался сюда ...
7 (*during*): **by day** днём; **by night** ночью
8 (*amount*): **to sell by the metre/kilo** продавать (*perf* продать) метрами/ килограммами; **she is paid by the hour** у неё почасовая оплата
9 (*Math, measure*) на +acc; **to multiply/ divide by three** умножать (*perf* умножить)/ делить (*perf* разделить) на три; **a room three metres by four** комната размером три метра на четыре
10 (*according to*) по +dat; **to play by the rules** играть (*impf*) по правилам; **it's all right by me** я не возражаю; **by law** по закону
11: **(all) by oneself** (*alone*) (совершенно) один (*f* одна, *pl* одни); (*unaided*) сам (*f* сама, *pl* сами); **I did it all by myself** я сделал всё один or сам; **he was standing by himself** он стоял один
12: **by the way** кстати, между прочим
▷ adv 1 see **pass** etc
2: **by and by** вскоре; **by and large** в целом

bye(-bye) ['baɪ('baɪ)] excl пока

bypass ['baɪpɑːs] n (*Aut*) объезд, окружная дорога; (*Med*) обходное шунтирование ▷ vt (*town*) объезжать (*perf* объехать)

by-product ['baɪprɔdʌkt] n (*Industry*) побочный продукт

byte [baɪt] n (*Comput*) байт

C [siː] n (Mus) до nt ind

C abbr = **Celsius**; **centigrade**

cab [kæb] n такси́ nt ind; (of truck etc) каби́на

cabaret ['kæbəreɪ] n кабаре́ nt ind

cabbage ['kæbɪdʒ] n капу́ста

cabin ['kæbɪn] n (on ship) каю́та; (on plane) каби́на

cabinet ['kæbɪnɪt] n шкаф; (also **display cabinet**) го́рка; (Pol) кабине́т (мини́стров)

cable ['keɪbl] n ка́бель m; (rope) кана́т; (metal) трос ▷ vt (message) телеграфи́ровать (impf/perf); **cable television** n ка́бельное телеви́дение

cactus ['kæktəs] (pl **cacti**) n ка́ктус

café ['kæfeɪ] n кафе́ nt ind

caffein(e) ['kæfiːn] n кофеи́н

cage [keɪdʒ] n (for animal) кле́тка

cagoule [kə'guːl] n дождеви́к

cake [keɪk] n (large) торт; (small) пиро́жное nt adj

calcium ['kælsɪəm] n ка́льций

calculate ['kælkjuleɪt] vt (figures, cost) подсчи́тывать (perf подсчита́ть); (distance) вычисля́ть (perf вы́числить); (estimate) рассчи́тывать (perf рассчита́ть)

calculation [kælkju'leɪʃən] n (see vb) подсчёт; вычисле́ние; расчёт

calculator ['kælkjuleɪtə'] n калькуля́тор

calendar ['kæləndə'] n календа́рь m

calf [kɑːf] (pl **calves**) n (of cow) телёнок; (Anat) икра́

calibre ['kælɪbə'] (US **caliber**) n кали́бр

call [kɔːl] vt называ́ть (perf назва́ть); (Tel) звони́ть (perf позвони́ть) +dat; (summon) вызыва́ть (perf вы́звать); (arrange) созыва́ть (perf созва́ть) ▷ vi (shout) крича́ть (perf кри́кнуть); (Tel) звони́ть (perf позвони́ть); (visit: also **call in**, **call round**) заходи́ть (perf зайти́) ▷ n (shout) крик; (Tel) звоно́к; **she is called Suzanne** её зову́т Сюза́нна; **the mountain is called Ben Nevis** гора́ называ́ется Бен Не́вис; **to be on call** дежу́рить (impf); **call back** vi (return) заходи́ть (perf зайти́) опя́ть; (Tel) перезва́нивать (perf перезвони́ть) ▷ vt (Tel) перезва́нивать (perf перезвони́ть) +dat; **call for** vt fus (demand) призыва́ть (perf призва́ть) к +dat; (fetch) заходи́ть (perf зайти́) за +instr; **call off** vt отменя́ть (perf отмени́ть); **call on** vt fus (visit) заходи́ть (perf зайти́) к +dat; (appeal to) призыва́ть (perf призва́ть) к +dat; **call out** vi крича́ть (perf кри́кнуть); **call centre** n центр приёма комме́рческих итп звонко́в в большо́м объёме

callous ['kæləs] adj безду́шный

calm [kɑːm] adj споко́йный; (place) ти́хий; (weather) безве́тренный ▷ n тишина́, поко́й ▷ vt успока́ивать (perf успоко́ить); **calm down** vt успока́ивать (perf успоко́ить) ▷ vi успока́иваться (perf успоко́иться)

calorie ['kælərɪ] n кало́рия

calves [kɑːvz] npl of **calf**

Cambodia [kæm'bəudɪə] n Камбо́джа

camcorder ['kæmkɔːdə'] n видеока́мера

came [keɪm] pt of **come**

camel ['kæməl] n верблю́д

camera ['kæmərə] n фотоаппара́т; (also **cine camera**, **movie camera**) кинока́мера; (TV) телека́мера; **cameraman** irreg n (Cinema) (кино)опера́тор; (TV) (теле)опера́тор; **camera phone** n камерафо́н m (моби́льный телефо́н со встро́енной фотовидеока́мерой)

camouflage ['kæməflɑːʒ] n (Mil) камуфля́ж, маскиро́вка ▷ vt маскирова́ть (perf замаскирова́ть)

camp [kæmp] n ла́герь m; (Mil) вое́нный городо́к ▷ vi разбива́ть (perf разби́ть) ла́герь; (go camping) жить (impf) в пала́тках

campaign [kæm'peɪn] n кампа́ния ▷ vi: **to campaign (for/against)** вести́ (impf) кампа́нию (за +acc/про́тив +gen)

camping ['kæmpɪŋ] n ке́мпинг; **to go camping** отправля́ться (perf отпра́виться) в похо́д

camp site n ке́мпинг

campus ['kæmpəs] n студе́нческий городо́к

can¹ [kæn] n (for food) консе́рвная ба́нка ▷ vt консерви́ровать (perf законсерви́ровать)

⬤ **KEYWORD**

can² [kæn] (negative **cannot**, **can't**, conditional, pt **could**) aux vb **1** (be able to) мочь (perf смочь); **you can do it** Вы смо́жете э́то сде́лать; **I'll help you all I can** я помогу́ Вам всем, чем смогу́; **I can't go on any longer** я бо́льше не могу́; **I can't see you** я не ви́жу Вас; **she couldn't sleep**

that night в ту ночь она́ не могла́ спать
2 (know how to) уме́ть (impf); **I can swim**
я уме́ю пла́вать; **can you speak Russian?**
Вы уме́ете говори́ть по-ру́сски?
3 (may) мо́жно; **can I use your phone?**
мо́жно от Вас позвони́ть?; **could I have a
word with you?** мо́жно с Ва́ми
поговори́ть?; **you can smoke if you like** Вы
мо́жете кури́ть, е́сли хоти́те; **can I help
you with that?** я могу́ Вам в э́том помо́чь?
4 (expressing disbelief, puzzlement): **it
can't be true!** (э́того) не мо́жет быть!;
what CAN he want? что же ему́ ну́жно?
5 (expressing possibility, suggestion): **he
could be in the library** он, мо́жет быть or
возмо́жно, в библиоте́ке; **she could have
been delayed** возмо́жно, что её
задержа́ли

Canada ['kænədə] n Кана́да
canal [kə'næl] n кана́л
canary [kə'nɛərɪ] n канаре́йка
cancel ['kænsəl] vt отменя́ть (perf
отмени́ть); (contract, cheque, visa)
аннули́ровать (impf/perf); **cancellation**
['kænsə'leɪʃən] n (see vb) отме́на;
аннули́рование
cancer ['kænsə'] n (Med) рак; **Cancer** Рак
candidate ['kændɪdeɪt] n претенде́нт; (in
exam) экзамену́емый(-ая) m(f) adj; (Pol)
кандида́т
candle ['kændl] n свеча́; **candlestick** n
подсве́чник
candy ['kændɪ] n (US) конфе́та
cane [keɪn] n (Bot) тростни́к; (stick) ро́зга
▷ vt (Brit) нака́зывать (perf наказа́ть)
ро́згами
cannabis ['kænəbɪs] n (drug) гаши́ш
canned [kænd] adj (fruit etc)
консерви́рованный
cannon ['kænən] (pl **cannon** or **cannons**)
n пу́шка
cannot ['kænɔt] = **can not** see **can²**
canoe [kə'nuː] n кано́э nt ind
canon ['kænən] n (Rel) кано́ник
can't [kænt] = **can not**
canteen [kæn'tiːn] n (in school etc)
столо́вая f adj
canter ['kæntə'] vi галопи́ровать (impf)
canvas ['kænvəs] n (also Art) холст; (for
tents) брезе́нт; (Naut) паруси́на ▷ adj
паруси́новый
canyon ['kænjən] n каньо́н
cap [kæp] n ке́пка; (of uniform) фура́жка;
(of pen) колпачо́к; (of bottle) кры́шка ▷ vt
(outdo) превосходи́ть (perf превзойти́)
capability [keɪpə'bɪlɪtɪ] n спосо́бность f
capable ['keɪpəbl] adj (person)
спосо́бный; **capable of sth/doing**
спосо́бный на что-н/+infin
capacity [kə'pæsɪtɪ] n ёмкость f; (of ship,
theatre etc) вмести́тельность f; (of person:
capability) спосо́бность f; (: role) роль f
cape [keɪp] n (Geo) мыс; (cloak) плащ

capital ['kæpɪtl] n (also **capital city**)
столи́ца; (money) капита́л; (also **capital
letter**) загла́вная бу́ква; **capitalism** n
капитали́зм; **capitalist** adj
капиталисти́ческий ▷ n капитали́ст;
capital punishment n сме́ртная казнь f
Capricorn ['kæprɪkɔːn] n Козеро́г
capsule ['kæpsjuːl] n ка́псула
captain ['kæptɪn] n команди́р; (of team,
in army) капита́н
caption ['kæpʃən] n по́дпись f
captivity [kæp'tɪvɪtɪ] n плен
capture ['kæptʃə'] vt захва́тывать (perf
захвати́ть); (animal) лови́ть (perf
пойма́ть); (attention) прико́вывать (perf
прикова́ть) ▷ n (of person, town) захва́т;
(of animal) пои́мка
car [kɑː'] n автомоби́ль m, маши́на; (Rail)
ваго́н
caramel ['kærəməl] n (sweet) караме́ль f
carat ['kærət] n кара́т
caravan ['kærəvæn] n (Brit) жило́й
автоприце́п; **caravan site** n (Brit)
площа́дка для стоя́нки жилы́х
автоприце́пов
carbohydrate [kɑːbəu'haɪdreɪt] n
углево́д
carbon ['kɑːbən] n углеро́д; **carbon
footprint** n показа́тель эми́ссии парнико́вых
га́зов; **carbon dioxide** [-daɪ'ɔksaɪd] n
двуо́кись f углеро́да

card [kɑːd] n карто́н; (also **playing card**)
игра́льная ка́рта; (also **greetings card**)
откры́тка; (also **visiting card, business
card**) визи́тная ка́рточка; **cardboard** n
карто́н
cardigan ['kɑːdɪgən] n жаке́т (вя́заный)
cardinal ['kɑːdɪnl] adj (importance,
principle) кардина́льный; (number)
коли́чественный ▷ n кардина́л
care [kɛə'] n (worry) забо́та; (of patient)
ухо́д; (attention) внима́ние ▷ vi: **to care
about** люби́ть (impf); **in sb's care** на
чьём-н попече́нии; **to take care (to do)**
позабо́титься (perf) (+infin); **to take care
of** забо́титься (perf позабо́титься) о +prp;
(problem) занима́ться (perf заня́ться)
+instr; **care of** для переда́чи +dat; **I don't
care** мне всё равно́; **I couldn't care less**
мне наплева́ть; **care for** vt fus
забо́титься (perf позабо́титься) о +prp; **he
cares for her** (like) он неравноду́шен к ней

career [kəˈrɪəʳ] n карье́ра

carefree [ˈkɛəfriː] adj беззабо́тный

careful [ˈkɛəful] adj осторо́жный;
(thorough) тща́тельный; **(be) careful!**
осторо́жно!, береги́сь!; **carefully** [ˈkɛəfə
lɪ] adv (see adj) осторо́жно; тща́тельно

careless [ˈkɛəlɪs] adj невнима́тельный;
(casual) небре́жный; (untroubled)
беззабо́тный

caretaker [ˈkɛəteɪkəʳ] n завхо́з

cargo [ˈkɑːɡəu] n (pl **cargoes**) n груз

car hire n (Brit) прока́т автомоби́лей

Caribbean [kærɪˈbiːən] n: **the Caribbean
(Sea)** Кари́бское мо́ре

caring [ˈkɛərɪŋ] adj забо́тливый

carnation [kɑːˈneɪʃən] n гвозди́ка

carnival [ˈkɑːnɪvl] n карнава́л; (US:
funfair) аттракцио́нный городо́к

carol [ˈkærəl] n (also **Christmas carol**)
рожде́ственский гимн

car park n (Brit) автостоя́нка

carpenter [ˈkɑːpɪntəʳ] n пло́тник

carpet [ˈkɑːpɪt] n ковёр ⊳ vt устила́ть
(perf устла́ть) коврами

carriage [ˈkærɪdʒ] n (Brit: Rail)
(пассажи́рский) ваго́н; (horse-drawn)
экипа́ж; (costs) сто́имость f перево́зки;
carriageway n (Brit) прое́зжая часть f
доро́ги

carrier [ˈkærɪəʳ] n (Med) носи́тель m;
(Comm) транспортиро́вщик; **carrier bag**
n (Brit) паке́т (для поку́пок)

carrot [ˈkærət] n (Bot) морко́вь f

carry [ˈkærɪ] vt (take) носи́ть/нести́ (impf);
(transport) вози́ть/везти́ (impf); (involve)
влечь (perf повле́чь) (за собо́й); (Med)
переноси́ть (impf) ⊳ vi (sound)
передава́ться (impf); **to get carried away
(by)** (fig) увлека́ться (perf увле́чься)
(+instr); **carry on** vi продолжа́ться (perf
продо́лжиться) ⊳ vt продолжа́ть (perf
продо́лжить); **carry out** vt (orders)
выполня́ть (perf вы́полнить);
(investigation) проводи́ть (perf провести́)

cart [kɑːt] n теле́га, пово́зка ⊳ vt (inf)
таска́ть/тащи́ть (impf)

carton [ˈkɑːtən] n карто́нная коро́бка;
(container) паке́т

cartoon [kɑːˈtuːn] n (drawing)
карикату́ра; (Brit: comic strip) ко́микс; (TV)
мультфи́льм

cartridge [ˈkɑːtrɪdʒ] n (in gun) ги́льза; (of
pen) (черни́льный) балло́нчик

carve [kɑːv] vt (meat) нареза́ть (perf
наре́зать); (wood, stone) ре́зать (impf) по
+dat

carving [ˈkɑːvɪŋ] n резно́е изде́лие

car wash n мо́йка автомоби́лей

case [keɪs] n слу́чай; (Med: patient)
больно́й(-ая) m(f) adj; (Law) (суде́бное)
де́ло; (investigation) рассле́дование; (for
spectacles) футля́р; (Brit: also **suitcase**)
чемода́н; (of wine) я́щик (содержа́щий 12
буты́лок); **in case (of)** в слу́чае (+gen); **in**
any **case** во вся́ком слу́чае; **just in case** на
вся́кий слу́чай

cash [kæʃ] n нали́чные pl adj (де́ньги)
⊳ vt: **to cash a cheque** обнали́чивать (perf
обнали́чить); **to pay (in) cash** плати́ть (perf
заплати́ть) нали́чными; **cash on delivery**
нало́женный платёж; **cash card** n
банкома́тная ка́рточка; **cash desk** n
(Brit) ка́сса; **cash dispenser** n (Brit)
банкома́т; **cashier** [kæˈʃɪəʳ] n касси́р

cashmere [ˈkæʃmɪəʳ] n кашеми́р

casino [kəˈsiːnəu] n казино́ nt ind

casserole [ˈkæsərəul] n рагу́ nt ind; (also
casserole dish) ла́тка

cassette [kæˈsɛt] n кассе́та

cast [kɑːst] (pt, pp **cast**) vt (light, shadow,
glance) броса́ть (perf бро́сить); (Fishing)
забра́сывать (perf забро́сить); (doubts)
се́ять (perf посе́ять) ⊳ n (Theat) соста́в
(исполни́телей); (Med: also **plaster cast**)
гипс; **to cast one's vote** отдава́ть (perf
отда́ть) свой го́лос

caster sugar [ˈkɑːstə-] n (Brit) са́харная
пу́дра

castle [ˈkɑːsl] n за́мок; (fortified)
кре́пость f; (Chess) ладья́, тура́

casual [ˈkæʒjul] adj (meeting) случа́йный;
(attitude) небре́жный; (clothes)
повседне́вный

casualty [ˈkæʒjultɪ] n (sb injured)
пострада́вший(-ая) m/f adj; (sb killed)
же́ртва; (department) травматоло́гия

cat [kæt] n (pet) ко́шка; (tomcat) кот; **big
cats** (Zool) коша́чьи pl adj

catalogue [ˈkætəlɔɡ] (US **catalog**) n
катало́г

catarrh [kəˈtɑːʳ] n ката́р

catastrophe [kəˈtæstrəfɪ] n катастро́фа

catch [kætʃ] (pt, pp **caught**) vt ловить
(perf пойма́ть); (bus etc) сади́ться (perf
сесть) на +acc; (breath: in shock) зата́ивать
(perf затаи́ть); (: after running)
передохну́ть (perf); (attention) привлека́ть
(perf привле́чь); (hear) ула́вливать (perf
улови́ть); (illness) подхва́тывать (perf
подхвати́ть) ⊳ vi (become trapped)
застрева́ть (perf застря́ть) ⊳ n (of fish)
уло́в; (of ball) захва́т; (hidden problem)
подво́х; (of lock) защёлка; **to catch sight of**
уви́деть (perf); **to catch fire** загора́ться
(perf загоре́ться); **catch on** vi
прижива́ться (perf прижи́ться); **catch up**
vi (fig) нагоня́ть (perf нагна́ть) ⊳ vt (also
catch up with) догоня́ть (perf догна́ть);
catching adj (Med) зара́зный

category [ˈkætɪɡərɪ] n катего́рия

cater [ˈkeɪtəʳ] vi: **to cater (for)**
организова́ть (impf/perf) пита́ние (для
+gen); **cater for** vt fus (Brit: needs, tastes)
удовлетворя́ть (perf удовлетвори́ть);
(: readers etc) обслу́живать (perf обслужи́ть)

cathedral [kəˈθiːdrəl] n собо́р

Catholic [ˈkæθəlɪk] adj католи́ческий ⊳ n
като́лик(-и́чка)

cattle ['kætl] *npl* скот *msg*

catwalk ['kætwɔːk] *n* помо́ст (*для пока́за мод*)

caught [kɔːt] *pt, pp of* **catch**

cauliflower ['kɔlɪflauəʳ] *n* цветна́я капу́ста

cause [kɔːz] *n* (*reason*) причи́на; (*aim*) де́ло ▷ *vt* явля́ться (*perf* яви́ться) причи́ной +*gen*

caution ['kɔːʃən] *n* осторо́жность *f*; (*warning*) предупрежде́ние, предостереже́ние ▷ *vt* предупрежда́ть (*perf* предупреди́ть)

cautious ['kɔːʃəs] *adj* осторо́жный

cave [keɪv] *n* пеще́ра; **cave in** *vi* (*roof*) обва́ливаться (*perf* обвали́ться)

caviar(e) ['kævɪɑːʳ] *n* икра́

cavity ['kævɪtɪ] *n* (*in tooth*) дупло́

cc *abbr* (= *cubic centimetre*) куби́ческий сантиме́тр

CCTV *n abbr* (= *closed-circuit television*) за́мкнутая телевизио́нная систе́ма

CD *n abbr* = **compact disc**; **CD player** прои́грыватель *m* для компа́кт-ди́сков; **CD-ROM** *n* компа́кт-диск ПЗУ

cease [siːs] *vi* прекраща́ться (*perf* прекрати́ться); **cease-fire** *n* прекраще́ние огня́

cedar ['siːdəʳ] *n* кедр

ceiling ['siːlɪŋ] *n* (*also fig*) потоло́к

celebrate ['sɛlɪbreɪt] *vt* пра́здновать (*perf* отпра́здновать) ▷ *vi* весели́ться (*perf* повесели́ться); **to celebrate Mass** соверша́ть (*perf* соверши́ть) прича́стие

celebration [sɛlɪ'breɪʃən] *n* (*event*) пра́здник; (*of anniversary etc*) пра́зднование

celebrity [sɪ'lɛbrɪtɪ] *n* знамени́тость *f*

celery ['sɛlərɪ] *n* сельдере́й

cell [sɛl] *n* (*in prison*) ка́мера; (*Bio*) кле́тка

cellar ['sɛləʳ] *n* подва́л; (*also* **wine cellar**) ви́нный по́греб

cello ['tʃɛləu] *n* виолонче́ль *f*

cellphone ['sɛlfəun] *n* моби́льный телефо́н

Celsius ['sɛlsɪəs] *adj*: **30 degrees Celsius** 30 гра́дусов по Це́льсию

Celtic ['kɛltɪk] *adj* ке́льтский

cement [sə'mɛnt] *n* цеме́нт

cemetery ['sɛmɪtrɪ] *n* кла́дбище

censor ['sɛnsəʳ] *n* це́нзор ▷ *vt* подверга́ть (*perf* подве́ргнуть) цензу́ре; **censorship** *n* цензу́ра

census ['sɛnsəs] *n* пе́репись *f*

cent [sɛnt] *n* цент; *see also* **per cent**

centenary [sɛn'tiːnərɪ] *n* столе́тие

center ['sɛntəʳ] *n, vb* (*US*) *see* **centre**

centigrade ['sɛntɪɡreɪd] *adj*: **30 degrees centigrade** 30 гра́дусов по Це́льсию

centimetre ['sɛntɪmiːtəʳ] (*US* **centimeter**) *n* сантиме́тр

centipede ['sɛntɪpiːd] *n* многоно́жка

central ['sɛntrəl] *adj* центра́льный; **this flat is very central** э́та кварти́ра

располо́жена бли́зко к це́нтру; **Central America** *n* Центра́льная Аме́рика; **central heating** *n* центра́льное отопле́ние

centre ['sɛntəʳ] (*US* **center**) *n* центр ▷ *vt* (*Phot, Typ*) центри́ровать (*impf/perf*)

century ['sɛntjurɪ] *n* век

ceramic [sɪ'ræmɪk] *adj* керами́ческий

cereal ['siːrɪəl] *n*: **cereals** зерновы́е *pl adj*; (*also* **breakfast cereal**) хло́пья *pl* к за́втраку

ceremony ['sɛrɪmənɪ] *n* церемо́ния; (*behaviour*) церемо́нии *fpl*; **with ceremony** со все́ми форма́льностями

certain ['sɜːtən] *adj* определённый; **I'm certain (that)** я уве́рен(, что); **certain days** определённые дни; **a certain pleasure** не́которое удово́льствие; **it's certain (that)** несомне́нно(, что); **in certain circumstances** при определённых обстоя́тельствах; **a certain Mr Smith** не́кий Ми́стер Смит; **for certain** наверняка́; **certainly** *adv* (*undoubtedly*) несомне́нно; (*of course*) коне́чно; **certainty** *n* (*assurance*) уве́ренность *f*; (*inevitability*) несомне́нность *f*

certificate [sə'tɪfɪkɪt] *n* свиде́тельство; (*doctor's etc*) спра́вка; (*diploma*) дипло́м

cf. *abbr* = **compare**

CFC *n abbr* (= *chlorofluorocarbon*) хлорфтороуглеро́д

chain [tʃeɪn] *n* цепь *f*; (*decorative, on bicycle*) цепо́чка; (*of shops, hotels*) сеть *f*; (*of events, ideas*) верени́ца ▷ *vt* (*also* **chain up**: *person*) прико́вывать (*perf* прикова́ть); (: *dog*) сажа́ть (*perf* посади́ть) на цепь; **a chain of mountains** го́рная цепь

chair [tʃɛəʳ] *n* стул; (*also* **armchair**) кре́сло; (*of university*) ка́федра; (*also* **chairperson**) председа́тель *m* ▷ *vt* председа́тельствовать (*impf*) на +*prp*; **chairlift** *n* кана́тный подъёмник; **chairman** *irreg n* председа́тель *m*; (*Brit: Comm*) президе́нт

chalet ['ʃæleɪ] *n* шале́ *m ind*

chalk [tʃɔːk] *n* мел

challenge ['tʃælɪndʒ] *n* вы́зов; (*task*) испыта́ние ▷ *vt* (*also Sport*) броса́ть (*perf* бро́сить) вы́зов +*dat*; (*authority, right etc*) оспа́ривать (*perf* оспо́рить); **to challenge sb to** вызыва́ть (*perf* вы́звать) кого́-н на +*acc*

challenging ['tʃælɪndʒɪŋ] *adj* (*tone, look*) вызыва́ющий; (*task*) тру́дный

chamber ['tʃeɪmbəʳ] *n* ка́мера; (*Pol*) пала́та; **chamber of commerce** Торго́вая Пала́та

champagne [ʃæm'peɪn] *n* шампа́нское *nt adj*

champion ['tʃæmpɪən] *n* чемпио́н; (*of cause*) побо́рник(-ица); (*of person*) защи́тник(-ица); **championship** *n* (*contest*) чемпиона́т; (*title*) зва́ние чемпио́на

chance [tʃɑːns] n шанс; (opportunity) возмо́жность f; (risk) риск ▷ vt рискова́ть (impf) +instr ▷ adj случа́йный; **to take a chance** рискну́ть (perf); **by chance** случа́йно; **to leave to chance** оставля́ть (perf оста́вить) на во́лю слу́чая

chancellor ['tʃɑːnsələʳ] n (Pol) ка́нцлер; **Chancellor of the Exchequer** n (Brit) Ка́нцлер казначе́йства

● **CHANCELLOR OF THE EXCHEQUER**
●
● **Chancellor of the Exchequer** — ка́нцлер
● казначе́йства. В Великобрита́нии он
● выполня́ет фу́нкции мини́стра
● фина́нсов.

chandelier [ʃændə'lɪəʳ] n люстра

change [tʃeɪndʒ] vt меня́ть (perf поменя́ть); (money: to other currency) обме́нивать (perf обменя́ть); (: for smaller currency) разме́нивать (perf разменя́ть) ▷ vi (alter) меня́ться (impf), изменя́ться (perf измени́ться); (one's clothes) переодева́ться (perf переоде́ться); (change trains etc) де́лать (perf сде́лать) переса́дку ▷ n (alteration) измене́ние; (difference) переме́на; (replacement) сме́на; (also **small** or **loose change**) ме́лочь f; (money returned) сда́ча; **to change sb into** превраща́ть (perf преврати́ть) кого́-н в +acc; **to change one's mind** переду́мывать (perf переду́мать); **to change gear** переключа́ть (perf переключи́ть) ско́рость; **for a change** для разнообра́зия

channel ['tʃænl] n кана́л; (Naut) тра́сса ▷ vt: **to channel into** направля́ть (perf напра́вить) на +acc ▷ adj: **the Channel Islands** Норма́ндские острова́ mpl; **the (English) Channel** Ла-Ма́нш; **the Channel Tunnel** тунне́ль m под Ла-Ма́ншем

chant [tʃɑːnt] n сканди́рование; (Rel) пе́ние

chaos ['keɪɒs] n ха́ос

chaotic [keɪ'ɒtɪk] adj хаоти́чный

chap [tʃæp] n (Brit: inf) па́рень m

chapel ['tʃæpl] n (in church) приде́л; (in prison etc) часо́вня; (Brit: also **non-conformist chapel**) протеста́нтская нонконформи́стская це́рковь

chapter ['tʃæptəʳ] n глава́; (in life, history) страни́ца

character ['kærɪktəʳ] n (personality) ли́чность f; (nature) хара́ктер; (in novel, film) персона́ж; (letter, symbol) знак; **characteristic** ['kærɪktə'rɪstɪk] n характе́рная черта́ ▷ adj: **characteristic (of)** характе́рный (для +gen)

charcoal ['tʃɑːkəul] n (fuel) древе́сный у́голь m

charge [tʃɑːdʒ] n (fee) пла́та; (Law) обвине́ние; (responsibility) отве́тственность f; (Mil) ата́ка ▷ vi атакова́ть (impf/perf) ▷ vt (battery, gun) заряжа́ть (perf заряди́ть); (Law): **to charge sb with** предъявля́ть (perf предъяви́ть) кому́-н обвине́ние в +prp; **charges** npl (Comm) де́нежный сбор msg; (Tel) телефо́нный тари́ф msg; **to reverse the charges** звони́ть (perf позвони́ть) по колле́кту; **to take charge of** (child) брать (perf взять) на попече́ние; (company) брать (perf взять) на себя́ руково́дство +instr; **to be in charge of** отвеча́ть (impf) за +acc; **who's in charge here?** кто здесь гла́вный?; **to charge (sb) (for)** проси́ть (perf попроси́ть) (у кого́-н) пла́ту (за +acc); **how much do you charge for ...?** ско́лько Вы про́сите за +acc?; **charge card** n креди́тная ка́рточка (определённого магази́на)

charity ['tʃærɪtɪ] n благотвори́тельная организа́ция; (kindness) милосе́рдие; (money, gifts) ми́лостыня

● **CHARITY SHOP**
●
● **Charity shop** — благотвори́тельный
● магази́н. В э́тих магази́нах рабо́тают
● волонтёры, продаю́щие поде́ржанную
● оде́жду, ста́рые кни́ги, предме́ты
● дома́шнего обихо́да. Получа́емая
● при́быль направля́ется в
● благотвори́тельные о́бщества, кото́рые
● э́ти магази́ны подде́рживают.

charm [tʃɑːm] n очарова́ние, обая́ние; (on bracelet etc) брело́к ▷ vt очаро́вывать (perf очарова́ть); **charming** adj очарова́тельный

chart [tʃɑːt] n гра́фик; (of sea) навигацио́нная ка́рта; (of stars) ка́рта звёздного не́ба ▷ vt наноси́ть (perf нанести́) на ка́рту; (progress) следи́ть (impf) за +instr; **charts** npl (Mus) хит-пара́д msg

charter ['tʃɑːtəʳ] vt фрахтова́ть (perf зафрахтова́ть) ▷ n ха́ртия; (Comm) уста́в; **chartered accountant** n (Brit) бухга́лтер вы́сшей квалифика́ции; **charter flight** n ча́ртерный рейс

chase [tʃeɪs] vt гоня́ться (impf) or гна́ться impf за (+instr) ▷ n пого́ня; **to chase away** or **off** прогоня́ть (perf прогна́ть)

chat [tʃæt] vi болта́ть (perf поболта́ть); (Comput) обща́ться (perf пообща́ться) в ча́те, писа́ть (perf написа́ть) в ча́те ▷ n бесе́да; (Comput) чат; **chat room** n (Internet) чат-ко́мната; **chat show** n (Brit) шо́у с уча́стием знамени́тостей

chatter ['tʃætəʳ] n (gossip) болтовня́

chauffeur ['ʃəufəʳ] n (персона́льный) шофёр

cheap [tʃiːp] adj дешёвый ▷ adv дёшево; **cheaply** adv дёшево

cheat [tʃiːt] vi (at cards) жу́льничать (impf); (in exam) спи́сывать (perf списа́ть)

▷ *vt*: **to cheat sb (out of £10)** надува́ть (*perf* наду́ть) кого́-н (на £10) ▷ *n* жу́лик

check [tʃɛk] *vt* прове́рить (*perf* прове́рить); (*halt*) уде́рживать (*perf* удержа́ть); (*curb*) сде́рживать (*perf* сдержа́ть); (*US*: *items*) отмеча́ть (*perf* отме́тить) ▷ *n* (*inspection*) прове́рка; (*US*: *bill*) счёт; (: *Comm*) = **cheque**; (*pattern*) кле́тка ▷ *adj* кле́тчатый; **check in** *vi* регистри́роваться (*perf* зарегистри́роваться) ▷ *vt* (*luggage*) сдава́ть (*perf* сдать); **check out** *vi* выпи́сываться (*perf* вы́писаться); **check up** *vi*: **to check up on** наводи́ть (*perf* навести́) спра́вки о +*prp*; **checking account** *n* (*US*) теку́щий счёт; **checkout** *n* контро́ль *m*, ка́сса; **checkroom** *n* (*US*) ка́мера хране́ния; **checkup** *n* осмо́тр

cheek [tʃiːk] *n* щека́; (*impudence*) на́глость *f*; (*nerve*) де́рзость *f*; **cheeky** *adj* наха́льный, на́глый

cheer [tʃɪəʳ] *vt* приве́тствовать (*perf* поприве́тствовать) ▷ *vi* одобри́тельно восклица́ть (*impf*); **cheers** *npl* (*of welcome*) приве́тственные во́згласы *mpl*; (*of approval*) одобри́тельные во́згласы *mpl*; **cheers!** (за) Ва́ше здоро́вье!; **cheer up** *vi* развесели́ться (*perf*), повеселе́ть (*perf*) ▷ *vt* развесели́ть (*perf*); **cheer up!** не грусти́те!; **cheerful** *adj* весёлый

cheese [tʃiːz] *n* сыр

chef [ʃɛf] *n* шеф-по́вар

chemical ['kɛmɪkl] *adj* хими́ческий ▷ *n* химика́т; (*in laboratory*) реакти́в

chemist ['kɛmɪst] *n* (*Brit*: *pharmacist*) фармаце́вт; (*scientist*) хи́мик; **chemistry** *n* хи́мия

cheque [tʃɛk] *n* (*Brit*) чек; **chequebook** *n* (*Brit*) че́ковая кни́жка; **cheque card** *n* (*Brit*) ка́рточка, подтвержда́ющая платёжеспосо́бность владе́льца

cherry ['tʃɛrɪ] *n* чере́шня; (*sour variety*) ви́шня

chess [tʃɛs] *n* ша́хматы *pl*

chest [tʃɛst] *n* грудь *f*; (*box*) сунду́к

chestnut ['tʃɛsnʌt] *n* кашта́н

chest of drawers *n* комо́д

chew [tʃuː] *vt* жева́ть (*impf*); **chewing gum** *n* жева́тельная рези́нка

chic [ʃiːk] *adj* шика́рный, элега́нтный

chick [tʃɪk] *n* цыплёнок; (*of wild bird*) птене́ц

chicken ['tʃɪkɪn] *n* ку́рица; (*inf*: *coward*) труси́шка *m/f*; **chickenpox** *n* ветря́нка

chief [tʃiːf] *n* (*of organization etc*) нача́льник ▷ *adj* гла́вный, основно́й; **chief executive** (*US* **chief executive officer**) *n* гла́вный исполни́тельный дире́ктор; **chiefly** *adv* гла́вным о́бразом

child [tʃaɪld] (*pl* **children**) *n* ребёнок; **do you have any children?** у Вас есть де́ти?; **childbirth** *n* ро́ды *pl*; **childhood** *n* де́тство; **childish** *adj* (*games, attitude*)

реба́ческий; (*person*) реба́чливый; **child minder** *n* (*Brit*) ня́ня; **children** ['tʃɪldrən] *npl of* **child**

Chile ['tʃɪlɪ] *n* Чи́ли *ind*

chill [tʃɪl] *n* (*Med*) просту́да ▷ *vt* охлажда́ть (*perf* охлади́ть); **to catch a chill** простужа́ться (*perf* простуди́ться)

chil(l)i ['tʃɪlɪ] (*US* **chili**) *n* кра́сный стручко́вый пе́рец

chilly ['tʃɪlɪ] *adj* холо́дный

chimney ['tʃɪmnɪ] *n* (дымова́я) труба́

chimpanzee [tʃɪmpæn'ziː] *n* шимпанзе́ *m ind*

chin [tʃɪn] *n* подборо́док

China ['tʃaɪnə] *n* Кита́й

china ['tʃaɪnə] *n* фарфо́р

Chinese [tʃaɪ'niːz] *adj* кита́йский ▷ *n inv* кита́ец(-а́янка)

chip [tʃɪp] *n* (*of wood*) ще́пка; (*of stone*) оско́лок; (*also* **microchip**) микросхе́ма, чип ▷ *vt* отбива́ть (*perf* отби́ть); **chips** *npl* (*Brit*) карто́фель *msg* фри; (*US*: *also* **potato chips**) чи́псы *mpl*

chiropodist [kɪ'rɔpədɪst] *n* (*Brit*) мозо́льный опера́тор *m/f*

chisel ['tʃɪzl] *n* (*for wood*) долото́; (*for stone*) зуби́ло

chives [tʃaɪvz] *npl* лук-ре́занец *msg*

chlorine ['klɔːriːn] *n* хлор

chocolate ['tʃɔklɪt] *n* шокола́д; (*sweet*) шокола́дная конфе́та

choice [tʃɔɪs] *n* вы́бор

choir ['kwaɪəʳ] *n* хор; (*area*) хо́ры *pl*

choke [tʃəuk] *vi* дави́ться (*perf* подави́ться); (*with smoke, anger*) задыха́ться (*perf* задохну́ться) ▷ *vt* (*strangle*) души́ть (задуши́ть *or* удуши́ть *perf*)

cholesterol [kə'lɛstərɔl] *n* холестери́н; **high cholesterol** с высо́ким содержа́нием холестери́на

choose [tʃuːz] (*pt* **chose**, *pp* **chosen**) *vt* выбира́ть (*perf* вы́брать); **to choose to do** реша́ть (*perf* реши́ть) +*infin*

chop [tʃɔp] *vt* (*wood*) наруби́ть (*perf* наруби́ть); (*also* **chop up**: *vegetables, meat*) ре́зать (наре́зать *or* поре́зать *perf*) ▷ *n* (*Culin*) ≈ отбивна́я (котле́та)

chord [kɔːd] *n* (*Mus*) акко́рд

chore [tʃɔːʳ] *n* (*burden*) повседне́вная обя́занность *f*; **household chores** дома́шние хло́поты

chorus ['kɔːrəs] *n* хор; (*refrain*) припе́в

chose [tʃəuz] *pt of* **choose**; **chosen** ['tʃəuzn] *pp of* **choose**

Christ [kraɪst] *n* Христо́с

Christian ['krɪstɪən] *adj* христиа́нский ▷ *n* христиани́н(-а́нка); **Christianity** [krɪstɪ'ænɪtɪ] *n* христиа́нство; **Christian name** *n* и́мя *nt*

Christmas ['krɪsməs] *n* Рождество́; **Happy** *or* **Merry Christmas!** Счастли́вого Рождества́!; **Christmas card** *n* рожде́ственская откры́тка

● **CHRISTMAS CRACKER**

● **Christmas cracker** — рожде́ственская
хлопу́шка. В отли́чие от обы́чной
хлопу́шки в неё завора́чиваются
бума́жная коро́на, шу́тка и ма́ленький
пода́рок. Механи́зм хлопу́шки
приво́дится в де́йствие, е́сли дёрнуть
за о́ба её конца́ одновреме́нно.
Раздаётся хлопо́к и пода́рок выпада́ет.

Christmas Day *n* день *m* Рождества́
Christmas Eve *n* Сочельник

● **CHRISTMAS PUDDING**

● **Christmas pudding** — рожде́ственский
пу́динг. Кекс, пригото́вленный на пару́ и
содержа́щий большо́е коли́чество
сушёных фру́ктов.

Christmas tree *n* (рожде́ственская) ёлка
chrome [krəʊm] *n* хром
chronic ['krɒnɪk] *adj* хрони́ческий
chubby ['tʃʌbɪ] *adj* пу́хлый
chuck [tʃʌk] *vt* (*inf*) швыря́ть (*perf* швырну́ть)
chuckle ['tʃʌkl] *vi* посме́иваться (*impf*)
chunk [tʃʌŋk] *n* (*of meat*) кусо́к
church [tʃəːtʃ] *n* це́рковь *f*; **churchyard**
n пого́ст
CIA *n abbr* (*US*) (= Central Intelligence
Agency) ЦРУ
CID *n abbr* (*Brit*) (= Criminal Investigation
Department) уголо́вный ро́зыск
cider ['saɪdə^r] *n* сидр
cigar [sɪ'gɑː^r] *n* сига́ра
cigarette [sɪgə'rɛt] *n* сигаре́та
cinema ['sɪnəmə] *n* кинотеа́тр
cinnamon ['sɪnəmən] *n* кори́ца
circle ['səːkl] *n* круг; (*Theat*) балко́н
circuit ['səːkɪt] *n* (*Elec*) цепь *f*; (*tour*)
турне́ *nt ind*; (*track*) трек
circular ['səːkjʊlə^r] *adj* (*plate, pond etc*)
кру́глый ▷ *n* циркуля́р
circulate ['səːkjʊleɪt] *vi* циркули́ровать
(*impf*) ▷ *vt* передава́ть (*perf* переда́ть)
circulation [səːkjʊ'leɪʃən] *n* (*Press*)
тира́ж; (*Med*) кровообраще́ние; (*Comm*)
обраще́ние; (*of air, traffic*) циркуля́ция
circumstances ['səːkəmstənsɪz] *npl*
обстоя́тельства *ntpl*
circus ['səːkəs] *n* (*show*) цирк
cite [saɪt] *vt* цити́ровать (*perf*
процити́ровать); (*Law*) вызыва́ть (*perf*
вы́звать) в суд
citizen ['sɪtɪzn] *n* (*of country*)
граждани́н(-а́нка); (*of town*) жи́тель(ница)
m(f); **citizenship** *n* гражда́нство
city ['sɪtɪ] *n* го́род; **the City** Си́ти *nt ind*

● **CITY**

● Э́тот райо́н Ло́ндона явля́ется его́
фина́нсовым це́нтром.

civic ['sɪvɪk] *adj* муниципа́льный; (*duties,
pride*) гражда́нский
civil ['sɪvl] *adj* гражда́нский; (*authorities*)
госуда́рственный; (*polite*) учти́вый;
civilian [sɪ'vɪlɪən] *adj* (*life*)
обще́ственный ▷ *n* ми́рный(-ая)
жи́тель(ница) *m(f)*; **civilian casualties**
же́ртвы среди́ ми́рного населе́ния
civilization [sɪvɪlaɪ'zeɪʃən] *n*
цивилиза́ция
civilized ['sɪvɪlaɪzd] *adj* культу́рный;
(*society*) цивилизо́ванный
civil: **civil servant** *n* госуда́рственный
слу́жащий *m adj*; **Civil Service** *n*
госуда́рственная слу́жба; **civil war** *n*
гражда́нская война́
claim [kleɪm] *vt* (*responsibility*) брать
(*perf* взять) на себя́; (*credit*) припи́сывать
(*perf* приписа́ть) себе́; (*rights, inheritance*)
претендова́ть (*impf*) или притяза́ть *impf* на
(+*acc*) ▷ *vi* (*for insurance*) де́лать (*perf*
сде́лать) страхову́ю зая́вку ▷ *n*
(*assertion*) утвержде́ние; (*for
compensation, pension*) зая́вка; (*to
inheritance, land*) прете́нзия, притяза́ние;
to claim (that) *or* **to be** утвержда́ть (*impf*),
что
clamp [klæmp] *n* зажи́м ▷ *vt* зажима́ть
(*perf* зажа́ть)
clan [klæn] *n* клан
clap [klæp] *vi* хло́пать (*impf*)
claret ['klærət] *n* бордо́ *nt ind*
clarify ['klærɪfaɪ] *vt* (*fig*) разъясня́ть (*perf*
разъясни́ть)
clarinet [klærɪ'nɛt] *n* кларне́т
clarity ['klærɪtɪ] *n* (*fig*) я́сность *f*
clash [klæʃ] *n* столкнове́ние; (*of events
etc*) совпаде́ние; (*of metal objects*)
звя́канье ▷ *vi* ста́лкиваться (*perf*
столкну́ться); (*colours*) не совмеща́ться
(*impf*); (*events etc*) совпада́ть (*perf*
совпа́сть) (по вре́мени); (*metal objects*)
звя́кать (*impf*)
class [klɑːs] *n* класс; (*lesson*) уро́к; (*of
goods: type*) разря́д; (*: quality*) сорт ▷ *vt*
классифици́ровать (*impf/perf*)
classic ['klæsɪk] *adj* класси́ческий ▷ *n*
класси́ческое произведе́ние; **classical**
adj класси́ческий
classification [klæsɪfɪ'keɪʃən] *n*
классифика́ция; (*category*) разря́д
classroom ['klɑːsrum] *n* класс
clatter ['klætə^r] *n* звя́канье; (*of hooves*)
цо́канье
clause [klɔːz] *n* (*Law*) пункт
claustrophobic [klɔːstrə'fəʊbɪk] *adj*:
she is claustrophobic она́ страда́ет
клаустрофо́бией
claw [klɔː] *n* ко́готь *m*; (*of lobster*) клешня́
clay [kleɪ] *n* гли́на
clean [kliːn] *adj* чи́стый; (*edge, fracture*)
ро́вный ▷ *vt* (*hands, face*) мыть (*perf*
вы́мыть); (*car, cooker*) чи́стить (*perf*
почи́стить); **clean out** *vt* (*tidy*) вычища́ть

(*perf* вычистить); **clean up** *vt* (*room*)
убира́ть (*perf* убра́ть); (*child*) мыть (*perf*
помы́ть); **cleaner** *n* убо́рщик(-ица);
(*substance*) мо́ющее сре́дство
cleanser [klɛnzəʳ] *n* очища́ющий лосьо́н
clear [klɪəʳ] *adj* я́сный; (*footprint, writing*)
чёткий; (*glass, water*) прозра́чный; (*road*)
свобо́дный; (*conscience, profit*) чи́стый
▷ *vt* (*space, room*) освобожда́ть (*perf*
освободи́ть); (*suspect*) опра́вдывать (*perf*
оправда́ть); (*fence etc*) брать (*perf* взять)
▷ *vi* (*sky*) проясня́ться (*perf* проясни́ться);
(*fog, smoke*) рассе́иваться (*perf*
рассе́яться) ▷ *adv*: **clear of** пода́льше от
+*gen*; **to make it clear to sb that** ... дава́ть
(*perf* дать) кому́-н поня́ть, что ...; **to clear
the table** убира́ть (*perf* убра́ть) со стола́;
clear up *vt* убира́ть (*perf* убра́ть);
(*mystery, problem*) разреша́ть (*perf*
разреши́ть); **clearance** *n* расчи́стка;
(*permission*) разреше́ние; **clearing** *n*
поля́на; **clearly** *adv* я́сно; (*obviously*)
я́вно, очеви́дно
clergy [ˈkləːdʒɪ] *n* духове́нство
clerk [klɑːk, (*US*) kləːrk] *n* (*Brit*) клерк,
делопроизводи́тель(ница) *m(f)*; (*US: sales
person*) продаве́ц(-вщи́ца)
clever [ˈklɛvəʳ] *adj* у́мный
cliché [ˈkliːʃeɪ] *n* клише́ *nt ind*, штамп
click [klɪk] *vt* (*tongue, heels*) щёлкать
(*perf* щёлкнуть) +*instr* ▷ *vi* (*device,
switch*) щёлкать (*perf* щёлкнуть); **click on**
vi (*Comput*) щёлкать (*perf* щёлкнуть)
client [ˈklaɪənt] *n* клие́нт
cliff [klɪf] *n* скала́, утёс
climate [ˈklaɪmɪt] *n* кли́мат; **climate
change** *n* измене́ние кли́мата
climax [ˈklaɪmæks] *n* кульмина́ция
climb [klaɪm] *vi* поднима́ться (*perf*
подня́ться); (*plant*) ползти́ (*impf*); (*plane*)
набира́ть (*perf* набра́ть) высоту́ ▷ *vt*
(*stairs*) взбира́ться (*perf* взобра́ться) по
+*prp*; (*tree, hill*) взбира́ться (*perf*
взобра́ться) +*acc* ▷ *n* подъём; **to climb
over a wall** перелеза́ть (*perf* переле́зть)
че́рез сте́ну; **climber** *n* альпини́ст(ка)
clinch [klɪntʃ] *vt* (*deal*) заключа́ть (*perf*
заключи́ть); (*argument*) разреша́ть (*perf*
разреши́ть)
cling [klɪŋ] *n* (*pt, pp* **clung**) *vi* (*clothes*)
прилега́ть (*impf*); **to cling to** вцепля́ться
(*perf* вцепи́ться) в +*acc*; (*fig*) цепля́ться
(*impf*) за +*acc*
clinic [ˈklɪnɪk] *n* кли́ника
clip [klɪp] *n* (*also* **paper clip**) скре́пка;
(*for hair*) зако́лка; (*TV, Cinema*) клип ▷ *vt*
(*fasten*) прикрепля́ть (*perf* прикрепи́ть);
(*cut*) подстрига́ть (*perf* подстри́чь);
clipping *n* (*Press*) вы́резка
cloak [kləuk] *n* (*cape*) плащ; **cloakroom**
n гардеро́б; (*Brit: WC*) убо́рная *f adj*
clock [klɔk] *n* (*timepiece*) часы́ *pl*;
clockwise *adv* по часово́й стре́лке;
clockwork *adj* (*toy*) заводно́й

clone [kləun] *n* (*Bio*) клон
close¹ [kləus] *adj* бли́зкий; (*writing*)
убо́ристый; (*contact, ties*) те́сный; (*watch,
attention*) прistáльный; (*weather, room*)
ду́шный ▷ *adv* бли́зко; **close to** (*near*)
бли́зкий к +*dat*; **close to** or **on** (*almost*)
бли́зко к +*dat*; **close by** or **at hand** ря́дом
close² [kləuz] *vt* закрыва́ть (*perf*
закры́ть); (*finalize*) заключа́ть (*perf*
заключи́ть); (*end*) заверша́ть (*perf*
заверши́ть) ▷ *vi* закрыва́ться (*perf*
закры́ться); (*end*) заверша́ться (*perf*
заверши́ться) ▷ *n* коне́ц; **close down** *vt*
закрыва́ть (*perf* закры́ть) ▷ *vi*
закрыва́ться (*perf* закры́ться); **closed** *adj*
закры́тый
closely [ˈkləuslɪ] *adv* при́стально;
(*connected, related*) те́сно
closet [ˈklɔzɪt] *n* (*cupboard*) шкаф
closure [ˈkləuʒəʳ] *n* (*of factory, road*)
закры́тие
clot [klɔt] *n* сгу́сток; (*in vein*) тромб
cloth [klɔθ] *n* ткань *f*; (*for cleaning etc*)
тря́пка
clothes [kləuðz] *npl* оде́жда *fsg*;
clothes peg (*US* **clothes pin**) *n*
прище́пка
clothing [ˈkləuðɪŋ] *n* = **clothes**
cloud [klaud] *n* о́блако; **cloudy** *adj*
(*sky*) о́блачный; (*liquid*) му́тный
clove [kləuv] *n* гвозди́ка; **clove of garlic**
до́лька чеснока́
clown [klaun] *n* кло́ун
club [klʌb] *n* клуб; (*weapon*) дуби́нка;
(*also* **golf club**) клю́шка; **clubs** *npl*
(*Cards*) тре́фы *fpl*
clue [kluː] *n* ключ; (*for police*) ули́ка;
I haven't a clue (я) поня́тия не име́ю
clump [klʌmp] *n* за́росли *fpl*
clumsy [ˈklʌmzɪ] *adj* неуклю́жий; (*object*)
неудо́бный
clung [klʌŋ] *pt, pp of* **cling**
cluster [ˈklʌstəʳ] *n* скопле́ние
clutch [klʌtʃ] *n* хва́тка; (*Aut*) сцепле́ние
▷ *vt* сжима́ть (*perf* сжать)
cm *abbr* (= *centimetre*) см (= *сантиме́тр*)
Co *abbr* = **company**; **county**
coach [kəutʃ] *n* (*bus*) авто́бус;
(*horse-drawn*) экипа́ж; (*of train*) ваго́н;
(*Sport*) тре́нер; (*Scol*) репети́тор ▷ *vt*
(*Sport*) тренирова́ть (*perf*
натренирова́ть); (*Scol*): **to coach sb for**
гото́вить (*perf* подгото́вить) кого́-н к +*dat*
coal [kəul] *n* у́голь *m*
coalition [kəuəˈlɪʃən] *n* коали́ция
coarse [kɔːs] *adj* гру́бый
coast [kəust] *n* бе́рег; (*area*) побере́жье;
coastal *adj* прибре́жный; **coastguard**
n офице́р береговой слу́жбы; **coastline**
n береговая ли́ния
coat [kəut] *n* пальто́ *nt ind*; (*on animal:
fur*) мех; (: *wool*) шерсть *f*; (*of paint*) слой
▷ *vt* покрыва́ть (*perf* покры́ть); **coat
hanger** *n* ве́шалка

cobweb ['kɔbwɛb] *n* паути́на
cocaine [kə'keɪn] *n* кокаи́н
cock [kɔk] *n* пету́х ▷ *vt* (*gun*) взводи́ть (*perf* взвести́); **cockerel** ['kɔkərl] *n* пету́х
Cockney ['kɔknɪ] *n* ко́кни

- **COCKNEY**

- Так называ́ют вы́ходцев из восто́чного
- райо́на Ло́ндона. Они́ говоря́т на
- осо́бом диале́кте англи́йского языка́.
- Ко́кни та́кже обознача́ет э́тот диале́кт.

cockpit ['kɔkpɪt] *n* каби́на
cockroach ['kɔkrəʊtʃ] *n* тарака́н
cocktail ['kɔkteɪl] *n* кокте́йль *m*; (*with fruit, prawns*) сала́т
cocoa ['kəʊkəʊ] *n* кака́о *nt ind*
coconut ['kəʊkənʌt] *n* коко́совый оре́х; (*flesh*) коко́с
COD *abbr* = **cash on delivery**; (*US*) (= **collect on delivery**) нало́женный платёж
cod [kɔd] *n* треска́ *f no pl*
code [kəʊd] *n* код; (*of behaviour*) ко́декс; **post code** почто́вый и́ндекс
coffee ['kɔfɪ] *n* ко́фе *m ind*; **coffee table** *n* кофе́йный сто́лик
coffin ['kɔfɪn] *n* гроб
cognac ['kɔnjæk] *n* конья́к
coherent [kəʊ'hɪərənt] *adj* свя́зный, стро́йный; **she was very coherent** её речь была́ о́чень свя́зной
coil [kɔɪl] *n* мото́к ▷ *vt* сма́тывать (*perf* смота́ть)
coin [kɔɪn] *n* моне́та ▷ *vt* приду́мывать (*perf* приду́мать)
coincide [kəʊɪn'saɪd] *vi* совпада́ть (*perf* совпа́сть); **coincidence** [kəʊ'ɪnsɪdəns] *n* совпаде́ние
coke [kəʊk] *n* кокс
colander ['kɔləndə'] *n* дуршла́г
cold [kəʊld] *adj* холо́дный ▷ *n* хо́лод; (*Med*) просту́да; **it's cold** хо́лодно; **I am** *or* **feel cold** мне хо́лодно; **to catch cold** *or* **a cold** простужа́ться (*perf* простуди́ться); **in cold blood** хладнокро́вно; **cold sore** *n* лихора́дка (*на губе́ и́ли носу́*)
colic ['kɔlɪk] *n* ко́лики *pl*
collapse [kə'læps] *vi* (*building, system, plans*) ру́шиться (*perf* ру́хнуть); (*table etc*) скла́дываться (*perf* сложи́ться); (*company*) разоря́ться (*perf* разори́ться); (*government*) разва́ливаться (*perf* развали́ться); (*Med: person*) свали́ться (*perf*) ▷ *n* (*of building*) обва́л; (*of system, plans*) круше́ние; (*of company*) разоре́ние; (*of government*) паде́ние; (*Med*) упа́док сил, колла́пс
collar ['kɔlə'] *n* воротни́к; (*for dog etc*) оше́йник; **collarbone** *n* ключи́ца
colleague ['kɔliːg] *n* колле́га *m/f*
collect [kə'lɛkt] *vt* собира́ть (*perf* собра́ть); (*stamps etc*) коллекциони́ровать

(*impf*); (*Brit: fetch*) забира́ть (*perf* забра́ть); (*debts etc*) взы́скивать (*perf* взыска́ть) ▷ *vi* (*crowd*) собира́ться (*perf* собра́ться); **to call collect** (*US*) звони́ть (*impf*) по колле́кту; **collection** [kə'lɛkʃən] *n* (*of stamps etc*) колле́кция; (*for charity, also Rel*) поже́ртвования *ntpl*; (*of mail*) вы́емка; **collective** *adj* коллекти́вный; **collector** *n* (*of stamps etc*) коллекционе́р; (*of taxes etc*) сбо́рщик
college ['kɔlɪdʒ] *n* учи́лище; (*of university*) ко́лледж; (*of technology etc*) институ́т
collision [kə'lɪʒən] *n* столкнове́ние
colon ['kəʊlən] *n* (*Ling*) двоето́чие; (*Anat*) пряма́я кишка́
colonel ['kəːnl] *n* полко́вник
colony ['kɔlənɪ] *n* коло́ния
colour ['kʌlə'] (*US* **color**) *n* цвет ▷ *vt* раскра́шивать (*perf* раскра́сить); (*dye*) кра́сить (*perf* покра́сить); (*fig: opinion*) окра́шивать (*perf* окра́сить) ▷ *vi* красне́ть (*perf* покрасне́ть); **skin colour** цвет ко́жи; **in colour** в цве́те; **colour in** *vt* раскра́шивать (*perf* раскра́сить); **coloured** *adj* цветно́й; **colour film** *n* цветна́я плёнка; **colourful** *adj* кра́сочный; (*character*) я́ркий; **colouring** *n* (*of skin*) цвет лица́; (*in food*) краси́тель; **colour television** *n* цветно́й телеви́зор
column ['kɔləm] *n* коло́нна; (*of smoke*) столб; (*Press*) ру́брика
coma ['kəʊmə] *n*: **to be in a coma** находи́ться (*impf*) в ко́ме
comb [kəʊm] *n* расчёска; (*ornamental*) гре́бень *m* ▷ *vt* расчёсывать (*perf* расчеса́ть); (*fig*) прочёсывать (*perf* прочеса́ть)
combat ['kɔmbæt] *n* бой; (*battle*) би́тва ▷ *vt* боро́ться (*impf*) про́тив +*gen*
combination [kɔmbɪ'neɪʃən] *n* сочета́ние, комбина́ция; (*code*) код
combine [kəm'baɪn] *vt* комбини́ровать (*perf* скомбини́ровать) ▷ *vi* (*groups*) объединя́ться (*perf* объедини́ться)

O **KEYWORD**

come [kʌm] (*pt* **came**, *pp* **come**) *vi*
1 (*move towards: on foot*) подходи́ть (*perf* подойти́); (: *by transport*) подъезжа́ть (*perf* подъе́хать); **to come running** подбега́ть (*perf* подбежа́ть)
2 (*arrive: on foot*) приходи́ть (*perf* прийти́); (: *by transport*) приезжа́ть (*perf* прие́хать); **he came running to tell us** он прибежа́л, сказа́ть нам; **are you coming to my party?** Вы придёте ко мне на вечери́нку?; **I've only come for an hour** я зашёл то́лько на час
3 (*reach*) доходи́ть (*perf* дойти́) до +*gen*; **to come to** (*power, decision*) приходи́ть (*perf* прийти́) к +*dat*

4 (*occur*): **an idea came to me** мне в го́лову пришла́ иде́я
5 (*be, become*): **to come into being** возника́ть (*perf* возни́кнуть); **to come loose** отходи́ть (*perf* отойти́); **I've come to like him** он стал мне нра́виться
come about *vi*: **how did it come about?** каки́м о́бразом э́то произошло́?, как э́то получи́лось?; **it came about through ...** э́то получи́лось из-за +*gen* ...
come across *vt fus* ната́лкиваться (*perf* натолкну́ться) на +*acc*
come away *vi* уходи́ть (*perf* уйти́); (*come off*) отходи́ть (*perf* отойти́)
come back *vi* возвраща́ться (*perf* возврати́ться), верну́ться (*perf*)
come by *vt fus* достава́ть (*perf* доста́ть)
come down *vi* (*price*) понижа́ться (*perf* пони́зиться); **the tree came down in the storm** де́рево снесло́ бу́рей; **the building will have to come down soon** зда́ние должны́ ско́ро снести́
come forward *vi* (*volunteer*) вызыва́ться (*perf* вы́зваться)
come from *vt fus*: **she comes from India** она́ из Йндии
come in *vi* (*person*) входи́ть (*perf* войти́); **to come in on** (*deal*) вступа́ть (*perf* вступи́ть) в +*acc*; **where does he come in?** в чём его́ роль?
come in for *vt fus* подверга́ться (*perf* подве́ргнуться) +*dat*
come into *vt fus* (*fashion*) входи́ть (*perf* войти́) в +*acc*; (*money*) насле́довать (*perf* унасле́довать)
come off *vi* (*button*) отрыва́ться (*perf* оторва́ться); (*handle*) отла́мываться (*perf* отлома́ться); (*can be removed*) снима́ться (*impf*); (*attempt*) удава́ться (*perf* уда́ться)
come on *vi* (*pupil*) де́лать (*perf* сде́лать) успе́хи; (*work*) продвига́ться (*perf* продви́нуться); (*lights etc*) включа́ться (*perf* включи́ться); **come on!** ну!, дава́йте!
come out *vi* выходи́ть (*perf* вы́йти); (*stain*) сходи́ть (*perf* сойти́)
come round *vi* очну́ться (*perf*), приходи́ть (*perf* прийти́) в себя́
come to *vi* = **come round**
come up *vi* (*sun*) всходи́ть (*perf* взойти́); (*event*) приближа́ться (*perf* прибли́зиться); (*questions*) возника́ть (*perf* возни́кнуть); **something important has come up** случи́лось что-то ва́жное
come up against *vt fus* ста́лкиваться (*perf* столкну́ться) с +*instr*
come up with *vt fus* (*idea, solution*) предлага́ть (*perf* предложи́ть)
come upon *vt fus* ната́лкиваться (*perf* натолкну́ться) на +*acc*

comeback ['kʌmbæk] *n*: **to make a comeback** (*actor etc*) обрета́ть (*perf* обрести́) но́вую популя́рность
comedian [kə'miːdɪən] *n* ко́мик

comedy ['kɒmɪdɪ] *n* коме́дия
comet ['kɒmɪt] *n* коме́та
comfort ['kʌmfət] *n* комфо́рт; (*relief*) утеше́ние ▷ *vt* утеша́ть (*perf* уте́шить); **comforts** *npl* (*luxuries*) удо́бства *ntpl*; **comfortable** *adj* комфорта́бельный, удо́бный; **to be comfortable** (*physically*) чу́вствовать (*impf*) себя́ удо́бно; (*financially*) жить (*impf*) в доста́тке; (*patient*) чу́вствовать (*impf*) себя́ норма́льно
comic ['kɒmɪk] *adj* коми́ческий, смешно́й ▷ *n* (*comedian*) ко́мик; (*Brit: magazine*) ко́микс
comma ['kɒmə] *n* запята́я *f adj*
command [kə'mɑːnd] *n* кома́нда; (*control*) контро́ль *m*; (*mastery*) владе́ние ▷ *vt* (*Mil*) кома́ндовать (*impf*) +*instr*
commemorate [kə'meməreɪt] *vt* (*with statue etc*) увекове́чивать (*perf* увекове́чить); (*with event etc*) отмеча́ть (*perf* отме́тить)
commence [kə'mɛns] *vt* приступа́ть (*perf* приступи́ть) к +*dat* ▷ *vi* начина́ться (*perf* нача́ться)
commend [kə'mɛnd] *vt* хвали́ть (*perf* похвали́ть); (*recommend*): **to commend sth to sb** рекомендова́ть (*perf* порекомендова́ть) что-н кому́-н
comment ['kɒmɛnt] *n* замеча́ние ▷ *vi*: **to comment (on)** комменти́ровать (*perf* прокомменти́ровать); **"no comment"** "возде́рживаюсь от коммента́риев"; **commentary** ['kɒməntərɪ] *n* (*Sport*) репорта́ж; **commentator** ['kɒmənteɪtəʳ] *n* коммента́тор
commerce ['kɒməːs] *n* комме́рция
commercial [kə'məːʃəl] *adj* комме́рческий ▷ *n* рекла́ма
commission [kə'mɪʃən] *n* зака́з; (*Comm*) комиссио́нные *pl adj*; (*committee*) коми́ссия ▷ *vt* зака́зывать (*perf* заказа́ть); **out of commission** неиспра́вный
commit [kə'mɪt] *vt* (*crime*) соверша́ть (*perf* соверши́ть); (*money*) выделя́ть (*perf* вы́делить); (*entrust*) вверя́ть (*perf* вве́рить); **to commit o.s.** принима́ть (*perf* приня́ть) на себя́ обяза́тельства; **to commit suicide** поко́нчить (*perf*) жизнь самоуби́йством; **commitment** *n* (*belief*) пре́данность *f*; (*obligation*) обяза́тельство
committee [kə'mɪtɪ] *n* комите́т
commodity [kə'mɔdɪtɪ] *n* това́р
common ['kɒmən] *adj* о́бщий; (*usual*) обы́чный; (*vulgar*) вульга́рный ▷ *npl*: **the Commons** (*also* **the House of Commons**: *Brit*) Пала́та *fsg* о́бщин; **to have sth in common (with sb)** име́ть (*impf*) что-н о́бщее (с кем-н); **it's common knowledge that** общеизве́стно, что; **to** *or* **for the common good** для всео́бщего бла́га; **commonly** *adv* обы́чно; **commonplace** *adj* обы́чный, обы́денный

■ **COMMONS**
●
● **House of Commons** — Пала́та о́бщин.
● Одна́ из пала́т брита́нского
● парла́мента. В ней заседа́ет 650
● вы́борных чле́нов парла́мента.

Commonwealth n (Brit): **the
Commonwealth** Содру́жество
communal ['kɔmju:nl] adj (shared)
о́бщий; (flat) коммуна́льный
commune ['kɔmju:n] n комму́на
communicate [kə'mju:nɪkeɪt] vt
передава́ть (perf переда́ть) ▷ vi: **to
communicate (with)** обща́ться (impf) (с
+instr)
communication [kəmju:nɪ'keɪʃən] n
коммуника́ция
communion [kə'mju:nɪən] n (also **Holy
Communion**) Свято́е Прича́стие
communism ['kɔmjunɪzəm] n коммуни́зм
communist ['kɔmjunɪst] adj
коммунисти́ческий ▷ n коммуни́ст(ка)
community [kə'mju:nɪtɪ] n
обще́ственность f; (within larger group)
о́бщина; **the business community** деловы́е
круги́; **community centre** n
≈ обще́ственный центр

■ **COMMUNITY SERVICE**
●
● **Community service** — трудова́я
● пови́нность. Для не́которых
● нaруши́телей зако́на така́я фо́рма
● наказа́ния заменя́ет тюре́мное
● заключе́ние.

commuter [kə'mju:tə^r] n челове́к,
кото́рый е́здит на рабо́ту из при́города в
го́род
compact [kəm'pækt] adj компа́ктный;
compact disc n компа́кт-диск
companion [kəm'pænjən] n
спу́тник(-ица)
company ['kʌmpənɪ] n компа́ния;
(Theat) тру́ппа; (companionship)
компа́ния, о́бщество; **to keep sb company**
составля́ть (perf соста́вить) кому́-н
компа́нию
comparable ['kɔmpərəbl] adj (size)
сопостави́мый
comparative [kəm'pærətɪv] adj (also
Ling) сравни́тельный; **comparatively**
adv сравни́тельно
compare [kəm'pɛə^r] vt: **to compare sb/
sth with** or **to** сра́внивать (perf сравни́ть)
кого́-н/что-н с +instr; (set side by side)
сопоставля́ть (perf сопоста́вить) кого́-н/
что-н с +instr ▷ vi: **to compare (with)**
соотноси́ться (impf) (с +instr)
comparison [kəm'pærɪsn] n
(see vt) сравне́ние; сопоставле́ние; **in
comparison (with)** по сравне́нию or в
сравне́нии (с +instr)

compartment [kəm'pɑ:tmənt] n купе́ nt
ind; (section) отделе́ние
compass ['kʌmpəs] n ко́мпас;
compasses npl (also **pair of
compasses**) ци́ркуль msg
compassion [kəm'pæʃən] n
сострада́ние
compatible [kəm'pætɪbl] adj
совмести́мый
compel [kəm'pɛl] vt вынужда́ть (perf
вы́нудить); **compelling** adj (argument)
убеди́тельный; (reason) настоя́тельный
compensate ['kɔmpənseɪt] vt: **to
compensate sb for sth** компенси́ровать
(impf/perf) кому́-н что-н ▷ vi: **to
compensate for** (distress, loss)
компенси́ровать (impf/perf)
compensation [kɔmpən'seɪʃən] n
компенса́ция
compete [kəm'pi:t] vi (in contest etc)
соревнова́ться (impf); **to compete (with)**
(companies) конкури́ровать (impf) (с
+instr); (rivals) сопе́рничать (impf) (с
+instr)
competent ['kɔmpɪtənt] adj (person)
компете́нтный
competition [kɔmpɪ'tɪʃən] n
соревнова́ние; (between firms)
конкуре́нция; (between rivals)
сопе́рничество
competitive [kəm'pɛtɪtɪv] adj (person)
честолюби́вый; (price)
конкурентоспосо́бный
competitor [kəm'pɛtɪtə^r] n (rival)
сопе́рник, конкуре́нт; (participant)
уча́стник(-ица) соревнова́ния
complacent [kəm'pleɪsnt] adj
безразли́чие
complain [kəm'pleɪn] vi: **to complain
(about)** жа́ловаться (perf пожа́ловаться)
(на +acc); **complaint** n жа́лоба; **to make
a complaint against** подава́ть (perf
пода́ть) жа́лобу на +acc
complement ['kɔmplɪmənt] vt
дополня́ть (perf допо́лнить)
complete [kəm'pli:t] adj по́лный;
(finished) заверше́нный ▷ vt (building,
task) заверша́ть (perf заверши́ть); (set)
комплектова́ть (perf укомплектова́ть);
(form) заполня́ть (perf запо́лнить);
completely adv по́лностью,
соверше́нно
completion [kəm'pli:ʃən] n (of building,
task) заверше́ние
complex ['kɔmplɛks] adj сло́жный ▷ n
ко́мплекс
complexion [kəm'plɛkʃən] n (of face)
цвет лица́
compliance [kəm'plaɪəns] n
(submission) послуша́ние; **compliance
with** сле́дование +dat
complicate ['kɔmplɪkeɪt] vt усложня́ть
(perf усложни́ть); **complicated** adj
сло́жный

complication [kɔmplɪˈkeɪʃən] n
осложне́ние

compliment [n ˈkɔmplɪmənt, vb
ˈkɔmplɪmɛnt] n комплиме́нт, хвала́ ▷ vt
хвали́ть (perf похвали́ть); **compliments**
npl (regards) наилу́чшие пожела́ния ntpl;
to compliment sb, pay sb a compliment
де́лать (perf сде́лать) кому́-н комплиме́нт;
complimentary [kɔmplɪˈmɛntərɪ] adj
(remark) ле́стный; (ticket etc) да́рственный

comply [kəmˈplaɪ] vi: **to comply (with)**
подчиня́ться (perf подчини́ться) (+dat)

component [kəmˈpəunənt] adj
составно́й ▷ n компоне́нт

compose [kəmˈpəuz] vt сочиня́ть (perf
сочини́ть); **to be composed of** состоя́ть
(impf) из +gen; **to compose o.s.**
успока́иваться (perf успоко́иться);
composer n компози́тор

composition [kɔmpəˈzɪʃən] n (structure)
соста́в; (essay) сочине́ние; (Mus)
компози́ция

composure [kəmˈpəuʒəʳ] n
самооблада́ние

compound [ˈkɔmpaund] n (Chem)
соедине́ние; (Ling) сло́жное сло́во;
(enclosure) ко́мплекс

comprehension [kɔmprɪˈhɛnʃən] n
понима́ние

comprehensive [kɔmprɪˈhɛnsɪv] adj
исче́рпывающий ▷ n (Brit: also
comprehensive school)
общеобразова́тельная шко́ла

● **COMPREHENSIVE SCHOOL**
●
● **Comprehensive school** —
● о́бщеобразова́тельная шко́ла. В
● Великобрита́нии э́то госуда́рственная
● шко́ла для дете́й в во́зрасте 11-18 лет.

comprise [kəmˈpraɪz] vt (also **be
comprised of**) включа́ть (impf) в себя́,
состоя́ть (impf) из +gen; (constitute)
составля́ть (perf соста́вить)

compromise [ˈkɔmprəmaɪz] n
компроми́сс ▷ vt компромети́ровать
(perf скомпромети́ровать) ▷ vi идти́ (perf
пойти́) на компроми́сс

compulsive [kəmˈpʌlsɪv] adj
патологи́ческий; (reading etc)
захва́тывающий

compulsory [kəmˈpʌlsərɪ] adj
(attendance) обяза́тельный; (redundancy)
принуди́тельный

computer [kəmˈpjuːtəʳ] n компью́тер;
computer game n компью́терная игра́

computing [kəmˈpjuːtɪŋ] n (as subject)
компью́терное де́ло

comrade [ˈkɔmrɪd] n това́рищ

con [kɔn] vt надува́ть (perf наду́ть) ▷ n
(trick) обма́н, надува́тельство

conceal [kənˈsiːl] vt укрыва́ть (perf
укры́ть); (keep back) скрыва́ть (perf скрыть)

concede [kənˈsiːd] vt признава́ть (perf
призна́ть)

conceited [kənˈsiːtɪd] adj высокоме́рный

conceive [kənˈsiːv] vt (idea) заду́мывать
(perf заду́мать) ▷ vi забере́менеть (perf)

concentrate [ˈkɔnsəntreɪt] vi
сосредото́чиваться (perf
сосредото́читься), концентри́роваться
(perf сконцентри́роваться) ▷ vt: **to
concentrate (on)** (energies)
сосредото́чивать (perf сосредото́чить) or
концентри́ровать (сконцентри́ровать
perf) (+prp на)

concentration [kɔnsənˈtreɪʃən] n
сосредото́чение, концентра́ция;
(attention) сосредото́ченность f; (Chem)
концентра́ция

concept [ˈkɔnsɛpt] n поня́тие

concern [kənˈsəːn] n (affair) де́ло; (worry)
трево́га, озабо́ченность f; (care) уча́стие;
(Comm) предприя́тие ▷ vt (worry)
беспоко́ить (impf), трево́жить (impf);
(involve) вовлека́ть (perf вовле́чь); **to be
concerned (about)** беспоко́иться (impf) (о
+prp); **concerning** prep относи́тельно
+gen

concert [ˈkɔnsət] n конце́рт

concession [kənˈsɛʃən] n (compromise)
усту́пка; (right) конце́ссия; (reduction)
льго́та

concise [kənˈsaɪs] adj кра́ткий

conclude [kənˈkluːd] vt зака́нчивать
(perf зако́нчить); (treaty, deal etc)
заключа́ть (perf заключи́ть); (decide)
приходи́ть (perf прийти́) к заключе́нию or
вы́воду

conclusion [kənˈkluːʒən] n заключе́ние;
(of speech) оконча́ние; (of events)
заверше́ние

concrete [ˈkɔŋkriːt] n бето́н ▷ adj
бето́нный; (fig) конкре́тный

concussion [kənˈkʌʃən] n сотрясе́ние
мо́зга

condemn [kənˈdɛm] vt осужда́ть (perf
осуди́ть); (building) бракова́ть (perf
забракова́ть)

condensation [kɔndɛnˈseɪʃən] n
конденса́ция

condition [kənˈdɪʃən] n состоя́ние;
(requirement) усло́вие ▷ vt формирова́ть
(perf сформирова́ть); (hair, skin)
обраба́тывать (perf обрабо́тать);
conditions npl (circumstances) усло́вия
ntpl; **on condition that** при усло́вии, что;
conditional adj усло́вный; **conditioner**
n (for hair) бальза́м; (for fabrics)
смягча́ющий раство́р

condom [ˈkɔndəm] n презервати́в

condone [kənˈdəun] vt потво́рствовать
(impf) +dat

conduct [n ˈkɔndʌkt, vb kənˈdʌkt] n (of
person) поведе́ние ▷ vt (survey etc)
проводи́ть (perf провести́); (Mus)
дирижи́ровать (impf); (Phys) проводи́ть

(*impf*); **to conduct o.s.** вести (*perf* повести) себя; **conductor** [kənˈdʌktəʳ] *n* (*Mus*) дирижёр; (*US: Rail*) контролёр; (*on bus*) кондуктор

cone [kəun] *n* конус; (*also* **traffic cone**) конусообразное дорожное заграждение; (*Bot*) шишка; (*ice-cream*) мороженое *nt adj* (*трубочка*)

confectionery [kənˈfɛkʃənəʳ] *n* кондитерские изделия *ntpl*

confer [kənˈfəːʳ] *vi* совещаться (*impf*) ▷ *vt*: **to confer sth (on sb)** (*honour*) оказывать (*perf* оказать) что-н (кому́-н); (*degree*) присуждать (*perf* присудить) что-н (кому́-н)

conference [ˈkɔnfərəns] *n* конференция

confess [kənˈfɛs] *vt* (*guilt, ignorance*) признавать (*perf* признать); (*sin*) исповедоваться (*perf* исповедаться) в +*prp* ▷ *vi* (*to crime*) признаваться (*perf* признаться); **confession** [kənˈfɛʃən] *n* признание; (*Rel*) исповедь *f*

confide [kənˈfaɪd] *vi*: **to confide in** доверяться (*perf* довериться) +*dat*

confidence [ˈkɔnfɪdns] *n* уверенность *f*; (*in self*) уверенность в себе; **in confidence** конфиденциально

confident [ˈkɔnfɪdənt] *adj* (*see n*) уверенный; уверенный в себе

confidential [kɔnfɪˈdɛnʃəl] *adj* конфиденциальный; (*tone*) доверительный

confine [kənˈfaɪn] *vt* (*lock up*) запирать (*perf* запереть); (*limit*): **to confine (to)** ограничивать (*perf* ограничить) (+*instr*); **confined** *adj* закрытый

confirm [kənˈfəːm] *vt* подтверждать (*perf* подтвердить); **confirmation** [kɔnfəˈmeɪʃən] *n* подтверждение

conflict [ˈkɔnflɪkt] *n* конфликт; (*of interests*) столкновение

conform [kənˈfɔːm] *vi*: **to conform (to)** подчиняться (*perf* подчиниться) (+*dat*)

confront [kənˈfrʌnt] *vt* (*problems*) сталкиваться (*perf* столкнуться) с +*instr*; (*enemy*) противостоять (*impf*) +*dat*; **confrontation** [kɔnfrənˈteɪʃən] *n* конфронтация

confuse [kənˈfjuːz] *vt* запутывать (*perf* запутать); (*mix up*) путать (*perf* спутать); **confused** *adj* (*person*) озадаченный

confusing [kənˈfjuːzɪŋ] *adj* запутанный

confusion [kənˈfjuːʒən] *n* (*perplexity*) замешательство; (*mix-up*) путаница; (*disorder*) беспорядок

congestion [kənˈdʒɛstʃən] *n* (*on road*) перегруженность *f*; (*in area*) перенаселённость *f*

congratulate [kənˈgrætjuleɪt] *vt*: **to congratulate sb (on)** поздравлять (*perf* поздравить) кого́-н (с +*instr*)

congratulations [kəngrætjuˈleɪʃənz] *npl* поздравления *ntpl*; **congratulations (on)** (*from one person*) поздравляю (с +*instr*);

(*from several people*) поздравляем (с +*instr*)

congregation [kɔngrɪˈgeɪʃən] *n* прихожане *mpl*, приход

congress [ˈkɔngrɛs] *n* конгресс; (*US*): **Congress** конгресс США; **congressman** *irreg n* (*US*) конгрессмен

conjunction [kənˈdʒʌnkʃən] *n* (*Ling*) союз

conjure [ˈkʌndʒəʳ] *vt* (*fig*) соображать (*perf* сообразить); **conjure up** *vt* (*memories*) пробуждать (*perf* пробудить)

connect [kəˈnɛkt] *vt* (*Elec*) подсоединять (*perf* подсоединить), подключать (*perf* подключить); (*fig: associate*) связывать (*perf* связать) ▷ *vi*: **to connect with** согласовываться (*perf* согласоваться) по расписанию с +*instr*; **to connect sb/sth (to)** соединять (*perf* соединить) кого́-н/что-н (с +*instr*); **he is connected with ...** он связан с +*instr* ...; **I am trying to connect you** (*Tel*) я пытаюсь подключить Вас; **connection** [kəˈnɛkʃən] *n* связь *f*; (*train etc*) пересадка

conquer [ˈkɔŋkəʳ] *vt* (*Mil*) завоёвывать (*perf* завоевать); (*overcome*) побороть (*perf*)

conquest [ˈkɔŋkwɛst] *n* (*Mil*) завоевание

cons [kɔnz] *npl see* **convenience; pro**

conscience [ˈkɔnʃəns] *n* совесть *f*

conscientious [kɔnʃɪˈɛnʃəs] *adj* добросовестный

conscious [ˈkɔnʃəs] *adj* (*deliberate*) сознательный; (*aware*): **to be conscious of sth/that** сознавать (*impf*) что-н/, что; **the patient was conscious** пациент находился в сознании; **consciousness** *n* сознание; (*of group*) самосознание

consecutive [kənˈsɛkjutɪv] *adj*: **on three consecutive occasions** в трёх случаях подряд; **on three consecutive days** три дня подряд

consensus [kənˈsɛnsəs] *n* единое мнение; **consensus (of opinion)** консенсус

consent [kənˈsɛnt] *n* согласие

consequence [ˈkɔnsɪkwəns] *n* следствие; **of consequence** (*significant*) значительный; **it's of little consequence** это не имеет большого значения; **in consequence** (*consequently*) следовательно, вследствие этого

consequently [ˈkɔnsɪkwəntlɪ] *adv* следовательно

conservation [kɔnsəˈveɪʃən] *n* (*also* **nature conservation**) охрана природы, природоохрана

conservative [kənˈsəːvətɪv] *adj* консервативный; (*estimate*) скромный; (*Brit: Pol*): **Conservative** консервативный ▷ *n* (*Brit*): **Conservative** консерватор

conservatory [kənˈsəːvətrɪ] *n* застеклённая веранда

conserve [kənˈsəːv] *vt* сохранять (*perf* сохранить); (*energy*) сберегать (*perf* сберечь) ▷ *n* варенье

consider [kən'sɪdə^r] vt (*believe*) считáть (*perf* посчитáть); (*study*) рассмáтривать (*perf* рассмотрéть); (*take into account*) учи́тывать (*perf* учéсть); (*regard*): **to consider that ...** полагáть (*impf*) или считáть (*impf*), что ...; **to consider sth** (*think about*) дýмать (*impf*) о чём-н; **considerable** *adj* значи́тельный; **considerably** *adv* значи́тельно; **considerate** *adj* (*person*) забóтливый; (*action*) внимáтельный; **consideration** [kənsɪdə'reɪʃən] *n* рассмотрéние, обдýмывание; (*factor*) соображéние; (*thoughtfulness*) внимáние; **considering** *prep* учи́тывая +*acc*

consignment [kən'saɪnmənt] *n* (*Comm*) пáртия

consist [kən'sɪst] *vi*: **to consist of** состоя́ть (*impf*) из +*gen*

consistency [kən'sɪstənsɪ] *n* послéдовательность *f*; (*of yoghurt etc*) консистéнция

consistent [kən'sɪstənt] *adj* послéдовательный

consolation [kənsə'leɪʃən] *n* утешéние

console [kən'səul] *vt* утешáть (*perf* утéшить)

consonant ['kənsənənt] *n* соглáсный *m* *adj*

conspicuous [kən'spɪkjuəs] *adj* замéтный

conspiracy [kən'spɪrəsɪ] *n* зáговор

constable ['kʌnstəbl] (*Brit*: also **police constable**) *n* (участкóвый) полицéйский *m* *adj*

constant ['kənstənt] *adj* постоя́нный; (*fixed*) неизмéнный; **constantly** *adv* постоя́нно

constipation [kənstɪ'peɪʃən] *n* запóр

constituency [kən'stɪtjuənsɪ] *n* (*area*) избирáтельный óкруг

constitute ['kənstɪtjuːt] *vt* (*represent*) явля́ться (*perf* яви́ться) +*instr*; (*make up*) составля́ть (*perf* состáвить)

constitution [kənstɪ'tjuːʃən] *n* (*of country, person*) конститýция; (*of organization*) устáв

constraint [kən'streɪnt] *n* (*restriction*) ограничéние

construct [kən'strʌkt] *vt* сооружáть (*perf* сооруди́ть); **construction** [kən'strʌkʃən] *n* (*of building etc*) сооружéние; (*structure*) констрýкция; **constructive** *adj* конструкти́вный

consul ['kənsl] *n* кóнсул; **consulate** ['kənsjulɪt] *n* кóнсульство

consult [kən'sʌlt] *vt* (*friend*) совéтоваться (*perf* посовéтоваться) с +*instr*; (*book, map*) справля́ться (*perf* спрáвиться) в +*prp*; **to consult sb (about)** (*expert*) консульти́роваться (*perf* проконсульти́роваться) с кем-н (о +*prp*); **consultant** *n* консультáнт; (*Med*) врач-консультáнт; **consultation** [kənsəl'teɪʃən] *n* (*Med*) консультáция; (*discussion*) совещáние

consume [kən'sjuːm] *vt* потребля́ть (*perf* потреби́ть); **consumer** *n* потреби́тель *m*

consumption [kən'sʌmpʃən] *n* потреблéние; (*amount*) расхóд

cont. *abbr* (= *continued*); **cont. on** продолжéние на +*prp*

contact ['kəntækt] *n* (*communication*) контáкт; (*touch*) соприкосновéние; (*person*) деловóй(-áя) знакóмый(-ая) *m(f)* *adj* ▷ *vt* свя́зываться (*perf* связáться) с +*instr*; **contact lenses** *npl* контáктные ли́нзы *fpl*; **contactless** *adj* бесконтáктный

contagious [kən'teɪdʒəs] *adj* зарáзный; (*fig*) заразительный

contain [kən'teɪn] *vt* (*hold*) вмещáть (*perf* вмести́ть); (*include*) содержáть (*impf*); (*curb*) сдéрживать (*perf* сдержáть); **to contain o.s.** сдéрживаться (*perf* сдержáться); **container** *n* контéйнер

contemplate ['kəntəmpleɪt] *vt* (*consider*) размышля́ть (*impf*) о +*prp*; (*look at*) созерцáть (*impf*)

contemporary [kən'tɛmpərərɪ] *adj* совремéнный ▷ *n* совремéнник(-ица)

contempt [kən'tɛmpt] *n* презрéние; **contempt of court** оскорблéние судá

contend [kən'tɛnd] *vt*: **to contend that** утверждáть (*impf*), что ▷ *vi*: **to contend with** (*problem etc*) борóться (*impf*) с +*instr*

content [*n* 'kəntɛnt, *adj, vb* kən'tɛnt] *n* содержáние ▷ *adj* довóльный ▷ *vt* (*satisfy*) удовлетворя́ть (*perf* удовлетвори́ть); **contents** *npl* (*of bottle etc*) содержи́мое *ntsg adj*; (*of book*) содержáние *ntsg*; (*table of*) **contents** оглавлéние; **contented** *adj* довóльный

contest [*n* 'kəntɛst, *vb* kən'tɛst] *n* (*sport*) соревновáние; (*beauty*) кóнкурс; (*for power etc*) борьбá ▷ *vt* оспáривать (*perf* оспóрить); (*election, competition*) борóться (*impf*) на +*prp*; **contestant** [kən'tɛstənt] *n* учáстник(-ница)

context ['kəntɛkst] *n* контéкст

continent ['kəntɪnənt] *n* континéнт, матери́к; **the Continent** (*Brit*) Еврóпа (*крóме брита́нских острово́в*)

continental [kəntɪ'nɛntl] *adj* (*Brit*) европéйский

● **CONTINENTAL BREAKFAST**
●
● **Continental breakfast** — европéйский
● зáвтрак. В европéйский зáвтрак вхóдит
● хлеб, мáсло и джем. Егó подаю́т в
● гости́ницах вмéсто традицио́нного
● зáвтрака из бекóна и яи́чницы.

continental quilt *n* (*Brit*) стёганое одея́ло

continual [kən'tɪnjuəl] *adj* непреры́вный,

постоя́нный; **continually** adv
непреры́вно, постоя́нно
continue [kən'tɪnjuː] vi (carry on)
продолжа́ться (impf); (after interruption:
talk) продолжа́ться (perf продо́лжиться);
(: person) продолжа́ть (perf продо́лжить)
▷ vt продолжа́ть (perf продо́лжить)
continuity [kɒntɪ'njuːɪtɪ] n
прее́мственность f
continuous [kən'tɪnjuəs] adj
непреры́вный; (line) сплошно́й
contraception [kɒntrə'sɛpʃən] n
предупрежде́ние бере́менности
contraceptive [kɒntrə'sɛptɪv] n
противозача́точное сре́дство,
контрацепти́в
contract [n 'kɒntrækt, vb kən'trækt] n
догово́р, контра́кт ▷ vi сжима́ться (perf
сжа́ться) ▷ vt (Med) заболева́ть (perf
заболе́ть) +instr; **contractor** [kən'træktə'ʳ]
n подря́дчик
contradict [kɒntrə'dɪkt] vt (person)
возража́ть (perf возрази́ть) +dat;
(statement) возража́ть (perf возрази́ть) на
+acc; **contradiction** [kɒntrə'dɪkʃən] n
противоре́чие
contrary ['kɒntrərɪ] adj противополо́жный
▷ n противополо́жность f; **on the contrary**
напро́тив, наоборо́т; **unless you hear to
the contrary** е́сли не бу́дет други́х
инстру́кций
contrast [n 'kɒntrɑːst, vb kən'trɑːst] n
контра́ст ▷ vt сопоставля́ть (perf
сопоста́вить); **in contrast to** or **with** по
контра́сту с +instr
contribute [kən'trɪbjuːt] vi (give) де́лать
(perf сде́лать) вклад ▷ vt (money, an
article) вноси́ть (perf внести́); **to contribute
to** (to charity) же́ртвовать (perf
поже́ртвовать) на +acc or для +gen; (to
paper) писа́ть (perf написа́ть) для +gen;
(to discussion) вноси́ть (perf внести́) вклад
в +prp; (to problem) усугубля́ть (perf
усугуби́ть)
contribution [kɒntrɪ'bjuːʃən] n
(donation) поже́ртвование, вклад; (to
debate, campaign) вклад; (to journal)
публика́ция
contributor [kən'trɪbjuːtə'ʳ] n (to appeal)
же́ртвователь m; (to newspaper) а́втор
control [kən'trəul] vt контроли́ровать
(impf) ▷ n (of country, organization)
контро́ль m; (of o.s.) самооблада́ние;
controls npl (of vehicle) управле́ние; (on
radio etc) ру́чки fpl настро́йки; **to control
o.s.** сохраня́ть (perf сохрани́ть)
самооблада́ние; **to be in control of**
контроли́ровать (impf); **everything is
under control** всё под контро́лем; **out of
control** неуправля́емый
controversial [kɒntrə'vəːʃl] adj
спо́рный; (person, writer) неоднозна́чный
controversy ['kɒntrəvəːsɪ] n
диску́ссия, спор

convenience [kən'viːnɪəns] n удо́бство;
at your convenience когда́ Вам бу́дет
удо́бно; **a flat with all modern
conveniences** or (Brit) **all mod cons**
кварти́ра со все́ми удо́бствами
convenient [kən'viːnɪənt] adj удо́бный
convent ['kɒnvənt] n (Rel) (же́нский)
монасты́рь m
convention [kən'vɛnʃən] n (custom)
усло́вность f; (conference) конфере́нция;
(agreement) конве́нция; **conventional**
adj традицио́нный; (methods, weapons)
обы́чный
conversation [kɒnvə'seɪʃən] n бесе́да,
разгово́р; **to have a conversation with sb**
разгова́ривать (impf) or бесе́довать
(побесе́довать perf) с кем-н
conversely [kɒn'vəːslɪ] adv наоборо́т
conversion [kən'vəːʃən] n обраще́ние;
(of weights) перево́д; (of substances)
превраще́ние
convert [vb kən'vəːt, n 'kɒnvəːt] vt
(person) обраща́ть (perf обрати́ть) ▷ n
новообращённый(-ая)m(f) adj; **to convert
sth into** превраща́ть (perf преврати́ть)
что-н в +acc
convey [kən'veɪ] vt передава́ть (perf
переда́ть); (cargo, person) перевози́ть
(perf перевезти́)
convict [vb kən'vɪkt, n 'kɒnvɪkt] vt
осужда́ть (perf осуди́ть) ▷ n ка́торжник;
conviction [kən'vɪkʃən] n (belief)
убежде́ние; (certainty) убеждённость f;
(Law) осужде́ние; (: previous) суди́мость f
convince [kən'vɪns] vt (assure) уверя́ть
(perf уве́рить); (persuade) убежда́ть (perf
убеди́ть); **convinced** adj: **convinced of/
that** убеждённый в +prp/, что
convincing [kən'vɪnsɪŋ] adj
убеди́тельный
convoy ['kɒnvɔɪ] n (of trucks) коло́нна;
(of ships) конво́й
cook [kuk] vt гото́вить (perf пригото́вить)
▷ vi (person) гото́вить (impf); (food)
гото́виться (impf) ▷ n по́вар; **cooker** n
плита́; **cookery** n кулинари́я; **cookery
book** n (Brit) пова́ренная or кулина́рная
кни́га; **cookie** n (esp US) пече́нье;
cooking n гото́вка; **I like cooking** я люблю́
гото́вить
cool [kuːl] adj прохла́дный; (dress,
clothes) лёгкий; (person: calm)
невозмути́мый; (: hostile) холо́дный; (inf:
great) круто́й ▷ vi (water, air) остыва́ть
(perf осты́ть); **cool!** (inf) здо́рово!
cooperate [kəu'ɔpəreɪt] vi (collaborate)
сотру́дничать (impf); (assist)
соде́йствовать (impf)
cooperation [kəuɔpə'reɪʃən] n (see vi)
коопера́ция, сотру́дничество; соде́йствие
cop [kɒp] n (Brit: inf) мент
cope [kəup] vi: **to cope with** справля́ться
(perf спра́виться) с +instr
copper ['kɒpə'ʳ] n (metal) медь f

copy ['kɔpɪ] n (duplicate) ко́пия; (of book etc) экземпля́р ▷ vt копи́ровать (perf скопи́ровать); **copyright** n а́вторское пра́во, копира́йт

coral ['kɔrəl] n кора́лл

cord [kɔːd] n (string) верёвка; (Elec) шнур; (fabric) вельве́т

corduroy ['kɔːdərɔɪ] n вельве́т

core [kɔː] n сердцеви́на; (of problem) суть f ▷ vt выреза́ть (perf вы́резать) сердцеви́ну +gen

coriander [kɔrɪ'ændə'] n (spice) ки́нза, кориа́ндр

cork [kɔːk] n про́бка; **corkscrew** n што́пор

corn [kɔːn] n (Brit) зерно́; (US: maize) кукуру́за; (on foot) мозо́ль f; **corn on the cob** поча́ток кукуру́зы

corner ['kɔːnə'] n у́гол; (Sport: also **corner kick**) угло́вой m adj (уда́р)

cornflour ['kɔːnflauə'] n (Brit) кукуру́зная мука́

coronary ['kɔrənərɪ] n (also **coronary thrombosis**) коро́нарный тромбо́з

coronation [kɔrə'neɪʃən] n корона́ция

coroner ['kɔrənə'] n (Law) ко́ронер (судья́, рассле́дующий причи́ны сме́рти, происше́дшей при подозри́тельных обстоя́тельствах)

corporal ['kɔːpərəl] adj: **corporal punishment** теле́сное наказа́ние

corporate ['kɔːpərɪt] adj корпорацио́нный; (ownership) о́бщий; (identity) корпорати́вный

corporation [kɔːpə'reɪʃən] n (Comm) корпора́ция

corps [kɔː'] (pl **corps**) n (also Mil) ко́рпус

corpse [kɔːps] n труп

correct [kə'rɛkt] adj пра́вильный; (proper) соотве́тствующий ▷ vt исправля́ть (perf испра́вить); (exam) проверя́ть (perf прове́рить); **correction** [kə'rɛkʃən] n исправле́ние; (mistake corrected) попра́вка

correspond [kɔrɪs'pɔnd] vi: **correspond (with)** (write) перепи́сываться (impf) (c +instr); (tally) согласо́вываться (impf) (c +instr); (equate): **to correspond (to)** соотве́тствовать (impf) (+dat); **correspondence** n (letters) перепи́ска; (: in business) корреспонде́нция; (relationship) соотноше́ние; **correspondent** n (Press) корреспонде́нт(ка)

corridor ['kɔrɪdɔː'] n коридо́р; (in train) прохо́д

corrupt [kə'rʌpt] adj прода́жный, коррумпи́рованный ▷ vt развраща́ть (perf разврати́ть); **corruption** [kə'rʌpʃən] n корру́пция, прода́жность f

cosmetic [kɔz'mɛtɪk] n (usu pl) косме́тика

cosmopolitan [kɔzmə'pɔlɪtn] adj (place) космополити́ческий

cost [kɔst] (pt, pp **cost**) n (price) сто́имость f ▷ vt сто́ить (impf) ▷ (pt, pp **costed**) (find out cost of) расчи́тывать (perf расчита́ть) сто́имость +gen; **costs** npl (Comm) расхо́ды mpl; (Law) суде́бные изде́ржки fpl; **how much does it cost?** ско́лько э́то сто́ит?; **to cost sb sth** (time, job) сто́ить (impf) кому́-н чего́-н; **at all costs** любо́й цено́й; **costly** adj (expensive) дорогостоя́щий; **cost of living** n сто́имость f жи́зни

costume ['kɔstjuːm] n костю́м; (Brit: also **swimming costume**) купа́льник, купа́льный костю́м

cosy ['kəuzɪ] (US **cozy**) adj (room, atmosphere) ую́тный

cot [kɔt] n (Brit) де́тская крова́тка; (US: camp bed) ко́йка

cottage ['kɔtɪdʒ] n котте́дж

cotton ['kɔtn] n (fabric) хло́пок, хлопчатобума́жная ткань f; (thread) (шве́йная) ни́тка; **cotton wool** n (Brit) ва́та

couch [kautʃ] n тахта́, дива́н

cough [kɔf] vi ка́шлять (impf) ▷ n ка́шель m

could [kud] pt of **can²**; **couldn't** ['kudnt] = **could not**

council ['kaunsl] n сове́т; **city or town council** муниципалите́т, городско́й сове́т; **council house** n (Brit) дом, принадлежа́щий муниципалите́ту; **councillor** n член муниципалите́та; **council tax** n (Brit) муниципа́льный нало́г

● COUNCIL ESTATE
●
● **Council estate** — муниципа́льный
● жило́й микрорайо́н. Дома́ в таки́х
● райо́нах стро́ятся на сре́дства
● муниципалите́та. Типовы́е постро́йки
● включа́ют многоэта́жные дома́ и́ли ряд
● однотипных примыка́ющих друг к
● дру́гу домо́в с сада́ми.

counsel ['kaunsl] n (advice) сове́т; (lawyer) адвока́т ▷ vt: **to counsel sth/sb to do** сове́товать (perf посове́товать) что-н/кому́-н +infin; **counsellor** n (advisor) сове́тник; (US: lawyer) адвока́т

count [kaunt] vt счита́ть (perf посчита́ть); (include) счита́ть (impf) ▷ vi счита́ть (perf сосчита́ть) (qualify) счита́ться (impf); (matter) име́ть (impf) значе́ние ▷ n подсчёт; (level) у́ровень m; **count on** vt fus рассчи́тывать (impf) на +acc; **countdown** n обра́тный счёт

counter ['kauntə'] n (in shop, café) прила́вок; (in bank, post office) сто́йка; (in game) фи́шка ▷ vt (oppose) опроверга́ть (perf опрове́ргнуть) ▷ adv: **counter to** в противове́с +dat

counterpart ['kauntəpɑːt] n (of person) колле́га m/f

countless ['kauntlıs] adj несчётный, бесчи́сленный

country ['kʌntrı] n страна́; (native land) ро́дина; (rural area) дере́вня; **countryside** n дере́вня, се́льская ме́стность f

county ['kauntı] n гра́фство

- **COUNTY**
- В Великобрита́нии, Ирла́ндии и США
- county — администрати́вно-
- территориа́льная едини́ца
- эквивале́нтная о́бласти и управля́емая
- ме́стным прави́тельством.

coup [kuː] n (pl **coups**) n (also **coup d'état**) госуда́рственный переворо́т

couple ['kʌpl] n (married couple) (супру́жеская) па́ра; (of people, things) па́ра; **a couple of** (some) па́ра +gen

coupon ['kuːpɔn] n (voucher) купо́н; (form) тало́н

courage ['kʌrıdʒ] n сме́лость f, хра́брость f; **courageous** [kə'reıdʒəs] adj сме́лый, хра́брый

courgette [kuə'ʒet] n (Brit) молодо́й кабачо́к

courier ['kurıər] n курье́р; (for tourists) руководи́тель m гру́ппы

course [kɔːs] n курс; (of events, time) ход; (of action) направле́ние; (of river) тече́ние; **first/last course** пе́рвое/сла́дкое блю́до; **of course** коне́чно

court [kɔːt] n (Law) суд; (Sport) корт; (royal) двор; **to take sb to court** подава́ть (perf пода́ть) на кого́-н в суд

courtesy ['kɜːtəsı] n ве́жливость f; **(by) courtesy of** благодаря́ любе́зности +gen

courtroom ['kɔːtruːm] n зал суда́

courtyard ['kɔːtjɑːd] n вну́тренний двор

cousin ['kʌzn] n (also **first cousin**: male) двою́родный брат; (: female) двою́родная сестра́

cover ['kʌvər] vt закрыва́ть (perf закры́ть); (with cloth) укрыва́ть (perf укры́ть); (distance) покрыва́ть (perf покры́ть); (topic) рассма́тривать (perf рассмотре́ть); (include) охва́тывать (perf охвати́ть); (Press) освеща́ть (perf освети́ть) ▷ n (for furniture, machinery) чехо́л; (of book etc) обло́жка; (shelter) укры́тие; **covers** npl (for bed) посте́льное бельё ntsg; **he was covered in** or **with** (mud) он был покры́т +instr; **to take cover** укрыва́ться (perf укры́ться); **under cover** в укры́тии; **under cover of darkness** под покро́вом темноты́; **cover up** vt закрыва́ть (perf закры́ть) ▷ vi (fig): **to cover up for sb** покрыва́ть (perf покры́ть) кого́-н; **coverage** n освеще́ние

cow [kau] n (also inf!) коро́ва (also !)

coward ['kauəd] n трус(и́ха); **cowardly** adj трусли́вый

cowboy ['kaubɔı] n ковбо́й

cozy ['kəuzı] adj (US) = **cosy**

crab [kræb] n краб

crack [kræk] n (noise) треск; (gap) щель f; (in dish, wall) тре́щина ▷ vt (whip, twig) щёлкать (perf щёлкнуть) +instr; (dish etc) раска́лывать (perf расколо́ть); (nut) коло́ть (perf расколо́ть); (problem) реша́ть (perf реши́ть); (code) разга́дывать (perf разгада́ть); (joke) отпуска́ть (perf отпусти́ть)

crackle ['krækl] vi потре́скивать (impf)

cradle ['kreıdl] n (crib) колыбе́ль f

craft [krɑːft] n (trade) ремесло́; (boat: pl inv) кора́бль f; **craftsman** irreg n реме́сленник; **craftsmanship** n (quality) вы́делка; (skill) мастерство́

cram [kræm] vt: **to cram sth with** набива́ть (perf наби́ть) что-н +instr; **to cram sth into** вти́скивать (perf вти́снуть) что-н в +acc

cramp [kræmp] n су́дорога; **cramped** adj те́сный

crane [kreın] n (Tech) (подъёмный) кран

crash [kræʃ] n (noise) гро́хот; (of car) ава́рия; (of plane, train) круше́ние ▷ vt разбива́ть (perf разби́ть) ▷ vi разбива́ться (perf разби́ться); (two cars) ста́лкиваться (perf столкну́ться); **crash course** n интенси́вный курс; **crash helmet** n защи́тный шлем

crate [kreıt] n деревя́нный я́щик; (for bottles) упако́вочный я́щик

crave [kreıv] vt, vi: **to crave sth** or **for sth** жа́ждать (impf) чего́-н

crawl [krɔːl] vi (move) по́лзать/ползти́ (impf) ▷ n (Sport) кроль f

craze [kreız] n пова́льное увлече́ние

crazy ['kreızı] adj сумасше́дший; **he's crazy about skiing** (inf) он поме́шан на лы́жах; **to go crazy** помеша́ться (perf)

cream [kriːm] n сли́вки pl; (cosmetic) крем ▷ adj (colour) кре́мовый; **creamy** adj (taste) сли́вочный

crease [kriːs] n (fold) скла́дка; (: in trousers) стре́лка; (in dress, on brow) морщи́на

create [kriː'eıt] vt (impression) создава́ть (созда́ть perf); (invent) твори́ть (impf), создава́ть (perf созда́ть)

creation [kriː'eıʃən] n созда́ние; (Rel) сотворе́ние

creative [kriː'eıtıv] adj тво́рческий

creature ['kriːtʃər] n (animal) существо́; (person) созда́ние

crèche [kreʃ] n (де́тские) я́сли pl

credentials [krı'denʃlz] npl (references) квалифика́ция f; (for identity) рекоменда́тельное письмо́ ntsg, рекоменда́ция fsg

credibility [kredı'bılıtı] n (see adj) правдоподо́бность f; авторите́т

credible ['krɛdɪbl] *adj* вероя́тный, правдоподо́бный; (*person*) авторите́тный

credit ['krɛdɪt] *n* (*Comm*) креди́т; (*recognition*) до́лжное *nt adj* ▷ *vt* (*Comm*) кредитова́ть (*impf/perf*); **to credit sb with sth** (*sense etc*) припи́сывать (*perf* приписа́ть) кому́-н что-н; **credits** *npl* (*Cinema, TV*) ти́тры *mpl*; **credit card** *n* креди́тная ка́рточка; **credit crunch** *n* креди́тный кри́зис

creek [kri:k] *n* у́зкий зали́в; (*US: stream*) руче́й

creep [kri:p] (*pt, pp* **crept**) *vi* (*person, animal*) кра́сться (*impf*) ▷ *n* (*inf*) подхали́м(ка)

crept [krɛpt] *pt, pp of* **creep**

crescent ['krɛsnt] *n* полуме́сяц

cress [krɛs] *n* кресс-сала́т

crest [krɛst] *n* (*of hill*) гре́бень *m*; (*of bird*) хохоло́к, гребешо́к; (*coat of arms*) герб

crew [kru:] *n* экипа́ж; (*TV, Cinema*) съёмочная гру́ппа

cricket ['krɪkɪt] *n* (*game*) кри́кет; (*insect*) сверчо́к

crime [kraɪm] *n* преступле́ние; (*illegal activity*) престу́пность *f*

criminal ['krɪmɪnl] *n* престу́пник(-ица) ▷ *adj* (*illegal*) престу́пный

crimson ['krɪmzn] *adj* мали́новый, тёмно-кра́сный

cripple ['krɪpl] *n* (*inf!*) кале́ка *m/f* ▷ *vt* (*person*) кале́чить (*perf* искале́чить)

crisis ['kraɪsɪs] (*pl* **crises**) *n* кри́зис

crisp [krɪsp] *adj* (*food*) хрустя́щий; (*weather*) све́жий; (*reply*) чёткий; **crisps** *npl* (*Brit*) чи́псы *pl*

criterion [kraɪ'tɪərɪən] (*pl* **criteria**) *n* крите́рий

critic ['krɪtɪk] *n* кри́тик; **critical** *adj* крити́ческий; (*person, opinion*) крити́чный; **he is critical** (*Med*) он в крити́ческом состоя́нии; **criticism** ['krɪtɪsɪzəm] *n* кри́тика; (*of book, play*) крити́ческий разбо́р; **criticize** ['krɪtɪsaɪz] *vt* критикова́ть (*impf*)

Croatia [krəu'eɪʃə] *n* Хорва́тия

crockery ['krɔkərɪ] *n* посу́да

crocodile ['krɔkədaɪl] *n* крокоди́л

crocus ['krəukəs] *n* шафра́н

crook [kruk] *n* (*criminal*) жу́лик; **crooked** ['krukɪd] *adj* криво́й; (*dishonest*) жуликова́тый; (*business*) жу́льнический

crop [krɔp] *n* (*сельскохозя́йственная*) культу́ра; (*harvest*) урожа́й; (*also* **riding crop**) плеть *f*

cross [krɔs] *n* крест; (*mark*) кре́стик; (*Bio*) по́месь *f* ▷ *vt* пересека́ть (*perf* пересе́чь), переходи́ть (*perf* перейти́); (*cheque*) кросси́ровать (*impf/perf*); (*arms etc*) скре́щивать (*perf* скрести́ть) ▷ *adj* серди́тый; **cross out** *vt* вычёркивать (*perf* вы́черкнуть); **crossing** *n*

перепра́ва; (*also* **pedestrian crossing**) перехо́д; **crossroads** *n* перекрёсток; **crossword** *n* кроссво́рд

crotch [krɔtʃ] *n* проме́жность *f*; **the trousers are tight in the crotch** брю́ки жмут в шагу́

crouch [krautʃ] *vi* приседа́ть (*perf* присе́сть)

crow [krəu] *n* (*bird*) воро́на

crowd [kraud] *n* толпа́; **crowded** *adj* (*area*) перенаселённый; **the room was crowded** ко́мната была́ полна́ люде́й; **crowdfunding** *n* краудфа́ндинг

crown [kraun] *n* коро́на; (*of head*) маку́шка; (*of hill*) верши́на; (*of tooth*) коро́нка ▷ *vt* коронова́ть (*impf/perf*); **the Crown** (Брита́нская) Коро́на

crucial ['kru:ʃl] *adj* реша́ющий; (*work*) ва́жный

crude [kru:d] *adj* (*materials*) сыро́й; (*fig: basic*) примити́вный; (*: vulgar*) гру́бый

cruel ['kruəl] *adj* жесто́кий; **cruelty** *n* жесто́кость *f*

cruise [kru:z] *n* круи́з ▷ *vi* крейси́ровать (*impf*)

crumb [krʌm] *n* (*of cake etc*) кро́шка

crumble ['krʌmbl] *vt* крощи́ть (*perf* раскроши́ть) ▷ *vi* осыпа́ться (*perf* осы́паться); (*fig*) ру́шиться (*perf* ру́хнуть)

crunch [krʌntʃ] *vt* (*food etc*) грызть (*perf* разгры́зть) ▷ *n* (*fig*): **the crunch** крити́ческий *or* реша́ющий моме́нт; **crunchy** *adj* хрустя́щий

crush [krʌʃ] *vt* (*squash*) выжима́ть (*perf* вы́жать); (*crumple*) мять (*perf* смять); (*defeat*) сокруша́ть (*perf* сокруши́ть); (*upset*) уничтожа́ть (*perf* уничто́жить) ▷ *n* (*crowd*) да́вка; **to have a crush on sb** сходи́ть (*impf*) с ума́ по кому́-н

crust [krʌst] *n* ко́рка; (*of earth*) кора́

crutch [krʌtʃ] *n* (*Med*) косты́ль *m*

cry [kraɪ] *vi* пла́кать (*impf*); (*also* **cry out**) крича́ть (*perf* кри́кнуть) ▷ *n* крик

crystal ['krɪstl] *n* (*glass*) хруста́ль; (*Chem*) криста́лл

cub [kʌb] *n* детёныш

Cuba ['kju:bə] *n* Ку́ба

cube [kju:b] *n* (*also Math*) куб ▷ *vt* возводи́ть (*perf* возвести́) в куб

cubicle ['kju:bɪkl] *n* (*at pool*) каби́нка

cuckoo ['kuku:] *n* куку́шка

cucumber ['kju:kʌmbə] *n* огуре́ц

cuddle ['kʌdl] *vt* обнима́ть (*perf* обня́ть) ▷ *vi* обнима́ться (*perf* обня́ться) ▷ *n* ла́ска

cue [kju:] *n* кий; (*Theat*) ре́плика

cuff [kʌf] *n* (*of sleeve*) манже́та; (*US: of trousers*) отворо́т; (*blow*) шлепо́к; **off the cuff** экспро́мтом

cuisine [kwɪ'zi:n] *n* ку́хня (*ку́шанья*)

cul-de-sac ['kʌldəsæk] *n* тупи́к

culprit ['kʌlprɪt] *n* (*person*) вино́вник(-вница)

cult [kʌlt] *n* (*also Rel*) культ

cultivate ['kʌltɪveɪt] vt (crop, feeling) культиви́ровать (impf); (land) возде́лывать (impf)

cultural ['kʌltʃərəl] adj культу́рный

culture ['kʌltʃər] n культу́ра

cunning ['kʌnɪŋ] n хи́трость f ▷ adj (crafty) хи́трый

cup [kʌp] n ча́шка; (as prize) ку́бок; (of bra) ча́шечка

cupboard ['kʌbəd] n шкаф

curator [kjuə'reɪtər] n храни́тель m

curb [kə:b] vt (powers etc) обу́здывать (perf обузда́ть) ▷ n (US: kerb) бордю́р

cure [kjʊəl] vt вылёчивать (perf вы́лечить); (Culin) обраба́тывать (perf обрабо́тать) ▷ n лека́рство; (solution) сре́дство

curfew ['kə:fju:] n коменда́нтский час

curiosity [kjuərɪ'ɔsɪtɪ] n (see adj) любопы́тство; любозна́тельность f

curious ['kjuərɪəs] adj любопы́тный; (interested) любозна́тельный

curl [kə:l] n (of hair) локон, завито́к ▷ vt (hair) завива́ть (perf зави́ть); (: tightly) закру́чивать (perf закрути́ть) ▷ vi (hair) ви́ться (impf); **curly** adj выющийся

currant ['kʌrnt] n (dried grape) изю́минка; **currants** (dried grapes) кишми́ш

currency ['kʌrnsɪ] n валю́та

current ['kʌrnt] n (of air, water) пото́к; (Elec) ток ▷ adj (present) теку́щий, совреме́нный; (accepted) общепри́нятый; **current account** n (Brit) теку́щий счёт; **current affairs** npl теку́щие собы́тия ntpl; **currently** adv в да́нный or настоя́щий моме́нт

curriculum [kə'rɪkjuləm] n (pl **curriculums** or **curricula**) n (Scol) (учёбная) програ́мма; **curriculum vitae** [kənkjuləm'vi:taɪ] n автобиогра́фия

curry ['kʌrɪ] n блю́до с ка́рри

curse [kə:s] n прокля́тие; (swearword) руга́тельство

curt [kə:t] adj ре́зкий

curtain ['kə:tn] n за́навес; (light) занаве́ска

curve [kə:v] n изги́б

cushion ['kuʃən] n поду́шка ▷ vt смягча́ть (perf смягчи́ть)

custard ['kʌstəd] n заварно́й крем

custody ['kʌstədɪ] n опёка; **to take into custody** брать (perf взять) под стра́жу

custom ['kʌstəm] n (traditional) тради́ция; (convention) обы́чай; (habit) привы́чка

customer ['kʌstəmər] n (of shop) покупа́тель(ница) m(f); (of business) клие́нт, зака́зчик

customs ['kʌstəmz] npl тамо́жня fsg

cut [kʌt] (pt, pp **cut**) vt (bread, meat) ре́зать (perf разре́зать); (hand, knee) ре́зать (perf поре́зать); (grass, hair) стричь (perf постри́чь); (text) сокраща́ть (perf

сократи́ть); (spending, supply) уре́зывать (perf уре́зать); (prices) снижа́ть (perf сни́зить) ▷ vi ре́зать (impf) ▷ n (in skin) поре́з; (in salary, spending) сниже́ние; (of meat) кусо́к; **cut down** vt (tree) сруба́ть (perf сруби́ть); (consumption) сокраща́ть (perf сократи́ть); **cut off** vt отреза́ть (perf отре́зать); (electricity, water) отключа́ть (perf отключи́ть); (Tel) разъединя́ть (perf разъедини́ть); **cut out** vt (remove) выреза́ть (perf вы́резать); (stop) прекраща́ть (perf прекрати́ть); **cut up** vt разреза́ть (perf разре́зать)

cute [kju:t] adj (sweet) ми́лый, преле́стный

cutlery ['kʌtlərɪ] n столо́вый прибо́р

cut-price (US **cut-rate**) adj по сни́женной цене́

cut-rate adj (US) = **cut-price**

cutting ['kʌtɪŋ] adj (edge) о́стрый; (remark etc) язви́тельный ▷ n (Brit: Press) вы́резка; (from plant) черено́к

CV n abbr = **curriculum vitae**

cyberbullying ['saɪbəbulɪɪŋ] n тра́вля в Интерне́те, кибербу́ллинг

cyberspace ['saɪbəspeɪs] n киберпростра́нство

cycle ['saɪkl] n цикл; (bicycle) велосипе́д

cyclone ['saɪkləun] n цикло́н

cylinder ['sɪlɪndər] n цили́ндр; (of gas) балло́н

cymbals ['sɪmblz] npl таре́лки fpl

cynical ['sɪnɪkl] adj цини́чный

Cyprus ['saɪprəs] n Кипр

cystitis [sɪs'taɪtɪs] n цисти́т

Czech [tʃɛk] adj че́шский ▷ n чех (че́шка); **Czech Republic** n: the Czech Republic Че́шская Респу́блика

D [diː] n (Mus) ре

dab [dæb] vt (eyes, wound) промокнуть (perf); (paint, cream) наносить (perf нанести)

dad [dæd] n (inf) папа m, папочка m; **daddy** n (inf) = dad

daffodil ['dæfədɪl] n нарцисс

daft [dɑːft] adj (ideas) дурацкий; (person) чокнутый

dagger ['dægəʳ] n кинжал

daily ['deɪlɪ] adj (dose) суточный; (routine) повседневный; (wages) дневной ⊳ n (also **daily paper**) ежедневная газета ⊳ adv ежедневно

dairy ['dɛərɪ] n (Brit: shop) молочный магазин; (for making butter) маслодельня; (for making cheese) сыроварня; **dairy farm** молочная ферма; **dairy products** молочные продукты mpl

daisy ['deɪzɪ] n маргаритка

dam [dæm] n дамба ⊳ vt перекрывать (perf перекрыть) дамбой

damage ['dæmɪdʒ] n (harm) ущерб; (dents etc) повреждение; (fig) вред ⊳ vt повреждать (perf повредить); (fig) вредить (perf повредить) +dat; **damages** npl (Law) компенсация fsg

damn [dæm] vt осуждать (perf осудить) ⊳ adj (inf. also **damned**) проклятый ⊳ n (inf): **I don't give a damn** мне плевать; **damn (it)!** чёрт возьми or побери!

damp [dæmp] adj (building, wall) сырой; (cloth) влажный ⊳ n сырость f ⊳ vt (also **dampen**) смачивать (perf смочить); (: fig) охлаждать (perf охладить)

dance [dɑːns] n танец; (social event) танцы mpl ⊳ vi танцевать (impf); **dancer** n танцовщик(-ица); (for fun) танцор

dandelion ['dændɪlaɪən] n одуванчик

danger ['deɪndʒəʳ] n опасность f; "danger!" "опасно!"; **he is in danger of losing his job** ему грозит потеря работы; **dangerous** adj опасный

Danish ['deɪnɪʃ] adj датский ⊳ npl: the **Danish** датчане

dare [dɛəʳ] vt: to dare sb to do вызывать (perf вызвать) кого-н +infin ⊳ vi: to dare (to) do сметь (perf посметь) +infin; I dare say смею заметить

daring ['dɛərɪŋ] adj (audacious) дерзкий; (bold) смелый

dark [dɑːk] adj тёмный; (complexion) смуглый ⊳ n: in the dark в темноте; **dark blue** etc тёмно-синий etc; **after dark** после наступления темноты; **darkness** n темнота; **darkroom** n тёмная комната, проявительная лаборатория

darling ['dɑːlɪŋ] adj дорогой(-ая) m(f) adj

dart [dɑːt] n (in game) дротик (для игры в дарт); (in sewing) вытачка; **darts** n дарт

dash [dæʃ] n (drop) капелька; (sign) тире nt ind ⊳ vt (throw) швырять (perf швырнуть); (shatter: hopes) разрушать (perf разрушить), разбивать (perf разбить) ⊳ vi: to dash towards рвануться (perf) к +dat

dashboard ['dæʃbɔːd] n (Aut) приборная панель f

dashcam ['dæʃkæm] n автомобильный видеорегистратор, видеорегистратор

data ['deɪtə] npl данные pl adj; **database** n база данных

date [deɪt] n (day) число, дата; (with friend) свидание; (fruit) финик ⊳ vt датировать (impf/perf); (person) встречаться (impf) с +instr; **date of birth** дата рождения; **to date** на сегодняшний день; **out of date** устарелый; (expired) просроченный; **up to date** современный; **dated** adj устарелый

daughter ['dɔːtəʳ] n дочь f; **daughter-in-law** n сноха

daunting ['dɔːntɪŋ] adj устрашающий

dawn [dɔːn] n (of day) рассвет

day [deɪ] n (period) сутки pl, день m; (daylight) день; (heyday) время nt; **the day before** накануне; **the day after** на следующий день; **the day after tomorrow** послезавтра; **the day before yesterday** позавчера; **the following day** на следующий день; **by day** днём; **daylight** n дневной свет; **day return** n (Brit) обратный билет (действительный в течение одного дня); **daytime** n день m

dazzle ['dæzl] vt (blind) ослеплять (perf ослепить)

DC abbr (= direct current) постоянный ток

dead [dɛd] adj мёртвый; (arm, leg) онемелый ⊳ adv (inf: completely) абсолютно; (inf: directly) прямо ⊳ npl: **the dead** мёртвые pl adj; (in accident, war) погибшие pl adj; **the battery is dead** батарейка села; **the telephone is dead** телефон отключился; **to shoot sb dead** застрелить (perf) кого-н; **dead tired** смертельно усталый or уставший; **dead end** n тупик; **deadline** n последний or предельный срок; **deadly** adj (lethal) смертоносный; **Dead Sea** n: the Dead Sea Мёртвое море

deaf [dɛf] adj (totally) глухой

deal [di:l] (pt, pp **dealt**) n (agreement) сделка ▷ vt (blow) наносить (perf нанести); (cards) сдавать (perf сдать); **a great deal (of)** очень много (+gen); **deal in** vt fus (Comm, drugs) торговать (impf) +instr; **deal with** vt fus иметь (impf) дело с +instr; (problem) решать (perf решить); (subject) заниматься (perf заняться) +instr; **dealt** [dɛlt] pt, pp of **deal**

dean [di:n] n (Scol) декан

dear [dɪəʳ] adj дорогой ▷ n: (my) dear (to man, boy) дорогой (мой); (to woman, girl) дорогая (моя) ▷ excl: dear me! о, Господи!; Dear Sir уважаемый господин; Dear Mrs Smith дорогая or уважаемая миссис Смит; **dearly** adv (love) очень; (pay) дорого

death [dɛθ] n смерть f; **death penalty** n смертная казнь f

debate [dɪ'beɪt] n дебаты pl ▷ vt (topic) обсуждать (perf обсудить)

debit ['dɛbɪt] vt: to debit a sum to sb or to sb's account дебетовать (impf/perf) сумму с кого-н or с чьего-н счёта; see also **direct debit**

debris ['dɛbriː] n обломки mpl, развалины fpl

debt [dɛt] n (sum) долг; to be in debt быть (impf) в долгу

debug ['di:bʌg] vt (Comput) отлаживать (perf отладить) +gen

decade ['dɛkeɪd] n десятилетие

decaffeinated [dɪ'kæfɪneɪtɪd] adj: decaffeinated coffee кофе без кофеина

decay [dɪ'keɪ] n разрушение

deceased [dɪ'siːst] n: the deceased покойный(-ая) m(f) adj

deceit [dɪ'siːt] n обман

deceive [dɪ'siːv] vt обманывать (perf обмануть)

December [dɪ'sɛmbəʳ] n декабрь m

decency ['diːsənsɪ] n (propriety) благопристойность f

decent ['diːsənt] adj (wages, meal) приличный; (behaviour, person) порядочный

deception [dɪ'sɛpʃən] n обман

deceptive [dɪ'sɛptɪv] adj обманчивый

decide [dɪ'saɪd] vt (settle) решать (perf решить) ▷ vi: to decide to do/that решать (perf решить) +infin/, что; to decide on останавливаться (perf остановиться) на +prp

decision [dɪ'sɪʒən] n решение

decisive [dɪ'saɪsɪv] adj решительный

deck [dɛk] n (Naut) палуба; (of cards) колода; (also record deck) проигрыватель m; top deck (of bus) верхний этаж; **deckchair** n шезлонг

declaration [dɛklə'reɪʃən] n (statement) декларация; (of war) объявление

declare [dɪ'klɛəʳ] vt (state) объявлять (perf объявить); (for tax) декларировать (impf/perf)

decline [dɪ'klaɪn] n (drop) падение; (in strength) упадок; (lessening) уменьшение; to be in or on the decline быть (impf) в упадке

decorate ['dɛkəreɪt] vt (room etc) отделывать (perf отделать); (adorn): to decorate (with) украшать (perf украсить) +instr

decoration [dɛkə'reɪʃən] n (on tree, dress) украшение; (medal) награда

decorator ['dɛkəreɪtəʳ] n обойщик

decrease ['diːkriːs] vt уменьшать (perf уменьшить) ▷ vi уменьшаться (perf уменьшиться) ▷ n: decrease (in) уменьшение (+gen)

decree [dɪ'kriː] n постановление

dedicate ['dɛdɪkeɪt] vt: to dedicate to посвящать (perf посвятить) +dat

dedication [dɛdɪ'keɪʃən] n (devotion) преданность f; (in book etc) посвящение

deduction [dɪ'dʌkʃən] n (conclusion) умозаключение; (subtraction) вычитание; (amount) вычет

deed [di:d] n (feat) деяние, поступок; (Law) акт

deep [di:p] adj глубокий; (voice) низкий ▷ adv: the spectators stood 20 deep зрители стояли в 20 рядов; the lake is 4 metres deep глубина озера — 4 метра; deep blue etc тёмно-синий etc; **deeply** adv глубоко

deer [dɪəʳ] n inv олень m

defeat [dɪ'fiːt] n поражение ▷ vt наносить (perf нанести) поражение +dat

defect ['diːfɛkt] n (in product) дефект; (of plan) недостаток; **defective** [dɪ'fɛktɪv] adj (goods) дефектный

defence [dɪ'fɛns] (US **defense**) n защита; (Mil) оборона

defend [dɪ'fɛnd] vt защищать (perf защитить); (Law) защищать (impf); **defendant** n подсудимый(-ая) m(f) adj, обвиняемый(-ая) m(f) adj; (in civil case) ответчик(-ица); **defender** n защитник

defense (US) = **defence**

defensive [dɪ'fɛnsɪv] adj (weapons, measures) оборонительный; (behaviour, manner) вызывающий ▷ n: he was on the defensive он был готов к обороне

defer [dɪ'fəːʳ] vt отсрочивать (perf отсрочить)

defiance [dɪ'faɪəns] n вызов; in defiance of вопреки +dat

defiant [dɪ'faɪənt] adj (person, reply) дерзкий; (tone) вызывающий

deficiency [dɪ'fɪʃənsɪ] n (lack) нехватка

deficient [dɪ'fɪʃənt] adj: to be deficient in (lack) испытывать (impf) недостаток в +prp

deficit ['dɛfɪsɪt] n (Comm) дефицит

define [dɪ'faɪn] vt определя́ть (perf
определи́ть); (word etc) дава́ть (perf дать)
определе́ние +dat

definite ['dɛfɪnɪt] adj определённый; **he
was definite about it** его́ мне́ние на э́тот
счёт бы́ло определённым; **definitely**
adv определённо; (certainly) несомне́нно

definition [dɛfɪ'nɪʃən] n (of word)
определе́ние

deflate [di:'fleɪt] vt (tyre, balloon)
спуска́ть (perf спусти́ть)

deflect [dɪ'flɛkt] vt (shot) отража́ть (perf
отрази́ть); (criticism) отклоня́ть (perf
отклони́ть); (attention) отвлека́ть (perf
отвле́чь)

defuse [di:'fju:z] vt разряжа́ть (perf
разряди́ть)

defy [dɪ'faɪ] vt (resist) оспа́ривать (perf
оспо́рить); (fig: description etc) не
поддава́ться (impf) +dat; **to defy sb to do**
(challenge) призыва́ть (perf призва́ть)
кого́-н +infin

degree [dɪ'gri:] n (extent) сте́пень f; (unit
of measurement) гра́дус; (Scol) (учёная)
сте́пень; **by degrees** постепе́нно; **to some
degree, to a certain degree** до не́которой
сте́пени

delay [dɪ'leɪ] vt (decision, event)
откла́дывать (perf отложи́ть); (person,
plane etc) заде́рживать (perf задержа́ть)
▷ vi ме́длить (impf) ▷ n заде́ржка; **to be
delayed** заде́рживаться (impf); **without
delay** незамедли́тельно

delegate [n 'dɛlɪgɪt, vb 'dɛlɪgeɪt] n
делега́т ▷ vt (task) поруча́ть (perf
поручи́ть)

deliberate [adj dɪ'lɪbərɪt, vb dɪ'lɪbəreɪt]
adj (intentional) наме́ренный; (slow)
нетороплйвый ▷ vi совеща́ться (impf);
(person) разду́мывать (impf);
deliberately adv (see adj) наме́ренно,
наро́чно; нетороплйво

delicacy ['dɛlɪkəsɪ] n то́нкость f; (food)
деликате́с

delicate ['dɛlɪkɪt] adj то́нкий; (problem)
деликатный; (health) хру́пкий

delicatessen [dɛlɪkə'tɛsn] n
гастроно́мия, магазин деликате́сов

delicious [dɪ'lɪʃəs] adj о́чень вку́сный;
(smell) восхити́тельный

delight [dɪ'laɪt] n (feeling) восто́рг ▷ vt
ра́довать (perf пора́довать); **to take (a)
delight in** находи́ть (impf) удово́льствие в
+prp; **delighted** adj: **(to be) delighted (at
or with)** (быть) (impf) в восто́рге (от
+gen); **he was delighted to see her** он был
рад ви́деть её

delightful adj восхити́тельный

delinquent [dɪ'lɪŋkwənt] adj
престу́пный

deliver [dɪ'lɪvəʳ] vt (goods) доставля́ть
(perf доста́вить); (letter) вруча́ть (perf
вручи́ть); (message) передава́ть (perf
переда́ть); (speech) произноси́ть (perf

произнести́); (baby) принима́ть (perf
приня́ть); **delivery** n (of goods)
доста́вка; (of baby) ро́ды pl; **to take
delivery of** получа́ть (perf получи́ть)

delusion [dɪ'lu:ʒən] n заблужде́ние

demand [dɪ'mɑ:nd] vt тре́бовать (perf
потре́бовать) +gen ▷ n (request, claim)
тре́бование; (Econ): **demand (for)** спрос
(на +acc); **to be in demand** (commodity)
по́льзоваться (impf) спро́сом; **on demand**
по тре́бованию; **demanding** adj (boss)
тре́бовательный; (child) тру́дный; (work:
requiring effort) тяжёлый

demise [dɪ'maɪz] n (fig) упа́док

demo ['dɛməu] n abbr (inf)
= **demonstration**

democracy [dɪ'mɔkrəsɪ] n (system)
демокра́тия; (country) демократи́ческая
страна́

democrat ['dɛməkræt] n демокра́т;
Democrat (US) член па́ртии демокра́тов;
democratic [dɛmə'krætɪk] adj
демократи́ческий; **Democratic Party** (US)
па́ртия демокра́тов

demolish [dɪ'mɔlɪʃ] vt сноси́ть (perf
снести́); (argument) разгроми́ть (perf)

demolition [dɛmə'lɪʃən] n (see vb) снос;
разгро́м

demon ['di:mən] n де́мон

demonstrate ['dɛmənstreɪt] vt
демонстри́ровать (perf
продемонстри́ровать) ▷ vi: **to
demonstrate (for/against)**
демонстри́ровать (impf) (за +acc/про́тив
+gen)

demonstration [dɛmən'streɪʃən] n
демонстра́ция

den [dɛn] n (of animal, person) ло́гово

denial [dɪ'naɪəl] n отрица́ние; (refusal)
отка́з

denim ['dɛnɪm] n джи́нсовая ткань f;
denims npl (jeans) джи́нсы pl

Denmark ['dɛnmɑ:k] n Да́ния

denounce [dɪ'nauns] vt (condemn)
осужда́ть (perf осуди́ть); (inform on)
доноси́ть (perf донести́) на +acc

dense [dɛns] adj (smoke, foliage etc)
густо́й; (inf: person) тупо́й

density ['dɛnsɪtɪ] n пло́тность f; **single/
double-density disk** диск с одина́рной/
двойно́й пло́тностью

dent [dɛnt] n (in metal) вмя́тина ▷ vt
(also **make a dent in**: car etc) оставля́ть
(perf оста́вить) вмя́тину на +acc

dental ['dɛntl] adj зубно́й

dentist ['dɛntɪst] n зубно́й врач,
стомато́лог

dentures ['dɛntʃəz] npl зубно́й проте́з
msg

deny [dɪ'naɪ] vt отрица́ть (impf);
(allegation) отверга́ть (perf отве́ргнуть);
(refuse): **to deny sb sth** отка́зывать (perf
отказа́ть) кому́-н в чём-н

deodorant [di:'əudərənt] n дезодора́нт

depart [dɪˈpɑːt] vi (person) отбывать (perf отбыть); (bus, train) отправляться (perf отправиться); (plane) улетать (perf улететь); **to depart from** (fig) отклоняться (perf отклониться) от +gen

department [dɪˈpɑːtmənt] n (in shop) отдел; (Scol) отделение; (Pol) ведомство, департамент; **department store** n универсальный магазин, универмаг

departure [dɪˈpɑːtʃəʳ] n (see vi) отъезд; отправление; вылет; **departure lounge** n зал вылета

depend [dɪˈpɛnd] vi: **to depend on** зависеть (impf) от +gen; (trust) полагаться (perf положиться) на +acc; **it depends** смотря по обстоятельствам, как получится; **depending on ...** в зависимости от +gen ...; **dependent** adj; **dependent (on)** зависимый (от +gen) ▷ n иждивенец(-нка)

depict [dɪˈpɪkt] vt изображать (perf изобразить)

deport [dɪˈpɔːt] vt депортировать (impf/perf), высылать (perf выслать)

deposit [dɪˈpɔzɪt] n (in account) депозит, вклад; (down payment) первый взнос, задаток; (of ore, oil) залежь f ▷ vt (money) помещать (perf поместить); (bag) сдавать (perf сдать); **deposit account** n депозитный счёт

depot [ˈdɛpəu] n (storehouse) склад; (for buses) парк; (for trains) депо nt ind; (US: station) станция

depress [dɪˈprɛs] vt (Psych) подавлять (impf), угнетать (impf); **depressed** adj (person) подавленный, угнетённый; (prices) сниженный; **depressed area** район, переживающий экономический упадок; **depressing** adj (news, outlook) удручающий; **depression** [dɪˈprɛʃən] n депрессия; (Meteorology) область f низкого давления

deprive [dɪˈpraɪv] vt: **to deprive sb of** лишать (perf лишить) кого-н +gen; **deprived** adj бедный; (family, child) обездоленный

depth [dɛpθ] n глубина; **in the depths of despair** в глубоком отчаянии; **to be out of one's depth** (in water) не доставать (impf) до дна

deputy [ˈdɛpjutɪ] n заместитель m; (Pol) депутат ▷ cpd: **deputy chairman** заместитель председателя; **deputy head** (Brit: Scol) заместитель директора

derelict [ˈdɛrɪlɪkt] adj заброшенный

derive [dɪˈraɪv] vt: **to derive (from)** (pleasure) получать (perf получить) (от +gen); (benefit) извлекать (perf извлечь) (из +gen)

descend [dɪˈsɛnd] vt (stairs) спускаться (perf спуститься) по +dat; (hill) спускаться (perf спуститься) с +gen ▷ vi (go down) спускаться (perf спуститься); **descendant** n потомок

descent [dɪˈsɛnt] n спуск; (Aviat) снижение; (origin) происхождение

describe [dɪsˈkraɪb] vt описывать (perf описать)

description [dɪsˈkrɪpʃən] n описание; (sort) род

desert [n ˈdɛzət, vb dɪˈzəːt] n пустыня ▷ vt покидать (perf покинуть) ▷ vi (Mil) дезертировать (impf/perf)

deserve [dɪˈzəːv] vt заслуживать (perf заслужить)

design [dɪˈzaɪn] n дизайн; (process: of dress) моделирование; (sketch: of building) проект; (pattern) рисунок ▷ vt (house, kitchen) проектировать (perf спроектировать); (product, test) разрабатывать (perf разработать)

designate [ˈdɛzɪgneɪt] vt (nominate) назначать (perf назначить); (indicate) обозначать (perf обозначить)

designer [dɪˈzaɪnəʳ] n (also **fashion designer**) модельер; (Art) дизайнер; (of machine) конструктор

desirable [dɪˈzaɪərəbl] adj (proper) желательный

desire [dɪˈzaɪəʳ] n желание ▷ vt (want) желать (impf)

desk [dɛsk] n (in office, study) (письменный) стол; (for pupil) парта; (in hotel, at airport) стойка; (Brit: also **cash desk**) касса

despair [dɪsˈpɛəʳ] n отчаяние ▷ vi: **to despair of sth/doing** отчаиваться (perf отчаяться) в чём-н/+infin

despatch [dɪsˈpætʃ] n, vt = **dispatch**

desperate [ˈdɛspərɪt] adj (action, situation) отчаянный; (criminal) отъявленный; **to be desperate** (person) быть (impf) в отчаянии; **to be desperate to do** жаждать (impf) +infin; **to be desperate for money** крайне нуждаться (impf) в деньгах; **desperately** adv отчаянно; (very) чрезвычайно

desperation [dɛspəˈreɪʃən] n отчаяние

despise [dɪsˈpaɪz] vt презирать (impf)

despite [dɪsˈpaɪt] prep несмотря на +acc

dessert [dɪˈzəːt] n десерт

destination [dɛstɪˈneɪʃən] n (of person) цель f; (of mail) место назначения

destined [ˈdɛstɪnd] adj: **he is destined to do** ему суждено +infin; **to be destined for** предназначаться (impf) для +gen

destiny [ˈdɛstɪnɪ] n судьба

destroy [dɪsˈtrɔɪ] vt уничтожать (perf уничтожить), разрушать (perf разрушить)

destruction [dɪsˈtrʌkʃən] n уничтожение, разрушение

destructive [dɪsˈtrʌktɪv] adj (capacity, force) разрушительный; (criticism) сокрушительный; (emotion) губительный

detached [dɪˈtætʃt] adj беспристрастный; **detached house** особняк

detail [ˈdiːteɪl] n подробность f, деталь f

▷ vt перечисля́ть (perf перечи́слить); **in detail** подро́бно, в деталя́х; **detailed** adj дета́льный, подро́бный

detain [dɪ'teɪn] vt заде́рживать (perf задержа́ть); (in hospital) оставля́ть (perf оста́вить)

detect [dɪ'tɛkt] vt обнару́живать (perf обнару́жить); (sense) чу́вствовать (perf почу́вствовать); **detection** [dɪ'tɛkʃən] n (discovery) обнаруже́ние; **detective** n сы́щик, детекти́в

detention [dɪ'tɛnʃən] n (imprisonment) содержа́ние под стра́жей; (arrest) задержа́ние; (Scol): **to give sb detention** оставля́ть (perf оста́вить) кого́-н по́сле уро́ков

● **DETENTION**
●
● В брита́нских шко́лах дете́й,
● наруша́ющих дисципли́ну, в ка́честве
● наказа́ния мо́гут оста́вить по́сле уро́ков
● в шко́ле.

deter [dɪ'təːʳ] vt уде́рживать (perf удержа́ть)

detergent [dɪ'təːdʒənt] n мо́ющее сре́дство

deteriorate [dɪ'tɪərɪəreɪt] vi ухудша́ться (perf ухудши́ться)

determination [dɪtəːmɪ'neɪʃən] n (resolve) реши́мость f; (establishment) установле́ние

determine [dɪ'təːmɪn] vt (find out) устана́вливать (perf установи́ть); (establish, dictate) определя́ть (perf определи́ть); **determined** adj реши́тельный, волево́й; **determined to do** по́лный реши́мости +infin

deterrent [dɪ'tɛrənt] n сре́дство сде́рживания, сде́рживающее сре́дство; **nuclear deterrent** сре́дство я́дерного сде́рживания

detour ['diːtuəʳ] n (also US) объе́зд

detract [dɪ'trækt] vi: **to detract from** умаля́ть (perf умали́ть)

detrimental [dɛtrɪ'mɛntl] adj: **detrimental to** вре́дный для +gen

devastating ['dɛvəsteɪtɪŋ] adj (weapon, storm) разруши́тельный; (news, effect) ошеломля́ющий

develop [dɪ'vɛləp] vt (idea, industry) развива́ть (perf разви́ть); (plan, resource) разраба́тывать (perf разрабо́тать); (land) застра́ивать (perf застро́ить); (Phot) проявля́ть (perf прояви́ть) ▷ vi (evolve, advance) развива́ться (perf разви́ться); (appear) проявля́ться (perf прояви́ться); **development** n разви́тие; (of resources) разрабо́тка; (of land) застро́йка

device [dɪ'vaɪs] n (apparatus) устро́йство, прибо́р

devil ['dɛvl] n дья́вол, чёрт

devious ['diːvɪəs] adj (person) лука́вый

devise [dɪ'vaɪz] vt разраба́тывать (perf разрабо́тать)

devote [dɪ'vəut] vt: **to devote sth to** посвяща́ть (perf посвяти́ть) что-н +dat; **devoted** adj (admirer, partner) пре́данный; **his book is devoted to Scotland** его́ кни́га посвящена́ Шотла́ндии

devotion [dɪ'vəuʃən] n пре́данность f; (Rel) поклоне́ние

devout [dɪ'vaut] adj (Rel) благочести́вый

dew [djuː] n роса́

diabetes [daɪə'biːtiːz] n диабе́т

diabetic [daɪə'bɛtɪk] n диабе́тик

diagnose [daɪəg'nəuz] vt (illness) диагности́ровать (impf/perf); (problem) определя́ть (perf определи́ть)

diagnosis [daɪəg'nəusɪs] (pl **diagnoses**) n диа́гноз

diagonal [daɪ'ægənl] adj диагона́льный

diagram ['daɪəgræm] n схе́ма

dial ['daɪəl] n (of clock) цифербла́т; (of radio) регуля́тор настро́йки ▷ vt (number) набира́ть (perf набра́ть)

dialect ['daɪəlɛkt] n диале́кт

dialling tone ['daɪəlɪŋ-] (US **dial tone**) n непреры́вный гудо́к

dialogue ['daɪəlɔg] (US **dialog**) n диало́г

diameter [daɪ'æmɪtəʳ] n диа́метр

diamond ['daɪəmənd] n алма́з; (cut diamond) бриллиа́нт; (shape) ромб; **diamonds** npl (Cards) бу́бны fpl

diaper ['daɪəpəʳ] n (US) подгу́зник

diarrhoea [daɪə'riːə] (US **diarrhea**) n поно́с

diary ['daɪərɪ] n (journal) дневни́к; (engagements book) ежедне́вник

dice [daɪs] npl inv (in game) ку́бик ▷ vt (perf наре́зать) ку́биками

dictate [dɪk'teɪt] vt диктова́ть (perf продиктова́ть)

dictator [dɪk'teɪtəʳ] n дикта́тор

dictionary ['dɪkʃənrɪ] n слова́рь m

did [dɪd] pt of **do**

didn't ['dɪdnt] = **did not**

die [daɪ] vi (person, emotion) умира́ть (perf умере́ть); (smile, light) угаса́ть (perf уга́снуть); **to be dying for sth/to do** до сме́рти хоте́ть (impf) чего́-н/+infin

diesel ['diːzl] n ди́зель m; (also **diesel oil**) ди́зельное то́пливо

diet ['daɪət] n дие́та

differ ['dɪfəʳ] vi: **to differ (from)** отлича́ться (impf) (от +gen); (disagree): **to differ about** расходи́ться (perf разойти́сь) в вопро́се +gen; **difference** n разли́чие; (in size, age) ра́зница; (disagreement) разногла́сие; **different** adj друго́й, ино́й; (various) разли́чный, ра́зный; **to be different from** отлича́ться (impf) от +gen; **differentiate** [dɪfə'rɛnʃɪeɪt] vi: **to differentiate (between)** проводи́ть (perf провести́) разли́чие (ме́жду +instr); **differently** adv (otherwise) ина́че,

по-дру́гому; (*in different ways*)
по-ра́зному

difficult ['dɪfɪkəlt] *adj* тру́дный,
тяжёлый; **difficulty** *n* тру́дность *f*,
затрудне́ние

dig [dɪg] (*pt, pp* **dug**) *vt* (*hole*) копа́ть (*perf*
вы́копать), рыть (*perf* вы́рыть); (*garden*)
копа́ть (*perf* вскопа́ть) ▷ *n* (*prod*) толчо́к;
(*excavation*) раско́пки *fpl*; **to dig one's nails
into** впива́ться (*perf* впи́ться) ногтя́ми в
+*acc*; **dig up** (*plant*) выка́пывать (*perf*
вы́копать); (*information*) раска́пывать
(*perf* раскопа́ть)

digest [daɪ'dʒɛst] *vt* (*food*) перева́ривать
(*perf* перевари́ть); (*facts*) усва́ивать (*perf*
усво́ить); **digestion** [dɪ'dʒɛstʃən] *n*
пищеваре́ние

digit ['dɪdʒɪt] *n* (*number*) ци́фра; **digital**
adj: **digital watch** электро́нные часы́ *mpl*

dignified ['dɪgnɪfaɪd] *adj* по́лный
досто́инства

dignity ['dɪgnɪtɪ] *n* досто́инство

dilemma [daɪ'lɛmə] *n* диле́мма

dilute [daɪ'luːt] *vt* (*liquid*) разбавля́ть
(*perf* разба́вить)

dim [dɪm] *adj* (*outline, memory*) сму́тный;
(*light*) ту́склый; (*room*) пло́хо
освещённый ▷ *vt* (*light*) приглуша́ть
(*perf* приглуши́ть)

dimension [daɪ'mɛnʃən] *n*
(*measurement*) измере́ние; (*also pl*: *scale,
size*) разме́ры *mpl*; (*aspect*) аспе́кт

diminish [dɪ'mɪnɪʃ] *vi* уменьша́ться (*perf*
уме́ньшиться)

din [dɪn] *n* гро́хот

dine [daɪn] *vi* обе́дать (*perf* пообе́дать);
diner *n* (*person*) обе́дающий(-ая) *m(f)
adj*; (*US*) дешёвый рестора́н

dinghy ['dɪŋgɪ] *n* (*also* **sailing dinghy**)
шлю́пка; (*also* **rubber dinghy**) надувна́я
ло́дка

dingy ['dɪndʒɪ] *adj* (*streets, room*)
мра́чный; (*clothes, curtains etc*)
замы́зганный

dining room ['daɪnɪŋ-] *n* столо́вая *f adj*

dinner ['dɪnəʳ] *n* (*evening meal*) у́жин;
(*lunch, banquet*) обе́д; **dinner jacket** *n*
смо́кинг; **dinner party** *n* зва́ный обе́д

dinosaur ['daɪnəsɔːʳ] *n* диноза́вр

dip [dɪp] *n* (*depression*) впа́дина; (*Culin*)
со́ус ▷ *vt* (*immerse*) погружа́ть (*perf*
погрузи́ть), окуна́ть (*perf* окуну́ть); (: *in
liquid*) мака́ть (*perf* макну́ть), обма́кивать
(*perf* обмакну́ть); (*Brit: Aut: lights*)
приглуша́ть (*perf* приглуши́ть) ▷ *vi*
(*ground, road*) идти́ (*perf* пойти́) под
укло́н; **to go for a dip** окуна́ться (*perf*
окуну́ться)

diploma [dɪ'pləumə] *n* дипло́м

diplomacy [dɪ'pləuməsɪ] *n* диплома́тия

diplomat ['dɪpləmæt] *n* диплома́т;
diplomatic [dɪplə'mætɪk] *adj* (*Pol*)
дипломати́ческий; (*tactful*)
дипломати́чный

dire [daɪəʳ] *adj* (*consequences*) злове́щий;
(*poverty, situation*) жу́ткий

direct [daɪ'rɛkt] *adj* прямо́й ▷ *adv*
пря́мо ▷ *vt* (*company, project etc*)
руководи́ть (*impf*) +*instr*; (*play, film*)
ста́вить (*perf* поста́вить); **to direct
(towards** *or* **at)** (*attention, remark*)
направля́ть (*perf* напра́вить) (на +*acc*); **to
direct sb to do** (*order*) веле́ть (*impf*)
кому́-н +*infin*; **can you direct me to ...?** Вы
не ука́жете, где нахо́дится ...?; **direct
debit** *n* (*Brit: Comm*) прямо́е дебетова́ние

direction [dɪ'rɛkʃən] *n* (*way*)
направле́ние; **directions** *npl*
(*instructions*) указа́ния *ntpl*; **to have a
good sense of direction** хорошо́
ориенти́роваться (*perf*); **directions for use**
инстру́кция

directly [dɪ'rɛktlɪ] *adv* пря́мо; (*at once*)
сейча́с же; (*as soon as*) как то́лько

director [dɪ'rɛktəʳ] *n* (*Comm*) дире́ктор;
(*of project*) руководи́тель *m*; (*TV, Cinema*)
режиссёр

directory [dɪ'rɛktərɪ] *n* спра́вочник

dirt [dəːt] *n* грязь *f*; **dirty** *adj* гря́зный
▷ *vt* па́чкать (*perf* испа́чкать)

disability [dɪsə'bɪlɪtɪ] *n*: (**physical**)
disability инвали́дность *f no pl*; **mental
disability** у́мственная неполноце́нность *f*

disabled [dɪs'eɪbld] *adj* (*mentally*)
у́мственно неполноце́нный; (*physically*):
disabled person инвали́д

disadvantage [dɪsəd'vɑːntɪdʒ] *n*
недоста́ток

disagree [dɪsə'griː] *vi* (*differ*)
расходи́ться (*perf* разойти́сь); **to disagree
(with)** (*oppose*) не соглаша́ться (*perf*
согласи́ться) (с +*instr*); **I disagree with you**
я с Ва́ми не согла́сен; **disagreement** *n*
разногла́сие; (*opposition*): **disagreement
with** несогла́сие с +*instr*

disappear [dɪsə'pɪəʳ] *vi* исчеза́ть (*perf*
исче́знуть); **disappearance** *n*
исчезнове́ние

disappoint [dɪsə'pɔɪnt] *vt*
разочаро́вывать (*perf* разочарова́ть);
disappointed *adj* разочаро́ванный;
disappointing *adj*: **the film is rather
disappointing** э́тот фильм не́сколько
разочаро́вывает; **disappointment** *n*
разочарова́ние

disapproval [dɪsə'pruːvəl] *n*
неодобре́ние

disapprove [dɪsə'pruːv] *vi*: **to disapprove
(of)** не одобря́ть (*impf*) (+*acc*)

disarm [dɪs'ɑːm] *vt* (*Mil*) разоружа́ть
(*perf* разоружи́ть); **disarmament** *n*
разоруже́ние

disaster [dɪ'zɑːstəʳ] *n* (*natural*) бе́дствие;
(*man-made, also fig*) катастро́фа

disastrous [dɪ'zɑːstrəs] *adj* губи́тельный

disbelief ['dɪsbə'liːf] *n* неве́рие

disc [dɪsk] *n* (*Anat*) межпозвоно́чный
хрящ; (*Comput*) = **disk**

discard [dɪsˈkɑːd] vt (object)
выбра́сывать (perf вы́бросить); (idea,
plan) отбра́сывать (perf отбро́сить)

discharge [vb dɪsˈtʃɑːdʒ, n ˈdɪstʃɑːdʒ] vt
(waste) выбра́сывать (perf вы́бросить);
(patient) выпи́сывать (perf вы́писать);
(employee) увольня́ть (perf уво́лить);
(soldier) демобилизова́ть (impf/perf) ▷ n
(Med) выделе́ние; (of patient) вы́писка; (of
employee) увольне́ние; (of soldier)
демобилиза́ция

discipline [ˈdɪsɪplɪn] n дисципли́на ▷ vt
дисциплини́ровать (impf/perf); (punish)
налага́ть (perf наложи́ть)
дисциплина́рное взыска́ние на +acc

disclose [dɪsˈkləuz] vt раскрыва́ть (perf
раскры́ть)

disco [ˈdɪskəu] n abbr (= discotheque)
дискоте́ка

discomfort [dɪsˈkʌmfət] n (unease)
нело́вкость f; (pain) недомога́ние

discontent [dɪskənˈtɛnt] n
недово́льство

discount [n ˈdɪskaunt, vb dɪsˈkaunt] n
ски́дка ▷ vt (Comm) снижа́ть (perf
сни́зить) це́ну на +acc; (idea, fact) не
принима́ть (perf приня́ть) в расчёт

discourage [dɪsˈkʌrɪdʒ] vt (dishearten)
препя́тствовать (perf воспрепя́тствовать);
to discourage sb from doing отгова́ривать
(perf отговори́ть) кого́-н +infin

discover [dɪsˈkʌvəʳ] vt обнару́живать
(perf обнару́жить); **discovery** n
откры́тие

discredit [dɪsˈkrɛdɪt] vt
дискредити́ровать (impf/perf)

discreet [dɪsˈkriːt] adj (tactful)
такти́чный; (careful) осмотри́тельный;
(barely noticeable) непримé́тный

discrepancy [dɪsˈkrɛpənsɪ] n
расхожде́ние

discretion [dɪsˈkrɛʃən] n (tact)
такти́чность f; **use your (own) discretion**
поступа́йте по своему́ усмотре́нию

discriminate [dɪsˈkrɪmɪneɪt] vi: **to
discriminate between** различа́ть (perf
различи́ть); **to discriminate against**
дискримини́ровать (impf/perf)

discrimination [dɪskrɪmɪˈneɪʃən] n
(bias) дискримина́ция; (discernment)
разбо́рчивость f

discuss [dɪsˈkʌs] vt обсужда́ть (perf
обсуди́ть); **discussion** [dɪsˈkʌʃən] n
(talk) обсужде́ние; (debate) диску́ссия

disease [dɪˈziːz] n боле́знь f

disgrace [dɪsˈɡreɪs] n позо́р ▷ vt
позо́рить (perf опозо́рить); **disgraceful**
adj позо́рный

disgruntled [dɪsˈɡrʌntld] adj
недово́льный

disguise [dɪsˈɡaɪz] n маскиро́вка ▷ vt
(object) маскирова́ть (perf
замаскирова́ть); **in disguise** (person)
переоде́тый; **to disguise (as)** (dress up)

переодева́ть (perf переоде́ть) (+instr);
(make up) гримирова́ть (perf
загримирова́ть) (под +acc)

disgust [dɪsˈɡʌst] n отвраще́ние ▷ vt
внуша́ть (perf внуши́ть) отвраще́ние +dat;
disgusting adj отврати́тельный

dish [dɪʃ] n блю́до; **to do** or **wash the
dishes** мыть (perf вы́мыть) посу́ду

dishonest [dɪsˈɔnɪst] adj нече́стный

dishwasher [ˈdɪʃwɔʃəʳ] n посудомо́ечная
маши́на

disillusion [dɪsɪˈluːʒən] vt
разочаро́вывать (perf разочарова́ть)

disinfectant [dɪsɪnˈfɛktənt] n
дезинфици́рующее сре́дство

disintegrate [dɪsˈɪntɪɡreɪt] vi (break up)
распада́ться (perf распа́сться)

disk [dɪsk] n диск

dislike [dɪsˈlaɪk] n (feeling) неприя́знь f
▷ vt не люби́ть (impf); **I dislike the idea**
мне не нра́вится э́та иде́я; **he dislikes
cooking** он не лю́бит гото́вить

dismal [ˈdɪzml] adj уны́лый, мра́чный;
(failure, performance) жа́лкий

dismantle [dɪsˈmæntl] vt разбира́ть
(perf разобра́ть)

dismay [dɪsˈmeɪ] n трево́га, смяте́ние
▷ vt приводи́ть (perf привести́) в
смяте́ние

dismiss [dɪsˈmɪs] vt (worker) увольня́ть
(perf уво́лить); (pupils, soldiers)
распуска́ть (perf распусти́ть); (Law)
прекраща́ть (perf прекрати́ть);
(possibility, idea) отбра́сывать (perf
отбро́сить); **dismissal** n (sacking)
увольне́ние

disorder [dɪsˈɔːdəʳ] n беспоря́док; (Med)
расстро́йство; **civil disorder** социа́льные
беспоря́дки

dispatch [dɪsˈpætʃ] vt (send) отправля́ть
(perf отпра́вить) ▷ n (sending) отпра́вка;
(Press) сообще́ние; (Mil) донесе́ние

dispel [dɪsˈpɛl] vt расе́ивать (perf
рассе́ять)

dispense [dɪsˈpɛns] vt (medicines)
приготовля́ть (perf пригото́вить);
dispense with vt fus обходи́ться (perf
обойти́сь) без +gen; **dispenser** n
торго́вый автома́т

disperse [dɪsˈpəːs] vt (objects)
рассе́ивать (perf рассе́ять); (crowd)
разгоня́ть (perf разогна́ть) ▷ vi
рассе́иваться (perf рассе́яться)

display [dɪsˈpleɪ] n демонстра́ция;
(exhibition) вы́ставка ▷ vt (emotion,
quality) выка́зывать (perf вы́казать);
(goods, exhibits) выставля́ть (perf
вы́ставить)

disposable [dɪsˈpəuzəbl] adj
однора́зовый

disposal [dɪsˈpəuzl] n (of goods)
реализа́ция; (of rubbish) удале́ние; **to
have sth at one's disposal** располага́ть
(impf) чем-н

dispose [dɪs'pəuz] *vi*: **dispose of**
избавля́ться (*perf* изба́виться) от +*gen*;
(*problem, task*) справля́ться (*perf*
спра́виться) с +*instr*

disposition [dɪspə'zɪʃən] *n* (*nature*) нрав

disproportionate [dɪsprə'pɔ:ʃənət] *adj*
(*excessive*) неопра́вданно большо́й;
disproportionate to несоизмери́мый с
+*instr*

dispute [dɪs'pju:t] *n* спор; (*domestic*)
ссо́ра; (*Law*) тя́жба ▷ *vt* оспа́ривать (*perf*
оспо́рить)

disregard [dɪsrɪ'gɑ:d] *vt* пренебрега́ть
(*perf* пренебре́чь)

disrupt [dɪs'rʌpt] *vt* наруша́ть (*perf*
нару́шить); **disruption** [dɪs'rʌpʃən] *n*
(*interruption*) наруше́ние

dissatisfaction [dɪssætɪs'fækʃən] *n*
недово́льство, неудовлетворённость *f*

dissatisfied [dɪs'sætɪsfaɪd] *adj*
неудовлетворённый; **dissatisfied (with)**
недово́льный (+*instr*)

dissent [dɪ'sɛnt] *n* инакомы́слие

dissolve [dɪ'zɔlv] *vt* (*substance*)
растворя́ть (*perf* раствори́ть);
(*organization, parliament*) распуска́ть (*perf*
распусти́ть); (*marriage*) расторга́ть (*perf*
расто́ргнуть) ▷ *vi* растворя́ться (*perf*
раствори́ться); **to dissolve in(to) tears**
залива́ться (*perf* зали́ться) слеза́ми

distance ['dɪstns] *n* (*in space*)
расстоя́ние; (*in sport*) диста́нция; (*in time*)
отдалённость *f*; **in the distance** вдалеке́,
вдали́; **from a distance** издалека́, и́здали

distant ['dɪstnt] *adj* (*place, time*) далёкий;
(*relative*) да́льний; (*manner*) отчуждённый

distinct [dɪs'tɪŋkt] *adj* (*clear*)
отчётливый; (*unmistakable*)
определённый; (*different*): **distinct (from)**
отли́чный (от +*gen*); **as distinct from** в
отли́чие от +*gen*; **distinction**
[dɪs'tɪŋkʃən] *n* (*difference*) отли́чие;
(*honour*) честь *f*; (*Scol*) ≈ "отли́чно";
distinctive *adj* своеобра́зный,
характе́рный; (*feature*) отличи́тельный

distinguish [dɪs'tɪŋgwɪʃ] *vt* различа́ть
(*perf* различи́ть); **to distinguish o.s.**
отлича́ться (*perf* отличи́ться);
distinguished *adj* ви́дный

distort [dɪs'tɔ:t] *vt* искажа́ть (*perf*
искази́ть)

distract [dɪs'trækt] *vt* отвлека́ть (*perf*
отвле́чь); **distracted** *adj* (*dreaming*)
невнима́тельный; (*anxious*)
встрево́женный;
distraction [dɪs'trækʃən] *n* (*diversion*)
отвлече́ние; (*amusement*) развлече́ние

distraught [dɪs'trɔ:t] *adj*: **distraught
(with)** обезу́мевший (от +*gen*)

distress [dɪs'trɛs] *n* отча́яние; (*through
pain*) страда́ние ▷ *vt* расстра́ивать (*perf*
расстро́ить), приводи́ть (*perf* привести́) в
отча́яние

distribute [dɪs'trɪbju:t] *vt* (*prizes*)

раздава́ть (*perf* разда́ть); (*leaflets*)
распространя́ть (*perf* распространи́ть);
(*profits, weight*) распределя́ть (*perf*
распредели́ть)

distribution [dɪstrɪ'bju:ʃən] *n* (*of goods*)
распростране́ние; (*of profits, weight*)
распределе́ние

distributor [dɪs'trɪbjutər] *n* (*Comm*)
дистрибью́тер

district ['dɪstrɪkt] *n* райо́н

distrust [dɪs'trʌst] *n* недове́рие ▷ *vt* не
доверя́ть (*impf*) +*dat*

disturb [dɪs'tə:b] *vt* (*person*) беспоко́ить
(*perf* побеспоко́ить); (*thoughts, peace*)
меша́ть (*perf* помеша́ть) +*dat*;
(*disorganize*) наруша́ть (*perf* нару́шить);
disturbance *n* расстро́йство; (*violent
event*) беспоря́дки *mpl*; **disturbed** *adj*
(*person: upset*) расстро́енный;
emotionally disturbed психи́чески
неуравнове́шенный; **disturbing** *adj*
трево́жный

ditch [dɪtʃ] *n* ров, кана́ва; (*for irrigation*)
кана́л ▷ *vt* (*inf: person, car*) броса́ть (*perf*
бро́сить); (: *plan*) забра́сывать (*perf*
забро́сить)

dive [daɪv] *n* (*from board*) прыжо́к (в
во́ду); (*underwater*) ныря́ние ▷ *vi* ныря́ть
(*impf*); **to dive into** (*bag, drawer etc*)
запуска́ть (*perf* запусти́ть) ру́ку в +*acc*;
(*shop, car etc*) ныря́ть (*perf* нырну́ть) в
+*acc*; **diver** *n* водола́з

diverse [daɪ'və:s] *adj* разнообра́зный

diversion [daɪ'və:ʃən] *n* (*Brit: Aut*)
объе́зд; (*of attention, funds*) отвлече́ние

diversity [daɪ'və:sɪtɪ] *n* разнообра́зие,
многообра́зие

divert [daɪ'və:t] *vt* (*traffic*) отводи́ть (*perf*
отвести́); (*funds, attention*) отвлека́ть (*perf*
отвле́чь)

divide [dɪ'vaɪd] *vt* (*split*) разделя́ть (*perf*
раздели́ть); (*Math*) раздела́ть (*perf*
раздели́ть); (*share out*) дели́ть (*perf*
подели́ть) ▷ *vi* дели́ться (*perf*
раздели́ться); (*road*) разделя́ться (*perf*
раздели́ться); **divided highway** *n* (*US*)
автотра́сса

divine [dɪ'vaɪn] *adj* боже́ственный

diving ['daɪvɪŋ] *n* ныря́ние; (*Sport*)
прыжки́ *mpl* в во́ду; **diving board** *n*
вы́шка (*для прыжко́в в во́ду*)

division [dɪ'vɪʒən] *n* (*also Math*) деле́ние;
(*sharing out*) разделе́ние; (*disagreement*)
разногла́сие; (*Comm*) подразделе́ние;
(*Mil*) диви́зия; (*Sport*) ли́га

divorce [dɪ'vɔ:s] *n* разво́д ▷ *vt* (*Law*)
разводи́ться (*perf* развести́сь) с +*instr*;
divorced *adj* разведённый; **divorcee**
[dɪvɔ:'si:] *n* разведённый(-ая) *m(f) adj*

DIY *n abbr* (*Brit*) (= *do-it-yourself*) сде́лай
сам

dizzy ['dɪzɪ] *adj*: **dizzy turn** *or* **spell**
при́ступ головокруже́ния

DJ *n abbr* (= *disc jockey*) диск-жоке́й

○ **KEYWORD**

do [du:] (*pt* **did**, *pp* **done**) *aux vb* **1** (*in negative constructions and questions*): **I don't understand** я не понима́ю; **she doesn't want it** она́ не хо́чет э́того; **didn't you know?** ра́зве Вы не зна́ли?; **what do you think?** что Вы ду́маете?

2 (*for emphasis*) действи́тельно; **she does look rather pale** она́ действи́тельно вы́глядит о́чень бле́дной; **oh do shut up!** да, замолчи́ же!

3 (*in polite expressions*) пожа́луйста; **do sit down** пожа́луйста, сади́тесь; **do take care!** пожа́луйста, береги́ себя́!

4 (*used to avoid repeating vb*): **she swims better than I do** она́ пла́вает лу́чше меня́ *or*, чем я; **do you read newspapers? — yes, I do/no, I don't** Вы чита́ете газе́ты? — да(, чита́ю)/нет(, не чита́ю); **she lives in Glasgow — so do I** она́ живёт в Гла́зго — и я то́же; **he didn't like it and neither did we** ему́ э́то не понра́вилось, и нам то́же; **who made this mess? — I did** кто здесь насори́л? — я; **he asked me to help him and I did** он попроси́л меня́ помо́чь ему́, что я и сде́лал

5 (*in tag questions*) не так *or* пра́вда ли? **you like him, don't you?** он Вам нра́вится, не так *or* пра́вда ли?; **I don't know him, do I?** я его́ не зна́ю, не так *or* пра́вда ли?

▷ *vt* **1** де́лать (*perf* сде́лать); **what are you doing tonight?** что Вы де́лаете сего́дня ве́чером?; **I've got nothing to do** мне не́чего де́лать; **what can I do for you?** чем могу́ быть поле́зен?; **we're doing "Othello" at school** (*studying*) мы прохо́дим "Оте́лло" в шко́ле; (*performing*) мы ста́вим "Оте́лло" в шко́ле; **to do one's teeth** чи́стить (*perf* почи́стить) зу́бы; **to do one's hair** причёсываться (*perf* причеса́ться); **to do the washing-up** мыть (*perf* помы́ть) посу́ду

2 (*Aut etc*): **the car was doing 100 (km/h)** маши́на шла со ско́ростью 100 км/ч; **we've done 200 km already** мы уже́ прое́хали 200 км; **he can do 100 km/h in that car** на э́той маши́не он мо́жет е́хать со ско́ростью 100 км/ч

▷ *vi* **1** (*act, behave*) де́лать (*perf* сде́лать); **do as I do** де́лайте, как я; **you did well to react so quickly** ты молоде́ц, что так бы́стро среаги́ровал

2 (*get on, fare*): **he's doing well/badly at school** он хорошо́/пло́хо у́чится; **the firm is doing well** дела́ в фи́рме иду́т успе́шно; **how do you do?** о́чень прия́тно

3 (*be suitable*) подходи́ть (*perf* подойти́); **will it do?** э́то подойдёт?

4 (*be sufficient*) хвата́ть (*perf* хвати́ть) +*gen*; **will ten pounds do?** деся́ти фу́нтов хва́тит?; **that'll do** э́того доста́точно; **that'll do!** (*in annoyance*) дово́льно!, хва́тит!; **to make do (with)** удовлетворя́ться (*perf* удовлетвори́ться) (+*instr*)

▷ *n* (*inf*): **we're having a bit of a do on Saturday** у нас бу́дет вечери́нка в суббо́ту; **it was a formal do** э́то был официа́льный приём

do away *vt fus* (*abolish*) поко́нчить (*perf*) с +*instr*

do up *vt* (*laces*) завя́зывать (*perf* завяза́ть); (*dress, buttons*) застёгивать (*perf* застегну́ть); (*room, house*) ремонти́ровать (*perf* отремонти́ровать)

do with *vt fus*: **I could do with a drink** я бы вы́пил чего́-нибудь; **I could do with some help** по́мощь мне бы не помеша́ла; **what has it got to do with you?** како́е э́то име́ет к Вам отноше́ние?; **I won't have anything to do with it** я не жела́ю име́ть к э́тому никако́го отноше́ния; **it has to do with money** э́то каса́ется де́нег

do without *vt fus* обходи́ться (*perf* обойти́сь) без +*gen*

dock [dɔk] *n* (*Naut*) док; (*Law*) скамья́ подсуди́мых; **docks** *npl* (*Naut*) док *msg*, верфь *fsg*

doctor ['dɔktə'] *n* (*Med*) врач; (*Scol*) до́ктор

document ['dɔkjumənt] *n* докуме́нт; **documentary** [dɔkju'mɛntəri] *n* документа́льный фильм; **documentation** [dɔkjumən'teɪʃən] *n* документа́ция

dodge [dɔdʒ] *vt* увёртываться (*perf* уверну́ться) от +*gen*

dodgy ['dɔdʒi] *adj* (*inf*): **dodgy character** подозри́тельный тип

does [dʌz] *vb see* **do**; **doesn't** ['dʌznt] = **does not**

dog [dɔg] *n* соба́ка ▷ *vt* пресле́довать (*impf*)

dole [dəul] *n* (*Brit*) посо́бие по безрабо́тице; **to be on the dole** получа́ть (*impf*) посо́бие по безрабо́тице

doll [dɔl] *n* (*also US: inf*) ку́кла

dollar ['dɔlə'] *n* до́ллар

dolphin ['dɔlfɪn] *n* дельфи́н

dome [dəum] *n* ку́пол

domestic [də'mɛstɪk] *adj* дома́шний; (*trade, politics*) вну́тренний; (*happiness*) семе́йный

dominant ['dɔmɪnənt] *adj* (*share, role*) преобла́дающий, домини́рующий; (*partner*) вла́стный

dominate ['dɔmɪneɪt] *vt* домини́ровать (*impf*) над +*instr*

dominoes ['dɔmɪnəuz] *n* (*game*) домино́ *nt ind*

donate [də'neɪt] *vt*: **to donate (to)** же́ртвовать (*perf* поже́ртвовать) (+*dat or* на +*acc*)

donation [də'neɪʃən] *n* поже́ртвование

done [dʌn] *pp of* **do**

donkey ['dɔŋkɪ] *n* осёл

donor ['dəunə'] *n* (*Med*) до́нор; (*to charity*) же́ртвователь(ница) *m(f)*

don't [dəunt] = **do not**

donut ['dəunʌt] n (US) = **doughnut**

doom [du:m] n рок ▷ vt: the plan was doomed to failure план был обречён на провал

door [dɔ:ʳ] n дверь f; **doorbell** n (дверной) звонок; **door handle** n дверная ручка; (of car) ручка двери; **doorstep** n порог; **doorway** n дверной проём

dope [dəup] n (inf: drug) гашиш; (: person) придурок ▷ vt (speck) вводить (perf ввести) наркотик +dat

dormitory ['dɔ:mɪtrɪ] n (room) общая спальня; (US: building) общежитие

DOS [dɔs] n abbr (Comput) (= disk operating system) ДОС (= дисковая операционная система), DOS

dosage ['dəusɪdʒ] n доза

dose [dəus] n (of medicine) доза

dot [dɔt] n точка; (speck) крапинка, пятнышко ▷ vt: dotted with усеянный +instr; on the dot минута в минуту

double ['dʌbl] adj двойной ▷ adv: to cost double стоить (impf) вдвое дороже ▷ n двойник ▷ vt удваивать (perf удвоить) ▷ vi (increase) удваиваться (perf удвоиться); on the double, or at the double (Brit) бегом; **double bass** n контрабас; **double bed** n двуспальная кровать f; **double-decker** n (also **double-decker bus**) двухэтажный автобус; **double glazing** n (Brit) двойные рамы fpl; **double room** n (in hotel) двухместный номер; **doubles** n (Tennis) пары fpl

doubt [daut] n сомнение ▷ vt сомневаться (impf); (mistrust) сомневаться (impf) в +prp, не доверять (impf) +dat; I doubt whether or if she'll come я сомневаюсь, что она придёт; **doubtful** adj сомнительный; **doubtless** adv несомненно

dough [dəu] n (Culin) тесто; **doughnut** (US **donut**) n пончик

dove [dʌv] n голубь m

down [daun] n (feathers) пух ▷ adv (motion) вниз; (position) внизу ▷ prep (towards lower level) (вниз) с +gen or по +dat; (along) (вдоль) по +dat ▷ vt (inf: drink) проглатывать (perf проглотить); down with the government! долой правительство!; **downfall** n падение; (from drinking etc) гибель f; **downhill** adv (face, look) вниз; to go downhill (person, business) идти (perf пойти) под гору; (road) идти (perf пойти) под уклон; **download** ['daunləud] n загрузка ▷ vt (Comput) загружать (perf загрузить) +gen; **downloadable** [daun'ləudəbl] adj (Comput) загружаемый; **downright** adj явный; (refusal) полный ▷ adv совершенно

Down's syndrome n синдром Дауна

down: **downstairs** adv (position) внизу; (motion) вниз; **downtown** adv (position) в центре; (motion) в центр; **downward** adj направленный вниз ▷ adv вниз; **downward trend** тенденция на понижение; **downwards** adv = **downward**

dozen ['dʌzn] n дюжина; a dozen books дюжина книг; **dozens of** десятки +gen

Dr abbr = **doctor**

drab [dræb] adj унылый

draft [drɑ:ft] n (first version) черновик; (US: Mil) призыв ▷ vt набрасывать (perf набросать); (proposal) составлять (perf составить); see also **draught**

drag [dræg] vt тащить (impf); (lake, pond) прочёсывать (perf прочесать) ▷ vi (time, event etc) тянуться (impf)

dragon ['drægn] n дракон; **dragonfly** n стрекоза

drain [dreɪn] n водосток, водоотвод; (fig): drain on (on resources) утечка +gen; (on health, energy) расход +gen ▷ vt (land, glass) осушать (perf осушить); (vegetables) сливать (perf слить); (wear out) утомлять (perf утомить) ▷ vi (liquid) стекать (perf стечь); **drainage** ['dreɪnɪdʒ] n (system) канализация; (process) дренаж, осушение; **draining board** (US **drainboard**) n сушка

drama ['drɑ:mə] n (also fig) драма; **dramatic** [drə'mætɪk] adj драматический; (increase etc) резкий; (change) разительный; **dramatist** n драматург

drank [dræŋk] pt of **drink**

drastic ['dræstɪk] adj (measure) решительный; (change) коренной

draught [drɑ:ft] (US **draft**) n (of air) сквозняк; on draught (beer) бочковое; **draughts** n (Brit) шашки pl

draw [drɔ:] (pt **drew**, pp **drawn**) vt (Art) рисовать (perf нарисовать); (Tech) чертить (perf начертить); (pull: cart) тащить (impf); (: curtains) задёргивать (perf задёрнуть); (gun, tooth) вырывать (perf вырвать); (attention) привлекать (perf привлечь); (crowd) собирать (perf собрать); (money) снимать (perf снять); (wages) получать (perf получить) ▷ vi (Sport) играть (perf сыграть) в ничью ▷ n (Sport) ничья; (lottery) лотерея; to draw near приближаться (perf приблизиться); **draw up** vi (train, bus etc) подъезжать (perf подъехать) ▷ vt (chair etc) придвигать (perf придвинуть); (document) составлять (perf составить); **drawback** n недостаток; **drawer** n ящик; **drawing** n (picture) рисунок; **drawing pin** n (Brit) (канцелярская) кнопка; **drawing room** n гостиная f adj

drawn [drɔ:n] pp of **draw**

dread [dred] n ужас ▷ vt страшиться (impf) +gen; **dreadful** adj ужасный, страшный

dream [dri:m] (pt, pp **dreamed** or **dreamt**) n сон; (ambition) мечта́ ▷ vt: I must have dreamt it мне э́то, наве́рное, присни́лось ▷ vi ви́деть (impf) сон; (wish) мечта́ть (impf)

dreary ['drɪərɪ] adj тоскли́вый

dress [drɛs] n (frock) пла́тье; (no pl: clothing) оде́жда ▷ vt одева́ть (perf оде́ть); (wound) перевя́зывать (perf перевяза́ть) ▷ vi одева́ться (perf оде́ться); **to get dressed** одева́ться (perf оде́ться); **dress up** vi наряжа́ться (perf наряди́ться); **dresser** n (Brit) буфе́т; (US: chest of drawers) туале́тный сто́лик; **dressing** n (Med) повя́зка; (Culin) запра́вка; **dressing gown** n (Brit) хала́т; **dressing room** n (Theat) (артисти́ческая) убо́рная f adj; (Sport) раздева́лка; **dressing table** n туале́тный сто́лик

drew [dru:] pt of **draw**

dried [draɪd] adj (fruit) сушёный; (milk) сухо́й

drift [drɪft] n (of current) ско́рость f; (of snow) зано́с, сугро́б; (meaning) смысл ▷ vi (boat) дрейфова́ть (impf); **snow had drifted over the road** доро́гу занесло́ сне́гом

drill [drɪl] n (drill bit) сверло́; (machine) дрель f; (: for mining etc) бура́в; (Mil) уче́ние ▷ vt (hole) сверли́ть (perf просверли́ть) ▷ vi (for oil) бури́ть (impf)

drink [drɪŋk] (pt **drank**, pp **drunk**) n напи́ток; (alcohol) (спиртно́й) напи́ток; (sip) глото́к ▷ vt пить (perf вы́пить) ▷ vi пить (impf); **to have a drink** вы́пить (perf); **I had a drink of water** я вы́пил воды́; **drink-driving** n вожде́ние в нетре́звом состоя́нии; **drinker** n пью́щий(-ая) m(f) adj; **drinking water** n питьева́я вода́

drip [drɪp] n ка́панье; (one drop) ка́пля; (Med) ка́пельница ▷ vi (water, rain) ка́пать (impf); **the tap is dripping** кран течёт

drive [draɪv] (pt **drove**, pp **driven**) n (journey) пое́здка; (also **driveway**) подъе́зд; (energy) напо́р; (campaign) кампа́ния; (Comput: also **disk drive**) дисково́д ▷ vt (vehicle) води́ть/вести́ (impf); (motor, wheel) приводи́ть (perf привести́) в движе́ние ▷ vi води́ть (perf вести́) (маши́ну); (travel) е́здить/е́хать (impf); **right-/left-hand drive** право-/левосторо́ннее управле́ние; **to drive sb to the airport** отвози́ть (perf отвезти́) кого́-н в аэропо́рт; **to drive sth into** (nail, stake) вбива́ть (perf вбить) что-н в +acc; **to drive sb mad** своди́ть (perf свести́) кого́-н с ума́; **driven** ['drɪvn] pp of **drive**; **driver** n води́тель m; (of train) машини́ст; **driver's license** n (US) (води́тельские) права́ nt pl; **driveway** n подъе́зд

driving ['draɪvɪŋ] n вожде́ние; **driving**

licence n (Brit) (води́тельские) права́ ntpl

drizzle ['drɪzl] n и́зморось f ▷ vi мороси́ть (impf)

drop [drɒp] n (of water) ка́пля; (reduction) паде́ние; (fall: distance) расстоя́ние (све́рху вниз) ▷ vt (object) роня́ть (perf урони́ть); (eyes) опуска́ть (perf опусти́ть); (voice, price) понижа́ть (perf пони́зить); (also **drop off**: passenger) выса́живать (perf вы́садить) ▷ vi па́дать (perf упа́сть); (wind) стиха́ть (perf сти́хнуть); **drops** npl (Med) ка́пли fpl; **drop off** vi (go to sleep) засыпа́ть (perf засну́ть); **drop out** vi (of game, deal) выходи́ть (perf вы́йти)

drought [draut] n за́суха

drove [drəuv] pt of **drive**

drown [draun] vt топи́ть (perf утопи́ть); (also **drown out**: sound) заглуша́ть (perf заглуши́ть) ▷ vi тону́ть (perf утону́ть)

drug [drʌg] n (Med) лека́рство; (narcotic) нарко́тик ▷ vt (person, animal) вводи́ть (perf ввести́) нарко́тик +dat; **to be on drugs** (impf) на нарко́тиках; **hard/ soft drugs** си́льные/сла́бые нарко́тики

● **DRUGSTORE**

● **Drugstore** — апте́ка. Америка́нские
● апте́ки сочета́ют в себе́ апте́ки и кафе́.
● В них продаю́т не то́лько лека́рства, но
● и космети́ческие това́ры, напи́тки и
● заку́ски.

drum [drʌm] n бараба́н; (for oil) бо́чка; **drums** npl (kit) уда́рные инструме́нты mpl; **drummer** n (in rock group) уда́рник

drunk [drʌŋk] pp of **drink** ▷ adj пья́ный ▷ n (also **drunkard**) пья́ница m/f; **drunkard** n (пья́ница m/f; **drunken** adj пья́ный

dry [draɪ] adj сухо́й; (lake, riverbed) вы́сохший; (humour) сде́ржанный; (lecture, subject) ску́чный ▷ vt (clothes, ground) суши́ть (perf вы́сушить); (surface) вытира́ть (perf вы́тереть) ▷ vi со́хнуть (perf вы́сохнуть); **dry-cleaner's** n химчи́стка

DSS n abbr (Brit) (= Department of Social Security) Министе́рство социа́льного обеспе́чения

dual ['djuəl] adj двойно́й; (function) дво́йственный; **dual carriageway** n (Brit) автотра́сса

dubious ['dju:bɪəs] adj сомни́тельный

Dublin ['dʌblɪn] n Ду́блин

duck [dʌk] n у́тка ▷ vi (also **duck down**) пригиба́ться (perf пригну́ться)

due [dju:] adj (expected) предполага́емый; (attention, consideration) до́лжный; **I am due £20** мне должны́ о́р полага́ется £20 ▷ n: **to give sb his** (or **her**) **due** отдава́ть (perf отда́ть) кому́-н до́лжное ▷ adv: **due north** пря́мо на се́вер; **dues** npl (for club etc) взно́сы *mpl*; **in due course** в своё вре́мя; **due to** из-за +*gen*; **he is due to go** он до́лжен идти́

duel ['djuəl] *n* дуэ́ль *f*

duet [dju:'ɛt] *n* дуэ́т

dug [dʌg] *pt, pp of* **dig**

duke [dju:k] *n* ге́рцог

dull [dʌl] *adj* (*light, colour*) ту́склый, мра́чный; (*sound*) глухо́й; (*pain, wit*) тупо́й; (*event*) ску́чный ▷ *vt* притупля́ть (*perf* притупи́ть)

dumb [dʌm] *adj* (*inf, pej: person*) тупо́й; (: *idea*) дура́цкий

dummy ['dʌmɪ] *n* (*tailor's model*) манеке́н; (*Brit: for baby*) со́ска, пусты́шка ▷ *adj* (*bullet*) холосто́й

dump [dʌmp] *n* (*also* **rubbish dump**) сва́лка; (*inf, pej: place*) дыра́ ▷ *vt* (*put down*) сва́ливать (*perf* свали́ть), выбра́сывать (*perf* вы́бросить); (*car*) броса́ть (*perf* бро́сить)

dungarees [dʌŋgə'ri:z] *npl* комбинезо́н *msg*

duplicate [*n, adj* 'dju:plɪkət, *vb* 'dju:plɪkeɪt] *n* дублика́т, ко́пия ▷ *adj* запасно́й ▷ *vt* копи́ровать (*perf* скопи́ровать); (*repeat*) дубли́ровать (*perf* продубли́ровать); **in duplicate** в двойно́м экземпля́ре

durable ['djuərəbl] *adj* про́чный

duration [djuə'reɪʃən] *n* продолжи́тельность *f*

during ['djuərɪŋ] *prep* (*in the course of*) во вре́мя +*gen*, в тече́ние +*gen*; (*from beginning to end*) в тече́ние +*gen*

dusk [dʌsk] *n* су́мерки *pl*

dust [dʌst] *n* пыль *f* ▷ *vt* вытира́ть (*perf* вы́тереть) пыль с +*gen*; **to dust with** (*cake etc*) посыпа́ть (*perf* посы́пать) +*instr*; **dustbin** *n* (*Brit*) му́сорное ведро́; **dusty** *adj* пы́льный

Dutch [dʌtʃ] *adj* голла́ндский ▷ *npl*: **the Dutch** голла́ндцы *mpl*; **they decided to go Dutch** (*inf*) они́ реши́ли, что ка́ждый бу́дет плати́ть за себя́

duty ['dju:tɪ] *n* (*responsibility*) обя́занность *f*; (*obligation*) долг; (*tax*) по́шлина; **on duty** на дежу́рстве; **off duty** вне слу́жбы; **duty-free** *adj* (*drink etc*) беспо́шлинный

duvet ['du:veɪ] *n* (*Brit*) одея́ло

dwarf [dwɔ:f] (*pl* **dwarves**) *n* (*inf!*) ка́рлик ▷ *vt* де́лать (*perf* сде́лать) кро́хотным; (*achievement*) умаля́ть (*perf* умали́ть)

dwell [dwɛl] (*pt, pp* **dwelt**) *vi* прожива́ть (*impf*); **dwell on** *vt fus* заде́рживаться (*perf* задержа́ться) на +*prp*

dye [daɪ] *n* краси́тель *m*, кра́ска ▷ *vt* кра́сить (*perf* покра́сить)

dying ['daɪɪŋ] *adj* (*person, animal*) умира́ющий

dynamic [daɪ'næmɪk] *adj* (*leader, force*) динами́чный

dynamite ['daɪnəmaɪt] *n* динами́т

E [i:] *n* (*Mus*) ми *nt ind*

each [i:tʃ] *adj, pron* ка́ждый; **each other** друг дру́га; **they hate each other** они́ ненави́дят друг дру́га; **they think about each other** они́ ду́мают друг о дру́ге; **they have two books each** у ка́ждого из них по две кни́ги

eager ['i:gəʳ] *adj* (*keen*) увлечённый; (*excited*) возбуждённый; **to be eager for/to do** жа́ждать (*impf*) +*gen*/+*infin*

eagle ['i:gl] *n* орёл

ear [ɪəʳ] *n* (*Anat*) у́хо; (*of corn*) ко́лос; **earache** *n* ушна́я боль *f*; **I have earache** у меня́ боли́т у́хо

earl [ə:l] *n* (*Brit*) граф

earlier ['ə:lɪəʳ] *adj* бо́лее ра́нний ▷ *adv* ра́ньше, ра́нее

early ['ə:lɪ] *adv* ра́но ▷ *adj* ра́нний; (*quick: reply*) незамедли́тельный; (*settlers*) пе́рвый; **early in the morning** ра́но у́тром; **to have an early night** ра́но ложи́ться (*perf* лечь) спать; **in the early spring, early in the spring** ра́нней весно́й; **in the early 19th century, early in the 19th century** в нача́ле 19-го ве́ка; **early retirement** *n*: **to take early retirement** ра́но уходи́ть (*perf* уйти́) на пе́нсию

earn [ə:n] *vt* (*salary*) зараба́тывать (*perf* зарабо́тать); (*interest*) приноси́ть (*perf* принести́); (*praise*) заслу́живать (*perf* заслужи́ть)

earnest ['ə:nɪst] *adj* (*person, manner*) серьёзный; (*wish, desire*) и́скренний; **in earnest** всерьёз

earnings ['ə:nɪŋz] *npl* за́работок *msg*

earring ['ɪərɪŋ] *n* серьга́

earth [ə:θ] *n* земля́; (*Brit: Elec*) заземле́ние ▷ *vt* (*Brit: Elec*) заземля́ть (*perf* заземли́ть); **Earth** (*planet*) Земля́; **earthquake** *n* землетрясе́ние

ease [i:z] *n* лёгкость *f*; (*comfort*) поко́й ▷ *vt* (*pain, problem*) облегча́ть (*perf* облегчи́ть); (tension) ослабля́ть (perf осла́бить); to ease sth into вставля́ть (perf вста́вить) что-н в +acc; to ease sth out of вынима́ть (perf вы́нуть) что-н из +gen; to ease o.s. into опуска́ться (perf опусти́ться) в +acc; at ease! (Mil) во́льно!

easily ['i:zɪlɪ] adv (see adj) легко́; непринуждённо; (without doubt) несомне́нно

east [i:st] n восто́к ▷ adj восто́чный ▷ adv на восто́к; **the East** Восто́к

Easter ['i:stə^r] n Па́сха; **Easter egg** n (chocolate) пасха́льное яйцо́

eastern ['i:stən] adj восто́чный

East Germany n (formerly) Восто́чная Герма́ния

easy ['i:zɪ] adj лёгкий; (manner) непринуждённый ▷ adv: **to take it** or **things easy** не напряга́ться (impf); **easy-going** adj (person) ужи́вчивый, покла́дистый

eat [i:t] (pt **ate**, pp **eaten**) vt есть (perf съесть) ▷ vi есть (impf)

EC n abbr (= European Community) ЕС (= Европе́йское соо́бщество)

ECB n abbr (= European Central Bank) Центра́льный банк Евро́пы

eccentric [ɪk'sɛntrɪk] adj эксцентри́чный

echo ['ɛkəu] (pl **echoes**) n э́хо ▷ vt (repeat) вто́рить (impf) +dat ▷ vi (sound) отдава́ться (perf отда́ться); **the room echoed with her laughter** в ко́мнате раздава́лся её смех

eclipse [ɪ'klɪps] n затме́ние

ecological [i:kə'lɔdʒɪkəl] adj экологи́ческий

ecology [ɪ'kɔlədʒɪ] n эколо́гия

economic [i:kə'nɔmɪk] adj экономи́ческий; (profitable) рента́бельный; **economical** adj эконо́мичный; (thrifty) эконо́мный; **economics** n (Scol) эконо́мика

economist [ɪ'kɔnəmɪst] n экономи́ст

economy [ɪ'kɔnəmɪ] n эконо́мика, хозя́йство; (financial prudence) эконо́мия; **economy class** n (Aviat) дешёвые поса́дочные места́

ecstasy ['ɛkstəsɪ] n (rapture) экста́з

ecstatic [ɛks'tætɪk] adj восто́рженный

eczema ['ɛksɪmə] n экзе́ма

edge [ɛdʒ] n край; (of knife etc) острие́ ▷ vt (trim) окаймля́ть (perf окайми́ть); **on edge** (fig) нерво́зный; **to edge away from** отходи́ть (perf отойти́) бочко́м от +gen

edgy ['ɛdʒɪ] adj нерво́зный

edible ['ɛdɪbl] adj съедо́бный

Edinburgh ['ɛdɪnbərə] n Эдинбу́рг

edit ['ɛdɪt] vt редакти́ровать (perf отредакти́ровать); (broadcast, film) монти́ровать (perf смонти́ровать); **edition** [ɪ'dɪʃən] n (of book) изда́ние; (of newspaper, programme) вы́пуск; **editor** n реда́ктор; (Press, TV) обозрева́тель m; **editorial** [ɛdɪ'tɔːrɪəl] adj редакцио́нный

▷ n редакцио́нная f adj (статья́)

educate ['ɛdjukeɪt] vt (teach) дава́ть (perf дать) образова́ние +dat; (instruct) просвеща́ть (perf просвети́ть)

education [ɛdju'keɪʃən] n (schooling) просвеще́ние, образова́ние; (teaching) обуче́ние; (knowledge) образова́ние; **educational** adj (institution) уче́бный; (staff) преподава́тельский; **educational policy** поли́тика в о́бласти просвеще́ния; **educational system** систе́ма образова́ния or просвеще́ния

eel [i:l] n у́горь m

eerie ['ɪərɪ] adj жу́ткий

effect [ɪ'fɛkt] n (result) эффе́кт; **to take effect** (drug) де́йствовать (perf подействовать); (law) вступа́ть (perf вступи́ть) в си́лу; **in effect** в су́щности; **effective** adj (successful) эффекти́вный; (actual) действи́тельный; **effectively** adv (successfully) эффекти́вно; (in reality) в су́щности, факти́чески

efficiency [ɪ'fɪʃənsɪ] n эффекти́вность f; де́льность f

efficient [ɪ'fɪʃənt] adj эффекти́вный; (person) де́льный

effort ['ɛfət] n уси́лие; (attempt) попы́тка; **effortless** adj (achievement) лёгкий

e.g. adv abbr (for example) (= exempli gratia) наприме́р

egg [ɛg] n яйцо́; **hard-boiled/soft-boiled egg** яйцо́ вкруту́ю/всмя́тку; **egg cup** n рю́мка для яйца́

ego ['i:gəu] n самолю́бие

Egypt ['i:dʒɪpt] n Еги́пет

eight [eɪt] n во́семь; **eighteen** n восемна́дцать; **eighteenth** [eɪ'ti:nθ] adj восемна́дцатый; **eighth** [eɪtθ] adj восьмо́й; **eightieth** adj восьмидеся́тый; **eighty** n во́семьдесят

Eire ['ɛərə] n Э́йре nt ind

either ['aɪðə^r] adj (one or other) любо́й (из двух); (both, each) ка́ждый ▷ adv та́кже ▷ pron: **either (of them)** любо́й (из них) ▷ conj: **either yes or no** ли́бо да, ли́бо нет; **on either side** на обе́их сторона́х; **I don't smoke — I don't either** я не курю́ — я то́же; **I don't like either** мне не нра́вится ни тот, ни друго́й; **there was no sound from either of the flats** ни из одно́й из кварти́р не доноси́лось ни зву́ка

elaborate [adj ɪ'læbərɪt, vb ɪ'læbəreɪt] adj сло́жный ▷ vt (expand) развива́ть (perf разви́ть); (refine) разраба́тывать (perf разрабо́тать) ▷ vi: **to elaborate on** (idea, plan) рассма́тривать (perf рассмотре́ть) в дета́лях

elastic [ɪ'læstɪk] n рези́нка ▷ adj (stretchy) эласти́чный

elbow ['ɛlbəu] n ло́коть m

elder ['ɛldə^r] adj ста́рший ▷ n (tree) бузина́; (older person): **elders** ста́ршие pl adj; **elderly** adj пожило́й ▷ npl: **the elderly** престаре́лые pl adj

eldest ['ɛldɪst] adj (са́мый) ста́рший ▷ n
ста́рший(-ая) m(f) adj

elect [ɪ'lɛkt] vt избира́ть (perf избра́ть)
▷ adj: **the president elect** и́збранный
президе́нт; **to elect to do** предпочита́ть
(perf предпоче́сть) +infin; **electoral** adj
избира́тельный; **electorate** n: **the
electorate** электора́т, избира́тели mpl

electric [ɪ'lɛktrɪk] adj электри́ческий;
electrical adj электри́ческий;
electrician [ɪlɛk'trɪʃən] n
электромонтёр, эле́ктрик; **electricity**
[ɪlɛk'trɪsɪtɪ] n электри́чество

electronic [ɪlɛk'trɔnɪk] adj электро́нный;
electronics n электро́ника

elegance ['ɛlɪɡəns] n элега́нтность f

elegant ['ɛlɪɡənt] adj элега́нтный

element ['ɛlɪmənt] n (also Chem)
элеме́нт; (of heater, kettle etc)
(электронагрева́тельный) элеме́нт; **the
elements** стихи́я fsg; **he is in his element**
он в свое́й стихи́и; **elementary**
[ɛlɪ'mɛntərɪ] adj элемента́рный; (school,
education) нача́льный

elephant ['ɛlɪfənt] n слон(и́ха)

elevator ['ɛlɪveɪtə^r] n (US) лифт

eleven [ɪ'lɛvn] n оди́ннадцать; **eleventh**
adj оди́ннадцатый

eligible ['ɛlɪdʒəbl] adj (for marriage)
подходя́щий; **to be eligible for** (qualified)
име́ть (impf) пра́во на +acc; (suitable)
подходи́ть (perf подойти́)

eliminate [ɪ'lɪmɪneɪt] vt исключа́ть (perf
исключи́ть); (team, contestant) выбива́ть
(perf вы́бить)

elm [ɛlm] n вяз

eloquent ['ɛləkwənt] adj (description,
person) красноречи́вый; (speech) я́ркий

else [ɛls] adv (other) ещё; **nothing else**
бо́льше ничего́; **somewhere else** (be)
где́-нибудь ещё; (go) куда́-нибудь ещё;
(come from) отку́да-нибудь ещё;
everywhere else везде́; **where else?**
(position) где ещё?; (motion) куда́ ещё?;
everyone else все остальны́е; **nobody else
spoke** бо́льше никто́ не говори́л; **or else
... а не то ...; **elsewhere** adv (be) в
друго́м or ино́м ме́сте; (go) в друго́е or
ино́е ме́сто

elusive [ɪ'lu:sɪv] adj неулови́мый

email ['i:meɪl] n электро́нная по́чта ▷ vt
(message) посыла́ть (perf посла́ть) по
электро́нной по́чте; **to email sb** писа́ть
(perf написа́ть) кому́-н по электро́нной
по́чте; **email address** а́дрес электро́нной
по́чты, электро́нный а́дрес

embankment [ɪm'bæŋkmənt] n (of
road, railway) на́сыпь f; (of river)
на́бережная f adj

embargo [ɪm'bɑ:gəu] (pl **embargoes**) n
эмба́рго nt ind

embark [ɪm'bɑ:k] vi: **to embark on**
(journey) отправля́ться (perf отпра́виться)
в +acc; (task) бра́ться (perf взя́ться);

(course of action) предпринима́ть (perf
предприня́ть)

embarrass [ɪm'bærəs] vt смуща́ть (perf
смути́ть); (Pol) ста́вить (perf поста́вить) в
затрудни́тельное положе́ние;
embarrassed adj смущённый;
embarrassing adj (position) нело́вкий,
неудо́бный; **embarrassment** n (feeling)
смуще́ние; (problem) затрудне́ние

embassy ['ɛmbəsɪ] n посо́льство

embrace [ɪm'breɪs] vt (person)
обня́ть; (include) охва́тывать (perf
охвати́ть) ▷ vi обнима́ться (impf)

embroidery n (stitching) вы́шивка;
(activity) вышива́ние

embryo ['ɛmbrɪəu] n (Bio) эмбрио́н

emerald ['ɛmərəld] n изумру́д

emerge [ɪ'mɜ:dʒ] vi (fact) всплыва́ть (perf
всплыть); (industry, society) появля́ться
(perf появи́ться); **to emerge from** (from
room, imprisonment) выходи́ть (perf
вы́йти) из +gen

emergency [ɪ'mɜ:dʒənsɪ] n
экстрема́льная ситуа́ция; **in an emergency**
в экстрема́льной ситуа́ции; **state of
emergency** чрезвыча́йное положе́ние;
emergency talks э́кстренные перегово́ры;
emergency exit n авари́йный вы́ход

emigrate ['ɛmɪgreɪt] vi эмигри́ровать
(impf/perf)

emigration [ɛmɪ'greɪʃən] n эмигра́ция

eminent ['ɛmɪnənt] adj ви́дный, зна́тный

emission [ɪ'mɪʃən] n (of gas) вы́брос; (of
radiation) излуче́ние

emoji [ɪ'məudʒɪ] n эмо́дзи nt ind

emoticon [ɪ'məutɪkɔn] n смайл

emotion [ɪ'məuʃən] n (feeling) чу́вство;
emotional adj эмоциона́льный; (issue)
волну́ющий

emphasis ['ɛmfəsɪs] (pl **emphases**) n
значе́ние; (in speaking) ударе́ние, акце́нт

emphasize ['ɛmfəsaɪz] vt подчёркивать
(perf подчеркну́ть)

empire ['ɛmpaɪə^r] n импе́рия

employ [ɪm'plɔɪ] vt нанима́ть (perf
наня́ть); (tool, weapon) применя́ть (perf
примени́ть); **employee** [ɪmplɔɪ'i:] n
рабо́тник; **employer** n работода́тель m;
employment n рабо́та; (availability of
jobs) за́нятость f

emptiness ['ɛmptɪnɪs] n пустота́

empty ['ɛmptɪ] adj пусто́й ▷ vt
(container) опорожня́ть (perf
опорожни́ть); (place, house etc)
опустоша́ть (perf опустоши́ть) ▷ vi
(house) пусте́ть (perf опусте́ть);
empty-handed adj с пусты́ми рука́ми

EMU n abbr = **European monetary union**

emulsion [ɪ'mʌlʃən] n (also **emulsion
paint**) эму́льсия, эмульсио́нная кра́ска

enable [ɪ'neɪbl] vt (make possible)
спосо́бствовать (impf) +dat; **to enable sb
to do** (allow) дава́ть (perf дать)
возмо́жность кому́-н +infin

enamel [ɪ'næməl] n эма́ль f

enchanting [ɪn'tʃɑːntɪŋ] adj обворожи́тельный

encl. abbr (on letters etc) (= enclosed, enclosure) приложе́ние

enclose [ɪn'kləuz] vt (land, space) огора́живать (perf огороди́ть); (object) заключа́ть (perf заключи́ть); **to enclose (with)** (letter) прилага́ть (perf приложи́ть) (к +dat); **please find enclosed a cheque for £100** здесь прилага́ется чек на £100

enclosure [ɪn'kləuzə'] n огоро́женное ме́сто

encore [ɔŋ'kɔː'] excl бис ⊳ n: **as an encore** на бис

encounter [ɪn'kauntə'] n встре́ча ⊳ vt встреча́ться (perf встре́титься) с +instr, (problem) ста́лкиваться (perf столкну́ться) с +instr

encourage [ɪn'kʌrɪdʒ] vt поощря́ть (perf поощри́ть); (growth) спосо́бствовать (impf) +dat; **to encourage sb to do** убежда́ть (impf) кого́-н +infin; **encouragement** n (see vt) поощре́ние; подде́ржка

encyclop(a)edia [ɛnsaɪkləu'piːdɪə] n энциклопе́дия

end [ɛnd] n коне́ц; (aim) цель f ⊳ vt (also **bring to an end, put an end to**) класть (perf положи́ть); коне́ц +dat, прекраща́ть (perf прекрати́ть) ⊳ vi (situation, activity, period) конча́ться (perf ко́нчиться); **in the end** в конце́ концо́в; **on end** (object) стоймя́; **for hours on end** часа́ми; **end up** vi: **to end up in** (place) ока́зываться (perf оказа́ться) в +prp; (in prison) угожда́ть (perf угоди́ть) в +prp; **we ended up taking a taxi** в конце́ концо́в мы взя́ли такси́

endanger [ɪn'deɪndʒə'] vt подверга́ть (perf подве́ргнуть) опа́сности; **an endangered species** вымира́ющий вид

endearing [ɪn'dɪərɪŋ] adj (smile) покоря́ющий; (person, behaviour) располага́ющий

endeavour [ɪn'dɛvə'] (US **endeavor**) n (attempt) попы́тка

ending ['ɛndɪŋ] n (of book etc) коне́ц

endless ['ɛndlɪs] adj бесконе́чный; (forest, beach) бескра́йний

endorse [ɪn'dɔːs] vt (cheque) распи́сываться (perf расписа́ться) на +prp; (document) де́лать (perf сде́лать) отме́тку на +prp; (proposal, candidate) подде́рживать (perf поддержа́ть); **endorsement** n (approval) подде́ржка; (Brit: Aut) отме́тка

endurance [ɪn'djuərəns] n выно́сливость f

endure [ɪn'djuə'] vt переноси́ть (perf перенести́) ⊳ vi вы́стоять (perf)

enemy ['ɛnəmɪ] adj вра́жеский; неприя́тельский ⊳ n враг; (opponent) проти́вник

energetic [ɛnə'dʒɛtɪk] adj энерги́чный

energy ['ɛnədʒɪ] n эне́ргия

enforce [ɪn'fɔːs] vt (law) следи́ть (impf) or проследи́ть perf за соблюде́нием (+gen)

engaged adj (couple) обручённый; (Brit: busy): **the line is engaged** ли́ния занята́; **he is engaged to** он обручён с +instr, **to get engaged** обруча́ться (perf обручи́ться)

engaged tone n (Brit: Tel) гудки́ pl "за́нято"

engagement n (appointment) договорённость f; (to marry) обруче́ние

engagement ring n обруча́льное кольцо́

engine ['ɛndʒɪn] n (Aut) дви́гатель m, мото́р; (Rail) локомоти́в

engineer [ɛndʒɪ'nɪə'] n (designer) инжене́р; (for repairs) меха́ник; (US: Rail) машини́ст; **engineering** n (Scol) инжене́рное де́ло; (design) техни́ческий диза́йн

England ['ɪŋglənd] n А́нглия

English ['ɪŋglɪʃ] adj англи́йский ⊳ n (Ling) англи́йский язы́к; ⊳ npl: **the English** (people) англича́не mpl; **Englishman** irreg n англича́нин

enhance [ɪn'hɑːns] vt (enjoyment, beauty) уси́ливать (perf уси́лить); (reputation) повыша́ть (perf повы́сить)

enjoy [ɪn'dʒɔɪ] vt люби́ть (impf); (have benefit of) облада́ть (impf) +instr, **to enjoy o.s.** хорошо́ проводи́ть (perf провести́) вре́мя; **to enjoy doing** люби́ть (impf) +infin; **enjoyable** adj прия́тный; **enjoyment** n удово́льствие

enlarge [ɪn'lɑːdʒ] vt увели́чивать (perf увели́чить) ⊳ vi: **to enlarge on** распространя́ться (impf) о +prp; **enlargement** n (Phot) увеличе́ние

enlist [ɪn'lɪst] vt (person) вербова́ть (perf завербова́ть); (support) заруча́ться (perf заручи́ться) +instr ⊳ vi: **to enlist in** (Mil) вербова́ться (perf завербова́ться) в +acc

enormous [ɪ'nɔːməs] adj грома́дный

enough [ɪ'nʌf] adj доста́точно +gen ⊳ pron доста́точно ⊳ adv: **big enough** доста́точно большо́й; **I've had enough!** с меня́ доста́точно or хва́тит!; **have you got enough work to do?** у Вас доста́точно рабо́ты?; **have you had enough to eat?** Вы нае́лись?; **that's enough, thanks** доста́точно, спаси́бо; **I've had enough of him** он мне надое́л; **enough!** дово́льно!; **strangely or oddly enough ...** как э́то ни стра́нно ...

enquire [ɪn'kwaɪə'] vt, vi = **inquire**

enrich [ɪn'rɪtʃ] vt обогаща́ть (perf обогати́ть)

en route [ɔn'ruːt] adv по пути́

ensure [ɪn'ʃuə'] vt обеспе́чивать (perf обеспе́чить)

entail [ɪn'teɪl] vt влечь (perf повле́чь) за собо́й

enter ['ɛntə'] vt (room, building) входи́ть

(*perf* войти́) в +*acc*; (*university, college*) поступа́ть (*perf* поступи́ть) в +*acc*; (*club, profession, contest*) вступа́ть (*perf* вступи́ть) в +*acc*; (*in book*) заноси́ть (*perf* занести́); (*Comput*) вводи́ть (*perf* ввести́) ▷ *vi* входи́ть (*perf* войти́); **to enter sb in** (*competition*) запи́сывать (*perf* записа́ть) кого́-н в +*acc*; **enter into** *vt fus* (*discussion, deal*) вступа́ть (*perf* вступи́ть) в +*acc*

enterprise ['ɛntəpraɪz] *n* (*company, undertaking*) предприя́тие; (*initiative*) предприи́мчивость *f*; **free/private enterprise** свобо́дное/ча́стное предпринима́тельство

enterprising ['ɛntəpraɪzɪŋ] *adj* (*person*) предприи́мчивый; (*scheme*) предпринима́тельский

entertain [ɛntə'teɪn] *vt* (*amuse*) развлека́ть (*perf* развле́чь); (*play host to*) принима́ть (*perf* приня́ть); (*idea*) разду́мывать (*impf*) над +*instr*; **entertainer** *n* эстра́дный арти́ст; **entertaining** *adj* занима́тельный, развлека́тельный; **entertainment** *n* (*amusement*) развлече́ние; (*show*) представле́ние

enthusiasm [ɪn'θu:zɪæzəm] *n* энтузиа́зм

enthusiastic [ɪnθu:zɪ'æstɪk] *adj*: **enthusiastic (about)** по́лный энтузиа́зма (по по́воду +*gen*)

entire [ɪn'taɪə'] *adj* весь; **entirely** *adv* по́лностью; (*for emphasis*) соверше́нно

entitled [ɪn'taɪtld] *adj*: **to be entitled to sth/to do** име́ть (*impf*) пра́во на что-н/+*infin*

entrance [*n* 'ɛntrns, *vb* ɪn'trɑ:ns] *n* (*way in*) вход; (*arrival*) появле́ние ▷ *vt* обвора́живать (*perf* обворожи́ть); **to gain entrance to** (*university*) поступа́ть (*perf* поступи́ть) в +*acc*; (*profession*) вступа́ть (*perf* вступи́ть) в +*acc*; **to make an entrance** появля́ться (*perf* появи́ться)

entrepreneur ['ɔntrəprə'nə:'] *n* предпринима́тель(ница) *m(f)*

entry ['ɛntrɪ] *n* вход; (*in register, accounts*) за́пись *f*; (*in reference book*) статья́; (*arrival: in country*) въезд; "**no entry**" "нет вхо́да"; (*Aut*) "нет въе́зда"

envelope ['ɛnvələup] *n* конве́рт

envious ['ɛnvɪəs] *adj* зави́стливый

environment [ɪn'vaɪərnmənt] *n* среда́; **the environment** окружа́ющая среда́; **environmental** [ɪnvaɪərn'mɛntl] *adj* экологи́ческий

envisage [ɪn'vɪzɪdʒ] *vt* предви́деть (*impf*)

envoy ['ɛnvɔɪ] *n* посла́нник

envy ['ɛnvɪ] *n* за́висть *f* ▷ *vt* зави́довать (*perf* позави́довать) +*dat*; **to envy sb sth** зави́довать (*perf* позави́довать) кому́-н из-за чего́-н

epic ['ɛpɪk] *n* эпопе́я; (*poem*) эпи́ческая поэ́ма ▷ *adj* эпоха́льный

epidemic [ɛpɪ'dɛmɪk] *n* эпиде́мия

epilepsy ['ɛpɪlɛpsɪ] *n* эпиле́псия

episode ['ɛpɪsəud] *n* эпизо́д

equal ['i:kwl] *adj* ра́вный; (*intensity, quality*) одина́ковый ▷ *n* ра́вный(-ая) *m(f)* *adj* ▷ *vt* (*number*) равня́ться (*impf*); **he is equal to** (*task*) ему́ по си́лам *or* по плечу́; **equality** [i:'kwɔlɪtɪ] *n* ра́венство, равнопра́вие; **equally** *adv* одина́ково; (*share*) по́ровну

equation [ɪ'kweɪʃən] *n* (*Math*) уравне́ние

equator [ɪ'kweɪtə'] *n* эква́тор

equip [ɪ'kwɪp] *vt*: **to equip (with)** (*person, army*) снаряжа́ть (*perf* снаряди́ть) (+*instr*); (*room, car*) обору́довать (*impf/perf*) (+*instr*); **to equip sb for** (*prepare*) гото́вить (*perf* подгото́вить) кого́-н к +*dat*; **equipment** *n* обору́дование

equivalent [ɪ'kwɪvələnt] *n* эквивале́нт ▷ *adj*: **equivalent (to)** эквивале́нтный (+*dat*)

era ['ɪərə] *n* э́ра

erase [ɪ'reɪz] *vt* стира́ть (*perf* стере́ть); **eraser** *n* рези́нка, ла́стик

erect [ɪ'rɛkt] *adj* (*posture*) прямо́й ▷ *vt* (*build*) воздвига́ть (*perf* воздви́гнуть), возводи́ть (*perf* возвести́); (*assemble*) ста́вить (*perf* поста́вить); **erection** [ɪ'rɛkʃən] *n* (*see vt*) возведе́ние; устано́вка; (*Physiol*) эре́кция

erosion [ɪ'rəuʒən] *n* эро́зия

erotic [ɪ'rɔtɪk] *adj* эроти́ческий

erratic [ɪ'rætɪk] *adj* (*attempts*) беспоря́дочный; (*behaviour*) сумасбро́дный

error ['ɛrə'] *n* оши́бка

erupt [ɪ'rʌpt] *vi* (*war, crisis*) разража́ться (*perf* разрази́ться); **the volcano erupted** произошло́ изверже́ние вулка́на; **eruption** [ɪ'rʌpʃən] *n* (*of volcano*) изверже́ние; (*of fighting*) взрыв

escalator ['ɛskəleɪtə'] *n* эскала́тор

escape [ɪs'keɪp] *n* (*from prison*) побе́г; (*from person*) бе́гство; (*of gas*) уте́чка ▷ *vi* убега́ть (*perf* убежа́ть); (*from jail*) бежа́ть (*impf/perf*); (*leak*) утека́ть (*perf* уте́чь) ▷ *vt* (*consequences etc*) избега́ть (*perf* избежа́ть) +*gen*; **his name escapes me** его́ и́мя вы́пало у меня́ из па́мяти; **to escape from** (*place*) сбега́ть (*perf* сбежа́ть) из/с +*gen*; (*person*) сбега́ть (*perf* сбежа́ть) от +*gen*; **he escaped with minor injuries** он отде́лался лёгкими уши́бами

escort [*n* 'ɛskɔ:t, *vb* ɪs'kɔ:t] *n* сопровожде́ние; (*Mil, Police*) конво́й; (: *one person*) конво́ир ▷ *vt* сопровожда́ть (*perf* сопроводи́ть)

especially [ɪs'pɛʃlɪ] *adv* осо́бенно

espionage ['ɛspɪənɑ:ʒ] *n* шпиона́ж

essay ['ɛseɪ] *n* (*Scol*) сочине́ние

essence ['ɛsns] *n* су́щность *f*; (*Culin*) эссе́нция

essential [ɪ'sɛnʃl] *adj* обяза́тельный, необходи́мый; (*basic*) суще́ственный ▷ *n* необходи́мое *nt adj*; **essentials** *npl* (*of* *subject*) осно́вы; **it is essential to ...** необходи́мо +*infin* ...; **essentially** *adv* в су́щности

establish [ɪsˈtæblɪʃ] *vt* (*organization*) учрежда́ть (*perf* учреди́ть); (*facts, contact*) устана́вливать (*perf* установи́ть); (*reputation*) утвержда́ть (*perf* утверди́ть) за собо́й; **establishment** *n* (*see vb*) учрежде́ние; установле́ние; утвержде́ние; (*shop etc*) заведе́ние; **the Establishment** исте́блишмент

estate [ɪsˈteɪt] *n* (*land*) поме́стье; (*Brit: also* **housing estate**) жило́й ко́мплекс; **estate agent** *n* (*Brit*) аге́нт по прода́же недви́жимости, риэ́лтор

estimate [*vb* ˈɛstɪmeɪt, *n* ˈɛstɪmət] *vt* (*reckon*) предвари́тельно подсчи́тывать (*perf* подсчита́ть); (*: cost*) оце́нивать (*perf* оцени́ть) ▷ *n* (*calculation*) подсчёт; (*assessment*) оце́нка; (*builder's etc*) сме́та

etc *abbr* (= *et cetera*) и т.д. (= и так да́лее)

eternal [ɪˈtəːnl] *adj* ве́чный

eternity [ɪˈtəːnɪtɪ] *n* ве́чность *f*

ethical [ˈɛθɪkl] *adj* (*relating to ethics*) эти́ческий; (*morally right*) эти́чный

ethics [ˈɛθɪks] *n*, *npl* э́тика *fsg*

Ethiopia [iːˈθɪəpɪə] *n* Эфио́пия

ethnic [ˈɛθnɪk] *adj* этни́ческий

etiquette [ˈɛtɪkɛt] *n* этике́т

EU *n abbr* (= *European Union*) ЕС, Евросою́з (= *Европе́йский сою́з*)

euro [ˈjuərəu] *n* е́вро *m ind*

Europe [ˈjuərəp] *n* Евро́па; **European** [juərəˈpiːən] *adj* европе́йский; **European Community** *n* Европе́йское соо́бщество; **European Union** *n* Европе́йский сою́з

evacuate [ɪˈvækjueɪt] *vt* (*people*) эвакуи́ровать (*impf/perf*); (*place*) освобожда́ть (*perf* освободи́ть)

evade [ɪˈveɪd] *vt* (*duties, question*) уклоня́ться (*perf* уклони́ться) от +*gen*; (*person*) избега́ть (*impf*) +*gen*

evaluate [ɪˈvæljueɪt] *vt* оце́нивать (*perf* оцени́ть)

eve [iːv] *n*: **on the eve of** накану́не +*gen*

even [ˈiːvn] *adj* (*level, smooth*) ро́вный; (*equal*) ра́вный; (*number*) чётный ▷ *adv* да́же; **even if** да́же е́сли; **even though** хотя́ и; **even more** ещё бо́льше; (+*adj*) ещё бо́лее; **even so** (и) всё же; **not even** да́же не; **I am even more likely to leave now** тепе́рь ещё бо́лее вероя́тно, что я уе́ду; **to break even** зака́нчивать (*perf* зако́нчить) без убы́тка; **to get even with sb** (*inf*) расквита́ться (*perf*) с кем-н

evening [ˈiːvnɪŋ] *n* ве́чер; **in the evening** ве́чером; **evening dress** *n* (*no pl: formal clothes*) вече́рний туале́т

event [ɪˈvɛnt] *n* (*occurrence*) собы́тие; (*Sport*) вид (соревнова́ния); **in the event of** в слу́чае +*gen*

eventual [ɪˈvɛntʃuəl] *adj* коне́чный; **eventually** *adv* в конце́ концо́в

ever [ˈɛvəʳ] *adv* (*always*) всегда́; (*at any*

time) когда́-либо, когда́-нибудь; **why ever not?** почему́ же нет?; **the best ever** са́мый лу́чший; **have you ever been to Russia?** Вы когда́-нибудь бы́ли в Росси́и?; **better than ever** лу́чше, чем когда́-либо; **ever since** с тех пор; **ever since our meeting** со дня на́шей встре́чи; **ever since we met** с тех пор как мы встре́тились; **ever since that day** с того́ дня; **evergreen** *n* вечнозелёный

KEYWORD

every [ˈɛvrɪ] *adj* **1** (*each*) ка́ждый; (*all*) все; **every one of them** ка́ждый из них; **every shop in the town was closed** все магази́ны го́рода бы́ли закры́ты
2 (*all possible*) вся́кий, вся́ческий; **we wish you every success** мы жела́ем Вам вся́ческих успе́хов; **I gave you every assistance** я помо́г Вам всем, чем то́лько возмо́жно; **I tried every option** я испро́бовал все вариа́нты; **I have every confidence in him** я в нём соверше́нно уве́рен; **he's every bit as clever as his brother** он столь же умён, как и его́ брат
3 (*showing recurrence*) ка́ждый; **every week** ка́ждую неде́лю; **every other car** ка́ждая втора́я маши́на; **she visits me every other/third day** она́ прихо́дит ко мне че́рез день/ка́ждые два дня; **every now and then** вре́мя от вре́мени

everybody [ˈɛvrɪbɔdɪ] *pron* (*each*) ка́ждый; (*all*) все *pl*

everyday [ˈɛvrɪdeɪ] *adj* (*daily*) ежедне́вный; (*common*) повседне́вный

everyone [ˈɛvrɪwʌn] *pron* = **everybody**

everything [ˈɛvrɪθɪŋ] *pron* всё

everywhere [ˈɛvrɪwɛəʳ] *adv* везде́, повсю́ду

evidence [ˈɛvɪdns] *n* (*proof*) доказа́тельство; (*testimony*) показа́ние; (*indication*) при́знаки *mpl*; **to give evidence** дава́ть (*perf* дать) (свиде́тельские) показа́ния

evident [ˈɛvɪdnt] *adj* очеви́дный; **evidently** *adv* очеви́дно

evil [ˈiːvl] *adj* (*person, spirit*) злой; (*influence*) дурно́й; (*system*) ги́бельный ▷ *n* зло

evoke [ɪˈvəuk] *vt* вызыва́ть (*perf* вы́звать)

evolution [iːvəˈluːʃən] *n* эволю́ция

evolve [ɪˈvɔlv] *vi* (*animal, plant*) эволюциони́ровать (*impf/perf*); (*plan, idea*) развива́ться (*perf* разви́ться)

ex- [ɛks] *prefix* (*former*) экс-, бы́вший

exact [ɪgˈzækt] *adj* то́чный ▷ *vt*: **to exact sth from** (*payment*) взы́скивать (*perf* взыска́ть) что-н с +*gen*; **exactly** *adv* то́чно

exaggerate [ɪgˈzædʒəreɪt] *vt, vi* преувели́чивать (*perf* преувели́чить)

exaggeration [ɪgzædʒə'reɪʃən] n преувеличе́ние

exam [ɪg'zæm] n abbr = **examination**

examination [ɪgzæmɪ'neɪʃən] n (inspection) изуче́ние; (consideration) рассмотре́ние; (Scol) экза́мен; (Med) осмо́тр

examine [ɪg'zæmɪn] vt (scrutinize) рассма́тривать (perf рассмотре́ть), изуча́ть (perf изучи́ть); (inspect) осма́тривать (perf осмотре́ть); (Scol) экзаменова́ть (perf проэкзаменова́ть); (Med) осма́тривать (perf осмотре́ть); **examiner** (Scol) n экзамена́тор

example [ɪg'zɑːmpl] n приме́р; **for example** наприме́р

exceed [ɪk'siːd] vt превыша́ть (perf превы́сить); **exceedingly** adv весьма́, чрезвыча́йно

excel [ɪk'sɛl] vi: **to excel (in** or **at)** отлича́ться (perf отличи́ться) (в +prp); **excellence** ['ɛksələns] n (in sport, business) мастерство́; (superiority) превосхо́дство; **excellent** ['ɛksələnt] adj отли́чный, превосхо́дный

except [ɪk'sɛpt] prep (also **except for**) кро́ме +gen ▷ vt: **to except sb (from)** исключа́ть (perf исключи́ть) кого́-н (из +gen); **except if/when** кро́ме тех слу́чаев, е́сли/когда́; **except that** кро́ме того́, что; **exception** [ɪk'sɛpʃən] n исключе́ние; **to take exception to** обижа́ться (perf оби́деться) на +acc; **exceptional** [ɪk'sɛpʃənl] adj исключи́тельный

excess [ɪk'sɛs] n избы́ток; **excess baggage** n изли́шек багажа́; **excessive** adj чрезме́рный

exchange [ɪks'tʃeɪndʒ] n (argument) перепа́лка ▷ vt: **to exchange (for)** (goods etc) обме́нивать (perf обменя́ть) (на +acc); **exchange (of)** обме́н (+instr); **exchange rate** n валю́тный or обме́нный курс

excite [ɪk'saɪt] vt возбужда́ть (perf возбуди́ть), волнова́ть (perf взволнова́ть); **to get excited** возбужда́ться (perf возбуди́ться), волнова́ться (perf взволнова́ться); **excitement** n (agitation) возбужде́ние; (exhilaration) волне́ние

exciting [ɪk'saɪtɪŋ] adj (news, opportunity) волну́ющий

exclude [ɪks'kluːd] vt исключа́ть (perf исключи́ть)

exclusion [ɪks'kluːʒən] n исключе́ние

exclusive [ɪks'kluːsɪv] adj (hotel, interview) эксклюзи́вный; (use, right) исключа́ть or исключа́я +acc; **exclusively** adv исключи́тельно

excruciating [ɪks'kruːʃɪeɪtɪŋ] adj мучи́тельный

excursion [ɪks'kəːʃən] n экску́рсия

excuse [n ɪks'kjuːs, vb ɪks'kjuːz] n оправда́ние ▷ vt (justify) опра́вдывать (perf оправда́ть); (forgive) проща́ть (perf прости́ть); **to make excuses for sb** опра́вдываться (impf) за кого́-н; **that's no excuse!** э́то не оправда́ние!; **to excuse sb from sth** освобожда́ть (perf освободи́ть) кого́-н от чего́-н; **excuse me!** извини́те!, прости́те!; (as apology) извини́те or прости́те (меня́)!; **if you will excuse me, I have to ...** с Ва́шего разреше́ния я до́лжен ...

execute ['ɛksɪkjuːt] vt (kill) казни́ть (impf/perf); (carry out) выполня́ть (perf вы́полнить)

execution [ɛksɪ'kjuːʃən] n (see vb) казнь f; выполне́ние

executive [ɪg'zɛkjutɪv] n (person) руководи́тель m; (committee) исполни́тельный о́рган ▷ adj (board, role) руководя́щий

exempt [ɪg'zɛmpt] adj: **exempt from** освобождённый от +gen ▷ vt: **to exempt sb from** освобожда́ть (perf освободи́ть) кого́-н от +gen

exercise ['ɛksəsaɪz] n (Sport) заря́дка, гимна́стика; (: for legs, stomach etc) (физи́ческое) упражне́ние; (also Scol, Mus) упражне́ние; (keep-fit) заря́дка; (physical) гимна́стика ▷ vt (patience) проявля́ть (perf прояви́ть); (authority, right) применя́ть (perf примени́ть); (dog) выгу́ливать (impf) ▷ vi (also **to take exercise**) упражня́ться (impf); **military exercises** вое́нные уче́ния

exert [ɪg'zəːt] vt (influence, pressure) ока́зывать (perf оказа́ть); (authority) применя́ть (perf примени́ть); **to exert o.s.** напряга́ться (perf напря́чься); **exertion** [ɪg'zəːʃən] n (effort) уси́лие

exhaust [ɪg'zɔːst] n (also **exhaust pipe**) выхлопна́я труба́; (fumes) выхлопны́е га́зы mpl ▷ vt (person) изнуря́ть (perf изнури́ть); (money, resources) истоща́ть (perf истощи́ть); (topic) исче́рпывать (perf исче́рпать); **exhausted** adj изнурённый, изнеможённый; **exhaustion** [ɪg'zɔːstʃən] n изнеможе́ние; **nervous exhaustion** не́рвное истоще́ние

exhibit [ɪg'zɪbɪt] n экспона́т ▷ vt (paintings) экспони́ровать (impf/perf), выставля́ть (perf вы́ставить); (quality, emotion) проявля́ть (perf прояви́ть); **exhibition** [ɛksɪ'bɪʃən] n (of paintings etc) вы́ставка

exhilarating [ɪg'zɪləreɪtɪŋ] adj волну́ющий

exile ['ɛksaɪl] n (banishment) ссы́лка, изгна́ние; (person) ссы́льный(-ая) m(f) adj, изгна́нник ▷ vt (abroad) высыла́ть (perf вы́слать)

exist [ɪg'zɪst] vi существова́ть (impf); **existence** n существова́ние; **existing** adj существу́ющий

exit ['ɛksɪt] n (way out) вы́ход; (on motorway) вы́езд; (departure) ухо́д

exotic [ɪg'zɔtɪk] adj экзоти́ческий

expand [ɪks'pænd] vt (area, business, influence) расширя́ть (perf расши́рить)
▷ vi (gas, metal, business) расширя́ться (perf расши́риться)

expansion [ɪks'pænʃən] n расшире́ние; (of economy) рост

expect [ɪks'pɛkt] vt ожида́ть (impf); (baby) ждать (impf); (suppose) полага́ть (impf) ▷ vi: **to be expecting** (be pregnant) ждать (impf) ребёнка; **expectation** [ɛkspɛk'teɪʃən] n (hope) ожида́ние

expedition [ɛkspə'dɪʃən] n экспеди́ция; (for pleasure) похо́д

expel [ɪks'pɛl] vt (from school etc) исключа́ть (perf исключи́ть); (from place) изгоня́ть (perf изгна́ть)

expenditure [ɪks'pɛndɪtʃəʳ] n (money spent) затра́ты fpl; (of energy, time, money) затра́та, расхо́д

expense [ɪks'pɛns] n (cost) сто́имость f; **expenses** npl (travelling etc expenses) расхо́ды mpl; (expenditure) затра́ты fpl; **at the expense of** за счёт +gen

expensive [ɪks'pɛnsɪv] adj дорого́й

experience [ɪks'pɪərɪəns] n (in job, of situation) о́пыт; (event, activity) слу́чай; (: difficult, painful) испыта́ние ▷ vt испы́тывать (perf испыта́ть), пережива́ть (perf пережи́ть); **experienced** adj о́пытный

experiment [ɪks'pɛrɪmənt] n экспериме́нт, о́пыт ▷ vi: **to experiment (with/on)** эксперименти́ровать (impf) (с +instr/на +prp); **experimental** [ɪkspɛrɪ'mɛntl] adj (methods, ideas) эксперимента́льный; (tests) про́бный

expert ['ɛkspə:t] n экспе́рт, специали́ст; **expert opinion/advice** мне́ние/сове́т экспе́рта or специали́ста; **expertise** [ɛkspə:'tiːz] n зна́ния ntpl и о́пыт

expire [ɪks'paɪəʳ] vi (run out) истека́ть (perf исте́чь); **my passport expires in January** срок де́йствия моего́ па́спорта истека́ет в январе́

explain [ɪks'pleɪn] vt объясня́ть (perf объясни́ть)

explanation [ɛksplə'neɪʃən] n объясне́ние

explicit [ɪks'plɪsɪt] adj я́вный, очеви́дный; (sex, violence) открове́нный

explode [ɪks'pləud] vi (bomb, person) взрыва́ться (perf взорва́ться); (population) ре́зко возраста́ть (perf возрасти́)

exploit [vb ɪks'plɔɪt, n 'ɛksplɔɪt] vt эксплуати́ровать (impf); (opportunity) испо́льзовать (impf/perf) ▷ n де́йствие; **exploitation** [ɛksplɔɪ'teɪʃən] n (see vt) эксплуата́ция; испо́льзование

explore [ɪks'plɔːʳ] vt (place) иссле́довать (impf/perf); (idea, suggestion) изуча́ть (perf изучи́ть); **explorer** n иссле́дователь(ница) m(f)

explosion [ɪks'pləuʒən] n взрыв;

population explosion демографи́ческий взрыв

explosive [ɪks'pləusɪv] adj (device, effect) взрывно́й; (situation) взрывоопа́сный; (person) вспы́льчивый ▷ n (substance) взры́вчатое вещество́; (device) взрывно́е устро́йство

export [n, cpd 'ɛkspɔ:t, vb ɛks'pɔːt] n (process) э́кспорт, вы́воз; (product) предме́т э́кспорта ▷ vt экспорти́ровать (impf/perf); (perf вы́везти) ▷ cpd (duty, licence) э́кспортный

expose [ɪks'pəuz] vt (object) обнажа́ть (perf обнажи́ть); (truth, plot) раскрыва́ть (perf раскры́ть); (person) разоблача́ть (perf разоблачи́ть); **to expose sb to sth** подверга́ть (perf подве́ргнуть) кого́-н чему́-н; **exposed** adj (place): **exposed (to)** откры́тый (+dat)

exposure [ɪks'pəuʒəʳ] n (of culprit) разоблаче́ние; (Phot) вы́держка, экспози́ция; **to suffer from exposure** (Med) страда́ть (perf пострада́ть) от переохлажде́ния

express [ɪks'prɛs] adj (clear) чёткий; (Brit: service) сро́чный ▷ n экспре́сс ▷ vt выража́ть (perf вы́разить); **expression** [ɪks'prɛʃən] n выраже́ние

exquisite [ɛks'kwɪzɪt] adj (perfect) изы́сканный

extend [ɪks'tɛnd] vt (visit, deadline) продлева́ть (perf продли́ть); (building) расширя́ть (perf расши́рить); (hand) протя́гивать (perf протяну́ть); (welcome) ока́зывать (perf оказа́ть) ▷ vi (land, road) простира́ться (impf); (period) продолжа́ться (perf продо́лжиться); **to extend an invitation to sb** приглаша́ть (perf пригласи́ть) кого́-н

extension [ɪks'tɛnʃən] n (of building) пристро́йка; (of time) продле́ние; (Elec) удлини́тель m; (Tel: in house) паралле́льный телефо́н; (: in office) доба́вочный телефо́н

extensive [ɪks'tɛnsɪv] adj обши́рный; (damage) значи́тельный

extent [ɪks'tɛnt] n (of area etc) протяжённость f; (of problem etc) масшта́б; **to some extent** до не́которой сте́пени; **to go to the extent of ...** доходи́ть (perf дойти́) до того́, что ...; **to such an extent that ...** до тако́й сте́пени, что ...

exterior [ɛks'tɪərɪəʳ] adj нару́жный ▷ n (outside) вне́шняя сторона́

external [ɛks'tə:nl] adj вне́шний

extinct [ɪks'tɪŋkt] adj (animal) вы́мерший; (plant) исче́знувший; **to become extinct** (animal) вымира́ть (perf вы́мереть); (plant) исчеза́ть (perf исче́знуть); **extinction** [ɪks'tɪŋkʃən] n (of animal) вымира́ние; (of plant) исчезнове́ние

extra ['ɛkstrə] adj (additional)

дополни́тельный; (spare) ли́шний ▷ adv
(in addition) дополни́тельно; (especially)
осо́бенно ▷ n (luxury) изли́шество;
(surcharge) допла́та

extract [vb ɪks'trækt, n 'ɛkstrækt] vt
извлека́ть (perf извле́чь); (tooth) удаля́ть
(perf удали́ть); (mineral) добыва́ть (perf
добы́ть); (money, promise) выта́гивать
(perf вы́тянуть) ▷ n (from novel,
recording) отры́вок

extraordinary [ɪks'trɔːdnrɪ] adj
незауря́дный, необыча́йный

extravagance [ɪks'trævəgəns] n (with
money) расточи́тельство

extravagant [ɪks'trævəgənt] adj (lavish)
экстрава́гантный; (wasteful: person)
расточи́тельный

extreme [ɪks'triːm] adj кра́йний;
(situation) экстрема́льный; (heat, cold)
сильне́йший ▷ n (of behaviour)
кра́йность f; **extremely** adv кра́йне

extrovert ['ɛkstrəvəːt] n экстрове́рт

eye [aɪ] n (Anat) глаз; (of needle) у́шко
▷ vt разгля́дывать (perf разгляде́ть); **to
keep an eye on** (person, object)
присма́тривать (perf присмотре́ть) за
+instr; (time) следи́ть (impf) за +instr;
eyebrow n бровь f; **eyelash** n
ресни́ца; **eyelid** n ве́ко; **eyeliner** n
каранда́ш для век; **eye shadow** n те́ни
fpl (для век); **eyesight** n зре́ние

F [ɛf] n (Mus) фа
F abbr = **Fahrenheit**
fabric ['fæbrɪk] n (cloth) ткань f
fabulous ['fæbjuləs] adj (inf) ска́зочный;
(extraordinary) невероя́тный
face [feɪs] n (of person, organization)
лицо́; (of clock) цифербла́т; (of mountain,
cliff) склон ▷ vt (fact) признава́ть (perf
призна́ть); **the house faces the sea** дом
обращён к мо́рю; **he was facing the door**
он был обращён лицо́м к две́ри; **we are
facing difficulties** нам предстоя́т
тру́дности; **face down** лицо́м вниз; **to
lose/save face** теря́ть (perf потеря́ть)/
спаса́ть (perf спасти́) репута́цию or лицо́;
to make or **pull a face** де́лать (perf
сде́лать) грима́су; **in the face of** (difficulties
etc) пе́ред лицо́м +gen; **on the face of it** на
пе́рвый взгляд; **face to face (with)** лицо́м к
лицу́ (с +instr); **face up to** vt fus
признава́ть (perf призна́ть); (difficulties)
справля́ться (perf спра́виться) с +instr;
face cloth n (Brit) махро́вая салфе́тка
(для лица́)
facial ['feɪʃl] adj: **facial expression**
выраже́ние лица́; **facial hair** во́лосы,
расту́щие на лице́
facilitate [fə'sɪlɪteɪt] vt спосо́бствовать
(impf/perf) +dat
facilities [fə'sɪlɪtɪz] npl усло́вия ntpl;
(buildings) помеще́ние ntsg; (equipment)
обору́дование ntsg; **cooking facilities**
усло́вия для приготовле́ния пи́щи
fact [fækt] n факт; **in fact** факти́чески
faction ['fækʃən] n (group) фра́кция
factor ['fæktə'] n (of problem) фа́ктор
factory ['fæktərɪ] n (for textiles) фа́брика;
(for machinery) заво́д
factual ['fæktjuəl] adj факти́ческий
faculty ['fækəltɪ] n спосо́бность f; (of
university) факульте́т
fad [fæd] n причу́да

fade [feɪd] vi (colour) выцвета́ть (perf вы́цвести); (light, hope, smile) угаса́ть (perf угасну́ть); (sound) замира́ть (perf замере́ть); (memory) тускне́ть (perf потускне́ть)

fag [fæg] n (Brit: inf) сигаре́та

Fahrenheit ['færənhaɪt] n Фаренге́йт

fail [feɪl] vt (exam, candidate) прова́ливать (perf провали́ть); (subj: memory) изменя́ть (perf измени́ть) +dat; (: person) подводи́ть (perf подвести́); (: courage) покида́ть (perf покину́ть) ▷ vi (candidate, attempt) прова́ливаться (perf провали́ться); (brakes) отка́зывать (perf отказа́ть); **my eyesight/health is failing** у меня́ слабе́ет зре́ние/здоро́вье; **to fail to do** (be unable) не мочь (perf смочь) +infin; **without fail** обяза́тельно, непреме́нно; **failing** n недоста́ток ▷ prep за неиме́нием +gen; **failure** n прова́л, неуда́ча; (Tech) ава́рия, вы́ход из стро́я; (person) неуда́чник(-ица)

faint [feɪnt] adj сла́бый; (recollection) сму́тный; (mark) едва́ заме́тный ▷ vi (Med) па́дать (perf упа́сть) в о́бморок; **to feel faint** чу́вствовать (perf почу́вствовать) сла́бость; **faintest** adj: **I haven't the faintest idea** я не име́ю ни мале́йшего поня́тия

fair [fɛəʳ] adj (person, decision) справедли́вый; (size, number) изря́дный; (chance, guess) хоро́ший; (skin, hair) све́тлый; (weather) хоро́ший, я́сный ▷ n (also **trade fair**) я́рмарка; (Brit: also **funfair**) аттракцио́ны mpl ▷ adv: **to play fair** вести́ (impf) дела́ че́стно; **fairground** n я́рмарочная пло́щадь f; **fairly** adv (justly) справедли́во; (quite) дово́льно

fairy ['fɛərɪ] n фе́я; **fairy tale** n ска́зка

faith [feɪθ] n (also Rel) ве́ра; **faithful** adj: **faithful (to)** ве́рный (+dat); **faithfully** adv ве́рно

fake [feɪk] n (painting, document) подде́лка ▷ adj фальши́вый, подде́льный ▷ vt (forge) подде́лывать (perf подде́лать); (feign) симули́ровать (impf)

fall [fɔːl] (pt **fell**, pp **fallen**) n паде́ние; (US: autumn) о́сень f ▷ vi па́дать (perf упа́сть); (government) пасть (perf); (rain, snow) па́дать (impf), выпада́ть (perf вы́пасть); **falls** npl (waterfall) водопа́д msg; **a fall of snow** снегопа́д; **to fall flat** (plan) прова́ливаться (perf провали́ться); **to fall flat (on one's face)** па́дать (perf упа́сть) ничко́м; **fall back on** vt fus прибега́ть (perf прибе́гнуть) к +dat; **fall down** vi (person) па́дать (perf упа́сть); (building) ру́шиться (perf ру́хнуть); **fall for** vt fus (trick, story) ве́рить (perf пове́рить) +dat; (person) влюбля́ться (perf влюби́ться) в +acc; **fall in** vi (roof) обва́ливаться (perf обвали́ться); **fall off** vi па́дать (perf упа́сть); (handle, button) отва́ливаться (perf отвали́ться); **fall out**

vi (hair, teeth) выпада́ть (perf вы́пасть); **to fall out with sb** ссо́риться (perf поссо́риться) с кем-н

fallen ['fɔːlən] pp of **fall**

false [fɔːls] adj (untrue, wrong) ло́жный; (insincere, artificial) фальши́вый; **false teeth** npl (Brit) иску́сственные зу́бы mpl

fame [feɪm] n сла́ва

familiar [fə'mɪlɪəʳ] adj (well-known) знако́мый; (intimate) дру́жеский; **he is familiar with** (subject) он знако́м с +instr

family ['fæmɪlɪ] n семья́; (children) де́ти pl

famine ['fæmɪn] n го́лод

famous ['feɪməs] adj знамени́тый

fan [fæn] n (folding) ве́ер; (Elec) вентиля́тор; (of famous person) покло́нник(-ица); (of sports team) боле́льщик(-ица); (: inf) фан ▷ vt (face) обма́хивать (perf обмахну́ть); (fire) раздува́ть (perf разду́ть)

fanatic [fə'nætɪk] n (extremist) фана́тик

fancy ['fænsɪ] n (whim) при́хоть f ▷ adj шика́рный ▷ vt (want) хоте́ть (perf захоте́ть); (imagine) вообража́ть (perf вообрази́ть); **to take a fancy to** увлека́ться (perf увле́чься) +instr; **he fancies her** (inf) она́ ему́ нра́вится; **fancy that!** представля́ете!; **fancy dress** n маскара́дный костю́м

fantastic [fæn'tæstɪk] adj фантасти́ческий; **that's fantastic!** замеча́тельно!, потряса́юще!

fantasy ['fæntəsɪ] n фанта́зия

far [fɑːʳ] adj (distant) да́льний ▷ adv (a long way) далеко́; (much) гора́здо; **at the far end** в да́льнем конце́; **at the far side** на друго́й стороне́; **the far left/right** (Pol) кра́йне ле́вый/пра́вый; **far away, far off** далеко́; **he was far from poor** он был далеко́ or отню́дь не бе́ден; **by far** намно́го; **go as far as the post office** дойди́те до по́чты; **as far as I know** наско́лько мне изве́стно; **how far?** (distance) как далеко́?

farce [fɑːs] n фарс

fare [fɛəʳ] n (in taxi, train, bus) сто́имость f прое́зда; **half/full fare** полсто́имости/ по́лная сто́имость прое́зда

Far East n: **the Far East** Да́льний Восто́к

farm [fɑːm] n фе́рма ▷ vt (land) обраба́тывать (perf обрабо́тать); **farmer** n фе́рмер; **farmhouse** n фе́рмерская уса́дьба; **farming** n (agriculture) се́льское хозя́йство; (of crops) выра́щивание; (of animals) разведе́ние; **farmyard** n фе́рмерский двор

farther ['fɑːðəʳ] adv да́лее

fascinating ['fæsɪneɪtɪŋ] adj (story) захва́тывающий; (person) очарова́тельный

fascination [fæsɪ'neɪʃən] n очарова́ние

fashion ['fæʃən] n (trend) мо́да; **in/out of fashion** в/не в мо́де; **in a friendly fashion** по-дру́жески; **fashionable** adj мо́дный;

fashion show n показ or демонстрация мод

fast [fɑːst] adv (quickly) быстро; (firmly: stick) прочно; (: hold) крепко ▷ n (Rel) пост ▷ adj быстрый; (car) скоростной; (colour) прочный; **to be fast** (clock) спешить (impf); **he is fast asleep** он крепко спит

fasten ['fɑːsn] vt закреплять (perf закрепить); (door) запирать (perf запереть); (shoe) завязывать (perf завязать); (coat, dress) застёгивать (perf застегнуть); (seat belt) пристёгивать (perf пристегнуть) ▷ vi (coat, belt) застёгиваться (perf застегнуться); (door) запираться (perf запереться)

fast food n быстро приготовленная еда

fat [fæt] adj толстый ▷ n жир

fatal ['feɪtl] adj (mistake) фатальный, роковой; (injury, illness) смертельный; **fatally** adv (injured) смертельно

fate [feɪt] n судьба, рок

father ['fɑːðə'] n отец; **father-in-law** n (wife's father) свёкор; (husband's father) тесть m

fatigue [fə'tiːg] n утомление

fatty ['fætɪ] adj (food) жирный

fault [fɔːlt] n (blame) вина; (defect: in person) недостаток; (: in machine) дефект; (Geo) разлом ▷ vt (criticize) придираться (impf) к +dat; **it's my fault** это моя вина; **to find fault with** придираться (perf придраться) к +dat; **I am at fault** я виноват; **faulty** adj (goods) испорченный; (machine) повреждённый

fauna ['fɔːnə] n фауна

favour ['feɪvə'] (US **favor**) n (approval) расположение; (help) одолжение ▷ vt (prefer: solution) оказывать (perf оказать) предпочтение +dat; (: pupil etc) выделять (perf выделить); (assist) благоприятствовать (impf) +dat; **to do sb a favour** оказывать (perf оказать) кому-н услугу; **in favour of** в пользу +gen; **favourable** adj благоприятный; **favourite** adj любимый ▷ n любимец; (Sport) фаворит

fawn [fɔːn] n молодой олень m

fax [fæks] n факс ▷ vt посылать (perf послать) факсом

FBI n abbr (US) (= Federal Bureau of Investigation) ФБР (= Федеральное бюро расследований)

fear [fɪə'] n (terror) страх; (less strong) боязнь f; (worry) опасение ▷ vt бояться (impf) +gen; **for fear of missing my flight** боясь опоздать на самолёт; **fearful** adj (person): **to be fearful of** бояться (impf) or страшиться impf (+gen); **fearless** adj бесстрашный

feasible ['fiːzəbl] adj осуществимый

feast [fiːst] n (banquet) пир

feat [fiːt] n подвиг

feather ['fɛðə'] n перо

feature ['fiːtʃə'] n особенность f, черта; (Press) очерк; (TV, Radio) передача ▷ vt: **to feature in** фигурировать (impf) в +prp; **features** npl (of face) черты fpl (лица); **feature film** n художественный фильм

February ['fɛbruərɪ] n февраль m

fed [fɛd] pt, pp of **feed**

federal ['fɛdərəl] adj федеральный

federation [fɛdə'reɪʃən] n федерация

fee [fiː] n плата; **school fees** плата за обучение

feeble ['fiːbl] adj хилый; (excuse) слабый

feed [fiːd] (pt, pp **fed**) n (fodder) корм; (Comput) лента, френд-лента ▷ vt кормить (perf накормить); **to feed sth into** (data) загружать (perf загрузить) что-н в +acc; (paper) подавать (perf подать) что-н в +acc; **feed on** vt fus питаться (impf) +instr

feel [fiːl] (pt, pp **felt**) vt (touch) трогать (perf потрогать); (experience) чувствовать (impf), ощущать (perf ощутить); **to feel (that)** (believe) считать (impf), что; **he feels hungry** он голоден; **she feels cold** ей холодно; **to feel lonely/better** чувствовать (impf) себя одиноко/лучше; **I don't feel well** я плохо себя чувствую; **the material feels like velvet** этот материал на ощупь как бархат; **I feel like ...** (want) мне хочется ...; **feel about for** vt fus: **to feel about for sth** искать (impf) что-н ощупью; **feeling** n чувство; (physical) ощущение

feet [fiːt] npl of **foot**

fell [fɛl] pt of **fall**

fellow ['fɛləu] n (man) парень m; (of society) действительный член ▷ cpd: **their fellow prisoners/students** их сокамерники/сокурсники; **fellowship** n (Scol) стипендия (для исследовательской работы)

felt [fɛlt] pt, pp of **feel** ▷ n фетр

female ['fiːmeɪl] n самка ▷ adj женский; (child) женского пола

feminine ['fɛmɪnɪn] adj (clothes, behaviour) женственный; (Ling) женского рода

feminist ['fɛmɪnɪst] n феминист(ка)

fence [fɛns] n (barrier) забор, изгородь f

fencing ['fɛnsɪŋ] n (Sport) фехтование

fend [fɛnd] vi: **to fend for o.s.** заботиться (perf позаботиться) о себе; **fend off** vt отражать (perf отразить)

fender ['fɛndə'] n (US: of car) крыло

fern [fəːn] n папоротник

ferocious [fə'rəuʃəs] adj (animal, attack) свирепый; (behaviour, heat) дикий

ferry ['fɛrɪ] n (also **ferryboat**) паром ▷ vt перевозить (perf перевезти)

fertile ['fəːtaɪl] adj (land, soil) плодородный; (imagination) богатый; (woman) способный к зачатию

fertilizer ['fəːtɪlaɪzə'] n удобрение

festival ['fɛstɪvəl] n (Rel) праздник; (Art, Mus) фестиваль m

festive ['fɛstɪv] adj (mood) пра́здничный; **the festive season** (Brit) ≈ Свя́тки pl

fetch [fɛtʃ] vt (object) приноси́ть (perf принести́); (person) приводи́ть (perf привести́); (by car) привози́ть (perf привезти́)

fête [feɪt] n благотвори́тельный база́р

fetus ['fi:təs] n (US) = **foetus**

feud [fju:d] n вражда́

fever ['fi:vər] n (temperature) жар; (disease) лихора́дка; **feverish** adj лихора́дочный; (person: with excitement) возбуждённый; **he is feverish** у него́ жар, его́ лихора́дит

few [fju:] adj (not many) немно́гие; (some) не́которые pl adj ▷ pron: (a) few немно́гие pl adj; **a few** (several) не́сколько +gen; **fewer** adj ме́ньше +gen

fiancé [fɪ'ɑ:nseɪ] n жени́х

fiancée [fɪ'ɑ:nseɪ] n неве́ста

fiasco [fɪ'æskəʊ] n фиа́ско nt ind

fibre ['faɪbər] (US fiber) n волокно́; (dietary) клетча́тка

fickle ['fɪkl] adj непостоя́нный

fiction ['fɪkʃən] n (Literature) худо́жественная литерату́ра; **fictional** adj (event, character) вы́мышленный

fiddle ['fɪdl] n (Mus) скри́пка; (swindle) надува́тельство ▷ vt (Brit: accounts) подде́лывать (perf подде́лать)

fidelity [fɪ'dɛlɪtɪ] n (loyalty) ве́рность f

field [fi:ld] n по́ле; (fig) о́бласть f

fierce [fɪəs] adj свире́пый; (fighting) я́ростный

fifteen [fɪf'ti:n] n пятна́дцать; **fifteenth** adj пятна́дцатый

fifth [fɪfθ] adj пя́тый ▷ n (fraction) пя́тая f adj; (Aut: also **fifth gear**) пя́тая ско́рость f

fiftieth ['fɪftɪɪθ] adj пятидеся́тый

fifty ['fɪftɪ] n пятьдеся́т

fig [fɪg] n инжи́р

fight [faɪt] (pt, pp fought) n дра́ка; (campaign, struggle) борьба́ ▷ vt (person) дра́ться (perf подра́ться) с +instr; (Mil) воева́ть (impf) с +instr; (illness, problem, emotion) боро́ться (impf) с +instr ▷ vi (people) воева́ть (impf); (Mil) воева́ть (impf); **to fight an election** уча́ствовать (impf) в предвы́борной борьбе́; **fighting** n (battle) бой; (brawl) дра́ка

figure ['fɪgər] n фигу́ра; (number) ци́фра ▷ vt (think) счита́ть (impf) ▷ vi (appear) фигури́ровать (impf); **figure out** vt понима́ть (perf поня́ть)

file [faɪl] n (dossier) де́ло; (folder) скоросшива́тель m; (Comput) файл ▷ vt (papers, document) подшива́ть (perf подши́ть); (Law: claim) подава́ть (perf пода́ть); (wood, fingernails) шлифова́ть (perf отшлифова́ть) ▷ vi: **to file in/past** входи́ть (perf войти́)/проходи́ть (perf пройти́) коло́нной; **in single file** в коло́нну по одному́

fill [fɪl] vi (room etc) наполня́ться (perf напо́лниться) ▷ vt (vacancy) заполня́ть (perf запо́лнить); (need) удовлетворя́ть (perf удовлетвори́ть) ▷ n: **to eat one's fill** наеда́ться (perf нае́сться); **to fill (with)** (container) наполня́ть (perf напо́лнить) (+instr); (space, area) заполня́ть (perf запо́лнить) (+instr); **fill in** vt (hole) заполня́ть (perf запо́лнить); **fill up** vt (container) наполня́ть (perf напо́лнить); (space) заполня́ть (perf запо́лнить) ▷ vi (Aut) заправля́ться (perf запра́виться)

fillet ['fɪlɪt] n филе́ nt ind

filling ['fɪlɪŋ] n (for tooth) пло́мба; (of pie) начи́нка; (of cake) просло́йка

film [fɪlm] n (Cinema) фильм; (Phot) плёнка; (of powder, liquid etc) то́нкий слой ▷ vt, vi снима́ть (perf снять); **film star** n кинозвезда́ m/f

filter ['fɪltər] n фильтр ▷ vt фильтрова́ть (perf профильтрова́ть)

filth [fɪlθ] n грязь f; **filthy** adj гря́зный

fin [fɪn] n (of fish) плавни́к

final ['faɪnl] adj (last) после́дний; (Sport) фина́льный; (ultimate) заключи́тельный; (definitive) оконча́тельный ▷ n (Sport) фина́л; **finals** npl (Scol) выпускны́е экза́мены mpl; **finale** [fɪ'nɑ:lɪ] n фина́л; **finalist** n финали́ст; **finally** adv (eventually) в конце́ концо́в; (lastly) наконе́ц

finance [faɪ'næns] n фина́нсы pl ▷ vt финанси́ровать (impf/perf); **finances** npl (personal) фина́нсы pl

financial [faɪ'nænʃəl] adj фина́нсовый

find [faɪnd] (pt, pp found) vt находи́ть (perf найти́); (discover) обнару́живать (perf обнару́жить) ▷ n нахо́дка; **to find sb at home** заста́ть (perf заста́ть) кого́-н до́ма; **to find sb guilty** (Law) признава́ть (perf призна́ть) кого́-н вино́вным(-ой); **find out** vt (fact, truth) узнава́ть (perf узна́ть); (person) разоблача́ть (perf разоблачи́ть) ▷ vi: **to find out about** узнава́ть (perf узна́ть) о +prp; **findings** npl (Law) заключе́ние ntsg; (in research) результа́ты mpl

fine [faɪn] adj прекра́сный; (delicate: hair, features) то́нкий; (sand, powder, detail) ме́лкий; (adjustment) то́чный ▷ adv (well) прекра́сно ▷ n штраф ▷ vt штрафова́ть (perf оштрафова́ть); **he's fine** (well) он чу́вствует себя́ хорошо́; (happy) у него́ всё в поря́дке; **the weather is fine** пого́да хоро́шая; **to cut it fine** (of time) оставля́ть (perf оста́вить) сли́шком ма́ло вре́мени

finger ['fɪŋgər] n па́лец ▷ vt тро́гать (perf потро́гать); **little finger** мизи́нец

finish ['fɪnɪʃ] n коне́ц; (Sport) фи́ниш; (polish etc) отде́лка ▷ vt зака́нчивать (perf зако́нчить), конча́ть (perf ко́нчить) ▷ vi зака́нчиваться (perf зако́нчиться); (person) зака́нчивать (perf зако́нчить); **to**

finish doing конча́ть (*perf* ко́нчить) +*infin*; **he finished third** (*in race etc*) он зако́нчил тре́тьим; **finish off** *vt* зака́нчивать (*perf* зако́нчить); (*kill*) прика́нчивать (*perf* прико́нчить); **finish up** *vt* (*food*) доеда́ть (*perf* дое́сть); (*drink*) допива́ть (*perf* допи́ть) ▷ *vi* (*end up*) конча́ть (*perf* ко́нчить)

Finland ['fɪnlənd] *n* Финля́ндия; **Gulf of Finland** Фи́нский зали́в

Finn [fɪn] *n* финн; **Finnish** *adj* фи́нский

fir [fəːʳ] *n* ель *f*

fire ['faɪəʳ] *n* (*flames*) ого́нь *m*, пла́мя *nt*; (*in hearth*) ого́нь *m*; (*accidental*) пожа́р; (*bonfire*) костёр ▷ *vt* (*gun etc*) вы́стрелить (*perf*) из +*gen*; (*arrow*) выпуска́ть (*perf* вы́пустить); (*stimulate*) разжига́ть (*perf* разже́чь); (*inf: dismiss*) увольня́ть (*perf* уво́лить) ▷ *vi* (*shoot*) вы́стрелить (*perf*); **the house is on fire** дом гори́т *or* в огне́; **fire alarm** *n* пожа́рная сигнализа́ция; **firearm** *n* огнестре́льное ору́жие *nt no pl*; **fire brigade** *n* пожа́рная кома́нда; **fire engine** *n* пожа́рная маши́на; **fire escape** *n* пожа́рная ле́стница; **fire-extinguisher** *n* огнетуши́тель *m*; **firefighter** *n* пожа́рный(-ая) *m(f) adj*, пожа́рник; **fireplace** *n* ками́н; **fire station** *n* пожа́рное депо́ *nt ind*; **firewood** *n* дрова́ *pl*; **fireworks** *npl* фейерве́рк *msg*

firm [fəːm] *adj* (*ground, decision, faith*) твёрдый; (*mattress*) жёсткий; (*grasp, body, muscles*) кре́пкий ▷ *n* фи́рма; **firmly** *adv* (*believe, stand*) твёрдо; (*grasp, shake hands*) кре́пко

first [fəːst] *adj* пе́рвый ▷ *adv* (*before all others*) пре́жде всего́; (*firstly*) во-пе́рвых ▷ *n* (*Aut: also* **first gear**) пе́рвая ско́рость *f*; (*Brit: Scol: degree*) дипло́м пе́рвой сте́пени; **at first** снача́ла; **first of all** пре́жде всего́; **first aid** *n* пе́рвая по́мощь *f*; **first-aid kit** *n* паке́т пе́рвой по́мощи; **first-class** *adj* (*excellent*) первокла́ссный; **first-class ticket** биле́т пе́рвого кла́сса; **first-class stamp** ма́рка пе́рвого кла́сса

first: **first-hand** *adj* непосре́дственный; **a first-hand account** расска́з очеви́дца; **first lady** *n* (*US*) пе́рвая ле́ди *f ind*; **firstly** *adv* во-пе́рвых; **first name** *n* и́мя *nt*; **first-rate** *adj* первокла́ссный

fiscal ['fɪskl] *adj* фиска́льный

fish [fɪʃ] *n inv* ры́ба ▷ *vt* (*river, area*) лови́ть (*impf*) ры́бу в +*prp*, рыба́чить (*impf*) в +*prp* ▷ *vi* (*commercially*) занима́ться (*impf*) рыболо́вством; (*as sport, hobby*) занима́ться (*impf*) ры́бной ло́влей; **to go fishing** ходи́ть/идти́ (*perf* пойти́) на рыба́лку; **fisherman** *irreg n* рыба́к

fist [fɪst] *n* кула́к

fit [fɪt] *adj* (*suitable*) приго́дный; (*healthy*) в хоро́шей фо́рме ▷ *vt* (*subj: clothes etc*) подходи́ть (*perf* подойти́) по разме́ру +*dat*, быть (*impf*) впо́ру +*dat* ▷ *vi* (*clothes*) подходи́ть (*perf* подойти́) по разме́ру, быть (*impf*) впо́ру; (*parts*) подходи́ть (*perf* подойти́) ▷ *n* (*Med*) припа́док; (*of coughing, giggles*) при́ступ; **fit to do** (*ready*) гото́вый +*infin*; **fit for** (*suitable for*) приго́дный для +*gen*; **a fit of anger** при́ступ гне́ва; **this dress is a good fit** э́то пла́тье хорошо́ сиди́т; **by fits and starts** уры́вками; **fit in** *vi* (*person, object*) впи́сываться (*perf* вписа́ться); **fitness** *n* (*Med*) состоя́ние здоро́вья; **fitting** *adj* (*thanks*) надлежа́щий; **fittings** *npl*: **fixtures and fittings** обору́дование *ntsg*

five [faɪv] *n* пять; **fiver** *n* (*inf: Brit*) пять фу́нтов; (*: US*) пять до́лларов

fix [fɪks] *vt* (*arrange: date*) назнача́ть (*perf* назна́чить); (*: amount*) устана́вливать (*perf* установи́ть); (*mend*) нала́живать (*perf* нала́дить) ▷ *n* (*inf*): **to be in a fix** влипа́ть (*perf* влипну́ть); **fixed** *adj* (*price*) твёрдый; (*ideas*) навя́зчивый; (*smile*) засты́вший

fixture ['fɪkstʃəʳ] *n see* **fittings**

fizzy ['fɪzɪ] *adj* шипу́чий, газиро́ванный

flag [flæg] *n* флаг

flair [flɛəʳ] *n* (*style*) стиль *m*; **a flair for** (*talent*) дар *or* тала́нт к +*dat*; **political flair** полити́ческий тала́нт

flak [flæk] *n* (*inf*) нахлобу́чка

flake [fleɪk] *n* (*of snow, soap powder*) хло́пья *pl*; (*of rust, paint*) слой

flamboyant [flæm'bɔɪənt] *adj* я́ркий, бро́ский; (*person*) колори́тный

flame [fleɪm] *n* (*of fire*) пла́мя *nt*

flank [flæŋk] *n* (*of animal*) бок; (*Mil*) фланг ▷ *vt*: **flanked by** ме́жду +*instr*

flannel ['flænl] *n* (*fabric*) флане́ль *f*; (*Brit: also* **face flannel**) махро́вая салфе́тка (*для лица́*)

flap [flæp] *n* (*of envelope*) отворо́т; (*of pocket*) кла́пан ▷ *vt* (*wings*) хло́пать *impf* +*instr*

flare [flɛəʳ] n (signal) сигнáльная ракéта; **flare up** vi вспыхивать (perf вспыхнуть)

flash [flæʃ] n вспышка; (also **news flash**) мóлния ▷ vt (light) (внезáпно) освещáть (perf освети́ть); (news, message) посылáть (perf послáть) мóлнией; (look) метáть (perf метнýть) ▷ vi (lightning, light, eyes) сверкáть (perf сверкнýть); (light on ambulance etc) мигáть (impf); **in a flash** мгновéнно; **to flash by** or **past** (sth) (person) мчáться (perf промчáться) мимо (чего-н); **flashlight** n фонáрь m, прожéктор

flask [flɑːsk] n (also **vacuum flask**) тéрмос

flat [flæt] adj (surface) плóский; (tyre) спýщенный; (battery) сéвший; (beer) вы́дохшийся; (refusal, denial) категори́ческий; (Mus: note) бемóльный; (rate, fee) еди́ный ▷ n (Brit: apartment) кварти́ра; (Aut: also **flat tyre**) спýщенная ши́на; (Mus) бемóль m; **to work flat out** выклáдываться (perf вы́ложиться) пóлностью

flatter [ˈflætəʳ] vt льсти́ть (perf польсти́ть) +dat

flavour [ˈfleɪvəʳ] (US **flavor**) vt (soup) приправля́ть (perf припрáвить) ▷ n (taste) вкус; (of ice-cream etc) при́вкус; **strawberry-flavoured** с клубни́чным при́вкусом

flaw [flɔː] n (in argument, character) недостáток, изъя́н; (in cloth, glass) дефéкт; **flawless** adj безупрéчный

flea [fliː] n блохá

flee [fliː] (pt, pp **fled**) vt (danger, famine) бежáть (impf) от +gen; (country) бежáть (impf/perf) из +gen ▷ vi спасáться (impf) бéгством

fleece [fliːs] n (sheep's coat) (овéчья) шкýра; (sheep's wool) овéчья шерсть f

fleet [fliːt] n (of ships) флот; (of lorries, cars) парк

fleeting [ˈfliːtɪŋ] adj мимолётный

Flemish [ˈflɛmɪʃ] adj фламáндский

flesh [flɛʃ] n (Anat) плоть f; (of fruit) мя́коть f

flew [fluː] pt of **fly**

flex [flɛks] n ги́бкий шнур ▷ vt (leg, muscles) размина́ть (perf размя́ть); **flexibility** [flɛksɪˈbɪlɪtɪ] n ги́бкость f; **flexible** [ˈflɛksɪbl] adj ги́бкий

flick [flɪk] vt (with finger) смáхивать (perf смахнýть); (ash) стря́хивать (perf стряхнýть); (whip) хлестнýть (perf) +instr; (switch) щёлкать (perf щёлкнуть) +instr

flicker [ˈflɪkəʳ] vi (light, flame) мерцáть (impf)

flight [flaɪt] n полёт; (of steps) пролёт (лéстницы)

flimsy [ˈflɪmzɪ] adj (shoes, clothes) лёгкий; (structure) непрóчный; (excuse, evidence) слáбый

fling [flɪŋ] (pt, pp **flung**) vt (throw) швыря́ть (perf швырнýть)

flip [flɪp] vt (coin) подбрáсывать (perf подбрóсить) щелчкóм

float [fləut] n (for fishing) поплавóк; (for swimming) пеноплáстовая доскá для обучáющихся плáвать; (money) размéнные дéньги pl ▷ vi (object, person: on water) плáвать (impf); (sound, cloud) плыть (impf) ▷ vt (idea, plan) пускáть (perf пусти́ть) в ход; **to float a company** выпускáть (perf вы́пустить) áкции компáнии на ры́нок

flock [flɔk] n (of sheep) стáдо; (of birds) стáя ▷ vi: **to flock to** стекáться (perf стéчься) в +prp

flood [flʌd] n (of water) наводнéние; (of letters, imports etc) потóк ▷ vt (subj: water) заливáть (perf зали́ть); (: people) наводня́ть (perf наводни́ть) ▷ vi (place) наполня́ться (perf напóлниться) водóй; **to flood into** (people, goods) хлы́нуть (perf) в/на +acc; **flooding** n наводнéние

floor [flɔːʳ] n (of room) пол; (storey) этáж; (of sea, valley) дно ▷ vt (subj: question, remark) сражáть (perf срази́ть); **ground** or **(US) first floor** пéрвый этáж; **floorboard** n половúца

flop [flɔp] n (failure) провáл

floppy [ˈflɔpɪ] n (also **floppy disk**) дискéта, ги́бкий диск

flora [ˈflɔːrə] n флóра; **floral** [ˈflɔːrl] adj (pattern) цветúстый

flour [ˈflauəʳ] n мукá

flourish [ˈflʌrɪʃ] vi (business) процветáть (impf); (plant) пы́шно расти́ (impf) ▷ n (bold gesture): **with a flourish** демонстрати́вно

flow [fləu] n (also Elec) потóк; (of blood, river) течéние ▷ vi течь (impf)

flower [ˈflauəʳ] n цветóк ▷ vi (plant, tree) цвести́ (impf); **flowers** цветы́; **flowerpot** n цветóчный горшóк

flown [fləun] pp of **fly**

flu [fluː] n (Med) грипп

fluent [ˈfluːənt] adj (linguist) свобóдно говоря́щий; (speech) бéглый; (writing) свобóдный; **he speaks fluent Russian, he's fluent in Russian** он свобóдно говори́т по-рýсски

fluff [flʌf] n (on jacket, carpet) ворс; **fluffy** adj (soft) пуши́стый

fluid [ˈfluːɪd] adj (movement) текýчий; (situation) перемéнчивый ▷ n жи́дкость f

fluke [fluːk] n (inf) удáча, везéние

flung [flʌŋ] pt, pp of **fling**

fluorescent [fluəˈrɛsnt] adj (dial, light) флюоресци́рующий

fluoride [ˈfluəraɪd] n фтори́д

flurry [ˈflʌrɪ] n (of snow) вихрь m; **a flurry of activity** бýрная дéятельность f

flush [flʌʃ] n (on face) румя́нец ▷ vt (drains, pipe) промывáть (perf промы́ть) ▷ vi (redden) зардéться (perf) ▷ adj: **flush**

with (*level*) на одно́м у́ровне с +*instr*; **to flush the toilet** спуска́ть (*perf* спусти́ть) во́ду в туале́те

flute [fluːt] *n* фле́йта

flutter ['flʌtəʳ] *n* (*of wings*) взмах

fly [flaɪ] (*pt* **flew**, *pp* **flown**) *n* (*insect*) му́ха; (*on trousers: also* **flies**) ширинка ▷ *vt* (*plane*) лета́ть (*impf*) на +*prp*; (*passengers, cargo*) перевози́ть (*perf* перевезти́); (*distances*) пролета́ть (*perf* пролете́ть), преодолева́ть (*perf* преодоле́ть) ▷ *vi* (*also fig*) лета́ть/лете́ть (*impf*); (*flag*) развева́ться (*impf*); **flying** *n* (*activity*) лётное де́ло ▷ *adj*: **a flying visit** кра́ткий визи́т; **with flying colours** блестя́ще

foal [fəul] *n* жеребёнок

foam [fəum] *n* пе́на; (*also* **foam rubber**) поролóн

focus ['fəukəs] (*pl* **focuses**) *n* (*Phot*) фóкус; (*of attention, argument*) средотóчие ▷ *vt* (*camera*) настра́ивать (*perf* настрóить) ▷ *vi*: **to focus (on)** (*Phot*) настра́иваться (*perf* настрóиться) (на +*acc*); **to focus on** (*fig*) сосредотáчиваться (*perf* сосредотóчиться) на +*prp*; **in focus** в фóкусе; **out of focus** не в фóкусе

foetus ['fiːtəs] (*US* **fetus**) *n* плод, зарóдыш

fog [fɔg] *n* тумáн; **foggy** *adj* тумáнный; **it's foggy** тумáнно

foil [fɔɪl] *n* (*metal*) фольгá

fold [fəuld] *n* (*crease*) склáдка; (: *in paper*) сгиб ▷ *vt* (*clothes, paper*) склáдывать (*perf* сложи́ть); (*arms*) скрéщивать (*perf* скрести́ть); **folder** *n* пáпка; (*ring-binder*) скоросшивáтель *m*; **folding** *adj* складнóй

foliage ['fəulɪɪdʒ] *n* листвá

folk [fəuk] *npl* лю́ди *pl*, нарóд *msg* ▷ *cpd* (*art, music*) нарóдный; **folks** *npl* (*inf*: *relatives*) бли́зкие *pl adj*; **folklore** ['fəuklɔːʳ] *n* фольклóр

follow ['fɔləu] *vt* (*leader, person*) слéдовать (*perf* послéдовать) за +*instr*; (*example, advice*) слéдовать (*perf* послéдовать) +*dat*; (*event, story*) следи́ть (*impf*) за +*instr*; (*route, path*) держáться (*impf*); (*on Twitter*) читáть (*impf*), фóлловить (*perf* зафóлловить) (*inf*) ▷ *vi* слéдовать (*perf* послéдовать); **to follow suit** (*fig*) слéдовать (*perf* послéдовать) примéру; **follow up** *vt* (*letter, offer*) рассмáтривать (*perf* рассмотрéть); (*case*) расслéдовать (*impf*); **follower** *n* (*of person, belief*) послéдователь(ница) *m(f)*; **following** *adj* слéдующий

fond [fɔnd] *adj* (*smile, look, parents*) лáсковый; (*memory*) прия́тный; **to be fond of** любúть (*impf*)

food [fuːd] *n* едá, пи́ща; **food poisoning** *n* пищевóе отравлéние; **food processor** *n* кýхонный комбáйн

fool [fuːl] *n* дурáк ▷ *vt* (*deceive*) обмáнывать (*perf* обманýть), одурáчивать (*perf* одурáчить); **foolish** *adj* глýпый; (*rash*) неосмотри́тельный

foot [fut] (*pl* **feet**) *n* (*of person*) ногá, ступня́; (*of animal*) ногá; (*of bed*) конéц; (*of cliff*) поднóжие; (*measure*) фут ▷ *vt*: **to foot the bill** плати́ть (*perf* заплати́ть); **on foot** пешкóм

● **FOOT**

● **Foot** — мéра длины́ рáвная 30,4 см.

foot: **footage** *n* (*Cinema: material*) кáдры *mpl*; **football** *n* футбóльный мяч; (*game*: *Brit*) футбóл; (: *US*) америкáнский футбóл; **footballer** *n* (*Brit*) футболи́ст; **foothills** *npl* предгóрья *ntpl*; **foothold** *n* (*on rock etc*) опóра; **footing** *n* (*fig*) оснóва; **to lose one's footing** (*fall*) теря́ть (*perf* потеря́ть) опóру; **footnote** *n* снóска; **footpath** *n* тропи́нка, дорóжка; **footprint** *n* след; **footwear** *n* óбувь *f*

◯ **KEYWORD**

for [fɔːʳ] *prep* **1** (*indicating destination*) в/на +*acc*; (*indicating intention*) за +*instr*; **the train for London** пóезд в *or* на Лóндон; **he left for work** он уéхал на рабóту; **he went for the paper/the doctor** он пошёл за газéтой/врачóм; **is this for me?** э́то мне *or* для меня́?; **there's a letter for you** Вам письмó; **it's time for lunch/bed** порá обéдать/спать

2 (*indicating purpose*) для +*gen*; **what's it for?** для чегó э́то?; **give it to me — what for?** дáйте мне э́то — зачéм *or* для чегó?; **to pray for peace** моли́ться (*impf*) за мир

3 (*on behalf of, representing*) **to speak for sb** говори́ть (*impf*) от лицá когó-н; **MP for Brighton** член парлáмента от Брáйтона; **he works for the government** он на госудáрственной слýжбе; **he works for a local firm** он рабóтает на мéстную фи́рму; **I'll ask him for you** я спрошý егó от Вáшего и́мени; **to do sth for sb** (*on behalf of*) дéлать (*perf* сдéлать) что-н за когó-н

4 (*because of*) из-за +*gen*; **for lack of funds** из-за отсýтствия средств; **for this reason** по э́той причи́не; **for some reason, for whatever reason** по какóй-то причи́не; **for fear of being criticized** боя́сь кри́тики; **to be famous for sth** быть (*impf*) извéстным чем-н

5 (*with regard to*) для +*gen*; **it's cold for July** для ию́ля сейчáс хóлодно; **he's tall for his age** для своегó вóзраста он высóкий; **a gift for languages** спосóбности к языкáм; **for everyone who voted yes, 50 voted no** на кáждый гóлос "за" прихóдится 50 голосóв "прóтив"

6 (*in exchange for, in favour of*) за +*acc*; **I sold it for £5** я прóдал э́то за £5; **I'm all for it** я целикóм и пóлностью за э́то

7 (*referring to distance*): **there are roadworks for five miles** на протяже́нии пяти миль произво́дятся доро́жные рабо́ты; **to stretch for miles** простира́ться (*impf*) на мно́го миль; **we walked for miles/for ten miles** мы прошли́ мно́го миль/де́сять миль

8 (*referring to time*) на +*acc*; (: *in past*): **he was away for 2 years** он был в отъе́зде 2 го́да, его́ не́ было 2 го́да; (: *in future*): **she will be away for a month** она́ уезжа́ет на ме́сяц; **can you do it for tomorrow?** Вы мо́жете сде́лать э́то к за́втрашнему дню?; **it hasn't rained for 3 weeks** уже́ 3 неде́ли не́ было дождя́; **for hours** часа́ми

9 (*with infinite clause*): **it is not for me to decide** не мне реша́ть; **there is still time for you to do it** у Вас ещё есть вре́мя сде́лать э́то; **for this to be possible ...** что́бы э́то осуществи́ть, ...

10 (*in spite of*) несмотря́ на +*acc*; **for all his complaints** несмотря́ на все его́ жа́лобы

11 (*in phrases*): **for the first/last time** в пе́рвый/после́дний раз; **for the time being** пока́
▷ *conj* (*rather formal*) и́бо

forbid [fə'bɪd] (*pt* **forbad(e)**, *pp* **forbidden**) *vt* запреща́ть (*perf* запрети́ть); **to forbid sb to do** запреща́ть (*perf* запрети́ть) кому́-н +*infin*

force [fɔːs] *n* (*also Phys*) си́ла ▷ *vt* (*compel*) вынужда́ть (*perf* вы́нудить), принужда́ть (*perf* прину́дить); (*push*) толка́ть (*perf* толкну́ть); (*break open*) взла́мывать (*perf* взлома́ть); **the Forces** (*Brit*: *Mil*) вооружённые си́лы *fpl*; **in force** в большо́м коли́честве; **to force o.s. to do** заставля́ть (*perf* заста́вить) себя́ +*infin*; **forced** *adj* (*landing*) вы́нужденный; (*smile*) принуждённый; **forceful** *adj* си́льный

ford [fɔːd] *n* (*in river*) брод

fore [fɔː] *n*: **to come to the fore** выдвига́ться (*perf* вы́двинуться)

forecast ['fɔːkɑːst] *n* прогно́з ▷ *vt* (*irreg like* **cast**) предска́зывать (*perf* предсказа́ть)

forecourt ['fɔːkɔːt] *n* (*of garage*) пере́дняя площа́дка

forefinger ['fɔːfɪŋɡə] *n* указа́тельный па́лец

forefront ['fɔːfrʌnt] *n*: **in** *or* **at the forefront of** (*movement*) в аванга́рде +*gen*

foreground ['fɔːɡraund] *n* пере́дний план

forehead ['fɔrɪd] *n* лоб

foreign ['fɔrɪn] *adj* (*language, tourist, firm*) иностра́нный; (*trade*) вне́шний; (*country*) зарубе́жный; **foreign person** иностра́нец(-нка); **foreigner** *n* иностра́нец(-нка); **foreign exchange** *n* (*system*) обме́н валю́ты; **Foreign Office**

n (*Brit*) министе́рство иностра́нных дел; **Foreign Secretary** *n* (*Brit*) мини́стр иностра́нных дел

foreman ['fɔːmən] *irreg n* (*Industry*) ма́стер

foremost ['fɔːməust] *adj* (*most important*) важне́йший ▷ *adv*: **first and foremost** в пе́рвую о́чередь, пре́жде всего́

forensic [fə'rensɪk] *adj* (*medicine, test*) суде́бный

foresee [fɔː'siː] (*irreg like* **see**) *vt* предви́деть (*impf/perf*); **foreseeable** *adj*: **in the foreseeable future** в обозри́мом бу́дущем

forest ['fɔrɪst] *n* лес; **forestry** *n* лесово́дство, лесни́чество

forever [fə'rɛvə] *adv* (*for good*) навсегда́, наве́чно; (*endlessly*) ве́чно

foreword ['fɔːwəːd] *n* предисло́вие

forgave [fə'ɡeɪv] *pt of* **forgive**

forge [fɔːdʒ] *vt* (*signature, money*) подде́лывать (*perf* подде́лать); **forgery** *n* подде́лка

forget [fə'ɡɛt] (*pt* **forgot**, *pp* **forgotten**) *vt* забыва́ть (*perf* забы́ть); (*appointment*) забыва́ть (*perf* забы́ть) о +*prp* ▷ *vi* забыва́ть (*perf* забы́ть); **forgetful** *adj* забы́вчивый

forgive [fə'ɡɪv] (*pt* **forgave**, *pp* **forgiven**) *vt* (*pardon*) проща́ть (*perf* прости́ть); **to forgive sb sth** проща́ть (*perf* прости́ть) кому́-н что-н; **to forgive sb for sth** (*excuse*) проща́ть (*perf* прости́ть) кого́-н за что-н; **I forgave him for doing it** я прости́л его́ за то, что он сде́лал э́то

forgot [fə'ɡɔt] *pt of* **forget**; **forgotten** *pp* *of* **forget**

fork [fɔːk] *n* ви́лка; (*for gardening*) ви́лы *pl*; (*in road, river, tree*) разветвле́ние

forlorn [fə'lɔːn] *adj* поки́нутый; (*hope, attempt*) тще́тный

form [fɔːm] *n* (*type*) вид; (*shape*) фо́рма; (*Scol*) класс; (*questionnaire*) анке́та; (*also* **booking form**) бланк ▷ *vt* (*make*) образо́вывать (*perf* образова́ть); (*organization, group*) формирова́ть (*perf* сформирова́ть); (*idea, habit*) выраба́тывать (*perf* вы́работать); **in top form** в прекра́сной фо́рме

formal ['fɔːməl] *adj* форма́льный; (*person, behaviour*) церемо́нный; (*occasion*) официа́льный; **formal clothes** официа́льная фо́рма оде́жды; **formality** [fɔː'mælɪtɪ] *n* форма́льность *f*; (*of person, behaviour*) церемо́нность *f*; (*of occasion*) официа́льность *f*

format ['fɔːmæt] *n* форма́т

formation [fɔː'meɪʃən] *n* формирова́ние

former ['fɔːmə] *adj* бы́вший; (*earlier*) пре́жний ▷ *n*: **the former ... the latter ...** пе́рвый ... после́дний ...; **formerly** *adv* ра́нее, ра́ньше

formidable ['fɔːmɪdəbl] *adj* (*opponent*) гро́зный; (*task*) серьёзнейший

formula ['fɔːmjulə] (pl **formulae** or **formulas**) n (Math, Chem) формула; (plan) схема

fort [fɔːt] n крепость f, форт

forthcoming adj предстоящий; (person) общительный

fortieth ['fɔːtɪɪθ] adj сороковой

fortnight ['fɔːtnaɪt] (Brit) n две недели; **fortnightly** adv раз в две недели ▷ adj: **fortnightly magazine** журнал, выходящий раз в две недели

fortress ['fɔːtrɪs] n крепость f

fortunate ['fɔːtʃənɪt] adj (event, choice) счастливый; (person) удачливый; **he was fortunate to get a job** на его счастье, он получил работу; **it is fortunate that ...** к счастью ...; **fortunately** adv к счастью; **fortunately for him** на его счастье

fortune ['fɔːtʃən] n (wealth) состояние; (also **good fortune**) счастье, удача; **ill fortune** невезение, неудача

forty ['fɔːtɪ] n сорок

forum ['fɔːrəm] n форум

forward ['fɔːwəd] adv вперёд ▷ n (Sport) нападающий(-ая) m(f) adj, форвард m ▷ vt (letter, parcel) пересылать (perf переслать) ▷ adj (position) передний; (not shy) дерзкий; **to move forward** (progress) продвигаться (perf продвинуться)

fossil ['fɔsl] n окаменелость f, ископаемое nt adj

foster ['fɔstəʳ] vt (child) брать (perf взять) на воспитание

fought [fɔːt] pt, pp of **fight**

foul [faul] adj гадкий, мёрзкий; (language) непристойный; (temper) жуткий ▷ n (Sport) нарушение ▷ vt (dirty) гадить (perf загадить)

found [faund] pt, pp of **find** ▷ vt (establish) основывать (perf основать); **foundation** n (base) основа; (organization) общество, фонд; (also **foundation cream**) крем под макияж; **foundations** npl (of building) фундамент msg; **founder** n основатель(ница) m(f)

fountain ['fauntɪn] n фонтан

four [fɔːʳ] n четыре; **on all fours** на четвереньках

fourteen ['fɔːtiːn] n четырнадцать; **fourteenth** adj четырнадцатый

fourth ['fɔːθ] adj четвёртый ▷ n (Aut: also **fourth gear**) четвёртая скорость f

fowl [faul] n птица

fox [fɔks] n лиса ▷ vt озадачивать (perf озадачить)

foyer ['fɔɪeɪ] n фойе nt ind

fraction ['frækʃən] n (portion) частица; (Math) дробь f; **a fraction of a second** доля секунды

fracture ['fræktʃəʳ] n перелом ▷ vt (bone) ломать (perf сломать)

fragile ['frædʒaɪl] adj хрупкий

fragment ['frægmənt] n фрагмент; (of glass) осколок, обломок

fragrance ['freɪgrəns] n благоухание

frail [freɪl] adj (person) слабый, немощный; (structure) хрупкий

frame [freɪm] n (of building, structure) каркас, остов; (of person) сложение; (of picture, window) рама; (of spectacles: also **frames**) оправа ▷ vt оформлять (perf оформить); **frame of mind** настроение; **framework** n каркас; (fig) рамки fpl

France [frɑːns] n Франция

franchise ['fræntʃaɪz] n (Pol) право голоса; (Comm) франшиза

frank [fræŋk] adj (discussion, person) откровенный; (look) открытый; **frankly** adv откровенно

frantic ['fræntɪk] adj иступлённый; (hectic) лихорадочный

fraud [frɔːd] n (person) мошенник; (crime) мошенничество

fraught [frɔːt] adj: **fraught with** чреватый +instr

fray [freɪ] vi трепаться (perf истрепаться); **tempers were frayed** все были на грани срыва

freak [friːk] adj странный, ненормальный ▷ n: **he is a freak** он со странностями

freckle ['frɛkl] n (usu pl) веснушка

free [friː] adj свободный; (costing nothing) бесплатный ▷ vt (prisoner etc) освобождать (perf освободить), выпускать (perf выпустить) (на свободу); (object) высвобождать (perf высвободить); **free (of charge), for free** бесплатно; **freedom** n свобода; **free kick** n (Football) свободный удар; **freelance** adj внештатный, работающий по договорам; **freely** adv (without restriction) свободно; (liberally) обильно; **free-range** adj: **free-range eggs** яйца от кур на свободном выгуле; **free will** n: **of one's own free will** по (своей) доброй воле

freeze [friːz] (pt **froze**, pp **frozen**) vi (weather) холодать (perf похолодать); (liquid, pipe, person) замерзать (perf замёрзнуть); (person: stop moving) застывать (perf застыть) ▷ vt замораживать (perf заморозить) ▷ n (on arms, wages) замораживание; **freezer** n морозильник

freezing ['friːzɪŋ] adj: **freezing (cold)** ледяной; n: **3 degrees below freezing** 3 градуса мороза or ниже нуля; **I'm freezing** я замёрз; **it's freezing** очень холодно

freight [freɪt] n фрахт

French [frɛntʃ] adj французский; ▷ npl: **the French** (people) французы mpl; **French fries** npl (US) картофель msg фри; **Frenchman** irreg n француз

frenzy ['frɛnzɪ] n (of violence) остервенение, бешенство

frequency ['friːkwənsɪ] n частота

frequent [adj 'fri:kwənt, vb frɪ'kwɛnt] adj
частый ▷ vt посещать (impf);
frequently adv часто
fresh [frɛʃ] adj свежий; (instructions,
approach) новый; **to make a fresh start**
начинать (perf начать) заново; **fresh in
one's mind** свежо в памяти; **fresher** n
(Brit: inf) первокурсник; **freshly** adv:
freshly made свежеприготовленный;
freshly painted свежевыкрашенный;
freshwater adj (lake) пресный; (fish)
пресноводный
fret [frɛt] vi волноваться (impf)
friction ['frɪkʃən] n трение; (fig) трения
ntpl
Friday ['fraɪdɪ] n пятница
fridge [frɪdʒ] n (Brit) холодильник
fried [fraɪd] pt, pp of **fry** ▷ adj жареный
friend [frɛnd] n (male) друг; (female)
подруга ▷ vt добавлять (perf добавить) в
друзья, зафрендить (perf) (inf); **friendly**
adj (person, smile etc) дружелюбный;
(government, country) дружественный;
(place, restaurant) приятный ▷ n (also
friendly match) товарищеский матч; **to
be friendly with** дружить (impf) с +instr; **to
be friendly to sb** относиться (perf
отнестись) к кому-н дружелюбно;
friendship n дружба
fright [fraɪt] n испуг; **to take fright**
испугаться (perf); **frighten** vt пугать
(perf испугать); **frightened** adj
испуганный; **to be frightened (of)** бояться
(impf) (+gen); **he is frightened by change**
его пугают изменения; **frightening** adj
страшный, устрашающий
fringe [frɪndʒ] n (Brit: of hair) чёлка; (on
shawl, lampshade etc) бахрома; (of forest
etc) край, окраина
frivolous ['frɪvələs] adj (conduct, person)
легкомысленный; (object, activity)
пустячный
frog [frɔg] n лягушка

O KEYWORD

from [frɔm] prep **1** (indicating starting
place, origin etc) из +gen, с +gen; (from a
person) от +gen; **he is from Cyprus** он с
Кипра; **from London to Glasgow** из
Лондона в Глазго; **a letter from my sister**
письмо от моей сестры; **a quotation from
Dickens** цитата из Диккенса; **to drink from
the bottle** пить (impf) из бутылки; **where
do you come from?** Вы откуда?
2 (indicating movement: from inside) из
+gen; (: away from) от +gen, с +gen; (: off)
с +gen; (: from behind) из-за +gen; **she ran from
the house** она выбежала из дома; **the car
drove away from the house** машина
отъехала от дома; **he took the magazine
from the table** он взял журнал со стола;
they got up from the table они встали
из-за стола

3 (indicating time) с +gen; **from two
o'clock to or until or till three (o'clock)** с
двух часов до трёх (часов); **from January
(to August)** с января (по август)
4 (indicating distance: position) от +gen;
(: motion) до +gen; **the hotel is one
kilometre from the beach** гостиница
находится в километре от пляжа; **we're
still a long way from home** мы ещё далеко
от дома
5 (indicating price, number etc: range) от
+gen; (: change) с +gen; **prices range from
£10 to £50** цены колеблются от £10 до
£50; **the interest rate was increased from
nine per cent to ten per cent** процентные
ставки повысились с девяти до десяти
процентов
6 (indicating difference) от +gen; **to be
different from sb/sth** отличаться (impf) от
кого-н/чего-н
7 (because of, on the basis of): **from what
he says** судя по тому, что он говорит;
from what I understand как я понимаю;
to act from conviction действовать (impf)
по убеждению; **he is weak from hunger**
он слаб от голода

front [frʌnt] n (of house, also fig) фасад;
(of dress) перед; (of train, car) передняя
часть f; (also **sea front**) набережная f adj;
(Mil, Meteorology) фронт ▷ adj
передний; **in front** вперёд; **in front of**
перед +instr; **front door** n входная
дверь f; **frontier** ['frʌntɪə'] n граница;
front page n первая страница (газеты)
frost [frɔst] n мороз; (also **hoarfrost**)
иней; **frostbite** n обморожение; **frosty**
adj (weather, night) морозный; (welcome,
look) ледяной
froth ['frɔθ] n (on liquid) пена
frown [fraun] n нахмуренный взгляд
froze [frəuz] pt of **freeze**; **frozen** pp of
freeze
fruit [fru:t] n inv фрукт; (fig) плод; **fruit
machine** n (Brit) игровой автомат
frustrate [frʌs'treɪt] vt (person, plan)
расстраивать (perf расстроить)
fry [fraɪ] (pt, pp **fried**) vt жарить (perf
пожарить); **frying pan** (US **fry-pan**) n
сковорода
ft abbr = **feet**; **foot**
fudge [fʌdʒ] n ≈ сливочная помадка
fuel ['fjuəl] n (for heating) топливо; (for
plane, car) горючее nt adj
fulfil [ful'fɪl] (US **fulfill**) vt (function,
desire, promise) исполнять (perf
исполнить); (ambition) осуществлять (perf
осуществить)
full [ful] adj полный; (skirt) широкий
▷ adv: **to know full well that** прекрасно
знать (impf), что; **at full volume/power** на
полную громкость/мощность; **I'm full (up)**
я сыт; **he is full of enthusiasm/hope** он
полон энтузиазма/надежды; **full details**

все дета́ли; **at full speed** на по́лной ско́рости; **a full two hours** це́лых два часа́; **in full** по́лностью; **full-length** adj (film, novel) полнометра́жный; (coat) дли́нный; (mirror) высо́кий; **full moon** n по́лная луна́; **full-scale** adj (attack, war, search etc) широкомасшта́бный; **full-time** adj, adv (study) на дневно́м отделе́нии; (work) на по́лной ста́вке; **fully** adv (completely) по́лностью, вполне́; **fully as big as** по кра́йней ме́ре тако́й же величины́, как

fumes [fjuːmz] npl испаре́ния ntpl, пары́ mpl

fun [fʌn] n: **what fun!** как ве́село!; **to have fun** весели́ться (perf повесели́ться); **he's good fun (to be with)** с ним ве́село; **for fun** для заба́вы; **to make fun of** подшу́чивать (perf подшути́ть) над +instr

function ['fʌŋkʃən] n фу́нкция; (product) произво́дная f adj; (social occasion) приём ▷ vi (operate) функциони́ровать (impf)

fund [fʌnd] n фонд; (of knowledge etc) запа́с; **funds** npl (money) (де́нежные) сре́дства ntpl, фо́нды mpl

fundamental [fʌndə'mɛntl] adj фундамента́льный

funeral ['fjuːnərəl] n по́хороны pl

fungus ['fʌŋgəs] (pl **fungi**) n (plant) гриб; (mould) пле́сень f

funnel ['fʌnl] n (for pouring) воро́нка; (of ship) труба́

funny ['fʌnɪ] adj (amusing) заба́вный; (strange) стра́нный, чудно́й

fur [fəːʳ] n мех

furious ['fjuərɪəs] adj (person) взбешённый; (exchange, argument) бу́рный; (effort, speed) неи́стовый

furnish ['fəːnɪʃ] vt (room, building) обставля́ть (perf обста́вить); **to furnish sb with sth** (supply) предоставля́ть (perf предоста́вить) что-н кому́-н; **furnishings** npl обстано́вка fsg

furniture ['fəːnɪtʃəʳ] n ме́бель f; **piece of furniture** предме́т ме́бели

furry ['fəːrɪ] adj пуши́стый

further ['fəːðəʳ] adj дополни́тельный ▷ adv (farther) да́льше; (moreover) бо́лее того́ ▷ vt (career, project) продвига́ть (perf продви́нуть), соде́йствовать (impf/ perf) +dat; **further education** n (Brit) профессиона́льно-техни́ческое образова́ние

● FURTHER EDUCATION
●
● **Further education** — сре́днее
● специа́льное образова́ние. Его́ мо́жно
● получи́ть в ко́лледжах. Обуче́ние
● прово́дится на осно́ве по́лного
● дневно́го ку́рса, почасово́го или
● вече́рнего ку́рса.

furthermore adv бо́лее того́
furthest ['fəːðɪst] superl of **far**

fury ['fjuərɪ] n я́рость f, бе́шенство

fuse [fjuːz] (US **fuze**) n (Elec) предохрани́тель m; (on bomb) фити́ль m

fusion ['fjuːʒən] n (of ideas, qualities) слия́ние; (also **nuclear fusion**) я́дерный си́нтез

fuss [fʌs] n (excitement) сумато́ха; (anxiety) суета́; (trouble) шум; **to make** or **kick up a fuss** поднима́ть (perf подня́ть) шум; **to make a fuss of sb** носи́ться (impf) с кем-н; **fussy** adj (nervous) суетли́вый; (choosy) ме́лочный, су́етный; (elaborate) вы́чурный

future ['fjuːtʃəʳ] adj бу́дущий ▷ n бу́дущее nt adj; (Ling: also **future tense**) бу́дущее вре́мя nt; **in (the) future** в бу́дущем; **in the near/immediate future** в недалёком/ближа́йшем бу́дущем

fuze [fjuːz] n (US) = **fuse**

fuzzy ['fʌzɪ] adj (thoughts, picture) расплы́вчатый; (hair) пуши́стый

g

g *abbr* (= *gram*) г (= *грамм*)

gadget ['gædʒɪt] *n* приспособле́ние

Gaelic ['geɪlɪk] *n* (*Ling*) га́льский язы́к

gag [gæg] *n* (*on mouth*) кляп ▷ *vt* вставля́ть (*perf* вста́вить) кляп +*dat*

gain [geɪn] *n* (*increase*) приро́ст ▷ *vt* (*confidence, experience*) приобрета́ть (*perf* приобрести́); (*speed*) набира́ть (*perf* набра́ть) ▷ *vi* (*benefit*): **to gain from sth** извлека́ть (*perf* извле́чь) вы́году из чего́-н; **to gain 3 pounds (in weight)** поправля́ться (*perf* попра́виться) на 3 фу́нта; **to gain on sb** догоня́ть (*perf* догна́ть) кого́-н

gala ['gɑːlə] *n* (*festival*) пра́зднество

galaxy ['gæləksɪ] *n* гала́ктика

gale [geɪl] *n* (*wind*) си́льный ве́тер; (*at sea*) штормово́й ве́тер

gallery ['gælərɪ] *n* (*also* **art gallery**) галере́я; (*in hall, church*) балко́н; (*in theatre*) галёрка

gallon ['gælən] *n* галло́н (4,5 ли́тра)

gallop ['gæləp] *vi* (*horse*) скака́ть (*impf*) (гало́пом), галопи́ровать (*impf*)

gamble ['gæmbl] *n* риско́ванное предприя́тие, риск ▷ *vt* (*money*) ста́вить (*perf* поста́вить) ▷ *vi* (*take a risk*) рискова́ть (*perf* рискну́ть); (*bet*) игра́ть (*impf*) в аза́ртные и́гры; **to gamble on sth** (*also fig*) де́лать (*perf* сде́лать) ста́вку на что-н; **gambler** *n* игро́к; **gambling** ['gæmblɪŋ] *n* аза́ртные и́гры *fpl*

game [geɪm] *n* игра́; (*match*) матч; (*esp Tennis*) гейм; (*also* **board game**) насто́льная игра́; (*Culin*) дичь *f* ▷ *adj* (*willing*): **game (for)** гото́вый (на +*acc*); **big game** кру́пный зверь

gammon ['gæmən] *n* (*bacon*) о́корок; (*ham*) ветчина́

gang [gæŋ] *n* ба́нда; (*of friends*) компа́ния

gangster ['gæŋstər] *n* га́нгстер

gap [gæp] *n* (*space*) промежу́ток; (: *between teeth*) щерби́на; (: *in time*) интерва́л; (*difference*) расхожде́ние; **generation gap** разногла́сия ме́жду поколе́ниями

garage ['gærɑːʒ] *n* гара́ж; (*petrol station*) запра́вочная ста́нция, бензоколо́нка

garbage ['gɑːbɪdʒ] *n* (*US: rubbish*) му́сор; (*inf: nonsense*) ерунда́; **garbage can** *n* (*US*) помо́йный я́щик

garden ['gɑːdn] *n* сад; **gardens** *npl* (*park*) парк *msg*; **gardener** *n* садово́д; (*employee*) садо́вник(-ица); **gardening** *n* садово́дство

garlic ['gɑːlɪk] *n* чесно́к

garment ['gɑːmənt] *n* наря́д

garnish ['gɑːnɪʃ] *vt* украша́ть (*perf* укра́сить)

garrison ['gærɪsn] *n* гарнизо́н

gas [gæs] *n* газ; (*US: gasoline*) бензи́н ▷ *vt* (*kill*) удуша́ть (*perf* удуши́ть) (*газом*)

gasoline ['gæsəliːn] *n* (*US*) бензи́н

gasp [gɑːsp] *n* (*breath*) вдох

gas station *n* (*US*) запра́вочная ста́нция, бензоколо́нка

gate [geɪt] *n* кали́тка; (*at airport*) вы́ход; **gates** *npl* воро́та; **gateway** *n* воро́та *pl*

gather ['gæðər] *vt* собира́ть (*perf* собра́ть); (*understand*) полага́ть (*impf*) ▷ *vi* (*assemble*) собира́ться (*perf* собра́ться); **to gather speed** набира́ть (*perf* набра́ть) ско́рость; **gathering** *n* собра́ние

gauge [geɪdʒ] *n* (*instrument*) измери́тельный прибо́р ▷ *vt* (*amount, quantity*) измеря́ть (*perf* изме́рить); (*fig*) оце́нивать (*perf* оцени́ть)

gave [geɪv] *pt of* **give**

gay [geɪ] *adj* (*cheerful*) весёлый; (*homosexual*): **gay bar** бар для голубы́х *or* гомосексуали́стов ▷ *n* гомосексуали́ст, голубо́й *m adj*; **he is gay** он гомосексуали́ст *or* голубо́й

gaze [geɪz] *n* (при́стальный) взгляд ▷ *vi*: **to gaze at sth** разгля́дывать (*impf*) что-н

GB *abbr* = **Great Britain**

GCSE *n abbr* (*Brit*) (= *General Certificate of Secondary Education*)

- **GCSE**
-
- GCSE — аттеста́т о сре́днем
- образова́нии. Шко́льники сдаю́т
- экза́мены для получе́ния э́того
- аттеста́та в во́зрасте 15-16 лет. Часть
- предме́тов, по кото́рым сдаю́тся
- экза́мены обяза́тельна, часть - по
- вы́бору. Одна́ко э́того аттеста́та не
- доста́точно для поступле́ния в
- университе́т.

gear [gɪər] *n* (*equipment, belongings etc*) принадле́жности *fpl*; (*Aut*) ско́рость *f*; (: *mechanism*) переда́ча ▷ *vt* (*fig*): **to gear sth to** приспоса́бливать (*perf* приспосо́бить) что-н к +dat; **top** or (US) **high/low gear** вы́сшая/ни́зкая ско́рость; **in gear** в зацепле́нии; **gearbox** n коро́бка переда́ч or скоросте́й; **gear lever** (US **gear shift**) n переключа́тель m скоросте́й

geese [giːs] npl of **goose**

gem [dʒɛm] n (stone) драгоце́нный ка́мень m, самоцве́т

Gemini ['dʒɛmɪnaɪ] n Близнецы́ mpl

gender ['dʒɛndə'] n (sex) пол; (Ling) род

gene [dʒiːn] n ген

general ['dʒɛnərl] n (Mil) генера́л ⊳ adj о́бщий; (movement, interest) всео́бщий; **in general** в о́бщем; **general election** n всео́бщие вы́боры mpl; **generally** adv вообще́; (+vb) обы́чно; **to become generally available** станови́ться (perf стать) общедосту́пным(-ой); **it is generally accepted that ...** общепри́знанно, что ...

generate ['dʒɛnəreɪt] vt (power, electricity) генери́ровать (impf), выраба́тывать (perf вы́работать); (excitement, interest) вызыва́ть (perf вы́звать); (jobs) создава́ть (perf созда́ть)

generation [dʒɛnə'reɪʃən] n поколе́ние; (of power) генери́рование; **for generations** из поколе́ния в поколе́ние

generator ['dʒɛnəreɪtə'] n генера́тор

generosity [dʒɛnə'rɔsɪtɪ] n ще́дрость f

generous ['dʒɛnərəs] adj (person: lavish) ще́дрый; (: unselfish) великоду́шный; (amount of money) значи́тельный

genetics [dʒɪ'nɛtɪks] n гене́тика

Geneva [dʒɪ'niːvə] n Жене́ва

genitals ['dʒɛnɪtlz] npl половы́е о́рганы mpl

genius ['dʒiːnɪəs] n (skill) тала́нт; (person) ге́ний

gent [dʒɛnt] n abbr (Brit: inf) = **gentleman**

gentle ['dʒɛntl] adj не́жный, ла́сковый; (nature, movement, landscape) мя́гкий

gentleman ['dʒɛntlmən] irreg n (man) джентльме́н

gently ['dʒɛntlɪ] adv (smile, treat, speak) не́жно, ла́сково; (curve, slope, move) мя́гко

gents [dʒɛnts] n: **the gents** мужско́й туале́т

genuine ['dʒɛnjuɪn] adj (sincere) и́скренний; (real) по́длинный

geographic(al) [dʒɪə'græfɪk(l)] adj географи́ческий

geography [dʒɪ'ɔgrəfɪ] n геогра́фия

geology [dʒɪ'ɔlədʒɪ] n геоло́гия

geometry [dʒɪ'ɔmətrɪ] n геоме́трия

Georgia ['dʒɔːdʒə] n Гру́зия; **Georgian** adj грузи́нский

geranium [dʒɪ'reɪnɪəm] n гера́нь f

geriatric [dʒɛrɪ'ætrɪk] adj гериатри́ческий

germ [dʒəːm] n (Med) микро́б

German ['dʒəːmən] adj неме́цкий ⊳ n

не́мец(-мка); **German measles** n (Brit) красну́ха

Germany ['dʒəːmənɪ] n Герма́ния

gesture ['dʒɛstjə'] n жест

○ **KEYWORD**

get [gɛt] (pt, pp **got**) (US) ⊳ (pp **gotten**) vi

1 (become) станови́ться (perf стать); **it's getting late** стано́вится по́здно; **to get old** старе́ть (perf постаре́ть); **to get tired** устава́ть (perf уста́ть); **to get cold** мёрзнуть (perf замёрзнуть); **to get annoyed easily** легко́ раздража́ться (impf); **he was getting bored** ему́ ста́ло ску́чно; **he gets drunk every weekend** он напива́ется ка́ждый выходно́й

2 (be): **he got killed** его́ уби́ли; **when do I get paid?** когда́ мне запла́тят?

3 (go): **to get to/from** добира́ться (perf добра́ться) до +gen/из +gen/с +gen; **how did you get here?** как Вы сюда́ добрали́сь?

4 (begin): **to get to know sb** узнава́ть (perf узна́ть) кого́-н; **I'm getting to like him** он начина́ет мне нра́виться; **let's get started** дава́йте начнём

⊳ modal aux vb: **you've got to do it** Вы должны́ э́то сде́лать

⊳ vt **1**: **to get sth done** сде́лать (perf) что-н; **to get the washing done** стира́ть (perf постира́ть); **to get the dishes done** мыть (помы́ть or вы́мыть perf) посу́ду; **to get the car started** or **to start** заводи́ть (perf завести́) маши́ну; **to get sb to do** заставля́ть (perf заста́вить) кого́-н +infin; **to get sb ready** собира́ть (perf собра́ть) кого́-н; **to get sth ready** гото́вить (perf пригото́вить) что-н; **to get sb drunk** напа́ивать (perf напои́ть) кого́-н; **she got me into trouble** она́ вовлекла́ меня́ в неприя́тности

2 (obtain: permission, results) получа́ть (perf получи́ть); (find: job, flat) находи́ть (perf найти́); (person: call) звать (perf позва́ть); (: pick up) забира́ть (perf забра́ть); (call out: doctor, plumber etc) вызыва́ть (perf вы́звать); (object: carry) приноси́ть (perf принести́); (: buy) покупа́ть (perf купи́ть); (: deliver) доставля́ть (perf доста́вить); **we must get him to hospital** мы должны́ доста́вить его́ в больни́цу; **do you think we'll get the piano through the door?** как Вы ду́маете, мы прота́щим пиани́но че́рез дверь?; **I'll get the car** я схожу́ за маши́ной; **can I get you something to drink?** Позво́льте предложи́ть Вам что́-нибудь вы́пить?

3 (receive) получа́ть (perf получи́ть); **to get a reputation for** приобрета́ть (perf приобрести́) дурну́ю репута́цию +instr; **what did you get for your birthday?** что Вам подари́ли на день рожде́ния?

4 (grab) хвата́ть (perf схвати́ть); (hit): **the bullet got him in the leg** пу́ля попа́ла ему́ в но́гу

5 (*catch, take*): **we got a taxi** мы взя́ли такси́; **did she get her plane?** она́ успе́ла на самолёт?; **what train are you getting?** каки́м по́ездом Вы е́дете?; **where do I get the train?** где мне сесть на по́езд?
6 (*understand*) понима́ть (*perf* поня́ть); (*hear*) расслы́шать (*perf*); **(do you) get it?** (*inf*) (тебе́) поня́тно?; **I've got it!** тепе́рь поня́тно!; **I'm sorry, I didn't get your name** прости́те, я не расслы́шал Ва́ше и́мя
7 (*have, possess*): **how many children have you got?** ско́лько у Вас дете́й?; **I've got very little time** у меня́ о́чень ма́ло вре́мени
get about vi (*news*) распространя́ться (*perf* распространи́ться); **I don't get about much now** (*go places*) тепе́рь я ма́ло где быва́ю
get along vi: **get along with** ла́дить (*impf*) с +*instr*; (*manage*) = **get by**; **I'd better be getting along** мне, пожа́луй, пора́ (идти́)
get at vt fus (*criticize*) придира́ться (*perf* придра́ться) к +*dat*; (*reach*) дотя́гиваться (*perf* дотяну́ться) до +*gen*
get away vi (*leave*) уходи́ть (*perf* уйти́); (*escape*) убега́ть (*perf* убежа́ть)
get away with vt fus: **he gets away with everything** ему́ всё схо́дит с рук
get back vi (*return*) возвраща́ться (*perf* возврати́ться), верну́ться (*perf*) ▷ vt получа́ть (*perf* получи́ть) наза́д *or* обра́тно
get by vi (*pass*) проходи́ть (*perf* пройти́); (*manage*): **to get by without** обходи́ться (*perf* обойти́сь) без +*gen*; **I will get by** (*manage*) я спра́влюсь
get down vt (*depress*) угнета́ть (*impf*) ▷ vi: **to get down from** слеза́ть (*perf* слезть) с +*gen*
get down to vt fus сади́ться (*perf* сесть) *or* бра́ться (*perf* взя́ться) за +*acc*
get in vi (*train*) прибыва́ть (*perf* прибы́ть), приходи́ть (*perf* прийти́); (*arrive home*) приходи́ть (*perf* прийти́); (*to concert, building*) попада́ть (*perf* попа́сть), проходи́ть (*perf* пройти́); **he got in by ten votes** он прошёл с большинство́м в де́сять голосо́в; **as soon as the bus arrived we all got in** как то́лько авто́бус подошёл, мы се́ли в него́
get into vt fus (*building*) входи́ть (*perf* войти́) в +*acc*; (*vehicle*) сади́ться (*perf* сесть) в +*acc*; (*clothes*) влеза́ть (*perf* влезть) в +*acc*; (*fight, argument*) вступа́ть (*perf* вступи́ть) в +*acc*; (*university, college*) поступа́ть (*perf* поступи́ть) в +*acc*; (*subj: train*) прибыва́ть (*perf* прибы́ть) в/на +*acc*; **to get into bed** ложи́ться (*perf* лечь) в посте́ль
get off vi (*escape*): **to get off lightly/with sth** отде́лываться (*perf* отде́латься) легко́/чем-н
▷ vt (*clothes*) снима́ть (*perf* снять)

▷ vt fus (*train, bus*) сходи́ть (*perf* сойти́) с +*gen*; (*horse, bicycle*) слеза́ть (*perf* слезть) с +*gen*
get on vi (*age*) старе́ть (*impf*); **how are you getting on?** как Ва́ши успе́хи?
get out vi (*leave*) выбира́ться (*perf* вы́браться); (*socialize*) выбира́ться (*perf* вы́браться) из до́ма
get out of vt fus (*duty*) отде́лываться (*perf* отде́латься) от +*gen*
get over vt fus (*illness*) преодолева́ть (*perf* преодоле́ть)
get round vt fus (*law, rule*) обходи́ть (*perf* обойти́); (*fig: person*) угова́ривать (*perf* уговори́ть)
get through vi (*Tel*) дозва́ниваться (*perf* дозвони́ться)
get through to vt fus (*Tel*) дозва́ниваться (*perf* дозвони́ться) до +*gen*
get together vi (*several people*) собира́ться (*perf* собра́ться) ▷ vt (*people*) собира́ть (*perf* собра́ть)
get up vi встава́ть (*perf* встать)
get up to vt fus (*Brit*) затева́ть (*perf* затея́ть); **they're always getting up to mischief** они́ всегда́ прока́зничают

ghastly ['gɑːstlɪ] *adj* ме́рзкий, омерзи́тельный
ghetto ['gɛtəʊ] *n* ге́тто *nt ind*
ghost [gəʊst] *n* (*spirit*) привиде́ние, при́зрак
giant ['dʒaɪənt] *n* (*in myths*) велика́н; (*fig: Comm*) гига́нт ▷ *adj* огро́мный
gift [gɪft] *n* (*present*) пода́рок; (*ability*) дар, тала́нт; **gifted** *adj* одарённый
gigantic [dʒaɪ'gæntɪk] *adj* гига́нтский
giggle ['gɪgl] *vi* хихи́кать (*impf*)
gills [gɪlz] *npl* (*of fish*) жа́бры *fpl*
gilt [gɪlt] *adj* позоло́ченный
gimmick ['gɪmɪk] *n* уло́вка, трюк
gin [dʒɪn] *n* джин
ginger ['dʒɪndʒər] *n* (*spice*) имби́рь *m*
giraffe [dʒɪ'rɑːf] *n* жира́ф
girl [gəːl] *n* (*child*) де́вочка; (*young unmarried woman*) де́вушка; (*daughter*) до́чка; **an English girl** молода́я англича́нка; **girlfriend** *n* подру́га
gist [dʒɪst] *n* суть *f*

○ **KEYWORD**

give [gɪv] (*pt* **gave**, *pt* **given**) *vt* **1** (*hand over*): **to give sb sth** *or* **sth to sb** дава́ть (*perf* дать) кому́-н что-н; **they gave her a book for her birthday** они́ подари́ли ей кни́гу на день рожде́ния
2 (*used with noun to replace verb*): **to give a sigh** вздыха́ть (*perf* вздохну́ть); **to give a shrug** передёргивать (*perf* передёрнуть) плеча́ми; **to give a speech** выступа́ть (*perf* вы́ступить) с ре́чью; **to give a lecture** чита́ть (*perf* прочита́ть) ле́кцию; **to give**

three cheers три́жды прокрича́ть (perf) "ура́"

3 (tell: news) сообща́ть (perf сообщи́ть); (advice) дава́ть (perf дать); **could you give him a message for me please? tell him that ...** переда́йте ему́, пожа́луйста, от меня́, что ...;

I've got a message to give you from your brother я до́лжен переда́ть тебе́ что-то от твоего́ бра́та

4: to give sb sth (clothing, food, right) дава́ть (perf дать) кому́-н что-н; (title) присва́ивать (perf присво́ить) кому́-н что-н; (honour, responsibility) возлага́ть (perf возложи́ть) на кого́-н что-н; **to give sb a surprise** удивля́ть (perf удиви́ть) кого́-н; **that's given me an idea** это навело́ меня́ на мысль

5 (dedicate: one's life) отдава́ть (perf отда́ть); **you'll need to give me more time** Вы должны́ дать мне бо́льше вре́мени; **she gave it all her attention** она́ отнесла́сь к э́тому с больши́м внима́нием

6 (organize: dinner etc) дава́ть (perf дать)
▷ vi **1** (stretch: fabric) растя́гиваться (perf растяну́ться)

2 (break, collapse) = **give way**

give away vt (money, object) отдава́ть (perf отда́ть); (bride) отдава́ть (perf отда́ть) за́муж

give back vt отдава́ть (perf отда́ть) обра́тно

give in vi (yield) сдава́ться (perf сда́ться)
▷ vt (essay etc) сдава́ть (perf сдать)

give off vt fus (smoke, heat) выделя́ть (impf)

give out vt (distribute) раздава́ть (perf разда́ть)

give up vi (stop trying) сдава́ться (perf сда́ться) ▷ vt (job, boyfriend) броса́ть (perf бро́сить); (idea, hope) оставля́ть (perf оста́вить); **to give up smoking** броса́ть (perf бро́сить) кури́ть;

to give o.s. up сдава́ться (perf сда́ться)

give way vi (rope, ladder) не выде́рживать (perf вы́держать); (wall, roof) обва́ливаться (perf обвали́ться); (floor) прова́ливаться (perf провали́ться); (chair) ру́хнуть (perf); (Brit: Aut) уступа́ть (perf уступи́ть) доро́гу; **his legs gave way beneath him** у него́ подкоси́лись но́ги

glacier ['glæsɪə^r] n ледни́к
glad [glæd] adj: **I am glad** я рад; **gladly** adv (willingly) с ра́достью
glamorous ['glæmərəs] adj шика́рный, роско́шный
glance [glɑːns] n (look) взгляд ▷ vi: **to glance at** взгля́дывать (perf взгляну́ть) на +acc
gland [glænd] n железа́
glare [gleə^r] n взгляд; (of light) сия́ние
glaring ['gleərɪŋ] adj я́вный, вопию́щий
glass [glɑːs] n (substance) стекло́;

(container, contents) стака́н; **glasses** npl (spectacles) очки́ ntpl
glaze [gleɪz] n (on pottery) глазу́рь f
gleam [gliːm] vi мерца́ть (impf)
glen [glɛn] n речна́я доли́на
glide [glaɪd] vi скользи́ть (impf); (Aviat) плани́ровать (impf); (bird) пари́ть (impf); **glider** n планёр
glimmer ['glɪmə^r] n (of interest, hope) про́блеск; (of light) мерца́ние
glimpse [glɪmps] n: **glimpse of** взгляд на +acc ▷ vt ви́деть (perf уви́деть) ме́льком, взгляну́ть (perf) на +acc
glint [glɪnt] vi блесте́ть (perf блесну́ть), мерца́ть (impf)
glitter ['glɪtə^r] vi сверка́ть (perf сверкну́ть)
global ['gləʊbl] adj (interest, attention) глоба́льный; **global warming** n глоба́льное потепле́ние
globe [gləʊb] n (world) земно́й шар; (model of world) гло́бус
gloom [gluːm] n мрак; (fig) уны́ние
glorious ['glɔːrɪəs] adj (sunshine, flowers) великоле́пный
glory ['glɔːrɪ] n (prestige) сла́ва
gloss [glɒs] n (shine) гля́нец, лоск; (also **gloss paint**) гля́нцевая кра́ска
glossary ['glɒsərɪ] n глосса́рий
glossy ['glɒsɪ] adj (photograph, magazine) гля́нцевый; (hair) блестя́щий
glove [glʌv] n перча́тка; **glove compartment** n перча́точный я́щик, барда́чок (inf)
glow [gləʊ] vi свети́ться (impf)
glucose ['gluːkəʊs] n глюко́за
glue [gluː] n клей ▷ vt: **to glue sth onto sth** прикле́ивать (perf прикле́ить) что-н на что-н

⬤ **KEYWORD**

go [gəʊ] (pt **went**, pp **gone**, pl **goes**) vi
1 (move: on foot) ходи́ть/идти́ (perf пойти́); (travel: by transport) е́здить/е́хать (perf пое́хать); **she went into the kitchen** она́ пошла́ на ку́хню; **he often goes to China** он ча́сто е́здит в Кита́й; **they are going to the theatre tonight** сего́дня ве́чером они́ иду́т в теа́тр
2 (depart: on foot) уходи́ть (perf уйти́); (: by plane) улета́ть (perf улете́ть); (: by train, car) уезжа́ть (perf уе́хать); **the plane goes at 6am** самолёт улета́ет в 6 часо́в утра́; **the train/bus goes at 6pm** по́езд/ авто́бус ухо́дит в 6 часо́в; **I must go now** мне на́до идти́
3 (attend): **to go to** ходи́ть (impf) в/на +acc; **she doesn't go to lectures/school** она́ не хо́дит на ле́кции/в шко́лу; **she went to university** она́ учи́лась в университе́те
4 (take part in activity): **to go dancing** ходи́ть/идти́ (perf пойти́) танцева́ть
5 (work): **is your watch going?** Ва́ши часы́

идут?; **the bell went** прозвенел звонок; **the tape recorder was still going** магнитофон всё ещё работал
6 (*become*): **to go pale** бледнеть (*perf* побледнеть); **to go mouldy** плесневеть (*perf* заплесневеть)
7 (*be sold*) расходиться (*perf* разойтись); **the books went for £10** книги разошлись по £10
8 (*fit, suit*): **to go with** подходить (*perf* подойти) к +*dat*
9 (*be about to, intend to*): **to go to do** собираться (*perf* собраться) +*infin*
10 (*time*) идти (*impf*)
11 (*event, activity*) проходить (*perf* пройти); **how did it go?** как всё прошло?
12 (*be given*) идти (*perf* пойти); **the proceeds will go to charity** прибыли пойдёт на благотворительные цели; **the job is to go to someone else** работу дадут кому-то другому
13 (*break etc*): **the fuse went** предохранитель перегорел; **the leg of the chair went** ножка стула сломалась
14 (*be placed*): **the milk goes in the fridge** молоко бывает в холодильнике
▷ *n* **1** (*try*) попытка; **to have a go** (*at doing*) делать (*perf* сделать) попытку (+*infin*)
2 (*turn*): **whose go is it?** (*in board games*) чей ход?
3 (*move*): **to be on the go** быть (*impf*) на ногах
go about *vi* (*also* **go around**: *rumour*) ходить (*impf*)
go ahead *vi* (*event*) продолжаться (*perf* продолжиться); **to go ahead with** (*project*) приступать (*perf* приступить) к +*dat*; **may I begin?** — **yes, do go ahead!** можно начинать? — да, давайте!
go along *vi* идти (*perf* пойти); **to go along with sb** (*accompany*) идти (*perf* пойти) с кем-н; (*agree*) соглашаться (*perf* согласиться) с кем-н
go away *vi* (*leave: on foot*) уходить (*perf* уйти); (: *by transport*) уезжать (*perf* уехать); **go away and think about it for a while** иди и подумай об этом
go back *vi* (*return, go again*) возвращаться (*perf* возвратиться), вернуться (*perf*); **we went back into the house** мы вернулись в дом; **I am never going back to her house again** я никогда больше не пойду к ней
go for *vt fus* (*fetch: paper, doctor*) идти (*perf* пойти) за +*instr*; (*choose, like*) выбирать (*perf* выбрать); (*attack*) набрасываться (*perf* наброситься) на +*acc*; **that goes for me too** ко мне это тоже относится
go in *vi* (*enter*) входить (*perf* войти), заходить (*perf* зайти)
go in for *vt fus* (*enter*) принимать (*perf* принять) участие в +*prp*; (*take up*) заняться (*perf*) +*instr*
go into *vt fus* (*enter*) входить (*perf* войти) в +*acc*; (*take up*) заняться (*perf*) +*instr*; **go into details** входить (*impf*) *or* вдаваться (*impf*) в подробности
go off *vi* (*leave: on foot*) уходить (*perf* уйти); (: *by transport*) уезжать (*perf* уехать); (*food*) портиться (*perf* испортиться); (*bomb*) взрываться (*perf* взорваться); (*gun*) выстреливать (*perf* выстрелить); (*alarm*) звонить (*perf* зазвонить); (*event*) проходить (*perf* пройти); (*lights*) выключаться (*perf* выключиться)
▷ *vt fus* разлюбить (*perf*)
go on *vi* (*discussion*) продолжаться (*impf*); (*continue*): **to go on** (*doing*) продолжать (*impf*) (+*infin*); **life goes on** жизнь продолжается; **what's going on here?** что здесь происходит?; **we don't have enough information to go on** у нас недостаточно информации
go on with *vt fus* продолжать (*perf* продолжить)
go out *vi* (*fire, light*) гаснуть (*perf* погаснуть); (*leave*): **to go out of** выходить (*perf* выйти) из +*gen*; **are you going out tonight?** Вы сегодня вечером куда-нибудь идёте?
go over *vi* идти (*perf* пойти)
▷ *vt fus* просматривать (*perf* просмотреть)
go through *vt fus* (*town etc: by transport*) проезжать (*perf* проехать) через +*acc*; (*files, papers*) просматривать (*perf* просмотреть)
go up *vi* (*ascend*) подниматься (*perf* подняться); (*price, level, buildings*) расти (*perf* вырасти)
go without *vt fus* обходиться (*perf* обойтись) без +*gen*

goal [gəʊl] *n* (*Sport*) гол; (*aim*) цель *f*;
goalkeeper *n* вратарь *m*, голкипер;
goalpost *n* боковая штанга, стойка ворот
goat [gəʊt] *n* (*billy*) козёл; (*nanny*) коза
god [gɒd] *n* (*fig*) божество, бог; **God** Бог;
godchild *n* крестник(-ица);
goddaughter *n* крестница; **goddess** *n* богиня; **godfather** *n* крёстный отец;
godmother *n* крёстная мать *f*; **godson** *n* крестник
goggles [ˈgɒglz] *npl* защитные очки *ntpl*
going [ˈgəʊɪŋ] *adj*: **the going rate** текущие расценки *fpl*
gold [gəʊld] *n* (*metal*) золото ▷ *adj* золотой; **gold reserves** золотой запас;
goldfish *n* серебряный карась *m*
golf [gɒlf] *n* гольф; **golf club** *n* (*stick*) клюшка (*в гольфе*); **golf course** *n* поле для игры в гольф
gone [gɒn] *pp of* **go**
gong [gɒŋ] *n* гонг

good [gʊd] adj хоро́ший; (pleasant)
прия́тный; (kind) до́брый ▷ n (virtue)
добро́; (benefit) по́льза; **goods** npl
(Comm) това́ры mpl; **good!** хорошо́!; **to
be good at** име́ть (impf) спосо́бности к
+dat; **it's good for you** э́то поле́зно (для
здоро́вья); **would you be good enough to
…?** не бу́дете ли Вы так добры́ +perf infin
…?; **a good deal (of)** большо́е коли́чество
(+gen); **a good many** мно́го +gen; **good
afternoon/evening!** до́брый день/ве́чер!;
good morning! до́брое у́тро! **good night!**
(on leaving) до свида́ния!; (on going to
bed) споко́йной or до́брой но́чи!; **it's no
good complaining** жа́ловаться
бесполе́зно; **for good** навсегда́; **goodbye**
excl до свида́ния; **to say goodbye (to)**
проща́ться (perf попроща́ться) (с +instr);
Good Friday n Страстна́я пя́тница;
good-looking adj краси́вый; **good-
natured** adj доброду́шный; (pet)
послу́шный; **goodness** n доброта́; **for
goodness sake!** ра́ди Бо́га!; **goodness
gracious!** Бо́же!, Госпо́дь!; **goodwill** n
(of person) до́брая во́ля

goose [ɡuːs] n (pl **geese**) n гусь(-сы́ня) m(f)
gooseberry ['ɡʊzbərɪ] n крыжо́вник m
no pl

gorge [ɡɔːdʒ] n тесни́на, (у́зкое) уще́лье
▷ vt: **to gorge o.s. (on)** наеда́ться (perf
нае́сться) (+gen)
gorgeous ['ɡɔːdʒəs] adj преле́стный
gorilla [ɡə'rɪlə] n гори́лла
gospel ['ɡɒspl] n (Rel) Ева́нгелие
gossip ['ɡɒsɪp] n (rumours) спле́тня;
(chat) разгово́ры mpl; (person)
спле́тник(-ица)

got [ɡɒt] pt, pp of **get**; **gotten** pp (US) of
get
govern ['ɡʌvən] vt (country) управля́ть
(impf) +instr; (event, conduct) руководи́ть
(impf) +instr
government ['ɡʌvnmənt] n
прави́тельство; (act) управле́ние
governor ['ɡʌvənə'] n (of state, colony)
губерна́тор; (of school etc) член
правле́ния

gown [ɡaʊn] n (dress) пла́тье; (of teacher,
judge) ма́нтия
GP n abbr (= general practitioner)
участко́вый терапе́вт
grab [ɡræb] vt хвата́ть (perf схвати́ть)
▷ vi: **to grab at** хвата́ться (perf
схвати́ться) за +acc
grace [ɡreɪs] n гра́ция, изя́щество; (Rel)
моли́тва (пе́ред едо́й); **5 days' grace** 5
дней отсро́чки; **graceful** adj (animal,
person) грацио́зный
gracious ['ɡreɪʃəs] adj (person, smile)
любе́зный ▷ excl: **(good) gracious!** Бо́же
пра́вый!
grade [ɡreɪd] n (Comm: quality) сорт;
(Scol: mark) оце́нка; (US: school year)
класс ▷ vt (rank, class) распределя́ть

(perf распредели́ть); (products)
сортирова́ть (perf рассортирова́ть);
grade crossing n (US)
железнодоро́жный перее́зд; **grade
school** n (US) нача́льная шко́ла
gradient ['ɡreɪdɪənt] n (of hill) укло́н
gradual ['ɡrædjʊəl] adj постепе́нный;
gradually adv постепе́нно
graduate [n 'ɡrædjʊɪt, vb 'ɡrædjʊeɪt] n
выпускни́к(-и́ца) ▷ vi: **to graduate from**
зака́нчивать (perf зако́нчить); **I graduated
last year** я зако́нчил университе́т в
про́шлом году́
graduation [ɡrædjʊ'eɪʃən] n (ceremony)
выпускно́й ве́чер
graffiti [ɡrə'fiːtɪ] n, npl графи́ти nt ind
grain [ɡreɪn] n (seed) зерно́; (no pl:
cereals) хле́бные зла́ки mpl; (of sand)
песчи́нка; (of salt) крупи́нка; (of wood)
волокно́
gram [ɡræm] n грамм
grammar ['ɡræmə'] n грамма́тика;
grammar school n (Brit) ≈ гимна́зия

○ **GRAMMAR SCHOOL**
○
○ В Великобрита́нии гимна́зии даю́т
○ сре́днее образова́ние. Ученики́
○ поступа́ют в них на ко́нкурсной осно́ве.
○ Число́ их невелико́. Одна́ко в США
○ **grammar school** называ́ются нача́льные
○ шко́лы.

gramme [ɡræm] n = **gram**
grand [ɡrænd] adj грандио́зный;
(gesture) велича́ственный; **grandchild**
(pl **grandchildren**) n внук(-у́чка);
granddad n (inf) де́душка m;
granddaughter n вну́чка; **grandfather**
n дед; **grandma** n (inf) бабу́ля,
ба́бушка; **grandmother** n ба́бушка;
grandparents npl де́душка m и
ба́бушка; **grandson** n внук
granite ['ɡrænɪt] n грани́т
granny ['ɡrænɪ] n (inf) = **grandma**
grant [ɡrɑːnt] vt (money, visa) выдава́ть
(perf вы́дать); (request) удовлетворя́ть
(perf удовлетвори́ть); (admit) признава́ть
(perf призна́ть) ▷ n (Scol) стипе́ндия;
(Admin) грант; **to take sb/sth for granted**
принима́ть (perf приня́ть) кого́-н/что-н как
до́лжное
grape [ɡreɪp] n виногра́д m no pl;
grapefruit (pl **grapefruit** or **grapefruits**)
n грейпфру́т
graph [ɡrɑːf] n (diagram) гра́фик;
graphic ['ɡræfɪk] adj (explicit)
вырази́тельный; (design)
изобрази́тельный; **graphics** n гра́фика
grasp [ɡrɑːsp] vt хвата́ть (perf схвати́ть)
▷ n (grip) хва́тка; (understanding)
понима́ние
grass [ɡrɑːs] n трава́; (lawn) газо́н;
grasshopper n кузне́чик

grate [greɪt] n камѝнная решётка ▷ vt (Culin) тере́ть (perf натере́ть) ▷ vi (metal, chalk): **to grate (on)** скрежета́ть (impf) (по +dat)

grateful ['greɪtful] adj благода́рный

grater ['greɪtə^r] n тёрка

gratitude ['grætɪtjuːd] n благода́рность f

grave [greɪv] n моги́ла f ▷ adj серьёзный

gravel ['grævl] n гра́вий

gravestone ['greɪvstəun] n надгро́бие

graveyard ['greɪvjɑːd] n кла́дбище

gravity ['grævɪtɪ] n тяготе́ние, притяже́ние; (seriousness) серьёзность f

gravy ['greɪvɪ] n (sauce) со́ус

gray [greɪ] adj (US) = **grey**

graze [greɪz] vi пасти́сь (impf) ▷ vt (scrape) цара́пать (perf оцара́пать)

grease [griːs] n (lubricant) сма́зка; (fat) жир ▷ vt сма́зывать (perf сма́зать)

greasy ['griːsɪ] adj жи́рный

great [greɪt] adj (large) большо́й; (heat, pain) си́льный; (city, man) вели́кий; (inf: terrific) замеча́тельный

Great Britain n Великобрита́ния

● **GREAT BRITAIN**
●
● В Великобрита́нию вхо́дят А́нглия,
● Шотла́ндия и Уэльс. Эти стра́ны вме́сте
● с Се́верной Ирла́ндией образу́ют
● **United Kingdom** — Соединённое
● Короле́вство (Великобрита́нии и
● Се́верной Ирла́ндии).

greatly adv о́чень; (influenced) весьма́

Greece [griːs] n Гре́ция

greed [griːd] n жа́дность f; (for power, wealth) жа́жда; **greedy** adj жа́дный

Greek [griːk] adj гре́ческий

green [griːn] adj зелёный ▷ n (colour) зелёный цвет; (grass) лужа́йка; **greens** npl (vegetables) зе́лень fsg; **greengrocer** n (Brit) зеленщи́к; (shop) овощно́й магази́н; **greenhouse** n тепли́ца; **greenhouse effect** n парнико́вый эффе́кт

Greenland ['griːnlənd] n Гренла́ндия

greet [griːt] vt приве́тствовать (perf поприве́тствовать), здоро́ваться (perf поздоро́ваться); (news) встреча́ть (perf встре́тить); **greeting** n приве́тствие

grew [gruː] pt of **grow**

grey [greɪ] (US **gray**) adj се́рый; (hair) седо́й; **greyhound** n борза́я f adj

grid [grɪd] n (pattern) се́тка; (grating) решётка; (Elec) еди́ная энергосисте́ма

grief [griːf] n го́ре

grievance ['griːvəns] n жа́лоба

grieve [griːv] vi горева́ть (impf); **to grieve for** горева́ть (impf) о +prp

grill [grɪl] n (on cooker) гриль m; (grilled food: also **mixed grill**) жа́ренные на гри́ле проду́кты mpl ▷ vt (Brit) жа́рить (perf пожа́рить) (на гри́ле)

grim [grɪm] adj (place, person) мра́чный, угрю́мый; (situation) тяжёлый

grime [graɪm] n (from soot, smoke) ко́поть f; (from mud) грязь f

grin [grɪn] n широ́кая улы́бка ▷ vi: **to grin (at)** широко́ улыба́ться (perf улыбну́ться) (+dat)

grind [graɪnd] (pt, pp **ground**) vt (coffee, pepper) моло́ть (perf смоло́ть); (US: meat) прокру́чивать (perf прокрути́ть); (knife) точи́ть (perf наточи́ть)

grip [grɪp] n хва́тка; (of tyre) сцепле́ние ▷ vt (object) схва́тывать (perf схвати́ть); (audience, attention) захва́тывать (perf захвати́ть); **to come to grips with** занима́ться (perf заня́ться) +instr; **gripping** adj захва́тывающий

grit [grɪt] n (stone) ще́бень m ▷ vt (road) посыпа́ть (perf посы́пать) ще́бнем; **to grit one's teeth** сти́скивать (perf сти́снуть) зу́бы

groan [grəun] n (of person) стон

grocer ['grəusə^r] n бакале́йщик; **groceries** npl бакале́я fsg; **grocer's (shop)** n бакале́йный магази́н, бакале́я

groin [grɔɪn] n пах

groom [gruːm] n (for horse) ко́нюх; (also **bridegroom**) жени́х ▷ vt (horse) уха́живать (impf) за +instr; **to groom sb for** (job) гото́вить (perf подгото́вить) кого́-н к +dat

groove [gruːv] n кана́вка

gross [grəus] adj вульга́рный; (neglect, injustice) вопию́щий; (Comm: income) валово́й; **grossly** adv чрезме́рно

grotesque [grə'tɛsk] adj гроте́скный

ground [graund] pt, pp of **grind** ▷ n (earth, land) земля́; (floor) пол; (US: also **ground wire**) заземле́ние; (usu pl: reason) основа́ние ▷ vt (US: Elec) заземля́ть (perf заземли́ть); **grounds** npl (of coffee) гу́ща fsg; **school grounds** шко́льная площа́дка; **sports ground** спорти́вная площа́дка; **on the ground** на земле́; **to the ground** (burnt) дотла́; **the plane was grounded by the fog** самолёт не мог подня́ться в во́здух из-за тума́на; **groundwork** n (preparation) фунда́мент, осно́ва; **to do the groundwork** закла́дывать (perf заложи́ть) фунда́мент

group [gruːp] n гру́ппа

grouse [graus] n inv (bird) (шотла́ндская) куропа́тка

grow [grəu] (pt **grew**, pp **grown**) vi расти́ (perf вы́расти); (become) станови́ться (perf стать) ▷ vt (roses, vegetables) выра́щивать (perf вы́растить); (beard, hair) отра́щивать (perf отрасти́ть); **grow up** vi (child) расти́ (perf вы́расти), взросле́ть (perf повзросле́ть)

growl [graul] vi (dog) рыча́ть (impf)

grown [grəun] pp of **grow**; **grown-up** n (adult) взро́слый(-ая) m(f) adj ▷ adj (son, daughter) взро́слый

growth [grəʊθ] n рост; (increase) прирост; (Med) опухоль f

grub [grʌb] n (larva) личинка; (inf: food) жратва

grubby [ˈgrʌbɪ] adj грязный

grudge [grʌdʒ] n недовольство; **to bear sb a grudge** затаивать (perf затаить) на кого-н обиду

gruelling [ˈgruəlɪŋ] (US **grueling**) adj изнурительный, тяжкий

gruesome [ˈgruːsəm] adj жуткий

grumble [ˈgrʌmbl] vi ворчать (impf)

grumpy [ˈgrʌmpɪ] adj сварливый

grunt [grʌnt] vi (pig) хрюкать (perf хрюкнуть); (person) бурчать (perf буркнуть)

guarantee [gærənˈtiː] n (assurance) поручительство; (warranty) гарантия ▷ vt гарантировать (impf/perf); **he can't guarantee (that) he'll come** он не может поручиться, что он придёт

guard [gɑːd] n (one person) охранник; (squad) охрана; (Brit: Rail) кондуктор; (Tech) предохранительное устройство; (also **fireguard**) предохранительная решётка (перед камином) ▷ vt (prisoner) охранять (impf); (secret) хранить (impf); **to guard (against)** (protect) охранять (impf) (от +gen); **to be on one's guard** быть (impf) настороже or начеку; **guard against** vt fus (prevent) предохранять (impf) от +gen; **guardian** n (Law) опекун

guerrilla [gəˈrɪlə] n партизан(ка)

guess [ges] vt (estimate) считать (perf сосчитать) приблизительно; (correct answer) угадывать (perf угадать) ▷ vi догадываться (perf догадаться) ▷ n догадка; **to take** or **have a guess** отгадывать (perf отгадать)

guest [gest] n (visitor) гость(я) m/f; (in hotel) постоялец(-лица); **guesthouse** n гостиница

guidance [ˈgaɪdəns] n (advice) совет

guide [gaɪd] n (in museum, on tour) гид, экскурсовод; (also **guidebook**) путеводитель m; (handbook) руководство ▷ vt (show around) водить (impf); (direct) направлять (perf направить); **guidebook** n путеводитель m; **guide dog** n собака-поводырь f; **guidelines** npl руководство ntsg

guild [gɪld] n гильдия

guilt [gɪlt] n (remorse) вина; (culpability) виновность f; **guilty** adj (person, expression) виноватый; (of crime) виновный

guinea pig [ˈgɪnɪ-] n морская свинка; (fig) подопытный кролик

guitar [gɪˈtɑːʳ] n гитара

gulf [gʌlf] n (Geo) залив; (fig) пропасть f

gull [gʌl] n чайка

gulp [gʌlp] vi нервно сглатывать (perf сглотнуть) ▷ vt (also **gulp down**) проглатывать (perf проглотить)

gum [gʌm] n (Anat) десна; (glue) клей; (also **chewing-gum**) жвачка (inf), жевательная резинка

gun [gʌn] n пистолет; (rifle, airgun) ружьё; **gunfire** n стрельба; **gunman** irreg n вооружённый бандит; **gunpoint** n: **at gunpoint** под дулом пистолета; **gunshot** n выстрел

gust [gʌst] n (of wind) порыв

gut [gʌt] n (Anat) кишка; **guts** npl (Anat) кишки fpl, внутренности fpl; (inf: courage) мужество ntsg

gutter [ˈgʌtəʳ] n (in street) сточная канава; (of roof) водосточный жёлоб

guy [gaɪ] n (inf: man) парень m; (also **guyrope**) палаточный шнур

gym [dʒɪm] n (also **gymnasium**) гимнастический зал; (also **gymnastics**) гимнастика; **gymnastics** [dʒɪmˈnæstɪks] n гимнастика

gynaecologist [gaɪnɪˈkɒlədʒɪst] (US **gynecologist**) n гинеколог

gypsy [ˈdʒɪpsɪ] n цыган(ка)

Half term — короткие каникулы. В середине триместров школьникам дают короткий перерыв в 3-4 дня.

hall [hɔːl] *n* (*in house*) прихожая *f adj*, холл; (*for concerts, meetings etc*) зал
hallmark ['hɔːlmɑːk] *n* проба; (*fig*) отличительная черта
Hallowe'en ['hæləu'iːn] *n* канун Дня всех святых

HALLOWE'EN

Этот праздник отмечают вечером 31 октября. По традиции это день ведьм и духов. Дети наряжаются в костюмы ведьм и вампиров, делают лампы из тыкв. С наступлением темноты они ходят по домам, играя в игру подобную русским Коробейникам. Если хозяева не дают детям конфет, они могут сыграть над ними шутку.

hallucination [həluːsɪ'neɪʃən] *n* галлюцинация
hallway ['hɔːlweɪ] *n* прихожая *f adj*, холл
halo ['heɪləu] *n* (*Rel*) нимб
halt [hɔːlt] *n* остановка ⊳ *vt* останавливать (*perf* остановить) ⊳ *vi* останавливаться (*perf* остановиться)
halve [hɑːv] *vt* (*reduce*) сокращать (*perf* сократить) наполовину; (*divide*) делить (*perf* разделить) пополам
halves [hɑːvz] *pl of* **half**
ham [hæm] *n* (*meat*) ветчина;
hamburger *n* гамбургер
hammer ['hæmə'] *n* молоток ⊳ *vi* (*on door etc*) колотить (*impf*) ⊳ *vt* (*nail*): **to hammer in** забивать (*perf* забить), вбивать (*perf* вбить); **to hammer sth into sb** (*fig*) вдалбливать (*perf* вдолбить) что-н кому-н
hamper ['hæmpə'] *vt* мешать (*perf* помешать) +*dat* ⊳ *n* (*basket*) большая корзина с крышкой
hamster ['hæmstə'] *n* хомяк
hand [hænd] *n* (*Anat*) рука, кисть *f*; (*of clock*) стрелка; (*worker*) рабочий *m adj* ⊳ *vt* (*give*) вручать (*perf* вручить); **to give** *or* **lend sb a hand** протягивать (*perf* протянуть) кому-н руку (помощи); **at hand** под рукой; **in hand** (*situation*) под контролем; (*time*) в распоряжении; **on hand** (*person, services etc*) в распоряжении; **I have the information to hand** я располагаю информацией; **on the one hand ..., on the other hand ...** с одной стороны ..., с другой стороны ...; **hand in** *vt* (*work*) сдавать (*perf* сдать); **hand out** *vt* раздавать (*perf* раздать); **hand over** *vt* передавать (*perf* передать), вручать (*perf* вручить); **handbag** *n* (дамская)

habit ['hæbɪt] *n* (*custom*) привычка; (*addiction*) пристрастие; (*Rel*) облачение
habitat ['hæbɪtæt] *n* среда обитания
hack [hæk] *vt* отрубать (*perf* отрубить) ⊳ *n* (*pej: writer*) писака *m/f*
had [hæd] *pt, pp of* **have**
haddock ['hædək] (*pl* **haddock** *or* **haddocks**) *n* треска
hadn't ['hædnt] = **had not**
haemorrhage ['hɛmərɪdʒ] (*US* **hemorrhage**) *n* кровотечение; **brain haemorrhage** кровоизлияние (в мозг)
Hague [heɪg] *n*: **The Hague** Гаага
hail [heɪl] *n* град ⊳ *vt* (*flag down*) подзывать (*perf* подозвать) ⊳ *vi*: **it's hailing** идёт град; **hailstone** *n* градина
hair [hɛə'] *n* волосы *pl*; (*of animal*) волосяной покров; **to do one's hair** причёсываться (*perf* причесаться); **hairbrush** *n* щётка для волос; **haircut** *n* стрижка; **hairdresser** *n* парикмахер; **hair dryer** [-draɪə'] *n* фен; **hair spray** *n* лак для волос; **hairstyle** *n* причёска; **hairy** *adj* (*person*) волосатый; (*animal*) мохнатый
half [hɑːf] (*pl* **halves**) *n* половина; (*also* **half pint**: *of beer etc*) полпинты *f*; (*on train, bus*) билет за полцены ⊳ *adv* наполовину; **one and a half** (*with m/nt nouns*) полтора +*gen sg*; (*with f nouns*) полторы +*gen sg*; **three and a half** три с половиной; **half a dozen (of)** полдюжины *f* (+*gen*); **half a pound (of)** полфунта *m* (+*gen*); **a week and a half** полторы недели; **half (of)** половина (+*gen*); **half the amount of** половина +*gen*; **to cut sth in half** разрезать (*perf* разрезать) что-н пополам; **half-hearted** *adj* ленивый; **half-hour** *n* полчаса *m*; **half-price** *adj, adv* за полцены; **half-time** *n* перерыв между таймами; **halfway** *adv* на полпути

су́мочка; **handbrake** n ручно́й то́рмоз; **handcuffs** npl нару́чники mpl; **handful** n (fig: of people) го́рстка; **hand-held** adj ручно́й

handicap ['hændɪkæp] n (infl:disability) физи́ческая неполноце́нность f; (disadvantage) препя́тствие ▷ vt препя́тствовать (perf воспрепя́тствовать) +dat

handkerchief ['hæŋkətʃɪf] n носово́й плато́к

handle ['hændl] n ру́чка ▷ vt (touch) держа́ть (impf) в рука́х; (deal with) занима́ться (impf) +instr; (: successfully) справля́ться (perf спра́виться) с +instr; (treat: people) обраща́ться (impf) с +instr; **to fly off the handle** (inf) срыва́ться (perf сорва́ться); **"handle with care"** "обраща́ться осторо́жно"

hand luggage n ручна́я кладь f

handmade ['hænd'meɪd] adj ручно́й рабо́ты; **it's handmade** э́то ручна́я рабо́та

handsome ['hænsəm] adj (man) краси́вый; (woman) интере́сный; (building, profit, sum) внуши́тельный

handwriting ['hændraɪtɪŋ] n по́черк

handy ['hændɪ] adj (useful) удо́бный; (close at hand) поблизо́сти

hang [hæŋ] (pt, pp **hung**) vt ве́шать (perf пове́сить) ▷ (pt, pp **hanged**) (execute) ве́шать (perf пове́сить) ▷ vi висе́ть (impf) ▷ n: **to get the hang of sth** (inf) разбира́ться (perf разобра́ться) в чём-н; **hang around** vi слоня́ться (impf), болта́ться (impf); **hang on** vi (wait) подожда́ть (impf); **hang up** vi (Tel) ве́шать (perf пове́сить) тру́бку ▷ vt ве́шать (perf пове́сить)

hangover ['hæŋəʊvə'] n (after drinking) похме́лье

happen ['hæpən] vi случа́ться (perf случи́ться), происходи́ть (perf произойти́); **I happened to meet him in the park** я случа́йно встре́тил его́ в па́рке; **as it happens** кста́ти

happily ['hæpɪlɪ] adv (luckily) к сча́стью; (cheerfully, gladly) ра́достно

happiness ['hæpɪnɪs] n (cheerfulness) сча́стье

happy ['hæpɪ] adj (pleased) счастли́вый; (cheerful) весёлый; **I am happy (with it)** (content) я дово́лен (э́тим); **he is always happy to help** он всегда́ рад помо́чь; **happy birthday!** с днём рожде́ния!

harassment ['hærəsmənt] n пресле́дование

harbour ['hɑːbə'] (US **harbor**) n га́вань f ▷ vt (hope, fear) зата́ивать (perf затаи́ть); (criminal, fugitive) укрыва́ть (perf укры́ть)

hard [hɑːd] adj (surface, object) твёрдый; (question, problem) тру́дный; (work, life) тяжёлый; (person) суро́вый; (facts, evidence) неопровержи́мый ▷ adv: **to work hard** мно́го и усе́рдно рабо́тать

(impf); **I don't have any hard feelings** я держу́ зла; **he is hard of hearing** он туг на́ ухо; **to think hard** хорошо́ поду́мать (perf); **to try hard to win** упо́рно добива́ться (impf) побе́ды; **to look hard at** смотре́ть (perf посмотре́ть) при́стально на +acc; **hardback** n кни́га в твёрдом переплёте; **hard disk** n жёсткий диск; **harden** vt (substance) де́лать (perf сде́лать) твёрдым(-ой); (attitude, person) ожесточа́ть (perf ожесточи́ть) ▷ vi (see vt) тверде́ть (perf затверде́ть); ожесточа́ться (perf ожесточи́ться)

hardly ['hɑːdlɪ] adv едва́; **hardly ever/anywhere** почти́ никогда́/нигде́

hardship ['hɑːdʃɪp] n тя́готы pl, тру́дности fpl

hard up adj (inf) нужда́ющийся; **I am hard up** я нужда́юсь

hardware ['hɑːdwɛə'] n (tools) скобяны́е изде́лия ntpl

hard-working [hɑːd'wɜːkɪŋ] adj усе́рдный

hardy ['hɑːdɪ] adj выно́сливый; (plant) морозоусто́йчивый

hare [hɛə'] n за́яц

harm [hɑːm] n (injury) теле́сное повреждéние, тра́вма; (damage) уще́рб ▷ vt (thing) поврежда́ть (perf повреди́ть); (person) наноси́ть (perf нанести́) вред +dat; **harmful** adj вре́дный; **harmless** adj безоби́дный

harmony ['hɑːmənɪ] n гармо́ния

harness ['hɑːnɪs] n (for horse) у́пряжь f; (for child) постро́мки fpl; (safety harness) привязны́е ремни́ mpl ▷ vt (horse) запряга́ть (perf запря́чь); (resources, energy) ста́вить (perf поста́вить) себе́ на слу́жбу

harp [hɑːp] n а́рфа

harsh [hɑːʃ] adj (sound, light, criticism) ре́зкий; (person, remark) жёсткий; (life, winter) суро́вый

harvest ['hɑːvɪst] n (time) жа́тва; (of barley, fruit) урожа́й ▷ vt собира́ть (perf собра́ть) урожа́й +gen

has [hæz] vb see **have**

hasn't ['hæznt] = **has not**

hassle ['hæsl] (inf) n моро́ка

haste [heɪst] n спе́шка; **hasten** ['heɪsn] vt торопи́ть (perf поторопи́ть) ▷ vi: **to hasten to do** торопи́ться (perf поторопи́ться) +infin

hastily ['heɪstɪlɪ] adv (see adj) поспе́шно; опроме́тчиво

hasty ['heɪstɪ] adj поспе́шный; (rash) опроме́тчивый

hat [hæt] n шля́па; (woolly) ша́пка

hatch [hætʃ] n (Naut: also **hatchway**) люк; (also **service hatch**) разда́точное окно́ ▷ vi (also **hatch out**) вылупля́ться (perf вы́лупиться)

hate [heɪt] vt ненави́деть (impf)

hatred ['heɪtrɪd] n не́нависть f

haul [hɔːl] vt (pull) таскáть/тащи́ть (impf)
▷ n (of stolen goods etc) добы́ча
haunt [hɔːnt] vt (fig) пресле́довать
(impf); **to haunt sb/a house** явля́ться (perf
яви́ться) кому́-н/в до́ме; **haunted** adj:
this house is haunted в э́том дом есть
привиде́ния

KEYWORD

have [hæv] (pt, pp **had**) aux vb **1 to have
arrived** прие́хать (perf); **have you already
eaten?** ты уже́ пое́л?; **he has been kind to
me** он был добр ко мне; **he has been
promoted** он получи́л повыше́ние по
слу́жбе; **has he told you?** он Вам сказа́л?;
having finished or **when he had finished ...**
зако́нчив or когда́ он зако́нчил ...
2 (in tag questions) не так ли; **you've done
it, haven't you?** Вы сде́лали э́то, не так ли?
3 (in short answers and questions): **you've
made a mistake — no I haven't/so I have**
Вы оши́блись — нет, не оши́бся/да,
оши́бся; **we haven't paid — yes we have!**
мы не заплати́ли — нет, заплати́ли!; **I've
been there before, have you?** я там уже́
был, а Вы?
▷ modal aux vb (be obliged): **I have (got)
to finish this work** я до́лжен зако́нчить э́ту
рабо́ту; **I haven't got** or **I don't have to
wear glasses** мне не на́до носи́ть очки́;
this has to be a mistake э́то, наверняка́,
оши́бка
▷ vt **1** (possess): **I** etc **have** у меня́ (есть)
etc +nom; **he has (got) blue eyes/dark hair**
у него́ голубы́е глаза́/тёмные во́лосы; **do
you have** or **have you got a car?** у Вас есть
маши́на?
2 (referring to meals etc): **to have dinner**
обе́дать (perf пообе́дать); **to have
breakfast** за́втракать (perf поза́втракать);
to have a cigarette выку́ривать (perf
вы́курить) сигаре́ту; **to have a glass of
wine** выпива́ть (perf вы́пить) бока́л вина́
3 (receive, obtain etc): **may I have your
address?** Вы мо́жете дать мне свой
а́дрес?; **you can have the book for £5**
бери́те кни́гу за £5; **I must have the report
by tomorrow** докла́д до́лжен быть у меня́
к за́втрашнему дню; **she is having a baby
in March** она́ бу́дет рожа́ть в ма́рте
4 (allow) допуска́ть (perf допусти́ть);
I won't have it! я э́того не допущу́!
5: I am having my television repaired мне
должны́ почини́ть телеви́зор; **to have sb
do** проси́ть (perf попроси́ть) кого́-н +infin;
he soon had them all laughing вско́ре он
заста́вил всех смея́ться
6 (experience, suffer): **I have flu/a
headache** у меня́ грипп/боли́т голова́; **to
have a cold** простужа́ться (perf
простуди́ться); **she had her bag stolen** у
неё укра́ли су́мку; **he had an operation** ему́
сде́лали опера́цию

7 (+n): **to have a swim** пла́вать (perf
попла́вать); **to have a rest** отдыха́ть (perf
отдохну́ть); **let's have a look** дава́йте
посмо́трим; **we are having a meeting
tomorrow** за́втра у нас бу́дет собра́ние;
let me have a try да́йте мне попро́бовать
have out vt: **to have it out with sb**
объясня́ться (perf объясни́ться) с кем-н;
she had her tooth out ей удали́ли зуб; **she
had her tonsils out** ей вы́резали гла́нды

haven ['heɪvn] n (fig) убе́жище
haven't ['hævnt] = **have not**
havoc ['hævək] n (chaos) ха́ос
hawk [hɔːk] n я́стреб
hay [heɪ] n се́но; **hay fever** n сенна́я
лихора́дка; **haystack** n стог се́на
hazard ['hæzəd] n опа́сность f ▷ vt: **to
hazard a guess** осме́ливаться (perf
осме́литься) предположи́ть; **hazardous**
adj опа́сный
haze [heɪz] n ды́мка; **heat haze** ма́рево
hazy ['heɪzɪ] adj тума́нный
he [hiː] pron он
head [hɛd] n (Anat) голова́; (mind) ум; (of
list, queue) нача́ло; (of table) глава́;
(Comm) руководи́тель(ница) m(f); (Scol)
дире́ктор ▷ vt возглавля́ть (perf
возгла́вить); **heads** or **tails** ≈ орёл или
ре́шка; **he is head over heels in love** он
влюблён по́ уши; **head for** vt fus (place)
направля́ться (perf напра́виться) в/на
+acc or к +dat; (disaster) обрека́ть (perf
обре́чь) себя́ на +acc; **headache** n
(Med) головна́я боль f; **heading** n
заголо́вок; **headlight** n фа́ра; **headline**
n заголо́вок; **head office** n
управле́ние; **headphones** npl нау́шники
mpl; **headquarters** npl штаб-кварти́ра
fsg; **headscarf** n косы́нка, (головно́й)
плато́к; **head teacher** n дире́ктор
шко́лы
heal [hiːl] vt выле́чивать (perf вы́лечить);
(damage) поправля́ть (perf попра́вить)
▷ vi (injury) зажива́ть (perf зажи́ть),
(damage) восстана́вливаться (perf
восстанови́ться)
health [hɛlθ] n здоро́вье; **health care** n
здравоохране́ние; **Health Service** n
(Brit): **the Health Service** слу́жба
здравоохране́ния; **healthy** adj
здоро́вый; (pursuit) поле́зный; (profit)
доста́точно хоро́ший
heap [hiːp] n (small) ку́ча; (large) гру́да
▷ vt: **to heap (up)** (stones, sand) сва́ливать
(perf свали́ть) в ку́чу; **to heap with sth**
(plate, sink) наполня́ть (perf напо́лнить)
чем-н; **heaps of** (inf) ку́ча fsg +gen
hear [hɪəʳ] (pt, pp **heard**) vt слы́шать (perf
услы́шать); (lecture, concert, case) слу́шать
(impf); **to hear about** слы́шать (perf
услы́шать) о +prp; **to hear from sb**
слы́шать (perf услы́шать) от кого́-н; **I can't
hear you** Вас не слы́шно; **heard** [hɜːd]

pt, pp of **hear**; **hearing** n (*sense*) слух; (*Law, Pol*) слушание; **hearing aid** n слуховой аппарат

heart [hɑ:t] n сердце; (*of problem, matter*) суть f; **hearts** npl (*Cards*) черви fpl; **to lose/take heart** пасть (*perf*)/не падать (*impf*) духом; **at heart** в глубине души; (**off**) **by heart** наизусть; **heart attack** n сердечный приступ, инфаркт; **heartbeat** n (*rhythm*) сердцебиение; **heartbroken** adj: **he is heartbroken** он убит горем

hearth [hɑ:θ] n очаг

heartless ['hɑ:tlɪs] adj бессердечный

hearty ['hɑ:tɪ] adj (*person, laugh*) задорный, весёлый; (*welcome, support*) сердечный; (*appetite*) здоровый

heat [hi:t] n тепло; (*extreme*) жар; (*of weather*) жара; (*excitement*) пыл; (*also* **qualifying heat**: *in race*) забег; (: *in swimming*) заплыв ▷ vt (*water, food*) греть (*perf* нагреть); (*house*) отапливать (*perf* отопить); **heat up** vi (*water, house*) согреваться (*perf* согреться) ▷ vt (*food, water*) подогревать (*perf* подогреть); (*room*) обогревать (*perf* обогреть); **heated** adj (*argument*) горячий; (*pool*) обогреваемый; **heater** n обогреватель m

heather ['hɛðəʳ] n вереск

heating ['hi:tɪŋ] n отопление

heat wave n период сильной жары

heaven ['hɛvn] n рай; **heavenly** adj (*fig*) райский

heavily ['hɛvɪlɪ] adv (*fall, sigh*) тяжело; (*drink, smoke, depend*) сильно; (*sleep*) крепко

heavy ['hɛvɪ] adj тяжёлый; (*rain, blow, fall*) сильный; (*build: of person*) грузный; **he is a heavy drinker/smoker** он много пьёт/курит

Hebrew ['hi:bru:] adj древнееврейский

Hebrides ['hɛbrɪdi:z] npl: **the Hebrides** Гебридские острова mpl

hectic ['hɛktɪk] adj (*day*) суматошный; (*activities*) лихорадочный

he'd [hi:d] = **he would; he had**

hedge [hɛdʒ] n живая изгородь f

hedgehog ['hɛdʒhɔg] n ёж

heed [hi:d] vt (*also* **take heed of**) принимать (*perf* принять) во внимание

heel [hi:l] n (*of foot*) пятка; (*of shoe*) каблук

hefty ['hɛftɪ] adj (*person, object*) здоровенный; (*profit, fine*) изрядный

height [haɪt] n (*of tree, of plane*) высота; (*of person*) рост; (*of power*) вершина; (*of season*) разгар; (*of luxury, taste*) верх; **heighten** vt усиливать (*perf* усилить)

heir [ɛəʳ] n наследник; **heiress** n наследница

held [hɛld] pt, pp of **hold**

helicopter ['hɛlɪkɔptəʳ] n вертолёт

hell [hɛl] n (*also fig*) ад; **hell!** (*inf*) чёрт!

he'll [hi:l] = **he will; he shall**

hello [hə'ləu] excl здравствуйте; (*informal*) привет; (*Tel*) алло

helmet ['hɛlmɪt] n (*of police officer, miner*) каска; (*also* **crash helmet**) шлем

help [hɛlp] n помощь f ▷ vt помогать (*perf* помочь) +dat; **help!** на помощь!, помогите!; **help yourself** угощайтесь; **he can't help it** он ничего не может поделать с этим; **helper** n помощник(-ица); **helpful** adj полезный; **helpless** adj беспомощный; **helpline** n телефон доверия

hem [hɛm] n (*of dress*) подол

hemorrhage ['hɛmərɪdʒ] n (*US*) = **haemorrhage**

hen [hɛn] n (*chicken*) курица

hence [hɛns] adv (*therefore*) следовательно, вследствие этого; **2 years hence** (*from now*) по истечении двух лет

hepatitis [hɛpə'taɪtɪs] n гепатит, болезнь f Боткина

her [hə:ʳ] pron (*direct*) её; (*indirect*) ей; (*after prep: +gen*) неё; (: *+instr, +dat, +prp*) ней; *see also* **me** ▷ adj её; (*referring to subject of sentence*) свой; *see also* **my**

herb [hə:b] n трава; (*as medicine*) лекарственная трава; **herbs** npl (*Culin*) зелень fsg

herd [hə:d] n стадо

here [hɪəʳ] adv (*location*) здесь; (*destination*) сюда; (*at this point: in past*) тут; **from here** отсюда; **"here!"** (*present*) "здесь!"; **here is ..., here are ...** вот ...

hereditary [hɪ'rɛdɪtrɪ] adj наследственный

heritage ['hɛrɪtɪdʒ] n наследие

hernia ['hə:nɪə] n грыжа

hero ['hɪərəu] (*pl* **heroes**) n герой; **heroic** [hɪ'rəuɪk] adj героический

heroin ['hɛrəuɪn] n героин

heroine ['hɛrəuɪn] n героиня

heron ['hɛrən] n цапля

herring ['hɛrɪŋ] n (*Zool*) сельдь f; (*Culin*) селёдка

hers [hə:z] pron её; (*referring to subject of sentence*) свой; *see also* **mine¹**

herself [hə:'sɛlf] pron (*reflexive, after prep: +acc, +gen*) себя; (: *+dat, +prp*) себе; (: *+instr*) собой; (*emphatic*) сама; (*alone*): **by herself** одна; *see also* **myself**

he's [hi:z] = **he is; he has**

hesitant ['hɛzɪtənt] adj нерешительный; **to be hesitant to do** не решаться (*impf*) +infin

hesitate ['hɛzɪteɪt] vi колебаться (*perf* поколебаться); (*be unwilling*) не решаться (*impf*)

hesitation [hɛzɪ'teɪʃən] n колебание

heterosexual ['hɛtərəu'sɛksjuəl] adj гетеросексуальный

heyday ['heɪdeɪ] n: **the heyday of** расцвет +gen

hi [haɪ] excl (*as greeting*) привет

hiccoughs ['hɪkʌps] npl = **hiccups**

hiccups ['hɪkʌps] npl: she's got (the) hiccups у неё икота

hide [haɪd] (pt **hid**, pp **hidden**) n (skin) шкура ▷ vt (object, person) прятать (perf спрятать); (feeling, information) скрывать (perf скрыть); (sun, view) закрывать (perf закрыть) ▷ vi: to hide (from sb) прятаться (perf спрятаться) (от кого-н)

hideous ['hɪdɪəs] adj жуткий; (face) омерзительный

hiding ['haɪdɪŋ] n (beating) порка; to be in hiding скрываться (impf)

hi-fi ['haɪfaɪ] n стереосистема

high [haɪ] adj высокий; (wind) сильный ▷ adv высоко; the building is 20 m high высота здания — 20 м; to be high (inf: on drugs etc) кайфовать (impf); high risk высокая степень риска; high in the air (position) высоко в воздухе; **highchair** n высокий стульчик (для маленьких детей); **higher education** n высшее образование; **high jump** n прыжок в высоту; **Highlands** npl: the Highlands Высокогорья ntpl (Шотландии); **highlight** n (of event) кульминация ▷ vt (problem, need) выявлять (perf выявить); **highly** adv очень; (paid) высоко; to speak highly of высоко отзываться (perf отозваться) о +prp; to think highly of быть (impf) высокого мнения о +prp; **highness** n: Her/His Highness Её/Его Высочество; **high-rise** adj высотный; **high school** n (Brit) средняя школа (для 11-18ти летних); (US) средняя школа (для 14-18ти летних)

● **HIGH SCHOOL**
●
● В Британии дети посещают среднюю
● школу в возрасте от 11 до 18 лет. В
● США школьники вначале посещают
● младшую среднюю школу, а затем, в
● возрасте от 14 до 18 лет, среднюю
● школу. Школьное образование
● обязательно до 16 лет.

high: **high season** n (Brit) разгар сезона; **high street** n (Brit) центральная улица; **highway** n (US) трасса, автострада; (main road) автострада

hijack ['haɪdʒæk] vt (plane, bus) угонять (perf угнать)

hike [haɪk] n: to go for a hike идти (perf пойти) в поход

hilarious [hɪ'lɛərɪəs] adj чрезвычайно смешной

hill [hɪl] n (small) холм; (fairly high) гора; (slope) склон; **hillside** n склон; **hilly** adj холмистый

him [hɪm] pron (direct) его; (indirect) ему; (after prep: +gen) него; (: +dat) нему; (: +instr) ним; (: +prp) нём; see also **me**; **himself** pron (reflexive, after prep: +acc,

+gen) себя; (: +dat, +prp) себе; (: +instr) собой; (emphatic) сам; (alone): by himself один; see also **myself**

hinder ['hɪndə'] vt препятствовать (perf воспрепятствовать) or мешать (perf помешать) +dat

hindsight ['haɪndsaɪt] n: with hindsight ретроспективным взглядом

Hindu ['hɪnduː] adj индусский

hinge [hɪndʒ] n (on door) петля

hint [hɪnt] n (suggestion) намёк; (tip) совет; (sign, glimmer) подобие

hip [hɪp] n бедро

hippopotamus [hɪpə'pɒtəməs] (pl **hippopotamuses** or **hippopotami**) n гиппопотам

hire ['haɪə'] vt (Brit: car, equipment) брать (perf взять) напрокат; (venue) снимать (perf снять), арендовать (impf/perf); (worker) нанимать (perf нанять) ▷ n (Brit: of car) прокат; for hire напрокат; **hire-purchase** n (Brit): to buy sth on hire-purchase покупать (perf купить) что-н в рассрочку

his [hɪz] adj его; (referring to subject of sentence) свой; see also **my** ▷ pron его; see also **mine¹**

hiss [hɪs] vi (snake, gas) шипеть (impf)

historian [hɪ'stɔːrɪən] n историк

historic(al) [hɪ'stɔrɪk(l)] adj исторический

history ['hɪstərɪ] n (of town, country) история

hit [hɪt] (pt **hit**) vt ударять (perf ударить); (target) попадать (perf попасть) в +acc; (collide with: car) сталкиваться (perf столкнуться) с +instr; (affect: person, services) ударять (perf ударить) по +dat ▷ n (Comput) посещение; (success): the play was a big hit пьеса пользовалась большим успехом; to hit it off (with sb) (inf) находить (perf найти) общий язык (с кем-н)

hitch [hɪtʃ] vt (also **hitch up**: trousers, skirt) подтягивать (perf подтянуть) ▷ n (difficulty) помеха; to hitch sth to (fasten) привязывать (perf привязать) что-н к +dat; (hook) прицеплять (perf прицепить) что-н к +dat; to hitch (a lift) ловить (perf поймать) попутку

hi-tech ['haɪ'tɛk] adj высокотехнический

HIV n abbr (= human immunodeficiency virus) ВИЧ (= вирус иммунодефицита человека); HIV-negative/positive с отрицательной/положительной реакцией на ВИЧ

hive [haɪv] n (of bees) улей

hoard [hɔːd] n (of food) (тайный) запас; (of treasure) клад ▷ vt (provisions) запасать (perf запасти); (money) копить (perf скопить)

hoarse [hɔːs] adj (voice) хриплый

hoax [həʊks] n (false alarm) ложная тревога

hob [hɔb] *n* ве́рхняя часть плиты́ с конфо́рками

hobby ['hɔbɪ] *n* хо́бби *nt ind*

hockey ['hɔkɪ] *n* хокке́й (на траве́)

hog [hɔg] *vt* (*inf*) завладева́ть (*perf* завладе́ть) +*instr*

hoist [hɔɪst] *n* подъёмник, лебёдка ▷ *vt* поднима́ть (*perf* подня́ть); **to hoist sth on to one's shoulders** взва́ливать (*perf* взвали́ть) что-н на пле́чи

hold [həuld] (*pt, pp* **held**) *vt* (*grip*) держа́ть (*impf*); (*contain*) вмеща́ть (*impf*); (*detain*) содержа́ть (*impf*); (*power, qualification*) облада́ть (*impf*) +*instr*; (*post*) занима́ть (*impf*); (*conversation, meeting*) вести́ (*perf* провести́); (*party*) устра́ивать (*perf* устро́ить) ▷ *vi* (*withstand pressure*) выде́рживать (*perf* вы́держать); (*be valid*) остава́ться (*perf* оста́ться) в си́ле ▷ *n* (*grasp*) захва́т; (*Naut*) трюм; (*Aviat*) грузово́й отсе́к; **to hold one's head up** высоко́ держа́ть (*impf*) го́лову; **to hold sb hostage** держа́ть (*impf*) кого́-н в ка́честве зало́жника; **hold the line!** (*Tel*) не кладите́ *or* ве́шайте тру́бку! **he holds you responsible for her death** он счита́ет Вас вино́вным в её сме́рти; **to catch** *or* **grab hold of** хвата́ться (*perf* схвати́ться) за +*acc*; **to have a hold over sb** держа́ть (*impf*) кого́-н в рука́х; **hold back** *vt* (*thing*) приде́рживать (*perf* придержа́ть); (*person*) уде́рживать (*perf* удержа́ть); (*information*) скрыва́ть (*perf* скрыть); **hold down** *vt* (*person*) уде́рживать (*perf* удержа́ть); **to hold down a job** уде́рживаться (*perf* удержа́ться) на рабо́те; **hold on** *vi* (*grip*) держа́ться (*impf*); (*wait*) ждать (*perf* подожда́ть); **hold on!** (*Tel*) не кладите́ *or* ве́шайте тру́бку!; **hold on to** *vt fus* (*for support*) держа́ться (*impf*) за +*acc*; (*keep: object*) приде́рживать (*perf* придержа́ть); (: *beliefs*) сохраня́ть (*perf* сохрани́ть); **hold out** *vt* (*hand*) протя́гивать (*perf* протяну́ть); (*hope, prospect*) сохраня́ть (*perf* сохрани́ть) ▷ *vi* (*resist*) держа́ться (*perf* продержа́ться); **hold up** *vt* (*raise*) поднима́ть (*perf* подня́ть); (*support*) подде́рживать (*perf* поддержа́ть); (*delay*) заде́рживать (*perf* задержа́ть); (*rob*) гра́бить (*perf* огра́бить); **holder** *n* (*container*) держа́тель *m*; (*of ticket, record*) облада́тель(ница) *m(f)*; **title holder** нося́щий(-ая) *m(f) adj* ти́тул

hole [həul] *n* (*in wall*) дыра́; (*in road*) я́ма; (*burrow*) нора́; (*in clothing*) ды́рка; (*in argument*) брешь *f*

holiday ['hɔlɪdeɪ] *n* (*Brit: from school*) кани́кулы *pl*; (: *from work*) о́тпуск; (*day off*) выходно́й день *m*; (*also* **public holiday**) пра́здник; **on holiday** (*from school*) на кани́кулах; (*from work*) в о́тпуске

Holland ['hɔlənd] *n* Голла́ндия

hollow ['hɔləu] *adj* (*container*) по́лый; (*log, tree*) дупли́стый; (*cheeks*) впа́лый; (*laugh*) нейскренний; (*claim, sound*) пусто́й ▷ *n* (*in ground*) впа́дина; (*in tree*) дупло́ ▷ *vt*: **to hollow out** выка́пывать (*perf* вы́копать)

holly ['hɔlɪ] *n* остроли́ст

holocaust ['hɔləkɔ:st] *n* (*nuclear*) истребле́ние; (*Jewish*) холоко́ст

holy ['həulɪ] *adj* свято́й

home [həum] *n* дом; (*area, country*) ро́дина ▷ *cpd* дома́шний; (*Econ, Pol*) вну́тренний; (*Sport*): **home team** хозя́ева *mpl* поля́ ▷ *adv* (*go, come*) домо́й; (*hammer etc*) в то́чку; **at home** до́ма; (*in country*) на ро́дине; (*in situation*) как у себя́ до́ма; **make yourself at home** чу́вствуйте себя́ как до́ма; **homeland** *n* ро́дина; **homeless** *adj* бездо́мный ▷ *npl*: **the homeless** бездо́мные *pl adj*; **homely** *adj* ую́тный; **home-made** *adj* (*food*) дома́шний; (*bomb*) самоде́льный; **Home Office** *n* (*Brit*): **the Home Office** ≈ Министе́рство вну́тренних дел; **home page** *n* электро́нная страни́ца *or* страни́чка; **Home Secretary** *n* (*Brit*) ≈ мини́стр вну́тренних дел; **homesick** *adj*: **to be homesick** (*for family*) скуча́ть (*impf*) по до́му; (*for country*) скуча́ть (*impf*) по ро́дине; **homework** *n* дома́шняя рабо́та, дома́шнее зада́ние

homicide ['hɔmɪsaɪd] *n* (*esp US*) уби́йство

homosexual [hɔməu'sɛksjuəl] *adj* гомосексуа́льный ▷ *n* гомосексуали́ст(ка)

honest ['ɔnɪst] *adj* че́стный; **honestly** *adv* че́стно; **honesty** *n* че́стность *f*

honey ['hʌnɪ] *n* (*food*) мёд; **honeymoon** *n* медо́вый ме́сяц; **honeysuckle** *n* жи́молость *f*

honorary ['ɔnərərɪ] *adj* почётный

honour ['ɔnə'] (*US* **honor**) *vt* (*person*) почита́ть (*impf*), чтить (*impf*); (*commitment*) выполня́ть (*perf* вы́полнить) ▷ *n* (*pride*) честь *f*; (*tribute, distinction*) по́честь *f*; **honourable** *adj* (*person, action*) благоро́дный

● **HONOURS DEGREE**
●
● **Honours degree** — (учёная) сте́пень.
● Большинство́ студе́нтов университе́та
● получа́ют учёную сте́пень. Така́я
● сте́пень вы́ше по у́ровню, чем так
● называ́емая "обы́чная сте́пень" или
● "зачёт".

hood [hud] *n* капюшо́н; (*US: Aut*) капо́т; (*of cooker*) вытяжно́й колпа́к

hoof [hu:f] (*pl* **hooves**) *n* копы́то

hook [huk] *n* крючо́к ▷ *vt* прицепля́ть (*perf* прицепи́ть)

hooligan ['hu:lɪgən] *n* хулига́н

hoop [hu:p] *n* о́бруч

hoover ['hu:vər] (Brit) n пылесо́с ▷ vt
пылесо́сить (perf пропылесо́сить)

hooves [hu:vz] npl of **hoof**

hop [hɔp] vi скака́ть (impf) на одно́й ноге́

hope [həup] vt, vi наде́яться (impf) ▷ n
наде́жда; **to hope that/to do** наде́яться
(impf), что/+infin; **I hope so/not** наде́юсь,
что да/нет; **hopeful** adj (person) по́лный
наде́жд; (situation) обнаде́живающий; **to
be hopeful of sth** наде́яться (impf) на
что-н; **hopefully** adv (expectantly) с
наде́ждой; **hopefully, he'll come back**
бу́дем наде́яться, что он вернётся;
hopeless adj (situation, person)
безнадёжный; **I'm hopeless at names** я не
в состоя́нии запомина́ть имена́

hops [hɔps] npl хмель msg

horizon [həˈraɪzn] n горизо́нт;
horizontal [hɔrɪˈzɔntl] adj
горизонта́льный

hormone ['hɔ:məun] n гормо́н

horn [hɔ:n] n (of animal) рог; (also
French horn) валто́рна; (Aut) гудо́к

horoscope ['hɔrəskəup] n гороско́п

horrendous [həˈrendəs] adj ужаса́ющий

horrible ['hɔrɪbl] adj ужа́сный

horrid ['hɔrɪd] adj проти́вный, ме́рзкий

horror ['hɔrər] n (alarm) у́жас; (dislike)
отвраще́ние; (of war) у́жасы mpl

horse [hɔ:s] n ло́шадь f; **horseback** adv:
on horseback верхо́м; **horsepower** n
лошади́ная си́ла; **horse racing** n ска́чки
fpl; **horseradish** n хрен

hose [həuz] n (also **hosepipe**) шланг

hospital ['hɔspɪtl] n больни́ца

hospitality [hɔspɪˈtælɪtɪ] n
гостеприи́мство

host [həust] n (at party, dinner) хозя́ин;
(TV, Radio) веду́щий m adj; **a host of** ма́сса
+gen, мно́жество +gen

hostage ['hɔstɪdʒ] n зало́жник(-ица)

hostel ['hɔstl] n общежи́тие; (for
homeless) прию́т; (also **youth hostel**)
молодёжная гости́ница

hostess ['həustɪs] n (at party, dinner etc)
хозя́йка; (TV, Radio) веду́щая f adj; (Brit:
also **air hostess**) стюарде́сса

hostile ['hɔstaɪl] adj (person, attitude)
вражде́бный; (conditions, environment)
неблагоприя́тный; (troops) вра́жеский

hostility [hɔˈstɪlɪtɪ] n вражде́бность f

hot [hɔt] adj (object, temper, argument)
горя́чий; (weather) жа́ркий; (spicy: food)
о́стрый; **she is hot** ей жа́рко; **it's hot**
(weather) жа́рко

hotel [həuˈtel] n гости́ница, оте́ль m

hotspot ['hɔtspɔt] n (Comput: also
wireless hotspot) хот-спо́т m

hot-water bottle [hɔtˈwɔ:tə-] n гре́лка

hound [haund] vt трави́ть (perf
затрави́ть) ▷ n го́нчая f adj

hour ['auər] n час; **hourly** adj (rate)
почасово́й; (service) ежечасный

house [n haus, vb hauz] n дом; (Theat)
зал ▷ vt (person) сели́ть (perf посели́ть);
(collection) размеща́ть (perf размести́ть);
at my house у меня́ до́ма; **the House of
Commons/Lords** (Brit) Пала́та о́бщин/
ло́рдов; **on the house** (inf) беспла́тно;
household n (inhabitants) домоча́дцы
mpl; (home) дом; **housekeeper** n
эконо́мка; **housewife** irreg n дома́шняя
хозя́йка, домохозя́йка; **housework** n
дома́шние дела́ ntpl

○ **HOUSE OF LORDS**
●
● **House of Lords** — Пала́та ло́рдов.
● Брита́нский парла́мент состои́т из двух
● пала́т: из Пала́ты о́бщин, чле́ны
● кото́рой избира́ются и Пала́ты ло́рдов,
● кото́рая в настоя́щее вре́мя пережива́ет
● пери́од рефо́рм. До неда́внего вре́мени
● её чле́ны не избира́лись.

housing ['hauzɪŋ] n жильё; **housing
estate** (US **housing project**) n
жили́щный ко́мплекс; (larger) жило́й
масси́в

hover ['hɔvər] vi (bird, insect) пари́ть
(impf); **hovercraft** n су́дно на
возду́шной поду́шке

○ **KEYWORD**

how [hau] adv **1** (in what way) как; **to
know how to do** уме́ть (impf) +infin; **to
know how to do** знать (impf), как +infin; **how did you like the
film?** как Вам понра́вился фильм?; **how
are you?** как дела́ or Вы?
2 ско́лько; **how much milk/many people?**
ско́лько молока́/челове́к?; **how long?** как
до́лго?, ско́лько вре́мени?; **how old are
you?** ско́лько Вам лет?; **how tall is he?**
како́го он ро́ста?; **how lovely/awful!** как
чуде́сно/ужа́сно!

howl [haul] vi (animal, wind) выть (impf);
(baby, person) реве́ть (impf)

HP n abbr (Brit) = **hire-purchase**

h.p. abbr (Aut) (= horsepower) л.с.
(= лошади́ная си́ла)

HQ abbr = **headquarters**

HTML abbr (= hypertext markup language)
ги́пертекст

hug [hʌg] vt обнима́ть (perf обня́ть);
(object) обхва́тывать (perf обхвати́ть)

huge [hju:dʒ] adj огро́мный, грома́дный

hull [hʌl] n (Naut) ко́рпус

hum [hʌm] vt напева́ть (impf) (без слов)
▷ vi (person) напева́ть (impf); (machine)
гуде́ть (perf прогуде́ть)

human ['hju:mən] adj челове́ческий ▷ n
(also **human being**) челове́к

humane [hju:ˈmeɪn] adj (treatment)
челове́чный

humanitarian [hju:mænɪˈtɛərɪən] adj
(aid) гуманита́рный; (principles) гума́нный

humanity [hjuːˈmænɪtɪ] *n* (*mankind*) челове́чество; (*humaneness*) челове́чность *f*, гума́нность *f*

human rights *npl* права́ *ntpl* челове́ка

humble [ˈhʌmbl] *adj* скро́мный ▷ *vt* сбива́ть (*perf* сбить) спесь с +*gen*

humidity [hjuːˈmɪdɪtɪ] *n* вла́жность *f*

humiliate [hjuːˈmɪlɪeɪt] *vt* унижа́ть (*perf* уни́зить)

humiliation [hjuːmɪlɪˈeɪʃən] *n* униже́ние

humorous [ˈhjuːmərəs] *adj* (*book*) юмористи́ческий; (*remark*) шутли́вый; **humorous person** челове́к с ю́мором

humour [ˈhjuːmə˞] (*US* **humor**) *n* ю́мор; (*mood*) настрое́ние ▷ *vt* ублажа́ть (*perf* ублажи́ть)

hump [hʌmp] *n* (*in ground*) буго́р; (*on back*) горб

hunch [hʌntʃ] *n* дога́дка

hundred [ˈhʌndrəd] *n* сто; **hundredth** *adj* со́тый

hung [hʌŋ] *pt, pp of* **hang**

Hungarian [hʌŋˈɡɛərɪən] *adj* венге́рский

Hungary [ˈhʌŋɡərɪ] *n* Ве́нгрия

hunger [ˈhʌŋɡə˞] *n* го́лод

hungry [ˈhʌŋɡrɪ] *adj* голо́дный; (*keen*): **hungry for** жа́ждущий +*gen*; **he is hungry** он го́лоден

hunt [hʌnt] *vt* (*animal*) охо́титься (*impf*) на +*acc*; (*criminal*) охо́титься (*impf*) за +*instr* ▷ *vi* (*Sport*) охо́титься (*impf*) ▷ *n* охо́та; (*for criminal*) ро́зыск; **to hunt (for)** (*search*) иска́ть (*impf*); **hunter** *n* охо́тник(-ица); **hunting** *n* охо́та

hurdle [ˈhəːdl] *n* препя́тствие; (*Sport*) барье́р

hurricane [ˈhʌrɪkən] *n* урага́н

hurry [ˈhʌrɪ] *n* спе́шка ▷ *vi* спеши́ть (*perf* поспеши́ть), торопи́ться (*perf* поторопи́ться) ▷ *vt* (*person*) подгоня́ть (*perf* подогна́ть), торопи́ть (*perf* поторопи́ть); **to be in a hurry** спеши́ть (*impf*), торопи́ться (*impf*); **hurry up** *vt* (*person*) подгоня́ть (*perf* подогна́ть), торопи́ть (*perf* поторопи́ть); (*process*) ускоря́ть (*perf* ускори́ть) ▷ *vi* торопи́ться (*perf* поторопи́ться); **hurry up!** поторопи́сь!, скоре́е!

hurt [həːt] (*pt, pp* **hurt**) *vt* причиня́ть (*perf* причини́ть) боль +*dat*; (*injure*) ушиба́ть (*perf* ушиби́ть); (*feelings*) задева́ть (*perf* заде́ть) ▷ *vi* (*be painful*) боле́ть (*impf*) ▷ *adj* (*offended*) оби́женный; (*injured*) ушибленный; **to hurt o.s.** ушиба́ться (*perf* ушиби́ться)

husband [ˈhʌzbənd] *n* муж

hush [hʌʃ] *n* тишина́; **hush!** ти́хо!, ти́ше!

husky [ˈhʌskɪ] *adj* (*voice*) хри́плый ▷ *n* ездова́я соба́ка

hut [hʌt] *n* (*house*) избу́шка, хи́жина; (*shed*) сара́й

hyacinth [ˈhaɪəsɪnθ] *n* гиаци́нт

hydrogen [ˈhaɪdrədʒən] *n* водоро́д

hygiene [ˈhaɪdʒiːn] *n* гигие́на

hygienic [haɪˈdʒiːnɪk] *adj* (*product*) гигиени́ческий

hymn [hɪm] *n* церко́вный гимн

hype [haɪp] *n* (*inf*) ажиота́ж

hyperlink [ˈhaɪpəlɪŋk] *n* гиперссы́лка

hypocritical [hɪpəˈkrɪtɪkl] *adj* лицеме́рный

hypothesis [haɪˈpɔθɪsɪs] (*pl* **hypotheses**) *n* гипо́теза

i

I [aɪ] pron я

ice [aɪs] n лёд; (*ice cream*) моро́женое nt adj ▷ vt покрыва́ть (*perf* покры́ть) глазу́рью; **iceberg** n а́йсберг; **ice cream** n моро́женое nt adj; **ice hockey** n хокке́й (на льду)

Iceland ['aɪslənd] n Исла́ндия

icing ['aɪsɪŋ] n глазу́рь f; **icing sugar** n (*Brit*) са́харная пу́дра (*для приготовле́ния глазу́ри*)

icon ['aɪkɔn] n (*Rel*) ико́на; (*Comput*) ико́нка

icy ['aɪsɪ] adj (*cold*) ледяно́й; (*road*) обледене́лый

I'd [aɪd] = **I would**; **I had**

idea [aɪ'dɪə] n иде́я

ideal [aɪ'dɪəl] n идеа́л ▷ adj идеа́льный

identical [aɪ'dɛntɪkl] adj индентти́чный

identification [aɪdɛntɪfɪ'keɪʃən] n определе́ние, идентифика́ция; (*of person, body*) опозна́ние; (**means of**) **identification** удостовере́ние ли́чности

identify [aɪ'dɛntɪfaɪ] vt определя́ть (*perf* определи́ть); (*person*) узнава́ть (*perf* узна́ть); (*body*) опознава́ть (*perf* опозна́ть); (*distinguish*) выявля́ть (*perf* вы́явить)

identity [aɪ'dɛntɪtɪ] n (*of person*) ли́чность f; (*of group, nation*) самосозна́ние

ideology [aɪdɪ'ɔlədʒɪ] n идеоло́гия

idiom ['ɪdɪəm] n (*phrase*) идио́ма

idiot ['ɪdɪət] n идио́т(ка)

idle ['aɪdl] adj пра́здный; (*lazy*) лени́вый; (*unemployed*) безрабо́тный; (*machinery, factory*) безде́йствующий; **to be idle** безде́йствовать (*impf*)

idol ['aɪdl] n куми́р; (*Rel*) и́дол

idyllic [ɪ'dɪlɪk] adj идилли́ческий

i.e. abbr (*that is*) (= *id est*) т.е. (= *то есть*)

if [ɪf] conj **1** (*conditional use*) е́сли; **if I finish early, I will ring you** е́сли я зако́нчу ра́но, я тебе́ позвоню́; **if I were you (I would …)** на Ва́шем ме́сте (я бы …)
2 (*whenever*) когда́
3 (*although*): **(even) if** да́же е́сли; **I'll get it done, (even) if it takes all night** я сде́лаю э́то, да́же е́сли э́то займёт у меня́ всю ночь
4 (*whether*) ли; **I don't know if he is here** я не зна́ю, здесь ли он; **ask him if he can stay** спроси́те, смо́жет ли он оста́ться
5: **if so/not** е́сли да/нет; **if only** е́сли бы то́лько; **if only I could** е́сли бы я то́лько мог; *see also* **as**

ignite [ɪg'naɪt] vt (*set fire to*) зажига́ть (*perf* заже́чь) ▷ vi загора́ться (*perf* загоре́ться)

ignition [ɪg'nɪʃən] n (*Aut*) зажига́ние

ignorance ['ɪgnərəns] n неве́жество

ignorant ['ɪgnərənt] adj неве́жественный; **ignorant of** (*a subject*) несве́дущий в +prp; (*unaware of*): **he is ignorant of that fact** он не зна́ет об э́том

ignore [ɪg'nɔ:] vt игнори́ровать (*impf/perf*); (*disregard*) пренебрега́ть (*perf* пренебре́чь)

I'll [aɪl] = **I will**; **I shall**

ill [ɪl] adj больно́й; (*effects*) дурно́й ▷ adv: **to speak ill (of sb)** ду́рно говори́ть (*impf*) (о ком-н); **he is ill** он бо́лен; **to be taken ill** заболева́ть (*perf* заболе́ть)

illegal [ɪ'li:gl] adj незако́нный; (*organization*) нелега́льный

illegible [ɪ'lɛdʒɪbl] adj неразбо́рчивый

illegitimate [ɪlɪ'dʒɪtɪmət] adj (*child*) внебра́чный; (*activities*) незако́нный, нелегити́мный

ill health [ɪl'hɛlθ] n плохо́е здоро́вье

illiterate [ɪ'lɪtərət] adj негра́мотный

illness ['ɪlnɪs] n боле́знь f

illuminate [ɪ'lu:mɪneɪt] vt (*light up*) освеща́ть (*perf* освети́ть)

illusion [ɪ'lu:ʒən] n (*false idea*) иллю́зия; (*trick*) фо́кус

illustrate ['ɪləstreɪt] vt иллюстри́ровать (*perf* проиллюстри́ровать)

illustration [ɪlə'streɪʃən] n иллюстра́ция

I'm [aɪm] = **I am**

image ['ɪmɪdʒ] n (*picture*) о́браз; (*public face*) и́мидж; (*reflection*) изображе́ние

imaginary [ɪ'mædʒɪnərɪ] adj (*creature, land*) вообража́емый

imagination [ɪmædʒɪ'neɪʃən] n воображе́ние

imaginative [ɪ'mædʒɪnətɪv] adj (*solution*) хитроу́мный; **he is very imaginative** он облада́ет бога́тым воображе́нием

imagine [ɪ'mædʒɪn] vt (*visualize*) представля́ть (*perf* предста́вить) (себе́),

воображ́ать (*perf* вообраз́ить); (*dream*)
воображ́ать (*perf* вообраз́ить); (*suppose*)
предполаѓать (*perf* предполож́ить)

imitate ['ımıteıt] *vt* подраж́ать (*impf*)
+*dat*, имит́ировать (*impf*)

imitation [ımı'teıʃən] *n* подраж́ание,
имит́ация

immaculate [ı'mækjulət] *adj*
безупр́ечный

immature [ımə'tjuər] *adj* незр́елый

immediate [ı'mi:dıət] *adj* (*reaction,
answer*) нем́едленный; (*need*)
безотлаѓательный; (*family*) ближ́айший;
immediately *adv* (*at once*) нем́едленно;
(*directly*) ср́азу

immense [ı'mɛns] *adj* огр́омный,
гром́адный

immigrant ['ımıgrənt] *n* иммигр́ант(ка)

immigration [ımı'greıʃən] *n*
иммигр́ация; (*also* **immigration control**)
иммиграци́онный контр́оль

imminent ['ımınənt] *adj* (*arrival,
departure*) немин́уемый

immoral [ı'mɔrl] *adj* амор́альный,
безнр́авственный

immortal [ı'mɔ:tl] *adj* бессм́ертный

immune [ı'mju:n] *adj*: **he is immune to**
(*disease*) у неѓо иммуните́т пр́отив +*gen*;
(*flattery, criticism etc*) он невоспри́имчив к
+*dat*; **immune system** *n* имм́унная
сист́ема

immunize ['ımjunaız] *vt*: **to immunize sb
(against)** д́елать (*perf* сд́елать) ком́у-н
прив́ивку (пр́отив +*gen*)

impact ['ımpækt] *n* (*of crash*) уд́ар;
(*force*) уд́арная с́ила; (*of law, measure*)
возд́ействие

impartial [ım'pɑ:ʃl] *adj* беспристр́астный

impatience [ım'peıʃəns] *n* нетерп́ение

impatient [ım'peıʃənt] *adj*
нетерпел́ивый; **to get** *or* **grow impatient**
тер́ять (*perf* потер́ять) терп́ение; **she was
impatient to leave** ей не терп́елось уйт́и

impeccable [ım'pɛkəbl] *adj*
безупр́ечный

impending [ım'pɛndıŋ] *adj* гряд́ущий

imperative [ım'pɛrətıv] *adj*: **it is
imperative that ...** необход́имо, чт́обы ...

imperfect [ım'pə:fıkt] *adj* (*system*)
несоверш́енный; (*goods*) деф́ектный

imperial [ım'pıərıəl] *adj* (*history, power*)
имп́ерский; (*Brit: measure*): **imperial
system** брит́анская сист́ема един́иц
измер́ения и в́еса

impersonal [ım'pə:sənl] *adj*
(*organization, place*) безл́икий

impersonate [ım'pə:səneıt] *vt* выдав́ать
(*perf* в́ыдать) себ́я за +*acc*

implement [*vb* 'ımplımɛnt, *n* 'ımplımənt]
vt провод́ить (*perf* провест́и) в жизнь ▷ *n*
(*for gardening*) ор́удие

implication [ımplı'keıʃən] *n* (*inference*)
сл́едствие

implicit [ım'plısıt] *adj* (*inferred*)

невы́раженный, имплиц́итный;
(*unquestioning*) безогово́рочный

imply [ım'plaı] *vt* (*hint*) намеќать (*perf*
намекн́уть); (*mean*) означ́ать (*impf*)

import [*vb* ım'pɔ:t, *n, cpd* 'ımpɔ:t] *vt*
импорт́ировать (*impf/perf*), ввоз́ить (*perf*
ввезт́и) ▷ *n* (*article*) импорт́ируемый
тов́ар; (*importation*) ́импорт ▷ *cpd*:
import duty/licence п́ошлина/лиц́ензия на
ввоз

importance [ım'pɔ:tns] *n* в́ажность *f*

important [ım'pɔ:tnt] *adj* в́ажный; **it's
not important** ́это нев́ажно

impose [ım'pəuz] *vt* (*restrictions, fine*)
налаѓать (*perf* налож́ить); (*discipline,
rules*) ввод́ить (*perf* ввест́и) ▷ *vi*
навя́зываться (*perf* навяз́аться)

imposing [ım'pəuzıŋ] *adj*
велич́ественный

impossible [ım'pɔsıbl] *adj* (*task,
demand*) невыполн́имый; (*situation,
person*) невынос́имый

impotent ['ımpətnt] *adj* бесс́ильный

impractical [ım'præktıkl] *adj* (*plan etc*)
нере́альный; (*person*) непракт́ичный

impress [ım'prɛs] *vt* (*person*)
производ́ить (*perf* произвест́и)
впечатл́ение на +*acc*; **to impress sth on sb**
внуш́ать (*perf* внуш́ить) что-н ком́у-н

impression [ım'prɛʃən] *n* впечатл́ение;
(*of stamp, seal*) отпеч́аток; (*imitation*)
имит́ация; **he is under the impression that
...** у неѓо создал́ось впечатл́ение, что ...

impressive [ım'prɛsıv] *adj*
впечатл́яющий

imprison [ım'prızn] *vt* заключ́ать (*perf*
заключ́ить) в тюрьм́у; **imprisonment** *n*
(тюр́емное) заключ́ение

improbable [ım'prɔbəbl] *adj*
невероя́тный

improve [ım'pru:v] *vt* улучш́ать (*perf*
улучш́ить) ▷ *vi* улучш́аться (*perf*
улучш́иться); (*pupil*) станов́иться (*perf*
стать) л́учше; **the patient improved**
больн́ому ст́ало л́учше; **improvement (in)** улучш́ение (+*gen*)

improvise ['ımprəvaız] *vt, vi*
импровиз́ировать (*impf/perf*)

impulse ['ımpʌls] *n* (*urge*) пор́ыв; **to act
on impulse** поддав́аться (*perf* подд́аться)
пор́ыву

impulsive [ım'pʌlsıv] *adj* (*person*)
импульс́ивный; (*gesture*) пор́ывистый

О **KEYWORD**

in [ın] *prep* **1** (*indicating position*) в/на
+*prp*; **in the house/garden** в д́оме/сад́у; **in
the street/Ukraine** на ́улице/Украи́не; **in
London/Canada** в Л́ондоне/Кан́аде; **in the
country** в дер́евне; **in town** в ѓороде; **in
here** здесь; **in there** там
2 (*indicating motion*) в/на +*acc*; **in the
house/room** в дом/ќомнату

3 (*indicating time: during*): **in spring/ summer/autumn/winter** весно́й/ле́том/ о́сенью/зимо́й; **in the morning/afternoon/ evening** у́тром/днём/ве́чером; **in the evenings** по вечера́м; **at 4 o'clock in the afternoon** в 4 часа́ дня
4 (*indicating time: in the space of*) за +*acc*; (: *after a period of*) че́рез +*acc*; **I did it in 3 hours** я сде́лал э́то за 3 часа́; **I'll see you in 2 weeks** уви́димся че́рез 2 неде́ли
5 (*indicating manner etc*): **in a loud/quiet voice** гро́мким/ти́хим го́лосом; **in English/ Russian** по-англи́йски/по-ру́сски, на англи́йском/ру́сском языке́
6 (*wearing*) в +*prp*; **the boy in the blue shirt** ма́льчик в голубо́й руба́шке
7 (*indicating circumstances*): **in the sun** на со́лнце; **in the rain** под дождём; **in the shade** в тени́; **a rise in prices** повыше́ние цен
8 (*indicating mood, state*) в +*prp*; **in despair** в отча́янии
9 (*with ratios, numbers*): **one in ten households** одна́ из десяти́ семе́й; **20 pence in the pound** 20 пе́нсов с ка́ждого фу́нта; **they lined up in twos** они́ вы́строились по дво́е; **a gradient of one in five** укло́н оди́н к пяти́
10 (*referring to people, works*) у +*gen*; **the disease is common in children** э́то заболева́ние ча́сто встреча́ется у дете́й; **in Dickens** у Ди́ккенса; **you have a good friend in him** в нём тебе́ хоро́ший друг
11 (*indicating profession etc*): **to be in publishing/advertising** занима́ться (*impf*) изда́тельским де́лом/рекла́мным би́знесом; **to be in teaching** рабо́тать (*impf*) учи́телем; **to be in the army** быть (*impf*) в а́рмии
12 (*with present participle*): **in saying this** говоря́ э́то; **in behaving like this, she ...** поступа́я таки́м о́бразом, она́ ...
▷ *adv*: **to be in** (*train, ship, plane*) прибыва́ть (*perf* прибы́ть); (*in fashion*) быть (*impf*) в мо́де; **is he in today?** он сего́дня здесь?; **he is not in today** его́ сего́дня нет; **he wasn't in yesterday** его́ вчера́ не́ бы́ло; **he'll be in later today** он бу́дет по́зже сего́дня; **to ask sb in** предлага́ть (*perf* предложи́ть) кому́-н войти́; **to run/walk in** вбега́ть (*perf* вбежа́ть)/входи́ть (*perf* войти́)
▷ *n*: **to know the ins and outs** знать (*impf*) все ходы́ и вы́ходы

in. *abbr* = **inch**
inability [ɪnə'bɪlɪtɪ] *n*: **inability (to do)** неспосо́бность *f* (+*infin*)
inaccurate [ɪn'ækjʊrət] *adj* нето́чный
inadequate [ɪn'ædɪkwət] *adj* недоста́точный; (*work*) неудовлетвори́тельный; (*person*) некомпете́нтный; **to feel inadequate** чу́вствовать (*impf*) себя́ не на у́ровне

inadvertently [ɪnəd'vəːtntlɪ] *adv* неча́янно, неумы́шленно
inappropriate [ɪnə'prəʊprɪət] *adj* (*unsuitable*) неподходя́щий; (*improper*) неуме́стный
inbox ['ɪnbɒks] *n* па́пка "Входя́щие"
Inc. *abbr* = **incorporated**
incapable [ɪn'keɪpəbl] *adj* (*helpless*) беспо́мощный; **incapable of sth/doing** неспосо́бный на что-н/+*infin*
incense [*n* 'ɪnsens, *vb* ɪn'sens] *n* ла́дан
▷ *vt* приводи́ть (*perf* привести́) в я́рость
incentive [ɪn'sentɪv] *n* сти́мул
inch [ɪntʃ] *n* дюйм

  ● **INCH**
  ●
  ● **Inch** – ме́ра длины́ ра́вная 2,54 см.

incidence ['ɪnsɪdns] *n* число́; **high incidence** высо́кий у́ровень
incident ['ɪnsɪdnt] *n* (*event*) слу́чай; **without incident** без происше́ствий; **incidentally** [ɪnsɪ'dentəlɪ] *adv* (*by the way*) кста́ти, ме́жду про́чим
inclination [ɪnklɪ'neɪʃən] *n* (*desire*) расположенность *f*; (*tendency*) скло́нность *f*
incline [*n* 'ɪnklaɪn, *vb* ɪn'klaɪn] *n* (*slope*) укло́н, накло́н ▷ *vi*: **he is inclined to ...** он скло́нен +*infin* ....; **he is inclined to depression** он скло́нен к депре́ссиям
include [ɪn'kluːd] *vt* включа́ть (*perf* включи́ть)
including [ɪn'kluːdɪŋ] *prep* включа́я +*acc*
inclusion [ɪn'kluːʒən] *n* включе́ние
inclusive [ɪn'kluːsɪv] *adj*: **inclusive of** включа́я +*acc*; **the price is fully inclusive** цена́ включа́ет в себя́ всё; **from March 1st to 5th inclusive** с 1-ого до 5-ого ма́рта включи́тельно
income ['ɪnkʌm] *n* дохо́д; **income support** *n* де́нежное посо́бие (*семьям с ни́зким дохо́дом*); **income tax** *n* подохо́дный нало́г
incompatible [ɪnkəm'pætɪbl] *adj* несовмести́мый
incompetence [ɪn'kɒmpɪtns] *n* некомпете́нтность *f*
incompetent [ɪn'kɒmpɪtnt] *adj* (*person*) некомпете́нтный; (*work*) неуме́лый
incomplete [ɪnkəm'pliːt] *adj* (*unfinished*) незавершённый; (*partial*) непо́лный
inconsistent [ɪnkən'sɪstnt] *adj* (*actions*) непосле́довательный; (*statement*) противоречи́вый; (*work*) неро́вный; **inconsistent with** (*beliefs, values*) несовмести́мый с +*instr*
inconvenience [ɪnkən'viːnjəns] *n* (*problem*) неудо́бство ▷ *vt* причиня́ть (*perf* причини́ть) беспоко́йство +*dat*
inconvenient [ɪnkən'viːnjənt] *adj* неудо́бный

incorporate [ɪn'kɔ:pəreɪt] vt (*contain*) включáть (*impf*) в себя́, содержáть (*impf*); **to incorporate (into)** включáть (*perf* включи́ть) (в +acc)

incorrect [ɪnkə'rɛkt] adj неве́рный, непрáвильный

increase [n 'ɪnkri:s, vb ɪn'kri:s] n: **increase (in), increase (of)** увеличе́ние (+gen) ▷ vi увели́чиваться (*perf* увели́читься) ▷ vt увели́чивать (*perf* увели́чить); (*price*) поднимáть (*perf* подня́ть)

increasingly adv (*with comparative*) всё; (*more intensely*) всё бóлее; (*more often*) всё чáще

incredible [ɪn'krɛdɪbl] adj невероя́тный

incur [ɪn'kə:ʳ] vt (*expenses, loss*) нести́ (*perf* понести́); (*debt*) накопи́ть (*perf*); (*disapproval, anger*) навлекáть (*perf* навле́чь) на себя́

indecent [ɪn'di:snt] adj непристóйный

indeed [ɪn'di:d] adv (*certainly*) действи́тельно, в сáмом де́ле; (*in fact, furthermore*) бóлее тогó; **this book is very interesting indeed** э́та кни́га весьмá интере́сная; **thank you very much indeed** большóе Вам спаси́бо; **he is indeed very talented** он на сáмом де́ле óчень талáнтлив; **yes indeed!** да, действи́тельно *or* конéчно!

indefinitely adv (*continue, wait*) бесконéчно; (*be closed, delayed*) на неопределённое врéмя

independence [ɪndɪ'pɛndns] n незави́симость f

independent [ɪndɪ'pɛndnt] adj незави́симый

index ['ɪndɛks] (*pl* **indexes**) n (*in book*) указáтель m; (*in library etc*) катáлог; **price index** и́ндекс цен

India ['ɪndɪə] n И́ндия; **Indian** adj инди́йский ▷ n инди́ец

indicate ['ɪndɪkeɪt] vt укáзывать (*perf* указáть) на +acc; (*mention*) укáзывать (*perf* указáть)

indication [ɪndɪ'keɪʃən] n знак; **all the indications are that ...** всё укáзывает на то, что ...

indicative [ɪn'dɪkətɪv] adj: **to be indicative of** свиде́тельствовать (*impf*) о +prp, укáзывать (*impf*) на +acc

indicator ['ɪndɪkeɪtəʳ] n (*Aut*) указáтель m поворóта; (*fig*) покáзатель m

indifference [ɪn'dɪfrəns] n безразли́чие, равноду́шие

indifferent [ɪn'dɪfrənt] adj безразли́чный, равноду́шный; (*mediocre*) посре́дственный

indigestion [ɪndɪ'dʒɛstʃən] n несварéние желу́дка

indignant [ɪn'dɪgnənt] adj: **indignant at sth/with sb** возмущённый чем-н/кем-н

indirect [ɪndɪ'rɛkt] adj (*way*) окóльный, обхóдный; (*answer*) уклóнчивый; (*effect*) побóчный; **indirect object** (*Ling*) кóсвенное дополнéние

indispensable [ɪndɪs'pɛnsəbl] adj (*object*) необходи́мый; (*person*) незамени́мый

individual [ɪndɪ'vɪdjuəl] n ли́чность f, индиви́дуум ▷ adj индивидуáльный; **certain individuals** отде́льные ли́чности; **individually** adv в отде́льности; (*responsible*) ли́чно

indoor ['ɪndɔ:ʳ] adj (*plant*) кóмнатный; (*pool*) закры́тый; **indoors** adv (*go*) в помещéние; (*be*) в помещéнии; **he stayed indoors all morning** он просиде́л дóма всё у́тро

induce [ɪn'dju:s] vt (*cause*) вызывáть (*perf* вы́звать); (*persuade*) побуждáть (*perf* побуди́ть); (*Med: birth*) стимули́ровать (*impf/perf*)

indulge [ɪn'dʌldʒ] vt (*desire, whim etc*) потвóрствовать (*impf*) +dat, потакáть (*impf*) +dat; (*person, child*) баловáть (*perf* избаловáть) ▷ vi: **to indulge in** бáловаться (*perf* побáловаться) +instr

industrial [ɪn'dʌstrɪəl] adj индустриáльный, промы́шленный; **industrial accident** несчáстный слу́чай на произвóдстве; **industrial estate** n (*Brit*) индустриáльный парк

industry ['ɪndəstrɪ] n (*manufacturing*) индустри́я, промы́шленность f no pl; **industries** npl óтрасли pl промы́шленности; **tourist/fashion industry** индустри́я тури́зма/мóды

inefficient [ɪnɪ'fɪʃənt] adj неэффекти́вный; (*machine*) непроизводи́тельный

inequality [ɪnɪ'kwɔlɪtɪ] n (*of system*) нерáвенство

inevitable [ɪn'ɛvɪtəbl] adj неизбéжный, неотврати́мый

inevitably [ɪn'ɛvɪtəblɪ] adv неизбéжно

inexpensive [ɪnɪk'spɛnsɪv] adj недорогóй

inexperienced [ɪnɪk'spɪərɪənst] adj неóпытный

inexplicable [ɪnɪk'splɪkəbl] adj необъясни́мый

infamous ['ɪnfəməs] adj (*person*) бесчéстный

infant ['ɪnfənt] n (*baby*) младéнец; (*young child*) ребёнок

INFANT SCHOOL

Infant school — подготови́тельная шкóла. В Великобритáнии такýю шкóлу посещáют дéти в вóзрасте от 5 (иногдá 4) до 7 лет.

infantry ['ɪnfəntrɪ] n пехóта

infect [ɪn'fɛkt] vt заражáть (*perf* зарази́ть); **infection** [ɪn'fɛkʃən] n

зара́за, инфе́кция; **infectious** [ɪnˈfɛkʃəs]
adj (disease) инфекцио́нный; (fig)
зарази́тельный

inferior [ɪnˈfɪərɪər] adj (position, status)
подчинённый; (goods) ни́зкого ка́чества

infertile [ɪnˈfəːtaɪl] adj беспло́дный

infertility [ɪnfəːˈtɪlɪtɪ] n беспло́дие

infested [ɪnˈfɛstɪd] adj: **the house is
infested with rats** дом киши́т кры́сами

infinite [ˈɪnfɪnɪt] adj бесконе́чный

infirmary [ɪnˈfəːmərɪ] n больни́ца

inflammation [ɪnfləˈmeɪʃən] n
воспале́ние

inflation [ɪnˈfleɪʃən] n инфля́ция

inflexible [ɪnˈflɛksɪbl] adj (rule,
timetable) жёсткий; (person) неги́бкий

inflict [ɪnˈflɪkt] vt: **to inflict sth on sb**
причиня́ть (perf причини́ть) что-н кому́-н

influence [ˈɪnfluəns] n (power) влия́ние;
(effect) возде́йствие ▷ vt влия́ть (perf
повлия́ть) на +acc; **under the influence of
alcohol** под возде́йствием алкого́ля

influential [ɪnfluˈɛnʃl] adj влия́тельный

influx [ˈɪnflʌks] n прито́к

inform [ɪnˈfɔːm] vt: **to inform sb of sth**
сообща́ть (perf сообщи́ть) кому́-о чём-н
▷ vi: **to inform on sb** доноси́ть (perf
донести́) на кого́-н

informal [ɪnˈfɔːml] adj (visit, invitation)
неофициа́льный; (discussion, manner)
непринуждённый; (clothes) бу́дничный

information [ɪnfəˈmeɪʃən] n
информа́ция, сообще́ние; **a piece of
information** сообще́ние

informative [ɪnˈfɔːmətɪv] adj
содержа́тельный

infrastructure [ˈɪnfrəstrʌktʃər] n
инфраструкту́ра

infuriating [ɪnˈfjuərɪeɪtɪŋ] adj
возмути́тельный

ingenious [ɪnˈdʒiːnjəs] adj хитроу́мный;
(person) изобрета́тельный

ingredient [ɪnˈɡriːdɪənt] n ингредие́нт;
(fig) составна́я часть f

inhabit [ɪnˈhæbɪt] vt населя́ть (impf);
inhabitant n жи́тель(ница) m(f)

inhale [ɪnˈheɪl] vt вдыха́ть (perf
вдохну́ть) ▷ vi де́лать (perf сде́лать)
вдох; (when smoking) затя́гиваться (perf
затяну́ться)

inherent [ɪnˈhɪərənt] adj: **inherent in or
to** прису́щий +dat

inherit [ɪnˈhɛrɪt] vt насле́довать (impf/
perf), унасле́довать (perf); **inheritance** n
насле́дство

inhibit [ɪnˈhɪbɪt] vt ско́вывать (perf
скова́ть); (growth) заде́рживать (perf
задержа́ть); **inhibition** [ɪnhɪˈbɪʃən] n
ско́ванность f no pl

initial [ɪˈnɪʃl] adj первонача́льный,
нача́льный ▷ n (also **initial letter**)
нача́льная бу́ква ▷ vt ста́вить (perf
поста́вить) инициа́лы на +prp; **initials** npl
(of name) инициа́лы mpl; **initially** adv

(at first) внача́ле, снача́ла

initiate [ɪˈnɪʃɪeɪt] vt (talks etc) класть (perf
положи́ть) нача́ло +dat, зачина́ть (impf);
(new member) посвяща́ть (perf посвяти́ть)

initiative [ɪˈnɪʃətɪv] n инициати́ва,
начина́ние; (enterprise) инициати́вность f;
to take the initiative брать (perf взять) на
себя́ инициати́ву

inject [ɪnˈdʒɛkt] vt (drugs, poison)
вводи́ть (perf ввести́); (patient): **to inject
sb with sth** де́лать (perf сде́лать) уко́л
чего́-н кому́-н; **to inject into** (money)
влива́ть (perf влить) в +acc; **injection**
[ɪnˈdʒɛkʃən] n уко́л; (of money) влива́ние

injure [ˈɪndʒər] vt (person, limb, feelings)
ра́нить (impf/perf); **injured** adj ра́неный

injury [ˈɪndʒərɪ] n ра́на; (industrial, sports)
тра́вма

injustice [ɪnˈdʒʌstɪs] n
несправедли́вость f

ink [ɪŋk] n (in pen) черни́ла pl

inland [ˈɪnlənd] adv (travel) вглубь;
Inland Revenue n (Brit) ≈ (Гла́вное)
нало́говое управле́ние

in-laws [ˈɪnlɔːz] npl (of woman) родня́ со
стороны́ му́жа; (of man) родня́ со стороны́
жены́

inmate [ˈɪnmeɪt] n (of prison)
заключённый(-ая) m(f) adj; (of asylum)
пацие́нт(ка)

inn [ɪn] n тракти́р

inner [ˈɪnər] adj вну́тренний; **inner city**
n центра́льная часть го́рода

innocence [ˈɪnəsns] n невино́вность f;
(naivety) неви́нность f

innocent [ˈɪnəsnt] adj невино́вный;
(naive) неви́нный

innovation [ɪnəuˈveɪʃən] n но́вшество

input [ˈɪnput] n (resources, money)
вложе́ние

inquest [ˈɪnkwɛst] n (into death)
(суде́бное) рассле́дование

inquire [ɪnˈkwaɪər] vi: **to inquire (about)**
наводи́ть (perf навести́) спра́вки (о +prp;
(health) справля́ться (perf спра́виться) о
+prp; **to inquire when/where**
осведомля́ться (perf осве́домиться) когда́/
где; **inquire into** vt fus рассле́довать
(impf/perf)

insane [ɪnˈseɪn] adj безу́мный,
сумасше́дший

insect [ˈɪnsɛkt] n насеко́мое nt adj

insecure [ɪnsɪˈkjuər] adj (person)
неуве́ренный в себе́

insecurity [ɪnsɪˈkjuərɪtɪ] n
неуве́ренность f в себе́

insensitive [ɪnˈsɛnsɪtɪv] adj
бесчу́вственный

insert [ɪnˈsəːt] vt: **to insert (into)**
вставля́ть (perf вста́вить) (в +acc); (piece
of paper) вкла́дывать (perf вложи́ть) (в
+acc)

inside [ˈɪnˈsaɪd] n вну́тренняя часть f

▷ adj вну́тренний ▷ adv (be) внутри́; (go) внутрь ▷ prep (position) внутри́ +gen; (motion) внутрь +gen; **inside ten minutes** в преде́лах десяти́ мину́т; **insides** npl (inf: stomach) вну́тренности fpl; **inside out** adv наизна́нку; (know) вдоль и поперёк

insight ['ɪnsaɪt] n: **insight (into)** понима́ние (+gen)

insignificant [ɪnsɪg'nɪfɪknt] adj незначи́тельный

insist [ɪn'sɪst] vi: **to insist (on)** наста́ивать (perf настоя́ть) (на +prp); **he insisted that I came** он настоя́л на том, что́бы я пришёл; **he insisted that all was well** он утвержда́л, что всё в поря́дке; **insistent** adj насто́йчивый

insomnia [ɪn'sɔmnɪə] n бессо́нница

inspect [ɪn'spɛkt] vt (equipment, premises) осма́тривать (perf осмотре́ть); **inspection** n [ɪn'spɛkʃən] n осмо́тр; **inspector** n (Admin, Police) инспе́ктор; (Brit: on buses, trains) контролёр

inspiration [ɪnspə'reɪʃən] n вдохнове́ние

inspire [ɪn'spaɪə*] vt (workers, troops) вдохновля́ть (perf вдохнови́ть); **to inspire sth (in sb)** внуша́ть (perf внуши́ть) что-н (кому́-н)

instability [ɪnstə'bɪlɪtɪ] n нестаби́льность f

install [ɪn'stɔ:l] vt (machine) устана́вливать (perf установи́ть); (official) ста́вить (perf поста́вить); **installation** [ɪnstə'leɪʃən] n (of machine, plant) устано́вка

instalment [ɪn'stɔ:lmənt] (US **installment**) n (of payment) взнос; (of story) часть f; **to pay in instalments** плати́ть (perf заплати́ть) в рассро́чку

instance ['ɪnstəns] n приме́р; **for instance** наприме́р; **in the first instance** в пе́рвую о́чередь

instant ['ɪnstənt] n мгнове́ние, миг ▷ adj (reaction, success) мгнове́нный; (coffee) раствори́мый; **come here this instant!** иди́ сюда́ сию́ же мину́ту!; **instantly** adv неме́дленно, сра́зу

instead [ɪn'stɛd] adv взаме́н ▷ prep: **instead of** вме́сто or взаме́н +gen

instinct ['ɪnstɪŋkt] n инсти́нкт; **by instinct** инстинкти́вно; **instinctive** [ɪn'stɪŋktɪv] adj инстинкти́вный

institute ['ɪnstɪtju:t] n (for research, teaching) институ́т; (professional body) ассоциа́ция ▷ vt (system, rule) учрежда́ть (perf учреди́ть)

institution [ɪnstɪ'tju:ʃən] n учрежде́ние; (custom, tradition) институ́т

instruct [ɪn'strʌkt] vt: **to instruct sb in sth** обуча́ть (perf обучи́ть) кого́-н чему́-н; **to instruct sb to do** поруча́ть (perf поручи́ть) кому́-н +infin; **instruction** [ɪn'strʌkʃən] n (teaching) обуче́ние; **instructions** npl (orders) указа́ния ntpl; **instructions (for use)** инстру́кция or

руково́дство (по примене́нию); **instructor** n (for driving etc) инстру́ктор

instrument ['ɪnstrumənt] n инструме́нт; **instrumental** [ɪnstru'mɛntl] adj: **to be instrumental in** игра́ть (perf сыгра́ть) существенную роль в +prp

insufficient [ɪnsə'fɪʃənt] adj недоста́точный

insulation [ɪnsju'leɪʃən] n (against cold) (тепло)изоля́ция

insulin ['ɪnsjulɪn] n инсули́н

insult [vb ɪn'sʌlt, n 'ɪnsʌlt] vt оскорбля́ть (perf оскорби́ть) ▷ n оскорбле́ние; **insulting** [ɪn'sʌltɪŋ] adj оскорби́тельный

insurance [ɪn'ʃuərəns] n страхова́ние; **insurance policy** n страхово́й по́лис

insure [ɪn'ʃuə*] vt: **to insure (against)** страхова́ть (perf застрахова́ть) (от +gen); **to insure (o.s.) against** страхова́ться (perf застрахова́ться) от +gen

intact [ɪn'tækt] adj (unharmed) неповреждённый; (whole) нетро́нутый

intake ['ɪnteɪk] n (of food, drink) потребле́ние; (Brit: of pupils, recruits) набо́р

integral ['ɪntɪgrəl] adj неотъе́млемый

integrate ['ɪntɪgreɪt] vt интегри́ровать (impf/perf) ▷ vi (groups, individuals) объединя́ться (perf объедини́ться)

integrity [ɪn'tɛgrɪtɪ] n (morality) че́стность f, поря́дочность f

intellect ['ɪntəlɛkt] n интелле́кт; **intellectual** [ɪntə'lɛktjuəl] adj интеллектуа́льный ▷ n интеллектуа́л

intelligence [ɪn'tɛlɪdʒəns] n ум; (thinking power) у́мственные способности fpl; (Mil etc) разве́дка

intelligent [ɪn'tɛlɪdʒənt] adj у́мный; (animal) разу́мный

intend [ɪn'tɛnd] vt: **to intend sth for** предназнача́ть (perf предназна́чить) что-н для +gen; **to intend to do** намерева́ться (impf) +infin

intense [ɪn'tɛns] adj (heat, emotion) си́льный; (noise, activity) интенси́вный

intensify [ɪn'tɛnsɪfaɪ] vt уси́ливать (perf уси́лить)

intensity [ɪn'tɛnsɪtɪ] n (of effort, sun) интенси́вность f

intensive [ɪn'tɛnsɪv] adj интенси́вный; **intensive care** интенси́вная терапи́я

intent [ɪn'tɛnt] n: **intent (on)** сосредото́ченный (на +prp); **to be intent on doing** (determined) стреми́ться (impf) +infin

intention [ɪn'tɛnʃən] n наме́рение; **intentional** adj наме́ренный

interact [ɪntər'ækt] vi: **to interact (with)** взаимоде́йствовать (impf) (с +instr); **interaction** [ɪntər'ækʃən] n взаимоде́йствие

intercom ['ɪntəkɔm] n селе́ктор

intercourse ['ɪntəkɔ:s] n (sexual) полово́е сноше́ние

interest ['ɪntrɪst] *n*: **interest (in)** интере́с (к +*dat*); (*Comm*: *sum of money*) проце́нты *mpl* ▷ *vt* интересова́ть (*impf*); **to interest sb in sth** заинтересо́вывать (*perf* заинтересова́ть) кого́-н в чём-н; **interested** *adj* заинтересо́ванный; **to be interested (in sth)** (*music etc*) интересова́ться (*impf*) (чем-н); **interesting** *adj* интере́сный

interfere [ɪntə'fɪə'] *vi*: **to interfere in** вме́шиваться (*perf* вмеша́ться) в +*acc*; **to interfere with** (*hinder*) меша́ть (*perf* помеша́ть) +*dat*; **interference** *n* вмеша́тельство

interim ['ɪntərɪm] *adj* (*government*) вре́менный; (*report*) промежу́точный ▷ *n*: **in the interim** тем вре́менем

interior [ɪn'tɪərɪə'] *n* (*of building*) интерье́р; (*of car, box etc*) вну́тренность *f* ▷ *adj* (*door, room etc*) вну́тренний; **interior department/minister** департа́мент/мини́стр вну́тренних дел

intermediate [ɪntə'miːdɪət] *adj* (*stage*) промежу́точный

internal [ɪn'təːnl] *adj* вну́тренний

international [ɪntə'næʃənl] *adj* междунаро́дный

internet ['ɪntənɛt] *n* Интерне́т; **internet café** *n* интерне́т-кафе́ *nt ind*; **internet service provider** *n* интерне́т-прова́йдер

interpret [ɪn'təːprɪt] *vt* (*explain*) интерпрети́ровать (*impf/perf*), толкова́ть (*impf*); (*translate*) переводи́ть (*perf* перевести́) (у́стно) ▷ *vi* переводи́ть (*perf* перевести́) (у́стно); **interpretation** [ɪntəːprɪ'teɪʃən] *n* интерпрета́ция, толкова́ние; **interpreter** *n* перево́дчик(-ица) (у́стный)

interrogation [ɪntɛrəu'geɪʃən] *n* допро́с

interrupt [ɪntə'rʌpt] *vt*, *vi* прерыва́ть (*perf* прерва́ть); **interruption** [ɪntə'rʌpʃən] *n* (*act*) прерыва́ние

interval ['ɪntəvl] *n* интерва́л; (*Brit: Sport*) переры́в; (: *Theat*) антра́кт; **at intervals** вре́мя от вре́мени

intervene [ɪntə'viːn] *vi* (*in conversation, situation*) вме́шиваться (*perf* вмеша́ться); (*event*) меша́ть (*perf* помеша́ть)

interview ['ɪntəvjuː] *n* (*see vt*) собесе́дование; интервью́ *nt ind* ▷ *vt* (*for job*) проводи́ть (*perf* провести́) собесе́дование с +*instr*; (*Radio, TV etc*) интервьюи́ровать (*impf/perf*), брать (*perf* взять) интервью́ у +*gen*

intimate ['ɪntɪmət] *adj* (*friend, relationship*) бли́зкий; (*conversation, atmosphere*) инти́мный; (*knowledge*) глубо́кий, непосре́дственный

intimidate [ɪn'tɪmɪdeɪt] *vt* запу́гивать (*perf* запуга́ть)

into ['ɪntu] *prep* **1** (*indicating motion*) в/на +*acc*; **into the house/garden** в дом/сад; **into the post office/factory** на по́чту/фа́брику; **research into cancer** иссле́дования в о́бласти ра́ковых заболева́ний; **he worked late into the night** он рабо́тал до по́здней но́чи **2** (*indicating change of condition, result*): **she has translated the letter into Russian** она́ перевела́ письмо́ на ру́сский язы́к; **the vase broke into pieces** ва́за разби́лась на ме́лкие кусо́чки; **they got into trouble for it** им попа́ло за э́то; **he lapsed into silence** он погрузи́лся в молча́ние; **to burst into tears** распла́каться (*perf*); **to burst into flames** вспы́хивать (*perf* вспы́хнуть)

intolerant [ɪn'tɔlərnt] *adj* нетерпи́мый

intranet ['ɪntrənɛt] *n* интране́т, лока́льная вычисли́тельная сеть

intricate ['ɪntrɪkət] *adj* (*pattern*) замыслова́тый; (*relationship*) сло́жный

intriguing [ɪn'triːgɪŋ] *adj* (*fascinating*) интригу́ющий

introduce [ɪntrə'djuːs] *vt* (*new idea, measure etc*) вводи́ть (*perf* ввести́); (*speaker, programme*) представля́ть (*perf* предста́вить); **to introduce sb (to sb)** представля́ть (*perf* предста́вить) кого́-н (кому́-н); **to introduce sb to** (*pastime etc*) знако́мить (*perf* познако́мить) кого́-н с +*instr*

introduction [ɪntrə'dʌkʃən] *n* введе́ние; (*to person, new experience*) знако́мство

introductory [ɪntrə'dʌktərɪ] *adj* (*lesson*) вступи́тельный

intrude [ɪn'truːd] *vi*: **to intrude (on)** вторга́ться (*perf* вто́ргнуться) (в/на +*acc*); **intruder** *n*: **there is an intruder in our house** к нам в дом кто-то вто́ргся

intuition [ɪntjuː'ɪʃən] *n* интуи́ция

inundate ['ɪnʌndeɪt] *vt*: **to inundate with** (*calls etc*) засыпа́ть (*perf* засы́пать) +*instr*

invade [ɪn'veɪd] *vt* (*Mil*) вторга́ться (*perf* вто́ргнуться) в +*acc*

invalid [*n* 'ɪnvəlɪd, *adj* ɪn'vælɪd] *n* инвали́д ▷ *adj* недействи́тельный

invaluable [ɪn'væljuəbl] *adj* неоцени́мый

invariably [ɪn'vɛərɪəblɪ] *adv* неизме́нно

invasion [ɪn'veɪʒən] *n* (*Mil*) вторже́ние

invent [ɪn'vɛnt] *vt* изобрета́ть (*perf* изобрести́); (*fabricate*) выду́мывать (*perf* вы́думать); **invention** [ɪn'vɛnʃən] *n* (*see vt*) изобрете́ние; вы́думка; **inventor** *n* изобрета́тель *m*

inventory ['ɪnvəntrɪ] *n* (*of house etc*) (инвентариза́цио́нная) о́пись *f*

inverted commas [ɪn'vəːtɪd-] *npl* (*Brit: Ling*) кавы́чки *fpl*

invest [ɪnˈvɛst] vt вкла́дывать (perf вложи́ть) ▷ vi: **to invest in** вкла́дывать (perf вложи́ть) де́ньги в +acc
investigate [ɪnˈvɛstɪɡeɪt] vt (accident, crime) рассле́довать (impf/perf)
investigation [ɪnvɛstɪˈɡeɪʃən] n рассле́дование
investment [ɪnˈvɛstmənt] n (activity) инвести́рование; (amount of money) инвести́ция, вклад
investor [ɪnˈvɛstəʳ] n инве́стор, вкла́дчик
invigilator [ɪnˈvɪdʒɪleɪtəʳ] n экзамена́тор, следя́щий за тем, что́бы студе́нты не спи́сывали во вре́мя экза́менов
invisible [ɪnˈvɪzɪbl] adj неви́димый
invitation [ɪnvɪˈteɪʃən] n приглаше́ние
invite [ɪnˈvaɪt] vt приглаша́ть (perf пригласи́ть); (discussion, criticism) побужда́ть (perf побуди́ть) к +dat; **to invite sb to do** предлага́ть (perf предложи́ть) кому́-н +infin
inviting [ɪnˈvaɪtɪŋ] adj соблазни́тельный
invoice [ˈɪnvɔɪs] n счёт, факту́ра ▷ vt выпи́сывать (perf вы́писать) счёт or факту́ру +dat
involve [ɪnˈvɔlv] vt (include) вовлека́ть (perf вовле́чь); (concern, affect) каса́ться (impf) +gen; **to involve sb (in sth)** вовлека́ть (perf вовле́чь) кого́-н (во что-н); **involvement** n (participation) прича́стность f; (enthusiasm) увлече́ние
iPod® [ˈaɪpɔd] n айпод m (inf)
IQ n abbr (= intelligence quotient) коэффицие́нт у́мственного разви́тия
IRA n abbr (= Irish Republican Army) ИРА (= Ирла́ндская республика́нская а́рмия)
Iran [ɪˈrɑːn] n Ира́н; **Iranian** [ɪˈreɪnɪən] adj ира́нский
Iraq [ɪˈrɑːk] n Ира́к; **Iraqi** adj ира́кский
Ireland [ˈaɪələnd] n Ирла́ндия
iris [ˈaɪrɪs] n (pl irises) n (Anat) ра́дужная оболо́чка (гла́за)
Irish [ˈaɪrɪʃ] adj ирла́ндский ▷ npl: **the Irish** ирла́ндцы; **Irishman** irreg n ирла́ндец
iron [ˈaɪən] n (metal) желе́зо; (for clothes) утю́г ▷ cpd желе́зный ▷ vt (clothes) гла́дить (perf погла́дить); **iron out** vt (fig: problems) ула́живать (perf ула́дить)
ironic(al) [aɪˈrɔnɪk(l)] adj ирони́ческий
ironing board n гла́дильная доска́
irony [ˈaɪrənɪ] n иро́ния
irrational [ɪˈræʃənl] adj неразу́мный, нерациона́льный
irregular [ɪˈrɛɡjuləʳ] adj (pattern) непра́вильной фо́рмы; (surface) неро́вный; (Ling) непра́вильный
irrelevant [ɪˈrɛləvənt] adj: **this fact is irrelevant** э́тот факт к де́лу не отно́сится
irresistible [ɪrɪˈzɪstɪbl] adj (urge, desire) непреодоли́мый; (person, thing) неотрази́мый
irresponsible [ɪrɪˈspɔnsɪbl] adj безотве́тственный

irrigation [ɪrɪˈɡeɪʃən] n ороше́ние, иррига́ция
irritable [ˈɪrɪtəbl] adj раздражи́тельный
irritate [ˈɪrɪteɪt] vt раздража́ть (perf раздражи́ть)
irritating [ˈɪrɪteɪtɪŋ] adj (sound etc) доса́дный; (person) неприя́тный
irritation [ɪrɪˈteɪʃən] n раздраже́ние
is [ɪz] vb see be
Islam [ˈɪzlɑːm] n (Rel) исла́м; **Islamic** [ɪzˈlæmɪk] adj исла́мский, мусульма́нский
island [ˈaɪlənd] n (Geo) о́стров
isn't [ˈɪznt] = is not
isolated adj (place, person) изоли́рованный; (incident) отде́льный
isolation [aɪsəˈleɪʃən] n изоля́ция
ISP n abbr = internet service provider
Israel [ˈɪzreɪl] n Изра́иль m; **Israeli** [ɪzˈreɪlɪ] adj изра́ильский
issue [ˈɪʃuː] n (problem, subject) вопро́с, пробле́ма; (of book, stamps etc) вы́пуск; (most important part): **the issue** суть f ▷ vt (newspaper) выпуска́ть (perf вы́пустить); (statement) де́лать (perf сде́лать); (equipment, documents) выдава́ть (perf вы́дать); **to be at issue** быть (impf) предме́том обсужде́ния; **to make an issue of sth** де́лать (perf сде́лать) пробле́му из чего́-н

⊙ **KEYWORD**

it [ɪt] pron **1** (specific subject) он (f она́, nt оно́) (direct object) его́ (f её) (indirect object) ему́ (f ей) (after prep: +gen) него́ (f неё); (: +dat) нему́ (f ней) (: +instr) ним (f ней); (: +prp) нём (f ней); **where is your car? — it's in the garage** где Ва́ша маши́на? — она́ в гараже́; **I like this hat, whose is it?** мне нра́вится э́та шля́па, чья она́?
2 э́то; (: indirect object) э́тому; **what kind of car is it? — it's a Lada** кака́я э́то маши́на? — э́то Ла́да; **who is it? — it's me** кто э́то? — э́то я
3 (after prep: +gen) э́того; (: +dat) э́тому; (: +instr) э́тим; (: +prp) э́том; **I spoke to him about it** я говори́л с ним об э́том; **why is it that ...?** отчего́ ...?; **what is it?** (what's wrong) что тако́е?
4 (impersonal): **it's raining** идёт дождь; **it's cold today** сего́дня хо́лодно; **it's interesting that ...** интере́сно, что ...; **it's 6 o'clock** сейча́с 6 часо́в; **it's the 10th of August** сего́дня 10-ое а́вгуста

Italian [ɪˈtæljən] adj италья́нский
italics [ɪˈtælɪks] npl (Typ) курси́в msg
Italy [ˈɪtəlɪ] n Ита́лия
itch [ɪtʃ] vi чеса́ться (impf); **he was itching to know our secret** ему́ не терпе́лось узна́ть наш секре́т; **itchy** adj: **I feel all itchy** у меня́ всё че́шется
it'd [ˈɪtd] = it had; it would

item ['aɪtəm] *n* предме́т; (*on agenda*) пункт; (*also* **news item**) сообще́ние

itinerary [aɪ'tɪnərərɪ] *n* маршру́т

it'll ['ɪtl] = **it shall; it will**

its [ɪts] *adj, pron* его́ (*f* её) (*referring to subject of sentence*) свой (*f* своя́, *nt* своё) *see also* **my**; **mine**¹

it's [ɪts] = **it has; it is**

itself [ɪt'sɛlf] *pron* (*reflexive*) себя́; (*emphatic: masculine*) сам по себе́; (*: feminine*) сама́ по себе́; (*: neuter*) само́ по себе́

ITV *n abbr* (*Brit: TV*) = **Independent Television**

I've [aɪv] = **I have**

ivory ['aɪvərɪ] *n* (*substance*) слоно́вая кость *f*

ivy ['aɪvɪ] *n* (*Bot*) плющ

j

jab [dʒæb] *n* (*Brit. inf: Med*) уко́л

jack [dʒæk] *n* (*Aut*) домкра́т; (*Cards*) вале́т

jacket ['dʒækɪt] *n* ку́ртка; (*of suit*) пиджа́к; (*of book*) суперобло́жка

jackpot ['dʒækpɔt] *n* джэк-пот, куш

jagged ['dʒægɪd] *adj* зубча́тый

jail [dʒeɪl] *n* тюрьма́ ▷ *vt* сажа́ть (*perf* посади́ть) (в тюрьму́)

jam [dʒæm] *n* (*preserve*) джем; (*also* **traffic jam**) про́бка ▷ *vt* (*passage*) забива́ть (*perf* заби́ть); (*mechanism*) закли́нивать (*perf* закли́нить) ▷ *vi* (*drawer*) застрева́ть (*perf* застря́ть); **to jam sth into** запи́хивать (*perf* запихну́ть) что-н в +*acc*

janitor ['dʒænɪtə'] *n* вахтёр

January ['dʒænjuərɪ] *n* янва́рь *m*

Japan [dʒə'pæn] *n* Япо́ния

Japanese [dʒæpə'ni:z] *n* япо́нец(-нка)

jar [dʒɑ:'] *n* ба́нка

jargon ['dʒɑ:gən] *n* жарго́н

javelin ['dʒævlɪn] *n* копьё

jaw [dʒɔ:] *n* че́люсть *f*

jazz [dʒæz] *n* джаз

jealous ['dʒɛləs] *adj* ревни́вый; **to be jealous of** (*possessive*) ревнова́ть (*impf*) к +*dat*; (*envious*) зави́довать (*impf*) +*dat*; **jealousy** *n* (*resentment*) ре́вность *f*; (*envy*) за́висть *f*

jeans [dʒi:nz] *npl* джи́нсы *pl*

jelly ['dʒɛlɪ] *n* желе́ *nt ind*; (*US*) джем; **jellyfish** *n* меду́за

jerk [dʒə:k] *n* (*jolt*) рыво́к ▷ *vt* дёргать (*perf* дёрнуть), рвану́ть (*perf*) ▷ *vi* дёргаться (*perf* дёрнуться); **the car jerked to a halt** маши́на ре́зко затормози́ла

jersey ['dʒə:zɪ] *n* (*pullover*) сви́тер

Jesus ['dʒi:zəs] *n* (*Rel*) Иису́с

jet [dʒɛt] *n* (*of gas, liquid*) струя́; (*Aviat*) реакти́вный самолёт; **jet lag** *n* наруше́ние су́точного режи́ма органи́зма по́сле дли́тельного полёта

jetty ['dʒɛtɪ] *n* прича́л

Jew [dʒu:] n еврей(ка)

jewel ['dʒu:əl] n драгоценный камень m; **jeweller** (US **jeweler**) n ювелир; **jewellery** (US **jewelry**) n драгоценности fpl, ювелирные изделия ntpl

Jewish ['dʒu:ɪʃ] adj еврейский

jigsaw ['dʒɪgsɔ:] n (also **jigsaw puzzle**) головоломка

job [dʒɔb] n работа; (task) дело; (inf: difficulty): **I had a job getting here!** я с трудом добрался сюда!; **it's not my job** это не моё дело; **it's a good job that ...** хорошо ещё, что ...; **jobless** adj безработный

jockey ['dʒɔkɪ] n жокей

jog [dʒɔg] vt толкать (perf толкнуть) ▷ vi бегать (impf) трусцой; **to jog sb's memory** подстёгивать (perf подстегнуть) чью-н память; **jogging** n бег трусцой

join [dʒɔɪn] vt (organization) вступать (perf вступить) в +acc; (put together) соединять (perf соединить); (group, queue) присоединяться (perf присоединиться) к +dat ▷ vi (rivers) сливаться (perf слиться); (roads) сходиться (perf сойтись); **join in** vi присоединяться (perf присоединиться) ▷ vt fus (work, discussion etc) принимать (perf принять) участие в +prp; **join up** vi (meet) соединяться (perf соединиться); (Mil) поступать (perf поступить) на военную службу

joiner ['dʒɔɪnə'] n (Brit) столяр

joint [dʒɔɪnt] n (Tech) стык; (Anat) сустав; (Brit: Culin) кусок (мяса); (inf: place) притон; (: of cannabis) скрутка с марихуаной, косяк ▷ adj совместный

joke [dʒəuk] n (gag) шутка, анекдот; (also **practical joke**) розыгрыш ▷ vi шутить (perf пошутить); **to play a joke on** шутить (perf пошутить) над +instr, сыграть (perf) шутку с +instr; **joker** n шутник; (Cards) джокер

jolly ['dʒɔlɪ] adj весёлый ▷ adv (Brit: inf) очень

jolt [dʒəult] n (jerk) рывок ▷ vt встряхивать (perf встряхнуть); (emotionally) потрясать (perf потрясти)

journal ['dʒə:nl] n журнал; (diary) дневник; **journalism** n журналистика; **journalist** n журналист(ка)

journey ['dʒə:nɪ] n поездка; (distance covered) путь m, дорога

joy [dʒɔɪ] n радость f; **joyrider** n человек, угоняющий машины ради развлечения

Jr abbr (in names) = **junior**

judge [dʒʌdʒ] n судья m ▷ vt (competition, person etc) судить (impf); (consider, estimate) оценивать (perf оценить)

judo ['dʒu:dəu] n дзюдо nt ind

jug [dʒʌg] n кувшин

juggle ['dʒʌgl] vi жонглировать (impf) ▷ vt (fig) жонглировать (impf) +instr

juice [dʒu:s] n сок; **juicy** ['dʒu:sɪ] adj сочный

July [dʒu:'laɪ] n июль m

jumble ['dʒʌmbl] n (muddle) нагромождение ▷ vt (also **jumble up**) перемешивать (perf перемешать); **jumble sale** n (Brit) благотворительная распродажа подержанных вещей

jumbo ['dʒʌmbəu] n (also **jumbo jet**) реактивный аэробус

jump [dʒʌmp] vi прыгать (perf прыгнуть); (start) подпрыгивать (perf подпрыгнуть); (increase) подскакивать (perf подскочить) ▷ vt (fence) перепрыгивать (perf перепрыгнуть) (через +acc), перескакивать (perf перескочить) (через +acc); (increase) скачок; **to jump the queue** (Brit) идти (perf пойти) без очереди

jumper ['dʒʌmpə'] n (Brit) свитер, джемпер; (US: dress) сарафан

junction ['dʒʌŋkʃən] n (Brit: of roads) перекрёсток; (: Rail) узел

June [dʒu:n] n июнь m

jungle ['dʒʌŋgl] n джунгли pl

junior ['dʒu:nɪə'] adj младший ▷ n младший(-ая) m(f) adj; **he's junior to me (by 2 years)**, **he's my junior (by 2 years)** он младше меня (на 2 года)

junk [dʒʌŋk] n барахло, хлам; **junk food** n еда, содержащая мало питательных веществ; **junkie** n (inf) наркоман; **junk mail** n незапрошенная почтовая реклама

jurisdiction [dʒuərɪs'dɪkʃən] n (Law) юрисдикция; (Admin) сфера полномочий

jury ['dʒuərɪ] n присяжные pl adj (заседатели)

just [dʒʌst] adj справедливый ▷ adv (exactly) как раз, именно; (only) только; (barely) едва; **he's just left** он только что ушёл; **it's just right** это как раз то, что надо; **just two o'clock** ровно два часа; **she's just as clever as you** она столь же умна, как и ты; **it's just as well (that) ...** и хорошо, (что) ...; **just as he was leaving** как раз когда он собрался уходить; **just before Christmas** перед самым Рождеством; **there was just enough petrol** бензина едва хватило; **just here** вот здесь; **he (only) just missed** он чуть не попал; **just listen!** ты только послушай!

justice ['dʒʌstɪs] n (Law: system) правосудие; (fairness) справедливость f; (US: judge) судья m; **to do justice to** (fig) отдавать (perf отдать) должное +dat

justification [dʒʌstɪfɪ'keɪʃən] n основание; (of action) оправдание

justify ['dʒʌstɪfaɪ] vt оправдывать (perf оправдать); **to justify o.s.** оправдываться (perf оправдаться)

juvenile ['dʒu:vənaɪl] n несовершеннолетний(-яя) m(f) adj, подросток ▷ adj детский

K

K *abbr* = **one thousand**; (*Comput*) (= *kilobyte*) К (= килоба́йт)

kangaroo [kæŋgə'ruː] *n* кенгуру́ *m ind*

karaoke [kɑːrə'əʊki] *n* карио́ки *ind*

karate [kə'rɑːtɪ] *n* карате́ *nt ind*

kebab [kə'bæb] *n* ≈ шашлы́к

keel [kiːl] *n* киль *m*

keen [kiːn] *adj* о́стрый; (*eager*) стра́стный, увлечённый; (*competition*) напряжённый; **to be keen to do** *or* **on doing** о́чень хоте́ть (*impf*) +*infin*; **to be keen on sth** увлека́ться (*impf*) чем-н

keep [kiːp] (*pt, pp* **kept**) *vt* (*receipt, money*) оставля́ть (*perf* оста́вить) себе́; (*store*) храни́ть (*impf*); (*preserve*) сохраня́ть (*perf* сохрани́ть); (*house, shop, family*) содержа́ть (*impf*); (*prisoner, chickens*) держа́ть (*impf*); (*accounts, diary*) вести́ (*impf*); (*promise*) сде́рживать (*perf* сдержа́ть) ⊳ *vi* (*in certain state or place*) оставля́ться (*perf* оста́ться); (*food*) сохраня́ться (*impf*); (*continue*): **to keep doing** продолжа́ть (*impf*) +*impf infin* ⊳ *n*: **he has enough for his keep** ему́ доста́точно на прожи́тие; **where do you keep the salt?** где у вас соль?; **he tries to keep her happy** он де́лает всё для того́, что́бы она́ была́ дово́льна; **to keep the house tidy** содержа́ть (*impf*) дом в поря́дке; **to keep sth to o.s.** держа́ть (*impf*) что-н при себе́; **to keep sth (back) from sb** скрыва́ть (*perf* скрыть) что-н от кого́-н; **to keep sth from happening** не дава́ть (*perf* дать) чему́-н случи́ться; **to keep time** (*clock*) идти́ (*impf*) то́чно; **keep on** *vi*: **to keep on doing** продолжа́ть (*impf*) +*impf infin*; **keep on (about)** не перестава́я говори́ть (*impf*) (о +*prp*); **keep out** *vt* не впуска́ть (*perf* впусти́ть); **"keep out"** "посторо́нним вход воспрещён"; **keep up** *vt* (*payments, standards*) подде́рживать (*impf*) ⊳ *vi*: **to keep up (with)** поспева́ть (*perf* поспе́ть) (за +*instr*), идти́ (*impf*) в но́гу (с +*instr*); **keep fit** *n* аэро́бика

kennel ['kɛnl] *n* конура́

Kenya ['kɛnjə] *n* Ке́ния

kept [kɛpt] *pt, pp of* **keep**

kerb [kəːb] *n* (*Brit*) бордю́р

kettle ['kɛtl] *n* ча́йник

key [kiː] *n* ключ; (*of piano, computer*) кла́виша ⊳ *cpd* ключево́й ⊳ *vt* (*also* **key in**) набира́ть (*perf* набра́ть) (на клавиату́ре); **keyboard** *n* клавиату́ра; **keyring** *n* брело́к

khaki ['kɑːkɪ] *n, adj* ха́ки *nt, adj ind*

kick [kɪk] *vt* (*person, table*) ударя́ть (*perf* уда́рить) ного́й; (*ball*) ударя́ть (*perf* уда́рить) ного́й по +*dat*; (*inf: habit, addiction*) поборо́ть (*perf*) ⊳ *vi* (*horse*) ляга́ться (*impf*) ⊳ *n* уда́р; **kick off** *vi*: **the match kicks off at 3pm** матч начина́ется в 3 часа́ (*в футбо́ле*)

kid [kɪd] *n* (*inf: child*) ребёнок; (*goat*) козлёнок

kidnap ['kɪdnæp] *vt* похища́ть (*perf* похи́тить)

kidney ['kɪdnɪ] *n* (*Med*) по́чка; (*Culin*) по́чки *fpl*

kill [kɪl] *vt* убива́ть (*perf* уби́ть); **to kill o.s.** поко́нчить (*perf*) с собо́й; **to be killed** (*in war, accident*) погиба́ть (*perf* поги́бнуть); **killer** *n* уби́йца *m/f*

kilo ['kiːləʊ] *n* килогра́мм, кило́ *nt ind* (*inf*); **kilogram(me)** ['kɪləʊgræm] *n* килогра́мм; **kilometre** ['kɪləmiːtə'] (*US* **kilometer**) *n* киломе́тр

kind [kaɪnd] *adj* до́брый ⊳ *n* тип, род; **in kind** (*Comm*) нату́рой; **a kind of** род +*gen*; **two of a kind** две ве́щи одного́ ти́па; **what kind of ...?** како́й ...?

kindergarten ['kɪndəgɑːtn] *n* де́тский сад

kindly ['kaɪndlɪ] *adj* (*smile*) до́брый; (*person, tone*) доброжела́тельный ⊳ *adv* (*smile, behave*) любе́зно, доброжела́тельно; **will you kindly give me his address** бу́дьте добры́, да́йте мне его́ а́дрес

kindness ['kaɪndnɪs] *n* (*quality*) доброта́

king [kɪŋ] *n* коро́ль *m*; **kingdom** *n* короле́вство; **the animal/plant kingdom** живо́тное/расти́тельное ца́рство; **kingfisher** *n* зиморо́док

kiosk ['kiːɔsk] *n* кио́ск; (*Brit: Tel*) телефо́нная бу́дка

kipper ['kɪpə'] *n* ≈ копчёная селёдка

kiss [kɪs] *n* поцелу́й ⊳ *vt* целова́ть (*perf* поцелова́ть) ⊳ *vi* целова́ться (*perf* поцелова́ться)

kit [kɪt] *n* (*also* **sports kit**) (спорти́вный) костю́м; (*equipment*) снаряже́ние; (*set of tools*) набо́р; (*for assembly*) компле́кт

kitchen ['kɪtʃɪn] *n* ку́хня

kite [kaɪt] *n* (*toy*) возду́шный змей

kitten ['kɪtn] *n* котёнок

kitty ['kɪtɪ] n (pool of money) общая касса

kiwi ['kiːwiː] n киви f ind

km abbr (= kilometre) км (= киломе́тр)

knack [næk] n спосо́бность f

knee [niː] n коле́но

kneel [niːl] (pt, pp **knelt**) vi (also **kneel down**: action) встава́ть (perf встать) на коле́ни; (: state) стоя́ть (impf) на коле́нях

knew [njuː] pt of **know**

knickers ['nɪkəz] npl (Brit) (же́нские) тру́сики mpl

knife [naɪf] (pl **knives**) n нож ▷ vt ра́нить (impf) ножо́м

knight [naɪt] n ры́царь m; (Chess) конь m

knit [nɪt] vt (garment) вяза́ть (perf связа́ть) ▷ vi вяза́ть (impf); (bones) сраста́ться (perf срасти́сь); **to knit one's brows** хму́рить (perf нахму́рить) бро́ви; **knitting** n вяза́нье; **knitting needle** n вяза́льная спи́ца

knives [naɪvz] npl of **knife**

knob [nɔb] n (on door) ру́чка; (on radio etc) кно́пка

knock [nɔk] vt (strike) ударя́ть (perf уда́рить); (bump into) ста́лкиваться (perf столкну́ться) с +instr; (inf: criticize) критикова́ть (impf) ▷ n (blow, bump) уда́р, толчо́к; (on door) стук; **to knock some sense into sb** учи́ть (perf научи́ть) кого́-н уму́-ра́зуму; **he knocked at** or **on the door** он постуча́л в дверь; **knock down** vt (person, price) сбива́ть (perf сбить); **knock out** vt (subj: person, drug) оглуша́ть (perf оглуши́ть); (Boxing) нокаути́ровать (perf); (defeat) выбива́ть (perf вы́бить); **knock over** vt сбива́ть (perf сбить)

knot [nɔt] n (also Naut) у́зел; (in wood) сучо́к ▷ vt завя́зывать (perf завяза́ть) узло́м

know [nəu] (pt **knew**, pp **known**) vt (facts, people) знать (impf); **to know how to do** уме́ть (impf) +infin; **to know about** or **of** знать (impf) о +prp; **know-all** n (Brit: inf: pej) всезна́йка m/f; **know-how** n ноу-ха́у nt ind; **knowingly** adv (purposely) созна́тельно; (smile, look) понима́юще

knowledge ['nɔlɪdʒ] n зна́ние; (things learnt) зна́ния ntpl; (awareness) представле́ние; **knowledgeable** adj зна́ющий; **he is very knowledgeable about art** он большо́й знато́к иску́сства

known [nəun] pp of **know**

knuckle ['nʌkl] n косты́шка

Korea [kə'rɪə] n Коре́я

Kosovan ['kɔsəvən] n косова́р

Kosovar ['kɔsəvaː'] n косова́р

Kosovo ['kɔsəvəu] n Ко́сово

L abbr (Brit: Aut) (= learner) учени́к

l abbr (= litre) л (= литр)

lab [læb] n abbr = **laboratory**

label ['leɪbl] n этике́тка, ярлы́к; (on suitcase) би́рка ▷ vt (see n) прикрепля́ть (perf прикрепи́ть) ярлы́к на +acc; прикрепля́ть (perf прикрепи́ть) би́рку к +dat

labor ['leɪbə'] n (US) = **labour**

laboratory [lə'bɔrətərɪ] n лаборато́рия

labour ['leɪbə'] (US **labor**) n (work) труд; (workforce) рабо́чая си́ла; (Med) ро́ды mpl; **to be in labour** рожа́ть (impf); **labourer** n неквалифици́рованный рабо́чий m adj

lace [leɪs] n (fabric) кру́жево; (of shoe) шнуро́к ▷ vt (shoe: also **lace up**) шнурова́ть (perf зашнурова́ть)

lack [læk] n (absence) отсу́тствие; (shortage) недоста́ток, нехва́тка ▷ vt: **she lacked self-confidence** ей не хвата́ло or не достава́ло уве́ренности в себе́; **through** or **for lack of** из-за недоста́тка +gen

lacquer ['lækə'] n лак

lad [læd] n па́рень m

ladder ['lædə'] n ле́стница; (Brit: in tights) спусти́вшиеся пе́тли fpl

ladle ['leɪdl] n поло́вник

lady ['leɪdɪ] n (woman) да́ма; **ladies and gentlemen ...** да́мы и господа́ ...; **young/old lady** молода́я/пожила́я же́нщина; **the ladies' (room)** же́нский туале́т; **ladybird** (US **ladybug**) n бо́жья коро́вка

lag [læg] n (period of time) заде́ржка

lager ['laːgə'] n све́тлое пи́во

laid [leɪd] pt, pp of **lay**

lain [leɪn] pp of **lie**

lake [leɪk] n о́зеро

lamb [læm] n (Zool) ягнёнок; (Culin) (молода́я) бара́нина

lame [leɪm] adj (person, animal) хромо́й; (excuse, argument) сла́бый

lament [lə'mɛnt] n плач ▷ vt оплакивать (perf оплакать)

lamp [læmp] n лампа; (street lamp) фонарь m; **lamppost** n (Brit) фонарный столб; **lampshade** n абажур

land [lænd] n земля ▷ vi (from ship) высаживаться (perf высадиться); (Aviat) приземляться (perf приземлиться) ▷ vt (plane) сажать (perf посадить); (goods) выгружать (perf выгрузить); **to land sb with sth** (inf) наваливать (perf навалить) что-н на кого-н; **landing** n (of house) лестничная площадка; (of plane) посадка, приземление; **landlady** n (of house, flat) домовладелица, хозяйка; (of pub) хозяйка; **landlord** n (of house, flat) домовладелец, хозяин; (of pub) хозяин; **landmark** n (наземный) ориентир; (fig) веха; **landowner** n землевладелец(-лица); **landscape** n (view, painting) пейзаж; (terrain) ландшафт; **landslide** n (Geo) оползень m; (Pol: also **landslide victory**) решительная победа

lane [leɪn] n (in country) тропинка; (of road) полоса; (Sport) дорожка

language ['læŋgwɪdʒ] n язык; **bad language** сквернословие

lantern ['læntən] n фонарь m

lap [læp] n (of time) промежуток; (Sport) круг

lapel [lə'pɛl] n лацкан

lapse [læps] n (bad behaviour) промах; (of time) промежуток; (of concentration) потеря

laptop ['læptɔp] n (also **laptop computer**) портативный компьютер, ноутбук m

lard [lɑːd] n свиной жир

larder ['lɑːdəʳ] n кладовая f adj

large [lɑːdʒ] adj большой; (major) крупный; **at large** (as a whole) в целом; (at liberty) на воле; **largely** adv по большей части, потому что ...; **large-scale** adj крупномасштабный

lark [lɑːk] n (bird) жаворонок

laryngitis [lærɪn'dʒaɪtɪs] n ларингит

laser ['leɪzəʳ] n лазер; **laser printer** n лазерный принтер

lash [læʃ] n (eyelash) ресница; (of whip) удар (хлыста) ▷ vt (also **lash against**: subj: rain, wind) хлестать (impf) о +acc; (tie): **to lash to** привязывать (perf привязать) к +dat

last [lɑːst] adj (most recent) прошлый; (final) последний ▷ adv в последний раз; (finally) в конце ▷ vi (continue) длиться (perf продлиться), продолжаться (impf); (keep: thing) сохраняться (perf сохраниться); (: person) держаться (perf продержаться); (suffice): **we had enough money to last us** нам хватило денег; **last year** в прошлом году; **last week** на прошлой неделе; **last night** (early) вчера

вечером; (late) прошлой ночью; **at last** наконец; **last but one** предпоследний; **lastly** adv наконец; **last-minute** adj последний

latch [lætʃ] n (on gate) задвижка; (on front door) замок m

late [leɪt] adj (late) поздний; (dead) покойный ▷ adv поздно; (behind time) с опозданием; **to be late** опаздывать (perf опоздать); **of late** в последнее время; **in late May** в конце мая; **latecomer** n опоздавший(-ая) m(f) adj; **lately** adv в последнее время

later ['leɪtəʳ] adj (time, date) более поздний; (meeting, version) последующий ▷ adv позже, позднее; **later on** впоследствии, позже; **he arrived later than me** он пришёл позже меня

latest ['leɪtɪst] adj самый поздний; (most recent) (самый) последний; (news) последний; **at the latest** самое позднее

lather ['lɑːðəʳ] n (мыльная) пена

Latin ['lætɪn] n (Ling) латинский язык ▷ adj: **Latin languages** романские языки; **Latin countries** страны южной Европы; **Latin America** n Латинская Америка

latitude ['lætɪtjuːd] n (Geo) широта

latter ['lætəʳ] adj последний ▷ n: **the latter** последний(-яя) m(f) adj

Latvia ['lætvɪə] n Латвия; **Latvian** adj латвийский ▷ n (Ling) латышский язык

laugh [lɑːf] n смех ▷ vi смеяться (impf); **for a laugh** (inf) для смеха; **laugh at** vt fus смеяться (perf посмеяться) над +instr; **laughter** n смех

launch [lɔːntʃ] n (of rocket, product) запуск ▷ vt (ship) спускать (perf спустить) на воду; (rocket) запускать (perf запустить); (attack, campaign) начинать (perf начать); (product) пускать (perf пустить) в продажу, запускать (perf запустить)

laundry ['lɔːndrɪ] n (washing) стирка

lava ['lɑːvə] n лава

lavatory ['lævətərɪ] n туалет

lavender ['lævəndəʳ] n лаванда

lavish ['lævɪʃ] adj (amount, hospitality) щедрый ▷ vt: **to lavish sth on sb** осыпать (perf осыпать) кого-н чем-н

law [lɔː] n закон; (professions): **(the) law** юриспруденция; (Scol) право; **it's against the law** это противозаконно; **lawful** adj законный

lawn [lɔːn] n газон; **lawn mower** n газонокосилка

lawsuit ['lɔːsuːt] n судебный иск

lawyer ['lɔːjəʳ] n (solicitor, barrister) юрист

lax [læks] adj (discipline) слабый; (standards) низкий; (morals, behaviour) распущенный

laxative ['læksətɪv] n слабительное nt adj

lay [leɪ] pt of **lie** ▷ adj (not expert) непрофессиональный; (Rel) мирской

▷ (pt, pp **laid**) vt (place) класть (perf
положи́ть); (table) накрыва́ть (perf
накры́ть); (на +acc); (carpet) стлать (perf
постели́ть); (cable) прокла́дывать (perf
проложи́ть); (egg) откла́дывать (perf
отложи́ть); **lay down** vt (object) класть
(perf положи́ть); (rules etc) устана́вливать
(perf установи́ть); (weapons) скла́дывать
(perf сложи́ть); **to lay down the law**
прика́зывать (perf приказа́ть); **lay off** vt
(workers) увольня́ть (perf уво́лить); **lay
on** vt (meal etc) устра́ивать (perf
устро́ить); **lay out** vt раскла́дывать (perf
разложи́ть)

lay-by ['leɪbaɪ] n (Brit) площа́дка для
вре́менной стоя́нки (на автодоро́ге)
layer ['leɪə'] n слой
layout ['leɪaut] n (of garden, building)
плани́ровка
lazy ['leɪzɪ] adj лени́вый
lb abbr (= pound) (weight) фунт

● LB

● **Pound** — ме́ра ве́са ра́вная 0,454 кг.

lead[1] [li:d] (pt, pp **led**) n (front position)
пе́рвенство, ли́дерство; (clue) нить f; (in
play, film) гла́вная роль f; (for dog)
поводо́к; (Elec) про́вод ▷ vt (competition,
market) лиди́ровать (impf) в +prp;
(opponent) опережа́ть (impf); (person,
group: guide) вести́ (perf повести́) ▷ vi
(activity, organization etc) руководи́ть
(impf) +instr ▷ vi (road, pipe) вести́
(impf); (Sport) лиди́ровать (impf); **to lead
the way** ука́зывать (perf указа́ть) путь;
lead away vt уводи́ть (perf увести́); **lead
on** vt води́ть (impf) за́ нос; **lead to** vt fus
вести́ (perf привести́) к +dat; **lead up to**
vt fus (events) приводи́ть (perf привести́)
к +dat; (topic) подводи́ть (perf подвести́) к
+dat
lead[2] [lɛd] n (metal) свине́ц; (in pencil)
графи́т
leader ['li:də'] n (of group, Sport) ли́дер;
leadership n руково́дство; (quality)
ли́дерские ка́чества ntpl
lead-free ['lɛdfri:] adj не содержа́щий
свинца́
leading ['li:dɪŋ] adj (most important)
веду́щий; (first, front) пере́дний
lead singer [li:d-] n соли́ст(ка)
leaf [li:f] (pl **leaves**) n лист
leaflet ['li:flɪt] n листо́вка
league [li:g] n ли́га; **to be in league with
sb** быть (impf) в сго́воре с кем-н
leak [li:k] n уте́чка; (hole) течь f ▷ vi
протека́ть (perf проте́чь); (liquid, gas)
проса́чиваться (perf просочи́ться) ▷ vt
(information) разглаша́ть (perf разгласи́ть)
lean [li:n] (pt, pp **leaned** or **leant**) adj
(person) сухоща́вый; (meat) по́стный ▷ vt:
to lean sth on or **against** прислоня́ть (perf

прислони́ть) что-н к +dat ▷ vi: **to lean
forward/back** наклоня́ться (perf
наклони́ться) вперёд/наза́д; **to lean
against** (wall) прислоня́ться (perf
прислони́ться) к +dat; (person) опира́ться
(perf опере́ться) на +acc; **to lean on** (chair)
опира́ться (perf опере́ться) о +acc; (rely
on) опира́ться (perf опере́ться) на +acc;
leant [lɛnt] pt, pp of **lean**
leap [li:p] (pt, pp **leaped** or **leapt**) n
скачо́к ▷ vi пры́гать (perf пры́гнуть);
(price, number) подска́кивать (perf
подскочи́ть); **leapt** [lɛpt] pp, pt of **leap**;
leap year n високо́сный год
learn [lə:n] (pt, pp **learned** or **learnt**) vt
(skill) учи́ться (perf научи́ться) +dat; (facts,
poem) учи́ть (perf вы́учить) ▷ vi учи́ться
(impf); **to learn about** or **of/that** ... (hear,
read) узнава́ть (perf узна́ть) о +prp/, что
...; **to learn about sth** (study) изуча́ть (perf
изучи́ть) что-н; **to learn (how) to do**
учи́ться (perf научи́ться) +impf infin;
learnt [lə:nt] pt, pp of **learn**
lease [li:s] n аре́ндный догово́р, аре́нда
▷ vt: **to lease sth (to sb)** сдава́ть (perf
сдать) что-н в аре́нду (кому́-н); **to lease
sth from sb** арендова́ть (impf/perf) or
брать (взять perf) в аре́нду у кого́-н
leash [li:ʃ] n поводо́к
least [li:st] adj: **the least** (+noun: smallest)
наиме́ньший; (: slightest: difficulty)
мале́йший ▷ adv (+vb) ме́ньше всего́;
(+adj) наиме́нее; **at least** по кра́йней
ме́ре; **not in the least** (as response)
отню́дь нет; (+vb, +adj) ниско́лько or
во́все не
leather ['lɛðə'] n ко́жа
leave [li:v] (pt, pp **left**) vt оставля́ть (perf
оста́вить), покида́ть (perf поки́нуть); (go
away from: on foot) уходи́ть (perf уйти́) из
+gen; (: by transport) уезжа́ть (perf уе́хать)
из +gen; (party, committee) выходи́ть (perf
вы́йти) из +gen ▷ vi (on foot) уходи́ть
(perf уйти́); (by transport) уезжа́ть (perf
уе́хать); (bus, train) выходи́ть (perf уйти́)
▷ n о́тпуск; **to leave sth to sb** (money,
property) оставля́ть (perf оста́вить) что-н
кому́-н; **to be left (over)** оставá́ться (perf
оста́ться); **on leave** в о́тпуске; **leave
behind** vt оставля́ть (perf оста́вить);
leave out vt (omit) пропуска́ть (perf
пропусти́ть); **he was left out** его́
пропусти́ли
leaves [li:vz] npl of **leaf**
lecture ['lɛktʃə'] n ле́кция ▷ vi чита́ть
(impf) ле́кции ▷ vt (scold): **to lecture sb
on** or **about** чита́ть (perf прочита́ть)
кому́-н ле́кцию по по́воду +gen; **to give a
lecture on** чита́ть (perf прочита́ть) ле́кцию
о +prp; **lecturer** n (Brit: Scol)
преподава́тель(ница) m(f)
led [lɛd] pt, pp of **lead**[1]
ledge [lɛdʒ] n вы́ступ; (of window)
подоко́нник

leek [liːk] n лук-порей no pl
left [lɛft] pt, pp of **leave** ▷ adj (of direction, position) левый ▷ n левая сторона ▷ adv (motion): **(to the) left** налево; (position): **(on the) left** слева; **the Left** (Pol) левые pl adj; **left-handed** adj: **he/she is left-handed** он/она левша; **left-wing** adj (Pol) левый
leg [lɛg] n (Anat) нога; (of insect, furniture) ножка; (also **trouser leg**) штанина; (of journey, race) этап
legacy ['lɛgəsɪ] n (in will) наследство; (fig) наследие
legal ['liːgl] adj (advice, requirement) юридический; (system, action) судебный; (lawful) законный; **legalize** vt узаконивать (perf узаконить); **legally** adv юридически; (by law) по закону
legend ['lɛdʒənd] n (story) легенда; (person) легендарная личность f; **legendary** adj легендарный
legislation [lɛdʒɪs'leɪʃən] n законодательство
legislative ['lɛdʒɪslətɪv] adj (Pol) законодательный
legitimate [lɪ'dʒɪtɪmət] adj законный, легитимный
leisure ['lɛʒər] n (also **leisure time**) досуг, свободное время nt; at (one's) **leisure** не спеша; **leisure centre** n спортивно-оздоровительный комплекс; **leisurely** adj неторопливый
lemon ['lɛmən] n (fruit) лимон; **lemonade** [lɛmə'neɪd] n лимонад
lend [lɛnd] (pt, pp **lent**) vt: **to lend sth to sb**, **lend sb sth** одалживать (perf одолжить) что-н кому-н
length [lɛŋθ] n (measurement) длина; (distance) протяжённость f; (piece: of wood, cloth etc) отрезок; (duration) продолжительность f; **at length** (for a long time) пространно; **lengthy** adj (text) длинный; (meeting) продолжительный; (explanation) пространный
lens [lɛnz] n (of glasses, camera) линза
Lent [lɛnt] n Великий Пост
lent [lɛnt] pt, pp of **lend**
lentil ['lɛntl] n чечевица no pl
Leo ['liːəu] n Лев
leopard ['lɛpəd] n леопард
leotard ['liːətɑːd] n трико nt ind
lesbian ['lɛzbɪən] adj лесбийский ▷ n лесбиянка
less [lɛs] adj (attention, money) меньше +gen ▷ adv (beautiful, clever) менее ▷ prep минус +nom; **less than** меньше or менее +gen; **less than half** меньше половины; **less than ever** меньше, чем когда-либо; **less and less** всё меньше и меньше; (+gen) всё меньше и менее; **the less ... the more** чем меньше ..., тем больше ...; **lesser** adj: **to a lesser extent** в меньшей степени
lesson ['lɛsn] n урок; **to teach sb a lesson**

(fig) проучить (perf) кого-н
let [lɛt] (pt, pp **let**) vt (Brit: lease) сдавать (perf сдать) (внаём); (allow): **to let sb do** разрешать (perf разрешить) or позволять (perf позволить) кому-н +infin; **let me try** дайте я попробую; **to let sb know about ...** давать (perf дать) кому-н знать о +prp ...; **let's go there** давай(те) пойдём туда; **let's do it!** давай(те) сделаем это; **"to let"** "сдаётся внаём"; **to let go of** отпускать (perf отпустить); **let down** vt (tyre etc) спускать (perf спустить); (fig: person) подводить (perf подвести); **let in** vt (water, air) пропускать (perf пропустить); (person) впускать (perf впустить); **let off** vt (culprit, child) отпускать (perf отпустить); (bomb) взрывать (perf взорвать); **let out** vt выпускать (perf выпустить); (sound) издавать (perf издать)
lethal ['liːθl] adj (weapon, chemical) смертоносный; (dose) смертельный
letter ['lɛtər] n письмо; (of alphabet) буква; **letter box** n (Brit) почтовый ящик

● **LETTER BOX**
●
● Помимо почтового ящика данное слово
● также обозначает прорезь во входной
● двери, в которую опускается
● корреспонденция.

lettuce ['lɛtɪs] n салат латук
leukaemia [luː'kiːmɪə] (US **leukemia**) n белокровие, лейкемия
level ['lɛvl] adj (flat) ровный ▷ n уровень m ▷ adv: **to draw level with** (person, vehicle) поравняться (perf) с +instr; **to be level with** быть (impf) на одном уровне с +instr
lever ['liːvər] n рычаг; (bar) лом; **leverage** n (fig: influence) влияние
levy ['lɛvɪ] n налог ▷ vt налагать (perf наложить)
liability [laɪə'bɪlətɪ] n (responsibility) ответственность f; (person, thing) обуза m/f; **liabilities** npl (Comm) обязательства ntpl
liable ['laɪəbl] adj: **liable for** (legally responsible) подсудный за +acc; **to be liable to** подлежать (impf) +dat; **he's liable to take offence** возможно, что он обидится
liar ['laɪər] n лжец, лгун(ья)
libel ['laɪbl] n клевета
liberal ['lɪbərl] adj (also Pol) либеральный; (large, generous) щедрый; **Liberal Democrat** n либерал-демократ; **the Liberal Democrats** (party) партия либерал-демократов
liberate ['lɪbəreɪt] vt освобождать (perf освободить)
liberation [lɪbə'reɪʃən] n освобождение

liberty ['lɪbətɪ] *n* свобо́да; **to be at liberty** (*criminal*) быть (*impf*) на свобо́де; **I'm not at liberty to comment** я не во́лен комменти́ровать; **to take the liberty of doing** позволя́ть (*perf* позво́лить) себе́ +*infin*

Libra ['li:brə] *n* Весы́ *pl*

librarian [laɪ'brɛərɪən] *n* библиоте́карь *m*

library ['laɪbrərɪ] *n* библиоте́ка

lice [laɪs] *npl of* **louse**

licence ['laɪsns] (*US* **license**) *n* (*permit*) лице́нзия; (*Aut: also* **driving licence**) (води́тельские) права́ *ntpl*

license ['laɪsns] (*US*) = **licence** ▷ *vt* выдава́ть (*perf* вы́дать) лице́нзию на +*acc*; **licensed** *adj* (*restaurant*) с лице́нзией на прода́жу спиртны́х напи́тков

lick [lɪk] *vt* (*stamp, fingers etc*) лиза́ть (*impf*), обли́зывать (*perf* облиза́ть); **to lick one's lips** обли́зываться (*perf* облиза́ться)

lid [lɪd] *n* кры́шка; (*also* **eyelid**) ве́ко

lie [laɪ] (*pt* **lay**, *pp* **lain**) *vi* (*be horizontal*) лежа́ть (*impf*); (*be situated*) лежа́ть (*impf*), находи́ться (*impf*); (*problem, cause*) заключа́ться (*impf*) ▷ (*pt, pp* **lied**) (*be untruthful*) лгать (*perf* солга́ть), врать (*perf* совра́ть) ▷ *n* (*untrue statement*) ложь *f no pl*; **to lie** or **be lying in first/last place** занима́ть (*impf*) пе́рвое/после́днее ме́сто; **lie down** *vi* (*motion*) ложи́ться (*perf* лечь); (*position*) лежа́ть (*impf*); **lie-in** *n* (*Brit*): **to have a lie-in** встава́ть (*perf* встать) попо́зже

lieutenant [lɛf'tenənt, (*US*) lu:'tenənt] *n* лейтена́нт

life [laɪf] (*pl* **lives**) *n* жизнь *f*; **lifeboat** *n* спаса́тельное су́дно; (*on ship*) спаса́тельная шлю́пка; **lifeguard** *n* спаса́тель *m*; **life jacket** *n* спаса́тельный жиле́т; **life preserver** (*US*) = **life jacket**; **lifestyle** *n* о́браз жи́зни; **lifetime** *n* (*of person*) жизнь *f*; (*of institution*) вре́мя *nt* существова́ния

lift [lɪft] *vt* поднима́ть (*perf* подня́ть); (*ban, sanctions*) снима́ть (*perf* снять) ▷ *vi* (*fog*) рассе́иваться (*perf* рассе́яться) ▷ *n* (*Brit*) лифт; **to give sb a lift** (*Brit: Aut*) подвози́ть (*perf* подвезти́) кого́-н

light [laɪt] (*pt, pp* **lit**) *n* свет; (*Aut*) фа́ра ▷ *vt* (*candle, fire*) зажига́ть (*perf* заже́чь); (*place*) освеща́ть (*perf* освети́ть) ▷ *adj* (*pale, bright*) све́тлый; (*not heavy*) лёгкий; **lights** *npl* (*also* **traffic lights**) светофо́р *msg*; **have you got a light?** (*for cigarette*) мо́жно у Вас прикури́ть?; **to come to light** выясня́ться (*perf* вы́ясниться); **in the light of** (*discussions etc*) в све́те +*gen*; **light up** *vi* (*face*) светле́ть (*perf* просветле́ть) ▷ *vt* (*illuminate*) освеща́ть (*perf* освети́ть); **light-hearted** *adj* (*person*) беспе́чный; (*question, remark*) несерьёзный; **lighthouse** *n* мая́к; **lighting** *n* освеще́ние; **lightly** *adv* (*touch, kiss*) слегка́; (*eat, treat*) легко́; (*sleep*) чу́тко; **to**

get off lightly легко́ отде́лываться (*perf* отде́латься)

lightning ['laɪtnɪŋ] *n* мо́лния

like [laɪk] *prep* как +*acc*; (*similar to*) похо́жий на +*acc* ▷ *vt* (*sweets, reading*) люби́ть (*impf*) ▷ *n*: **and the like** и тому́ подо́бное; **he looks like his father** он похо́ж на своего́ отца́; **what does she look like?** как она́ вы́глядит?; **what's he like?** что он за челове́к?; **there's nothing like …** ничто́ не мо́жет сравни́ться с +*instr* …; **do it like this** де́лайте э́то так; **that's just like him** (*typical*) э́то на него́ похо́же; **it is nothing like …** э́то совсе́м не то, что …; **I like/liked him** он мне нра́вится/ понра́вился; **I would like, I'd like** мне хоте́лось бы, я бы хоте́л; **would you like a coffee?** хоти́те ко́фе?; **his likes and dislikes** его́ вку́сы; **likeable** *adj* симпати́чный

likelihood ['laɪklɪhud] *n* вероя́тность *f*

likely ['laɪklɪ] *adj* вероя́тный; **she is likely to agree** она́, вероя́тно, согласи́тся; **not likely!** (*inf*) ни за что́!

likewise ['laɪkwaɪz] *adv* та́кже; **to do likewise** поступа́ть (*perf* поступи́ть) таки́м же о́бразом

lilac ['laɪlək] *n* сире́нь *f no pl*

lily ['lɪlɪ] *n* ли́лия

limb [lɪm] *n* (*Anat*) коне́чность *f*

lime [laɪm] *n* (*fruit*) лайм; (*tree*) ли́па; (*chemical*) и́звесть *f*

limelight ['laɪmlaɪt] *n*: **to be in the limelight** быть (*impf*) в це́нтре внима́ния

limestone ['laɪmstəun] *n* известня́к

limit ['lɪmɪt] *n* преде́л; (*restriction*) лими́т, ограниче́ние ▷ *vt* (*production, expense etc*) лимити́ровать (*impf/perf*), ограни́чивать (*perf* ограни́чить); **limited** *adj* ограни́ченный

limousine ['lɪməzi:n] *n* лимузи́н

limp [lɪmp] *vi* хрома́ть (*impf*) ▷ *adj* (*person, limb*) бесси́льный; (*material*) мя́гкий

line [laɪn] *n* ли́ния; (*row*) ряд; (*of writing, song*) строка́, стро́чка; (*wrinkle*) морщи́на; (*wire*) про́вод; (*fig: of thought*) ход; (*of business, work*) о́бласть *f* ▷ *vt* (*road*) выстра́иваться (*perf* вы́строиться) вдоль +*gen*; (*clothing*) подбива́ть (*perf* подби́ть); (*container*) выкла́дывать (*perf* вы́ложить) изнутри́; **hold the line please!** пожа́луйста, не клади́те тру́бку!; **to cut in line** (*US*) идти́ (*perf* пойти́) без о́череди; **in line with** (*in keeping with*) в соотве́тствии с +*instr*; **line up** *vi* выстра́иваться (*perf* вы́строиться) ▷ *vt* (*order*) выстра́ивать (*perf* вы́строить)

linen ['lɪnɪn] *n* (*sheets etc*) бельё

liner ['laɪnə'] *n* (*ship*) ла́йнер; (*also* **bin liner**) целофа́новый мешо́к для мусорного ведра́

linger ['lɪŋgə'] *vi* уде́рживаться (*perf* удержа́ться); (*person*) заде́рживаться (*perf* задержа́ться)

lingerie [ˈlænʒəriː] n жéнское (нúжнее) бельё

linguist [ˈlɪŋgwɪst] n (language specialist) лингвúст; **linguistics** [lɪŋˈgwɪstɪks] n языкознáние, лингвúстика

lining [ˈlaɪnɪŋ] n (cloth) подклáдка

link [lɪŋk] n связь f; (of chain) звенó ▷ vt (join) соединя́ть (perf соединúть); (associate): **to link with** or **to** свя́зывать (perf связáть) с +instr; **link up** vt (systems) соединя́ть (perf соединúть) ▷ vi соединя́ться (perf соединúться)

lion [ˈlaɪən] n лев

lip [lɪp] n (Anat) губá; **lip-read** vi читáть (impf) с губ; **lipstick** n (губнáя) помáда

liqueur [lɪˈkjʊər] n ликёр

liquid [ˈlɪkwɪd] n жúдкость f ▷ adj жúдкий

liquor [ˈlɪkər] n (esp US) спиртнóе nt adj, спиртнóй напúток

Lisbon [ˈlɪzbən] n Лиссабóн

lisp [lɪsp] n шепеля́вость f

list [lɪst] n спúсок ▷ vt (enumerate) перечисля́ть (perf перечúслить); (write down) составля́ть (perf состáвить) спúсок +gen

listen [ˈlɪsn] vi: **to listen (to sb/sth)** слýшать (impf) (когó-н/чтó-н)

lit [lɪt] pt, pp of **light**

liter [ˈliːtər] n (US) = **litre**

literacy [ˈlɪtərəsɪ] n грáмотность f

literal [ˈlɪtərl] adj буквáльный; **literally** adv буквáльно

literary [ˈlɪtərərɪ] adj литерату́рный

literate [ˈlɪtərət] adj (able to read and write) грáмотный

literature [ˈlɪtrɪtʃər] n литература

Lithuania [lɪθjuˈeɪnɪə] n Литвá; **Lithuanian** adj литóвский

litre [ˈliːtər] (US **liter**) n литр

litter [ˈlɪtər] n (rubbish) мýсор; (Zool) помёт, вы́водок

little [ˈlɪtl] adj мáленький; (younger) млáдший; (short) корóткий ▷ adv мáло; **a little (bit)** немнóго; **little by little** понемнóгу

live [vb lɪv, adj laɪv] vi жить (impf) ▷ adj (animal, plant) живóй; (broadcast) прямóй; (performance) пéред пýбликой; (bullet) боевóй; (Elec) под напряжéнием; **to live with sb** жить (impf) с кем-н; **he lived to (be) a hundred** он дожúл до стá лет; **live on** vt fus (food) жить (impf) на +prp; (salary) жить (impf) на +acc; **live up to** vt fus опрáвдывать (perf оправдáть)

livelihood [ˈlaɪvlɪhud] n срéдства ntpl к существовáнию

lively [ˈlaɪvlɪ] adj живóй; (place, event) оживлённый

liver [ˈlɪvər] n (Anat) пéчень f; (Culin) печёнка

lives [laɪvz] npl of **life**

livestock [ˈlaɪvstɔk] n скот

living [ˈlɪvɪŋ] adj живóй ▷ n: **to earn** or

make a living зарабáтывать (perf заработáть) на жизнь; **living room** n гостúная f adj

lizard [ˈlɪzəd] n á́щерица

load [ləud] n (of person, animal) нóша; (of vehicle) груз; (weight) нагрýзка ▷ vt (also **load up (with):** goods) грузúть (perf погрузúть); (gun, camera) заряжáть (perf зарядúть); **to load (with)** (also **load up:** vehicle, ship) загружáть (perf загрузúть) (+instr); **loads of, a load of** (inf) кýча +gen; **a load of rubbish** (inf) сплошнáя чепухá; **loaded** adj (gun) заряженный; **loaded question** вопрóс с подтéкстом or подвóхом

loaf [ləuf] (pl **loaves**) n (bread) буханка

loan [ləun] n заём; (money) ссýда ▷ vt давáть (perf дать) взаймы́; (money) ссужáть (perf ссудúть); **to take sth on loan** брать (perf взять) чтó-н на врéмя

loathe [ləuð] vt ненавúдеть (impf)

loaves [ləuvz] npl of **loaf**

lobby [ˈlɔbɪ] n (of building) вестибю́ль m; (pressure group) лóбби nt ind ▷ vt склоня́ть (perf склонúть) на свою́ стóрону

lobster [ˈlɔbstər] n омáр

local [ˈləukl] adj мéстный; **locals** npl мéстные pl adj (жúтели); **local authorities** npl мéстные влáсти fpl; **local government** n мéстное управлéние; **locally** adv (live, work) поблúзости

locate [ləuˈkeɪt] vt определя́ть (perf определúть) расположéние or местонахождéние +gen; **to be located in** (situated) располагáться (impf), находúться (impf) в/на +prp

location [ləuˈkeɪʃən] n (place) расположéние, местонахождéние; **on location** (Cinema) на натýре

loch [lɔx] n (Scottish) óзеро

lock [lɔk] n (on door etc) замóк; (on canal) шлюз; (of hair) лóкон ▷ vt запирáть (perf заперéть) ▷ vi (door) запирáться (perf запирáться); (wheels) тормозúть (perf затормозúть); **lock in** vt: **to lock sb in** запирáть (perf заперéть) когó-н; **lock up** vt (criminal etc) упрятывать (perf упрятать); (house) запирáть (perf заперéть) ▷ vi запирáться (perf запирáться)

locker [ˈlɔkər] n шкáфчик

locomotive [ləukəˈməutɪv] n локомотúв

lodge [lɔdʒ] n приврáтницкая f adj; **lodger** n квартирáнт(ка)

loft [lɔft] n чердáк

log [lɔg] n брeвнó; (for fire) полéно; (account) журнáл ▷ vt (event, fact) регистрúровать (perf зарегистрúровать); **log in** vi (Comput) входúть (perf войтú); **log off** vi (Comput) выходúть (perf выйти) из систéмы; **log on** vi (Comput) входúть (perf войтú) в систéму

logic [ˈlɔdʒɪk] n лóгика; **logical** adj

(*based on logic*) логи́ческий; (*reasonable*) логи́чный

login ['lɔgɪn] *n* (*Comput*) и́мя (*nt*) по́льзователя

logo ['ləʊgəʊ] *n* эмбле́ма

London ['lʌndən] *n* Ло́ндон

lone [ləʊn] *adj* (*person*) одино́кий

loneliness ['ləʊnlɪnɪs] *n* одино́чество

lonely ['ləʊnlɪ] *adj* (*person, childhood*) одино́кий; (*place*) уединённый

long [lɔŋ] *adj* дли́нный; (*in time*) до́лгий ▷ *adv* (*see adj*) дли́нно; до́лго ▷ *vi*: to **long for sth/to do** жа́ждать (*impf*) чего́-н/+infin; **so** *or* **as long as you don't mind** е́сли то́лько Вы не возража́ете; **don't be long!** не заде́рживайтесь!; **how long is the street?** какова́ длина́ э́той у́лицы?; **how long is the lesson?** ско́лько дли́тся уро́к?; **6 metres long** длино́й в 6 ме́тров; **6 months long** продолжи́тельностью в 6 ме́сяцев; **all night (long)** всю ночь (напролёт); **he no longer comes** он бо́льше не прихо́дит; **long before** задо́лго до +*gen*; **long after** до́лгое вре́мя по́сле +*gen*; **before long** вско́ре; **at long last** наконе́ц; **long-distance** *adj* (*travel*) да́льний

longitude ['lɔŋgɪtjuːd] *n* долгота́

long: **long jump** *n* прыжо́к в длину́; **long-life** *adj* консерви́рованный; (*battery*) продлённого де́йствия; **long-standing** *adj* долголе́тний; **long-term** *adj* долгосро́чный

look [lʊk] *vi* (*see*) смотре́ть (*perf* посмотре́ть); (*glance*) взгляну́ть (*perf*); (*seem, appear*) вы́глядеть (*impf*) ▷ *n* (*glance*) взгляд; (*appearance*) вид; (*expression*) выраже́ние; **looks** *npl* (*also* **good looks**) краси́вая вне́шность *fsg*; **to look south/(out) onto the sea** (*face*) выходи́ть (*impf*) на юг/на мо́ре; **look after** *vt fus* (*care for*) уха́живать (*impf*) за +*instr*; (*deal with*) забо́титься (*impf*) о +*prp*; **look around** *vt fus* = **look round**; **look at** *vt fus* смотре́ть (*perf* посмотре́ть) на +*acc*; (*read quickly*) просма́тривать (*perf* просмотре́ть); **look back** *vi* (*turn around*) огля́дываться (*perf* огляну́ться) (на +*acc*); **look down on** *vt fus* (*fig*) смотре́ть (*impf*) свысока́ на +*acc*; **look for** *vt fus* иска́ть (*impf*); **look forward to** *vt fus*: **to look forward to sth** ждать (*impf*) чего́-н с нетерпе́нием; **we look forward to hearing from you** (с нетерпе́нием) ждём Ва́шего отве́та; **look into** *vt fus* рассле́довать (*impf/perf*); **look on** *vi* (*watch*) наблюда́ть (*impf*); **look out** *vi* (*beware*): **to look out (for)** остерега́ться (*impf*) (+*gen*); **to look out (of)** (*glance out*) вы́глянуть (*perf* вы́глянуть) (в +*acc*); **look out for** *vt fus* (*search for*) стара́ться (*perf* постара́ться) найти́; **look round** *vt fus* (*museum etc*) осма́тривать (*perf* осмотре́ть); **look through** *vt fus*

(*papers*) просма́тривать (*perf* просмотре́ть); (*window*) смотре́ть (*perf* посмотре́ть) в +*acc*; **look to** *vt fus* (*rely on*) ждать (*impf*) от +*gen*; **look up** *vi* поднима́ть (*perf* подня́ть) глаза́; (*situation*) идти́ (*perf* пойти́) к лу́чшему ▷ *vt* (*fact*) смотре́ть (*perf* посмотре́ть); **lookout** *n* (*person*) наблюда́тель(ница) *m(f)*; (*point*) наблюда́тельный пункт; **to be on the lookout for sth** присма́тривать (*impf*) что-н

loop [luːp] *n* пе́тля ▷ *vt*: **to loop sth round sth** завя́зывать (*perf* завяза́ть) что-н пе́тлей вокру́г чего́-н

loose [luːs] *adj* свобо́дный; (*knot, grip, connection*) сла́бый; (*hair*) распу́щенный ▷ *n*: **to be on the loose** быть (*impf*) в бега́х; **the handle is loose** ру́чка расшата́лась; **to set loose** (*prisoner*) освобожда́ть (*perf* освободи́ть); **loosen** *vt* (*belt, screw, grip*) ослабля́ть (*perf* осла́бить)

loot [luːt] *n* (*inf*) награ́бленное *nt adj* ▷ *vt* (*shops, homes*) разграбля́ть (*perf* разгра́бить)

lord [lɔːd] *n* (*Brit: peer*) лорд; (*Rel*): **the Lord** Госпо́дь *m*; **my Lord** мило́рд; **good Lord!** Бо́же пра́вый!

lorry ['lɔrɪ] *n* (*Brit*) грузови́к

lose [luːz] (*pt, pp* **lost**) *vt* теря́ть (*perf* потеря́ть); (*contest, argument*) прои́грывать (*perf* проигра́ть) ▷ *vi* (*in contest, argument*) прои́грывать (*perf* проигра́ть); **loser** *n* (*in contest*) проигра́вший(-ая) *m(f) adj*

loss [lɔs] *n* поте́ря; (*sense of bereavement*) утра́та; (*Comm*) убы́ток; **heavy losses** тяжёлые поте́ри *fpl*; **to be at a loss** теря́ться (*perf* растеря́ться)

lost [lɔst] *pt, pp* *of* **lose** ▷ *adj* пропа́вший; **to get lost** заблуди́ться (*perf*)

lot [lɔt] *n* (*of people, goods*) па́ртия; (*at auction*) лот; **a lot** (*of*) (*many*) мно́го (+*gen*); **the lot** (*everything*) всё; **lots of ...** мно́го +*gen* ...; **I see a lot of him** мы с ним ча́сто ви́димся; **I read/don't read a lot** я мно́го/ма́ло чита́ю; **a lot bigger/more expensive** намно́го *or* гора́здо бо́льше/ доро́же; **to draw lots (for sth)** тяну́ть (*impf*) жре́бий (для чего́-н)

lotion ['ləʊʃən] *n* лосьо́н

lottery ['lɔtərɪ] *n* лотере́я

loud [laʊd] *adj* (*noise, voice, laugh*) гро́мкий; (*support, condemnation*) громогла́сный; (*clothes*) крича́щий ▷ *adv* гро́мко; **out loud** вслух; **loudly** *adv* (*speak, laugh*) гро́мко; (*support*) громогла́сно; **loudspeaker** *n* громкоговори́тель *m*

lounge [laʊndʒ] *n* (*in house, hotel*) гости́ная *f adj*; (*at airport*) зал ожида́ния

louse [laʊs] (*pl* **lice**) *n* (*insect*) вошь *f*

love [lʌv] *vt* люби́ть (*impf*) ▷ *n*: **love (for)** любо́вь *f* (к +*dat*); **to love to do** люби́ть

(*impf*) +*infin*; **I'd love to come** я бы с
удово́льствием пришёл; **"love (from)
Anne"** "лю́бящая Вас А́нна"; **to fall in love
with** влюбля́ться (*perf* влюби́ться) в +*acc*;
he is in love with her он в неё влюблён; **to
make love** занима́ться (*perf* заня́ться)
любо́вью; **"fifteen love"** (*Tennis*)
"пятна́дцать — ноль"; **love affair** *n*
рома́н; **love life** *n* инти́мная жизнь *f*
lovely ['lʌvlɪ] *adj* (*beautiful*) краси́вый;
(*delightful*) чуде́сный
lover ['lʌvəʳ] *n* любо́вник(-ица); (*of art etc*)
люби́тель(ница) *m(f)*
loving ['lʌvɪŋ] *adj* не́жный
low [ləʊ] *adj* ни́зкий; (*quiet*) ти́хий;
(*depressed*) пода́вленный ▷ *adv* (*fly*)
ни́зко; (*sing: quietly*) ти́хо ▷ *n* (*Meteorology*)
ни́зкое давле́ние; **we are (running) low on
milk** у нас оста́лось ма́ло молока́; **an
all-time low** небыва́ло ни́зкий у́ровень
lower ['ləʊəʳ] *adj* (*bottom: of two things*)
ни́жний; (*less important*) ни́зший ▷ *vt*
(*object*) спуска́ть (*perf* спусти́ть); (*level,
price*) снижа́ть (*perf* сни́зить); (*voice*)
понижа́ть (*perf* пони́зить); (*eyes*) опуска́ть
(*perf* опусти́ть)

● **LOWER SIXTH**
●
● **Lower sixth** — ни́жняя ступе́нь
● шко́льного квалификацио́нного ку́рса.
● Э́тот курс дли́тся два го́да, в тече́ние
● кото́рых шко́льники гото́вятся к
● квалификацио́нным экза́менам,
● даю́щим пра́во поступле́ния в
● университе́т.

low-fat ['ləʊ'fæt] *adj* обезжи́ренный
loyal ['lɔɪəl] *adj* ве́рный; (*Pol*) лоя́льный;
loyalty *n* ве́рность *f*; (*Pol*) лоя́льность *f*;
loyalty card *n* ≈ диско́нтная ка́рта
LP *n abbr* (= *long-playing record*)
долгоигра́ющая пласти́нка

● **L-PLATES**
●
● **L-plates** — бе́лая табли́чка, на кото́рую
● нанесена́ кра́сная бу́ква **L**,
● обознача́ющая **Learner** – Учени́к. Таки́е
● табли́чки помеща́ются на за́днем или
● ветрово́м стекле́ автомоби́лей,
● води́тели кото́рых прохо́дят курс по
● вожде́нию.

Ltd *abbr* (*Comm*) (= *limited (liability)
company*) компа́ния с ограни́ченной
отве́тственностью
luck [lʌk] *n* (*also* **good luck**) уда́ча; **bad
luck** неуда́ча; **good luck!** уда́чи (Вам)!;
hard *or* **tough luck!** не повезло́!; **luckily**
adv к сча́стью; **lucky** *adj* (*situation,
object*) счастли́вый; (*person*) уда́чливый;
he is lucky at cards/in love ему́ везёт в
ка́ртах/любви́

lucrative ['lu:krətɪv] *adj* при́быльный,
дохо́дный; (*job*) высокоопла́чиваемый
ludicrous ['lu:dɪkrəs] *adj* смехотво́рный
luggage ['lʌgɪdʒ] *n* бага́ж
lukewarm ['lu:kwɔ:m] *adj* слегка́
тёплый; (*fig*) прохла́дный
lull [lʌl] *n* зати́шье ▷ *vt*: **to lull sb to sleep**
убаю́кивать (*perf* убаю́кать) кого́-н; **to lull
sb into a false sense of security** усыпля́ть
(*perf* усыпи́ть) чью-н бди́тельность
lullaby ['lʌləbaɪ] *n* колыбе́льная *f adj*
luminous ['lu:mɪnəs] *adj* (*digit, star*)
светя́щийся
lump [lʌmp] *n* (*of clay, snow*) ком; (*of
butter, sugar*) кусо́к; (*bump*) ши́шка;
(*growth*) о́пухоль *f* ▷ *vt*: **to lump together**
меша́ть (*perf* смеша́ть) в (одну́) ку́чу; **a
lump sum** единовре́менно
выпла́чиваемая су́мма; **lumpy** *adj*
(*sauce*) комкова́тый
lunatic ['lu:nətɪk] *adj* (*behaviour*)
безу́мный
lunch [lʌntʃ] *n* обе́д; **lunch time** *n*
обе́денное вре́мя *nt*, обе́д
lung [lʌŋ] *n* лёгкое *nt adj*; **lung cancer** рак
лёгких
lure [luəʳ] *vt* зама́нивать (*perf* замани́ть);
to lure sb away from отвлека́ть (*perf
отвле́чь) кого́-н от +*gen*
lush [lʌʃ] *adj* (*healthy*) пы́шный
lust [lʌst] *n* (*sexual desire*) по́хоть *f*;
(*greed*) жа́жда: **lust (for)** жа́жда (к +*dat*)
Luxembourg ['lʌksəmbə:g] *n*
Люксембу́рг
luxurious [lʌg'zjʊərɪəs] *adj* роско́шный
luxury ['lʌkʃərɪ] *n* (*great comfort*)
ро́скошь *f*; (*treat*) роско́шество
lyrics ['lɪrɪks] *npl* текст *msg* (*пе́сни*)

m *abbr* (= metre) м (= метр); = **mile**; **million**

MA *n abbr* = **Master of Arts**

mac [mæk] *n* (*Brit: inf*) макинтош

macaroni [mækə'rəunɪ] *n* макароны *pl*

Macedonia [mæsɪ'dəunɪə] *n* Македония

machine [mə'ʃiːn] *n* машина; (*also* **sewing machine**) машинка; **machine gun** *n* пулемёт; **machinery** [mə'ʃiːnərɪ] *n* оборудование; (*Pol*) механизм

mackerel ['mækrl] *n inv* скумбрия

mackintosh ['mækɪntɒʃ] *n* = **mac**

mad [mæd] *adj* сумасшедший, помешанный; (*angry*) бешеный; (*keen*): **he is mad about** он помешан на +*prp*

madam ['mædəm] *n* (*form of address*) мадам *f ind*, госпожа

made [meɪd] *pt, pp of* **make**

madman ['mædmən] *irreg n* сумасшедший *m adj*

madness ['mædnɪs] *n* безумие

Madrid [mə'drɪd] *n* Мадрид

Mafia ['mæfɪə] *n*: **the Mafia** мафия

magazine [mægə'ziːn] *n* журнал

maggot ['mægət] *n* личинка (насекомых)

magic ['mædʒɪk] *n* магия; **magical** *adj* магический; (*experience, evening*) волшебный; **magician** [mə'dʒɪʃən] *n* (*conjurer*) фокусник

magistrate ['mædʒɪstreɪt] *n* (*Law*) мировой судья *m*

magnet ['mægnɪt] *n* магнит; **magnetic** [mæg'netɪk] *adj* магнитный; (*personality*) притягательный

magnificent [mæg'nɪfɪsnt] *adj* великолепный

magnify ['mægnɪfaɪ] *vt* увеличивать (*perf* увеличить); (*sound*) усиливать (*perf* усилить); **magnifying glass** *n* увеличительное стекло, лупа

mahogany [mə'hɒɡənɪ] *n* красное дерево

maid [meɪd] *n* (*in house*) служанка;

(*in hotel*) горничная *f adj*

maiden name *n* девичья фамилия

mail [meɪl] *n* почта ▷ *vt* отправлять (*perf* отправить) по почте; (*Comput*): **to mail sb** писать (*perf* написать) кому-н по электронной почте; **mailbox** *n* (*US: letter box*) почтовый ящик; **mail order** *n* заказ товаров по почте

main [meɪn] *adj* главный ▷ *n*: **gas/water main** газопроводная/водопроводная магистраль *f*; **mains** *npl* сеть *fsg*; **main meal** обед; **mainland** *n*: **the mainland** материк; **mainly** *adv* главным образом; **mainstream** *n* господствующая направление

maintain [meɪn'teɪn] *vt* (*friendship, system, momentum*) поддерживать (*perf* поддержать); (*building*) обслуживать (*impf*); (*affirm: belief, opinion*) утверждать (*impf*)

maintenance ['meɪntənəns] *n* (*of friendship, system*) поддержание; (*of building*) обслуживание; (*Law: alimony*) алименты *pl*

maize [meɪz] *n* кукуруза, маис

majesty ['mædʒɪstɪ] *n*: **Your Majesty** Ваше Величество

major ['meɪdʒə] *adj* (*important*) существенный

majority [mə'dʒɔrɪtɪ] *n* большинство

make [meɪk] (*pt, pp* **made**) *vt* делать (*perf* сделать); (*clothes*) шить (*perf* сшить); (*manufacture*) изготовлять (*perf* изготовить); (*meal*) готовить (*perf* приготовить); (*money*) зарабатывать (*perf* заработать); (*profit*) получать (*perf* получить) ▷ *n* (*brand*) марка; **to make sb do** (*force*) заставлять (*perf* заставить) кого-н +*infin*; **2 and 2 make 4** (*equal*) 2 плюс 2 равняется четырём; **to make sb unhappy** расстраивать (*perf* расстроить) кого-н; **to make a noise** шуметь (*impf*); **to make the bed** стелить (*perf* постелить) постель; **to make a fool of sb** делать (*perf* сделать) из кого-н дурака; **to make a profit** получать (*perf* получить) прибыль; **to make a loss** нести (*perf* понести) убыток; **to make it** (*arrive*) успевать (*perf* успеть); **let's make it Monday** давайте договоримся на понедельник; **to make do with/without** обходиться (*perf* обойтись) +*instr*/без +*gen*; **make for** *vt fus* (*place*) направляться (*perf* направиться) к +*dat*/в +*acc*; **make out** *vt* (*decipher*) разбирать (*perf* разобрать); (*see*) различать (*perf* различить); (*write out*) выписывать (*perf* выписать); (*understand*) разбираться (*perf* разобраться) в +*prp*; **make up** *vt fus* (*constitute*) составлять (*perf* составить) ▷ *vt* (*invent*) выдумывать (*perf* выдумать) ▷ *vi* (*after quarrel*) мириться (*perf* помириться); (*with cosmetics*): **to make (o.s.) up** делать (*perf* сделать) макияж; **make up for** *vt fus* (*mistake*) заглаживать (*perf* загла́дить); (*loss*) восполня́ть (*perf* восполни́ть); **maker** *n* (*of goods*) изготови́тель *m*; **makeshift** *adj* вре́менный; **make-up** *n* косме́тика, макия́ж; (*Theat*) грим

making ['meɪkɪŋ] *n* (*of programme*) созда́ние; **to have the makings of** име́ть (*impf*) зада́тки +*gen*

malaria [mə'lɛərɪə] *n* маляри́я

male [meɪl] *n* (*human*) мужчи́на *m*; (*animal*) саме́ц ▷ *adj* мужско́й; (*child*) мужско́го по́ла

malicious [mə'lɪʃəs] *adj* зло́бный, злой

malignant [mə'lɪgnənt] *adj* (*Med*) злока́чественный

mall [mɔːl] *n* (*also* **shopping mall**) ≈ торго́вый центр

mallet ['mælɪt] *n* деревя́нный молото́к

malnutrition [mælnju:'trɪʃən] *n* недоеда́ние

malt [mɔːlt] *n* (*grain*) со́лод; (*also* **malt whisky**) солодо́вое ви́ски *nt ind*

mammal ['mæml] *n* млекопита́ющее *nt adj*

mammoth ['mæməθ] *adj* (*task*) колосса́льный

man [mæn] (*pl* **men**) *n* мужчи́на *m*; (*person, mankind*) челове́к ▷ *vt* (*machine*) обслу́живать (*impf*); (*post*) занима́ть (*perf* заня́ть); **an old man** стари́к; **man and wife** муж и жена́

manage ['mænɪdʒ] *vi* (*get by*) обходи́ться (*perf* обойти́сь) ▷ *vt* (*business, organization*) руководи́ть (*impf*) +*instr*, управля́ть (*impf*) +*instr*; (*shop, restaurant*) заве́довать (*impf*) +*instr*; (*economy*) управля́ть (*impf*) +*instr*; (*workload, task*) справля́ться (спра́виться (*impf*)) с +*instr*; **I managed to convince him** мне удало́сь убеди́ть его́; **management** *n* (*body*) руково́дство; (*act*): **management (of)** управле́ние (+*instr*); **manager** *n* (*of business, organization*) управля́ющий *m adj*, ме́неджер; (*of shop*) заве́дующий *m adj*; (*of pop star*) ме́неджер; (*Sport*) гла́вный тре́нер; **manageress** [mænɪdʒə'rɛs] *n* (*of shop*) заве́дующая *f adj*; **managerial** [mænɪ'dʒɪərɪəl] *adj* (*role*) руководя́щий; **managerial staff** руководя́щий аппара́т

managing director ['mænɪdʒɪŋ-] *n* управля́ющий дире́ктор

mandarin ['mændərɪn] *n* (*also* **mandarin orange**) мандари́н

mandate ['mændeɪt] *n* (*Pol*) полномо́чие

mandatory ['mændətərɪ] *adj* обяза́тельный

mane [meɪn] *n* гри́ва

maneuver [mə'nu:vər] *n, vb* (*US*) = **manoeuvre**

mango ['mæŋgəu] (*pl* **mangoes**) *n* ма́нго *nt ind*

mania ['meɪnɪə] *n* (*also Psych*) ма́ния

maniac ['meɪnɪæk] *n* манья́к

manic ['mænɪk] *adj* безу́мный, маниака́льный

manifest ['mænɪfɛst] *vt* проявля́ть (*perf* прояви́ть) ▷ *adj* очеви́дный, я́вный

manifesto [mænɪ'fɛstəu] *n* манифе́ст

manipulate [mə'nɪpjuleɪt] *vt* манипули́ровать (*impf*) +*instr*

mankind [mæn'kaɪnd] *n* челове́чество

manly ['mænlɪ] *adj* му́жественный

man-made ['mæn'meɪd] *adj* иску́сственный

manner ['mænər] *n* (*way*) о́браз; (*behaviour*) мане́ра; **manners** *npl* (*conduct*) мане́ры *fpl*; **all manner of things/people** всевозмо́жные ве́щи/лю́ди; **in a manner of speaking** в не́котором ро́де

manoeuvre [mə'nu:vər] (*US* **maneuver**) *vt* передвига́ть (*perf* передви́нуть); (*manipulate*) маневри́ровать (*impf*) +*instr* ▷ *vi* маневри́ровать (*impf*) ▷ *n* манёвр

manpower ['mænpauər] *n* рабо́чая си́ла

mansion ['mænʃən] *n* особня́к

manslaughter ['mænslɔ:tər] *n* непредумы́шленное уби́йство

mantelpiece ['mæntlpi:s] *n* ками́нная доска́

manual ['mænjuəl] *adj* ручно́й ▷ *n* посо́бие; **manual worker** чернорабо́чий(-ая) *m(f) adj*

manufacture [mænju'fæktʃər] *vt* (*goods*) изготовля́ть (*perf* изгото́вить), производи́ть (*perf* произвести́) ▷ *n* изготовле́ние, произво́дство; **manufacturer** *n* изготови́тель *m*, производи́тель *m*

manure [mə'njuər] *n* наво́з

manuscript ['mænjuskrɪpt] *n* (*old text*) манускри́пт; (*before printing*) ру́копись *f*

many ['mɛnɪ] *adj* (*a lot of*) мно́гие ▷ *pron* (*several*) мно́гие *pl adj*; **a great many** о́чень мно́го +*gen*; **how many?** ско́лько?; **many a time** мно́го раз; **in many cases** во мно́гих слу́чаях; **many of us** мно́гие из нас

map [mæp] *n* ка́рта; (*of town*) план

maple ['meɪpl] *n* клён

mar [mɑ:r] *vt* по́ртить (*perf* испо́ртить)

marathon ['mærəθən] *n* марафо́н

marble ['mɑ:bl] *n* (*stone*) мра́мор

March [mɑ:tʃ] *n* март

march [mɑ:tʃ] *vi* марширова́ть (*perf* промарширова́ть) ▷ *n* марш

mare [mɛər] *n* кобы́ла

margarine [mɑ:dʒə'ri:n] *n* маргари́н

margin ['mɑ:dʒɪn] *n* (*on page*) поля́ *ntpl*; (*of victory*) преиму́щество; (*of defeat*) ме́ньшинство; (*also* **profit margin**) ма́ржа, чи́стая при́быль *f no pl*; **marginal** *adj* незначи́тельный

marigold ['mærɪgəuld] *n* ноготки́ *mpl*

marijuana [mærɪ'wɑ:nə] *n* марихуа́на

marina [mə'ri:nə] *n* мари́на, при́стань *f* для яхт

marine [mə'ri:n] *adj* морско́й; (*engineer*)

судовой ⊳ n (Brit) служащий m adj военно-морского флота; (US) морской пехотинец

marital ['mærɪtl] adj супружеский; **marital status** семейное положение

maritime ['mærɪtaɪm] adj морской

mark [mɑːk] n (symbol) значок, пометка; (stain) пятно; (of shoes etc) след; (token) знак; (Brit: Scol) отметка, оценка ⊳ vt (occasion) отмечать (perf отметить); (with pen) помечать (perf пометить); (subj: shoes, tyres) оставлять (perf оставить) след на +prp; (furniture) повреждать (perf повредить); (clothes, carpet) ставить (perf поставить) пятно на +prp; (place, time) указывать (perf указать); (Brit: Scol) проверять (perf проверить); **marked** adj заметный; **marker** n (sign) знак; (bookmark) закладка; (pen) фломастер

market ['mɑːkɪt] n рынок ⊳ vt (promote) рекламировать (impf); (sell) выпускать (perf выпустить) в продажу; **marketing** n маркетинг; **market research** n маркетинговые исследования ntpl

marmalade ['mɑːməleɪd] n джем (цитрусовый)

maroon [mə'ruːn] vt: **we were marooned** мы были отрезаны от внешнего мира

marquee [mɑː'kiː] n маркиза, палаточный павильон

marriage ['mærɪdʒ] n брак; (wedding) свадьба; **marriage certificate** n свидетельство о браке

married ['mærɪd] adj (man) женатый; (woman) замужняя; (couple) женатые; (life) супружеский

marrow ['mærəu] n (Bot) кабачок; (also **bone marrow**) костный мозг

marry ['mærɪ] vt (subj: man) жениться (impf/perf) на +prp; (: woman) выходить (perf выйти) замуж за +acc; (: priest) венчать (perf обвенчать); (also **marry off**: son) женить (impf/perf); (: daughter) выдавать (perf выдать) замуж ⊳ vi: **to get married** (man) жениться (impf); (woman) выходить (perf выйти) замуж; (couple) жениться (perf пожениться)

Mars [mɑːz] n Марс

marsh [mɑːʃ] n болото

marshal ['mɑːʃl] n (at public event) распорядитель(ница) m(f) ⊳ vt (support) упорядочивать (perf упорядочить); **police marshal** (US) начальник полицейского участка

martyr ['mɑːtər] n мученик(-ица)

marvellous (US **marvelous**) ['mɑːvləs] adj восхитительный, изумительный

Marxist ['mɑːksɪst] adj марксистский ⊳ n марксист(ка)

marzipan ['mɑːzɪpæn] n марципан

mascara [mæs'kɑːrə] n тушь f для ресниц

mascot ['mæskət] n талисман

masculine ['mæskjulɪn] adj мужской; (Ling) мужского рода

mash [mæʃ] vt делать (perf сделать) пюре из +gen

mask [mɑːsk] n маска ⊳ vt (feelings) маскировать (impf)

mason ['meɪsn] n (also **stone mason**) каменщик; (also **freemason**) масон, вольный каменщик; **masonry** n (каменная) кладка

mass [mæs] n (also Phys) масса; (Rel): **Mass** причастие ⊳ cpd массовый; **masses** npl (народные) массы fpl; **masses of** (inf) масса fsg +gen, уйма fsg +gen

massacre ['mæsəkər] n массовое убийство, резня

massage ['mæsɑːʒ] n массаж ⊳ vt (rub) массировать (impf)

massive ['mæsɪv] adj массивный; (support, changes) огромный

mass media n inv средства ntpl массовой информации

mast [mɑːst] n мачта

master ['mɑːstər] n (also fig) хозяин ⊳ vt (control) владеть (perf овладеть) +instr; (learn, understand) овладевать (perf овладеть) +instr; **Master Smith** (title) господин or мастер Смит; **Master of Arts/ Science** ≈ магистр гуманитарных/ естественных наук; **masterpiece** n шедевр

masturbation [mæstə'beɪʃən] n мастурбация

mat [mæt] n коврик; (also **doormat**) дверной коврик; (also **table mat**) подставка ⊳ adj = **matt**

match [mætʃ] n спичка; (Sport) матч; (equal) ровня m/f ⊳ vt (subj: colours) сочетаться (impf) c +instr; (correspond to) соответствовать (impf) +dat ⊳ vi (colours, materials) сочетаться (impf); **to be a good match** (colours, clothes) хорошо сочетаться (impf); **they make** or **are a good match** они хорошая пара; **matching** adj сочетающийся

mate [meɪt] n (inf: friend) друг; (animal) самец(-мка); (Naut) помощник капитана ⊳ vi спариваться (perf спариться)

material [mə'tɪərɪəl] n материал ⊳ adj материальный; **materials** npl (equipment) принадлежности fpl; **building materials** строительные материалы; **materialize** vi материализоваться (impf/ perf), осуществляться (perf осуществиться)

maternal [mə'təːnl] adj материнский

maternity [mə'təːnɪtɪ] n материнство

mathematics [mæθə'mætɪks] n математика

maths [mæθs] n abbr = **mathematics**

matron ['meɪtrən] n (in hospital) старшая медсестра; (in school) (школьная) медсестра

matt [mæt] adj матовый

matter ['mætə'] n де́ло, вопро́с; (substance, material) вещество́ ⊳ vi име́ть (impf) значе́ние; **matters** npl (affairs, situation) дела́ ntpl; **reading matter** (Brit) материа́л для чте́ния; **what's the matter?** в чём де́ло?; **no matter what** несмотря́ ни на что; **as a matter of course** как само́ собо́й разуме́ющееся; **as a matter of fact** со́бственно говоря́; **it doesn't matter** э́то не ва́жно

mattress ['mætrɪs] n матра́с

mature [mə'tjʊə'] adj (person) зре́лый; (cheese, wine) вы́держанный ⊳ vi (develop) развива́ться (perf разви́ться); (grow up) взросле́ть (perf повзросле́ть); (cheese) зреть or созрева́ть (perf созре́ть); (wine) выста́иваться (perf вы́стояться)

maturity [mə'tjʊərɪtɪ] n зре́лость f

maximum ['mæksɪməm] (pl **maxima** or **maximums**) adj максима́льный ⊳ n ма́ксимум

May [meɪ] n май

● **MAY DAY**

▪ **May Day** — Первома́й. По тради́ции в э́тот день пра́зднуется нача́ло весны́.

may [meɪ] (conditional **might**) vi (to show possibility): **I may go to Russia** я, мо́жет быть, пое́ду в Росси́ю; (to show permission): **may I smoke/come?** мо́жно закури́ть/мне прийти́?; **it may or might rain** мо́жет пойти́ дождь; **you may or might as well go now** Вы, пожа́луй, мо́жете идти́ сейча́с; **come what may** будь что бу́дет

maybe ['meɪbiː] adv мо́жет быть

mayhem ['meɪhɛm] n погро́м

mayonnaise [meɪə'neɪz] n майоне́з

mayor [mɛə'] n мэр

○ **KEYWORD**

me [miː] pron **1** (direct) меня́; **he loves me** он лю́бит меня́; **it's me** э́то я
2 (indirect) мне; **give me them** or **them to me** да́йте их мне
3 (after prep: +gen) меня́; (: +dat, +prp) мне; (: +instr) мной; **it's for me** (on answering phone) э́то мне
4 (referring to subject of sentence: after prep: +gen) себя́; (: +dat) себе́; (: +instr) собо́й; (: +prp) себе́; **I took him with me** я взял его́ с собо́й

meadow ['mɛdəʊ] n луг

meagre ['miːgə'] (US **meager**) adj ску́дный

meal [miːl] n еда́ no pl; (afternoon) обе́д; (evening) у́жин; **during meals** во вре́мя еды́, за едо́й

mean [miːn] n (pt, pp **meant**) adj (miserly) скупо́й; (unkind) вре́дный; (vicious) по́длый ⊳ vt (signify) зна́чить (impf), означа́ть (impf); (refer to) име́ть (impf) в виду́ ⊳ n (average) середи́на; **means** npl (way) спо́соб msg, сре́дство ntsg; (money) сре́дства ntpl; **by means of** посре́дством +gen, с по́мощью +gen; **by all means!** пожа́луйста!; **do you mean it?** Вы э́то серьёзно?; **to mean to do** (intend) намерева́ться (impf) +infin; **to be meant for** предназнача́ться (impf) для +gen; **meaning** n (purpose, value) смысл; (definition) значе́ние; **meaningful** adj (result, occasion) значи́тельный; (glance, remark) многозначи́тельный; **meaningless** adj бессмы́сленный; **meant** [mɛnt] pt, pp of **mean**; **meantime** adv (also **in the meantime**) тем вре́менем, ме́жду тем; **meanwhile** adv = **meantime**

measles ['miːzlz] n корь f

measure ['mɛʒə'] vt измеря́ть (perf изме́рить) ⊳ n ме́ра; (of whisky etc) по́рция; (also **tape measure**) руле́тка, сантиме́тр ⊳ vi: **the room measures 10 feet by 20** пло́щадь ко́мнаты 10 фу́тов на 20; **measurements** npl ме́рки fpl, разме́ры mpl

meat [miːt] n мя́со; **cold meats** (Brit) холо́дные мясны́е заку́ски pl

mechanic [mɪ'kænɪk] n меха́ник; **mechanical** adj механи́ческий

mechanism ['mɛkənɪzəm] n механи́зм

medal ['mɛdl] n меда́ль f; **medallist** (US **medalist**) n медали́ст(ка)

meddle ['mɛdl] vi: **to meddle in** вме́шиваться (perf вмеша́ться) в +acc; **to meddle with sth** вторга́ться (perf вто́ргнуться) во что-н

media ['miːdɪə] n or npl: **the media** сре́дства ntpl ма́ссовой информа́ции, ме́диа ⊳ npl see **medium**

mediaeval [mɛdɪ'iːvl] adj = **medieval**

mediate ['miːdɪeɪt] vi (arbitrate) посре́дничать (impf)

medical ['mɛdɪkl] adj медици́нский ⊳ n медосмо́тр

medication [mɛdɪ'keɪʃən] n лека́рство, лека́рственный препара́т

medicine ['mɛdsɪn] n (science) медици́на; (drug) лека́рство

medieval [mɛdɪ'iːvl] adj средневеко́вый

mediocre [miːdɪ'əʊkə'] adj заура́дный, посре́дственный

meditation [mɛdɪ'teɪʃən] n (Rel) медита́ция

Mediterranean [mɛdɪtə'reɪnɪən] adj: **the Mediterranean (Sea)** Средизе́мное мо́ре

medium ['miːdɪəm] adj (pl **media** or **mediums**) adj сре́дний ⊳ n (means) сре́дство

meek [miːk] adj кро́ткий

meet [miːt] (pt, pp **met**) vt встреча́ть (perf встре́тить); (obligations) выполня́ть (*perf* выполнить); (*problem*) сталкиваться (*perf* столкнуться) с +*instr*; (*need*) удовлетворять (*perf* удовлетворить) ▷ *vi* (*people*) встречаться (*perf* встретиться); (*lines, roads*) пересекаться (*perf* пересечься); **meet with** *vt fus* (*difficulty*) сталкиваться (*perf* столкнуться) с +*instr*; (*success*) пользоваться (*impf*) +*instr*; (*approval*) находить (*perf* найти); **meeting** *n* встреча; (*at work, of committee etc*) заседание; (*Pol: also* **mass meeting**) митинг; **she's at a meeting** она на заседании

melancholy ['mɛlənkəlɪ] *adj* (*smile*) меланхолический

melody ['mɛlədɪ] *n* мелодия

melon ['mɛlən] *n* дыня

melt [mɛlt] *vi* таять (*perf* растаять) ▷ *vt* (*snow, butter*) топить (*perf* растопить)

member ['mɛmbəʳ] *n* (*also Anat*) член; **Member of Parliament** (*Brit*) член парламента; **membership** *n* (*members*) члены *mpl*; (*status*) членство; **membership card** *n* членский билет

meme [miːm] *n* мем

memento [mə'mɛntəu] *n* сувенир

memo ['mɛməu] *n* (*Admin: instruction*) директива

memorable ['mɛmərəbl] *adj* памятный

memorial [mɪ'mɔːrɪəl] *n* памятник ▷ *cpd* мемориальный

memorize ['mɛməraɪz] *vt* заучивать (*perf* заучить) (наизусть)

memory ['mɛmərɪ] *n* память *f*; (*recollection*) воспоминание; **in memory of** в память о +*prp*; **memory card** *n* (*Comput*) карта памяти

men [mɛn] *npl of* **man**

menace ['mɛnɪs] *n* (*threat*) угроза

mend [mɛnd] *vt* ремонтировать (*perf* отремонтировать), чинить (*perf* починить); (*clothes*) чинить (*perf* починить) ▷ *n*: **to be on the mend** идти (*impf*) на поправку; **to mend one's ways** исправляться (*perf* исправиться)

meningitis [mɛnɪn'dʒaɪtɪs] *n* менингит

menopause ['mɛnəupɔːz] *n* климактерический период, климакс

menstruation [mɛnstru'eɪʃən] *n* менструация

menswear ['mɛnzwɛəʳ] *n* мужская одежда

mental ['mɛntl] *adj* (*ability, exhaustion*) умственный; (*image*) мысленный; (*illness*) душевный, психический; (*arithmetic, calculation*) в уме; **mentality** [mɛn'tælɪtɪ] *n* менталитет, умонастроение

mention ['mɛnʃən] *n* упоминание ▷ *vt* упоминать (*perf* упомянуть); **don't mention it!** не за что!

menu ['mɛnjuː] *n* (*also Comput*) меню *nt ind*

MEP *n abbr* (*Brit*) (= *Member of the European Parliament*) член Европейского парламента

mercenary ['məːsɪnərɪ] *adj* корыстный ▷ *n* наёмник

merchant ['məːtʃənt] *n* торговец

merciless ['məːsɪlɪs] *adj* беспощадный

mercury ['məːkjurɪ] *n* (*metal*) ртуть *f*

mercy ['məːsɪ] *n* милосердие; **to be at sb's mercy** быть (*impf*) во власти кого-н

mere [mɪəʳ] *adj*: **she's a mere child** она всего лишь ребёнок; **his mere presence irritates her** само его присутствие раздражает её; **merely** *adv* (*simply*) просто; (*just*) только

merge [məːdʒ] *vt* сливать (*perf* слить), объединять (*perf* объединить) ▷ *vi* (*also Comm*) сливаться (*perf* слиться); (*roads*) сходиться (*perf* сойтись); **merger** *n* (*Comm*) слияние

meringue [mə'ræŋ] *n* безе *nt ind*

merit ['mɛrɪt] *n* достоинство ▷ *vt* заслуживать (*perf* заслужить)

merry ['mɛrɪ] *adj* весёлый; **Merry Christmas!** С Рождеством!, Счастливого Рождества!

mesh [mɛʃ] *n* (*net*) сеть *f*

mess [mɛs] *n* (*in room*) беспорядок; (*of situation*) неразбериха; (*Mil*) столовая *f adj*; **to be in a mess** (*untidy*) быть (*impf*) в беспорядке; **mess up** *vt* (*spoil*) портить (*perf* испортить)

message ['mɛsɪdʒ] *n* сообщение; (*note*) записка; (*of play, book*) идея; **to leave sb a message** (*note*) оставлять (*perf* оставить) кому-н записку; **can I give him a message?** ему что-нибудь передать?

messenger ['mɛsɪndʒəʳ] *n* курьер, посыльный *m adj*

Messrs *abbr* (*on letters*) (= *messieurs*) гг. (= *господа*)

messy ['mɛsɪ] *adj* (*untidy*) неубранный

met [mɛt] *pt, pp of* **meet**

metabolism [mɛ'tæbəlɪzəm] *n* метаболизм, обмен веществ

metal ['mɛtl] *n* металл

metaphor ['mɛtəfəʳ] *n* метафора

meteor ['miːtɪəʳ] *n* метеор

meteorology [miːtɪə'rɔlədʒɪ] *n* метеорология

meter ['miːtəʳ] *n* (*instrument*) счётчик; (*US: unit*) = **metre**

method ['mɛθəd] *n* (*way*) метод, способ; **methodical** [mɪ'θɔdɪkl] *adj* методичный

meticulous [mɪ'tɪkjuləs] *adj* тщательный

metre ['miːtəʳ] (*US meter*) *n* метр

metric ['mɛtrɪk] *adj* метрический

metropolitan [mɛtrə'pɔlɪtn] *adj* столичный

Mexico ['mɛksɪkəu] *n* Мексика

mice [maɪs] *npl of* **mouse**

micro: **microphone** *n* микрофон; **microscope** *n* микроскоп; **microwave** *n* (*also* **microwave oven**) микроволновая печь *f*

mid [mɪd] *adj*: **in mid May/afternoon** в

середи́не ма́я/дня; **in mid air** в во́здухе;
midday n по́лдень m
middle ['mɪdl] n середи́на ▷ adj
сре́дний; **in the middle of** посреди́ +gen;
middle-aged adj сре́дних лет; **Middle
Ages** npl: **the Middle Ages** сре́дние века́
mpl; **middle-class** adj: **middle-class
people/values** лю́ди/це́нности сре́днего
кла́сса; **Middle East** n: **the Middle East**
Бли́жний Восто́к
midge [mɪdʒ] n мо́шка
midnight ['mɪdnaɪt] n по́лночь f
midst [mɪdst] n: **in the midst of** посреди́
+gen
midway [mɪd'weɪ] adv: **midway
(between)** на полпути́ (ме́жду +instr);
midway through в середи́не +gen
midweek [mɪd'wiːk] adv в середи́не
неде́ли
midwife ['mɪdwaɪf] (pl **midwives**) n
акуше́рка
might [maɪt] vb see **may**
mighty [maɪtɪ] adj могу́щий
migraine ['miːgreɪn] n мигре́нь f
migrant ['maɪgrənt] adj: **migrant worker**
рабо́чий-мигра́нт
migration [maɪ'greɪʃən] n мигра́ция
mike [maɪk] n abbr = **microphone**
mild [maɪld] adj мя́гкий; (interest)
сла́бый; (infection) лёгкий; **mildly**
['maɪldlɪ] adv (see adj) мя́гко; слегка́;
легко́; **to put it mildly** мя́гко говоря́
mile [maɪl] n ми́ля; **mileage** n
коли́чество миль; **milestone** n
≈ километро́вый столб; (fig) ве́ха

military ['mɪlɪtərɪ] adj вое́нный ▷ n: **the
military** вое́нные pl adj
militia [mɪ'lɪʃə] n (наро́дное) ополче́ние
milk [mɪlk] n молоко́ ▷ vt (cow) дои́ть
(perf подои́ть); (fig) эксплуати́ровать
(impf); **milky** adj моло́чный
mill [mɪl] n (factory: making cloth)
фа́брика; (: making steel) заво́д; (for
coffee, pepper) ме́льница
millimetre (US **millimeter**) ['mɪlɪmiːtə']
n миллиме́тр
million ['mɪljən] n миллио́н; **millionaire**
[mɪljə'nɛə'] n миллионе́р
mime [maɪm] n пантоми́ма ▷ vt
изобража́ть (perf изобрази́ть) же́стами
mimic ['mɪmɪk] vt (subj: comedian)
пароди́ровать (perf)
min. abbr (= minute) мин.(.) (= мину́та)
mince [mɪns] vt (meat) пропуска́ть (perf
пропусти́ть) че́рез мясору́бку ▷ n (Brit)
(мясно́й) фарш

mind [maɪnd] n (intellect) ум ▷ vt (look
after) смотре́ть (impf) за +instr; (object to):
I don't mind the noise шум меня́ не
беспоко́ит; **it's always on my mind** э́то не
выхо́дит у меня́ из головы́; **to keep** or
bear sth in mind име́ть (impf) что-н в
виду́; **to make up one's mind** реша́ться
(perf реши́ться); **to my mind ...** по моему́
мне́нию ...; **I don't mind** мне всё равно́;
mind you, ... име́йте в виду́ ...; **never
mind!** ничего́!; **mindless** adj (violence)
безду́мный; (job) механи́ческий

KEYWORD

mine¹ [maɪn] pron **1** мой (f моя́, nt моё,
pl мои́); **that book is mine** э́та кни́га моя́;
that house is mine э́тот дом мой; **this is
mine** э́то моё; **an uncle of mine** мой дя́дя
2 (referring back to subject) свой (f своя́,
nt своё, pl свой); **may I borrow your pen?
I have forgotten mine** мо́жно взять Ва́шу
ру́чку? я забы́л свою́

mine² [maɪn] n (for coal) ша́хта;
(explosive) ми́на ▷ vt (coal) добыва́ть
(perf добы́ть); **minefield** n ми́нное
по́ле; **miner** n шахтёр
mineral ['mɪnərəl] n минера́л; (ore)
поле́зное ископа́емое nt adj; **mineral
water** n минера́льная вода́
miniature ['mɪnətʃə'] adj миниатю́рный
minibus ['mɪnɪbʌs] n микроавто́бус

minimal ['mɪnɪml] adj минима́льный
minimize ['mɪnɪmaɪz] vt (reduce)
своди́ть (perf свести́) к ми́нимуму; (play
down) преуменьша́ть (perf
преуме́ньшить)
minimum ['mɪnɪməm] (pl **minima**) n
ми́нимум ▷ adj минима́льный
mining ['maɪnɪŋ] n (industry) у́гольная
промы́шленность f
minister ['mɪnɪstə'] n (Brit) мини́стр;
(Rel) свяще́нник
ministry ['mɪnɪstrɪ] n (Brit: Pol)
министе́рство

minor ['maɪnə^r] *adj* (*injuries*)
незначи́тельный; (*repairs*) ме́лкий ▷ *n*
(*Law*) несовершенноле́тний(-яя) *m(f) adj*;
minority [maɪ'nɔrɪtɪ] *n* меньшинство́

mint [mɪnt] *n* (*Bot*) мя́та; (*sweet*) мя́тная
конфе́та ▷ *vt* чека́нить (*perf* отчека́нить);
in mint condition в прекра́сном состоя́нии

minus ['maɪnəs] *n* (*also* **minus sign**)
ми́нус ▷ *prep*: **12 minus 6 equals 6** 12
ми́нус 6 равня́ется 6; **minus 24 (degrees)**
ми́нус 24 гра́дуса

minute[1] [maɪ'nju:t] *adj* (*tiny*)
тща́тельный

minute[2] ['mɪnɪt] *n* мину́та; **minutes** *npl*
(*of meeting*) протоко́л *msg*; **at the last
minute** в после́днюю мину́ту

miracle ['mɪrəkl] *n* чу́до

miraculous [mɪ'rækjuləs] *adj* чуде́сный

mirror ['mɪrə^r] *n* зе́ркало

misbehave [mɪsbɪ'heɪv] *vi* пло́хо себя́
вести́ (*impf*)

miscarriage ['mɪskærɪdʒ] *n* (*Med*)
вы́кидыш; **miscarriage of justice** суде́бная
оши́бка

miscellaneous [mɪsɪ'leɪnɪəs] *adj*
(*subjects, items*) разнообра́зный

mischief ['mɪstʃɪf] *n* озорство́;
(*maliciousness*) зло

mischievous ['mɪstʃɪvəs] *adj* (*naughty,
playful*) озорно́й

misconception [mɪskən'sɛpʃən] *n*
заблужде́ние, ло́жное представле́ние

misconduct [mɪs'kɔndʌkt] *n* дурно́е
поведе́ние; **professional misconduct**
наруше́ние служе́бной дисципли́ны

miserable ['mɪzərəbl] *adj* (*unhappy*)
несча́стный; (*unpleasant*) скве́рный;
(*donation, conditions*) жа́лкий; (*failure*)
позо́рный

misery ['mɪzərɪ] *n* (*unhappiness*)
невзго́да; (*wretchedness*) жа́лкое
существова́ние

misfortune [mɪs'fɔ:tʃən] *n* несча́стье

misguided [mɪs'gaɪdɪd] *adj* (*person*)
неве́рно ориенти́рованный; (*ideas*)
оши́бочный

misinterpret [mɪsɪn'tə:prɪt] *vt* неве́рно
интерпрети́ровать (*impf/perf*) *or*
толкова́ть (истолкова́ть *perf*)

mislead [mɪs'li:d] (*irreg like* **lead**[1]) *vt*
вводи́ть (*perf* ввести́) в заблужде́ние;
misleading *adj* обма́нчивый

misprint ['mɪsprɪnt] *n* опеча́тка

Miss [mɪs] *n* мисс *f ind*

miss [mɪs] *vt* (*train, bus etc*) пропуска́ть
(*perf* пропусти́ть); (*target*) не попада́ть
(*perf* попа́сть) в +*acc*; (*person, home*)
скуча́ть (*impf*) по +*dat*; (*chance, opportunity*)
упуска́ть (*perf* упусти́ть) ▷ *vi* (*person*)
прома́хиваться (*perf* промахну́ться) ▷ *n*
про́мах; **you can't miss my house** мой дом
невозмо́жно не заме́тить; **miss out** *vt*
(*Brit*) пропуска́ть (*perf* пропусти́ть)

missile ['mɪsaɪl] *n* (*Mil*) раке́та

missing ['mɪsɪŋ] *adj* пропа́вший; (*tooth,
wheel*) недоста́ющий; (*absent*) отсу́тствовать
(*impf*); **to be missing** пропа́сть (*perf*); **to be
missing, go missing** пропада́ть (*perf*
пропа́сть) без вести

mission ['mɪʃən] *n* (*also Pol, Rel*) ми́ссия;
missionary *n* миссионе́р(ка)

mist [mɪst] *n* (*light*) ды́мка

mistake [mɪs'teɪk] (*irreg like* **take**) *n*
оши́бка ▷ *vt* (*be wrong about*) ошиба́ться
(*perf* ошиби́ться) в +*prp*; **by mistake** по
оши́бке; **to make a mistake** ошиба́ться
(*perf* ошиби́ться), де́лать (*perf* сде́лать)
оши́бку; **to mistake A for B** принима́ть
(*perf* приня́ть) A за Б; **mistaken** *pp of*
mistake ▷ *adj*: **to be mistaken**
ошиба́ться (*perf* ошиби́ться)

mistletoe ['mɪsltəu] *n* оме́ла

● **MISTLETOE**

●

● В Великобрита́нии и США э́то расте́ние
● испо́льзуется как рожде́ственское
● украше́ние. По обы́чаю под оме́лой
● полага́ется целова́ться.

mistook [mɪs'tuk] *pt of* **mistake**

mistress ['mɪstrɪs] *n* (*also fig*) хозя́йка;
(*lover*) любо́вница

mistrust [mɪs'trʌst] *vt* не доверя́ть
(*impf*) +*dat* ▷ *n*: **mistrust (of)** недове́рие
(к +*dat*)

misty ['mɪstɪ] *adj* (*day*) тума́нный

misunderstand [mɪsʌndə'stænd] (*irreg
like* **stand**) *vt* непра́вильно понима́ть
(*perf* поня́ть) ▷ *vi* не понима́ть (*perf*
поня́ть); **misunderstanding** *n*
недоразуме́ние

misuse [*n* mɪs'ju:s, *vb* mɪs'ju:z] *n* (*of
power, funds*) злоупотребле́ние ▷ *vt*
злоупотребля́ть (*perf* злоупотреби́ть)
+*instr*

mix [mɪks] *vt* (*cake, cement*) заме́шивать
(*perf* замеси́ть) ▷ *n* смесь *f* ▷ *vi* (*people*):
to mix (with) обща́ться (*impf*) (с +*instr*); **to
mix sth (with sth)** сме́шивать (*perf*
смеша́ть) что-н (с чем-н); **mix up** *vt*
(*combine*) переме́шивать (*perf*
перемеша́ть); (*confuse: people*) пу́тать
(*perf* спу́тать); (: *things*) пу́тать (*perf*
перепу́тать); **mixer** *n* (*for food*) ми́ксер;
mixture ['mɪkstʃə^r] *n* смесь *f*; **mix-up** *n*
пу́таница

mm *abbr* (= *millimetre*) мм (= миллиме́тр)

moan [məun] *n* (*cry*) стон ▷ *vi* (*inf:
complain*): **to moan (about)** ныть (*impf*) (о
+*prp*)

moat [məut] *n* ров

mob [mɔb] *n* (*crowd*) толпа́

mobile ['məubaɪl] *adj* подви́жный ▷ *n*
(*toy*) подвесно́е декорати́вное
украше́ние; (*phone*) моби́льный телефо́н,
моби́льник (*inf*); **mobile phone** *n*
моби́льный телефо́н

mobility [məuˈbɪlɪtɪ] n подви́жность f
mobilize [ˈməubɪlaɪz] vt мобилизова́ть
(impf/perf)
mock [mɔk] vt (ridicule) издева́ться
(impf) над +instr ▷ adj (fake) ло́жный;
mockery n издева́тельство; **to make a**
mockery of sb/sth выставля́ть (perf
вы́ставить) кого́-н/что-н на посме́шище
mod cons npl abbr (Brit) = **modern**
conveniences
mode [məud] n (of life) о́браз; (of
transport) вид
model [ˈmɔdl] n моде́ль f, маке́т; (also
fashion model) моде́ль,
манеке́нщик(-ица) (also **artist's model**)
нату́рщик(-ица) ▷ adj (ideal) образцо́вый
modem [ˈməudem] n (Comput) моде́м
moderate [adj ˈmɔdərət, vb ˈmɔdəreɪt] adj
(views, amount) уме́ренный; (change)
незначи́тельный ▷ vt умеря́ть (perf
уме́рить)
moderation [mɔdəˈreɪʃən] n
уме́ренность f
modern [ˈmɔdən] adj совреме́нный
modest [ˈmɔdɪst] adj скро́мный;
modesty n скро́мность f
modification [mɔdɪfɪˈkeɪʃən] n (see vt)
модифика́ция; видоизмене́ние
modify [ˈmɔdɪfaɪ] vt (vehicle, engine)
модифици́ровать (impf/perf); (plan)
видоизменя́ть (perf видоизмени́ть)
moist [mɔɪst] adj вла́жный; **moisture** n
вла́га
mold [məuld] n, vb (US) = **mould**
mole [məul] n (spot) ро́динка; (Zool) крот
molecule [ˈmɔlɪkjuːl] n моле́кула
mom [mɔm] n (US) = **mum**
moment [ˈməumənt] n моме́нт,
мгнове́ние; **for a moment** на мгнове́ние;
at that moment в э́тот моме́нт; **at the**
moment в настоя́щий моме́нт;
momentary adj мгнове́нный
momentous [məuˈmentəs] adj
знамена́тельный
momentum [məuˈmentəm] n (fig)
дви́жущая си́ла; **to gather** or **gain**
momentum набира́ть (perf набра́ть) си́лу
mommy [ˈmɔmɪ] n (US) = **mummy**
monarch [ˈmɔnək] n мона́рх; **monarchy**
n мона́рхия
monastery [ˈmɔnəstərɪ] n монасты́рь m
Monday [ˈmʌndɪ] n понеде́льник
monetary [ˈmʌnɪtərɪ] adj де́нежный
money [ˈmʌnɪ] n де́ньги pl; **to make**
money (person) зараба́тывать (perf
зарабо́тать) де́ньги; (make a profit) де́лать
(perf сде́лать) де́ньги
mongrel [ˈmʌŋɡrəl] n дворня́га
monitor [ˈmɔnɪtə'] n монито́р; (Comput)
монито́р ▷ vt (broadcasts, pulse) следи́ть
(impf) за +instr
monk [mʌŋk] n мона́х
monkey [ˈmʌŋkɪ] n обезья́на
monopoly [məˈnɔpəlɪ] n монопо́лия

monotonous [məˈnɔtənəs] adj
однообра́зный, моното́нный
monster [ˈmɔnstə'] n чудо́вище, монстр
month [mʌnθ] n ме́сяц; **monthly** adj
ежеме́сячный; (ticket) ме́сячный ▷ adv
ежеме́сячно
monument [ˈmɔnjumənt] n (memorial)
па́мятник, монуме́нт
mood [muːd] n настрое́ние; (of crowd)
настро́й; **to be in a good/bad mood** быть
(impf) в хоро́шем/плохо́м настрое́нии;
moody adj (temperamental): **she is a very**
moody person у неё о́чень переме́нчивое
настрое́ние
moon [muːn] n луна́; **moonlight** n
лу́нный свет
moor [muə'] n ве́ресковая пу́стошь f
moose [muːs] n inv лось m
mop [mɔp] n (for floor) шва́бра; (of hair)
копна́ ▷ vt (floor) мыть (вы́мыть or
помы́ть perf) (шва́брой); (eyes, face)
вытира́ть (perf вы́тереть)
moped [ˈməuped] n мопе́д
moral [ˈmɔrl] adj мора́льный; (person)
нра́вственный ▷ n (of story) мора́ль f;
morals npl (values) нра́вы mpl
morale [mɔˈrɑːl] n мора́льный дух
morality [məˈrælɪtɪ] n нра́вственность f
morbid [ˈmɔːbɪd] adj (imagination)
ненорма́льный; (ideas) жу́ткий

🔘 **KEYWORD**

more [mɔː'] adj 1 (greater in number etc)
бо́льше +gen; **I have more friends than**
enemies у меня́ бо́льше друзе́й, чем
враго́в
2 (additional) ещё; **do you want (some)**
more tea? хоти́те ещё ча́ю?; **is there any**
more wine? вино́ ещё есть?; **I have no**
or **I don't have any more money** у меня́
бо́льше нет де́нег; **it'll take a few more**
weeks э́то займёт ещё не́сколько неде́ль
▷ pron 1 (greater amount): **more than ten**
бо́льше десяти́; **we've sold more than a**
hundred tickets мы про́дали бо́лее ста
биле́тов; **it costs more than we expected**
э́то сто́ит бо́льше, чем мы ожида́ли
2 (further or additional amount): **is there**
any more? ещё есть?; **there's no more**
бо́льше ничего́ нет; **a little more** ещё
немно́го or чуть-чу́ть; **many/much more**
намно́го/гора́здо бо́льше
▷ adv (+vb) бо́льше; **I like this picture**
more э́та карти́на мне нра́вится бо́льше
2: **more dangerous/difficult (than)** бо́лее
опа́сный/тру́дный(, чем)
3: **more economically (than)** бо́лее
экономи́чно(, чем); **more easily/quickly**
(than) ле́гче/быстре́е(, чем); **more and**
more (excited, friendly) всё бо́лее и бо́лее;
he grew to like her more and more она́
нра́вилась ему́ всё бо́льше и бо́льше;
more or less бо́лее и́ли ме́нее; **she is more**

beautiful than ever она прекра́снее, чем когда́-либо; **he loved her more than ever** он люби́л её бо́льше, чем когда́-либо; **the more ..., the better** чем бо́льше ..., тем лу́чше; **once more** ещё раз; **I'd like to see more of you** мне хоте́лось бы ви́деть тебя́ ча́ще

moreover [mɔːˈrəuvəᵊ] *adv* бо́лее того́

morgue [mɔːg] *n* морг

morning [ˈmɔːnɪŋ] *n* у́тро; (*between midnight and 3 a.m.*) ночь *f* ▷ *cpd* у́тренний; **in the morning** у́тром; **3 o'clock in the morning** 3 часа́ но́чи; **7 o'clock in the morning** 7 часо́в утра́

Morse [mɔːs] *n* (*also* **Morse code**) а́збука Мо́рзе

mortal [ˈmɔːtl] *adj* (*man, sin*) сме́ртный; (*deadly*) смерте́льный

mortar [ˈmɔːtəᵊ] *n* (*cement*) цеме́нтный раство́р

mortgage [ˈmɔːgɪdʒ] *n* ипоте́чный креди́т ▷ *vt* закла́дывать (*perf* заложи́ть)

Moscow [ˈmɔskəu] *n* Москва́

Moslem [ˈmɔzləm] *adj, n* = **Muslim**

mosque [mɔsk] *n* мече́ть *f*

mosquito [mɔsˈkiːtəu] (*pl* **mosquitoes**) *n* кома́р

moss [mɔs] *n* мох

○ **KEYWORD**

most [məust] *adj* **1** (*almost all: countable nouns*) большинство́ +*gen*; (: *uncountable and collective nouns*) бо́льшая часть +*gen*; **most cars** большинство́ маши́н; **most milk** бо́льшая часть молока́; **in most cases** в большинстве́ слу́чаев
2 (*largest, greatest*): **who has the most money?** у кого́ бо́льше всего́ де́нег?; **this book has attracted the most interest among the critics** э́та кни́га вы́звала наибо́льший интере́с у кри́тиков ▷ *pron* (*greatest quantity, number: countable nouns*) большинство́; (: *uncountable and collective nouns*) бо́льшая часть *f*; **most of the houses** большинство́ домо́в; **most of the cake** бо́льшая часть то́рта; **do the most you can** де́лайте всё, что Вы мо́жете; **I ate the most** я съел бо́льше всех; **to make the most of sth** максима́льно испо́льзовать (*impf/perf*) что-н; **at the (very) most** са́мое бо́льшее ▷ *adv* (+*vb: with inanimate objects*) бо́льше всего́; (: *with animate objects*) бо́льше всех; (+*adv*) исключи́тельно; (+*adj*) са́мый, наибо́лее; **I liked him the most** он понра́вился мне бо́льше всех; **what do you value most, wealth or health?** что Вы бо́льше всего́ це́ните, бога́тство и́ли здоро́вье?

mostly [ˈməustlɪ] *adv* бо́льшей ча́стью, в основно́м

MOT *n abbr* (*Brit*) = **Ministry of Transport; MOT** (**test**) техосмо́тр

● **MOT**
●
● По зако́ну автомоби́ли, кото́рым
● бо́льше трёх лет, должны́ ежего́дно
● проходи́ть техосмо́тр.

motel [məuˈtɛl] *n* моте́ль *m*

moth [mɔθ] *n* мотылёк

mother [ˈmʌðəᵊ] *n* мать *f* ▷ *vt* (*pamper*) ня́нчиться (*impf*) с +*instr* ▷ *adj*: **mother country** ро́дина, родна́я страна́; **motherhood** *n* матери́нство; **mother-in-law** *n* (*wife's mother*) тёща; (*husband's mother*) свекро́вь *f*; **mother tongue** *n* родно́й язы́к

● **MOTHER'S DAY**
●
● Mother's Day — День Ма́тери.
● Отмеча́ется в четвёртое воскресе́нье
● Вели́кого Поста́. В э́тот день
● поздравле́ния и пода́рки получа́ют
● то́лько ма́мы.

motif [məuˈtiːf] *n* (*design*) орна́мент

motion [ˈməuʃən] *n* (*movement, gesture*) движе́ние; (*proposal*) предложе́ние; **motionless** *adj* неподви́жный

motivation [məutɪˈveɪʃən] *n* (*drive*) целеустремлённость *f*

motive [ˈməutɪv] *n* моти́в, побужде́ние

motor [ˈməutəᵊ] *n* мото́р ▷ *cpd* (*trade*) автомоби́льный; **motorbike** *n* мотоци́кл; **motorcycle** *n* мотоци́кл; **motorist** *n* автомобили́ст; **motorway** *n* (*Brit*) автомагистра́ль *f*, автостра́да

motto [ˈmɔtəu] (*pl* **mottoes**) *n* деви́з

mould [məuld] (*US* **mold**) *n* (*cast*) фо́рма; (*mildew*) пле́сень *f* ▷ *vt* (*substance*) лепи́ть (*perf* вы́лепить); (*fig: opinion, character*) формирова́ть (*perf* сформирова́ть); **mouldy** *adj* (*food*) заплесневе́лый

mound [maund] *n* (*heap*) ку́ча

mount [maunt] *vt* (*horse*) сади́ться (*perf* сесть) на +*acc*; (*display*) устра́ивать (*perf* устро́ить); (*jewel*) оправля́ть (*perf* опра́вить); (*picture*) обрамля́ть (*perf* обрами́ть); (*stair*) всходи́ть (*perf* взойти́) по +*dat* ▷ *vi* (*increase*) расти́ (*impf*) ▷ *n*: **Mount Ararat** гора́ Арара́т; **mount up** *vi* нака́пливаться (*perf* накопи́ться)

mountain [ˈmauntɪn] *n* гора́ ▷ *cpd* го́рный; **mountain bike** *n* велосипе́д, для езды́ по пересечённой ме́стности; **mountainous** *adj* го́рный, гори́стый

mourn [mɔːn] *vt* (*death*) опла́кивать (*impf*) ▷ *vi*: **to mourn** скорбе́ть (*impf*) по +*dat* или о +*prp*; **mourning** *n* тра́ур; **in mourning** в тра́уре

mouse [maus] (*pl* **mice**) *n* (*also Comput*)

мышь f; **mouse mat** n ко́врик для
мы́ши; **mouse pad** n = **mouse mat**
moustache [məsˈtɑːʃ] (US **mustache**) n
усы́ mpl
mouth [mauθ] n рот; (of cave, hole) вход;
(of river) у́стье; **mouthful** n (of food)
кусо́чек; (of drink) глото́к; **mouth organ**
n губна́я гармо́шка; **mouthpiece** n
(Mus) мундшту́к; (Tel) микрофо́н
move [muːv] n (movement) движе́ние; (in
game) ход; (of house) перее́зд; (of job)
перехо́д ▷ vt передвига́ть (perf
передви́нуть); (piece: in game) ходи́ть
(perf пойти́) +instr; (arm etc) дви́гать (perf
дви́нуть) +instr; (person: emotionally)
тро́гать (perf тро́нуть), растро́гать (perf)
▷ vi дви́гаться (perf дви́нуться); (things)
дви́гаться (impf); (also **move house**)
переезжа́ть (perf перее́хать); **get a move
on!** поторопли́вайтесь!; **move about** vi
(change position) передвига́ться (perf
передви́нуться), перемеща́ться (perf
перемести́ться); (travel) переезжа́ть
(impf) с ме́ста на ме́сто; **move around** vi
= **move about**; **move away** vi: to move
away (from) (leave) уезжа́ть (perf уе́хать)
(из +gen); (step away) отходи́ть (perf
отойти́) (от +gen); **move in** vi (police,
soldiers) входи́ть (perf войти́); **to move
in(to)** (house) въезжа́ть (perf въе́хать) (в
+acc); **move out** vi (of house) выезжа́ть
(perf вы́ехать); **move over** vi (to make
room) подвига́ться (perf подви́нуться);
move up vi (be promoted) продвига́ться
(perf продви́нуться) по слу́жбе;
movement n движе́ние; (between fixed
points) передвиже́ние; (in attitude, policy)
сдвиг
movie [ˈmuːvɪ] n (кино)фи́льм; **to go to
the movies** ходи́ть/идти́ (perf пойти́) в
кино́
moving [ˈmuːvɪŋ] adj (emotional)
тро́гательный; (mobile) подви́жный
mow [məu] (pt **mowed**, pp **mowed** or
mown) vt (grass) подстрига́ть (perf
подстри́чь)
MP n abbr = **Member of Parliament**
MP3 abbr MP3; **MP3 player** n
MP3-пле́ер m
mph abbr = **miles per hour**
Mr [ˈmɪstə*] n: **Mr Smith** (informal) ми́стер
Смит; (formal) г-н Смит (= господи́н Смит)
Mrs [ˈmɪsɪz] n: **Mrs Smith** (informal)
ми́ссис Смит; (formal) г-жа Смит
(= госпожа́ Смит)
Ms [mɪz] n = **Miss; Mrs**

• **Ms**
•
• Да́нное сокраще́ние употребля́ется
• гла́вным о́бразом в пи́сьменном языке́
• и заменя́ет **Miss** и **Mrs**. Употребля́я его́,
• вы не ука́зываете, за́мужем же́нщина
• и́ли нет.

MSP n abbr (= Member of the Scottish
Parliament) член шотла́ндского
парла́мента

◯ **KEYWORD**

much [mʌtʃ] adj мно́го +gen; **we haven't
got much time** у нас не так мно́го
вре́мени; **how much** ско́лько +gen; **how
much money do you need?** ско́лько де́нег
Вам ну́жно?; **he's spent so much money
today** он сего́дня потра́тил так мно́го
де́нег; **I have as much money as you (do)** у
меня́ сто́лько же де́нег, ско́лько у Вас;
I don't have as much time as you (do) у
меня́ нет сто́лько вре́мени, ско́лько у Вас
▷ pron мно́го, мно́гое; **much is still
unclear** мно́гое ещё нея́сно; **there isn't
much to do here** здесь не́чего де́лать;
how much does it cost? — too much
ско́лько э́то сто́ит? — сли́шком до́рого;
how much is it? ско́лько э́то сто́ит?, почём
э́то? (разг)
▷ adv **1** (greatly, a great deal) о́чень;
thank you very much большо́е спаси́бо;
**we are very much looking forward to your
visit** мы о́чень ждём Ва́шего прие́зда; **he
is very much a gentleman** он настоя́щий
джентльме́н; **however much he tries**
ско́лько бы он ни стара́лся; **I try to help as
much as possible** or **as I can** я стара́юсь
помога́ть как мо́жно бо́льше or ско́лько
могу́; **I read as much as ever** я чита́ю
сто́лько же, ско́лько пре́жде; **he is as
much a member of the family as you** он
тако́й же член семьи́, как и Вы
2 (by far) намно́го, гора́здо; **I'm much
better now** мне сейча́с намно́го or
гора́здо лу́чше; **it's much the biggest
publishing company in Europe** э́то са́мое
кру́пное изда́тельство в Евро́пе
3 (almost) почти́; **the view today is much
as it was 10 years ago** вид сего́дня почти́
тако́й же, как и 10 лет наза́д; **how are you
feeling? — much the same** как Вы себя́
чу́вствуете? — всё так же

muck [mʌk] n (dirt) грязь f
mud [mʌd] n грязь f
muddle [ˈmʌdl] n (mix-up) пу́таница,
неразбери́ха; (mess) беспоря́док ▷ vt
(also **muddle up**: person) запу́тывать
(perf запу́тать); (: things) переме́шивать
(perf перемеша́ть)
muddy [ˈmʌdɪ] adj гря́зный
muffled [ˈmʌfld] adj приглушённый
mug [mʌg] n кру́жка; (inf: face) мо́рда;
(: fool) ду́рень m ▷ vt гра́бить (perf
огра́бить) (на у́лице)
mule [mjuːl] n (Zool) мул
multinational [mʌltɪˈnæʃənl] adj
междунаро́дный
multiple [ˈmʌltɪpl] adj (injuries)
многочи́сленный ▷ n (Math) кра́тное

число; **multiple collision** столкновéние нéскольких автомобилей; **multiple sclerosis** n рассéянный склерóз

multiplication [mʌltɪplɪˈkeɪʃən] n умножéние

multiply [ˈmʌltɪplaɪ] vt умножáть (perf умнóжить) ▷ vi размножáться (perf размнóжиться)

multistorey [ˈmʌltɪˈstɔːrɪ] adj (Brit) многоэтáжный

mum [mʌm] (Brit: inf) n мáма ▷ adj: **to keep mum about sth** помáлкивать (impf) о чём-н

mumble [ˈmʌmbl] vt бормотáть (perf проборомотáть) ▷ vi бормотáть (impf)

mummy [ˈmʌmɪ] n (Brit: inf) мамýля, мáма; (corpse) мýмия

mumps [mʌmps] n свинка

munch [mʌntʃ] vt, vi жевáть (impf)

municipal [mjuːˈnɪsɪpl] adj муниципáльный

mural [ˈmjuərl] n фрéска, настéнная рóспись f

murder [ˈməːdə] n убийство (умышленное) ▷ vt убивáть (perf убить) (умышленно); **murderer** n убийца m/f

murky [ˈməːkɪ] adj (street, night) мрáчный; (water) мýтный

murmur [ˈməːmə] n (of voices, waves) рóпот ▷ vt, vi шептáть (impf)

muscle [ˈmʌsl] n мышца, мýскул

muscular [ˈmʌskjulə] adj (pain, injury) мышечный; (person) мýскулистый

museum [mjuːˈzɪəm] n музéй

mushroom [ˈmʌʃrum] n гриб

music [ˈmjuːzɪk] n мýзыка; **musical** adj музыкáльный; (sound, tune) мелодичный ▷ n мюзикл; **musician** [mjuːˈzɪʃən] n музыкáнт

Muslim [ˈmʌzlɪm] n мусульмáнин(-нка) ▷ adj мусульмáнский

mussel [ˈmʌsl] n мидия

must [mʌst] n (need) необходимость f ▷ aux vb (necessity): **I must go** мне нáдо or нýжно идти; (obligation): **I must do it** я дóлжен это сдéлать; (probability): **he must be there by now** он дóлжен ужé быть там; **you must come and see me soon** Вы обязáтельно должны скóро ко мне зайти; **why must he behave so badly?** отчегó он так плóхо себя ведёт?

mustache [ˈmʌstæʃ] n (US) = **moustache**

mustard [ˈmʌstəd] n горчица

mustn't [ˈmʌsnt] = **must not**

mute [mjuːt] adj (silent) безмóлвный

mutilate [ˈmjuːtɪleɪt] vt (person) увéчить (perf изувéчить); (thing) урóдовать (perf изурóдовать)

mutiny [ˈmjuːtɪnɪ] n мятéж, бунт

mutter [ˈmʌtə] vt, vi бормотáть (impf)

mutton [ˈmʌtn] n барáнина

mutual [ˈmjuːtʃuəl] adj (feeling, help) взаимный; (friend, interest) óбщий;

mutual understanding взаимопонимáние

muzzle [ˈmʌzl] n (of dog) мóрда; (of gun) дýло; (for dog) намóрдник ▷ vt (dog) надевáть (perf надéть) намóрдник на +acc

 KEYWORD

my [maɪ] adj **1** мой; (referring back to subject of sentence) свой; **this is my house/car** это мой дом/моя машина; **is this my pen or yours?** это моя рýчка или Вáша?; **I've lost my key** я потерял свой ключ
2 (with parts of the body etc): **I've washed my hair/cut my finger** я помыл гóлову/порéзал пáлец

KEYWORD

myself [maɪˈsɛlf] pron **1** (reflexive): **I've hurt myself** я ушибся; **I consider myself clever** я считáю себя ýмным; **I am ashamed of myself** мне стыдно за моё поведéние
2 (complement): **she's the same age as myself** онá одногó вóзраста со мной
3 (after prep: +gen) себя; (: +dat, +prp) себé; (: +instr) собóй; **I wanted to keep the book for myself** я хотéл остáвить книгу себé; **I sometimes talk to myself** иногдá я сам с собóй разговáриваю; **(all) by myself** (alone) сам; **I made it all by myself** я всё это сдéлал сам
4 (emphatic) сам; **I myself chose the flowers** я сам выбирáл цветы

mysterious [mɪsˈtɪərɪəs] adj таинственный

mystery [ˈmɪstərɪ] n (puzzle) загáдка

mystical [ˈmɪstɪkl] adj мистический

myth [mɪθ] n миф; **mythology** [mɪˈθɔlədʒɪ] n мифолóгия

n

n/a abbr (= not applicable) не применяется

nag [næg] vt (scold) пилить (impf)

nail [neɪl] n ноготь m; (Tech) гвоздь m
▷ vt: **to nail sth to** прибивать (perf
прибить) что-н к +dat; **nail polish** n лак
для ногтей

naive [naɪˈiːv] adj наивный

naked [ˈneɪkɪd] adj голый

name [neɪm] n (of person) имя nt; (of
place, object) название; (of pet) кличка
▷ vt называть (perf назвать); **what's your
name?** как Вас зовут?; **my name is Peter**
меня зовут Питер; **what's the name of this
place?** как называется это место?; **by
name** по имени; **in the name of** (for the
sake of) во имя +gen; (representing) от
имени +gen; **namely** adv а именно

nanny [ˈnænɪ] n няня

nap [næp] n (sleep) короткий сон

napkin [ˈnæpkɪn] n (also **table napkin**)
салфетка

nappy [ˈnæpɪ] n (Brit) подгузник

narrative [ˈnærətɪv] n история, повесть f

narrator [nəˈreɪtəʳ] n (in book)
рассказчик(-ица); (in film) диктор

narrow [ˈnærəu] adj узкий; (majority,
advantage) незначительный ▷ vi (road)
сужаться (perf сузиться); (gap, difference)
уменьшаться (perf уменьшиться) ▷ vt: **to
narrow sth down to** сводить (perf свести)
что-н к +dat; **to have a narrow escape** едва
спастись (perf)

nasal [ˈneɪzl] adj (voice) гнусавый

nasty [ˈnɑːstɪ] adj (unpleasant)
противный; (malicious) злобный;
(situation, wound) скверный

nation [ˈneɪʃən] n народ; (state) страна;
(native population) нация

national [ˈnæʃənl] adj национальный;
National Health Service n (Brit)
государственная служба
здравоохранения; **National Insurance**
n (Brit) государственное страхование;
nationalist adj националистический;
nationality [næʃəˈnælɪtɪ] n (status)
гражданство; (ethnic group) народность f

nationwide [ˈneɪʃənwaɪd] adj
общенародный ▷ adv по всей стране

native [ˈneɪtɪv] n (local inhabitant)
местный(-ая) житель(ница) m(f) ▷ adj
(indigenous) коренной, исконный; (of
one's birth) родной; (innate) врождённый;
a native of Russia уроженец(-нка) России;
a native speaker of Russian
носитель(ница) m(f) русского языка

NATO [ˈneɪtəu] n abbr (= North Atlantic
Treaty Organization) НАТО

natural [ˈnætʃrəl] adj (behaviour)
естественный; (aptitude, materials)
природный; (disaster) стихийный;
naturally adv естественно; (innately) от
природы; (in nature) естественным
образом; **naturally, I refused** естественно,
я отказался

nature [ˈneɪtʃəʳ] n (also **Nature**) природа;
(character) натура; (sort) характер; **by
nature** (person) по натуре; (event, thing)
по природе

naughty [ˈnɔːtɪ] adj (child)
непослушный, озорной

nausea [ˈnɔːsɪə] n тошнота

naval [ˈneɪvl] adj военно-морской

navel [ˈneɪvl] n пупок

navigate [ˈnævɪgeɪt] vt (Naut, Aviat)
управлять (impf) +instr ▷ vi определять
(perf определить) маршрут

navigation [nævɪˈgeɪʃən] n (science)
навигация; (action): **navigation (of)**
управление (+instr)

navy [ˈneɪvɪ] n военно-морской флот;
navy(-blue) adj тёмно-синий

Nazi [ˈnɑːtsɪ] n нацист(ка)

NB abbr (note well) (= nota bene) нотабене

near [nɪəʳ] adj близкий ▷ adv близко
▷ prep (also **near to**: space) возле +gen,
около +gen; (: time) к +dat, около +gen;
nearby adj близлежащий ▷ adv
поблизости; **nearly** adv почти; **I nearly
fell** я чуть (было) не упал

neat [niːt] adj (person, place) опрятный;
(work) аккуратный; (clear: categories)
чёткий; (esp US: inf) классный; **neatly**
adv (dress) опрятно; (work) аккуратно;
(sum up) чётко

necessarily [ˈnɛsɪsrɪlɪ] adv неизбежно

necessary [ˈnɛsɪsrɪ] adj неоходимый;
(inevitable) обязательный, неизбежный;
it's not necessary это не обязательно; **it is
necessary to/that ...** необходимо +infin/
чтобы ...

necessity [nɪˈsɛsɪtɪ] n необходимость f;
necessities npl (essentials) предметы
mpl первой необходимости

neck [nɛk] n (Anat) шея; (of garment)
ворот; (of bottle) горлышко; **necklace**
[ˈnɛklɪs] n ожерелье

need [niːd] n потре́бность f; (deprivation) нужда́; (necessity): **need (for)** нужда́ (в +prp) ▷ vt: **I need time/money** мне ну́жно вре́мя/нужны́ де́ньги; **there's no need to worry** не́зачем волнова́ться; **I need to see him** мне на́до or ну́жно с ним уви́деться; **you don't need to leave yet** Вам ещё не пора́ уходи́ть

needle [niːdl] n игла́, иго́лка; (for knitting) спи́ца ▷ vt (fig: inf) подка́лывать (perf подколо́ть)

needless [niːdlɪs] adj изли́шний; **needless to say** само́ собо́й разуме́ется

needn't [niːdnt] = **need not**

needy [niːdɪ] adj нужда́ющийся

negative [nɛgətɪv] adj (also Elec) отрица́тельный ▷ n (Phot) негати́в

neglect [nɪˈglɛkt] vt (child, work) забра́сывать (perf забро́сить); (garden, health) запуска́ть (perf запусти́ть); (duty) пренебрега́ть (perf пренебре́чь) ▷ n: **neglect (of)** невнима́ние (к +dat); **in a state of neglect** в запусте́нии

negotiate [nɪˈgəʊʃɪeɪt] vt (treaty, deal) заключа́ть (perf заключи́ть); (obstacle) преодолева́ть (perf преодоле́ть); (corner) огиба́ть (perf обогну́ть) ▷ vi: **to negotiate (with sb for sth)** вести́ (impf) перегово́ры (с кем-н о чём-н)

negotiation [nɪgəʊʃɪˈeɪʃən] n (of treaty, deal) заключе́ние; (of obstacle) преодоле́ние; **negotiations** перегово́ры mpl

negotiator [nɪˈgəʊʃɪeɪtəʳ] n уча́стник перегово́ров

neighbour [ˈneɪbəʳ] (US **neighbor**) n сосе́д(ка); **neighbourhood** n (place) райо́н; (people) сосе́ди mpl; **neighbouring** adj сосе́дний

neither [ˈnaɪðəʳ] adj ни тот, ни друго́й ▷ conj: **I didn't move and neither did John** ни я, ни Джон не дви́нулись с ме́ста ▷ pron: **neither of them came** ни тот ни друго́й не пришёл, ни оди́н из них не пришёл; **neither version is true** ни та ни друга́я ве́рсия не верна́; **neither ... nor ...** ни ..., ни ...; **neither good nor bad** ни хорошо́, ни пло́хо

neon [ˈniːɔn] n нео́н

nephew [ˈnɛvjuː] n племя́нник

nerve [nəːv] n (Anat) нерв; (courage) вы́держка; (impudence) на́глость f

nervous [ˈnəːvəs] adj не́рвный; **to be** or **feel nervous** не́рвничать (impf); **nervous breakdown** n не́рвный срыв

nest [nɛst] n гнездо́

net [nɛt] n (also fig) сеть f; (Sport) се́тка; (Comput): **the Net** Сеть f ▷ adj (Comm) чи́стый ▷ vt (fish) лови́ть (perf пойма́ть) в сеть; (profit) приноси́ть (perf принести́)

Netherlands [ˈnɛðələndz] npl: **the Netherlands** Нидерла́нды pl

nett [nɛt] adj = **net**

nettle [ˈnɛtl] n крапи́ва

network [ˈnɛtwəːk] n сеть f

neurotic [njuəˈrɔtɪk] adj неврастени́чный

neutral [ˈnjuːtrəl] adj нейтра́льный ▷ n (Aut) холосто́й ход

never [ˈnɛvəʳ] adv никогда́; **never in my life** никогда́ в жи́зни; **nevertheless** adv тем не ме́нее

new [njuː] adj (brand new) но́вый; (recent) неда́вний; **newborn** adj новорождённый; **newcomer** n новичо́к; **newly** adv неда́вно

news [njuːz] n (good, bad) но́вость f, изве́стие; **a piece of news** но́вость f; **the news** (Radio, TV) но́вости fpl; **news agency** n информацио́нное аге́нтство; **newsletter** n информацио́нный бюллете́нь m; **newsreader** n ди́ктор (програ́ммы новосте́й)

New Year n Но́вый год; **Happy New Year!** С Но́вым го́дом!; **New Year's Day** n пе́рвое января́; **New Year's Eve** n кану́н Но́вого го́да

New Zealand [njuːˈziːlənd] n Но́вая Зела́ндия

next [nɛkst] adj сле́дующий; (adjacent) сосе́дний ▷ adv пото́м, да́лее ▷ prep: **next to** ря́дом с +instr, во́зле +gen; **next time** в сле́дующий раз; **the next day** на сле́дующий день; **next year** в бу́дущем or сле́дующем году́; **in the next 15 minutes** в ближа́йшие 15 мину́т; **next to nothing** почти́ ничего́; **next please!** сле́дующий, пожа́луйста!; **next door** adv по сосе́дству, ря́дом ▷ adj (neighbour) ближа́йший; **next of kin** n ближа́йший ро́дственник

NHS n abbr (Brit) = **National Health Service**

nibble [ˈnɪbl] vt надку́сывать (perf надкуси́ть)

nice [naɪs] adj прия́тный, хоро́ший; (attractive) симпати́чный; **to look nice** хорошо́ вы́глядеть (impf); **that's very nice of you** о́чень ми́ло с Ва́шей стороны́

nick [nɪk] n (in skin) поре́з; (in surface) зару́бка ▷ vt (inf: steal) ута́скивать (perf утащи́ть); **in the nick of time** как раз во́время

nickel [ˈnɪkl] n ни́кель m; (US: coin) моне́та в 5 це́нтов

nickname [ˈnɪkneɪm] n кли́чка, про́звище ▷ vt прозыва́ть (perf прозва́ть)

nicotine [ˈnɪkətiːn] n никоти́н

niece [niːs] n племя́нница

night [naɪt] n ночь f; (evening) ве́чер; **at night, by night** но́чью; **all night long** ночь напролёт; **in** or **during the night** но́чью; **last night** вчера́ но́чью; (evening) вчера́ ве́чером; **the night before last** позапро́шлой но́чью; (evening) позавчера́ ве́чером; **nightdress** n ночна́я руба́шка

nightlife [ˈnaɪtlaɪf] n ночна́я жизнь f

nightly ['naɪtlɪ] *adj* (*every night*)
ежено́щный ⊳ *adv* ежено́щно
nightmare ['naɪtmeər] *n* кошма́р
nil [nɪl] *n* нуль *m*; (*Brit: score*) ноль *m*
nine [naɪn] *n* де́вять; **nineteen** *n*
девятна́дцать; **nineteenth** *adj*
девятна́дцатый; **ninetieth** *adj*
девяно́стый; **ninety** *n* девяно́сто; **ninth**
[naɪnθ] *adj* девя́тый
nip [nɪp] *vt* (*pinch*) щипа́ть (*perf*
ущипну́ть); (*bite*) куса́ть (*perf* укуси́ть)
⊳ *vi* (*Brit: inf*): **to nip out** выска́кивать
(*perf* вы́скочить)
nipple ['nɪpl] *n* (*Anat*) сосо́к
nitrogen ['naɪtrədʒən] *n* азо́т

⊙ **KEYWORD**

no [nəu] (*pl* **noes**) *adv* (*opposite of "yes"*)
нет; **are you coming? — no (I'm not)** Вы
придёте? — нет(, не приду́); **no thank you**
нет, спаси́бо
⊳ *adj* (*not any*): **I have no money/books** у
меня́ нет де́нег/книг; **it is of no importance
at all** э́то не име́ет никако́го значе́ния; **no
system is totally fair** никака́я систе́ма не
явля́ется по́лностью справедли́вой; **"no
entry"** "вход воспрещён"; **"no smoking"**
"не кури́ть"
⊳ *n*: **there were twenty noes** два́дцать
голосо́в бы́ло "про́тив"

nobility [nəu'bɪlɪtɪ] *n* (*class*) знать *f*,
дворя́нство
noble ['nəubl] *adj* (*aristocratic*)
дворя́нский, зна́тный; (*high-minded*)
благоро́дный
nobody ['nəubədɪ] *pron* никто́; **there is
nobody here** здесь никого́ нет
nod [nɔd] *vi* кива́ть (*impf*) ⊳ *n* киво́к
⊳ *vt*: **to nod one's head** кива́ть (*perf*
кивну́ть) голово́й; **nod off** *vi* задрема́ть
(*perf*)
noise [nɔɪz] *n* шум
noisy ['nɔɪzɪ] *adj* шу́мный
nominal ['nɔmɪnl] *adj* номина́льный
nominate ['nɔmɪneɪt] *vt* (*propose*): **to
nominate sb (for)** выставля́ть (*perf*
вы́ставить) кандидату́ру кого́-н (на +*acc*);
(*appoint*): **to nominate sb (to/as)**
назнача́ть (*perf* назна́чить) кого́-н (на
+*acc*/+*instr*)
nomination [nɔmɪ'neɪʃən] *n* (*see vb*)
выставле́ние; назначе́ние
nominee [nɔmɪ'niː] *n* кандида́т
non- [nɔn] *prefix* не-
none [nʌn] *pron* (*person*) никто́, ни оди́н;
(*thing: countable*) ничто́, ни оди́н;
(: *uncountable*) ничего́; **none of you** никто́
or ни оди́н из вас; **I've none left** у меня́
ничего́ не оста́лось
nonetheless ['nʌnðə'lɛs] *adv* тем не
ме́нее, всё же
nonfiction [nɔn'fɪkʃən] *n*

документа́льная литерату́ра
nonsense ['nɔnsəns] *n* ерунда́, чепуха́
non-smoker [nɔn'sməukər] *adj*
некуря́щий *m adj*
noodles ['nuːdlz] *npl* вермише́ль *fsg*
noon [nuːn] *n* по́лдень *m*
no-one ['nəuwʌn] *pron* = **nobody**
nor [nɔːr] *conj* = **neither** ⊳ *adv see*
neither
norm [nɔːm] *n* но́рма
normal ['nɔːml] *adj* норма́льный;
normally *adv* (*usually*) обы́чно;
(*properly*) норма́льно
north [nɔːθ] *n* се́вер ⊳ *adj* се́верный
⊳ *adv* (*go*) на се́вер; (*be*) к се́веру; **North
Africa** *n* Се́верная А́фрика; **North
America** *n* Се́верная Аме́рика;
northeast *n* се́веро-восто́к; **northern**
['nɔːðən] *adj* се́верный; **Northern
Ireland** *n* Се́верная Ирла́ндия; **North
Pole** *n* Се́верный по́люс; **North Sea** *n*
Се́верное мо́ре; **northwest** *n*
се́веро-за́пад
Norway ['nɔːweɪ] *n* Норве́гия
Norwegian [nɔː'wiːdʒən] *adj*
норве́жский
nose [nəuz] *n* нос; (*sense of smell*) нюх,
чутьё; **nosebleed** *n* носово́е
кровотече́ние; **nosey** ['nəuzɪ] *adj* (*inf*)
= **nosy**
nostalgia [nɔs'tældʒɪə] *n* ностальги́я
nostalgic [nɔs'tældʒɪk] *adj* (*memory,
film*) ностальги́ческий; **to be nostalgic (for)**
испы́тывать (*impf*) ностальги́ю (по +*dat*),
тоскова́ть (*impf*) по +*dat*
nostril ['nɔstrɪl] *n* ноздря́
nosy ['nəuzɪ] *adj* (*inf*): **to be nosy** сова́ть
(*impf*) нос в чужи́е дела́
not [nɔt] *adv* нет; (*before verbs*) не; **he is
not** *or* **isn't at home** его́ нет до́ма; **he
asked me not to do it** он попроси́л меня́
не де́лать э́того; **you must not** *or* **you
mustn't do that** (*forbidden*) э́того нельзя́
де́лать; **it's too late, isn't it?** уже́ сли́шком
по́здно, не пра́вда ли?; **not that ...** не то,
что́бы ...; **not yet** нет ещё, ещё нет; **not
now** не сейча́с; *see also* **all**; **only**
notably ['nəutəblɪ] *adv* (*particularly*)
осо́бенно; (*markedly*) заме́тно
notch [nɔtʃ] *n* насе́чка
note [nəut] *n* (*record*) за́пись *f*; (*letter*)
запи́ска; (*also* **footnote**) сно́ска; (*also*
banknote) банкно́та; (*Mus*) но́та; (*tone*)
тон ⊳ *vt* (*observe*) замеча́ть (*perf*
заме́тить); (*also* **note down**) запи́сывать
(*perf* записа́ть); **notebook** *n* записна́я
кни́жка; **noted** *adj* изве́стный; **notepad**
n блокно́т; **notepaper** *n* пи́счая бума́га
nothing ['nʌθɪŋ] *n* ничто́; (*zero*) ноль *m*;
he does nothing он ничего́ не де́лает;
there is nothing to do/be said де́лать/
сказа́ть не́чего; **nothing new/much/of the
sort** ничего́ но́вого/осо́бенного/
подо́бного; **for nothing** да́ром

notice ['nəutɪs] n (announcement)
объявле́ние; (warning) предупрежде́ние
▷ vt замеча́ть (perf заме́тить); **to take
notice of** обраща́ть (perf обрати́ть)
внима́ние на +acc; **at short notice** без
предупрежде́ния; **until further notice**
впредь до дальне́йшего уведомле́ния;
noticeable adj заме́тный; **notice board**
n доска́ объявле́ний
notification [nəutɪfɪ'keɪʃən] n
уведомле́ние
notify ['nəutɪfaɪ] vt: **to notify sb (of sth)**
уведомля́ть (perf уве́домить) кого́-н (о
чём-н)
notion ['nəuʃən] n (idea) поня́тие;
(opinion) представле́ние
notorious [nəu'tɔːrɪəs] adj печа́льно
изве́стный
noun [naun] n (и́мя nt) существи́тельное
nt adj
nourish ['nʌrɪʃ] vt пита́ть (impf); (fig)
взра́щивать (perf взрасти́ть);
nourishment n (food) пита́ние
novel ['nɔvl] n рома́н ▷ adj
оригина́льный; **novelist** n романи́ст(ка);
novelty n (newness) новизна́; (object)
нови́нка
November [nəu'vɛmbəʳ] n ноя́брь m
novice ['nɔvɪs] n (in job) новичо́к
now [nau] adv тепе́рь, сейча́с ▷ conj:
now (that) ... тепе́рь, когда́ ...; **right now**
пря́мо сейча́с; **by now** к настоя́щему
вре́мени; **now and then** or **again** вре́мя от
вре́мени; **from now on** отны́не, впредь;
until now до сих пор; **nowadays** adv в
на́ши дни
nowhere ['nəuwɛəʳ] adv (be) нигде́; (go)
никуда́
nuclear ['njuːklɪəʳ] adj я́дерный
nucleus ['njuːklɪəs] n (pl **nuclei**) n ядро́
nude [njuːd] adj обнажённый, наго́й ▷ n:
in the nude в обнажённом ви́де
nudge [nʌdʒ] vt подта́лкивать (perf
подтолкну́ть)
nuisance ['njuːsns] n доса́да; (person)
зану́да; **what a nuisance!** кака́я доса́да!
numb [nʌm] adj онеме́вший; **to go numb**
неме́ть (perf онеме́ть)
number ['nʌmbəʳ] n но́мер; (Math)
число́; (written figure) ци́фра; (quantity)
коли́чество ▷ vt (pages etc) нумерова́ть
(perf пронумерова́ть); (amount to)
насчи́тывать (impf); **a number of**
не́сколько +gen, ряд +gen; **numberplate**
n (Brit) номерно́й знак
numerical [njuː'mɛrɪkl] adj (value)
числово́й; **in numerical order** по номера́м
numerous ['njuːmərəs] adj
многочи́сленный; **on numerous occasions**
многокра́тно
nun [nʌn] n мона́хиня
nurse [nəːs] n медсестра́; (also **male
nurse**) медбра́т ▷ vt (patient) уха́живать
(impf) за +instr

nursery ['nəːsərɪ] n (institution) я́сли pl;
(room) де́тская f adj; (for plants) пито́мник;
nursery rhyme n де́тская пе́сенка;
nursery school n де́тский сад
nursing ['nəːsɪŋ] n (profession)
профе́ссия медсестры́; **nursing home** n
ча́стный дом для престаре́лых
nurture ['nəːtʃəʳ] vt (child, plant)
выра́щивать (perf вы́растить)
nut [nʌt] n (Bot) оре́х; (Tech) га́йка;
nutmeg n муска́тный оре́х
nutrient ['njuːtrɪənt] n пита́тельное
вещество́
nutrition [njuː'trɪʃən] n (nourishment)
пита́тельность f; (diet) пита́ние
nutritious [njuː'trɪʃəs] adj пита́тельный
nylon ['naɪlɔn] n нейло́н ▷ adj
нейло́новый

oak [əuk] *n* дуб ▷ *adj* дубо́вый

OAP *n abbr* (*Brit*) = **old age pensioner**

oar [ɔːʳ] *n* весло́

oasis [əu'eɪsɪs] (*pl* **oases**) *n* оа́зис

oath [əuθ] *n* (*promise*) кля́тва; (: *Law*)
прися́га; (*swear word*) прокля́тие; **on**
(*Brit*) *or* **under oath** под прися́гой

oats [əuts] *npl* овёс *msg*

obedience [ə'biːdɪəns] *n* повинове́ние,
послуша́ние

obedient [ə'biːdɪənt] *adj* послу́шный

obese [əu'biːs] *adj* ту́чный

obey [ə'beɪ] *vt* подчиня́ться (*perf*
подчини́ться) +*dat*, повинова́ться (*impf/
perf*) +*dat*

obituary [ə'bɪtjuərɪ] *n* некроло́г

object [*n* 'ɔbdʒɪkt, *vb* əb'dʒɛkt] *n* (*thing*)
предме́т; (*aim, purpose*) цель *f*; (*of
affection, desires*) объе́кт; (*Ling*)
дополне́ние ▷ *vi*: **to object (to)**
возража́ть (*perf* возрази́ть) (про́тив +*gen*);
money is no object де́ньги — не
пробле́ма; **objection** [əb'dʒɛkʃən] *n*
возраже́ние; **I have no objection to ...** я не
име́ю никаки́х возраже́ний про́тив +*gen*
...; **objective** [əb'dʒɛktɪv] *adj*
объекти́вный ▷ *n* цель *f*

obligation [ɔblɪ'geɪʃən] *n* обяза́тельство

obligatory [ə'blɪgətərɪ] *adj*
обяза́тельный

oblige [ə'blaɪdʒ] *vt* обя́зывать (*perf*
обяза́ть); (*force*): **to oblige sb to do**
обя́зывать (*perf* обяза́ть) кого́-н +*infin*; **I'm
much obliged to you for your help**
(*grateful*) я о́чень обя́зан Вам за Ва́шу
по́мощь

oblivious [ə'blɪvɪəs] *adj*: **to be oblivious
of** *or* **to** не сознава́ть (*impf*) +*gen*

obnoxious [əb'nɔkʃəs] *adj*
отврати́тельный

oboe ['əubəu] *n* гобо́й

obscene [əb'siːn] *adj* непристо́йный

obscure [əb'skjuəʳ] *adj* (*little known*)
непримётный; (*incomprehensible*)
сму́тный ▷ *vt* (*view etc*) загора́живать
(*perf* загороди́ть); (*truth etc*) затемня́ть
(*perf* затемни́ть)

observant [əb'zəːvnt] *adj*
наблюда́тельный

observation [ɔbzə'veɪʃən] *n*
наблюде́ние; (*remark*) замеча́ние

observe [əb'zəːv] *vt* (*watch*) наблюда́ть
(*impf*) за +*instr*; (*comment*) замеча́ть (*perf*
заме́тить); (*abide by*) соблюда́ть (*perf*
соблюсти́); **observer** *n* наблюда́тель *m*

obsession [əb'sɛʃən] *n* страсть *f*,
одержи́мость *f*

obsessive [əb'sɛsɪv] *adj* стра́стный,
одержи́мый

obsolete ['ɔbsəliːt] *adj* устаре́вший

obstacle ['ɔbstəkl] *n* препя́тствие

obstinate ['ɔbstɪnɪt] *adj* упря́мый

obstruct [əb'strʌkt] *vt* (*road, path*)
загора́живать (*perf* загороди́ть); (*traffic,
progress*) препя́тствовать (*perf*
воспрепя́тствовать) +*dat*; **obstruction**
[əb'strʌkʃən] *n* (*of law*) обстру́кция;
(*object*) препя́тствие

obtain [əb'teɪn] *vt* приобрета́ть (*perf*
приобрести́)

obvious ['ɔbvɪəs] *adj* очеви́дный;
obviously *adv* очеви́дно; (*of course*)
разуме́ется; **obviously not** разуме́ется, нет

occasion [ə'keɪʒən] *n* (*time*) раз; (*case,
opportunity*) слу́чай; (*event*) собы́тие;
occasional *adj* ре́дкий, нечастый;
occasionally *adv* и́зредка

occupant ['ɔkjupənt] *n* (*long-term*)
обита́тель(ница) *m(f)*

occupation [ɔkju'peɪʃən] *n* заня́тие;
(*Mil*) оккупа́ция

occupy ['ɔkjupaɪ] *vt* занима́ть (*perf*
заня́ть); (*country, attention*) захва́тывать
(*perf* захвати́ть); **to occupy o.s. with sth**
занима́ться (*perf* заня́ться) чем-н

occur [ə'kəːʳ] *vi* происходи́ть (*perf*
произойти́), случа́ться (*perf* случи́ться);
(*exist*) встреча́ться (*perf* встре́титься); **to
occur to sb** приходи́ть (*perf* прийти́)
кому́-н в го́лову; **occurrence** *n* (*event*)
происше́ствие

ocean ['əuʃən] *n* океа́н

o'clock [ə'klɔk] *adv*: **it is five o'clock**
сейча́с пять часо́в

October [ɔk'təubəʳ] *n* октя́брь *m*

octopus ['ɔktəpəs] *n* осьмино́г

odd [ɔd] *adj* (*strange*) стра́нный,
необы́чный; (*uneven*) нечётный; (*not
paired*) непа́рный; **60-odd** шестьдеся́т с
ли́шним; **at odd times** времена́ми; **I was
the odd one out** я был ли́шний; **oddly**
adv (*behave, dress*) стра́нно; **see also
enough**; **odds** *npl* (*in betting*) ста́вки *fpl*;
to be at odds (with) быть (*impf*) не в
лада́х (с +*instr*)

odour ['əudəʳ] (*US* **odor**) *n* за́пах

KEYWORD

of [ɔv, əv] *prep* **1** (*expressing belonging*): **the history of Russia** история России; **a friend of ours** наш друг; **a boy of 10** мальчик десяти лет; **that was kind of you** это было очень любезно с Вашей стороны; **a man of great ability** человек больших способностей; **the city of New York** город Нью-Йорк; **south of London** к югу от Лондона
2 (*expressing quantity, amount, dates etc*): **a kilo of flour** килограмм муки; **how much of this material do you need?** сколько такой ткани Вам нужно?; **there were three of them** (*people*) их было трое; (*objects*) их было три; **three of us stayed** трое из нас остались; **the 5th of July** 5-ое июля; **on the 5th of July** 5-ого июля
3 (*from*) из +*gen*; **the house is made of wood** дом сделан из дерева

 KEYWORD

off [ɔf] *adv* **1** (*referring to distance, time*): **it's a long way off** это далеко отсюда; **the city is 5 miles off** до города 5 миль; **the game is 3 days off** до игры осталось 3 дня
2 (*departure*): **to go off to Paris/Italy** уезжать (*perf* уехать) в Париж/Италию; **I must be off** мне пора (идти)
3 (*removal*): **to take off one's hat/clothes** снимать (*perf* снять) шляпу/одежду; **the button came off** пуговица оторвалась; **ten per cent off** (*Comm*) скидка в десять процентов
4: **to be off** (*on holiday*) быть (*impf*) в отпуске; **I'm off on Fridays** (*day off*) у меня выходной по пятницам; **he was off on Friday** (*absent*) в пятницу его не было на работе; **I have a day off** у меня отгул; **to be off sick** не работать (*impf*) по болезни
▷ *adj* **1** (*not on*) выключенный; (: *tap*) закрытый; (*disconnected*) отключённый
2 (*cancelled: meeting, match*) отменённый; (: *agreement*) расторгнутый
3 (*Brit*): **to go off** (*milk*) прокисать (*perf* прокиснуть; (*cheese, meat*) портиться (*perf* испортиться)
4: **on the off chance** на всякий случай; **to have an off day** вставать (*perf* встать) с левой ноги
▷ *prep* **1** (*indicating motion*) с +*gen*; **to fall off a cliff** упасть (*perf*) со скалы
2 (*distant from*) от +*gen*; **it's just off the M1** это недалеко от автострады M1; **it's five km off the main road** это в пяти км от шоссе
3: to be off meat (*dislike*) разлюбить (*perf*) мясо

offence [əˈfɛns] (*US* **offense**) *n* (*crime*) правонарушение; **to take offence at** обижаться (*perf* обидеться) на +*acc*

offend [əˈfɛnd] *vt* (*person*) обижать (*perf* обидеть); **offender** *n* правонарушитель(ница) *m(f)*
offense [əˈfɛns] *n* (*US*) = **offence**
offensive [əˈfɛnsɪv] *adj* (*remark, behaviour*) оскорбительный ▷ *n* (*Mil*) наступление; **offensive weapon** орудие нападения
offer [ˈɔfəʳ] *n* предложение ▷ *vt* предлагать (*perf* предложить)
office [ˈɔfɪs] *n* (*firm*) офис; (*room*) кабинет; **doctor's office** (*US*) кабинет врача; **to take office** (*person*) вступать (*perf* вступить) в должность
officer [ˈɔfɪsəʳ] *n* (*Mil*) офицер; (*also* **police officer**) полицейский *m adj*; (: *in Russia*) милиционер
official [əˈfɪʃl] *adj* официальный ▷ *n* (*of organization*) должностное лицо; **government official** официальное лицо
off-licence [ˈɔflaɪsns] *n* (*Brit*) винный магазин
off-line [ɔfˈlaɪn] *adj* (*Comput*) в оффлайн (*m ind*), оффлайновый; (: *работать*) автономный; (*switched off*) отключённый
off-peak [ˈɔfˈpiːk] *adj* (*heating, electricity*) непиковый
offset [ˈɔfsɛt] *irreg vt* уравновешивать (*perf* уравновесить)
offshore [ɔfˈʃɔːʳ] *adj* (*oilrig, fishing*) морской; (*Comm*) оффшорный; **offshore wind** ветер с берега
offspring [ˈɔfsprɪŋ] *n inv* отпрыск
often [ˈɔfn] *adv* часто; **how often …?** как часто …?; **more often than not** чаще всего; **as often as not** довольно часто; **every so often** время от времени
oil [ɔɪl] *n* масло; (*petroleum*) нефть *f*; (*for heating*) печное топливо ▷ *vt* смазывать (*perf* смазать); **oily** *adj* (*rag*) промасленный; (*skin*) жирный
ointment [ˈɔɪntmənt] *n* мазь *f*
O.K. [ˈəuˈkeɪ] *excl* (*inf*) хорошо, ладно
old [əuld] *adj* старый; **how old are you?** сколько Вам лет?; **he's 10 years old** ему 10 лет; **old man** старик; **old woman** старуха; **older brother** старший брат; **old age** *n* старость *f*; **old-fashioned** *adj* старомодный
olive [ˈɔlɪv] *n* (*fruit*) маслина, оливка ▷ *adj* оливковый; **olive oil** *n* оливковое масло
Olympic Games® *npl* (*also* **the Olympics**) Олимпийские игры *fpl*
omelet(te) [ˈɔmlɪt] *n* омлет
omen [ˈəumən] *n* предзнаменование
ominous [ˈɔmɪnəs] *adj* зловещий
omit [əuˈmɪt] *vt* пропускать (*perf* пропустить)

 KEYWORD

on [ɔn] *prep* **1** (*position*) на +*prp*; (*motion*)

на +*acc*; **the book is on the table** кни́га на столе́; **to put the book on the table** класть (*perf* положи́ть) кни́гу на стол; **on the left** сле́ва; **the house is on the main road** дом стои́т у шоссе́

2 (*indicating means, method, condition etc*): **on foot** пешко́м; **on the plane/train** (*go*) на самолёте/по́езде; (*be*) в самолёте/по́езде; **on the radio/television** по ра́дио/телеви́зору; **she's on the telephone** она́ разгова́ривает по телефо́ну; **to be on medication** принима́ть (*impf*) лека́рства; **to be on holiday/business** быть (*impf*) в о́тпуске/командиро́вке

3 (*referring to time*): **on Friday** в пя́тницу; **on Fridays** по пя́тницам; **on June 20th** 20-ого ию́ня; **a week on Friday** че́рез неде́лю, счита́я с пя́тницы; **on arrival** по прие́зде; **on seeing this** уви́дев это

4 (*about, concerning*) о +*prp*; **information on train services** информа́ция о расписа́нии поездо́в; **a book on physics** кни́га по фи́зике

▷ *adv* **1** (*referring to dress*) в +*prp*; **to have one's coat on** быть (*impf*) в пальто́; **what's she got on?** во что она́ была́ оде́та?; **she put her boots/hat on** она́ наде́ла сапоги́/шля́пу

2 (*further, continuously*) да́льше, да́лее; **to walk on** идти́ (*impf*) да́льше

▷ *adj* **1** (*functioning, in operation*) включённый; (: *tap*) откры́тый; **is the meeting still on?** (*not cancelled*) собра́ние состои́тся?; **there's a good film on at the cinema** в кинотеа́тре идёт хоро́ший фильм

2: **that's not on!** (*inf: of behaviour*) так не пойдёт *or* не годи́тся!

once [wʌns] *adv* (оди́н) раз; (*formerly*) когда́-то, одна́жды ▷ *conj* как то́лько; **at once** сра́зу же; (*simultaneously*) вме́сте; **once a week** (оди́н) раз в неде́лю; **once more** ещё раз; **once and for all** раз и навсегда́

oncoming [ˈɔnkʌmɪŋ] *adj* встре́чный

🔵 **KEYWORD**

one [wʌn] *n* оди́н (*f* одна́, *nt* одно́, *pl* одни́); **one hundred and fifty** сто пятьдеся́т; **one day there was a knock at the door** одна́жды разда́лся стук в дверь; **one by one** оди́н за други́м

▷ *adj* **1** (*sole*) еди́нственный; **the one book which …** еди́нственная кни́га, кото́рая …

2 (*same*) оди́н; **they all belong to the one family** они́ все из одно́й семьи́

▷ *pron* **1**: **I'm the one who told him** это я сказа́л ему́; **this one** э́тот (*f* э́та, *nt* э́то); **that one** тот (*f* та, *nt* то); **I've already got one** у меня́ уже́ есть

2: **one another** друг дру́га; **do you ever see one another?** Вы когда́-нибудь ви́дитесь?; **they didn't dare look at one another** они́ не сме́ли взгляну́ть друг на дру́га

3 (*impersonal*): **one never knows** никогда́ не зна́ешь; **one has to do it** на́до сде́лать это; **to cut one's finger** поре́зать (*perf*) (себе́) па́лец

one: **one-off** *n* (*Brit: inf*) едини́чный слу́чай; **oneself** *pron* (*reflexive*) себя́; (*emphatic*) сам; (*after prep: +acc, +gen*) себя́; (: +*dat*) себе́; (: +*instr*) собо́й; (: +*prp*) себе́; **to hurt oneself** ушиба́ться (*perf* ушиби́ться); **to keep sth for oneself** держа́ть (*impf*) что-н при себе́; **to talk to oneself** разгова́ривать (*impf*) с (сами́м) собо́й; **one-sided** *adj* односторо́нний; (*contest*) нера́вный; **one-way** *adj*: **one-way street** у́лица с односторо́нним движе́нием

ongoing [ˈɔngəʊɪŋ] *adj* продолжа́ющийся

onion [ˈʌnjən] *n* лук

on-line [ɔnˈlaɪn] *adj* онла́йновый; **to go on-line** включа́ться (*perf* включи́ться) в сеть

only [ˈəʊnlɪ] *adv* то́лько ▷ *adj* еди́нственный ▷ *conj* то́лько; **not only … but also …** не то́лько …, но и …

onset [ˈɔnsɛt] *n* наступле́ние

onward(s) [ˈɔnwəd(z)] *adv* вперёд, да́льше; **from that time onward(s)** с тех пор

opaque [əʊˈpeɪk] *adj* ма́товый

open [ˈəʊpn] *adj* откры́тый ▷ *vt* открыва́ть (*perf* откры́ть) ▷ *vi* открыва́ться (*perf* откры́ться); (*book, debate etc*) начина́ться (*perf* нача́ться); **in the open (air)** на откры́том во́здухе; **open up** *vt* открыва́ть (*perf* откры́ть) ▷ *vi* открыва́ться (*perf* откры́ться); **opening** *adj* (*speech, remarks etc*) вступи́тельный ▷ *n* (*gap, hole*) отве́рстие; (*job*) вака́нсия; **openly** *adv* откры́то; **open-minded** *adj* (*person*) откры́тый; **open-plan** *adj*: **open-plan office** о́фис с откры́той планиро́вкой

opera [ˈɔpərə] *n* о́пера

operate [ˈɔpəreɪt] *vt* управля́ть (*impf*) +*instr* ▷ *vi* де́йствовать (*impf*); (*Med*): **to operate (on sb)** опери́ровать (*perf* проопери́ровать) (кого́-н)

operation [ɔpəˈreɪʃən] *n* опера́ция; (*of machine: functioning*) рабо́та; (: *controlling*) управле́ние; **to be in operation** де́йствовать (*impf*); **he had an operation** (*Med*) ему́ сде́лали опера́цию; **operational** [ɔpəˈreɪʃənl] *adj*: **the machine was operational** маши́на функциони́ровала

operative [ˈɔpərətɪv] *adj* (*law etc*) де́йствующий

operator [ˈɔpəreɪtə'] n (Tel)
телефони́ст(ка); (Tech) опера́тор

opinion [əˈpɪnjən] n мне́ние; **in my
opinion** по моему́ мне́нию, по-мо́ему;
opinion poll n опро́с обще́ственного
мне́ния

opponent [əˈpəunənt] n оппоне́нт,
проти́вник(-ница); (Sport) проти́вник

opportunity [ɔpəˈtjuːnɪtɪ] n
возмо́жность f; **to take the opportunity
of doing** по́льзоваться (perf
воспо́льзоваться) слу́чаем, что́бы +infin

oppose [əˈpəuz] vt проти́виться (perf
воспроти́виться) +dat; **to be opposed to
sth** проти́виться (impf) чему́-н; **as
opposed to** в противополо́жность
+dat

opposite [ˈɔpəzɪt] adj противополо́жный
▷ adv напро́тив ▷ prep напро́тив +gen
▷ n: **the opposite** (say, think, do etc)
противополо́жное nt adj

opposition [ɔpəˈzɪʃən] n оппози́ция; **the
Opposition** (Pol) оппозицио́нная па́ртия

oppress [əˈprɛs] vt угнета́ть (impf)

opt [ɔpt] vi: **to opt for** избира́ть (perf
избра́ть); **to opt to do** реша́ть (perf
реши́ть) +infin; **opt out** vi: **to opt out of**
выходи́ть (perf вы́йти) из +gen

optician [ɔpˈtɪʃən] n окули́ст

optimism [ˈɔptɪmɪzəm] n оптими́зм

optimistic [ɔptɪˈmɪstɪk] adj
оптимисти́чный

optimum [ˈɔptɪməm] adj оптима́льный

option [ˈɔpʃən] n (choice) возмо́жность f,
вариа́нт; **optional** adj необяза́тельный

or [ɔː'] conj и́ли; (otherwise): **or (else)** а то,
ина́че; (with negative): **he hasn't seen or
heard anything** он ничего́ не ви́дел и не
слы́шал

oral [ˈɔːrəl] adj у́стный; (medicine)
ора́льный ▷ n у́стный экза́мен

orange [ˈɔrɪndʒ] n апельси́н ▷ adj
(colour) ора́нжевый

orbit [ˈɔːbɪt] n орби́та ▷ vt обраща́ться
(perf обрати́ться) вокру́г +gen

orchard [ˈɔːtʃəd] n сад (фрукто́вый)

orchestra [ˈɔːkɪstrə] n орке́стр

orchid [ˈɔːkɪd] n орхиде́я

ordeal [ɔːˈdiːl] n испыта́ние

order [ˈɔːdə'] n зака́з; (command) прика́з;
(sequence, discipline) поря́док ▷ vt
зака́зывать (perf заказа́ть); (command)
прика́зывать (perf приказа́ть) +dat; (also
put in order) располага́ть (perf
расположи́ть) по поря́дку; **in order** в
поря́дке; **in order to do** для того́ что́бы
+infin; **out of order** (not in sequence) не по
поря́дку; (not working) неиспра́вный; **to
order sb to do** прика́зывать (perf
приказа́ть) кому́-н +infin; **order form** n
бланк зака́за; **orderly** n (Med) санита́р
▷ adj (room) опря́тный; (system)
упоря́доченный

ordinary [ˈɔːdnrɪ] adj обы́чный,

обыкнове́нный; (mediocre) зауря́дный;
out of the ordinary необыкнове́нный

ore [ɔː'] n руда́

organ [ˈɔːgən] n (Anat) о́рган; (Mus)
орга́н; **organic** [ɔːˈgænɪk] adj (fertilizer)
органи́ческий; (food) экологи́чески
чи́стый; **organism** n органи́зм

organization [ɔːgənaɪˈzeɪʃən] n
организа́ция

organize [ˈɔːgənaɪz] vt организо́вывать
(impf/perf), устра́ивать (perf устро́ить)

orgasm [ˈɔːgæzəm] n орга́зм

oriental [ɔːrɪˈɛntl] adj восто́чный

origin [ˈɔrɪdʒɪn] n происхожде́ние;
original [əˈrɪdʒɪnl] adj первонача́льный;
(new) оригина́льный; (genuine)
по́длинный; (imaginative) самобы́тный
▷ n по́длинник, оригина́л; **originally**
[əˈrɪdʒɪnəlɪ] adv первонача́льно;
originate [əˈrɪdʒɪneɪt] vi: **to originate
from** происходи́ть (perf произойти́) от/из
+gen; **to originate in** зарожда́ться (perf
зароди́ться) в +prp

ornament [ˈɔːnəmənt] n (decorative
object) украше́ние; **ornamental**
[ɔːnəˈmɛntl] adj декорати́вный

ornate [ɔːˈneɪt] adj декорати́вный

orphan [ˈɔːfn] n сирота́ m/f

orthodox [ˈɔːθədɔks] adj
ортодокса́льный; **the Russian Orthodox
Church** Ру́сская правосла́вная це́рковь

orthopaedic [ɔːθəˈpiːdɪk] (US
orthopedic) adj ортопеди́ческий

ostrich [ˈɔstrɪtʃ] n стра́ус

other [ˈʌðə'] adj друго́й ▷ pron: **the other
(one)** друго́й(-а́я) m(f) adj, друго́е nt adj
▷ adv: **other than** кро́ме +gen; **others** npl
(other people) други́е pl adj; **the others**
остальны́е pl adj; **the other day** на днях;
otherwise adv (differently) ина́че,
по-друго́му; (apart from that) в остально́м
▷ conj а то, ина́че

otter [ˈɔtə'] n вы́дра

ought [ɔːt] (pt **ought**) aux vb: **I ought to
do it** мне сле́дует э́то сде́лать; **this ought
to have been corrected** э́то сле́довало
испра́вить; **he ought to win** он до́лжен
вы́играть

ounce [auns] n у́нция

● OUNCE
●
● Ounce — ме́ра ве́са ра́вная 28,349 г.

our [ˈauə'] adj наш; see also **my**; **ours**
pron наш; (referring to subject of
sentence) свой; see also **mine¹**; **ourselves**
pl pron (reflexive, complement) себя́;
(after prep: +acc, +gen) себя́; (: +dat, +prp)
себе́; (: +instr) собо́й; (emphatic) са́ми;
(alone): **(all) by ourselves** са́ми; **let's keep it
between ourselves** дава́йте оста́вим э́то
ме́жду на́ми; see also **myself**

oust [aust] vt изгоня́ть (perf изгна́ть)

◯ **KEYWORD**

out [aut] *adv* **1** (*not in*): **they're out in the garden** они в саду; **out in the rain/snow** под дождём/снéгом; **out here** здесь; **out there** там; **to go out** выходи́ть (*perf* вы́йти); **out loud** гро́мко
2 (*not at home, absent*): **he is out at the moment** его́ сейча́с нет (до́ма); **let's have a night out on Friday** дава́йте пойдём куда́-нибудь в пя́тницу ве́чером!
3 (*indicating distance*) в +*prp*; **the boat was ten km out (from the shore)** кора́бль находи́лся в десяти́ км от бе́рега
4 (*Sport*): **the ball is out** мяч за преде́лами по́ля
▷ *adj* **1:** **to be out** (*unconscious*) быть (*impf*) без созна́ния; (*out of bounds*) выбыва́ть (*perf* вы́быть); (*flowers*) распуска́ться (*perf* распусти́ться); (*news, secret*) станови́ться (*perf* стать) изве́стным(-ой); (*fire, light, gas*) ту́хнуть (*perf* поту́хнуть), га́снуть (*perf* пога́снуть); **to go out of fashion** выходи́ть (*perf* вы́йти) из мо́ды
2 (*finished*): **before the week was out** до оконча́ния неде́ли
3: to be out to do (*intend*) намерева́ться (*impf*) +*infin*; **to be out in one's calculations** (*wrong*) ошиба́ться (*perf* ошиби́ться) в расчётах
▷ *prep* **1** (*outside, beyond*) из +*gen*; **to go out of the house** выходи́ть (*perf* вы́йти) из до́ма; **to be out of danger** (*safe*) быть (*impf*) вне опа́сности
2 (*cause, motive*): **out of curiosity** из любопы́тства; **out of fear/joy/boredom** от стра́ха/ра́дости/ску́ки; **out of grief** с го́ря; **out of necessity** по необходи́мости
3 (*from, from among*) из +*gen*
4 (*without*): **we are out of sugar/petrol** у нас ко́нчился са́хар/бензи́н

outbreak ['autbreɪk] *n* (*of disease, violence*) вспы́шка; (*of war*) нача́ло
outburst ['autbə:st] *n* взрыв
outcast ['autkɑːst] *n* изго́й
outcome ['autkʌm] *n* исхо́д
outcry ['autkraɪ] *n* негодова́ние, проте́ст
outdated [aut'deɪtɪd] *adj* (*customs, ideas*) отжи́вший; (*technology*) устаре́лый
outdoor [aut'dɔːʳ] *adj* на откры́том во́здухе; (*pool*) откры́тый; **outdoors** *adv* на у́лице, на откры́том во́здухе
outer ['autəʳ] *adj* нару́жный; **outer space** *n* косми́ческое простра́нство
outfit ['autfɪt] *n* (*clothes*) костю́м
outgoing ['autgəuɪŋ] *adj* (*extrovert*) общи́тельный; (*president, mayor etc*) уходя́щий
outing ['autɪŋ] *n* похо́д
outlaw ['autlɔː] *vt* объявля́ть (*perf* объяви́ть) вне зако́на
outlay ['autleɪ] *n* затра́ты *fpl*

outlet ['autlɛt] *n* (*hole*) выходно́е отве́рстие; (*pipe*) сток; (*Comm: also* **retail outlet**) торго́вая то́чка; (*for emotions*) вы́ход
outline ['autlaɪn] *n* (*shape*) ко́нтур, очерта́ния *ntpl*; (*sketch, explanation*) набро́сок ▷ *vt* (*fig*) опи́сывать (*perf* описа́ть)
outlook ['autluk] *n* (*attitude*) взгля́д *mpl*, воззре́ния *ntpl*; (*prospects*) перспекти́вы *fpl*
outnumber [aut'nʌmbəʳ] *vt* чи́сленно превосходи́ть (*perf* превзойти́)
out-of-date [autəv'deɪt] *adj* (*clothes*) немо́дный; (*equipment*) устаре́лый
out-of-the-way ['autəvðə'weɪ] *adj* (*place*) глуби́нный
outpatient ['autpeɪʃənt] *n* амбулато́рный(-ая) пацие́нт(ка)
output ['autput] *n* вы́работка, проду́кция; (*Comput*) выходны́е да́нные *pl*
outrage ['autreɪdʒ] *n* (*emotion*) возмуще́ние ▷ *vt* возмуща́ть (*perf* возмути́ть); **outrageous** [aut'reɪdʒəs] *adj* возмути́тельный
outright [*adv* aut'raɪt, *adj* 'autraɪt] *adv* (*win, own*) абсолю́тно; (*refuse, deny*) наотре́з; (*ask*) пря́мо ▷ *adj* (*winner, victory*) открове́нный; (*refusal, hostility*) откры́тый; **to be killed outright** погиба́ть (*perf* поги́бнуть) сра́зу
outset ['autsɛt] *n* нача́ло
outside [aut'saɪd] *n* нару́жная сторона́ ▷ *adj* нару́жный, вне́шний ▷ *adv* (*be*) снару́жи; (*go*) нару́жу ▷ *prep* вне +*gen*, за преде́лами +*gen*; (*building*) у +*gen*; (*city*) под +*instr*; **outsider** *n* (*stranger*) посторо́нний(-яя) *m(f) adj*
outskirts ['autskə:ts] *npl* окра́ины *fpl*
outspoken [aut'spəukən] *adj* открове́нный
outstanding [aut'stændɪŋ] *adj* (*exceptional*) выдаю́щийся; (*unfinished*) незако́нченный; (*unpaid*) неопла́ченный
outward ['autwəd] *adj* вне́шний; **the outward journey** пое́здка туда́
outweigh [aut'weɪ] *vt* переве́шивать (*perf* переве́сить)
oval ['əuvl] *adj* ова́льный
ovary ['əuvərɪ] *n* яи́чник
oven ['ʌvn] *n* (*domestic*) духо́вка

◯ **KEYWORD**

over ['əuvəʳ] *adv* **1** (*across*): **to cross over** переходи́ть (*perf* перейти́); **over here** здесь; **over there** там; **to ask sb over** (*to one's house*) приглаша́ть (*perf* пригласи́ть) кого́-н в го́сти *or* к себе́
2 (*indicating movement from upright*): **to knock/turn sth over** сбива́ть (*perf* сбить)/ перевора́чивать (*perf* переверну́ть) что-н; **to fall over** па́дать (*perf* упа́сть); **to bend**

over нагибáться (*perf* нагнýться)
3 (*finished*): **the game is over** игрá окóнчена; **his life is over** егó закóнчилась жизнь
4 (*excessively*) слúшком, чересчýр
5 (*remaining: money, food etc*): **there are 3 over** остáлось 3
6: all over (*everywhere*) вездé, повсю́ду; **over and over** (*again*) снóва и снóва
▷ *prep* **1** (*on top of*) на +*prp*; (*above, in control of*) над +*instr*
2 (*on(to) the other side of*) чéрез +*acc*; **the pub over the road** паб чéрез дорóгу
3 (*more than*) свы́ше +*gen*, бóльше +*gen*; **she is over 40** ей бóльше 40; **over and above** намнóго бóльше, чем
4 (*in the course of*) в течéние +*gen*, за +*acc*; **over the winter** зá зиму, в течéние зимы; **let's discuss it over dinner** давáйте обсýдим э́то за обéдом; **the work is spread over two weeks** рабóта рассчúтана на две недéли

overall [*adj, n* 'əuvərɔːl, *adv* əuvə'rɔːl] *adj* óбщий ▷ *adv* (*in general*) в цéлом *or* óбщем; (*altogether*) целикóм ▷ *n* (*Brit*) халáт; **overalls** *npl* (*clothing*) комбинезóн *msg*; **overall majority** подавля́ющее большинствó
overboard ['əuvəbɔːd] *adv*: **to fall overboard** пáдать (*perf* упáсть) зá борт
overcast ['əuvəkɑːst] *adj* хмýрый, пáсмурный
overcoat ['əuvəkəut] *n* пальтó *nt ind*
overcome [əuvə'kʌm] (*irreg like* **come**) *vt* (*problems*) преодолевáть (*perf* преодолéть)
overcrowded [əuvə'kraudɪd] *adj* переполненный
overdo [əuvə'duː] (*irreg like* **do**) *vt* (*work, exercise*) перестарáться (*perf*) в +*prp*; (*interest, concern*) утрúровать (*impf*)
overdose ['əuvədəus] *n* передозирóвка
overdraft ['əuvədrɑːft] *n* перерасхóд, овердрáфт
overdrawn [əuvə'drɔːn] *adj*: **he is overdrawn** он превы́сил кредúт своегó текýщего счёта
overdue [əuvə'djuː] *adj* (*change, reform etc*) запоздáлый
overgrown [əuvə'grəun] *adj* (*garden*) зарóсший
overhead [*adv* əuvə'hɛd, *adj, n* 'əuvəhɛd] *adv* наверхý, над головóй; (*in the sky*) в нéбе ▷ *adj* (*lighting*) вéрхний; (*cable, railway*) надзéмный ▷ *n* (*US*) = **overheads**; **overheads** *npl* (*expenses*) накладны́е расхóды *mpl*
overhear [əuvə'hɪəʳ] (*irreg like* **hear**) *vt* (*случáйно*) подслýшать (*perf*)
overlap [əuvə'læp] *vi* находúть (*impf*) одúн на другóй; (*fig*) частúчно совпадáть (*perf* совпáсть)
overleaf [əuvə'liːf] *adv* на оборóте

overload [əuvə'ləud] *vt* (*also Elec, fig*) перегружáть (*perf* перегрузúть)
overlook [əuvə'luk] *vt* (*place*) выходúть (*impf*) на +*acc*; (*problem*) упускáть (*perf* упустúть) из вúду; (*behaviour*) закрывáть (*perf* закры́ть) глазá на +*acc*
overnight [əuvə'naɪt] *adv* (*during the night*) зá ночь; (*fig*) в одночáсье, срáзу; **to stay overnight** ночевáть (*perf* переночевáть)
overpowering [əuvə'pauərɪŋ] *adj* (*heat, stench*) невыносúмый
overrun [əuvə'rʌn] *irreg vi* (*meeting*) затя́гиваться (*perf* затянýться)
overseas [əuvə'siːz] *adv* (*live, work*) за рубежóм *or* гранúцей; (*go*) за рубéж *or* гранúцу ▷ *adj* (*market, trade*) внéшний; (*student, visitor*) инострáнный
oversee [əuvə'siː] (*irreg like* **see**) *vt* следúть (*impf*) за +*instr*
overshadow [əuvə'ʃædəu] *vt* (*place, building etc*) возвышáться (*impf*) над +*instr*; (*fig*) затмевáть (*perf* затмúть)
oversight ['əuvəsaɪt] *n* недосмóтр
overt [əu'vəːt] *adj* откры́тый
overtake [əuvə'teɪk] (*irreg like* **take**) *vt* (*Aut*) обгоня́ть (*perf* обогнáть)
overthrow [əuvə'θrəu] (*irreg like* **throw**) *vt* свергáть (*perf* свéргнуть)
overtime ['əuvətaɪm] *n* сверхурóчное врéмя *nt*
overturn [əuvə'təːn] *vt* (*car, chair*) перев오рáчивать (*perf* перевернýть); (*decision, plan*) отвергáть (*perf* отвéргнуть); (*government, system*) свергáть (*perf* свéргнуть)
overweight [əuvə'weɪt] *adj* тýчный
overwhelm [əuvə'wɛlm] *vt* (*subj: feelings, emotions*) переполня́ть (*perf* переполнúть); **overwhelming** *adj* (*victory, defeat*) пóлный; (*majority*) подавля́ющий; (*feeling, desire*) всепобеждáющий
owe [əu] *vt*: **she owes me £500** онá должнá мне £500; **he owes his life to that man** он обя́зан своéй жúзнью э́тому человéку
owing to ['əuɪŋ-] *prep* вслéдствие +*gen*
owl [aul] *n* совá
own [əun] *vt* владéть (*impf*) +*instr* ▷ *adj* сóбственный; **he lives on his own** он живёт одúн; **to get one's own back** оты́грываться (*perf* отыгрáться); **own up** *vi*: **to own up to sth** признавáться (*perf* признáться) в чём-н; **owner** *n* владéлец(-лица); **ownership** *n*: **ownership (of)** владéние (+*instr*)
ox [ɔks] (*pl* **oxen**) *n* бык
oxygen ['ɔksɪdʒən] *n* кислорóд
oyster ['ɔɪstəʳ] *n* ýстрица
oz. *abbr* = **ounce**
ozone ['əuzəun] *n* озóн

p

p *abbr* (*Brit*) = **penny, pence**

PA *n abbr* (= *personal assistant*) референт, личный секретарь *m*

pa [pɑː] *n* (*inf*) папа *m*

p.a. *abbr* = **per annum**

pace [peɪs] *n* (*step*) шаг; (*speed*) темп ▷ *vi*: **to pace up and down** ходить (*impf*) взад вперёд; **to keep pace with** идти (*impf*) в ногу с +*instr*; **pacemaker** *n* (*Med*) ритмизатор сердца

Pacific [pə'sɪfɪk] *n*: **the Pacific (Ocean)** Тихий океан

pack [pæk] *n* (*packet*) пачка; (*of wolves*) стая; (*also* **backpack**) рюкзак; (*of cards*) колода ▷ *vt* (*fill*) паковать (*perf* упаковать); (*cram*): **to pack into** набивать (*perf* набить) в +*acc* ▷ *vi*: **to pack (one's bags)** укладываться (*perf* уложиться)

package ['pækɪdʒ] *n* пакет; (*also* **package deal**: *Comm*) пакет предложений; **package holiday** *n* (*Brit*) организованный отдых по путёвке

packet ['pækɪt] *n* (*of cigarettes etc*) пачка; (*of crisps*) пакет

packing ['pækɪŋ] *n* прокладочный материал; (*act*) упаковка

pact [pækt] *n* пакт

pad [pæd] *n* (*of paper*) блокнот; (*soft material*) прокладка ▷ *vt* (*cushion, soft toy etc*) набивать (*perf* набить)

paddle ['pædl] *n* (*oar*) байдарочное весло; (*US: bat*) ракетка ▷ *vt* управлять (*impf*) +*instr* ▷ *vi* (*in sea*) шлёпать (*impf*)

paddock ['pædək] *n* (*field*) выгон

padlock ['pædlɔk] *n* (*висячий*) замок

paedophile ['piːdəufaɪl] (*US* **pedophile**) *n* педофил

page [peɪdʒ] *n* страница; (*also* **pageboy**) паж ▷ *vt* (*in hotel etc*) вызывать (*perf* вызвать) (по селектору)

paid [peɪd] *pt, pp of* **pay**

pain [peɪn] *n* боль *f*; **to be in pain**

страдать (*impf*) от боли; **to take pains to do** стараться (*perf* постараться) изо всех сил +*infin*; **painful** *adj* мучительный; **my back is painful** у меня болит спина; **painkiller** *n* болеутоляющее *nt adj* (средство); **painstaking** *adj* кропотливый

paint [peɪnt] *n* краска ▷ *vt* красить (*perf* покрасить); (*picture, portrait*) рисовать (*perf* нарисовать), писать (*perf* написать); **to paint the door blue** красить (*perf* покрасить) дверь в голубой цвет; **painter** *n* (*artist*) художник(-ица); (*decorator*) маляр; **painting** *n* картина; (*activity: of artist*) живопись *f*; (: *of decorator*) малярное дело

pair [pɛəʳ] *n* пара

pajamas [pə'dʒɑːməz] *npl* (*US*) = **pyjamas**

pal [pæl] *n* (*inf*) дружок

palace ['pæləs] *n* дворец

pale [peɪl] *adj* бледный

Palestine ['pælɪstaɪn] *n* Палестина

palm [pɑːm] *n* (*also* **palm tree**) пальма; (*of hand*) ладонь *f* ▷ *vt*: **to palm sth off on sb** (*inf*) подсовывать (*perf* подсунуть) что-н кому-н

pamphlet ['pæmflət] *n* брошюра; (*political, literary etc*) памфлет

pan [pæn] *n* (*also* **saucepan**) кастрюля; (*also* **frying pan**) сковорода

pancake ['pænkeɪk] *n* (*thin*) блин; (*thick*) оладья

panda ['pændə] *n* панда, бамбуковый медведь *m*

pane [peɪn] *n*: **pane (of glass)** (*in window*) оконное стекло

panel ['pænl] *n* (*of wood, glass etc*) панель *f*; (*of experts*) комиссия; **panel of judges** жюри *nt ind*

panic ['pænɪk] *n* паника ▷ *vi* паниковать (*impf*)

panorama [pænə'rɑːmə] *n* панорама

pansy ['pænzɪ] *n* анютины глазки *pl*

panther ['pænθəʳ] *n* пантера

pantomime ['pæntəmaɪm] *n* (*Brit*) рождественское театрализованное представление

■ **PANTOMIME**

■
■ **Pantomime** — рождественское
■ представление. Комедии с богатым
■ музыкальным оформлением,
■ написанные по мотивам известных
■ сказок, таких как "Золушка", "Кот в
■ сапогах" и др. Они предназначены
■ главным образом для детей. Театры
■ ставят их в Рождество.

pants [pænts] *npl* (*Brit: underwear*) трусы *pl*; (*US: trousers*) брюки *pl*

paper ['peɪpəʳ] *n* бумага; (*also* **newspaper**) газета; (*exam*) письменный

экза́мен; (*essay: at conference*) докла́д;
(: *in journal*) статья́; (*also* **wallpaper**) обо́и
pl ▷ adj бума́жный ▷ vt окле́ивать (*perf*
окле́ить) обо́ями; **papers** npl (*also*
identity papers) докуме́нты mpl;
paperback n кни́га в мя́гкой обло́жке;
paperclip n (канцеля́рская) скре́пка;
paperwork n бума́жная волоки́та
paprika ['pæprɪkə] n кра́сный мо́лотый
пе́рец
par [pɑː[ʳ]] n: **to be on a par with** быть
(*impf*) на ра́вных с +instr
parachute ['pærəʃuːt] n парашю́т
parade [pə'reɪd] n ше́ствие; (*Mil*) пара́д
▷ vi (*Mil*) идти́ (*impf*) стро́ем
paradise ['pærədaɪs] n (*also fig*) рай
paradox ['pærədɔks] n парадо́кс
paraffin ['pærəfɪn] n (*Brit*: *also* **paraffin
oil**) кероси́н
paragraph ['pærəgrɑːf] n абза́ц
parallel ['pærəlel] adj паралле́льный;
(*fig: similar*) аналоги́чный ▷ n
паралле́ль f
paralysis [pə'rælɪsɪs] n (*Med*) парали́ч
paranoid ['pærənɔɪd] adj (*person*)
парано́идный
parasite ['pærəsaɪt] n парази́т
parcel ['pɑːsl] n (*package*) свёрток; (*sent
by post*) посы́лка
pardon ['pɑːdn] n (*Law*) поми́лование
▷ vt (*Law*) ми́ловать (*perf* поми́ловать);
pardon me!, I beg your pardon! прошу́
проще́ния!; **(I beg your) pardon?, (US)
pardon me?** (*what did you say?*) прости́те,
не расслы́шал
parent ['pɛərənt] n роди́тель(ница) m(f);
parents npl (*mother and father*) роди́тели
mpl; **parental** [pə'rɛntl] adj
роди́тельский
Paris ['pærɪs] n Пари́ж
parish ['pærɪʃ] n (*Rel*) прихо́д
park [pɑːk] n парк ▷ vt ста́вить (*perf*
поста́вить), паркова́ть (*perf*
припаркова́ть) ▷ vi паркова́ться (*perf*
припаркова́ться)
parking ['pɑːkɪŋ] n (*of vehicle*) парко́вка;
(*space to park*) стоя́нка; "**no parking**"
"стоя́нка запрещена́"; **parking lot** n
(*US*) (а́вто)стоя́нка
parliament ['pɑːləmənt] n парла́мент;
parliamentary [pɑːlə'mɛntərɪ] adj
парла́ментский
parole [pə'rəul] n: **he was released on
parole** (*Law*) он был освобождён под
че́стное сло́во
parrot ['pærət] n попуга́й
parsley ['pɑːslɪ] n петру́шка
parsnip ['pɑːsnɪp] n пастерна́к
(посевно́й)
part [pɑːt] n (*section, division*) часть f;
(*component*) дета́ль f; (*role*) роль f;
(*episode*) се́рия; (*US: in hair*) пробо́р
▷ adv = **partly** ▷ vt разделя́ть (*perf*
раздели́ть); (*hair*) расчёсывать (*perf*

расчеса́ть) на пробо́р ▷ vi (*people*)
расстава́ться (*perf* расста́ться); (*crowd*)
расступа́ться (*perf* расступи́ться); **to take
part in** принима́ть (*perf* приня́ть) уча́стие
в +prp; **to take sb's part** (*support*)
станови́ться (*perf* стать) на чью-н сто́рону;
for my part с мое́й стороны́; **for the most
part** бо́льшей ча́стью; **part with** vt fus
расстава́ться (*perf* расста́ться) с +instr
partial ['pɑːʃl] adj (*incomplete*)
части́чный; **I am partial to chocolate** (*like*)
у меня́ пристра́стие к шокола́ду
participant [pɑː'tɪsɪpənt] n
уча́стник(-ица)
participate [pɑː'tɪsɪpeɪt] vi: **to participate
in** уча́ствовать (*impf*) в +prp
particle ['pɑːtɪkl] n части́ца
particular [pə'tɪkjulə[ʳ]] adj (*distinct,
special*) осо́бый; (*fussy*) приверед́ливый;
particulars npl (*personal details*) да́нные
pl adj; **in particular** в ча́стности;
particularly adv осо́бенно
parting ['pɑːtɪŋ] n разделе́ние; (*farewell*)
проща́ние; (*Brit: in hair*) пробо́р ▷ adj
проща́льный
partition [pɑː'tɪʃən] n (*wall, screen*)
перегоро́дка
partly ['pɑːtlɪ] adv части́чно
partner ['pɑːtnə[ʳ]] n партнёр(ша);
(*spouse*) супру́г(а); (*Comm, Sport, Cards*)
партнёр; **partnership** n (*Comm:
company*) това́рищество; (: *with person*)
партнёрство; (*Pol*) сою́з
part-time ['pɑːt'taɪm] adj (*work*)
почасово́й; (*staff*) на почасово́й ста́вке
▷ adv: **to work part-time** быть (*impf*) на
почасово́й ста́вке; **to study part-time**
обуча́ться (*impf*) по непо́лной програ́мме
party ['pɑːtɪ] n па́ртия; (*celebration:
formal*) ве́чер; (: *informal*) вечери́нка;
(*group: rescue*) отря́д; (: *of tourists etc*)
гру́ппа ▷ cpd (*Pol*) парти́йный; **birthday
party** пра́зднование дня рожде́ния, день
рожде́ния
pass [pɑːs] vt (*time*) проводи́ть (*perf*
провести́); (*hand over*) передава́ть (*perf*
переда́ть); (*go past: on foot*) проходи́ть
(*perf* пройти́); (: *by transport*) проезжа́ть
(*perf* прое́хать); (*overtake: vehicle*)
обгоня́ть (*perf* обогна́ть); (*exam*) сдава́ть
(*perf* сдать); (*law, proposal*) принима́ть
(*perf* приня́ть) ▷ vi (*go past: on foot*)
проходи́ть (*perf* пройти́); (: *by transport*)
проезжа́ть (*perf* прое́хать); (*in exam*)
сдава́ть (*perf* сдать) экза́мен ▷ n (*permit*)
про́пуск; (*Geo*) перева́л; (*Sport*) пас,
переда́ча; (*Scol: also* **pass mark**): **to get a
pass** получа́ть (*perf* получи́ть) зачёт;
pass by vi (*on foot*) проходи́ть (*perf*
пройти́); (*by transport*) проезжа́ть (*perf*
прое́хать); **pass on** vt передава́ть (*perf*
переда́ть)
passage ['pæsɪdʒ] n (*also Anat*) прохо́д;
(*in book*) отры́вок; (*journey*) путеше́ствие

passenger ['pæsɪndʒəʳ] n пассажи́р(ка)
passer-by [pɑːsə'baɪ] (pl **passers-by**) n
прохо́жий(-ая) m(f) adj
passion ['pæʃən] n страсть f; **passionate**
adj стра́стный
passive ['pæsɪv] adj пасси́вный
passport ['pɑːspɔːt] n па́спорт
password ['pɑːswəːd] n паро́ль m
past [pɑːst] prep ми́мо +gen; (beyond) за
+instr; (later than) по́сле +gen ▷ adj
(government etc) пре́жний; (week, month
etc) про́шлый ▷ n про́шлое nt adj; (Ling):
the past (tense) проше́дшее вре́мя ▷ adv:
to run past пробега́ть (perf пробежа́ть)
ми́мо; **ten/quarter past eight** де́сять
мину́т/че́тверть девя́того; **for the past few
days** за после́дние не́сколько дней
pasta ['pæstə] n макаро́нные изде́лия
ntpl
paste [peɪst] n (wet mixture) па́ста; (glue)
кле́йстер; (Culin) паште́т ▷ vt (paper etc)
наноси́ть (perf нанести́) клей на +acc
pastel ['pæstl] adj пасте́льный
pastime ['pɑːstaɪm] n
времяпрепровожде́ние
pastry ['peɪstrɪ] n (dough) те́сто
pasture ['pɑːstʃəʳ] n па́стбище
pat [pæt] vt (dog) ласка́ть (perf
приласка́ть) ▷ n: **to give sb/o.s. a pat on
the back** (fig) хвали́ть (perf похвали́ть)
кого́-н/себя́
patch [pætʃ] n (of material) запла́та; (also
eye patch) повя́зка; (area) пятно́; (repair)
запла́та ▷ vt (clothes) лата́ть (perf
залата́ть); **to go through a bad patch**
пережива́ть (impf) тру́дные времена́; **bald
patch** лы́сина; **patchy** adj (colour)
пятни́стый; (information, knowledge etc)
отры́вочный
pâté ['pæteɪ] n (Culin) паште́т
patent ['peɪtnt] n пате́нт ▷ vt (Comm)
патентова́ть (perf запатентова́ть)
paternal [pə'təːnl] adj (love, duty)
отцо́вский
path [pɑːθ] n (trail, track) тропа́,
тропи́нка; (concrete, gravel etc) доро́жка;
(trajectory) ли́ния движе́ния
pathetic [pə'θɛtɪk] adj жа́лостный; (very
bad) жа́лкий
patience ['peɪʃns] n (quality) терпе́ние
patient ['peɪʃnt] n пацие́нт(ка) ▷ adj
терпели́вый
patio ['pætɪəu] n па́тио m ind,
вну́тренний дво́рик
patriotic [pætrɪ'ɔtɪk] adj патриоти́чный;
(song etc) патриоти́ческий
patrol [pə'trəul] n патру́ль m ▷ vt
патрули́ровать (impf)
patron ['peɪtrən] n (client) (постоя́нный)
клие́нт; (benefactor: of charity) шеф,
покрови́тель m; **patron of the arts**
покрови́тель(ница) m(f) иску́сств
pattern ['pætən] n (design) узо́р;
(Sewing) вы́кройка

pause [pɔːz] n переры́в; (in speech) па́уза
▷ vi де́лать (perf сде́лать) переры́в; (in
speech) па́узу
pave [peɪv] vt мости́ть (perf вы́мостить);
to pave the way for (fig) прокла́дывать
(perf проложи́ть) путь для +gen;
pavement n (Brit) тротуа́р
pavilion [pə'vɪlɪən] n (Sport) павильо́н
paw [pɔː] n (of animal) ла́па
pawn [pɔːn] n (Chess, fig) пе́шка ▷ vt
закла́дывать (perf заложи́ть);
pawnbroker n ростовщи́к(-и́ца)
pay [peɪ] (pt, pp **paid**) n зарпла́та ▷ vt
(sum of money, wage) плати́ть (perf
заплати́ть); (debt, bill) плати́ть (perf
уплати́ть) ▷ vi (be profitable) окупа́ться
(perf окупи́ться); **to pay attention (to)**
обраща́ть (perf обрати́ть) внима́ние (на
+acc); **to pay sb a visit** наноси́ть (perf
нанести́) кому́-н визи́т; **pay back** vt
возвраща́ть (perf возврати́ть), верну́ть
(perf); (person) отпла́чивать (perf
отплати́ть); **pay for** vt fus плати́ть (perf
заплати́ть) за +acc; (fig) поплати́ться
(perf) за +acc; **pay in** vt вноси́ть (perf
внести́); **pay off** vt (debt) выпла́чивать
(perf вы́платить); (creditor)
рассчи́тываться (perf рассчита́ться) с
+instr; (person) рассчи́тывать (perf
рассчита́ть) ▷ vi окупа́ться (perf
окупи́ться); **pay up** vi рассчи́тываться
(perf рассчита́ться) (спо́лна); **payable** adj
(cheque); **payable to** подлежа́щий упла́те
на и́мя +gen; **payment** n (act) платёж,
упла́та; (amount) вы́плата
PC n abbr (= personal computer) ПК
(= персона́льный компью́тер); (Brit)
= **police constable**; **politically correct**
pc abbr = **per cent**
pea [piː] n (Bot, Culin) горо́х m no pl
peace [piːs] n (not war) мир; (calm)
поко́й; **peaceful** adj (calm) ми́рный
peach [piːtʃ] n пе́рсик
peacock ['piːkɔk] n павли́н
peak [piːk] n верши́на, пик; (of cap)
козырёк
peanut ['piːnʌt] n ара́хис
pear [pɛəʳ] n гру́ша
pearl [pəːl] n жемчу́жина; **pearls** npl
же́мчуг
peasant ['pɛznt] n крестья́нин(-нка)
peat [piːt] n торф
pebble ['pɛbl] n га́лька no pl
peck [pɛk] vt (subj: bird) клева́ть (impf);
(: once) клю́нуть (perf) ▷ n (kiss) поцелу́й
peculiar [pɪ'kjuːlɪəʳ] adj (strange)
своеобра́зный; (unique): **peculiar to**
сво́йственный +dat
pedal ['pɛdl] n педа́ль f ▷ vi крути́ть
(impf) педа́ли
pedestal ['pɛdəstl] n пьедеста́л
pedestrian [pɪ'dɛstrɪən] n пешехо́д
pedigree ['pɛdɪɡriː] n родосло́вная f adj
▷ cpd поро́дистый

pedophile ['pi:dəufaɪl] n (US)
= **paedophile**

pee [pi:] vi (inf) пи́сать (perf попи́сать)

peel [pi:l] n кожура́ ▷ vt (vegetables,
fruit) чи́стить (perf почи́стить) ▷ vi (paint)
лупи́ться (perf облупи́ться); (wallpaper)
отстава́ть (perf отста́ть); (skin)
шелуши́ться (impf)

peep [pi:p] n (look) взгляд укра́дкой ▷ vi
взгля́дывать (perf взгляну́ть)

peer [pɪə'] n (Brit: noble) пэр; (equal)
ро́вня m/f; (contemporary) рове́сник(-ица)
▷ vi: **to peer at** всма́триваться (perf
всмотре́ться) в +acc

peg [peg] n (for coat etc) крючо́к; (Brit:
also **clothes peg**) прище́пка

pejorative [pɪ'dʒɒrətɪv] adj
уничижи́тельный

pelvis ['pelvɪs] n таз

pen [pen] n ру́чка; (felt-tip) флома́стер;
(enclosure) заго́н

penalty ['penltɪ] n наказа́ние; (fine)
штраф; (Sport) пена́льти m ind

pence [pens] npl of **penny**

pencil ['pensl] n каранда́ш

pending ['pendɪŋ] prep впредь до +gen,
в ожида́нии +gen ▷ adj (lawsuit, exam
etc) предстоя́щий

penetrate ['penɪtreɪt] vt (subj: person,
light) проника́ть (perf прони́кнуть) в/на
+acc

penguin ['peŋgwɪn] n пингви́н

penicillin [penɪ'sɪlɪn] n пеницилли́н

peninsula [pə'nɪnsjulə] n полуо́стров

penis ['pi:nɪs] n пе́нис, полово́й член

penknife ['pennaɪf] n перочи́нный нож

penniless ['penɪlɪs] adj без гроша́

penny ['penɪ] (pl **pennies** or **pence**) n
(Brit) пе́нни nt ind, пенс

pension ['penʃən] n пе́нсия; **pensioner**
n (Brit: also **old age pensioner**)
пенсионе́р(ка)

pentagon ['pentəgən] n (US): **the
Pentagon** Пентаго́н

penultimate [pe'nʌltɪmət] adj
предпосле́дний

people ['pi:pl] npl (persons) лю́ди pl;
(nation, race) наро́д; **several people came**
пришло́ не́сколько челове́к; **people say
that …** говоря́т, что …

pepper ['pepə'] n пе́рец ▷ vt (fig): **to
pepper with** забра́сывать (perf заброса́ть)
+instr; **peppermint** n (sweet) мя́тная
конфе́та

per [pə:'] prep (of amounts) на +acc; (of
price) за +acc; (of charge) с +gen; **per
annum/day** в год/день; **per person** на
челове́ка

perceive [pə'si:v] vt (realize) осознава́ть
(perf осозна́ть)

per cent n проце́нт

percentage [pə'sentɪdʒ] n проце́нт

perception [pə'sepʃən] n (insight)
понима́ние

perch [pə:tʃ] vi: **to perch (on)** (bird)
сади́ться (perf сесть) (на +acc); (person)
приса́живаться (perf присе́сть) (на +acc)

percussion [pə'kʌʃən] n уда́рные
инструме́нты mpl

perennial [pə'renɪəl] adj (fig) ве́чный

perfect [adj 'pə:fɪkt, vb pə'fɛkt] adj
соверше́нный, безупре́чный; (weather)
прекра́сный; (utter: nonsense etc)
соверше́нный ▷ vt (technique)
соверше́нствовать (perf
усоверше́нствовать); **perfection**
[pə'fɛkʃən] n соверше́нство; **perfectly**
['pə:fɪktlɪ] adv (well, all right) вполне́

perform [pə'fɔ:m] vt (task, operation)
выполня́ть (perf вы́полнить); (piece of
music) исполня́ть (perf испо́лнить); (play)
игра́ть (perf сыгра́ть) ▷ vi (well, badly)
справля́ться (perf спра́виться);
performance n (of actor, athlete etc)
выступле́ние; (of musical work)
исполне́ние; (of play, show)
представле́ние; (of car, engine, company)
рабо́та; **performer** n исполни́тель(ница)
m(f)

perfume ['pə:fju:m] n духи́ pl

perhaps [pə'hæps] adv мо́жет быть,
возмо́жно

perimeter [pə'rɪmɪtə'] n пери́метр

period ['pɪərɪəd] n (length of time)
пери́од; (Scol) уро́к; (esp US: full stop)
то́чка; (Med) менструа́ция ▷ adj
(costume, furniture) стари́нный;
periodical [pɪərɪ'ɔdɪkl] n (magazine)
периоди́ческое изда́ние ▷ adj
периоди́ческий

perish ['perɪʃ] vi (person) погиба́ть (perf
поги́бнуть)

perk [pə:k] n (inf) дополни́тельное
преиму́щество

perm [pə:m] n пермане́нт, хими́ческая
зави́вка

permanent ['pə:mənənt] adj
постоя́нный; (dye, ink) сто́йкий

permission [pə'mɪʃən] n позволе́ние,
разреше́ние

permit [vb pə'mɪt, n 'pə:mɪt] vt позволя́ть
(perf позво́лить) ▷ n разреше́ние

persecute ['pə:sɪkju:t] vt пресле́довать
(impf)

persecution [pə:sɪ'kju:ʃən] n
пресле́дование

persevere [pə:sɪ'vɪə'] vi упо́рствовать
(impf)

persist [pə'sɪst] vi: **to persist (in doing)**
наста́ивать (perf настоя́ть) (на том, что́бы
+infin); **persistent** adj
непрекраща́ющийся; (smell) сто́йкий;
(person) упо́рный

person ['pə:sn] n челове́к; **in person**
ли́чно; **personal** adj ли́чный; **personal
computer** n персона́льный компью́тер;
personality [pə:sə'nælɪtɪ] n хара́ктер;
(famous person) знамени́тость f;

personally adv ли́чно; **to take sth personally** принима́ть (perf приня́ть) что-н на свой счёт
personnel [pə:sə'nɛl] n персона́л, штат; (Mil) ли́чный соста́в
perspective [pə'spɛktɪv] n (Archit, Art) перспекти́ва; (way of thinking) ви́дение; **to get sth into perspective** (fig) смотре́ть (perf посмотре́ть) на что-н в и́стинном све́те
perspiration [pə:spɪ'reɪʃən] n пот
persuade [pə'sweɪd] vt: **to persuade sb to do** убежда́ть (perf убеди́ть) or угова́ривать (perf уговори́ть) кого- н +infin
persuasion [pə'sweɪʒən] n убежде́ние
persuasive [pə'sweɪsɪv] adj (argument) убеди́тельный; (person) насто́йчивый
perverse [pə'və:s] adj (contrary) вре́дный
pervert [vb pə'və:t, n 'pə:və:t] vt (person, mind) развраща́ть (perf разврати́ть), растлева́ть (perf растли́ть); (truth, sb's words) извраща́ть (perf изврати́ть) ⊳ n (also **sexual pervert**) (полово́й) извраще́нец
pessimism ['pɛsɪmɪzəm] n пессими́зм
pessimistic [pɛsɪ'mɪstɪk] adj пессимисти́чный
pest [pɛst] n (insect) вреди́тель m; (fig: nuisance) зану́да m/f
pester ['pɛstə'] vt пристава́ть (perf приста́ть) к +dat
pesticide ['pɛstɪsaɪd] n пестици́д
pet [pɛt] n дома́шнее живо́тное nt adj
petal ['pɛtl] n лепесто́к
petite [pə'ti:t] adj миниатю́рный
petition [pə'tɪʃən] n (signed document) пети́ция
petrified ['pɛtrɪfaɪd] adj (fig) оцепене́вший; **I was petrified** я оцепене́л
petrol ['pɛtrəl] (Brit) n бензи́н; **two/four-star petrol** низкоокта́новый/высокоокта́новый бензи́н
petroleum [pə'trəʊlɪəm] n нефть f
petty ['pɛtɪ] adj (trivial) ме́лкий; (small-minded) ограни́ченный
pew [pju:] n скамья́ (в це́ркви)
phantom ['fæntəm] n фанто́м
pharmacist ['fɑ:məsɪst] n фармаце́вт
pharmacy ['fɑ:məsɪ] n (shop) апте́ка
phase [feɪz] n фа́за ⊳ vt: **to phase sth in** поэта́пно вводи́ть (perf ввести́) что-н; **to phase sth out** поэта́пно ликвиди́ровать (impf/perf) что-н
PhD n abbr (= Doctor of Philosophy) до́ктор филосо́фии
pheasant ['fɛznt] n фаза́н
phenomena [fə'nɔmɪnə] npl of **phenomenon**
phenomenal [fə'nɔmɪnl] adj феномена́льный
phenomenon [fə'nɔmɪnən] (pl **phenomena**) n явле́ние, феноме́н
philosopher [fɪ'lɔsəfə'] n фило́соф

philosophical [fɪlə'sɔfɪkl] adj филосо́фский
philosophy [fɪ'lɔsəfɪ] n филосо́фия
phobia ['fəʊbjə] n фо́бия, страх
phone [fəʊn] n телефо́н ⊳ vt звони́ть (perf позвони́ть) +dat; **to be on the phone** говори́ть (impf) по телефо́ну; (possess phone) име́ть (impf) телефо́н; **phone back** vt перезва́нивать (perf перезвони́ть) +dat ⊳ vi перезва́нивать (perf перезвони́ть); **phone up** vt звони́ть (perf позвони́ть) +dat; **phone book** n телефо́нная кни́га; **phone box** n (Brit) телефо́нная бу́дка; **phone call** n телефо́нный звоно́к; **phonecard** n телефо́нная ка́рта
phonetics [fə'nɛtɪks] n фоне́тика
phoney ['fəʊnɪ] adj фальши́вый
photo ['fəʊtəʊ] n фотогра́фия; **photocopier** ['fəʊtəʊkɔpɪə'] n (machine) ксе́рокс, копирова́льная маши́на; **photocopy** n ксероко́пия, фотоко́пия ⊳ vt фотокопи́ровать (perf сфотокопи́ровать), ксерокопи́ровать (impf/perf); **photograph** n фотогра́фия ⊳ vt фотографи́ровать (perf сфотографи́ровать); **photographer** [fə'tɔgrəfə'] n фото́граф; **photography** [fə'tɔgrəfɪ] n фотогра́фия
phrase [freɪz] n фра́за ⊳ vt формули́ровать (perf сформули́ровать)
physical ['fɪzɪkl] adj физи́ческий; (world, object) материа́льный; **physically** adv физи́чески
physician [fɪ'zɪʃən] n (esp US) врач
physicist ['fɪzɪsɪst] n фи́зик
physics ['fɪzɪks] n фи́зика
physiotherapy [fɪzɪəʊ'θɛrəpɪ] n физиотерапи́я
physique [fɪ'zi:k] n телосложе́ние
pianist ['pi:ənɪst] n пиани́ст(ка)
piano [pɪ'ænəʊ] n пиани́но, фортепья́но nt ind
pick [pɪk] n (also **pickaxe**) кирка́ ⊳ vt (select) выбира́ть (perf вы́брать); (gather: fruit, flowers) собира́ть (perf собра́ть); (remove) рвать (impf); (lock) взла́мывать (perf взлома́ть); **take your pick** выбира́йте; **to pick one's nose/teeth** ковыря́ть (impf) в носу́/зуба́х; **to pick a quarrel (with sb)** иска́ть (impf) по́вод для ссо́ры (с кем-н); **pick out** vt (distinguish) разгляде́ть (perf); (select) отбира́ть (perf отобра́ть); **pick up** vi (improve) улучша́ться (perf улу́чшиться) ⊳ vt (lift) поднима́ть (perf подня́ть); (arrest) забира́ть (perf забра́ть); (collect: person: by car) заезжа́ть (perf зае́хать) за +instr; (passenger) подбира́ть (perf подобра́ть); (language, skill etc) усва́ивать (perf усво́ить); (Radio) лови́ть (perf пойма́ть); **to pick up speed** набира́ть (perf набра́ть) ско́рость; **to pick o.s. up** (after falling) поднима́ться (perf подня́ться)

pickle ['pɪkl] n (*also* **pickles**) соле́нья ntpl ▷ vt (*in vinegar*) маринова́ть (*perf* замаринова́ть); (*in salt water*) соли́ть (*perf* засоли́ть)

pickpocket ['pɪkpɔkɪt] n вор-карма́нник

picnic ['pɪknɪk] n пикни́к

picture ['pɪktʃəʳ] n карти́на; (*photo*) фотогра́фия; (*TV*) изображе́ние ▷ vt (*imagine*) рисова́ть (*perf* нарисова́ть) карти́ну +gen; **pictures** npl: **the pictures** (*Brit: inf*) кино́ nt ind

picturesque [pɪktʃə'rɛsk] adj живопи́сный

pie [paɪ] n пиро́г; (*small*) пирожо́к

piece [piːs] n (*portion, part*) кусо́к; (*component*) дета́ль f ▷ vt: **to piece together** (*information*) свя́зывать (*perf* связа́ть); (*object*) соединя́ть (*perf* соедини́ть); **a piece of clothing** вещь, предме́т оде́жды; **a piece of advice** сове́т; **to take to pieces** (*dismantle*) разбира́ть (*perf* разобра́ть)

pier [pɪəʳ] n пирс

pierce [pɪəs] vt протыка́ть (*perf* проткну́ть), прока́лывать (*perf* проколо́ть)

pig [pɪg] n (*also fig*) свинья́

pigeon ['pɪdʒən] n го́лубь m

pigtail ['pɪgteɪl] n коси́чка

pike [paɪk] n inv (*fish*) щу́ка

pile [paɪl] n (*large heap*) ку́ча, гру́да; (*neat stack*) сто́пка; (*of carpet*) ворс ▷ vi: **to pile into** (*vehicle*) набива́ться (*perf* наби́ться) в +acc; **to pile out of** (*vehicle*) выва́ливаться (*perf* вы́валиться) из +gen; **pile up** vt (*objects*) сва́ливать (*perf* свали́ть) в ку́чу ▷ vi громозди́ться (*impf*); (*problems, work*) нака́пливаться (*perf* накопи́ться)

piles [paɪlz] npl (*Med*) геморро́й msg

pilgrimage ['pɪlgrɪmɪdʒ] n пало́мничество

pill [pɪl] n табле́тка; **the pill** (*contraceptive*) противозача́точные pl adj (*also fig*)

pillar ['pɪləʳ] n (*Archit*) столб, коло́нна

pillow ['pɪləu] n поду́шка; **pillowcase** n на́волочка

pilot ['paɪlət] n (*Aviat*) пило́т, лётчик ▷ cpd (*scheme, study etc*) эксперимента́льный ▷ vt (*aircraft*) управля́ть (*impf*) +instr

pimple ['pɪmpl] n прыщ, пры́щик

PIN [pɪn] n (= *personal identification number*) (*also* **PIN number**) персона́льный идентификацио́нный но́мер

pin [pɪn] n (*for clothes, papers*) була́вка ▷ vt прика́лывать (*perf* приколо́ть); **pins and needles** (*fig*) колотьё; **to pin sth on sb** (*fig*) возлага́ть (*perf* возложи́ть) что-н на кого́-н; **pin down** vt: **to pin sb down** (*fig*) принужда́ть (*perf* прину́дить) кого́-н

pinch [pɪntʃ] n (*small amount*) щепо́тка ▷ vt щипа́ть (*perf* ущипну́ть); (*inf: steal*) стащи́ть (*perf*); **at a pinch** в кра́йнем слу́чае

pine [paɪn] n (*tree, wood*) сосна́

pineapple ['paɪnæpl] n анана́с

pink [pɪŋk] adj ро́зовый

pint [paɪnt] n пи́нта

● **PINT**

● Одна́ пи́нта равна́ 0,568 л.

pioneer [paɪə'nɪəʳ] n (*of science, method*) первооткрыва́тель m, нова́тор

pious ['paɪəs] adj набо́жный

pip [pɪp] n (*of grape, melon*) ко́сточка; (*of apple, orange*) зёрнышко

pipe [paɪp] n (*for water, gas*) труба́; (*for smoking*) тру́бка ▷ vt (*water, gas, oil*) подава́ть (*perf* пода́ть); **pipes** npl (*also* **bagpipes**) волы́нка fsg

pirate ['paɪərət] n (*sailor*) пира́т ▷ vt (*video tape, cassette*) незако́нно распространя́ть (*perf* распространи́ть)

Pisces ['paɪsiːz] n Ры́бы fpl

pistol ['pɪstl] n пистоле́т

pit [pɪt] n (*in ground*) я́ма; (*also* **coal pit**) ша́хта; (*quarry*) карье́р ▷ vt: **to pit one's wits against sb** состяза́ться (*impf*) в уме́ с кем-н

pitch [pɪtʃ] n (*Brit: Sport*) по́ле; (*Mus*) высота́; (*level*) у́ровень m

pitiful ['pɪtɪful] adj жа́лкий

pity ['pɪtɪ] n жа́лость f ▷ vt жале́ть (*perf* пожале́ть)

pizza ['piːtsə] n пи́цца

placard ['plækɑːd] n плака́т

place [pleɪs] vt (*put*) помеща́ть (*perf* помести́ть); (*identify: person*) вспомина́ть (*perf* вспо́мнить) ▷ n ме́сто; (*home*): **at his place** у него́ (до́ма); **to place an order with sb for sth** (*Comm*) зака́зывать (*perf* заказа́ть) что-н у кого́-н; **to take place** происходи́ть (*perf* произойти́); **out of place** (*inappropriate*) неуме́стный; **in the first place** (*first of all*) во-пе́рвых; **to change places with sb** меня́ться (*perf* поменя́ться) места́ми с кем-н

placid ['plæsɪd] adj (*person*) ти́хий

plague [pleɪg] n (*Med*) чума́; (*fig: of locusts etc*) наше́ствие ▷ vt (*fig: subj: problems*) осажда́ть (*perf* осади́ть)

plaice [pleɪs] n inv ка́мбала

plain [pleɪn] adj просто́й; (*unpatterned*) гла́дкий; (*clear*) я́сный, поня́тный ▷ adv (*wrong, stupid etc*) я́вно ▷ n (*Geo*) равни́на; **plainly** adv я́сно

plan [plæn] n план ▷ vt плани́ровать (*perf* заплани́ровать); (*draw up plans for*) плани́ровать (*impf*) ▷ vi плани́ровать (*impf*)

plane [pleɪn] n (*Aviat*) самолёт; (*fig: level*) план

planet ['plænɪt] n плане́та

plank [plæŋk] n (*of wood*) доска́

planning ['plænɪŋ] n (*of future, event*) плани́рование; (*also* **town planning**) планиро́вка

plant [plɑːnt] n (Bot) расте́ние; (factory) заво́д; (machinery) устано́вка ▷ vt (seed, garden) сажа́ть (perf посади́ть); (field) засе́ивать (perf засе́ять); (bomb, evidence) подкла́дывать (perf подложи́ть); **plantation** [plæn'teɪʃən] n (of tea, sugar etc) планта́ция; (of trees) лесонасажде́ние

plaque [plæk] n (on teeth) налёт; (on building) мемориа́льная доска́

plaster ['plɑːstə'] n (for walls) штукату́рка; (also **plaster of Paris**) гипс; (Brit: also **sticking plaster**) пла́стырь m ▷ vt (wall, ceiling) штукату́рить (perf оштукату́рить); (cover): **to plaster with** заштукату́ривать (perf заштукату́рить) +instr

plastic ['plæstɪk] n пластма́сса ▷ adj (made of plastic) пластма́ссовый

plate [pleɪt] n (dish) таре́лка

plateau ['plætəʊ] (pl **plateaus** or **plateaux**) n плато́ nt ind

platform ['plætfɔːm] n (at meeting) трибу́на; (at station) помо́ст; (for landing, loading on etc) площа́дка; (Rail, Pol) платфо́рма

plausible ['plɔːzɪbl] adj убеди́тельный

play [pleɪ] n пье́са ▷ vt (subj: children: game) игра́ть (impf) в +acc; (sport, cards) игра́ть (perf сыгра́ть) в +acc; (opponent) игра́ть (perf сыгра́ть) с +instr; (part, piece of music) игра́ть (perf сыгра́ть); (instrument) игра́ть (impf) на +prp; (tape, record) ста́вить (perf поста́вить) ▷ vi игра́ть (impf); **play down** vt не заостря́ть (impf) внима́ние на +prp; **player** n (Sport) игро́к; **playful** adj (person) игри́вый; **playground** n (in park) де́тская площа́дка; (in school) игрова́я площа́дка; **playgroup** n де́тская гру́ппа; **playtime** n (Scol) переме́на; **playwright** n драмату́рг

plc abbr (Brit) (= public limited company) публи́чная компа́ния с ограни́ченной отве́тственностью

plea [pliː] n (personal request) мольба́; (public request) призы́в; (Law) заявле́ние

plead [pliːd] vt (ignorance, ill health etc) ссыла́ться (perf сосла́ться) на +acc ▷ vi (Law): **to plead guilty/not guilty** признава́ть (perf призна́ть) себя́ вино́вным(-ой)/невино́вным(-ой); (beg): **to plead with sb** умоля́ть (impf) кого́-н

pleasant ['plɛznt] adj прия́тный

please [pliːz] excl пожа́луйста ▷ vt угожда́ть (perf угоди́ть) +dat; **please yourself!** (inf) как Вам уго́дно!; **do as you please** де́лайте как хоти́те; **he is difficult/ easy to please** ему́ тру́дно/легко́ угоди́ть; **pleased** adj: **pleased (with)** дово́льный (+instr); **pleased to meet you** о́чень прия́тно

pleasure ['plɛʒə'] n удово́льствие; **it's a pleasure** не сто́ит; **to take pleasure in** получа́ть (perf получи́ть) удово́льствие от +gen

pleat [pliːt] n скла́дка

pledge [plɛdʒ] n обяза́тельство ▷ vt (money) обя́зываться (perf обяза́ться) дать; (support) обя́зываться (perf обяза́ться) оказа́ть

plentiful ['plɛntɪful] adj оби́льный

plenty ['plɛntɪ] n (enough) изоби́лие; **plenty of** (food, money etc) мно́го +gen; (jobs, people, houses) мно́жество +gen; **we've got plenty of time to get there** у нас доста́точно вре́мени, что́бы туда́ добра́ться

pliers ['plaɪəz] npl плоскогу́бцы pl

plight [plaɪt] n му́ки fpl

plot [plɔt] n (conspiracy) за́говор; (of story) сюже́т; (of land) уча́сток ▷ vt (plan) замышля́ть (замы́слить impf); (Math) наноси́ть (perf нанести́) ▷ vi (conspire) составля́ть (perf соста́вить) за́говор

plough [plaʊ] (US **plow**) n плуг ▷ vt паха́ть (perf вспаха́ть)

ploy [plɔɪ] n уло́вка

pluck [plʌk] vt (eyebrows) выщи́пывать (perf вы́щипать); (instrument) перебира́ть (impf) стру́ны +gen; **to pluck up courage** набира́ться (perf набра́ться) хра́брости or му́жества

plug [plʌg] n (Elec) ви́лка, штёпсель m; (in sink, bath) про́бка ▷ vt (hole) затыка́ть (perf заткну́ть); (inf: advertise) реклами́ровать (perf разреклами́ровать); **plug in** vt (Elec) включа́ть (perf включи́ть) в розе́тку

plum [plʌm] n сли́ва

plumber ['plʌmə'] n водопрово́дчик, сле́сарь-санте́хник

plumbing ['plʌmɪŋ] n (piping) водопрово́д и канализа́ция; (trade, work) слеса́рное де́ло

plummet ['plʌmɪt] vi: **to plummet (down)** (price, amount) ре́зко па́дать (perf упа́сть)

plump [plʌmp] adj по́лный, пу́хлый ▷ vi: **to plump for** (inf) выбира́ть (perf вы́брать)

plunge [plʌndʒ] n (fig: of prices etc) ре́зкое паде́ние ▷ vt (knife) мета́ть (perf метну́ть); (hand) выбра́сывать (perf вы́бросить) ▷ vi (fall) ру́хнуть (perf); (dive) броса́ться (perf бро́ситься); (fig: prices etc) ре́зко па́дать (perf упа́сть); **to take the plunge** (fig) отва́живаться (perf отва́житься)

plural ['pluərl] n мно́жественное число́

plus [plʌs] n, adj плюс ind ▷ prep: **ten plus ten is twenty** де́сять плюс де́сять — два́дцать; **ten/twenty plus** (more than) де́сять/два́дцать с ли́шним

plywood ['plaɪwud] n фане́ра

PM abbr (Brit) = **Prime Minister**

p.m. adv abbr (= post meridiem) по́сле полу́дня

pneumonia [njuː'məʊnɪə] n воспале́ние лёгких, пневмони́я

PO Box n abbr (= Post Office Box) абоне́нтский or почто́вый я́щик

pocket ['pɔkɪt] n карма́н; (fig: small area) уголо́к ▷ vt класть (perf положи́ть) себе́ в карма́н; **to be out of pocket** (Brit) быть (impf) в убы́тке

podcast ['pɔdkæst] n подка́ст ▷ vi выпуска́ть (perf вы́пустить) подка́ст

poem ['pəʊɪm] n (long) поэ́ма; (short) стихотворе́ние

poet ['pəʊɪt] n (male) поэ́т; (female) поэте́сса; **poetic** [pəʊ'ɛtɪk] adj поэти́ческий; **poetry** n поэ́зия

poignant ['pɔɪnjənt] adj пронзи́тельный

point [pɔɪnt] n (of needle, knife etc) остриё, ко́нчик; (purpose) смысл; (significant part) суть f; (particular position) то́чка; (detail, moment) моме́нт; (stage in development) ста́дия; (score) очко́; (Elec: also **power point**) розе́тка ▷ vt (show, mark) ука́зывать (perf указа́ть) ▷ vi: **to point at** ука́зывать (perf указа́ть) на +acc; **points** npl (Rail) стре́лка fsg; **to be on the point of doing** собира́ться (impf) +infin; **I made a point of visiting him** я счёл необходи́мым посети́ть его́; **to get/miss the point** понима́ть (perf поня́ть)/не понима́ть (perf поня́ть) суть; **to come to the point** доходи́ть (perf дойти́) до су́ти; **there's no point in doing** нет смы́сла +infin; **to point sth at sb** (gun etc) наце́ливать (perf наце́лить) что-н на кого́-н; **point out** vt ука́зывать (perf указа́ть) на +acc; **point to** vt fus ука́зывать (perf указа́ть) на +acc; **point-blank** adv (refuse) наотре́з; (say, ask) напрями́к ▷ adj: **at point-blank range** в упо́р; **pointed** adj о́стрый; (fig: remark) язви́тельный; **pointless** adj бессмы́сленный; **point of view** n то́чка зре́ния

poison ['pɔɪzn] n яд ▷ vt отравля́ть (perf отрави́ть); **poisonous** adj (toxic) ядови́тый

poke [pəʊk] vt (with stick etc) ты́кать (perf ткну́ть); **to poke sth in(to)** (put) втыка́ть (perf воткну́ть) что-н в +acc

poker ['pəʊkə'] n кочерга́; (Cards) по́кер

Poland ['pəʊlənd] n По́льша

polar ['pəʊlə'] adj поля́рный; **polar bear** n бе́лый медве́дь m

pole [pəʊl] n (stick) шест; (telegraph pole) столб; (Geo) по́люс; **pole vault** n прыжки́ mpl с шесто́м

police [pə'li:s] npl поли́ция fsg; (in Russia) мили́ция fsg ▷ vt патрули́ровать (impf); **policeman** irreg n полице́йский m adj; **police officer** n полице́йский m adj; **police station** n полице́йский уча́сток; (in Russia) отделе́ние мили́ции; **policewoman** irreg n (же́нщина-) полице́йский m adj

policy ['pɔlɪsɪ] n поли́тика; (also **insurance policy**) по́лис

polio ['pəʊlɪəʊ] n полиомиели́т

Polish ['pəʊlɪʃ] adj по́льский

polish ['pɔlɪʃ] n (for furniture) (полирова́льная) па́ста; (for shoes) гутали́н; (for floor) масти́ка; (shine, also fig) лоск ▷ vt (furniture etc) полирова́ть (perf отполирова́ть); (floors, shoes) натира́ть (perf натере́ть); **polished** adj (style) отто́ченный

polite [pə'laɪt] adj ве́жливый

political [pə'lɪtɪkl] adj полити́ческий; (person) полити́чески акти́вный, политизи́рованный; **politically** adv полити́чески; **politically correct** полити́чески корре́ктный

politician [pɔlɪ'tɪʃən] n поли́тик, полити́ческий де́ятель m

politics ['pɔlɪtɪks] n поли́тика; (Scol) политоло́гия

poll [pəʊl] n (also **opinion poll**) опро́с; (usu pl: election) вы́боры mpl ▷ vt (number of votes) набира́ть (perf набра́ть)

pollen ['pɔlən] n пыльца́

pollute [pə'lu:t] vt загрязня́ть (perf загрязни́ть)

pollution [pə'lu:ʃən] n загрязне́ние; (substances) загрязни́тель m

polo neck ['pəʊləʊ-] n (also **polo neck sweater** or **jumper**) сви́тер с кру́глым воротнико́м

polyester [pɔlɪ'ɛstə'] n (fabric) полиэфи́рное волокно́

polystyrene [pɔlɪ'staɪri:n] n пенопла́ст

polythene ['pɔlɪθi:n] n полиэтиле́н

pomegranate ['pɔmɪɡrænɪt] n (Bot) грана́т

pompous ['pɔmpəs] adj (pej: person, style) напы́щенный, чва́нный

pond [pɔnd] n пруд

ponder ['pɔndə'] vt обду́мывать (perf обду́мать)

pony ['pəʊnɪ] n по́ни m ind; **ponytail** n (hairstyle) хвост, хво́стик

poodle ['pu:dl] n пу́дель m

pool [pu:l] n (puddle) лу́жа; (pond) пруд; (also **swimming pool**) бассе́йн; (fig: of light, paint) пятно́; (Sport, Comm) пул ▷ vt объединя́ть (perf объедини́ть); **pools** npl (also **football pools**) футбо́льный тотализа́тор; **typing pool**, (US) **secretary pool** машинопи́сное бюро́ nt ind

poor [puə'] adj (not rich) бе́дный; (bad) плохо́й; ▷ npl: **the poor** (people) беднота́ fsg, бе́дные pl adj; **poor in** (resources etc) бе́дный +instr; **poorly** adv пло́хо ▷ adj: **she is feeling poorly** она́ пло́хо себя́ чу́вствует

pop [pɔp] n (also **pop music**) поп-му́зыка; (inf: US: father) па́па m; (sound) хлопо́к ▷ vi (balloon) ло́паться (perf ло́пнуть) ▷ vt (put quickly): **to pop sth into/onto** забра́сывать (perf забро́сить) что-н в +acc/на +acc; **pop in** vi загля́дывать (perf загляну́ть), заска́кивать (perf заскочи́ть); **pop up** vi вылеза́ть (*perf* вы́лезти); **popcorn** *n* возду́шная кукуру́за, попко́рн

pope [pəup] *n*: **the Pope** Па́па *m* ри́мский

poplar ['pɒplə] *n* то́поль *m*

poppy ['pɒpɪ] *n* мак

pop star *n* поп-звезда́ *m/f*

popular ['pɒpjulə] *adj* популя́рный; **popularity** [pɒpju'lærɪtɪ] *n* популя́рность *f*

population [pɒpju'leɪʃən] *n* (*of town, country*) населе́ние

porcelain ['pɔːslɪn] *n* фарфо́р

porch [pɔːtʃ] *n* крыльцо́; (*US*) вера́нда

pore [pɔːʳ] *n* по́ра

pork [pɔːk] *n* свини́на

porn [pɔːn] *n* (*inf*) порногра́фия

pornographic [pɔːnə'græfɪk] *adj* порнографи́ческий

pornography [pɔː'nɔgrəfɪ] *n* порногра́фия

porridge ['pɔrɪdʒ] *n* овся́ная ка́ша

port [pɔːt] *n* (*harbour*) порт; (*wine*) портве́йн; **port of call** порт захо́да

portable ['pɔːtəbl] *adj* порта́тивный

porter ['pɔːtəʳ] *n* (*doorkeeper*) портье́ *m ind*, швейца́р; (*for luggage*) носи́льщик

portfolio [pɔːt'fəulɪəu] *n* (*Art*) па́пка

portion ['pɔːʃən] *n* (*part*) часть *f*; (*equal part*) до́ля; (*of food*) по́рция

portrait ['pɔːtreɪt] *n* портре́т

portray [pɔː'treɪ] *vt* изобража́ть (*perf* изобрази́ть)

Portugal ['pɔːtjugl] *n* Португа́лия

Portuguese [pɔːtju'giːz] *adj* португа́льский

pose [pəuz] *n* по́за ▷ *vt* (*question*) ста́вить (*perf* поста́вить); (*problem, danger*) создава́ть (*perf* созда́ть) ▷ *vi* (*pretend*): **to pose as** выдава́ть (*perf* вы́дать) себя́ за +*acc*; **to pose for** пози́ровать (*impf*) для +*gen*

posh [pɔʃ] *adj* (*inf: hotel etc*) фешене́бельный; (*: person, behaviour*) великосве́тский

position [pə'zɪʃən] *n* положе́ние; (*of house, thing*) расположе́ние, ме́сто; (*job*) до́лжность *f*; (*in competition, race*) ме́сто; (*attitude*) пози́ция ▷ *vt* располага́ть (*perf* расположи́ть)

positive ['pɒzɪtɪv] *adj* (*affirmative*) положи́тельный; (*certain*) уве́ренный, убеждённый; (*definite: decision, policy*) определённый

possess [pə'zɛs] *vt* владе́ть (*impf*) +*instr*; (*quality, ability*) облада́ть (*impf*) +*instr*; **possession** [pə'zɛʃən] *n* (*state of possessing*) владе́ние; **possessions** *npl* (*belongings*) ве́щи *fpl*; **to take possession of** вступа́ть (*perf* вступи́ть) во владе́ние +*instr*; **possessive** *adj* (*quality*) со́бственнический; (*person*) ревни́вый; (*Ling*) притяжа́тельный

possibility [pɒsɪ'bɪlɪtɪ] *n* возмо́жность *f*

possible ['pɒsɪbl] *adj* возмо́жный; **it's possible** э́то возмо́жно; **as soon as possible** как мо́жно скоре́е

possibly ['pɒsɪblɪ] *adv* (*perhaps*) возмо́жно; **if you possibly can** е́сли то́лько Вы мо́жете; **I cannot possibly come** я ника́к не смогу́ прийти́

post [pəust] *n* (*Brit: mail*) по́чта; (*pole*) столб; (*job, situation, also Comput*) пост ▷ *vt* (*Brit: mail*) посыла́ть (*perf* посла́ть), отправля́ть (*perf* отпра́вить) (по по́чте); **postage** *n* почто́вые расхо́ды *mpl*; **postal** *adj* почто́вый; **postcard** *n* (почто́вая) откры́тка; **postcode** *n* (*Brit*) почто́вый и́ндекс

poster ['pəustəʳ] *n* афи́ша, плака́т; (*for advertising*) по́стер

postgraduate ['pəust'grædjuət] *n* аспира́нт(ка) ▷ *adj*: **postgraduate study** аспиранту́ра

postman ['pəustmən] *irreg n* почтальо́н

post office *n* почто́вое отделе́ние, отделе́ние свя́зи; (*organization*): **the Post Office** ≈ Министе́рство свя́зи

postpone [pəus'pəun] *vt* откла́дывать (*perf* отложи́ть)

posture ['pɒstʃəʳ] *n* (*of body*) оса́нка

pot [pɒt] *n* (*for cooking, flowers*) горшо́к; (*also teapot*) (зава́рочный) ча́йник; (*also coffeepot*) кофе́йник; (*bowl, container*) ба́нка ▷ *vt* (*plant*) сажа́ть (*perf* посади́ть); **a pot of tea** ча́йник ча́я

potato [pə'teɪtəu] (*pl* **potatoes**) *n* карто́фель *m no pl*, карто́шка (*inf*); (*single potato*) карто́фелина

potent ['pəutnt] *adj* мо́щный; (*drink*) кре́пкий

potential [pə'tɛnʃl] *adj* потенциа́льный ▷ *n* потенциа́л

pottery ['pɒtərɪ] *n* кера́мика; (*factory*) фа́брика керами́ческих изде́лий; (*small*) керами́ческий цех

potty ['pɒtɪ] *adj* (*inf: mad*) чо́кнутый ▷ *n* (*for child*) горшо́к

pouch [pautʃ] *n* (*for tobacco*) кисе́т; (*for coins*) кошелёк; (*Zool*) су́мка

poultry ['pəultrɪ] *n* (*birds*) дома́шняя пти́ца; (*meat*) пти́ца

pounce [pauns] *vi*: **to pounce on** набра́сываться (*perf* набро́ситься) на +*acc*

pound [paund] *n* (*money, weight*) фунт; **pound sterling** фунт сте́рлингов

● **POUND**
●
● **Pound** — ме́ра ве́са ра́вная 0,454 кг.

pour [pɔːʳ] *vt* (*liquid*) налива́ть (*perf* нали́ть); (*dry substance*) насыпа́ть (*perf* насы́пать) ▷ *vi* (*water etc*) ли́ться (*impf*); (*rain*) лить (*impf*); **to pour sb some tea** налива́ть (*perf* нали́ть) кому́-н ча́й; **pour in** *vi* (*people*) вали́ть (*perf* повали́ть); (*news, letters etc*) сы́паться (*perf* посы́паться); **pour out** *vi* (*people*) вали́ть (*perf* повали́ть) ▷ *vt* (*drink*) налива́ть (*perf* нали́ть); (*fig: thoughts etc*) излива́ть (*perf* изли́ть)

pout [paut] *vi* надува́ть (*perf* наду́ть) гу́бы, ду́ться (*perf* наду́ться)

poverty ['pɔvətɪ] *n* бе́дность *f*

powder ['paudə^r] *n* порошо́к; (*also* face **powder**) пу́дра

power ['pauə^r] *n* (*authority*) власть *f*; (*ability, opportunity*) возмо́жность *f*; (*legal right*) полномо́чие; (*of engine*) мо́щность *f*; (*electricity*) (электро)эне́ргия; **to be in power** находи́ться (*impf*) у вла́сти; **powerful** *adj* могу́чий; (*person, organization*) могу́щественный; (*argument, engine*) мо́щный; **powerless** *adj* бесси́льный; **power station** *n* электроста́нция

pp *abbr* = **pages**

PR *n abbr* = **public relations**

practical ['præktɪkl] *adj* (*not theoretical*) практи́ческий; (*sensible, viable*) практи́чный; (*good with hands*) уме́лый; **practically** *adv* практи́чески

practice ['præktɪs] *n* пра́ктика; (*custom*) привы́чка ▷ *vt, vi* (*US*) = **practise**; **in practice** на пра́ктике; **I am out of practice** я разучи́лся

practise ['præktɪs] (*US* **practice**) *vt* (*piano etc*) упражня́ться (*impf*) на +*acc*; (*sport, language*) отраба́тывать (*perf* отрабо́тать); (*custom*) приде́рживаться (*impf*) +*gen*; (*craft*) занима́ться (*impf*) +*instr*; (*religion*) испове́довать (*impf*) ▷ *vi* (*Mus*) упражня́ться (*impf*); (*Sport*) тренирова́ться (*impf*); (*lawyer, doctor*) практикова́ть (*impf*); **to practise law/medicine** занима́ться (*impf*) адвока́тской/ враче́бной пра́ктикой

practising ['præktɪsɪŋ] *adj* (*Christian etc*) на́божный; (*doctor, lawyer*) практику́ющий

practitioner [præk'tɪʃənə^r] *n* терапе́вт

pragmatic [præg'mætɪk] *adj* (*reason etc*) прагмати́ческий

praise [preɪz] *n* (*approval*) похвала́ ▷ *vt* хвали́ть (*perf* похвали́ть)

pram [præm] *n* (*Brit*) де́тская коля́ска

prawn [prɔːn] *n* креве́тка

pray [preɪ] *vi* моли́ться (*perf* помоли́ться); **to pray for/that** моли́ться (*impf*) за +*acc/*, что́бы; **prayer** [prɛə^r] *n* моли́тва

preach [priːtʃ] *vi* пропове́довать (*impf*) ▷ *vt* (*sermon*) произноси́ть (*perf* произнести́); **preacher** *n* пропове́дник(-ица)

precarious [prɪ'kɛərɪəs] *adj* риско́ванный

precaution [prɪ'kɔːʃən] *n* предосторо́жность *f*

precede [prɪ'siːd] *vt* предше́ствовать (*impf*) +*dat*; **precedent** ['prɛsɪdənt] *n* прецеде́нт

preceding [prɪ'siːdɪŋ] *adj* предше́ствующий

precinct ['priːsɪŋkt] *n* (*US: in city*) райо́н, префекту́ра; **pedestrian precinct** (*Brit*) пешехо́дная зо́на; **shopping precinct** (*Brit*) торго́вый центр

precious ['prɛʃəs] *adj* це́нный; (*stone*) драгоце́нный

precise [prɪ'saɪs] *adj* то́чный; **precisely** *adv* (*accurately*) то́чно; (*exactly*) ро́вно

precision [prɪ'sɪʒən] *n* то́чность *f*

predator ['prɛdətə^r] *n* хи́щник

predecessor ['priːdɪsɛsə^r] *n* предше́ственник(-ица)

predicament [prɪ'dɪkəmənt] *n* затрудни́тельное положе́ние

predict [prɪ'dɪkt] *vt* предска́зывать (*perf* предсказа́ть); **predictable** *adj* предска́зуемый; **prediction** [prɪ'dɪkʃən] *n* предсказа́ние

predominantly [prɪ'dɔmɪnəntlɪ] *adv* преиму́щественно

preface ['prɛfəs] *n* предисло́вие

● **PREFECT**
●
● **Prefect** — ста́роста шко́лы. Ста́ростами
● мо́гут быть то́лько старшекла́ссники.
● Они́ помога́ют учителя́м подде́рживать
● в шко́ле дисципли́ну.

prefer [prɪ'fəː^r] *vt* предпочита́ть (*perf* предпоче́сть); **preferable** ['prɛfrəbl] *adj* предпочти́тельный; **preferably** ['prɛfrə blɪ] *adv* предпочти́тельно; **preference** ['prɛfrəns] *n* (*liking*): **to have a preference for** предпочита́ть (*impf*)

prefix ['priːfɪks] *n* приста́вка

pregnancy ['prɛgnənsɪ] *n* бере́менность *f*

pregnant ['prɛgnənt] *adj* бере́менная; (*remark, pause*) многозначи́тельный; **she is 3 months pregnant** она́ на четвёртом ме́сяце бере́менности

prehistoric ['priːhɪs'tɔrɪk] *adj* доистори́ческий

prejudice ['prɛdʒudɪs] *n* (*dislike*) предрассу́док; (*preference*) предвзя́тость *f*, предубежде́ние

preliminary [prɪ'lɪmɪnərɪ] *adj* предвари́тельный

prelude ['prɛljuːd] *n* прелю́дия

premature ['prɛmətʃuə^r] *adj* преждевре́менный; (*baby*) недоно́шенный

premier ['prɛmɪə^r] *adj* лу́чший ▷ *n* премье́р(-мини́стр)

première ['prɛmɪɛə^r] *n* премье́ра

premises ['prɛmɪsɪz] *npl* (*of business*) помеще́ние *ntsg*; **on the premises** в помеще́нии

premium ['priːmɪəm] *n* пре́мия; **to be at a premium** по́льзоваться (*impf*) больши́м спро́сом

premonition [prɛmə'nɪʃən] *n* предчу́вствие

preoccupied [prɪˈɔkjupaɪd] *adj*
озабо́ченный

preparation [prɛpəˈreɪʃən] *n* (*activity*)
подгото́вка; (*of food*) приготовле́ние;
preparations *npl* (*arrangements*)
приготовле́ния *ntpl*

prepare [prɪˈpɛəʳ] *vt* подгота́вливать (*perf*
подгото́вить); (*meal*) гото́вить (*perf*
пригото́вить) ▷ *vi*: **to prepare for**
гото́виться (*perf* подгото́виться) к +*dat*;
prepared *adj* гото́вый; **prepared for**
(*ready*) гото́вый к +*dat*

preposition [prɛpəˈzɪʃən] *n* предло́г

prescribe [prɪˈskraɪb] *vt* (*Med*)
пропи́сывать (*perf* прописа́ть)

prescription [prɪˈskrɪpʃən] *n* (*Med: slip
of paper*) реце́пт; (: *medicine*) лека́рство
(*назна́ченное врачо́м*)

presence [ˈprɛzns] *n* прису́тствие; (*fig*)
нару́жность *f*; **in sb's presence** в
прису́тствии кого́-н

present [*adj, n* ˈprɛznt, *vb* prɪˈzɛnt] *adj*
(*current*) ны́нешний, настоя́щий; (*in
attendance*) прису́тствующий ▷ *n* (*gift*)
пода́рок ▷ *vt* представля́ть (*perf*
предста́вить); (*Radio, TV*) вести́ (*impf*); **the
present** (*time*) настоя́щее *nt adj*; **at present**
в настоя́щее вре́мя; **to give sb a present**
дари́ть (*perf* подари́ть) кому́-н пода́рок;
to present sth to sb, present sb with sth
(*prize etc*) вруча́ть (*perf* вручи́ть) что-н
кому́-н; (*gift*) преподноси́ть (*perf*
преподнести́) что-н кому́-н; **to present sb
(to)** (*introduce*) представля́ть (*perf*
предста́вить) кого́-н (+*dat*)

presentation [prɛznˈteɪʃən] *n* (*of report
etc*) изложе́ние; (*appearance*) вне́шний
вид; (*also* **presentation ceremony**)
презента́ция

present-day *adj* сего́дняшний,
ны́нешний

presenter [prɪˈzɛntəʳ] *n* (*Radio, TV*)
веду́щий(-ая) *m(f) adj*; (: *of news*) ди́ктор

presently *adv* вско́ре; (*now*) в настоя́щее
вре́мя

preservation [prɛzəˈveɪʃən] *n* (*act: of
building, democracy*) сохране́ние

preservative [prɪˈzəːvətɪv] *n* (*for food*)
консерва́нт; (*for wood*) пропи́точный
соста́в

preserve [prɪˈzəːv] *vt* сохраня́ть (*perf*
сохрани́ть); (*food*) консерви́ровать (*perf*
законсерви́ровать) ▷ *n* (*usu pl: jam*)
варе́нье

preside [prɪˈzaɪd] *vi*: **to preside (over)**
председа́тельствовать (*impf*) (на +*prp*)

president [ˈprɛzɪdənt] *n* (*Pol, Comm*)
президе́нт; **presidential** [prɛzɪˈdɛnʃl] *adj*
президе́нтский; **presidential candidate**
кандида́т в президе́нты; **presidential
adviser** сове́тник президе́нта

press [prɛs] *n* (*also* **printing press**)
печа́тный стано́к ▷ *vt* (*hold together*)
прижима́ть (*perf* прижа́ть); (*push*)

нажима́ть (*perf* нажа́ть); (*iron*) гла́дить
(*perf* погла́дить); (*pressurize: person*)
вынужда́ть (*perf* вы́нудить); **the press**
(*newspapers, journalists*) пре́сса; **to press
sth on sb** (*insist*) навя́зывать (*perf*
навяза́ть) что-н кому́-н; **to press sb to do**
or **into doing** вынужда́ть (*perf* вы́нудить)
кого́-н +*infin*; **to press for** (*change etc*)
наста́ивать (*perf* настоя́ть) на +*prp*; **press
ahead** *vi*: **press ahead with** продолжа́ть
(*perf* продо́лжить); **press on** *vi*
продолжа́ть (*impf*); **press conference** *n*
пресс-конфере́нция; **pressing** *adj*
(*urgent*) неотло́жный

pressure [ˈprɛʃəʳ] *n* давле́ние; (*stress*)
напряже́ние; **to put pressure on sb (to do)**
ока́зывать (*perf* оказа́ть) давле́ние *or*
нажи́м на кого́-н (+*infin*); **pressure group**
n инициати́вная гру́ппа

prestige [prɛsˈtiːʒ] *n* прести́ж

prestigious [prɛsˈtɪdʒəs] *adj*
прести́жный

presumably [prɪˈzjuːməblɪ] *adv* на́до
полага́ть

presume [prɪˈzjuːm] *vt*: **to presume (that)**
(*suppose*) предполага́ть (*perf*
предположи́ть), что

pretence [prɪˈtɛns] (*US* **pretense**) *n*
притво́рство; **under false pretences** под
ло́жным предло́гом

pretend [prɪˈtɛnd] *vi*: **to pretend that**
притворя́ться (*perf* притвори́ться), что;
he pretended to help он сде́лал вид, что
помога́ет; **he pretended to be asleep** он
притвори́лся, что спит

pretense [prɪˈtɛns] *n* (*US*) = **pretence**

pretentious [prɪˈtɛnʃəs] *adj*
претенцио́зный

pretext [ˈpriːtɛkst] *n* предло́г

pretty [ˈprɪtɪ] *adj* (*person*) хоро́шенький;
(*thing*) краси́вый ▷ *adv* (*quite*)
дово́льно

prevail [prɪˈveɪl] *vi* (*be current*)
преоблада́ть (*impf*), превали́ровать
(*impf*); (*gain influence*) оде́рживать (*perf*
одержа́ть) верх; **prevailing** *adj* (*wind*)
преоблада́ющий

prevent [prɪˈvɛnt] *vt* (*accident etc*)
предотвраща́ть (*perf* предотврати́ть),
предупрежда́ть (*perf* предупреди́ть); **to
prevent sb from doing** меша́ть (*perf*
помеша́ть) кому́-н +*infin*; **prevention**
[prɪˈvɛnʃən] *n* предотвраще́ние,
предупрежде́ние; **preventive** *adj* (*Pol:
measures*) превенти́вный; (*medicine*)
профилакти́ческий

preview [ˈpriːvjuː] *n* (*of film*) (закры́тый)
просмо́тр; (*of exhibition*) вернисаж

previous [ˈpriːvɪəs] *adj* преды́дущий;
previous to до +*gen*; **previously** *adv*
(*before*) ра́нее; (*in the past*) пре́жде

prey [preɪ] *n* добы́ча

price [praɪs] *n* цена́ ▷ *vt* оце́нивать (*perf*
оцени́ть); **priceless** *adj* (*diamond,*

painting etc) бесце́нный; **price list** _n_
прейскура́нт

prick [prɪk] _n_ (_pain_) уко́л ▷ _vt_ (_make hole in_) прока́лывать (_perf_ проколо́ть); (_finger_) коло́ть (_perf_ уколо́ть); **to prick up one's ears** навостри́ть (_perf_) у́ши

prickly ['prɪklɪ] _adj_ колю́чий

pride [praɪd] _n_ го́рдость f; (_pej: arrogance_) горды́ня ▷ _vt:_ **to pride o.s. on** горди́ться (_impf_) +_instr_

priest [priːst] _n_ свяще́нник

primarily ['praɪmərɪlɪ] _adv_ в пе́рвую о́чередь

primary ['praɪmərɪ] _adj_ (_task_) первостепе́нный, первоочередно́й ▷ _n_ (_US: Pol_) предвари́тельные вы́боры _mpl_; **primary school** _n_ (_Brit_) нача́льная шко́ла

prime [praɪm] _adj_ (_most important_) гла́вный, основно́й; (_best quality_) первосо́ртный; (_example_) я́ркий ▷ _n_ расцве́т ▷ _vt_ (_fig: person_) подгота́вливать (_perf_ подгото́вить); **Prime Minister** _n_ премье́р-мини́стр

primitive ['prɪmɪtɪv] _adj_ (_early_) первобы́тный; (_unsophisticated_) примити́вный

primrose ['prɪmrəuz] _n_ первоцве́т

prince [prɪns] _n_ принц; (_Russian_) князь _m_; **princess** [prɪn'sɛs] _n_ принце́сса; (_Russian: wife_) княги́ня; (: _daughter_) княжна́

principal ['prɪnsɪpl] _adj_ гла́вный, основно́й ▷ _n_ (_of school, college_) дире́ктор; (_of university_) ре́ктор

principle ['prɪnsɪpl] _n_ при́нцип; (_scientific law_) зако́н; **in principle** в при́нципе; **on principle** из при́нципа

print [prɪnt] _n_ (_Typ_) шрифт; (_Art_) эста́мп, гравю́ра; (_Phot, fingerprint_) отпеча́ток; (_footprint_) след ▷ _vt_ (_book etc_) печа́тать (_perf_ напеча́тать); (_cloth_) набива́ть (_perf_ наби́ть); (_write in capitals_) писа́ть (_perf_ написа́ть) печа́тными бу́квами; **this book is out of print** э́та кни́га бо́льше не издаётся; **printer** _n_ (_machine_) при́нтер; (_firm: also_ **printer's**) типогра́фия

prior ['praɪə^r] _adj_ (_previous_) пре́жний; (_more important_) гла́внейший; **to have prior knowledge of sth** знать (_impf_) о чём-н зара́нее; **prior to** до +_gen_

priority [praɪ'ɔrɪtɪ] _n_ (_most urgent task_) первоочередна́я зада́ча; (_most important thing, task_) приорите́т; **to have priority (over)** име́ть (_impf_) преиму́щество (пе́ред +_instr_)

prison ['prɪzn] _n_ тюрьма́ ▷ _cpd_ тюре́мный; **prisoner** _n_ (_in prison_) заключённый(-ая) _m(f) adj_; (_captured person_) пле́нный(-ая) _m(f) adj_; **prisoner of war** _n_ военнопле́нный _m adj_

privacy ['prɪvəsɪ] _n_ уедине́ние

private ['praɪvɪt] _adj_ (_property, industry_) ча́стный; (_discussion, club_) закры́тый;

(_belongings, life_) ли́чный; (_thoughts, plans_) скры́тый; (_secluded_) уединённый; (_secretive, reserved_) за́мкнутый; (_confidential_) конфиденциа́льный; **"private"** (_on door_) "посторо́нним вход воспрещён"; **in private** конфиденциа́льно

privatize ['praɪvɪtaɪz] _vt_ приватизи́ровать (_impf/perf_)

privilege ['prɪvɪlɪdʒ] _n_ привиле́гия

prize [praɪz] _n_ приз ▷ _adj_ первокла́ссный ▷ _vt_ (высоко́) цени́ть (_impf_)

pro [prəu] _prep_ за +_acc_ ▷ _n:_ **the pros and cons** за и про́тив

probability [prɔbə'bɪlɪtɪ] _n:_ **probability of/that** вероя́тность f +_gen_/того́, что; **in all probability** по всей вероя́тности

probable ['prɔbəbl] _adj_ вероя́тный

probably ['prɔbəblɪ] _adv_ вероя́тно

probation [prə'beɪʃən] _n_ (_Law_) усло́вное осужде́ние; (_employee_) испыта́тельный срок

probe [prəub] _vt_ (_investigate_) рассле́довать (_impf/perf_); (_poke_) прощу́пывать (_perf_ прощу́пать)

problem ['prɔbləm] _n_ пробле́ма

procedure [prə'siːdʒər] _n_ процеду́ра

proceed [prə'siːd] _vi_ (_activity, event, process_) продолжа́ться (_perf_ продо́лжиться); (_person_) продвига́ться (_perf_ продви́нуться); **to proceed with** (_continue_) продолжа́ть (_perf_ продо́лжить); **to proceed to do** продолжа́ть (_perf_ продо́лжить) +_infin_; **proceedings** _npl_ (_events_) мероприя́тия _ntpl_; (_Law_) суде́бные разбира́тельства _ntsg_; **proceeds** ['prəusiːdz] _npl_ поступле́ния _ntpl_

process ['prəusɛs] _n_ проце́сс ▷ _vt_ обраба́тывать (_perf_ обрабо́тать); **in the process** в проце́ссе

procession [prə'sɛʃən] _n_ проце́ссия

proclaim [prə'kleɪm] _vt_ провозглаша́ть (_perf_ провозгласи́ть)

prod [prɔd] _vt_ (_push_) ты́кать (_perf_ ткнуть) ▷ _n_ тычо́к

produce [_vb_ prə'djuːs, _n_ 'prɔdjuːs] _vt_ производи́ть (_perf_ произвести́); (_Chem_) выраба́тывать (_perf_ вы́работать); (_evidence, argument_) представля́ть (_perf_ предста́вить); (_bring or take out_) предъявля́ть (_perf_ предъяви́ть); (_play, film_) ста́вить (_perf_ поста́вить) ▷ _n_ (_Agr_) (сельскохозя́йственная) проду́кция; **producer** [prə'djuːsər] _n_ (_of film, play_) режиссёр-постано́вщик, продю́сер

product ['prɔdʌkt] _n_ (_thing_) изде́лие; (_food, result_) проду́кт

production [prə'dʌkʃən] _n_ (_process_) произво́дство; (_amount produced_) проду́кция; (_Theat_) постано́вка

productive [prə'dʌktɪv] _adj_ производи́тельный, продукти́вный

productivity [prɔdʌk'tɪvɪtɪ] _n_ производи́тельность f, продукти́вность f

profession [prə'fɛʃən] n профе́ссия;
  professional adj профессиона́льный
professor [prə'fɛsər] n (Brit) профе́ссор;
  (US) преподава́тель(ница) m(f)
profile ['prəufaɪl] n (of face, also Comput)
  про́филь m; (article) о́черк; **profile
  picture** n фотогра́фия про́филя, фо́то
  про́филя (inf)
profit ['prɔfɪt] n при́быль f, дохо́д ▷ vi:
  to profit by or **from** (fig) извлека́ть (perf
  извле́чь) вы́году из +gen; **profitable** adj
  при́быльный; (fig) вы́годный
profound [prə'faund] adj глубо́кий
program(me) ['prəugræm] n програ́мма
  ▷ vt программи́ровать (perf
  запрограмми́ровать); **programmer** n
  программи́ст(ка)
progress [n 'prəugrɛs, vb prə'grɛs] n
  (advances, changes) прогре́сс;
  (development) разви́тие ▷ vi
  прогресси́ровать (impf); (continue)
  продолжа́ться (perf продо́лжиться); **the
  match is in progress** матч идёт;
  progressive [prə'grɛsɪv] adj
  прогресси́вный; (gradual) постепе́нный
prohibit [prə'hɪbɪt] vt запреща́ть (perf
  запрети́ть)
project [n 'prɔdʒɛkt, vb prə'dʒɛkt] n
  прое́кт ▷ vt (plan, estimate)
  проекти́ровать (perf запроекти́ровать)
  ▷ vi (jut out) выступа́ть (perf вы́ступить);
  projection [prə'dʒɛkʃən] n (estimate)
  перспекти́вная оце́нка; **projector**
  [prə'dʒɛktər] n (Cinema) кинопрое́ктор;
  (also **slide projector**) прое́ктор
prolific [prə'lɪfɪk] adj плодови́тый
prolong [prə'lɔŋ] vt продлева́ть (perf
  продли́ть)
promenade [prɔmə'nɑːd] n промена́д
prominent ['prɔmɪnənt] adj
  выдаю́щийся
promiscuous [prə'mɪskjuəs] adj
  развра́тный
promise ['prɔmɪs] n (vow) обеща́ние;
  (talent) потенциа́л; (hope) наде́жда ▷ vi
  (vow) дава́ть (perf дать) обеща́ние ▷ vt:
  to promise sb sth, promise sth to sb
  обеща́ть (perf пообеща́ть) что-н кому́-н;
  to promise (sb) to do/that обеща́ть (perf
  пообеща́ть) (кому́-н) +infin/, что; **to
  promise well** подава́ть (impf) больши́е
  наде́жды; **promising** ['prɔmɪsɪŋ] adj
  многообеща́ющий
promote [prə'məut] vt (employee)
  повыша́ть (perf повы́сить) (в до́лжности);
  (product, pop star) реклами́ровать (impf/
  perf); (ideas) подде́рживать (perf
  поддержа́ть); **promotion** [prə'məuʃən] n
  (at work) повыше́ние (в до́лжности); (of
  product, event) рекла́ма
prompt [prɔmpt] adj незамедли́тельный
  ▷ vt (cause) побужда́ть (perf побуди́ть);
  (when talking) подска́зывать (perf
  подсказа́ть) ▷ adv: **at 8 o'clock prompt**

ро́вно в 8 часо́в; **to prompt sb to do**
  побужда́ть (perf побуди́ть) кого́-н +infin;
  promptly adv (immediately)
  незамедли́тельно; (exactly) то́чно
prone [prəun] adj: **prone to** (inclined to)
  скло́нный к +dat
pronoun ['prəunaun] n местоиме́ние
pronounce [prə'nauns] vt (word)
  произноси́ть (perf произнести́);
  (declaration, verdict) объявля́ть (perf
  объяви́ть); (opinion) выска́зывать (perf
  вы́сказать)
pronunciation [prənʌnsɪ'eɪʃən] n (of
  word) произноше́ние
proof [pruːf] n (evidence) доказа́тельство
  ▷ adj: **this vodka is 70% proof** э́то
  семидесятигра́дусная во́дка
prop [prɔp] n (support) подпо́рка ▷ vt
  (also **prop up**) подпира́ть (perf
  подпере́ть); **to prop sth against**
  прислоня́ть (perf прислони́ть) что-н к
  +dat; **props** npl (Theat) реквизи́т msg
propaganda [prɔpə'gændə] n
  пропага́нда
propeller n пропе́ллер
proper ['prɔpər] adj (real) настоя́щий;
  (correct) до́лжный, надлежа́щий; (socially
  acceptable) прили́чный; **properly** adv
  (eat, study) как сле́дует; (behave)
  прили́чно, до́лжным о́бразом
property ['prɔpətɪ] n (possessions)
  со́бственность f; (building and land)
  недви́жимость f; (quality) сво́йство
prophecy ['prɔfɪsɪ] n проро́чество
proportion [prə'pɔːʃən] n (part) часть f,
  до́ля; (ratio) пропо́рция, соотноше́ние;
  proportional adj: **proportional (to)**
  пропорциона́льный (+dat)
proposal [prə'pəuzl] n предложе́ние
propose [prə'pəuz] vt (plan, toast)
  предлага́ть (perf предложи́ть); (motion)
  выдвига́ть (perf вы́двинуть) ▷ vi (offer
  marriage): **to propose (to sb)** де́лать (perf
  сде́лать) предложе́ние (кому́-н); **to
  propose sth/to do** or **doing** предполага́ть
  (impf) что-н/+infin
proposition [prɔpə'zɪʃən] n (statement)
  утвержде́ние; (offer) предложе́ние
proprietor [prə'praɪətər] n
  владе́лец(-лица)
prose [prəuz] n (not poetry) про́за
prosecute ['prɔsɪkjuːt] vt: **to prosecute
  sb** пресле́довать (impf) кого́-н в суде́бном
  поря́дке
prosecution [prɔsɪ'kjuːʃən] n (Law:
  action) суде́бное пресле́дование;
  (: accusing side) обвине́ние
prosecutor [prɔsɪkjuːtər] n
  обвини́тель m
prospect ['prɔspɛkt] n перспекти́ва;
  prospects npl (for work etc) перспекти́вы
  fpl; **prospective** [prə'spɛktɪv] adj (future)
  бу́дущий; (potential) возмо́жный;
prospectus [prə'spɛktəs] n проспе́кт

prosper ['prɔspə'] vi преуспева́ть (perf преуспе́ть); **prosperity** [prɔ'spɛrɪtɪ] n процвета́ние; **prosperous** adj преуспева́ющий

prostitute ['prɔstɪtjuːt] n проститу́тка

protect [prə'tɛkt] vt защища́ть (perf защити́ть); **protection** [prə'tɛkʃən] n защи́та; **protective** adj защи́тный; (person) забо́тливый, бе́режный

protein ['prəutiːn] n бело́к, протеи́н

protest [n 'prəutɛst, vb prə'tɛst] n проте́ст ▷ vi: **to protest about/against** протестова́ть (impf) по по́воду +gen/ про́тив +gen ▷ vt (insist): **to protest that** заявля́ть (perf заяви́ть), что

Protestant ['prɔtɪstənt] n протеста́нт(ка)

proud [praud] adj: **proud (of)** го́рдый (+instr)

prove [pruːv] vt дока́зывать (perf доказа́ть) ▷ vi: **to prove (to be)** оказа́ться (impf/perf) +instr; **to prove o.s.** проявля́ть (perf прояви́ть) себя́

proverb ['prɔvɜːb] n посло́вица

provide [prə'vaɪd] vt обеспе́чивать (perf обеспе́чить) +instr; **to provide sb with sth** обеспе́чивать (perf обеспе́чить) кого́-н чем-н; **provide for** vt fus (person) обеспе́чивать (perf обеспе́чить); **provided (that)** conj при усло́вии, что

providing [prə'vaɪdɪŋ] conj = **provided (that)**

province ['prɔvɪns] n о́бласть f

provincial [prə'vɪnʃəl] adj провинциа́льный

provision [prə'vɪʒən] n (supplying) обеспе́чение; (of contract, agreement) положе́ние; **provisions** npl (food) прови́зия fsg; **provisional** adj вре́менный

provocative [prə'vɔkətɪv] adj (remark, gesture) провокацио́нный

provoke [prə'vəuk] vt провоци́ровать (perf спровоци́ровать)

proximity [prɔk'sɪmɪtɪ] n бли́зость f

proxy ['prɔksɪ] n: **by proxy** по дове́ренности

prudent ['pruːdnt] adj благоразу́мный

prune [pruːn] n черносли́в m no pl ▷ vt подреза́ть (perf подре́зать)

PS abbr = **postscript**

pseudonym ['sjuːdənɪm] n псевдони́м

psychiatric [saɪkɪ'ætrɪk] adj психиатри́ческий

psychiatrist [saɪ'kaɪətrɪst] n психиа́тр

psychic ['saɪkɪk] adj (person) яснови́дящий

psychological [saɪkə'lɔdʒɪkl] adj психологи́ческий

psychologist [saɪ'kɔlədʒɪst] n психо́лог

psychology [saɪ'kɔlədʒɪ] n психоло́гия

PTO abbr (= please turn over) смотри́ на оборо́те

pub [pʌb] n паб, пивна́я f adj

puberty ['pjuːbətɪ] n полова́я зре́лость f

public ['pʌblɪk] adj обще́ственный; (statement, action etc) публи́чный ▷ n: **the public** (everyone) обще́ственность f, наро́д; **to make public** предава́ть (perf преда́ть) гла́сности; **in public** публи́чно

publication [pʌblɪ'keɪʃən] n публика́ция, изда́ние

publicity [pʌb'lɪsɪtɪ] n (information) рекла́ма, па́блисити nt ind; (attention) шуми́ха

publicize ['pʌblɪsaɪz] vt предава́ть (perf преда́ть) гла́сности

public: publicly adv публи́чно; **public opinion** n обще́ственное мне́ние; **public relations** npl вне́шние свя́зи fpl, свя́зи с обще́ственностью; **public school** n (Brit) ча́стная шко́ла; (US) госуда́рственная шко́ла

publish ['pʌblɪʃ] vt издава́ть (perf изда́ть); (Press: letter, article) публикова́ть (perf опубликова́ть); **publisher** n (company) изда́тельство; **publishing** n (profession) изда́тельское де́ло

pudding ['pudɪŋ] n пу́динг; (Brit: dessert) сла́дкое nt adj; **black pudding**, (US) **blood pudding** кровяна́я колбаса́

puddle ['pʌdl] n лу́жа

puff [pʌf] n (of wind) дунове́ние; (of cigarette, pipe) затя́жка; (of smoke) клуб

pull [pul] vt тяну́ть (perf потяну́ть); (trigger) нажима́ть (perf нажа́ть) на +acc; (curtains etc) заде́ргивать (perf задёрнуть) ▷ vi (tug) тяну́ть (impf) ▷ n: **to give sth a pull** (tug) тяну́ть (perf потяну́ть) что-н; **to pull to pieces** разрыва́ть (perf разорва́ть) на ча́сти; **to pull o.s. together** брать (perf взять) себя́ в ру́ки; **to pull sb's leg** (fig) разы́грывать (perf разыгра́ть) кого́-н; **pull down** vt (building) сноси́ть (perf снести́); **pull in** vi (crowds, people) привлека́ть (perf привле́чь); **pull out** vt (extract) выта́скивать (perf вы́тащить) ▷ vi: **to pull out (from)** (Aut: from kerb) отъезжа́ть (perf отъе́хать) (от +gen); **pull up** vi (stop) остана́вливаться (perf останови́ться) ▷ vt (plant) вырыва́ть (perf вы́рвать) (с ко́рнем)

pulley ['pulɪ] n шкив

pullover ['puləuvə'] n сви́тер, пуло́вер

pulpit ['pulpɪt] n ка́федра

pulse [pʌls] n (Anat) пульс

puma ['pjuːmə] n пу́ма

pump [pʌmp] n насо́с; (also **petrol pump**) бензоколо́нка ▷ vt кача́ть (perf накача́ть); (extract: oil, water, gas) выка́чивать (perf вы́качать)

pumpkin ['pʌmpkɪn] n ты́ква

pun [pʌn] n каламбу́р

punch [pʌntʃ] n уда́р; (for making holes) дыроко́л; (drink) пунш ▷ vt (hit): **to punch sb/sth** ударя́ть (perf уда́рить) кого́-н/что-н кулако́м

punctual ['pʌŋktjuəl] adj пунктуа́льный

punctuation [pʌŋktju'eɪʃən] n пунктуа́ция

puncture ['pʌŋktʃəʳ] n (Aut) прокол ▷ vt прокалывать (perf проколоть)
punish ['pʌnɪʃ] vt: **to punish sb (for sth)** наказывать (perf наказать) кого-н (за что-н); **punishment** n наказание
pupil ['pju:pl] n (Scol) ученик(-йца); (of eye) зрачок
puppet ['pʌpɪt] n марионетка
puppy ['pʌpɪ] n (young dog) щенок
purchase ['pə:tʃɪs] n покупка ▷ vt покупать (perf купить)
pure [pjuəʳ] adj чистый; **purely** adv чисто; **purify** ['pjuərɪfaɪ] vt очищать (perf очистить); **purity** ['pjuərɪtɪ] n чистота
purple ['pə:pl] adj фиолетовый
purpose ['pə:pəs] n цель f; **on purpose** намеренно
purr [pə:ʳ] vi мурлыкать (impf)
purse [pə:s] n (Brit) кошелёк; (US: handbag) сумка ▷ vt: **to purse one's lips** поджимать (perf поджать) губы
pursue [pə'sju:] vt преследовать (impf); (fig: policy) проводить (impf); (: interest) проявлять (impf)
pursuit [pə'sju:t] n (of person, thing) преследование; (of happiness, wealth etc) поиски mpl; (pastime) занятие
push [puʃ] n (shove) толчок ▷ vt (press) нажимать (perf нажать); (shove) толкать (perf толкнуть); (promote) проталкивать (perf протолкнуть) ▷ vi (press) нажимать (perf нажать); (shove) толкаться (impf); (fig): **to push for** требовать (perf потребовать) +acc or +gen; **push through** vt (measure, scheme) проталкивать (perf протолкнуть); **push up** vt (prices) повышать (perf повысить)
put [put] (pt, pp put) vt ставить (perf поставить); (thing: horizontally) класть (perf положить); (person: in institution) помещать (perf поместить); (: in prison) сажать (perf посадить); (idea, feeling) выражать (perf выразить); (case, view) излагать (perf изложить); **I put it to you that ...** я говорю Вам, что ...; **put across** vt (ideas etc) объяснять (perf объяснить); **put away** vt (store) убирать (perf убрать); **put back** vt (replace) класть (perf положить) на место; (postpone) откладывать (perf отложить); (delay) задерживать (perf задержать); **put by** vt откладывать (perf отложить); **put down** vt (place) ставить (perf поставить); (: horizontally) класть (perf положить); (note down) записывать (perf записать); (suppress, humiliate) подавлять (perf подавить); (animal: kill) умерщвлять (perf умертвить); **to put sth down to** (attribute) объяснять (perf объяснить) что-н +instr; **put forward** vt (ideas) выдвигать (perf выдвинуть); **put in** vt (application, complaint) подавать (perf подать); (time, effort) вкладывать (perf вложить);

put off vt (delay) откладывать (perf отложить); (discourage) отталкивать (perf оттолкнуть); (switch off) выключать (perf выключить); **put on** vt (clothes) надевать (perf надеть); (make-up, ointment etc) накладывать (perf наложить); (light etc) включать (perf включить); (kettle, record, dinner) ставить (perf поставить); (assume: look) напускать (perf напустить); (behaviour) принимать (perf принять); **to put on weight** поправляться (perf поправиться); **put out** vt (fire) тушить (perf потушить); (candle, cigarette, light) гасить (perf погасить); (rubbish) выносить (perf вынести); (one's hand) вытягивать (perf вытянуть); **put through** vt (person, call) соединять (perf соединить); (plan, agreement) выполнять (perf выполнить); **put up** vt (building, tent) ставить (perf поставить); (umbrella) раскрывать (perf раскрыть); (hood) надевать (perf надеть); (poster, sign) вывешивать (perf вывесить); (price, cost) поднимать (perf поднять); (guest) помещать (perf поместить); **put up with** vt fus мириться (impf) с +instr
puzzle ['pʌzl] n (game, toy) головоломка
puzzling ['pʌzlɪŋ] adj запутанный
pyjamas [pɪ'dʒɑːməz] (US pajamas) npl: **(a pair of) pyjamas** пижама fsg
pylon ['paɪlən] n пилон, опора
pyramid ['pɪrəmɪd] n (Geom) пирамида

q

quadruple [kwɔ'dru:pl] *vt* увеличивать (*perf* увеличить) в четыре раза ▷ *vi* увеличиваться (*perf* увеличиться) в четыре раза

quaint [kweɪnt] *adj* чудной

quake [kweɪk] *vi* трепетать (*impf*)

qualification [kwɔlɪfɪ'keɪʃən] *n* (*usu pl: academic, vocational*) квалификация; (*skill, quality*) качество; **what are your qualifications?** какая у Вас квалификация?

qualified ['kwɔlɪfaɪd] *adj* (*trained*) квалифицированный; **I'm not qualified to judge that** я не компетентен судить об этом

qualify ['kwɔlɪfaɪ] *vt* (*modify: make more specific*) уточнять (*perf* уточнить); (: *express reservation*) оговаривать (*perf* оговорить) ▷ *vi*: **to qualify as an engineer** получать (*perf* получить) квалификацию инженера; **to qualify (for)** (*benefit etc*) иметь (*impf*) право (на +*acc*); (*in competition*) выходить (*perf* выйти) в +*acc*

quality ['kwɔlɪtɪ] *n* качество; (*property: of wood, stone*) свойство

quantity ['kwɔntɪtɪ] *n* количество

quarantine ['kwɔrntiːn] *n* карантин

quarrel ['kwɔrl] *n* ссора ▷ *vi*: **to quarrel (with)** ссориться (*perf* поссориться) (с +*instr*)

quarry ['kwɔrɪ] *n* карьер; (*for stone*) каменоломня

quarter ['kwɔːtər] *n* четверть *f*; (*of year, town*) квартал; (*US: coin*) двадцать пять центов ▷ *vt* делить (*perf* разделить) на четыре части; **quarters** *npl* (*for living*) помещение *ntsg*; (: *Mil*) казармы *fpl*; **a quarter of an hour** четверть *f* часа; **quarterly** *adj* (*meeting*) (еже)квартальный; (*payment*) (по)квартальный ▷ *adv* (*see adj*) ежеквартально; поквартально

quartz [kwɔːts] *n* кварц

quay [kiː] *n* (*also* **quayside**) пристань *f*

queasy ['kwiːzɪ] *adj*: **I feel a bit queasy** меня немного мутит

queen [kwiːn] *n* королева; (*Cards*) дама; (*Chess*) ферзь *m*

queer [kwɪər] *adj* (*odd*) странный

quench [kwɛntʃ] *vt*: **to quench one's thirst** утолять (*perf* утолить) жажду

query ['kwɪərɪ] *n* вопрос ▷ *vt* подвергать (*perf* подвергнуть) сомнению

quest [kwɛst] *n* поиск

question ['kwɛstʃən] *n* вопрос; (*doubt*) сомнение ▷ *vt* (*interrogate*) допрашивать (*perf* допросить); (*doubt*) усомниться (*perf*) в +*prp*; **beyond question** бесспорно; **that's out of the question** об этом не может быть и речи; **questionable** *adj* сомнительный; **question mark** *n* вопросительный знак; **questionnaire** [kwɛstʃə'nɛər] *n* анкета

queue [kjuː] (*Brit*) *n* очередь *f* ▷ *vi* (*also* **queue up**) стоять (*impf*) в очереди

quick [kwɪk] *adj* быстрый; (*clever: person*) сообразительный; (: *mind*) живой; (*brief*) краткий; **be quick!** быстро!; **quickly** *adv* быстро

quid [kwɪd] *n inv* (*Brit: inf*) фунт (*стерлингов*)

quiet ['kwaɪət] *adj* тихий; (*peaceful, not busy*) спокойный; (*without fuss*) сдержанный ▷ *n* (*silence*) тишина; (*peace*) покой; **quietly** *adv* тихо; (*calmly*) спокойно

quilt [kwɪlt] *n* (*also* **continental quilt**) стёганое одеяло

quit [kwɪt] (*pt, pp* **quit** *or* **quitted**) *vt* бросать (*perf* бросить) ▷ *vi* (*give up*) сдаваться (*perf* сдаться); (*resign*) увольняться (*perf* уволиться)

quite [kwaɪt] *adv* (*rather*) довольно; (*entirely*) совершенно; (*almost*): **the flat's not quite big enough** квартира недостаточно большая; **quite a few** довольно много; **quite (so)!** верно!, (вот) именно!

quits [kwɪts] *adj*: **let's call it quits** будем квиты

quiver ['kwɪvər] *vi* трепетать (*impf*)

quiz [kwɪz] *n* (*game*) викторина ▷ *vt* расспрашивать (*perf* расспросить)

quota ['kwəutə] *n* квота

quotation [kwəu'teɪʃən] *n* цитата; (*estimate*) цена (продавца)

quote [kwəut] *n* цитата; (*estimate*) цена ▷ *vt* цитировать (*perf* процитировать); (*figure, example*) приводить (*perf* привести); (*price*) назначать (*perf* назначить); **quotes** *npl* (*quotation marks*) кавычки *fpl*

r

rabbi ['ræbaɪ] n равви́н

rabbit ['ræbɪt] n (male) кро́лик; (female) крольчи́ха

rabies ['reɪbi:z] n бе́шенство, водобоя́знь f

RAC n abbr (Brit) (= Royal Automobile Club) Короле́вская автомоби́льная ассоциа́ция

race [reɪs] n (species) ра́са; (competition) го́нки fpl; (: running) забе́г; (: swimming) заплы́в; (: horse race) ска́чки fpl; (for power, control) борьба́ ▷ vt (horse) гнать (impf) ▷ vi (compete) принима́ть (perf приня́ть) уча́стие в соревнова́нии; (hurry) мча́ться (impf); (pulse) учаща́ться (perf участи́ться); **racecourse** n ипподро́м; **racehorse** n скакова́я ло́шадь f

racial ['reɪʃl] adj ра́совый

racing ['reɪsɪŋ] n (horse racing) ска́чки fpl; (motor racing) го́нки fpl

racism ['reɪsɪzəm] n раси́зм

racist ['reɪsɪst] adj раси́стский ▷ n расист(ка)

rack [ræk] n (shelf) по́лка; (also **luggage rack**) бага́жная по́лка; (also **roof rack**) бага́жник (на кры́ше автомоби́ля); (for dishes) суши́лка для посу́ды ▷ vt: she was racked by pain её терза́ла боль; to **rack one's brains** лома́ть (impf) го́лову

racket ['rækɪt] n (Sport) раке́тка; (noise) гвалт; (con) жу́льничество; (extortion) рэ́кет

radar ['reɪdɑːʳ] n рада́р

radiation [reɪdɪ'eɪʃən] n (radioactive) радиа́ция, радиоакти́вное излуче́ние; (of heat, light) излуче́ние

radiator ['reɪdɪeɪtəʳ] n радиа́тор, батаре́я; (Aut) радиа́тор

radical ['rædɪkl] adj радика́льный

radio ['reɪdɪəu] n (broadcasting) ра́дио nt ind; (for transmitting and receiving) радиопереда́тчик ▷ vt (person) свя́зываться (perf связа́ться) по ра́дио с +instr; **on the radio** по ра́дио; **radioactive** adj радиоакти́вный; **radio station** n радиоста́нция

radish ['rædɪʃ] n реди́ска; **radishes** реди́с msg

RAF n abbr (Brit) (= Royal Air Force) ≈ BBC (= Вое́нно-возду́шные си́лы Великобрита́нии)

raffle ['ræfl] n (веще́вая) лотере́я

raft [rɑːft] n плот

rag [ræg] n тря́пка; (pej: newspaper) газете́нка; **rags** npl (clothes) лохмо́тья pl

rage [reɪdʒ] n (fury) бе́шенство, я́рость f ▷ vi (person) свире́пствовать (impf); (storm, debate) бушева́ть (impf); **it's all the rage** (in fashion) все помеша́лись на э́том

ragged ['rægɪd] adj (edge) зазу́бренный; (clothes) потрёпанный

raid [reɪd] n (Mil) рейд; (criminal) налёт; (by police) обла́ва, рейд ▷ vt (see n) соверша́ть (perf соверши́ть) рейд на +acc; соверша́ть (perf соверши́ть) налёт на +acc

rail [reɪl] n (on stairs, bridge etc) пери́ла pl; **rails** npl (Rail) ре́льсы mpl; **by rail** по́ездом; **railing(s)** n(pl) (iron fence) решётка fsg; **railroad** n (US) = **railway**; **railway** n (Brit) желе́зная доро́га ▷ cpd железнодоро́жный; **railway line** n (Brit) железнодоро́жная ли́ния; **railway station** n (Brit: large) железнодоро́жный вокза́л; (: small) железнодоро́жная ста́нция

rain [reɪn] n дождь m ▷ vi: **it's raining** идёт дождь; **in the rain** под дождём, в дождь; **rainbow** n ра́дуга; **raincoat** n плащ; **rainfall** n (measurement) у́ровень m оса́дков; **rainy** adj (day) дождли́вый

raise [reɪz] n (esp US) повыше́ние ▷ vt (lift, produce) поднима́ть (perf подня́ть); (increase, improve) повыша́ть (perf повы́сить); (doubts: subj: person) выска́зывать (perf вы́сказать); (: results) вызыва́ть (perf вы́звать); (rear: family) воспи́тывать (perf воспита́ть); (get together: army, funds) собира́ть (perf собра́ть); (: loan) изы́скивать (perf изыска́ть); **to raise one's voice** повыша́ть (perf повы́сить) го́лос

raisin ['reɪzn] n изю́минка; **raisins** npl изю́м m no pl

rake [reɪk] n (tool) гра́бли pl ▷ vt (garden) разра́внивать (perf разровня́ть) (гра́блями); (leaves, hay) сгреба́ть (perf сгрести́)

rally ['rælɪ] n (Pol etc) манифеста́ция; (Aut) (а́вто)ра́лли nt ind; (Tennis) ра́лли nt ind ▷ vt (supporters) спла́чивать (perf сплоти́ть) ▷ vi (supporters) спла́чиваться (perf сплоти́ться)

ram [ræm] n бара́н ▷ vt (crash into) тара́нить (perf протара́нить); (push: bolt) задвига́ть (*perf* задви́нуть); (: *fist*) дви́нуть (*perf*) +*instr*

RAM *n abbr* (*Comput*) (= *random access memory*) ЗУПВ (= *запомина́ющее устро́йство с произво́льной вы́боркой*)

ramble ['ræmbl] *vi* (*walk*) броди́ть (*impf*); (*talk: also* **ramble on**) зану́дствовать (*impf*)

rambling ['ræmblɪŋ] *adj* (*speech*) несвя́зный

ramp [ræmp] *n* скат, укло́н; **on ramp** (*US: Aut*) въезд на автостра́ду; **off ramp** (*US: Aut*) съезд с автостра́ды

rampage [ræm'peɪdʒ] *n*: **to be on the rampage** бу́йствовать (*impf*)

ran [ræn] *pt of* **run**

ranch [rɑːntʃ] *n* ра́нчо *nt ind*

random ['rændəm] *adj* случа́йный ▷ *n*: **at random** наугад

rang [ræŋ] *pt of* **ring**

range [reɪndʒ] *n* (*series: of proposals*) ряд; (: *of products*) ассортиме́нт *m no pl*; (: *of colours*) га́мма; (*of mountains*) цепь *f*; (*of missile*) да́льность *f*, ра́диус де́йствия; (*of voice*) диапазо́н; (*Mil: also* **shooting range**) стре́льбище ▷ *vt* (*place in a line*) выстра́ивать (*perf* вы́строить) ▷ *vi*: **to range over** (*extend*) простира́ться (*impf*); **to range from ... to ...** колеба́ться (*impf*) от +*gen* ... до +*gen* ...

ranger ['reɪndʒə*r*] *n* (*in forest*) лесни́к; (*in park*) смотри́тель(ница) *m(f)*

rank [ræŋk] *n* (*in row*) ряд; (*Mil*) шере́нга; (*status*) чин, ранг; (*Brit: also* **taxi rank**) стоя́нка такси́ ▷ *vi*: **to rank among** чи́слиться (*impf*) среди́ +*gen* ▷ *vt*: **I rank him sixth** я ста́влю его́ на шесто́е ме́сто; **the rank and file** (*fig*) рядовы́е чле́ны *mpl*

ransom ['rænsəm] *n* вы́куп; **to hold to ransom** (*fig*) держа́ть (*impf*) в зало́жниках

rant [rænt] *vi*: **to rant and rave** рвать (*impf*) и мета́ть (*impf*)

rap [ræp] *vi*: **to rap on a door/table** стуча́ть (*perf* постуча́ть) в дверь/по столу́

rape [reɪp] *n* изнаси́лование ▷ *vt* наси́ловать (*perf* изнаси́ловать)

rapid ['ræpɪd] *adj* стреми́тельный; **rapidly** *adv* стреми́тельно

rapist ['reɪpɪst] *n* наси́льник

rapport [ræ'pɔː*r*] *n* взаимопонима́ние

rare [rɛə*r*] *adj* ре́дкий; (*steak*) крова́вый; **rarely** *adv* ре́дко, нечасто

rash [ræʃ] *adj* опроме́тчивый ▷ *n* (*Med*) сыпь *f no pl*

raspberry ['rɑːzbərɪ] *n* мали́на *f no pl*

rat [ræt] *n* (*also fig*) кры́са

rate [reɪt] *n* (*speed*) ско́рость *f*; (: *of change, inflation*) темп; (*of interest*) ста́вка; (*ratio*) у́ровень *m*; (*price: at hotel etc*) расце́нка ▷ *vt* (*value*) оце́нивать (*perf* оцени́ть); (*estimate*) расце́нивать (*perf* расцени́ть); **rates** *npl* (*Brit: property tax*) нало́г *msg* на недви́жимость; **to rate sb as** счита́ть (*impf*) кого́-н +*instr*; **to rate sth as**

расце́нивать (*perf* расцени́ть) что-н как

rather ['rɑːðə*r*] *adv* (*quite, somewhat*) дово́льно; (*to some extent*) не́сколько; (*more accurately*): **or rather** верне́е сказа́ть; **it's rather expensive** (*quite*) э́то дово́льно до́рого; **there's rather a lot** дово́льно мно́го; **I would rather go** я, пожа́луй, пойду́; **I'd rather not leave** я бы не хоте́л уходи́ть; **rather than** (+*n*) а не +*nom*, вме́сто +*gen*; **rather than go to the park, I went to the cinema** вме́сто того́ чтобы идти́ в парк, я пошёл в кино́

rating ['reɪtɪŋ] *n* оце́нка, рейтинг; **ratings** *npl* (*Radio, TV*) рейтинг *msg*

ratio ['reɪʃɪəu] *n* соотноше́ние; **in the ratio of one hundred to one** в соотноше́нии сто к одному́

ration ['ræʃən] *n* (*allowance: of food*) рацио́н, паёк; (: *of petrol*) но́рма ▷ *vt* норми́ровать (*impf/perf*); **rations** *npl* (*Mil*) рацио́н *msg*

rational ['ræʃənl] *adj* разу́мный, рациона́льный

rattle ['rætl] *n* дребезжа́ние; (*of train, car*) громыха́ние; (*for baby*) погрему́шка ▷ *vi* (*small objects*) дребезжа́ть (*impf*) ▷ *vt* (*shake noisily*) сотряса́ть (*perf* сотрясти́); (*fig: unsettle*) нерви́ровать (*impf*); **to rattle along** (*car, bus*) прогромыха́ть (*impf*); **the wind rattled the windows** о́кна дребезжа́ли от ве́тра

rave [reɪv] *vi* (*in anger*) бесноваться (*impf*), бушева́ть (*impf*); (*Med*) бре́дить (*impf*); (*with enthusiasm*): **to rave about** восторга́ться (*impf*) +*instr*

raven ['reɪvən] *n* во́рон

ravine [rə'viːn] *n* уще́лье

raw [rɔː] *adj* сыро́й; (*unrefined: sugar*) нерафини́рованный; (*sore*) све́жий; (*inexperienced*) зелёный; (*weather, day*) промо́зглый; **raw material** *n* сырьё *nt no pl*

ray [reɪ] *n* луч; (*of heat*) пото́к

razor ['reɪzə*r*] *n* бри́тва; **safety razor** безопа́сная бри́тва; **electric razor** электробри́тва

Rd *abbr* = **road**

re [riː] *prep* относи́тельно +*gen*

reach [riːtʃ] *vt* (*place, end, agreement*) достига́ть (*perf* дости́гнуть *or* дости́чь) +*gen*; (*conclusion, decision*) приходи́ть (*perf* прийти́) к +*dat*; (*be able to touch*) достава́ть (*perf* доста́ть); (*by telephone*) свя́зываться (*perf* связа́ться) с +*instr* ▷ *vi*: **to reach into** запуска́ть (*perf* запусти́ть) ру́ку в +*acc*; **out of/within reach** вне/в преде́лах досяга́емости; **within reach of the shops** недалеко́ от магази́нов; "**keep out of the reach of children**" "бере́чь от дете́й"; **to reach for** протя́гивать (*perf* протяну́ть) ру́ку к +*dat*; **to reach up** протя́гивать (*perf* протяну́ть) ру́ку вверх; **reach out** *vt* протя́гивать (*perf* протяну́ть) ▷ *vi*: **to reach out for sth**

протя́гивать (*perf* протяну́ть) ру́ку за чем-н

react [rɪ'ækt] *vi* (*Chem*): **to react (with)** вступа́ть (*perf* вступи́ть) в реа́кцию (с +*instr*); (*Med*): **to react (to)** реаги́ровать (*impf*) (на +*acc*); (*respond*) реаги́ровать (*perf* отреаги́ровать) (на +*acc*); (*rebel*): **to react (against)** восстава́ть (*perf* восста́ть) (про́тив +*gen*); **reaction** [rɪ'ækʃən] *n* (*Chem*) реа́кция; (*also Med, Pol*): **reaction (to/against)** реа́кция (на +*acc*/про́тив +*gen*); **reactions** *npl* (*reflexes*) реа́кция *fsg*; **reactor** *n* (*also* **nuclear reactor**) реа́ктор

read¹ [rɛd] *pt, pp of* **read²**
read² [riːd] (*pt, pp* **read**) *vt* чита́ть (прочита́ть *or* проче́сть *perf*); (*mood*) определя́ть (*perf* определи́ть); (*thermometer etc*) снима́ть (*perf* снять) показа́ния с +*gen*; (*Scol*) изуча́ть (*impf*) ▷ *vi* (*person*) чита́ть (*impf*); (*text etc*) чита́ться (*impf*); **read out** *vt* зачи́тывать (*perf* зачита́ть); **reader** *n* (*of book, newspaper etc*) чита́тель(ница) *m(f)*

readily ['rɛdɪlɪ] *adv* (*willingly*) с гото́вностью; (*easily*) легко́

reading ['riːdɪŋ] *n* (*of books etc*) чте́ние; (*on thermometer etc*) показа́ние

ready ['rɛdɪ] *adj* гото́вый ▷ *vt*: **to get sb/ sth ready** гото́вить (*perf* подгото́вить) кого́-н/что-н; **to get ready** гото́виться (*perf* пригото́виться)

real [rɪəl] *adj* настоя́щий; (*leather*) натура́льный; **in real terms** реа́льно; **real estate** *n* недви́жимость *f*; **realistic** [rɪə'lɪstɪk] *adj* реалисти́ческий; **reality** [riː'ælɪtɪ] *n* реа́льность *f*, действи́тельность *f*; **in reality** на са́мом де́ле, в реа́льности

realization [rɪəlaɪ'zeɪʃən] *n* (*see vt*) осозна́ние; осуществле́ние

realize ['rɪəlaɪz] *vt* (*understand*) осознава́ть (*perf* осозна́ть); (*fulfil*) осуществля́ть (*perf* осуществи́ть)

really ['rɪəlɪ] *adv* (*very*) о́чень; (*actually*): **what really happened?** что произошло́ в действи́тельности *or* на са́мом де́ле?; **really?** (*with interest*) действи́тельно?, пра́вда?; (*expressing surprise*) неуже́ли?

realm [rɛlm] *n* (*fig: of activity, study*) о́бласть *f*, сфе́ра

reappear [riːə'pɪəʳ] *vi* сно́ва появля́ться (*perf* появи́ться)

rear [rɪəʳ] *adj* за́дний ▷ *n* (*back*) за́дняя часть *f* ▷ *vt* (*cattle, family*) выра́щивать (*perf* вы́растить) ▷ *vi* (*also* **rear up**) станови́ться (*perf* стать) на дыбы́

rearrange [riːə'reɪndʒ] *vt* (*objects*) переставля́ть (*perf* переста́вить); (*order*) изменя́ть (*perf* измени́ть)

reason ['riːzn] *n* (*cause*) причи́на; (*ability to think*) ра́зум, рассу́док; (*sense*) смысл ▷ *vi*: **to reason with sb** убежда́ть (*impf*) кого́-н; **it stands to reason that ...**

разуме́ется, что ...; **reasonable** *adj* разу́мный; (*quality*) неплохо́й; (*price*) уме́ренный; **reasonably** *adv* (*sensibly*) разу́мно; (*fairly*) дово́льно; **reasoning** *n* рассужде́ние

reassurance [riːə'ʃuərəns] *n* (*comfort*) подде́ржка

reassure [riːə'ʃuəʳ] *vt* (*comfort*) утеша́ть (*perf* уте́шить); **to reassure sb of** заверя́ть (*perf* заве́рить) кого́-н в +*prp*

rebate ['riːbeɪt] *n* обра́тная вы́плата

rebel [*n* 'rɛbl, *vb* rɪ'bɛl] *n* бунта́рь(-рка) *m(f)* ▷ *vi* восстава́ть (*perf* восста́ть); **rebellion** [rɪ'bɛljən] *n* восста́ние; **rebellious** [rɪ'bɛljəs] *adj* (*child, behaviour*) стропти́вый; (*troops*) мяте́жный

rebuild [riː'bɪld] (*irreg like* **build**) *vt* (*town, building*) перестра́ивать (*perf* перестро́ить); (*fig*) восстана́вливать (*perf* восстанови́ть)

recall [rɪ'kɔːl] *vt* вспомина́ть (*perf* вспо́мнить); (*parliament, ambassador etc*) отзыва́ть (*perf* отозва́ть)

receipt [rɪ'siːt] *n* (*document*) квита́нция; (*act of receiving*) получе́ние; **receipts** *npl* (*Comm*) де́нежные поступле́ния *ntpl*, платежи́ *mpl*

receive [rɪ'siːv] *vt* получа́ть (*perf* получи́ть); (*criticism*) встреча́ть (*perf* встре́тить); (*visitor, guest*) принима́ть (*perf* приня́ть); **receiver** *n* (*Tel*) (телефо́нная) тру́бка; (*Comm*) ликвида́тор (неплатёжеспосо́бной компа́нии)

recent ['riːsnt] *adj* неда́вний; **recently** *adv* неда́вно

reception [rɪ'sɛpʃən] *n* (*in hotel*) регистра́ция; (*in office, hospital*) приёмная *f adj*; (*in health centre*) регистрату́ра; (*party, also Radio, TV*) приём; **receptionist** *n* (*in hotel, hospital*) регистра́тор; (*in office*) секрета́рь *m*

recession [rɪ'sɛʃən] *n* (*Econ*) спад

recipe ['rɛsɪpɪ] *n* (*also fig*) реце́пт

recipient [rɪ'sɪpɪənt] *n* получа́тель *m*

recital [rɪ'saɪtl] *n* (*concert*) со́льный конце́рт

recite [rɪ'saɪt] *vt* (*poem*) деклами́ровать (*perf* продеклами́ровать)

reckless ['rɛkləs] *adj* безотве́тственный

reckon ['rɛkən] *vt* (*calculate*) счита́ть (посчита́ть *or* сосчита́ть *perf*); (*think*): **I reckon that ...** я счита́ю, что ...

reclaim [rɪ'kleɪm] *vt* (*demand back*) тре́бовать (*perf* потре́бовать) обра́тно; (*land: from sea*) отвоёвывать (*perf* отвоева́ть)

recognition [rɛkəg'nɪʃən] *n* призна́ние; (*of person, place*) узнава́ние; **he has changed beyond recognition** он измени́лся до неузнава́емости

recognize ['rɛkəgnaɪz] *vt* признава́ть (*perf* призна́ть); (*symptom*) распознава́ть (*perf* распознáть); **to recognize (by)** (*person, place*) узнавáть (*perf* узнáть) (по +*dat*)

recollection [rɛkə'lɛkʃən] *n* воспоминáние, пáмять *f*

recommend [rɛkə'mɛnd] *vt* рекомендовáть (*perf* порекомендовáть); **recommendation** [rɛkəmɛn'deɪʃən] *n* рекомендáция

reconcile ['rɛkənsaɪl] *vt* (*people*) мирить (*perf* помирить); (*facts, beliefs*) примирять (*perf* примирить); **to reconcile o.s. to sth** смиряться (*perf* смириться) с чем-н

reconsider [ri:kən'sɪdər] *vt* пересмáтривать (*perf* пересмотрéть)

reconstruct [ri:kən'strʌkt] *vt* перестрáивать (*perf* перестрóить); (*event, crime*) воспроизводить (*perf* воспроизвести), реконструировать (*impf/perf*)

record [*vb* rɪ'kɔ:d, *n, adj* 'rɛkɔ:d] *vt* (*in writing, on tape*) запи́сывать (*perf* записáть); (*register: temperature, speed etc*) регистри́ровать (*perf* зарегистри́ровать) ▷ *n* (*written account*) зáпись *f*; (*of meeting*) протокóл; (*of attendance*) учёт; (*Mus*) пласти́нка; (*history: of person, company*) репутáция; (*also* **criminal record**) суди́мость *f*; (*Sport*) рекóрд ▷ *adj*: **in record time** в рекóрдное врéмя; **off the record** (*speak*) неофициáльно; **recorder** [rɪ'kɔ:dər] *n* (*Mus*) англи́йская флéйта; **recording** [rɪ'kɔ:dɪŋ] *n* зáпись *f*; **record player** [-'pleɪər] *n* прои́грыватель *m*

recount [rɪ'kaunt] *vt* (*story*) повéдать (*perf*); (*event*) повéдать (*perf*) о +*prp*

recover [rɪ'kʌvər] *vt* получáть (*perf* получи́ть) обрáтно; (*Comm*) возмещáть (*perf* возмести́ть) ▷ *vi* (*get better*): **to recover (from)** поправляться (*perf* попрáвиться) (пóсле +*gen*); **recovery** *n* (*Med*) выздоровлéние; (*Comm*) подъём; (*of stolen items*) возвращéние; (*of lost items*) обнаружéние

recreation [rɛkrɪ'eɪʃən] *n* (*leisure activities*) развлечéние

recruit [rɪ'kru:t] *n* (*Mil*) новобрáнец, призывни́к ▷ *vt* (*into organization, army*) вербовáть (*perf* завербовáть); (*into company*) нанимáть (*perf* нанять); (*new*) **recruit** (*in company*) нóвый сотрудник; (*in organization*) нóвый член; **recruitment** *n* (*Mil*) вербóвка; (*by company*) набóр (на рабóту)

rectangle ['rɛktæŋgl] *n* прямоугóльник

rectangular [rɛk'tæŋgjulər] *adj* прямоугóльный

rectify ['rɛktɪfaɪ] *vt* исправлять (*perf* испрáвить)

recur [rɪ'kə:r] *vi* повторяться (*perf* повтори́ться)

recycle [ri:'saɪkl] *vt* перерабáтывать (*perf* переработáть)

red [rɛd] *n* крáсный цвет; (*pej: Pol*) крáсный(-ая) *m(f) adj* ▷ *adj* крáсный; (*hair*) ры́жий; **to be in the red** имéть (*impf*) задóлженность; **Red Cross** *n* Крáсный Крест; **redcurrant** *n* крáсная сморóдина *f no pl*

redeem [rɪ'di:m] *vt* (*situation, reputation*) спасáть (*perf* спасти́); (*debt*) выплáчивать (*perf* вы́платить)

redhead ['rɛdhɛd] *n* ры́жий(-ая) *m(f) adj*

reduce [rɪ'dju:s] *vt* сокращáть (*perf* сократи́ть); **to reduce sb** доводи́ть (*perf* довести́) когó-н до слёз; **to reduce sb to silence** заставлять (*perf* застáвить) когó-н замолчáть; **he was reduced to stealing** он дошёл до тогó, что стал воровáть

reduction [rɪ'dʌkʃən] *n* (*in price*) ски́дка; (*in numbers*) сокращéние

redundancy [rɪ'dʌndənsɪ] (*Brit*) *n* сокращéние (штáтов)

redundant [rɪ'dʌndnt] *adj* (*Brit: unemployed*) увóленный; (*useless*) изли́шний; **he was made redundant** егó сократи́ли

reed [ri:d] *n* (*Bot*) тростни́к

reef [ri:f] *n* риф

reel [ri:l] *n* катушка; (*of film, tape*) бобина

ref [rɛf] *n abbr* (*Sport: inf*) = **referee**

refer [rɪ'fə:r] *vt*: **to refer sb to** (*doctor etc*) отсылáть (*perf* отослáть) когó-н +*dat*; (*doctor*) направлять (*perf* напрáвить) когó-н к +*dat*; **refer to** *vt fus* упоминáть (*perf* упомянуть) о +*prp*; (*relate to*) относи́ться (*impf*) к +*dat*; (*consult*) обращáться (*perf* обрати́ться) к +*dat*

referee [rɛfə'ri:] *n* (*Sport*) рефери́ *m ind*, судья *m*; (*Brit: for job*) лицó, дающее рекомендáцию ▷ *vt* суди́ть (*impf*)

reference ['rɛfrəns] *n* (*mention*) упоминáние; (*in book, paper*) ссылка; (*for job: letter*) рекомендáция; **with reference to** (*in letter*) ссылаясь на +*acc*

refine [rɪ'faɪn] *vt* (*sugar*) рафини́ровать (*impf/perf*); (*oil*) очищáть (*perf* очи́стить); (*theory, task*) совершéнствовать (*perf* усовершéнствовать); **refined** *adj* (*person, taste*) утончённый

reflect [rɪ'flɛkt] *vt* отражáть (*perf* отрази́ть) ▷ *vi* (*think*) раздумывать (*impf*); **reflect on** *vt* (*discredit*) отражáться (*perf* отрази́ться) на +*acc*; **reflection** [rɪ'flɛkʃən] *n* отражéние; (*thought*) раздумье; (*comment*): **reflection on** суждéние о +*prp*; **on reflection** взвéсив все обстоятельства

reflex ['ri:flɛks] *n* рефлéкс

reform [rɪ'fɔ:m] *n* (*of law, system*) рефóрма ▷ *vt* (*character*) преобразовáть (*impf/perf*); (*system*) реформи́ровать (*impf/perf*)

refrain [rɪ'freɪn] *n* (*of song*) припéв ▷ *vi*: **to refrain from commenting** воздéрживаться (*perf* воздержáться) от комментáриев

refresh [rɪ'frɛʃ] vt освежа́ть (perf освежи́ть); **refreshing** adj (sleep) освежа́ющий; (drink) тонизи́рующий; **refreshments** npl заку́ски fpl и напи́тки mpl

refrigerator [rɪ'frɪdʒəreɪtə^r] n холоди́льник

refuge ['rɛfjuːdʒ] n (shelter) убе́жище, прибе́жище; **to take refuge in** находи́ть (perf найти́) прибе́жище в +prp

refugee [rɛfju'dʒiː] n бе́женец(-нка)

refund [n 'riːfʌnd, vb rɪ'fʌnd] n возмеще́ние ▷ vt возмеща́ть (perf возмести́ть)

refurbish [riː'fəːbɪʃ] vt ремонти́ровать (perf отремонти́ровать)

refusal [rɪ'fjuːzəl] n отка́з

refuse¹ [rɪ'fjuːz] vt (offer, gift) отка́зываться (perf отказа́ться) от +gen; (permission) отка́зывать (perf отказа́ть) в +prp ▷ vi отка́зываться (perf отказа́ться); **to refuse to do** отка́зываться (perf отказа́ться) +infin

refuse² ['rɛfjuːs] n му́сор

regain [rɪ'geɪn] vt (power, position) вновь обрета́ть (perf обрести́)

regard [rɪ'gɑːd] n (esteem) уваже́ние ▷ vt (consider) счита́ть (impf); (view, look on): **to regard with** относи́ться (perf отнести́сь) с +instr; **to give one's regards to** передава́ть (perf переда́ть) покло́ны +dat; **as regards, with regard to** что каса́ется +gen, относи́тельно +gen; **regarding** prep относи́тельно +gen; **regardless** adv (continue) несмотря́ ни на что́; **regardless of** несмотря́ на +acc, не счита́ясь с +instr

reggae ['rɛgeɪ] n ра́гги m ind

regiment ['rɛdʒɪmənt] n полк

region ['riːdʒən] n (area: of country) регио́н; (: smaller) райо́н; (Admin, Anat) о́бласть f; **in the region of** (fig) в райо́не +gen; **regional** adj (organization) областно́й, региона́льный; (accent) ме́стный

register ['rɛdʒɪstə^r] n (census, record) за́пись f; (Scol) журна́л; (also **electoral register**) спи́сок избира́телей ▷ vt регистри́ровать (perf зарегистри́ровать); (subj: meter etc) пока́зывать (perf показа́ть) ▷ vi регистри́роваться (perf зарегистри́роваться); (as student) запи́сываться (perf записа́ться); (make impression) запечатлева́ться (perf запечатле́ться) в па́мяти; **registered** adj (letter) заказно́й; **Registered Trademark** n зарегистри́рованный това́рный знак

registrar ['rɛdʒɪstrɑː^r] n регистра́тор

registration [rɛdʒɪs'treɪʃən] n регистра́ция; (Aut: also **registration number**) (регистрацио́нный) но́мер автомоби́ля

registry office ['rɛdʒɪstrɪ-] n (Brit) ≈ ЗАГС (отде́л за́писей гражда́нского состоя́ния)

regret [rɪ'grɛt] n сожале́ние ▷ vt сожале́ть (impf) о +prp; (death) скорбе́ть (impf) о +prp; **regrettable** adj приско́рбный, досто́йный сожале́ния

regular ['rɛgjulə^r] adj регуля́рный; (even) ро́вный (symmetrical) пра́вильный; (usual: time) обы́чный ▷ n (in café, restaurant) завсегда́тай; (in shop) клие́нт; **regularly** adv регуля́рно; (symmetrically: shaped etc) пра́вильно

regulate ['rɛgjuleɪt] vt регули́ровать (perf отрегули́ровать)

regulation [rɛgju'leɪʃən] n регули́рование; (rule) пра́вило

rehabilitation ['riːəbɪlɪ'teɪʃən] n (of addict) реабилита́ция; (of criminal) интегра́ция

rehearsal [rɪ'həːsəl] n репети́ция

rehearse [rɪ'həːs] vt репети́ровать (perf отрепети́ровать)

reign [reɪn] n ца́рствование ▷ vi (monarch) ца́рствовать (impf); (fig) цари́ть (impf)

reimburse [riːɪm'bəːs] vt возмеща́ть (perf возмести́ть)

rein [reɪn] n (for horse) вожжа́

reincarnation [riːɪnkɑː'neɪʃən] n (belief) переселе́ние душ

reindeer ['reɪndɪə^r] n inv се́верный оле́нь m

reinforce [riːɪn'fɔːs] vt (strengthen) укрепля́ть (perf укрепи́ть); (back up) подкрепля́ть (perf подкрепи́ть)

reinstate [riːɪn'steɪt] vt восстана́вливать (perf восстанови́ть) в пре́жнем положе́нии

reject [vb rɪ'dʒɛkt, n 'riːdʒɛkt] vt отклоня́ть (perf отклони́ть), отверга́ть (perf отве́ргнуть); (political system) отверга́ть (perf отве́ргнуть); (candidate) отклоня́ть (perf отклони́ть); (goods) бракова́ть (perf забракова́ть) ▷ n (product) некондицио́нное изде́лие; **rejection** [rɪ'dʒɛkʃən] n отклоне́ние

rejoice [rɪ'dʒɔɪs] vi: **to rejoice at** or **over** ликова́ть (impf) по по́воду +gen

relate [rɪ'leɪt] vt (tell) переска́зывать (perf пересказа́ть); (connect): **to relate sth to** относи́ть (perf отнести́) что-н к +dat ▷ vi: **to relate to** (person) сходи́ться (perf сойти́сь) с +instr; (subject, thing) относи́ться (perf отнести́сь) к +dat; **related** adj: **related (to)** (person) состоя́щий в родстве́ (с +instr); (animal, language) ро́дственный (с +instr); **they are related** они́ состоя́т в родстве́; **relating to** [rɪ'leɪtɪŋ-] prep относи́тельно +gen

relation [rɪ'leɪʃən] n (member of family) ро́дственник(-ица); (connection) отноше́ние; **relations** npl (dealings) сноше́ния mpl; (relatives) ро́дственники mpl, родня́ fsg; **relationship** n (between two people, countries) (взаимо-) отноше́ния ntpl; (between two things, affair) связь f

relative ['rɛlətɪv] n (family member) ро́дственник(-ица) ▷ adj (comparative) относи́тельный; **relative to** (in relation to) относя́щийся к +dat; **relatively** adv относи́тельно

relax [rɪ'læks] vi рассла́бля́ться (perf рассла́биться) ▷ vt (grip, rule, control) ослабля́ть (perf осла́бить); (person) расслабля́ть (perf рассла́бить); **relaxation** [ri:læk'seɪʃən] n о́тдых; (of muscle) расслабле́ние; (of grip, rule, control) ослабле́ние; **relaxed** adj непринуждённый, рассла́бленный; **relaxing** adj (holiday) расслабля́ющий

relay [n 'ri:leɪ, vb rɪ'leɪ] n (race) эстафе́та ▷ vt передава́ть (perf переда́ть)

release [rɪ'li:s] n (from prison) освобожде́ние; (of gas, book, film) вы́пуск ▷ vt (see n) освобожда́ть (perf освободи́ть); выпуска́ть (perf вы́пустить); (Tech: catch, spring etc) отпуска́ть (perf отпусти́ть)

relentless [rɪ'lɛntlɪs] adj (effort) неосла́бный; (rain) продолжи́тельный; (determined) неуста́нный

relevant ['rɛləvənt] adj актуа́льный; **relevant to** относя́щийся к +dat

reliable [rɪ'laɪəbl] adj надёжный; (information) достове́рный

relic ['rɛlɪk] n (of past etc) рели́квия

relief [rɪ'li:f] n облегче́ние; (aid) по́мощь f

relieve [rɪ'li:v] vt (pain, suffering) облегча́ть (perf облегчи́ть); (fear, worry) уменьша́ть (perf уме́ньшить); (colleague, guard) сменя́ть (perf смени́ть); **to relieve sb of sth** освобожда́ть (perf освободи́ть) кого́-н от чего́-н; **relieved** adj: **to feel relieved** чу́вствовать (perf почу́вствовать) облегче́ние

religion [rɪ'lɪdʒən] n рели́гия

religious [rɪ'lɪdʒəs] adj религио́зный

relish ['rɛlɪʃ] n (Culin) припра́ва; (enjoyment) наслажде́ние ▷ vt наслажда́ться (perf наслади́ться) +instr, смакова́ть (impf)

reluctance [rɪ'lʌktəns] n нежела́ние

reluctant [rɪ'lʌktənt] adj неохо́тный; (person): **he is reluctant to go there** он идёт туда́ неохо́тно; **reluctantly** adv неохо́тно

rely on [rɪ'laɪ-] vt fus (count on) рассчи́тывать (impf) на +acc; (trust) полага́ться (perf положи́ться) на +acc

remain [rɪ'meɪn] vi остава́ться (perf оста́ться); **remainder** n оста́ток; **remaining** adj сохрани́вшийся, оста́вшийся; **remains** npl (of meal) оста́тки mpl; (of building) разва́лины fpl; (of body) оста́нки mpl

remand [rɪ'mɑ:nd] n: **on remand** взя́тый под стра́жу ▷ vt: **he was remanded in custody** он был взят под стра́жу

remark [rɪ'mɑ:k] n замеча́ние ▷ vt замеча́ть (perf заме́тить); **remarkable** adj замеча́тельный

remedy ['rɛmədɪ] n (cure) сре́дство ▷ vt исправля́ть (perf испра́вить)

remember [rɪ'mɛmbəʳ] vt (recall) вспомина́ть (perf вспо́мнить); (bear in mind) по́мнить (impf)

remind [rɪ'maɪnd] vt: **to remind sb to do** напомина́ть (perf напо́мнить) кому́-н +infin; **to remind sb of sth** напомина́ть (perf напо́мнить) кому́-н о чём-н; **she reminds me of her mother** она́ напомина́ет мне свою́ мать; **reminder** n напомина́ние

reminiscent [rɛmɪ'nɪsənt] adj: **to be reminiscent of sth** напомина́ть (perf напо́мнить) что-н

remnant ['rɛmnənt] n оста́ток

remorse [rɪ'mɔ:s] n раска́яние

remote [rɪ'məut] adj (place, time) отдалённый; **remote control** n дистанцио́нное управле́ние; **remotely** adv отдалённо; **I'm not remotely interested** я ниско́лько не заинтересо́ван

removal [rɪ'mu:vəl] n удале́ние; (Brit: of furniture) перево́зка

remove [rɪ'mu:v] vt (take away) убира́ть (perf убра́ть); (clothing, employee) снима́ть (perf снять); (stain) удаля́ть (perf удали́ть); (problem, doubt) устраня́ть (perf устрани́ть)

Renaissance [rɪ'neɪsɑ̃:s] n: **the Renaissance** (History) Возрожде́ние

render ['rɛndəʳ] vt (assistance) ока́зывать (perf оказа́ть); (harmless, useless) де́лать (perf сде́лать) +instr

rendezvous ['rɒndɪvu:] n (meeting) свида́ние; (place) ме́сто свида́ния

renew [rɪ'nju:] vt возобновля́ть (perf возобнови́ть); **renewable** [ri:'nju:əbl] adj (energy) возобновля́емый

renovate ['rɛnəveɪt] vt модернизи́ровать (impf/perf); (building) де́лать (perf сде́лать) капита́льный ремо́нт в +prp

renowned [rɪ'naund] adj просла́вленный

rent [rɛnt] n кварти́рная пла́та ▷ vt (take for rent: house) снима́ть (perf снять); (: television, car) брать (perf взять) напрока́т; (also **rent out**: house) сдава́ть (perf сдать; внаём); (: television, car) дава́ть (perf дать) напрока́т; **rental** n (charge) пла́та за прока́т

rep [rɛp] n abbr (Comm) = **representative**
repair [rɪ'pɛər] n ремонт ▷ vt (clothes, shoes) чинить (perf починить); (car) ремонтировать (perf отремонтировать); **in good/bad repair** в хорошем/плохом состоянии
repay [ri:'peɪ] (irreg like **pay**) vt (money, debt) выплачивать (perf выплатить); (person) уплачивать (perf уплатить) +dat; **to repay sb (for sth)** (favour) отплачивать (perf отплатить) кому-н (за что-н); **repayment** n выплата
repeat [rɪ'pi:t] vt повторять (perf повторить) ▷ vi повторяться (perf повториться) ▷ n (Radio, TV) повторение; **repeatedly** adv неоднократно
repellent [rɪ'pɛlənt] n: **insect repellent** репеллент
repercussions [ri:pə'kʌʃənz] npl последствия ntpl
repetition [rɛpɪ'tɪʃən] n (repeat) повторение
repetitive [rɪ'pɛtɪtɪv] adj повторяющийся
replace [rɪ'pleɪs] vt (put back) класть (perf положить) обратно; (: vertically) ставить (perf поставить) обратно; (take the place of) заменять (perf заменить); **replacement** n замена
replay [n 'ri:pleɪ, vb ri:'pleɪ] n (of match) переигровка; (of film) повторный показ ▷ vt (match, game) переигрывать (perf переиграть); (part of tape) повторно проигрывать (perf проиграть)
replica ['rɛplɪkə] n (copy) копия
reply [rɪ'plaɪ] n ответ ▷ vi отвечать (perf ответить)
report [rɪ'pɔ:t] n (account) доклад, отчёт; (Press, TV etc) репортаж; (statement) сообщение; (Brit: also **school report**) отчёт об успеваемости ▷ vt сообщать (perf сообщить) о +prp; (event, meeting) докладывать (perf доложить) о +prp; (person) доносить (perf донести) на +acc ▷ vi (make a report) докладывать (perf доложить); **to report to sb** (present o.s.) являться (perf явиться) к кому-н; (be responsible to) быть (impf) под началом кого-н; **to report that** сообщать (perf сообщить), что; **reportedly** adv как сообщают; **reporter** n репортёр
represent [rɛprɪ'zɛnt] vt (person, nation) представлять (perf представить); (view, belief) излагать (perf изложить); (constitute) представлять (impf) собой; (idea, emotion) символизировать (impf/perf); (describe): **to represent sth as** изображать (perf изобразить) что-н как; **representation** [rɛprɪzɛn'teɪʃən] n (state) представительство; (picture, statue) изображение; **representative** n представитель m ▷ adj представительный

repress [rɪ'prɛs] vt подавлять (perf подавить); **repression** [rɪ'prɛʃən] n подавление
reprimand ['rɛprɪmɑ:nd] n выговор ▷ vt делать (perf сделать) выговор +dat
reproduce [ri:prə'dju:s] vt воспроизводить (perf воспроизвести) ▷ vi размножаться (perf размножиться)
reproduction [ri:prə'dʌkʃən] n воспроизведение; (Art) репродукция
reptile ['rɛptaɪl] n пресмыкающееся nt adj (животное)
republic [rɪ'pʌblɪk] n республика; **Republican** n (US: Pol) республиканец(-нка)
reputable ['rɛpjutəbl] adj (person) уважаемый; **reputable company** компания с хорошей репутацией
reputation [rɛpju'teɪʃən] n репутация
request [rɪ'kwɛst] n (polite demand) просьба; (formal demand) заявка ▷ vt: **to request sth of or from sb** просить (perf попросить) что-н у кого-н
require [rɪ'kwaɪər] vt (subj: person) нуждаться (impf) в +prp; (: thing, situation) требовать (impf); (order): **to require sth of sb** требовать (perf потребовать) что-н от кого-н; **we require you to complete the task** мы требуем, чтобы Вы завершили работу; **requirement** n (need, want) потребность f
rescue ['rɛskju:] n спасение ▷ vt: **to rescue (from)** спасать (perf спасти) (от +gen); **to come to sb's rescue** приходить (perf прийти) кому-н на помощь
research [rɪ'sə:tʃ] n исследование ▷ vt исследовать (impf/perf)
resemblance [rɪ'zɛmbləns] n сходство
resemble [rɪ'zɛmbl] vt походить (impf) на +acc
resent [rɪ'zɛnt] vt (fact) негодовать (impf) против +gen; (person) негодовать (impf) на +acc; **resentful** adj негодующий; **I am resentful of his behaviour** его поведение приводит меня в негодование; **resentment** n негодование
reservation [rɛzə'veɪʃən] n (booking) предварительный заказ; (doubt) сомнение; (for tribe) резервация
reserve [rɪ'zə:v] n (store) резерв, запас; (also **nature reserve**) заповедник; (Sport) запасной игрок; (restraint) сдержанность f ▷ vt (look, tone) сохранять (perf сохранить); (seats, table etc) заказывать (perf заказать); **in reserve** в резерве or запасе; **reserved** adj (restrained) сдержанный
reservoir ['rɛzəvwɑ:r] n (of water) водохранилище
reshuffle [rɪ:'ʃʌfl] n: **Cabinet reshuffle** перетасовка or перестановки fpl в кабинете министров
residence ['rɛzɪdəns] n (home) резиденция; (length of stay) пребывание

resident ['rɛzɪdənt] n (of country, town) (постоя́нный(-ая)) жи́тель(ница) m(f); (in hotel) прожива́ющий(-ая) m(f) adj ▷ adj (population) постоя́нный

residential [rɛzɪ'dɛnʃəl] adj (area) жило́й; (course, college) с прожива́нием

resign [rɪ'zaɪn] vi (from post) уходи́ть (perf уйти́) в отста́вку ▷ vt (one's post) оставля́ть (perf оста́вить) c +gen; **to resign o.s. to** смиря́ться (perf смири́ться) c +instr; **resignation** [rɛzɪg'neɪʃən] n отста́вка; (acceptance) поко́рность f, смире́ние

resin ['rɛzɪn] n смола́

resist [rɪ'zɪst] vt сопротивля́ться (impf) +dat; (temptation) устоя́ть (perf) пе́ред +instr; **resistance** n (opposition) сопротивле́ние; (to illness) сопротивля́емость f

resolution [rɛzə'luːʃən] n (decision) реше́ние; (: formal) резолю́ция; (determination) реши́мость f; (of problem, difficulty) разреше́ние

resolve [rɪ'zɔlv] n реши́тельность f ▷ vt (problem, difficulty) разреша́ть (perf разреши́ть) ▷ vi: **to resolve to do** реша́ть (perf реши́ть) +infin

resort [rɪ'zɔːt] n (town) куро́рт; (recourse) прибега́ние ▷ vi: **to resort to** прибега́ть (perf прибе́гнуть) к +dat; **the last resort** после́дняя наде́жда; **in the last resort** в кра́йнем слу́чае

resource [rɪ'zɔːs] n ресу́рс; **resourceful** adj изобрета́тельный, нахо́дчивый

respect [rɪs'pɛkt] n уваже́ние ▷ vt уважа́ть (impf); **respects** npl (greetings) почте́ние ntsg; **with respect to, in respect of** в отноше́нии +gen; **in this respect** в э́том отноше́нии; **respectable** adj прили́чный; (morally correct) респекта́бельный; **respectful** adj почти́тельный

respective [rɪs'pɛktɪv] adj: **he drove them to their respective homes** он отвёз их обо́их по дома́м; **respectively** adv соотве́тственно

respond [rɪs'pɔnd] vi (answer) отвеча́ть (perf отве́тить); (react): **to respond to** (pressure, criticism) реаги́ровать (perf отреаги́ровать) на +acc

response [rɪs'pɔns] n (answer) отве́т; (reaction) резона́нс, о́тклик

responsibility [rɪspɔnsɪ'bɪlɪtɪ] n (liability) отве́тственность f; (duty) обя́занность f

responsible [rɪs'pɔnsɪbl] adj: **responsible (for)** отве́тственный (за +acc)

responsive [rɪs'pɔnsɪv] adj (child, nature) отзы́вчивый; **responsive to** (demand, treatment) восприи́мчивый к +dat

rest [rɛst] n (relaxation, pause) о́тдых; (stand, support) подста́вка ▷ vi (relax, stop) отдыха́ть (perf отдохну́ть) ▷ vt (head, eyes etc) дава́ть (perf дать) о́тдых +dat; (lean): **to rest sth against** прислоня́ть

(perf прислони́ть) что-н к +dat; **the rest** (remainder) остально́е nt adj; **the rest of them** остальны́е (из них); **to rest on** (person) опира́ться (perf опере́ться) на +acc; (idea) опира́ться (impf) на +acc; (object) лежа́ть (impf) на +prp; **rest assured that ...** бу́дьте уве́рены, что ...; **it rests with him to ...** на нём лежи́т обя́занность +infin ...; **to rest one's eyes** or **gaze on** остана́вливать (perf останови́ть) (свой) взгляд на +acc

restaurant ['rɛstərɔn] n рестора́н

restless ['rɛstlɪs] adj беспоко́йный

restoration [rɛstə'reɪʃən] n (of building etc) реставра́ция; (of order, health) восстановле́ние

restore [rɪ'stɔː] vt (see n) реставри́ровать (perf отреставри́ровать); восстана́вливать (perf восстанови́ть); (stolen property) возвраща́ть (perf возврати́ть); (to power) верну́ть (perf)

restrain [rɪs'treɪn] vt сде́рживать (perf сдержа́ть); (person): **to restrain sb from doing** не дава́ть (perf дать) кому́-н +infin; **restraint** n (moderation) сде́ржанность f; (restriction) ограниче́ние

restrict [rɪs'trɪkt] vt ограни́чивать (perf ограни́чить); **restriction** [rɪs'trɪkʃən] n: **restriction (on)** ограниче́ние (на +acc)

result [rɪ'zʌlt] n результа́т ▷ vi: **to result in** зака́нчиваться (perf зако́нчиться) +instr; **as a result of** в результа́те +gen

resume [rɪ'zjuːm] vt (work, journey) возобновля́ть (perf возобнови́ть) ▷ vi продолжа́ть (perf продо́лжить)

résumé ['reɪzjuːmeɪ] n резюме́ nt ind; (US: for job) автобиогра́фия

retail ['riːteɪl] adj ро́зничный ▷ adv в ро́зницу; **retailer** n ро́зничный торго́вец

retain [rɪ'teɪn] vt (keep) сохраня́ть (perf сохрани́ть)

retaliation [rɪtælɪ'eɪʃən] n (against attack) отве́тный уда́р; (against ill-treatment) возме́здие

retarded [rɪ'tɑːdɪd] adj (development, growth) заме́дленный

retire [rɪ'taɪə] vi (give up work) уходи́ть (perf уйти́) на пе́нсию; (withdraw) удаля́ться (perf удали́ться); (go to bed) удаля́ться (perf удали́ться) на поко́й; **retired** adj: **he is retired** он на пе́нсии; **retirement** n вы́ход or ухо́д на пе́нсию

retreat [rɪ'triːt] n (place) убе́жище; (withdrawal) ухо́д; (Mil) отступле́ние ▷ vi отступа́ть (perf отступи́ть)

retrieve [rɪ'triːv] vt (object) получа́ть (perf получи́ть) обра́тно; (honour) восстана́вливать (perf восстанови́ть); (situation) спаса́ть (perf спасти́)

retrospect ['rɛtrəspɛkt] n: **in retrospect** в ретроспе́кции; **retrospective** [rɛtrə'spɛktɪv] adj (law, tax) име́ющий обра́тную си́лу

return [rɪ'tə:n] n (from, to place) возвраще́ние; (of sth stolen etc) возвра́т; (Comm) дохо́д ▷ cpd (journey, ticket) обра́тный ▷ vi возвраща́ться (perf возврати́ться), верну́ться (perf) ▷ vt возвраща́ть (perf возврати́ть), верну́ть (perf); (Law: verdict) выноси́ть (perf вы́нести); (Pol: candidate) избира́ть (perf избра́ть); (ball) отбива́ть (perf отби́ть); **in return (for)** в отве́т (на +acc); **many happy returns (of the day)!** с днём рожде́ния!; **to return to** (consciousness) приходи́ть (perf прийти́) в +acc; (power) верну́ться (perf) к +dat

reunion [ri:'ju:nɪən] n (reuniting) воссоедине́ние; (party) встре́ча

revamp [ri:'væmp] vt обновля́ть (perf обнови́ть)

reveal [rɪ'vi:l] vt (make known) обнару́живать (perf обнару́жить); (make visible) открыва́ть (perf откры́ть); **revealing** adj (action, statement) показа́тельный; (dress) откры́тый

revel ['rɛvl] vi: **to revel in sth** упива́ться (impf) чем-н; **to revel in doing** обожа́ть (impf) +infin

revelation [rɛvə'leɪʃən] n (fact) откры́тие

revenge [rɪ'vɛndʒ] n месть f; **to take revenge on, revenge o.s. on** мстить (perf отомсти́ть) +dat

revenue ['rɛvənju:] n дохо́ды mpl

Reverend ['rɛvərənd] adj: **the Reverend** его́ преподо́бие

reversal [rɪ'və:sl] n радика́льное измене́ние; (of roles) переме́на

reverse [rɪ'və:s] n (opposite) противополо́жность f; (of coin, medal) оборо́тная сторона́; (of paper) оборо́т; (Aut: also **reverse gear**) обра́тный ход ▷ adj (opposite) обра́тный ▷ vt (order, position, decision) изменя́ть (perf измени́ть); (process, trend) пово́рачивать (perf поверну́ть) вспять ▷ vi (Brit: Aut) дава́ть (perf дать) за́дний ход; **in reverse order** в обра́тном поря́дке; **to reverse a car** дава́ть (perf дать) за́дний ход; **to reverse roles** меня́ться (perf поменя́ться) роля́ми

revert [rɪ'və:t] vi: **to revert to** (to former state) возвраща́ться (perf возврати́ться) к +dat; (Law: money, property) переходи́ть (perf перейти́) к +dat

review [rɪ'vju:] n (of situation, policy etc) пересмо́тр; (of book, film etc) реце́нзия; (magazine) обозре́ние ▷ vt (situation, policy etc) пересма́тривать (perf пересмотре́ть); (book, film etc) рецензи́ровать (perf отрецензи́ровать)

revise [rɪ'vaɪz] vt (manuscript) перераба́тывать (perf перерабо́тать); (opinion, law) пересма́тривать (perf пересмотре́ть) ▷ vi (Scol) повторя́ть (perf повтори́ть)

revision [rɪ'vɪʒən] n (see vb)

перерабо́тка; пересмо́тр; повторе́ние

revival [rɪ'vaɪvl] n (recovery) оживле́ние; (of interest, faith) возрожде́ние

revive [rɪ'vaɪv] vt (person) возвраща́ть (perf возврати́ть) к жи́зни; (economy, industry) оживля́ть (perf оживи́ть); (tradition, interest etc) возрожда́ть (perf возроди́ть) ▷ vi (see vt) приходи́ть (perf прийти́) в созна́ние; оживля́ться (perf оживи́ться); возрожда́ться (perf возроди́ться)

revolt [rɪ'vəult] n (rebellion) восста́ние ▷ vi (rebel) восстава́ть (perf восста́ть) ▷ vt вызыва́ть (perf) отвраще́ние у +gen; **revolting** adj отврати́тельный

revolution [rɛvə'lu:ʃən] n револю́ция; (of wheel, earth etc) оборо́т; **revolutionary** adj революцио́нный ▷ n революционе́р(ка)

revolve [rɪ'vɔlv] vi (turn) враща́ться (impf); (fig): **to revolve (a)round** враща́ться (impf) вокру́г +gen

revolver [rɪ'vɔlvə'] n револьве́р

reward [rɪ'wɔ:d] n награ́да ▷ vt: **to reward (for)** (effort) вознагражда́ть (perf вознагради́ть) (за +acc); **rewarding** adj: **this work is rewarding** э́та рабо́та прино́сит удовлетворе́ние

rewind [ri:'waɪnd] (irreg like **wind**[2]) vt перема́тывать (perf перемота́ть)

rewrite [ri:'raɪt] (irreg like **write**) vt (rework) перепи́сывать (perf переписа́ть)

rheumatism ['ru:mətɪzəm] n ревмати́зм

rhinoceros [raɪ'nɔsərəs] n носоро́г

rhubarb ['ru:bɑ:b] n реве́нь m

rhyme [raɪm] n ри́фма; (in poetry) разме́р

rhythm ['rɪðm] n ритм

rib [rɪb] n (Anat) ребро́

ribbon ['rɪbən] n ле́нта; **in ribbons** (torn) в кло́чья

rice [raɪs] n рис

rich [rɪtʃ] adj бога́тый; (clothes, jewels) роско́шный; (food, colour, life) насы́щенный; (abundant): **rich in** бога́тый +instr; ▷ npl: **the rich** (rich people) бога́тые pl adj

rid [rɪd] (pt, pp **rid**) vt: **to rid sb of sth** избавля́ть (perf изба́вить) кого́-н от чего́-н; **to get rid of** избавля́ться (perf изба́виться) или отде́лываться (perf отде́латься) от +gen

ridden ['rɪdn] pp of **ride**

riddle ['rɪdl] n (conundrum) зага́дка ▷ vt: **riddled with** (holes, bullets) изрешечённый +instr; (guilt, doubts) по́лный +gen; (corruption) прони́занный +instr

ride [raɪd] (pt **rode**, pp **ridden**) n пое́здка ▷ vi (as sport) е́здить (impf) верхо́м; (go somewhere, travel) е́здить/е́хать (пое́хать perf) ▷ vt (horse) е́здить/е́хать (impf) верхо́м на +prp; (bicycle, motorcycle) е́здить/е́хать (impf) на +prp; (distance) проезжа́ть (perf прое́хать); **a 5 mile ride**

поездка в 5 миль; **to take sb for a ride** (*fig*)
прокатить (*perf*) кого-н; **rider** *n* (*on horse*) наездник(-ица); (*on bicycle*) велосипедист(ка); (*on motorcycle*) мотоциклист(ка)

ridge [rɪdʒ] *n* (*of hill*) гребень *m*

ridicule ['rɪdɪkju:l] *vt* высмеивать (*perf* высмеять)

ridiculous [rɪ'dɪkjuləs] *adj* смехотворный; **it's ridiculous** это смешно

riding ['raɪdɪŋ] *n* верховая езда

rife [raɪf] *adj*: **to be rife** (*corruption*) процветать (*impf*); **to be rife with** (*rumours, fears*) изобиловать (*impf*) +*instr*

rifle ['raɪfl] *n* (*Mil*) винтовка; (*for hunting*) ружьё

rift [rɪft] *n* (*also fig*) трещина

rig [rɪg] *n* (*also oil rig*) буровая установка ▷ *vt* подтасовывать (*perf* подтасовать) результаты +*gen*

right [raɪt] *adj* правильный; (*person, time, size*) подходящий; (*fair, just*) справедливый; (*not left*) правый ▷ *n* (*entitlement*) право; (*not left*) правая сторона ▷ *adv* (*correctly*) правильно; (*not to the left*) направо ▷ *vt* (*ship*) выравнивать (*perf* выровнять); (*car*) ставить (*perf* поставить) на колёса; (*fault, situation*) исправлять (*perf* исправить); (*wrong*) устранять (*perf* устранить) ▷ *excl* так, хорошо; **she's right** она права; **that's right!** (*answer*) правильно!; **is that clock right?** эти часы правильно идут?; **on the right** справа; **you are in the right** правда за Вами; **by rights** по справедливости; **right and wrong** хорошее и дурное; **right now** сейчас же; **right away** сразу же; **rightful** *adj* законный; **rightly** *adv* (*with reason*) справедливо; **right of way** *n* (*path etc*) право прохода; (*Aut*) право проезда; **right-wing** *adj* (*Pol*) правый

rigid ['rɪdʒɪd] *adj* (*structure, control*) жёсткий; (*fig: attitude etc*) косный

rigorous ['rɪgərəs] *adj* жёсткий; (*training*) серьёзный

rim [rɪm] *n* (*of glass, dish*) край; (*of spectacles*) ободок; (*of wheel*) обод

rind [raɪnd] *n* (*of bacon, cheese*) корка; (*of lemon, orange etc*) кожура

ring [rɪŋ] (*pt* **rang**, *pp* **rung**) *n* (*of metal, smoke*) кольцо; (*of people, objects, light*) круг; (*of spies, drug dealers etc*) сеть *f*; (*for boxing*) ринг; (*of circus*) арена; (*of doorbell, telephone*) звонок ▷ *vi* звонить (*perf* позвонить); (*doorbell*) звенеть (*impf*); (*also* **ring out**: *voice, shot*) раздаваться (*perf* раздаться) ▷ *vt* (*Brit: Tel*) звонить (*perf* позвонить) +*dat*; **to give sb a ring** (*Brit: Tel*) звонить (*perf* позвонить) кому-н; **my ears are ringing** у меня звенит в ушах; **to ring the bell** звонить (*impf*) в звонок; **ring up** *vt* (*Brit*) звонить (*perf* позвонить) +*dat*; **ringtone** ['rɪŋtəun] *n* (*on mobile*) мелодия для мобильного телефона

rink [rɪŋk] *n* (*for skating*) каток

rinse [rɪns] *vt* полоскать (*perf* прополоскать) ▷ *n*: **to give sth a rinse** ополаскивать (*perf* ополоснуть) что-н

riot ['raɪət] *n* (*disturbance*) беспорядки *mpl*, бесчинства *ntpl* ▷ *vi* бесчинствовать (*impf*); **to run riot** буйствовать (*impf*)

rip [rɪp] *n* разрыв ▷ *vt* (*paper, cloth*) разрывать (*perf* разорвать) ▷ *vi* разрываться (*perf* разорваться)

ripe [raɪp] *adj* спелый, зрелый

ripple ['rɪpl] *n* рябь *f no pl*, зыбь *f no pl*; (*of laughter, applause*) волна

rise [raɪz] (*pt* **rose**, *pp* **risen**) *n* (*slope*) подъём; (*increase*) повышение; (*fig: of state, leader*) возвышение ▷ *vi* подниматься (*perf* подняться); (*prices, numbers, voice*) повышаться (*perf* повыситься); (*sun, moon*) всходить (*perf* взойти); (*also* **rise up**: *rebels*) восставать (*perf* восстать); (*in rank*) продвигаться (*perf* продвинуться); **rise to power** приход к власти; **to give rise to** вызывать (*perf* вызвать); **to rise to the occasion** оказываться (*perf* оказаться) на высоте положения; **risen** ['rɪzn] *pp of* **rise**

rising ['raɪzɪŋ] *adj* (*number, prices*) растущий; (*sun, moon*) восходящий

risk [rɪsk] *n* риск ▷ *vt* (*endanger*) рисковать (*impf*) +*instr*; (*chance*) рисковать (*perf* рискнуть) +*instr*; **to take a risk** рисковать (*perf* рискнуть), идти (*perf* пойти) на риск; **to run the risk of doing** рисковать (*impf*) +*infin*; **at risk** в опасной ситуации; **to put sb/sth at risk** подвергать (*perf* подвергнуть) кого-н/что-н риску; **at one's own risk** на свой (страх и) риск; **risky** *adj* рискованный

rite [raɪt] *n* обряд; **last rites** последнее причастие

ritual ['rɪtjuəl] *adj* ритуальный ▷ *n* (*Rel*) обряд; (*procedure*) ритуал

rival ['raɪvl] *n* соперник(-ица); (*in business*) конкурент ▷ *adj* (*business*) конкурирующий ▷ *vt* соперничать (*impf*) с +*instr*; **rival team** команда соперника; **rivalry** *n* (*in sport, love*) соперничество; (*in business*) конкуренция

river ['rɪvəʳ] *n* река ▷ *cpd* (*port, traffic*) речной; **up/down river** вверх/вниз по реке

road [rəud] *n* дорога, путь *m*; (*in town*) дорога; (*motorway etc*) дорога, шоссе *nt ind* ▷ *cpd* (*accident*) дорожный; **major/minor road** главная/второстепенная дорога; **road sense** чувство дороги; **road junction** пересечение дорог, перекрёсток; **roadblock** *n* дорожное заграждение; **road rage** *n* хулиганское поведение на автодороге; **roadside** *n* обочина

roam [rəum] *vi* скитаться (*impf*)

roar [rɔːʳ] *n* рёв; (*of laughter*) взрыв ▷ *vi* реветь (*impf*); **to roar with laughter** хохотать (*impf*)

roast [rəust] n (of meat) жарко́е nt adj
▷ vt (meat, potatoes) жа́рить (perf
зажа́рить)

rob [rɔb] vt гра́бить (perf огра́бить); **to
rob sb of sth** красть (perf укра́сть) что-н у
кого́-н; (fig) лиша́ть (perf лиши́ть) кого́-н
чего́-н; **robber** n граби́тель m; **robbery**
n ограбле́ние, грабёж

robe [rəub] n (for ceremony etc) ма́нтия;
(also **bath robe**) ба́нный хала́т; (US) плед

robin ['rɔbɪn] n (Zool) заря́нка

robot ['rəubɔt] n ро́бот

robust [rəu'bʌst] adj (person) кре́пкий

rock [rɔk] n (substance) (го́рная) поро́да;
(boulder) валу́н; (US: small stone)
ка́мешек; (Mus: also **rock music**) рок ▷ vt
(swing) кача́ть (impf); (shake) шата́ть
(impf) ▷ vi (object) кача́ться (impf),
шата́ться (impf); (person) кача́ться (impf);
on the rocks (drink) со льдом; (marriage
etc) на гра́ни распа́да; **rock and roll** n
рок-н-ро́лл

rocket ['rɔkɪt] n раке́та

rocky ['rɔkɪ] adj (hill) скали́стый; (path,
soil) камени́стый; (unstable) ша́ткий

rod [rɔd] n прут; (also **fishing rod**)
у́дочка

rode [rəud] pt of **ride**

rodent ['rəudnt] n грызу́н

rogue [rəug] n плут

role [rəul] n роль f; **role model** n
приме́р (для подража́ния)

roll [rəul] n (of paper, cloth etc) руло́н; (of
banknotes) сви́ток; (also **bread roll**)
бу́лочка; (register, list) спи́сок; (of drums)
бой; (of thunder) раска́т ▷ vt (ball, stone
etc) ката́ть/кати́ть (impf); (also **roll up**:
string) скру́чивать (perf скрути́ть);
(: sleeves, eyes) зака́тывать (perf
закати́ть); (cigarette) свёртывать (perf
сверну́ть); (also **roll out**: pastry)
раска́тывать (perf раската́ть) ▷ vi (also
roll along: ball, car etc) кати́ться (impf);
(ship) кача́ться (impf); **roll up** vt (carpet,
newspaper) свора́чивать (perf сверну́ть);
roller n (for hair) бигуди́ pl ind; **roller
skates** npl ро́лики mpl, ро́ликовые
коньки́ mpl; **rolling pin** n ска́лка

ROM [rɔm] n abbr (Comput) ПЗУ (=
постоя́нное запомина́ющее устро́йство)

Roman ['rəumən] adj ри́мский; **Roman
Catholic** adj (ри́мско-)католи́ческий ▷ n
като́лик(-и́чка)

romance [rə'mæns] n (love affair, novel)
рома́н; (charm) рома́нтика

Romania [rəu'meɪnɪə] n Румы́ния;
Romanian adj румы́нский

romantic [rə'mæntɪk] adj романти́чный;
(play, story etc) романти́ческий

Rome [rəum] n Рим

roof [ru:f] n (pl **roofs**) n кры́ша; **the roof of
the mouth** нёбо

room [ru:m] n (in house) ко́мната; (in

school) класс; (in hotel) но́мер; (space)
ме́сто; **rooms** npl (lodging) кварти́ра fsg;
"**rooms to let**", (US) "**rooms for rent**"
"сдаю́тся ко́мнаты"; **single/double room**
(in hotel) одноме́стный/двухме́стный
но́мер

root [ru:t] n ко́рень m; **roots** npl (family
origins) ко́рни mpl

rope [rəup] n верёвка ▷ vt (also **rope
off**: area) отгора́живать (perf отгороди́ть)
верёвкой; **to know the ropes** (fig) знать
(impf), что к чему́; **to rope to** привя́зывать
(perf привяза́ть) верёвкой к +dat; **to rope
together** свя́зывать (perf связа́ть)
верёвкой

rose [rəuz] pt of **rise** ▷ n ро́за

rosemary ['rəuzmərɪ] n розмари́н

rosy ['rəuzɪ] adj (face, cheeks) румя́ный;
(situation) ра́достный; (future) ра́дужный

rot [rɔt] n (result) гниль f ▷ vt гнои́ть
(perf сгнои́ть) ▷ vi гнить (perf сгни́ть)

rota ['rəutə] n расписа́ние дежу́рств

rotate [rəu'teɪt] vt враща́ть (impf); (crops,
jobs) чередова́ть (impf) ▷ vi враща́ться
(impf)

rotten ['rɔtn] adj гнило́й; (meat, eggs)
ту́хлый; (inf: unpleasant) ме́рзкий; (inf:
bad) пога́ный; **to feel rotten** (ill)
чу́вствовать (impf) себя́ пога́но

rouble ['ru:bl] (US **ruble**) n рубль m

rough [rʌf] adj гру́бый; (surface)
шерохова́тый; (terrain) пересечённый;
(person, manner) ре́зкий; (sea) бу́рный;
(town, area) опа́сный; (plan, work)
черново́й; (guess) приблизи́тельный ▷ vt:
to rough it ограни́чивать (perf
ограни́чить) себя́ ▷ adv: **to sleep rough**
(Brit) ночева́ть (impf) где придётся;
roughly adv гру́бо; (approximately)
приблизи́тельно

Roumania etc = **Romania** etc

round [raund] adj кру́глый ▷ n (duty:
of police officer, doctor) обхо́д; (game:
of cards, golf) па́ртия; (in competition)
тур; (of ammunition) компле́кт; (of talks,
also Boxing) ра́унд ▷ vt огиба́ть (perf
обогну́ть) ▷ prep (surrounding) вокру́г
+gen; (approximately) о́коло +gen: **round about three
hundred** где-то о́коло трёхсот ▷ adv: **all
round** круго́м, вокру́г; **a round of applause**
взрыв аплодисме́нтов; **a round of drinks**
по бока́лу на ка́ждого; **round his neck/the
table** вокру́г его́ ше́и/стола́; **the shop is
just round the corner** (fig) до магази́на
руко́й пода́ть; **to go round the back**
обходи́ть (perf обойти́) сза́ди; **to walk
round the room** ходи́ть (impf) по ко́мнате;
to go round to sb's (house) ходи́ть/идти́
(impf) к кому́-н; **there's enough to go
round** хва́тит на всех; **round off** vt
(speech etc) заверша́ть (perf заверши́ть);
round up vt (cattle, people) сгоня́ть (perf
согна́ть); (price, figure) округля́ть (perf
округли́ть); **roundabout** n (Brit: Aut)

кольцева́я тра́нспортная развя́зка; (: *at fair*) карусе́ль *f* ▷ *adj*: **in a roundabout way** око́льным путём; **roundup** *n* (*of information*) сво́дка

rouse [rauz] *vt* (*wake up*) буди́ть (*perf* разбуди́ть); (*stir up*) возбужда́ть (*perf* возбуди́ть)

route [ru:t] *n* (*way*) путь *m*, доро́га; (*of bus, train etc*) маршру́т

routine [ru:'ti:n] *adj* (*work*) повседне́вный; (*procedure*) обы́чный ▷ *n* (*habits*) распоря́док; (*drudgery*) рути́на; (*Theat*) но́мер

row¹ [rəu] *n* (*way*) ряд ▷ *vi* грести́ (*impf*) ▷ *vt* управля́ть (*impf*) +*instr*; **in a row** (*fig*) подря́д

row² [rau] *n* (*noise*) шум; (*dispute*) сканда́л; (*inf: scolding*) нагоня́й ▷ *vi* сканда́лить (*perf* поскандалить)

rowing ['rəuɪŋ] *n* гре́бля

royal ['rɔɪəl] *adj* короле́вский; **royalty** *n* (*royal persons*) чле́ны *mpl* короле́вской семьи́; (*payment*) (а́вторский) гонора́р

rpm *abbr* (= *revolutions per minute*) оборо́ты в мину́ту

RSVP *abbr* (= *répondez s'il vous plaît*) про́сим отве́тить на приглаше́ние

rub [rʌb] *vt* (*part of body*) тере́ть (*perf* потере́ть); (*object: to clean*) тере́ть (*impf*); (: *to dry*) вытира́ть (*perf* вы́тереть); (*hands: also* **rub together**) потира́ть (*perf* потере́ть) ▷ *n*: **to give sth a rub** (*polish*) натира́ть (*perf* натере́ть) что-н; **to rub sb up** or (*US*) **rub sb the wrong way** раздража́ть (*perf* раздражи́ть) кого́-н

rubber ['rʌbə'] *n* (*substance*) рези́на, каучу́к; (*Brit: eraser*) рези́нка, ла́стик

rubbish ['rʌbɪʃ] *n* му́сор; (*junk*) хлам; (*fig: pej: nonsense*) ерунда́, чушь *f*; (: *goods*) дрянь *f*

rubble ['rʌbl] *n* обло́мки *mpl*

rouble ['ru:bl] *n* (*US*) = **rouble**

ruby ['ru:bɪ] *n* руби́н

rucksack ['rʌksæk] *n* рюкза́к

rudder ['rʌdə'] *n* руль *m*

rude [ru:d] *adj* (*impolite*) гру́бый; (*unexpected*) жесто́кий

rug [rʌg] *n* ко́врик; (*Brit: blanket*) плед

rugby ['rʌgbɪ] *n* (*also* **rugby football**) ре́гби *nt ind*

rugged ['rʌgɪd] *adj* (*landscape*) скали́стый; (*features*) гру́бый; (*character*) прямо́й

ruin ['ru:ɪn] *n* (*destruction: of building, plans*) разруше́ние; (*downfall*) ги́бель *f*; (*bankruptcy*) разоре́ние ▷ *vt* (*building, hopes, plans*) разруша́ть (*perf* разру́шить); (*future, health, reputation*) губи́ть (*perf* погуби́ть); (*person: financially*) разоря́ть (*perf* разори́ть); (*spoil: clothes*) по́ртить (*perf* испо́ртить); **ruins** *npl* (*of building*) разва́лины *fpl*, руи́ны *fpl*

rule [ru:l] *n* (*norm, regulation*) пра́вило; (*government*) правле́ние ▷ *vt* (*country,*

people) пра́вить (*impf*) +*instr* ▷ *vi* (*leader, monarch etc*) пра́вить (*impf*); **as a rule** как пра́вило; **rule out** *vt* (*exclude*) исключа́ть (*perf* исключи́ть); **ruler** *n* прави́тель(ница) *m(f)*; (*instrument*) лине́йка

ruling ['ru:lɪŋ] *adj* (*party*) пра́вящий ▷ *n* (*Law*) постановле́ние

rum [rʌm] *n* ром

Rumania *etc* = **Romania** *etc*

rumble ['rʌmbl] *n* (*of traffic, thunder*) гул

rumour ['ru:mə'] (*US* **rumor**) *n* слух ▷ *vt*: **it is rumoured that ...** хо́дят слу́хи, что ...

run [rʌn] (*pt* **ran**, *pp* **run**) *n* (*fast pace*) бег; (*journey*) пое́здка; (*Skiing*) тра́сса; (*Cricket, Baseball*) очко́; (*in tights etc*) спусти́вшиеся пе́тли *fpl* ▷ *vi* бе́гать/ бежа́ть (*impf*); (*flee*) бежа́ть (*impf/perf*), сбега́ть (*perf* сбежа́ть); (*work: machine*) рабо́тать (*impf*); (*bus, train*) ходи́ть (*impf*); (*play, show*) идти́ (*impf*); (: *contract*) дли́ться (*impf*); (*in election*) баллоти́роваться (*perf*) ▷ *vt* (*race, distance*) пробега́ть (*perf* пробежа́ть); (*business, hotel*) управля́ть (*impf*) +*instr*; (*competition, course*) организова́ть (*impf/ perf*); (*house*) вести́ (*impf*); (*Comput: program*) выполня́ть (*perf* вы́полнить); (*water*) пуска́ть (*perf* пусти́ть); (*bath*) наполня́ть (*perf* напо́лнить); (*Press: feature*) печа́тать (*perf* напеча́тать); **in the long run** в коне́чном ито́ге; **to be on the run** скрыва́ться (*impf*); **to run sth along** or **over** (*hand, fingers*) проводи́ть (*perf* провести́) чем-н по +*dat*; **I'll run you to the station** я подвезу́ Вас до ста́нции; **run about** *vi* бе́гать (*impf*); **run around** *vi* = **run about**; **run away** *vi* убега́ть (*perf* убежа́ть); **run down** *vt* (*production, industry*) свора́чивать (*perf* сверну́ть); (*Aut: hit*) сбива́ть (*perf* сбить); (*criticize*) поноси́ть (*impf*); **to be run down** (*person*) выбива́ться (*perf* вы́биться) из сил; **run in** *vt* (*Brit: car*) обка́тывать (*perf* обката́ть); **run into** *vt fus* (*meet: person*) ста́лкиваться (*perf* столкну́ться) с +*instr*; (: *trouble*) ната́лкиваться (*perf* натолкну́ться) на +*acc*; (*collide with*) вреза́ться (*perf* вре́заться) в +*acc*; **run off** *vt* (*copies*) де́лать (*perf* сде́лать), отсня́ть (*perf*) ▷ *vi* (*person, animal*) сбега́ть (*perf* сбежа́ть); **run out** *vi* (*person*) выбега́ть (*perf* вы́бежать); (*liquid*) вытека́ть (*perf* вы́течь); (*lease, visa*) истека́ть (*perf* исте́чь); (*money*) иссяка́ть (*perf* исся́кнуть); **my passport runs out in July** срок де́йствия моего́ па́спорта истека́ет в ию́ле; **run out of** *vt fus*: **I've run out of money/petrol** or (*US*) **gas** у меня́ ко́нчились де́ньги/ко́нчился бензи́н; **run over** *vt* (*Aut*) дави́ть (*perf* задави́ть); **run through** *vt fus* пробега́ть (*perf* пробежа́ть); (*rehearse*) прогоня́ть (*perf* прогна́ть); **run up** *vt*: **to run up a debt**

аккумули́ровать (*impf/perf*) долги́; **to run up against** (*difficulties*) ста́лкиваться (*perf* столкну́ться) с +*instr*; **runaway** *adj* (*truck, horse etc*) потеря́вший управле́ние

rung [rʌŋ] *pp of* **ring** ▷ *n* (*of ladder*) ступе́нька

runner ['rʌnəʳ] *n* (*in race: person*) бегу́н(ья); (: *horse*) скаку́н; (*on sledge, for drawer etc*) по́лоз; **runner-up** *n* финали́ст (*заня́вший второ́е ме́сто*)

running ['rʌnɪŋ] *n* (*sport*) бег; (*of business*) руково́дство ▷ *adj* (*water: to house*) водопрово́дный; **he is in/out of the running for sth** ему́ сули́т/не сули́т что-н; **6 days running** 6 дней подря́д

runny ['rʌnɪ] *adj* (*honey, egg*) жи́дкий; (*nose*) сопли́вый

run-up ['rʌnʌp] *n* (*to event*) преддве́рие

runway ['rʌnweɪ] *n* взлётно-поса́дочная полоса́

rupture ['rʌptʃəʳ] *n* (*Med*) гры́жа

rural ['ruərl] *adj* се́льский

rush [rʌʃ] *n* (*hurry*) спе́шка; (*Comm: sudden demand*) большо́й спрос; (*of water*) пото́к; (*of emotion*) прили́в ▷ *vt*: **to rush one's meal/work** второпя́х съеда́ть (*perf* съесть)/де́лать (*perf* сде́лать) рабо́ту ▷ *vi* (*person*) бежа́ть (*impf*); (*air, water*) хлы́нуть (*perf*); **rushes** *npl* (*Bot*) камы́ш *mpl*; **rush hour** *n* час пик

Russia ['rʌʃə] *n* Росси́я; **Russian** *adj* (*native Russian*) ру́сский; (*belonging to Russian Federation*) росси́йский ▷ *n* ру́сский(-ая) *m(f) adj*; (*Ling*) ру́сский язы́к

rust [rʌst] *n* ржа́вчина ▷ *vi* ржаве́ть (*perf* заржаве́ть)

rusty ['rʌstɪ] *adj* ржа́вый; (*fig: skill*) подзабы́тый

ruthless ['ruːθlɪs] *adj* беспоща́дный

rye [raɪ] *n* рожь *f*

Sabbath ['sæbəθ] *n* (*Christian*) воскресе́нье

sabotage ['sæbətɑːʒ] *n* сабота́ж ▷ *vt* (*machine, building*) выводи́ть (*perf* вы́вести) из стро́я; (*plan, meeting*) саботи́ровать (*impf/perf*)

sachet ['sæʃeɪ] *n* паке́тик

sack [sæk] *n* (*bag*) мешо́к ▷ *vt* (*dismiss*) увольня́ть (*perf* уво́лить); **to give sb the sack** увольня́ть (*perf* уво́лить) кого́-н (с рабо́ты); **I got the sack** меня́ уво́лили (с рабо́ты)

sacred ['seɪkrɪd] *adj* свяще́нный; (*place*) свято́й

sacrifice ['sækrɪfaɪs] *n* же́ртва; (*Rel*) жертвоприноше́ние ▷ *vt* (*fig*) же́ртвовать (*perf* поже́ртвовать) +*instr*

sad [sæd] *adj* печа́льный

saddle ['sædl] *n* седло́

sadistic [sə'dɪstɪk] *adj* сади́стский

sadly ['sædlɪ] *adv* (*unhappily*) печа́льно, гру́стно; (*unfortunately*) к сожале́нию; (*seriously: mistaken, neglected*) серьёзно

sadness ['sædnɪs] *n* печа́ль *f*, грусть *f*

s.a.e. *abbr* (*Brit*) (= *stamped addressed envelope*) надпи́санный конве́рт с ма́ркой

safari [sə'fɑːrɪ] *n*: **to go on safari** проводи́ть (*perf* провести́) о́тпуск в сафа́ри

safe [seɪf] *adj* (*place, subject*) безопа́сный; (*return, journey*) благополу́чный; (*bet*) надёжный ▷ *n* сейф; **to be safe** находи́ться (*impf*) в безопа́сности; **safe from** (*attack*) защищённый от +*gen*; **safe and sound** цел и невреди́м; **(just) to be on the safe side** на вся́кий слу́чай; **safely** *adv* (*assume, say*) с уве́ренностью; (*drive, arrive*) благополу́чно; **safety** *n* безопа́сность *f*; **safety pin** англи́йская була́вка

sage [seɪdʒ] *n* (*herb*) шалфе́й

Sagittarius [sædʒɪ'tɛərɪəs] *n* Стреле́ц

said [sɛd] *pt, pp of* **say**

sail [seɪl] *n* парус ▷ *vt* (*boat*) плавать/плыть (*impf*) на +*prp* ▷ *vi* (*passenger, ship*) плавать/плыть (*impf*); (*also* **set sail**) отплывать (*perf* отплыть); **to go for a sail** ехать (*perf* поехать) кататься на лодке; **sailing** *n* (*Sport*) парусный спорт; **sailor** *n* моряк, матрос

saint [seɪnt] *n* святой(-ая) *m(f) adj*

sake [seɪk] *n*: **for the sake of sb/sth, for sb's/sth's sake** ради кого-н/чего-н

salad [ˈsæləd] *n* салат

salami [səˈlɑːmɪ] *n* салями *f ind*

salary [ˈsælərɪ] *n* зарплата (= *заработная плата*)

sale [seɪl] *n* (*act*) продажа; (*with discount*) распродажа; (*auction*) торги *mpl*; **sales** *npl* (*amount sold*) объём *msg* продажи; **"for sale"** "продаётся"; **on sale** в продаже; **salesman** *irreg n* (*also* **travelling salesman**) торговый агент

saliva [səˈlaɪvə] *n* слюна

salmon [ˈsæmən] *n inv* (*Zool*) лосось *m*; (*Culin*) лососина

salon [ˈsælɒn] *n* салон; **beauty salon** косметический салон

salt [sɔːlt] *n* соль *f*; **salty** *adj* солёный

salute [səˈluːt] *n* (*Mil*) салют ▷ *vt* (*Mil*) отдавать (*perf* отдать) честь +*dat*; (*fig*) приветствовать (*impf*)

salvage [ˈsælvɪdʒ] *n* (*saving*) спасение ▷ *vt* (*also fig*) спасать (*perf* спасти)

same [seɪm] *adj* такой же; (*identical*) одинаковый ▷ *pron*: **the same** тот же (самый), (*f* та же (самая), *nt* то же (самое), *pl* те же (самые)); **the same book as** та же (самая) книга, что и; **at the same time** (*simultaneously*) в это же время; (*yet*) в то же время; **all** *or* **just the same** всё равно; **to do the same (as sb)** делать (*perf* сделать) то же (самое) (, что и кто-н); **Happy New Year! — the same to you!** С Новым годом! — Вас также!

sample [ˈsɑːmpl] *n* (*of work, goods*) образец ▷ *vt* (*food, wine*) пробовать (*perf* попробовать); **to take a blood/urine sample** брать (*perf* взять) кровь/мочу на анализ

sanction [ˈsæŋkʃən] *n* (*approval*) санкция ▷ *vt* (*approve*) санкционировать (*impf/perf*); **sanctions** *npl* (*severe measures*) санкции *fpl*

sanctuary [ˈsæŋktjuərɪ] *n* (*for animals*) заповедник; (*for people*) убежище

sand [sænd] *n* песок ▷ *vt* (*also* **sand down**) ошкуривать (*perf* ошкурить)

sandal [ˈsændl] *n* сандалия

sandpaper [ˈsændpeɪpə^r] *n* наждачная бумага

sandstone [ˈsændstəun] *n* песчаник

sandwich [ˈsændwɪtʃ] *n* бутерброд ▷ *vt*: **sandwiched between** зажатый между +*instr*; **cheese/ham sandwich** бутерброд с сыром/ветчиной

sandy [ˈsændɪ] *adj* песчаный

sane [seɪn] *adj* разумный

sang [sæŋ] *pt of* **sing**

sanity [ˈsænɪtɪ] *n* (*of person*) рассудок; (*sense*) разумность *f*

sank [sæŋk] *pt of* **sink**

Santa Claus [sæntəˈklɔːz] *n* (*in Britain etc*) Санта-Клаус; (*in Russia*) ≈ Дед Мороз

sap [sæp] *n* (*Bot*) сок ▷ *vt* (*strength*) высасывать (*perf* высосать); (*confidence*) отбирать (*perf* отобрать)

sapphire [ˈsæfaɪə^r] *n* сапфир

sarcasm [ˈsɑːkæzm] *n* сарказм

sarcastic [sɑːˈkæstɪk] *adj* саркастичный

sardine [sɑːˈdiːn] *n* сардина

sat [sæt] *pt, pp of* **sit**

satellite [ˈsætəlaɪt] *n* спутник; (*Pol: country*) сателлит; **satellite dish** *n* спутниковая антенна

satin [ˈsætɪn] *adj* атласный

satire [ˈsætaɪə^r] *n* сатира

satisfaction [sætɪsˈfækʃən] *n* (*pleasure*) удовлетворение; (*refund, apology etc*) возмещение

satisfactory [sætɪsˈfæktərɪ] *adj* удовлетворительный

satisfy [ˈsætɪsfaɪ] *vt* удовлетворять (*perf* удовлетворить); (*convince*) убеждать (*perf* убедить); **to satisfy sb (that)** убеждать (*perf* убедить) кого-н (в том, что)

Saturday [ˈsætədeɪ] *n* суббота

sauce [sɔːs] *n* соус; **saucepan** *n* кастрюля

saucer [ˈsɔːsə^r] *n* блюдце

Saudi Arabia [saudɪəˈreɪbɪə] *n* Саудовская Аравия

sauna [ˈsɔːnə] *n* сауна, финская баня

sausage [ˈsɔsɪdʒ] *n* (*for cooking*) сарделька, сосиска

savage [ˈsævɪdʒ] *adj* свирепый

save [seɪv] *vt* (*rescue*) спасать (*perf* спасти); (*economize on*) экономить (*perf* сэкономить); (*put by*) сберегать (*perf* сберечь); (*keep: receipts, file*) сохранять (*perf* сохранить); (*: seat, place*) занимать (*perf* занять); (*work, trouble*) избавлять (*perf* избавить) от +*gen*; (*Sport*) отбивать (*perf* отбить), отражать (*perf* отразить) ▷ *vi* (*also* **save up**) копить (*perf* скопить) деньги ▷ *prep* помимо +*gen*

savings [ˈseɪvɪŋz] *npl* (*money*) сбережения *ntpl*

savour [ˈseɪvə^r] (*US* **savor**) *vt* (*food, drink*) смаковать (*impf*); (*experience*) наслаждаться (*perf* насладиться) +*instr*; **savoury** *adj* несладкий

saw [sɔ:] (*pt* **sawed**, *pp* **sawed** or **sawn**) *vt* пили́ть (*impf*) ▷ *n* пила́ ▷ *pt of* **see**; **sawdust** *n* опи́лки *pl*

saxophone ['sæksəfəʊn] *n* саксофо́н

say [seɪ] (*pt, pp* **said**) *vt* говори́ть (*perf* сказа́ть) ▷ *n*: **to have one's say** выража́ть (*perf* вы́разить) своё мне́ние; **to say yes** соглаша́ться (*perf* согласи́ться); **to say no** отка́зываться (*perf* отказа́ться); **could you say that again?** повтори́те, пожа́луйста; **that is to say** то есть; **that goes without saying** э́то само́ собо́й разуме́ется; **saying** *n* погово́рка

scab [skæb] *n* (*on wound*) струп

scaffolding ['skæfəldɪŋ] *n* леса́ *mpl*

scald [skɔ:ld] *n* ожо́г ▷ *vt* ошпа́ривать (*perf* ошпа́рить)

scale [skeɪl] *n* шкала́; (*usu pl: of fish*) чешуя́ *f no pl*; (*Mus*) га́мма; (*of map, project etc*) масшта́б ▷ *vt* взбира́ться (*perf* взобра́ться) на +*acc*; **scales** *npl* (*for weighing*) весы́ *pl*; **on a large scale** в широ́ком масшта́бе

scalp [skælp] *n* скальп

scalpel ['skælpl] *n* ска́льпель *m*

scampi ['skæmpɪ] *npl* (*Brit*) паниро́ванные креве́тки *fpl*

scan [skæn] *vt* (*examine*) обсле́довать (*perf*); (*read quickly*) просма́тривать (*perf* просмотре́ть); (*Radar*) скани́ровать (*impf*) ▷ *n* (*Med*) скани́рование; **ultrasound scan** ультразву́к

scandal ['skændl] *n* сканда́л; (*gossip*) спле́тни *fpl*; (*disgrace*) позо́р

Scandinavia [skændɪ'neɪvɪə] *n* Сканди́навия

scapegoat ['skeɪpgəʊt] *n* козёл отпуще́ния

scar [skɑ:] *n* шрам; (*fig*) тра́вма ▷ *vt* травми́ровать (*impf/perf*); **his face is scarred** у него́ на лице́ шрам

scarce [skɛəs] *adj* ре́дкий; **to make o.s. scarce** (*inf*) исчеза́ть (*perf* исче́знуть); **scarcely** *adv* (*hardly*) едва́ ли; (*with numbers*) то́лько

scare [skɛəʳ] *n* (*fright*) испу́г; (*public fear*) трево́га, па́ника ▷ *vt* пуга́ть (*perf* испуга́ть); **there was a bomb scare at the station** опаса́лись, что на ста́нции подло́жена бо́мба; **scarecrow** *n* (огоро́дное) чу́чело; **scared** *adj* испу́ганный, напу́ганный; **he was scared** он испуга́лся *or* был испу́ган

scarf [skɑ:f] (*pl* **scarfs** or **scarves**) *n* шарф; (*also* **headscarf**) плато́к

scarves [skɑ:vz] *npl of* **scarf**

scary ['skɛərɪ] *adj* стра́шный

scatter ['skætəʳ] *vt* (*papers, seeds*) разбра́сывать (*perf* разброса́ть) ▷ *vi* рассыпа́ться (*perf* рассы́паться)

scenario [sɪ'nɑ:rɪəu] *n* сцена́рий

scene [si:n] *n* (*Theat, fig*) сце́на; (*of crime, accident*) ме́сто; (*sight, view*) карти́на; **scenery** *n* (*Theat*) декора́ции *fpl*; (*landscape*) пейза́ж

scenic ['si:nɪk] *adj* живопи́сный

scent [sɛnt] *n* (*smell*) за́пах; (*track, also fig*) след; (*perfume*) духи́ *pl*

sceptical ['skɛptɪkl] (*US* **skeptical**) *adj* (*person*) скепти́чный; (*remarks*) скепти́ческий

schedule ['ʃɛdju:l, (*US*) 'skɛdju:l] *n* (*timetable*) расписа́ние, гра́фик; (*list of prices, details etc*) пе́речень *m* ▷ *vt* (*timetable*) распи́сывать (*perf* расписа́ть); (*visit*) назнача́ть (*perf* назна́чить); **on schedule** по расписа́нию *or* гра́фику; **to be ahead of schedule** опережа́ть (*perf* опереди́ть) гра́фик; **to be behind schedule** отстава́ть (*perf* отста́ть) от гра́фика

scheme [ski:m] *n* (*plan, idea*) за́мысел; (*plot*) про́иски *pl*, ко́зни *pl*; (*pension plan etc*) план

schizophrenic [skɪtsə'frɛnɪk] *adj* шизофрени́ческий

scholar ['skɔləʳ] *n* (*learned person*) учёный *m adj*; **scholarship** *n* (*grant*) стипе́ндия

school [sku:l] *n* шко́ла; (*US: inf*) университе́т; (*Brit: college*) институ́т ▷ *cpd* шко́льный; **schoolboy** *n* шко́льник; **schoolchildren** *npl* шко́льники *mpl*; **schoolgirl** *n* шко́льница; **schooling** *n* шко́льное образова́ние

science ['saɪəns] *n* нау́ка; (*in school*) естествозна́ние; **science fiction** *n* нау́чная фанта́стика

scientific [saɪən'tɪfɪk] *adj* нау́чный

scientist ['saɪəntɪst] *n* учёный *m adj*

scissors ['sɪzəz] *npl*: **(a pair of) scissors** но́жницы *pl*

scold [skəuld] *vt* брани́ть (*perf* вы́бранить), руга́ть (*perf* отруга́ть)

scone [skɔn] *n* (*Culin*) кекс

scooter ['sku:təʳ] *n* (*also* **motor scooter**) мопе́д; (*toy*) самока́т

scope [skəup] *n* (*opportunity*) просто́р; (*of plan, undertaking*) масшта́б

score [skɔ:ʳ] *n* (*in game, test*) счёт ▷ *vt* (*goal*) забива́ть (*perf* заби́ть); (*point*) набира́ть (*perf* набра́ть); (*in test*) получа́ть (*perf* получи́ть) ▷ *vi* (*in game*) набира́ть (*perf* набра́ть) очки́; (*Football*) забива́ть (*perf* заби́ть) гол; **scores of** деся́тки +*gen*; **on that score** на э́тот счёт; **to score six out of ten** набира́ть (*perf* набра́ть) шесть ба́ллов из десяти́; **score out** *vt* вычёркивать (*perf* вы́черкнуть); **scoreboard** *n* табло́ *nt ind*

scorn [skɔ:n] *n* презре́ние ▷ *vt* презира́ть (*impf*)

Scorpio ['skɔ:pɪəu] *n* Скорпио́н

scorpion ['skɔ:pɪən] *n* скорпио́н

Scot [skɔt] *n* шотла́ндец(-дка)

Scotch [skɔtʃ] *n* (шотла́ндское) ви́ски *nt ind*

Scotland ['skɔtlənd] *n* Шотла́ндия

Scots [skɔts] *adj* шотла́ндский
Scottish ['skɔtɪʃ] *adj* шотла́ндский
scout [skaut] *n* (*Mil*) разве́дчик; (*also*
boy scout) (бой)ска́ут
scramble ['skræmbl] *vi*: **to scramble out
of** выкара́бкиваться (*perf* вы́карабкаться)
из +*gen*; **to scramble for** дра́ться (*perf*
подра́ться) за +*acc*; **scrambled eggs** *npl*
яи́чница-болту́нья
scrap [skræp] *n* (*of paper*) клочо́к; (*of
information*) обры́вок; (*of material*)
лоску́т; (*also* **scrap metal**) металлоло́м,
металли́ческий лом ▷ *vt* (*machines etc*)
отдава́ть (*perf* отда́ть) на слом; (*plans etc*)
отка́зываться (*perf* отказа́ться) от +*gen*;
scraps *npl* (*of food*) объе́дки *mpl*
scrape [skreɪp] *vt* (*remove*) соска́бливать
(*perf* соскобли́ть); (*rub against*) цара́пать
(*perf* поцара́пать), обдира́ть (*perf*
ободра́ть) ▷ *vi*: **to scrape through** (*exam
etc*) пролеза́ть (*perf* проле́зть) на +*prp*
scratch [skrætʃ] *n* цара́пина ▷ *vt*
цара́пать (*perf* поцара́пать); (*an itch*)
чеса́ть (*perf* почеса́ть) ▷ *vi* чеса́ться (*perf*
почеса́ться); **from scratch** с нуля́; **to be up
to scratch** быть (*impf*) на до́лжном
у́ровне
scream [skri:m] *n* вопль *m*, крик ▷ *vi*
вопи́ть (*impf*), крича́ть (*impf*)
screen [skri:n] *n* экра́н; (*barrier, also fig*)
ши́рма ▷ *vt* (*protect, conceal*) заслоня́ть
(*perf* заслони́ть); (*show: film etc*)
выпуска́ть (*perf* вы́пустить) на экра́н;
(*check: candidates etc*) проверя́ть (*perf*
прове́рить); **screening** *n* (*Med*)
профилакти́ческий осмо́тр; **screenplay**
n сцена́рий; **screen saver** *n*
скринсе́йвер
screw [skru:] *n* винт ▷ *vt* (*fasten*)
приви́нчивать (*perf* привинти́ть); **to screw
sth in** зави́нчивать (*perf* завинти́ть) что-н;
screwdriver *n* отве́ртка
scribble ['skrɪbl] *vt* черкну́ть (*perf*) ▷ *vi*
исчёркивать (*perf* исчёркать)
script [skrɪpt] *n* (*Cinema etc*) сцена́рий;
(*Arabic etc*) шрифт
scroll [skrəul] *n* сви́ток ▷ *vt*: **to scroll up/
down** переме́щать (*perf* перемести́ть)
наве́рх/вниз
scrub [skrʌb] *vt* скрести́ (*impf*)
scruffy ['skrʌfɪ] *adj* потрёпанный
scrutiny ['skru:tɪnɪ] *n* тща́тельное
изуче́ние *or* рассмотре́ние
sculptor ['skʌlptə] *n* ску́льптор
sculpture ['skʌlptʃəʳ] *n* скульпту́ра
scum [skʌm] *n* пе́на; (*inf. pej: people*)
подо́нки *mpl*
sea [si:] *n* мо́ре ▷ *cpd* морско́й; **by sea**
(*travel*) мо́рем; **on the sea** (*town*) на мо́ре;
out to sea, out at sea в мо́ре; **seafood** *n*
ры́бные блю́да *ntpl*; **seafront** *n*
на́бережная *f adj*; **seagull** *n* ча́йка
seal [si:l] *n* (*Zool*) тюле́нь *m*; (*stamp*)
печа́ть *f* ▷ *vt* (*envelope*) запеча́тывать

(*perf* запеча́тать); (*opening*) заде́лывать
(*perf* заде́лать)
sea level *n* у́ровень *m* мо́ря
seam [si:m] *n* (*of garment*) шов
search [sə:tʃ] *n* по́иск; (*for criminal*)
ро́зыск; (*of sb's home etc*) о́быск ▷ *vt*
обы́скивать (*perf* обыска́ть) ▷ *vi*: **to
search for** иска́ть (*impf*); **in search of** в
по́исках +*gen*
seasick ['si:sɪk] *adj*: **to be seasick**
страда́ть (*impf*) морско́й боле́знью
seaside ['si:saɪd] *n* взмо́рье
season ['si:zn] *n* вре́мя *nt* го́да; (*for
football, of films etc*) сезо́н ▷ *vt* (*food*)
заправля́ть (*perf* запра́вить); **seasonal**
adj сезо́нный; **seasoning** *n* припра́ва
seat [si:t] *n* (*chair, place*) сиде́нье; (*in
theatre, parliament*) ме́сто; (*of trousers*)
зад ▷ *vt* (*subj: venue*) вмеща́ть (*perf*
вмести́ть); **to be seated** сиде́ть (*impf*);
seat belt *n* привязно́й реме́нь *m*
seaweed ['si:wi:d] *n* во́доросли *fpl*
sec. *abbr* = **second²**
secluded [sɪ'klu:dɪd] *adj* уединённый
second¹ [sɪ'kɔnd] *vt* (*Brit: employee*)
командирова́ть (*impf*)
second² ['sɛkənd] *adj* второ́й ▷ *adv*
(*come*) вторы́м; (*when listing*) во-вторы́х
▷ *n* (*unit of time*) секу́нда; (*Aut: also*
second gear) втора́я ско́рость *f*; (*Comm*)
некондицио́нный това́р; (*Brit: Scol*)
дипло́м второ́го кла́сса ▷ *vt* (*motion*)
подде́рживать (*perf* поддержа́ть);
secondary *adj* втори́чный; **secondary
school** *n* сре́дняя шко́ла; **second-class**
adj второразря́дный; **second-class stamp**
ма́рка второ́го кла́сса

second: **second-hand** *adj* поде́ржанный,
сэ́конд-хэнд *ind*; **secondly** *adv*
во-вторы́х; **second-rate** *adj* (*film*)
посре́дственный; (*restaurant*)
второразря́дный; **second thoughts** *npl*:
to have second thoughts (about doing)
сомнева́ться (*impf*) (сле́дует ли +*infin*); **on
second thoughts** *or* (*US*) **thought** по
зре́лом размышле́нии
secrecy ['si:krəsɪ] *n* секре́тность *f*
secret ['si:krɪt] *adj* секре́тный, та́йный;
(*admirer*) та́йный ▷ *n* секре́т, та́йна; **in
secret** (*do, meet*) секре́тно, та́йно
secretary ['sɛkrətərɪ] *n* секрета́рь *m*;
Secretary of State (for) (*Brit*) ≈ мини́стр
(+*gen*)
secretive ['si:krətɪv] *adj* (*pej: person*)

скры́тный; **he is secretive about his plans** он де́ржит свои́ пла́ны в секре́те

secret service n секре́тная слу́жба

sect [sɛkt] n се́кта

section ['sɛkʃən] n (part) часть f; (of population, company) се́ктор; (of document, book) разде́л

sector ['sɛktə^r] n (part) се́ктор

secular ['sɛkjulə^r] adj све́тский

secure [sɪ'kjuə^r] adj (safe: person, money, job) надёжный; (firmly fixed: rope, shelf) про́чный ▷ vt (fix: rope, shelf etc) (про́чно) закрепи́ть (perf закрепи́ть); (get: job, loan etc) обеспе́чивать (perf обеспе́чить)

security [sɪ'kjuərɪtɪ] n (protection) безопа́сность f; (for one's future) обеспе́ченность f

sedate [sɪ'deɪt] adj (person) степе́нный; (pace) разме́ренный ▷ vt дава́ть (perf дать) седати́вное or успокои́тельное сре́дство

sedative ['sɛdɪtɪv] n седати́вное or успокои́тельное сре́дство

seduce [sɪ'dju:s] vt соблазня́ть (perf соблазни́ть)

seductive [sɪ'dʌktɪv] adj (look, voice) обольсти́тельный; (offer) соблазни́тельный

see [si:] (pt saw, pp seen) vt ви́деть (perf уви́деть) ▷ vi ви́деть (impf); (find out) выясня́ть (perf вы́яснить); **to see that** (ensure) следи́ть (perf проследи́ть), что́бы; **see you soon!** пока́!, до ско́рого!; **see off** vt провожа́ть (perf проводи́ть); **see through** vt доводи́ть (perf довести́) до конца́ ▷ vt fus ви́деть (impf) наскво́зь +acc; **see to** vt fus позабо́титься (perf) о +prp

seed [si:d] n се́мя nt; **to go to seed** (fig) сдать (perf)

seeing ['si:ɪŋ] conj: **seeing (that)** поско́льку, так как

seek [si:k] (pt, pp sought) vt иска́ть (impf)

seem [si:m] vi каза́ться (perf показа́ться); **there seems to be ...** ка́жется, что име́ется ...; **he seems to be tired** он ка́жется уста́лым; **seemingly** adv по-ви́димому; (important) как представля́ется

seen [si:n] pp of **see**

segment ['sɛgmənt] n (of population) се́ктор; (of orange) до́лька

seize [si:z] vt хвата́ть (perf схвати́ть); (power, hostage, territory) захва́тывать (perf захвати́ть); (opportunity) по́льзоваться (perf воспо́льзоваться) +instr

seizure ['si:ʒə^r] n (Med) при́ступ; (of power) захва́т; (of goods) конфиска́ция

seldom ['sɛldəm] adv ре́дко

select [sɪ'lɛkt] adj (school, area) эли́тный ▷ vt (choose) выбира́ть (perf вы́брать); **selection** [sɪ'lɛkʃən] n (process) отбо́р;

(range) вы́бор; (medley) подбо́рка;

selective adj (person) разбо́рчивый; (not general) избира́тельный

self [sɛlf] (pl **selves**) n: **he became his usual self again** он стал опя́ть сами́м собо́й ▷ prefix само-; **self-assured** adj самоуве́ренный; **self-catering** adj (Brit): **self-catering holiday** туристи́ческая путёвка, в кото́рую включа́ется прое́зд и жильё; **self-centred** (US **self-centered**) adj эгоцентри́чный; **self-confidence** n уве́ренность f в себе́; **self-conscious** adj (nervous) засте́нчивый; **self-control** n самооблада́ние; **self-defence** (US **self-defense**) n самозащи́та, самооборо́на; **in self-defence** защища́я себя́; **self-employed** adj рабо́тающий на себя́; **selfie** n сéлфи nt ind; **self-interest** n коры́сть f; **selfish** adj эгоисти́ческий; **self-pity** n жа́лость f к (самому́) себе́; **self-respect** n самоуваже́ние; **self-service** adj: **self-service restaurant** кафе́ nt ind с самообслу́живанием

sell [sɛl] (pt, pp **sold**) vt продава́ть (perf прода́ть) ▷ vi продава́ться (impf); **to sell at** or **for 10 pounds** продава́ться (impf) по 10 фу́нтов; **sell off** vt распродава́ть (perf распрода́ть); **sell out** vi (book etc) расходи́ться (perf разойти́сь); (shop): **to sell out of sth** распродава́ть (perf прода́ть) что-н; **the tickets are sold out** все биле́ты про́даны

Sellotape ['sɛləuteɪp] n (Brit) клéйкая ле́нта

selves [sɛlvz] pl of **self**

semester [sɪ'mɛstə^r] n (esp US) семе́стр

semi- ['sɛmɪ] prefix полу-

● **SEMI**
●
● Semi — полуособня́к. В
● Великобрита́нии мно́гие се́мьи живу́т в
● полуособняка́х - два двухэта́жных до́ма
● име́ют одну́ о́бщую сте́ну, но
● отде́льный вход и сад.

semi: **semicircle** n полукру́г; **semicolon** n то́чка с запято́й; **semifinal** n полуфина́л

seminar ['sɛmɪnɑ:^r] n семина́р

senate ['sɛnɪt] n сена́т

senator ['sɛnɪtə^r] n (US etc) сена́тор

send [sɛnd] (pt, pp **sent**) vt посыла́ть (perf посла́ть); **send away** vt (letter, goods) отсыла́ть (perf отосла́ть); (visitor) прогоня́ть (perf прогна́ть); **send back** vt посыла́ть (perf посла́ть) обра́тно; **send for** vt fus (by post) зака́зывать (perf заказа́ть); (person) посыла́ть (perf посла́ть) за +instr; **send off** vt (letter) отправля́ть (perf отпра́вить); (Brit: Sport) удаля́ть (perf удали́ть); **send out** vt (invitation) рассыла́ть (perf разосла́ть);

(*signal*) посыла́ть (*perf* посла́ть); **sender** *n* отправи́тель *m*

senile ['si:naɪl] *adj* маразмати́ческий

senior ['si:nɪə'] *adj* (*staff, officer*) ста́рший; (*manager, consultant*) гла́вный; **to be senior to sb** (*in rank*) быть (*impf*) вы́ше кого́-н по положе́нию; **she is 15 years his senior** она́ ста́рше его́ на 15 лет; **senior citizen** *n* (*esp Brit*) пожило́й челове́к, челове́к пенсио́нного во́зраста

sensation [sɛn'seɪʃən] *n* (*feeling*) ощуще́ние; (*great success*) сенса́ция; **sensational** *adj* (*wonderful*) потряса́ющий; (*dramatic*) сенсацио́нный

sense [sɛns] *vt* чу́вствовать (*perf* почу́вствовать), ощуща́ть (*perf* ощути́ть) ▷ *n* (*feeling*) чу́вство, ощуще́ние; **it makes sense** в э́том есть смысл; **the senses** пять чувств; **senseless** *adj* бессмы́сленный; (*unconscious*) бесчу́вственный; **sense of humour** (*US* **sense of humor**) *n* чу́вство ю́мора

sensible ['sɛnsɪbl] *adj* разу́мный; (*shoes*) практи́чный

sensitive ['sɛnsɪtɪv] *adj* чувстви́тельный; (*understanding*) чу́ткий; (*issue*) щекотли́вый

sensual ['sɛnsjuəl] *adj* чу́вственный

sensuous ['sɛnsjuəs] *adj* (*lips*) чу́вственный; (*material*) не́жный

sent [sɛnt] *pt, pp of* **send**

sentence ['sɛntns] *n* (*Ling*) предложе́ние; (*Law*) пригово́р ▷ *vt*: **to sentence sb to** пригова́ривать (*perf* приговори́ть) кого́-н к +*dat*

sentiment ['sɛntɪmənt] *n* (*tender feelings*) чу́вство; (*opinion*) настрое́ние; **sentimental** [sɛntɪ'mɛntl] *adj* сентимента́льный

separate [*adj* 'sɛprɪt, *vb* 'sɛpəreɪt] *adj* отде́льный; (*ways*) ра́зный ▷ *vt* (*split up*: *people*) разлуча́ть (*perf* разлучи́ть); (: *things*) разделя́ть (*perf* раздели́ть); (*distinguish*) различа́ть (*perf* различи́ть) ▷ *vi* расходи́ться (*perf* разойти́сь); **separately** ['sɛprɪtlɪ] *adv* отде́льно, по отде́льности; **separation** [sɛpə'reɪʃən] *n* (*being apart*) разлу́ка; (*Law*) разде́льное прожива́ние

September [sɛp'tɛmbə'] *n* сентя́брь *m*

septic ['sɛptɪk] *adj* заражённый

sequel ['si:kwl] *n* продолже́ние

sequence ['si:kwəns] *n* после́довательность *f*

Serbia ['sə:bɪə] *n* Се́рбия

Serbo-Croat ['sə:bəu'krəuæt] *adj* се́рбо-хорва́тский

sergeant ['sɑ:dʒənt] *n* сержа́нт

serial ['sɪərɪəl] *n* (*TV, Radio*) сериа́л; (*Press*) произведе́ние в не́скольких частя́х

series ['sɪərɪz] *n inv* се́рия

serious ['sɪərɪəs] *adj* серьёзный; **are you serious (about it?)** Вы (э́то) серьёзно?; **seriously** *adv* серьёзно

sermon ['sə:mən] *n* про́поведь *f*

servant ['sə:vənt] *n* слуга́(-жа́нка) *m(f)*

serve [sə:v] *vt* (*company, country*) служи́ть (*impf*) +*dat*; (*customer*) обслу́живать (*perf* обслужи́ть); (*subj*: *train etc*) обслу́живать (*impf*); (*apprenticeship*) проходи́ть (*perf* пройти́); (*prison term*) отбыва́ть (*perf* отбы́ть) ▷ *vi* (*Tennis*) подава́ть (*perf* пода́ть) ▷ *n* (*Tennis*) пода́ча; **it serves him right** поде́лом ему́; **to serve on** (*jury, committee*) состоя́ть (*impf*) в +*prp*; **to serve as/for** служи́ть (*perf* послужи́ть) +*instr*/вме́сто +*gen*

service ['sə:vɪs] *n* (*help*) услу́га; (*in hotel*) обслу́живание, се́рвис; (*Rel*) слу́жба; (*Aut*) техобслу́живание; (*Tennis*) пода́ча ▷ *vt* (*car*) проводи́ть (*perf* провести́) техобслу́живание +*gen*; **services** *npl*: **the Services** (*Mil*) Вооружённые си́лы *fpl*; **military** *or* **national service** вое́нная слу́жба; **train service** железнодоро́жное сообще́ние; **postal service** почто́вая связь

serviette [sə:vɪ'ɛt] *n* (*Brit*) салфе́тка

session ['sɛʃən] *n* (*of treatment*) сеа́нс; **recording session** за́пись *f*; **to be in session** (*court etc*) заседа́ть (*impf*)

set [sɛt] (*pt, pp* **set**) *n* (*collection*) набо́р; (*of pans, clothes*) компле́кт; (*also* **television set**) телеви́зор; (*Tennis*) сет; (*Math*) мно́жество; (*Cinema, Theat*: *stage*) сце́на ▷ *adj* (*fixed*) устано́вленный; (*ready*) гото́вый ▷ *vt* (*place*: *vertically*) ста́вить (*perf* поста́вить); (: *horizontally*) класть (*perf* положи́ть); (*table*) накрыва́ть (*perf* накры́ть); (*time*) назнача́ть (*perf* назна́чить); (*price, record*) устана́вливать (*perf* установи́ть); (*alarm, task*) ста́вить (*perf* поста́вить); (*exam*) составля́ть (*perf* соста́вить) ▷ *vi* (*sun*) сади́ться (*perf* сесть), заходи́ть (*perf* зайти́); (*jam*) густе́ть (*perf* загусте́ть); (*jelly, concrete*) застыва́ть (*perf* засты́ть); **to set to music** класть (*perf* положи́ть) на му́зыку; **set on fire** поджига́ть (*perf* подже́чь); **to set free** освобожда́ть (*perf* освободи́ть); **set about** *vt fus* (*task*) приступа́ть (*perf* приступи́ть) к +*dat*; **set aside** *vt* (*money*) откла́дывать (*perf* отложи́ть); (*time*) выделя́ть (*perf* вы́делить); **set back** *vt* (*progress*) заде́рживать (*perf* задержа́ть); **to set sb back £5** обойти́сь (*perf* обойти́сь) кому́-н в £5; **set off** *vi* отправля́ться (*perf* отпра́виться) ▷ *vt* (*bomb*) взрыва́ть (*perf* взорва́ть); (*alarm*) приводи́ть (*perf* привести́) в де́йствие; (*events*) повлека́ть (*perf* повле́чь) (за собо́й); **set out** *vt* выставля́ть (*perf* вы́ставить) ▷ *vi* (*depart*): **to set out (from)** отправля́ться (*perf* отпра́виться) (из +*gen*); **to set out to do** намерева́ться (*impf*) +*infin*; **set up** *vt* (*organization*) учрежда́ть (*perf* учреди́ть); **setback** *n* неуда́ча

settee [sɛ'ti:] *n* дива́н

setting ['sɛtɪŋ] n (background)
обстано́вка; (position: of controls)
положе́ние

settle ['sɛtl] vt (argument, problem)
разреша́ть (perf разреши́ть); (matter)
ула́живать (perf ула́дить); (bill)
рассчи́тываться (perf рассчита́ться) с
+instr ▷ vi (dust, sediment) оседа́ть (perf
осе́сть); (also **settle down**)
обосно́вываться (perf обоснова́ться);
(: live sensibly) остепеня́ться (perf
остепени́ться); (: calm down)
успока́иваться (perf успоко́иться); to
settle for sth соглаша́ться (perf
согласи́ться) на что-н; to **settle on sth**
остана́вливаться (perf останови́ться) на
чём-н; **settle in** vi осва́иваться (perf
осво́иться); **settlement** n (payment)
упла́та; (agreement) соглаше́ние; (village,
colony) поселе́ние; (of conflict)
урегули́рование

seven ['sɛvn] n семь; **seventeen** n
семна́дцать; **seventeenth** adj
семна́дцатый; **seventh** adj седьмо́й;
seventieth adj семидеся́тый; **seventy** n
се́мьдесят

sever ['sɛvə'] vt (artery, pipe) перереза́ть
(perf перере́зать); (relations) прерыва́ть
(perf прерва́ть)

several ['sɛvərl] adj не́сколько +gen
▷ pron не́которые pl adj; **several of us**
не́которые из нас

severe [sɪ'vɪə'] adj (shortage, pain, winter)
жесто́кий; (damage) серьёзный; (stern)
жёсткий

sew [səu] (pt sewed, pp sewn) vt, vi шить
(impf)

sewage ['su:ɪdʒ] n сто́чные во́ды fpl;
sewage system канализа́ция

sewer ['su:ə'] n канализацио́нная труба́

sewing ['səuɪŋ] n шитьё; **sewing
machine** n шве́йная маши́нка

sewn [səun] pp of **sew**

sex [sɛks] n (gender) пол; (lovemaking)
секс; to **have sex with sb** переспа́ть (perf
с кем-н); **sexist** adj сексистский; **he is
sexist** он — сексист; **sexual** adj
полово́й; **sexual equality** ра́венство
поло́в; **sexual harassment** сексуа́льное
пресле́дование; **sexy** adj сексуа́льный;
(woman) сексопи́льная

shabby ['ʃæbɪ] adj (clothes) потрёпанный;
(treatment) недосто́йный

shack [ʃæk] n лачу́га

shade [ʃeɪd] n (shelter) тень f; (for lamp)
абажу́р; (of colour) отте́нок ▷ vt (shelter)
затеня́ть (perf затени́ть); (eyes) заслоня́ть
(perf заслони́ть); **in the shade** в тени́

shadow ['ʃædəu] n тень f ▷ vt (follow)
сле́довать (impf) как тень за +instr;
shadow cabinet n (Brit) теневой
кабине́т

shady ['ʃeɪdɪ] adj (place, trees) тени́стый;
(fig: dishonest) тёмный

shaft [ʃɑ:ft] n (of mine, lift) ша́хта; (of
light) сноп

shake [ʃeɪk] (pt shook, pp shaken) vt
трясти́ (impf); (bottle) взба́лтывать (perf
взболта́ть); (building) сотряса́ть (perf
сотрясти́); (weaken: beliefs, resolve)
пошатну́ть (perf); (upset, surprise)
потряса́ть (perf потрясти́) ▷ vi (voice)
дрожа́ть (impf); to **shake one's head**
кача́ть (perf покача́ть) голово́й; to **shake
hands with sb** жать (perf пожа́ть) кому́-н
ру́ку; to **shake with** трясти́сь (impf) от
+gen; **shake off** vt стря́хивать (perf
стряхну́ть); (fig: pursuer) избавля́ться
(perf изба́виться) от +gen; **shake up** vt
(fig: organization) встря́хивать (perf
встряхну́ть)

shaky ['ʃeɪkɪ] adj (hand, voice) дрожа́щий

shall [ʃæl] aux vb: **I shall go** я пойду́; **shall
I open the door?** (мне) откры́ть дверь?; **I'll
get some water, shall I?** я принесу́ воды́,
да?

shallow ['ʃæləu] adj (water) ме́лкий; (box)
неглубо́кий; (breathing, also fig)
пове́рхностный

sham [ʃæm] n притво́рство

shambles ['ʃæmblz] n неразбери́ха

shame [ʃeɪm] n (embarrassment) стыд;
(disgrace) позо́р ▷ vt позо́рить (perf
опозо́рить); **it is a shame that/to do** жаль,
что/+infin; **what a shame!** кака́я жа́лость!,
как жаль!; **shameful** adj позо́рный;
shameless adj бессты́дный

shampoo [ʃæm'pu:] n шампу́нь m ▷ vt
мыть (помы́ть или вы́мыть perf) шампу́нем

shan't [ʃɑ:nt] = **shall not**

shape [ʃeɪp] n фо́рма ▷ vt (ideas, events)
формирова́ть (perf сформирова́ть); (clay)
лепи́ть (perf слепи́ть); to **take shape**
обрета́ть (perf обрести́) фо́рму

share [ʃɛə'] n до́ля; (Comm) а́кция ▷ vt
(books, cost) дели́ть (perf подели́ть);
(toys) дели́ться (perf подели́ться) +instr;
(features, qualities) разделя́ть (impf);
(opinion, concern) разделя́ть (perf
раздели́ть); **share out** vt дели́ть (perf
раздели́ть); **shareholder** n акционе́р

shark [ʃɑ:k] n аку́ла

sharp [ʃɑ:p] adj о́стрый; (sound) ре́зкий;
(Mus) дие́з ind ▷ adv (precisely): **at 2
o'clock sharp** ро́вно в два часа́; **he is very
sharp** у него́ о́чень о́стрый ум; **sharpen**
vt (pencil, knife) точи́ть (perf поточи́ть);
sharpener n (also **pencil sharpener**)
точи́лка; **sharply** adv ре́зко

shatter ['ʃætə'] vt (vase, hopes)
разбива́ть (perf разби́ть); (upset: person)
потряса́ть (perf потрясти́) ▷ vi би́ться
(perf разби́ться)

shave [ʃeɪv] vt брить (perf побри́ть) ▷ vi
бри́ться (perf побри́ться) ▷ n: to **have a
shave** бри́ться (perf побри́ться)

shawl [ʃɔ:l] n шаль f

she [ʃi:] pron она́

shed [ʃɛd] (*pt, pp* **shed**) *n* (*in garden*)
сарай ▷ *vt* (*skin, load*) сбрасывать (*perf*
сбросить); (*tears*) лить (*impf*)

she'd [ʃiːd] = **she had; she would**

sheep [ʃiːp] *n inv* овца; **sheepdog** *n*
овчарка

sheer [ʃɪə^r] *adj* (*utter*) сущий; (*steep*)
отвесный

sheet [ʃiːt] *n* (*on bed*) простыня;
(*of paper, glass etc*) лист; (*of ice*)
полоса

sheik(h) [ʃeɪk] *n* шейх

shelf [ʃɛlf] (*pl* **shelves**) *n* полка

shell [ʃɛl] *n* (*of mollusc*) раковина; (*of
egg, nut*) скорлупа; (*explosive*) снаряд;
(*of building*) каркас; (*of ship*) корпус ▷ *vt*
(*peas*) лущить (*perf* облущить); (*Mil*)
обстреливать (*perf* обстрелять)

she'll [ʃiːl] = **she will; she shall**

shellfish [ʃɛlfɪʃ] *n inv* (*crab*) рачки *pl*;
(*scallop*) моллюски *mpl*

shelter [ʃɛltə^r] *n* (*refuge*) приют;
(*protection*) укрытие ▷ *vt* (*protect*)
укрывать (*perf* укрыть); (*hide*) давать
(*perf* дать) приют +*dat* ▷ *vi* укрываться
(*perf* укрыться); **sheltered** *adj* (*life*)
беззаботный; (*spot*) защищённый

shelves [ʃɛlvz] *npl of* **shelf**

shepherd [ʃɛpəd] *n* пастух

sheriff [ʃɛrɪf] *n* (*US*) шериф

sherry [ʃɛrɪ] *n* херес

she's [ʃiːz] = **she is; she has**

shield [ʃiːld] *n* щит; (*trophy*) трофей
▷ *vt*: **to shield (from)** заслонять (*perf*
заслонить) (от +*gen*)

shift [ʃɪft] *n* (*in direction, conversation*)
перемена; (*in policy, emphasis*) сдвиг; (*at
work*) смена ▷ *vt* передвигать (*perf*
передвинуть), перемещать (*perf*
переместить) ▷ *vi* перемещаться (*perf*
переместиться)

shin [ʃɪn] *n* голень *f*

shine [ʃaɪn] (*pt, pp* **shone**) *n* блеск ▷ *vi*
(*sun, light*) светить (*impf*); (*eyes, hair*)
блестеть (*impf*) ▷ *vt*: **to shine a torch on
sth** направлять (*perf* направить) фонарь
на что-н

shiny [ʃaɪnɪ] *adj* блестящий

ship [ʃɪp] *n* корабль *m* ▷ *vt* (*by ship*)
перевозить (*perf* перевезти) по морю;
(*send*) отправлять (*perf* отправить),
экспедировать (*impf/perf*); **shipment** *n*
(*goods*) партия; **shipping** *n* (*of cargo*)
перевозка; **shipwreck** *n* (*ship*) судно,
потерпевшее крушение ▷ *vt*: **to be
shipwrecked** терпеть (*perf* потерпеть)
кораблекрушение; **shipyard** *n*
(судостроительная) верфь *f*

shirt [ʃəːt] *n* (*man's*) рубашка; (*woman's*)
блуза; **in (one's) shirt sleeves** в одной
рубашке

shit [ʃɪt] *excl* (*infl*) чёрт!, блин!

shiver [ʃɪvə^r] *n* дрожь *f* ▷ *vi* дрожать
(*impf*)

shock [ʃɔk] *n* (*start, impact*) толчок;
(*Elec, Med*) шок; (*emotional*) потрясение
▷ *vt* (*upset*) потрясать (*perf* потрясти);
(*offend*) возмущать (*perf* возмутить),
шокировать (*impf/perf*); **shocking** *adj*
(*outrageous*) возмутительный; (*dreadful*)
кошмарный

shoe [ʃuː] *n* (*for person*) туфля; (*for horse*)
подкова; **shoes** (*footwear*) обувь *fsg*;
shoelace *n* шнурок

shone [ʃɔn] *pt, pp of* **shine**

shook [ʃuk] *pt of* **shake**

shoot [ʃuːt] (*pt, pp* **shot**) *n* (*Bot*) росток,
побег ▷ *vt* (*gun*) стрелять (*impf*) из +*gen*;
(*bird, robber etc: kill*) застреливать (*perf*
застрелить); (: *wound*) выстрелить (*perf*)
в +*acc*; (*film*) снимать (*perf* снять) ▷ *vi*: **to
shoot (at)** стрелять (*perf* выстрелить) (в
+*acc*); (*Football etc*) бить (*impf*) (по +*dat*);
shoot down *vt* (*plane*) сбивать (*perf*
сбить); **shooting** *n* (*shots, attack*)
стрельба; (*Hunting*) охота

shop [ʃɔp] *n* магазин; (*also* **workshop**)
мастерская *f adj* ▷ *vi* (*also* **go shopping**)
ходить (*impf*) по магазинам, делать (*perf*
сделать) покупки; **shopkeeper** *n*
владелец(-лица) магазина; **shoplifting** *n*
кража товаров (*из магазинов*); **shopping**
n (*goods*) покупки *fpl*; **shopping centre**
(*US* **shopping center**) *n* торговый
центр; **shopping mall** *n* (*esp US*)
= **shopping centre**

shore [ʃɔː^r] *n* берег

short [ʃɔːt] *adj* короткий; (*in height*)
невысокий; (*curt*) резкий; (*insufficient*)
скудный; **we are short of milk** у нас мало
молока; **in short** короче говоря; **it is short
for ...** это сокращение от +*gen* ...; **to cut
short** (*speech, visit*) прерывать (*perf*
прервать); **everything short of ...** всё,
кроме +*gen* ...; **short of doing** кроме как
+*infin*; **to fall short of** не выполнять (*perf*
выполнить); **we're running short of time** у
нас заканчивается время; **to stop short**
застывать (*perf* застыть) на месте; **to stop
short of doing** не осмеливаться (*perf*
осмелиться) +*infin*; **shortage** *n*: **a
shortage of** нехватка +*gen*, дефицит +*gen*;
short cut *n* (*on journey*) короткий
путь *m*; **shortfall** *n* недостаток;
shorthand *n* (*Brit*) стенография;
short-lived *adj* кратковременный,
недолгий; **shortly** *adv* вскоре; **shorts**
npl: **(a pair of) shorts** шорты *pl*;
short-sighted *adj* (*Brit*) близорукий;
short story *n* рассказ; **short-term** *adj*
(*effect*) кратковременный

shot [ʃɔt] *pt, pp of* **shoot** ▷ *n* (*of gun*)
выстрел; (*Football*) удар; (*injection*) укол;
(*Phot*) снимок; **a good/poor shot** (*person*)
меткий/плохой стрелок; **like a shot** мигом;
shotgun *n* дробовик

should [ʃud] *aux vb*: **I should go now** я
должен идти; **I should go if I were you** на

Ва́шем ме́сте я бы пошёл; **I should like to** я бы хоте́л

shoulder ['ʃəʊldə'] n (Anat) плечо́ ▷ vt (fig) принима́ть (perf приня́ть) на себя́; **shoulder blade** n лопа́тка

shouldn't ['ʃʊdnt] = should not

shout [ʃaʊt] n крик ▷ vt выкри́кивать (perf вы́крикнуть) ▷ vi (also shout out) крича́ть (impf)

shove [ʃʌv] vt толка́ть (perf толкну́ть); (inf: put): **to shove sth in** запи́хивать (запиха́ть or запихну́ть perf) что-н в +acc

shovel ['ʃʌvl] n лопа́та ▷ vt (snow, coal) грести́ (perf лопа́той)

show [ʃəʊ] (pt showed, pp shown) n (of emotion) проявле́ние; (semblance) подо́бие; (exhibition) вы́ставка; (Theat) спекта́кль m; (TV) програ́мма, шо́у nt ind ▷ vt пока́зывать (perf показа́ть); (courage etc) проявля́ть (perf прояви́ть) ▷ vi (be evident) проявля́ться (perf прояви́ться); **for show** для ви́ду; **to be on show** (exhibits etc) выставля́ться (impf); **show in** (person) проводи́ть (perf провести́); **show off** vi хва́статься (impf) ▷ vt (display) хва́статься (perf похва́статься) +instr; **show out** vt (person) провожа́ть (perf проводи́ть) к вы́ходу; **show up** vi (against background) видне́ться (impf); (fig) обнару́живаться (perf обнару́житься); (inf: turn up) явля́ться (perf яви́ться) ▷ vt (uncover) выявля́ть (perf вы́явить); **show business** n шо́у-би́знес

shower ['ʃaʊə'] n (also shower bath) душ; (of rain) кратковре́менный дождь m ▷ vi принима́ть (perf приня́ть) душ ▷ vt: **to shower sb with** (gifts, abuse etc) осыпа́ть (perf осы́пать) кого́-н +instr; **to have** or **take a shower** принима́ть (perf приня́ть) душ; **shower gel** n гель m для ду́ша

show: **showing** n (of film) пока́з, демонстра́ция; **show jumping** n конку́р; **shown** pp of show; **show-off** n (inf) хвасту́н(ья); **showroom** n демонстрацио́нный зал

shrank [ʃræŋk] pt of shrink

shred [ʃred] n (usu pl) клочо́к ▷ vt кроши́ть (perf накроши́ть)

shrewd [ʃruːd] adj проница́тельный

shriek [ʃriːk] n визг ▷ vi визжа́ть (impf)

shrimp [ʃrɪmp] n (ме́лкая) креве́тка

shrine [ʃraɪn] n святы́ня; (tomb) ра́ка

shrink [ʃrɪŋk] (pt shrank, pp shrunk) vi (cloth) сади́ться (perf сесть); (profits, audiences) сокраща́ться (perf сократи́ться); (also shrink away) отпря́нуть (perf)

shrivel ['ʃrɪvl] (also shrivel up) vt высу́шивать (perf вы́сушить) ▷ vi высыха́ть (perf вы́сохнуть)

shroud [ʃraʊd] vt: **shrouded in mystery** оку́танный та́йной

● **SHROVE TUESDAY**
●
● **Shrove Tuesday** — Ма́сленица. За
● Ма́сленицей сле́дует пе́рвый день
● Вели́кого Поста́. По тради́ции на
● Ма́сленицу пеку́т блины́.

shrub [ʃrʌb] n куст

shrug [ʃrʌg] vi: **to shrug (one's shoulders)** пожима́ть (perf пожа́ть) плеча́ми; **shrug off** vt отма́хиваться (perf отмахну́ться) от +gen

shrunk [ʃrʌŋk] pp of shrink

shudder ['ʃʌdə'] vi содрога́ться (perf содрогну́ться)

shuffle ['ʃʌfl] vt тасова́ть (perf стасова́ть) ▷ vi: **to shuffle (one's feet)** волочи́ть (impf) но́ги

shun [ʃʌn] vt избега́ть (impf) +gen

shut [ʃʌt] (pt, pp shut) vt закрыва́ть (perf закры́ть) ▷ vi (factory) закрыва́ться (perf закры́ться); **shut down** vt (factory etc) закрыва́ть (perf закры́ть) ▷ vi (factory) закрыва́ться (perf закры́ться); **shut off** vt (supply etc) перекрыва́ть (perf перекры́ть); **shut up** vi (keep quiet) заткну́ться (perf) ▷ vt (keep quiet) затыка́ть (perf заткну́ть) рот +dat; **shutter** n (on window) ста́вень m; (Phot) затво́р

shuttle ['ʃʌtl] n (plane) самолёт-челно́к; (also space shuttle) шатл; (also shuttle service) регуля́рное сообще́ние

shy [ʃaɪ] adj (timid) засте́нчивый, стесни́тельный; (reserved) осторо́жный

Siberia [saɪ'bɪərɪə] n Сиби́рь f

sick [sɪk] adj (ill) больно́й; (humour) скве́рный; **he is/was sick** (vomiting) его́ рвёт/вы́рвало; **I feel sick** меня́ тошни́т; **I'm sick of arguing/school** меня́ тошни́т от спо́ров/шко́лы; **sickening** adj проти́вный, тошнотво́рный

sickly ['sɪklɪ] adj (child) хи́лый; (smell) тошнотво́рный

sickness ['sɪknɪs] n (illness) боле́знь f; (vomiting) рво́та

side [saɪd] n сторона́; (of body) бок; (team) кома́нда, сторона́; (of hill) склон ▷ adj (door etc) боково́й; **sideboard** n буфе́т; **side effect** n побо́чное де́йствие; **side street** n переу́лок; **sidewalk** n (US) тротуа́р; **sideways** adv (go in, lean) бо́ком; (look) и́скоса

siege [siːdʒ] n оса́да

sieve [sɪv] n (Culin) си́то ▷ vt просе́ивать (perf просе́ять)

sift [sɪft] vt просе́ивать (perf просе́ять)

sigh [saɪ] n вздох ▷ vi вздыха́ть (perf вздохну́ть)

sight [saɪt] n (faculty) зре́ние; (spectacle) зре́лище, вид; (on gun) прице́л; **in sight** в по́ле зре́ния; **out of sight** из ви́да; **sightseeing** n: **to go sightseeing** осма́тривать (perf осмотре́ть) достопримеча́тельности

sign [saɪn] n (notice) вы́веска; (with hand) знак; (indication, evidence) при́знак ▷ vt (document) подпи́сывать (perf подписа́ть); **to sign sth over to sb** передава́ть (perf переда́ть) что-н кому́-н; **sign on** vi (Brit: as unemployed) отмеча́ться (perf отме́титься) как безрабо́тный; (for course) регистри́роваться (perf зарегистри́роваться); **sign up** vi (Mil) нанима́ться (perf наня́ться); (for course) регистри́роваться (perf зарегистри́роваться) ▷ vt нанима́ть (perf наня́ть)

signal ['sɪgnl] n сигна́л ▷ vi сигнализи́ровать (impf/perf); **to signal to** подава́ть (perf пода́ть) знак +dat

signature ['sɪgnətʃəʳ] n по́дпись f

significance [sɪg'nɪfɪkəns] n значе́ние

significant [sɪg'nɪfɪkənt] adj (amount, discovery) значи́тельный

signify ['sɪgnɪfaɪ] vt (represent) означа́ть (impf)

silence ['saɪləns] n тишина́ ▷ vt заставля́ть (perf заста́вить) замолча́ть

silent ['saɪlənt] adj безмо́лвный; (taciturn) молчали́вый; (film) немо́й; **to remain silent** молча́ть (impf)

silhouette [sɪlu:'ɛt] n силуэ́т

silk [sɪlk] n шёлк ▷ adj шёлковый

silly ['sɪlɪ] adj глу́пый

silver ['sɪlvəʳ] n серебро́ ▷ adj сере́бристый

SIM card ['sɪm-] n (Tel) СИМ-ка́рта

similar ['sɪmɪləʳ] adj: **similar (to)** схо́дный (с +instr), подо́бный (+dat); **similarity** [sɪmɪ'lærɪtɪ] n схо́дство; **similarly** adv (in a similar way) подо́бным о́бразом

simmer ['sɪməʳ] vi (Culin) туши́ться (impf)

simple ['sɪmpl] adj просто́й; (foolish) недалёкий

simplicity [sɪm'plɪsɪtɪ] n (see adj) простота́; недалёкость f

simplify ['sɪmplɪfaɪ] vt упроща́ть (perf упрости́ть)

simply ['sɪmplɪ] adv про́сто

simulate ['sɪmjuleɪt] vt изобража́ть (perf изобрази́ть)

simultaneous [sɪməl'teɪnɪəs] adj одновре́менный; **simultaneously** adv одновре́менно

sin [sɪn] n грех ▷ vi греши́ть (perf согреши́ть)

since [sɪns] adv с тех пор ▷ conj (time) с тех пор как; (because) так как ▷ prep: **since July** с ию́ля; **since then, ever since** с тех пор; **it's two weeks since I wrote** уже́ две неде́ли с (тех пор) как я написа́л; **since our last meeting** со вре́мени на́шей после́дней встре́чи

sincere [sɪn'sɪəʳ] adj и́скренний

sing [sɪŋ] (pt **sang**, pp **sung**) vt, vi петь (perf спеть)

singer ['sɪŋəʳ] n певе́ц(-ви́ца)

singing ['sɪŋɪŋ] n пе́ние

single ['sɪŋgl] adj (person) одино́кий; (individual) одино́чный; (not double) одина́рный ▷ n (Brit: also **single ticket**) биле́т в оди́н коне́ц; (record) со́льник; **not a single person** ни оди́н челове́к; **single out** vt (choose) выделя́ть (perf вы́делить); **single-minded** adj целеустремлённый; **single room** n (in hotel) одноме́стный но́мер

singular ['sɪŋgjuləʳ] adj необыкнове́нный ▷ n (Ling) еди́нственное число́

sinister ['sɪnɪstəʳ] adj злове́щий

sink [sɪŋk] (pt **sank**, pp **sunk**) n ра́ковина ▷ vt (ship) топи́ть (perf потопи́ть); (well) рыть (perf вы́рыть); (foundations) врыва́ть (perf врыть) ▷ vi (ship) тону́ть (потону́ть perf or затону́ть perf); (heart, spirits) па́дать (perf упа́сть); (also **sink back**, **sink down**) отки́дываться (perf отки́нуться); **to sink sth into** (teeth, claws etc) вонза́ть (perf вонзи́ть) что-н в +acc; **sink in** vi (fig): **it took a long time for her words to sink in** её слова́ дошли́ до меня́ неско́ро

sinus ['saɪnəs] n (Anat) па́зуха

sip [sɪp] n ма́ленький глото́к ▷ vt потя́гивать impf

sir [səʳ] n сэр, господи́н; **Sir John Smith** Сэр Джон Смит

siren ['saɪərn] n сире́на

sister ['sɪstəʳ] n сестра́; (Brit: Med) (медици́нская or мед-) сестра́; **sister-in-law** n (brother's wife) неве́стка; (husband's sister) золо́вка; (wife's sister) своя́ченица

sit [sɪt] (pt, pp **sat**) vi (sit down) сади́ться (perf сесть); (be sitting) сиде́ть (impf); (assembly) заседа́ть (impf) ▷ vt (exam) сдава́ть (perf сдать); **sit down** vi сади́ться (perf сесть); **sit up** vi (after lying) сади́ться (perf сесть)

sitcom ['sɪtkɔm] n abbr (TV) (= situation comedy) коме́дия положе́ний

site [saɪt] n (place) ме́сто; (also **building site**) строи́тельная площа́дка

sitting ['sɪtɪŋ] n (of assembly etc) заседа́ние; (in canteen) сме́на; **sitting room** n гости́ная f adj

situated ['sɪtjueɪtɪd] adj: **to be situated** находи́ться (impf), располага́ться (impf)

situation [sɪtju'eɪʃən] n ситуа́ция, положе́ние; (job) ме́сто; (location) положе́ние; **"situations vacant"** (Brit) "вака́нтные места́"

six [sɪks] n шесть; **sixteen** n шестна́дцать; **sixteenth** adj шестна́дцатый; **sixth** adj шесто́й; **sixtieth** adj шестидеся́тый; **sixty** n шестьдеся́т

● SIXTH FORM

● Sixth form — квалификацио́нный курс.
Э́тот курс состои́т из двух ступене́й –
ни́жней и ве́рхней. Курс дли́тся два
го́да и предлага́ется на вы́бор
шко́льникам, кото́рые к 16 года́м
заверши́ли обяза́тельную шко́льную
програ́мму. В тече́ние двух лет ученики́
гото́вятся к выпускны́м экза́менам,
даю́щим пра́во на поступле́ние в
университе́т.

size [saɪz] n разме́р; (extent) величина́,
масшта́б; **sizeable** adj поря́дочный

skate [skeɪt] n (also **ice skate**) конёк;
(also **roller skate**) ро́ликовый конёк,
ро́лик ▷ vi ката́ться (impf) на конька́х

skating ['skeɪtɪŋ] n (for pleasure) ката́ние
на конька́х

skeleton ['skelɪtn] n (Anat) скеле́т;
(outline) схе́ма

sketch [sketʃ] n эски́з, набро́сок; (outline)
набро́сок; (Theat, TV) сце́нка, скетч ▷ vt
(draw) набросáть (impf); (also **sketch
out**) обрисо́вывать (perf обрисова́ть) в
о́бщих черта́х

ski [skiː] n лы́жа ▷ vi ката́ться (impf) на
лы́жах

skid [skɪd] vi (Aut) идти́ (perf пойти́)
ю́зом

skier ['skiːər] n лы́жник(-ица)

skiing ['skiːɪŋ] n (for pleasure) ката́ние на
лы́жах

skilful ['skɪlful] (US **skillful**) adj
иску́сный, уме́лый; (player) техни́чный

skill [skɪl] n (ability, dexterity) мастерство́;
(in computing etc) на́вык; **skilled** adj
(able) иску́сный; (worker)
квалифици́рованный

skim [skɪm] vt (milk) снима́ть (perf снять)
сли́вки с +gen; (glide over) скользи́ть
(impf) над +instr ▷ vi: **to skim through**
пробега́ть (perf пробежа́ть)

skin [skɪn] n (of person) ко́жа; (of animal)
шку́ра; (of fruit, vegetable) кожура́; (of
grape, tomato) ко́жица ▷ vt (animal)
снима́ть (perf снять) шку́ру с +gen;
skinny adj то́щий

skip [skɪp] n (Brit: container) скип ▷ vi
подпры́гивать (perf подпры́гнуть); (with
rope) скака́ть (impf) ▷ vt (miss out)
пропуска́ть (perf пропусти́ть)

skipper ['skɪpər] n (Naut) шки́пер,
капита́н; (Sport) капита́н

skirt [skɜːt] n ю́бка ▷ vt обходи́ть (perf
обойти́)

skull [skʌl] n че́реп

skunk [skʌŋk] n (animal) скунс

sky [skaɪ] n не́бо; **skyscraper** n
небоскрёб

slab [slæb] n плита́

slack [slæk] adj (rope) прови́сший;
(discipline) сла́бый; (security) плохо́й

slam [slæm] vt (door) хло́пать (perf
хло́пнуть) +instr ▷ vi (door)
захло́пываться (perf захло́пнуться)

slang [slæŋ] n (informal language) сленг;
(jargon) жарго́н

slant [slɑːnt] n накло́н; (fig: approach) укло́н

slap [slæp] n шлепо́к ▷ vt шлёпать (perf
шлёпнуть); **to slap sb across the face**
дава́ть (perf дать) кому́-н пощёчину; **to
slap sth on sth** (paint etc) ля́пать (perf
наля́пать) что-н на что-н

slash [slæʃ] vt ре́зать (perf поре́зать); (fig:
prices) уре́зывать (perf уре́зать)

slate [sleɪt] n (material) сла́нец; (tile)
кро́вельная пли́тка (из гли́нистого
сла́нца) ▷ vt (fig) разноси́ть (perf
разнести́) в пух и прах

slaughter ['slɔːtər] n (of animals) убо́й;
(of people) резня́, бо́йня ▷ vt (see n)
забива́ть (perf заби́ть); истребля́ть (perf
истреби́ть)

slave [sleɪv] n раб(ы́ня); **slavery** n
ра́бство

Slavonic [sləˈvɔnɪk] adj славя́нский

sleazy ['sliːzɪ] adj (place) запу́щенный

sledge [sledʒ] n са́ни pl; (for children)
са́нки pl

sleek [sliːk] adj (fur) лосня́щийся; (hair)
блестя́щий

sleep [sliːp] (pt, pp **slept**) n сон ▷ vi
спать (impf); (spend night) ночева́ть (perf
переночева́ть); **to go to sleep** засыпа́ть
(perf засну́ть); **sleep in** vi просыпа́ть
(perf проспа́ть); **sleeper** n (Rail: train)
по́езд со спа́льными ваго́нами; (: berth)
спа́льное ме́сто; **sleeping bag** n
спа́льный мешо́к; **sleepy** adj со́нный

sleet [sliːt] n мо́крый снег

sleeve [sliːv] n (of jacket etc) рука́в; (of
record) конве́рт

slender ['slendər] adj (figure) стро́йный;
(majority) небольшо́й

slept [slept] pt, pp of **sleep**

slice [slaɪs] n (of meat) кусо́к; (of bread,
lemon) ло́мтик ▷ vt (bread, meat etc)
нареза́ть (perf наре́зать)

slick [slɪk] adj (performance) гла́дкий;
(salesman, answer) бо́йкий ▷ n (also **oil
slick**) плёнка не́фти

slide [slaɪd] (pt, pp **slid**) n (in playground)
де́тская го́рка; (Phot) слайд; (Brit: also
hair slide) зако́лка ▷ vt задвига́ть (perf
задви́нуть) ▷ vi скользи́ть (impf)

slight [slaɪt] adj хру́пкий; (small)
незначи́тельный; (: error) ме́лкий; (accent,
pain) сла́бый ▷ n униже́ние; **not in the
slightest** ниско́лько; **slightly** adv (rather)
слегка́

slim [slɪm] adj (figure) стро́йный; (chance)
сла́бый ▷ vi худе́ть (perf похуде́ть)

slimy ['slaɪmɪ] adj (pond) и́листый

sling [slɪŋ] (pt, pp **slung**) n (Med)
перевя́зь f ▷ vt (throw) швыря́ть (perf
швырну́ть)

slip [slɪp] n (mistake) про́мах; (underskirt) ни́жняя ю́бка; (of paper) поло́ска ▷ vt сова́ть (perf су́нуть); (slide) скользи́ть (скользну́ть f); (lose balance) поскользну́ться (perf); (decline) снижа́ться (perf сни́зиться); to give sb the slip ускольза́ть (perf ускользну́ть) от кого́-н; a slip of the tongue огово́рка; to slip sth on/off надева́ть (perf наде́ть)/сбра́сывать (perf сбро́сить) что-н; to slip into (room etc) скользну́ть (perf) в +acc; to slip out of (room etc) выска́льзывать (perf вы́скользнуть) из +gen; **slip away** vi ускольза́ть (perf ускользну́ть); **slip in** vt сова́ть (perf су́нуть) ▷ vi (errors) закра́дываться (perf закра́сться)

slipper ['slɪpə'] n та́почка

slippery ['slɪpərɪ] adj ско́льзкий

slit [slɪt] (pt, pp slit) n (cut) разре́з; (in skirt) шли́ца; (opening) щель f ▷ vt разреза́ть (perf разре́зать)

slog [slɔg] n: it was a hard slog э́то была́ тяжёлая рабо́та

slogan ['slǝugǝn] n ло́зунг

slope [slǝup] n склон; (gentle hill) укло́н; (slant) накло́н

sloppy ['slɔpɪ] adj (work) халту́рный

slot [slɔt] n (in machine) про́резь f, паз ▷ vt: to slot sth into опуска́ть (perf опусти́ть) что-н в +acc

Slovakia [slǝu'vækɪǝ] n Слова́кия

slow [slǝu] adj ме́дленный; (stupid) тупо́й ▷ adv ме́дленно ▷ vt (also **slow down, slow up**: vehicle) замедля́ть (perf заме́длить) ▷ vi (traffic) замедля́ться (perf заме́длиться); (car, train etc) сбавля́ть (perf сба́вить) ход; my watch is (20 minutes) slow мои́ часы́ отстаю́т (на 20 мину́т); **slowly** adv ме́дленно; **slow motion** n: in slow motion в заме́дленном де́йствии

slug [slʌg] n (Zool) сли́зень m

sluggish ['slʌgɪʃ] adj вя́лый

slum [slʌm] n трущо́ба

slump [slʌmp] n (economic) спад; (in profits, sales) паде́ние

slung [slʌŋ] pt, pp of **sling**

slur [slǝ:'] vt (words) мя́млить (perf промя́млить) ▷ n (fig): **slur (on)** пятно́ (на +prp)

sly [slaɪ] adj лука́вый

smack [smæk] n (slap) шлепо́к ▷ vt хло́пать (perf хло́пнуть); (child) шлёпать (perf отшлёпать) ▷ vi: to smack of отдава́ть (impf) +instr

small [smɔ:l] adj ма́ленький; (quantity, amount) небольшо́й, ма́лый

smart [smɑ:t] adj (neat, tidy) опря́тный; (clever) толко́вый ▷ vi (also fig) жечь (impf); **smart phone** n смартфо́н

smash [smæʃ] n (collision: also **smash-up**) ава́рия ▷ vt разбива́ть (perf разби́ть); (Sport: record) побива́ть (perf поби́ть) ▷ vi (break) разбива́ться (perf

разби́ться); to smash against or into (collide) вреза́ться (perf вре́заться) в +acc; **smashing** adj (inf) потряса́ющий

smear [smɪə'] n (trace) след; (Med: also **smear test**) мазо́к ▷ vt (spread) ма́зать (perf нама́зать)

smell [smɛl] (pt, pp **smelt** or **smelled**) n за́пах; (sense) обоня́ние ▷ vt чу́вствовать (perf почу́вствовать) за́пах +gen ▷ vi (food etc) па́хнуть (impf); to smell (of) (unpleasant) воня́ть (impf) (+instr); **smelly** adj воню́чий, злово́нный

smelt [smɛlt] pt, pp of **smell**

smile [smaɪl] n улы́бка ▷ vi улыба́ться (perf улыбну́ться)

smirk [smǝ:k] n (pej) ухмы́лка

smog [smɔg] n смог

smoke [smǝuk] n дым ▷ vi (person) кури́ть (impf); (chimney) дыми́ться (impf) ▷ vt (cigarettes) кури́ть (perf вы́курить); **smoked** adj (bacon, fish) копчёный; (glass) ды́мчатый; **smoker** n (person) куря́щий(-ая) m(f) adj, кури́льщик(-щица); **smoking** ['smǝukɪŋ] n (act) куре́ние; "no smoking" "не кури́ть"; **smoky** ['smǝukɪ] adj ды́мный

smooth [smu:ð] adj гла́дкий; (sauce) однородный; (flavour) мя́гкий; (movement) пла́вный; **smoothie** n сму́зи m ind

smother ['smʌðə'] vt (fire) туши́ть (perf потуши́ть); (person) души́ть (perf задуши́ть); (emotions) подавля́ть (perf подави́ть)

smudge [smʌdʒ] n пятно́ ▷ vt разма́зывать (perf разма́зать)

smug [smʌg] adj дово́льный

smuggle ['smʌgl] vt (goods) провози́ть (perf провезти́) (контраба́ндой)

smuggling ['smʌglɪŋ] n контраба́нда

snack [snæk] n заку́ска

snag [snæg] n поме́ха

snail [sneɪl] n ули́тка

snake [sneɪk] n змея́

snap [snæp] adj (decision etc) момента́льный ▷ vt (break) разла́мывать (perf разломи́ть); (fingers) щёлкнуть +instr ▷ vi (break) разла́мываться (perf разломи́ться); (speak sharply) крича́ть (impf); to snap shut (trap, jaws etc) защёлкиваться (perf защёлкнуться); **snap up** vt расхва́тывать (perf расхвата́ть); **snapshot** n сни́мок

snarl [snɑ:l] vi рыча́ть (impf)

snatch [snætʃ] n обры́вок ▷ vt (grab) хвата́ть (perf схвати́ть); (handbag) вырыва́ть (perf вы́рвать); (child) похища́ть (perf похи́тить); (opportunity) урыва́ть (perf урва́ть)

sneak [sni:k] vi: to sneak into проска́льзывать (perf проскользну́ть) в +acc; to sneak out of выска́льзывать (perf вы́скользнуть) из +gen; to sneak up on я́бедничать (perf ная́бедничать) на +acc; **sneakers** npl кроссо́вки fpl

sneer [snɪəʳ] *vi* (*mock*): **to sneer at** глуми́ться (*impf*) над +*instr*

sneeze [sniːz] *vi* чиха́ть (*perf* чихну́ть)

sniff [snɪf] *n* (*sound*) сопе́ние ▷ *vi* шмы́гать (*perf* шмыгну́ть) но́сом; (*when crying*) всхли́пывать (*impf*) ▷ *vt* ню́хать (*impf*)

snip [snɪp] *vt* ре́зать (*perf* поре́зать)

sniper ['snaɪpəʳ] *n* сна́йпер

snob [snɔb] *n* сноб

snooker ['snuːkəʳ] *n* сну́кер

snore [snɔːʳ] *vi* храпе́ть (*impf*)

snorkel ['snɔːkl] *n* тру́бка (ныря́льщика)

snow [snəu] *n* снег ▷ *vi*: **it's snowing** идёт снег; **snowball** *n* снежо́к; **snowdrift** *n* сугро́б; **snowman** *n irreg* снегови́к, сне́жная ба́ба

SNP *n abbr* = **Scottish National Party**

snub [snʌb] *vt* пренебрежи́тельно обходи́ться (*perf* обойти́сь) с +*instr*

snug [snʌg] *adj* (*place*) ую́тный; (*well-fitting*) облега́ющий

⬤ **KEYWORD**

so [səu] *adv* **1** (*thus, likewise*) так; **if this is so** е́сли э́то так; **if so** е́сли так; **while she was so doing, he ...** пока́ она́ э́то де́лала, он ...; **I didn't do it — you did so!** я не де́лал э́того — а вот и сде́лал!; **you weren't there — I was so!** тебя́ там не́ было — а вот и был!; **I like him — so do I** он мне нра́вится — мне то́же; **I'm still at school — so is he** я ещё учу́сь в шко́ле — он то́же; **so it is!** и действи́тельно!, и пра́вда!; **I hope/think so** наде́юсь/ду́маю, что так; **so far** пока́; **how do you like the book so far?** ну, как Вам кни́га?

2 (*in comparisons*: +*adv*) насто́лько, так; (: +*adj*) насто́лько, тако́й; **so quickly (that)** насто́лько *or* так бы́стро(, что); **so big (that)** тако́й большо́й(, что); **she's not so clever as her brother** она́ не так умна́, как её брат

3 (*describing degree, extent*) так; **I've got so much work** у меня́ так мно́го рабо́ты; **I love you so much** я тебя́ так люблю́; **thank you so much** спаси́бо Вам большо́е; **I'm so glad to see you** я так рад Вас ви́деть; **there are so many books I would like to read** есть так мно́го книг, кото́рые я бы хоте́л прочесть; **so ... that ...** так ... что ...

4 (*about*) о́коло +*gen*; **ten or so** о́коло десяти́; **I only have an hour or so** у меня́ есть о́коло ча́са

5 (*phrases*): **so long!** (*inf: goodbye*) пока́! ▷ *conj* **1** (*expressing purpose*): **so as to do** что́бы +*infin*; **I brought this wine so that you could try it** я принёс э́то вино́, что́бы Вы могли́ его́ попро́бовать

2 (*expressing result*) так что; **so I was right** так что, я был прав; **so you see, I could have stayed** так что, ви́дите, я мог бы оста́ться

soak [səuk] *vt* (*drench*) промочи́ть (*perf*); (*steep*) зама́чивать (*perf* замочи́ть) ▷ *vi* (*steep*) отмока́ть (*perf* впита́ть); **soak up** *vt* впи́тывать (*perf* впита́ть) (в себя́)

soap [səup] *n* мы́ло; **soap opera** *n* (*TV*) мы́льная о́пера

soar [sɔːʳ] *vi* (*price, temperature*) подска́кивать (*perf* подскочи́ть)

sob [sɔb] *n* рыда́ние ▷ *vi* рыда́ть (*impf*)

sober ['səubəʳ] *adj* тре́звый; (*colour, style*) сде́ржанный

soccer ['sɔkəʳ] *n* футбо́л

sociable ['səuʃəbl] *adj* общи́тельный

social ['səuʃl] *adj* (*history, structure etc*) обще́ственный, социа́льный; **he has a good social life** он мно́го обща́ется с людьми́; **socialism** *n* социали́зм; **socialist** *n* социали́ст ▷ *adj* социалисти́ческий; **socialize** *vi*: **to socialize (with)** обща́ться (*impf*) (с +*instr*); **socially** *adv*: **to visit sb socially** заходи́ть (*perf* зайти́) к кому́-н по-дру́жески; **socially acceptable** социа́льно прие́млемый; **social media** *n* социа́льные се́ти; **social networking** [-'nɛtwəːkɪŋ] *n* взаимоде́йствие посре́дством социа́льных сете́й с други́ми их уча́стниками; **social security** (*Brit*) *n* социа́льная защи́та; **social work** *n* социа́льная рабо́та

society [sə'saɪətɪ] *n* о́бщество

sociology [səusɪ'ɔlədʒɪ] *n* социоло́гия

sock [sɔk] *n* носо́к

socket ['sɔkɪt] *n* глазни́ца; (*Brit: Elec: in wall*) розе́тка

soda ['səudə] *n* (*also* **soda water**) со́довая *f adj*; (*US: also* **soda pop**) газиро́вка

sodium ['səudɪəm] *n* на́трий

sofa ['səufə] *n* дива́н

soft [sɔft] *adj* мя́гкий; **soft drink** *n* безалкого́льный напи́ток; **softly** *adv* (*gently*) мя́гко; (*quietly*) ти́хо; **software** *n* програ́мма, програ́ммное обеспе́чение

soggy ['sɔgɪ] *adj* (*ground*) сыро́й

soil [sɔɪl] *n* (*earth*) по́чва; (*territory*) земля́ ▷ *vt* па́чкать (*perf* запа́чкать)

solar ['səuləʳ] *adj* со́лнечный

sold [səuld] *pt, pp of* **sell**

soldier ['səuldʒəʳ] *n* (*Mil*) солда́т

sole [səul] *n* (*of foot*) подо́шва; (*of shoe*) подо́шва, подмётка ▷ *n inv* (*fish*) па́лтус ▷ *adj* (*unique*) еди́нственный; **solely** *adv* то́лько

solemn ['sɔləm] *adj* торже́ственный

solicitor [sə'lɪsɪtəʳ] *n* (*Brit*) адвока́т

solid ['sɔlɪd] *adj* (*not hollow*) це́льный; (*not liquid*) твёрдый; (*reliable*) про́чный; (*entire*) це́лый; (*gold*) чи́стый ▷ *n* твёрдое те́ло; **solids** *npl* твёрдая пи́ща *fsg*

solitary ['sɔlɪtərɪ] *adj* одино́кий; (*empty*) уединённый; (*single*) едини́чный

solitude ['sɔlɪtjuːd] *n* уедине́ние, одино́чество

solo ['səuləu] *n* со́ло *nt ind* ▷ *adv* (*fly*) в одино́чку; (*play*) со́ло; **soloist** *n* соли́ст(ка)
soluble ['sɔljubl] *adj* раствори́мый
solution [sə'luːʃən] *n* (*answer*) реше́ние; (*liquid*) раство́р
solve [sɔlv] *vt* (*problem*) разреша́ть (*perf* разреши́ть); (*mystery*) раскрыва́ть (*perf* раскры́ть)
solvent ['sɔlvənt] *adj* платёжеспосо́бный ▷ *n* раствори́тель *m*
sombre ['sɔmbə'] (*US* **somber**) *adj* мра́чный

⭕ **KEYWORD**

some [sʌm] *adj* **1** (*a certain amount or number of*): **would you like some tea/ biscuits?** хоти́те ча́ю/пече́нья?; **there's some milk in the fridge** в холоди́льнике есть молоко́; **he asked me some questions** он за́дал мне не́сколько вопро́сов; **there are some people waiting to see you** Вас ждут каки́е-то лю́ди
2 (*certain: in contrasts*) не́который; **some people say that ...** не́которые говоря́т, что ...
3 (*unspecified*) како́й-то; **some woman phoned you** Вам звони́ла кака́я-то же́нщина; **we'll meet again some day** мы когда́-нибудь опя́ть встре́тимся; **shall we meet some day next week?** дава́йте встре́тимся ка́к-нибудь на сле́дующей неде́ле!
▷ *pron* (*a certain number: people*) не́которые *pl*, одни́ *pl*; **some took the bus, and some walked** не́которые пое́хали на авто́бусе, а не́которые пошли́ пешко́м; **I've got some** (*books etc*) у меня́ есть не́сколько; **who would like a piece of cake? — I'd like some** кто хо́чет кусо́к то́рта? — я хочу́; **I've read some of the book** я прочёл часть кни́ги
▷ *adv* о́коло; **some ten people** о́коло десяти́ челове́к

somebody ['sʌmbədɪ] *pron* = **someone**
somehow ['sʌmhau] *adv* (*in some way: in future*) ка́к-нибудь; (: *in past*) ка́к-то; (*for some reason*) почему́-то, каки́м-то о́бразом
someone ['sʌmwʌn] *pron* (*specific person*) кто́-то; (*unspecified person*) кто́-нибудь; **I saw someone in the garden** я ви́дел кого́-то в саду́; **someone will help you** Вам кто́-нибудь помо́жет
something ['sʌmθɪŋ] *pron* (*something specific*) что́-то; (*something unspecified*) что́-нибудь; **there's something wrong with my car** что́-то случи́лось с мое́й маши́ной; **would you like something to eat/drink?** хоти́те чего́-нибудь пое́сть/вы́пить?; **I have something for you** у меня́ ко́е-что для Вас есть

sometime ['sʌmtaɪm] *adv* (*in future*) когда́-нибудь; (*in past*) когда́-то, ка́к-то
sometimes ['sʌmtaɪmz] *adv* иногда́
somewhat ['sʌmwɔt] *adv* не́сколько
somewhere ['sʌmwɛə'] *adv* (*be: somewhere specific*) где́-то; (: *anywhere*) где́-нибудь; (*go: somewhere specific*) куда́-то; (: *anywhere*) куда́-нибудь; (*come from*) отку́да-то; **it's somewhere or other in Scotland** э́то где́-то в Шотла́ндии; **is there a post office somewhere around here?** здесь где́-нибудь есть по́чта?; **let's go somewhere else** дава́йте пое́дем куда́-нибудь в друго́е ме́сто
son [sʌn] *n* сын
song [sɔŋ] *n* пе́сня
son-in-law ['sʌnɪnlɔː] *n* зять *m*
soon [suːn] *adv* (*in a short time*) ско́ро; (*early*) ра́но; **soon (afterwards)** вско́ре; *see also* **as**; **sooner** *adv* скоре́е; **I would sooner do that** я бы скоре́е сде́лал э́то; **sooner or later** ра́но и́ли по́здно
soothe [suːð] *vt* успока́ивать (*perf* успоко́ить)
sophisticated [sə'fɪstɪkeɪtɪd] *adj* изощрённый; (*refined*) изы́сканный
soprano [sə'prɑːnəu] *n* сопра́но *f ind*
sordid ['sɔːdɪd] *adj* (*place*) убо́гий; (*story etc*) гну́сный
sore [sɔː'] *n* я́зва, боля́чка ▷ *adj* (*esp US: offended*) оби́женный; (*painful*): **my arm is sore, I've got a sore arm** у меня́ боли́т рука́; **it's a sore point** (*fig*) э́то больно́е ме́сто
sorrow ['sɔrəu] *n* печа́ль *f*, грусть *f*
sorry ['sɔrɪ] *adj* плаче́вный; **I'm sorry** мне жаль; **sorry!** извини́те, пожа́луйста!; **sorry?** (*pardon*) прости́те?; **I feel sorry for him** мне его́ жаль *или* жа́лко
sort [sɔːt] *n* (*type*) сорт ▷ *vt* (*mail*) сортирова́ть (*perf* рассортирова́ть); (*also* **sort out**: *papers, belongings etc*) разбира́ть (*perf* разобра́ть); (: *problems*) разбира́ться (*perf* разобра́ться) в +*prp*
so-so ['səusəu] *adv* так себе́
sought [sɔːt] *pt, pp of* **seek**
soul [səul] *n* (*spirit, person*) душа́
sound [saund] *adj* (*healthy*) здоро́вый; (*safe, not damaged*) це́лый; (*secure: investment*) надёжный; (*reliable, thorough*) соли́дный; (*sensible: advice*) разу́мный ▷ *n* звук ▷ *vt* (*alarm*) поднима́ть (*perf* подня́ть) ▷ *vi* звуча́ть (*impf*) ▷ *adv*: **he is sound asleep** он кре́пко спит; **I don't like the sound of it** мне э́то не нра́вится; **soundtrack** *n* му́зыка (*из кинофи́льма*)
soup [suːp] *n* суп
sour ['sauə'] *adj* ки́слый; (*fig: bad-tempered*) угрю́мый
source [sɔːs] *n* (*also fig*) исто́чник
south [sauθ] *n* юг ▷ *adj* ю́жный ▷ *adv* (*go*) на юг; (*be*) на ю́ге; **South America** *n* Ю́жная Аме́рика; **southeast** *n*

юго-восто́к; **southern** ['sʌðən] *adj*
ю́жный; **South Pole** *n*: the South Pole
Ю́жный по́люс; **southwest** *n* ю́го-за́пад
souvenir [su:vəˈnɪəʳ] *n* сувени́р
sovereign ['sɔvrɪn] *n* (*ruler*)
госуда́рь(-ры́ня) *m(f)*
Soviet ['səuvɪət] *adj* сове́тский; **the
Soviet Union** (*formerly*) Сове́тский Сою́з
sow[1] [sau] *n* (*pig*) свинья́
sow[2] [səu] (*pt* **sowed**, *pp* **sown**) *vt* (*also
fig*) се́ять (*perf* посе́ять)
soya ['sɔɪə] (*US* **soy**) *adj* со́евый
spa [spa:] *n* (*US*: also **health spa**) во́ды *fpl*
space [speɪs] *n* простра́нство; (*small
place, room*) ме́сто; (*beyond Earth*) ко́смос;
(*interval, period*) промежу́ток ▷ *cpd*
косми́ческий ▷ *vt* (*also* **space out**:
payments, visits) распределя́ть (*perf*
распредели́ть); **spacecraft** *n*
косми́ческий кора́бль *m*; **spaceship** *n*
= **spacecraft**
spacious ['speɪʃəs] *adj* просто́рный
spade [speɪd] *n* (*tool*) лопа́та; (*child's*)
лопа́тка; **spades** *npl* (*Cards*) пи́ки *fpl*
spaghetti [spəˈgɛtɪ] *n* спаге́тти *pl ind*
Spain [speɪn] *n* Испа́ния
spam [spæm] *n* (*Comput*) спам
(*бесполезная информация, обычно
реклама, по электронной почте*), на
Интерне́те
span [spæn] *pt of* **spin** ▷ *n* (*of hand,
wings*) разма́х; (*in time*) промежу́ток ▷ *vt*
охва́тывать (*perf* охвати́ть)
Spanish ['spænɪʃ] *adj* испа́нский; ▷ *npl*:
the Spanish испа́нцы *mpl*
spank [spæŋk] *vt* шлёпать (*perf*
отшлёпать)
spanner ['spænəʳ] *n* (*Brit*) (га́ечный) ключ
spare [spɛəʳ] *adj* (*free: time, seat*)
свобо́дный; (*surplus*) ли́шний; (*reserve*)
запасно́й ▷ *vt* (*trouble, expense*)
избавля́ть (*perf* изба́вить) от +*gen*; (*make
available*) выделя́ть (*perf* вы́делить);
(*refrain from hurting*) щади́ть (*perf*
пощади́ть); **I have some time to spare** у
меня́ есть немно́го свобо́дного вре́мени;
to have money to spare име́ть (*impf*)
ли́шние де́ньги; **spare time** *n*
свобо́дное вре́мя *nt*
spark [spa:k] *n* (*also fig*) и́скра
sparkle ['spa:kl] *n* блеск ▷ *vi* (*diamonds,
water, eyes*) сверка́ть (*impf*)
sparkling ['spa:klɪŋ] *adj* (*wine*) игри́стый
sparrow ['spærəu] *n* воробе́й
sparse [spa:s] *adj* ре́дкий
spasm ['spæzəm] *n* (*Med*) спазм
spat [spæt] *pt, pp of* **spit**
spate [speɪt] *n* (*fig*): **a spate of** пото́к +*gen*
speak [spi:k] (*pt* **spoke**, *pp* **spoken**) *vi*
говори́ть (*impf*); (*make a speech*)
выступа́ть (*perf* вы́ступить) ▷ *vt* (*truth*)
говори́ть (*perf* сказа́ть); **to speak to sb**
разгова́ривать (*impf*) *or* говори́ть (*impf*) с
кем-н; **to speak of** *or* **about** говори́ть

(*impf*) о +*prp*; **speaker** *n* (*in public*)
ора́тор; (*also* **loudspeaker**)
громкоговори́тель *m*
spear [spɪəʳ] *n* копьё
special ['spɛʃl] *adj* (*important*) осо́бый,
осо́бенный; (*edition, adviser, school*)
специа́льный; **specialist** *n* специали́ст;
speciality [spɛʃɪˈælɪtɪ] *n* (*dish*)
фи́рменное блю́до; (*subject*)
специализа́ция; **specialize** *vi*: **to
specialize (in)** специализи́роваться (*impf/
perf*) (в/на +*prp*); **specially** *adv*
(*especially*) осо́бенно
species ['spi:ʃi:z] *n inv* вид
specific [spəˈsɪfɪk] *adj* специфи́ческий,
определённый; **specifically** *adv*
(*exactly*) точне́е; (*specially*) специа́льно
specify ['spɛsɪfaɪ] *vt* уточня́ть (*perf*
уточни́ть)
specimen ['spɛsɪmən] *n* (*example*)
экземпля́р; (*sample*) образе́ц; **a specimen
of urine** моча́ для ана́лиза
speck [spɛk] *n* (*of dirt*) пя́тнышко; (*of
dust*) крупи́ца, крупи́нка
spectacle ['spɛktəkl] *n* (*scene, event*)
зре́лище; **spectacles** *npl* (*glasses*) очки́
pl
spectacular [spɛkˈtækjuləʳ] *adj*
впечатля́ющий, порази́тельный
spectator [spɛkˈteɪtəʳ] *n* зри́тель(ница)
m(f)
spectrum ['spɛktrəm] *n* (*pl* **spectra**) *n*
спектр
speculate ['spɛkjuleɪt] *vi* (*Comm*)
спекули́ровать (*impf*); (*guess*): **to
speculate about** стро́ить (*impf*)
предположе́ния о +*prp*
sped [spɛd] *pt, pp of* **speed**
speech [spi:tʃ] *n* речь *f*; **speechless** *adj*:
I was speechless with anger от гне́ва я
лиши́лся да́ра ре́чи; **she looked at him,
speechless** она́ посмотре́ла на него́ в
онеме́нии
speed [spi:d] (*pt, pp* **sped**) *n* (*rate*)
ско́рость *f*; (*promptness*) быстрота́ ▷ *vi*
(*move*): **to speed along/by** мча́ться (*perf*
промча́ться) по +*dat*/ми́мо +*gen*; **at full** *or*
top speed на по́лной *or* преде́льной
ско́рости; **speed up** ▷ (*pt, pp* **speeded
up**) *vi* ускоря́ться (*perf* ускори́ться) ▷ *vt*
ускоря́ть (*perf* ускори́ть); **speeding** *n*
превыше́ние ско́рости; **speed limit** *n*
преде́л ско́рости; **speedometer**
[spɪˈdɔmɪtəʳ] *n* спидо́метр; **speedy** *adj*
(*prompt*) ско́рый
spell [spɛl] (*pt, pp* **spelt** *or* **spelled**) *n*
(*also* **magic spell**) колдовство́; (*period of
time*) пери́од ▷ *vt* (*also* **spell out**)
произноси́ть (*perf* произнести́) по
бу́квам; (*fig*: *explain*) разъясня́ть (*perf*
разъясни́ть) ▷ *vi*: **he can't spell** у него́
плоха́я орфогра́фия; **spelling** *n*
орфогра́фия, правописа́ние
spend [spɛnd] (*pt, pp* **spent**) *vt* (*money*)

тра́тить (*perf* потра́тить); (*time, life*)
проводи́ть (*perf* провести́)
sperm [spəːm] *n* спе́рма
sphere [sfɪəʳ] *n* сфе́ра
spice [spaɪs] *n* (*pepper, salt etc*) спе́ция
spicy ['spaɪsɪ] *adj* (*food*) о́стрый; (: *with a strong flavour*) пря́ный
spider ['spaɪdəʳ] *n* пау́к
spike [spaɪk] *n* (*point*) остриё
spill [spɪl] (*pt, pp* **spilt** *or* **spilled**) *vt* (*liquid*) пролива́ть (*perf* проли́ть), разлива́ть (*perf* разли́ть) ▷ *vi* (*liquid*) пролива́ться (*perf* проли́ться), разлива́ться (*perf* разли́ться)
spin [spɪn] (*pt, pp* **spun**) *n* (*trip in car*) ката́ние; (*Aviat*) што́пор; (*Pol*) укло́н, тенде́нция ▷ *vt* (*Brit: clothes*) выжима́ть (*perf* вы́жать) (в стира́льной маши́не) ▷ *vi* (*make thread*) прясть (*impf*); (*person, head*) кружи́ться (*impf*)
spinach ['spɪnɪtʃ] *n* шпина́т
spinal ['spaɪnl] *adj* (*relating to the spine*) позвоно́чный; (*relating to the spinal cord*) спинномозгово́й; **spinal injury** поврежде́ние позвоно́чника; **spinal cord** *n* спинно́й мозг
spine [spaɪn] *n* (*Anat*) позвоно́чник; (*thorn*) колю́чка, игла́
spiral ['spaɪərl] *n* спира́ль *f*
spire ['spaɪəʳ] *n* шпиль *m*
spirit ['spɪrɪt] *n* дух; (*soul*) душа́; **spirits** *npl* (*alcohol*) спиртны́е напи́тки *mpl*, спиртно́е *ntsg adj*; **in good/low spirits** в хоро́шем/подавленном настрое́нии
spiritual ['spɪrɪtjuəl] *adj* духо́вный
spit [spɪt] (*pt, pp* **spat**) *n* (*saliva*) слюна́ ▷ *vi* (*person*) плева́ть (*perf* плю́нуть); (*fire, hot oil*) бры́згать (*impf*); (*inf: rain*) мороси́ть (*impf*)
spite [spaɪt] *n* зло́ба, злость *f* ▷ *vt* досажда́ть (*perf* досади́ть) +*dat*; **in spite of** несмотря́ на +*acc*; **spiteful** *adj* зло́бный
splash [splæʃ] *n* (*sound*) всплеск ▷ *vt* бры́згать (*perf* бры́знуть) ▷ *vi* (*also* **splash about**) плеска́ться (*impf*)
splendid ['splendɪd] *adj* великоле́пный
splinter ['splɪntəʳ] *n* (*of wood*) ще́пка; (*of glass*) оско́лок; (*in finger*) зано́за
split [splɪt] (*pt, pp* **split**) *n* (*crack, tear*) тре́щина; (*Pol, fig*) раско́л ▷ *vt* (*atom, piece of wood*) расщепля́ть (*perf* расщепи́ть); (*Pol, fig*) раска́лывать (*perf* расколо́ть); (*work, profits*) дели́ть (*perf* раздели́ть) ▷ *vi* (*divide*) расщепля́ться (*perf* расщепи́ться), разделя́ться (*perf* раздели́ться); **split up** *vi* (*couple*) расходи́ться (*perf* разойти́сь); (*group*) разделя́ться (*perf* раздели́ться)
spoil [spɔɪl] (*pt, pp* **spoilt** *or* **spoiled**) *vt* по́ртить (*perf* испо́ртить)
spoke [spəuk] *pt of* **speak** ▷ *n* (*of wheel*) спи́ца; **spoken** *pp of* **speak**
spokesman ['spəuksmən] *irreg n* представи́тель *m*

spokeswoman ['spəukswumən] *irreg n* представи́тельница
sponge [spʌndʒ] *n* гу́бка; (*also* **sponge cake**) бискви́т
sponsor ['spɔnsəʳ] *n* спо́нсор ▷ *vt* финанси́ровать (*impf/perf*), спонси́ровать (*impf/perf*); (*applicant*) поруча́ться (*perf* поручи́ться) за +*acc*; **sponsorship** *n* спо́нсорство

◦ **SPONSORSHIP**
◦
◦ В Великобрита́нии спонси́рование
◦ явля́ется распространённым спо́собом
◦ сбо́ра де́нег на благотвори́тельность.
◦ При́нято выполня́ть ра́зного ро́да
◦ зада́чи, наприме́р, пла́вание, ходьба́ на
◦ дли́нную диста́нцию или да́же
◦ похуде́ние. Предполо́жим, вы хоти́те
◦ собра́ть де́ньги для благотвори́тельной
◦ организа́ции, финанси́рующей
◦ иссле́дования ра́ковых заболева́ний.
◦ Вы заявля́ете, что пройдёте пешко́м 10
◦ миль и про́сите знако́мых, друзе́й и тд
◦ спонси́ровать ва́ше реше́ние, же́ртвуя
◦ де́ньги в по́льзу э́той
◦ благотвори́тельной организа́ции.

spontaneous [spɔn'teɪnɪəs] *adj* (*gesture*) спонта́нный, непосре́дственный; (*demonstration*) стихи́йный
spoon [spuːn] *n* ло́жка; **spoonful** *n* (по́лная) ло́жка
sport [spɔːt] *n* (*game*) спорт *m no pl*; **sportsman** *irreg n* спортсме́н; **sportswoman** *irreg n* спортсме́нка; **sporty** *adj* спорти́вный
spot [spɔt] *n* (*mark*) пятно́; (*dot: on pattern*) кра́пинка; (*on skin*) пры́щик; (*place*) ме́сто ▷ *vt* замеча́ть (*perf* заме́тить); **a spot of bother** ме́лкая неприя́тность *f*; **spots of rain** ка́пли дождя́; **on the spot** (*in that place*) на ме́сте; (*immediately*) в тот же моме́нт; **spotless** *adj* чисте́йший; **spotlight** *n* проже́ктор
spouse [spaus] *n* супру́г(а)
sprang [spræŋ] *pt of* **spring**
sprawl [sprɔːl] *vi* (*person*) разва́ливаться (*perf* развали́ться); (*place*) раски́дываться (*perf* раски́нуться)
spray [spreɪ] *n* (*drops of water*) бры́зги *pl*; (*hair spray*) аэрозо́ль *m* ▷ *vt* опры́скивать (*perf* опры́скать)
spread [spred] (*pt, pp* **spread**) *n* (*range*) спектр; (*distribution*) распростране́ние; (*Culin: butter*) бутербро́дный маргари́н; (*inf: food*) пир ▷ *vt* (*lay out*) расстила́ть (*perf* расстели́ть); (*scatter*) разбра́сывать (*perf* разброса́ть); (*butter*) нама́зывать (*perf* нама́зать); (*wings*) расправля́ть (*perf* распра́вить); (*arms*) раскрыва́ть (*perf* раскры́ть); (*workload, wealth*) распределя́ть (*perf* распредели́ть) ▷ *vi* (*disease, news*) распространя́ться (*perf*

распространи́ться); **spread out** vi (move apart) рассыпа́ться (perf рассы́паться); **spreadsheet** n (крупноформа́тная) электро́нная табли́ца

spree [spri:] n разгу́л

spring [sprɪŋ] (pt **sprang**, pp **sprung**) n (coiled metal) пружи́на; (season) весна́; (of water) исто́чник, родни́к ▷ vi (leap) пры́гать (perf пры́гнуть); **in spring** весно́й; **to spring from** (stem from) происходи́ть (perf произойти́) из +gen

sprinkle [ˈsprɪŋkl] vt (salt, sugar) посыпа́ть (perf посы́пать) +instr; **to sprinkle water on sth, sprinkle sth with water** опры́скивать (perf опры́скать) что-н водо́й

sprint [sprɪnt] n (race) спринт ▷ vi (run fast) стреми́тельно бе́гать/бежа́ть (impf)

sprung [sprʌŋ] pp of **spring**

spun [spʌn] pt, pp of **spin**

spur [spəːʳ] n (fig) сти́мул ▷ vt (also **spur on**) пришпо́ривать (perf пришпо́рить); **to spur sb on to** побужда́ть (perf побуди́ть) кого́-н к +dat; **on the spur of the moment** вдруг, не разду́мывая

spy [spaɪ] n шпио́н ▷ vi: **to spy on** шпио́нить (impf) за +instr

Sq. abbr = **square**

squabble [ˈskwɔbl] vi вздо́рить (perf повздо́рить)

squad [skwɔd] n (Mil, Police) отря́д; (Sport) кома́нда

squadron [ˈskwɔdrn] n (Aviat) эскадри́лья

square [skwɛəʳ] n (shape) квадра́т; (in town) пло́щадь f ▷ adj квадра́тный ▷ vt (reconcile, settle) ула́живать (perf ула́дить); **a square meal** соли́дный обе́д; **2 metres square** 2 ме́тра в ширину́, 2 ме́тра в длину́; **2 square metres** 2 квадра́тных ме́тра

squash [skwɔʃ] n (Brit: drink) напи́ток; (Sport) сквош ▷ vt дави́ть (perf раздави́ть)

squat [skwɔt] adj призе́мистый ▷ vi (also **squat down**: position) сиде́ть (impf) на ко́рточках; (: motion) сади́ться (perf сесть) на ко́рточки

squeak [skwiːk] vi (door) скрипе́ть (perf скри́пнуть); (mouse) пища́ть (perf пи́скнуть)

squeal [skwiːl] vi визжа́ть (impf)

squeeze [skwiːz] n (of hand) пожа́тие; (Econ) ограниче́ние ▷ vt сжима́ть (perf сжать); (juice) выжима́ть (perf вы́жать)

squid [skwɪd] n кальма́р

squint [skwɪnt] n (Med) косогла́зие

squirrel [ˈskwɪrəl] n бе́лка

squirt [skwəːt] vi бры́згать (perf бры́знуть) ▷ vt бры́згать (perf бры́знуть) +instr

Sr abbr (in names) = **senior**

St abbr (= saint) св.; (= street) ул. (= у́лица)

stab [stæb] vt наноси́ть (perf нанести́) уда́р +dat; (kill): **to stab sb (to death)** заре́зать (perf) кого́-н ▷ n (of pain) уко́л; (inf: try): **to have a stab at doing** пыта́ться (perf попыта́ться) +infin

stability [stəˈbɪlɪtɪ] n усто́йчивость f, стаби́льность f

stable [ˈsteɪbl] adj стаби́льный, усто́йчивый ▷ n (for horse) коню́шня

stack [stæk] n (of wood, plates) шта́бель m; (of papers) ки́па ▷ vt (also **stack up**: chairs etc) скла́дывать (perf сложи́ть)

stadium [ˈsteɪdɪəm] n (pl **stadia** or **stadiums**) n (Sport) стадио́н

staff [stɑːf] n (workforce) штат, сотру́дники mpl; (Brit: Scol: also **teaching staff**) преподава́тельский соста́в or коллекти́в ▷ vt: **the firm is staffed by 5 people** на фи́рму рабо́тает 5 челове́к

stag [stæg] n (Zool) саме́ц оле́ня

stage [steɪdʒ] n (in theatre) сце́на; (platform) подмо́стки pl; (point, period) ста́дия ▷ vt (play) ста́вить (perf поста́вить); (demonstration) устра́ивать (perf устро́ить); **in stages** поэта́пно, по эта́пам

stagger [ˈstægəʳ] vt (amaze) потряса́ть (perf потрясти́); (holidays etc) распи́сывать (perf расписа́ть) ▷ vi: **he staggered along the road** он шёл по доро́ге шата́ясь; **staggering** adj потряса́ющий, порази́тельный

stagnant [ˈstægnənt] adj (water) стоя́чий; (economy) засто́йный

stain [steɪn] n пятно́ ▷ vt (mark) ста́вить (perf поста́вить) пятно́ на +acc; **stainless steel** n нержаве́ющая сталь f

stair [stɛəʳ] n (step) ступе́нь f, ступе́нька; **stairs** npl (steps) ле́стница fsg; **staircase** n ле́стница; **stairway** = **staircase**

stake [steɪk] n (post) кол; (investment) до́ля ▷ vt (money, reputation) рискова́ть (perf рискну́ть) +instr; **his reputation was at stake** его́ репута́ция была́ поста́влена на ка́рту; **to stake a claim (to)** притяза́ть (impf) (на +acc)

stale [steɪl] adj (bread) чёрствый; (food) несве́жий; (air) за́тхлый

stalk [stɔːk] n (of flower) сте́бель m; (of fruit) черешо́к

stall [stɔːl] n (in market) прила́вок; (in stable) сто́йло ▷ vi: **I stalled (the car)** у меня́ загло́хла маши́на; **stalls** npl (Brit: Theat) парте́р msg

stamina [ˈstæmɪnə] n сто́йкость f, вы́держка

stammer [ˈstæməʳ] n заика́ние

stamp [stæmp] n (Post) ма́рка; (rubber stamp) печа́ть f, штамп; (mark, also fig) печа́ть f ▷ vi (also **stamp one's foot**) то́пать (perf то́пнуть) (ного́й) ▷ vt (mark) клейми́ть (perf заклейми́ть); (: with rubber stamp) штампова́ть (perf проштампова́ть)

stampede [stæmˈpiːd] n да́вка

stance [stæns] n (also fig) пози́ция

stand [stænd] (pt, pp **stood**) n (stall) ларёк, кио́ск; (at exhibition) стенд; (Sport) трибу́на; (for umbrellas) сто́йка; (for coats, hats) ве́шалка ▷ vi (be upright) стоя́ть (impf); (rise) встава́ть (perf встать);

(*remain: decision, offer*) оставаться (*perf* остаться) в силе; (*in election etc*) баллотироваться (*impf*) ▷ vt (*place: object*) ставить (*perf* поставить); (*tolerate, withstand*) терпеть (*perf* стерпеть), выносить (*perf* вынести); **to make a stand against sth** выступать (*perf* выступить) против чего-н; **to stand for parliament** (*Brit*) баллотироваться (*impf*) в парламент; **to stand at** (*value, score etc*) составлять (*perf* составить) на +*prp*; **stand by** vi (*be ready*) быть (*impf*) наготове ▷ vt fus не отступать (*perf* отступить) от +*gen*; **stand for** vt fus (*signify*) обозначать (*impf*); (*represent*) представлять (*impf*); **I won't stand for it** я этого не потерплю; **stand out** vi (*be obvious*) выделяться (*perf* выделиться); **stand up** vi (*rise*) вставать (*perf* встать); **stand up for** vt fus (*defend*) стоять (*perf* постоять) за +*acc*; **stand up to** vt fus оказывать (*perf* оказать) сопротивление +*dat*

standard ['stændəd] n (*level*) уровень m; (*norm, criterion*) стандарт ▷ adj (*normal: size etc*) стандартный; **standards** npl (*morals*) нравы mpl; **standard of living** n уровень m жизни

standpoint ['stændpɔɪnt] n позиция

standstill ['stændstɪl] n: **to be at a standstill** (*negotiations*) быть (*impf*) в тупике; **to come to a standstill** (*negotiations*) заходить (*perf* зайти) в тупик; (*traffic*) стать (*perf*)

stank [stæŋk] pt of **stink**

staple ['steɪpl] n (*for papers*) скоба ▷ adj (*food etc*) основной ▷ vt (*fasten*) сшивать (*perf* сшить)

star [stɑ:ʳ] n звезда ▷ vi: **to star in** играть (*perf* сыграть) главную роль в +*prp* ▷ vt: **the film stars my brother** главную роль в фильме играет мой брат; **stars** npl: **the stars** (*horoscope*) звёзды fpl

starch [stɑ:tʃ] n (*also Culin*) крахмал

stare [stɛəʳ] vi: **to stare at** (*deep in thought*) пристально смотреть (*impf*) на +*acc*; (*amazed*) таращиться (*impf*) на +*acc*

stark [stɑ:k] adj (*bleak*) голый ▷ adv: **stark naked** совершенно голый

start [stɑ:t] n начало; (*Sport*) старт; (*in fright*) вздрагивание; (*advantage*) преимущество ▷ vt (*begin, found*) начинать (*perf* начать); (*cause*) вызывать (*perf* вызвать); (*engine*) заводить (*perf* завести) ▷ vi (*begin*) начинаться (*perf* начаться); (*begin moving*) отправляться (*perf* отправиться); (*engine, car*) заводиться (*perf* завестись); (*jump: in fright*) вздрагивать (*perf* вздрогнуть); **to start doing** or **to do** начинать (*perf* начать) +*impf infin*; **start off** vi (*begin*) начинаться (*perf* начаться); (*begin moving*) трогаться (*perf* тронуться); (*leave*) отправляться (*perf* отправиться); **start out** vi (*leave*) отправляться (*perf*

отправиться); **start up** vi (*engine, car*) заводиться (*perf* завестись) ▷ vt (*business*) начинать (*perf* начать); (*car, engine*) заводить (*perf* завести); **starter** n (*Brit: Culin*) закуска; **starting point** n (*for journey*) отправной пункт

startle ['stɑ:tl] vt вспугивать (*perf* вспугнуть)

startling ['stɑ:tlɪŋ] adj поразительный

starvation [stɑ:'veɪʃən] n голод

starve [stɑ:v] vi (*to death*) умирать (*perf* умереть) от голода; (*be very hungry*) голодать (*impf*) ▷ vt (*person, animal*) морить (*perf* заморить) голодом

state [steɪt] n (*condition*) состояние; (*government*) государство ▷ vt (*say, declare*) констатировать (*impf/perf*); **the States** (*Geo*) Соединённые Штаты mpl; **to be in a state** быть (*impf*) в панике

statement ['steɪtmənt] n (*declaration*) заявление

statesman ['steɪtsmən] irreg n государственный деятель m

static ['stætɪk] adj (*not moving*) статичный, неподвижный

station ['steɪʃən] n станция; (*larger railway station*) вокзал; (*also police station*) полицейский участок ▷ vt (*position: guards etc*) выставлять (*perf* выставить)

stationary ['steɪʃnərɪ] adj (*vehicle*) неподвижный

stationery ['steɪʃnərɪ] n канцелярские принадлежности fpl

statistic [stə'tɪstɪk] n статистик; **statistics** n (*science*) статистика

statue ['stætju:] n статуя

stature ['stætʃəʳ] n (*size*) рост

status ['steɪtəs] n статус; (*importance*) значение; **the status quo** статус-кво m ind

statutory ['stætjutrɪ] adj установленный законом

staunch [stɔ:ntʃ] adj преданный, непоколебимый

stay [steɪ] n пребывание ▷ vi (*remain*) оставаться (*perf* остаться); (*with sb, as guest*) гостить (*impf*); (*in place*) останавливаться (*perf* остановиться); **to stay at home** оставаться (*perf* остаться) дома; **to stay put** не двигаться (*perf* двинуться) с места; **to stay the night** ночевать (*perf* переночевать); **stay in** vi (*at home*) оставаться (*perf* остаться) дома; **stay on** vi оставаться (*perf* остаться); **stay out** vi (*of house*) отсутствовать (*impf*); **stay up** vi (*at night*) не ложиться (*impf*) (спать)

steadily ['stɛdɪlɪ] adv (*firmly*) прочно; (*constantly, fixedly*) постоянно

steady ['stɛdɪ] adj (*constant*) стабильный; (*boyfriend, speed*) постоянный; (*person*) уравновешенный; (*firm: hand etc*) твёрдый; (*look, voice*) ровный ▷ vt (*object*) придавать (*perf* придать) устойчивость +dat; (nerves, voice) совладать (perf) с +instr

steak [steɪk] n филе nt ind; (fried beef) бифштекс

steal [sti:l] (pt **stole**, pp **stolen**) vt воровать (perf своровать), красть (perf украсть) ▷ vi воровать (impf), красть (impf); (creep) красться (impf)

steam [sti:m] n пар ▷ vt (Culin) парить (impf) ▷ vi (give off steam) выделять (impf) пар

steel [sti:l] n сталь f ▷ adj стальной

steep [sti:p] adj крутой; (price) высокий ▷ vt (food) вымачивать (perf вымочить); (clothes) замачивать (perf замочить)

steeple ['sti:pl] n шпиль m

steer [stɪəʳ] vt (vehicle, person) направлять (perf направить) ▷ vi маневрировать (impf); **steering wheel** n руль m

stem [stɛm] n (of plant) стебель m; (of glass) ножка ▷ vt (stop) останавливать (perf остановить); **stem from** vt fus произрастать (perf произрасти) из +gen

step [stɛp] n (also fig) шаг; (of stairs) ступень f, ступенька ▷ vi (forward, back) ступать (perf ступить); **steps** npl (Brit) = **stepladder**; **to be in/out of step (with)** идти (impf) в ногу/не в ногу (с +instr); **step down** vi (fig: resign) уходить (perf уйти) в отставку; **step on** vt fus (walk on) наступать (perf наступить) на +acc; **step up** vt (increase) усиливать (perf усилить); **stepbrother** n сводный брат; **stepdaughter** n падчерица; **stepfather** n отчим; **stepladder** n (Brit) стремянка; **stepmother** n мачеха; **stepsister** n сводная сестра; **stepson** n пасынок

stereo ['stɛrɪəu] n (system) стереосистема

stereotype ['stɪərɪətaɪp] n стереотип

sterile ['stɛraɪl] adj бесплодный; (clean) стерильный

sterilize ['stɛrɪlaɪz] vt стерилизовать (impf/perf)

sterling ['stə:lɪŋ] n (Econ) фунт стерлингов; **sterling silver** серебро 925-ой пробы

stern [stə:n] adj суровый

stew [stju:] n (meat) тушёное мясо ▷ vt тушить (perf потушить)

steward ['stju:əd] n (on plane) бортпроводник; **stewardess** n (on plane) стюардесса, бортпроводница

stick [stɪk] (pt, pp **stuck**) n (of wood) палка; (walking stick) трость f ▷ vt (with glue etc) клеить (perf приклеить); (inf: put) совать (perf сунуть); (thrust) втыкать (perf воткнуть) ▷ vi (become attached) приклеиваться (perf приклеиться); (in mind) засесть (perf); **stick out** vi (ears) торчать (impf); **stick up for** vt fus (person) заступаться (perf заступиться) за +acc; (principle) отстаивать (perf отстоять); **sticker** n наклейка; **sticky** adj (hands etc) липкий; (label) клейкий; (situation) щекотливый

stiff [stɪf] adj (brush) жёсткий; (person) деревянный; (zip) тугой; (manner, smile) натянутый; (competition) жёсткий; (: sentence) суровый; (strong: drink) крепкий; (: breeze) сильный ▷ adv до смерти

stifling ['staɪflɪŋ] adj (heat) удушливый

stigma ['stɪgmə] n (fig) клеймо

still [stɪl] adj тихий ▷ adv (up to this time) всё ещё; (even, yet) ещё; (nonetheless) всё-таки, тем не менее

stimulate ['stɪmjuleɪt] vt стимулировать (impf/perf)

stimulus ['stɪmjuləs] (pl **stimuli**) n (encouragement) стимул

sting [stɪŋ] (pt, pp **stung**) n (from insect) укус; (from plant) ожог; (organ: of wasp etc) жало ▷ vt (also fig) уязвлять (perf уязвить) ▷ vi (insect, animal) жалиться (impf); (plant) жечься (impf); (eyes, ointment etc) жечь (impf)

stink [stɪŋk] (pt **stank**, pp **stunk**) vi смердеть (impf), вонять (impf) (inf)

stir [stə:ʳ] n (fig) шум, сенсация ▷ vt (tea etc) мешать (perf помешать); (fig: emotions) волновать (perf взволновать) ▷ vi (move) шевелиться (perf пошевелиться); **stir up** vt (trouble) вызывать (perf вызвать); **stir-fry** vt быстро обжаривать (perf обжарить)

stitch [stɪtʃ] n (Sewing) стежок; (Knitting) петля; (Med) шов ▷ vt (sew) шить (perf сшить); (Med) зашивать (perf зашить); **I have a stitch in my side** у меня колет в боку

stock [stɔk] n (supply) запас; (Agr) поголовье; (Culin) бульон; (Finance: usu pl) ценные бумаги fpl ▷ adj (reply, excuse etc) дежурный ▷ vt (have in stock) иметь (impf) в наличии; **stocks and shares** акции и ценные бумаги; **to be in/out of stock** иметься (impf)/не иметься (impf) в наличии; **to take stock of** (fig) оценивать (perf оценить); **stockbroker** n (Comm) фондовый брокер; **stock exchange** n фондовая биржа

stocking ['stɔkɪŋ] n чулок

stock market n (Brit) фондовая биржа

stole [stəul] pt of **steal**; **stolen** pp of **steal**

stomach ['stʌmək] n (Anat) желудок; (belly) живот ▷ vt (fig) переносить (perf перенести)

stone [stəun] n (also Med) камень m; (pebble) камешек; (in fruit) косточка; (Brit: weight) стоун (14 фунтов) ▷ adj каменный

● **STONE**
●
● Stone — мера веса равная 6,35 кг.

stood [stud] pt, pp of **stand**

stool [stu:l] n табурет(ка)

stoop [stu:p] vi (also **stoop down**: bend) наклоняться (perf наклониться), нагибаться (perf нагнуться)

stop [stɒp] n остано́вка; (Ling: also **full stop**) то́чка ▷ vt остана́вливать (perf останови́ть); (prevent: also **put a stop to**) прекраща́ть (perf прекрати́ть) ▷ vi (person, clock) остана́вливаться (perf останови́ться); (rain, noise etc) прекраща́ться (perf прекрати́ться); **to stop doing** перестава́ть (perf переста́ть) +infin; **stop by** vi заходи́ть (perf зайти́); **stoppage** ['stɒpɪdʒ] n (strike) забасто́вка

storage ['stɔːrɪdʒ] n хране́ние

store [stɔː] n (stock, reserve) запа́с; (depot) склад; (Brit: large shop) универма́г; (esp US: shop) магази́н ▷ vt храни́ть (impf); **in store** в бу́дущем

storey ['stɔːrɪ] (US **story**) n эта́ж

storm [stɔːm] n (also fig) бу́ря; (of criticism) шквал; (of laughter) взрыв ▷ vt (attack: place) штурмова́ть (impf); **stormy** adj (fig) бу́рный; **stormy weather** нена́стье

story ['stɔːrɪ] n исто́рия; (lie) вы́думка, ска́зка; (US) = **storey**

stout [staut] adj (strong: branch etc) кре́пкий; (fat) доро́дный; (resolute: friend, supporter) сто́йкий

stove [stəuv] n печь f, пе́чка

St Petersburg [sənt'piːtəzbəːg] n Санкт-Петербу́рг

straight [streɪt] adj прямо́й; (simple: choice) я́сный ▷ adv пря́мо; **to put** or **get sth straight** (make clear) вноси́ть (perf внести́) я́сность во что-н; **straight away, straight off** (at once) сра́зу (же); **straighten** vt (skirt, tie, bed) поправля́ть (perf попра́вить); **straightforward** adj (simple) просто́й; (honest) прямо́й

strain [streɪn] n (pressure) нагру́зка; (Med: physical) растяже́ние; (: mental) напряже́ние ▷ vt (back etc) растя́гивать (perf растяну́ть); (voice) напряга́ть (perf напря́чь); (stretch: resources) перенапряга́ть (perf перенапря́чь) по +dat; (Culin) проце́живать (perf процеди́ть); **strained** adj (muscle) растя́нутый; (laugh, relations) натя́нутый

strand [strænd] n нить f; (of hair) прядь f; **stranded** adj: **to be stranded** застрева́ть (perf застря́ть)

strange [streɪndʒ] adj стра́нный; (not known) незнако́мый; **strangely** adv (act, laugh) стра́нно; see also **enough**; **stranger** n (unknown person) незнако́мец, посторо́нний(-яя) m(f) adj

strangle ['stræŋgl] vt (also fig) души́ть (perf задуши́ть)

strap [stræp] n реме́нь m; (of dress) брете́лька; (of watch) ремешо́к

strategic [strə'tiːdʒɪk] adj стратеги́ческий

strategy ['strætɪdʒɪ] n страте́гия

straw [strɔː] n соло́ма; (drinking straw) соло́минка; **that's the last straw!** э́то после́дняя ка́пля!

strawberry ['strɔːbərɪ] n клубни́ка f no pl; (wild) земляни́ка f no pl

stray [streɪ] adj (animal) бродя́чий; (bullet) шально́й ▷ vi заблуди́ться (perf); (thoughts) блужда́ть (impf)

streak [striːk] n (stripe) полоса́

stream [striːm] n ручёй; (of people, vehicles, questions) пото́к ▷ vi (liquid) течь (impf), ли́ться (impf); **to stream in/out** (people) вали́ть (perf повали́ть) толпо́й в +acc/из +gen

street [striːt] n у́лица

strength [streŋθ] n си́ла; (of girder, knot etc) про́чность f; **strengthen** vt (building, machine) укрепля́ть (perf укрепи́ть); (fig: group) пополня́ть (perf пополни́ть); (: argument) подкрепля́ть (perf подкрепи́ть)

strenuous ['strenjuəs] adj (exercise) уси́ленный; (efforts) напряжённый

stress [stres] n (pressure) давле́ние, напряже́ние; (mental strain) стресс; (emphasis) ударе́ние ▷ vt (point, need etc) де́лать (perf сде́лать) ударе́ние на +acc; (syllable) ста́вить (perf поста́вить) ударе́ние на +acc

stretch [stretʃ] n (area) отре́зок, простра́нство ▷ vt (pull) натя́гивать (perf натяну́ть) ▷ vi (person, animal) потя́гиваться (perf потяну́ться); (extend): **to stretch to** or **as far as** простира́ться (impf) до +gen; **stretch out** vi растя́гиваться (perf растяну́ться) ▷ vt (arm etc) протя́гивать (perf протяну́ть)

stretcher ['stretʃəʳ] n носи́лки pl

strict [strɪkt] adj стро́гий; (precise: meaning) то́чный; **strictly** adv (severely) стро́го; (exactly) то́чно

stride [straɪd] (pt **strode**, pp **stridden**) n (step) шаг ▷ vi шага́ть (impf)

strike [straɪk] (pt, pp **struck**) n (of workers) забасто́вка; (Mil: attack) уда́р ▷ vt (hit: person, thing) ударя́ть (perf уда́рить); (subj: idea, thought) осеня́ть (perf осени́ть); (oil etc) открыва́ть (perf откры́ть) месторожде́ние +gen; (bargain, deal) заключа́ть (perf заключи́ть) ▷ vi (workers) бастова́ть (impf); (disaster, illness) обру́шиваться (perf обру́шиться); (clock) бить (perf проби́ть); **to be on strike** (workers) бастова́ть (impf); **to strike a match** зажига́ть (perf заже́чь) спи́чку; **striker** n забасто́вщик(-ица); (Sport) напада́ющий(-ая) m(f) adj

striking ['straɪkɪŋ] adj порази́тельный

string [strɪŋ] (pt, pp **strung**) n верёвка; (Mus: for guitar etc) струна́; (of beads) ни́тка ▷ vt: **to string together** свя́зывать (perf связа́ть); **strings** npl (Mus) стру́нные инструме́нты mpl; **to string out** растя́гивать (perf растяну́ть)

strip [strɪp] n полоса́, поло́ска ▷ vt (undress) раздева́ть (perf разде́ть); (paint) обдира́ть (perf ободра́ть), сдира́ть (perf содра́ть); (*also* **strip down**: *machine*) разбира́ть (*perf* разобра́ть) ▷ *vi*: раздева́ться (*perf* разде́ться)

stripe [straip] *n* поло́ска; (*Police, Mil*) петли́ца; **striped** *adj* полоса́тый

stripper ['strɪpə'] *n* стриптизёрка

strive [straɪv] (*pt* **strove**, *pp* **striven**) *vi*: **to strive for sth/to do** стреми́ться (*impf*) к чему́-н/+*infin*

strode [strəud] *pt of* **stride**

stroke [strəuk] *n* (*also Med*) уда́р; (*Swimming*) стиль *m* ▷ *vt* гла́дить (*perf* погла́дить); **at a stroke** одни́м ма́хом

stroll [strəul] *n* прогу́лка ▷ *vi* прогу́ливаться (*perf* прогуля́ться), проха́живаться (*perf* пройти́сь)

strong [strɔŋ] *adj* си́льный; **they are 50 strong** их 50; **stronghold** *n* (*fig*) опло́т, тверды́ня

strove [strəuv] *pt of* **strive**

struck [strʌk] *pt, pp of* **strike**

structure ['strʌktʃə'] *n* структу́ра

struggle ['strʌgl] *n* (*fight*) борьба́ ▷ *vi* (*try hard*) си́литься (*impf*), прилага́ть (*perf* приложи́ть) больши́е уси́лия; (*fight*) боро́ться (*impf*); (: *to free o.s.*) сопротивля́ться (*impf*)

strung [strʌŋ] *pt, pp of* **string**

stub [stʌb] *n* (*of cheque, ticket etc*) корешо́к; (*of cigarette*) окуро́к ▷ *vt*: **to stub one's toe** бо́льно спотыка́ться (*perf* споткну́ться)

stubble ['stʌbl] *n* (*on chin*) щети́на

stubborn ['stʌbən] *adj* (*determination, child*) упря́мый, упо́рный

stuck [stʌk] *pt, pp of* **stick** ▷ *adj*: **to be stuck** застря́ть (*perf*)

stud [stʌd] *n* (*on clothing etc*) кно́пка, заклёпка; (*earring*) серьга́ со штифто́м; (*on sole of boot*) шип ▷ *vt* (*fig*): **studded with** усы́панный +*instr*

student ['stju:dənt] *n* (*at university*) студе́нт(ка); (*at school*) уча́щийся(-аяся) *m(f) adj* ▷ *adj* студе́нческий; (*at school*) учени́ческий

studio ['stju:dɪəu] *n* сту́дия

study ['stʌdɪ] *n* (*activity*) учёба; (*room*) кабине́т ▷ *vt* изуча́ть (*perf* изучи́ть) ▷ *vi* учи́ться (*perf*)

stuff [stʌf] *n* (*things*) ве́щи *fpl*; (*substance*) вещество́ ▷ *vt* набива́ть (*perf* наби́ть); (*Culin*) начина́ть (*perf* начини́ть), фарширова́ть (*perf* нафарширова́ть); (*inf*: *push*) запи́хивать (*perf* запиха́ть); **stuffing** *n* наби́вка; (*Culin*) начи́нка, фарш; **stuffy** *adj* (*room*) ду́шный; (*person, ideas*) чо́порный

stumble ['stʌmbl] *vi* спотыка́ться (*perf* споткну́ться); **to stumble across** *or* **on** (*fig*) натыка́ться (*perf* наткну́ться) на +*acc*

stump [stʌmp] *n* (*of tree*) пень *m*; (*of limb*) обру́бок ▷ *vt* озада́чивать (*perf* озада́чить)

stun [stʌn] *vt* (*subj*: *news*) потряса́ть (*perf* потрясти́), ошеломля́ть (*perf* ошеломи́ть); (: *blow on head*) оглуша́ть (*perf* оглуши́ть)

stung [stʌŋ] *pt, pp of* **sting**

stunk [stʌŋk] *pp of* **stink**

stunning ['stʌnɪŋ] *adj* (*fabulous*) потряса́ющий

stupid ['stju:pɪd] *adj* глу́пый; **stupidity** [stju:'pɪdɪtɪ] *n* глу́пость *f*

sturdy ['stə:dɪ] *adj* кре́пкий

stutter ['stʌtə'] *n* заика́ние ▷ *vi* заика́ться (*impf*)

style [staɪl] *n* стиль *m*

stylish ['staɪlɪʃ] *adj* сти́льный, элега́нтный

subconscious [sʌb'kɔnʃəs] *adj* подсозна́тельный

subdued [sʌb'dju:d] *adj* (*light*) приглушённый; (*person*) подавленный

subject [*n* 'sʌbdʒɪkt, *vb* səb'dʒɛkt] *n* (*topic*) те́ма; (*Scol*) предме́т; (*Ling*) подлежа́щее *nt adj* ▷ *vt*: **to subject sb to sth** подверга́ть (*perf* подве́ргнуть) кого́-н чему́-н; **to be subject to** (*tax*) подлежа́ть (*impf*) +*dat*; (*law*) подчиня́ться (*impf*) +*dat*; **subjective** [səb'dʒɛktɪv] *adj* субъекти́вный

submarine [sʌbmə'ri:n] *n* подво́дная ло́дка

submission [səb'mɪʃən] *n* (*state*) подчине́ние, повинове́ние; (*of plan etc*) пода́ча

submit [səb'mɪt] *vt* (*proposal, application etc*) представля́ть (*perf* предста́вить) на рассмотре́ние ▷ *vi*: **to submit to sth** подчиня́ться (*perf* подчини́ться) чему́-н

subordinate [sə'bɔ:dɪnət] *adj*: **to be subordinate to** (*in rank*) подчиня́ться (*impf*) +*dat* ▷ *n* подчинённый(-ая) *m(f) adj*

subscribe [səb'skraɪb] *vi*: **to subscribe to** (*opinion, fund*) подде́рживать (*perf* поддержа́ть); (*magazine etc*) подпи́сываться (*perf* подписа́ться) на +*acc*

subscription [səb'skrɪpʃən] *n* (*to magazine etc*) подпи́ска

subsequent ['sʌbsɪkwənt] *adj* после́дующий; **subsequent to** вслед +*dat*; **subsequently** *adv* впосле́дствии

subside [səb'saɪd] *vi* (*feeling, wind*) утиха́ть (*perf* ути́хнуть); (*flood*) убыва́ть (*perf* убы́ть)

subsidiary [səb'sɪdɪərɪ] *n* (*also* **subsidiary company**) доче́рняя компа́ния

subsidy ['sʌbsɪdɪ] *n* субси́дия, дота́ция

substance ['sʌbstəns] *n* (*product, material*) вещество́

substantial [səb'stænʃl] *adj* (*solid*) про́чный, основа́тельный; (*fig: reward, meal*) соли́дный

substitute ['sʌbstɪtju:t] *n* (*person*) заме́на; (: *Football etc*) запасно́й *m adj* (игро́к); (*thing*) замени́тель *m* ▷ *vt*: **to substitute A for B** заменя́ть (*perf* замени́ть) А на Б

substitution [sʌbstɪ'tju:ʃən] *n* (*act*) заме́на

subtitle ['sʌbtaɪtl] *n* (*in film*) субти́тр

subtle ['sʌtl] *adj* (*change*) то́нкий, едва́ улови́мый; (*person*) то́нкий, иску́сный

subtract [səb'trækt] *vt* вычита́ть (*perf* вы́честь)

suburb ['sʌbə:b] *n* при́город; **the suburbs** (*area*) при́город *msg*; **suburban** [sə'bə:bən] *adj* при́городный

subway ['sʌbweɪ] *n* (*US*) метро́ *nt ind*, подзе́мка (*inf*); (*Brit*: *underpass*) подзе́мный перехо́д

succeed [sək'si:d] *vi* (*plan etc*) удава́ться (*perf* уда́ться), име́ть (*impf*) успе́х; (*person*: *in career etc*) преуспева́ть (*perf* преуспе́ть) ▷ *vt* (*in job, order*) сменя́ть (*perf* смени́ть); **he succeeded in finishing the article** ему́ удало́сь зако́нчить статью́

success [sək'sɛs] *n* успе́х, уда́ча; **the book was a success** кни́га име́ла успе́х; **he was a success** он доби́лся успе́ха; **successful** *adj* (*venture*) успе́шный; **he was successful in convincing her** ему́ удало́сь убеди́ть её; **successfully** *adv* успе́шно

succession [sək'sɛʃən] *n* (*series*) череда́, ряд; (*to throne etc*) насле́дование; **in succession** подря́д

successive [sək'sɛsɪv] *adj* (*governments*) сле́дующий оди́н за други́м

successor [sək'sɛsə'] *n* прее́мник(-ица); (*to throne*) насле́дник(-ица)

succumb [sə'kʌm] *vi* (*to temptation*) поддава́ться (*perf* подда́ться)

such [sʌtʃ] *adj* тако́й ▷ *adv*: **such a long trip** така́я дли́нная пое́здка; **such a book** така́я кни́га; **such books** таки́е кни́ги; **such a lot of** тако́е мно́жество +*gen*; **such as** (*like*) таки́е как; **as such** как таково́й; **such-and-such** *adj* таки́е-то и таки́е-то

suck [sʌk] *vt* (*bottle, sweet*) соса́ть (*impf*)

sudden ['sʌdn] *adj* внеза́пный; **all of a sudden** внеза́пно, вдруг; **suddenly** *adv* внеза́пно, ...

sudoku [su'dəuku:] *n* судо́ку *nt ind*

sue [su:] *vt* предъявля́ть (*perf* предъяви́ть) иск +*dat*

suede [sweɪd] *n* за́мша

suffer ['sʌfə'] *vt* (*hardship etc*) переноси́ть (*perf* перенести́); (*pain*) страда́ть (*impf*) от +*gen* ▷ *vi* (*person, results etc*) страда́ть (*perf* пострада́ть); **to suffer from** страда́ть (*impf*) +*instr*; **suffering** *n* (*hardship*) страда́ние

suffice [sə'faɪs] *vi*: **this suffices to ...** э́того доста́точно, ...

sufficient [sə'fɪʃənt] *adj* доста́точный

suffocate ['sʌfəkeɪt] *vi* задыха́ться (*perf* задохну́ться)

sugar ['ʃugə'] *n* са́хар

suggest [sə'dʒɛst] *vt* (*propose*) предлага́ть (*perf* предложи́ть); (*indicate*) предполага́ть (*perf* предположи́ть); **suggestion** [sə'dʒɛstʃən] *n* (*see vt*) предложе́ние; предположе́ние

suicide ['suɪsaɪd] *n* (*death*) самоуби́йство; *see also* **commit**

suit [su:t] *n* костю́м; (*Law*) иск; (*Cards*) масть *f* ▷ *vt* (*be convenient, appropriate*) подходи́ть (*perf* подойти́) +*dat*; (*colour, clothes*) идти́ (*impf*) +*dat*; **to suit sth to** (*adapt*) приспоса́бливать (*perf* приспосо́бить) что-н к +*dat*; **they are well suited** (*couple*) они́ хорошо́ друг дру́гу подхо́дят; **suitable** *adj* подходя́щий

suitcase ['su:tkeɪs] *n* чемода́н

suite [swi:t] *n* (*of rooms*) апартаме́нты *mpl*; (*furniture*): **bedroom/dining room suite** спа́льный/столо́вый гарниту́р

sulfur ['sʌlfə'] *n* (*US*) = **sulphur**

sulk [sʌlk] *vi* зло́бствовать (*impf*), ду́ться (*impf*) (*inf*)

sulphur ['sʌlfə'] (*US* **sulfur**) *n* се́ра

sultana [sʌl'tɑ:nə] *n* кишми́ш

sum [sʌm] *n* (*calculation*) арифме́тика, вычисле́ние; (*amount*) су́мма; **sum up** *vt* (*describe*) сумми́ровать (*impf/perf*) ▷ *vi* подводи́ть (*perf* подвести́) ито́г

summarize ['sʌməraɪz] *vt* сумми́ровать (*impf/perf*)

summary ['sʌmərɪ] *n* (*of essay etc*) кра́ткое изложе́ние

summer ['sʌmə'] *n* ле́то ▷ *adj* ле́тний; **in summer** ле́том; **summertime** *n* (*season*) ле́то, ле́тняя пора́

summit ['sʌmɪt] *n* (*of mountain*) верши́на, пик; (*also* **summit meeting**) встре́ча на вы́сшем у́ровне, са́ммит

sun [sʌn] *n* со́лнце; **sunbathe** *vi* загора́ть (*impf*); **sunburn** *n* со́лнечный ожо́г

Sunday ['sʌndɪ] *n* воскресе́нье

sunflower ['sʌnflauə'] *n* (*Bot*) подсо́лнечник

sung [sʌŋ] *pp of* **sing**

sunglasses ['sʌnglɑ:sɪz] *npl* солнцезащи́тные очки́ *pl*

sunk [sʌŋk] *pp of* **sink**

sun: sunlight *n* со́лнечный свет; **sunny** *adj* (*weather, place*) со́лнечный; **sunrise** *n* восхо́д (со́лнца); **sunset** *n* зака́т, захо́д (со́лнца); **sunshine** *n* со́лнечный свет; **in the sunshine** на со́лнце; **sunstroke** *n* со́лнечный уда́р; **suntan** *n* зага́р

super ['su:pə'] *adj* мирово́й, потряса́ющий

superb [su:'pə:b] *adj* превосхо́дный, великоле́пный

superficial [su:pə'fɪʃəl] *adj* пове́рхностный; (*wound*) лёгкий

superintendent [su:pərɪn'tɛndənt] *n* (*Police*) нача́льник

superior [su'pɪərɪə'] *adj* (*better*) лу́чший; (*more senior*) вышестоя́щий; (*smug*) высокоме́рный ▷ *n* нача́льник

supermarket ['su:pəmɑ:kɪt] *n* суперма́ркет, универса́м

supernatural [su:pə'nætʃərəl] *adj* сверхъесте́ственный

superpower ['su:pəpauə'] *n* (*Pol*) вели́кая держа́ва, сверхдержа́ва

superstition [suːpəˈstɪʃən] n суеве́рие
superstitious [suːpəˈstɪʃəs] adj суеве́рный
supervise [ˈsuːpəvaɪz] vt (person, activity) кури́ровать (impf); (dissertation) руководи́ть (impf)
supervision [suːpəˈvɪʒən] n руково́дство, надзо́р
supervisor [ˈsuːpəvaɪzəʳ] n (of workers) нача́льник; (Scol) нау́чный руководи́тель(ница) m(f)
supper [ˈsʌpəʳ] n у́жин
supple [ˈsʌpl] adj (person, body) ги́бкий; (leather) упру́гий
supplement [ˈsʌplɪmənt] n (of vitamins) доба́вка, дополне́ние; (of book, newspaper etc) приложе́ние ▷ vt добавля́ть (perf доба́вить) к +dat
supplier [səˈplaɪəʳ] n поставщи́к
supply [səˈplaɪ] n (see vt) поста́вка; снабже́ние; (stock) запа́с ▷ vt (goods) поставля́ть (perf поста́вить); (gas) снабжа́ть (perf снабди́ть); **to supply sb with sth** (see vt) поставля́ть (perf поста́вить) что-н кому́-н/чему́-н; снабжа́ть (perf снабди́ть) кого́-н/что-н чем-н; **supplies** npl (food) запа́сы mpl продово́льствия
support [səˈpɔːt] n (moral, financial etc) подде́ржка; (Tech) опо́ра ▷ vt (morally) подде́рживать (perf поддержа́ть); (financially: family etc) содержа́ть (impf); (football team etc) боле́ть (impf) за +acc; (hold up) подде́рживать (impf); (theory etc) подтвержда́ть (perf подтверди́ть); **supporter** n (Pol etc) сторо́нник(-ица); (Sport) боле́льщик(-ица)
suppose [səˈpəuz] vt полага́ть (impf), предполага́ть (perf предположи́ть); **he was supposed to do it** (duty) он до́лжен был э́то сде́лать; **supposedly** [səˈpəuzɪdlɪ] adv я́кобы
supposing [səˈpəuzɪŋ] conj предположим, допустим
suppress [səˈpres] vt (revolt) подавля́ть (perf подави́ть)
supreme [suˈpriːm] adj (in titles) Верхо́вный; (effort, achievement) велича́йший
surcharge [ˈsəːtʃɑːdʒ] n дополни́тельный сбор
sure [ʃuəʳ] adj (certain) уве́ренный; (reliable) ве́рный; **to make sure of sth/that** удостоверя́ться (perf удостове́риться) в чём-н/, что; **sure!** (okay) коне́чно!; **sure enough** и пра́вда or впра́вду; **surely** adv (certainly) наверняка́
surf [səːf] vt (Comput) ла́зить (impf) по +dat, серфи́ть (impf)
surface [ˈsəːfɪs] n пове́рхность f ▷ vi всплыва́ть (perf всплыть)
surfing [ˈsəːfɪŋ] n сёрфинг
surge [səːdʒ] n (increase) рост; (fig: of emotion) прили́в
surgeon [ˈsəːdʒən] n (Med) хиру́рг

surgery [ˈsəːdʒərɪ] n (treatment) хирурги́я, хирурги́ческое вмеша́тельство; (Brit: room) кабине́т; (: time) приём; **to undergo surgery** переноси́ть (perf перенести́) опера́цию
surname [ˈsəːneɪm] n фами́лия
surpass [səːˈpɑːs] vt (person, thing) превосходи́ть (perf превзойти́)
surplus [ˈsəːpləs] n (of trade, payments) акти́вное са́льдо nt ind ▷ adj (stock, grain) избы́точный
surprise [səˈpraɪz] n удивле́ние; (unexpected event) неожи́данность f ▷ vt (astonish) удивля́ть (perf удиви́ть); (catch unawares) застава́ть (perf заста́ть) враспло́х
surprising [səˈpraɪzɪŋ] adj (situation, announcement) неожи́данный; **surprisingly** adv удиви́тельно
surrender [səˈrɛndəʳ] n сда́ча, капитуля́ция ▷ vi (army, hijackers etc) сдава́ться (perf сда́ться)
surround [səˈraund] vt (subj: walls, hedge etc) окружа́ть (impf); (Mil, Police etc) окружа́ть (perf окружи́ть); **surrounding** adj (countryside) окружа́ющий, окре́стный; **surroundings** npl (place) окре́стности fpl; (conditions) окруже́ние ntsg
surveillance [səːˈveɪləns] n наблюде́ние
survey [vb səˈveɪ, n ˈsəːveɪ] vt (scene, work etc) осма́тривать (perf осмотре́ть) ▷ n (of land) геодези́ческая съёмка; (of house) инспе́кция; (of habits etc) обзо́р; **surveyor** [səˈveɪəʳ] n (of land) геодези́ст; (of house) инспе́ктор
survival [səˈvaɪvl] n выжива́ние
survive [səˈvaɪv] vi выжива́ть (perf вы́жить), уцеле́ть (perf); (custom etc) сохраня́ться (perf сохрани́ться) ▷ vt (person) пережива́ть (perf пережи́ть); (illness) переноси́ть (perf перенести́)
survivor [səˈvaɪvəʳ] n (of illness, accident) вы́живший(-ая) m(f) adj
suspect [vb səsˈpɛkt, n, adj ˈsʌspɛkt] vt подозрева́ть (impf) ▷ n подозрева́емый(-ая) m(f) adj ▷ adj подозри́тельный
suspend [səsˈpɛnd] vt (delay) приостана́вливать (perf приостанови́ть); (stop) прерыва́ть (perf прерва́ть); (from employment) отстраня́ть (perf отстрани́ть); **suspenders** npl (Brit) подвя́зки fpl; (US) подтя́жки fpl
suspense [səsˈpɛns] n трево́га, напряже́ние; **to keep sb in suspense** держа́ть (impf) кого́-н во взве́шенном состоя́нии
suspension [səsˈpɛnʃən] n (from job, team) отстране́ние; (Aut) амортиза́тор; (of payment) приостановле́ние
suspicion [səsˈpɪʃən] n подозре́ние
suspicious [səsˈpɪʃəs] adj подозри́тельный
sustain [səsˈteɪn] vt подде́рживать (perf поддержа́ть); (losses) нести́ (perf понести́);

(*injury*) получа́ть (*perf* получи́ть);
sustainable adj (*development, progress*)
стаби́льный, усто́йчивый
swallow ['swɔləʊ] n (*Zool*) ла́сточка ⊳ vt
(*food, pills*) глота́ть (*perf* проглоти́ть); (*fig*)
подавля́ть (*perf* подави́ть)
swam [swæm] pt of **swim**
swamp [swɔmp] n топь f ⊳ vt (*with
water*) залива́ть (*perf* зали́ть); (*fig: person*)
зава́ливать (*perf* завали́ть)
swan [swɔn] n ле́бедь m
swap [swɔp] n обме́н ⊳ vt: **to swap (for)**
(*exchange (for)*) меня́ть (*perf* обменя́ть)
(на +acc); (*replace (with)*) меня́ть (*perf*
поменя́ть) (на +acc)
swarm [swɔːm] n (*of bees*) рой; (*of
people*) тьма
sway [sweɪ] vi кача́ться (*perf* качну́ться)
⊳ vt: **to be swayed by** поддава́ться (*perf*
подда́ться) на +acc
swear [sweəʳ] (pt **swore**, pp **sworn**) vi
(*curse*) скверносло́вить (*impf*), руга́ться
(*perf* вы́ругаться) ⊳ vt кля́сться (*perf*
покля́сться)
sweat [swɛt] n пот ⊳ vi потеть (*perf*
вспоте́ть); **sweater** n сви́тер; **sweatshirt**
n спорти́вный сви́тер; **sweaty** adj
(*clothes*) пропоте́вший; (*hands*) по́тный
swede [swiːd] n (*Brit*) брю́ква
Sweden ['swiːdn] n Шве́ция
Swedish ['swiːdɪʃ] adj шве́дский; ⊳ npl:
the Swedish шве́ды
sweep [swiːp] (pt, pp **swept**) vt (*with
brush*) мести́ or подмета́ть (*perf* подмести́);
(*with arm*) сма́хивать (*perf* смахну́ть);
(*subj: current*) сноси́ть (*perf* снести́),
смыва́ть (*perf* смыть) ⊳ vi (*wind*)
бушева́ть (*impf*)
sweet [swiːt] n (*candy*) конфе́та; (*Brit:
Culin*) сла́дкое nt adj no pl, сла́дости fpl
⊳ adj сла́дкий; (*kind, attractive*) ми́лый;
sweet corn n кукуру́за
swell [swɛl] (pt **swelled**, pp **swollen** or
swelled) n (*of sea*) волне́ние ⊳ adj (*US:
inf*) мирово́й ⊳ vi (*numbers*) расти́ (*perf*
вы́расти); (*also swell up: face, ankle etc*)
опуха́ть (*perf* опу́хнуть), вздува́ться (*perf*
взду́ться); **swelling** n (*Med*) о́пухоль f,
взду́тие
swept [swɛpt] pt, pp of **sweep**
swift [swɪft] adj стреми́тельный
swim [swɪm] (pt **swam**, pp **swum**) vi
пла́вать/плыть (*impf*); (*as sport*) пла́вать
(*impf*); (*head*) идти́ (*perf* пойти́) кру́гом;
(*room*) плыть (*perf* поплы́ть) ⊳ vt
переплыва́ть (*perf* переплы́ть); (*a length*)
проплыва́ть (*perf* проплы́ть); **swimmer** n
пловец́-вчи́ка) n пла́вание;
swimming costume n (*Brit*) купа́льный
костю́м; **swimming pool** n пла́вательный
бассе́йн; **swimming trunks** npl пла́вки
pl; **swimsuit** n купа́льник
swing [swɪŋ] (pt, pp **swung**) n (*in
playground*) каче́ли pl; (*change: in

opinions etc) крен, поворо́т ⊳ vt (*arms*)
разма́хивать (*impf*) +instr; (*legs*) болта́ть
(*impf*) +instr; (*also swing round: vehicle
etc*) развора́чивать (*perf* разверну́ть) ⊳ vi
кача́ться (*impf*); (*also swing round:
vehicle etc*) развора́чиваться (*perf
развернуться); **to be in full swing** (*party
etc*) быть (*impf*) в по́лном разга́ре
swirl [swəːl] vi кружи́ться (*impf*)
Swiss [swɪs] adj швейца́рский
switch [swɪtʃ] n (*for light, radio etc*)
выключа́тель m; (*change*) переключе́ние
⊳ vt (*change*) переключа́ть (*perf*
переключи́ть); **switch off** vt выключа́ть
(*perf* вы́ключить); **switch on** vt включа́ть
(*perf* включи́ть); **switchboard** n (*Tel*)
коммута́тор
Switzerland ['swɪtsələnd] n Швейца́рия
swivel ['swɪvl] vi (*also swivel round*)
повора́чиваться (*impf*)
swollen ['swəʊlən] pp of **swell**
sword [sɔːd] n меч
swore [swɔːʳ] pt of **swear**
sworn [swɔːn] pp of **swear** ⊳ adj
(*statement, evidence*) да́нный под
прися́гой; (*enemy*) закля́тый
swum [swʌm] pp of **swim**
swung [swʌŋ] pt, pp of **swing**
syllable ['sɪləbl] n слог
syllabus ['sɪləbəs] n (*учебная*) програ́мма
symbol ['sɪmbl] n (*sign*) знак;
(*representation*) си́мвол; **symbolic(al)**
[sɪm'bɔlɪk(l)] adj символи́ческий
symmetrical [sɪ'mɛtrɪkl] adj
симметри́чный
symmetry ['sɪmɪtrɪ] n симме́трия
sympathetic [sɪmpə'θɛtɪk] adj (*person*)
уча́стливый; (*remark, opinion*)
сочу́вственный; (*likeable: character*)
прия́тный, симпати́чный; **to be
sympathetic to(wards)** (*supportive of*)
сочу́вствовать (*impf*) +dat
sympathize ['sɪmpəθaɪz] vi: **to sympathize
with** сочу́вствовать (*impf*) +dat
sympathy ['sɪmpəθɪ] n (*pity*) сочу́вствие,
уча́стие; **with our deepest sympathy** с
глубоча́йшими соболе́знованиями; **to
come out in sympathy** (*workers*) бастова́ть
(*impf*) в знак солида́рности
symphony ['sɪmfənɪ] n симфо́ния
symptom ['sɪmptəm] n симпто́м
synagogue ['sɪnəgɔg] n синаго́га
syndicate ['sɪndɪkɪt] n (*of people,
businesses*) синдика́т
syndrome ['sɪndrəʊm] n синдро́м
synonym ['sɪnənɪm] n сино́ним
synthetic [sɪn'θɛtɪk] adj (*materials*)
синтети́ческий, иску́сственный
syringe [sɪ'rɪndʒ] n шприц
syrup ['sɪrəp] n (*juice*) сиро́п; (*also
golden syrup*) (све́тлая or же́лтая) па́тока
system ['sɪstəm] n систе́ма; **systematic**
[sɪstə'mætɪk] adj системати́ческий

ta [tɑː] *excl* (*Brit: inf*) спаси́бо

table ['teɪbl] *n* (*furniture*) стол; (*Math, Chem etc*) табли́ца; **to lay** *or* **set the table** накрыва́ть (*perf* накры́ть) на стол; **table of contents** оглавле́ние; **tablecloth** *n* ска́терть *f*; **table lamp** *n* насто́льная ла́мпа; **tablemat** *n* подста́вка (*под столовые приборы*); **tablespoon** *n* столо́вая ло́жка

tablet ['tæblɪt] *n* (*Comput*) планше́т

table tennis *n* насто́льный те́ннис

tabloid ['tæblɔɪd] *n* табло́ид, малоформа́тная газе́та

- **TABLOID**
-
- Так называ́ют популя́рные
- малоформа́тные газе́ты. Они́ содержа́т
- мно́го фотогра́фий, больши́е заголо́вки
- и коро́ткие статьи́. Табло́иды освеща́ют
- сканда́льные исто́рии, жизнь звёзд
- шо́у-би́знеса и спорти́вные но́вости.

taboo [tə'buː] *n* табу́ *nt ind* ▷ *adj* запрещённый

tack [tæk] *n* (*nail*) гвоздь *m* с широ́кой шля́пкой

tackle ['tækl] *n* (*for fishing etc*) снасть *f*; (*for lifting*) сло́жный блок; (*Sport*) блокиро́вка ▷ *vt* (*difficulty*) справля́ться (*perf* спра́виться) с +*instr*; (*fight, challenge*) схвати́ться (*perf*) с +*instr*; (*Sport*) блокиро́вать (*impf/perf*)

tacky ['tækɪ] *adj* (*sticky*) ли́пкий; (*pej: cheap*) дешёвый

tact [tækt] *n* такт, такти́чность *f*; **tactful** *adj* такти́чный

tactics ['tæktɪks] *npl* та́ктика *fsg*

tactless ['tæktlɪs] *adj* беста́ктный

tag [tæg] *n* (*label*) этике́тка, ярлы́к

tail [teɪl] *n* (*of animal, plane*) хвост; (*of shirt*) коне́ц; (*of coat*) пола́ ▷ *vt* сади́ться

(*perf* сесть) на хвост +*dat*; **tails** *npl* (*suit*) фрак *msg*

tailor ['teɪləʳ] *n* (мужско́й) портно́й *m adj*

take [teɪk] (*pt* **took**, *pp* **taken**) *vt* брать (*perf* взять); (*photo, measures*) снима́ть (*perf* снять); (*shower, decision, drug*) принима́ть (*perf* приня́ть); (*notes*) де́лать (*perf* сде́лать); (*grab: sb's arm etc*) хвата́ть (*perf* схвати́ть); (*require: courage, time*) тре́бовать (*perf* потре́бовать); (*tolerate: pain etc*) переноси́ть (*perf* перенести́); (*hold: passengers etc*) вмеща́ть (*perf* вмести́ть); (*on foot: person*) отводи́ть (*perf* отвести́); (: *thing*) относи́ть (*perf* отнести́); (*by transport: person, thing*) отвози́ть (*perf* отвезти́); (*exam*) сдава́ть (*perf* сдать); **to take sth from** (*drawer etc*) вынима́ть (*perf* вы́нуть) что-н из +*gen*; (*steal from: person*) брать (*perf* взять) что-н у +*gen*; **I take it that ...** как я понима́ю, ...; **take apart** *vt* разбира́ть (*perf* разобра́ть); **take away** *vt* (*remove*) убира́ть (*perf* убра́ть); (*carry off*) забира́ть (*perf* забра́ть); (*Math*) отнима́ть (*perf* отня́ть); **take back** *vt* (*return: thing*) относи́ть (*perf* отнести́) обра́тно; (: *person*) отводи́ть (*perf* отвести́) обра́тно; (*one's words*) брать (*perf* взять) наза́д; **take down** *vt* (*building*) сноси́ть (*perf* снести́); (*note*) запи́сывать (*perf* записа́ть); **take in** *vt* (*deceive*) обма́нывать (*perf* обману́ть); (*understand*) воспринима́ть (*perf* восприня́ть); (*lodger, orphan*) брать (*perf* взять); **take off** *vi* (*Aviat*) взлета́ть (*perf* взлете́ть) ▷ *vt* (*remove*) снима́ть (*perf* снять); **take on** *vt* (*work, employee*) брать (*perf* взять); (*opponent*) сража́ться (*perf* срази́ться) с +*instr*; **take out** *vt* (*invite*) води́ть/вести́ (*perf* повести́) в; (*remove*) вынима́ть (*perf* вы́нуть); **to take sth out of** (*drawer, pocket etc*) вынима́ть (*perf* вы́нуть) что-н из +*gen*; **don't take your anger out on me!** не вымеща́й свой гнев на мне!; **take over** *vt* (*business*) поглоща́ть (*perf* поглоти́ть); (*country*) захва́тывать (*perf* захвати́ть) власть в +*prp* ▷ *vi*: **to take over from sb** сменя́ть (*perf* смени́ть) кого́-н; **take to** *vt fus*: **she took to him at once** он ей сра́зу понра́вился; **take up** *vt* (*hobby*) заня́ться (*perf*) +*instr*; (*job*) бра́ться (*perf* взя́ться) за +*acc*; (*idea, story*) подхва́тывать (*perf* подхвати́ть); (*time, space*) занима́ть (*perf* заня́ть); **I'll take you up on that!** ловлю́ Вас на сло́ве!; **takeaway** *n* (*Brit: food*) еда́ на вы́нос; **takeoff** *n* (*Aviat*) взлёт; **takeover** *n* (*Comm*) поглоще́ние

takings ['teɪkɪŋz] *npl* (*Comm*) вы́ручка *fsg*

tale [teɪl] *n* расска́з; **to tell tales** (*fig*) я́бедничать (*perf* ная́бедничать)

talent ['tælnt] *n* тала́нт; **talented** *adj* тала́нтливый

talk [tɔːk] *n* (*speech*) докла́д;

(*conversation, interview*) бесе́да, разгово́р; (*gossip*) разгово́ры *mpl* ▷ *vi* (*speak*) говори́ть (*impf*); (*to sb*) разгова́ривать (*impf*); **talks** *npl* (*Pol etc*) перегово́ры *pl*; **to talk about** говори́ть (*perf* поговори́ть *or* разгова́ривать *impf* о (+*prp*); **to talk sb into doing** угова́ривать (*perf* уговори́ть) кого́-н +*infin*; **to talk sb out of sth** отгова́ривать (*perf* отговори́ть) кого́-н от чего́-н; **to talk shop** говори́ть (*impf*) о дела́х; **talk over** *vt* (*problem*) обгова́ривать (*perf* обговори́ть)

tall [tɔ:l] *adj* высо́кий; **he is 6 feet tall** его́ рост — 6 фу́тов

tambourine [tæmbə'ri:n] *n* (*Mus*) тамбури́н, бу́бен

tame [teɪm] *adj* ручно́й; (*fig*) вя́лый

tampon ['tæmpɔn] *n* тампо́н

tan [tæn] *n* (*also* **suntan**) зага́р

tandem ['tændəm] *n* (*cycle*) танде́м; **in tandem** (*together*) совме́стно, вме́сте

tangerine [tændʒə'ri:n] *n* мандари́н

tank [tæŋk] *n* (*water tank*) бак; (: *large*) цисте́рна; (*for fish*) аква́риум; (*Mil*) танк

tanker ['tæŋkə^r] *n* (*ship*) та́нкер; (*truck, Rail*) цисте́рна

tanned [tænd] *adj* загоре́лый

tantrum ['tæntrəm] *n* исте́рика

tap [tæp] *n* (водопрово́дный) кран; (*gentle blow*) стук ▷ *vt* (*hit*) стуча́ть (*perf* постуча́ть) по +*dat*; (*resources*) испо́льзовать (*impf/perf*); (*telephone, conversation*) прослу́шивать (*impf*)

tape [teɪp] *n* (*also* **magnetic tape**) (магни́тная) плёнка; (*cassette*) кассе́та; (*sticky tape*) кле́йкая ле́нта ▷ *vt* (*record*) запи́сывать (*perf* записа́ть); (*stick*) закле́ивать (*perf* закле́ить) кле́йкой ле́нтой; **tape recorder** *n* магнитофо́н

tapestry ['tæpɪstrɪ] *n* (*object*) гобеле́н

tar [tɑ:] *n* дёготь *m*

target ['tɑ:gɪt] *n* цель *f*

tariff ['tærɪf] *n* (*on goods*) тари́ф; (*Brit*: *in hotels etc*) прейскура́нт

tarmac ['tɑ:mæk] *n* (*Brit*: *on road*) асфа́льт

tart [tɑ:t] *n* (*Culin*: *large*) пиро́г ▷ *adj* (*flavour*) те́рпкий

tartan ['tɑ:tn] *adj* (*rug, scarf etc*) кле́тчатый

task [tɑ:sk] *n* зада́ча; **to take sb to task** отчи́тывать (*perf* отчита́ть) кого́-н

taste [teɪst] *n* вкус; (*sample*) про́ба; (*fig*: *glimpse, idea*) представле́ние ▷ *vt* про́бовать (*perf* попро́бовать) ▷ *vi*: **to taste of** *or* **like** име́ть (*impf*) вкус +*gen*; **you can taste the garlic (in the dish)** (в блю́де) чу́вствуется чесно́к; **in bad/good taste** в дурно́м/хоро́шем вку́се; **tasteful** *adj* элега́нтный; **tasteless** *adj* безвку́сный

tasty ['teɪstɪ] *adj* (*food*) вку́сный

tatters ['tætəz] *npl*: **in tatters** (*clothes*) изо́рванный в кло́чья

tattoo [tə'tu:] *n* (*on skin*) татуиро́вка

taught [tɔ:t] *pt, pp of* **teach**

taunt [tɔ:nt] *n* издева́тельство ▷ *vt* (*person*) издева́ться (*impf*) над +*instr*

Taurus ['tɔ:rəs] *n* Теле́ц

taut [tɔ:t] *adj* (*thread etc*) туго́й; (*skin*) упру́гий

tax [tæks] *n* нало́г ▷ *vt* (*earnings, goods etc*) облага́ть (*perf* обложи́ть) нало́гом; (*fig*: *memory, patience*) напряга́ть (*perf* напря́чь); **tax-free** *adj* (*goods, services*) не облага́емый нало́гом

taxi ['tæksɪ] *n* такси́ *nt ind*

taxpayer ['tækspeɪə^r] *n* налогоплате́льщик(-щица)

TB *n abbr* = **tuberculosis**

tea [ti:] *n* чай; (*Brit*: *meal*) у́жин; **high tea** (*Brit*) (по́здний) обе́д

teach [ti:tʃ] (*pt, pp* **taught**) *vi* преподава́ть (*impf*) ▷ *vt*: **to teach sb sth, teach sth to sb** учи́ть (*perf* научи́ть) кого́-н чему́-н; (*in school*) преподава́ть (*impf*) что-н кому́-н; **teacher** *n* учи́тель(ница) *m(f)*; **teaching** *n* (*work*) преподава́ние

team [ti:m] *n* (*of people*) кома́нда

teapot ['ti:pɔt] *n* (зава́рочный) ча́йник

tear¹ [tɛə^r] (*pt* **tore**, *pp* **torn**) *n* дыра́, ды́рка ▷ *vt* (*rip*) рвать (*perf* порва́ть) ▷ *vi* (*rip*) рва́ться (*perf* порва́ться)

tear² [tɪə^r] *n* слеза́; **in tears** в слеза́х; **tearful** *adj* запла́канный

tease [ti:z] *vt* дразни́ть (*impf*)

teaspoon ['ti:spu:n] *n* ча́йная ло́жка

teatime ['ti:taɪm] *n* у́жин

tea towel *n* (*Brit*) посу́дное полоте́нце

technical ['tɛknɪkl] *adj* (*terms, advances*) техни́ческий

technician [tɛk'nɪʃən] *n* те́хник

technique [tɛk'ni:k] *n* те́хника

technology [tɛk'nɔlədʒɪ] *n* те́хника; (*in particular field*) техноло́гия

teddy (bear) ['tɛdɪ(-)] *n* (плю́шевый) ми́шка

tedious ['ti:dɪəs] *adj* ну́дный

tee [ti:] *n* подста́вка для мяча́ (в го́льфе)

teenage ['ti:neɪdʒ] *adj* (*problems*) подростко́вый; (*fashion*) тине́йджеровский; **teenage children** подро́стки *mpl*; **teenager** *n* подро́сток, тине́йджер

teens [ti:nz] *npl*: **to be in one's teens** быть (*impf*) в подростко́вом во́зрасте

teeth [ti:θ] *npl of* **tooth**

teetotal ['ti:'təutl] *adj* непью́щий, тре́звый

telecommunications ['tɛlɪkə-mju:nɪ'keɪʃənz] *n* телекоммуника́ции *fpl*

telegram ['tɛlɪɡræm] *n* телегра́мма

telephone ['tɛlɪfəun] *n* телефо́н ▷ *vt* (*person*) звони́ть (*perf* позвони́ть) +*dat*; **he is on the telephone** (*talking*) он говори́т по телефо́ну; **are you on the telephone?** (*possessing phone*) у Вас есть телефо́н?; **telephone call** *n* телефо́нный звоно́к; **there is a telephone call for Peter** Пи́тера про́сят к телефо́ну; **telephone directory** n телефо́нный спра́вочник; **telephone number** n но́мер телефо́на, телефо́н (inf)

telesales ['tɛlɪseɪlz] n телефо́нная рекла́ма

telescope ['tɛlɪskəup] n телеско́п

television ['tɛlɪvɪʒən] n телеви́дение; (set) телеви́зор; **on television** по телеви́дению

tell [tɛl] (pt, pp **told**) vt (say) говори́ть (perf сказа́ть); (relate) расска́зывать (perf рассказа́ть); (distinguish): **to tell sth from** отлича́ть (perf отличи́ть) что-н от +gen ▷ vi (have an effect): **to tell (on)** ска́зываться (perf сказа́ться) (на +prp); **to tell sb to do** говори́ть (perf сказа́ть) кому́-н +infin; **tell off** vt: **to tell sb off** отчи́тывать (perf отчита́ть) кого́-н; **teller** n (in bank) касси́р

telly ['tɛlɪ] n abbr (Brit: inf) (= **television**) те́лик

temper ['tɛmpəʳ] n (nature) нрав; (mood) настрое́ние; (fit of anger) гнев; **to be in a temper** быть (impf) в раздражённом состоя́нии; **to lose one's temper** выходи́ть (perf вы́йти) из себя́

temperament ['tɛmprəmənt] n темпера́мент; **temperamental** [tɛmprə'mɛntl] adj темпера́ментный; (fig) капри́зный

temperature ['tɛmprətʃəʳ] n температу́ра; **he has** or **is running a temperature** у него́ температу́ра, он температу́рит (inf)

temple ['tɛmpl] n (Rel) храм; (Anat) висо́к

temporary ['tɛmpərərɪ] adj вре́менный

tempt [tɛmpt] vt соблазня́ть (perf соблазни́ть), искуша́ть (impf); **to tempt sb into doing** соблазня́ть (perf соблазни́ть) кого́-н +infin; **temptation** [tɛmp'teɪʃən] n собла́зн, искуше́ние; **tempting** adj (offer) соблазни́тельный

ten [tɛn] n де́сять

tenant ['tɛnənt] n съёмщик(-мщица)

tend [tɛnd] vt (crops, patient) уха́живать (impf) за +instr ▷ vi: **to tend to do** име́ть (impf) скло́нность +infin

tendency ['tɛndənsɪ] n (habit) скло́нность f; (trend) тенде́нция

tender ['tɛndəʳ] adj не́жный; (sore) чувстви́тельный ▷ n (Comm: offer) предложе́ние ▷ vt (apology) приноси́ть (perf принести́); **legal tender** (money) зако́нное платёжное сре́дство; **to tender one's resignation** подава́ть (perf пода́ть) в отста́вку

tendon ['tɛndən] n сухожи́лие

tennis ['tɛnɪs] n те́ннис

tenor ['tɛnəʳ] n (Mus) те́нор

tense [tɛns] adj напряжённый

tension ['tɛnʃən] n напряже́ние

tent [tɛnt] n пала́тка

tentative ['tɛntətɪv] adj (person, smile) осторо́жный; (conclusion, plans) сде́ржанный

tenth [tɛnθ] adj деся́тый ▷ n (fraction) одна́ деся́тая f adj

tepid ['tɛpɪd] adj (liquid) теплова́тый

term [tə:m] n (expression) те́рмин; (period in power etc) срок; (Scol: in school) че́тверть f; (: at university) триме́стр ▷ vt (call) называ́ть (perf назва́ть); **terms** npl (conditions) усло́вия ntpl; **in abstract terms** в абстра́ктных выраже́ниях; **in the short term** в ближа́йшем бу́дущем; **in the long term** в перспекти́ве; **to be on good terms with sb** быть (impf) в хоро́ших отноше́ниях с кем-н; **to come to terms with** примиря́ться (perf примири́ться) с +instr

terminal ['tə:mɪnl] adj неизлечи́мый ▷ n (Elec) кле́мма, зажи́м; (Comput) термина́л; (also **air terminal**) аэровокза́л, термина́л; (Brit: also **coach terminal**) авто́бусный вокза́л

terminate ['tə:mɪneɪt] vt прекраща́ть (perf прекрати́ть)

terminology [tə:mɪ'nɔlədʒɪ] n терминоло́гия

terrace ['tɛrəs] n терра́са; **the terraces** (Brit: standing areas) трибу́ны fpl; **terraced** adj (garden) терра́сный; **terraced house** дом в ряду́ примыка́ющих друг к дру́гу одноти́пных домо́в

terrain [tɛ'reɪn] n ландша́фт

terrible ['tɛrɪbl] adj ужа́сный

terribly ['tɛrɪblɪ] adv ужа́сно

terrific [tə'rɪfɪk] adj (thunderstorm, speed etc) колосса́льный; (time, party etc) потряса́ющий

terrify ['tɛrɪfaɪ] vt ужаса́ть (perf ужасну́ть)

territorial [tɛrɪ'tɔ:rɪəl] adj территориа́льный

territory ['tɛrɪtərɪ] n террито́рия; (fig) о́бласть f

terror ['tɛrəʳ] n у́жас; **terrorism** n террори́зм; **terrorist** n террори́ст(ка)

test [tɛst] n (trial, check) прове́рка, тест; (of courage etc) испыта́ние; (Med) ана́лиз; (Chem) о́пыт; (Scol) контро́льная рабо́та, тест; (also **driving test**) экза́мен на води́тельские права́ ▷ vt проверя́ть (perf прове́рить); (courage) испы́тывать (perf испыта́ть); (Med) анализи́ровать (perf проанализи́ровать)

testicle ['tɛstɪkl] n яи́чко

testify ['tɛstɪfaɪ] vi (Law) дава́ть (perf дать) показа́ния; **to testify to sth** свиде́тельствовать (impf) о чём-н

testimony ['tɛstɪmənɪ] n (Law) показа́ние, свиде́тельство; (clear proof): **to be (a) testimony to** явля́ться (perf яви́ться) свиде́тельством +gen

test tube n проби́рка

text [tɛkst] n текст; (*on mobile phone*)
SMS nt ▷ vt писа́ть (*perf* написа́ть)
SMS; **textbook** n учéбник; **text
message** n тéкстовое сообщéние,
SMS nt ind

texture [ˈtɛkstʃəʳ] n (*structure*) строéние,
структу́ра; (*feel*) факту́ра

than [ðæn] conj чем; (*with numerals*)
бóльше +gen, бóлее +gen; **I have less
work than you** у меня́ мéньше рабóты,
чем у Вас; **more than once** не раз; **more
than three times** бóлее or бóльше трёх
раз

thank [θæŋk] vt благодари́ть (*perf*
поблагодари́ть); **thank you (very much)**
(большóе) спаси́бо; **thank God!** слáва
Бóгу!; **thanks** npl благодáрность fsg
▷ excl спаси́бо; **many thanks, thanks a lot**
большóе спаси́бо; **thanks to** благодаря́
+dat

 KEYWORD

that [ðæt] (*pl* **those**) adj (*demonstrative*)
тот (*f* та, *nt* то); **that man** тот мужчи́на;
**which book would you like? — that one
over there** каку́ю кни́гу Вы хоти́те? —
вон ту; **I like this film better than that one**
мне э́тот фильм нрáвится бóльше, чем
тот
▷ pron **1** (*demonstrative*) э́то; **who's/
what's that?** кто/что э́то?; **is that you?**
э́то Вы?; **we talked of this and that**
мы говори́ли об э́том и о том or сём;
that's what he said вот что он сказáл;
what happened after that? а что
произошлó пóсле э́того?; **that is (to say)**
то есть
2 (*direct object*) котóрый (*f* котóрую, *nt*
котóрое, *pl* котóрые) (*indirect object*)
котóрому (*f* котóрой, *pl* котóрым) (*after
prep*: +acc) котóрый (*f* котóрую, *nt*
котóрое, *pl* котóрые) (: +gen) котóрого
(*f* котóрой, *pl* котóрых) (: +dat) котóрому
(*f* котóрой, *pl* котóрым) (: +instr) котóрым
(*f* котóрой, *pl* котóрыми) (: +prp) котóром
(*f* котóрой, *pl* котóрых); **the theory that
we discussed** теóрия, кото́рую мы
обсуждáли; **all (that) I have** всё, что у
меня́ есть
3 (*of time*) когдá; **the day (that) he died**
день, когдá он умер
▷ conj что; (*introducing purpose*) чтóбы;
he thought that I was ill он ду́мал, что я
был бóлен; **she suggested that I phone
you** онá предложи́ла, чтóбы я Вам
позвони́л
▷ adv (*demonstrative*): **I can't work that
much** я не могу́ так мнóго рабóтать; **it
can't be that bad** не так уж всё плóхо; **the
wall's about this high** стенá приме́рно вот
такóй высоты́

thaw [θɔ:] n óттепель f

 KEYWORD

the [ði:, ðə] def art **1**: **the books/children
are at home** кни́ги/дéти дóма; **the rich and
the poor** богáтые pl adj и бéдные pl adj; **to
attempt the impossible** (*perf*
попытáться) сдéлать невозмóжное
2 (*in titles*): **Elizabeth the First** Елизавéта
Пéрвая
3 (*in comparisons*): **the more ... the more**
... чем бóльше ..., тем бóльше ...; (+adj)
чем бóлее ..., тем бóлее ...

theatre [ˈθɪətəʳ] (*US* **theater**) n теáтр;
(*Med*: also **operating theatre**)
операцио́нная f adj

theft [θɛft] n крáжа

their [ðɛəʳ] adj их; (*referring to subject of
sentence*) свой; *see also* **my**; **theirs** pron
их; (*referring to subject of sentence*) свой;
see also **mine¹**

them [ðɛm] pron (*direct*) их; (*indirect*) им;
(*after prep*: +gen, +prp) них; (: +dat) ним;
(: +instr) ни́ми; **a few of them** нéкоторые
из них; **give me a few of them** дáйте мне
нéсколько из них; *see also* **me**

theme [θi:m] n тéма

themselves [ðəmˈsɛlvz] pl pron
(*reflexive*) себя́; (*emphatic*) сáми; (*after
prep*: +gen) себя́; (: +dat, +prp) себé;
(: +instr) собóй; (*alone*): **(all) by themselves**
одни́; **they shared the money between
themselves** они́ раздели́ли дéньги мéжду
собóй; *see also* **myself**

then [ðɛn] adv потóм; (*at that time*) тогдá
▷ conj (*therefore*) тогдá ▷ adj (*at the time*)
тогдáшний; **from then on** с тех пор; **by
then** к тому́ врéмени; **if ... then ...** éсли ...
то ...

theology [θɪˈɔlədʒɪ] n теолóгия,
богослóвие

theory [ˈθɪərɪ] n теóрия; **in theory**
теорети́чески

therapist [ˈθɛrəpɪst] n врач

therapy [ˈθɛrəpɪ] n терапи́я

 KEYWORD

there [ðɛəʳ] adv **1**: **there is some milk in
the fridge** в холоди́льнике есть молокó;
there is someone in the room в кóмнате
ктó-то есть; **there were many problems**
бы́ло мнóго проблéм; **there will be a lot of
people at the concert** на концéрте бу́дет
мнóго нарóду; **there was a book/there
were flowers on the table** на столé лежáла
кни́га/стоя́ли цветы́; **there has been an
accident** произошлá авáрия
2 (*referring to place: motion*) тудá;
(: *position*) там; (: *closer*) тут; **I agree
with you there** тут or в э́том я с тобóй
соглáсен; **there you go!** (*inf*) вот!;
there he is! вот он!; **get out of there!**
уходи́ оттýда!

thereabouts [ˈðɛərəˈbauts] adv (place) поблизости; (amount) около этого

thereafter [ðɛərˈɑːftəʳ] adv с того времени

thereby [ˈðɛəbaɪ] adv таким образом

therefore [ˈðɛəfɔːʳ] adv поэтому

there's [ˈðɛəz] = there is; there has

thermal [ˈθəːml] adj (springs) горячий; (underwear) утеплённый

thermometer [θəˈmɔmɪtəʳ] n термометр, градусник

these [ðiːz] pl adj, pron эти

thesis [ˈθiːsɪs] (pl theses) n (Scol) диссертация

they [ðeɪ] pron они; they say that ... говорят, что ...; they'd = they had; they would; they'll = they shall; they will; they're = they are; they've = they have

thick [θɪk] adj (in shape) толстый; (in consistency) густой; (inf: stupid) тупой ▷ n: in the thick of the battle в самой гуще битвы; the wall is 20 cm thick толщина стены — 20 см; **thicken** vi (plot) усложниться (perf усложниться) ▷ vt (sauce etc) делать (perf сделать) гуще; **thickness** n (size) толщина

thief [θiːf] (pl thieves) n вор(овка)

thigh [θaɪ] n бедро

thin [θɪn] adj тонкий; (person, animal) худой; (soup, sauce) жидкий ▷ vt: to thin (down) (sauce, paint) разбавлять (perf разбавить)

thing [θɪŋ] n вещь f; **things** npl (belongings) вещи fpl; **poor thing** бедняжка m/f; the best thing would be to ... самое лучшее было бы +infin ...; how are things? как дела?

think [θɪŋk] (pt, pp thought) vt (reflect, believe) думать (impf); to think of (come up with) приводить (perf привести); (consider) думать (perf подумать) о +prp; **what did you think of them?** что Вы о них думаете?; to think about думать (perf подумать) о +prp; I'll think about it я подумаю об этом; I am thinking of starting a business я думаю начать бизнес; I think so/not я думаю, что да/нет; to think well of sb думать (impf) о ком-н хорошо; **think over** vt обдумывать (perf обдумать); **think up** vt придумывать (perf придумать)

third [θəːd] adj третий ▷ n (fraction) треть f, одна третья f adj; (Aut: also third gear) третья скорость f; (Brit: Scol) диплом третьей степени; **thirdly** adv в-третьих; **Third World** n: the Third World Третий мир

thirst [θəːst] n жажда; **thirsty** adj: I am thirsty я хочу or мне хочется пить

thirteen [θəːˈtiːn] n тринадцать; **thirteenth** adj тринадцатый

thirtieth [ˈθəːtɪɪθ] adj тридцатый

thirty [ˈθəːtɪ] n тридцать

KEYWORD

this [ðɪs] (pl these) adj (demonstrative) этот (f эта, nt это); this man этот мужчина; which book would you like? — this one please какую книгу Вы хотите? — вот эту, пожалуйста
▷ pron (demonstrative) этот (f эта, nt это); who/what is this? кто/что это?; this is where I live вот здесь я живу; this is what he said вот, что он сказал; this is Mr Brown это мистер Браун
▷ adv (demonstrative): this high/long вот такой высоты/длины; the dog was about this big собака была вот такая большая; we can't stop now we've gone this far теперь, когда мы так далеко зашли, мы не можем остановиться

thistle [ˈθɪsl] n чертополох

thorn [θɔːn] n шип, колючка

thorough [ˈθʌrə] adj (search, wash) тщательный; (knowledge, research) основательный; (person) скрупулёзный; **thoroughly** adv полностью, тщательно; (very: satisfied) совершенно вполне; (: ashamed) совершенно

those [ðəuz] pl adj, pron те

though [ðəu] conj хотя ▷ adv впрочем, однако

thought [θɔːt] pt, pp of think ▷ n мысль f; (reflection) размышление; (opinion) соображение; **thoughtful** adj (deep in thought) задумчивый; (serious) подуманный, глубокий; (considerate) внимательный; **thoughtless** adj бездумный

thousand [ˈθauzənd] n тысяча; two thousand две тысячи; five thousand пять тысяч; thousands of тысячи +gen; **thousandth** adj тысячный

thrash [θræʃ] vt пороть (perf выпороть); (inf: defeat) громить (perf разгромить)

thread [θrɛd] n (yarn) нить f, нитка; (of screw) резьба; (Comput) ветка дискуссии ▷ vt (needle) продевать (perf продеть) нитку в +acc

threat [θrɛt] n угроза; **threaten** vi (storm, danger) грозить (impf) ▷ vt: to threaten sb with угрожать (impf) or грозить (pringrozить perf) кому-н +instr; to threaten to do угрожать (impf) or грозить (пригрозить perf) +infin

three [θriː] n три; **three-dimensional** adj (object) трёхмерный; **three-piece suite** n мягкая мебель f

threshold [ˈθrɛʃhəuld] n порог

threw [θruː] pt of throw

thrill [θrɪl] n (excitement) восторг; (fear) трепет ▷ vt приводить (perf привести) в трепет, восхищать (perf восхитить); to be thrilled быть (impf) в восторге; **thriller** n триллер; **thrilling** adj захватывающий

throat [θrəut] n горло; I have a sore

throat у меня болит горло
throne [θrəun] n трон
through [θru:] prep (space) через +acc; (time) в течение +gen; (by means of) через +acc, посредством +gen; (because of) из-за +gen ▷ adj (ticket, train) прямой ▷ adv насквозь; **he is absent through illness** он отсутствовал по болезни; **to put sb through to sb** (Tel) соединять (perf соединить) кого-н с кем-н; **to be through with** покончить (perf) с +instr; "**no through road**" (Brit) "нет сквозного проезда"; **throughout** prep (place) по +dat; (time) в течение +gen ▷ adv везде, повсюду
throw [θrəu] (pt **threw**, pp **thrown**) n бросок ▷ vt (object) бросать (perf бросить); (fig: person) сбивать (perf сбить) с толку; **to throw a party** закатывать (perf закатить) вечер; **throw away** vt (rubbish) выбрасывать (perf выбросить); (money) бросать (impf) на ветер; **throw off** vt сбрасывать (perf сбросить); **throw out** vt (rubbish, person) выбрасывать (perf выбросить); (idea) отвергать (perf отвергнуть); **throw up** vi (vomit): **he threw up** его вырвало
thrush [θrʌʃ] n (Zool) дрозд
thrust [θrʌst] (pt, pp **thrust**) n (Tech) движущая сила ▷ vt толкать (perf толкнуть)
thud [θʌd] n глухой стук
thug [θʌg] n (criminal) хулиган
thumb [θʌm] n (Anat) большой палец (кисти) ▷ vt: **to thumb a lift** (inf) голосовать (impf) (на дороге)
thump [θʌmp] n (blow) удар; (sound) глухой стук ▷ vt (person) стукнуть (perf) ▷ vi (heart etc) стучать (impf)
thunder [ˈθʌndəʳ] n гром; **thunderstorm** n гроза
Thursday [ˈθəːzdɪ] n четверг
thus [ðʌs] adv итак, таким образом
thwart [θwɔːt] vt (person) чинить (impf) препятствия +dat; (plans) расстраивать (perf расстроить)
thyme [taɪm] n тимьян, чабрец
tick [tɪk] n (of clock) тиканье; (mark) галочка, птичка; (Zool) клещ ▷ vi (clock) тикать (impf) ▷ vt отмечать (perf отметить) галочкой; **in a tick** (Brit: inf) мигом
ticket [ˈtɪkɪt] n билет; (price tag) этикетка; (also **parking ticket**) штраф за нарушение правил парковки
tickle [ˈtɪkl] vt щекотать (perf пощекотать) ▷ vi щекотать (impf)
ticklish [ˈtɪklɪʃ] adj (problem) щекотливый; (person): **to be ticklish** бояться (impf) щекотки
tide [taɪd] n (in sea) прилив и отлив; (fig: of events) волна; (of fashion, opinion) направление; **high tide** полная вода, высшая точка прилива; **low tide** малая

вода, низшая точка отлива; **tide over** vt: **this money will tide me over till Monday** на эти деньги я смогу продержаться до понедельника
tidy [ˈtaɪdɪ] adj опрятный; (mind) аккуратный ▷ vt (also **tidy up**) прибирать (perf прибрать)
tie [taɪ] n (string etc) шнурок; (Brit: also **necktie**) галстук; (fig: link) связь f; (Sport) ничья ▷ vt завязывать (perf завязать) ▷ vi (Sport) играть (perf сыграть) вничью; **to tie sth in a bow** завязывать (perf завязать) что-н бантом; **to tie a knot in sth** завязывать (perf завязать) что-н узлом; **tie up** vt (dog, boat) привязывать (perf привязать); (prisoner, parcel) связывать (perf связать); **I'm tied up at the moment** (busy) сейчас я занят
tier [tɪəʳ] n (of stadium etc) ярус; (of cake) слой
tiger [ˈtaɪgəʳ] n тигр
tight [taɪt] adj (rope) тугой; (shoes, bend, clothes) узкий; (security) усиленный; (schedule, budget) жёсткий ▷ adv (hold, squeeze) крепко; (shut) плотно; **money is tight** у меня туго с деньгами; **tighten** vt (rope) натягивать (perf натянуть); (screw) затягивать (perf затянуть); (grip) сжимать (perf сжать); (security) усиливать (perf усилить) ▷ vi (grip) сжиматься (perf сжаться); (rope) натягиваться (perf натянуться); **tightly** adv (grasp) крепко; **tights** npl (Brit) колготки pl
tile [taɪl] n (on roof) черепица; (on floor) плитка
till [tɪl] n касса ▷ prep, conj = **until**
tilt [tɪlt] vt наклонять (perf наклонить); (head) склонять (perf склонить) ▷ vi наклоняться (perf наклониться)
timber [ˈtɪmbəʳ] n (wood) древесина
time [taɪm] n время nt; (occasion) раз ▷ vt (measure time of) засекать (perf засечь) время +gen; (fix moment for) выбирать (perf выбрать) время для +gen; **a long time** долго; **a long time ago** давно; **for the time being** пока; **four at a time** по четыре; **from time to time** время от времени; **at times** временами; **in time** (soon enough) вовремя; (after some time) со временем; (Mus: play) в такт; **in a week's time** через неделю; **in no time** в два счёта; **any time** (whenever) в любое время; (as response) не за что; **on time** вовремя; **five times five** пятью пять; **what time is it?** который час?; **to have a good time** хорошо проводить (perf провести) время; **time limit** n предельный срок; **timely** adj своевременный; **timer** n (time switch) таймер; **timetable** n расписание
timid [ˈtɪmɪd] adj робкий
timing [ˈtaɪmɪŋ] n: **the timing of his resignation was unfortunate** выбор времени для его отставки был неудачен

tin [tɪn] n (material) о́лово; (container) (жестяна́я) ба́нка; (: Brit: can) консе́рвная ба́нка; **tinfoil** n фольга́

tinker ['tɪŋkə'] n (infl) бродя́чий луди́льщик

tinned [tɪnd] adj (Brit) консерви́рованный

tin-opener ['tɪnəupnə'] n (Brit) консе́рвный нож

tinted ['tɪntɪd] adj (hair) подкра́шеный; (spectacles, glass) ды́мчатый

tiny ['taɪnɪ] adj кро́шечный

tip [tɪp] n (of pen etc) ко́нчик; (gratuity) чаевы́е pl adj; (Brit: for rubbish) сва́лка; (advice) сове́т ▷ vt (waiter) дава́ть (perf дать) на чай +dat; (tilt) наклоня́ть (perf наклони́ть); (also **tip over**) опроки́дывать (perf опроки́нуть); (also **tip out**) выва́ливать (perf вы́валить)

tiptoe ['tɪptəu] n: **on tiptoe** на цы́почках

tire ['taɪə'] n (US) = **tyre** ▷ vt утомля́ть (perf утоми́ть) ▷ vi устава́ть (perf уста́ть); **tired** adj уста́лый; **to be tired of sth** устава́ть (perf уста́ть) от чего́-н

tiring ['taɪərɪŋ] adj утоми́тельный

tissue ['tɪʃu:] n бума́жная салфе́тка; (Anat, Bio) ткань f

tit [tɪt] n (Zool) сини́ца; **tit for tat** зуб за зуб

title ['taɪtl] n (of book etc) назва́ние; (rank, in sport) ти́тул

⊙ **KEYWORD**

to [tu:, tə] prep 1 (direction) в/на +acc; **to drive to school/the station** е́здить/е́хать (perf пое́хать) в шко́лу/на ста́нцию; **to the left** нале́во; **to the right** напра́во

2 (as far as) до +gen; **from Paris to London** от Пари́жа до Ло́ндона; **to count to ten** счита́ть (perf посчита́ть) до десяти́

3 (with expressions of time): **a quarter to five** без че́тверти пять

4 (for, of) к +dat; **the key to the front door** ключ (к) входно́й две́ри; **a letter to his wife** письмо́ жене́; **she is secretary to the director** она́ секрета́рь дире́ктора

5 (expressing indirect object): **to give sth to sb** дава́ть (perf дать) что-н кому́-н; **to talk to sb** разгова́ривать (impf) or говори́ть (impf) с кем-н; **what have you done to your hair?** что Вы сде́лали со свои́ми волоса́ми?

6 (in relation to) к +dat; **three goals to two** три: два; **X miles to the gallon** ≈ X ли́тров на киломе́тр; **30 roubles to the dollar** 30 рубле́й за до́ллар

7 (purpose, result) к +dat; **to my surprise** к моему́ удивле́нию; **to come to sb's aid** приходи́ть (perf прийти́) кому́-н на по́мощь

▷ with vb 1: **to want/try to do** хоте́ть (perf захоте́ть)/пыта́ться (perf попыта́ться) +infin; **he has nothing to lose** ему́ не́чего

теря́ть; **I am happy to ...** я сча́стлив +infin ...; **ready to use** гото́вый к употребле́нию; **too old/young to ...** сли́шком стар/мо́лод, что́бы +infin ...

2 (with vb omitted): **I don't want to** я не хочу́; **I don't feel like going — you really ought to** мне не хо́чется идти́ — но, Вы должны́

3 (purpose, result) что́бы +infin; **I did it to help you** я сде́лал э́то, что́бы помо́чь Вам

▷ adv: **to push the door to, pull the door to** закрыва́ть (perf закры́ть) дверь

toad [təud] n (Zool) жа́ба; **toadstool** n (Bot) пога́нка

toast [təust] n тост ▷ vt (Culin) поджа́ривать (perf поджа́рить); (drink to) пить (perf вы́пить) за +acc; **toaster** n то́стер

tobacco [tə'bækəu] n таба́к

today [tə'deɪ] adv, n сего́дня

toddler ['tɔdlə'] n малы́ш

toe [təu] n (of foot) па́лец (ноги́); (of shoe, sock) носо́к ▷ vt: **to toe the line** (fig) соотве́тствовать (impf)

toffee ['tɔfɪ] n ири́ска, тяну́чка

together [tə'gɛðə'] adv вме́сте; (at same time) одновреме́нно; **together with** вме́сте с +instr

toilet ['tɔɪlət] n унита́з; (Brit: room) туале́т ▷ cpd туале́тный; **toiletries** npl туале́тные принадле́жности fpl

token ['təukən] n (sign, souvenir) знак; (substitute coin) жето́н ▷ adj (strike, payment etc) символи́ческий; **book/gift token** (Brit) кни́жный/пода́рочный тало́н; **record token** (Brit) тало́н на пласти́нку

told [təuld] pt, pp of **tell**

tolerant ['tɔlərnt] adj: **tolerant (of)** терпи́мый (к +dat)

tolerate ['tɔlərеɪt] vt терпе́ть (impf)

toll [təul] n (of casualties etc) число́; (tax, charge) сбор, пла́та

tomato [tə'mɑ:təu] (pl **tomatoes**) n помидо́р

tomb [tu:m] n моги́ла; **tombstone** n надгро́бная плита́, надгро́бие

tomorrow [tə'mɔrəu] adv, n за́втра; **the day after tomorrow** послеза́втра; **tomorrow morning** за́втра у́тром

ton [tʌn] n (Brit) дли́нная то́нна; (US: also **short ton**) коро́ткая то́нна; (also **metric ton**) метри́ческая то́нна; **tons of** (inf) у́йма +gen

tone [təun] n (of voice, colour) тон ▷ vi (colours: also **tone in**) сочета́ться (impf); **tone up** vt (muscles) укрепля́ть (perf укрепи́ть)

tongue [tʌŋ] n язы́к

tonic ['tɔnɪk] n (Med) тонизи́рующее сре́дство; (also **tonic water**) то́ник

tonight [tə'naɪt] adv (this evening) сего́дня ве́чером; (this night) сего́дня но́чью ▷ n (see adv) сего́дняшний ве́чер;

сего́дняшняя ночь f

tonsil ['tɔnsl] n (usu pl) минда́лина;
tonsillitis [tɔnsɪ'laɪtɪs] n тонзилли́т

too [tu:] adv (excessively) сли́шком; (also:
referring to subject) та́кже, то́же;
(: referring to object) та́кже; **too much, too
many** сли́шком мно́го

took [tuk] pt of **take**

tool [tu:l] n (instrument) инструме́нт

tooth [tu:θ] (pl **teeth**) n (Anat) зуб; (Tech)
зубе́ц; **toothache** n зубна́я боль f;
toothbrush n зубна́я щётка;
toothpaste n зубна́я па́ста

top [tɔp] n (of mountain) верши́на; (of
tree) верху́шка; (of head) маку́шка; (of
page, list etc) нача́ло; (of ladder, cupboard,
table, box) верх; (lid: of box, jar) кры́шка;
(: of bottle) про́бка; (also: **spinning top**)
юла́, волчо́к ▷ adj (shelf, step) ве́рхний;
(marks) вы́сший; (scientist) веду́щий ▷ vt
(poll, vote) лиди́ровать (impf) в +prp; (list)
возглавля́ть (perf возгла́вить); (exceed:
estimate etc) превыша́ть (perf превы́сить);
on top of (above: be) на +prp; (: put) на
+acc; (in addition to) сверх +gen; **from top
to bottom** све́рху до́низу; **top up** (US **top
off**) vt (bottle) долива́ть (perf доли́ть)

topic ['tɔpɪk] n те́ма; **topical** adj
актуа́льный

topless ['tɔplɪs] adj обнажённый до
по́яса

topple ['tɔpl] vt (overthrow) ски́дывать
(perf ски́нуть) ▷ vi опроки́дываться (perf
опроки́нуться)

torch [tɔ:tʃ] n (with flame) фа́кел; (Brit:
electric) фона́рь m

tore [tɔ:ʳ] pt of **tear**[1]

torment [n 'tɔ:mɛnt, vb tɔ:'mɛnt] n
муче́ние ▷ vt му́чить (impf)

torn [tɔ:n] pp of **tear**[1]

tornado [tɔ:'neɪdəu] (pl **tornadoes**) n
смерч

torpedo [tɔ:'pi:dəu] (pl **torpedoes**) n
торпе́да

torrent ['tɔrnt] n пото́к; **torrential**
[tɔ'rɛnʃl] adj проливно́й

tortoise ['tɔ:təs] n черепа́ха

torture ['tɔ:tʃəʳ] n пы́тка ▷ vt пыта́ть
(impf)

Tory ['tɔ:rɪ] (Brit: Pol) adj консервати́вный
▷ n то́ри m/f ind, консерва́тор

toss [tɔs] vt (throw) подки́дывать (perf
подки́нуть), подбра́сывать (perf
подбро́сить); (head) отки́дывать (perf
отки́нуть) ▷ vi: **to toss and turn**
воро́чаться (impf); **to toss a coin**
подбра́сывать (perf подбро́сить) моне́ту;
to toss up to do подбра́сывать (perf
подбро́сить) моне́ту, что́бы +infin

total ['təutl] adj (number, workforce etc)
о́бщий; (failure, wreck etc) по́лный ▷ n
о́бщая су́мма ▷ vt (add up) скла́дывать
(perf сложи́ть); (add up to) составля́ть
(perf соста́вить)

totalitarian [təutælɪ'tɛərɪən] adj (Pol)
тоталита́рный

totally ['təutəlɪ] adv по́лностью;
(unprepared) соверше́нно

touch [tʌtʃ] n (sense) осяза́ние;
(approach) мане́ра; (detail) штрих;
(contact) прикоснове́ние ▷ vt (with hand,
foot) каса́ться (perf косну́ться) +gen,
тро́гать (perf тро́нуть); (tamper with)
тро́гать (impf); (make contact with)
прикаса́ться (perf прикосну́ться) к +dat,
дотра́гиваться (perf дотро́нуться) до
+gen; (move: emotionally) тро́гать (perf
тро́нуть); **there's been a touch of frost**
подморо́зило; **to get in touch with sb**
свя́зываться (perf связа́ться) с кем-н; **to
lose touch** (friends) теря́ть (perf потеря́ть)
связь; **touch on** vt fus каса́ться (perf
косну́ться) +gen; **touched** adj (moved)
тро́нутый; **touching** adj тро́гательный;
touchline n бокова́я ли́ния

tough [tʌf] adj (hard-wearing) кре́пкий,
про́чный; (person: physically)
выно́сливый; (: mentally) сто́йкий;
(difficult) тяжёлый

tour ['tuəʳ] n (journey) пое́здка; (of town,
factory etc) экску́рсия; (by pop group etc)
гастро́ли pl ▷ vt (country, city) объезжа́ть
(perf объе́хать); (factory) обходи́ть (perf
обойти́)

tourism ['tuərɪzm] n тури́зм

tourist ['tuərɪst] n тури́ст(ка) ▷ cpd
(attractions, season) туристи́ческий

tournament ['tuənəmənt] n турни́р

tow [təu] vt вози́ть/везти́ (impf) на
букси́ре; **"on or (US) in tow"** (Aut) "на
букси́ре"

toward(s) [tə'wɔ:d(z)] prep к +dat;
toward(s) doing с тем что́бы +infin

towel ['tauəl] n (also **hand towel**)
полоте́нце для рук; (also **bath towel**)
ба́нное полоте́нце

tower ['tauəʳ] n ба́шня; **tower block** n
(Brit) ба́шня, высо́тный дом

town [taun] n го́род; **to go to town** (fig)
разоря́ться (perf разори́ться); **town
centre** n центр (го́рода); **town hall** n
ра́туша

toxic ['tɔksɪk] adj токси́чный

toy [tɔɪ] n игру́шка

trace [treɪs] n след ▷ vt (draw)
переводи́ть (perf перевести́); (follow)
просле́живать (perf проследи́ть); (find)
разы́скивать (perf разыска́ть)

track [træk] n след; (path) тропа́; (of
bullet etc) траекто́рия; (Rail)
(железнодоро́жный) путь m; (song, also
Sport) доро́жка ▷ vt (follow) идти́ (impf)
по сле́ду +gen; **to keep track of** следи́ть
(impf) за +instr; **track down** vt (prey)
высле́живать (perf вы́следить); (person)
оты́скивать (perf отыска́ть); **tracksuit** n
трениро́вочный костю́м

tractor ['træktəʳ] n тра́ктор

trade [treɪd] n (activity) торго́вля; (skill, job) ремесло́ ▷ vi (do business) торгова́ть (impf) ▷ vt: **to trade sth (for sth)** обме́нивать (perf обменя́ть) что-н (на что-н); **trade in** vt (car etc) предлага́ть (perf предложи́ть) для встре́чной прода́жи; **trademark** n торго́вый знак; **trader** n торго́вец; **tradesman** irreg n (shopkeeper) торго́вец, ла́вочник; **trade union** n профсою́з (= профессиона́льный сою́з)

tradition [trə'dɪʃən] n тради́ция; **traditional** adj (also fig) традицио́нный

traffic ['træfɪk] n движе́ние; (of drugs) нелега́льная торго́вля; **traffic jam** n про́бка, зато́р; **traffic lights** npl светофо́р msg; **traffic warden** n (Brit) регулиро́вщик парко́ва́ния маши́н на городски́х у́лицах

tragedy ['trædʒədɪ] n траге́дия

tragic ['trædʒɪk] adj траги́ческий

trail [treɪl] n (path) доро́жка, тропи́нка; (track) след; (of smoke, dust) шлейф ▷ vt (drag) волочи́ть (impf); (follow) сле́довать (impf) по пята́м за +instr ▷ vi (hang loosely) волочи́ться (impf); (in game, contest) волочи́ться (impf) в хвосте́, отстава́ть (impf); **trailer** n (Aut) прице́п; (US: caravan) автоприце́п; (Cinema) рекла́мный ро́лик, ано́нс

train [treɪn] n по́езд; (of dress) шлейф ▷ vt (apprentice, doctor etc) обуча́ть (perf обучи́ть), гото́вить (impf); (athlete, mind) тренирова́ть (impf); (dog) дрессирова́ть (perf вы́дрессировать) ▷ vi учи́ться (perf обучи́ться); (Sport) тренирова́ться (impf); **one's train of thought** ход чьих-н мы́слей; **to train sb as** учи́ть (perf обучи́ть) кого́-н на +acc; **to train sth on** (camera etc) направля́ть (perf напра́вить) что-н на +acc; **trainee** n (hairdresser) учени́к; **trainee teacher** практика́нт(ка); **trainer** n (coach) тре́нер; (of animals) дрессиро́вщик(-щица); **trainers** npl (shoes) кроссо́вки fpl; **training** n (for occupation) обуче́ние, подгото́вка; (Sport) трениро́вка; **to be in training** (Sport) тренирова́ться (impf)

trait [treɪt] n черта́

traitor ['treɪtər] n преда́тель(ница) m(f)

tram [træm] n (Brit) трамва́й

tramp [træmp] n (person) бродя́га m/f

trample ['træmpl] vt: **to trample (underfoot)** раста́птывать (perf растопта́ть)

trampoline ['træmpəliːn] n бату́т

tranquil ['træŋkwɪl] adj безмяте́жный

transaction [træn'zækʃən] n опера́ция

transatlantic ['trænzət'læntɪk] adj трансатланти́ческий

transcript ['trænskrɪpt] n (typed) распеча́тка; (hand-written) ру́копись f

transfer ['trænsfər] n перево́д; (Pol: of power) переда́ча; (Sport) перехо́д; (design) переводна́я карти́нка ▷ vt (employees, money) переводи́ть (perf перевести́); (Pol: power) передава́ть (perf переда́ть)

transform [træns'fɔːm] vt (completely) преобразо́вывать (perf преобразова́ть); (alter) преобража́ть (perf преобрази́ть); **transformation** [trænsfə'meɪʃən] n (see vt) преобразова́ние; преображе́ние

transfusion [træns'fjuːʒən] n (also **blood transfusion**) перелива́ние кро́ви

transit ['trænzɪt] n транзи́т; **in transit** (people, things) при перево́зке, в транзи́те

transition [træn'zɪʃən] n перехо́д

translate [trænz'leɪt] vt: **to translate (from/into)** переводи́ть (perf перевести́) (с +gen/на +acc)

translation [trænz'leɪʃən] n перево́д

translator [trænz'leɪtər] n перево́дчик(-ица)

transmission [trænz'mɪʃən] n переда́ча

transmit [trænz'mɪt] vt передава́ть (perf переда́ть); **transmitter** n переда́тчик

transparent [træns'pærnt] adj прозра́чный

transplant [n 'trænsplɑːnt, vb træns'plɑːnt] n переса́дка ▷ vt (Med, Bot) переса́живать (perf пересади́ть)

transport [n 'trænspɔːt, vb træns'pɔːt] n тра́нспорт; (of people, goods) перево́зка ▷ vt (carry) перевози́ть (perf перевезти́)

transportation ['trænspɔː'teɪʃən] n транспортиро́вка, перево́зка; (means of transport) тра́нспорт

transvestite [trænz'vɛstaɪt] n трансвести́т

trap [træp] n лову́шка, западня́ ▷ vt лови́ть (perf пойма́ть) в лову́шку; (confine) запира́ть (perf запере́ть)

trash [træʃ] n му́сор; (pej, fig) дрянь f

trauma ['trɔːmə] n тра́вма; **traumatic** [trɔː'mætɪk] adj (fig) мучи́тельный

travel ['trævl] n (travelling) путеше́ствия ntpl ▷ vi (for pleasure) путеше́ствовать (impf); (commute) е́здить (impf); (news, sound) распространя́ться (perf распространи́ться) ▷ vt (distance: by transport) проезжа́ть (perf прое́хать); **travels** npl (journeys) разъе́зды mpl; **travel agent** n турате́нт; **traveller** (US **traveler**) n путеше́ственник(-ица); **traveller's cheque** (US **traveler's check**) n доро́жный чек

tray [treɪ] n (for carrying) подно́с; (on desk) корзи́нка

treacherous ['trɛtʃərəs] adj (person) вероло́мный; (look, action) преда́тельский; (ground, tide) кова́рный

treacle ['triːkl] n пато́ка

tread [trɛd] (pt **trod**, pp **trodden**) n (of stair) ступе́нь f; (of tyre) проте́ктор ▷ vi ступа́ть (impf)

treason ['triːzn] n изме́на

treasure ['trɛʒər] n сокро́вище ▷ vt

дорожи́ть (*impf*) +*instr*; (*thought*) леле́ять (*impf*); **treasures** *npl* (*art treasures etc*) сокро́вища *ntpl*; **treasurer** *n* казначе́й

treasury ['trɛʒərɪ] *n*: **the Treasury**, (*US*) **the Treasury Department** Госуда́рственное Казначе́йство

treat [tri:t] *n* (*present*) удово́льствие ⊳ *vt* (*person, object*) обраща́ться (*impf*) с +*instr*; (*patient, illness*) лечи́ть (*impf*); **to treat sb to sth** угоща́ть (*perf* угости́ть) кого́-н чем-н; **treatment** *n* (*attention, handling*) обраще́ние; (*Med*) лече́ние

treaty ['tri:tɪ] *n* соглаше́ние

treble ['trɛbl] *vt* утра́ивать (*perf* утро́ить) ⊳ *vi* утра́иваться (*perf* утро́иться)

tree [tri:] *n* де́рево

trek [trɛk] *n* (*trip*) похо́д, перехо́д

tremble ['trɛmbl] *vi* дрожа́ть (*impf*)

tremendous [trɪ'mɛndəs] *adj* (*enormous*) грома́дный; (*excellent*) великоле́пный

trench [trɛntʃ] *n* кана́ва; (*Mil*) транше́я, око́п

trend [trɛnd] *n* (*tendency*) тенде́нция; (*of events, fashion*) направле́ние; **trendy** *adj* мо́дный

trespass ['trɛspəs] *vi*: **to trespass on** (*private property*) вторга́ться (*perf* вто́ргнуться) в +*acc*; "**no trespassing**" "прохо́д воспрещён"

trial ['traɪəl] *n* (*Law*) проце́сс, суд; (*of machine etc*) испыта́ние; **trials** *npl* (*bad experiences*) перипети́и *fpl*; (*Law*) под судо́м; **by trial and error** ме́тодом проб и оши́бок

triangle ['traɪæŋgl] *n* (*Math, Mus*) треуго́льник

triangular [traɪ'æŋgjulə*] *adj* треуго́льный

tribe [traɪb] *n* пле́мя *nt*

tribunal [traɪ'bju:nl] *n* трибуна́л

tribute ['trɪbju:t] *n* (*compliment*) дань *f*; **to pay tribute to** отдава́ть (*perf* отда́ть) дань +*dat*

trick [trɪk] *n* (*magic trick*) фо́кус; (*prank*) подво́х; (*skill, knack*) приём ⊳ *vt* проводи́ть (*perf* провести́); **to play a trick on sb** разы́грывать (*perf* разыгра́ть) кого́-н; **that should do the trick** э́то должно́ срабо́тать

trickle ['trɪkl] *n* (*of water etc*) стру́йка ⊳ *vi* (*water, rain etc*) струи́ться (*impf*)

tricky ['trɪkɪ] *adj* (*job*) непросто́й; (*business*) хи́трый; (*problem*) ка́верзный

trifle ['traɪfl] *n* (*small detail*) пустя́к ⊳ *adv*: **a trifle long** чуть длиннова́т

trigger ['trɪgə*] *n* (*of gun*) куро́к

trim [trɪm] *adj* (*house, garden*) ухо́женный; (*figure*) подтя́нутый ⊳ *vt* (*cut*) подравня́ть (*perf* подровня́ть); (*decorate*): **to trim (with)** отде́лывать (*perf* отде́лать) (+*instr*) ⊳ *n*: **to give sb a trim** подра́внивать (*perf* подровня́ть) во́лосы кому́-н

trip [trɪp] *n* (*journey*) пое́здка; (*outing*) экску́рсия ⊳ *vi* (*stumble*) споткну́ться (*perf* споткну́ться); **on a trip** на экску́рсии; **trip up** *vi* (*stumble*) споткну́ться (*perf* споткну́ться) ⊳ *vt* (*person*) ста́вить (*perf* подста́вить) подно́жку +*dat*

triple ['trɪpl] *adj* тройно́й

tripod ['traɪpɔd] *n* трено́га

triumph ['traɪʌmf] *n* (*satisfaction*) торжество́; (*achievement*) триу́мф ⊳ *vi*: **to triumph (over)** торжествова́ть (*perf* восторжествова́ть) (над +*instr*); **triumphant** [traɪ'ʌmfənt] *adj* (*team, wave*) торжеству́ющий; (*return*) побе́дный

trivial ['trɪvɪəl] *adj* тривиа́льный

trod [trɔd] *pt of* **tread**; **trodden** *pp of* **tread**

trolley ['trɔlɪ] *n* теле́жка; (*also* **trolley bus**) тролле́йбус

trombone [trɔm'bəun] *n* тромбо́н

troop [tru:p] *n* (*of soldiers*) отря́д; (*of people*) гру́ппа; **troops** *npl* (*Mil*) войска́ *ntpl*

trophy ['trəufɪ] *n* трофе́й

tropical ['trɔpɪkl] *adj* тропи́ческий

trot [trɔt] *n* рысь *f* (*спо́соб бе́га*)

trouble ['trʌbl] *n* (*difficulty*) затрудне́ние; (*worry, unrest*) беспоко́йство; (*bother, effort*) хло́поты *pl* ⊳ *vt* (*worry*) беспоко́ить (*perf* побеспоко́ить); (*disturb*) беспоко́ить (*perf* побеспоко́ить) ⊳ *vi*: **to trouble to do** побеспоко́иться (*perf*) +*infin*; **troubles** *npl* (*personal*) неприя́тности *fpl*; **to be in trouble** (*ship, climber etc*) быть (*impf*) в беде́; **I am in trouble** у меня́ неприя́тности; **to have trouble doing** с трудо́м +*infin*; **troubled** *adj* (*person*) встрево́женный; (*times*) сму́тный; (*country*) многострада́льный; **troublemaker** *n* смутья́н; **troublesome** *adj* (*child*) озорно́й

trough [trɔf] *n* (*also* **drinking trough**) коры́то; (*also* **feeding trough**) корму́шка; (*low point*) впа́дина

trousers ['trauzəz] *npl* брю́ки *pl*; **short trousers** шо́рты *pl*

trout [traut] *n inv* (*Zool*) форе́ль *f*

truant ['truənt] *n* (*Brit*): **to play truant** прогу́ливать (*perf* прогуля́ть) уро́ки

truce [tru:s] *n* переми́рие

truck [trʌk] *n* (*lorry*) грузови́к; (*Rail*) платфо́рма

true [tru:] *adj* и́стинный; (*accurate: likeness*) то́чный; (*loyal*) ве́рный; **to come true** сбыва́ться (*perf* сбы́ться); **it is true** э́то пра́вда *or* ве́рно

truly ['tru:lɪ] *adv* по-настоя́щему; (*truthfully*) по пра́вде говоря́; **yours truly** (*in letter*) и́скренне Ваш

trumpet ['trʌmpɪt] *n* (*Mus*) труба́

trunk [trʌŋk] *n* (*of tree*) ствол; (*of elephant*) хо́бот; (*case*) доро́жный сунду́к; (*US: Aut*) бага́жник; **trunks** *npl* (*also* **swimming trunks**) пла́вки *pl*

trust [trʌst] n (faith) дове́рие; (responsibility) долг; (Law) дове́рительная со́бственность f ▷ vt (rely on, have faith in) доверя́ть (impf) +dat; (hope): **to trust (that)** полага́ть (impf), что; (entrust): **to trust sth to sb** доверя́ть (perf дове́рить) что-н кому́-н; **to take sth on trust** принима́ть (perf приня́ть) что-н на ве́ру; **trusted** adj пре́данный; **trustworthy** adj надёжный

truth [tru:θ] n пра́вда; (principle) и́стина; **truthful** adj правди́вый

try [traɪ] n (attempt) попы́тка; (Rugby) прохо́д с мячо́м ▷ vt (test) про́бовать (perf попро́бовать); (Law) суди́ть (impf); (patience) испы́тывать (impf); (key, door) про́бовать (perf попро́бовать); (attempt): **to try to do** стара́ться (perf постара́ться) or пыта́ться (perf попыта́ться) +infin ▷ vi (make effort) стара́ться (impf); **to have a try** про́бовать (perf попро́бовать); **try on** vt (dress etc) примеря́ть (perf приме́рить); **trying** adj утоми́тельный

tsar [zɑː] n царь m

T-shirt [ˈtiːʃəːt] n футбо́лка

tub [tʌb] n (container) бо́чка; (bath) ва́нна

tube [tjuːb] n (pipe) тру́бка; (container) тю́бик; (Brit: underground train) метро́ nt ind; (for tyre) ка́мера

tuberculosis [tjubəːkjuˈləusɪs] n туберкулёз

tuck [tʌk] vt (put) су́нуть (perf)

Tuesday [ˈtjuːzdɪ] n вто́рник

tug [tʌg] n (ship) букси́р ▷ vt дёргать (perf дёрнуть)

tuition [tjuːˈɪʃən] n (Brit) обуче́ние; (US: fees) пла́та за обуче́ние; **private tuition** ча́стные уро́ки

tulip [ˈtjuːlɪp] n тюльпа́н

tumble [ˈtʌmbl] n паде́ние ▷ vi (fall: person) вали́ться (perf свали́ться)

tumbler [ˈtʌmblə] n бока́л

tummy [ˈtʌmɪ] n (inf) живо́т

tumour [ˈtjuːmə] n (US **tumor**) (Med) о́пухоль f

tuna [ˈtjuːnə] n inv (also **tuna fish**) туне́ц

tune [tjuːn] n (melody) моти́в ▷ vt настра́ивать (perf настро́ить); (Aut) нала́живать (perf нала́дить); **the guitar is in/out of tune** гита́ра настро́ена/ расстро́ена; **to sing in tune** петь (impf) в лад; **to sing out of tune** фальши́вить (impf); **to be in/out of tune with** (fig) быть (impf) в ладу́/не в ладу́ с +instr; **tune in** vi (Radio, TV): **to tune in (to)** настра́иваться (perf настро́иться) (на +acc)

tunic [ˈtjuːnɪk] n ту́ника

tunnel [ˈtʌnl] n (passage) тунне́ль m

turf [təːf] n (grass) дёрн

Turkey [ˈtəːkɪ] n Ту́рция

turkey [ˈtəːkɪ] n инде́йка

Turkish [ˈtəːkɪʃ] adj туре́цкий

turmoil [ˈtəːmɔɪl] n смяте́ние; **in turmoil** в смяте́нии

turn [təːn] n поворо́т; (chance) о́чередь f; (inf: Med) вы́вих ▷ vt повора́чивать (perf поверну́ть) ▷ vi (object) повора́чиваться (perf поверну́ться); (person: look back) обора́чиваться (perf оберну́ться); (reverse direction) развора́чиваться (perf разверну́ться); (become): **he's turned forty** ему́ испо́лнилось со́рок; **a good/bad turn** до́брая/плоха́я услу́га; **"no left turn"** (Aut) "нет ле́вого поворо́та"; **it's your turn** твоя́ о́чередь; **in turn** по о́череди; **to take turns at sth** де́лать (impf) что-н по о́череди; **to turn nasty** озлобля́ться (perf озло́биться); **turn away** vi отвора́чиваться (perf отверну́ться) ▷ vt (business, applicant) отклоня́ть (perf отклони́ть); **turn back** vi повора́чивать (perf поверну́ть) наза́д ▷ vt (person) верну́ть (perf); (vehicle) развора́чивать (perf разверну́ть); **to turn back the clock** (fig) поверну́ть (perf) вре́мя вспять; **turn down** vt (request) отклоня́ть (perf отклони́ть); (heating) уменьша́ть (perf уме́ньшить) пода́чу +gen; **turn in** vi (inf) идти́ (perf пойти́) на боковску́ю; **turn off** vi свора́чивать (perf сверну́ть) ▷ vt выключа́ть (perf вы́ключить); **turn on** vt включа́ть (perf включи́ть); **turn out** vt (light, gas) выключа́ть (perf вы́ключить); (produce) выпуска́ть (perf вы́пустить) ▷ vi (troops, voters) прибыва́ть (perf прибы́ть); **to turn out to be** ока́зываться (perf оказа́ться) +instr; **turn over** vi (person) перевора́чиваться (perf переверну́ться) ▷ vt (object, page) перевора́чивать (perf переверну́ть); **turn round** vi (person, vehicle) развора́чиваться (perf разверну́ться); **turn up** vi (person) объявля́ться (perf объяви́ться); (lost object) находи́ться (perf найти́сь) ▷ vt (collar) поднима́ть (perf подня́ть); (radio) де́лать (perf сде́лать) гро́мче; (heater) увели́чивать (perf увели́чить) пода́чу +gen; **turning** n поворо́т; **turning point** n (fig) поворо́тный пункт, перело́мный моме́нт

turnip [ˈtəːnɪp] n (Bot, Culin) ре́па

turnout [ˈtəːnaut] n: **there was a high turnout for the local elections** в ме́стных вы́борах при́няло уча́стие мно́го люде́й

turnover [ˈtəːnəuvə] n (Comm) оборо́т; (: of staff) теку́честь f

turquoise [ˈtəːkwɔɪz] adj (colour) бирюзо́вый

turtle [ˈtəːtl] n черепа́ха

tutor [ˈtjuːtə] n преподава́тель(ница) m(f); (private tutor) репети́тор; **tutorial** [tjuːˈtɔːrɪəl] n (Scol) семина́р

TV n abbr (= television) ТВ (= телеви́дение)

tweed [twiːd] n твид

tweet [twiːt] vi писа́ть (perf написа́ть) твит, тви́тить (perf тви́тнуть) (inf) ▷ n твит

twelfth [twɛlfθ] adj двена́дцатый

twelve [twɛlv] *n* двена́дцать; **at twelve (o'clock)** в двена́дцать (часо́в)

twentieth ['twɛntɪɪθ] *adj* двадца́тый

twenty ['twɛntɪ] *n* два́дцать

twice [twaɪs] *adv* два́жды; **twice as much** вдво́е бо́льше

twig [twɪg] *n* сучо́к

twilight ['twaɪlaɪt] *n* (*evening*) су́мерки *mpl*

twin [twɪn] *adj* (*towers*) па́рный ▷ *n* близне́ц ▷ *vt*: **to be twinned with** (*towns etc*) быть (*impf*) побрати́мами с +*instr*; **twin sister** сестра́-близне́ц; **twin brother** брат-близне́ц

twinkle ['twɪŋkl] *vi* мерца́ть (*impf*); (*eyes*) сверка́ть (*impf*)

twist [twɪst] *n* (*action*) закру́чивание; (*in road, coil, flex*) вито́к; (*in story*) поворо́т ▷ *vt* (*turn*) изгиба́ть (*perf* изогну́ть); (*injure: ankle etc*) выви́хивать (*perf* вы́вихнуть); (*fig: meaning, words*) искажа́ть (*perf* искази́ть), коверка́ть (*perf* исковерка́ть) ▷ *vi* (*road, river*) извива́ться (*impf*)

twitch [twɪtʃ] *n* (*nervous*) подёргивание

two [tuː] *n* два *m/nt* (*f* две); **to put two and two together** (*fig*) сообража́ть (*perf* сообрази́ть) что к чему́

type [taɪp] *n* тип; (*Typ*) шрифт ▷ *vt* (*letter etc*) печа́тать (*perf* напеча́тать); **typewriter** *n* пи́шущая маши́нка

typhoid ['taɪfɔɪd] *n* брюшно́й тиф

typhoon [taɪ'fuːn] *n* тайфу́н

typical ['tɪpɪkl] *adj*: **typical (of)** типи́чный (для +*gen*)

typing ['taɪpɪŋ] *n* маши́нопись *f*

typist ['taɪpɪst] *n* машини́стка

tyre ['taɪəʳ] (*US* **tire**) *n* ши́на

tzar [zɑːʳ] *n* = **tsar**

UFO *n abbr* (= *unidentified flying object*) НЛО (= *неопо́знанный лета́ющий объе́кт*)

ugly ['ʌglɪ] *adj* (*person, dress etc*) уро́дливый, безобра́зный; (*dangerous: situation*) скве́рный

UK *n abbr* = **United Kingdom**

Ukraine [juː'kreɪn] *n* Украи́на

Ukrainian [juː'kreɪnɪən] *adj* украи́нский

ulcer ['ʌlsəʳ] *n* я́зва

ultimate ['ʌltɪmət] *adj* (*final*) оконча́тельный, коне́чный; (*greatest*) преде́льный; **ultimately** *adv* в коне́чном ито́ге; (*basically*) в преде́льном счёте

ultimatum [ʌltɪ'meɪtəm] (*pl* **ultimatums** *or* **ultimata**) *n* ультима́тум

ultraviolet ['ʌltrə'vaɪəlɪt] *adj* (*light etc*) ультрафиоле́товый

umbrella [ʌm'brɛlə] *n* (*for rain, sun*) зонт, зо́нтик

umpire ['ʌmpaɪəʳ] *n* судья́ *m*, рефери́ *m ind*

UN *n abbr* = **United Nations**

unable [ʌn'eɪbl] *adj* неспосо́бный; **he is unable to pay** он неспосо́бен заплати́ть

unanimous [juː'nænɪməs] *adj* единоду́шный

unarmed [ʌn'ɑːmd] *adj* безору́жный

unattached [ʌnə'tætʃt] *adj* (*person*) одино́кий

unattractive [ʌnə'træktɪv] *adj* непривлека́тельный

unavoidable [ʌnə'vɔɪdəbl] *adj* (*delay*) неизбе́жный

unaware [ʌnə'wɛəʳ] *adj*: **to be unaware of** не подозрева́ть (*impf*) о +*prp*; (*fail to notice*) не осознава́ть (*impf*)

unbearable [ʌn'bɛərəbl] *adj* невыноси́мый

unbeatable [ʌn'biːtəbl] *adj* (*price, quality*) непревзойдённый

unbelievable [ʌnbɪ'liːvəbl] *adj* невероя́тный

uncanny [ʌnˈkænɪ] adj (resemblance, knack) необъясни́мый; (silence) жу́ткий

uncertain [ʌnˈsəːtn] adj (unsure): **uncertain about** неуве́ренный относи́тельно +gen; **in no uncertain terms** без обиняко́в, вполне́ определённо; **uncertainty** n (not knowing) неопределённость f; (often pl: doubt) сомне́ние

unchanged [ʌnˈtʃeɪndʒd] adj (orders, habits) неизме́нный

uncle [ˈʌŋkl] n дя́дя m

uncomfortable [ʌnˈkʌmfətəbl] adj неудо́бный; (unpleasant) гнету́щий

uncommon [ʌnˈkɔmən] adj (rare, unusual) необы́чный

unconditional [ʌnkənˈdɪʃənl] adj (acceptance, obedience) безусло́вный; (discharge, surrender) безогово́рочный

unconscious [ʌnˈkɔnʃəs] adj без созна́ния; (unaware): **unconscious of** не сознаю́щий +gen

uncontrollable [ʌnkənˈtrəuləbl] adj (child, animal) неуправля́емый; (laughter) неудержи́мый

unconventional [ʌnkənˈvɛnʃənl] adj нетрадицио́нный

uncover [ʌnˈkʌvəʳ] vt открыва́ть (perf откры́ть); (plot, secret) раскрыва́ть (perf раскры́ть)

undecided [ʌndɪˈsaɪdɪd] adj (person) коле́блющийся; **he is undecided as to whether we will go** он не реши́л пойдёт ли он

undeniable [ʌndɪˈnaɪəbl] adj (fact, evidence) неоспори́мый

under [ˈʌndəʳ] adv (go, fly etc) вниз ▷ prep (position) под +instr; (motion) под +acc; (less than: cost, pay) ме́ньше +gen; (according to) по +dat; (during) при +prp; **children under 16** де́ти до 16-ти лет; **under there** там внизу́; **under repair** в ремо́нте

undercover [ʌndəˈkʌvəʳ] adj та́йный

underestimate [ˈʌndərˈɛstɪmeɪt] vt недооце́нивать (perf недооцени́ть)

undergo [ʌndəˈgəu] (irreg like **go**) vt (repair) проходи́ть (perf пройти́); (operation) переноси́ть (perf перенести́); (change) претерпева́ть (perf претерпе́ть)

undergraduate [ʌndəˈgrædjuɪt] n студе́нт(ка)

underground [ˈʌndəgraund] adv (work) под землёй ▷ adj (car park) подзе́мный; (activities) подпо́льный ▷ n: **the underground** (Brit: Rail) метро́ nt ind; (Pol) подпо́лье

underline [ʌndəˈlaɪn] vt подчёркивать (perf подчеркну́ть)

undermine [ʌndəˈmaɪn] vt (authority) подрыва́ть (perf подорва́ть)

underneath [ʌndəˈniːθ] adv внизу́ ▷ prep (position) под +instr; (motion) под +acc

underpants [ˈʌndəpænts] npl (men's) трусы́ pl

underprivileged [ʌndəˈprɪvɪlɪdʒd] adj (family) неиму́щий

understand [ʌndəˈstænd] (irreg like **stand**) vt (perf поня́ть); (believe): **to understand that** полага́ть (impf), что; **understandable** adj поня́тный; **understanding** adj понима́ющий ▷ n понима́ние; (agreement) договорённость f

understatement [ˈʌndəsteɪtmənt] n: **that's an understatement!** э́то сли́шком мя́гко ска́зано!

understood [ʌndəˈstud] pt, pp of **understand** ▷ adj (agreed) согласо́ванный; (implied) подразумева́емый

undertake [ʌndəˈteɪk] (irreg like **take**) vt (task, duty) брать (perf взять) на себя́; **to undertake to do** обя́зываться (perf обяза́ться) +infin

undertaker [ˈʌndəteɪkəʳ] n владе́лец похоро́нного бюро́

underwater [ʌndəˈwɔːtəʳ] adv под водо́й ▷ adj подво́дный

underwear [ˈʌndəwɛəʳ] n ни́жнее бельё

underworld [ˈʌndəwəːld] n (of crime) престу́пный мир

undesirable [ʌndɪˈzaɪərəbl] adj нежела́тельный

undisputed [ˈʌndɪsˈpjuːtɪd] adj неоспори́мый

undo [ʌnˈduː] (irreg like **do**) vt (laces, strings) развя́зывать (perf развяза́ть); (buttons) расстёгивать (perf расстегну́ть); (spoil) губи́ть (perf погуби́ть)

undoubtedly adv несомне́нно, бесспо́рно

undress [ʌnˈdrɛs] vt раздева́ть (perf разде́ть) ▷ vi раздева́ться (perf разде́ться)

uneasy [ʌnˈiːzɪ] adj (feeling) трево́жный; (peace, truce) напряжённый; **he is** or **feels uneasy** он неспоко́ен

unemployed [ʌnɪmˈplɔɪd] adj безрабо́тный ▷ npl: **the unemployed** безрабо́тные pl adj

unemployment [ʌnɪmˈplɔɪmənt] n безрабо́тица

uneven [ʌnˈiːvn] adj неро́вный

unexpected [ʌnɪksˈpɛktɪd] adj неожи́данный; **unexpectedly** adv неожи́данно

unfair [ʌnˈfɛəʳ] adj: **unfair (to)** несправедли́вый (к +dat)

unfaithful [ʌnˈfeɪθful] adj неве́рный

unfamiliar [ʌnfəˈmɪliəʳ] adj незнако́мый

unfashionable [ʌnˈfæʃnəbl] adj немо́дный

unfavourable [ʌnˈfeɪvrəbl] (US **unfavorable**) adj неблагоприя́тный

unfinished [ʌnˈfɪnɪʃt] adj незако́нченный

unfit [ʌn'fɪt] *adj* (*physically*): **she is unfit** она в плохой спортивной форме; **he is unfit for the job** он непригоден для этой работы

unfold [ʌn'fəʊld] *vt* (*sheets, map*) разворачивать (*perf* развернуть) ▷ *vi* (*situation*) разворачиваться (*perf* развернуться)

unfollow [ʌn'fɒləʊ] *vt* отписываться (*perf* отписаться) от +*gen*, отменять (*perf* отменить) подписку на +*acc*

unforgettable [ʌnfə'gɛtəbl] *adj* незабываемый

unfortunate [ʌn'fɔːtʃənət] *adj* (*unlucky*) несчастный; (*regrettable*) неудачный; **unfortunately** *adv* к сожалению

unfriend [ʌn'frɛnd] *vt* удалять (*perf* удалить) из списка друзей; отфрендить (*perf*) (*inf*)

unfriendly [ʌn'frɛndlɪ] *adj* недружелюбный

unhappy [ʌn'hæpɪ] *adj* несчастный; **unhappy with** (*dissatisfied*) недовольный +*instr*

unhealthy [ʌn'hɛlθɪ] *adj* нездоровый

unhurt [ʌn'həːt] *adj* невредимый

unidentified [ʌnaɪ'dɛntɪfaɪd] *adj* анонимный; *see also* **UFO**

uniform ['juːnɪfɔːm] *n* форма ▷ *adj* единообразный; (*temperature*) постоянный

uninhabited [ʌnɪn'hæbɪtɪd] *adj* необитаемый

unintentional [ʌnɪn'tɛnʃənəl] *adj* неумышленный

union ['juːnjən] *n* (*unification*) объединение; (*also* **trade union**) профсоюз ▷ *cpd* профсоюзный

unique [juː'niːk] *adj* уникальный

unit ['juːnɪt] *n* (*single whole*) целое *nt adj*; (*measurement*) единица; (*of furniture etc*) секция

unite [juː'naɪt] *vt* объединять (*perf* объединить) ▷ *vi* объединяться (*perf* объединиться); **united** *adj* объединённый; (*effort*) совместный; **United Kingdom** *n* Соединённое Королевство; **United Nations (Organization)** *n* (Организация) Объединённых Наций; **United States (of America)** *n* Соединённые Штаты (Америки)

unity ['juːnɪtɪ] *n* единство

universal [juːnɪ'vəːsl] *adj* универсальный

universe ['juːnɪvəːs] *n* вселенная *f adj*

university [juːnɪ'vəːsɪtɪ] *n* университет

unjust [ʌn'dʒʌst] *adj* несправедливый

unkind [ʌn'kaɪnd] *adj* недобрый; (*behaviour*) злобный

unknown [ʌn'nəʊn] *adj* неизвестный

unlawful [ʌn'lɔːful] *adj* незаконный

unleash [ʌn'liːʃ] *vt* (*fig: feeling*) давать (*perf* дать) волю +*dat*; (: *force*) развязывать (*perf* развязать)

unless [ʌn'lɛs] *conj* если не; **he won't come, unless we ask** он не придёт, если мы не попросим

unlike [ʌn'laɪk] *adj* (*not alike*) непохожий ▷ *prep* (*different from*) в отличие от +*gen*

unlikely [ʌn'laɪklɪ] *adj* (*not likely*) маловероятный

unlimited [ʌn'lɪmɪtɪd] *adj* неограниченный

unload [ʌn'ləʊd] *vt* (*box, car*) разгружать (*perf* разгрузить)

unlucky [ʌn'lʌkɪ] *adj* невезучий; (*object*) несчастливый; **he is unlucky** он невезучий, ему не везёт

unmarried [ʌn'mærɪd] *adj* (*man*) неженатый, холостой; (*woman*) незамужняя

unmistak(e)able [ʌnmɪs'teɪkəbl] *adj* (*voice, sound*) характерный

unnatural [ʌn'nætʃrəl] *adj* неестественный

unnecessary [ʌn'nɛsəsərɪ] *adj* ненужный

UNO *n abbr* (= *United Nations Organization*) ООН (= Организация Объединённых Наций)

unofficial [ʌnə'fɪʃl] *adj* неофициальный

unpack [ʌn'pæk] *vi* распаковываться (*perf* распаковаться) ▷ *vt* распаковывать (*perf* распаковать)

unpleasant [ʌn'plɛznt] *adj* неприятный

unpopular [ʌn'pɒpjʊləʳ] *adj* непопулярный

unprecedented [ʌn'prɛsɪdəntɪd] *adj* беспрецедентный

unpredictable [ʌnprɪ'dɪktəbl] *adj* непредсказуемый

unqualified [ʌn'kwɒlɪfaɪd] *adj* неквалифицированный; (*total*) совершённый

unravel [ʌn'rævl] *vt* (*fig: mystery*) разгадывать (*perf* разгадать)

unreal [ʌn'rɪəl] *adj* (*not real*) нереальный

unrealistic ['ʌnrɪə'lɪstɪk] *adj* нереалистичный

unreasonable [ʌn'riːznəbl] *adj* неразумный; (*length of time*) нереальный

unrelated [ʌnrɪ'leɪtɪd] *adj* (*incident*) изолированный, отдельный; **to be unrelated** (*people*) не состоять (*impf*) в родстве

unreliable [ʌnrɪ'laɪəbl] *adj* ненадёжный

unrest [ʌn'rɛst] *n* волнения *ntpl*

unruly [ʌn'ruːlɪ] *adj* неуправляемый

unsafe [ʌn'seɪf] *adj* опасный

unsatisfactory ['ʌnsætɪs'fæktərɪ] *adj* неудовлетворительный

unsettled [ʌn'sɛtld] *adj* (*person*) беспокойный; **the weather is unsettled** погода не установилась

unsightly [ʌn'saɪtlɪ] *adj* неприглядный

unskilled [ʌn'skɪld] *adj* неквалифицированный

unstable [ʌn'steɪbl] *adj* (*government*)

нестаби́льный; (*person: mentally*)
неуравнове́шенный
unsteady [ʌnˈstɛdɪ] *adj* нетвёрдый
unsuccessful [ʌnsəkˈsɛsful] *adj*
(*attempt*) безуспе́шный; (*writer*)
неуда́вшийся; **to be unsuccessful (in sth)**
терпе́ть (*perf* потерпе́ть) неуда́чу (в
чём-н); **your application was unsuccessful**
Ва́ше заявле́ние не при́нято
unsuitable [ʌnˈsuːtəbl] *adj*
неподходя́щий
unsure [ʌnˈʃuəʳ] *adj* неуве́ренный; **he is
unsure of himself** он неуве́рен в себе́
untidy [ʌnˈtaɪdɪ] *adj* неопря́тный
until [ənˈtɪl] *prep* до +*gen* ▷ *conj* пока́
не; **until he comes** пока́ он не придёт;
until now/then до сих/тех пор
unused¹ [ʌnˈjuːzd] *adj* (*not used*)
неиспо́льзованный
unused² [ʌnˈjuːst] *adj*: **he is unused to it**
он к э́тому не привы́к; **she is unused to
flying** она́ не привы́кла лета́ть
unusual [ʌnˈjuːʒuəl] *adj* необы́чный;
(*exceptional*) необыкнове́нный
unveil [ʌnˈveɪl] *vt* (*statue*) открыва́ть (*perf*
откры́ть)
unwanted [ʌnˈwɔntɪd] *adj* (*child,
pregnancy*) нежела́нный
unwell [ʌnˈwɛl] *adj*: **to feel unwell**
чу́вствовать (*impf*) себя́ пло́хо; **he is
unwell** он пло́хо себя́ чу́вствует, он
нездоро́в
unwilling [ʌnˈwɪlɪŋ] *adj*: **to be unwilling
to do** не хоте́ть (*impf*) +*infin*
unwind [ʌnˈwaɪnd] (*irreg like* wind²) *vi*
(*relax*) расслабля́ться (*perf* расслаби́ться)
unwise [ʌnˈwaɪz] *adj* неблагоразу́мный

🔘 **KEYWORD**

up [ʌp] *prep* (*motion*) на +*acc*; (*position*) на
+*prp*; **he went up the stairs/the hill** он
подня́лся по ле́стнице/на́ гору; **the cat
was up a tree** ко́шка была́ на де́реве; **they
live further up this street** они́ живу́т
да́льше на э́той у́лице; **he has gone up to
Scotland** он пое́хал в Шотла́ндию
▷ *adv* **1** (*upwards, higher*): **up in the sky/
the mountains** высоко́ в не́бе/в гора́х; **put
the picture a bit higher up** пове́сьте
карти́ну повы́ше; **up there** (*up above*) там
наверху́
2: **to be up** (*out of bed*) встава́ть (*perf*
встать); (*prices, level*) поднима́ться (*perf*
подня́ться); **the tent is up** пала́тка
устано́влена
3: **up to** (*as far as*) до +*gen*; **up to now** до
сих пор
4: **to be up to** (*depending on*) зави́сеть
(*impf*) от +*gen*; **it's not up to me to decide**
не мне реша́ть; **it's up to you** э́то на Ва́ше
усмотре́ние
5: **to be up to** (*inf: be doing*) затева́ть
(*impf*); (*be satisfactory*) соотве́тствовать

(*impf*) +*dat*, отвеча́ть (*impf*) +*dat*; **he's not
up to the job** он не справля́ется с э́той
рабо́той; **his work is not up to the required
standard** его́ рабо́та не соотве́тствует
тре́буемым станда́ртам; **what's she up to
these days?** а что она́ тепе́рь поде́лывает?
▷ *n*: **ups and downs** (*in life, career*) взлёты
mpl и паде́ния *ntpl*

upbringing [ˈʌpbrɪŋɪŋ] *n* воспита́ние
update [ʌpˈdeɪt] *vt* (*records*) обновля́ть
(*perf* обнови́ть)
upgrade [ʌpˈgreɪd] *vt* (*house, equipment*)
модернизи́ровать (*impf/perf*); (*employee*)
повыша́ть (*perf* повы́сить) (в до́лжности)
upheaval [ʌpˈhiːvl] *n* переворо́т
uphill [ʌpˈhɪl] *adj* (*fig*) тяжёлый,
напряжённый ▷ *adv* вверх; **to go uphill**
поднима́ться (*perf* подня́ться) в го́ру
upholstery [ʌpˈhəulstərɪ] *n* оби́вка
upload [ʌpˈləud] *vt* загружа́ть (*perf*
загрузи́ть), выкла́дывать (*perf* вы́ложить)
upon [əˈpɔn] *prep* (*position*) на +*prp*;
(*motion*) на +*acc*
upper [ˈʌpəʳ] *adj* ве́рхний
upright [ˈʌpraɪt] *adj* (*vertical*)
вертика́льный
uprising [ˈʌpraɪzɪŋ] *n* восста́ние
uproar [ˈʌprɔːʳ] *n* (*protest*) возмуще́ние;
(*shouts*) го́мон, кри́ки *mpl*
upset [*vb, adj* ʌpˈsɛt, *n* ˈʌpsɛt] (*irreg like*
set) *vt* (*glass etc*) опроки́дывать (*perf*
опроки́нуть); (*routine*) наруша́ть (*perf*
нару́шить); (*person, plan*) расстра́ивать
(*perf* расстро́ить) ▷ *adj* расстро́енный
▷ *n*: **I have a stomach upset** (*Brit*) у меня́
расстро́йство желу́дка
upside down [ˈʌpsaɪd-] *adv* вверх
нога́ми; (*turn*) вверх дном
upstairs [ʌpˈstɛəz] *adv* (*be*) наверху́; (*go*)
наве́рх ▷ *adj* ве́рхний ▷ *n* ве́рхний эта́ж
up-to-date [ˈʌptəˈdeɪt] *adj* (*information*)
после́дний; (*equipment*) нове́йший
upward [ˈʌpwəd] *adj*: **upward movement/
glance** движе́ние/взгляд вверх ▷ *adv*
= **upwards**; **upwards** *adv* вверх; (*more
than*): **upwards of** свы́ше +*gen*
uranium [juəˈreɪnɪəm] *n* ура́н
urban [ˈəːbən] *adj* городско́й
urge [əːdʒ] *n* потре́бность *f* ▷ *vt*: **to urge
sb to do** настоя́тельно проси́ть (*perf*
попроси́ть) кого́-н +*infin*
urgency [ˈəːdʒənsɪ] *n* (*of task etc*)
неотло́жность *f*; (*of tone*) насто́йчивость *f*
urgent [ˈəːdʒənt] *adj* (*message*) сро́чный;
(*need*) насу́щный, неотло́жный; (*voice*)
насто́йчивый
urine [ˈjuərɪn] *n* моча́
US *n abbr* (= *United States*) США
(= Соединённые Шта́ты Аме́рики)
us [ʌs] *pron* (*direct*) нас; (*indirect*) нам;
(*after prep*: +*gen*, +*prp*) нас; (: +*dat*) нам;
(: +*instr*) на́ми; **a few of us** не́которые из
нас; *see also* **me**

USA n abbr (= United States of America) США (= *Соединённые Штаты Аме́рики*)

USB stick [juː ɛs biː-] n (USB-) флеш-накопи́тель m, флеш-ди́ск, флёшка (*inf*)

use [vb juːz, n juːs] vt (*object, tool*) по́льзоваться (*impf*) +instr, испо́льзовать (*impf/perf*); (*phrase*) употребля́ть (*perf* употреби́ть) ▷ n (*using*) испо́льзование, употребле́ние; (*usefulness*) по́льза; (*purpose*) примене́ние; **she used to do it** она́ когда́-то занима́лась э́тим; **what's this used for?** для чего́ э́то испо́льзуется?; **to be used to** привы́кнуть (*perf*) к +dat; **to be in use** употребля́ться (*impf*), быть (*impf*) в употребле́нии; **to be out of use** не употребля́ться (*impf*); **of use** поле́зный; **it's no use** (э́то) бесполе́зно; **use up** (*food*) расхо́довать (*perf* израсхо́довать); **used** [juːzd] adj (*car*) поде́ржанный; **useful** [ˈjuːsful] adj поле́зный; **useless** [ˈjuːslɪs] adj (*unusable*) неприго́дный; (*pointless*) бесполе́зный; **user** [ˈjuːzəʳ] n по́льзователь m; **user-friendly** adj просто́й в испо́льзовании

USSR n abbr (*formerly*) (= Union of Soviet Socialist Republics) СССР (= *Сою́з Сове́тских Социалисти́ческих Респу́блик*)

usual [ˈjuːʒuəl] adj (*time, place etc*) обы́чный; **as usual** как обы́чно; **usually** adv обы́чно

utensil [juːˈtɛnsl] n инструме́нт; (*for cooking*) принадле́жность f

utility [juːˈtɪlɪtɪ] n: **public utilities** коммуна́льные услу́ги fpl

utilize [ˈjuːtɪlaɪz] vt утилизи́ровать (*impf/perf*)

utmost [ˈʌtməust] adj велича́йший ▷ n: **to do one's utmost** де́лать (*perf* сде́лать) всё возмо́жное

utter [ˈʌtəʳ] adj (*amazement*) по́лный; (*conviction*) глубо́кий; (*rubbish*) соверше́нный ▷ vt (*words*) произноси́ть (*perf* произнести́); **utterly** adv соверше́нно

U-turn [ˈjuːˈtəːn] n (*Aut*) разворо́т на 180 гра́дусов

vacancy [ˈveɪkənsɪ] n (*Brit: job*) вака́нсия; (*room*) свобо́дный но́мер

vacant [ˈveɪkənt] adj (*room, seat*) свобо́дный; (*look*) пусто́й

vacation [vəˈkeɪʃən] n (*esp US: holiday*) о́тпуск; (*Brit: Scol*) кани́кулы pl

vaccine [ˈvæksiːn] n вакци́на

vacuum [ˈvækjum] n (*empty space*) ва́куум ▷ vt пылесо́сить (*perf* пропылесо́сить); **vacuum cleaner** n пылесо́с

vagina [vəˈdʒaɪnə] n влага́лище

vague [veɪg] adj (*blurred: memory, outline*) сму́тный; (*look*) рассе́янный; (*idea, instructions, answer*) неопределённый

vain [veɪn] adj (*useless*) тщесла́вный; (*useless*) тще́тный; **in vain** тще́тно, напра́сно

valid [ˈvælɪd] adj (*ticket, document*) действи́тельный; (*reason, argument*) ве́ский

valley [ˈvælɪ] n доли́на

valuable [ˈvæljuəbl] adj це́нный; (*time*) драгоце́нный; **valuables** npl (*jewellery etc*) це́нности fpl

value [ˈvæljuː] n це́нность f ▷ vt оце́нивать (*perf* оцени́ть); (*appreciate*) цени́ть (*impf*); **values** npl (*principles*) це́нности fpl

valve [vælv] n (*also Med*) кла́пан

vampire [ˈvæmpaɪəʳ] n вампи́р

van [væn] n (*Aut*) фурго́н

vandalism [ˈvændəlɪzəm] n вандали́зм

vanilla [vəˈnɪlə] n вани́ль f

vanish [ˈvænɪʃ] vi исчеза́ть (*perf* исче́знуть)

vanity [ˈvænɪtɪ] n тщесла́вие

vape [veɪp] vi кури́ть (*impf*) электро́нную сигаре́ту, па́рить (*impf*), ве́йпить (*impf*) (*inf*)

vapour [ˈveɪpəʳ] (*US* vapor) n пар

variable [ˈvɛərɪəbl] adj (*likely to change*)

изме́нчивый; (*able to be changed: speed*) переме́нный

variation [vɛərɪˈeɪʃən] *n* (*change*) измене́ние; (*different form*) вариа́ция

varied [ˈvɛərɪd] *adj* разнообра́зный

variety [vəˈraɪətɪ] *n* разнообра́зие; (*type*) разнови́дность *f*

various [ˈvɛərɪəs] *adj* (*different, several*) разли́чный

varnish [ˈvɑːnɪʃ] *n* (*product*) лак; (*also* **nail varnish**) лак для ногте́й ▷ *vt* (*wood, table*) лакирова́ть (*perf* отлакирова́ть); (*nails*) кра́сить (*perf* покра́сить)

vary [ˈvɛərɪ] *vt* разнообра́зить (*impf*) ▷ *vi* (*sizes, colours*) различа́ться (*impf*); (*become different*): **to vary with** (*weather etc*) меня́ться (*impf*) в зави́симости от +*gen*

vase [vɑːz] *n* ва́за

vast [vɑːst] *adj* (*knowledge, area*) обши́рный; (*expense*) грома́дный

VAT [væt] *n abbr* (*Brit*) (= **value-added tax**) НДС (= *нало́г на доба́вленную сто́имость*)

vault [vɔːlt] *n* (*tomb*) склеп; (*in bank*) сейф, храни́лище ▷ *vt* (*also* **vault over**) перепры́гивать (*perf* перепры́гнуть) че́рез +*acc*

VCR *n abbr* = **video cassette recorder**

VDU [ˈviːdiːˈjuː] *n abbr* (= *visual display unit*) монито́р, диспле́й *m*

veal [viːl] *n* (*Culin*) теля́тина

veer [vɪər] *vi* (*vehicle*) свора́чивать (*perf* сверну́ть); (*wind*) меня́ть (*perf* поменя́ть) направле́ние

vegetable [ˈvɛdʒtəbl] *n* (*Bot*) о́вощ ▷ *adj* (*oil etc*) расти́тельный; (*dish*) овощно́й

vegetarian [vɛdʒɪˈtɛərɪən] *n* вегетариа́нец(-а́нка) ▷ *adj* вегетариа́нский

vegetation [vɛdʒɪˈteɪʃən] *n* (*plants*) расти́тельность *f*

vehicle [ˈviːɪkl] *n* автотра́нспортное сре́дство; (*fig*) сре́дство, ору́дие

veil [veɪl] *n* вуа́ль *f*

vein [veɪn] *n* (*of leaf*) жи́лка; (*Anat*) ве́на; (*of ore*) жи́ла

velvet [ˈvɛlvɪt] *n* ба́рхат ▷ *adj* ба́рхатный

vendor [ˈvɛndəʳ] *n*: **street vendor** у́личный(-ая) торго́вец(-вка)

vengeance [ˈvɛndʒəns] *n* мще́ние, возме́здие; **with a vengeance** (*fig*) отча́янно

venison [ˈvɛnɪsn] *n* оле́нина

venom [ˈvɛnəm] *n* (*also fig*) яд

vent [vɛnt] *n* (*also* **air vent**) вентиляцио́нное отве́рстие ▷ *vt* (*fig*) дава́ть (*perf* дать) вы́ход +*dat*

ventilation [vɛntɪˈleɪʃən] *n* вентиля́ция

venture [ˈvɛntʃəʳ] *n* предприя́тие ▷ *vt* (*opinion*) осме́ливаться (*perf* осме́литься) на +*acc* ▷ *vi* осме́ливаться (*perf* осме́литься); **business venture** предприя́тие

venue [ˈvɛnjuː] *n* ме́сто проведе́ния

verb [vəːb] *n* глаго́л

verbal [ˈvəːbl] *adj* (*spoken*) у́стный

verdict [ˈvəːdɪkt] *n* (*Law*) верди́кт; (*fig: opinion*) заключе́ние

verge [vəːdʒ] *n* (*Brit: of road*) обо́чина; **to be on the verge of sth** быть (*impf*) на гра́ни чего́-н

verify [ˈvɛrɪfaɪ] *vt* (*confirm*) подтвержда́ть (*perf* подтверди́ть); (*check*) сверя́ть (*perf* све́рить)

versatile [ˈvəːsətaɪl] *adj* (*person*) разносторо́нний; (*substance, machine etc*) универса́льный

verse [vəːs] *n* (*poetry, in Bible*) стих; (*part of poem*) строфа́

version [ˈvəːʃən] *n* (*form*) вариа́нт; (*account: of events*) ве́рсия

versus [ˈvəːsəs] *prep* про́тив +*gen*

vertical [ˈvəːtɪkl] *adj* вертика́льный

very [ˈvɛrɪ] *adv* о́чень ▷ *adj* са́мый; **the very book which ...** та са́мая кни́га, кото́рая ...; **thank you very much** большо́е (Вам) спаси́бо; **very much better** гора́здо лу́чше; **I very much hope so** я о́чень наде́юсь на э́то; **the very last** са́мый после́дний; **at the very least** как ми́нимум

vessel [ˈvɛsl] *n* (*ship*) су́дно; (*bowl*) сосу́д; **blood vessel** кровено́сный сосу́д

vest [vɛst] *n* (*Brit: underwear*) ма́йка; (*US: waistcoat*) жиле́т

vet [vɛt] *n abbr* (*Brit*) (= **veterinary surgeon**) ветерина́р ▷ *vt* (*check*) проверя́ть (*perf* прове́рить); (*approve*) одобря́ть (*perf* одо́брить)

veteran [ˈvɛtərn] *n* (*of war*) ветера́н

veterinary [ˈvɛtrɪnərɪ] *adj* ветерина́рный

veto [ˈviːtəu] (*pl* **vetoes**) *n* ве́то *nt ind* ▷ *vt* (*Pol, Law*) налага́ть (*perf* наложи́ть) ве́то на +*acc*

via [ˈvaɪə] *prep* че́рез +*acc*

viable [ˈvaɪəbl] *adj* жизнеспосо́бный

vibrate [vaɪˈbreɪt] *vi* вибри́ровать (*impf*)

vibration [vaɪˈbreɪʃən] *n* вибра́ция

vicar [ˈvɪkəʳ] *n* (*Rel*) прихо́дский свяще́нник

vice [vaɪs] *n* поро́к; (*Tech*) тиски́ *pl*

vice-chairman [vaɪsˈtʃɛəmən] *irreg n* замести́тель *m* председа́теля

vice versa [ˈvaɪsɪˈvəːsə] *adv* наоборо́т

vicinity [vɪˈsɪnɪtɪ] *n*: **in the vicinity (of)** вблизи́ (от +*gen*)

vicious [ˈvɪʃəs] *adj* (*attack, blow*) жесто́кий; (*words, look, dog*) злой; **vicious circle** поро́чный круг

victim [ˈvɪktɪm] *n* же́ртва

victor [ˈvɪktəʳ] *n* победи́тель(ница) *m(f)*

victorious [vɪkˈtɔːrɪəs] *adj* (*team*) победоно́сный; (*shout*) побе́дный

victory [ˈvɪktərɪ] *n* побе́да

video [ˈvɪdɪəu] *cpd* ви́део *ind* ▷ *n* (*also* **video film**) видеофи́льм; (*also* **video cassette**) видеокассе́та; (*also* **video cassette recorder**) видеомагнитофо́н; (*also* **video camera**) видеока́мера; **video**

game n видеоигра; **videophone** n видеотелефон; **video recorder** n видеомагнитофон; **video tape** n видеолента

vie [vaɪ] vi: **to vie with sb/for sth** состязаться (impf) с кем-н/в чём-н

Vienna [vɪˈɛnə] n Вена

view [vjuː] n (sight, outlook) вид; (opinion) взгляд ▷ vt рассматривать (perf рассмотреть); **in full view (of)** на виду (у +gen); **in view of the bad weather/the fact that** ввиду плохой погоды/того, что; **in my view** на мой взгляд; **viewer** n (person) зритель(ница) m(f); **viewfinder** n (Phot) видоискатель m; **viewpoint** n (attitude) точка зрения; (place) место обозрения

vigilant [ˈvɪdʒɪlənt] adj бдительный

vigorous [ˈvɪgərəs] adj (action, campaign) энергичный

vile [vaɪl] adj гнусный, омерзительный

villa [ˈvɪlə] n вилла

village [ˈvɪlɪdʒ] n деревня

villain [ˈvɪlən] n (in novel etc) злодей; (Brit: criminal) преступник

vine [vaɪn] n (with grapes) (виноградная) лоза

vinegar [ˈvɪnɪgəʳ] n уксус

vineyard [ˈvɪnjɑːd] n виноградник

vintage [ˈvɪntɪdʒ] cpd (comedy, performance etc) классический; (wine) марочный

vinyl [ˈvaɪnl] n винил

viola [vɪˈəulə] n (Mus) альт

violation [vaɪəˈleɪʃən] n (of agreement etc) нарушение

violence [ˈvaɪələns] n (brutality) насилие

violent [ˈvaɪələnt] adj (behaviour) жестокий; (death) насильственный; (debate, criticism) ожесточённый

violet [ˈvaɪələt] adj фиолетовый ▷ n (plant) фиалка

violin [vaɪəˈlɪn] n (Mus) скрипка

VIP n abbr (= very important person) особо важное лицо

virgin [ˈvəːdʒɪn] n девственница ▷ adj (snow, forest etc) девственный

Virgo [ˈvəːgəu] n Дева

virtually [ˈvəːtjuəlɪ] adv фактически, практически

virtual reality [ˈvəːtjuəl-] n (Comput) виртуальная реальность f

virtue [ˈvəːtjuː] n (moral correctness) добродетель f; (advantage) преимущество; (good quality) достоинство; **by virtue of** благодаря +dat

virus [ˈvaɪərəs] n (Med) вирус

visa [ˈviːzə] n (for travel) виза

visibility [vɪzɪˈbɪlɪtɪ] n видимость f

visible [ˈvɪzəbl] adj видимый; (results, growth) очевидный

vision [ˈvɪʒən] n (sight) зрение; (foresight) провидение, видение

visit [ˈvɪzɪt] n посещение, визит ▷ vt (person, place) посещать (perf посетить);

(elderly, patient) навещать (perf навестить); **visitor** n (person visiting) гость(я) m(f); (in public place) посетитель(ница) m(f); (in town etc) приезжий(-ая) m(f) adj

visual [ˈvɪzjuəl] adj (image) зрительный; **visualize** vt представлять (perf представить)

vital [ˈvaɪtl] adj (question) жизненный; (problem) насущный; (full of life: person) деятельный, полный жизни; (organization) жизнедеятельный; **it is vital ...** необходимо ...; **vitality** [vaɪˈtælɪtɪ] n (liveliness) живость f

vitamin [ˈvɪtəmɪn] n витамин

vivid [ˈvɪvɪd] adj (description, colour) яркий; (memory) отчётливый; (imagination) живой

vlog [vlɔg] n видеоблог, влог; **vlogger** n видеоблогер

vocabulary [vəuˈkæbjulərɪ] n (words known) словарный запас

vocal [ˈvəukl] adj (articulate) речистый

vocation [vəuˈkeɪʃən] n призвание

vodka [ˈvɔdkə] n водка

voice [vɔɪs] n голос ▷ vt (opinion) высказывать (perf высказать); **voice mail** n (system) голосовая почта; (device) автоответчик

void [vɔɪd] n (emptiness) пустота; (hole) провал ▷ adj (invalid) недействительный

volatile [ˈvɔlətaɪl] adj (situation) изменчивый; (person) неустойчивый; (liquid) летучий

volcano [vɔlˈkeɪnəu] n (pl **volcanoes**) n вулкан

volleyball [ˈvɔlɪbɔːl] n волейбол

voltage [ˈvəultɪdʒ] n (Elec) напряжение

volume [ˈvɔljuːm] n (amount) объём; (book) том; (sound level) громкость f

voluntarily [ˈvɔləntrɪlɪ] adv добровольно

voluntary [ˈvɔləntərɪ] adj (willing) добровольный; (unpaid) общественный

volunteer [vɔlənˈtɪəʳ] n (unpaid helper) добровольный(-ая) помощник(-ица), волонтёр; (to army etc) доброволец ▷ vt (information) предлагать (perf предложить) ▷ vi (for army etc) идти (perf пойти) добровольцем; **to volunteer to do** вызываться (perf вызваться) +infin

vomit [ˈvɔmɪt] n рвота ▷ vi: **he vomited** его вырвало

vote [vəut] n (indication of opinion) голосование; (votes cast) число поданных голосов; (right to vote) право голоса ▷ vi голосовать (perf проголосовать) ▷ vt (Labour etc) голосовать (perf проголосовать) за +acc; (elect): **he was voted chairman** он был избран председателем; (propose): **to vote that** предлагать (perf предложить), чтобы; **to put sth to the vote, take a vote on sth** ставить (perf поставить) что-н на

голосова́ние; **vote of thanks**
благода́рственная речь *f*; **to pass a vote of
confidence/no confidence** выража́ть (*perf*
вы́разить) во́тум дове́рия/недове́рия; **to
vote for** *or* **in favour of/against** голосова́ть
(*perf* проголосова́ть) за +*acc*/про́тив +*gen*;
voter *n* избира́тель(ница) *m(f)*

voting ['vəutɪŋ] *n* голосова́ние

voucher ['vautʃə^r] *n* (*with petrol,
cigarettes etc*) ва́учер

vow [vau] *n* кля́тва ⊳ *vt*: **to vow to do/
that** кля́сться (*perf* покля́сться) +*infin*/,
что; **vows** *npl* (*Rel*) обе́т *msg*

vowel ['vauəl] *n* гла́сный *m adj*

voyage ['vɔɪɪdʒ] *n* (*by ship*) пла́вание; (*by
spacecraft*) полёт

vulgar ['vʌlgə^r] *adj* (*rude*) вульга́рный;
(*tasteless*) по́шлый

vulnerable ['vʌlnərəbl] *adj* (*position*)
уязви́мый; (*person*) рани́мый; **he is
vulnerable to ...** он подве́ржен +*dat* ...

vulture ['vʌltʃə^r] *n* (*Zool*) гриф

wade [weɪd] *vi*: **to wade through** (*water*)
пробира́ться (*perf* пробра́ться) че́рез +*acc*

wage [weɪdʒ] *n* (*also* **wages**) зарпла́та
⊳ *vt*: **to wage war** вести́ (*impf*) войну́

wail [weɪl] *n* (*of person*) вопль *m* ⊳ *vi*
(*person*) вопи́ть (*impf*); (*siren*) выть (*impf*)

waist [weɪst] *n* та́лия; **waistcoat** *n*
(*Brit*) жиле́т

wait [weɪt] *vi* ждать (*impf*) ⊳ *n*
ожида́ние; **to keep sb waiting** заставля́ть
(*perf* заста́вить) кого́-н ждать; **I can't wait
to go home** (*fig*) мне не те́рпится пойти́
домо́й; **to wait for sb/sth** ждать (*impf*)
кого́-н/чего́-н; **we had a long wait for the
bus** мы до́лго жда́ли авто́буса; **wait on**
vt fus (*serve*) обслу́живать (*perf*
обслужи́ть); **waiter** *n* официа́нт;
waiting list *n* о́чередь *f*, спи́сок
очереднико́в; **waiting room** *n* (*in
surgery*) приёмная *f adj*; (*in station*) зал
ожида́ния; **waitress** *n* официа́нтка

wake [weɪk] (*pt* **woke** *or* **waked**, *pp*
woken *or* **waked**) *vt* (*also* **wake up**)
буди́ть (*perf* разбуди́ть) ⊳ *vi* (*also* **wake
up**) просыпа́ться (*perf* просну́ться) ⊳ *n*
бде́ние (у гро́ба); (*Naut*) кильва́тер; **in the
wake of** (*fig*) всле́дствие +*gen*

Wales [weɪlz] *n* Уэ́льс

walk [wɔːk] *n* (*hike*) похо́д; (*shorter*)
прогу́лка; (*gait*) похо́дка; (*path*) тропа́
⊳ *vi* (*go on foot*) ходи́ть/идти́ (*impf*)
(пешко́м); (*baby*) ходи́ть (*impf*); (*for
pleasure, exercise*) гуля́ть (*impf*) ⊳ *vt*
(*distance*) проходи́ть (*perf* пройти́); (*dog*)
выгу́ливать (*perf* вы́гулять); **10 minutes'
walk from here** в 10-ти мину́тах ходьбы́
отсю́да; **walk out** *vi* (*audience*)
демонстрати́вно покида́ть (*perf* поки́нуть)
зал; (*workers*) забастова́ть (*perf*); **walker**
n (*hiker*) тури́ст(ка); **walking stick** *n*
трость *f*

wall [wɔːl] *n* стена́

wallet ['wɒlɪt] n бума́жник

wallpaper ['wɔːlpeɪpə'] n обо́и pl ▷ vt окле́ивать (perf окле́ить) обо́ями

walnut ['wɔːlnʌt] n (nut) гре́цкий оре́х; (wood) оре́х

walrus ['wɔːlrəs] (pl **walrus** or **walruses**) n морж

waltz [wɔːls] n вальс

wander ['wɒndə'] vi (person) броди́ть (impf); (mind, thoughts) блужда́ть (impf) ▷ vt броди́ть (impf) по +dat

want [wɒnt] vt (wish for) хоте́ть (impf) +acc or +gen; (need) нужда́ться (impf) в +prp ▷ n: **for want of** за недоста́тком +gen; **to want to do** хоте́ть (impf) +infin; **I want you to apologize** я хочу́, что́бы Вы извини́лись; **wanted** adj (criminal etc) разы́скиваемый

war [wɔː'] n война́; **to declare war (on)** объявля́ть (perf объяви́ть) войну́ (+dat)

ward [wɔːd] n (Med) пала́та; (Brit: Pol) о́круг; (Law) ребёнок, под опе́кой; **ward off** vt (attack, enemy) отража́ть (perf отрази́ть); (danger, illness) отвраща́ть (perf отврати́ть)

warden ['wɔːdn] n (of park, reserve) смотри́тель(ница) m(f); (of prison) нача́льник; (of youth hostel) коменда́нт

wardrobe ['wɔːdrəub] n шифонье́р, платяно́й шкаф; (clothes) гардеро́б; (Theat) костюме́рная f adj

warehouse ['wɛəhaus] n склад

warfare ['wɔːfɛə'] n вое́нные or боевы́е де́йствия ntpl

warm [wɔːm] adj тёплый; (thanks, supporter) горя́чий; (heart) до́брый; **it's warm today** сего́дня тепло́; **I'm warm** мне тепло́; **warm up** vi (person, room) согрева́ться (perf согре́ться); (water) нагрева́ться (perf нагре́ться); (athlete) размина́ться (perf размя́ться) ▷ vt разогрева́ть (perf разогре́ть); **the weather warmed up** на у́лице потепле́ло; **warmly** adv (applaud) горячо́; (dress, welcome) тепло́; **warmth** n тепло́

warn [wɔːn] vt: **to warn sb (not) to do/of/ that** предупрежда́ть (perf предупреди́ть) кого́-н (не) +infin/о +prp/, что; **warning** n предупрежде́ние

warrant ['wɔrnt] n (also **search warrant**) о́рдер на о́быск; **warranty** n гара́нтия

Warsaw ['wɔːsɔː] n Варша́ва

warship ['wɔːʃɪp] n вое́нный кора́бль m

wart [wɔːt] n борода́вка

wartime ['wɔːtaɪm] n: **in wartime** в вое́нное вре́мя

wary ['wɛərɪ] adj: **to be wary of sb/sth** относи́ться (impf) к кому́-н/чему́-н с опа́ской

was [wɔz] pt of **be**

wash [wɔʃ] n мытьё; (clothes) сти́рка; (washing programme) режи́м сти́рки (в стира́льной маши́не); (of ship) пе́нистый след ▷ vt (hands, body) мыть (perf помы́ть); (clothes) стира́ть (perf постира́ть); (face) умыва́ть (perf умы́ть) ▷ vi (person) мы́ться (perf помы́ться); (sea etc): **to wash over sth** перека́тываться (perf перекати́ться) че́рез что-н; **to have a wash** помы́ться (perf); **to give sth a wash** помы́ть (perf) что-н; (clothes) постира́ть (perf) что-н; **wash off** vi отмыва́ться (perf отмы́ться); (stain) отсти́рываться (perf отстира́ться); **wash up** vi (Brit) мыть (perf вы́мыть) посу́ду; (US) мы́ться (perf помы́ться); **washer** n ша́йба; **washing** n сти́рка; **washing-up** n (гря́зная) посу́да

wasn't ['wɔznt] = **was not**

wasp [wɔsp] n оса́

waste [weɪst] n (act) тра́та; (rubbish) отхо́ды mpl; (also **waste land**: in city) пусты́рь m ▷ adj (rejected, damaged) брако́ванный; (left over) отрабо́танный ▷ vt растра́чивать (perf растра́тить); (opportunity) упуска́ть (perf упусти́ть); **wastes** npl пусты́ня fsg; **waste paper** испо́льзованная бума́га; **wastepaper basket** n корзи́на для (нену́жной) бума́г

watch [wɔtʃ] n (also **wristwatch**) (нару́чные) часы́ pl; (act of watching) наблюде́ние ▷ vt (also наблюда́ть (impf) за +instr; (match, programme) смотре́ть (perf посмотре́ть); (events, weight, language) следи́ть (impf) за +instr; (be careful of: person) остерега́ться (impf) +gen; (look after) смотре́ть (impf) за +instr ▷ vi (take care) смотре́ть (impf); (keep guard) дежу́рить (impf); **watch out** vi остерега́ться (perf остере́чься)

water ['wɔːtə'] n вода́ ▷ vt полива́ть (perf поли́ть) ▷ vi (eyes) слези́ться (impf); **in British waters** в брита́нских во́дах; **water down** vt разбавля́ть (perf разба́вить (водо́й); (fig) смягча́ть (perf смягчи́ть); **watercolour** (US **watercolor**) n (picture) акваре́ль f; **waterfall** n водопа́д; **watering can** n ле́йка; **watermelon** n арбу́з; **waterproof** adj непромока́емый

watt [wɔt] n ватт

wave [weɪv] n волна́; (of hand) взмах ▷ vi (signal) маха́ть (impf); (branches) кача́ться (impf); (flag) развева́ться (impf) ▷ vt маха́ть (impf) +instr; (stick, gun) разма́хивать (impf) +instr; **wavelength** n (Radio) длина́ волны́; **they are on the same wavelength** (fig) они́ смо́трят на ве́щи одина́ково

wax [wæks] n (polish) воск; (: for floor) масти́ка; (for skis) мазь f; (in ear) се́ра ▷ vt (floor) натира́ть (perf натере́ть) масти́кой; (car) натира́ть (perf натере́ть) во́ском; (skis) ма́зать (perf сма́зать) ма́зью

way [weɪ] n (route) путь m, доро́га; (manner, method) спо́соб; (usu pl: habit) привы́чка; **which way? — this way** куда́? — сюда́; **is it a long way from here?** э́то далеко́ отсю́да?; **which way do we go now?** куда́ нам тепе́рь идти́?; **on the way** (en route) по пути́ or доро́ге; **to be on one's way** быть (impf) в пути́; **to go out of one's way to do** стара́ться (perf постара́ться) изо всех сил +infin; **to be in sb's way** стоя́ть (impf) на чьём-н пути́; **to lose one's way** заблуди́ться (perf); **the plan is under way** план осуществля́ется; **in a way** в изве́стном смы́сле; **in some ways** в не́которых отноше́ниях; **no way!** (inf) ни за что!; **by the way ...** кста́ти ..., ме́жду про́чим ...; **"way in"** (Brit) "вход"; **"way out"** (Brit) "вы́ход"; **"give way"** (Brit: Aut) "уступи́те доро́гу"

WC n abbr (= water closet) туале́т

we [wiː] pron мы

weak [wiːk] adj сла́бый; **to grow weak** слабе́ть (perf ослабе́ть); **weaken** vi (person) смягча́ться (perf смягчи́ться) ▷ vt (government, person) ослабля́ть (perf осла́бить); **weakness** n сла́бость f; **to have a weakness for** име́ть (impf) сла́бость к +dat

wealth [wɛlθ] n (money, resources) бога́тство; (of details, knowledge etc) оби́лие; **wealthy** adj бога́тый

weapon ['wɛpən] n ору́жие

wear [wɛər] (pt wore, pp worn) n (use) но́ска; (damage) изно́с ▷ vi (last) носи́ться (impf); (rub through) изна́шиваться (perf износи́ться) ▷ vt (generally) носи́ть (impf); (put on) надева́ть (perf наде́ть); (damage) изна́шивать (perf износи́ть); **he was wearing his new shirt** на нём была́ его́ но́вая руба́шка; **wear down** vt (resistance) сломи́ть (perf); **wear out** vt (shoes, clothing) изна́шивать (perf износи́ть)

weary ['wɪərɪ] adj утомлённый ▷ vi: **to weary of** утомля́ться (perf утоми́ться) от +gen

weasel ['wiːzl] n (Zool) ла́ска

weather ['wɛðər] n пого́да ▷ vt (crisis) выде́рживать (perf вы́держать); **I am under the weather** мне нездоро́вится; **weather forecast** n прогно́з пого́ды

weave [wiːv] (pt wove, pp woven) vt (cloth) ткать (perf сотка́ть)

web [wɛb] n паути́на; (fig) сеть f; **web address** n а́дрес в Интерне́т, веб-а́дрес; **webcam** n Интерне́т-ка́мера, веб-ка́мера; **web page** n электро́нная страни́ца, страни́ца на интерне́те; **website** n сайт

wed [wɛd] (pt, pp wedded) vi венча́ться (perf обвенча́ться)

we'd [wiːd] = we had; we would

wedding ['wɛdɪŋ] n сва́дьба; (in church) венча́ние; **silver/golden wedding** сере́бряная/золота́я сва́дьба

wedge [wɛdʒ] n клин ▷ vt закрепля́ть (perf закрепи́ть) кли́ном; (pack tightly): **to wedge in** вти́скивать (perf вти́снуть) в +acc

Wednesday ['wɛnzdɪ] n среда́

wee [wiː] adj (Scottish) ма́ленький

weed [wiːd] n сорня́к ▷ vt поло́ть (perf вы́полоть)

week [wiːk] n неде́ля; **a week today** че́рез неде́лю; **a week on Friday** в сле́дующую пя́тницу; **weekday** n бу́дний день m; **weekend** n выходны́е pl adj (дни), суббо́та и воскресе́нье; **weekly** adv еженеде́льно ▷ adj еженеде́льный

weep [wiːp] (pt, pp wept) vi (person) пла́кать (impf)

weigh [weɪ] vt взве́шивать (perf взве́сить) ▷ vi ве́сить (impf); **weigh down** vt отягоща́ть (perf отяготи́ть); (fig) тяготи́ть (impf)

weight [weɪt] n вес; (for scales) ги́ря; **to lose weight** худе́ть (perf похуде́ть); **to put on weight** поправля́ться (perf попра́виться)

weir [wɪər] n (in river) запру́да

weird [wɪəd] adj (strange) стра́нный, дикови́нный

welcome ['wɛlkəm] adj жела́нный ▷ n (hospitality) приём; (greeting) приве́тствие ▷ vt (also bid welcome) приве́тствовать (impf); **thank you — you're welcome!** спаси́бо — пожа́луйста!

weld [wɛld] vt сва́ривать (perf свари́ть)

welfare ['wɛlfɛər] n (well-being) благополу́чие; (US: social aid) социа́льное посо́бие; **welfare state** n госуда́рство всео́бщего благостостоя́ния

well [wɛl] n (for water) коло́дец; (also oil well) (нефтяна́я) сква́жина ▷ adv хорошо́ ▷ excl (anyway) ну; (so) ну вот ▷ adj: **he is well** он здоро́в; **as well** та́кже; **I woke well before dawn** я просну́лся задо́лго до рассве́та; **I've brought my anorak as well as a jumper** кро́ме сви́тера я взял ещё и ку́ртку; **well done!** молоде́ц!; **get well soon!** поправля́йтесь скоре́е!; **he is doing well at school** в шко́ле он успева́ет; **the business is doing well** би́знес процвета́ет; **well up** vi (tears) наверну́ться (perf)

we'll [wiːl] = we will; we shall

well-dressed ['wɛl'drɛst] adj хорошо́ оде́тый

wellies ['wɛlɪz] npl = wellingtons

wellingtons ['wɛlɪŋtənz] npl (also **wellington boots**) рези́новые сапоги́ mpl

well-known ['wɛl'nəun] adj изве́стный

well-off ['wɛl'ɔf] adj обеспе́ченный

Welsh [wɛlʃ] adj уэ́льский ▷ npl: **the Welsh** (people) уэ́льсцы mpl, валли́йцы mpl; **Welshman** irreg n уэ́льсец, валли́ец; **Welshwoman** n irreg валли́йка, жи́тельница Уэ́льса

went [wɛnt] *pt of* **go**

wept [wɛpt] *pt, pp of* **weep**

were [wəːʳ] *pt of* **be**

we're [wɪəʳ] = **we are**

weren't [wəːnt] = **were not**

west [wɛst] *n* за́пад ▷ *adj* за́падный ▷ *adv* на за́пад; **the West** (*Pol*) За́пад; **western** *adj* за́падный ▷ *n* (*Cinema*) ве́стерн

wet [wɛt] *adj* (*damp, rainy*) вла́жный, сыро́й; (*soaking*) мо́крый; **to get wet** мо́кнуть (*perf* промо́кнуть)

we've [wiːv] = **we have**

whale [weɪl] *n* кит

wharf [wɔːf] (*pl* **wharves**) *n* при́стань *f*

⭕ **KEYWORD**

what [wɔt] *adj* **1** (*interrogative: direct, indirect*) како́й (*f* кака́я, *nt* како́е, *pl* каки́е); **what books do you need?** каки́е кни́ги Вам нужны́?; **what size is the dress?** како́го разме́ра э́то пла́тье?

2 (*emphatic*) како́й (*f* кака́я, *nt* како́е, *pl* каки́е); **what a lovely day!** како́й чуде́сный день!; **what a fool I am!** како́й же я дура́к! ▷ *pron* **1** (*interrogative*) что; **what are you doing?** что Вы де́лаете?; **what are you talking about?** о чём Вы говори́те?; **what is it called?** как э́то называ́ется?; **what about me?** а как же я?; **what about doing …?** как насчёт того́, что́бы +*infin* …?

2 (*relative*) что; **I saw what was on the table** я ви́дел, что бы́ло на столе́; **tell me what you're thinking about** скажи́те мне, о чём Вы ду́маете; **what you say is wrong** то, что Вы говори́те, неве́рно ▷ *excl* (*disbelieving*) что; **I've crashed the car — what!** я разби́л маши́ну — что!

whatever [wɔtˈɛvəʳ] *adj* (*any*) любо́й; **whatever book** люба́я кни́га ▷ *pron* (*any*) всё; (*regardless of*) что бы ни; **whatever you do …** что бы ты не де́лал …; **whatever the reason …** какова́ бы ни была́ причи́на …; **do whatever is necessary/you want** де́лайте всё, что необходи́мо/хоти́те; **whatever happens** что бы ни случи́лось; **there is no reason whatever** нет никако́й причи́ны; **nothing whatever** абсолю́тно ничего́

whatsoever [wɔtsəuˈɛvəʳ] *adj*: **there is no reason whatsoever** нет никако́й причи́ны

wheat [wiːt] *n* пшени́ца

wheel [wiːl] *n* (*of car etc*) колесо́; (*also* **steering wheel**) руль *m*; **wheelbarrow** *n* та́чка; **wheelchair** *n* инвали́дная коля́ска

wheeze [wiːz] *vi* хрипе́ть (*impf*)

when [wɛn] *adv, conj* когда́; **when you've read the book …** когда́ Вы прочита́ете кни́гу …

whenever [wɛnˈɛvəʳ] *adv* в любо́е вре́мя ▷ *conj* (*any time*) когда́ то́лько; (*every time that*) ка́ждый раз, когда́

where [wɛəʳ] *adv* (*position*) где; (*motion*) куда́ ▷ *conj* где; **where … from?** отку́да …?; **this is where …** э́то там, где …; **whereabouts** [*adv* wɛərəˈbauts, *n* ˈwɛərəbauts] *adv* (*position*) где; (*motion*) куда́ ▷ *n* местонахожде́ние; **whereas** *conj* тогда́ *or* в то вре́мя как; **whereby** *adv* (*formal*) посре́дством чего́; **wherever** [wɛərˈɛvəʳ] *conj* (*no matter where*): **wherever he was** где бы он ни был; (*not knowing where*): **wherever that is** где бы то ни бы́ло *or* (*interrogative: position*) где же; (*: motion*) куда́ же; **wherever he goes** куда́ бы он ни шёл

whether [ˈwɛðəʳ] *conj* ли; **I doubt whether she loves me** я сомнева́юсь, лю́бит ли она́ меня́; **I don't know whether to accept this proposal** я не зна́ю, приня́ть ли э́то предложе́ние; **whether you go or not** пойдёте Вы и́ли нет

⭕ **KEYWORD**

which [wɪtʃ] *adj* **1** (*interrogative: direct, indirect*) како́й (*f* кака́я, *nt* како́е, *pl* каки́е); **which picture would you like?** каку́ю карти́ну Вы хоти́те?; **which books are yours?** каки́е кни́ги Ва́ши?; **which one?** како́й? (*f* кака́я, *nt* како́е); **I've got two pens, which one do you want?** у меня́ есть две ру́чки, каку́ю Вы хоти́те?; **which one of you did it?** кто из Вас э́то сде́лал?

2: in which case в тако́м слу́чае; **by which time** к тому́ вре́мени ▷ *pron* **1** (*interrogative*) како́й (*f* кака́я, *nt* како́е, *pl* каки́е); **there are several museums, which shall we visit first?** здесь есть не́сколько музе́ев. В каку́ю мы пойдём снача́ла?; **which do you want, the apple or the banana?** что Вы хоти́те — я́блоко и́ли бана́н?; **which of you are staying?** кто из Вас остаётся?

2 (*relative*) кото́рый (*f* кото́рая, *nt* кото́рое, *pl* кото́рые); **the apple which is on the table** я́блоко, кото́рое лежи́т на столе́; **the news was bad, which is what I had feared** ве́сти бы́ли плохи́е, чего́ я и опаса́лся; **I had lunch, after which I decided to go home** я пообе́дал, по́сле чего́ я реши́л пойти́ домо́й; **I made a speech, after which nobody spoke** я вы́ступил с ре́чью, по́сле кото́рой никто́ ничего́ не сказа́л

whichever [wɪtʃˈɛvəʳ] *adj* (*any*) любо́й; (*regardless of*) како́й бы ни; **take whichever book you prefer** возьми́те любу́ю кни́гу; **whichever book you take** каку́ю бы кни́гу Вы ни взя́ли

while [waɪl] *n* (*period of time*) вре́мя *nt* ▷ *conj* пока́, в то вре́мя как; (*although*)

хотя́; **for a while** ненадо́лго; **while away**
vt: **to while away the time** корота́ть (perf
скорота́ть) вре́мя
whim [wɪm] n при́хоть f
whine [waɪn] vi (person, animal) скули́ть
(impf); (engine, siren) выть (impf)
whip [wɪp] n кнут, хлыст; (Pol: person)
организа́тор парла́ментской фра́кции
▷ vt (person, animal) хлеста́ть (impf);
(cream, eggs) взбива́ть (perf взбить);
to whip sth out выхва́тывать (perf
вы́хватить) что-н; **to whip sth away**
вырыва́ть (perf вы́рвать) что-н
whirl [wɜːl] vi кружи́ться (impf),
враща́ться (impf)
whisk [wɪsk] n (Culin) ве́нчик ▷ vt
(Culin) взбива́ть (perf взбить); **to whisk sb
away** or **off** увози́ть (perf увезти́) кого́-н
whiskers ['wɪskəz] npl (of animal) усы́
mpl; (of man) бакенба́рды fpl
whisky ['wɪskɪ] (US, Ireland **whiskey**) n
ви́ски nt ind
whisper ['wɪspə'] n шёпот ▷ vi
шепта́ться (impf) ▷ vt шепта́ть (impf)
whistle ['wɪsl] n (sound) свист; (object)
свисто́к ▷ vi свисте́ть (perf сви́стнуть)
white [waɪt] adj бе́лый ▷ n (colour)
бе́лый цвет; (person): **White** бе́лый(-ая)
m(f) adj; (of egg, eye) бело́к; **whitewash**
n (paint) известко́вый раство́р (для
побе́лки) ▷ vt (building) бели́ть (perf
побели́ть); (fig: incident) обеля́ть (perf
обели́ть)
whiting ['waɪtɪŋ] n inv хек
whizz [wɪz] vi: **to whizz past** or **by**
проноси́ться (perf пронести́сь) ми́мо

○ **KEYWORD**

who [huː] pron 1 (interrogative) кто; **who
is it?, who's there?** кто э́то or там?; **who
did you see there?** кого́ Вы там ви́дели?
2 (relative) кото́рый (f кото́рая, nt кото́рое,
pl кото́рые); **the woman who spoke to me**
же́нщина, кото́рая говори́ла со мной

whole [həul] adj це́лый ▷ n (entire unit)
це́лое nt adj; (all): **the whole of Europe** вся
Евро́па; **on the whole, as a whole** в це́лом;
wholemeal adj (Brit): **wholemeal flour**
мука́ гру́бого помо́ла; **wholemeal bread**
хлеб из муки́ гру́бого помо́ла; **wholesale**
adj (price) опто́вый; (destruction)
ма́ссовый ▷ adv (buy, sell) о́птом
wholly ['həulɪ] adv по́лностью, целико́м

○ **KEYWORD**

whom [huːm] pron 1 (interrogative: +acc,
+gen) кого́; (: +dat) кому́; (: +instr) кем;
(: +prp) ком; **whom did you see there?** кого́
Вы там ви́дели?; **to whom did you give the
book?** кому́ Вы отда́ли кни́гу?
2 (relative: +acc) кото́рого (f кото́рую,

pl кото́рых) (: +gen) кото́рого (f кото́рой,
pl кото́рых) (: +dat) кото́рому (f кото́рой,
pl кото́рым) (: +instr) кото́рым (f кото́рой,
pl кото́рыми) (: +prp) кото́ром (f кото́рой,
pl кото́рых); **the man whom I saw/to
whom I spoke** челове́к, кото́рого я ви́дел/с
кото́рым я говори́л

whore [hɔː'] n (inf: pej) шлю́ха

○ **KEYWORD**

whose [huːz] adj 1 (possessive:
interrogative) чей (f чья, nt чьё, pl чьи);
whose book is this?, whose is this book?
чья э́то кни́га?
2 (possessive: relative) кото́рый (f
кото́рая, nt кото́рое, pl кото́рые); **the
woman whose son you rescued** же́нщина,
сы́на кото́рой Вы спасли́
▷ pron чей (f чья, nt чьё, pl чьи); **whose is
this?** э́то чьё?; **I know whose it is** я зна́ю,
чьё э́то

why [waɪ] adv, conj почему́ ▷ excl: **why,
it's you!** как, э́то Вы?; **why is he always
late?** почему́ он всегда́ опа́здывает?; **I'm
not going — why not?** я не пойду́ —
почему́?; **why not do it now?** почему́ бы
не сде́лать э́то сейча́с?; **I wonder why he
said that** интере́сно, почему́ он э́то
сказа́л; **that's not why I'm here** я здесь не
по э́той причи́не; **that's why** вот почему́;
there is a reason why I want to see him у
меня́ есть причи́на для встре́чи с ним;
why, it's obvious/that's impossible! но
ведь э́то же очеви́дно/невозмо́жно!
wicked ['wɪkɪd] adj зло́бный, злой;
(mischievous: smile) лука́вый
wide [waɪd] adj широ́кий ▷ adv: **to open
wide** широ́ко открыва́ть (perf откры́ть); **to
shoot wide** стреля́ть (impf) ми́мо це́ли;
the bridge is 3 metres wide ширина́ моста́
— 3 ме́тра; **widely** adv (believed, known)
широ́ко; (travelled) мно́го; (differing)
значи́тельно; **widen** vt расширя́ть (perf
расши́рить) ▷ vi расширя́ться (perf
расши́риться); **wide open** adj широко́
раскры́тый; **widespread** adj (belief etc)
широко́ распространённый
widow ['wɪdəu] n вдова́; **widower** n
вдове́ц
width [wɪdθ] n ширина́
wield [wiːld] vt (power) облада́ть (impf)
+instr
wife [waɪf] (pl **wives**) n жена́
Wi-Fi ['waɪfaɪ] n беспроводна́я связь
wig [wɪg] n пари́к
wild [waɪld] adj (animal, plant, guess)
ди́кий; (weather, sea) бу́рный; (person,
behaviour) бу́йный; **wilds** npl (the wilds
(remote area) ди́кие места́ ntpl; **in the
wilds of** в дебря́х +gen; **wilderness**
['wɪldənɪs] n ди́кая ме́стность f; (desert)

пусты́ня; **wildlife** n ди́кая приро́да;
wildly adv (behave) бу́йно, ди́ко; (applaud)
бу́рно; (hit) нейстово; (guess) наобу́м

⭕ **KEYWORD**

will [wɪl] aux vb **1** (forming future tense):
I **will finish it tomorrow** я зако́нчу э́то
за́втра; I **will be working all morning** я
бу́ду рабо́тать всё у́тро; I **will have
finished it by tomorrow** я зако́нчу э́то к
за́втрашнему дню; I **will always remember
you** я бу́ду по́мнить тебя́ всегда́; **will you
do it? — yes, I will/no, I won't** Вы сде́лаете
э́то? — да, сде́лаю/нет, не сде́лаю; **the car
won't start** маши́на ника́к не заво́дится
2 (in conjectures, predictions): **he will** or
he'll be there by now он, наве́рное, уже́
там; **mistakes will happen** оши́бки
неизбе́жны
3 (in commands, requests, offers): **will you
be quiet!** а ну́-ка, поти́ше!; **will you help
me?** Вы мне не помо́жете?; **will you have
a cup of tea?** не хоти́те ли ча́шку ча́я?
▷ vt (pt, pp **willed**): **to will o.s. to do**
заставля́ть (perf заста́вить) себя́ +infin; **to
will sb to do** заклина́ть (impf) кого́-н
+infin
▷ n (volition) во́ля; (testament) завеща́ние

willing ['wɪlɪŋ] adj (agreed) согла́сный;
(enthusiastic) усе́рдный; **he's willing to do
it** он гото́в сде́лать э́то; **willingly** adv с
гото́вностью, охо́тно
willow ['wɪləʊ] n (tree) и́ва
willpower ['wɪlpaʊə'] n си́ла во́ли
wilt [wɪlt] vi ни́кнуть (perf пони́кнуть)
win [wɪn] (pt, pp **won**) n побе́да ▷ vt
выи́грывать (perf вы́играть); (support,
popularity) завоёвывать (perf завоева́ть)
▷ vi побежда́ть (perf победи́ть),
выи́грывать (perf вы́играть); **win over** vt
(person) покоря́ть (perf покори́ть)
wind¹ [wɪnd] n ве́тер; (Med) га́зы mpl
▷ vt: **the blow winded him** от уда́ра у него́
захвати́ло дух
wind² [waɪnd] (pt, pp **wound**) vt (rope,
thread) мота́ть (perf смота́ть); (toy, clock)
заводи́ть (perf завести́) ▷ vi (road, river)
ви́ться (impf); **wind up** vt (toy, clock)
заводи́ть (perf завести́); (debate)
заверша́ть (perf заверши́ть)
windfall ['wɪndfɔːl] n (money)
неожи́данный дохо́д
wind farm n ветряна́я электроста́нция
windmill ['wɪndmɪl] n ветряна́я
ме́льница
window ['wɪndəʊ] n окно́; (in shop)
витри́на; **windowsill** [-sɪl] n
подоко́нник
windscreen ['wɪndskriːn] n ветрово́е
стекло́
windy ['wɪndɪ] adj ве́треный; **it's windy
today** сего́дня ве́трено

wine [waɪn] n вино́
wing [wɪŋ] n (also Aut) крыло́; **wings**
npl (Theat) кули́сы fpl
wink [wɪŋk] n подми́гивание ▷ vi
подми́гивать (perf подмигну́ть), мига́ть
(perf мигну́ть); (light) мига́ть (perf
мигну́ть)
winner ['wɪnə'] n победи́тель(ница) m(f)
winter ['wɪntə'] n (season) зима́; **in
winter** зимо́й
wipe [waɪp] n: **to give sth a wipe**
протира́ть (perf протере́ть) что-н ▷ vt
(rub) вытира́ть (perf вы́тереть); (erase)
стира́ть (perf стере́ть); **wipe out** vt (city,
population) стира́ть (perf стере́ть) с лица́
земли́
wire ['waɪə'] n про́волока; (Elec) про́вод;
(telegram) телегра́мма ▷ vt (person)
телеграфи́ровать (impf/perf) +dat; (Elec:
also **wire up**) подключа́ть (perf
подключи́ть); **to wire a house** де́лать (perf
сде́лать) (электро)прово́дку в до́ме
wireless ['waɪəlɪs] adj беспроводно́й
wiring ['waɪərɪŋ] n (электро)прово́дка
wisdom ['wɪzdəm] n му́дрость f
wise [waɪz] adj му́дрый
...wise [waɪz] suffix: timewise в смы́сле
вре́мени
wish [wɪʃ] n жела́ние ▷ vt жела́ть (perf
пожела́ть); **best wishes** (for birthday etc)
всего́ наилу́чшего; **with best wishes** (in
letter) с наилу́чшими пожела́ниями; **to
wish sb goodbye** проща́ться (perf
попроща́ться) с кем-н; **he wished me well**
он пожела́л мне всего́ хоро́шего; **to wish
to do** хоте́ть (impf) +infin; **I wish him to
come** я хочу́, что́бы он пришёл; **to wish
for** жела́ть (perf пожела́ть) +acc or +gen
wistful ['wɪstful] adj тоскли́вый
wit [wɪt] n (wittiness) остроу́мие;
(intelligence: also **wits**) ум, ра́зум
witch [wɪtʃ] n ве́дьма

⭕ **KEYWORD**

with [wɪð, wɪθ] prep **1** (accompanying, in
the company of) с +instr; **I spent the day
with him** я провёл с ним день; **we stayed
with friends** мы останови́лись у друзе́й;
I'll be with you in a minute я освобожу́сь
че́рез мину́ту; **I'm with you** (I understand)
я Вас понима́ю; **she is really with it** (inf:
fashionable) она́ о́чень сти́льная; (: aware)
она́ всё сообража́ет
2 (descriptive) с +instr; **a girl with blue
eyes** де́вушка с голубы́ми глаза́ми; **a skirt
with a silk lining** ю́бка на шёлковой
подкла́дке
3 (indicating manner) с +instr; (indicating
cause) от +gen; (indicating means): **to
write with a pencil** писа́ть (impf)
карандашо́м; **with tears in her eyes** со
слеза́ми на глаза́х; **red with anger**
кра́сный от гне́ва; **you can open the door**

with this key Вы мо́жете откры́ть дверь э́тим ключо́м; **to fill sth with water** наполня́ть (*perf* напо́лнить) что-н водо́й

withdraw [wɪθˈdrɔː] (*irreg like* draw) *vt* (*object*) извлека́ть (*perf* извле́чь); (*remark*) брать (*perf* взять) наза́д; (*offer*) снима́ть (*perf* снять) ▷ *vi* (*troops, person*) уходи́ть (*perf* уйти́); **to withdraw money from an account** снима́ть (*perf* снять) де́ньги со счёта; **withdrawal** *n* (*of offer, remark*) отка́з; (*of troops*) вы́вод; (*of money*) сня́тие; **withdrawn** *pp of* **withdraw** ▷ *adj* за́мкнутый

wither [ˈwɪðəʳ] *vi* (*plant*) вя́нуть (*perf* завя́нуть)

withhold [wɪθˈhəuld] (*irreg like* hold) *vt* (*money*) уде́рживать (*perf* удержа́ть); (*information*) ута́ивать (*perf* утаи́ть)

within [wɪðˈɪn] *prep* (*place, distance, time*) внутри́ +gen, в преде́лах +gen ▷ *adv* внутри́; **within reach** в преде́лах досяга́емости; **within sight (of)** в по́ле зре́ния (+gen); **the finish is within sight** коне́ц не за гора́ми

without [wɪðˈaut] *prep* без +gen; **without a hat** без шля́пы; **without saying a word** не говоря́ ни сло́ва; **without looking** не гля́дя; **to go without sth** обходи́ться (*perf* обойти́сь) без чего́-н

withstand [wɪθˈstænd] (*irreg like* stand) *vt* выде́рживать (*perf* вы́держать)

witness [ˈwɪtnɪs] *n* свиде́тель(ница) *m(f)* ▷ *vt* (*event*) быть (*impf*) свиде́телем(-льницей) +gen; (*document*) заверя́ть (*perf* заве́рить)

witty [ˈwɪtɪ] *adj* остроу́мный

wives [waɪvz] *npl of* wife

wobble [ˈwɔbl] *vi* (*legs*) трясти́сь (*impf*); (*chair*) шата́ться (*impf*)

woe [wəu] *n* го́ре

woke [wəuk] *pt of* wake; **woken** *pp of* wake

wolf [wulf] (*pl* wolves) *n* волк

woman [ˈwumən] (*pl* women) *n* же́нщина

womb [wuːm] *n* ма́тка

women [ˈwɪmɪn] *npl of* woman

won [wʌn] *pt, pp of* win

wonder [ˈwʌndəʳ] *n* (*feeling*) изумле́ние ▷ *vi*: **I wonder whether you could tell me ...** не мо́жете ли Вы сказа́ть мне ...; **I wonder why he is late** интере́сно, почему́ он опозда́л; **to wonder at** удивля́ться (*impf*) +dat; **to wonder about** разду́мывать (*impf*) о +prp; **it's no wonder (that)** не удиви́тельно(, что); **wonderful** *adj* (*excellent*) чуде́сный

won't [wəunt] = will not

wood [wud] *n* (*timber*) де́рево; (*forest*) лес; **wooden** *adj* (*object*) деревя́нный; (*fig*) дубо́вый; **woodwork** *n* (*skill*) столя́рное де́ло

wool [wul] *n* (*material, yarn*) шерсть *f*; to

pull the wool over sb's eyes (*fig*) пуска́ть (*impf*) пыль в глаза́ кому́-н; **woollen** (*US* **woolen**) *adj* шерстяно́й; **woolly** (*US* **wooly**) *adj* шерстяно́й; (*fig: ideas*) расплы́вчатый; (: *person*) вя́лый

word [wəːd] *n* сло́во; (*news*) слух ▷ *vt* формули́ровать (*perf* сформули́ровать); **in other words** други́ми слова́ми; **to break/keep one's word** наруша́ть (*perf* нару́шить)/держа́ть (*perf* сдержа́ть) своё сло́во; **to have words with sb** име́ть (*impf*) кру́пный разгово́р с кем-н; **wording** *n* формулиро́вка; **word processor** *n* те́кстовый проце́ссор

wore [wɔːʳ] *pt of* wear

work [wəːk] *n* рабо́та; (*Art, Literature*) произведе́ние ▷ *vi* рабо́тать (*impf*); (*medicine etc*) де́йствовать (*perf* поде́йствовать) ▷ *vt* (*clay*) рабо́тать (*impf*) с +instr; (*wood, metal*) рабо́тать (*impf*) по +dat; (*land*) обраба́тывать (*perf* обрабо́тать); (*mine*) разраба́тывать (*perf* разрабо́тать); (*machine*) управля́ть (*impf*) +instr; (*miracle*) соверша́ть (*perf* соверши́ть); **he has been out of work for three months** он был без рабо́ты три ме́сяца; **to work loose** (*part*) расша́тываться (*perf* расшата́ться); (*knot*) сла́бнуть (*perf* осла́бнуть); **work on** *vt fus* (*task*) рабо́тать (*impf*) над +instr; (*person*) рабо́тать (*impf*) с +instr; (*principle*) исходи́ть (*impf*) из +gen; **work out** *vi* (*plans etc*) удава́ться (*perf* уда́ться) ▷ *vt* (*problem*) разреша́ть (*perf* разреши́ть); (*plan*) разраба́тывать (*perf* разрабо́тать); **it works out at £100** (*cost*) выхо́дит £100; **worker** *n* (*in factory*) рабо́чий(-ая) *m(f)* adj; (*in community etc*) рабо́тник(-ница); **workforce** *n* рабо́чая си́ла; **working-class** *adj* рабо́чий; **workman** *irreg n* (квалифици́рованный) рабо́чий *m* adj; **workshop** *n* мастерска́я *f* adj, цех; (*session*) семина́р; (*Theat, Mus*) сту́дия

world [wəːld] *n* мир ▷ *adj* мирово́й; **to think the world of sb** быть (*impf*) о́чень высо́кого мне́ния о ком-н; **world champion** чемпио́н ми́ра; **World Wide Web** *n* Всеми́рная Паути́на

worm [wəːm] *n* (*Zool*) червь *m*

worn [wɔːn] *pp of* wear ▷ *adj* (*carpet*) потёртый; **worn-out** *adj* (*object*) изно́шенный; (*person*) измо́танный

worried [ˈwʌrɪd] *adj* обеспоко́енный, встрево́женный

worry [ˈwʌrɪ] *n* (*anxiety*) беспоко́йство, волне́ние ▷ *vi* беспоко́иться (*impf*), волнова́ться (*impf*) ▷ *vt* (*person*) беспоко́ить (*perf* обеспоко́ить), волнова́ть (*perf* взволнова́ть); **worrying** *adj* трево́жный

worse [wəːs] *adj* ху́дший ▷ *adv* ху́же ▷ *n* ху́дшее *nt adj*; **a change for the worse** ухудше́ние; **worsen** *vi* ухудша́ться (*perf* уху́дшиться); **worse off** adj (financially) бо́лее бе́дный

worship ['wə:ʃɪp] n поклоне́ние, преклоне́ние ▷ vt поклоня́ться (impf) +dat, преклоня́ться (impf) пе́ред +instr

worst [wə:st] adj наиху́дший ▷ adv ху́же всего́ ▷ n наиху́дшее nt adj; **at worst** в ху́дшем слу́чае

worth [wə:θ] adj: **to be worth** сто́ить (impf); **it's worth it** э́то того́ сто́ит; **worthless** adj никчёмный; **worthwhile** adj сто́ящий

worthy ['wə:ðɪ] adj: **worthy (of)** досто́йный (+gen)

⚪ **KEYWORD**

would [wud] aux vb **1** (conditional tense): **I would tell you if I could** я бы сказа́л Вам, е́сли бы мог; **if you asked him he would do it** е́сли Вы его́ попро́сите, (то) он сде́лает э́то; **if you had asked him he would have done it** е́сли бы Вы попроси́ли его́, (то) он бы сде́лал э́то
2 (in offers, invitations, requests): **would you like a cake?** не хоти́те (ли) пирога́?; **would you ask him to come in?** пожа́луйста, пригласи́те его́ войти́!; **would you open the window please?** откро́йте, пожа́луйста, окно́!
3 (in indirect speech): **I said I would do it** я сказа́л, что сде́лаю э́то; **he asked me if I would stay with him** он попроси́л меня́ оста́ться с ним; **he asked me if I would resit the exam if I failed** он спроси́л меня́, бу́ду ли я пересдава́ть экза́мен, е́сли я провалю́сь
4 (emphatic): **it WOULD have to snow today!** и́менно сего́дня до́лжен пойти́ снег!; **you WOULD say that, wouldn't you!** Вы, коне́чно, э́то ска́жете!
5 (insistence): **she wouldn't behave** она́ ника́к не хоте́ла хорошо́ себя́ вести́
6 (conjecture): **it would have been midnight** должно́ быть, была́ по́лночь; **it would seem so** должно́, быть, так; **it would seem that ...** похо́же, что ...
7 (indicating habit): **he would come here on Mondays** он (обы́чно) приходи́л сюда́ по понеде́льникам

wouldn't ['wudnt] = **would not**
wound¹ [waund] pt, pp of **wind²**
wound² [wu:nd] n ра́на ▷ vt ра́нить (impf/perf)
wove [wəuv] pt of **weave**; **woven** pp of **weave**
wrap [ræp] vt (also **wrap up**) завора́чивать (perf заверну́ть); (wind): **to wrap sth round sth** (tape etc) обора́чивать (perf оберну́ть) что-н вокру́г чего́-л;
wrapper n (on chocolate) обёртка
wreath [ri:θ] n (for dead) вено́к
wreck [rɛk] n (vehicle, ship) обло́мки mpl

▷ vt (car) разбива́ть (perf разби́ть); (stereo) лома́ть (perf слома́ть); (weekend) по́ртить (perf испо́ртить); (relationship) разруша́ть (perf разру́шить); (life, health) губи́ть (perf погуби́ть); **wreckage** n обло́мки mpl; (of building) разва́лины fpl

wren [rɛn] n крапи́вник

wrench [rɛntʃ] n (Tech) га́ечный ключ; (tug) рыво́к; (fig) тоска́ ▷ vt (twist) вывёртывать (perf вы́вернуть); **to wrench sth from sb** вырыва́ть (perf вы́рвать) что-н у кого́-л

wrestle ['rɛsl] vi (Sport): **to wrestle (with sb)** боро́ться (impf) (с кем-н)

wrestling ['rɛslɪŋ] n борьба́

wretched ['rɛtʃɪd] adj несча́стный

wriggle ['rɪgl] vi (also **wriggle about**: worm) извива́ться (impf); (: person) ёрзать (impf)

wring [rɪŋ] (pt, pp **wrung**) vt (hands) лома́ть (impf); (also **wring out**: clothes) выжима́ть (perf вы́жать); (fig): **to wring sth out of sb** выжима́ть (perf вы́жать) что-н из кого́-л

wrinkle ['rɪŋkl] n (on face) морщи́на ▷ vt (nose etc) мо́рщить (perf смо́рщить) ▷ vi (skin etc) мо́рщиться (perf смо́рщиться)

wrist [rɪst] n (Anat) запя́стье

write [raɪt] (pt **wrote**, pp **written**) vt (letter, novel etc) писа́ть (perf написа́ть); (cheque, receipt) выпи́сывать (perf вы́писать) ▷ vi писа́ть (impf); **to write to sb** писа́ть (perf написа́ть) кому́-н; **write down** vt (note) писа́ть (perf написа́ть); **write off** vt (debt) спи́сывать (perf списа́ть); (plan) отменя́ть (perf отмени́ть); **writer** n писа́тель m

writing ['raɪtɪŋ] n (words written) на́дпись f; (of letter, article) (на)писа́ние; (also **handwriting**) по́черк; **writing is his favourite occupation** бо́льше всего́ он лю́бит писа́ть; **in writing** в пи́сьменном ви́де

written ['rɪtn] pp of **write**

wrong [rɔŋ] adj непра́вильный; (information) неве́рный; (immoral) дурно́й ▷ adv непра́вильно ▷ n (injustice) несправедли́вость f ▷ vt нехорошо́ поступа́ть (perf поступи́ть) с +instr; **you are wrong to do it** э́то нехорошо́ с Ва́шей стороны́; **you are wrong about that, you've got it wrong** Вы непра́вы; **who is in the wrong?** чья э́то вина́?; **what's wrong?** в чём де́ло?; **to go wrong** (plan) не удава́ться (perf уда́ться); **right and wrong** хоро́шее и дурно́е

wrote [rəut] pt of **write**

wrung [rʌŋ] pt, pp of **wring**

WWW n abbr = **World Wide Web**

X y

Xmas ['ɛksməs] *n abbr* = **Christmas**
X-ray ['ɛksreɪ] *n* (*ray*) рентге́новские лучи́
mpl; (*photo*) рентге́новский сни́мок ▷ *vt*
просве́чивать (*perf* просвети́ть)
(рентге́новскими луча́ми)
xylophone ['zaɪləfəʊn] *n* ксилофо́н

yacht [jɒt] *n* я́хта
yard [jɑːd] *n* (*of house etc*) двор;
(*measure*) ярд

- **YARD**
- Yard — ме́ра длины́ ра́вная 90,14 см.

yawn [jɔːn] *n* зево́к ▷ *vi* зева́ть (*perf*
зевну́ть)
year [jɪəʳ] *n* год; **he is eight years old** ему́
во́семь лет; **an eight-year-old child**
восьмиле́тний ребёнок; **yearly** *adj*
ежего́дный ▷ *adv* ежего́дно
yearn [jəːn] *vi*: **to yearn for sth** тоскова́ть
(*impf*) по чему́-н; **to yearn to do** жа́ждать
(*impf*) +*infin*
yeast [jiːst] *n* дро́жжи *pl*
yell [jɛl] *vi* вопи́ть (*impf*)
yellow ['jɛləʊ] *adj* жёлтый
yes [jɛs] *particle* да; (*in reply to negative*)
нет ▷ *n* проголосова́вший(-ая) *m(f) adj*
"за"; **to say yes** говори́ть (*perf* сказа́ть) да
yesterday ['jɛstədɪ] *adv* вчера́ ▷ *n*
вчера́шний день *m*; **yesterday morning/
evening** вчера́ у́тром/ве́чером; **all day
yesterday** вчера́ весь день
yet [jɛt] *adv* ещё, до сих пор ▷ *conj*
одна́ко, всё же; **the work is not finished
yet** рабо́та ещё не око́нчена; **the best yet**
са́мый лу́чший на сего́дняшний день; **as
yet** ещё пока́
yew [juː] *n* (*tree*) тис
yield [jiːld] *n* (*Agr*) урожа́й *m* ▷ *vt*
(*surrender*) сдава́ть (*perf* сдать); (*produce*)
приноси́ть (*perf* принести́) ▷ *vi*
(*surrender*) отступа́ть (*perf* отступи́ть);
(*US: Aut*) уступа́ть (*perf* уступи́ть)
доро́гу
yog(h)ourt ['jəʊgət] *n* йо́гурт
yog(h)urt ['jəʊgət] *n* = **yog(h)ourt**
yolk [jəʊk] *n* желто́к

you [ju:] *pron* **1** (*subject*: *familiar*) ты;
(: *polite*) Вы; (: *2nd person pl*) вы; **you
English are very polite** вы, англича́не,
о́чень ве́жливы; **you and I will stay here**
мы с тобо́й/Ва́ми оста́немся здесь
2 (*direct*: *familiar*) тебя́; (: *polite*) Вас;
(: *2nd person pl*) вас; **I love you** я тебя́/Вас
люблю́
3 (*indirect*: *familiar*) тебе́; (: *polite*) Вам;
(: *2nd person pl*) вам; **I'll give you a present**
я тебе́/Вам что́-нибудь подарю́
4 (*after prep*: +*gen*: *familiar*) тебя́; (: *polite*)
Вас; (: *2nd person pl*) вас; (: +*dat*: *familiar*)
тебе́; (: *polite*) Вам; (: *2nd person pl*) вам;
(: +*instr*: *familiar*) тобо́й; (: *polite*) Ва́ми;
(: *2nd person pl*) ва́ми; (: +*prp*: *familiar*)
тебе́; (: *polite*) Вас; (: *2nd person pl*) вас;
they've been talking about you они́
говори́ли о тебе́/Вас
5 (*after prep*: *referring to subject of sentence*:
+*gen*) себя́; (: +*dat*, +*prp*) себе́; (: +*instr*)
собо́й; **will you take the children with you?**
Вы возьмёте дете́й с собо́й?; **she's
younger than you** она́ моло́же тебя́/Вас
6 (*impersonal*: *one*): **you never know what
can happen** никогда́ не зна́ешь, что мо́жет
случи́ться; **you can't do that!** так нельзя́!;
fresh air does you good све́жий во́здух
поле́зен для здоро́вья

you'd [ju:d] = **you had**; **you would**
you'll [ju:l] = **you shall**; **you will**
young [jʌŋ] *adj* молодо́й; (*child*)
ма́ленький ▷ *npl* (*of animal*) молодня́к
msg; **the young** (*people*) молодёжь *f*;
youngster *n* ребёнок
your [jɔ:ʳ] *adj* (*familiar*) твой; (*polite*) Ваш;
(*2nd person pl*) ваш; *see also* **my**
you're [juəʳ] = **you are**
yours [jɔ:z] *pron* (*familiar*) твой; (*polite*)
Ваш; (*2nd person pl*) ваш; (*referring to
subject of sentence*) свой; **is this yours?**
э́то твоё/Ва́ше?; **yours sincerely, yours
faithfully** и́скренне Ваш; *see also* **mine**[1]
yourself [jɔ:'sɛlf] *pron* (*reflexive*) себя́;
(*after prep*: +*gen*) себя́; (: +*dat*, +*prp*) себе́;
(: +*instr*) собо́й; (*emphatic*) сам (*f* сама́, *pl*
са́ми) (*alone*) сам, оди́н; (**all**) **by yourself**
ты сам *or* оди́н; **you yourself told me** Вы
са́ми сказа́ли мне; *see also* **myself**
yourselves [jɔ:'sɛlvz] *pl pron* (*reflexive*)
себя́; (*after prep*: +*gen*) себя́; (: +*dat*, +*prp*)
себе́; (: +*instr*) собо́й; (*emphatic*) са́ми;
(*alone*) са́ми, одни́; (**all**) **by yourselves**
са́ми, одни́; **talk amongst yourselves for a
moment** поговори́те ме́жду собо́й пока́;
see also **myself**
youth [ju:θ] *n* (*young days*) ю́ность *f*,
мо́лодость *f*; (*young people*) молодёжь *f*;
(*young man*) ю́ноша *m*; **youthful** *adj*
ю́ношеский; (*person, looks*) ю́ный
you've [ju:v] = **you have**

zeal [zi:l] *n* рве́ние
zebra ['zi:brə] *n* зе́бра; **zebra crossing**
n (*Brit*) зе́бра, пешехо́дный перехо́д
zero ['zɪərəu] *n* ноль *m*, нуль *m*
zest [zest] *n* (*for life*) жа́жда; (*of orange*)
це́дра
zigzag ['zɪgzæg] *n* зигза́г
zinc [zɪŋk] *n* цинк
zip [zɪp] *n* (*also* **zip fastener**) мо́лния
▷ *vt* (*also* **zip up**) застёгивать (*perf*
застегну́ть) на мо́лнию; **zipper** *n* (*US*)
= **zip**
zodiac ['zəudɪæk] *n* зодиа́к
zone [zəun] *n* зо́на
zoo [zu:] *n* зоопа́рк
zoology [zu:'ɔlədʒɪ] *n* зооло́гия
zoom [zu:m] *vi*: **to zoom past** мелька́ть
(*perf* промелькну́ть) ми́мо; **zoom lens** *n*
объекти́в с переме́нным фо́кусным
расстоя́нием

TABLES OF RUSSIAN IRREGULAR FORMS

The following tables show the irregular forms of certain Russian words which appear in the dictionary text. For all tables, where there are alternatives given under the accusative, these are the animate forms which are identical with the genitive.

Nouns

Table 1

	мать	
	Singular	*Plural*
Nom	мать	ма́тери
Acc	мать	матере́й
Gen	ма́тери	матере́й
Dat	ма́тери	матеря́м
Instr	ма́терью	матеря́ми
Prp	о ма́тери	о матеря́х

Table 2

	дочь	
	Singular	*Plural*
Nom	дочь	до́чери
Acc	дочь	дочере́й
Gen	до́чери	дочере́й
Dat	до́чери	дочеря́м
Instr	до́черью	дочерьми́
Prp	о до́чери	о дочеря́х

Table 3

	путь	
	Singular	*Plural*
Nom	путь	пути́
Acc	путь	пути́
Gen	пути́	путе́й
Dat	пути́	путя́м
Instr	путём	путя́ми
Prp	о пути́	о путя́х

Table 4

	вре́мя	
	Singular	*Plural*
Nom	вре́мя	времена́
Acc	вре́мя	времена́
Gen	вре́мени	времён
Dat	вре́мени	времена́м
Instr	вре́менем	времена́ми
Prp	о вре́мени	о временах

(NB. Similarly with nouns like и́мя, пле́мя etc)

Pronouns

Table 5

	m	*f*	*nt*	*pl*
Nom	чей	чья	чьё	чьи
Acc	чей/чьего́	чью	чьё	чьи/чьих
Gen	чьего́	чьей	чьего́	чьих
Dat	чьему́	чьей	чьему́	чьим
Instr	чьим	чьей *or* чье́ю	чьим	чьи́ми
Prp	о чьём	о чьей	о чьём	о чьих

Table 6a

Nom	я	ты	он	она́	оно́
Acc/Gen	меня́	тебя́	его́	её	его́
Dat	мне	тебе́	ему́	ей	ему́
Instr	мной *or* мно́ю	тобо́й *or* тобо́ю	им	ей *or* е́ю	им
Prp	обо мне	о тебе́	о нём	о ней	о нём

(NB. The reflexive personal pronoun себя́ declines like тебя́)

Table 6b

Nom	мы	вы	они́
Acc/Gen	нас	вас	их
Dat	нам	вам	им
Instr	на́ми	ва́ми	и́ми
Prp	о нас	о вас	о них

Table 7

Nom	кто	что
Acc	кого́	что
Gen	кого́	чего́
Dat	кому́	чему́
Instr	кем	чем
Prp	о ком	о чём

(NB. Similarly with никто́, ничто́ etc)

Table 8

	m	f	nt	pl
Nom	мой	моя́	моё	мои́
Acc	мой/моего́	мою́	моё	мои́/мои́х
Gen	моего́	мое́й	моего́	мои́х
Dat	моему́	мое́й	моему́	мои́м
Instr	мои́м	мое́й or мое́ю	мои́м	мои́ми
Prp	о моём	о мое́й	о моём	о мои́х

(NB. твой declines like мой, as does the reflexive possessive pronoun свой)

Table 9

	m	f	nt	pl
Nom	наш	на́ша	на́ше	на́ши
Acc	наш/на́шего	на́шу	на́ше	на́ши/на́ших
Gen	на́шего	на́шей	на́шего	на́ших
Dat	на́шему	на́шей	на́шему	на́шим
Instr	на́шим	на́шей or на́шею	на́шим	на́шими
Prp	о на́шем	о на́шей	о на́шем	о на́ших

(NB. ваш declines like наш. The possessive pronouns его́, её and их are invariable)

Table 10

	m	f	nt	pl
Nom	э́тот	э́та	э́то	э́ти
Acc	э́тот/э́того	э́ту	э́то	э́ти/э́тих
Gen	э́того	э́той	э́того	э́тих
Dat	э́тому	э́той	э́тому	э́тим
Instr	э́тим	э́той or э́тою	э́тим	э́тими
Prp	об э́том	об э́той	об э́том	об э́тих

Table 11

	m	f	nt	pl
Nom	тот	та	то	те
Acc	тот/того́	ту	то	те/тех
Gen	того́	той	того́	тех
Dat	тому́	той	тому́	тем
Instr	тем	той or то́ю	тем	те́ми
Prp	о том	о той	о том	о тех

Table 12

	m	f	nt	pl
Nom	сей	сия́	сие́	сии́
Acc	сей/сего́	сию́	сие́	сии́/сих
Gen	сего́	сей	сего́	сих
Dat	сему́	сей	сему́	сим
Instr	сим	сей or се́ю	сим	си́ми
Prp	о сём	о сей	о сём	о сих

Table 13

	m	f	nt	pl
Nom	весь	вся	всё	все
Acc	весь/всего́	всю	всё	все/всех
Gen	всего́	всей	всего́	всех
Dat	всему́	всей	всему́	всем
Instr	всем	всей or все́ю	всем	все́ми
Prp	обо всём	обо всей	обо всём	обо всех

Verbs

Table 14

хоте́ть		
	Present	Past
я	хочу́	хоте́л/хоте́ла
ты	хо́чешь	хоте́л/хоте́ла
он	хо́чет	хоте́л
она́	хо́чет	хоте́ла
оно́	хо́чет	хоте́ло
мы	хоти́м	хоте́ли
вы	хоти́те	хоте́ли
они́	хотя́т	хоте́ли

(NB. Similarly with verbs such as расхоте́ть, захоте́ть etc)

Table 15

есть			
	Present	Past	Imperative
я	ем	ел/е́ла	
ты	ешь	ел/е́ла	
он	ест	ел	
она́	ест	е́ла	
оно́	ест	е́ло	
мы	еди́м	е́ли	
вы	еди́те	е́ли	
они́	едя́т	е́ли	
			е́шь(те)

(NB. Similarly with verbs such as съесть, пое́сть, перее́сть etc)

Table 16

дать			
	Present	Past	Imperative
я	дам	дал/дала́	
ты	дашь	дал/дала́	
он	даст	дал	
она́	даст	дала́	
оно́	даст	да́ло	
мы	дади́м	да́ли	
вы	дади́те	да́ли	
они́	даду́т	да́ли	
			да́й(те)

(NB. Similarly with verbs such as переда́ть, изда́ть, отда́ть, разда́ть etc)

Table 17

чтить			
	Present	Past	Imperative
я	чту	чтил/чти́ла	
ты	чтишь	чтил/чти́ла	
он	чтит	чтил	
она́	чтит	чти́ла	
оно́	чтит	чти́ло	
мы	чтим	чти́ли	
вы	чти́те	чти́ли	
они́	чтут/чтят	чти́ли	
			чти́(те)

(NB. Similarly with verbs such as почти́ть etc)

Table 18

идти́			
	Present	Past	Imperative
я	иду́	шёл/шла	
ты	идёшь	шёл/шла	
он	идёт	шёл	
она́	идёт	шла	
оно́	идёт	шло	
мы	идём	шли	
вы	идёте	шли	
они́	иду́т	шли	
			иди́(те)

(NB. Similarly with verbs such as прийти́, уйти́, отойти́, зайти́ etc)

Table 19

е́хать			
	Present	Past	Imperative
я	е́ду	е́хал/е́хала	
ты	е́дешь	е́хал/е́хала	
он	е́дет	е́хал	
она́	е́дет	е́хала	
оно́	е́дет	е́хало	
мы	е́дем	е́хали	
вы	е́дете	е́хали	
они́	е́дут	е́хали	
			поезжа́й(те)

(NB. Similarly with verbs such as прие́хать, перее́хать, уе́хать, въе́хать)

Table 20

	Present	Past	Imperative
	бежа́ть		
я	бегу́	бежа́л/бежа́ла	
ты	бежи́шь	бежа́л/бежа́ла	
он	бежи́т	бежа́л	
она́	бежи́т	бежа́ла	
оно́	бежи́т	бежа́ло	
мы	бежи́м	бежа́ли	
вы	бежи́те	бежа́ли	
они́	бегу́т	бежа́ли	
			беги́(те)

(NB. Similarly with verbs such as побежа́ть, убежа́ть, прибежа́ть etc)

Table 21

	Present	Past	Imperative
	быть		
я	бу́ду	был/была́	
ты	бу́дешь	был/была́	
он	бу́дет	был	
она́	бу́дет	была́	
оно́	бу́дет	бы́ло	
мы	бу́дем	бы́ли	
вы	бу́дете	бы́ли	
они́	бу́дут	бы́ли	
			бу́дь(те)

(NB. Not used in present tense, except есть in certain cases)

Numerals

Table 22

	m	f	nt	pl
Nom	оди́н	одна́	одно́	одни́
Acc	оди́н/одного́	одну́	одно́	одни́/одни́х
Gen	одного́	одно́й	одного́	одни́х
Dat	одному́	одно́й	одному́	одни́м
Instr	одни́м	одно́й or одно́ю	одни́м	одни́ми
Prp	об одно́м	об одно́й	об одно́м	об одни́х

Table 23

	m	f	nt
Nom	два	две	два
Acc	два/двух	две/двух	два/двух
Gen	двух	двух	двух
Dat	двум	двум	двум
Instr	двумя́	двумя́	двумя́
Prp	о двух	о двух	о двух

Table 24

	три	четы́ре
Nom	три	четы́ре
Acc	три/трёх	четы́ре/четырёх
Gen	трёх	четырёх
Dat	трём	четырём
Instr	тремя́	четырьмя́
Prp	о трёх	о четырёх

Table 25

	о́ба	о́ба
	m/nt	f
Nom	о́ба	о́бе
Acc	о́ба/обо́их	о́бе/обе́их
Gen	обо́их	обе́их
Dat	обо́им	обе́им
Instr	обо́ими	обе́ими
Prp	об обо́их	об обе́их

Table 26

	пять	пятьдеся́т
Nom	пять	пятьдеся́т
Acc	пять	пятьдеся́т
Gen	пяти́	пяти́десяти
Dat	пяти́	пяти́десяти
Instr	пятью́	пятью́десятью
Prp	о пяти́	о пяти́десяти

(NB. The numerals шесть to два́дцать plus три́дцать decline like пять; шестьдеся́т, се́мьдесят and во́семьдесят decline like пятьдеся́т)

Table 27

	со́рок	сто
Nom	со́рок	сто
Acc	со́рок	сто
Gen	сорока́	ста
Dat	сорока́	ста
Instr	сорока́	ста
Prp	о сорока́	о ста

(NB. девяно́сто declines like сто. After мно́го and не́сколько the genitive form is сот, the dative plural is стам, the instrumental plural is ста́ми, and the prepositional plural is стах)

Table 28

	две́сти	три́ста	четы́реста	пятьсо́т
Nom	две́сти	три́ста	четы́реста	пятьсо́т
Acc	две́сти	три́ста	четы́реста	пятьсо́т
Gen	двухсо́т	трёхсо́т	четырёхсо́т	пятисо́т
Dat	двумста́м	трёмста́м	четырёмста́м	пятиста́м
Instr	двумяста́ми	тремяста́ми	четырьмяста́ми	пятьюста́ми
Prp	о двухста́х	о трёхста́х	о четырёхста́х	о пятиста́х

(NB. шестьсо́т, семьсо́т, восемьсо́т and девятьсо́т decline like пятьсо́т)

Table 29

	ты́сяча	
	Singular	*Plural*
Nom	ты́сяча	ты́сячи
Acc	ты́сячу	ты́сячи
Gen	ты́сячи	ты́сяч
Dat	ты́сяче	ты́сячам
Instr	ты́сячей *or* ты́сячью	ты́сячами
Prp	о ты́сяче	о ты́сячах

Table 30a

	дво́е	тро́е	че́тверо
Nom	дво́е	тро́е	че́тверо
Acc	дво́е/двои́х	тро́е/трои́х	че́тверо/четверы́х
Gen	двои́х	трои́х	четверы́х
Dat	двои́м	трои́м	четверы́м
Instr	двои́ми	трои́ми	четверы́ми
Prp	о двои́х	о трои́х	о четверы́х

Table 30b

	пя́теро	ше́стеро	се́меро
Nom	пя́теро	ше́стеро	се́меро
Acc	пя́теро/пятеры́х	ше́стеро/шестеры́х	се́меро/семеры́х
Gen	пятеры́х	шестеры́х	семеры́х
Dat	пятеры́м	шестеры́м	семеры́м
Instr	пятеры́ми	шестеры́ми	семеры́ми
Prp	о пятеры́х	о шестеры́х	о семеры́х

(NB. Other collective numerals decline like че́тверо)